A DIGEST

OF THE

GENERAL STATUTE LAWS

OF THE

STATE OF TEXAS:

TO WHICH ARE SUBJOINED

THE REPEALED LAWS OF THE REPUBLIC AND STATE OF TEXAS,

BY, THROUGH, OR UNDER WHICH RIGHTS HAVE ACCRUED;

ALSO,

THE COLONIZATION LAWS

OF

MEXICO, COAHUILA AND TEXAS, WHICH WERE IN FORCE BEFORE THE DECLARATION OF INDEPENDENCE BY TEXAS.

PREPARED BY

WILLIAMSON S. OLDHAM AND GEORGE W. WHITE.

PUBLISHED BY AUTHORITY OF THE LEGISLATURE.

THE LAWBOOK EXCHANGE, LTD.
Clark, New Jersey

ISBN 1-58477-438-X

Lawbook Exchange edition 2004, 2024

The quality of this reprint is equivalent to the quality of the original work.

The Lawbook Exchange, Ltd.
33 Terminal Avenue
Clark, New Jersey 07066-1321

Please see our website for a selection of our other publications and fine facsimile reprints of classic works of legal history:
www.lawbookexchange.com

Library of Congress Cataloging-in-Publication Data

Oldham, William Simpson, 1813-1868
A digest of the general statute laws of the State of Texas : to which are subjoined the repealed laws of the Republic and State of Texas, by, through, or under which rights have accrued : also, the colonization laws of Mexico, Coahuila and Texas, which were in force before the declaration of independence by Texas / prepared by Williamson S. Oldham and George W. White.
p. cm.
Originally published: Austin, Tex. : Printed by J. Marshall & Co., 1859.
"Published by authority of the legislature."
Includes bibliographical references and index.
ISBN 1-58477-438-X (cloth: alk. paper)
1. Law—Texas—Digests. 2. Law—Mexico—Colonies. I. White, George W. II. Title.

KFT1238.O42 2004
348.764'026'09034—dc22 2004041401

Printed in the United States of America on acid-free paper

A DIGEST

OF THE

GENERAL STATUTE LAWS

OF THE

STATE OF TEXAS:

TO WHICH ARE SUBJOINED

THE REPEALED LAWS OF THE REPUBLIC AND STATE OF TEXAS,

BY, THROUGH, OR UNDER WHICH RIGHTS HAVE ACCRUED;

ALSO,

THE COLONIZATION LAWS

OF

MEXICO, COAHUILA AND TEXAS, WHICH WERE IN FORCE BEFORE THE DECLARATION OF INDEPENDENCE BY TEXAS.

PREPARED BY

WILLIAMSON S. OLDHAM AND GEORGE W. WHITE.

PUBLISHED BY AUTHORITY OF THE LEGISLATURE.

AUSTIN, TEXAS:

PRINTED BY JOHN MARSHALL & CO., AT THE STATE GAZETTE OFFICE.

1859.

AN ACT TO PROVIDE FOR A DIGEST OF THE LAWS OF TEXAS.

SECTION 1. *Be it enacted by the Legislature of the State of Texas*, That the Governor of this State be and is hereby authorised to receive proposals for the furnishing, for the use of the State, of five thousand copies of a new and revised Digest of all the General Statute Laws of this State down to and including those passed at the present session of the Legislature. Such Digest shall be printed upon paper of a quality not inferior to that of Hartley's Digest, and as far as practicable, it shall follow the plan of Hartley's Digest, or improve upon the same, and be put up in law sheep binding of the same character. It shall in addition conform to the following requisites: Besides the laws in force, it shall contain the appropriate titles in smaller type, and the repealed laws of the Republic and State of Texas, by, through, or under which, rights have accrued; also, the colonization laws of Mexico and Coahuila and Texas, which were in force before the Declaration of Independence by Texas. Marginal notes indicating the subject of each Section, and containing references to laws upon the same subject, if there be such, and at the foot of each page, referring to the decisions of the Supreme Court in which there have been judicial interpretations of the Act or Section to which such notes are attached.

SEC. 2. The Governor shall appoint a time to enter into a contract for such Digest, and give sixty days' notice of the same; at the expiration of which, he shall consider such proposals as shall be presented, and enter into a contract on the part of the State, as may be most to its interest, with such person or persons as are qualified for the execution of the work; provided, that the cost of such Digest shall not exceed four dollars for each copy.

SEC. 3. The person to whom such contract is awarded, shall enter into bond with two or more good securities, to the satisfaction of the Governor, in the sum of ten thousand dollars for the faithful performance of the contract. The contract shall require the delivery of said five thousand copies at the Office of the Secretary of State in the city of Austin, on or before the fourth day of July, 1859; and when the same shall have been delivered, the Secretary of State shall certify the fact to the Comptroller, who shall, when he receives such certificate, and also a certificate signed by any two of the judges of the Supreme Court, that the said Digest conforms to the requirements of this Act, shall issue his warrant for the amount due to the contractor according to the terms of his contract with the State, and the Treasurer shall pay the same. The Secretary of State shall immediately thereafter, cause copies of said Digest to be delivered and distributed as the General Laws of the State are now required to be.

SEC. 4. That the sum of twenty thousand dollars, or so much thereof as may be necessary, be and the same is hereby appropriated out of any money not otherwise appropriated, to carry out the provisions of this Act; and that this Act take effect and be in force from and after its passage.

Approved, 15th February, 1858.

PREFACE.

This Digest was compiled and published under the provisions of the Act of the Legislature of the 15th February, A. D., 1858. It includes "all the General Statute Laws of this State down to, and including those passed at the present (last) session of the Legislature."

It also contains "all the Repealed Laws of the Republic and State of Texas, by, through, or under which rights have accrued;" also, "the Colonization Laws of Mexico and of the State of Coahuila and Texas, which were in force before the Declaration of Independence by Texas."

It will be seen that the alphabetical arrangement of the Digest of the late Mr. Hartley, has been preserved as far as possible. The profession has grown familiar with that arrangement, and it was therefore deemed important to observe it in this new Digest. In other respects the plan of Brightly's Digest of the Statutes of the United States has been adopted.

The date of each act, and the time it took effect, is given in the margin, the numbering of the sections is in brackets, and the articles are numbered as in Hartley's Digest.

Under our contract with the State we had but thirteen months in which to prepare and publish the work. We have used every effort not only to comply with our contract in point of time, but to make a Digest acceptable to the profession in Texas. That there are defects in it, we doubt not, but we hope that due allowance will be made for the short period to which its preparation was limited.

The whole work has been prepared, printed and bound in this city, and as such it is submitted to the legal profession.

It will be seen that the act of the Legislature requires that two of the Judges of the Supreme Court shall approve the work. The following letters from Chief Justice Wheeler and Associate Justice Bell, have been furnished in compliance with that provision. The work would also have been submitted to Judge Roberts for his opinion upon it, but his remote residence from Austin (at Tyler) prevented it.

AUSTIN, 1859.

INDEPENDENCE, July 2, 1859.

MESSRS. OLDHAM & WHITE:

Gentlemen—I have before me, in the sheets you sent by the hand of Mr. Searcy, 752 pages of the Digest prepared by you under the provisions of "An Act to provide for a Digest of the Laws of Texas," approved Feb. 15th, 1858.

In so far as I can judge, from the cursory examination I have been enabled to give it, I think you have well performed the work of compiling the Digest, in conformity to the requirements of the statute.

Professing no peculiar qualifications to judge of the mechanical execution of the work, it will not be expected that I should express an opinion upon that part of the work.

Very respectfully, your obedient servant,

R. T. WHEELER.

AUSTIN, June 20, 1859.

MESSRS. OLDHAM & WHITE:

Gentlemen—At your request, I have examined your Digest, prepared by you in pursuance of the provisions of the Act of 15th February, 1858, entitled "An Act to provide for a Digest of the Laws of Texas."

I think it was not the intention of the Legislature to require the Judges of the Supreme Court to certify concerning the mechanical execution of the Digest. On such a subject my own opinion is worth but little, and in any but a very clear case, would be given with much diffidence. I do not hesitate, however, to say, that the mechanical execution of your Digest seems to me to be highly creditable to the State, and in all respects as good as the Legislature could have contemplated. I think no work of the same kind has been published in the United States, with which your Digest will not bear a very favorable comparison.

Your own part of the work is such as the legal profession will expect from you.

I find that you have preserved, as far as practicable, the plan of Hartley's Digest, with which the lawyers of Texas have long been familiar, and you have made many improvements upon Mr. Hartley's very valuable work.

I think your work is a very full compliance with all the requirements of the Act of 15th February, 1858, above referred to, and that it will be received with much applause by the legal profession in Texas.

You are at liberty to use this note as the certificate contemplated by the third section of the Act of 15th February, 1858, so far as my opinion of your work is concerned.

I have the honor, gentlemen, to be, with much respect,

Your obedient servant,
JAMES H. BELL,
Associate Justice, Supreme Court.

THE

CONSTITUTION

OF THE

UNITED STATES OF AMERICA.

Preamble.

We, the People of the United States, in order to form a more perfect union, establish justice, insure domestic tranquility, provide for the common defence, promote the general welfare, and secure the blessings of liberty to ourselves and our posterity, do ordain and establish this Constitution for the United States of America.

ARTICLE I.

Legislative power.

Sect. I. All legislative powers herein granted, shall be vested in a congress of the United States, which shall consist of a senate and house of representatives.

House of representatives.

Sect. II. 1. The house of representatives shall be composed of members chosen every second year by the people of the several states; and the electors in each state shall have the qualifications requisite for electors of the most numerous branch of the state legislature.

Qualification of members.

2. No person shall be a representative who shall not have attained to the age of twenty-five years, and been seven years a citizen of the United States, and who shall not, when elected, be an inhabitant of that state in which he shall be chosen.

Apportionment of representatives and direct taxes. Census.

3. Representatives and direct taxes shall be apportioned among the several states which may be included within this union, according to their respective numbers; which shall be determined by adding to the whole number of free persons, including those bound to service for a term of years, and excluding Indians not taxed, three-fifths of all other persons. The actual enumeration shall be made within three years after the first meeting of the congress of the United States, and within every subsequent term of ten years, in such manner as they shall by law direct. The number of representatives shall not exceed one for every thirty thousand, but each state shall have at least one representative; and until such enumeration shall be made, the state of New Hampshire shall be entitled to choose three, Massachusetts eight, Rhode Island and Providence Plantations one, Connecticut five, New York six, New Jersey four, Pennsylvania eight, Delaware one, Maryland six, Virginia ten, North Carolina five, South Carolina five, and Georgia three.

Number of representatives.

Vacancies.

4. When vacancies happen in the representation from any state, the executive authority thereof shall issue writs of election to fill such vacancies.

Officers. Impeachments.

5. The house of representatives shall choose their speaker and other officers; and shall have the sole power of impeachment.

Senate.

Sect. III. 1. The senate of the United States shall be composed of two senators from each state, chosen by the legislature thereof, for six years; and each senator shall have one vote.

Classification.

2. Immediately after they shall be assembled, in consequence of the first election, they shall be divided, as equally as may be, into three classes. The seats of the senators of the first class shall be vacated at the expiration of the second year, of the second class at the expiration of the fourth year, and of the third class at the expiration of the sixth year, so that one-third may be chosen every second year; and if vacancies happen by resignation, or otherwise, during the recess of

Vacancies.

Art. 1. Sec. 3.

the legislature of any state, the executive thereof may make temporary appointments until the next meeting of the legislature, which shall then fill such vacancies.

Qualifications.

3. No person shall be a senator who shall not have attained to the age of thirty years, and been nine years a citizen of the United States, and who shall not, when elected, be an inhabitant of that state for which he shall be chosen.

President of Senate.

4. The vice president of the United States shall be president of the senate, but shall have no vote, unless they be equally divided.

Officers, and president *pro tem.*

5. The senate shall choose their other officers, and also a president *pro tempore*, in the absence of the vice president, or when he shall exercise the office of president of the United States.

Trial of impeachments.

6. The senate shall have the sole power to try all impeachments. When sitting for that purpose, they shall be on oath or affirmation. When the president of the United States is tried, the chief justice shall preside; and no person shall be convicted without the concurrence of two-thirds of the members present.

Judgment.

7. Judgment in cases of impeachment shall not extend further than to removal from office, and disqualification to hold and enjoy any office of honor, trust or profit, under the United States; but the party convicted shall nevertheless be liable and subject to indictment, trial, judgment and punishment according to law.

Election of members of congress.

SECT. IV. 1. The times, places and manner of holding elections for senators and representatives, shall be prescribed in each state by the legislature thereof; but the congress may at any time by law make or alter such regulations, except as to the places of choosing senators.

To meet annually.

2. The congress shall assemble at least once in every year; and such meeting shall be on the first Monday in December, unless they shall by law appoint a different day.

Powers of each house.

SECT. V. 1. Each house shall be the judge of the elections, returns and qualifications of its own members, and a majority of each shall constitute a quorum to do business; but a smaller number may adjourn from day to day, and may be authorized to compel the attendance of absent members, in such manner, and under such penalties, as each house may provide.

Power to punish and expel.

2. Each house may determine the rules of its proceedings, punish its members for disorderly behavior, and with the concurrence of two-thirds, expel a member.

Journals. Yeas and nays.

3. Each house shall keep a journal of its proceedings, and from time to time publish the same, excepting such parts as may, in their judgment, require secrecy; and the yeas and nays of the members of either house, on any question, shall, at the desire of one-fifth of those present, be entered on the journal.

Adjournments.

4. Neither house, during the session of congress, shall, without the consent of the other, adjourn for more than three days, nor to any other place than that in which the two houses shall be sitting.

Compensation. Privileges.

SECT. VI. 1. The senators and representatives shall receive a compensation for their services, to be ascertained by law, and paid out of the treasury of the United States. They shall, in all cases, except treason, felony and breach of the peace, be privileged from arrest, during their attendance at the session of their respective houses, and in going to, and returning from, the same; and for any speech or debate in either house, they shall not be questioned in any other place.

Exclusion from office.

2. No senator or representative shall, during the time for which he was elected, be appointed to any civil office under the authority of the United States, which shall have been created, or the emoluments whereof shall have been increased, during such time; and no person holding any office under the United States, shall be a member of either house during his continuance in office.

Revenue bills.

SECT. VII. 1. All bills for raising revenue shall originate in the house of representatives; but the senate may propose or concur with amendments as on other bills.

Manner of passing. Veto power.

2. Every bill which shall have passed the house of representatives and the senate, shall, before it become a law, be presented to the president of the United States; if he approve, he shall sign it, but if not, he shall return it, with his objections, to that house in which it shall have originated, who shall enter the objections at large on their journal, and proceed to reconsider it. If, after such reconsideration, two-thirds of that house shall agree to pass the bill, it shall be sent, together with the objections, to the other house, by which it shall likewise be reconsidered, and if approved by two-thirds of that house, it shall become a law. But in all such cases the votes of both houses shall be determined by yeas and nays, and the names of the persons voting for and against the bill shall be entered on the journal of each house respectively. If any bill shall not be returned by the president within ten days, (Sundays excepted,) after it shall have been presented to him, the same shall be a law, in like manner as if he had signed it, unless the congress by their adjournment prevent its return, in which case it shall not be a law.

Joint orders, resolutions, &c.

3. Every order, resolution or vote, to which the concurrence of the senate and house of representatives may be necessary, (except on a question of adjournment,) shall be presented to the president of the United States: and before the same shall take effect, shall be approved by him, or being disapproved by him, shall be re-passed by two-thirds of the senate and house of representatives, according to the rules and limitations prescribed in the case of a bill.

General powers.

SECT. VIII. 1. The congress shall have power,

Taxation.

2. To lay and collect taxes, duties, imposts and excises, to pay the debts, and provide for the common defence and general welfare of the United States; but all duties, imposts and excises shall be uniform throughout the United States:

Loans.

3. To borrow money on the credit of the United States:

Commerce.

4. To regulate commerce with foreign nations, and among the several states, and with the Indian tribes:

Naturalization. Bankruptcy.

5. To establish an uniform rule of naturalization; and uniform laws on the subject of bankruptcies throughout the United States:

Weights, Coin, &c.

6. To coin money, regulate the value thereof, and of foreign coin; and fix the standard of weights and measures:

Counterfeiting.

7. To provide for the punishment of counterfeiting the securities and current coin of the United States:

Post offices

8. To establish post offices and post roads:

Patents and copyrights.

9. To promote the progress of science and useful arts, by securing for limited times, to authors and inventors, the exclusive right to their respective writings and discoveries:

Courts.

10. To constitute tribunals inferior to the supreme court:

Piracies, &c.

11. To define and punish piracies and felonies committed on the high seas, and offences against the law of nations:

War.

12. To declare war, grant letters of marque and reprisal, and make rules concerning captures on land and water:

Army.

13. To raise and support armies; but no appropriation of money to that use shall be for a longer term than two years:

Navy.

14. To provide and maintain a navy:

15. To make rules for the government and regulation of the land and naval forces:

Militia.

16. To provide for calling forth the militia to execute the laws of the Union, suppress insurrections and repel invasions:

17. To provide for organizing, arming, and disciplining the militia, and for governing such part of them as may be employed in the service of the United States, reserving to the states respectively, the appointment of the officers, and the authority of training the militia according to the discipline prescribed by congress:

Exclusive legislation.

18. To exercise exclusive legislation, in all cases whatsoever, over such district (not exceeding ten miles square) as may by cession of particular states, and the acceptance of congress, become the seat of the government of the United States; and to exercise like authority over all places purchased by the consent of the legislature of the state in which the same shall be, for the erection of forts, magazines, arsenals, dock-yards and other needful buildings: And,

Laws for carrying out vested powers.

19. To make all laws which shall be necessary and proper for carrying into execution the foregoing powers, and all other powers vested by this constitution in the government of the United States, or in any department or officer thereof.

Slave trade.

SECT. IX. 1. The migration or importation of such persons as any of the states now existing shall think proper to admit, shall not be prohibited by the congress prior to the year one thousand eight hundred and eight; but a tax or duty may be imposed on such importation, not exceeding ten dollars for each person.

Habeas corpus.

2. The privilege of the writ of *habeas corpus* shall not be suspended, unless when in cases of rebellion or invasion the public safety may require it.

Ex post facto laws.

3. No bill of attainder or *ex post facto* law shall be passed.

Direct taxes.

4. No capitation, or other direct tax, shall be laid, unless in proportion to the *census* or enumeration herein before directed to be taken.

State exports. Port duties.

5. No tax or duty shall be laid on articles exported from any state. No preference shall be given by any regulation of commerce or revenue to the ports of one state over those of another; nor shall vessels bound to, or from, one state be obliged to enter, clear or pay duties in another.

Receipts and expenditures.

6. No money shall be drawn from the treasury, but in consequence of appropriations made by law; and a regular statement and account of the receipts and expenditures of all public money shall be published from time to time.

Title and receipt of

7. No title of nobility shall be granted by the United States; and no person holding any office of profit or trust under them, shall, without the consent of the

Presents prohibited. congress, accept of any present, emolument, office or title of any kind whatever, from any king, prince or foreign state.

Limitation of the powers of the states. SECT. X. 1. No state shall enter into any treaty, alliance or confederation; grant letters of marque and reprisal; coin money; emit bills of credit; make anything but gold and silver coin a tender in payment of debts; pass any bill of attainder, *ex post facto* law, or law impairing the obligation of contracts, or grant any title of nobility.

Imposts. 2. No state shall, without the consent of the congress, lay any imposts or duties on imports or exports, except what may be absolutely necessary for executing its inspection laws; and the net produce of all duties and imposts, laid by any state on imports or exports, shall be for the use of the treasury of the United States; and all such laws shall be subject to the revision and control of the congress. No state shall, without the consent of congress, lay any duty of tonnage, keep troops or ships of war, in time of peace, enter into any agreement or compact with another state, or with a foreign power, or engage in war, unless actually invaded, or in such imminent danger as will not admit of delay.

Tonnage duties. Troops and ships of war. Compacts. War.

ARTICLE II.

President. SECT. I. 1. The executive power shall be vested in a president of the United States of America. He shall hold his office during the term of four years, and together with the vice president, chosen for the same term, be elected as follows:

Term of office.

Mode of election. 2. Each state shall appoint, in such manner as the legislature thereof may direct, a number of electors equal to the whole number of senators and representatives to which the state may be entitled in the congress; but no senator or representative, or person holding an office of trust or profit under the United States, shall be appointed an elector.

3. [The electors shall meet in their respective states, and vote by ballot for two persons, of whom one at least shall not be an inhabitant of the same state with themselves. And they shall make a list of all the persons voted for, and of the number of votes for each; which list they shall sign and certify, and transmit sealed to the seat of the government of the United States, directed to the president of the senate. The president of the senate shall, in the presence of the senate and house of representatives, open all the certificates, and the votes shall then be counted. The person having the greatest number of votes shall be the president, if such number be a majority of the whole number of electors appointed; and if there be more than one who have such majority, and have an equal number of votes, then the house of representatives shall immediately choose by ballot one of them for president; and if no person have a majority, then from the five highest on the list the said house shall in like manner choose the president. But in choosing the president, the votes shall be taken by states, the representation from each state having one vote; a quorum for this purpose shall consist of a member or members from two-thirds of the states, and a majority of all the states shall be necessary to a choice. In every case, after the choice of the president, the person having the greatest number of votes of the electors shall be the vice president. But if there should remain two or more who have equal votes, the senate shall choose from them by ballot the vice president.]

Time of election. 4. The congress may determine the time of choosing the electors, and the day on which they shall give their votes; which day shall be the same throughout the United States.

Qualifications of the president. 5. No person except a natural born citizen, or a citizen of the United States at the time of the adoption of this constitution, shall be eligible to the office of president; neither shall any person be eligible to that office who shall not have attained to the age of thirty-five years, and been fourteen years a resident within the United States.

Vacancy, how supplied. 6. In case of the removal of the president from office, or of his death, resignation or inability to discharge the powers and duties of the said office, the same shall devolve on the vice president, and the congress may by law provide for the case of removal, death, resignation, or inability, both of the president and vice president, declaring what officer shall then act as president, and such officer shall act accordingly until the disability be removed, or a president shall be elected.

His compensation. 7. The president shall, at stated times, receive for his services a compensation, which shall neither be increased nor diminished during the period for which he shall have been elected, and he shall not receive within that period any other emolument from the United States, or any of them.

Oath of office. 8. Before he enter on the execution of his office, he shall take the following oath or affirmation:

"I do solemnly swear, (or affirm,) that I will faithfully execute the office of president of the United States, and will, to the best of my ability, preserve, protect and defend the constitution of the United States."

Powers and duties.

SECT. II. 1. The president shall be commander-in-chief of the army and navy of the United States, and of the militia of the several states, when called into the actual service of the United States; he may require the opinion, in writing, of the principal officer in each of the executive departments, upon any subject relating to the duties of their respective offices, and he shall have power to grant reprieves and pardons for offences against the United States, except in cases of impeachment.

Treaties. Appointing power.

2. He shall have power, by and with the advice and consent of the senate, to make treaties, provided two-thirds of the senators present concur; and he shall nominate, and by and with the advice and consent of the senate, shall appoint ambassadors, other public ministers and cousuls, judges of the supreme court, and all other officers of the United States, whose appointments are not herein otherwise provided for, and which shall be established by law. But the Congress may by law vest the appointment of such inferior officers, as they think proper, in the president alone, in the courts of law, or in the heads of departments.

Power to fill vacancies.

3. The president shall have power to fill up all vacancies that may happen during the recess of the Senate, by granting commissions which shall expire at the end of their next session.

Further powers.

SECT. III. He shall, from time to time, give to the congress information of the state of the Union, and recommend to their consideration such measures as he shall judge necessary and expedient. He may, on extraordinary occasions, convene both houses, or either of them; and in case of disagreement between them, with respect to the time of adjournment, he may adjourn them to such time as he shall think proper. He shall receive ambassadors and other public ministers. He shall take care that the laws be faithfully executed: and shall commission all the officers of the United States.

Impeachments.

SECT. IV. The president, vice president, and all civil officers of the United States, shall be removed from office on impeachment for, and conviction of, treason, bribery, or other high crimes and misdemeanors.

ARTICLE III.

Judiciary. Tenure and compensation.

SECT. I. The judicial power of the United States shall be vested in one supreme court, and in such inferior courts as the congress may, from time to time, ordain and establish. The judges, both of the supreme and inferior courts, shall hold their offices during good behavior: and shall, at stated times, receive for their services, a compensation, which shall not be diminished during their continuance in office.

Judicial powers.

SECT. II. 1. The judicial power shall extend to all cases, in law and equity, arising under this Constitution, the laws of the United States, and treatises made, or which shall be made under their authority; to all cases affecting ambassadors, other public ministers, and consuls; to all cases of admiralty and maritime jurisdiction; to controversies to which the United States shall be a party; to controversies between two or more states; between a state and citizens of another state; between citizens of different states; between citizens of the same state claiming lands under grants of different states, and between a state, or the citizens thereof, and foreign states, citizens or subjects.

Jurisdiction of the supreme court.

2. In all cases affecting ambassadors, other public ministers and consuls, and those in which a state shall be party, the supreme court shall have original jurisdiction. In all the other cases before mentioned, the supreme court shall have appellate jurisdiction, both as to law and fact, with such exceptions and under such regulations as the congress shall make.

Trial for crimes.

3. The trial of all crimes, except in cases of impeachment, shall be by jury; and such trial shall be held in the state where the said crimes shall have been committed; but when not committed within any state, the trial shall be at such place or places as the congress may by law have directed.

Treason. Witnesses

SECT. III. 1. Treason against the United States shall consist only in levying war against them, or in adhering to their enemies, giving them aid and comfort. No person shall be convicted of treason unless on the testimony of two witnesses to the same overt act, or on confession in open court.

Punishment.

2. The congress shall have power to declare the punishment of treason, but no attainder of treason shall work corruption of blood, or forfeitute, except during the life of the person attainted.

ARTICLE IV.

SECT. I. Full faith and credit shall be given in each state to the public acts,

Art. 4. Sec. 2.

State records, &c. records, and judicial proceedings of every other state. And the congress may, by general laws, prescribe the manner in which such acts, records and proceedings shall be proved, and the effect thereof.

Privileges of citizens. SECT. II. 1. The citizens of each state shall be entitled to all privileges and immunities of citizens in the several states.

Fugitives from justice. 2. A person charged in any state with treason, felony or other crime, who shall flee from justice, and be found in another state, shall, on demand of the executive authority of the state from which he fled, be delivered up, to be removed to the state having jurisdiction of the crime.

Fugitives from labor. 3. No person held to service or labor in one state, under the laws thereof, escaping into another, shall, in consequence of any law or regulation therein, be discharged from such service or labor, but shall be delivered up on claim of the party to whom such service or labor may be due.

New States. SECT. III. 1. New states may be admitted by the congress into this Union: but no new state shall be formed or erected within the jurisdiction of any other state; nor any state be formed by the junction of two or more states, or parts of states, without the consent of the legislatures of the states concerned, as well as of the congress.

Territories. 2. The congress shall have power to dispose of and make all needful rules and regulations respecting the territory or other property belonging to the United States; and nothing in this constitution shall be so construed as to prejudice any claims of the United States, or of any particular state.

Republican form of government, &c., guarantied SECT. IV. The United States shall guarantee to every state in this Union a republican form of Government, and shall protect each of them against invasion; and on application of the legislature, or of the executive, (when the legislature cannot be convened,) against domestic violence.

ARTICLE V.

Amendments. The congress, whenever two-thirds of both houses shall deem it necessary, shall propose amendments to this constitution, or, on the application of the legislatures of two-thirds of the several states, shall call a convention for proposing amendments, which, in either case, shall be valid to all intents and purposes, as part of this constitution, when ratified by the legislatures of three-fourths of the several states, or by conventions in three-fourths thereof, as the one or the other mode of ratification may be proposed by the congress; provided, that no amendment, which may be made prior to the year one thousand eight hundred and eight, shall in any manner affect the first and fourth clauses in the ninth section of the first article; and that no state, without its consent, shall be deprived of its equal suffrage in the senate.

ARTICLE VI.

Debts. 1. All debts contracted, and engagements entered into, before the adoption of this constitution, shall be as valid against the United States, under this constitution, as under the confederation.

Supreme law of the land. 2. This constitution, and the laws of the United States, which shall be made in pursuance thereof, and all treaties made, or which shall be made, under the authority of the United States, shall be the supreme law of the land; and the judges in every state shall be bound thereby, any thing in the constitution or laws of any state to the contrary notwithstanding.

Oaths of office. No religious test. 3. The senators and representatives before mentioned, and the members of the several state legislatures, and all executive and judicial officers, both of the United States and of the several states, shall be bound, by oath or affirmation, to support this constitution; but no religious test shall ever be required as a qualification to any office or public trust under the United States.

ARTICLE VII.

Ratification The ratification of the conventions of nine states shall be sufficient for the establishment of this constitution between the states so ratifying the same.

Done in convention, by the unanimous consent of the states present, the seventeenth day of September, in the year of our Lord one thousand seven hundred and eighty-seven, and of the Independance of the United States of America the twelfth. In witness whereof, we have hereunto subscribed our names.

GEORGE WASHINGTON, *President*,
And deputy from Virginia.

New Hampshire.
John Langdon,
Nicholas Gilman.

Connecticut
William Samuel Johnson,
Roger Sherman.

Massachusetts.
Nathaniel Gorham,
Rufus King.
New Jersey.
William Livingston,
David Brearly,
William Patterson,
Jonathan Dayton.
Pennsylvania.
Benjamin Franklin,
Thomas Mifflin,
Pennsylvania.
Robert Morris,
George Clymer,
Thomas Fitzsimons,
Jared Ingersoll,
James Wilson,
Gouverneur Morris.
Delaware.
George Read,
Gunning Bedford, jun.,
John Dickinson,
Richard Bassett,
Jacob Broom.

New York.
Alexander Hamilton.

Maryland.
James McHenry,
Daniel of St. Thomas Jenifer,
Daniel Carroll.

Virginia.
John Blair,
James Madison, jun.
North Carolina.
William Blount,
Richard Dobbs Spaight,
Hugh Williamson.
South Carolina.
John Rutledge,
Charles Cotesworth Pinckney,
Charles Pinckney,
Pierce Butler.
Georgia.
William Few,
Abraham Baldwin.

Attest: William Jackson, Secretary.

AMENDMENTS TO THE CONSTITUTION.

ART. I. Congress shall make no law respecting an establishment of religion, or prohibiting the free exercise thereof; or abridging the freedom of speech, or of the press; or the right of the people peaceably to assemble, and to petition the government for a redress of grievances. Freedom of religion, of speech, of the press, and right of petition.

ART. II. A well regulated militia being necessary to the security of a free state, the right of the people to keep and bear arms shall not be infringed. Right to bear arms.

ART. III. No soldier shall, in time of peace, be quartered in any house without the consent of the owner; nor in time of war, but in a manner to be prescribed by law. Quartering of troops.

ART. IV. The right of the people to be secure in their persons, houses, papers, and effects, against unreasonable searches and seizures, shall not be violated; and no warrants shall issue, but upon probable cause, supported by oath or affirmation, and particularly describing the place to be searched, and the persons or things to be seized. Searches and seizures. Warrants

ART. V. No person shall be held to answer for a capital or otherwise infamous crime, unless on a presentment or indictment of a grand jury, except in cases arising in the land or naval forces, or in the militia, when in actual service, in time of war or public danger; nor shall any person be subject for the same offence to be twice put in jeopardy of life or limb; nor shall be compelled, in any criminal case, to be witness against himself; nor be deprived of life, liberty or property, without due process of law; nor shall private property be taken for public use without just compensation. Trials for crimes. Rights of property.

ART. VI. In all criminal prosecutions, the accused shall enjoy the right to a speedy and public trial, by an impartial jury of the state and district wherein the crime shall have been committed, which district shall have been previously ascertained by law, and to be informed of the nature and cause of the accusation; to be confronted with the witnesses against him; to have compulsory process for obtaining witnesses in his favor; and to have the assistance of counsel for his defence. Rights of defendants in criminal cases.

ART. VII. In suits at common law, where the value in controversy shall exceed twenty dollars, the right of trial by jury shall be preserved; and no fact tried by a jury shall be otherwise re-examined in any court of the United States than according to the rules of the common law. Trials in civil cases.

ART. VIII. Excessive bail shall not be required, nor excessive fines imposed, nor cruel and unusual punishments inflicted. Bail, fines, &c.

ART. IX. The enumeration in the constitution of certain rights, shall not be construed to deny or disparage others retained by the people. Reserved rights.

ART. X. The powers not delegated to the United States by the constitution, nor prohibited by it to the states, are reserved to the states respectively or to the people. Powers not delegated, reserved.

Limitation of judicial power.

ART. XI. The judicial power of the United States shall not be construed to extend to any suit in law or equity commenced or prosecuted against one of the United States, by citizens of another state, or by citizens or subjects of any foreign state.

Election of president and vice president.

ART. XII. 1. The electors shall meet in their respective states, and vote by ballot for president and vice president, one of whom, at least, shall not be an inhabitant of the same state with themselves; they shall name in their ballots the person voted for as president, and in distinct ballots the person voted for as vice president; and they shall make distinct lists of all persons voted for as president, and of all persons voted for as vice president, and of the number of votes for each, which list they shall sign and certify, and transmit sealed to he seat of the government of the United States, directed to the president of the senate; the president of the senate shall, in the presence of the senate and house of representatives, open all the certificates, and the votes shall then be counted; the person having the greatest number of votes for president shall be the president, if such number be a majority of the whole number of electors appointed; and if no person have such majority, then from the persons having the highest numbers, not exceeding three, on the list of those voted for as president, the house of representatives shall choose immediately by ballot the president. But in choosing the president, the votes shall be taken by states, the representation from each state having one vote; a quorum for this purpose shall consist of a member or members from two-thirds of the states, and a majority of all the states shall be necessary to a choice. And if the house of representatives shall not choose a president whenever the right of choice shall devolve upon them, before the fourth day of March next following, then the vice president shall act as president, as in the case of the death or other constitutional disability of the president.

2. The person having the greatest number of votes as vice president shall be the vice president, if such number be a majority of the whole number of electors appointed; and if no person have a majority, then from the two highest numbers on the list the senate shall choose the vice president: a quorum for the purpose shall consist of two-thirds of the whole number of senators, and a majority of the whole number shall be necessary to a choice.

3. But no person constitutionally ineligible to the office of president shall be eligible to that of vice president of the United States.

ARTICLES OF ANNEXATION.[a]

JOINT RESOLUTION

(OF THE CONGRESS OF THE UNITED STATES)

FOR ANNEXING TEXAS TO THE UNITED STATES.

Consent of Congress given to annexation of Texas as a State.

RESOLVED, by the Senate and House of Representatives of the United States of America in Congress assembled, That Congress doth consent that the territory properly included within, and rightly belonging to the Republic of Texas, may be erected into a new State, to be called the State of Texas, with a republican form of government, to be adopted by the people of said republic, by deputies in convention assembled, with the consent of the existing government, in order that the same may be admitted as one of the States of this Union.

Conditions and guarantees.

Boundaries to be adjusted by United States.

State constitution to be adopted and presented.

What to be ceded to the United States.

State Constitution, Art. 13, Sec. 8.

What to be retained.

Public debt of Texas not to become a charge upon the United States.

New States may be formed out of Texas territory

2. And be it further resolved, That the foregoing consent of Congress is given upon the following conditions, and with the following guarantees, to wit: *First.* Said State to be formed, subject to the adjustment by this government of all questions of boundary that may arise with other governments; and the constitution thereof, with the proper evidence of its adoption by the people of said Republic of Texas, shall be transmitted to the President of the United States, to be laid before Congress for its final action, on or before the first day of January, one thousand eight hundred and forty-six. *Second.* Said State, when admitted into the Union, after ceding to the United States, all public edifices, fortifications, barracks, ports and harbours, navy and navy-yards, docks, magazines, arms, armaments, and all other property and means pertaining to the public defence belonging to the said Republic of Texas, shall retain all the public funds, debts, taxes, and dues of every kind, which may belong to or be due and owing said Republic; and shall also retain all the vacant and unappropriated lands lying within its limits, to be applied to the payment of the debts and liabilities of said Republic of Texas, and the residue of said lands, after discharging said debts and liabilities, to be disposed of as said State may direct; but in no event are said debts and liabilities to become a charge upon the government of the United States. *Third.* New States, of convenient size, not exceeding four in number, in addition to said state of Texas, and having sufficient population, may hereafter, by the consent of said State, be formed out of the territory thereof, which shall be entitled to admission under the provisions of the Federal Constitution. And such States as may be formed out of that portion of said territory lying south of thirty-six degrees thirty minutes north latitude, commonly known as the Missouri Compromise Line, shall be admitted into the Union, with or without slavery, as the people of each State asking admission may desire. And in such State or States as shall be formed out of said territory north of said Missouri Compromise Line, slavery, or involuntary servitude, (except for crime,) shall be prohibited.

Alternative of negotiation left to the President of United States.

3. And be it further resolved, That if the President of the United States shall, in his judgment and discretion, deem it most advisable, instead of proceeding to submit the foregoing resolution to the Republic of Texas, as an overture on the part of the United States for admission, to negotiate with that Republic; then,

(a) Until the organization of the State Government, the 16th February, 1846, neither the Constitution nor laws of the United States were in force in the limits of Texas. The revenue laws of the Republic continued in force until that date. Cocke *v* Calkin & Co., 1 Tex. Rep. 542. The State *v* Williams Ext., 8 Tex. Rep. 384. The State of Texas was admitted into the Union on the 29th December, 1845, and from that day the laws of the United States were extended over it. Consequently, on the 30th of January, 1846, the revenue laws of Texas were not in force there. Calkin & Co., *v* Cocke. 14 Howard's Rep.

Terms upon which Texas shall be admitted as a State.

Be it resolved, that a State, to be formed out of the present Republic of Texas, with suitable extent and boundaries, and with two Representatives in Congress, until the next apportionment of representation, shall be admitted into the Unior, by virtue of this act, on an equal footing with the existing States, as soon as the terms and conditions of such admission, and the cession of the remaining Texian territory to the United States shall be agreed upon by the governments of Texas and the United States: And that the sum of one hundred thousand dollars be, and the same is hereby, appropriated to defray the expenses of missions and negotiations, to agree upon the terms of said admission and cession, either by treaty to be submitted to the Senate, or by articles to be submitted to the two Houses of Congress, as the President may direct.

Appropriation for expenses of negotiation.

Approved, March 1, 1845.

JOINT RESOLUTION.

(OF THE CONGRESS OF THE REPUBLIC OF TEXAS),

GIVING THE CONSENT OF THE EXISTING GOVERNMENT TO THE ANNEXATION OF TEXAS TO THE UNITED STATES.

Preamble.

WHEREAS, the Government of the United States hath proposed the following terms, guarantees and conditions, on which the people and territory of the Republic of Texas may be erected into a new State, to be called the State of Texas, and admitted as one of the States of the American Union, to wit:

[Here follow the first and second Sections of the resolution of the Congress of the United States, see page 9.]

And whereas, by said terms, the consent of the existing government of Texas is required—Therefore,

Consent of Texas given to annexation as a State.

Be it resolved by the Senate and House of Representatives of the Republic of Texas in Congress assembled, That the Government of Texas doth consent, that the people and territory of the Republic of Texas may be erected into a new State, to be called the State of Texas, with a republican form of government, to be adopted by the people of said Republic, by deputies in convention assembled, in order that the same may be admitted as one of the States of the American Union; and said consent is given on the terms, guarantees and conditions set forth in the preamble to this joint resolution.

Consent to President's proclamation calling convention, and election of deputies thereto.

SECT. 2. Be it further resolved, That the proclamation of the President of the Republic of Texas, bearing date May fifth, eighteen hundred and forty-five, and the election of deputies to sit in convention at Austin, on the fourth day of July next, for the adoption of a Constitution for the State of Texas, had in accordance therewith, hereby receives the consent of the existing Government of Texas.

President to furnish American Minister, and convention, with copy of this joint resolution.

SECT. 3. Be it further resolved, That the President of Texas is hereby requested immediately to furnish the Government of the United States, through their accredited minister near the Government, with a copy of this joint resolution; also to furnish the Convention to assemble at Austin, on the fourth of July next, a copy of the same. And the same shall take effect from and after its passage.

Approved, June 23, 1845.

IN CONVENTION OF THE PEOPLE OF THE REPUBLIC OF TEXAS. JULY 4, 1845

AN ORDINANCE.

Preamble reciting the official action of Congress and President of the U. S. and of the Pres't and Congress of Texas in regard to annexation.

WHEREAS, the Congress of the United States of America has passed resolutions providing for the annexation of Texas to that Union, which resolutions were approved by the President of the United States on the first day of March, one thousand eight hundred and forty-five; and whereas the President of the United States has submitted to Texas the first and second sections of the said resolution as the basis upon which Texas may be admitted as one of the States of the said Union; and whereas the existing government of the Republic of Texas has assented to the proposals thus made, the terms and conditions of which are as follows:

[Here follow the first and second Sections of the resolution of the Congress of the United States, see page 9.]

Now, in order to manifest the assent of the people of this Republic as required in the above-recited portions of the said resolutions; We, the deputies of the people of Texas in Convention assembled, in their name, and by their authority, do ordain and declare, that we assent to, and accept the proposals, conditions, and guarantees contained in the first and second sections of the resolution of the Congress of the United States aforesaid.

Done at the City of Austin, Republic of Texas, July 4th, 1845.

THO. J. RUSK, *President.*

Phil. M. Cuny, H. G. Runnels, Robert M. Forbes, Sam. Lusk, Jno. Caldwell. Jose Antonio Navarro, Geo. Wm. Brown, Gustavus A. Everts, Lemuel Dale Evans, J. B. Miller, R. E. B. Baylor, J. S. Mayfield, R. Bache, James Love, Wm. L. Hunter, John D. Anderson, Isaac Parker, P. O. Lumpkin, Francis Moore, Jr., Isaac W. Brashear, Alexander M'Gowan, Isaac Van Zandt, S. Holland, Edward Clark, Geo. W. Smyth, James Armstrong, John M. Lewis, James Scott, Archibald M'Neill, A. C. Horton, Israel Standefer, Jos. L. Hogg, Chas. S. Taylor, David Gage, Henry J. Jewett, Cavitt Armstrong, James Power, Albert H. Latimer, Wm. C. Young, J. Pinckney Henderson, Nicholas H. Darnell, Emery Rains, A. W. O. Hicks, James M. Burroughs, H. L. Kinney, William L. Cazneau, A. S. Cunningham, Abner S. Lipscomb, John Hemphill, Van R. Irion, Volney E. Howard, E. H. Tarrant, Francis M. White, James Davis, George T. Wood, G. W. Wright, H. R. Latimer, W. B. Ochiltree, Oliver Jones, B. C. Bagby, Chs. Bellinger Stewart.

Attest.

JAS. H. RAYMOND,
Secretary of the Convention.

JOINT RESOLUTION

(OF THE CONGRESS OF THE UNITED STATES, DECEMBER 29, 1845,)

FOR THE ADMISSION OF THE STATE OF TEXAS INTO THE UNION.

Preamble. WHEREAS the Congress of the United States, by a joint resolution approved March the first, eighteen hundred and forty-five, did consent that the territory properly included within, and rightfully belonging to, the Republic of Texas, might be erected into a new State, to be called the State of Texas, with a republican form of government, to be adopted by the people of said Republic, by deputies in convention assembled, with the consent of the existing government, in order that the same might be admitted as one of the States of the Union; which consent of Congress was given upon certain conditions specified in the first and second sections of said joint resolution; and whereas the people of the said Republic of Texas, by deputies in convention assembled, with the consent of the existing government, did adopt a constitution, and erect a new State with a republican form of government, and, in the name of the people of Texas, and by their authority, did ordain and declare that they assented to, and accepted the proposals, conditions, and guarantees contained in said first and second sections of said resolution: and whereas the said constitution, with the proper evidence of its adoption by the people of the Republic of Texas, has been transmitted to the President of the United States and laid before Congress, in conformity to the provisions of said joint resolution: therefore,

Texas admitted into the Union. Resolved, by the Senate and House of Representatives of the United States of America, in Congress assembled, That the State of Texas shall be one, and is hereby declared to be one, of the United States of America, and admitted into the Union on an equal footing with the original States in all respects whatever.

To be entitled to two Representatives. SECT. 2. And be it further resolved, That until the Representatives in Congress shall be apportioned according to an actual enumeration of the inhabitants of the United States, the State of Texas shall be entitled to choose two Representatives.

CONSTITUTION

OF

THE STATE OF TEXAS.

WE, THE PEOPLE OF THE REPUBLIC OF TEXAS, acknowledging with gratitude the grace of God, in permitting us to make [a] choice of our form of government, do in accordance with the provisions of the Joint Resolutions for annexing Texas to the United States, approved March 1st, one thousand eight hundred and forty-five, ordain and establish this Constitution. Preamble.

ARTICLE I. BILL OF RIGHTS.

That the general, great, and essential principles of Liberty and Free Government may be recognized and established we declare that— Object of Bill of Rights.

SECT. 1. All political power is inherent in the people, and all free governments are founded on their authority, and instituded for their benefit; and they have at all times the unalienable right to alter, reform, or abolish their form of government, in such manner as they may think expedient. Political power.

SECT. 2. All freemen, when they form a social compact, have equal rights; and no man, or set of men, is entitled to exclusive separate public emoluments or privileges, but in consideration of public services. Equal rights asserted—exclusive privileges denied.

SECT. 3. No religous test shall ever be required as a qualification to any office or public trust in this State. No religious test.

SECT. 4. All men have a natural and indefeasible right to worship God according to the dictates of their own consciences: no man shall be compelled to attend, erect, or support any place of worship, or to maintain any ministry against his consent: no human authority ought, in any case whatever, to control or interfere with the rights of conscience in matters of religion; and no preference shall ever be given by law to any religious societies or mode of worship. But it shall be the duty of the Legislature to pass such laws as [may] shall be necessary to protect every religious denomination in the peaceable enjoyment of their own mode of public worship. Religious liberty and toleration.

SECT. 5. Every citizen shall be at liberty to speak, write, or publish his opinions on any subject, being responsible for the abuse of that privilege: and no law shall ever be passed curtailing the liberty of speech or of the press. Liberty of speech and of the press

SECT. 6. In prosecutions for the publication of papers investigating the official conduct of officers, or men, in a public capacity, or when the matter published is proper for public information, the truth thereof may be given in evidence. And in all indictments for libels, the jury shall have the right to determine the law and the facts, under the direction of the court, as in other cases. Evidence in prosecution for libel. Rights of jury in trial for libel.

SECT. 7. The people shall be secure in their [persons] houses, papers, and possessions from all unreasonable seizures or sea[r]ches; and no warrant to search any place or to seize any person or thing, shall issue, without describing them as near as may be, nor without probable cause supported by oath or affirmation. Protection against searches & seizures.

Rights of accused persons. SECT. 8. In all criminal prosecutions, the accused shall have a speedy public trial, by an impartial jury: he shall not be compelled to give evidence against himself; he shall have the right of being heard by himself or counsel, or both; shall be confronted with the witnesses against him, and shall have compulsory process for obtaining witnesses in his favour: and no person shall be holden to answer for any criminal charge, but on indictment or information (*a*) except in cases arising in the land or naval forces, or offences against the laws regulating the militia

Bail in certain cases. SECT. 9. All prisoners shall be bailable by sufficient sureties, unless for capital offences, when the proof is evident or the presumption great; but this provision shall not be so construed as to prohibit bail after indictment found, upon an examination of the evidence by a Judge of the Supreme or District Court, upon the return of the [a] writ of *habeas corpus*, returnable in the county where the offence is committed.

Writ of habeas corpus. SECT. 10. The privileges of the writ of *habeas corpus* shall not be suspended, except when in case of rebellion or invasion the public safety may require it.

Excessive bail, fines, & punishments forbid. Open Court. SECT. 11. Excessive bail shall not be required, nor excessive fines imposed, nor cruel or unusual punishment inflicted. All courts shall be open, and every person, for an injury done him in his lands, goods, person, or reputation, shall have remedy by due course of law.

No trial after acquital Trial by jury inviolate SECT. 12. No person, for the same offence, shall be twice put in jeopardy of life or limb, nor shall a person be again put upon trial for the same offence after a verdict of not guilty;(*b*) and the right of trial by jury shall remain inviolate.

Right to bear arms. SECT. 13. Every citizen shall have the right to keep and bear arms, in the lawful defence of himself or the State.

Bill of attainder, contracts, &c. Property for public use. SECT. 14. No bill of attainder, ex post facto law, retroactive law, or any law impairing the obligation of contracts,(*c*) shall be made, and no person's property shall be taken or applied to public use, without adequate compensation being made, unless by the consent of such person.

Imprison-m't for debt SECT. 15. No person shall ever be imprisoned for debt.

Trial by law in all cases. SECT. 16. No citizen of this State shall be deprived of life, liberty, property, or privileges, outlawed, exiled, or in any manner disfranchised, except by due course of the law of the land.

Military authority. SECT. 17. The military shall at all times be subordinate to the civil authority.

Perpetuities, monopolies, primogeniture, &c. SECT. 18. Perpetuities and monopolies are contrary to the genius of a free government, and shall never be allowed: nor shall the law of primogeniture or entailments ever be in force in this State.

Right of assembling and of petition. SECT. 19. The citizens shall have the right, in a peaceable manner, to assemble together for their common good, and to apply to those invested with the power[s] of government for redress of grievances, or other purposes, by petition, address, or remonstrance.

Suspension of laws. SECT. 20. No power of suspending laws in this State shall be exercised, except by the Legislature, or its authority.

The rights shall be excepted out of the general powers of gov't. SECT. 21. To guard against transgressions of the high powers herein delegated, we declare that everything in this "Bill of Rights" is excepted out of the general powers of government, and shall for ever remain inviolate, and all laws contrary thereto, or to the following provisions, shall be void.

ARTICLE II. DIVISION OF THE POWERS OF GOVERNMENT.

Departm'ts of govern- SECT. 1. The powers of the Government of the State of Texas shall be divided into three distinct departments, and each of them be confided to a separate body

(*a*) The word information implies no particular form; it requires nothing more than that the accused shall be informed therein of the nature of the offence of which he is charged and put on his trial. Clepper *v.* the State, 4 Tex. Rep., 242. The terms, "indictment or information," are not synonymous or convertible words. Ibid.

(*b*) A verdict of not guilty puts a final termination to a criminal prosecution. No new trial or appeal can be had after. State *v.* Burns, 3 Tex. Rep. 118.

(*c*) Laws affecting the remedy are not generally within the scope of retrospective laws, or laws impairing the obligation of contracts; but they may become so by impairing or destroying a right. Paschal *v.* Perez, 7 Tex. Rep. 348. DeCordova *v.* City of Galveston, 4 Tex. Rep. 470. Sutherland *v.* DeLeon, 1 Tex. Rep. 250. A bankrupt law of a state, which discharges the person of the debtor and his future acquisitions, is not a law impairing the obligation of contracts, so far as it respects debts contracted subsequent to the passage of such law. Beers & Smith *v.* Rhea, 5 Tex. Rep. 349. See also Alley *v.* Denson, 8 Tex. Rep. 297.

of magistracy—to-wit: those which are Legislative to one, those which are Executive to another, and those which are Judicial to another; and no person, or collection of persons, being of one of those departments, shall exercise any power, properly attached to either of the others, except in the instances herein expressly permitted. ment defined

ARTICLE III. LEGISLATIVE DEPARTMENT.

SECT. 1. Every free male person who shall have attained the age of twenty-one years, and who shall be a citizen of the United States, or who is at the time of the adoption of this Constitution by the Congress of the United States, a citizen of the Republic of Texas, and shall have resided in this State one year next preceding an election, and the last six months within the district, county, city or town, in which he offers to vote (Indians not taxed, Africans and descendants of Africans excepted), shall be deemed a qualified elector: and should such qualified elector happen to be in any other county, situated in the district in which he resides, at the time of an election, he shall be permitted to vote for any district officer, provided that the qualified electors shall be permitted to vote anywhere in the State for State officers, and provided further that no soldier, seaman, or marine in the Army or Navy of the United States, shall be entitled to vote at any election created by this Constitution. Qualifications of electors. Where votes may be cast.

SECT. 2. All free male persons over the age of twenty-one years (Indians not taxed, Africans and descendants of Africans excepted), who shall have resided six months in Texas, immediately preceding the acceptance of this Constitution by the Congress of the United States shall be deemed qualified electors. Qualified electors.

SECT. 3. Electors in all cases shall be privileged from arrest during their attendance at elections, and in going to and returning from the same, except in cases of treason, felony, or breach of the peace. Privileges of electors.

SECT. 4. The Legislative powers of this State shall be vested in two distinct branches; the one to be styled the Senate, and the other the House of Representatives, and both together the "Legislature of the State of Texas." The style of the [all] laws shall be, "Be it enacted by the Legislature of the State of Texas." (*a*) The Legislature. Style of laws.

SECT. 5. The members of the House of Representatives shall be chosen by the qualified electors, and their term of office shall be two years from the day of the general election; and the sessions of the Legislature shall be biennial, at such times as shall be prescribed by law. Representatives, term of office. Biennial sessions.

SECT. 6. No person shall be a Representative, unless he be a citizen of the United States, or at the time of the adoption of this Constitution a citizen of the Republic of Texas, and shall have been an inhabitant of this State two years next preceding his election, and the last year thereof a citizen of the county, city or town, for which he shall be chosen, and shall have attained the age of twenty-one years, at the time of his election. Qualifications for Representatives. See sections 25, 26 and 27 of this Art.

SECT. 7. All elections by the people shall be held at such time and places in the several counties, cities or towns, as are now, or may hereafter be designated by law. Elections generally.

SECT. 8. The Senators shall be chosen by the qualified electors for the term of four years; and shall be divided by lot into two classes [as] nearly equal as can be. The seats of Senators of the first class shall be vacated at the expiration of the first two years; and of the second class at the expiration of four years; so that one-half thereof shall be chosen biennially thereafter. Senators—their term of office. Classification of.

SECT. 9. Such mode of classifying new additional Senators shall be observed, as will as nearly as possible preserve an equality of number in each class. New Senators, how classified.

SECT. 10. When a Senatorial district shall be composed of two or more counties, it shall not be separated by any county belonging to another district. Senatorial districts.

SECT. 11. No person shall be a Senator unless he be a citizen of the United States, or at the time of the acceptance of this Constitution by the Congress of the United States, a citizen of the Republic of Texas, and shall have been an inhabitant of this State three years next preceding the election; and the last year thereof a resident of the district for which he shall be chosen, and have attained the age of thirty years. Qualifications for Senators. See sec. 25, 26 and 27 of this Art.

SECT. 12. The House of Representatives, when assembled, shall elect a Speaker and its other officers, and the Senate shall choose a President for the time being, and its other officers. Each House shall judge of the qualifications and elections Organization of the two Houses. Qualifications. Con-

[*a*] This clause of the Constitution is inapplicable to a "resolution, order, or vote," as contradistinguished from a "Bill." The State v Delesdenier 7 Tex. R. 76.

tested elections. Quorum. Adjournments — of its own members, but contested elections shall be determined in such manner as shall be directed by law: two-thirds of each House shall constitute a quorum to do business, but a smaller number may adjourn from day to day, and compel the attendance of absent members, in such manner, and under such penalties as each House may provide.

Rules. Power over members. — SECT. 13. Each House may determine the rules of its own proceedings, punish members for disorderly conduct, and with the consent of two-thirds, expel a member, but not a second time for the same offence.

Journals. — SECT. 14. Each House shall keep a journal of its own proceedings, and publish the same; and the yeas and nays of the members of either House, on any question, shall, at the desire of any three members present be entered on the journal[s].

Vacancies in the Legislature. — SECT. 15. When vacancies happen in either House, the Governor, or the person exercising the power of the Governor, shall issue writs of election to fill such vacancies.

Members' privileges. — SECT. 16. Senators and Representatives shall, in all cases, except in treason, felony, or breach of the peace, be privileged from arrest during the session of the Legislature, and in going to and returning from the same, allowing one day for every twenty miles, such member may reside from the place at which the Legislature is convened.

Punishments. — SECT. 17. Each House may punish by imprisonment during the session, any person not a member, for disrespectful or disorderly conduct, in its presence, or for obstructing any of its proceedings: provided, such imprisonment shall not at any one time exceed forty-eight hours.

Open doors — SECT. 18. The doors of each House shall be kept open.

Adjournment, &c. — SECT. 19. Neither House shall, without the consent of the other, adjourn for more than three days; nor to any other place than that in which they may be sitting, without the concurrence of both Houses.

Passage of bills. — SECT. 20. Bills may originate in either House, and be amended, altered, or rejected by the other; but no bill shall have the force of a law, until on three several days it be read in each House, and free discussion be allowed thereon, unless in case of great emergency, four-fifths of the House in which the bill shall be pending, may deem it expedient to dispense with this rule; and every bill having passed both Houses, shall be signed by the Speaker and President of their respective Houses.

Bills for revenue. — SECT. 21. All bills for raising revenue shall originate in the House of Representatives, but the Senate may amend or reject them as other bids.

Rejected bills. — SECT. 22. After a bill or resolution has been rejected by either branch of the Legislature, no bill or resolution containing the same substance shall be passed into a law during the same session.

Compensation of members. See Sec. 34 of this Art. — SECT. 23. Each member of the Legislature shall receive from the public Treasury a compensation for his services, which may be increased or diminished by law; but no increase of compensation shall take effect during the session at which such increase shall be made.

Ineligibility of members to other offices. President pro tem. of Senate, Speaker of the House. — SECT. 24. No Senator or Representative shall, during the term for which he may be elected, be eligible to any civil office of profit under this State, which shall have been created, or the emoluments of which may have been increased during such term; and no member of either House of the Legislature shall, during the term for which he is elected, be eligible to any office or place, the appointment to which may be made in whole or in part, by either branch of the Legislature; nor shall the members thereof be capable of voting for a member of their own body, for any office whatever, except it be in such cases as are herein provided. The President for the time being of the Senate, and Speaker of the House of Representatives, shall be elected from their respective bodies.

Holders of lucrative offices ineligible. No two offices of trust or profit to be held by the same person. — SECT. 25. No Judge of any Court of law or equity, Secretary of State, Attorney-General, Clerk of any court of record, Sheriff, or Collector, or any person holding a lucrative office under the United States, or this State, or any foreign government, shall be eligible to the Legislature; nor shall at the same time hold or exercise any two offices, agencies, or appointments of trust or profit, under this State: provided, that officers of the militia, to which there is attached no annual salary, or the office of Justice of the Peace shall not be deemed lucrative.(a)

Collectors and holders — SECT. 26. No person who at any time may have been a Collector of taxes, or who may have been otherwise entrusted with public money, shall be eligible to

(a) The act of the Legislature which requires the Coroner, where the Sheriff is disqualified, or there is no Sheriff, to perform certain duties appertaining to the office of Sheriff, is not unconstitutional. Powell v. Wilson, 16 Tex. R. 59.

the Legislature, or to any office of profit or trust under the State Government, until he shall have obtained a discharge for the amount of such collections, and for all public moneys with which he may have [been] entrusted. *of public money ineligible.*

SECT. 27. Ministers of the Gospel, being by their profession dedicated to God and the care of souls, ought not to be diverted from the great duties of their functions; therefore, no Minister of the Gospel, or priest of any denomination whatever, shall be eligible to the Legislature. *Ministers ineligble.*

SECT. 28. Elections for Senators and Representatives shall be general throughout the State, and shall be regulated by law. *Certain elections general.*

SECT. 29. The Legislature shall at their first meeting, and in the year one thousand eight hundred and forty-eight and fifty, and every eight years thereafter, cause an enumeration to be made of all the free inhabitants (Indians not taxed, Africans and descendants of Africans excepted) of the State, designating particularly the number of qualified electors; and the whole number of Representatives shall at the several periods of making such enumeration be fixed by the Legislature, and apportioned among the several counties, cities or towns, according to the number of free population in each; and shall not be less than forty-five, nor more than ninety. *Census. Apportionment of Representatives.*

SECT. 30. Until the first enumeration and apportionment under this Constitution, the following shall be the apportionment of Representatives amongst the several counties, viz.:

The county of Montgomery shall elect four Representatives; the counties [of] Red River, Harrison, Nacogdoches, Harris and Washington, shall elect three Representatives each; the counties of Fannin, Lamar, Bowie, Shelby, San Augustine, Rusk, Houston, Sabine, Liberty, Robertson, Galveston, Brazoria, Fayette, Colorado, Austin, Gonzales and Bexar, two Representatives each; the counties of Jefferson, Jasper, Brazos, Milam, Bastrop, Travis, Matagorda, Jackson, Fort Bend, Victoria, Refugio, Goliad and San Patricio, one Representative each. *Temporary apportionment of Representatives.*

SECT. 31. The whole number of Senators shall at the next session after the several periods of making the enumeration, be fixed by the Legislature, and apportioned among the several districts to be established by law, according to the number of qualified electors, and shall never be less than nineteen, nor more than thirty-three. *Apportionment of Senators.*

SECT. 32. Until the first enumeration, as provided for by this Constitution, the Senatorial districts shall be as follows, to-wit: the counties of Fannin and Lamar shall constitute the first district, and shall elect one Senator; the counties of Red River and Bowie the second district, and elect one Senator; the counties of Fannin, Lamar, Red River and Bowie, conjointly shall elect one Senator; the county of Harrison, the third district, shall elect one Senator; the counties of Nacogdoches, Rusk and Houston, the fourth district, shall elect two Senators; the counties of San Augustine and Shelby, the fifth district, shall elect one Senator; the counties of Sabine and Jasper, the sixth district, shall elect one Senator; the counties of Liberty and Jefferson, the seventh district, shall elect one Senator; the counties of Robertson and Brazos, the eighth district, shall elect one Senator; the county of Montgomery, the ninth district, shall elect one Senator; the county of Harris, the tenth district, shall elect one Senator; the county of Galveston, the eleventh district, shall elect one Senator; the counties of Brazoria and Matagorda, the twelfth district, shall elect one Senator; the counties of Austin and Fort Bend, the thirteenth district, shall elect one Senator; the counties of Colorado and Fayette, the fourteenth district, shall elect one Senator; the counties of Bastrop and Travis, the fifteenth district, shall elect one Senator; the counties of Washington and Milam, the sixteenth district, shall elect one Senator; the counties of Victoria, Gonzales and Jackson, the seventeenth district, shall elect one Senator; the county of Bexar, the eighteenth district, shall elect one Senator; and the counties of Goliad, Refugio and San Patricio, the nineteenth district, shall elect one Senator. *Temporary apportionment of Senators.*

SECT. 33. The first session of the Legislature, after the adoption of this Constitution by the Congress of the United States, shall be held at the City of Austin, the present seat of government, and thereafter, until the year one thousand eight hundred and fifty; after which period the seat of government shall be permanently located by the people. *Seat of Government.*

SECT. 34. The members of the Legislature shall, at their first session, receive from the Treasury of the State, as their compensation, three dollars for each day *Compensation of* members of Legislature. they shall be in attendance on, and three dollars for every twenty-five miles travelling to and from the place of convening the Legislature.

Election for seat of government. SECT. 35. In order to settle permanently the seat of government, an election shall be holden throughout the State, at the usual places of holding elections, on the first Monday in March, one thousand eight hundred and fifty; which shall be conducted according to law, at which time the people shall vote for such place as they may see proper for the seat of government. The returns of said election to be transmitted to the Governor by the first Monday in June: if either place voted for shall have a majority of the whole number of votes cast, then the same shall be the permanent seat of Government until the year one thousand eight hundred and seventy, unless the State shall sooner be divided. But in case neither place voted for shall have the majority of the whole number of votes given in, then the Governor shall issue his proclamation for an election to be holden in the same manner, on the first Monday in October one thousand eight hundred and fifty, between the two places having the highest number of votes at the first election. The election shall be conducted in the same manner as at the first, and the returns made to the Governor, and the place having the highest number of votes shall be the seat of government for the time herein before provided.

ARTICLE IV. JUDICIAL DEPARTMENT.

Judicial power. SECT. 1. The judicial power of this State shall be vested in one Supreme Court, in District Courts, and in such inferior courts as the Legislature may from time to time ordain and establish; and such jurisdiction may be vested in corporation courts as may be deemed necessary, and be directed by law.

Supreme Court. SECT. 2. The Supreme Court shall consist of a Chief Justice and two Associates, any two of whom shall form a quorum.

Jurisdiction of Supreme Court. SECT. 3. The Supreme Court shall have appellate jurisdiction only, which shall be co-extensive with the limits of the State; but in criminal cases, and in appeals from interlocutory judgments, with such exceptions and under such regulations as the Legislature shall make.(*a*) Judges of may issue writs. And the Supreme Court and Judges thereof shall have power to issue the writ of *habeas corpus*, and under such regulations as may be prescribed by law may issue writs of *mandamus*, and such other writs as shall be necessary to enforce its own jurisdiction, and also compel a Judge of the District Court to proceed to trial and judgment in a cause. Sessions. And the Supreme Court shall hold its sessions once every year, between the months of October and June inclusive, at not more than three places in the State.

Clerks of Supreme Court. SECT. 4. The Supreme Court shall appoint its own Clerks, who shall hold their offices for four years, and be subject to removal by the said court for neglect of duty, misdemeanor in office, and such other causes as may be prescribed by law.

See Amendment. SECT. 5. The Governor shall nominate, and by and with the advice and consent of two-thirds of the Senate, shall appoint the Judges of the Supreme and District Courts, and they shall hold their offices for six years.

Judicial districts and Judges. SECT. 6. The State shall be divided into convenient judicial districts. For each district there shall be elected [appointed] a Judge who shall reside in the same, and hold the Courts at one place in each county, and at least twice in each year, in such manner as may be prescribed by law.(*b*)

Salaries of Judges. Art. 7, Sec. 36. SECT. 7. The Judges of the Supreme Court shall receive a salary not less than two thousand dollars annually, and the Judges of the District Court a salary not less than seventeen hundred and fifty dollars annually; and the salaries of the Judges shall not be increased or diminished during their continuance in office.

Removal from office. SECT. 8. The Judges of the Supreme and District Courts shall be removed by the Governor, on the address of two-thirds of each House of the Legislature, for wilful neglect of duty or other reasonable cause which shall not be sufficient ground for impeachment: provided, however, that the cause or causes for which such removal shall be required, shall be stated at length in such address, and entered on the journals of each House; and provided further, that the cause or causes shall be notified to the Judge so intended to be removed; and he shall be admitted to

(*a*) There having been no legislation upon the subject, the Supreme Court cannot entertain an appeal from an interlocutory judgment. Gross *v.* McClaren, 8 Tex. Rep., 341; Robinson *v.* Baillieul, 2 Tex. Rep., 160. In giving the right of appeal generally, under this constitutional provision, the Legislature had the power to except contempts. Floyd *v.* The State, 7 Tex. Rep., 215.

(*b*) The time and manner of holding the courts must be prescribed by law. The Constitution confers no discretion on the Judge. Doss *v.* Wagoner, 3 Tex. Rep., 515.

a hearing in his own defence before any vote for such address shall pass: And in all such cases, the vote shall be taken by yeas and nays, and entered on the journals of each House respectively.

Judges to be conservators of the peace. Style of process, &c.

SECT. 9. All Judges of the Supreme and District Courts shall, by virtue of their offices be conservators of the peace throughout the State. The style of all writs and process shall be "The State of Texas." All prosecutions shall be carried on in the name and by the authority of the "State of Texas," and conclude, "against the peace and dignity of the State."(*a*)

Jurisdiction and powers of District Courts.

SECT. 10. The District Court shall have original jurisdiction of all criminal cases, of all suits in behalf of the State to recover penalties, forfeitures, and escheats, and of all cases of divorce, and of all suits, complaints and pleas whatever, without regard to any distinction between law and equity, when the matter in controversy shall be valued at, or amount to one hundred dollars, exclusive of interest; and the said courts, or the Judges thereof, shall have power to issue all writs necessary to enforce their own jurisdiction and to* give them a general superintendence and control over inferior jurisdictions.(*b*) And in the trial of all criminal cases, the jury trying the same shall find and assess the amount of punishment to be inflicted, or fine imposed; except in capital cases, and where the punishment or fine imposed shall be specifically imposed by law.

Jury to assess certain fines.

Clerk of District Court.

SECT. 11. There shall be a Clerk of the District Court for each county, who shall be elected by the qualified voters for members of the Legislature, and who shall hold his office for four years, subject to removal by information, or by presentment of a grand jury and conviction by a petit jury. In case of vacancy, the Judge of the district have the power to appoint a Clerk, until a regular election can be held.(*c*)

Attorney General. See amendment.

SECT. 12. The Governor shall nominate and by and with the advice and consent of two-thirds of the Senate appoint an Attorney-General, who shall hold his office for two years, and there shall be elected by joint vote of both Houses of the Legislature, a District Attorney for each district, who shall hold his office for two years; and the duties, salaries and perquisites of the Attorney-General and District Attorneys, shall be prescribed by law.

Justices of the Peace, Sheriff, Coroner, and Constables. Term. Certain officers commissioned.

SECT. 13. There shall be appointed for each county a convenient number of Justices of the Peace, one Sheriff, one Coroner, and a sufficient number of Constables, who shall hold their offices for two years, to be elected by the qualified voters of the district or county, as the Legislature may direct. Justices of the Peace, Sheriffs, and Coroners shall be commissioned by the Governor. The Sheriff shall not be eligible more than four years in every six.

Judges shall not sit. Special judges to sit in Supreme Court, may be appointed by the Governor.

SECT. 14. No Judge shall sit in any case wherein he may be interested, or where either of the parties may be connected with him by affinity or consanguinity, within such degrees as may be prescribed by law, or where he shall have been of counsel in the cause. When the Supreme Court or any two of its members shall be thus disqualified to hear and determine any cause or causes in said Court, or when no judgment can be rendered in any case or cases in said Court, by reason

* This word "to," in the original, is crossed out by a pencil mark.

(*a*) An indictment which does not conclude "against the peace and dignity of the State," should be quashed. The State *v.* Durst, 7 Tex. Rep., 74.

(*b*) This section gives to the District Courts all the jurisdiction known to the common law and chancery courts of England, not incompatible with the Constitution of the United States and of this State, and laws under them. Newson *v.* Chrisman, 9 Tex. Rep., 113.

The jurisdiction conferred upon the District Courts is not exclusive—a concurrent jurisdiction may be conferred by statute upon inferior courts. Johnson *v.* Happell, 4 Tex. Rep., 96; Love & Chappell *v.* McIntyre, 3 Tex. Rep., 10; Clepper *v.* The State, 4 Tex. Rep., 242.

If the aggregate of the indebtedness is within the jurisdiction of the court it is sufficient, though neither item alone is of a sufficient amount. Mays *v.* Lewis, 4 Tex. Rep., 38; Lott *v.* Adams, ib., 426; Ferguson *v.* Calton, 8 Tex. Rep., 283; Lander *v.* Rounsaville, 12 Tex. Rep., 195.

The amount claimed in the petition is the sum in controversy, and determines the jurisdiction. Graham *v.* Roder, 5 Tex. Rep., 141.

Where the sum claimed is within the jurisdiction, and there is no plea to the jurisdiction, the court may give judgment for a less sum, unless the plaintiff improperly sought to give jurisdiction where it did not rightfully belong. Austin & Clapp *v.* Jordan, 5 Tex. Rep., 130; Graham *v.* Roder, ib., 141; Watts *v.* Harding, ib., 386; Bonner *v.* Watson, 6 Tex. Rep., 172; Sherwood *v.* Douthet, ib., 224; Bridge *v.* Ballew, 11 Tex. Rep., 269; Blakenship *v.* Adkins, 12 Tex. Rep., 536.

The District Courts have no appellate jurisdiction under this section of the Constitution. Titus *v.* Latimer, 5 Tex. Rep., 433; O'Brien *v.* Dunn, ib., 570; Able *v.* Bloomfield, 6 Tex. Rep., 263; Thomas *v.* The State, 9 Tex. Rep., 324.

(*c*) The term "regular election," as above used, means an election provided for by law to fill that vacancy. Banton *v* Wilson, 4 Tex. Rep., 400.

The incumbent, although elected to fill a vacancy, is entitled to hold the office for the full period. Ibid.

In District Courts by the parties. Judges may exchange districts, &c. Disqualification of inferior tribunals.

of the equal division of opinion of said Judges, the same shall be certified to the Governor of the State, who shall immediately commission the requisite number of persons learned in the law for the trial and determination of said case or cases. When the Judges of the District Court are thus disqualified, the parties may, by consent, appoint a proper person to try the said case; and the Judges of the said courts, may exchange districts, or hold courts for each other, when they may deem it expedient, and shall do so when directed by law. The disqualification of Judges of inferior tribunals, shall be remedied as may hereafter be by law prescribed.

Inferior Courts.

SECT. 15. Inferior tribunals shall be established in each county for appointing guardians, granting letters testamentary and of administration; for settling the accounts of executors, administrators, and guardians, and for the transaction of business appertaining to estates; and the District Courts shall have original and appellate jurisdiction, and general control over the said inferior tribunals, and original jurisdiction and control over executors, administrators, guardians, and minors, under such regulations as may be prescribed by law.(*a*)

Right of trial by jury in equity cases.

SECT. 16. In the trial of all causes in equity in the District Court, the plaintiff or defendant, shall, upon application made in open court, have the right of trial by jury, to be governed by the rules and regulations prescribed in trials at law.(*b*)

Justices' jurisdiction.

SECT. 17. Justices of the Peace shall have such civil and criminal jurisdiction as shall be provided for by law.(*c*)

Trial by jury before inferior tribunals.

SECT. 18. In all causes arising out of a contract, before any inferior judicial tribunal, when the amount in controversy shall exceed ten dollars, the plaintiff or defendant shall upon application to the presiding officer have the right of trial by jury.

Accused entitled to jury trial in inferior tribunals in all cases, where, &c.

SECT. 19. In all cases where Justices of the Peace, or other judicial officers of inferior tribunals shall have jurisdiction in the trial of causes, where the penalty for the violation of a law is fine or imprisonment (except in cases of contempt) the accused shall have the right of trial by jury.(*d*)

ARTICLE V. EXECUTIVE DEPARTMENT.

Executive power.

SECT. 1. The supreme executive power of this State shall be vested in the Chief Magistrate, who shall be styled the Governor of the State of Texas.

Election of Governor.

SECT. 2. The Governor shall be elected by the qualified electors of the State, at the time and places of elections for members of the Legislature.

Returns of election.

SECT. 3. The returns of every election for Governor, until otherwise provided by law, shall be made out, sealed up, and transmitted to the Seat of Government, and directed to the Speaker of the House of Representatives, who shall, during the first week of the session of the Legislature thereafter, open and publish them, in the presence of both Houses of the Legislature; the person having the highest number of votes, and being constitutionally eligible, shall be declared by the Speaker, under the direction of the Legislature to be Governor; but if two or more persons shall have the highest and an equal number of votes, one of them shall be immediately chosen Governor by joint vote of both Houses of the Legislature. Contested elections for Governor shall be determined by both Houses of the Legislature.

In case of a tie. Contested elections for Governor.

Gubernatorial term, and qualifications of Governor.

SECT. 4. The Governor shall hold his office for the term of two years from the regular time of installation, and until his successor shall be duly qualified, but shall not be eligible for more than four years in any term of six years; he shall be at least thirty years of age, shall be a citizen of the United States, or a citizen of the State of Texas, at the time of the adoption of this Constitution, and shall have resided in the same three years immediately preceding his election.

Salary.

SECT. 5. He shall, at stated times, receive a compensation for his services which

(*a*) The Probate Court cannot transcend the powers conferred upon it by the Constitution and laws enacted in pursuance of it. Francis *v* Northcote, 6 Tex. Rep. 185.
The District Court has original jurisdiction to arrest a fraudulent combination between an administrator and others. Dobbin *v* Bryan, 5 Tex. Rep., 276. Smith *v* Smith, 11 Tex. Rep., 102. May suspend an executor and appoint a receiver. Long *v* Wortham, 4 Tex. Rep., 381.
Under the Constitution the law provides two modes for revising the proceedings of the Probate Courts by the District Courts; by appeal and certiorari. Cain *v* Haas, 18 Tex. Rep., 616.

(*b*) The province of the jury is the same in equity as at law. Carter *v* Carter, 5 Tex. Rep., 93.

(*c*) It is competent for the Legislature to confer jurisdiction on Justices' Courts concurrent with that of the District Courts under the Constitution. Johnson *v* Happell, 4 Tex, Rep., 96. Clepper *v* The State, Ibid. 242.

(*d*) This section applies to Mayor's Courts. Burns *v* The Town of La Grange, 17 Tex. Rep., 415. Smith *v* San Antonio, Ibid. 643.

shall not be increased or diminished, during the term for which he shall have been elected. The first Governor shall receive an annual salary of two thousand dollars and no more. See Art. 7, Sect. 26.

SECT. 6. The Governor shall be Commander-in-chief of the army and navy of this State and of the militia, except when they shall be called into the service of the United States. Commander-in-chief.

SECT. 7. He may require information in writing from the officers of the Executive Department, on any subject relating to the duties of their respective offices. May require information to be given.

SECT. 8. He may by proclamation on extraordinary occasions convene the Legislature at the Seat of Government, or at a different place, if that should be in the actual possession of a public enemy. In case of disagreement between the two Houses, with respect to adjournment, he may adjourn them to such time as he shall think proper, not beyond the day of the next regular meeting of the Legislature. May convene and adjourn Legislature in certain cases.

SECT. 9. He shall from time to time, give to the Legislature information, in writing, of the state of the Government, and recommend to their consideration such measures as he may deem expedient. Shall communicate with the Legislature.

SECT. 10. He shall take care that the laws be faithfully executed. Shall see laws exect'd

SECT. 11. In all criminal cases, except in those of treason and impeachment, he shall have power, after conviction, to grant reprieves and pardons; and under such rules as the Legislature may prescribe, he shall have power to remit fines and forfeitures. In cases of treason, he shall have power by and with the advice and consent of the Senate, to grant reprieves, and pardons, and he may, in the recess of the Senate, respite the sentence, until the end of the next session of the Legislature. May grant reprieves and pardons and remit fines and forfeitures, but in cases of treason.

SECT. 12. There shall also be a Lieutenant-Governor, who shall be chosen at every election for Governor, by the same persons, and in the same manner, continue in office for the same time, and possess the same qualifications. In voting for Governor and Lieutenant-Governor, the electors shall distinguish for whom they vote as Governor, and for whom as Lieutenant-Governor. The Lieutenant-Governor shall, by virtue of his office, be President of the Senate, and have, when in committee of the whole, a right to debate and vote on all questions, and when the Senate is equally divided to give the casting vote. In case of the death, resignation, removal from office, inability or refusal of the Governor to serve, or of his impeachment or absence from the State, the Lieutenant-Governor shall exercise the powers and authority appertaining to the office of Governor, until another be chosen at the periodical election, and be duly qualified, or until the Governor impeached, absent, or disabled, shall be acquitted, return, or his disability be removed. Lieutenant Governor. Election, His right and duties as such. When shall act as Governor.

SEC. 13. Whenever the government shall be administered by the Lieutenant-Governor, or he shall be unable to attend as President of the Senate, the Senate shall elect one of their own members as President for the time being. And if, during the vacancy of the office of Governor, the Lieutenant-Governor shall die, resign, refuse to serve, or be removed from office, or be unable to serve, or if he shall be impeached, or absent from the State, the President of the Senate for the time being, shall in like manner administer the government, until he shall be superceded by a Governor, or Lieutenant-Governor; the Lieutenant-Governor shall, whilst he acts as President of the Senate, receive for his services the same compensation which shall be allowed to the Speaker of the House of Representatives, and no more, and during the time he administers the government as Governor, shall receive the same compensation which the Governor would have received had he been employed in the duties of his office, and no more. The President for the time being of the Senate shall, during the time he administers the government, receive in like manner the same compensation which the Governor would have received, had he been employed in the duties of his office. If the Lieutenant-Governor shall be required to administer the government, and shall, whilst in such administration die, resign, or be absent from the State, during the recess of the Legislature, it shall be the duty of the Secretary of State to convene the Senate for the purpose of choosing a President for the time being. President of Senate while Lieutenant Governor acts as Governor. President pro tem of Senate shall act as Governor, when Compensation of Lt. Governor. Compensation of President pro tem. of Senate while acting as Governor. In case of death, &c. of Lieut. Gov., acting as Gov. during recess of Senate.

SECT. 14. There shall be a seal of the State, which shall be kept by the Governor and used by him officially. The said seal shall be a star of five points, encircled by an olive and live oak branches, and the words "The State of Texas." State seal.

Commissions. SECT. 15. All commissions shall be in the name and by the authority of the State of Texas, be sealed with the State Seal, signed by the Governor and attested by the Secretary of State.

Secretary of State. Term of office. Duties. SECT. 16. There shall be a Secretary of State who shall be appointed by the Governor, by and with the advice and consent of the Senate, and shall continue in office during the term of service of the Governor elect. He shall keep a fair register of all official acts and proceedings of the Governor, and shall when required, lay the same and all papers, minutes, and vouchers, relative thereto, before the Legislature, or either House thereof, and shall perform such other duties as may be required of him by law.

Approval of laws. Veto power. SECT. 17. Every bill which shall have passed both Houses of the Legislature shall be presented to the Governor; if he approve, he shall sign it; but if not, he shall return it with his objections to the House in which it shall have originated, who shall enter the objections at large upon the journals and proceed to reconsider it; if, after such reconsideration two-thirds of the members present shall agree to pass the bill, it shall be sent, with the objections, to the other House, by which it shall likewise be re-considered; if approved by two-thirds of the members present, of that House, it shall become a law: but in such cases the votes of both Houses shall be determined by yeas and nays, and the names of the members voting for or against the bill, shall be entered on the journals of each House respectively; if Bills not returned to become laws. any bill shall not be returned by the Governor within five days, Sundays excepted, after it shall have been presented to him, the same shall be a law, in like manner, as if he had signed it. Every bill presented to the Governor one day previous to the adjournment of the Legislature, and not returned to the House in which it originated before its adjournment, shall become a law, and have the same force and effect as if signed by the Governor.

Joint resolutions, orders, &c., to be approved by the Governor. SECT. 18. Every order, resolution or vote, to which the concurrence of both Houses of the Legislature may be necessary, except on questions of adjournment, shall be presented to the Governor, and before it shall take effect, be approved by him, or being disapproved, shall be re-passed by both Houses, according to the rules and limitations prescribed in the case of a bill.

Notaries public. SECT. 19. The Governor, by and with the advice and consent of two-thirds of the Senate, shall appoint a convenient number of Notaries Public, not exceeding six for each county, who in addition to such duties as are prescribed by law, shall discharge such other duties as the Legislature may from time to time prescribe.

Nominations. SECT. 20. Nominations to fill all vacancies that may have occurred during the recess, shall be made to the Senate during the first ten days of its session. And should any nomination so made be rejected, the same individual shall not again be nominated during the session to fill the same office. And should the Governor fail to make nominations to fill any vacancy during the session of the Senate, such vacancy shall not be filled by the Governor until the next meeting of the Senate.

Governor's residence. SECT. 21. The Governor shall reside during the session of the Legislature, at the place where the session may be held, and at all other times wherever, in their opinion, the public good may require.

Governor to hold no other office. SECT. 22. No person holding the office of Governor, shall hold any other office or commission, civil or military.

Treasurer. Comptroller of accounts, &c. See amendment. SECT. 23. A State Treasurer and Comptroller of public accounts shall be biennially elected, by the joint ballot of both Houses of the Legislature, and in case of vacancy in either of said offices, during the recess of the Legislature, such vacancy shall be filled by the Governor, which appointment shall continue until the close of the next session of the Legislature thereafter.

ARTICLE VI. MILITIA.

Militia to be organized and disciplined. SECT. 1. The Legislature shall provide by law for organizing and disciplining the militia of this State, in such manner as they shall deem expedient, not incompatible with the Constitution and laws of the United States in relation thereto.

Scruples to bear arms. SECT. 2. Any person who conscientiously scruples to bear arms shall not be compelled to do so, but shall pay an equivalent for personal service.

SECT. 3. No licensed Minister of the Gospel shall be required to perform military duty, work on roads, or serve on juries in this State. Ministers of the Gospel free from services.

SECT. 4. The Governor shall have power to call forth the militia to execute the laws of the State, to suppress insurrections and to repel invasions. Governor may call out the militia.

ARTICLE VII. GENERAL PROVISIONS.

SECT. 1. Members of the Legislature and all officers, before they enter upon the duties of their offices, shall take the following oath or affirmation: "I, (A. B.) do solemnly swear (or affirm) that I will faithfully and impartially discharge and perform all the duties incumbent on me as ——————, according to the best of my skill and ability, agreeably to the Constitution and laws of the United States, and of this State: And I do further solemnly swear, (or affirm) that, since the adoption of this Constitution by the Congress of the United States, I, being a citizen of this State, have not fought a duel with deadly weapons, within this State nor out of it, nor have I sent or accepted a challenge to fight a duel with deadly weapons, nor have I acted as second in carrying a challenge, or aided, advised or assisted, any person thus offending—so help me God." Official oath. Duelling oath.

SECT. 2. Treason against this State shall consist only in levying war against it' or in adhering to its enemies—giving them aid and comfort; and no person shall be convicted of treason, unless on the testimony of two witnesses to the same overt act, or his own confession in open court. Treason.

SECT. 3. Every person shall be disqualified from holding any office of trust or profit in this State, who shall have been convicted of having given or offered a bribe to procure his election or appointment. Bribery.

SECT. 4. Laws shall be made to exclude from office, serving on juries, and from the right of suffrage, those who shall hereafter be convicted of bribery, perjury, forgery, or other high crimes. The privilege of free suffrage shall be supported by laws regulating elections, and prohibiting, under adequate penalties, all undue influence thereon from power, bribery, tumult, or other improper practice. Criminals excluded from privileges. Free suffrage secured.

SECT. 5. Any citizen of this State, who shall, after the adoption of this Constitution, fight a duel with deadly weapons, or send or accept a challenge to fight a duel with deadly weapons, either within the State or out of it, or who shall act as second, or knowingly aid and assist, in any manner, those thus offending, shall be deprived of holding any office of trust or profit under this State. Persons fighting or aiding in a duel, excluded from office.

SECT. 6. In all elections by the people the vote shall be by ballot, until the Legislature shall otherwise direct; and in all elections by the Senate and House of Representatives, jointly or separately, the vote shall be given *viva voce*, except in the election of their officers. Popular elections. Legislative elections.

SECT. 7. The Legislature shall provide by law for the compensation of all officers, servants, agents and public contractors, not provided for by this Constitution, and shall not grant extra compensation to any officer, agent, servant, or public contractor, after such public service shall have been performed, or contract entered into for the performance of the same; nor grant by appropriation or otherwise, any amount of money out of the Treasury of the State, to any individual on a claim real or pretended, where the same shall not have been provided for by pre-existing law: Provided, that nothing in this section shall be so construed as to affect the claims of persons against the Republic of Texas, heretofore existing. Compensation of officers, &c. Appropriations.

SECT. 8. No money shall be drawn from the Treasury but in pursuance of specific appropriations made by law; nor shall any appropriation of money be made for a longer term than two years, except for purposes of education; and no appropriation for private or individual purposes, or for purposes of internal improvement, shall be made, without the concurrence of two-thirds of both Houses of the Legislature. A regular statement and account of the receipts and expenditures of all public money shall be published annually in such manner as shall be prescribed by law. And in no case shall the Legislature have the power to issue "Treasury Warrants," "Treasury Notes," or paper of any description intended to circulate as money. Appropriations. Accounts published annually. Paper money prohibited.

SECT. 9. All civil officers shall reside within the State; and all district or county officers, within their districts or counties; and shall keep their offices at such places therein as may be required by law. Residence of officers.

Duration of offices. SECT. 10. The duration of all offices not fixed by this Constitution shall never exceed four years.

Absence from the State. SECT. 11. Absence on the business of this State, or of the United States, shall not forfeit a residence once obtained, so as to deprive any one of the right of suffrage, or of being elected, or appointed to any office, under the exceptions contained in this Constitution.

Deductions for neglect of duty. SECT. 12. The Legislature shall have power to provide for deductions from the salaries of public officers, who may neglect the performance of any duty that may be assigned them by law.

Members of Congress, and others, ineligible. SECT. 13. No member of Congress, nor person holding or exercising any office of profit or trust under the United States, or either of them, or under any foreign power, shall be eligible as a member of the Legislature, or hold or exercise any office of profit or trust under this State.

Change of venue. Penitentiary. SECT. 14. The Legislature shall provide for a change of venue in civil and criminal cases; and for the erection of a Penitentiary at as early a day as practicable.

Arbitration SECT. 15. It shall be the duty of the Legislature to pass such laws as may be necessary and proper, to decide differences by arbitration, when the parties shall elect that method of trial.

Revision and digest of laws. SECT. 16. Within five years after the adoption of this Constitution, the laws civil and criminal shall be revised, digested, arranged, and published, in such manner as the Legislature shall direct; and a like revision, digest, and publication, shall be made every ten years thereafter.

Lotteries. SECT. 17. No lottery shall be authorized by this State; and the buying or selling of lottery tickets within this State is prohibited.

Divorce. SECT. 18. No divorce shall be granted by the Legislature.

Marital rights. SECT. 19. All property both real and personal of the wife, owned or claimed by her before marriage, and that acquired afterwards by gift, devise, or descent, shall be her separate property; and laws shall be passed more clearly defining the rights of the wife, in relation as well to her separate property, as that held in common with her husband. Laws shall also be passed providing for the registration of the wife's separate property.(*a*)

Rights of property and action acquired under the Republic, &c. SECT. 20. The rights of property and of action, which have been acquired under the Constitution and laws of the Republic of Texas, shall not be divested; nor shall any rights or actions, which have been divested, barred, or declared null and void, by the Constitution and laws of the Republic of Texas, be re-invested, revis[v]ed or reinstated, by this Constitution; but the same shall remain precisely in the situation which they were before the adoption of this Constitution.(*b*)

Void titles, claims, and grants. SECT. 21. All claims, locations, surveys, grants and titles to land, which are declared null and void by the Constitution of the Republic of Texas, are, and the same shall remain forever null and void.

Property exempt from forced sale. SECT. 22. The Legislature shall have power to protect by law from forced sale, a certain portion of the property of all heads of families. The homestead of a family not to exceed two hundred acres of land, (not included in a town or city,) or any town or city lot or lots, in value not to exceed two thousand dollars, shall not be subject to forced sale, for any debts hereafter contracted, nor shall the owner, if a married man, be at liberty to alienate the same, unless by the consent of the wife, in such manner as the Legislature may hereafter point out.(*c*)

(*a*) The above mandate to the Legislature, to pass laws, cannot, in any degree, have been intended to abridge the rights of the wife, in her separate estate. The Legislature has no constitutional power to declare that the title of the wife to her property, shall be divested for want of registration, or that it shall be subjected to the debts of her husband. Edrington *v.* Mayfield and wife, 5 Tex. Rep. 363.

(*b*) The extent of the operation of this section is, that if the rights were of a character to be beyond the control of the Legislature, before the adoption of the Constitution, they should so continue; if otherwise, they should be subject to the action of the Legislature, in like manner as they had been under the Constitution and laws of the Republic. Warren *v.* Shuman, 5 Tex. Rep. 441.

(*c*) The homestead cannot be sold under a decree foreclosing a mortgage. Sampson & Keene *v.* Williamson, 6 Tex. Rep. 102. The valuation is placed on the lots themselves. Wood & wife *v.* Wheeler, 7 Tex. Rep. 13. North *v.* Shearn & wife, 15 Tex. Rep. 174. The constitutional limitation is not to the number but to the value of the lots. Pryor *v.* Stone, 19 Tex. Rep. 371. Hancock *v.* Morgan, 17 Tex. Rep. 582. A vacant lot separated by a street from the residence, and never used, is not protected as part of the homestead. Methery *v.* Walker, 17 Tex. Rep. 593. A homestead necessarily includes the idea of a house for a residence. Franklin *v.* Coffee, 18 Tex. Rep. 413. As to the acquisition, continuance and forfeiture, of the homestead exemption, see Ibid. Taylor *v.* Boulware, 17 Tex. Rep. 74. Edmiston *v.* Long, 17 Tex. Rep. 135. Merchant *v.* Perez, 11 Tex. Rep. 20. Trawick *v.* Harris, 8 Tex. Rep. 312.

SECT. 23. The Legislature shall provide in what cases officers shall continue to perform the duties of their offices, until their successors shall be duly qualified. Cases when officers shall hold over.

SECT. 24. Every law enacted by the Legislature shall embrace but one object, and that shall be expressed in the title. Laws to embrace but one object.

SECT. 25. No law shall be revised or amended by reference to its title; but in such case the act revised, or section amended, shall be re-enacted and published at length. Amendment of laws.

SECT. 26. No person shall hold or exercise at the same time, more than one civil office of emolument, except that of Justice of the Peace. No person hold more than one office except.

SECT. 27. Taxation shall be equal and uniform throughout the State.—All property in this State shall be taxed in proportion to its value, to be ascertained as directed by law, except such property as two-thirds of both Houses of the Legislature may think proper to exempt from taxation. The Legislature shall have power to lay an income tax, and to tax all persons pursuing any occupation, trade or profession: Provided that the term occupation, shall not be construed to apply to pursuits, either agricultural or mechanical.(*d*) Taxation.

SECT. 28. The Legislature shall have power to provide by law for exemption from taxation, two hundred and fifty dollars' worth of the household furniture or other property belonging to each family in this State. Property exempt from taxation.

SECT. 29. The Assessor and Collector of taxes, shall be appointed in such manner, and under such regulations, as the Legislature may direct. Assessors & Collectors of taxes.

SECT. 30. No corporate body shall hereafter be created, renewed, or extended, with banking or discounting privileges. Banking prohibited.

SECT. 31. No private corporation shall be created, unless the bill creating it shall be passed by two-thirds of both Houses of the Legislature; and two-thirds of the Legislature shall have power to revoke and repeal all private corporations, by making compensation for the franchise. And the State shall not be part owner of the stock, or property, belonging to any corporation. Two-thirds Leg. may pass or repeal acts for corporation State not own stock.

SECT. 32. The Legislature shall prohibit by law individuals from issuing bills, checks, promissory notes, or other paper to circulate as money. All paper money prohibited.

SECT. 33. The aggregate amount of debts hereafter contracted by the Legislature, shall never exceed the sum of one hundred thousand dollars, except in case of war, to repel invasion, or suppress insurrections. And in no case shall any amount be borrowed, except by a vote of two-thirds of both houses of the Legislature. State debts. Loans.

SECT. 34. The Legislature shall at the first session thereof, and may at any subsequent session, establish new counties for the convenience of the inhabitants of such new county or counties. Provided, that no new county shall be established, which shall reduce the county or counties, or either of them, from which it shall be taken, to a less area than nine hundred square miles (except the county of Bowie) unless by consent of two-thirds of the Legislature, nor shall any county be laid off of less contents. Every new county as to the right of suffrage and representation, shall be considered as part of the county or counties from which it was taken until entitled by numbers to the right of separate representation. New counties.

SECT. 35. No soldier shall in time of peace be quartered in the house or within the enclosure of any individual without the consent of the owner, nor in time of war, but in a manner prescribed by law. Quartering of soldiers.

SECT. 36. The salaries of the Governor, and Judges of the Supreme and District Courts, are hereby fixed at the minimum established in the Constitution, and shall not be increased for ten years. Salaries of Governors & judges. Art 4 Sec 7. Art 5 Sec 5.

MODE OF AMENDING THE CONSTITUTION.

SECT. 37. The Legislature, whenever two-thirds of each House shall deem it necessary, may propose amendments to this Constitution: which proposed amendments shall be duly published in the public prints of the State, at least three Mode of amending Constitution.

(*d*) The mode in which the power to tax occupations is to be exercised, is to be determined by the Legislature, and not to be questioned by the Courts. The State *v* Stephens, 4 Tex. Rep., 137.

months before the next general election of Representatives, for the consideration of the people, and it shall be the duty of the several returning officers, at the next election which shall be thus holden, to open a poll for and make a return to, the Secretary of State, of the names of all those voting for Representatives, who have voted on such proposed amendments, and if thereupon it shall appear that a majority of all the citizens of this State, voting for Representatives have voted in favor of such proposed amendments, and two-thirds of each House of the next Legislature, shall after such election, and before another ratify the same amendments by yeas and nays, they shall be valid to all intents and purposes, as parts of this Constitution; Provided, that the said proposed amendments shall at each of the said sessions have been read on three several days, in each House.

ARTICLE VIII. SLAVES.

Emancipation of slaves. Immigrants shall not be prohibited from bringing their slaves. Laws may be passed concerning emancipation of, and against introduction. Treatment Introduction of, as merchandize

SECT. 1. The Legislature shall have no power to pass laws for the emancipation of slaves without the consent of their owners, nor without paying their owners previous to such emancipation, a full equivalent in money for the slaves so emancipated.—They shall have no power to prevent emigrants to this State from bringing with them such persons as are deemed slaves, by the laws of any of the United States, so long as any person of the same age or description shall be continued in slavery by the laws of this State: Provided, that such slave be the *bona fide* property of such emigrants—provided also that laws shall be passed to inhibit the introduction into this State of slaves who have committed high crimes in other states or territories. They shall have the right to pass laws to permit the owners of slaves to emancipate them, saving the rights of creditors, and preventing them from becoming a public charge. (*a*) They shall have full power to pass laws, which will oblige the owners of slaves to treat them with humanity, to provide for their necessary food and clothing, to abstain from all injuries to them extending to life or limb; and in case of their neglect or refusal to comply with the directions of such laws, to have such slave or slaves taken from such owner, and sold for the benefit of such owner or owners. They may pass laws to prevent slaves from being brought into this State as merchandize only.

Trial by jury secured to slaves.

SECT. 2. In the prosecution of slaves for crimes of a higher grade than petit larceny, the Legislature shall have no power to deprive them of an impartial trial by a petit jury.

Offences against life or person of slaves.

SECT. 3 Any person who shall maliciously dismember, or deprive a slave of life, shall suffer such punishment as would be inflicted, in case the like offence had been committed upon a free white person, and on the like proof—except in case of insurrection of such slave.

ARTICLE IX. IMPEACHMENT.

Impeachment.

SECTION 1. The power of impeachment shall be vested in the House of Representatives.

Trial of impeachments

SECT. 2. Impeachment of the Governor, Lieutenant-Governor, Attorney-General, Secretary of State, Treasurer, Comptroller, and of the Judges of the District Courts, shall be tried by the Senate.

Senate shall try impeachments.

SECT. 3. Impeachments of Judges of the Supreme Court, shall be tried by the Senate. When sitting as a Court of Impeachment,the Senators shall be upon oath or affirmation; and no person shall be convicted without the concurrence of two-thirds of the Senators presnt.

Extent of judgment.

SECT. 4. Judgment, in cases of impeachment, shall extend only to removal from office, and disqualification from holding any office of honor, trust, or profit, under this State; but the parties convicted shall, nevertheless, be subject to indictment, trial, and punishment, according to law.

Officers impeached shall be suspended.

SECT. 5. All officers against whom articles of impeachment may be preferred, shall be suspended from the exercise of the duties of their office, during the pendency of such impeachment:. The appointing power may make a provisional appointment to fill the vacancy occasioned by the suspension of an officer, until the decision on the impeachment.

(*a*) A bequest of slaves, upon trust that they be carried to a free State, or to the colony of Liberia, where they may enjoy their freedom, does not conflict with the Constitution. Purvis *v* Sherrod, 12 Tex. Rep., 140.

SECT. 6. The Legislature shall provide for the trial, punishment, and removal from office, of all other officers of the State by indictment or otherwise. Laws made for trial, &c. of officers.

ARTICLE X. EDUCATION.

SECTION 1. A general diffusion of knowledge being essential to the preservation of the rights and liberties of the people, it shall be the duty of the Legislature of this State to make suitable provisions for the support and maintenance of public schools. Public schools.

SECT. 2. The Legislature shall as early as practicable establish free schools throughout the State, and shall furnish means for their support, by taxation on property: And it shall be the duty of the Legislature to set apart not less than one-tenth of the annual revenue of the State derivable from taxation, as a perpetual fund, which fund shall be appropriated to the support of free public schools, and no law shall ever be made diverting said fund to any other use; and until such time as the Legislature shall provide for the establishment of such schools in the several Districts of the State, the fund thus created shall remain as a charge against the State passed to the credit of the free common school fund. Provision for free schools by taxation. One tenth of annu'l revenue to be set apart &c.

SECT. 3. All public lands which have been heretofore, or which may hereafter be granted for public schools, to the various counties, or other political divisions in this State, shall not be alienated in fee, nor disposed of otherwise than by lease for a term not exceeding twenty years, in such manner as the Legislature may direct. Scho'l lands to be leased only.

SECT. 4. The several counties in this State which have not received their quantum of lands for the purposes of education shall be entitled to the same quantity heretofore appropriated by the Congress of the Republic of Texas to other counties. Sch'ol lands to counties not received

ARTICLE XI.

SECT. 1. All certificates for head-right claims to land, issued to fictitious persons, or which were forged, and all locations and surveys thereon, are, and the same were null and void from the beginning. Fraudulent land claims

SECT. 2 The District Courts shall be opened until the first day of July, one thousand eight hundred and forty-seven, for the establishment of certificates for head-rights, not recommended by the Commissioners appointed under the act, to detect fraudulent land certificates, and to provide for issuing patents to legal claimants; and the parties suing shall produce the like proof, and be subjected to the requisitions which were necessary, and were prescribed by law to sustain the original application for the said certificates, and all certificates above referred to, not established or sued upon before the period limited, shall be barred, and the said certificates, and all locations and surveys thereon, shall be for ever null and void—and all re-locations made on such surveys, shall not be disturbed until the certificates are established as above directed. Courts to be open for establishment of certain land claims, until a certain period. After that time all declared null and void.

ARTICLE XII. LAND OFFICE.

SECT. I. There shall be one General Land Office in the State, which shall be at the Seat of Government, where all titles which have heretofore emanated, or may hereafter emanate from Government, shall be registered; and the Legislature may establish from time to time such subordinate offices as they may deem requisite. General land office. Subordinate offices.

ARTICLE XIII. SCHEDULE.

SECT. 1. That no inconvenience may arise from a change of separate natural [national] Government to a State Government, it is declared, that all process, which shall be issued in the name of the Republic of Texas, prior to the organization of the State Government under this Constitution, shall be as valid as if issued in the name of the State of Texas. Process issued under Republic to be valid.

SECT. 2. The validity of all bonds and recognizances, executed in conformity with the Constitution and laws of the Republic of Texas, shall not be impaired by the change of government, but may be sued for and recovered in the name of the Governor of the State of Texas, and all criminal prosecutions or penal actions, which shall have arisen, prior to the organization of the State Government under this Constitution, in any of the courts of the Republic of Texas, shall be prosecu- Bonds, proceedings, &c. to be valid. Prosecutions.

ted to judgment and execution in the name of said State.(*a*) All suits at law and equity which may be depending in any of the courts of the Republic of Texas, prior to the organization of the State Government under this Constitution shall be transferred to the proper court of the State, which shall have jurisdiction of the subject-matter thereof.(*b*)

Suits depending in courts of the Republic.

Laws to be continued in force, if, &c.

SECT. 3. All laws and parts of laws now in force in the Republic of Texas, which are not repugnant to the Constitution of the United States, the joint resolutions for annexing Texas to the United States, or to the provisions of this Constitution, shall continue and remain in force, as the laws of this State, until they expire by their own limitation, or shall be altered or repealed by the Legislature thereof.

Fines, forfeitures, and escheats which accrued to the Republic.

SECT. 4. All fines, penalties, forfeitures and escheats, which shall have accrued to the Republic of Texas under the Constitution and laws, shall accrue to the State of Texas; and the Legislature shall by law provide a method for determining what lands may have been forfeited or escheated.(*c*)

Vote to be taken on Constitution.

SECT. 5. Immediately after the adjournment of this Convention, the President of the Republic shall issue his proclamation, directing the Chief Justices of the several counties of this Republic, and the several Chief Justices and their associates are hereby required to cause polls to be opened in their respective counties, at the established precincts, on the second Monday in October next, for the purpose of taking the sense of the people of Texas, in regard to the adoption or rejection of this Constitution, and the votes of all persons entitled to vote under the existing laws or this Constitution shall be received. Each voter shall express his opinion by declaring a "*viva voice*"* for "the Constitution accepted," or "the Constitution rejected," or some words clearly expressing the intention of the voter; and at the same time the vote shall be taken in like manner for and against annexation. The election shall be conducted in conformity with the existing laws regulating elections, and the Chief Justices of the several counties shall carefully and promptly make duplicate returns of said polls, one of which [shall] be transmitted to the Secretary of State of the Republic of Texas, and the other deposited in the Clerk's office of the County Court.

Vote to be counted.

Result to be proclaimed by the President.

SECT. 6. Upon the receipt of the said returns, or on the second Monday in November next, if the returns be not sooner made, it shall be the duty of the President, in presence of such officers of his cabinet as may be present, and of all persons who may choose to attend to compare the votes given for the ratification or rejection of this Constitution, and if it should appear, from the returns, that a majoriy of all the votes given, is for the adoption of the Constitution, then it shall be the duty of the President to make proclamation of that fact, and thenceforth this Constitution shall be ordained and established as the Constitution of the State, to go into operation and be of force and effect from and after the organization of the State Government, under this Constitution; and the President of this Republic is authorized and required to transmit to the President of the United States duplicate copies of this Constitution, properly authenticated, together with certified statements of the number of votes given for the ratification thereof, and the number for rejection; one of which copies shall be transmitted by mail, and one copy by special messenger, in sufficient time to reach the seat of government of the United States early in December next.

Copies of Constitution to be transmitted to the President of the U. States.

Election for Governor Lieutenant-Governor, and members of the Legislature

SECT. 7. Should this Constitution be accepted by the people of Texas, it shall be the duty of the President, on or before the second Monday in November next, to issue his proclamation, directing and requiring elections to be holden in all the counties of this Republic, on the third Monday in December next, for the office of Governor, Lieutenant Governor, members of the Senate and House of Representatives of the State Legislature, in accordance with the apportionment of representation directed by this Constitution. The returns for members of the Legislature of this State, shall be made to the Department of State of this Republic, and those for Governor and Lieutenant Governor shall be addressed to the Speaker of the House of Representatives, endorsed "Election Returns of County for Governor," and directed to the Department of State; and should from any

* A pencil line has been drawn through the letter *i* in the word *voice* in the original.

(*a*) A recognizance payable to Anson Jones, President of the Republic, under the Republic, can be enforced in the name of the State.

(*b*) Appeals from justices' courts pending in the District Courts, at the adoption of the Constitution, were transferred to the District Courts by virtue of the section, Sasse v. Schmidt, 6 Tex. R., 144.

(*c*) No method having yet been provided by law to determine what lands have been forfeited, the courts must wait the lead of the political authority before they can act. Hancock v. McKinney, 7 Tex. R., 384; Swift v Herrera, 9 Tex. R., 263.

cause whatever, the Chief Justices of counties fail to cause to be holden any of the polls or elections provided for by this Constitution at the times and places herein directed, the people of the precincts where such failure exists, are are* hereby authorized to choose managers, judges, and other officers to conduct said elections.

SECT. 8. Immediately on the President of this Republic receiving official information of the acceptance of this Constitution by the Congress of the United States, he shall issue his proclamation, convening at an early day the Legislature of the State of Texas, at the seat of government established under this Constitution; and after the said Legislature shall have organized, the Speaker of the House of Representatives shall, in presence of both branches of the Legislature, open the returns of the elections for Governor and Lieutenant Governor, count and compare the votes, and declare the names of the persons who shall be elected to the offices of Governor and Lieutenant Governor, who shall forthwith be installed in their respective offices; and the Legislature shall proceed as early as practicable to elect Senators to represent this State in the Senate of the United States, and also provide for the election of Representatives to the Congress of the United States. The Legislature shall also adopt such measures as may be required to cede to the United States, at the proper time, all public edifices, fortifications, barracks, ports, harbors, navy and navy-yards, docks, magazines, arms and armaments, and all other property and means pertaining to the public defence, now belonging to the Republic of Texas, and to make the necessary preparations for transferring to the said United States, all custom houses and other places for the collection of impost duties and other foreign revenues.

Legislature to be convened and State government organized. Senators and Representatives in Congress to be elected. Cession to be made to the U. S.

SECT. 9. It shall be the duty of the President of Texas, immediately after the inauguration of the Governor, to deliver to him all records, public money, documents, archives, and public property of every description whatsoever, under the control of the executive branch of the government; and the Governor shall dispose of the same in such manner as the Legislature may direct.

President to deliver over the government and public property to the Governor.

SECT. 10. That no inconvenience may result from the change of government, it is declared that the laws of this Republic, relative to the duties of officers, both civil and military of the same, shall remain in full force, and the duties of their several offices shall be performed in conformity with the existing laws, until the organization of the government of the State under this Constitution, or until the first day of the meeting of the Legislature. That then the offices of President, Vice-President of the President's Cabinet, Foreign Ministers, Charges and agents, and others repugnannt to this Constitution, shall be superceded by the same; and that all others shall be holden and exercised until they expire by their own limitation, or be superceded by the authority of this Constitution, or laws made in pursuance thereof.

Laws defining the duties of officers to remain in force until, &c. Officers repugnant to this Constitution superseded. Other officers continued, &c.

SECT. 11. In case of any disability on the part of the President of the Republic of Texas to act as herein required, it shall be the duty of the Secretary of State of the Republic of Texas; and in case of disability on the part of the Secretary of State, then it shall be the duty of the Attorney-General of the Republic of Texas to perform the duties assigned to the President.

Secretary of State or Attorney-General to act in case of disability of the President.

SECT. 12. The first general election for Governor, Lieutenant-Governor, and members of the Legislature, after the organization of the government, shall take place on the first Monday in November, one thousand eight hundred and forty-seven, and shall be held biennially thereafter, on the first Monday in November, until otherwise provided by the Legislature. And the Governor and Lieutenant-Governor, elected in December next, shall hold their offices until the installation in office of the Governor and Lieutenant-Governor to be elected in the year one thousand eight hundred and forty-seven.

Time of general election for Governor and Lieutenant Governor.

SECT. 13. The ordinance passed by the Convention on the fourth day of July, assenting to the overtures for the annexation of Texas to the United States, shall be attached to this Constitution and form a part of the same.

Ordinance 4th of July, 1845, made a part of this Constitution.

Done in Convention, by the Deputies of the people of Texas, at the City of Austin, this twenty-seventh day of August, in the year of our Lord one thousand eight hundred and forty-five. In testimony whereof, we have hereunto subscribed our names.

THO. J. RUSK, *President.*

* This word is crossed out by a pencil mark upon the original roll.

John D. Anderson, James Armstrong, Cavitt Armstrong, B. C. Bagby, R. E. B. Baylor, R. Bache, I. W. Brashear, Geo. Wm. Brown, Jas. M. Burroughs, Jno. Caldwell, William L. Cazeneau, Edward Clark, A. S. Cunningham, Phil. M. Cuny, Nicholas H. Darnell, James Davis, Lemuel Dale Evans, Gustavus A. Everts, Robert M. Forbes, David Gage, John Hemphill, J. Pinckney Henderson, A. W. O. Hicks, Jos. L. Hogg, A. C. Horton, Volney E. Howard, Spearman Holland, Wm. L. Hanter, Van R. Irion, Henry J. Jewett, Oliver Jones, H. L. Kinney, Albert H. Latimer, Henry R. Latimer, John M. Lewis, James Love, P. O. Lumpkin, Sam. Lusk, Abner S. Lipscomb, James S. Mayfield, A. M'Gowan, Archibald M'Neill, J. B. Miller, Francis Moore, Jr., J. Antonio Navarro, W. B. Ochiltree, Isaac Parker, James Power, Emery Rains, H. G. Rains, H. G. Runnels, James Scott, Geo. W. Smyth, Israel Standefer, Chas. Bellinger Stewart, E. H. Tarrant, Isaac Van Zandt, Francis M. White, Geo. T. Wood, G. W. Wright, Wm. Cock Young.

Attest, JAMES H. RAYMOND,
Secretary of the Convention.

AMENDMENT TO THE CONSTITUTION.

SECT. 1. Be it resolved by the Legislature of the State of Texas, That the Constitution of the State of Texas be so altered and amended that the Judges of the Supreme Court, Judges of the District Courts, Attorney-General, District Attorneys, Comptroller of Public Accounts, Treasurer of the State, and the Commissioner of the General Land Office, shall, at the expiration of their respective terms of office, or in case a vacancy may occur in either of them, by death, resignation, or otherwise, after this amendment takes effect, and thereafter, be elected by the qualified electors of the State, in the manner prescribed by law.

SECT. 2. Be it further resolved, That the election for District Judges and District Attorneys shall be confined to their respective districts.

Approved, January 16, 1850.

AN ORDINANCE.(*a*)

Preamble. WHEREAS, various contracts have been entered into by the President of the Republic of Texas, with divers individuals, with the expressed intention of colonizing an enormous amount of the public domain of Texas; and

Whereas, it is believed that said contracts are unconstitutional, and therefore void from the beginning, and if carried out would operate as a monopoly of upwards of seven millions of acres of the public domain of Texas, in the hands of a few individuals—when, in truth, the citizen soldiers and creditors of the Republic of Texas had, by the laws and Constitution of said Republic, a clear and indisputable previously subsisting right to locate upon the public domain thus attempted to be assigned to said contractors:—

Attorney-General or District Attorney to institute legal proceedings against colonization contractors. SECT. 1. Therefore it is hereby ordained and declared, That it shall be the duty of the Attorney-General of this State, or the District Attorney of the district in which any portion of the colonies may be situate, as soon as the organization of the State shall be completed, to institute legal proceedings against all colony contractors who have entered into contracts with the President of Texas; and if upon such investigation, it shall be found that any such contract was unconstitutional, illegal or fraudulent, or that the conditions of the same have not been complied with according to its terms, such contract shall be adjudged and decreed null and void: Provided, however, that all actual settlers under any such contract shall be entitled to their quantity of land as colonists—not to exceed six hundred and forty acres to the head of a family, and three hundred and twenty acres to a single man. And in all suits brought by or against any contractors, or any person claiming under, by or through them, or either of them, it shall be lawful for the adverse claimant to set forth any plea that it would have been competent for the

(*a*) We think it clear from doubt that the Ordinance appended to the Constitution is a part of the fundamental law of the land. It is of equal authority with the Constitution, and of binding force upon all the departments of the government of the State. Stewart *v.* Crosby, 15 Tex., Rep., 546.

State to plead; and the party may introduce testimony to prove the claim or title to have been forfeited, as well for frauds, or illegality, or unconstitutionality, as on account of a failure to comply with the conditions of the original grant or contract; and any such pleas shall be deemed good and valid in law, in all such suit or suits in this State.

SECT. 2. Be it further ordained, That the Legislature is hereby restrained from extending any contract for settling a colony, and from relieving any contractor from the failure of the conditions, or the forfeiture accruing from non-compliance with the contract. Contracts not to be extended. Contractors to have no relief.

SECT. 3. And be it further enacted, That this ordinance shall be presented to the people, for their adoption or rejection, at the same time that this Constitution shall be presented to them, and the returns of the votes taken on this ordinance shall be made to the office of the Secretary of State of the Republic of Texas, at the same time the votes for the Constitution may be returned. Ordinance to be adopted or rejected at the same time with Constitution.

Adopted in Convention, this twenty-seventh day of August, one thousand eight hundred and forty-five.

THOS. J. RUSK, *President.*

Attest,
JAMES H. RAYMOND,
Secretary of the Convention.

A DIGEST

OF THE

CIVIL STATUTES OF A GENERAL NATURE

OF THE STATE OF TEXAS.

ADOPTION.

Art. 1. [1] Any person wishing to adopt another as his or her legal heir, may do so by filing in the office of the Clerk of the County Court in which county he or she may reside, a statement in writing, by him or her signed and duly authenticated or acknowledged, as deeds are required to be: which statement shall recite in substance, that he or she adopts the person named therein as his or her legal heir; and the same shall be admitted to record in said office. Act of January 16, 1850. Take effect March 23, 1850. Mode of adoption.

Art. 2. [2] Such statement in writing, signed and authenticated, or acknowledged and recorded as aforesaid, shall entitle the party so adopted to all the rights and privileges, both in law and equity, of a legal heir of the party so adopting him or her: provided, however, that if the party adopting such person have, at the time of such adoption, or shall thereafter have a child or children, begotten in lawful wedlock, such adopted child or children shall in no case inherit more than the one-fourth of the estate of the party adopting him or her, which can be disposed of by will. Right of adopted heir. In case of subsequent children.

ALIENS.

Art. 3. [1] Any alien, being a free white person, shall have and enjoy in the State of Texas, such rights as are, or shall be, accorded to American citizens by the laws of the nation to which such alien shall belong, or by the treaties of such nation with the United States. Act of February 13, 1854. Civil rights of aliens.

May take and hold property by devise or descent.

ART. 4. [2] Aliens may take and hold any property, real or personal, in this State, by devise or descent from any alien or citizen, in the same manner in which citizens of the United States may take and hold real or personal estate by devise or descent within the country of such alien.

Resident aliens may acquire property.

ART. 5. [3] Any alien, being a free white person, who shall become a resident of this State, and shall, in conformity with the naturalization laws of the United States, have declared his intention to become a citizen of the United States, shall have the right to acquire and hold real estate in this State, in the same manner as if he was a citizen of the United States.

Repealing section.

ART. 6. [4] The ninth section of an act entitled "An act to regulate the descent and distribution of intestates' estates," approved March eighteenth, eighteen hundred and forty-eight, is hereby repealed, so far as the same may be inconsistent with this act; and this act shall take effect and be in force from and after its passage.

ARBITRATION. (*a*)

Act of 25th April, 1846.

Agreement in writing.

ART. 7. [1] All persons consenting to submit any dispute, controversy, or right of action, supposed to have accrued to either party, may, by an agreement in writing by them signed as plaintiff and defendant, and filing the same with a Justice of the Peace, or if the amount in dispute and claimed exceed in value one hundred dollars, with the Clerk of the District Court, entitle themselves to the benefits and provisions of this act; and the decision of any controversy, dispute, or right of action, made by arbitration according to the provisions of this act, shall be without appeal, unless the right to the same be reserved in the agreement filed, as above provided.

No appeal unless reserved.

ART. 8. [2] It shall be the duty of each and every Justice of the Peace, whenever a civil suit is brought before him, to offer to the election of parties therein, on, appearance, an adjustment of the same, according to the provisions of this act; as also, in the case of their agreeing to such adjustment, the choice of reserving or not the right of appeal.

Justices must propose arbitration.

ART. 9. [3] When such agreement is filed, the Justice of the Peace, or the District Clerk shall forthwith assign a day of trial for the cause, not less than two days thereafter, (*b*) and issue such process for witnesses as either party may desire.

Day of trial.

ART. 10. [4] Each party shall choose an arbitrator, who shall be over the age of twenty-one years, competent to serve as a juror, not related to either

Arbitrators to be chosen—qualifications.

(*a*) Unless the provisions of the act be observed, the award will not have the effect of a statutory award. Cox *v.* Gidding, 9 Tex. R. 44.

An injunction will not be granted against an award, which has been made a judgment of court under this act, where no fraud is alleged. Jones *v.* Frosh, 4 Tex. 202.

The statute should be liberally construed. Parties must substantially pursue its provisions, or the award cannot be made the judgment of a court. Owen *v.* Withee, 3 Tex. R. 161.

A reference to arbitrators is a waiver of any claim for seizure of property, under a distress warrant, issued without bond or affidavit. Mabry *v.* Little, 19 Tex. R. 337.

An administrator has no power to submit to arbitration, claims of his intestate. Johnson *v.* Cheney, 17 Tex. R. 336.

(*b*) When the record shows that a day of trial was appointed, the court will presume that it was done according to law, unless it is shown affirmatively that it was not. Offeciers *v.* Dirks, 2 Tex. 468.

party by consanguinity or affinity, and disinterested in the result of the cause submitted for his decision.

ART. 11. [5] On the day of trial the Justice or Clerk shall administer an oath to the said arbitrators, in substance as follows, to wit: That they will fairly and impartially decide the matter in dispute, according to the evidence adduced, and in accordance with the rules of law and equity applicable to the facts proved;(*c*) said Justice or Clerk shall, also, administer the necessary oaths to witnesses, and to the parties, if desired by the arbitrators. Oath of.

ART. 12. [6] If the arbitrators, chosen as aforesaid, cannot agree, the arbitrators shall select an umpire; and in case they disagree in the choice of an umpire, the Justice or Clerk may appoint an umpire, who shall be competent to serve as an arbitrator, and who shall in like manner be sworn. Umpire.

ART. 13. [7] The decisions of the arbitrators, if before a Justice of the Peace, shall be recorded as a judgment in his court, and on which execution may issue, as in ordinary cases of judgments obtained before Justices of the Peace: if before the Clerk, he shall file the same, and a judgment shall be entered thereon at the first regular term of the court thereafter:(*d*) but should either party appeal from the decision of the arbitrators, the appellant shall file his application with the Clerk of the District Court, within the first three days of said court, wherein the case shall be tried *de novo;* on which execution may issue, as in other judgments rendered by the District Court: the said judgments shall carry costs as in other cases. Award to be recorded. Proceedings on appeal. Execution.

ART. 14. [8] After an agreement filed, as provided in the first section of this act, the parties thereto shall be bound to this mode of trial under the following penalty, to wit: said agreement may be pleaded as a bar to any suit thereafter brought by a plaintiff in the agreement, for the same cause of action, when such plaintiff has refused to proceed under such agreement; and said agreement may be pleaded as a bar to any right claimed or defence set up by a defendant in the agreement, who refused to proceed therein, where such right or defence existed at the time of filing of said agreement. Penalty refusing to comply with agreement.

(*c*) The Clerk is not required, by law, to make a record of the form of the oath, the substance only being expressed in the act. Offeciers *v.* Dirks, 2 Tex. 468.

Going into the investigation without notice, or refusing sufficient time to procure necessary testimony, will vitiate an award. Green *v.* Franklin, 1 Tex. R. 497.

If the record does not show affirmatively, that the parties had notice of the time and place of meeting of the arbitrators, no exceptions being taken in the court below, the appellate court will presume that such notice was given. Hooper *v.* Brinson, 2 Tex. R. 185.

The awards of arbitrators have always been looked upon with peculiar favor. Green *v.* Franklin, *supra.*

Nothing will be presumed against an award. Every presumption not contradicted by proof will be admitted. Ibid.

(*d*) The consent of parties, either before or after an award, is necessary to its being made the judgment of a court. Without proof to the contrary, consent will be presumed. Edrington *v.* League, 1 Tex. R. 64.

An award may be set aside on the ground of fraud, partiality, misconduct, or gross mistake, on the part of the arbitrators, to the manifest injury of the party complaining—Payne *v.* Metz, 14 Tex. R. 56; otherwise the award is conclusive of all matters submitted to the arbitrators. Jones *v.* Frosh, 6 Tex. R. 202.

ATTACHMENT.

Act of March 11, 1848.

Upon return of not found attachment may be issued.

Defendant failing to plead.

ART. 15. [1] Whenever a writ shall issue from any of the courts of this State, commanding the Sheriff or other officer to summon any person to answer to any civil suit in said court, and the said officer shall return that the defendant is not to be found in his county, the plaintiff may sue out a writ of attachment, to be levied of the property of such defendant, returnable in the same manner as original writs: and if the said officer shall return any property by him attached, and the defendant shall fail to appear and plead within the time limited by the law regulating pleadings, the plaintiff shall be entitled to judgment as in ordinary suits; and the property so attached, if not replevied, or released by special bail, shall remain in the custody of the sheriff or other officer, until final judgment.

Bond not security for costs.

ART. 16. [2] The bonds given upon which attachments are issued, shall not be construed as security for costs.

Judges &c. may issue.

ART. 17. [3] The Judges and Clerks of the District Courts and Justices of the Peace may issue said judicial attachments, returnable to their respective courts.(b)

For affidavit see Art. 43.

Bond to be given.

ART. 18. [5] The plaintiff, his agent or attorney, shall, at the time of making such affidavit, give bond, with two or more good and sufficient sureties, payable to the defendant in at least double the amount sworn to be due, conditioned that plaintiff will prosecute his suit to effect and pay such damages as shall be adjudged against him for wrongfully suing out such attachment.(c)

Bond may be put in suit.

ART. 19. [6] Said bond may be put in suit in the same manner as other bonds.

Upon filing affidavit and bond writ to issue.

Property to remain with officer.

How replevied.

ART. 20. [7] Upon such affidavit and bond being filed, it shall be the duty of said District Judge, Clerk, or Justice of the Peace, to issue an attachment against the property of the debtor, wherever the same may be found, or so much thereof as shall be sufficient to satisfy the demand and costs of plaintiff which property shall remain in the hands of the officer attaching the same until final judgment, unless the same shall be replevied or released by special bail; and should the defendant fail to replevy the property so attached within fifteen days after the levying of the attachment, the plaintiff in the attachment shall have the right of replevying the same upon giving bond to the defendant in double the amount of the value of the property attached, with good and suffi-

(a) Attachment laws and proceedings under them are in all courts subjected to the strictest scrutiny. Chevalier *v.* Williams & Co., 2 Tex. Rep., 239.

It has been the uniform rule of this court never to extend their provisions by liberal intendment. Givens *v.* Taylor & Hart, 6 Tex. Rep., 315.

The remedy by attachment is summary in its action, and the plaintiff must comply with all the incidents appertaining to this stringent mode of redress. Wooster *v.* McGee, 1 Tex. Rep., 17.

(b) Neither personal service nor by publication upon the defendant is required in judicial attachments.—Briggs *v.* Smith, 13 Tex. Rep., 269.

Bond must be given to procure a judicial attachment as in an original attachment. Ibid. A judgment by default, upon such attachment, without bond, was reversed. Ibid.

(c) A bond which is not entitled of any action, and does not correctly describe the parties to the suit, is defective. Schrimpf *v.* McArdle, 13 Tex. Rep., 368.

If the agent had no authority to sign the name of the principal to the bond, the attachment may be quashed on that account. Ibid. The objection must be taken by plea in abatement, and not by motion to quash. Messner *v.* Hutchins, 17 Tex. Rep., 597; Messner *v.* Lewis, 20 Tex. Rep., 221.

The Clerk must judge of the sufficiency of the bond, and approve it as a predicate to his action. He need not make a formal entry of his approval. Griffith *v.* Robinson, 19 Tex. Rep., 219.

cient security, conditioned for the forthcoming of the property to abide the result of the suit.

Art. 21. [8] The same proceedings shall be had thereon as in judicial attachments. Same proceedings as judicial attachments.

Art. 22. [9] Every original attachment issued without affidavit and bond taken as aforesaid, shall be abated on motion of defendant. Issued without affidavit & bond to be abated.

Art. 23. [10] The bond aforesaid shall not be void for want of form: Provided it contains all essential matters. Bond not void for want of form.

Art. 24. [11] Attachments may be levied on defendant's property, and the manner of executing an attachment on personal property shall be, by the officer going to the house in which, or to the person in whose possession the property of the defendant is supposed to be, and then and there declaring in the presence of one or more credible persons of the neighborhood that he attaches said property.(a) How levied.

Art. 25. [12] The defendant shall have the right to replevy the property so attached, by giving bond, payable to the plaintiff, with two or more sufficient sureties, for the amount of the debt and interest thereon, or at his election, for the value of the property so attached, conditioned, that if the defendant be condemned in the action, he or some other person for him, shall return the specific property attached to satisfy the judgment that may be rendered; and should the defendant fail to replevy the property attached, within the time prescribed in section seventh, then the plaintiff shall have the right to replevy the same, as prescribed in said section. Any officer taking any such bond shall endorse thereon the value of the property replevied, and unless the property so attached shall be replevied, or unless claim be made to it, and bond given to try the right of the same, as provided by law, or unless the defendant give special bail as provided for by this act, such property shall remain in the custody of the officer attaching the same, to satisfy the judgment that may be rendered, and the said replevin bond, or bond for the trial of the right of property, or bond given as special bail, shall be lodged with the Clerk of the Court, or Justice of the Peace where the attachment is returnable: and should the obligors in any such replevin bond neglect to deliver the property attached, or so much thereof as may be sufficient, to the proper officer of the Court, for the satisfaction of the final judgment that may be rendered in the attachment, within ten days after the final judgment shall be rendered, such bond shall forthwith be endorsed by said officer as forfeited; and, if the judgment is against the defendant, the Clerk or Justice of the Peace with whom the same is lodged, shall forthwith issue execution in favor of the plaintiff, against all the obligors in such replevin bond for the full penalty thereof, unless such penalty shall be for a greater amount than the judgment, with interest and costs, against the defendant in attachment, in which case, such execution shall be issued against such obligors for the amount of such judgment, interest and costs; if the judgment shall be against the plaintiff in any case where he may have replevied the property, the Clerk or Justice of the Peace with whom such replevin bond is lodged, shall forthwith issue execution in favor of the defendant against all the obligors in such replevin bond, for the value of such property, with legal interest, from the date of the bond. And should the obligors in any such bond, for the trial of the right of property, where the claimant fails to establish his right, neglect to deliver the property attached, or so much thereof as may be sufficient, to the proper officer of the Court, to satisfy

Defendant may replevy. Condition of bond. Officer to endorse on bond. Property to remain with officer unless. Bond to be lodged with Clerk or Justice. Execution to issue on bond when.

(a) The return executed by "levying the within attachment in presence of John B. Costa and A. B. McGill, on lots No. 3, &c.," is sufficient. Morgan v. Johnson, 15 Tex. R., 568. Messner v. Hutchins, 17 Tex. R., 597. Messner v. Lewis, 20 Tex. R., 221.

the final judgment that may be rendered against the defendant in attachment, within ten days after the failure of the claimant to establish his right thereto, then, the like proceedings shall be had against the obligors in such bond, for the trial of the right of property, as is herein provided for replevin bonds.

Officers may require indemnifying bond.

ART. 26. [13] Whenever an officer shall levy an attachment it shall be at his own risk, and such officer may for his own indemnification require the plaintiff in attachment to execute and deliver to him a bond of indemnity to secure him, if it should afterwards appear that the property levied upon by him does not belong to the defendant.

Deft. may give special bail. Property released by special bail.

ART. 27. [14] Any person against whose property an attachment has issued, his agent or attorney, may, at any time before final judgment, upon giving special bail, with good and sufficient sureties, for the amount of the debt and interest, recover possession of the property so attached from the person in whose hands it may be, but the giving such special bail shall be deemed an appearance of the defendant, and the suit shall thereupon proceed as in ordinary cases, but if the plaintiff recover, he shall have judgment against all the obligors in the bail bond.

Attachment may issue tho' debt not due.

ART. 28. [15] Special bail put in as above provided for shall release the property so attached.

Judgment not to be rendered till due.

ART. 29. [16] A writ of attachment may issue in all cases against the property of a debtor legally subject to attachment, although the debt or demand of the plantiff be not due, and the same proceedings shall be had thereon as in other cases of attachments, except that no final judgment shall be rendered against the defendant, until the debt or demand of the plaintiff shall become due; (*e*) but if the property so attached be of a wasting or perishing nature, then the same shall by order of the Judge, or Justice of the Peace, to whose court the attachment is returnable, be sold, giving a credit on the sale until the debt or demand of the plaintiff shall become due, on the purchaser's giving bond, with two or more sufficient sureties, payable to the plaintiff, for the payment of the purchase-money; which bond shall be lodged with the other papers in the cause, and if the money is not paid at the expiration of the time given, the Clerk or Justice of the Peace, with whom such bond is lodged, shall issue execution against the principal and sureties, or either of them, and the money when collected shall be paid into the hands of the Clerk or Justice of the Peace, to abide the final decision of the cause.

If property perishable to be sold.

What property to be sold and when.

ART. 30. [17] When any property attached on the oath of the plaintiff, his agent or attorney, be certified to any District Judge or Justice of the Peace to whose court the attachment is returnable, to be likely to be wasted or destroyed by keeping, and if the person to whom it belongs, his agent or attorney, shall not within thirty days after the levy of the attachment, replevy or release the same by special bail, then such property shall, by order of such Judge or Justice of the Peace, be sold at public sale by the officer who levied the writ, in the same manner as sales by execution, and the said officer shall, within five days after such sale, return the order of sale to the Court or Justice of the Peace to which the attachment is returnable, with his proceedings thereon, and also at the time of making such return, shall pay over into the hands of the Clerk or Justice of the Peace, all moneys arising from such sale, which moneys shall be subject to the judgment of the suit.

Judgment not to be rendered un-

ART. 31. [18] No judgment shall be rendered in suit by attachment unless

(*e*) Where part of the claim is not due at the time the suit is brought, and the attachment is quashed, the suit abates as to the amount not due, but may proceed as to the balance. Sydnor *v.* Totman, 6 Tex. R. 189.

the citation or summons has been served in the ordinary mode, or by publication in the manner provided for by law. less service personal or by publication.

ART. 32. [21] Whenever judgment shall be rendered against any garnishee in the manner provided for by this act, he shall have the right at any time, within ten days after final judgment entered against him as garnishee, to deliver the money and effects for which judgment was so entered, to the proper officer of the court, in discharge of himself. Garnishee may deliver money and effects in court.

ART. 33. [22] If upon the examination of any garnishee, it shall appear that there is any of defendant's effects in the hands of any other person who has not been summoned, or that any other person is indebted to the defendant, the Court or Justice of the Peace shall, upon application, issue a judicial attachment or garnishment, to be served as in other cases of attachment and garnishment, and like proceedings shall be had thereon as in other cases of attachment and garnishment. Effects in hands of persons not summoned other persons indebted to defenant.

ART. 34. [23] The defendant may in all cases, show by competent proof, that the garnishee is indebted to him in a greater amount than he is willing to admit on oath. Deft. may show garnishee indetb'd in greater amount.

ART. 35. [25] Every garnishee shall be allowed out of the effects and moneys attached, a reasonable compensation for his attendance, and in case no effects or moneys are attached in the hands of the garnishee, said compensation shall be taxed against the party causing such garnishee to be summoned. Compensation garnishee.

ART. 36. [26] The following form of bond and writ may be used. Know all men that ——— as principal, and ——— as sureties, do hereby acknowledge ourselves bound to pay to ——— the sum of —— dollars, and —— cents, conditioned that A. B. plaintiff in attachment against C. D. defendant, will prosecute his suit with effect, and that he will pay such damages as shall be adjudged against him, for wrongfully suing out said attachment. Witness our hands and scrawls by way of seals, this —— day of ——— A. D. 18—. Form of Bond.

The State of Texas, County of ——— To the Sheriff of the County of ——— Greeting: We command you that you attach so much of the property of C. D., if to be found in your county, repleviable on security, as shall be of value sufficient to make —— dollars and —— cents, and costs, to satisfy the demand of A. B., and such property so attached in your hands to keep and secure, that the same may be liable to further proceedings thereupon to be had at ———, so as to compel the said C. D., to appear and plead to the complaint of the said A. B., when and where you shall make known how you have executed this writ. Form of writ.

ART. 37. [27] All writs of attachment shall be signed and dated by the officer issuing the same, and when issued by a Judge or Clerk of the District Court, shall have the seal of the court affixed. Writs to be signed and dated, sealed when issued by Judge or Clerk.

ART. 38. [28] No attachment shall be issued by any Judge or Clerk of the District Court, unless the plaintiff in the suit shall first file his petition in the same manner as in other suits. Petition to be filed.

ART. 39. [1] Where a judicial or original attachment has been issued, the plaintiff may apply to the officer who issued the same, for a writ of garnishment against any person supposed to be indebted to, or supposed to have any of the effects of, the defendant, commanding the Sheriff or other proper officer of the county where such person may reside, to summon him as a garnishee, to appear before the District Court or Justice of the Peace where the attachment is returnable, on the first day of Act of January 16th 1850, Take effect March 23, 1850. Writ of Garnishment.

the first term of the court, or on the return of the attachment, if returnable before a Justice of the Peace, then to answer upon oath, what he is indebted to the defendant, or what effects of the defendant he has in his possession, and had at the time of serving of the garnishment, and what credits and effects there are of the defendant in the hands of any other person, and what person, to the best of his knowledge or belief; and it shall be lawful at any time after the answer of the garnishee shall have been filed, and after final judgment shall have been rendered against the defendant in attachment, for the court or Justice of the Peace, to enter up a judgment against the garnishee, for all sums of money acknowledged by him to be due to the defendant, and for all effects of the defendant, acknowledged to be in his possession, or so much thereof as may be sufficient to satisfy the judgment of the plaintiff and costs: or if the garnishee be a resident of the county where the original suit is brought, it shall be lawful for the court or the Justice of the Peace in like manner to enter up a judgment against such garnishee, for all sums of money that may be proved to be due from him to the defendant, and for all effects of the defendant proved to be in his possession, or so much thereof, as will be sufficient to satisfy the judgment of the plaintiff and costs: and if such garnishee shall fail, or refuse, to deliver to the proper officer of the court, all sums of money and effects, for which such judgment was entered against him, or so much thereof as may be sufficient to satisfy the judgment of the plaintiff and costs, when demanded by such officer, he shall make return to the court or Justice of the Peace, of such failure or refusal; whereupon it shall be the duty of the Clerk or Justice of the Peace, to issue execution against such garnishee, in accordance with the terms of the judgment rendered against him.

What judgment may be rendered against garnishee.

Garnishee resident of county.

ART. 40. [2] Where any garnishee who is a resident of the county where the original suit is brought, shall be summoned in the manner aforesaid, and shall fail to answer on oath, as directed by this act, before final judgment shall have been rendered against the defendant in attachment, it shall be lawful for the court or Justice of the Peace, after calling the garnishee, to render judgment against him for such sum as judgment may have been rendered for against the defendant in attachment.

Garnishee's answer, how controverted.

Garnishee how tried.

ART. 41. [3] The plaintiff, wishing to controvert the garnishee's answer, may do so, by making oath, that he believes the same to be incorrect; whereupon, if the garnishee resides in the county in which the original suit is brought, an issue shall be formed under the direction of the court, and tried as in other suits; but if the garnishee is a resident of any other county, the plaintiff may file a copy of the judgment in the original suit, together with a copy of said controverted answer and oath, in any court of the county, in which the garnishee resides, that has jurisdiction of an amount equal to that demanded in the original suit; when, it shall be the duty of the Justice of the Peace, or the Clerk of the court, in whose office such copies are filed, to docket the same as an original suit, and issue a citation against the garnishee, as in other suits: and upon the return of such citation served, an issue shall be formed under the direction of the court or Justice of the Peace, as the case may be, and tried in like manner as the same might have been done in the court in which the original suit was brought, if the garnishee had been a resident of the county where such original suit was brought.

Garnishee out of county. Answer how obtained.

ART. 42. [4] When a garnishee resides in a county, other than that in which the original suit is brought, if he shall fail to appear and answer on oath, in obedience to the writ of garnishment, it shall be lawful for the court or Justice of the Peace, on motion of the plaintiff, to issue a commission to any officer authorized to take depositions in the county in which the garnishee resides, requiring him to cite said garnishee to come before him, and answer such garnishment under oath: and should said garnishee appear and answer, it shall be the duty of the officer, receiving such commission, to return the same together with [the] answers of the garnishee certified to under his hand and official seal, to the court or Justice from whence it issued: but should the garnishee fail or refuse to apper and answer under oath, when so cited by the officer to whom any such commission shall have been sent, then such officer shall return such commission with the citation, and service endorsed thereon, together with a certificate of such failure or refusal, attested by his hand and official seal, to the court or Justice from whence such commission issued, whereupon, it shall be lawful for such court or Justice, to proceed against such garnishee in like manner, as if he were a resident of the county, in which the original suit was brought, and had failed to appear and answer. Refusing to answer.

SEC. 31. That in all cases, where a judicial attachment shall hereafter issue, if at any time before the trial, the defendant by himself, or by his attorney, shall appear and answer the suit, he may, on motion, have said attachment set aside and vacated, and the property attached, released; but nothing in this thirty-first section, shall in any manner affect or control the proceedings on original attachments. Judicial attachment answer vacated on motion.

ART. 43. [1] The Judges and Clerks of the District Courts and Justice of the Peace, may issue original attachments, returnable to their respective Courts, upon the party applying for the same, his Agent or Attorney making an affidavit in writing, stating that the defendant is justly indebted to the plaintiff and the amount of the demand; also, that the defendant is not a resident of this State, or that he is about to remove out of this State, or that he secretes himself so that the ordinary process of law cannot be served on him; or that he is about to remove his property beyond this State, or that he is about to remove his property beyond the county in which the suit is to be or has been commenced, or that he is about to transfer or secrete, or has transferred or secreted his property for the purpose of defrauding his creditors, and that thereby the plaintiff will probably lose his debt, and he shall also swear that the attachment is not sued out for the purpose of injuring the defendant. (*a*) Act of July 24, 1856. Who may issue attachments and when. Oath.

ATTORNEYS AND COUNSELLORS AT LAW.

ART. 44. [1] Any person who, in vacation, wishes to be allowed to practice as an attorney and counsellor at law, shall make application to the Judge of the District Court, or to a Judge of the Supreme Court, and shall produce a Act of May 12, 1846. Qualifications of

(*a*) It is not sufficient for the affidavit to state that affiant has good reason to believe, and does believe, that the defendant is about to remove, &c. It must be positive as to the fact. Sydnor *v.* Totman, 6 Texas R. 189.

There need not be an affidavit apart from the petition. It is sufficient if the petition contain all the requisites of the affidavit and be sworn to. Watts *v.* Harding, 5 Tex. R. 386.

The facts set forth in the affidavit are not traversable. Cloud *v.* Smith, 1 Tex. R. 611.

An affidavit which is in strict conformity to Section 4 of the Act regulating attachments is a virtual compliance with the 143 Section of the Act to regulate proceedings in the District Courts. Primrose *v.* Roden, 14 Tex. R. 1. See Morgan *v.* Johnson, 15 Tex. R. 568. Seawell *v.* Lowry, 16 Tex. R. 47.

Where the ground of attachment is that the defendant secretes himself so that the ordinary process of law cannot be served upon him, it need not be added that the plaintiff will probably lose his debt. Messner *v.* Hutchins, 17 Tex. R. 597.

In an affidavit that the defendant secretes himself so that the ordinary process of law cannot be served upon him, need not state that he is a resident of the State.—Griffith *v.* Robinson, 19 Tex. R. 219.

In an affidavit, "that the defendant is about to remove out of the State," it need not be added that the plaintiff will thereby lose his debt. Wright *v.* Smith, 19 Tex. R. 297. See Messner *v.* Lewis, 20 Tex. R. 221.

attorneys, and how licensed temporarily in vacation.

certificate from the County Court of the county in which he resides, that he has been a resident of the State at least six months, that he is twenty-one years of age, and that he has a good reputation for moral character and honorable deportment; whereon the Judge shall proceed to examine the applicant, and if satisfied of his legal attainments, shall give him a certificate of the same; under which, if given by a Judge of the District Court, he shall be authorized to practice in the District and inferior Courts of that district, until the next succeeding term of the District Court of the county in which the applicant resides; and if given by a Supreme Judge, he shall be authorized to practice in the Supreme Court until its next regular term.(a)

Permanent license how granted in term time.

ART. 45. [2] During the term of any District Court, or of the Supreme Court, upon application in writing of any person desiring to obtain a permanent license to practice as attorney and counsellor at law in the courts of the State, accompanied with a certificate from the County Court, of the character specified in the first section, the court shall as soon as convenient, appoint a committee of three or more practicing attorneys of good standing, and set a day for the examination of the applicant, on which day the committee so appointed shall in open court proceed to examine the applicant, and if they, or a majority of them, and the court are satisfied of his legal qualifications, a report of that fact shall on the next day be made by the committee, and recorded by the Clerk, and thereon the Court shall order the Clerk to make out a license for the applicant, which shall be signed by the court and tested by the Clerk, under the seal of the court; under which when delivered, if granted by the District Court, the party shall be authorized to practice in any District or inferior Court of the State, and if by the Supreme Court, then in any court of the State.

Imigrants from other States may be licensed.

ART. 46. [3] Any person who immigrates to this State from any other State of the Union, with a view of permanently residing therein, may be admitted to practice as attorney and counsellor at law, upon producing a license from any Circuit or District Court, or Supreme Court of the State from which he emigrated, and also producing satisfactory evidence to the Judge or court to whom he applies, that he is a man of good reputation for moral character and honorable deportment, and shall not be subject to the requisites of residence prescribed in the first section of this act.

Oath to be administered.

ART. 47. [4] Before delivering to any person the certificate or license provided for in the preceding sections, the Judge or Clerk of the Court shall administer to the applicant the oath or affirmation prescribed by the Constitution of the State, which shall be entered on the license or certificate by the officer administering it; and upon the delivery of any permanent license, the Clerk of the Court granting it shall enrol the name of the person admitted on the records of the court.

Convicted persons shall not obtain license. If licensed shall be stricken from roll.

ART. 48. [5] No person convicted of bribery, perjury, forgery, larceny, or other felony, or of treason against this State or the United States, shall be capable of obtaining a license as attorney and counsellor at law; or if licensed, any Court of Record in which such person may practice, shall on proof of a conviction of any crime in this section named, supersede his license, and strike the name of such person from the roll of attorneys.

Officers of courts shall not practice.

ART. 49. [6] No Judge of the Supreme or District Courts, Sheriffs or Deputy Sheriffs, Coroners, Clerks of Courts, or Constables, shall be allowed to appear or plead as an attorney in any Court of Record in this State; nor shall

(a) The act which authorizes an attorney to appear by brief in the Supreme Court, means attorneys who are known to the Court as members of the Supreme Court bar. Thom v. Lawson, 6 Tex. Rep., 240.

any county or probate Judge, be allowed to appear in any case or suit originating in the court of which he is or may have been a Judge during the pendency of such suit.

ART. 50. [7] Any person not already licensed as an attorney at law, according to laws heretofore in force, who shall offer or attempt to practice as an attorney and counsellor at law, without obtaining a license, in the manner directed by this act, shall for every such offence, forfeit and pay a fine of not less than fifty, nor more than five hundred dollars, to be recovered by information or plaint of any person who informs in any court of the county having jurisdiction, one-half to the use of the informer, and the other to the county treasury: Provided, that nothing herein contained be so construed as to prevent or deprive any citizen of the right personally to prosecute or defend any suit in which he may be a party.

Penalty for practicing without license. (*Quere.* Is not this section repealed by the Penal Code?)

ART. 51. [8] Any attorney or counsellor at law who shall be guilty of any fraudulent or dishonorable conduct, or of any mal-practice, shall be liable to be suspended or stricken from the roll of attorneys at the discretion of the court; and any attorney who may be stricken from the roll, shall not afterwards be allowed to practice in any court of the State, unless reinstated on appeal to the Supreme Court.(*a*)

For certain acts to be stricken from roll.

Act of Feb. 11, 1854.

ART. 52. [1] Any prosecution under the fifth and eighth sections of this act, or for a contempt involving fraudulent or dishonorable conduct, or mal-practice, may be instituted by motion or information of any two or more practicing attorneys of any court in which the party prosecuted may practice; of which motion or information a copy shall be served on the defendant at least five days before the trial thereof; and the motion or information shall be made and carried on in the name of the State of Texas.

Prosecution for contempt.

ART. 53. [2] Each attorney and counsellor at law shall be subject to fine or imprisonment by any court in which he may practice, for misbehavior or contempt offered to such court; but no court shall strike an attorney and counsellor at law from the rolls for contempt, unless it involve fraudulent or dishonorable conduct, or mal-practice, in which case proceedings may be had as directed in the preceding section; and any attorney or counsellor at law who may be charged with contempt in the District Court, shall have the right to a trial by jury, should he demand it, and may plead not guilty as in prosecutions for misdemeanors, whereupon a jury shall be empanneled to try the cause, and if the jury find the accused guilty, they shall assess the punishment, and the court shall enter judgment in accordance with the verdict of the jury.

Fine and imprisonment for contempt.—Trial by jury for certain acts of contempt.

Act of May 12, 1846.

ART. 54. [11] Each attorney and counsellor who receives or collects money for his client and refuses to pay over the same when demanded, may be proceeded against by motion of the party injured or his attorney, before the District Court of the county in which such attorney or counsellor usually resides, or in which he resided when he collected or received the money, notice of which motion, with a copy thereof, shall be served on such party at least five days before the trial thereof; and in case the motion be sustained, judgment shall be rendered against the defendant for the amount by him collected or received, with legal interest, and also, not less than ten, nor more than twenty, per cent. damages on the principal sum; and if the evidence in the opinion of the court exhibits dishonorable or fraudulent conduct, then the court may, in its discretion, also adjudge that the defendant be suspended or stricken from the roll of attorneys.

Penalty for failing to pay over client's money.

(*b*) An attorney was stricken from the roll for representing the plaintiff in a divorce case without authority. Wilson *v.* The State, 6 Tex. Rep., 55.

Allowed to inspect papers and records.

ART. 55. [12] Each attorney and counsellor at law practicing in any court, shall be allowed, at all reasonable times, to inspect the papers and records relating to any suit or other matter in which he may be interested, without being required to take copies thereof; but no person whatever shall be allowed to take any papers out of the office to which they belong, without the permission of the clerk or keeper of the records; and the party withdrawing said papers, shall leave a descriptive receipt for the same.

Act of January 11, 1856.

May make affidavit in suits.

ART. 56. [1] Whenever in the commencement or progress of any suit or judicial proceeding, it may be necessary or proper for any party to such suit or proceeding to make an affidavit therein, such affidavit may be made by an Agent or Attorney at Law of the party to such suit or proceeding, and any affidavit so made by such Agent or Attorney shall have the same force and effect as if made by the principal.

ATTORNEY-GENERAL.

Act of May 11, 1846.

Duties.

ART. 57. [1] It shall be the duty of the Attorney-General to prosecute and defend all actions in the Supreme Court of the State, in which the State may be interested; and also to perform such other duties as may be prescribed by the constitution and laws of the State.

Failure to attend court—penalty.

ART. 58. [2] If any Attorney-General shall fail, from any cause, to attend said court at any of its sessions, his salary shall be liable to such deduction as may be prescribed by law.

To advise Dist. Attorneys.

ART. 59. [3] The Attorney-General shall counsel and advise the several District Attorneys in the State, in the prosecution and defence of all actions in the District Courts, wherein the State is interested, whenever requested by them so to do; and it shall be the duty of the Attorney-General to appear and defend the interests of the State, in any suits now pending, or which may be hereafter instituted, in the District Court, by empressarios for the settlement of their claims.

Report annually to Governor.

ART. 60. [4] It shall be the duty of the Attorney-General to report to the Governor on the first Monday of December, annually, and at such other times as he may require, the number of indictments which have been found by grand juries in this State for the preceding year; the offences charged therein; the number of arraignments, convictions, and acquittals, for each offence; the number of indictments which have been disposed of without the intervention of a petit jury, with the cause and manner of such disposition; and also a summary of the judgments rendered on conviction, specifying the offence, the nature and amount of penalties imposed, and the amount of fines collected.

Shall require reports from Dist. Attorneys.

ART. 61. [5] He shall require the several District Attorneys to communicate to him, semi-annually, at the close of the courts of their respective districts, in such form as he may prescribe, all the information necessary for his compliance with the requisitions of the fourth section.

ART. 62. [6] He shall transmit to the proper District Attorneys, with such instructions as he may deem necessary, all certified accounts, bonds, or other demands, which may have been delivered to him, by the Comptroller of Public Accounts, for prosecution and suit. Transmit instructions to Dist. Att'y.

ART. 63. [7] He shall require the several District Attorneys to report to him semi-annually, at the close of the courts of their respective districts, in such form as he may prescribe, precise information of the situation of all suits instituted by them, for the collection of public money. Shall require reports of District Att'ys of suits for public money.

ART. 64. [8] He shall report to the Comptroller of Public Accounts annually, on the last day of October, and at such other times as the Comptroller may require, a full and correct statement of the situation of all suits instituted for the collection of public money. Report to Comptroller.

ART. 65. [9] The Attorney-General shall, at the request of the Governor, Secretary of State, Comptroller of Public Accounts, State Treasurer, Assessor or Collector of Taxes, or Treasurer of any county, give an opinion in writing, in all cases touching the public interest, or concerning the revenue or expenses of the State. Give opinion in writing to public officers.

ART. 66. [10] He shall, whenever requested by the Comptroller of Public Accounts, prepare proper forms for contracts, obligations, and other instruments which may be wanted for the use of the State. Prepare forms of contracts.

ART. 67. [11] All money received by the Attorney-General, for debts due or penalties forfeited to the State, shall be paid by him into the Treasury, immediately after the receipt thereof. Pay money into Treasury.

ART. 68. [12] The Attorney-General shall keep in proper books, to be provided for that purpose, at the expense of the State, a register of all his official acts and opinions, of all actions and demands, prosecuted or defended by him or any District Attorney, in which any portion of the revenue of the State is involved, and of all proceedings had in relation thereto; and shall deliver the same to his successor in office. Keep books and register opinions and acts.

ART. 69. [13] It shall be the duty of the Attorney-General of this State to file the petition or information, and institute legal proceedings against all colony contractors who have entered into contracts with any President of the Republic of Texas; which proceedings may be commenced in any District Court for any county where the whole or any portion of territory embraced in any colony may be situate. Institute suits against Colony Contractors.

ART. 70. [14] No admission, agreement, or waiver, made by the Attorney-General, in any action or suit in which the Republic of Texas or the State is a party, shall prejudice the rights of the State. Rights of State shall not be prejudiced.

ART. 71. [15] The Attorney-General shall reside at, and keep his office at, the seat of Government. Reside and keep office at the seat of government.

ART. 72. [1] Whenever a vacancy may occur in the office of Attorney-General by death, resignation, or otherwise, it shall be the duty of the Governor, whenever the interest of the state may require it, to appoint counsel to represent the State; which counsel, so appointed, shall hold his appointment until an Attorney-General can be elected and qualified, and no longer, and shall be entitled to receive, as compensation for his services, at the same rate as is by law allowed to the Attorney-General. Act of January 11, 1850. In case of vacancy.

BANKRUPTCY.(a)

Act of January 19, 1841.

Who may become.

ART. 73. [1] Any citizen of this Republic, or resident therein, if a male, being twenty-one years old, or if a feme sole, being eighteen years old, or over, desiring to yield his or her estate for the satisfaction of creditors, and obtain exoneration from existing debts and pecuniary liabilities, may do so [in] observance of the following rules:

Petition and oath.

ART. 74.—RULE 1. He or she may present his or her petition to the Chief Justice of the county of his or her residence, stating as nearly as recollected, the names and additions of his or her creditors, and sums payable to them, (which statement shall not avail as an admission of the validity or amount thereof,) and praying the benefit of this act; thereon shall be an oath, or affirmation, signed by the petitioner, and to be taken before the said Judge, in these words: "I, ——, swear (or affirm) that my preceding petition is preferred in good faith, in order to a just transfer of my estate to my creditors; that I have not aliened, given, lent, leased, encumbered, covered or secreted, any of my estate, real, mixed or personal, or in possession, expectancy or action, with intent to delay, defeat or defraud my creditors; that there is not in the possession of any person or persons, natural or conventional, and known to me, any of my estate on secret or collusive trust, condition or contingency, directly or indirectly, for my present or future benefit; and that the deed of transfer, now executed to my trustees in bankruptcy, contains a full exhibition of all such of my estate, as now known to or remembered by me." If this be false when taken, the petitioner shall be subject to prosecution and punishment for perjury.

Notice to be published.

ART. 75.—RULE 2. This petition shall be preceded by a notice, three weeks successively published in some gazette of said county, or of the next nearest county having a gazette, in substance thus: "Before the Chief Justice of —— county, on the —— day of ——, I will apply for discharge in bankruptcy." The printer's certificate of the due publication, with one insertion subjoined, shall accompany the petition, and be sufficient evidence of publication.

ART. 76.—RULE 3. On the day notified, or second or third day next afterwards, if circumstances require, the said oath or affirmation shall be administered to the petitioner by the said Chief Justice, on his solemn explanation of its terms, import, and effects; and concurrently the petitioner shall sign, seal and deliver, before the Chief Justice, a deed in this form and substance: "Deed of conveyance and assignment by me —— to ——, trustees for the use of my creditors in bankruptcy: I convey to said trustees and their successors, all my estate, real, mixed and personal, whether in possession, expectancy, action or trust, to be held, collected, applied and

Shall make deed to trustees.

(a) A bankrupt or insolvent law of a State, which discharges the person of the debtor and his future acquisitions, is not a law impairing the obligations of contracts, so far as it respects debts contracted subsequent to the passage of that law. Beers & Smith v. Rhea, 5 Tex. Rep. 349. A discharge under such law, is not a good plea in bar to an action on a contract made *without* such state, nor when made *in* the state with a citizen of another state. Ibid.

distributed by them in satisfaction of all my creditors, according to the rules, conditions and limitations, of the act creating a system of bankruptcy; and this conveyance and assignment embraces whatever of such of my estate as may not be recollected and herein enumerated. The estate transferred is the following: [here let it be described.] Yet, out of the above, I am allowed to except, and do reserve for my support, the following: [here the reservation allowed in the fourth rule, is to be specified.] And I, with said trustees, hereunto set my name and seal, the —— day of ——." A majority of the designated creditors may nominate, in writing, the three trustees to be appointed, or otherwise they shall be selected by the said Chief Justice; the deed being signed, sealed and delivered, before the said Chief Justice, and certified by him, shall be considered as delivered for registration in the said Chief Justice's court on the day of its date; shall be recorded by the register within three months next afterwards, and shall be effectual from its date, as against subsequent creditors, purchasers, or donees.(*a*) Deed to be recorded.

Art. 77.—Rule 4. The reservation to the petitioner shall be, if a married man with wife and a child or children, or a wife only, or a child or children only to support, or if a feme sole, with or without a child or children, in full property, his or her homestead, with fifty acres of his or her lands, if he or she have so much, and if not, then all of his or her lands, with the improvements thereon; the fifty acres (if so much there be,) to be selected by him or her; also one year's provisions, one or more of the cows and calves, not exceeding three, and one or more of the horses, not exceeding two, mules or stock sufficient to work the reserved premises, one or more beds and bedding, and a sufficiency of household and kitchen furniture and farming utensils, according to the number and condition of the family; and at the allotment of the said Chief Justice, also in full property, the apparel of the family, and the professional books or tools, and implements of the art or trade of the petitioner—always reserving the family Bible, and giving to the wife or feme sole, in separate property, her musical instruments. If the petitioner be a single man, without a child to support, or grandchild, he shall have only one year's occupation of his homestead, one year's provisions, and horse, saddle and accoutrements, his apparel, professional books or tools, and implements of his art or trade. If any of the things reserved be not of the estate, there is to be no equivalent, except only in respect to the year's provisions, if not on hand, to be fixed by the Chief Justice. This reservation shall be exempt from existing debt and pecuniary liability, and from future levy, distress or attachment, unless it be charged by the act of the owner specially. If, at the reservation, there be any lien on the estate by judgment or decree, without being rendered specific by levy, it shall be discharged, and the creditor by judgment or decree, shall be remitted to priority of satisfaction out of the estate transferred in bankruptcy. If there be on any of the estate a specific lien by levy, the reservation shall be formed out of such of the estate as is not so bound. Reservation to bankrupt.

Art. 78.—Rule 5. When the oath shall have been taken, and deed delivered, the Chief Justice shall grant to the petitioner a discharge, thus:—"Republic of Texas, ——— county, ——— before me ———, Chief Justice of said county, this ——— day ———, has made conveyance and assignment to ———, trustees in bankruptcy of his (or her) estate: wherefore he (or she) is fully and for ever discharged from all of his (or her) existing debts and pecuniary liabilities, and exonerated from any suit, arrest, proceeding, levy, distress, attachment, hindrance, or molestation by or from any one, more or all of his or her present creditor or creditors. Witness my name and the Discharge.

(*a*) The assignment transfers the whole estate of the debtor, whether described in the deed or not. Smith *v.* Talbot, 18 Tex. Rep. 774.

seal of my Court, this ——— day of ———;" and this discharge shall have the effect it declares, in all courts, in all places, with and before all officers and persons, and to all intents and purposes. It shall be recorded by the Register, and on affidavit of the loss of the original, a certified copy by the Register shall be of equal force.

Power and duty of trustees.

ART. 79.—RULE 6. The said deed shall impart to the trustees, any two or one of them, power to take possession and fiduciary ownership of all the tangible estate of the bankrupt, wheresoever situated or found; to demand, receive, and acquit for anything, or debt of such estate in the hand of any person, and to the end of obtaining possession, and the exertion of the delegated fiduciary control over the same, shall have the like power, privileges and rights, which the principal had prior to the transfer. If a suit be requisite, it shall be in the name:—"The Trustees of a bankrupt." In the event of a succession in the commission, there need be no suggestion or revivor. On the death, dismission, resignation, removal or vacancy in the commission, the Chief Justice shall appoint a successor or successors, by noting and signing the appointment on the margin of the record of the deed, and on the deed itself, if presented; and the certificate of the Chief Justice, or of the Register, of the succession, shall be sufficient evidence thereof. In the like name, and without suggestion of succession or revivor, the trustees may be impleaded and defined, if sued in respect of any of the trust estate. The trustees thus may sue to recover any of such estate, whether mentioned in the deed and withheld, or not enumerated therein by accident, or fraudulently, collusively or colourably, conveyed, assured, assigned, given, loaned or bargained, or in any manner encumbered or covered, with intent to hinder, delay, defraud or defeat the creditors of the bankrupt, and all such fraudulent, collusive, or colourable disposition, shall be held utterly void. If, in any suit prosecuted or defended by the trustees, they wish the usual appeal, it shall be granted without security. They are not to be chargeable out of their own proper estates, for any costs or moneys adjudged against them in any such suit, but payment thereof shall be adjudged to be made out of the trust fund, namely: of the costs entirely, and of any pecuniary recovery on a claim against the bankrupt to be paid ratably. The trustees, or any of them, may be sued individually, for culpable neglect or mismanagement of the trust estate, or any fraudulent waste, conversion or embezzlement thereof, if desired by a majority of the designated creditors, and such suit shall be in the name: "The creditors of ———, a bankrupt," without using their personal names, and the recovery shall be for the ratable benefit of all the creditors, according to the principles in this act, prescribed for distribution: and shall be levied of the proper estate of the trustee or trustees sued and inculpated.

Creditors may give directions.

ART. 80.—RULE 7. The designated creditors of the bankrupt may agree unanimously in giving written directions to the trustees, concerning the management, sale, or disposition of the transferred estate, only postponing distribution until after the lapse of one year, for the exhibition of claims against the same, and as much longer as may be requisite for the admission or adjudication thereof, and a just participation of the valid claimants. In the absence of such direction, the trustees, on the first sale day of the Sheriff of the county, where the real or tangible estate is situated, after the lapse of three months for perishable estate, and of six months for slaves and lands, shall, at the court house, within the Sheriff's hours of sale, make public each vendue of the trust estate, by tracts, lots, parcels or particulars, as is lawful and requisite to valid Sheriff's sales, including in the sale in the proper county, the landed reservation as subject to the occupation of the bankrupt, which is not to be interrupted, making conveyance or assignment of the bankrupt's title to the vendees, they presenting for signature the proper deeds. If a bid

In absence of directions, trustees to sell.

be not promptly paid, there is to be a re-sale on that or the next day; and any deficit in the re-sale shall be paid by the first vendee, otherwise he shall be immediately sued thereon: all subsequent Sheriff's sale days shall be regular days for sales by the trustees of farther trust estate coming to their hands. Re-sale, if bid not promptly paid.

ART. 81.—RULE 8. If, between the grant of commission, and any of such days of sale, there shall be, in consequence of changes in the condition and circumstances of the country, as shall manifestly so enhance the value of estates as to render it probable that the trust estate will be more than sufficient to satisfy the creditors thereof, and the bankrupt, or his personal representatives or heirs shall so desire, he or they may apply to the Chief Justice granting the commission, for a rule on the trustees to sell only a sufficient portion of the trust estate, who, on five days' citation to the trustees, or any two of them, may make such order thereon as may seem just and equitable. If, upon a partial sale or sales, the debts of the bankrupt and the expenses of the commission shall be satisfied, the residue of the trust estate shall revert in the bankrupt or his proper legal representative, and shall be restored. Change in value of property. Partial sale to be made.

ART. 82.—RULE 9. On the grant of their commission, the trustees shall publish, three weeks successively, in a gazette of their county, or the next nearest county having a gazette, a notice thus: "The Chief Justice of ——— county, Texas, on the —— day of ——, committed to us the estate of ———, a bankrupt: therefore, after three, and six months, at the sale days of the Sheriff, our sales will be had. If claims against the trust estate be not presented to us within one year next after the above date, they will be barred." The printer's certificate, as in the second rule, shall be full evidence.(a) Publication by trustees to creditors.

ART. 83.—RULE 10. The trustees may recognise as valid and payable, any claim under the signature or written recognition of the bankrupt, or whose justness is known to them, provided, the creditor allow any just discount, set-off, payment or equity against it, if any; and in adjusting a debt due to the trust fund, they may allow any such discount, set-off, payment or equity; or in either case, if not fully satisfied with such mode of liquidation, they may resort to or require suit, and therein the principle of compensation and defalcation here declared shall be applied. No signature or admission of debt or liability, made by the bankrupt subsequent to the commission, shall be received in either mode. The trustees shall make a list of the designated and other disclosed creditors; and when the balances or amounts payable to them shall be ascertained by adjustment or adjudication, shall enter them on the list. At the end of one year next after the commission, after paying the costs and expenses of the commission, and reserving five per centum on the amount collected for their compensation, they shall distribute the residue on hand among the ascertained valid creditors, ratably, according to the respective balances or amounts ascertained to be due, reserving like proportions to meet the claims still in litigation, paying to each its share, on being established, and retaining the shares of rejected claims for further distribution among those established. Thus they shall proceed at the end of the succeeding year, when all claims shall have been adjusted, and the debts collected, and tangible estate reduced to money, full and final distribution as aforesaid, shall be made The only preference claims are the costs and necessary expenses of the commission, the compensation of the trustees, then the pecuniary recoveries had against the bankrupt prior to the commission, and not rendered specific by levy, as aforesaid; then any debt or debts due to the Republic by judgment Distribution. First year. Creditors paid pro rata. Succeeding year.

(a) The act is deficient in details, but its intention is, that creditors shall present their claims promptly, viz: within the limits of one year is manifest. Smith v. Talbot, 18 Tex. Rep. 774.

or decree, or for taxes; but this priority of the government shall be only such as now exists according to the laws in force; and in the relative application thereof, the dates of the admission of the claims of the general creditors by the trustees, and the adjudication of the others of such claims shall be regarded equally as the dates of adjudication or priority in regard to such claim of the government among the general creditors; except as excepted, there is to be no preference, but they are to be satisfied out of the residuum, ratably, in proportion to the ascertained amounts due to them. If there be a surplus after paying all, it shall be refunded to the bankrupt.

Surplus paid to bankrupt.

Trustees ruled to account.

ART. 84.—RULE 11. The trustees, from time to time, may be ruled by the Chief Justice granting the commission, by citation or attachment, out of, and returnable into his County Court, on five days' service thereof, to render such account as may be deemed requisite, touching the commission; and at the close thereof, a general exposition to be recorded; and so, on such process and service he shall have full power to adjust controversies, as between the trustees, to suspend or remove any one or more of them, appointing successors, or requiring security, if it shall seem proper; and in all things to exert such judicial supervision over the commission as shall be needful to keep its operation within the intent and scope of this act.

May be removed.

Proceedings to be recorded.

ART. 85.—RULE 12. The action of the said Chief Justice, in his court, or in vacation, touching the commission, shall be entered on the minutes, or other memorials of the probate branch of his court, the deed excepted, which is to be registered as aforesaid: the commission shall have its number, file, and index, in the series, and according to the time of occurrence, among the estates of decedents and wards; and the office fees and charges on the commission shall be those for analogous services, proceedings and items, in the probate department and registry of deeds.

Commission filed, and charges.

Act of 1841. Take effect March 17, 1841.

Bankrupts and insolvents emigrating to Texas

ART. 86. [1] Any person or persons, who may have, or may hereafter emigrate to, and become a citizen or citizens of this Republic, and who shall have yielded and given up his or their property in satisfaction of his or their debts, under the bankrupt, insolvent, or assignment laws of the state or country from which he or they may have so emigrated, or shall have otherwise, honestly, and in good faith, disposed of his or their property, in payment and satisfaction of his or their debts as aforesaid, by the said person producing a properly authenticated certificate, from the state or country from which he emigrates, of the fact of having taken the benefit of the assignment or insolvent law, which certificate shall be certified to by an authorized consul, or an accredited agent of this Republic: Provided, that the person so applying, shall be allowed twelve months from the time of pleading his insolvency to procure the certificate aforesaid, that he or they have so yielded, given up, or disposed of all his or their property as aforesaid, and obtaining the certificate to that effect, shall be as fully and perfectly exempt, and discharged from all and every debt, and pecuniary liability contracted previous to his or their having taken the benefit of the law as aforesaid: Provided, however, that said certificate shall not bar the rights of creditors, upon proof of fraud or falsity of said oath; and if said oath be false when taken, the person or persons so swearing falsely, shall be subject to prosecution and punishment for perjury.

Twelve months to obtain certificate.

No bar in case of fraud or false oath.

BILLS OF EXCHANGE, PROMISSORY NOTES, AND WRITTEN INSTRUMENTS.

[*See Discounts and Set-off—Principal and Surety.*]

ART. 87. [2] Any person to whom any of the aforesaid negotiable instruments may have been assigned, may, thereupon, maintain any action in his own name, which the original obligee, or payee, might have brought; but he shall not only allow all just discounts against himself, but, if he obtained the same after it became due, he shall also allow all just discounts against the assignor, before notice of the assignment was given to the defendant: but should he obtain such instrument before its maturity by giving for it a valuable consideration, and without notice of any discount or defence against it, then he shall be compelled to allow only the just discounts against himself. (*a*)

Act of January 25th, 1840. Take effect 16th March, 1840.

Assignee may maintain action in his own name

Discounts, when allowed.

ART. 88. [3] The obligee or assignee of any bond, or other written instrument, may transfer to another, by assignment, all the interest which he may have in the same; and an assignee of any of them may maintain an action in his own name; but, as this section has no reference to negotiable instruments, he shall allow every discount and defence against the same, which it would have been subject to in the hands of any previous owner, before notice of the assignment was given to the defendant; and, in order to hold the assignor as security for the payment of the instrument, the assignee shall use due diligence to collect the same. (*b*)

Assignee of instrument not negotiable.

Discounts.

Due diligence.

ART. 89. [4] The assignee or assignees, his, her, or their executors or administrators, of any of the instruments mentioned in the preceding sections* of this act, shall be entitled to recover from any previous assignor or assignors, his, her, or their executors or administrators: provided, that in any suit brought against a remote assignor, or remote assignors, his, her, or their executors or administrators, he, she, or they, shall be subject only to such recovery, and shall have the benefit of the same defence as if the suit had been instituted by any intermediate assignee or asssignees; and provided, also, that no joint action shall be commenced against any two or more assignors, unless when they shall be joint assignors.

Suits against assignors.

ART. 90. [5] When a suit shall be instituted by any assignee or assignees of any of the aforesaid instruments, the assignment or assignments thereof shall be regarded as fully proved, until the defendant or defendants shall deny in his plea that the same are genuine, and, moreover, shall file, with the papers of the

Assignments proved unless

(*a*) The first and second sections of the act comprehend all negotiable paper. Knight *v.* Holloman, 6 Tex. Rep. 153.

(*b*) The third section of the act comprehends all instruments not embraced in the first and second sections. Knight *v.* Holloman, 6 Tex. Rep. 153; Durst *v.* Swift, 11 Tex. Rep. 273. It is not necessary for the assignee to aver and prove himself an assignee for value, although the note have no words of availability. Ibid. Thompson *v.* Cartwright, 1 Tex. Rep. 87. McMullin *v.* Croft, 2 Tex. Rep. 397. Smith *v.* Clopton, 4 Tex. Rep. 109. Butler *v.* Robertson, 11 Tex. Rep. 142. The assignment of a contract in writing gives the assignee the legal title under the statute; and he may sue in his own name, although he may be a mere trustee, for the benefit of the assignor. Divene *v.* Martin, 15 Tex. Rep. 25. The holder of an instrument not negotiable, may maintain suit in his own name; but he must show his right to the paper, either by endorsement or proof of ownership. Marlin *v.* Manning, 2 Tex. Rep. 357.

* This word was enrolled "section" and afterwards altered, doubtlessly, by the enrolling committee.—COMPS.

denied by plea and affidavit.

cause, an affidavit, stating that he or they have good cause to believe, and verily do believe, that one or more of such assignments were forged. (*a*)

When assignor may be sued before drawer.

ART. 91. [6] The assignor or endorser of any of the beforementioned instruments may be sued without the necessity of previously suing the drawer, maker or obligor, when he may either reside beyond the limits of the Republic, or in such part of the same that he cannot be reached by the ordinary process of the law, or when he may be notoriously insolvent. (*b*)

Parol waiver of due diligence inadmissible.

ART. 92. [7] Parol testimony shall be inadmissible to prove that the assignor drawer, or endorser, released the owner of any of the aforesaid instruments from his obligation to use due diligence to collect the same.

Act of April 3, 1846. Take effect from passage.

Partial failure of consideration may be pleaded, when.

ART. 93. [1] The defendant or defendants in any action at law or equity, that may be hereafter instituted upon any bond, note, covenant, or other agreement in writing, in any court within this State, may plead a partial failure of consideration, where such bond, note, covenant, or other agreement in writing, shall remain in the possession of the original payee; or when it shall have been transferred or assigned after the maturity thereof; or when the defendant or defendants may prove a knowledge of such failure of consideration on the part of the holder, prior to said maturity [transfer?] (*c*)

Act of March 29, 1848. Take effect from passage.

Liability of drawer or endorser. How fixed without protest.

ART. 94. [1] The holder of any bill of exchange or promissory note, assignable or negotiable by law, may secure and fix the liabilities of any drawer or endorser of such bill of exchange, and every endorser of such promissory note, without protest or notice, by instituting suit against the acceptor of such bill of exchange, or against the maker of such promissory note, before the first term of the District Court to which suit can be brought, after the right of action shall accrue; (*d*) or by instituting suit before the second term of said court after the right of action shall accrue, and showing good cause why suit was not instituted before the first term next after the right of action accrued.

Same in Justice's court.

ART. 95. [2] Whenever the amount of such bill of exchange or promissory note shall be within the jurisdiction of a Justice of the Peace, the holder thereof may secure and fix the liability of any drawer or endorser, by instituting suit against the acceptor or maker within sixty days next after the right of action shall accrue.

Liability of drawer and endorser for non-acceptance.

Of endorser.

ART. 96. [3] The drawer of any bill of exchange which shall not be accepted when presented for acceptance, shall be immediately liable for the payment thereof; (*e*) and the holder of such bill may secure and fix the liability of any endorser thereof, by instituting suit against such drawer, within the time and in the manner prescribed by the first and second sections of this act.

(*a*) This section is not confined to assignments written on the instruments, but includes assignments by separate deeds. Durst *v.* Swift, 11 Tex. Rep. 273. Where the assignment is made by an agent, it is not necessary for the plaintiff to prove the authority of the agent, unless denied by affidavit. Herndon *v.* Ennis, 18 Tex. Rep. 410.

(*b*) Grayson *v.* Taylor, 14 Tex. 672. The principal being dead, suit may be brought against the surety in the first instance. Scott *v.* Dewees, 2 Tex. Rep. 153. Meriwether *v.* Lewis, Ibid. 340. Ennis et al. *v.* Crump, 6 Tex. Rep. 85. One of several promisors not signing as surety, cannot plead that he is surety, to avail himself of this act. Ritter *v.* Hamilton, 4 Tex. Rep. 325. Lewis H*v.* Riggs, 9 Tex. Rep. 164. Cook *v.* Southwick, Ibid. 61 e must have contracted and be sued as surety. Ennis5. & Reynolds *v.* Crump, 6 Tex. Rep. 85.

(*c*) The defendant may show a partial failure under a plea of total failure of consideration. Mercer *v.* Hall, 2 Tex. Rep. 284. A plea impeaching the consideration in whole, or in part, of a note in writing under seal, must be supported by affidavit. Clopton *v.* Pridgen, 8 Tex. Rep. 308.

(*d*) The court will, *ex officio*, take notice of the term to which the suit is brought, and whether to the first term of the court after the cause of action accrued. Hutchins *v.* Flintge, et al, 2 Tex. R. 473. Elliot *v.* Wiggins, 16 Tex. Rep. 596.

The fact of the maker's insolvency renders the indorser liable at once, and it is not necessary to sue the maker. Insall *v.* Robson, 16 Tex. Rep. 128. Rawdon *v.* Barton, 4 Tex. Rep. 289. The diligence prescribed as requisite to charge the endorser or drawer of negotiable paper, is substituted for the demand and notice required by the law merchant. Whatever will excuse the plaintiff from averring demand and notice, will excuse him from the use of the diligence prescribed by the statute. Dunum *v.* Headrick, 4 Tex. Rep. 495. Hutchins *v.* Flintge *et al.*, 1 Tex. Rep. 473. Frosh *v.* Holmes, 8 Tex. Rep. 29. The liability of a drawer or indorser of a bill drawn in this State and payable in another State or country, may be fixed by suit to the first term of the court, &c., as in case of an inland bill. Raymond *v.* Holmes, 11 Tex. Rep. 54.

Whether due diligence has been used is a question for the jury. Bailey *v.* Heald, 14 Tex. Rep. 226.

(*e*) Thatcher *v.* Mills, 14 Tex. Rep. 13.

ART. 97. [4] The holder of any such bill of exchange or promissory note, may also secure and fix the liability of any drawer or endorser of such bill of exchange or promissory note, for the payment thereof, without suit against the acceptor, drawer, or maker, by procuring such bill or note to be regularly protested by some Notary Public of any county, for non-acceptance or non-payment, and giving notice of such protest to such drawer or endorser, according to the usage and custom of merchants. Protest and notice by Notary.

ART. 98. [5] It shall be the duty of every Notary Public, who shall protest any bill of exchange or promissory note, for non-acceptance or non-payment, to set forth in his protest and in his notarial record, a full and true statement of what shall have been done by him in relation thereto, according to the facts, by specifying therein whether demand was made of the sum of money in such bill or note specified; of whom, and when, and where, such demand was made. It shall also be his duty to make the requisite notices of protest for the drawers and endorsers who are sought to be made liable; and when any such notice shall be served by him, he shall note in his protest and notarial record, on whom and when such notice was served; and when such notice shall be deposited in the post office by him, he shall specify when and where mailed, and to whom and where directed: and such protest, or a copy of such notarial record, certified under the hand and seal of such Notary Public, shall be admitted in all the courts of this State, as evidence of the facts therein set forth. Protest, how made. Notarial record. Notice to drawers and endorsers. Protest or copy of record evidence.

ART. 99. [6] Three days of grace shall be allowed on all bills of exchange and promissory notes, assignable and negotiable by law: (*a*) provided, that the fourth, fifth and sixth sections of this sct shall extend only to contracts between merchant and merchant, their factors and agents. Days of grace.

ART. 100. [1] The holder of any protested draft or bill of exchange, drawn within the limits of this State, upon any person or persons living beyond the limits of this State, shall, after having fixed the liability of the drawer or endorsor of any such draft or bill of exchange, as provided for in the act of March twentieth, eighteen hundred and forty-eight, be entitled to recover and receive ten per cent. on the amount of such draft or bill, as damages, together with interest and costs of suit thereon accruing: provided, that the provisions of this act shall not be so construed as to embrace drafts drawn by persons other than merchants, upon their agents or factors. Act of Dec. 24, 1851. Ten per cent. damages on protested drafts or bills.

(*a*) Days of grace are not allowed upon a promissory note, it not being made to appear that it was a contract between merchant and merchant, their factors or agents. Oliphant *v.* Dallas, 15 Tex. 138.

BLIND—INSTITUTION FOR THE EDUCATION OF.

ART. 101. [1] The sum of ten thousand dollars be, and the same is hereby appropriated and set apart for the establishment of an Institution for the Education of the Blind of Texas, which shall be located at the City of Austin. Act of August 16, 1856. Take effect from date. Appropriation for.

ART. 102. [2] A board of five Trustees shall be appointed by the Governor, whose duty it shall be to administer the funds of said Institution, and provide Trustees appointed—rent building.

for its going into operation as soon as practicable, by renting a suitable building and appointing such superintendent and other officers as may be required for the successful management of said Institution.

Money paid on order. ART. 103. [3] The said sum of ten thousand dollars shall be paid on the order of said Trustees, approved and countersigned by the Governor, out of any money in the Treasury not otherwise appropriated, as the actual current expenses of maintaining the Institution shall accrue; provided, that not more than five thousand dollars shall be expended in any one year.

Annual reports by Trustees. ART. 104. [4] Said Trustees shall be and they are hereby required to make full and accurate annual reports to the Governor of the State, showing the condition and progress of the Institution, with a full exhibit of all expenditures, and it shall be the duty of the Governor to lay the same before the Legislature.

Act of Feb. 11, 1858. Take effect from passage. Money appropriated. ART. 105. [1] The sum of twelve thousand five hundred dollars, or so much thereof as may be necessary, be and the same is hereby appropriated out of any unappropriated moneys in the Treasury, for the purchase and improvement of a site for the permanent location of the Institution for the instruction of the Blind of the State.

Paid out on order. ART. 106. [2] The said sum of twelve thousand and five hundred dollars shall be paid on the order of the Trustees, approved and countersigned by the Governor, out of any money in the Treasury not otherwise appropriated, so soon as they shall have made the herein authorized purchase.

Permanent location. ART. 107. [3] The Trustees of said Institution for the Blind shall be required, first, to examine carefully the tracts or lots of land belonging to the State in and around Austin, and if they can procure a suitable situation thereon for the permanent location of said Institution, they are hereby required to do so. But if the interests of the State and the Institution can, in their judgment, be better promoted by the purchase of any other than the property of the State, then they are hereby authorized to make said purchase.

Trustees to contract for improvements. ART. 108. [4] Said Trustees, after having made a selection for the permanent location of the Blind school, as directed by this Act, may contract for such improvements thereon as may be necessary for the present comfort and necessities of the pupils of said Institution, and that they may use any overplus of the appropriation made by this Act, that may remain after purchasing a site for the said school, for that purpose: provided, that no improvement shall be made upon any property so purchased, until said purchase shall be ratified by the Legislature.

Trustees to report purchase to Governor. ART. 109. [5] Said Trustees shall be and are hereby required to report to the Governor, so soon as they shall make said purchase; shall make a full and fair exhibit of said purchase and expenditures, and it shall be the duty of the Governor to lay the same before the Legislature at its next session.

Expenditures for buildings. ART. 110. [6] Should the Trustees select a location upon property belonging to the State, as directed under the provisions of the first part of the third section of this Act, they shall, under the direction of the Governor, Comptroller, and Secretary of State, expend the twelve thousand five hundred dollars, or so much thereof as may be necessary, for the purpose of erecting thereon suitable buildings for said Institution.

BOUNDARIES OF THE STATE.

ART. 111. [1] From and after the passage of this Act, the civil and political jurisdiction of this Republic be, and is hereby declared to extend to the following boundaries, to wit: beginning at the mouth of the Sabine River, and running west along the Gulf of Mexico three leagues from land, to the mouth of the Rio Grande, thence up the principal stream of said river to its source, thence due north to the forty-second degree of north latitude, thence along the boundary line as defined in the treaty between the United States and Spain, to the beginning: and that the President be, and is hereby authorized and required to open a negotiation with the Government of the United States of America, so soon as in his opinion the public interest requires it, to ascertain and define the boundary line as agreed upon in said treaty. Act of Dec. 19, 1836. Take effect from passage. Boundary of the Republic

ART. 112. [1] In accordance with the consent of the Congress of the United States, given by an Act of said Congress, approved July 5th, 1848, the Eastern Boundary of the State of Texas be, and the same is hereby extended so as to include within the limits of the State of Texas, the western half of Sabine Pass, Sabine Lake, and Sabine River from its mouth as far north as the thirty-second degree of north latitude; and that the several counties of this State, bounded by said Sabine Pass, Sabine Lake and Sabine River from its mouth as far north as the thirty-second degree of north latitude, shall have and exercise jurisdiction over such portions of the western half of said Pass, Lake and River as are opposite to said counties respectively; and this Act shall take effect from and after its passage. Act of Nov. 24, 1849. Take effect from passage. Eastern boundary of the State extended.

ART. 113. WHEREAS, said propositions are contained in the first section of said act, in the following words, to wit: "Be it enacted by the Senate and House of Representatives of the United States of America in Congress assembled, That the following propositions shall be, and the same hereby are, offered to the State of Texas, which, when agreed to by the said State, in an Act passed by the General Assembly, shall be binding and obligatory upon the United States and upon the said State of Texas: provided, the said agreement by the said General Assembly shall be given on or before the first day of December, eighteen hundred and fifty. Act of Nov. 25, 1850. Take effect from passage.

First: The State of Texas will agree that her boundary on the north shall commence at the point at which the meridian of one hundred degrees west from Greenwich is intersected by the parallel of thirty-six degrees thirty minutes north latitude, and shall run from said point due west to the meridian of one hundred and three degrees west from Greenwich; thence her boundary shall run due south to the thirty-second degree of north latitude; thence on the said parallel of thirty-two degrees of north latitude to the Rio Bravo del Norte; and thence with the channel of said river to the Gulf of Mexico. Proposition of Congress to settle the North-Western boundary.

Second: The State of Texas cedes to the United States all her claim to territory exterior to the limits and boundaries which she agrees to establish by the first article of this agreement.

Therefore, 1*st*. *Be it enacted by the Legislature of the State of Texas*, That the State of Texas hereby agrees to and accepts said propositions; and it is hereby declared that the said State shall be bound by the terms thereof, according to their true import and meaning. Proposition accepted.

CHANGE OF NAME.

Act of Feb. 5, 1856.

Take effect from passage.

Person may apply to District Court to change name.

ART. 114. [1] Hereafter when any person, acting in his or her own right, or a minor, under the age of twenty-one years, shall desire to change either his or her christian, or sir-name, or both, and to adopt another name instead thereof, shall file his or her application in the District Court, of the county of his or her residence, setting forth the causes which induce him or her to desire a change of name and to adopt another, whereupon the Judge of the said court, if in his opinion it should be for the interest or benefit of the applicant to change his or her name, and to adopt another, shall by a judgment of said court order that the adopted name of the party shall be substituted for the original name.

When and how a minor's name may be changed

ART. 115. [2] Whenever it shall be the interest of any minor, under the age of twenty-one years, to change his or her name, and to adopt another name instead of the original name, the guardian, or next friend of said minor, shall file his or her application in the District Court of the county of the said minor's residence, setting forth the causes which induce the minor to desire to change the original name, accompanied with the full name which the minor wishes to adopt. Whereupon the Judge of said court, if the facts contained in the application shall satisfy him that it will be for the benefit and interest of the minor to change his or her name and to adopt another, shall grant authority to change his or her original name, and to adopt another instead thereof.

Change of name not to release responsibility or defeat rights.

ART. 116. [3] Whenever any person shall change his or her original name, and adopt another instead thereof, it shall not operate so as to release the person from any responsibility which he or she may have incurred by the original name, nor shall it operate by said change of name to defeat or destroy any rights of property or action which the person had or held in his original name.

CITY RECORDER.

Act of Jan. 4, 1841.

Board of Aldermen to fill vacancy.

ART. 117. From and after the passage of this act, whenever the office of Recorder in either of the incorporated towns or cities of the Republic shall become vacant by resignation or other cause, the Board of Aldermen shall have power to elect a successor.

COMMISSIONERS TO TAKE DEPOSITIONS, ETC.(a)

ART. 118. [1] The Governor of the State of Texas is hereby authorized to name, appoint, and commission one or more persons, in each, or such of the other States of the United States, or the District of Columbia, as he may deem expedient, which Commissioners shall continue in office during the pleasure of the Governor, and shall have authority to take the acknowledgments and proofs of the execution of any deed, mortgage, or other conveyance of any lands, tenements, or hereditaments, and also to take the examination of married women as to their relinquishment of any right, title, or interest, which theymay have in any lands lying or being in this State.

Act of May 8, 1846. Took effect 26th June, 1846.

Governor may appoint—term of office—powers.

ART. 119. [2] Any contract, letter of attorney, or other writing, under seal, to be used or recorded in this State, and such acknowledgment or proof, taken or made in the manner directed by the laws of this State, and certified by any one of said Commissioners, before whom the same shall be taken or made, under his seal—which certificate shall be endorsed on or annexed to said deed or instrument aforesaid,—shall have the same effect and be as good and valid in law for all purposes, as if the same had been made or taken as now required by law.

May take acknowledgments—how certified.

ART. 120. [3] Every Commissioner appointed by virtue of this act shall have full power and authority to administer an oath or affirmation to any person who shall be willing and desirous to make such oath or affirmation before him: and such affidavit or affirmation made before such Commissioner, shall be, and is hereby declared to be, as good and effectual, to all intents and purposes, as if taken by any officer in this State competent to take the same.

May administer oaths.

ART. 121. [4] Every Commissioner appointed as aforesaid, before he shall proceed to perform any duty under and by virtue of this law, shall take and subscribe an oath or affirmation before the clerk of any court of record in the city or county in which such Commissioner may reside, well and faithfully to execute and perform all the duties of such Commissioner, under and by virtue of this act, or the laws of this State; which oath or affirmation, certified to by the clerk, under his hand and seal of office, shall be filed in the office of Secretary of this State.

Shall take oath to perform duties.

Oath to file in Secretary of State's office.

ART. 122. [5] Every Commissioner appointed under this act shall have power and authority to take depositions under a commission issued to him according to law, from any court in this State, to be used as evidence in any cause pending in a court of the same, when returned as prescribed by law.

May take depositions.

(a) A Commissioner appointed under this act has authority to take and certify an oath in authentication of a claim against the estate of a deceased person.—Greenwood *v.* Woodward, 18 Tex. Rep., 1; Hailey *v.* McGee, 19 Tex. Rep., 107.

He has authority to take and certify the answers of a party to a suit to interrogatories propounded by the adverse party. Lovett *v.* Casey, 17 Tex. Rep., 594; Walker *v.* Burbridge, ibid, 650.

COMMON SCHOOLS.

I. SCHOOL LANDS.

Act of January 26, 1839. In force from passage. Three leagues granted to each county.

ART. 123. [1] Each county of this Republic shall have three leagues of land surveyed and set apart for the purpose of establishing a primary school or academy in said county; which said land shall be located and surveyed by the County Surveyor, or his deputy in each county, and be paid the fees now allowed under the land law, out of the county treasury: provided there is that quantity of good vacant land in the counties: and further provided, that said land may be surveyed in any sized tracts; provided, that said land shall not be surveyed in tracts less than one hundred and sixty acres.

Proviso.

When to be surveyed out of county.

ART. 124. [2] Where there is not a sufficient quantity of good land that is vacant in any county, the County Court of such county or counties shall be, and they are hereby, empowered and required to have surveyed, upon any of the vacant lands of this Republic, said quantity of land, and pay the expenses of the land out of the county treasury.

Surveyor's return to be recorded and sent to Com. Land Office.

ART. 125. [3] When said lands are surveyed in accordance with this act, the Surveyor shall return a correct description of the same, with the field notes of the survey, to the Clerk of the County Court, who shall record the same, and forward a transcript of the same to the Commissioner of the General Land Office after it is recorded, with his certificate and the seal of office thereto attached; and when the lands so surveyed are not situated in the county for which it is surveyed, the description and field notes shall be recorded in the county where it is surveyed as well as in the county for which it is surveyed, and forwarded to the Land Office as above described.

ART. 126. [6] None of the lands appropriated and set apart by this act, for the purpose of education, shall be disposed of in any manner except by lease, until the expiration of three years, and none of said lands shall be disposed of by lease for a longer term than three years. Not to be disposed of until three years, except.

ART. 127. [2] It shall be the duty of the said School Commissioners, as early after the passage of this act as may be convenient, to cause to be located and surveyed, by some legal surveyor or surveyors, the three leagues of land appropriated to each of the counties of this Republic, by an act of Congress passed the 26th day of January, in the year 1839, entitled "An act appropriating certain lands for the establishment of a general system of education," provided the same have not been previously surveyed and located; and if any part of the said three leagues of land have been already surveyed and located, and due returns made thereof according to the provisions of the aforesaid act, then the said Commissioners shall cause to be located and surveyed, so much more land as will, including the parts surveyed and returned as aforesaid, amount to three leagues. Act of February 5, 1840. Took effect 16th March, 1840. School Com. to cause lands to located and surveyed.

ART. 128. [3] The County Treasurer of any of the counties of this Republic shall pay, upon the warrant of the Chief Justice, certifying under his hand that so much is due for surveying school lands for said county, to said surveyor or surveyors, so much money as the said warrant shall require: provided, that in no case the expense of said surveying and locating shall be greater than at the rate of one hundred dollars per league. County Treasurer to pay surveying fees when.

ART. 129. [4] The said Board of School Commissioners be, and they are hereby, authorized to cause to be surveyed, in such manner as is prescribed by the before cited act, one additional league of land, in the manner therein described; which said additional lands the said Board of Commissioners may, in their discretion, at any time, sell and convey to any person or persons whatever, and apply the proceeds of the same, or any part thereof, to the purchase of the necessary scientific endowments—one-half for the use and benefit of an academic school of each county, and the remainder distributed equally among the various common school districts which may be laid off in their respective counties. One additional league to be sold for what purpose.

ART. 130. [1] Each and every county in this State, which has been established and organized since the sixteenth day of February, in the year one thousand eight hundred and forty-six, or which may hereafter be established and organized by law, shall have surveyed and set apart four leagues of land for the purposes of education; which locations and surveys may be made upon any vacant and unappropriated lands within the limits of the State. Act of Jan. 16, 1850. In force from passage. Four leagues granted to new counties.

ART. 131. [2] The lands so donated, shall be located and surveyed in conformity to an act entitled "An act appropriating certain lands for the establishment of a general system of education," approved January 26th, 1839, and the provisions of the same shall apply to the lands when so located. How located and surveyed.

II. SCHOOL FUND.

[*See Constitution, Art.* 10.]

ART. 132. [2] One-tenth of the annual revenue of the State be and the same is set apart for the purposes of education, to be drawn from the treasury in accordance with such laws as may be enacted. Act of Feb. 11, 1850. In force from passage. One-tenth annual revenue.

ART. 133. [1] The Comptroller is hereby authorized and empowered to Act of Dec. 20, 1850.

State bonds to issue bearing interest. issue, in the name of the State, State bonds, signed by the Governor and countersigned by the Comptroller, to the amount of thirty-six thousand dollars, bearing five per cent. interest from date of issue.

Act of December 2, 1850. To remain in Treasury to the credit of school fund. ART. 134. [2] Said bonds shall be deposited in the Treasury of the State, and remain as a charge against the State, passed to the credit of the free common school fund.

Act of Jan. 31, 1854. Two million five per cent. bonds. ART. 135. [1] The sum of two millions of dollars of the five per cent. bonds of the United States, now remaining in the Treasury of the State, be set apart as a school fund, for the support and maintenance of public schools, which shall be called the Special School Fund, and the interest arising therefrom shall be apportioned and distributed for the support of schools as herein provided.

Act of Aug. 29, 1856. ART. 136. [1] The Treasurer of the State be authorized and required to transfer to the general or State account, the specie now in the Treasury, to the credit of the general School Fund account, and replace the same from the one million five hundred and seventy-five thousand dollars, United States Bonds, now standing to the credit of the State account; and it is hereby made the duty of the State Treasurer, annually on the first day of July in each year, to transfer the specie then standing to the credit of the school fund, received from one-tenth taxes to State account, and replace the same with United States' Bonds from the State account, unless otherwise provided by law; that the Special School Fund of two millions dollars, created by "An act to establish a system of schools," passed January 31st, 1854, and that the General School Fund, derivable from one-tenth taxes, be, and the same are blended and made one; and the interest arising from the United States Bonds, constituting said fund, and the interest arising from all moneys set aside for school purposes, be, and the same is hereby appropriated to the respective counties, for the use and benefit of the children of said counties, between the age of six and eighteen years, as herein provided.

Specie transfered to State account replaced by U. S. bonds.

Appropriated to counties for use of schools.

III.—SCHOOL SYSTEM.

Act of Jan. 31, 1854. Commissioners—their duties. ART. 137. [2.] The Chief Justice and County Commissioners shall constitute a Board of School Commissioners for each county, whose duty it shall be, during the year eighteen hundred and fifty-four, to form their respective counties into school districts of convenient size, and number the same, so that each district in a county shall be known by its appropriate number: provided, however, that in forming said districts the convenience of neighborhoods shall be regarded as much as possible, and each school district shall contain a sufficient number of children for the maintenance of a school. They shall, also, at the same time, order an election by the qualified voters of each school district, for three Trustees for each district, giving ten days notice of said election, by posting up advertisements of the same at one public place at least, in each district, stating fully the time and places of holding, and the object of said election.

Person to hold election appointed. ART. 138. [3] It shall be the duty of the Chief Justice to appoint a suitable person in each district to preside at the election in his district, who shall make his returns within ten days to the Chief Justice of the county, and the said elections shall, in all other respects, be governed by the laws regulating elections.

ART. 139. [4] The District Trustees, so elected, shall select from their number a chairman, who shall, whenever it may be deemed necessary, call a meeting of the trustees, and preside at their deliberations, and perform such other duties as may hereafter be assigned him. Chairman of trustees duties.

ART. 140. [7] It shall be the duty of the District Trustees to fix the time and place for holding an election in their respective districts (for the location or selection of school houses within their respective districts) and to appoint a presiding officer. That the chairman of the board of trustees shall cause written notices of said election to be posted up for at least five days next preceding the election, in three public places in each school district. That the returns of said election shall be made within five days to the chairman of the said board, who shall examine the same in the presence of his co-trustees; and a majority of the votes polled in a district shall be necessary to the permanent location of a school house; and no change of the location of a school house thus located shall be made, except by a majority of two-thirds of those voting in such election, taken after due notice as above provided. School houses—how located.

ART. 141. [8] No money shall be drawn from the county treasury for school purposes in any school district, until the people of such district shall have provided a good and substantial school house, with the necessary seats and other fixtures, and that the money appropriated by this act shall be applied only towards the payment of teachers for each school. School house to be provided before money is drawn.

ART. 142. [9] It shall be the duty of the school trustees for each district, as early as practicable after their election, by giving due notice, to call a meeting of all the patrons of the school in the district, and a majority of those present shall indicate to the trustees the length of time during the year they desire a school, the kind of teacher they want, and the amount of salary they are willing to pay. It shall be the duty of said trustees to observe, as far as possible, such instructions, to employ teachers of suitable moral character and qualifications, to visit from time to time the district school or schools under their charge, to expel a pupil for misconduct, to examine all complaints between teacher and pupil of a serious character, to discharge a teacher for incapacity or improper conduct, and generally to exercise supervision over the affairs of the school within their district. Term of school and teacher's salary settled by patrons. Duty of trustees.

ART. 143. [11] It shall be the duty of said trustees, upon receiving the shares of the school fund to which their school district is entitled, to apply the same towards the payment of the teacher's salary, and the remainder of said salary, if any, to apportion equally among the patrons of the school according to the number of pupils and the time sent by each to the school; and if any such patron should neglect or refuse to pay his share of the salary apportioned as aforesaid, said trustees may institute suit against him or her for the amount of money due, and the tabular statement furnished them, under oath, by the teacher, and mentioned in the preceding section of this act, shall be *prima facie* evidence of such indebtedness. (*See Art.* 155.) Funds applied to payment of teacher's salary.

ART. 144. [12] If any patron or patrons of the school are unable to pay their share of the salary apportioned as aforesaid, and the said trustees be satisfied of the fact, it shall be the duty of said trustees to make out a list of all such patrons in the district, together with the amount of money due from each for tuition, and forward the same under their own proper signatures to the Chief Justice of the county. Patron unable to pay.

ART. 145. [13] The Chief Justice of each county shall annually furnish the Treasurer of the State with a statement under his hand and seal of the county, of the amount of money due for tuition from all such patrons as are exempt Chief Justice of county to furnish Treasurer annual statement.

under the preceding section of this act in the county, according to the lists returned by the school trustees. And the Treasurer of the State is hereby authorized and required to pay said amounts of money due from the patrons so exempt, out of the school fund derivable from taxation and created by the Constitution of the State, and he shall distribute the same in manner and form as provided in the sixth section of this act. (*See Art.* 150.)

Trustees to be elected annually. Incorporated.

ART. 146. [15] The trustees of each school district shall be elected annually after the year eighteen hundred and fifty-four, on the first Monday in September, in the manner herein provided; that they shall be a body corporate and politic by the corporate name of the Trustees of Common School District No.——, (filling the blank with the number of the district,) and for the purposes for which they are created, may sue and be sued, hold and dispose of property, and do such acts and things as are incidental and necessary to the performance of their duties.

Chairman to apply for funds.

ART. 147. [17] It shall be the duty of the chairman of the board of trustees for each school district, to present, at least once a year, his application to the Chief Justice of his county for such amounts of said fund as his district may be entitled to receive, according to the number of children between the ages heretofore prescribed within his district, and also present his application to the Chief Justice annually for the amount of money due his district for the tuition of children exempt from tuition fees; and the said Chief Justice, hav ing duly informed himself that the same is correct, shall draw upon the County Treasurer an order, under his hand and seal of the County Court, for the amount or amounts so due and demanded.

Trustees may employ teacher in primary department of college when—

ART. 148. [18] Nothing in this act shall prevent the trustees of any school district, after being instructed by a majority of the patrons of schools in such district, from employing the teacher of a primary department in any college or academy, and converting such primary department into a common school for such district.

Act of Aug 29, 1856.

Census of white population between six and eighteen, each year.

ART. 149. [2] It shall be the duty of the Assessor and Collector of each county in the State, during each and every year hereafter, to make out a list of all the free white population in his county, between the ages of six and eighteen years, and transmit the same under his official signature to the County Clerk of the county, and a certified copy to the Treasurer of the State, on or before the first day of July in each and every year.

List to be filed and preserved by Clerk.

ART. 150. [3] It shall be the duty of the Clerk of the County Court to file and preserve in his office the list aforesaid, furnished by the Assessor and Collector. It shall be the duty of the Treasurer of the State to ascertain from the abstracts transmitted to him by the Assessor and Collector, the aggregate population between the ages of six and eighteen years. And the fund appropriated by this act shall be apportioned among the different counties in the State, according to the number of scholastic population in each county, subject to the order of the County Courts, and payable to the respective County Treasurers, upon the order of the County Court, under the hand of the Chief-Justice and seal of the Court, or such amount be placed to the credit of the Assessor and Collector of Taxes of such county, upon his payment into the Treasury of his county, the amount so appropriated to such county, and filing the receipt of the county Treasurer acknowledged by the said Treasurer before the Clerk of the County Court, and by the said Clerk, duly certified under his hand and the seal of his Court, with the Treasurer of the State.

How funds apportioned and paid.

Compensation to Assessor.

ART. 151. [8] The Assessor and Collector of each county, for the year 1856 and all succeeding years, shall receive for his compensation, for discharging the duties imposed upon him by this act, twelve cents per child for two hundred children and less; eight cents per child for all less than three hundred and more than two hundred; six cents per child for all less than four hundred and more than three hundred; five cents per child for all less than five hundred and more than four hundred; four cents per child for all less than a thousand and more than five hundred; three cents per child for two thousand and more than one thousand; two cents for all over two thousand. And should the Assessor and Collector refuse or fail to take and report the census of the children as required by this act, he shall forfeit the whole of the compensation allowed, and be fined not less than twenty-five nor more than one hundred dollars, at the discretion of the County Court; and in case of failure from any cause whatever, of the Assessor and Collector, in making a report of the census of his respective county, to the County Clerk, on or before the first day of July, in each year, the County Court shall be authorized to appoint some suitable person to perform said labor, who shall be entitled to the same compensation as allowed to Assessors and Collectors, under this act; provided, he makes his returns by the first day of September following. Assessors and Collectors, or other persons appointed to take the census of scholastic population, shall not be entitled to compensation for their services, unless their returns are made within the time prescribed by this act.

When County Court may appoint census takers.

ART. 152. [9] The counties which have not heretofore received their share of the Special School fund for either years 1854 or 1855 from failure to make returns of their scholastic population, shall be entitled to receive the same upon the following basis, to wit: Those counties that made returns for the year 1854, but none for 1855, shall be allowed an addition of five per cent to the returns of 1854, and the result be placed to the credit of such counties as their share of the fund for 1855. Those counties that made returns for 1855, but failed for the year 1854, five per cent shall be deducted from the return of 1855, and the result be placed to the credit of such counties as their share of the fund for 1854. Those counties that have failed entirely to make returns, shall, upon their making due returns for some present year, be allowed a credit for the years so failing, by deducting from the number of children for the year returned, such an annual percentage of increase as the aggregate returns of all the counties shown to be increase back to the year 1854. When the Assessor and Collector, or person appointed under the provisions of the previous section, shall fail to make and have on file in the Treasurer's office, by the first of the fiscal month of the Treasury, of each year, returns of the scholastic population of their respective counties, the census returns of such counties, for the previous year, shall be taken as the basis of distribution to such counties and the amount so set aside shall be paid to such counties without regard to returns that may be made to the Treasurer's office, after the date above mentioned.

What Counties to receive share of School Fund.

When census returns not made, basis.

ART. 153. [10] The Treasurer of the State shall send to each County Court and to each Assessor and Collector, a copy of this law, and require from each Court an annual report of the number of Schools, the number of children, the disposition of the fund, and such other information as will give a correct idea of the condition of the schools.

State Treasurer to send this law to County Court and to Assessor, and require report.

ART. 154. [1] All Schools which avail themselves of the benefits of this act, are declared to be Public Schools; and the County Court of each county shall annually apportion the School Fund among the children of scholastic age, who attend such Public Schools in the following manner:

Act of Feb. 5, 1858.

Public Schools—funds to be appropriated.

They shall first pay the tuition of all children whose parents or guardians are unable to pay the same; of orphans whose tuition has not been paid, and of the children of widows who have no greater amount of property than is secured by

Payments for what.

the Constitution and laws of the State, from forced sale, and who choose to avail themselves of the benefits of this act.

Balance. After paying as aforesaid, the tuition of those classes of children, the balance of the fund shall be apportioned among the paying patrons of the several Public Schools, in proportion to the time each child has attended School, without regard to the amount which may have been paid to the teachers by each paying patron.

See Act of Feb. 5, 1858. Teacher's Report. ART. 155. [2] Every teacher who claims the benefit of this act shall make a report to the County Court setting forth:

1st. The names of all the patrons of his School.

2nd. The names of all the scholars who attend his School.

3d. The number of days which each and every scholar has attended School.

4th. The amount which has been paid by the patrons of the School, upon the tuition of each and every scholar.

5th. The names of all such persons, being patrons of the School, as are entitled to the benefit of this act, whether on account of inability to pay, or as paying patrons entitled to a *pro-rata* interest in the distribution of the fund. The report thus furnished shall be examined, revised and corrected by the County Court, in such manner as to show with accuracy the names of such children as are orphans or the children of widows, and whose tuition has not been paid, and the names of the paying patrons, and the full amount of all tuition money paid from all sources, and no School shall receive any benefit under this act, which has not been taught at least three consecutive months, which shall be established by the oath of the teacher, sustained by the evidence of two respectable paying patrons of the School.

Bond of County Treasurer. ART. 156. [3] The County Treasurer of each county shall give bond, with two or more securities, payable to the county, in twice the amount of the School Fund to which the county shall be entitled, so soon as the Chief Justice shall be notified by the Treasurer of the State of the amount to which his county is entitled, which bond shall be conditioned, that he will, well and faithfully, keep an account of the money to him committed, as a School Fund for his county, and pay over the same, only upon the order of the Chief Justice of the county, under his hand and the seal of the County Court. He shall keep an accurate account of all moneys received and paid out by him, to register and number all orders by him paid or accepted to be paid. He shall, To be renewed when. between the first and tenth of the fiscal month of the Treasury of each year, (*See Fiscal Year*,) renew his bond; and all suits upon such bonds shall be in the name of the county, and in other respects they shall be governed by the laws regulating the bonds of County Treasurer.

State Treasurer ex-officio Superintendent. Duties of. ART. 157. [4] The Treasurer of the State shall be *ex-officio* Superintendent of Schools. It shall be his duty, after the first day of the fiscal month, in each and every year, to record the abstracts of children of lawful age in different counties, apportion the money as herein contemplated, distributing to the several counties the amount to which each is entitled, according to its scholastic population. And it shall be the duty of the Treasurer to keep a correct account of all the moneys and matters appertaining to the School Fund, and report to the Governor annually, at the close of the fiscal year, the condition of the School Fund, distribution of moneys, and such suggestions in regard to the school system as may be deemed advisable. That the fiscal scholastic year (*See Fiscal Year*,) shall commence and end upon the fiscal year of the State Treasury; that the County Court of each county, after ascertaining the scholastic population, shall make a return of the same to the State Treasurer, who, upon the order of the County Court, under the seal of their offices, shall pay over to said County Courts, or their order, their distributive shares of the interest of the School Fund.

Art. 158. [5] The County Courts shall allow, as the regular rate of tuition, a sum not to exceed ten cents per day for each scholar who may take the benefit of this act, and the act to which this act is a supplement. Rate of tuition.

Art. 159. [6] The amonnt which any teacher may be entitled to receive under the provisions of this act, shall be paid to him by the County Treasurer, upon the order of the Chief Justice, and when a distribution is ordered among the paying patrons of a School, under the provisions of this act, there shall be appointed by the County Court at least two responsible householders, patrons of the respective Schools, who shall distribute the fund to each one entitled under the provisions of this law, and make a report of their action to the Court at its next session. Amount how paid to teacher.

Art. 160. [7] In every case where a School claiming the benefit of this act, is attended by scholars who reside in a county, other than that in which the School is taught, the teacher of such School may report to the County Courts of the several counties, where the scholars reside, and shall be entitled to a distributive share of the county School Fund in the same manner as if the School were taught in the county of the residence of such scholars. Scholars from other County.

Art. 161. [8] There shall be appointed by the County Court of each county, a Board of School Examiners, consisting of three persons, who shall, upon application, examine all persons proposing to teach Public Schools within the limits thereof, and upon finding upon such examination, such applicant properly qualified to discharge the duties of a teacher, shall grant him or her a certificate, stating the branches he or she is qualified to teach; and no person shall draw any of the money set apart for School purposes under the provisions of the School law, unless authorized by certificate as herein provided, to teach a Public School. School Examiners, duties.

Art. 162. [9] The provisions of this act, so far as relates to the apportionment to be made by the County Courts, shall extend only to such children as are actually sent to schools of the State within the county; and no School shall be entitled to the benefits of this act, unless the English language is principally taught therein. Apportionment under this act extends to only, &c.

Art. 163. [10] The Treasurer of the State shall furnish forms for reports of teachers, and of the several County Courts, and County Treasurer, which forms shall be followed in making their several reports. And the said Treasurer shall cause a sufficient number of said forms, together with this law, to be printed, as will furnish ten copies for each County Court in the State. State Treasurer to furnish forms &c.

Art. 164. [11] Any teacher of a Public School who has taught the same for three months, and desires to avail himself of the benefit of this law, may apply to the County Court in advance of the annual apportionment of the School Fund to be made by them, and upon such showing as will satisfy the County Court, that the same can be done without risk of interfering with the annual apportionment afterwards to be made, the said County Court may order a partial payment to be made to such teacher, of the amount to which he would be entitled under this law. What teachers may receive pay in advance of apportionment.

COMPTROLLER OF PUBLIC ACCOUNTS.

Act of April 11, 1846. Took effect from passage.

Bond and oath.

ART. 165. [1] The first Comptroller of the State of Texas shall, within twenty days from and after the passage of this act, and every subsequent Comptroller shall, within twenty days after he shall have received notice of his election, and before he enters upon the duties of his office, give a bond, payable to the Governor of the State of Texas and his successors in office, for the use of the State, in the sum of seventy-five thousand dollars, with not less than six good securities, to be approved of by the Governor of the State of Texas, conditioned that he will faithfully execute the duties of his office; and shall take and subscribe to the oath prescribed by the Constitution, which, together with the bond, shall be deposited in the office of the Secretary of State; which said bond shall not be void on the first recovery of part or of the whole of the penalty, but shall thereafter continue in force for the whole amount of the penalty thereof, and may be sued on from time to time, and shall be deemed to extend to the faithful performance of the duties of his trust until his successor shall be duly qualified, and shall have entered upon the duties of his office.

General duties.

ART. 166. [2] It shall be the duty of the Comptroller of public accounts to superintend the fiscal concerns of the State, and manage the same in the manner required by law; he shall also perform such official acts as were required of the Secretary of the Treasurer under the Republic of Texas, when not otherwise provided for by law.

Shall make exhibits to Governor.

ART. 167. [3] He shall exhibit to the Governor, on the first Monday of December of each year, and at such other times as he shall require, an exact and complete statement of the funds of the State, of its revenues, and of the public expenditures during the preceding year, (or for such other time as may be required,) with a detailed estimate of the expenditures to be defrayed from the Treasury for the ensuing year, specifying therein each object of expenditure, and distinguishing between such as are provided for by special or general appropriations and such as are required to be provided for by law, and showing the means from which such expenditures are to be defrayed.

Shall keep accounts of the State.

ART. 168. [4] He shall keep and state all accounts between this State and the United States, and all other accounts in which the State is interested, and suggest plans for the improvement and management of the public revenue.

Shall superintend the collection of moneys.

ART. 169. [5] He shall examine and settle the accounts of all persons indebted to the State, and certify the amount or balance to the Treasurer, and direct and superintend the collection of all moneys due the State.

ART. 170. [6] He shall audit the claims of all persons against the State in cases where the provisions for the payment thereof have been made by law, unless the auditing of any such claims shall be otherwise specially provided for. Shall audit claims.

ART. 171. [7] He shall require all persons who shall have received any moneys belonging to the State, and shall not have accounted therefor, to settle their accounts; and shall from time to time require all persons receiving moneys, or having the disposition or management of any property of the State, of which an account is kept in his office, to render statements thereof to him. Shall require receivers of public moneys to account.

ART. 172. [8] He shall draw warrants on the Treasurer for the payment of all moneys directed by law to be paid out of the Treasury; and no warrant shall be drawn unless authorized by law; and every warrant shall refer to the law under which it is drawn, and no warrant shall be issued in favor of any person, or the agent or assignee of any person indebted to the State, until such debt be paid. Draw warrants on the Treasury

ART. 173. [9] He shall preserve the books, records, papers, and other things belonging to his office, and deliver the same without injury or damage to his successor. Shall preserve books of his office.

ART. 174. [10] He shall number each and every warrant he shall draw upon the Treasurer of the State; the numbers shall begin with one, at the commencement of each fiscal year, and proceed progressively to the end thereof; they shall specify on what particular account they are drawn; and he shall take a receipt for every such warrant from the person receiving the same, to be deposited in the files of his office. Warrants to be numbered and receipts taken.

ART. 175. [11] He shall furnish the Treasurer of the State, at the close of every month, with a report specifying the warrants that have been drawn during each month, their numbers, their several amounts, and the names of the persons to whom payable. Report monthly to Treasurer number of warrants.

ART. 176. [12] He shall prescribe and furnish the forms to be used by all persons in the collection of the public revenue, and the mode and manner of keeping and stating their accounts. Forms to collectors.

ART. 177. [13] He shall require all accounts presented to him for settlement, not otherwise provided for by law, to be certified to by affidavit, taken before some Notary Public, touching the correctness of the same, or by oath or affirmation, which may be administered by himself in any case in which he may deem it necessary. Shall require accounts to be sworn to.

ART. 178. [14] He shall remit or make an allowance to every Tax Collector in the auditing of his accounts for all sums of money which in his judgment have been illegally assessed. Taxes illegally assessed.

ART. 179. [15] The accounts of the Comptroller against the State shall not be passed to the Treasurer until approved by the Secretary of State. Accounts approved by Secretary of State.

ART. 180. [16] The Comptroller shall from time to time cause to be published, at the expense of the State, in one or more of the newspapers printed therein, such instructions relating to the payment of moneys due this State, or the duties to be performed by the Assessors and Collectors thereof, as he may deem necessary. Instructions to Collectors.

ART. 181. [17] All liens, mortgages, bonds, and other sureties for money given to this State, or any officer, and being for the use of the State, unless otherwise specially directed, shall be deposited in the office of the Comptroller. Obligations to the State deposited in office.

ART. 182. [18] He shall procure, at the expense of the State, a seal, with

Seal of office. the words, "Comptroller's Office, State of Texas," engraved around the margin, and a star with five points in the centre thereof, which shall be used as the seal of the Comptroller's office in the authentication of all his official acts, except warrants drawn on the Treasurer of the State.

Annual accounts. See Fiscal Year. ART. 183. [19] The accounts of the Comptroller shall be annually closed on the last day of October, and he shall exhibit all books, papers, vouchers, and all other matters pertaining to his office, for the examination of either branch of the Legislature, or any committee which may be by them appointed, whenever required by them so to do.

Treasurer's disbursements. Warrants cancelled. ART. 184. [20] The Comptroller shall examine the disbursements of the Treasurer, at the end of each quarter, and shall, together with the Treasurer, cancel the warrants which have been paid, in such manner as to prevent their future circulation, and shall examine if the receipts acknowledged by the Treasurer, during the quarter, correspond with the deposits, and if the balance of money reported to be in his possession is actually in his hands.

Act of Feb. 10, 1852. Took effect from passage. Chief Clerk—oath, bond, and duties of. ART. 185. [1] There shall be created the office of Chief Clerk of the Comptroller's office, who, before entering upon the duties of his office, shall be required to take the oath prescribed by the Constitution, and give bond in the sum of ten thousand dollars, conditioned for the faithful performance of his duties; whose duty it shall be to keep the books of said office, and discharge the duties of the Comptroller, whenever said office may become vacant by death, resignation or otherwise, or when the Comptroller may be unavoidably absent, or incapable from sickness to discharge said duties.

Act of Aug. 29, 1856. Took effect from passage. Comptroller to perform duties of Auditor and Comptroller. ART. 186. [1] The Comptroller of Public Accounts be, and he is hereby authorized and required to perform all the duties required of the Auditor and Comptroller, under the provisions of an act entitled "An Act relating to lost certificates of Public Debt of the late Republic of Texas," approved February 7th, 1853. And he shall also issue warrants on all claims which have passed the Legislature since the first of January, 1856.

CONGRESSIONAL DISTRICTS.

Act of February 11, 1850. Took effect from March 23, 1850. First District. ART. 187. [1] The territory comprised within the limits of the following named counties shall compose the first Congressional District of the State of Texas, and shall elect one Representative to the Congress of the United States, to wit:—Anderson, Angelina, Bowie, Cass, Cherokee, Collin, Cooke, Dallas, Denton, Fannin, Grayson, Harrison, Henderson, Hopkins, Houston, Hunt, Jasper, Jefferson, Kaufman, Lamar, Liberty, Nacogdoches, Newton, Panola, Polk, Red River, Rusk, Sabine, San Augustine, Shelby, Smith, Titus, Tyler, Trinity, Upshur, Van Zandt, and Wood.

Second District. ART. 188. [2] The territory comprised within the limits of the following named counties shall compose the second Congressional District of the State of Texas, and shall elect one Representative to the Congress of the United States, to wit:—Austin, Bastrop, Bell, Bexar, Brazoria, Brazos, Burleson, Caldwell, Calhoun, Cameron, Colorado, Comal, De Witt, Ellis, El Paso, Falls, Fayette, Fort Bend, Galveston, Gillespie, Goliad, Gonzales, Grimes, Guadaloupe, Hays, Harris, Jackson, Kinney, Lavaca, Leon, Limestone, Matagorda, McLennan, Medina, Milam, Montgomery, Navarro, Nueces, Presidio, Refugio, Robertson, San Patricio, Santa Fe, Starr, Tarrant, Travis, Victoria, Uvalde, Walker, Washington, Webb, Williamson, Wharton, and Worth.

CONSTABLE.

ART. 189. [1] There shall be elected by the qualified electors of each Justice's precinct of this State, one Constable, who shall hold his office for two years, and until his successor shall be elected and qualified; should a vacancy occur in the office of Constable, an election shall be ordered by the Chief Justice of the County Court, to fill the vacancy, and the person elected shall continue in office until a Constable shall be elected at the next regular election for county officers, and qualified according to law. Act of May 12, 1846. Took effect July 13, 1846. One in each Justice's precinct. Term of office. Vacancy.

ART. 190. [2] Every person who may be elected to the office of Constable, shall, before entering upon the duties of the office, give a bond with two or more good and sufficient securities, to be approved by the County Court of his county, for such sum as may be directed by said Court, not less than five nor more than fifteen hundred dollars, payable to the Governor and his successors in office, conditioned for the faithful performance of all the duties required of him by law; and shall also take and subscribe the oath of office prescribed by the Constitution, which shall be endorsed on said bond, together with the certificate of the officer administering the same; which bond and oath shall be recorded in the office of the Clerk of the County Court, and deposited in said office; said bond shall not be void on the first recovery, but may be sued on from time to time, in the name of the party injured, until the whole amount thereof is recovered. Bond and oath.

ART. 191. [3] Whenever any of the securities of a Constable shall die, remove permanently from the State, or become insolvent, or whenever the County Court shall deem the securities of any Constable to be insufficient, said Court shall cite said Constable to appear at a time to be named in such citation, not less than twenty nor more than thirty days after issuing such citation, and give a new bond with good and sufficient security; and if such Constable shall neglect or refuse so to do, his office shall be declared vacant. Bond to be renewed when.

ART. 192. [4] Whenever any person elected Constable, shall neglect or refuse to give bond, and take the oath of office as required by this act, within twenty days after notice of his election, the office shall be deemed vacant. Neglecting to qualify.

ART. 193. [7] When any Constable shall meet with resistance in the execution of any lawful process, or in the arrest of offenders, he may call to his aid any citizen of the county who may be convenient; and any person who shall fail or refuse to obey such call, may be fined as for a contempt, by any Justice of the Peace, in a sum not exceeding ten dollars, on motion of such Constable, three days' notice thereof having been given to the party accused. May call assistance. Penalty for refusing to assist.

ART. 194. [8] Each Constable shall execute and return according to law all process, warrants, and precepts to him directed by any lawful officer, and shall attend upon all Justices' Courts held in his precinct, and shall perform all such other duties as may be required of him by law. Shall execute process. Attend Justices' courts.

ART. 195. [9] If any Constable shall fail to pay to the proper person any Failing to pay over money collected. money collected by him, by virtue of any execution, within ten days after the same may be demanded, he shall forfeit to such person double the amount collected, to be recovered on motion of the person to whom the same belongs, before the Justice who issued such execution, against the said Constable and his securities, jointly and severally, they having ten days' notice of such motion.

Failure to return execution. ART. 196. [10] If any Constable shall fail to return any execution within the time prescribed by law, he shall forfeit and pay to the plaintiff in such execution the whole amount thereof, to be recovered with costs, on motion, before the Justice who issued such execution, against the said Constable and his securities, jointly and severally, they having ten days' notice of such motion.

Failure to execute and return process. ART. 197. [11] If any Constable shall fail or refuse to execute and return, according to law, any process, warrant, or precept to him lawfully directed, he shall be fined for a contempt, on motion of the party injured, before the Justice who issued such process, warrant, or precept, in any sum not less than ten dollars, nor more than one hundred, with costs, which fine shall be for the benefit of the party injured; and said Constable shall have ten days' notice of such motion.

Failing to pay over money. ART. 198. [12] If any Constable shall receive from any person, any bonds, bills, notes, or accounts for collection, and shall give his receipt therefor, in his official capacity, and shall fail to pay to such person, on demand, any amount he may have collected on the same, such Constable and his securities shall be responsible on his official bond, for all such amounts as he may have collected on such bonds, bills, notes, or accounts not paid over.

Unfinished business. ART. 199. [13] Whenever any Constable shall vacate his office, all unfinished business remaining in his hands, shall be transferred to his successor, and completed by him in same manner as if commenced by himself.

May execute process thro'-out his county. ART. 200. [14] Every Constable may execute any process, civil or criminal, issued by a Justice of the Peace, or Coroner, throughout his county.

CONVEYANCES.

[*See Registration.*]

I. GENERALLY.

II. OF SEPARATE PROPERTY OF MARRIED WOMEN.

I. GENERALLY.

Act of Feb. 5, 1840.

Freehold estates, how passed. ART. 201. [1] No estate of inheritance or freehold, or for a term of more than five years, in lands and tenements, shall be conveyed from one to another, unless the conveyance be declared by writing, sealed and delivered; and any instrument to which the person making the same shall affix a scroll, by way of seal, shall be adjudged and holden to be of the same force and obligation as if it were actually sealed(*a*): provided, the person making the same shall, in the

(*a*) Using the words "in testimony whereof I have hereunto set my hand and seal," or other equivalent expression in the attestation clause of the instrument, with a scroll appended, is a sufficient recognition of the scroll, as the seal of the party making the instrument. Flemming *v.* Powell, 1 Tex. Rep., 225. English *v.* Helms 4 Tex. Rep. 228. Clopton *v.* Pridgen, 8 Tex. Rep. 308.

body of the instrument, recognize such scroll as having been affixed by way of seal; nor shall such conveyance be good against a purchaser for valuable consideration, not having notice thereof; nor any creditor, unless the same writing be acknowledged by the party or parties who shall have sealed and delivered it, or proved by two witnesses to be his, her, or their act, before the County Court of the county in which the land conveyed, or some part thereof, lieth; or in the manner hereinafter directed, and be lodged with the Clerk of the County Court to be recorded. (See Scroll or Seal.) Creditors and subsequent purchasers.

ART. 202. [14] All alienations of real estate, made by any person purporting to pass or assure a greater right or estate than such person may lawfully pass or assure, shall operate as alienations of so much of the right and estates in such lands, tenements or hereditaments, as such person might lawfully convey; but shall not pass or bar the residue of said right or estate purporting to be conveyed or assured; nor shall the alienation of any particular estate on which any remainder may depend, whether such alienation be by deed or will, nor shall the union of such particular estate with the inheritance by purchase or by descent, so operate as to defeat, impair, or, in any wise, to affect such remainder. Operation of grant of greater estate than the grantor had right to convey.

ART. 203. [15] Every estate in lands which shall hereafter be granted, conveyed, or devised to one, although other words heretofore necessary at common law to transfer an estate, in fee simple, be not added, shall be deemed a fee simple, if a less estate be not limited by express words, or do not appear to have been granted, conveyed or devised by construction, or operation of law. Words to pass fee simple.

ART. 204. [16] The following form or purport of a release, or the said form in substance, shall, to all intents and purposes, be valid and effectual to convey from one person to another, the fee simple of any land or real estate, if the same be executed in the presence of, and subscribed by two or more credible witnesses:

"The Republic of Texas.

"Know all men by these presents, that I, ——— ———, of the ———, in the Republic aforesaid, in consideration of ——— dollars and cents, to me paid by ——— ——— of ———, have granted, bargained, sold and released, and by these presents do grant, bargain, sell and release, unto the said ——— ———, all that (here describe the premises,) together with all and singular the rights, members, hereditaments and appurtenances to the same belonging, or in anywise incident or appertaining, to have and to hold, all and singular, the premises abovementioned, unto the said ——— ———, his heirs and assigns, forever; and I do hereby bind myself, my heirs, executors and administrators, to warrant and forever defend all and singular the said premises unto the said——— ———, his heirs and assigns, against every person whomsoever, lawfully claiming or to claim the same, or any part thereof. Form.

"Witness my hand and seal this ——— day of ———in the year of———.

"Signed, sealed and delivered }
in presence of ——— } [L. S.]"

Provided, That no person shall be obliged to insert the clause of warranty, or be restrained from inserting any clause or clauses in conveyances hereafter to be made, that may be deemed proper and advisable by the purchaser and seller; and that other forms not contravening the laws of the land shall not be invalidated. Other forms and clauses valid.

ART. 205. [17] All conveyances by commissioners, sheriffs, or other officers legally authorized to sell land, hereafter to be made, for lands sold in virtue of any decree, or judgment of any court within this Republic, shall be and they are hereby declared to be good and effectual for passing the absolute By sheriffs and other officers.

title to such lands to the purchasers thereof, and all persons claiming under them, any law (to) the contrary notwithstanding; saving to the Republic, and to all and every person or persons, bodies politic and corporate, their respective heirs and successors, other than the parties to such conveyances, decrees or judgments, and those claiming under them, all such right, title, interest and demand, they, every or any of them, would have had in case this act had not been made.

Estates *in futuro.*

ART. 206. [18] An estate of freehold or inheritance may be made, to commence, *in futuro*, by deed, in like manner as by will.

II. OF THE HOMESTEAD AND SEPARATE PROPERTY OF MARRIED WOMEN.(*a*)

[*See Marital Rights—Constitution, General Provisions—Sections* 19, 22.]

Act of April 30, 1846. Took effect 22d June 1846.

Separate property of wife and homestead, how conveyed.

ART. 207. [1] When a husband and his wife have signed and sealed any deed or other writing, purporting to be a conveyance of any estate, or interest in any land, slave or slaves, or other effects, the separate property of the wife, or of the homestead of the family,(*b*) or other property exempted by law from execution, if the wife appear before any Judge of the Supreme or District Court, or Notary Public, and being privily examined by such officer, apart from her husband, shall declare that she did freely and willingly sign and seal the said writing, to be then shown and explained to her, and wishes not to retract it, and shall acknowledge the said deed or writing, so again shown to her, to be her act, thereupon such Judge or Notary shall certify such privy examination, acknowledgment and declaration, under his hand and seal, by a certificate annexed to said writing, to the following effect or substance, viz.:

State of Texas, County of ——. Before me, ——, Judge of, or Notary Public of —— county, personally appeared ——, wife of ——, parties to a certain deed or writing, bearing date on the —— day of ——, and hereto annexed, and having been examined by me privily and apart from her husband, and having the same fully explained to her, she, the said ——, acknowledged the same to be her act and deed, and declared that she had willingly signed, sealed, and delivered the same, and that she wished not to retract it; to certify which, I hereto sign my name and affix my seal, this —— day of ——, A. D. ——. [SEAL.]

But any certificate showing that the requisites of the law have been complied with, shall be as valid as the form here prescribed; and such deed or conveyance, so certified, shall pass all the right, title and interest which the husband and wife, or either of them, may have in or to the property therein conveyed.(*c*)

(*a*) The conveyance of a married woman, made under the forms of law, is as valid as if made by a single woman, and its effects can be avoided only by showing mistake, fraud, or duress. Callahan *v.* Patterson, 4 Tex. Rep., 61. She may in the mode provided for in the statute, pass her whole estate for the payment of her husband's debts, or encumber her estate to a less extent. Hollis & wife *v.* Francois & Border, 5 Tex. Rep., 195.

The mortgage by the wife of her separate property, for the benefit of the husband, should be closely scrutinized, and be free from symptoms of fraud, coercion, or undue influence. Shelby *v.* Burtis, 18 Tex. Rep., 644.

Undue influence on the part of the husband from which the wife will be relieved, arises mainly from some exertion of power over her person and property, so as virtually to deprive her of her capacity as a free agent, and not where an appeal is merely made to her sympathies. Ibid.

The statute applies to the transfer of the most insignificant article. Hollis & wife *v.* Francois & Border, 5 Tex. Rep., 195.

(*b*) The privy examination of the wife apart from her husband, is indispensable to the conveyance of her separate property. Callahan *v.* Patterson, 4 Tex. Rep., 61. Taylor *v.* Hall, 20 Tex. Rep., 211.

The statute does not expressly declare void any other mode of conveyance. It seems from its terms to have but one object in view, and that was to secure the freedom of will and action on the part of the married woman; and where the proof is clear as to the freedom of will on her part, and the transaction commends itself in point of equity to the conscience of the Court—particularly if the party contracting with the wife cannot be restored to his former position—the conveyance will be sustained notwithstanding the want of a privy examination under the statute. Womack *v.* Womack, 8 Tex. Rep., 397.

It seems that the Notary's certificate must be conclusive as to the facts therein stated, unless fraud or imposition is alleged. Hartley *v.* Frosh, 6 Tex. Rep., 208.

(*c*) A married woman who has withdrawn from this State, and domiciliated in another State, cannot claim the benefit of the homestead exemption. Trawick *v.* Harris, 8 Tex. Rep., 312. A mechanic furnished materials and built a house for another, without contracting under the statute for a lien, and the latter moved into it and occupied it as a homestead. It was held that the mechanic retained no lien upon the property. Merchant *v.* Perez, 11 Tex. Rep., 20.

ART. 208. [2] When a husband and wife have signed and sealed any deed, of the character described in the first section of this act, out of this State, but within the United States or any of their territories, if the wife appear before any Judge of a court of record having a seal, in any of said States or Territories, and be examined, and make the declarations and acknowledgments provided for in said section, and such Judge shall make a certificate thereof in the manner provided for in said section, and attest the same under his hand and the seal of his court, such deed shall have the same force and effect as if the same had been done in this State, before any of the officers named in said section; and when any such deed shall have been signed and sealed out of the United States, such examinations, declarations and acknowledgments may be taken or made before any public Minister, Charge d'Affaires, or Consul of the United States, and the certificate of such Minister, Charge d'Affaires, or Consul, in the manner and form provided for in said section, and attested under their hand and official seal, shall have the same force and effect as if such examination, declaration, and acknowledgment had been taken, or made and certified in this State, before any of the officers named in said first section. When deed executed out of State.

ART. 208a. [3] This act is intended to apply to the property mentioned in the twenty-second section of the seventh article of the Constitution, as well as to the property owned or claimed by the wife before marriage, and that acquired afterwards by purchase, gift, devise, or descent. Application of this law.

CORONER.

ART. 209. [1] There shall be elected by the qualified electors of each county of this State, one Coroner, who shall hold his office for two years, and until his successor shall be elected and qualified: should a vacancy occur in the office of Coroner, an election shall be ordered by the Chief Justice to fill the vacancy; and the person elected shall continue in office until a Coroner shall be elected, at the next regular election for county officers, and qualify according to law. Act of May 13, 1846. Took effect from July 13, 1846. One in each county. Term of office, vacancy.

ART. 210. [2] Every person who may be elected to the office of Coroner, shall, before entering upon the duties of the office, give a bond with two or more good and sufficient securities, to be approved by the County Court of his county, for such sum as may be directed by such court, not less than two nor more than five thousand dollars, payable to the Governor and his successors in office, conditioned for the faithful performance of all the duties required of him by law, by virtue of his office; and shall also take and subscribe the oath of office prescribed by the Constitution, which shall be endorsed on said bond, together with the certificate of the officer administering the same; which bond and oath shall be recorded in the office of the Clerk of the County Court, and deposited in said office: said bond shall not be void on the first recovery, but may be sued on from time to time, in the name of any person injured, until the whole amount thereof is recovered. Bond and oath

ART. 211. [3] Whenever any of the securities of a coroner shall die, remove permanently from the State, or become insolvent; or whenever the County Court shall deem the Coroner's securities to be insufficient, said Court shall cite said Coroner to appear at a time to be named in such citation, not less

New Bond, when to be given or. than twenty nor more than thirty days after issuing such citation, and give a new bond with good and sufficient security; and if such Coroner shall neglect or refuse so to do, his office shall be declared vacant.

Neglect to qualify, office vacant. ART. 212. [4] Whenever any person elected Coroner shall neglect or refuse to give bond, and take the oath of office as required by this act, within twenty days after notice of his election, the office shall be deemed vacant.

When to perform duties of Sheriff. ART. 213. [7] It shall be the duty of each Coroner to execute and return all process, of whatever nature the same may be, where the Sheriff is a party, and in all cases where just exceptions can be taken to the Sheriff or his deputies, or where there is no Sheriff. (*a*)

Same. ART. 214. [8] In all cases, upon affidavit filed with the Clerk of any court in this State, of the partiality, prejudice, consanguinity, or affinity, of the Sheriff of any county, where suit is brought or to be brought, or shall have commenced, the Clerk shall issue and direct the original or other process in the suit to the Coroner, who shall execute the same and attend to the suit throughout, in the same manner as the Sheriff should do in like cases.

Same powers and same penalties when performing Sheriff's duties. ART. 215. [9] In all cases where the Coroner is required to perform any duties appertaining to the office of Sheriff, he shall have the same power and authority as a Sheriff could have in like cases; and he shall be subject to like penalties for any refusal or neglect to perform such duties, to be enforced in the same manner; and he shall be entitled to the same fees as Sheriffs would be, to be collected in the same manner.

(*a*) When there is no Sheriff, or the Sheriff is a party, the Clerk may act upon his own knowledge in issuing process to the Coroner. Oliphant *v.* Dallas, 15 Tex. Rep. 138.

The Coroner is not authorized to serve a citation in error, unless the petition alleges some legal objection to the Sheriff, or that there is no Sheriff. Mays *et al. v.* Forbes, 11 Tex. Rep. 284.

COTTON WEIGHER.

Act of Sept. 1, 1856. Take effect from passage. To be appointed—where—duties—term of office—vacancy. ART. 216. [1] There shall be appointed by the Governor, at Indianola and Lavaca, in the county of Calhoun, and at Houston, in Harris county, and at Richmond, in Fort Bend county, and at Galveston, in the county of Galveston, respectively, one fit and competent person to superintend the weighing, with his own scales or balances, of such cotton brought to market in the usual bales or packages, as he may be required to weigh. He shall hold his office for three years, subject to removal at any time for gross and palpable misconduct. When a vacancy may occur, by death, resignation, removal from office, or from the county, it shall be filled by the Governor, and the person receiving the appointment shall hold said office three years from the date of his commission. The Governor may make similar appointments, at his discretion, under the provisions of this act, in any other port or ports of this State.

Oath, powers, and duties. ART. 217. [2] Every person so appointed, before entering upon the duties of his office, shall take an oath before any officer in the county, authorized to administer oaths, faithfully and impartially to execute the duties of his office, and to make true returns; he shall be in readiness at all times, in business hours, to discharge the duties of his office; he shall have power to appoint and employ one or more deputies, who shall be sworn to perform the duties, and for whose acts the principal shall be liable. He shall keep a

Deputies.

memorandum record of all cotton weighed by him, shall certify the weight in detail, and at the request of purchaser or seller, the merchantable condition of cotton weighed by him.

Liable to indictment--for causes. Penalty.

Art. 218. [3] He shall be liable to indictment and conviction in any court of competent jurisdiction, for malfeasance in office, and for fraud, and on conviction, shall be removed from office, and be fined in the discretion of the jury, not less than one hundred nor more than one thousand dollars; he shall also be liable in damages, to the party injured.

Scales--balances--weights--mark bales.

Art. 219. [4] He shall keep accurate and well adjusted scales or balances, and accurate weights, and shall mark with ink, in legible characters, on each bale, the weight thereof, and the initials of his name and office.

Fees.

Art. 220. [5] He shall be allowed, for each bale weighed, marked and certified by him, eight cents, and shall not be obliged to deliver the cotton so weighed, marked and certified, until said charge be paid and satisfied.

Other persons prohibited. Penalty.

Art. 221. [6] It shall not be lawful for any person other than a regularly appointed Weighmaster to weigh any cotton offered for sale in said ports, and any person so offending shall be liable to indictment by the Grand Jury of the county, and on conviction, to a fine of one dollar for each and every bale so unlawfully weighed, and imprisonment in the county jail, not less than ten nor more than ninety days, either or both of which punishments may be inflicted at the discretion of the jury; provided, that nothing herein shall be construed to prevent any person weighing his or her or their own cotton.

COUNTIES.

I. ORGANIZATION OF.

Act of April 11, 1846. In force from date.

To be divided into convenient precincts.

Art. 222. [1] It shall be the duty of the Chief Justice, and any two of the County Commissioners of each and every county in this State, immediately after the receipt of this act, to lay off and divide their respective counties into convenient precincts for the election of Justices of the Peace and Constables, defining particularly the boundaries of such precincts, and also, to appoint a convenient place in each precinct where elections shall be held; of all which they shall cause the county Clerk to make a record.

Same of new

Art. 223. [2] It shall be the duty of the Chief Justice and any two of the

counties made in 1846. County Commissioners of every county in this State, from which any new county has been taken at this session of the Legislature, or from which the greater portion of any new county has been taken, to lay off and divide such new counties into convenient precincts for the election of Justices of the Peace and Constables, defining particularly the boundaries of such precincts, and also to appoint a convenient place in each precinct where elections shall be held; of all which they shall cause a record to be made, which they shall send to the Chief Justice of such new county, when elected.

Where no Chief Justice or County Commissioners. ART. 224. [6] In counties where there are no County Commissioners, the Chief Justice and any two Justices of the Peace, shall perform all the duties required of the Chief Justice and County Commissioners in the first two sections of this act; and in counties where there is no Chief Justice, then the Sheriff shall perform all the duties required of Chief Justices by the provisions of this act.

Incumbents to continue in office until when. ART. 225. [7] The present incumbents of all county offices shall continue in office, and perform all the duties required of them by law, until their successors, or officers performing similar duties, shall be elected under the provisions of this act, and enter upon the discharge of their duties, when they shall hand over to their successors, or officers performin similar duties, all books, papers, and other effects, belonging to their respective offices; and until the new counties established by this Legislature shall be organized under the provisions of this act, they shall be considered as forming a part of the county or counties from which they were taken.

II. ORGANIZATION OF NEW COUNTIES.

Act of March 20, 1848. Took effect from passage.

New counties. ART. 226. [1] Whenever any new county shall hereafter be established, it shall be the duty of the County Court from which the territory of such new county, or the greater part thereof, was taken, at least one month previous to the general election for county officers, next after such new county shall have been established, to lay off and divide such new county into convenient precincts, for the election of Justices of the Peace and Constables, defining particularly the boundaries of such precincts; and also, to designate convenient places in such new county, where elections shall be held: of all which they shall cause a record to be made by the Clerk, and a copy thereof shall be transmitted to the Chief Justice of such new county, when elected.

Chief Justice of former county to order election. ART. 227. [2] It shall be the duty of the Chief Justice of every county of this State, from which any new county has been so taken, at least one month previous to the general election of county officers, next after such new county has been established, to order an election to be held in such new county, on said general election day, for all county officers authorized to be elected by the people of such new county, and to appoint a presiding officer for each place designated in such new county for holding elections; such order of elections shall specify the number of precincts, their boundaries, and the officers to be elected in such county. Such presiding officers shall hold such elections in accordance with the laws regulating elections, and shall make their returns to the Chief Justice who ordered such election, who shall open and examine such returns and give certificates to the persons elected.

When office of Chief Justice is vacant. ART. 228. [3] In all cases where the office of Chief Justice shall be vacant, any two of the County Commissioners shall be authorized to perform all the duties required of Chief Justices by the provisions of this act.

III. INCORPORATION OF NEW COUNTIES.

Act of May 11, 1846. Took effect June 22, 1846.

ART. 229. [1] Each county which now exists, or which may be hereafter established in this State, shall be a body corporate and politic. Each county a body corporate.

ART. 230. [2] All suits brought by or against any of the counties of this State, shall be brought in the name of or against the county of (naming the county), and by that name they may sue and be sued, plead and be impleaded, defend and be defended, in any court of record or other place where justice may be administered: provided, however, that no county shall be sued, unless the claim upon which such suit is founded shall have first been presented to the County Court for allowance, and such court shall have neglected or refused to audit and allow the same. Suits by or against.

ART. 231. [4] All suits against a county shall be instituted and prosecuted to final judgment in some court of competent jurisdiction within such county. To be sued in their own county.

ART. 232. [5] In suits against any county, all process and notices issued in such suits, shall be served on the Chief Justice of such county, and the original suit shall be served either during the sitting of the County Court, or so as a term of said court will intervene between the day of service and the return day thereof. Service of process on.

ART. 233. [6] In all suits instituted by or against any county, the inhabitants of the county so suing or being sued, may be jurors or witnesses, if otherwise competent and qualified according to law. Inhabitants may be jurors.

ART. 234. [7] No execution shall be issued on any judgment against any county; but when a judgment shall be rendered against a county, it shall be the duty of the County Court of such county to settle and pay such judgment in like manner, and *pro rata* with other claims of a similar description are settled and paid by said court. Execution not to issue against.

ART. 235. [8] All deeds, grants, and conveyances heretofore made, or which may be hereafter made and duly acknowledged, or proven, and recorded as other deeds of conveyance to any county, or to the courts or commissioners of any county, or any other person or persons, by whatever form of conveyance, for the use and benefit of any county, shall be good and valid to all intents and purposes, to vest in such county in fee simple or otherwise, all such right, title, interest, and estate as the grantor in any such deed or conveyance had at the time of the execution thereof, in the lands conveyed and was intended thereby to be conveyed. Deeds, grants, &c., to.

ART. 236. [10] All notes, bonds, bills, contracts, covenants, agreements, or writings, made or to be made, whereby any person is or shall be bound to any county, or to the court or commissioners of any county, or to any other person or persons, in whatever form, for the payment of any debt or duty, or the performance of any matter or thing to the use of any county, shall be valid and effectual, to all intents and purposes, to vest in said county all rights, interests, and actions which would be vested in any individual if any such contract had been made directly to him. Notes, bonds, &c., to.

ART. 237. [11] Suits may be commenced and prosecuted on such notes, bonds, bills, contracts, covenants, agreements and writings, in the name of such county, as is provided in this act, or in the name of the person to whom they were made, for the use of the county, as fully and effectually as any person may or can sue on like notes, bills, contracts, covenants, agreements, or writings made to him. Suits on notes, &c.

Costs where plaintiff fails to recover more than County Court allowed him.

ART. 238. [13] When the plaintiff in any suit against a county shall fail to recover a greater amount than the County Court of such county shall have allowed to such plaintiff, on the presentation of his account to such court, such plaintiff shall pay all costs of said suit.

IV. COUNTY LINES.

Act of May 12, 1846. Took effect June 22, 1846.

Boundaries to be run and marked.

ART. 239. [1] Whenever it shall appear to the satisfaction of any County Court, that the boundaries of the county are not sufficiently special and well ascertained, such court shall appoint some competent person to proceed and ascertain, survey, and mark such line; and the court, in the order making the said appointment, shall specify the line to be run, and the time when the same shall be run, and the place of commencement.

Notice to adjoining county.

ART. 240. [2] It shall be the duty of the court making such order, to cause a copy thereof to be presented to the County Court of the adjoining county, or the county interested, at least ten days before the time appointed for the running and marking such line; whereupon, such court, on receiving a copy of such order, shall appoint a competent person, resident in such county, to proceed at the time and place appointed and assist in running and marking such line.

Duty of persons appointed.

ART. 241. [3] The person so appointed shall proceed at the time and place appointed, to ascertain, survey, and mark the line designated in such order, and make return thereof to the County Court of their respective counties.

Map and plot.

ART. 242. [4] Each person so appointed, shall return to the County Court of his county, a map or plot of the line so run and marked.

If person appointed fail to attend—marked line to true line.

ART. 243. [5] If either of the persons appointed to run and mark such line, shall fail to attend at the time and place appointed, the one in attendance shall proceed alone to perform the duties assigned him, and make his report to the County Court, which being approved by such court, shall be recorded as evidence of the line in question, and the line so surveyed and marked, shall thereafter be regarded as the true line of the county.

Expenses.

ART. 244. [6] The expenses of running and marking any such line shall be divided and paid equally by the counties interested; and each person appointed to run and mark any such line, shall be allowed the sum of two dollars per mile for each mile run: provided, in all instances, that any line run as above directed, shall be made in conformity with the existing laws creating and defining said county boundaries.

COUNTY COURT.

[*Constitution, Art.* 4, *Sec.* 15.]

ESTATES OF DECEASED PERSONS.

I. ORGANIZATION AND JURISDICTION.

II. CHIEF JUSTICE AND COUNTY COMMISSIONERS.

III. CLERK.

IV. GENERAL PROVISIONS.

I. ORGANIZATION AND JURISDICTION.

Act of March 16, 1848. Took effect August 7, 1848.

There shall be, in each county, one court.

ART. 245. [1] There shall be, in each county of this State, an inferior court, to be styled "The County Court," which shall be composed of one Chief Justice.(*a*)

Powers of the court as a Court of Probate.

ART. 246. [2] The said Court shall have the power to take probate of wills, to appoint guardians, to grant letters testamentary, and of administration; to settle the accounts of executors, administrators, and guardians; to transact all business appertaining to the estates of deceased persons, minors, idiots, lunatics, and persons *non compos mentis;* and the settlement, partition, and distribution of such estates: which powers shall be exercised in the manner prescribed by law. (*b*)

ART. 247. [3] The said Courts shall have power to lay off and divide their

(*a*) The County Court is a court of record, having common law jurisdiction within the meaning of the act of Congress; and as such, has power to issue letters of naturalization under said acts. *Ex parte* Burkhardt, 16 Tex. Rep. 470.

(*b*) The powers of the County Court as a Court of Probate, being limited by express law, its authority is restricted to the enumerated subjects Francis *v.* Northcote, 6 Tex. Rep. 185.

May establish precincts, places of election, ferries and roads. respective counties into convenient precincts for the election of Justices of the Peace and Constables; to establish places in such precincts where elections shall be held; to establish public ferries in their respective counties, wherever the public interest may require; to license ferrymen, and regulate the tolls to be charged at all public ferries in their counties; to lay out and establish, change and discontinue, public roads and highways; to build bridges; to appoint overseers and apportion hands to work on public roads, highways, and bridges; and said courts shall have and exercise general control and superintendence over all roads, highways, bridges and ferries in their counties: said courts shall, also, have power, and it shall be their duty, to provide courthouses, jails, and all necessary public buildings; to allow and settle all county accounts, and direct their payment in such manner, and at such times, as may meet the public interest; to try contested elections for county officers; to appoint patrols for their respective counties, whenever, in their opinion, the public welfare may require it; and to exercise general jurisdiction over police matters in their respective counties: and it shall be the duty of said courts to provide for the support of indigent persons resident in the county, who cannot support themselves, and for the burial of paupers. (*a*)

May appoint overseers.

Shall provide public buildings

Shall try contested elections.

Indigent persons.

May levy a tax. Art. 248. [4] The said County Courts shall have power to levy and collect a tax, for county purposes, upon all subjects of taxation in their respective counties, on which a tax may be levied by the State: provided said tax shall not exceed, in any one year, one-half the amount of the tax levied by the State on such subjects of taxation; and provided, also, that such tax shall be apportioned in the same manner as the State tax: and the said tax upon all subjects of taxation, other than trades and occupations and professions, shall be assessed and collected by the Assessor and Collector of State taxes, in the same manner as the State tax, and shall be paid by him into the county treasury; and all of said taxes upon trades, occupations and professions shall be collected by the County Treasurer, in the same manner as the State tax upon such subjects is collected; and the County Treasurer shall have the same power to enforce the collection of such taxes for the counties, as the Assessor and Collector has for the State.

How apportioned.

By whom and how collected.

Statement of annual expenditures and receipts shall be published or posted. Art. 249. [5] The said courts shall examine and adjust the accounts and books of the County Treasurer, and shall annually cause a detailed statement of all the receipts, expenditures and debts of their respective counties to be printed in some newspaper printed in the county, or to be posted up in some conspicuous place in the office of the Clerk of said court.

Court vested with power of County and Land Commissioners. Art. 250. [6] The said courts shall have and exercise all the powers which, by law, are vested in County Courts or Boards of County Commissioners, or Chief and Associate Justices as Land Commissioners.

Seal of the Court. Art. 251. [7] Each County Court of this State shall have a seal, whereon shall be engraved the words "County Court, ——— County, Texas", the blank to be filled with the name of the county; which seal shall be kept in the Clerk's office, and shall be used in the authentication of all official acts of said court, or of the Clerk of said court, or of the Chief Justice of said court, or of the County Commissioners when performing any of the duties of the Chief Justice which they are authorized to perform, in all cases where a seal shall be necessary for the authentication of any of said acts.

The Court may issue all process necessary to enforce its jurisdiction. Art. 252. [8] Each County Court shall have full power and authority to issue all such notices, citations, writs, and process, as may be necessary for the proper execution of the powers and duties imposed upon such courts, and to

(*a*) Public charity, under this act, is confined to indigents resident in the county, who are unable to support themselves, and does not extend to transient persons. Upshur County *v.* Yeury, 19 Tex. Rep. 126.

enforce its jurisdiction; and all such notices, citations, writs, and process, shall be dated and signed by the Clerk, and, when not otherwise directed by law, shall be executed at least five days before the return day thereof, which shall be specified in the same: provided, however, that subpœnas for witnesses may be executed and returned forthwith; and all such citations, writs, and process, other than subpœnas for witnesses, shall have the seal of such court affixed thereto; and all such citations, writs, subpœnas, and process, may be directed to any lawful officer of this State, whose duty it shall be to execute and return the same.

By whom signed, and when to be executed.

Must have the seal of the court

ART. 253. [9] The County Courts shall have like power to punish contempts as the District Courts can or may have and exercise.

Power to punish contempts. [See Art. 381.]

ART. 254. [10] Each County Court shall cause to be procured, and kept in the Clerk's office, suitable books, in which it shall be the duty of the Clerk to record all the proceedings of each term of the court; which record shall be read over and signed by the Chief Justice, or the member of the court presiding, at the end of each term; and the Clerk shall also record all the proceedings of such court that are authorized to take place in the vacation between the terms; and such records shall be read over on the first day of the term of the proper court next after such proceedings took place, and shall be signed by the Chief Justice or member of the court presiding.

Suitable books. Minutes.

Proceedings in vacation.

II. CHIEF JUSTICE AND COUNTY COMMISSIONERS.

ART. 255. [11] There shall be elected, by the qualified electors of each county in this State, on the first Monday in August, 1848, and every two years thereafter, one Chief Justice and four County Commissioners; who shall each hold their offices for a term of two years, and until their successors respectively shall be elected and qualified: in case of a vacancy in either of said offices, before the expiration of the term of two years from his election, an election shall be ordered to fill such office, for the unexpired term; and the person so elected, shall continue to discharge the duties of his office until his successor shall be elected and qualified: provided, however, that not more than one of said Commissioners shall be a resident of the same Justice's precinct; and at any regular election, the four persons having the highest number of votes, and resident in different precincts, shall be declared to be elected; and at an election to fill a vacancy, the person having the highest number of votes and not resident in a precinct where there is already one of said Commissioners, shall be declared to be elected: provided, also, that when any county shall not have as many as four precincts, then only two of said Commissioners may be elected from any one precinct.—(*See Elections.*)

Chief Justice and County Comm'rs shall be elected.

Term of office.

Vacancy, how filled.

Residence of Com'r.

Election of, how determined.

ART. 256. [12] Neither the Chief Justice, or any of said County Commissioners, shall enter upon the duties of their offices, until they shall have first taken and subscribed the oath of office prescribed by the Constitution, before some officer authorized to administer oaths; which oath, together with the certificate of the officer who administered the same, shall be filed and recorded in the Clerk's office of the County Court: and if either of said officers shall neglect to accept and qualify as aforesaid, within ten days after he is declared duly elected, his election shall be deemed void, and another election shall be ordered to fill the office.

Oath of office.

Must qualify in ten days.

III. CLERK.

Clerk—election of and term of office.

ART. 257. [13] There shall be elected by the qualified electors of each county of this State, on the first Monday in August, 1848, and every two years thereafter, a Clerk of said County Court, who shall hold his office for a term of two years, and until his successor is elected and qualified: in case of a vacancy in said office of Clerk, before the expiration of the term of two years from the regular election, an election shall be ordered to fill such vacancy, for the unexpired term; and the person so elected shall continue to perform the duties of his office until his successor shall be elected and qualified.

Election of, in case of vacancy.

Bond and oath of office.

ART. 258. [14] Every person elected Clerk of the County Court, before entering upon the duties of the office, shall enter into bond, with two or more good and sufficient sureties, to be approved by the Chief Justice, in a sum not less than two thousand dollars, payable to the Governor of the State, and his successors in office, conditioned that the person so elected shall well and truly discharge and perform all the duties of the office of Clerk of the County Court; and shall also take and subscribe the oath of office prescribed bv the Constitution, before some officer authorized to administer oaths, which shall be endorsed on, or attached to, said bond, together with the certificate of the officer who adminstered the same; such bond and oath shall be recorded in the County Clerk's office, and shall be deposited with the Clerk of the District Court of the county: such bond shall not be void on the first recovery, but may be sued on from time to time, in the name or names of any person or persons injured by a breach thereof, until the whole penalty shall have been recovered.

Bond shall not be void on the first recovery.

Shall have the custody of books and papers.

ART. 259. [15] The said Clerk shall have the custody of all the minutes, records, books, and papers belonging or appertaining to the County Courts, and Probate Courts, that have heretofore existed in their respective counties; and it shall be their duty to attend to the arrangement and preservation of the same.

May appoint a deputy.

ART. 260 [16] The Clerks of the several County Courts of this State shall have power, by writing, under their hand and seal, to appoint a deputy, for whose official acts they shall be responsible; and such deputy shall take and subscribe the oath of office prescribed by the Constitution, before some officer authorized to administer oaths, which shall be endorsed on or attached to the appointment, together with the certificate of the officer who administered the same; and such appointment and oath shall be recorded with the county records, and deposited with the Clerk of the District Court of the county.

Deputy shall take the oath of office.

Absence, inability, or unwillingness of the Clerk to attend.

ART. 261. [17] If, from any cause, the Clerk of the County Court is absent from the county seat, or is unable or unwilling to attend to the duties of his office, and he has no deputy; or if any duties are required to be done in the office of said Clerk, before an election can be had to fill a vacancy, the Chief Justice may, by an order entered on the minutes of the court, either in vacation or term time, appoint a Clerk *pro tem.* for said court; and any person appointed shall take the oath and give bond, in like manner as herein provided for Clerks who are elected; but such appointment shall, in no case, continue in force for more than thirty days.

Clerk *pro tem.* may be appointed, when.

Books, &c. shall be delivered to Clerk.

ART. 262. [18] Whenever the office of Clerk of the County Court shall become vacant, all books, records, papers and effects, belonging or appertaining to such office, shall be delivered to the person who may be appointed, or elected and qualified to fill such vacancy, when demanded by him; and any person having possession of any such books, records, papers and effects, who shall neglect to deliver them to the person so appointed, or elected and qualified, when demanded by him, may be cited to appear before the Chief Justice, either in term time or in vacation, to show cause why he should not so deliver such books, records, papers and effects; and on the return of such citation, served, the Chief Justice may cause the person so neglecting to be arrested and imprisoned until he shall so deliver such books, records, papers and effects, unless good cause can be shown why the same should not be done. Penalty for refusing.

IV. GENERAL PROVISIONS.

ART. 263. [19] When in the record of any order, judgment, or decree of the County Court, there shall be any mistake, and there shall be any papers on file in said court whereby such record may be safely amended, the Chief Justice may cause the same to be amended in open court according to the truth and justice of the case; but in all such cases the person or persons to be affected by such amendment shall have notice of the application for such amendment. In cases of mistake, record may be amended. Party affected shall have notice.

ART. 264. [20] The regular terms of the County Court shall commence and be held at the courthouse of each county in this State on the last Monday in every month, for the probate of wills, the granting of letters testamentary of administration and of guardianship, and the transaction of all business growing out of or connected with the powers and jurisdiction of the County Courts, over executors, administrators and guardians, and the estates of deceased persons, minors, idiots, lunatics, and persons *non compos mentis*; such terms shall be held by the Chief Justice without the assistance of any of the County Commissioners, and may be continued from day to day for one week, but not longer; and the Chief Justice shall have the authority to transact such business growing out of, or connected with, such powers and jurisdiction during the vacation between said terms of said court as may be authorized by law; provided, that the County Court of Washington county shall commence and be held on the first Monday in every month for the purposes above specified. Act of Feb. 16, 1852. Took effect March 1, 1852. Time of holding the Probate Court. Shall be held by Chief Justice, and continue one week. Time of holding in Washington county.

ART. 265. [21] A regular term of the County Court shall commence and be held at the court house of each county in this State, on the third Monday in February, May, August, and November, in every year, for the transaction of all business growing out of, or connected with, the powers and jurisdiction of the County Court, over all matters other than those named in the second and twentieth sections of this act; such terms shall be held by the Chief Justice, with the assistance of any two or more of the County Commissioners, and may continue for three days, but not longer; and special terms of said court may be held in like manner, and for like purposes as provided for in this section, at such other times as the Chief Justice may appoint; provided, however, that no county tax shall be levied, unless at some one of the regular terms, and with the assent of the Chief Justice and three of the County Commissioners, or the assent of the four Commissioners. Act of May 16, 1848. County Court—by whom and when held—term. When tax may be levied.

ART. 266. [22] The Chief Justice and County Commissioners each receive three dollars for every day they may be necessarily engaged in attendance on any regular term of said court that they are required to hold, to be paid out of the county treasury, but they shall not be paid for any special term. Act of Feb. 11, 1854. Took effect from date. Compensation of Chief Justice and Co. Com'rs

Act of May 16, 1848.

In case of vacancy in office of Chief Justice, County Com'rs may act.

ART. 267. [23] During any vacancy in the office of Chief Justice, any two of the County Commissioners shall have power to hold all such courts as the Chief Justice can hold; and to do and to perform all such official acts as he can do and perform.

Office of Clerk shall be declared vacant—when.

ART. 268. [24] If any person who has been elected or appointed Clerk of the County Court, shall neglect to give bond and take the oath of office within ten days after he shall have been declared elected or appointed, the office shall be deemed vacant, and a new election ordered or a new appointment made.

May adminitster oaths.

ART. 269. [26] The Chief Justices, County Commissioners, Clerks of the County Courts, and their deputies, shall have power to administer oaths of office, and all other oaths and affirmations, and give certificates thereof.

Chief Justice shall have power to take acknowledgment of deeds, &c.

ART. 270. [27] The Chief Justice of the County Court shall have power to take the acknowledgment and proof of all instruments of writing for the purpose of being recorded; and they shall also have power to examine and take the acknowledgment of married women, to all deeds of their separate property, and all deeds to property, for the sale of which their consent is required, in like manner, and under the same rules and regulations as are provided for Notaries Public; and all acts so done by any Chief Justice of a County Court, in this State, shall have the same force and effect as if done by a Notary Public.

Books and papers of probate shall be transferred to the County Court.

ART. 271. [28] All books, records, papers and effects, belonging or appertaining to the County and Probate Courts of the different counties of this State shall be transferred to the County Court established by this act, and the said County Court shall have and exercise all the powers conferred by law on County Courts, which are not herein enumerated; and the various officers of said court shall have and exercise all the powers not herein enumerated, which are conferred by law on such officers; and such powers shall be exercised in accordance with the laws conferring them, and the provisions of this act.

Act of Dec. 29 1849. Took effect from passage.

When two of County Commissioners may perform duties of Chief Justice.

(See Art. 267.)

ART. 272. [1] Whenever the office of Chief Justice of any County Court in this State is vacant, or whenever the Chief Justice of any County Court in this State shall be absent from the county, or unable to discharge the duties of his office, or shall be disqualified from attending to the duties of his office, by reason of interest, or from any other cause, then any two of the County Commissioners of such county shall have power to do and perform all the duties of Chief Justice of the County Court.

Suits by or against county.

ART. 273. [3] It shall be the duty of the County Court of each county in this State, to take and order suitable measures for prosecuting and defending all suits brought by or against such county.

Commissioners to sell real estate of county—deed how executed, effect of.

ART. 274. [9] The County Court may, by an order to be entered in the minutes of said court, appoint a commissioner to sell and dispose of any real estate of the county at public auction; and the deed of such commissioner, made in conformity to the order of said court, under his proper hand and seal, for and in behalf of the county, duly acknowledged, and proven, and recorded, shall be sufficient, to all intents and purposes, to convey to the purchasers all the right, title and interest, and estate whatever, which the county may have in and to the premises to be conveyed: provided, however, that nothing contained in this act shall authorize the County Court of any county to dispose of any lands given, donated, or granted to such county for the purposes of [illegible]ation in any other manner than shall be directed by law.

Proviso

ART. 275. [12] The County Courts may appoint an agent or agents to make any contract on behalf of the county for the erection or repairing of any county buildings, and to superintend their erection or repairing, or for any other purpose authorized by law, and the contracts or acts of such agent or agents, duly executed and done for and on behalf of the county, and within his powers, shall be valid and effectual to bind such county to all intents and purposes.

County agents for building—contracts by.

ART. 276. [1] The regular quarterly terms of the County Courts of the various counties for the transaction of all business growing out of, or connected with the powers and jurisdiction of the County Courts, over matters other than those named in the second and twentieth sections of the act of March 16th, 1848, entitled "An act to organize County Courts," may continue for one week, but not longer.

Act of Jan. 19, 1858. Took effect from date.

Regular quarterly terms may continue one week.

ART. 277. [1] In all cases where the records of any county in this State have become, or may become defaced, worn, or in any condition endangering their preservation in a safe and legible form, it shall be lawful for the County Court of such county to procure good and well bound books or book, as the case may be, and require the County Clerk to transcribe or have transcribed by a sworn deputy, the records contained in such book or books, in a plain legible hand, and when so transcribed they shall be carefully compared with the original record by the County Court, and the clerk or person transcribing the same. When found to be truly and correctly transcribed, the Chief Justice, Clerk, and at least two of the County Commissioners shall certify under their official oath of office at the conclusion of the record, with the impress of the county seal affixed on the same page, to the correctness of the same, reciting the number of pages contained in said book from one to the highest number: after which said transcribed records shall have all the force and effect in law and equity as the original records: provided, that the original books shall continue to be kept and preserved in the office of such County Clerk.

Act of Jan. 20, 1858. Took effect from passage.

When lawful to transcribe defaced records.

Transcripts—how authenticated.

ART. 278. [2] The County Clerk or person making such transcript or transcripts shall be entitled to such compensation for said services as may be allowed him by the County Court, in no case to exceed the sum of fifteen cents for each hundred words.

Compensation of Clerk for transcribing.

COUNTY SEATS.

ART. 279. [1] A majority of two-thirds of the votes of the qualified voters of a county shall be required to remove the seat of justice in any of the counties of this Republic, that now are or hereafter may be established: provided, however, that if in any county the seat of justice should be established at a greater distance than five miles from the centre of said county, a majority of all the votes shall be sufficient for its removal: provided such removal shall be within the limits of five miles from the centre of said county.(a)

Act of May 9, 1838. Took effect from passage.

Removal of.

(a) There is no contract within the purview of the Constitution, either with the purchasers of property or the donors of property, upon condition of the establishment of a county seat at a particular place, that the county seat shall not be removed from such place; nor has any one a vested right in the continuance of a county seat at a particular place. County seats may be removed by either a special act of the Legislature, or under the general law, without compensation to the owners of property. Alley *et al.* *v.* Denson—Chief Justice—8 Tex. Rep. 297. Bass *v.* Fontleroy, 11 Tex. Rep. 698. Walker *v.* Tarrant County, 20 Tex. Rep. 16.

In order to remove a county seat to a place within five miles of the centre of the county, from a place not within five miles, a majority of all the votes cast is only required. Ibid.

Chief Justice to order an election when.

ART. 280. [2] When, in the opinion of the Chief Justice of any county, the necessary number of inhabitants apply by petition or otherwise for a removal of the seat of justice,(*a*) it shall be the duty of the said Chief Justice to order an election for that purpose, giving due notice thereof, which election shall be held at the same places, and conducted in the same manner as elections for members of Congress; and the result of said election shall establish the seat of justice, in accordance with the provisions of the first section of this Act.

Act of April 11, 1846. Took effect from passage. Places of holding court until established.

ART. 281. [8] Until the county seats of new counties are established, as required by law, the courts of such new counties shall be held at such places as may be appointed by the County Courts thereof.

COUNTY OFFICES KEPT AT.

Act of March 16, 1848. Took effect Apr. 29, 1848. County offices to be kept at.

ART. 282. [1] The Sheriffs, Clerks of the District Court, and Clerks of the County Court of the several counties of this State, shall be, and they are hereby required to keep their several offices at the county seats of their respective counties.

Deput's of Sheriffs and Clerks.

ART. 283. [2] In all cases, where the said Sheriff and Clerks do not reside at the county seats of their respective counties, they shall be, and are hereby required to have deputies in their several offices, residing at said county seats.

Act of May 13, 1846. Treas'r's office.

ART. 284. [11] The County Treasurer shall keep his office at the county seat of his county.

COUNTY TREASURER.

Act of May 13, 1846. Took effect from date. Bond and oath. See Art. 297.

ART. 285. [2] Every person who shall be appointed to the office of County Treasurer, shall, within twenty days after receiving notice of his appointment, and before entering upon the duties of his office, give a bond to the County Court of his county and their successors in office, for the use of the county, with at least two good and sufficient sureties, to be approved of by the Chief Justice of his county, in such sum as they may deem necessary, conditioned that such Treasurer shall faithfully execute the duties of his office, and pay over, according to law, all moneys which shall come into his hands as County Treasurer, and render a just and true account thereof to the said court, at each and every regular term of said court; and such Treasurer shall take and subscribe the oath prescribed by the Constitution, which, together with the bond, shall be deposited in the County Clerk's office of his county.

Duties.

ART. 286. [3] It shall be the duty of the County Treasurer to receive all moneys belonging to the county, from whatever source they may be derived,

(*a*) The Chief Justice is the judge of what shall be a sufficient number of petitioners to authorize the ordering of an election. Alley *et al.* *v.* Denson—Chief Justice—8 Tex. Rep. 297.

and to pay and apply the same as required by law, in such manner as the County Court of his county may require and direct.

ART. 287. [4] The County Treasurer shall keep a just and true account of the receipts and expenditures of all moneys which shall come into his hands by virtue of his office, and of the debts due to and from his county; and direct prosecutions according to law, for the recovery of all debts that may be due to his county, and superintend the collection thereof. Shall keep accounts, superintend collection of debts, &c.

ART. 288. [5] The County Treasurer shall render a detailed report at every regular term of the County Court of his county, of all the moneys received and disbursed by him, of all debts due to and from his county, and of all other proceedings in his office, and shall exhibit to said Board at every such term, all his books and accounts for their inspection, and all vouchers relating to the same, to be audited and allowed. Report to County Court.

ART. 289. [6] He shall deliver the moneys, securities, and all other property of the county in his hands, together with all documents, instruments of writing, papers and books, belonging to, or for the use of the county, to his successor in office, and perform all other such acts as may be required of him by said County Court. Deliver over to successor, &c.

ART. 290. [7] The County Treasurer shall not pay any money out of the County Treasury, except in pursuance of a certificate or warrant from some officer authorized by law to issue the same; and if such Treasurer shall have any doubt of the legality or propriety of any order, decree, certificate, or warrant, presented to him for payment, he shall not pay the same, but shall make report thereof to the County Court for their consideration and direction. Pay money on warrant or certificate.

ART. 291. [8] It shall be the duty of the County Treasurer to examine the accounts, dockets, and records of the Clerks, Sheriff, Coroner, and Tax Collector of his county, for the purpose of ascertaining whether any moneys, of right belonging to his county, are in their hands, which have not been accounted for and paid over according to law, and shall report the same to the County Court at their next term, to the end that suit may be instituted for the recovery thereof. Ascertain county funds in hands of county officers.

ART. 292. [9] The County Treasurer shall receive and may retain in his hands such commission, not exceeding five per centum, upon the amount received and disbursed by him, as the County Court in their discretion may allow. Commissions.

ART. 293. [10] The County Treasurer may, at any time, be removed from office for malpractice, incompetence, or refusal to act, by the County Court, upon due notice given him, with a specification of the cause or causes upon which it is sought to effect such removal, of the time and place of investigation, and after a fair and impartial hearing in his behalf. How and for what removed from office.

ART. 294. [11] The County Treasurer shall keep his office at the county seat of his county. Keep office at county seat.

ART. 295. [1] There shall be elected by the qualified voters of every county of this State, on the first Monday in August, eighteen hundred and fifty, and every two years thereafter, a County Treasurer, whose term of office shall be two years from the day of election, and who shall continue to discharge the duties of said office until his successor shall be duly qualified. Act of Jan. 26, 1850. Took effect March 23, 1850. Elected by the people when. Term of office.

ART. 296. [2] In case of a vacancy in said office from any cause, it shall be the duty of the Chief Justice of the county in which such vacancy may Vacancy to be filled.

occur, immediately to order an election to fill the unexpired term for which said officer was elected.

Bond and oath. See Art. 285. ART. 297. [3] The County Treasurers of the several counties in this State shall, before entering upon the duties of their office, take the oath prescribed by law for all public officers, and shall enter into bond in such sum not less than two thousand dollars, and with such security, as the Chief Justice of the County Court shall direct.

COURT OF CLAIMS.

I. COMMISSIONER AND CLERKS.

II. POWERS AND DUTIES.

III. COMMISSIONER OF THE GENERAL LAND OFFICE—DUTY OF IN REGARD TO CLAIMS.

IV. CLAIMS AND CLAIMANTS.

V. GENERAL PROVISIONS.

I. COMMISSIONER AND CLERKS.

Act of January 16, 1858. Took effect from passage. Election and salary of Com- ART. 299. [1] There shall be elected by a joint vote of the Legislature, a "Commissioner of Claims," who shall hold his office until the first day of September, A. D., 1859. He shall keep his office at the city of Austin, and shall receive an annual salary of two thousand, two hundred and fifty dollars.

Before he enters upon the discharge of the duties of his office, he shall enter into bond with two or more good and sufficient sureties, in the sum of twenty thousand dollars, made payable to the Governor of the State of Texas, and his successors in office, conditioned that he will well and truly discharge all the duties, required of him by law, which bond shall be approved by the Governor, and by him filed in the office of the Secretary of State. He shall be allowed one Chief Clerk, to be appointed by him, (*See Salaries*,) * * * * * * * * and one assistant clerk, who shall receive an annual salary of nine hundred dollars. If from any cause a vacancy shall occur, in said office of Commissioner of Claims, during the recess of the Legislature, the Governor shall fill the same by appointment.

missioner. Bond to be given. Shall have two clerks. Vacancy how filled.

Art. 300. [9] If the duties imposed upon the Commissioner, by the provisions of this act, shall require the aid of an additional clerk, it shall be his duty to make the same known to the Governor, whose duty it shall be to employ and appoint such clerk, whose salary shall not exceed one thousand dollars.

When an additional clerk allowed. By whom appointed.

Art. 301. [1] The Commissioner of Claims be, and he is hereby authorized to employ an additional Clerk whenever the business of the office may require it, at a salary of seventy-five dollars per month, who shall continue in office only so long as his services may be required.

Act of August 15, 1856. Took effect from passage. Salary of additional clerk.

II. POWERS AND DUTIES OF COMMISSIONER.

Art. 302. [3] It shall be the duty of said Commissioner of Claims, to keep a register of every certificate presented to him under the provisions of the next preceding section, stating its number and date, by whom, and to whom it was issued, the quantity of land it calls for, whether it is a bounty, donation, or headright certificate. If it is a bounty, or donation certificate, he shall state for what service it was issued. If it is a headright certificate, he shall state whether it is a conditional or an unconditional one, and of what class. If it was issued to an assignee, he shall state the name of the assignor and assignee; he shall also state by whom it was presented, and who is represented to be the owner of it at the time; he shall also write across the face of each certificate, the word "registered," and sign his name, with the date of its registery.

Act of August 1, 1856. Took effect from passage. Certificates shall be presented and registered. See Art. 322.

Art. 303. [10] The said Commissioner of Claims shall hereafter perform all the duties required of the Commissioner of the General Land Office, under the provisions of an act to provide for the liquidation of the public debt of the Republic of Texas, approved February 11th, 1850.

When Commissioner shall perform the duties of Commissioner of the Land Office.

Art. 304. [11] The Commissioner of Claims shall also perform all the duties required of the Commissioner of the General Land Office, under the provision of an act authorizing the issuing of duplicates, land warrants, discharges, and certificates for headright claims upon certain conditions, approved 14th January, 1840, and also under the provisions of an act to amend the 1st Sec. of an act approved 14th January, 1840, entitled An Act authorising the issuing duplicate land warrants, discharges and certificates for headright claims upon certain conditions, approved May 11th, 1846. He shall be authorized to i ue duplicate, bounty and donation certificates, in the ame manner that the Secretary of war, or Adjutant General could have done at any time heretofore: provided, the applicant for a duplicate shall comply with all the requi ite prescribed in said two acts, and shall also prove by the testimony of at lea t

Shall issue duplicate certificates, warrants and discharges. Proof to be made before issuing.

two credible witnesses or record evidence, that the original certificate which is said to have been lost or destroyed, did, in fact, issue; and shall also prove that the original has not been returned to the General Land Office, and shall also prove his identity and residence by the same number of witnesses; and provided also, that if the original certificate was issued to an assignee, the assignment and the identity and residence of the parties and witnesses thereto, shall be proved in the same manner.

When certificate for unlocated balance may issue.

ART. 305. [12] Whenever any person shall desire to procure a certificate for an unlocated balance, of any certificate upon which a patent has issued, he may procure from the Commissioner of the General Land Office, a certificate showing that he is entitled to such unlocated balance, and also fully describing the original certificate, and how much thereof has been patented, and upon the presentation thereof to said Commissioner of Claims, he shall record it, and issue a new certificate, for such unlocated balance. Such new certificate shall be countersigned by the Commissioner of the General Land Office, and may then be located, surveyed and patented as other genuine certificates. The Commissioner of Claims shall keep a descriptive register of all such new certificates issued by him.

Register of same to be kept.

Duty of the Commissioner when a certificate is registered and deemed doubtful, or on failure to approve the same.

ART. 306. [13] Whenever a certificate shall be presented to the Commissioner of Claims for registry only, and he shall have reason to believe that it was improperly issued, from any cause, he shall, after registering it, write his belief across the face of it, with the date and his signature, before returning it; and also, whenever a certificate shall be presented to him for his approval, and he shall fail to approve it for any cause, he shall write across the face of it the reason why he fails to approve it, with the date and his signature.

Shall procure and file copies of muster rolls.

ART. 307. [15] It shall be the duty of the Commissioner of Claims, to procure all duplicates and copies of muster rolls of the companies that have heretofore served in the Republic or State of Texas, with such evidence in regard to their authenticity, as can be obtained, and file the same in his office, for the purpose of aiding him in detecting frauds that have heretofore been practiced upon the Government, or that hereafter may be attempted.

Shall report to Governor and Commissioner of Land Office.

ART. 308. [17] Said Commissioner of Claims shall report weekly to the Commissioner of the General Land Office, a descriptive list of all certificates which he has issued and approved for the week previous, and he shall annually make a report, on the first day of October, to the Governor, of the number and description of certificates that he has issued and approved for the year previous.

Fee for issuing certificate.

ART. 309. [18] He shall demand and receive a fee of one dollar for each duplicate certificate and for each certificate for an unlocated balance, and for each certificate to a Railroad Company, and for each certificate, as a reward or bonus for the building of a steamboat, steamship, or other vessel, that he may issue. He shall also demand and receive a fee of five dollars for each certificate for one league and labor; three dollars for each certificate of twelve hundred and eighty acres, or over that amount, and less than one league and labor, and two dollars for each certificate for less than twelve hundred and eighty acres, that he may issue as head-rights, and no fee shall be demanded for any original bounty or donation certificate. He shall enter all such fees, and by whom paid, in a book, to be kept for that purpose, and shall account for and pay over all such fees quarterly, to the State Treasurer.

Shall be paid to the Treasurer.

Seal.

ART. 310. [19] He shall procure a seal for the authentication of all instruments of writing emanating from his office, which shall have a star of five points in the centre, and the words, "Commissioner of Claims, Texas," around the star.

ART. 311. [21] The said Commissioner of Claims shall, hereafter, issue all land certificates to Railroad Companies, which the Commissioner of the General Land Office is authorized or required to issue under any law of the State; and also all land certificates that the Commissioner of the General Land Office is authorized or required to issue under the provisions of an act, to encourage the building of steamboats, steamships, and other vessels in the State of Texas, approved 3rd February, 1854, and all applications for such certificates shall, hereafter, be presented to said Commissioner of Claims, in the same manner as they were heretofore required to be presented to the Commissioner of the General Land Office, and the said Commissioner of Claims shall issue all such certificates in like manner, and under like restrictions as the Commissioner of the General Land Office, was heretofore required to issue them. Shall issue certificates to Railroad and Steamboat Companies

ART. 312. [23] The said Commissioner of Claims shall not act as the agent of any person for the prosecution of a claim of any description against the Republic or State of Texas; nor as the agent of any person in locating lands or procuring patents for lands; nor as the agent for any person in or about the registry; approval, or issuance of any land certificate whatever; nor shall he hereafter purchase any interest in any claim for land or money against the Republic or State of Texas; and if he shall violate any of the provisions of this section, he shall, on conviction therefor, be fined in a sum not less than two thousand dollars, and shall thereafter be ineligible to hold any office in this State. Shall not act as agent of any person, or prosecute claims, &c. Penalty for so doing.

ART. 313. [3] The sixth section of said act shall hereafter read as follows: whenever a land certificate is presented to the said Commissioner of Claims for his approval, under the provisions of this act, he shall register it as directed by the third section of this act, if it has not already been registered, and if it is a headright certificate, he shall compare it with a report of the Clerk of the Board of Land Commissioners, or of the Court by which it purports to have been issued, and if satisfied that it is a genuine certificate, he shall write across the face of it the word "approved," with the date of its approval, and sign his name thereto. If, however, such certificate was issued to an assignee, and he shall have reason to believe the assignment thereof was forged, he shall withhold his approval, until the assignment is proved to be genuine by the evidence of at least two credible witnesses, before the Commissioner, or by deposition taken before any officer authorized to take depositions under the laws of this State, and until the identity and residence of the parties and witnesses to such assignment is proved in the same manner. If such a certificate is a bounty or donation certificate, and the Commissioner has in his office any record or paper showing it to be a genuine one, or if the evidence of at least two credible witnesses, taken as above, is produced to him, that it is a genuine one, he shall file such evidence, and shall write across the face of the certificate the word "approved," with the date of its approval, and sign his name thereto. Act of Jan'y 16, 1858. Took effect from passage. Duty of Commissioner when certificates are presented. Assignment of, when and how to be proved.

Provided, however, that he shall hold his approval from any bounty or donation certificate issued to an assignee since the 29th day of November, A. D., 1851, until the genuineness of the assignment, and the identity and residence of the parties and witnesses thereto, shall be proved by the testimony of at least two credible witnesses, in the manner herein prescribed or otherwise established to the satisfaction of the Commissioner, and should the Commissioner of Claims, upon such investigation and examination of any such bounty, or donation, headright or other certificate, issued to an assignee, be satisfied that the original grantee was entitled to said certificate, and no Assignment of certain certificates shall be proven.

When approved for the benefit of grantee. satisfactory evidence of the genuineness of the assignment shall be presented, he shall endorse said certificate "approved for the benefit of the original grantee," giving the name; and patent shall not issue on any such claim, until the rightful owner thereof is proved before the Commissioner of Claims, or the person performing the duties of said office. In all cases where certificates shall be approved under the provisions of this section, the said Commissioner shall note the approval with the date thereof in the margin of his register, opposite the entry of the certificate. And any individual holding a headright certificate, which may be rejected, or refused to be approved by the Commissioner of Claims, shall have the right within twelve months from the time of such rejection, to bring suit in the District Court of the county, in which said certificate issued, for the establishment of the same, which suit shall be brought and conducted in the manner prescribed for the establishment of certificates not recommended by the act of February 4th, 1841, entitled "an act supplementary to an act to detect fraudulent land certificates, and provide for the issuing of patents to legal claimants." And all certificates which shall have been presented for registry, shall be presented for approval on or before the first day of September, 1858, or the same shall be null and void.

Date of approval to be noted.

Suit may be bro't in twelve months to establish rejected headright certificates.

This act not to extend to unrecommended certificates included in 2d Sec. of 11th Art. of the Constitution.

Provided, This act shall not be construed to give jurisdiction either to the Commissioner of Claims or the District Courts for the re-establishment of any unrecommended certificate embraced within the purview of the second section of the eleventh article of the Constitution. Nor shall this act authorize the Commissioner of Claims to approve any unconditional headright certificates unless it shall appear from the records of his office, or other satisfactory evidence that the corresponding conditional certificate was regularly issued, where such conditional certificate was required by law to be issued.

Certain duplicates shall not be issued.

ART. 314. [5] No duplicate of a conditional certificate, Poe certificate, or of the Discharge, shall hereafter be issued. Nor shall a duplicate Military Warrant be issued to the heirs of a deceased person until after the first day of September, A. D., 1858. And all the heirs, who are of age, shall make affidavit before some officer authorized to administer oaths, using a seal, that they have no knowledge that the deceased transferred his right to said claim during his life-time; nor have they transferred their right thereto since his death. That from and after the first day of September, A. D., 1858, duplicates may issue to the heirs of deceased persons as in other cases.

Adult heirs to make oath in certain cases.

Duplicates to heirs may issue after Sept., 1858.

Certificate for unlocated balance shall not issue, unless.

ART. 315. [6] No certificate for an unlocated balance of a certificate, which has in part been patented, shall be issued unless the original certificate has been approved, or issued by said Commissioner of Claims; but this section does not apply to certificates for unlocated balances of such certificates as are not by law required to be presented to and approved by said Commissioner.

Shall approve certain augmentations.

ART. 316. [7] Said Commissioner of Claims shall be authorized to approve all augmentation certificates which were issued under the act of 4th January, 1841, to persons for marrying in this country previous to 1st January, 1842, in the same manner as other genuine headright certificates are approved.

Business, how conducted and disposed of.

ART. 317. [8] The business of said office shall be conducted as nearly as is consistent with its organization and powers, in the same manner as the business of the General Land Office; and to this end the Commissioner shall act upon claims in the order in which they may reach his office, by mail or otherwise; he shall correspond with, and fully inform the applicants as to their business in his Court, and transmit to them all the papers as directed. He shall cross all interrogatories that may be filed in his Court, and cross-examine all witnesses; and he shall dispose of interrogatories when crossed, as directed by the person filing the same. He shall, when applications are made for an unlocated balance of a land certificate, or lost certificates, or for any other purpose whatever, which may require a certificate or any other information from the General Land Office, correspond with and obtain the information required from that office. This section shall be so construed as to secure the objects for which it is framed, to wit: To relieve persons having business in said Court from employing agents or attorneys to conduct the routine of business incident upon their applications.

ART. 318. [11] On the first day of September, A. D., 1859, the Commissioner of Claims shall deliver to the Comptroller, all the books, papers and archives, in and belonging to the office of Co missioner of Claims, and the same shall become a part of the archives of the Comptroller's office. Archives to be delivered to Comptroller.

III. COMMISSIONER GENERAL LAND OFFICE, DUTY OF IN REGARD TO CLAIMS.

ART. 319. [4] It shall be the duty of the Commissioner of the General Land Office, as early as practicable after the passage of this act, to furnish said Commissioner of Claims with a register of every land certificate that has been returned to his office, except headright certificates of the first and second class, which have been returned as genuine and legal claims, by the Commissioner appointed under "An Act to detect fraudulent land certificates, and to provide for issuing patents to legal claimants," approved 29th January, 1840, and certificates issued under some special act of the Congress of the Republic of Texas, or of the Legislature of this State, and certificates issued to colonists of Peters' Colony; Mercer's Colony; Castro's Colony; Fisher and Millers Colony; and the colonists of the German Emigration Company, and certificates issued for premium lands in said colonies, and certificates isued to companies incorporated under the laws of this State, for purposes of internal improvements, and to persons for building vessels, under the provisions of an act of February 3d, 1854, entitled "An Act to encourage the building of steamboats, steamships, and other vessels in the State of Texas," and certificates for unlocated balances heretofore issued,—which register shall state the number, and date of each certificate, by whom and to whom issued,—the quantity of Land called for, whether it is bounty, donation, or headright certificate. If it is a bounty, or donation certificate, it shall state for what service it was issued—if it is a headright certificate, it shall state whether it is a conditional or an unconditional one, and of what class. If it was issued to an assignee, it shall state the name of the assignor and assignee, and afterwards he shall furnish each week, to said Commissioner of Claims, a similar register of all certificates of the above description, which have been returned during the previous week, and which had not been previously registered by the Commissioner of Claims. Act of August 1, 1856. Took effect from passage. Shall furnish to Comr. of Claims a register of certain land certificates. Shall furnish weekly report of returns.

ART. 320. [5] It shall be the duty of the Commissioner of the General Land Office, to make out, and retain in his office, certified copies of all the reports which have heretofore been made, or may hereafter be made, to his office, by the Clerks of the Boards of Land Commissioners, and of the District and County Courts of the several counties of the Republic and the State of Texas, and to transfer the original reports to the Commissioner of Claims; and also a certified list of all the certificates issued under the provisions of an Act for the relief of the heirs of those who fell with Fannin, Ward, Travis, Grant, and Johnson, during the war with Mexico, in the years 1835 and 1836, approved February 9th, 1850, to the office of the Commissioner of Claims, immediately after he shall have entered upon his duties; and the said certified list of certificates shall have the same force and effect in the office of said Commissioner of Claims, as if it was an original record of his office. Shall retain copies and transfer certain orginal reports. Shall transfer a list of certificates issued to heirs of those who fell under Fannin and others.

After the said Commissioner of Claims shall have entered upon the discharge of his duties, the Commissioner of the General Land Office shall not issue a patent upon any land certificate, except headright certificates of the first and second class, which have been returned as genuine and legal by the Commissioners appointed under the provisions of "An Act to detect fraudulent land certificates, and to provide for the issuing of patents to legal claimants," approved 29th January, 1840, and certificates issued under some special act of the Congress of the Republic of Texas, or of the Legislature of this State, and certificates issued to colonists of Peter's Colony; Mercer's Colony; Castro's Colony; Fisher and Miller's Colony; and the colonists of the German Emigration Company; and certificates issued for premium lands in said colonies, and certificates issued to companies incorporated under the laws of this State, for the purposes of internal improvements, and to persons for building vessels under the provisions of the act of February 3d, 1854, entitled "An Act to encourage the building of steamboats, steamships, and other vessels in the State of Texas, and certificates for unlocated balances heretofore issued, and pre-emption certificates, until it shall have been presented to and approved by the Commissioner of Claims.

Certain certificates to be approved before patenting.

Shall furnish copies of certain muster rolls.

ART. 321. [9] The Commissioner of the General Land Office shall, as early as practicable after the passage of this act, furnish to said Commissioner of Claims, certified copies of those copies of the muster rolls of the several companies that were under the command of Fannin and Ward, and also of those copies of the lists of the names of those who fell in the Alamo, with Travis and with Grant, and under the command of Johnson, during the war with Mexico, in the year 1836, which were furnished by the Adjutant General to the Commissioner of the General Land Office, under the provisions of an act for the relief of the heirs of those who fell with Fannin, Ward, Travis, Grant and Johnson, during the war with Mexico, in the years 1835 and 1836, approved February 9th, 1850; which copies, when furnished, shall have the same force and effect in the office of said Commissioner of Claims, as if they were original records in his office. And the said Commissioner of Claims shall hereafter perform all the duties of the Adjutant General under the provisions of said recited act; provided, however, that no certificate shall hereafter be issued under the provisions of said act, unless the applicant shall prove his identity, and residence by the testimony of, at least two credible witnesses, in the manner herein prescribed; and provided, also, that no certificate shall be issued in the name of an assignee under said act.

Copy shall be evidence.

Identity of applicant how proven.

IV. CLAIMS AND CLAIMANTS.

Act of January 16, 1858. Took effect from passage.

What certificates required to be presented.

ART. 322. [2] All land certificates of every description, except headright certificates of the first and second classes, which have been returned as genuine and legal, by the Commissioners appointed, under an act to detect fraudulent land certificates, and to provide for issuing patents to legal claimants, approved 29th January A. D. 1840, and certificates issued under some special act of the Congress of the Republic of Texas, or of the Legislature of this State, and certificates to the colonists of Peters' Colony, Mercer's Colony, Castro's Colony, Fisher and Miller's Colony and the Colonists of the German Emigration Company, and certificates, issued for premium lands in said Colonies, and certificates issued to companies incorporated under the laws of this State, for the purpose of internal improvement, and to persons for building vessels under the provisions of the act of February 3d, A. D. 1854, entitled an act to encourage the builing of steamboats, steamships, and other vessels in the State of Texas, and pre-emption certificates and certificates issued under the provisions of an act to open and establish a national road, passed February 5th, 1844, and certificates for unlocated balances of any of the above enumerated certificates, shall be presented to said Commissioner of Claims for registry within two years, from and after the first day of September A. D. 1856, or they shall be forever barred from location surveys and patent. And any such certificates which have been entered, surveyed or located and filed in any District Surveyor's office, or returned to the General Land Office, or filed in any suit in any District Court, may be withdrawn from said office or court, for the purpose of being presented to said Commissioner of Claims, without in any manner affecting or violating said entry, location, or survey, or the right of the party claiming under any such certificates, in any such suit.

Within what time.

May be withdrawn from certain officers for approval.

ART. 323. [4] Any grantee of a conditional headright certificate, or his heirs, executors, or administrators, may apply, by a motion in writing, to the District Court of the county in which such conditional certificate was issued, for a corresponding unconditional certificate, which shall be granted by such Court upon such proof as would have authorized its issuance by any Officer, Board, or Court of the Republic or State of Texas, under the laws in force at any time previous to the 1st day of November, A. D. 1853. And upon further proof, by the certificate of the Commissioner of the General Land Office, under his seal of office, that such conditional certificate was duly reported to his office by the proper officer, and that no corresponding unconditional certificate appears, from the records or files of his office, to have been granted or issued, and upon a like certificate of the Commissioner of Claims, that such unconditional certificate does not appear, from the records or files of his office, to have been issued. The said unconditional certificates, when granted by any District Court, may be issued by the clerk thereof, under his seal of office, and attested and approved by the presiding Judge, but shall require no other or further approval for location, survey or patent. Provided, however, that no certificate shall issue to an assignee, under the provisions of this act. The clerks of the District Court shall each, at the close of every term, report to the Commissioner of the General Land Office all certificates issued by him under the provisions of this act. The District Attorneys of the Districts in which any such applications may be made, shall represent the State therein, and the same may, on the motion of the applicant, be taken up and disposed of at any time when the Court is not engaged in the trial of a cause. All claims for such unconditional certificates not presented to the proper District Courts for allowance, on or before the first of October, A. D. 1859, shall be forever barred. All original applications for headright certificates shall be presented to said Commissioner of Claims with the best evidence it is in the power of the applicants to produce, in regard to their right to the land for which they apply, together with proof of their identity and residence by at least two credible witnesses; and it shall be the duty of said Commissioner to report to the Legislature, for its action, a list of all such applications, with the evidence in support thereof, and his opinion in regard thereto, and such applications not presented on or before the first day of September, A. D. 1858, shall be forever barred.

Unconditional headrights, how obtained.

Clerk shall issue certificate, when

Not to issue in name of assignee.

Time of application to the court.

Application for original headrights, when to be made and proof taken.

ART. 324. [1] Any person entitled to bounty or donation lands for military services under the laws of the Republic and State of Texas, who has not heretofore received a certificate, warrant, or patent therefor, or who may have lost such warrant, and on application for a duplicate, cannot prove the existence of the original by any other than his own oath, or the heirs of such person, if he be dead, may apply to the Commissioner of Claims, and establish their rights to the same, by proof such as would have authorized the issue of a certificate or duplicate warrant in such case by any officer of the Republic or State of Texas, under the laws in force prior to the first day of November,

Act of Feb. 13 1858. Took effect from passage.

Duplicates of bounty and donation certificates, when to issue.

1853, and by proof of his or their identity and residence by two credible witnesses, examined before said Commissioner, or before some officer authorized to take depositions: provided, no duplicate bounty or donation warrant shall be issued unless the existence of the corresponding original be established to the satisfaction of the Commissioner by record proof or the evidence of at least two credible witnesses. But the certificate or warrant in such case shall not issue until after the first day of September, 1858, nor shall the provisions of this act apply to the claims of the heirs of those who fell with Fannin, Ward, Travis, Grant and Johnson, in 1835 and 1836, which are otherwise provided for, nor shall any warrant or certificate issue to an assignee.

This act not to extend to heirs of those who fell under Fannin & others.

When s shall b ed.

ART. 325. [2] All applications for bounty or donation land not filed with the Commissioner of Claims on or before the first day of September, 1858, shall be forever barred.

V. GENERAL PROVISIONS.

Act of August 1, 1856. Took effect from passage. Governor may appoint commissioners to examine certain records. Report shall be made. Compensation.

ART. 326. [14] The Governor shall be, and he is hereby authorized to appoint three discreet persons, with powers to examine the records of any of the Boards of Land Commissioners, and of the District and County Courts of any county in this State, and to examine persons in regard to the manner in which such records have been kept, and make a full report of their proceedings whenever in his opinion the public interest will be subserved by such examination, and the persons so appointed shall be entitled to receive from the State the sum of three dollars each, for every day they may be necessarily employed under their appointments.

Evidence shall be reduced to writing.

ART. 327. [16] All oral evidence submitted to said Commissioner of Claims, shall be reduced to writing, and signed by the party giving it, and shall then be sworn to before said Commissioner, or his clerk, who shall be authorized to administer oaths in all cases required in the discharge of the duties of their office, and all such evidence, and all other testimony issued before said Commissioner, shall be filed and preserved by him.

Clerks to report certificates issued.

ART. 328. [20] The several clerks of the District and County Courts of this State, shall hereafter report to the said Commissioner of Claims, all certificates for land obtained from their courts, in the same manner that they were heretofore required to report them to the Commissioner of the General Land Office.

A list of Burleson's regiment at San Jacinto, and copies of certain muster rolls made evidence in Court of Claims.

ART. 329. [22] The list of persons composing the regiment under the command of Edward Burleson, at the battle of San Jacinto, which is now in the possession of the Governor of this State, together with the affidavit of Captain Jesse Billingsley, attached thereto, proving its authenticity, and also the manuscript book, now in possession of the Governor, purporting to contain copies of certain muster rolls that were heretofore in the Adjutant General's Office, shall be deposited in the office of the said Commissioner of Claims, and may be used by him as evidence upon which to approve bounty, and donation certificates heretofore issued by the Adjutant General of this State, and by the Secretary of War of the late Republic of Texas.

Books and pa- p of Auditor to be transferred.

ART. 330. [27] All the books, papers and archives, in and belonging to the Auditor's office, shall be turned over to the Commissioner of Claims mentioned in this act, and become a part of the archives of his office.

ART. 331. The Commissioner of Claims be, and he is hereby authorized to use two of the rooms in the basement story of the Capitol, for the transaction of the business of his office. Act of August 11, 1856. Office rooms of Commissioner.

ART. 332. [10] All the postage incident to the correspondence of said Court shall, like that of the General Land Office, be paid by the State, and under the same regulations. Act of January 16, 1858. Postage.

ART. 333. [12] From and after the first day of September, A. D. 1859, the Comptroller shall do and perform all the duties then appertaining to the office of Commissioner of Claims, under the provisions of an act entitled "an act to ascertain the legal claims for money and lands against the State," passed August 1st, 1856, and under the provisions of this act. And thereafter the Comptroller shall not act as the agent of any person for the prosecution of a claim of any description, against the Republic or State of Texas; nor as the agent of any person in locating lands, or procuring patents for lands; nor as the agent of any person in and about the registry, approval, or issuance of any land certificate whatever; nor shall he thereafter purchase any interest in any claim for land or money against the Republic of Texas, or State of Texas; and if he shall violate any of the provisions of this section, he shall, on conviction therefor, be fined in a sum not less than two thousand dollars, and shall thereafter be ineligible to hold any office in this State. After Sept. '59 Comptroller to perform duties of Commissioner. Not to act as agent, &c. Penalty for

ART. 334. [13] Every county and district surveyor in this State, shall, on the first day of May next, and every three months thereafter, return to the Commissioner of Claims a full and complete list of all certificates for land, of whatever character, then in his office, specifying the same by number and quantity, stating to whom and by whom issued, and whether duplicated or original, and the name of the then owner or claimants; and if duplicate, the number of the original, and by whom and to whom the original issued; and whether said certificates are located or unlocated. And any surveyor who shall fail to make such return, under oath, shall be liable to a penalty of five hundred dollars. And it shall be the duty of the Commissioner of Claims to give information to the several District Attorneys of every violation of the provisions of this section; and it shall be the duty of the District Attorney to institute suit against the defaulting surveyor for the recovery of such penalty; and the certificate of the Commissioner of Claims that the surveyor has failed to make such returns, shall be sufficient evidence of the fact. County and District Surveyors shall return list of certificates in their offices. Penalty for failure. Commissioner to give information to District Attorneys of failure.

ART. 335. [14] All claims for land for military services, not presented to the Commissioner of Claims on or before the first day of September, 1858, shall also be forever barred; but when any claim for land, military or otherwise, is presented on or before that day, proof to establish the same may be subsequently taken, until the first day of January, 1859, and not thereafter. Proof of claim filed, when to be taken.

DEAF AND DUMB INSTITUTION.

ART. 336. [1] The sum of ten thousand dollars be, and the same is hereby appropriated and set apart for the establishment of an institution for the education of the Deaf and Dumb of Texas, which shall be located at the city of Austin. Act of August 26, 1856. Took effect from passage. $10,000 set apart for.

Five Trustees—Superintendent.

ART. 337. [2] A Board of five Trustees shall be appointed by the Governor, whose duty it shall be to administer the funds of said institution, and provide for its going into operation as soon as practicable, by renting a suitable building and appointing such Superintendent and other officers as may be required for the successful management of said institution.

Money, when and how to be paid.

ART. 338. [3] Said sum of ten thousand dollars shall be paid on the order of said Trustees, approved and countersigned by the Governor, out of any money in the treasury, not otherwise appropriated, as the actual current expenses of maintaining the institution shall accrue: provided, that not more than five thousand dollars shall be expended in any one year.

Annual reports by Trustees.

ART. 339. [4] Said Trustees shall be, and they are hereby required to make full and accurate annual reports to the Governor of the State, showing the condition and progress of the institution, with a full exhibit of all expenditures, and it shall be the duty of the Governor to lay the same before the Legislature.

Act of 1858.

Appropriation of $7,500.

ART. 340. [1] The sum of seven thousand and five hundred dollars be, and the same is hereby appropriated out of any unappropriated monies in the treasury, for the purpose of providing a permanent location for the Deaf and Dumb Institution of the State.

Permanent location.

ART. 341. [2] The Trustees of said institution shall be, and they are hereby authorized to examine carefully the several tracts or lots of land in and around the city of Austin, belonging to the State, and if they can procure a suitable situation for the permanent location of said institution thereon they are hereby required to do so, and expend the sum hereby appropriated in the erection of suitable buildings for the accommodation of the pupils. But if in their judgment the interests of the State and the institution can be better promoted by the purchase of any other than the property of the State, then, they are hereby authorized to make such purchase, if it can be done on reasonable terms, and expend the residue of this appropriation in fitting up or improving the same, if necessary to be done: provided, that all their acts in relation to this matter shall be subject to the approval and satisfaction of the Governor of the State.

Money, when to be paid.

ART. 342. [3] The said sum of seven thousand and five hundred dollars shall be paid, on the order of the Trustees, approved and countersigned by the Governor, out of any monies in the treasury not otherwise appropriated, so soon as it may be required.

Property purchased reported to Governor.

ART. 343. [4] The said Trustees, if they purchase property for the location of the institution be, and they are hereby required to report to the Governor, so soon as they shall have made such purchase. They shall make a fair and full exhibit of such purchase to him, and it shall be the duty of the Governor to lay the same before the Legislature at its next session.

DESCENTS AND DISTRIBUTION OF ESTATES.

[*See Aliens—Wills—Estates of Deceased Persons.*]

ART. 344. [1] The estates of suicides shall descend and vest as in cases of natural death. If any person shall be killed by casualty, there shall be no forfeiture by reason thereof. Act of March 18, 1848. In force from passage. Estates of suicides—deodands abolished.

ART. 345. [2] When any person having title to any estate of inheritance, real, personal, or mixed, shall die intestate, as to such estate, and shall leave no surviving husband or wife, it shall descend and pass in parcenary to his or her kindred, male and female, in the following course, that is to say: 1st. To his or her children and their descendants, if any there be. 2dly. If there be no children nor their descendants, then to his or her father and mother, in equal portions: but if only the father or mother survive the intestate, then his or her estate shall be divided into two equal portions, one of which shall pass to such survivor, and the other half shall pass to the brothers and sisters (*a*) of the deceased, and to their descendants, or to such of them as there be; but if there be none such, then the whole estate shall be inherited by the surviving father or mother. 3dly. If there be neither father nor mother, then the whole of such estate shall pass to the brothers and sisters of the intestate, and to their descendants, or to such of them as there be. 4thly. If there be none of the kindred aforesaid, then the inheritance shall be divided into two moieties, one of which shall go to the paternal and the other to the maternal kindred, in the following course, that is to say: to the grandfather and grandmother, in equal portions; but if only one of these be living, then the estate shall be divided into two equal parts, one of which shall go to such survivor, and the other shall go to the descendant or descendants of such deceased grandfather or grandmother. If there be no such descendants, then the whole estate shall be inherited by the surviving grandfather or grandmother. If there be no surviving grandfather or grandmother, then the whole of such estate shall go to their descendants, or to such of them as there be, and so on without end, passing in like manner to the nearest lineal ancestors and their descendants, or to such of them as there be. Person dying intestate leaving no husband or wife.

ART. 346. [3] There shall be no distinction in regulating the descent and distribution of intestates' estates between property which may have been derived by such intestate by gift, devise, or descent, from the father, and that which may have been derived by gift, devise, or descent, from the mother; and all the estate to which such intestate may have had title, at the time of death, shall descend and vest in the heirs of such person, in the same manner as if he or she had been the original purchaser thereof. Estate to descend as if intestate had been the original purchaser.

ART. 347. [4] When any person having title to any estate of inheritance, real, personal, or mixed, shall die intestate as to such estate, and shall leave a surviving husband or wife, the estate of such intestate shall descend and pass Surviving husband or wife.

(*a*) Where the deceased leaves brothers and sisters of the half blood and none of the whole blood, the former inherit the same as if they were of the whole blood. Marlow *v.* King, 17 Tex. Rep. 177. Where there are kindred of the whole blood and of the half blood, the latter inherit half as much as the former. Lee *et al. v.* Smith *et al.* 18 Tex. Rep. 141.

as follows: 1st. If the deceased have a child or children, or their descendants, the surviving husband or wife shall take one-third of the personal estate, not to include slaves, and the balance of such personal estate shall go to the child or children of the deceased and their descendants—the surviving husband or wife shall also be entitled to an estate for life, in one-third of the land and slaves of the intestate, with remainder to the child or children of the intestate and their descendants. 2dly. If the deceased have no child or children, or their descendants, then the surviving husband or wife shall be entitled to all the personal estate of the intestate, not to include slaves, and to one-half of the lands and slaves of the intestate, without remainder to any person or persons, and the other half shall pass and be inherited according to the rules of descent and distribution, as prescribed in the foregoing sections of this act.; provided, however, that if the deceased have neither surviving father nor mother, nor surviving brothers and sisters or their descendants, then the surviving husband or wife shall be entitled to the whole of the estate of such intestate, real, personal and mixed.

Right of inheritance, to whom.

ART. 348. [5] No right of inheritance shall accrue to any person whatever, other than to children of the intestate, unless they be in being, and capable in law to take as heirs at the time of the intestate's death.

Collaterals of the half blood.

ART. 349. [6] In cases before mentioned, where the inheritance is directed to pass to the collateral kindred of the intestate, if part of such collateral be of the whole blood, and the other part of the half blood only, of the intestate, those of the half blood shall inherit only half so much as those of the whole blood; but if all be of the half blood, they shall have whole portions. (*a*)

Per capita and per stirpes.

ART. 350. [7] Where the children of the intestate's brothers and sisters, uncles and aunts, or any other relations of the deceased standing in the same degree, come into the partition, they shall take "*per capita*," that is to say, by persons; and where a part of them being dead, and a part living, the issue of those dead have right to partition, such issue shall take "*per stirpes*," or by stocks, that is to say, the shares of their deceased parents.

Hotchpotch.

ART. 351. [8] Where any of the children of a person dying intestate, or their issue, shall have received from such intestate, in his lifetime, any real, personal or mixed estate, by way of advancement, and shall choose to come into the partition and distribution of the estate with the other parceners and distributees, such advancement, of real, personal and mixed estate, shall be brought into hotchpotch with the whole estate, real, personal, or mixed, descended; and such party returning such advancement, as aforesaid, shall, thereupon, be entitled to his, her, or their proper portion of the whole estate so descended, real, personal and mixed; and provided, that it shall be sufficient to account for the property so brought into hotchpotch at the time it was advanced; and when money or negroes shall have been advanced, the interest of the one, or the increase of the other, need not be brought into hotchpotch. (*b*)

Alienage of ancestors no bar—nine years to aliens to take possession. [*See Aliens.*]

ART. 352. [9] In making title to land by descent, it shall be no bar to a party, that any ancestor through whom he derives his descent from the intestate, is or hath been an alien; and every alien, to whom any land may be devised or may descend, shall have nine years to become a citizen of the State, and take possession of such land, or shall have nine years to sell the same, before it shall be declared forfeited, or shall escheat to the Government. (*c*)

(*a*) Lee *et al.* v. Smith *et al.* 18 Tex. Rep. 141.

(*b*) Parker *v.* Parker, 10 Tex. Rep. 83.

(*c*) The limitation of nine years in which aliens are allowed to become citizens and take possession, or sell, is not confined to the question of forfeiture and escheat, between the heir and the Government, but over-rides the general law of limitations; and if the heir becomes a citizen within nine years, he recovers the estate, not only against the State, but also against adverse possessors, although he do not "take possession or sue within the nine years," unless, in the latter case, his claim should be barred by the general law of limitations, by the lapse of time after he became a citizen. Cryer *v.* Andrews, 11 Tex. Rep. 170.

ART. 353. [10] Where a man, having by a woman a child or children, shall afterwards intermarry with such woman, such child or children, if recognized by him, shall thereby be legitimated, and made capable of inheriting his estate. The issue, also, in marriages deemed null in law, shall nevertheless be legitimate. (a) Children legitimated by marriage of parents.

ART. 354. [11] Bastards shall be capable of inheriting from and through their mothers, and of transmitting estates; and shall, also, be entitled to distributive shares of the personal estates of any of their kindred on the part of their mothers, in like manner as if they had been lawfully begotten of such mothers. Bastards.

ART. 355. [12] When two or more persons hold an estate, real, personal, or mixed, jointly, and one joint tenant dies before severance, his interest in said joint estate shall not survive to the remaining joint tenant or joint tenants, but shall descend to and be vested in the heirs or legal representatives of such deceased joint tenant, in the same manner as if his interest had been severed and ascertained. Joint tenants.

ART. 356. [3] This act shall not be construed to alter or change, in any manner, the mode now pointed out by law, for distributing the common property of the husband and wife, upon the death of one of them. Community property not affected by this act.

(a) The expressions in which this section is embodied, are too perspicuous to require comment. The issue of marriages deemed null in law, without regard to the grounds of nullity, are legitimated; and are, consequently, endowed with all the rights of the legitimate issue. Hartwell v. Jackson, 6 Tex. Rep. 576.

DISCOUNT AND SET-OFF AND RECONVENTION.

[*See Bills of Exchange, Promissory Notes and Written Instruments.*]

ART. 357. [1] When any suit shall be commenced and prosecuted, in any court within this Republic, for any debt due by judgment, bond, bill or otherwise, the defendant shall have liberty, upon trial thereof, to make all the discounts he can against such debt; and upon proof thereof, the same shall be allowed in court. (a) Act of Feb'ry 5, 1840. Took effect March 16, 1840. Defendant may plead, &c.

ART. 358. [2] In every action in which a defendant shall desire to prove any payment or set-off, he shall file with his plea an account, stating distinctly the nature of such payment or set-off, and the several items thereof; and on failure to do so, he shall not be entitled to prove before the jury such payment or set-off, unless the same be so plainly and particularly described in the plea, as to give the plaintiff full notice of the character thereof. (b) Requisites of plea.

(a) If the subject matter of a set-off is not barred at the commencement of the suit, and was then a debt due from the plaintiff to the defendant, it will be good although barred at the time the answer is filed.

Set-offs must be mutual and due in the same right with the debt sued for. A joint debt cannot be set-off against a separate demand, nor a separate debt against a joint one. Allbright et al. v. Aldrich et al., 2 Tex. Rep. 166. Henderson v. Gilliam & Co., 12 Tex. Rep. 71. But it may be otherwise where it is alleged that the party against whom the set-off is pleaded is insolvent. Hanchett v. Gray, 7 Tex. Rep. 549.

The object of the law in allowing set-offs, is to avoid a multiplicity of actions. Thomas v. Thomas' adm'r, 3 Tex. Rep. 270.

The plea of set-off is not admissible against the State. 10 Tex. Rep. 315. Bates v. The Republic, 2 Tex. Rep. 616. Borden v. Houston, 2 Tex. Rep 594.

See Hall v. Hall, 11 Tex. Rep. 526, and Smally v. Trammel, ib. 10. As to set-offs against suits by administrators, also Guthrie v. Guthrie, 17 Tex. Rep. 541.

(b) The District Court struck out a plea, alleging "that the notes sued on have been fully paid, satisfied, and discharged on or about, &c.," as being defective under the statute, held erroneous. Holliman v. Rogers, 6 Tex. Rep. 91. Hall v. Hodge, 2 Tex. Rep. 323.

Set-off obtained after suit bro't.

ART. 359. [3] No defendant shall be allowed to offset any discount or demand against the plaintiff's cause of action, which he may have become entitled to or procured, after suit instituted, so as to defeat the action, and deprive the plaintiff of his costs of suit: provided, that the defendant can, in every case, plead any legal discounts or set-offs which he may have up to the time of making his defence according to the rules of pleading; but the court shall, in all cases, when it appears that the defendant's discounts or set-offs were obtained after the institution of suit, give judgment for the amonnt which is proved to be actually due the plaintiff (if any there be,) together with his costs of suit expended in that behalf.(*a*)

When plaintiff's demand is reduced below jurisdiction by set-off—by payment—when set-off exceeds demand.

ART. 360. [4] Whenever any plaintiff may institute his suit for, and establish, a demand in any court having jurisdiction of the same, and his claims be reduced by set-off to an amount not within the jurisdiction of the court, judgment still shall be given for the amount due the plaintiff, and for costs of suit; should the set-off of the defendant exceed the amount established by the plaintiff, then judgment shall be given in favor of the defendant, for the amount that his claim may exceed that of the plaintiff, but the plaintiff shall recover the costs of the suit;(*b*) but should the claim of the plaintiff be reduced to a sum not within the jurisdiction of the court, by payment, then judgment shall be given in favor of the plaintiff for the balance due; but the defendant shall recover the costs of the suit; and when the defendant may have claim against the plaintiff, similar in its nature (but they need not be of the same degree) to that of the plaintiff, he shall be permitted to file in his answer a plea of reconvention, setting forth the amount due him, and judgment shall be given in favor of that party who may establish the largest claim, for the excess of his claim over that of his opponent and for costs.(*c*)

Plea of reconvention.

Set-off not allowed against unliquidated damages.

ART. 361. [5] If the plaintiff's cause of action be brought on a claim for unliquidated or uncertain damages, founded on a tort or breach of covenant, the defendant shall not be permitted to set-off or discount any debt due him by the plaintiff; and if the suit be founded on a certain demand, the defendant shall not be permitted to set-off unliquidated or uncertain damages, founded on a tort or breach of covenant, on the part of the plaintiff.(*d*)

Uncertain damages not set-off.

(*a*) The defendant may plead in set-off any claim acquired before pleading it; if acquired after suit brougnt, the plaintiff recovers costs. Thomas *v.* Young, 5 Tex. Rep. 253. Gaines *v.* Salmon, 16 Tex. Rep. 311. The apparent legal holder of a note may plead it in set-off, although the real interest be in another, ib.; Parrott *v.* Underwood, 10 Tex. Rep. 48. A judgment by defendant against plaintiff, upon which an appeal is pending, cannot be set-off. Weatherred *v.* Mays, 1 Tex. Rep. 472.

(*b*) Where the defendant's set-off exceeds the plaintiff's demand, it is error in the court to render judgment in favor of the defendant for costs. Hall *v.* Hodge, 2 Tex. Rep. 323. Weatherred *v.* Mays, 1 Tex. Rep. 472.

(*c*) The defendant may plead in reconvention all matters necessarily connected with the main action, and incident to the same. Walcott *v.* Hendrick, 6 Tex. Rep. 406. Castro *v.* Gentiley, 11 Tex. Rep. 28. As to particular cases for the plea, see Hammond *v.* Belcher, 10 Tex. Rep. 271. Parrott *v.* Underwood, 10 Tex. Rep. 48. Cannon *v.* Hemphill, 7 Tex. Rep. 184. Eggery *v.* Power, 5 Tex. Rep. 501. Stewart *v.* Insall, 9 Tex. Rep. 397. Bradford *v.* Hamilton, 7 Tex. Rep. 55. McCoy *v.* Jones, 9 Tex. Rep. 363. Carlin *v.* Hudson, 12 Tex. Rep. 202. Flanagan *v.* Ward, ib. 209. Peiser *v.* Cushman, 13 Tex. Rep. 390. Sterrett *v.* Houston, 14 Tex. Rep. 153. Cyrus *v.* Hicks, 20 Tex. Rep. 483. Ashworth *v.* Dark, ib., 825. Brady *v.* Price, 19 Tex. Rep. 285. Oldham *v.* Erhart, 18 Tex. Rep. 147. Clegg *v.* Varnell, ib., 294. Philips *v.* Patillo, ib., 518. Griffin *v.* Chubb, 16 Tex. Rep. 219. Hancock *v.* Dimon, 17 Tex. Rep. 369.

(*d*) A claim for unliquidated damages for a breach of contract, may be set-off against an open account for goods sold and delivered. Rodman *v.* Harris, 20 Tex. Rep. 31.

DISTRICT ATTORNEY.

Act of May 13, 1846.

Bond required of.

ART. 362. [1] Each District Attorney before entering on the duties of his office, shall give a bond payable to the Governor and his successors in office, for the use of the State, in the sum of five thousand dollars, to be approved by the District Judge of their respective districts, with not less than two sureties, conditioned that he will faithfully pay over in the manner prescribed in this act, all money which he may collect for the use of the State; and shall take and subscribe the oath prescribed by the Constitution, which, together with the bond, shall be deposited in the office of the Comptroller of Public Accounts; which bond shall not be void on the first recovery, but may be sued on from time to time.

Oath of.

Duties of.

ART. 363. [2] It shall be the duty of each District Attorney to attend all terms of the District Court in the district in which he may have been elected, to conduct all prosecutions for crimes and offences cognizable in such court, to prosecute and defend all other actions in which this State is interested, and to perform such other duties as may be prescribed by the Constitution and laws of the State. They shall severally reside within the district for which they were elected, and shall notify the Attorney-General and Comptroller of Public Accounts of the county of their residence.(a)

Residence

Failing to attend court, penalty.

ART. 364. [3] When any District Attorney shall fail to attend any of the terms of the court above specified, his salary shall be liable to such deduction as may be prescribed by law.

Report to Attorney-General semi-annually.

ART. 365. [4] Each District Attorney shall report to the Attorney-General semi-annually, at the close of the courts of their respective districts, in such form as he may prescribe, the number of indictments which have been found by the grand juries in his district for the preceding half year, specifying the offences charged therein, the number of arraignments, convictions, and acquittals for each offence, the number of indictments which have been disposed of without the intervention of a petit jury, with the cause and manner of such disposition, and also a summary of the judgments rendered on such convictions, specifying the offence, the nature and amount of the penalty imposed, and the amount of fines and penalties collected.

Shall give information when required by Attorney-General.

ART. 366. [5] The District Attorneys shall, from time to time, give to the Attorney-General such information as he may require as to their official acts.

Opinions to Assessor, Collector and County Treasurer.

ART. 367. [6] Each District Attorney, at the request of any Assessor or Collector of Taxes, or County Treasurer, in the district for which he may have been elected, shall give an opinion in writing in all cases touching the public interest, or concerning the revenue of the State.

ART. 368. [7] Each District Attorney shall give such directions to the

(a) In the absence of the District Attorney, the Court has the power to appoint an Attorney to represent the State. The State v. Johnson, 12 Texas Rep, 231.

Directions to Clerks and Sheriffs. District Clerks and Sheriffs in the several counties of their respective districts as he may deem necessary to insure the collection of all money for which judgments may have been rendered in favor of the State.

Receipt for money of State. ART. 369. [8] It shall be the duty of the several District Attorneys, whenever they collect any money for the use of the State, to deliver to the officer or person paying the same, duplicate receipts therefor.

File account with Comptroller. ☞ART. 370. [9] Each District Attorney shall, on or before the last day of October, in each year, file in the office of the Comptroller of Public Accounts, an account in writing, verified by his affidavit, of all money received by him by virtue of his office during the preceding year, and payable by law into the Treasury of the State, and shall, at the same time, pay such money into the Treasury, retaining the commissions thereon allowed by law.

Same with County Treasurer. ART. 371. [10] Each District Attorney shall also file a like account, verified in like manner, in the office of the County Treasurer of each county in his district, of all money received by him in such county by virtue of his office, during the preceding year and payable by law into the Treasury of the State.

Failing to give bond. ART. 372. [11] Should any person who may have been elected District Attorney fail, on or before the first day of the first term of the first District Court in his district, to enter into bond, as required by this act, it shall be the duty of the Judge of the District Court of said district to appoint some other competent person to discharge, pro tempore, the duties assigned by this act to said officer: provided, however, that such appointment shall in no instance extend beyond the term of the said District Court in any one county.

Shall not be counsel. ART. 373. [12] No District Attorney shall act as attorney or counsel for any party to an action wherein such party is charged with a crime, with a misdemeanor, or a breach of a penal statute, nor where the interest of such party is adverse to that of the State.

Admissions of, not to prejudice State. ART. 374. [13] No admission made by the District Attorney in any suit or action in which the State is a party, shall operate to prejudice the interests of the State.

Keep official register. ART. 375. [14] Each District Attorney shall keep in proper books, to be procured for that purpose, at the expense of the State, a Register of all his official acts and reports, and of all actions and demands prosecuted or defended by him, of all proceedings had in relation thereto; and shall deliver the same over to his successor in office.

Act of Jan. 11, 1848. Salary. ART. 376 [1] The several District Attorneys of this State shall receive an annual salary of five hundred dollars, to be paid quarterly.

DISTRICT COURT.

[*See Const., Art.* 4., *Sections* 1, 10.]

I. ORGANIZATION, POWERS AND JURISDICTION OF THE DISTRICT COURT.

II. DISTRICT CLERK.

III. VENUE.

IV. INSTITUTION OF SUITS—PROCESS AND SERVICE.

V. PLEADINGS.

VI. TRIAL AND CONTINUANCE.

VII. DISCONTINUANCE.

VIII. EVIDENCE.

1. *Witnesses.*

2. *Depositions.*

3. *Records, Office Copies and Written Instruments of Evidence.*

4. *Interrogatories to Opposite Party.*

IX. CHALLENGE OF JURORS.

X. CHARGE OF THE COURT, BILLS OF EXCEPTIONS, AND NON-SUIT.

XI. VERDICT.

XII. JUDGMENT.

XIII. NEW TRIAL AND ARREST OF JUDGMENT.

XIV. MOTIONS.

XV. COSTS.

I. ORGANIZATION, POWERS AND JURISDICTION OF THE DISTRICT COURTS.

Act of May 11, 1846. Took effect June 22, 1846.

Judges to be conservators of the peace.

ART. 377. [2] The Judges of the District Courts shall, by virtue of their offices, be conservators of the peace throughout the State, and the District Courts shall have original jurisdicrion of all criminal cases, of all suits in behalf of the State, to recover penalties, forfeitures, and escheats, and of all suits against the State, which are or may be allowed by law, and shall have power to hear and determine all prosecutions in the name of the State, by indictment, information, or presentment, for treason, murder, or other felonies, crimes, and misdemeanors, committed within their respective jurisdictions, except such as may be exclusively cognizable before Justices of the Peace, or other courts of the State, and shall in criminal cases, have and exercise all the powers incident and belonging to courts of oyer and terminer, and general jail delivery; also of all suits for the recovery of land, of all cases of divorce and alimony, and of all suits, complaints and pleas whatever, without regard to any distinction whatever, between law and equity, when the matter in controversy shall be valued at or amount to one hundred dollars or more, exclusive of interest; and generally to do and perform all other acts pertaining to courts of general jurisdiction.(a)

Jurisdiction, original.

Act of May 11, 1846. Took effect 22d June, 1846.

Appellate jurisdiction.

When to exercise original jurisdiction in probate matters.

ART. 378. [3] The District Courts shall have and exercise appellate jurisdiction and general control over such inferior tribunals as have been or may be established in each county, for appointing guardians, granting letters testamentary and of administration, for settling the accounts of executors, administrators, and guardians, and for the transaction of business appertaining to estates; and original jurisdiction in probate matters, only in cases where the Judge or Clerk of Probate is interested.(b)

Judges may grant writs of habeas corpus, mandamus, &c.

ART. 379. [4] The Judges of the District Courts, and each of them, either in vacation or term time, shall have authority to grant on petition to them therefor, writs of habeas corpus, mandamus, injunction, sequestration, error and supersedeas, and all other remedial writs, known to the law, returnable according to law: provided, that no mandamus shall be granted on an ex parte hearing, and any peremptory mandamus granted without notice, shall be deemed void: and further provided, that all writs of mandamus, sued out against the heads of any of the departments or bureaux of government, shall be returnable before the District Court of the county in which the seat of government may be.(c)

Mandamus, when to be granted and where returnable.

Upon notice, may give judgment against Sheriffs, or other officer, for money collected

ART. 380. [5] The said courts shall have power to hear and determine all motions, three days' notice being given to the adverse party, against sheriffs, coroners, or other officers, for money received under execution or other process or order of court, which shall not have been paid to the party entitled to the same, his agent or attorney, on demand, or for other defalcation of duty, and also all motions against attorneys and counsellors at law, and give judgment and order execution, according to the laws in such cases made and provided.

(a) The jurisdiction of the District Court is general. Drummond *v.* The Republic, 2 Tex Rep. 156. It includes all the jurisdiction known to the Common Law and chancery courts of England, not inconsistent with the Constitution of the United States and of this State, and laws under them. Newson *v.* Chrisman, 9 Tex. Rep. 113. The amount claimed in the petition is the sum in controversy, and determines the jurisdiction. Graham *v.* Roder, 5 Tex. Rep. 141. If the demand declared on is within the jurisdiction of the court, judgment may be given for an amount, under the jurisdiction, unless the plaintiff in stating his demand improperly sought to give jurisdiction where it did not rightfully belong. Tarbox & Brown *v.* Kennon, 3 Tex. Rep. 7. The District Courts, and Courts of Justices of the Peace, have concurrent jurisdiction, where the amount in controversy is one hundred dollars exclusive of interest. Love & Chappell *v.* McIntyre, 3 Tex. Rep. 10. Johnson *v.* Happell, 4 Tex. Rep. 96. The District Court has jurisdiction of a suit on two promissory notes, amounting in the aggregate to one hundred dollars exclusive of interest. Lott *v.* Adams, 4 Tex. Rep. 426. Mays *v.* Lewis, Ibid. 38. It has no jurisdiction of a note reduced by payment to less than one hundred dollars, exclusive of interest. Swigley *v.* Dickson, 2 Tex. Rep. 192.

(b) The District Court has jurisdiction independent of the 15th section of the 4th article of the Constitution, to act directly and originally upon exeutors, administrators and guardians, to prevent fraudulent combinations, that might result in the destruction of the rights of those interested in the estate. Newson, guardian, *v.* Chrisman, 9 Tex. Rep. 113. Dobbin *v.* Bryan, 5 Tex. Rep. 276. Long et al. *v.* Wortham, 4 Tex. R. 381. Smith *v.* Smith, 11 Tex. Rep. 102. Under the Constitution the law provides two modes of revising the proceedings of the Probate Courts, by the District Courts, by appeal and certiorari. Cain *v.* Haas, 18 Tex. Rep. 616.

(c) The writ of mandamus lies, as a private remedy, to compel the heads of departments to perform a duty, in cases where the duty is plain and where there is no discretion. Com. Gen. Land Office *v.* Smith, 5 Tex. Rep. 471. Glasscock *v.* The Com'r, &c., 3 Tex. Rep. 51. It will issue to an officer only where the duty to be performed is ministerial in its character; but not where the exercise of judgment and discretion are required, Ibid. A mandamus will not be issued where it appears that it would affect persons who are not before the court, and where the rights of those persons have not been determined in a previous suit, ibid. It is not allowed in cases where the law affords other adequate means of redress; nor in any case, except to perform a duty clearly defined by law—involving no discretion, nor leaving any alternative. Cullem, adm'x *v.* Latimer, 4 Tex. Rep. 329. It is a rule that all persons principally interested in the defence must be included in the rule to show cause, ibid. A mandamus is a proper writ to restore one to an office from which he has been illegally ousted, or to put a party in possession of an office which is illegally detained from him, and to cause the books, papers and archives thereof to be delivered to him. Banton *v.* Wilson, 4 Tex. Rep. 400. As to other cases, see Bracken *v.* Wells, 3 Tex. Rep. 88. Auditorial Board *v.* Arles, 15 Tex. Rep. 72. The granting of a writ of *habeas corpus* is not a matter of course in this State. Jordan *v.* The State, 14 Tex. Rep. 436. It does not lie to revise the action of a court of a competent jurisdiction, in cases of contempt, Ibid.

ART. 381. [6] Said courts shall have power to impose a fine, not exceeding one hundred dollars, for contempt of court, and may, in their discretion, imprison any person guilty of contempt not exceeding three days. May fine and imprison for contempt.

ART. 382. [7] The District Judges, when the appropriate relief is prayed for, may grant all such orders, writs or other process necessary to obtain such relief, and may, also, so frame the judgments of the court as to afford all the relief which may be required by the nature of the case, and which is granted by courts of law or equity.(*a*) May grant writs of relief.

ART. 383. [8] The District Courts of each county in this State shall have a seal, with a star of five points in the centre, and the words "District Court of —— County, Texas," engraved thereon; an impresssion of which seal shall be attached to all writs and other process (except subpœnas) issuing from said court, and shall be used in the authentication of all official acts of the Clerk; said seal shall be procured by the County Court of the county, and until procured, the seals heretofore in use, or private seals may be used.(*b*) Seal of the court shall be attached to process.

ART. 384. [9] Should the Judge of any District Court not appear at the time appointed for holding the same, the Sheriff of the county, or in his absence, or in case of vacancy in that office, the Coroner shall adjourn the court from day to day for three days, and if the Judge should not appear on the morning of the fourth day, then he shall adjourn the court until the next court in course. Act of May 11, 1846. Sheriff to adjourn court from day to day.

ART. 385. [11] The Judges in any case, civil or criminal, in which a party may swear that he is too poor to employ counsel, shall appoint counsel for such party, who shall attend to the cause in behalf of such party without any fee or reward. When a party be too poor to employ counsel, Judge to appoint.

ART. 386. [12] The records of the respective courts of each preceding day of the session, shall be read in open court on the morning of the succeeding day, except on the last day of the term, on which day they shall be read and signed by the Judge presiding, in open court. Record to be read and signed in open court.

ART. 387. [17] It shall be the duty of the Judges of each court to cause the judgments, sentences and decrees of the court to be carried into execution agreeably to law. Judges to have judgments, &c., executed.

ART. 388. [15] When any Judge of the District Court may be interested in causes pending in his district, or where any of the parties may be connected with him by consanguinity or affinity within the third degree, or when the Judge has been of counsel in the causes, he may exchange districts with any Judge who is not subject to like disabilities; any Judge may hold courts with any other District Judge, and exchange of districts may be made whenever the Judges exchanging may deem expedient. Judges may exchange districts.

ART. 389. [16] When any Judge is disqualified, the parties may, by consent, choose and appoint some other person to try the cause, and the acts and decisions of such person so appointed, shall be as valid as if done by the Judge. Special Judge may be appointed, when.

Act of Dec. 30, 1840. Took effect March 17, 1841.

ART. 389*a*. [1] If any Judge of any of the judicial districts of the Republic shall fail, neglect or refuse to hold his court at the time and place as

(*a*) Process calling on a party to answer to a suit, which is not under a seal, is void, and can exact no obedience. Frosch *v.* Schlumpf, 2 Tex. Rep. 422. The copy of the petition which is served upon the defendant is not required to be sealed. Thomas *v.* Womack, 13 Tex. Rep. 580.

(*b*) By this section of the statute the court is invested with all powers necessary to afford such appropriate relief as may be prayed for; and is also empowered to so frame the judgment of the court as to afford all the relief which may be required by the nature of the case, and is grantable by courts or law and equity. Hipp *v.* Huchett, 4 Tex. Rep. 20.

Penalty for failing to hold court. required by law, he shall for each and every court that he may so fail, neglect or refuse to hold in his district as aforesaid, forfeit to the government the sum of five hundred dollars, to be deducted from his annual salary.

(See Const. Art. 7, sec. 12.) [2] The Judge so failing to hold his court or courts as aforesaid, shall make and subscribe his affidavit in writing, that such failure resulted alone from sickness, or the public enemy, (provided nothing herein shall operate upon a Judge for not holding his court in a depopulated county that rendered him unable to attend,) which said affidavit shall be attached to his draft on the treasury.

[3] In every case where the Judge of the District Court shall fail to attend and hold his court as now provided by law, the Chief Justice of the county in which such failure occurs shall forthwith report the same, under his seal of office, to the Secretary of the Treasury; which report shall be a sufficient voucher for the Treasurer to withhold the amount specified in this act for such failure, except such excuse is presented as herein provided for, anything in the laws to the contray notwithstanding.

II. CLERK—DISTRICT.

Act of Dec. 5th 1849. Took effect from passage.

One Clerk of Dist. Court to be elected, &c. ART. 390. [1] There shall be elected by the qualified voters for members of the Legislature, on the first Monday in August, in the year eighteen hundred and fifty, one Clerk of the District Court in each and every county in the State of Texas, where four years shall have elapsed since the election of the incumbent in the office of District Clerk.

Time of celection and term of office. ART. 391. [2] On the first Monday in August, in the year eighteen hundred and fifty, and on the first Monday in August every two years thereafter, a regular election shall be held in each and every county where vacancies have already occured, or may hereafter occur, in the office of the Clerk of the District Court, by death, resignation, removal, or the laps of four years from the date of the incumbent's election.(*a*).

In case of vacancy, Judge to appoint. ART. 392. [3] In each and every county where a vacancy in the office of Clerk of the District Court now exists, or may hereafter occur, before the first Monday in August, in the year eighteen hundred and fifty, or between the times specified in this Act for holding regular elections to fill the vacancies in said office, the Judge of the District Court, in vacation or in term time, shall appoint some suitable person Clerk of the District Court, to fill said office until the first regular election thereafter is held according to the provisions of this Act. The order making the appointment shall be entered on the minutes of the District Court, at the first term held in such county after the said appointment; and the Clerk so appointed, shall give bond in the manner now prescribed by law.

Act of May 11th 1846.

Clerks shall give bond, &c. ART. 393. [20] The Clerks of the District Courts shall give bond with security to be approved by the County Court, payable to the Governor of the State of Texas and his successors in office, in the sum of five thousand dollars for the safe keeping of the records, and the faithful discharge of the duties of his office, and shall also take and subscribe the oath of office required by the Constitution, which shall be endorsed on his bond, and the bond and affidavit

(*a*) Vacancies can only be filled by appointment by the District Judge, until the next regular election for Clerks, the time for which are established by the act. Carolan *v.* McDonald, 15 Tex. Rep 327.

A Clerk elected to fill a vacancy, is elected to hold the office, for the full term of four years. Banton *v.* Wilson, 4 Tex. Rep. 400.

so taken and approved shall be filed and recorded in the office of the Clerk of the County Court, a certified copy of which bond may be put in suit, in the name of the Governor of the State, for the use of the party or parties injured, and shall not become void on the recovery of part of the penalty thereof, but shall be deemed to extend to the faithful discharge of the duties of his office, and may be sued on from time to time by the party or parties injured, until the whole amount of the penalty is recovered. May be sued on and not to be void on first recovery.

ART. 394. [2] Each Clerk elected or appointed, shall have power to appoint one or more deputies, by a written appointment, under his hand and seal of the court, which shall be filed and recorded in the office of the Clerk of the County Court. Clerk may appoint a deputy.

ART. 395. [22] The Clerks shall have the custody of all the minutes, records, books, papers and seals now deposited, or that may hereafter be deposited in their respective offices, and it shall be their duty carefully to attend to the arrangement and preservation of the same, and the court shall order the procurement of the necessary presses, cases, and office furniture, books and stationary and seal, at the expense of the respective counties. To have custody of books.

ART. 396. [23] Clerks elected or appointed, and their deputies, shall have power to administer oaths in all cases required in the discharge of the duties of their office.(*a.*) May administer oaths.

ART. 397. [24] It shall be the duty of the Clerks of the District Courts to keep a fair record of all acts done, and proceedings had in their respective courts, to enter all judgments of the court under the direction of the Judge, and also of executions issued, and returns thereon made, in the record books furnished for those purposes. To keep a fair record, enter judgments, executions issued, &c.

ART. 398. [25] The Clerks of the District Court, at the expiration of each term, shall make out a statement of all fines imposed, penalties and forfeitures incurred, and judgments rendered at such court, in behalf of the State, and to report the same to the Comptroller of Public Accounts. When to return list of fines, &c., to Comp'ler.

March 16, 1848. Took effect Apl. 29, 1848.

ART. 399. [1] The Sheriffs, Clerks of the District Court, and Clerks of the County Court of the several counties of this State, shall be, and they are hereby required to keep their several offices at the county seats of their respective counties. Clerks and Sheriffs offices where keep

ART. 400. [2] In all cases where the said Sheriffs, and Clerks do not reside at the county seats of their respective counties, they shall be, and are hereby required, to have deputies in their several offices, residing at said county seats. Deputy to reside, &c.

III. VENUE.

Act of May 13, 1846. Took effect June 22d 1846.

ART. 401. [12] No person who is an inhabitant of this State shall be sued out of the county where he has his domicil, except in the following cases, viz: First—in case of married women, who must be sued in the county where her husband has his domicil; second—in case the defendant is a transient person, in which case he may be sued in whatever county he may be found; third—in cases where there may be two or more defendants, residing in different counties, in which cases the plaintiff may institute suit in any county where any of such County in which suit shall be brought.

(*a*) The statute confers upon the Clerk authority, to administer all requsite oaths, in proceedings, appertaining to the Court of which he is Clerk. Smith *v.* Wilson, 15 Tex. Rep. 132.

He has no authority to administer an oath to a petition for a certiorari to a Justice of the Peace of another county and returnable to the District Court of such other county. Carlee *v.* Smith, 8 Tex. Rep. 134.

defendants may reside; fourth—in cases where a person has contracted to perform an obligation in any particular county, in which case suit may be instituted in that county, or where the defendant has his domicil; fifth—in cases of executors, administrators or guardians of an estate, or trustees, who must be sued in the county in which the estate is administered; sixth—in cases of fraud, and also in cases of defalcation of public officers, in which cases suit may be instituted in the county where the fraud was committed, or where the defalcation occurred, or where the defendant has his domicil; seventh—where the defendant has committed some crime or offence for which a civil action in damages may be commenced, in which cases suit may be instituted in the county where the crime or offence was committed, or in the county where the defendant has his domicil: provided, that prosecutions by the State for crime or offence, shall always be in the county where such crime or offence was committed; eighth—in cases where the suit is for a slave, animal, or other movable property, in which cases suit may be instituted in whatever county such property may be found, or where the defendant resides; ninth—in cases where the defendant has inherited an estate, concerning which suit is commenced, in which case suit may be instituted in the county where the estate principally lies; tenth—in cases for the foreclosure of mortgages, in which cases suit may be instituted in the courts where the mortgaged property or any part thereof may be; eleventh—in cases where the recovery of land, or damages thereto, is the object of a suit, in which cases suit must be instituted where the land or a part thereof is situated.(*a.*)

Act of May 11, 1846.

ART. 402. [14] The District Courts may order a change of venue for the trial of any suit, civil or criminal, under the rules and regulations prescribed by law.

Act of Jan. 14. 1841.

Venue may be changed on affidavit.

When and to whom granted.

ART. 403. [1] The Judges of the District Courts of their respective districts shall have power to change the venue for the trial of any suit; civil or criminal, on good and sufficient cause set forth and duly supported by oath or affirmation of three disinterested citizens of the Republic; the sufficiency of which evidence shall be determined by the presiding Judge; and when a change of venue shall be allowed in any suit. the trial thereof shall be adjourned to the nearest adjoining county which is free from the like exceptions: provided, That such change of venue shall in no instance be allowed more than once to each party in the same cause or suit. And in all criminal prosecutions, the right of the change of venue shall be confined to the party prosecuted.

(*a*) A suit for damages, for a *trespass de bonis asportatis*, the suit must be in the county of the defendant's residence. Illies *v.* Knight. 3 Tex. Rep. 312.

Where there are several defendants suit may be instituted in the county of the residence of any one of them. Raymond et al *v.* Holmes, 11 Tex. Rep. 54, Randon *v.* Barton, 4 Tex. Rep. 239.

Where a defendant has contracted to perform an obligation in a particular county, suit may be brought either in that county, or the county of his residence.—Durst *v.* Swift 11 Tex Rep 273

The provision, which requires action for the recovery of lands and damages thereto to be brought in the county where the land lies, is a privilege of the defendant, and if the objection, that the suit is brought in another county, is not taken at the proper time it will be waived. Morris *v.* Runnels, 12 Tex. Rep. 175.—Ryan et al *v.* Jackson et al 11 Tex. Rep. 391.

Where the recovery of land, or damages thereto is the object of the suit, it may be brought in any county where part of the land lies although the adverse party claims only part of the land, which lies in another county. Ibid.

Where suit is brought to annul a Probate sale and to remove a cloud &c., it is not necessary the suit should be brought in the county where the land lies. Finch's heirs *v.* Edmondson et al 9 Tex. Rep. 504, Morris *v.* Runnels 12 Tex. Rep. 175.

Suit for the specific performance of a contract for the sale of land must be brought in the county of defendant's residence. Miller admr *v.* Rusk, 17 Tex. Rep. 170.

A suit to foreclose a mortgage may be brought either in the county where the property is situated or that of the defendant's domicil. Kinney *v.* McCleod, 9 Tex. Rep. 78.

Executors, Administrators, Guardians and Trustees *must* be sued in the county where the estate is administered, no matter what may be the subject in controversy. Neill *v.* Owen admr. 3 Tex. Rep. 145, Richardson and wife *v.* Wells admr. Ibid 223.

A *scire facias*, simply to revive a judgment may be brought in the county where the judgment remains of record. Perkins *v.* Hume, 10 Tex. Rep. 50.

The word "domicil" in the statute means residence. Brown *v.* Boulden, 18 Tex. Rep. 431.

If the defendant is in the act of removing from one county to another, and his affairs are in such a state that it cannot be certainly known in which county he resides in fact, suit may be brought in either. Ibid.

At all event, if he has had his residence, in one county for a considerable time, anterior to the bringing of the suit, that, for the purposes of the suit, ought to be held the place of his residence, until he has effected an actual and complete change of residence. Ibid.

ART. 404. [1] Whenever any one of the District Judges of the State of Texas shall be disqualified by law from trying or setting in any case pending before him, and the parties shall fail to appoint by consent a proper person to try said case, it shall be the duty of such Judge, upon the motion of any party or his attorney, interested in the cause, to change the venue of such case from the county in which he may be residing, to the county out of his district, the county seat of which shall be nearest to the county seat at which said cause is pending or any county the parties may agree.(*a*) Act of Feb. 13, 1854. May be changed if Judge disqualified. [See art's 388, 389.]

IV. INSTITUTION OF SUITS—PROCESS AND SERVICE.

ART. 405. [2] No civil suit shall be instituted, nor shall any process be had in any suit, on Sundays, except in cases of attachment or sequestration. Act of May 13, 1846. Shall not be commenced on Sunday, except.

ART. 406. [3] All civil suits in the District Court shall be commenced by petition filed in the office of the clerk of the District Court.(*b*) Suits by petition.

ART. 407. [6] The clerk or deputy, receiving such petition, shall endorse thereon, the day on which it is filed, and also the number thereof, and shall enter the suit in a docket, to be kept for that purpose, in the order in which it is filed, stating in a convenient form, the number of the suit, the names of the parties and their attorneys, the object of the suit, the officer's return, and all subsequent proceedings in the suit, specifying the time they were had. Date of filing petition to be endorsed on &c.

ART. 408. [9] It shall be the duty of the clerk, when a petition is filed and the regulations hereinafter provided, are complied with, to issue a writ or citation, directed to the sheriff or other proper officer of the county or counties in which the petition alleges that the defendants are, requiring him to summon the defendants to appear at the proper term of the court, then and there to answer the plaintiff's petition, a certified copy of which shall accompany each writ or citation; and if there be more than one defendant, the clerk shall issue a writ or citation to each, accompanied with a copy of the petition; provided, that when suit is instituted in any court of this State against any corporation or body politic, service of said writ or citation, with a copy of the petition, on the Chief Justice, Mayor, President, Secretary or Treasurer thereof, shall be a sufficient service on said corporation or body politic.(*c*) Act of Feb. 6, 1854. Clerk to issue citation and copy of petition. How served on corporations.

ART. 409. [10] The style of all writs and process shall be—"The State of Texas," and shall be tested in the name of the clerk of the court from which it is issued: it shall also state the name of the parties to the suit, the time and place of holding the court; shall be dated and signed by the clerk, with the seal of the court affixed; excepting subpœnas, which may be issued without the seal; and the clerk issuing any process, shall mark thereon the day on which it issued.(*d*) Act of May 13, 1846. Style of process and duty of clerk.

(*a*) It is incumbent on the plaintiff, or party prosecuting the suit, in cases of change of venue, to cause the case to be transferred as early as conveniently practicable, or within a reasonable time. Ponton *v.* Bellows, 13 Tex. Rep. 254.

(*b*) The petition stating the cause of action is a prerequisite to all other proceedings in a civil suit. A judgment by confession, before the filing of the petition, is fatally defective. Montgomery *v.* Barnett, 8 Tex. Rep., 143. Dikes *v.* Monroe, 15 Tex. Rep., 236.

(*c*.) The citation must contain a statement of the names of the parties to the suit. Little *v.* Marler, 8 Tex. Rep., 107. Where there are several defendants, a citation requiring the sheriff to summon one to appear and answer the plaintiff's petition exhibited against him, a copy of which accompanies this writ, is bad. Ibid.

The proper practice is to issue a citation for each defendant, requiring the proper sheriff to summon him to answer the petition of the plaintiff or plaintiffs, (by name,) exhibited against himself and his co-defendants, naming them. Ibid. Where there are several defendants, the names of all must be stated in the citation, which is required to be issued to each of the defendants. Burleson *v.* Henderson, 4 Tex. Rep., 49. Anderson *v.* Brown, 16 Tex. Rep. 554.

(*d*) For the construction as to what the process shall contain, see the cases cited in the preceding note.

A writ to which the clerk omitted to affix the seal of the court, was after its return amended, by affixing the

Service may be waived.

ART. 410. [13] Any party to a suit, his agent or attorney, may waive the necessity of the issuance or the service of any writ or process required to be served on him in the suit, and accept such service therof; provided, that such waiver or acceptance shall be made in writing, signed by such party, his agent, or attorney, and filed among the papers of the suit, as a record. (*a*)

Arts. 416, 417, & notes.

ART. 411. [14] The sheriff, or other officer, receiving any process, shall endorse thereon the day on which he received it, and shall execute the same where not otherwise directed by the writ, or citation, by delivering to the party or parties in person, upon whom he is required to serve it, a copy thereof, and a copy of the petition accompanying it, if there be one, if the party can be found; when the process directs other mode of service, it shall be executed according to the requirements of the process.

Mode of serving process against sheriff.

ART. 412. [21] Process against a sheriff shall be issued to and served by the coroner of the county, if there be one, but if there be no coroner, or if he be unable to act, then such process may be issued to and served by any constable of the county, the return thereof always to be in the same mode as directed for service by sheriffs.

Party served shall obey process.

ART. 412.a [22] Every party upon whom any valid process is served, shall obey the requisites of such process under such penalty as may be prescribed by law.

Coroner to serve process when.

ART. 413. [7] It shall be the duty of each coroner to execute and return all process, of whatever nature the same may be, where the sheriff is a party, and in all cases where just exceptions can be taken to the sheriff or his deputies, or where there is no sheriff. (*b*)

When sheriff is related, &c., coroner shall act.

ART. 414. [8] In all cases upon affidavit filed with the clerk of any court in this State, of the partiality, prejudice, consanguinity, or affinity of the sheriff of any county, where suit is brought or to be brought, or shall have commenced, the clerk shall issue and direct the original or other process in the suit to the coroner, who shall execute the same and attend to the suit throughout, in the same manner as the sheriff should do in like cases.

When citation to be served and returned.

ART. 415. [10] All civil writs and citations (except subpœnas for witnesses and notices,) shall be returnable on the first day of the term of the court after the issuance thereof; and in order to compel the defendant to plead at the return term of the court, the writ of citation shall be served at least five days before the first day of said return term, exclusive of the days of service and return; and if the writ be issued too late, or cannot be served at least five days before the first day of said return term, exclusive of the days of service and return, the sheriff or other officer, to whom the same is directed, shall proceed, nevertheless, to serve the same, at any time before the return day thereof; which service shall compel the defendant to plead at the first term after the return thereof.

seal, *nunc pro tune*. Cartwright *v.* Chabert, 3 Tex. Rep., 261.

An execution commencing, "The State of Texas, county of Austin: To the sheriff of said county," &c. It was held that the name of the county might be rejected as surplusage. That had the objection been taken *in limine*, the execution might have been quashed or amended. Portis *v.* Parker, 8 Tex. Rep., 23.

Where the petition gives the names of the parties correctly, the citation which does not follow it by giving the name in full, or the firmname of co-plaintiffs, is not calculated to surprise the defendant, and an objection upon that ground cannot be sustained. Cummings *et al. v.* Rice & Nichols, 9 Tex. Rep., 527. Dikes *v.* Monroe & Brother, 15 Tex. Rep., 236.

(*a*) It has been the constant practice to render judgments by default where there has been a written waiver of process, or acceptance of service by the defendant without other proof of its genuiness than its having been filed among the papers of the suit. Crain, et al. *v.* Griffis, 14 Tex. Rep. 358.

"I acknowledge service, this 3rd November, 1858," written on the citation and signed by the defendant, is sufficient evidence of service under the statute without any return by the sheriff. Metz, et al., *v.* Bremond, et al., 13 Tex. Rep. 394. Jewett et al. *v.* Miller et al., 19 Tex. Rep. 290. The acceptance of service must be signed by the party in person or an attorney; or, if by any other person, his authority must be proven.—Fowler *v.* Morrill, 8 Tex. Rep. 153.

(*b*) When there is no sheriff, or the sheriff is a party, the clerk may act upon his own knowledge in issuing the process to the coroner. Oliphant *v.* Dallas, 15 Tex. Rep. 138.

ART. 416. [11] The return of the sheriff, or other officer, shall be made in writing on the back of the process, or attached thereto, stating fully the time and manner of service, and shall be signed by him officially. (*a*) The return shall be in writing.

ART. 417. [14] Every sheriff and deputy sheriff shall endorse on all process and precepts coming to their hands, the day on which they received them, the manner in which they executed them, and the day when they executed them, and shall sign their return officially. (*a*) Act of May 12, 1846. Requisites of an return.

ART. 418. [13] If the plaintiff, his agent, or attorney, shall, at the time of instituting his suit, or at any time during the progress thereof, make affidavit before the clerk of the court, that the defendant is not a resident of this State, or that he is absent from this State, or that he is a transient person, or that his residence is unknown to the affiant, the clerk of the court shall issue a citation to the proper officer (which citation shall contain a brief statement of the cause of action,) commanding the said officer to summon the defendant, by making publication of the citation in some newspaper published in the county where the writ issued, if there be a newspaper published in said county, but if not, then in the nearest county where a newspaper is published, for four weeks previous to the return day of such process. (*b*) Act of March 16, 1848. When service may be had by publication.

ART. 419. [14] If the plaintiff, his agent, or attorney, shall, at the time of instituting his suit, or at any time during the progress thereof, make affidavit that the names of the heirs, successors, or legal representatives of any deceased person, party to such suit, are unknown to the affiant, the clerk of the court shall issue a like writ, directed to the proper officer, commanding him to summon such heirs, successors, or legal representatives, whose names are unknown, (giving the name of the original deceased party, their ancestor,) by making publication of the citation in some newspaper published in the county where the writ issued, if there be a newspaper published in said county, but if not, then in the nearest county where a newspaper is published, for eight weeks previous to the return day of such process; when such notice is given and no appearance is entered within the time allowed for pleading, the court shall appoint an attorney to defend in behalf of such heirs, successors, and legal representatives, and proceed as in other cases. (*c*) Publication to unknown heirs, &c. When court shall appoint an attorney for.

ART. 420. [18] Any mistake, or informality, in a return, may be corrected by the officer at any time, under the direction of the court. (*d*) Act of May 13, 1846. Amendment of return.

ART. 421. [19] When any process shall have been improperly served, or shall not have been returned, or shall have been returned without service, it Alias, when to issue.

(*a*) The provisions of the statute, as to the mode of service and fulness of return, are as plain as they are imperative. They prescribe the mode, by which the court acquires jurisdiction over the person of the defendant, and as this is necessary to give validity to its acts and judgments, the regulations on the subject should be strictly observed by the officer charged with the duty, and by the tribunal before which the matters in controversy are to be determined. Roberts *v.* Stockslager, 4 Tex. Rep. 307.

A return, "left a copy of the writ, with a true copy of the petition," is insufficient. Ibid. The following return was held insufficient: "Came to hand January 4th, 1849. In obedience I command this writ to be published." Signed by the sheriff. Appended to the citation was the affidavit made by the publisher of a newspaper published in the county, stating that publication had been made for eight successive weeks, in said paper, in obedience to the requirements of the citation.—Goodlove, et al., *v.* Gray, 7 Tex. Rep. 483. See also Blossman *v.* Letchford, et al., 17 Tex. Rep. 647, for a defective return of service by publication. For other cases of the return of personal service held insufficient, see Hart *v.* Clifton, 19 Tex. Rep. 56. Stevens *v.* Price, 16 Tex. Rep. 572.

(*b*) The statute authorizing service by publication, in certain events extends to all suits, including suits for divorce. Hare *v.* Hare, 10 Tex. Rep. 355. It does not authorize service of citation upon unknown, non-resident defendants, not being the heirs, successors, or legal representatives of a deceased party. Bailey *v.* Morgan, 13 Tex. Rep. 342. The jurisdiction of the court in cases by publication, is dependent upon the fact of the defendant's non-residence, &c., and not upon the affidavit of the plaintiff of the fact. The affidavit is but *prima facie* evidence of the fact, and may be rebutted by proof to the contrary. Kitchen *v.* Crawford, 13 Tex. Rep. 516. In service by publication, and trial *ex parte*, it is error if there be no affidavit that the defendant is a non-resident of the state, or a transient person, or that his residence is unknown. Doty *v.* Moore, 16 Tex. Rep. 591. As to sheriff's return of service by publication, see Blossman *v.* Letchford, 17 Tex. Rep. 647. Where it appears from the petition, that the plaintiff and defendant are both non-residents of the State, and the proceeding is not *in rem*, as by attachment, or otherwise, the defendant cannot be cited by publication. Ward *v.* Lathrop and Lathrop, 4 Tex. Rep. 180. Where an affidavit was made for publication and attachment, and the attachment is not prosecuted, it is not a valid objection to the judgment that the affidavit was insufficient for the attachment, though not for publication. Wyser *v.* Calhoun, et al., 11 Tex. Rep. 323.

(*c*) As to service and return, see Blossman *v.* Letchford, 17 Tex. Rep. 647.

(*d*) For cases in which returns were allowed to be amended, see Flemming *v.* Powell, 2 Tex. R[illegible] Porter *v.* Miller, 7 Tex. Rep. 468.

shall be the duty of the clerk, upon the application of any party interested, his agent, or attorney, to issue other process, directed to the sheriff or other officer of the same or any other county, as the party applying may direct.

Officers failing to perform their duties may be fined.

ART. 422. [20] Every clerk, sheriff, or other officer failing, or neglecting, or refusing to perform any duty directed by this act, shall be liable to fine for contempt, in a sum not less than ten nor more than one hundred dollars, at the discretion of the court having cognizance of the same, and also to damages with costs, at the suit or action of any person injured.

No writ of *quia timet*, attachment, &c., to issue, unless.

ART. 423. [143] No writ of *quia timet*, attachment, or any other original writ or process, whereby the property of any citizen of this State shall be ordered to be seized or taken into custody, shall be issued by any civil officer of this State, or by order of any Judge of the same, unless the party applying for such writ or process, shall first make affidavit in writing of the truth of the matter set forth in his or her petition, and shall file in the clerk's office of the court where the same is to be sued out and entered, a bond with good security, and in a sum at least double the value of the property to be seized and taken, or of the debts and damages claimed to be due; conditioned to pay all costs and damages which the party against whom such suit or process may be sued out shall sustain, by reason of the wrongfully and unjustly suing out of the same: provided, that this section shall not be construed to prevent the issuing of attachments by justices of the peace, under the provisions of any statute authorizing such attachments: and provided also, that it shall not be so construed, as to prevent the issuing of any writ or process, to compel the attendance of defaulting witnesses or jurors in any court or tribunal, to which they may have been legally summoned, or to any writ or process authorized by law in criminal cases.

V. PLEADINGS.

Act of March 31, 1846.

Party to suit may appear in person.

ART. 424. [1] In all suits hereafter pending in any court in this State, either plaintiff or defendant shall be permitted to appear therein, in person, and prosecute or defend the same.

Petition may be filed by plaintiff or Attorney—what it shall contain.

ART. 425. [5] The petition may be filed by the plaintiff or attorney, and shall set forth clearly the names of the parties(*a*) and their residence,(*b*) if known, with a full and clear statement of the cause of action and such other allegations, pertinent to the cause, as he may deem necessary to sustain the suit,(*c*) and also a full statement of the nature of the relief he requests of the court.(*d*)

Answer of defendant.

ART. 426. [29] The defendant in his answer may plead as many several matters, whether of law or fact, as he shall think necessary for his defence, and

(*a*) A mistake in setting out the names of a partnership, plaintiffs in the petition may be corrected, by amendment, after a plea in abatement filed. Tousey *v.* Butler, 9 Tex. Rep., 525. The statute requires that the petition shall set forth the names of the parties; but it does not prescribe who shall be made parties. Jackson *v.* Alexander, 8 Tex. Rep., 109.

(*b*) A petition describing the plaintiff as "a resident of the State of Tennessee," was held sufficient under the statute Harper *v.* Nichol, 13 Tex. Rep., 151.—The requirement that the residence of the parties shall be stated, does not apply where the defendant is a transient person. Baker *v.* Wofford, 4 Tex. Rep., 122.

(*c*) The petition, with us, should be "a plain, straightforward statement of the cause of action, without repetition or circumlocution." McClelland *v.* Smith, 3 Tex. Rep., 210. The party should state the facts on which he intends to rely, with such circumstantial accuracy as to apprize the opposite party of what is intended to be proved on the trial. Caldwell *v.* Haley, Ibid, 317. Mims *v.* Mitchell, 1 Tex. Rep., 443. Ramsey *v.* McCauly. 2 Tex. Rep., 189. Carter & Hunt *v.* Wallace, Ibid, 206. Wright *v.* Wright, 3 Tex. Rep., 168. Jones *v.* Frosh, 6 Tex. Rep., 202. Holman *v.* Criswell, 13 Tex. Rep., 38. Pinchain *v.* Collard, Ibid, 333. Boynton *v.* Tidwell, 19 Tex. Rep., 118. Blount *v.* Ralston, 20 Tex. Rep. 132.

The cases above cited tend to establish our system of pleading under the statute, rather than to give a construction to it.

(*d*) Where the statute prescribes the specific relief which shall be granted, a petition for different specific relief and no general prayer is not demurrable. Hipp *v.* Huchett, 4 Tex, Rep., 20.

which may be pertinent to the cause: provided, that he shall file them all at the same time, and in due order of pleading.(*a*)

ART. 427. [30] No plea of *non est factum* shall be received or admitted from any party other than such as are sued as the representatives of other persons, unless the party pleading the same shall make affidavit to the truth thereof; and no plea of *non est factum* shall be received or admitted from any person sued as the representative of another, unless some suspicion be cast on the instrument upon which such plea is founded, by the affidavit of such representative.(*b*) Shall be admitted, unless no plea of *non est factum*.

ART. 428. When any party to a suit or action, either as principal or security, maker or endorser, founded on any bond, bill, promissory note, or other written contract, covenant or agreement whatsoever, shall deny his signature, he shall be required to do the same under oath.(*b*) Act of Jan. 28, 1839. Must be sworn to.

ART. 429. [1] In all cases in which a suit has been instituted for the recovery of an amount due upon such bond, bill, prommissory note, contract, or other writing obligatory, and such suit is now pending in any of the courts of this Republic, or in cases in which any such suit shall hereafter be instituted, the execution of the instrument shall be regarded as proved, and the plea of "non est factum" shall be considered as unavailing, until the defendant, or in case there be more defendants than one, at least one of them, shall have made oath before the court in which the case is pending, that he or they never executed the said instrument, nor authorized any person to execute it for him or them.(*b*) Act of January 26, 1839. Same subject. See Seals and Scrolls.

ART. 430. [52] In any suit founded on any instrument or note in writing, under the seal of the party charged therewith, the defendant may, by special plea, impeach or inquire into the consideration thereof, in the same manner as if such writing had not been sealed; but no pleas impeaching the consideration of any instrument or note in writing, under seal, shall be admitted, unless supported by the affidavit of the defendant, or some person for him, stating that the facts set forth in said plea, are true, as far as stated of his own knowledge, and that he believes them to be true, as far as stated, from the information of others.(*c*) Act of May 13, 1846. Plea impeaching consideration of promise under seal, must be sworn to.

ART. 431. [31] No plea in abatement, except a plea to the jurisdiction of the court, or where the truth of the plea appears of record, shall be received or admitted, unless the party pleading the same, or some other person for him, shall make affidavit to the truth thereof.(*d*) Abatement, when plea in, shall be sworn to.

ART. 432. [32] All the pleas filed shall be taken up and disposed of by the court in due order of pleading, under the direction of the court.(*e*) Pleas, how disposed of.

ART. 433. [33] All pleas in abatement, and all other dilatory pleas or

(*a*) A plea in abatement cannot be received after an answer to the merits. Drake *v.* Brander, 8 Tex. Rep., 352.

(*b*) Under the plea of *non est factum* not sworn to, the defendant will not be permitted to disprove the execution of the instrument. Drew *v.* Harrison & Brothers, 12 Tex. Rep. 279. Such a plea denying the execution of the note sued, or the partnership of the defendants, who are charged to have executed it, is a nullity. Ibid.

The statute does not dispense with the production of the note upon the trial, although its execution is not denied under oath. Matossy *v.* Frosh, 9 Tex. Rep., 610.

The affidavit of one charged as the representative of a succession, to the best of his knowledge and belief, is a compliance with the statute. Tarpley *v.* Poage's Adm'r, 2 Tex. Rep. 139.

(*c*) Under the plea of total failure of consideration, the defendant may show a partial failure. Mercer *v.* Hall, 2 Tex. Rep., 284. If a plea impeaching the consideration is filed, unsupported by affidavit, the plaintiff must except or move to strike it out, or he will be deemed to have waived the affidavit. Williams *v.* Bailes, 9 Tex. Rep. 61. The statute is inapplicable to cases where the plaintiff must show a valuable consideration as a prerequisite to a decree. Short *v.* Price, 17 Tex. Rep., 397.

(*d*) The statute prescribes no form of the oath or affirmation required in the verification of the plea in abatement. Chevallier *v.* Williams & Co., 2 Tex. Rep., 239. The affidavit to the truth of the plea, must be to affiant's actual knowledge of the facts, not to the best of his knowledge and belief. Wilson *v.* Adams, 15 Tex. Rep. 323.

(*e*) Pleas in abatement should be disposed of before an issue on the merits. Holstein *v.* Gardner, 16 Tex. Rep. 114.

Dilatory pleas, when to be disposed of. demurrers, not involving the merits of the cause, shall be determined during the term at which they are filed, if the term of court continue long enough.

Amendment of pleadings. ART. 434. [34] The pleadings in all suits may be amended under the direction of the court, and upon such terms as it may prescribe, at any time before the parties announce themselves ready for trial, and not thereafter; but no amendment shall prevent a suit from being tried at the same term it may be If it operate as a surprise. made, unless the court be satisfied that such amendment operate as a surprise to the opposite party.(*a*)

Exception of *non tenure*, effect of. ART. 435. [50] By an exception of *non tenure*, of part of any lands or tenements, for which any suit or action may be instituted, the suit shall not be abated, but for the quantity of which *non tenure* shall be alleged.

Partnership presumed unless denied, &c. ART. 436. [88] In suits brought by partners, it shall not be necessary to prove the partnership, unless the defendant shall in his answer deny that the plaintiffs are partners, or carry on business as described in the petition, which denial shall not be admitted or received unless verified by the affidavit of the party making it.(*b*)

VI. TRIAL AND CONTINUANCE.

Act of May 13, 1846.

Suits disposed of in the order filed, unless. ART. 437. [93] All suits in which answers are filed in due time, shall be tried or disposed of in the order in which they stand on the docket, or were filed, unless otherwise ordered by the court, with the consent of the parties or their attorneys.

When business shall stand continued. ART. 438. [95] If from any cause a District Court shall not be held at the time prescribed by law, or if from any cause the business before the court be not determined before the adjournment thereof, such business, of whatsoever nature, so undetermined, shall stand continued until the next succeeding term.

Act of March 16, 1848. Took effect August 1, 1848.

Pleas must be filed before application for continuance. ART. 439. [15] No application for continuance shall be heard before the defendant files his defence, nor shall any continuance be allowed unless by operation of law, or by consent of the parties, or for sufficient cause supported by affidavit: On the first application for continuance, if the cause of continuance be the want of testimony material to the case, the party applying for the same shall make affidavit that he has used due diligence to procure said testimony, stating such diligence: On the second application for continuance, What shall be sufficient cause. if the cause of continuance be the want of testimony material to the case, the same shall be shown, and that the party applying has used due diligence to procure said testimony, and state such diligence; the cause of failure, if known; that the testimony cannot be obtained from any other source; and if it be for the absence of a witness, he shall state the name and residence of the witness, and what he expects to prove by him; and that the continuance is not sought for delay, but that justice may be done.(*c*)

(*a*) After a plea of misnomer in abatement, the plaintiff may correct the mistake by amendment.—Cartwright *v.* Chabert, 3 Tex. Rep., 261. If the amendment is not asked before the trial is gone into, the Judge has no egal authority to grant it Love & Chappell *v.* McIntyre, 3 Tex. Rep. 10. The terms on which an amendment is made, are at the discretion of the court, which should always be exercised in a way as not to operate as a surprise on the other party Turner *v.* Lambeth, 2 Tex. Rep., 365. For cases of amendment, see Lewin *v.* Houston, 8 Tex. Rep., 94. Connell *v.* Chandler, 11 Tex. Rep., 249. Johnston *v.* Marshall, 14 Tex. Rep., 490. Coles *v.* Kelsey, 2 Tex. Rep., 541. Thomas *v.* Young, 5 Tex. Rep. 253. Tulane *v.* McKee, 10 Tex. Rep., 335. Croft *v.* Rains, 10 Tex. Rep. 520. Hollis *v.* Border, Ibid, 360. Jennings *v.* Moss. 4 Tex. Rep., 452. Hutchins *v.* Wade, 20 Tex. Rep., 7. Heard *v.* Lockett, Ibid, 162. Donald *v.* Tinnon, Ibid, 245. Sims *v.* Redding, Ibid, 386. Dowell *v.* Winters, Ibid, 793.

(*b*) A plea which denies the partnership of plaintiffs who sue as partners, is a nullity, and may be disregarded by the plaintiffs unless sworn to. Lee *v.* Hamilton, 12 Tex. Rep., 413.

(*c*) The affidavit should not be so general in its terms as to make it impossible to have a conviction for perjury in case it be wilfully false. Mays *v.* Lewis, 4 Tex. Rep., 38. When a party has announced himself ready for trial, it is, in general, too late to move for a continuance. Cotton *v.* The State, 4 Tex. Rep., 260

VII. DISCONTINUANCE.

Act of May 13, 1846.

Suit may be dismissed in vacation, when.

ART. 440. [28] The plaintiff or his attorney may enter a discontinuance on the docket of the Clerk in vacation, in any suit wherein the defendant has not answered, on the payment of all costs that have accrued theron.

When some of defendants are served in time and others not.

ART. 441. [45] When there are several defendants in a suit, and some of them are served with process, in due time, and others not so served, the plaintiff may either discontinue, as to those not so served, and proceed against those that are, or he may continue the suit until the next term of the court, and take new process against those not served; and no defendant against whom any suit may be discontinued, according to the provision of this section, shall be thereby exonerated from any liability, under which he was, but may at any time be proceeded against, as if no such suit had been brought, and no such discontinuance entered as to such defendant: provided, that this section shall not be so construed as to allow a plaintiff to discontinue, as to the principal, and take judgment against the endorser, or surety (who is) jointly sued. (*a*)

Discontinuance not to operate as a release.

Judgment must be rendered against principal at the same time of surety.

ART. 442. [46] The principal and the endorser or surety upon any instrument in writing, may be joined in the same suit; but no judgment in any such suit shall be rendered against the endorser or surety, unless judgment is at the same time rendered against the principal, except where the plaintiff discontinues as to the principal, because he resides beyond the limits of the State, or because he is insolvent; in which cases he may discontinue and take judgment.

VIII. EVIDENCE.

1. *Witnesses.*

Act of May 13, 1846.

Subpœnas, &c., and notices, may issue at any time.

ART. 443. [16] Subpœnas for witnesses and necessary notices in the course of a suit, may be executed and returned at any time before the trial of a suit in which they are issued; subpœnas shall be served by being read to the witness, and service thereof may be accepted by any witness, in writing on the back thereof.

Subpoenas may issue at request of partes.

ART. 444. [61] In all suits, civil or criminal, the Clerk shall, at the request of either party, their agent or attorney, issue subpœna for witnesses, directed to the Sheriff or other officer of the county where such witnesses reside; which subpœnas shall state the names of the parties to the suit, the time and place, when and where, such witnesses are required to appear, and the parties at whose instance such witnesses are summoned.

Failing to attend, may be fined.

ART. 445. [62] Every witness summoned in any suit, shall attend the court from day to day, and from term to term, until discharged by the court, or party summoning him; and if any witness, after being duly summoned, shall fail to attend, he may be fined by the court, in any sum not exceeding one hundred dollars, and an attachment may issue against the body of such

If the terms of the statute are complied with on the first and second application, the court can exercise no discretionary power; it must be granted. Hipp *v.* Bissell, 3 Tex. Rep., 18. Prewett *v.* Everett, 10 Tex. Rep., 283. The refusal of a continuance may be assigned for error. Hensley *v.* Lytle, 5 Tex. Rep., 497. If improperly granted it cannot be revised. Sweeney *v.* Jarvis, 6 Tex. Rep., 36. In the first application, the facts constituting due diligence must be shown. Mays *v.* Lewis, *supra.*

(*a*) It is competent to dismiss as to one of several defendants not served, and proceed against those served, whether the liability of the defendants be joint and several or joint only. Ellis *v.* Park, 8 Tex. Rep. 205. Williams *v.* McNeil, 5 Tex. Rep. 381. Where judgment is taken against all the defendants, one of whom is not served, from which all the defendants prosecuted a writ of error, the judgment may be reformed; dismissing the suit as to the one not sued, and affirming the judgment as to the others. Saffold *v.* Navarro, 15 Tex. Rep. 76. Where husband and wife are jointly sued, the plaintiff cannot dismiss as to the husband not served, and take judgment against the wife. Parker *v.* Hobgood, 16 Tex. Rep. 249. The plaintiff cannot dismiss as to the maker of a note and take judgment against the endorser, who is jointly sued with him. Campbell *v.* Beckwith, 17 Tex. Rep. 439.

witness, to compel his attendance: provided, however, that no such fine shall be imposed, nor shall such attachment issue in a civil suit, until it shall be shown to the court by affidavit of the party, his agent, or attorney, that reasonable compensation and mileage has been tendered or paid to such witness.

Compensation of witnesses.

ART. 446 [63] Witnesses shall be allowed a compensation of one dollar for each and every day they may be in attendance on the court, and six cents for every mile they may have to travel in going to and returning therefrom, which shall be paid on the certificate of the Clerk, by the party summoning them; which certificate shall be given on the affidavit of the witness, before the Clerk; and such compensation and mileage of witnesses shall be taxed in the bill of costs, against the party cast. (*a*)

Witness refusing to give evidence.

ART. 447. [64] Any witness refusing to give evidence may be committed to the county jail, there to remain without bail, until he shall consent to give evidence.

Witnesses, who are incompetent.

ART. 448. [65] All Negroes and Indians, and all persons of mixed blood, descended from negro ancestry, to the third generation inclusive, though one ancestor of each generation may have been a white person, shall be incapable of being a witness in any case whatever, except for or against each other. (*b*)

Privileged from arrest.

ART. 449. [66.] Witnesses shall be privileged from arrest, except in cases of treason or felony or misdemeanor, during their attendance at court, and in going to and returning therefrom, allowing one day for each twenty-five miles from their place of abode.

Act of February 5, 1858. Took effect July 1, 1858.

When surety of party may be a witness. Not necessary to except to charge of court.

ART. 450 [8] The competency of a witness who is surety for cost, or in any other manner, bound for a party to the suit, may be restored by the substitution of other good security, that it shall not be necessary to except to any charge of the court given to the jury on the trial of a cause to entitle a party to assign error theron. (*c*)

Witness against county, town, &c., who are competent.

ART. 451. [9] An inhabitant of a county, city, or town, or member of a corporation or religious society, is competent to testify upon either side in any suit involving the rights of such county, city, town, corporation, or society.

2. *Depositions.*

Act of May 13, 1846.

ART. 452. [67] Depositions of witnesses, in civil suits, residing in the State, may be taken in the following cases: first, where the witness is about to leave the State, or the county where the suit is to be tried; second, where a witness by reason of age, sickness, or official [duty?] shall be unable to attend the court; third, where the witness resides without the county in which the suit is pending; (*d*) fourth, where the witness is a female; and such deposition shall be taken in the following manner, viz: the party wishing to take such depositions, shall file interrogatories in the court where the suit is pending, and shall cause the opposite party, his agent, [or attorney?] to be served with a copy thereof, and also with a notice that he will apply to the Clerk of such court for a commission to take the answers of the witnesses to said interrogatories: such notice shall state where the witness resides, and the suit in which

Notice &c., to be filed, and copy served.

(*a*) In the absence of any statute upon the subject, witnesses may claim their fees, and the same be taxed in the bill of costs, at any time before the issue of execution; but not afterwards. Hardy *v.* De Leon, 7 Tex. Rep. 466. Under the statute, witnesses have a claim for their fees directly against the party summoning them, and may maintain an action for them as soon as the service is rendered. Flores *v.* Thorn, 8 Tex. Rep. 377.

(*b*) Negro testimony is inadmissible in all cases, except for and against each other. Rice *v.* Lemon, 16 Tex. Rep. 593.

(*c*) Under the act of 1848, (Hart. Dig. 803,) supplied by the above section, it was held that a "new bond must be given, covering all the requirements of the law as to the original bond." Drake *v.* Brander, 8 Tex. Rep. 351. The court has no power to release a security for costs, except for the purposes specified in the act. Hickey *v.* Rhine, 16 Tex. Rep. 576.

(*d*) If the witness moves into the county after his deposition has been taken, it may, nevertheless, be given in evidence. Abels *v.* Miller, 12 Tex. Rep. 109. As to waiver of service, see Moore *v.* Gammel, 13 Tex. Rep. 120.

the deposition is to be used: on or after the fifth day after the service of such notice and copy of interrogatories, it shall be the duty of the Clerk, upon application of the parties filing such interrogatories, his agent, or attorney, to issue a commission directed to any Chief Justice, Notary Public, or Clerk of the District Court, residing in the county where it is stated in the notice such witness resides, requiring him to cause such witness to appear before him, and to take his answers under oath, to such interrogatories, a certified copy of which shall be annexed to said commission; such commission shall be signed by the Clerk issuing the same, and sealed with the seal of the court. (*a*) When commission shall issue.

ART. 453. [68] Upon the receipt of such commission, by any Chief Justice, Notary Public, or Clerk of the District Court of the county to which it is directed, unless the witness shall voluntarily appear, it shall be his duty to issue a subpœna, directed to the Sheriff or other officer of the county, requiring him to summon the witness to appear and answer interrogatories, at a time and place to be named in such subpœna; and if such witness, after being duly summoned, shall fail to appear, or having appeared, shall refuse to answer the interrogatories, the said Chief Justice, Notary Public, or Clerk, shall have power to issue an attachment against such witness, and to fine and imprison him in like manner as by this act the District Court is empowered to do in like cases. Duty of Com'r upon receipt of commission.

ART. 454. [69] Upon the appearance of the witness voluntarily, or in obedience to a subpœna, it shall be the duty of the said Chief Justice, Notary Public, or Clerk of the District Court, to take the answers of the witness to such interrogatories, which shall be reduced to writing, and shall be signed and sworn to by the witness; the officer taking such answers, shall certify, under his hand and seal, that they were signed and sworn to by the witness, before him; and shall seal them up in an envelope, with the interrogatories and the commission, with his name across the seal, and endorsed on the envelope, the names of the parties to the suit, and the names of the witnesses, and shall direct the package to the Clerk of the court from which the commission issued. (*b*) Duty of Com'r when the witness appears. Mode of returning

ART. 455. [71] When a witness in any civil suit resides beyond the limits of the State, either party may take his deposition by filing interrogatories in the court where the suit is pending, and serving a notice, with a copy of such interrogatories, upon the opposite party, his agent or attorney, in the same manner as required for the depositions of witnesses residing in the State; and on or after the fifth day of the service of such notice, and a copy of interrogatories, it shall be the duty of the Clerk with whom such interrogatories are filed, upon the application of the party filing them, his agent or attorney, to issue a commission, directed to any Judge of any Court of Record within the State or county, where it is stated in the notice that such witness resides, requiring such Judge to cause the witness to come before him, and to take his answers to said interrogatories, a certified copy of which shall be annexed to such commission; the commission shall be signed by the Clerk issuing it, and sealed with the seal of the court: the Judge to whom any such commission is directed, upon the appearance of the witness before him, shall take his answers to the interrogatories, which shall be reduced to writing, and shall be signed and sworn to by the witness; when the Judge taking them shall certify, under his hand and the seal of his court, that the answers were signed and sworn to by the witness, before him, (*c*) and seal them up in an envelope, with the Of witness residing beyond the State. Duty of Com'r when witness appears.

(*a*) A Deputy Clerk of the District Court is not authorized by law to take depositions. Hughes *v.* Prewett, 5 Tex. Rep. 264. Urquhart *v.* Burleson, 6 Tex. Rep. 502.

(*b*) The certificate of the officer should state that the answers were signed and sworn to before him, in compliance with the statute. Chapman *v.* Allen, 15 Tex. Rep. 278.

(*c*) A certificate under his seal, by the Judge, stating that the witness swore to and signed the depositions, and then a certificate, under the seal of the court, that the court was one of record, and that he was the sole and presiding Judge, was held to be a compliance with the statute. Greenwood *v.* Woodward, 18 Tex. Rep. 1.

interrogatories and the commission, with his name across the seal, endorse and direct the envelope in like manner as is required for depositions taken within the State: and all depositions so taken, may be returned into court in like manner as depositions taken within the State.

Act of March 16, 1848. To whom commission may be directed out of this State.

ART. 456. [20] Commissions to take the depositions of witnesses residing beyond the limits of the State, may be directed to any Notary Public or Clerk of a Court of Record within the State or county where it is stated in the notice that such witness resides; and all such commissions shall be executed and returned in like manner as they are required to be executed and returned by a Judge of a Court of Record: and depositions so taken and returned, shall be governed by the same rules as are provided for other depositions in the District Court.

Act of May 13, 1846. Cross-interrogatories may be filed.

ART. 457. [72] In any suit where one party may file interrogatories for the purpose of taking the depositions of a witness, the opposite party may file cross-interrogatories, at any time before the commission issues, and a certified copy of such interrogatories shall be attached to the commission by the Clerk issuing the same, and all such cross-interrogatories shall be answered, signed, sworn and certified to in like manner and form as the answers to the interrogatories, and shall be sealed up and returned with them.

Where answer is not pertinent.

ART. 458. [73] If any deposition shall contain any testimony not pertinent to the interrogatories and cross-interrogatories propounded, such testimony shall be deemed surplusage, and shall be stricken out by the court.

When parties have joint interest in.

ART. 459. [76] Both parties shall be considered as having a joint interest to [in?] all depositions, when cross-interrogatories have been filed and answered, and either party shall have the right to use such depositions on the trial.(*a*)

How and when to be opened.

ART. 460. [77] Depositions, after being returned to court, may be opened by the Clerk at the request of either party or his counsel; and the Clerk shall endorse on such depositions, upon what day and at whose request they were opened, signing his name thereto; and they shall remain on file for the inspection of either party.

Objection to form and manner of taking, how to be made.

ART. 461. [78] No objections to the form of depositions, or to the manner of taking them, in any suit, shall be heard, unless they are in writing, and notice thereof is given to the opposite counsel, before the trial of the suit commences: provided, said depositions shall have been filed in the court at least one entire day before the day on which the trial commences.(*b*)

When notice to take depositions may be made by publication.

ART. 462. [79] In all civil suits where it shall be shown to the court, by affidavit filed therein, that either party is beyond the jurisdiction of the court, or that he cannot be found, or has deceased since the commencement of the suit, and such death has been suggested at a prior term of the court, so that the notice and copy of interrogatories cannot be served upon him, for the purpose of taking depositions, and such party has no attorney of record upon whom they can be served; or if he be deceased, and if the persons entitled to claim by or through such deceased defendant, have not made themselves parties to the suit, and are unknown, the party wishing to take depositions may file

(*a*) If cross-interrogatories be not filed, the party at whose instance the commission was issued, may decline on the trial to read the deposition, and the opposite party will have no right to read it. Norvell *v.* Oury, 13 Tex. Rep. 31. Harris *v.* Leavitt, 16 Tex. Rep. 340.

(*b*) Objections to the form and manner cannot be taken orally at the trial. Croft *v.* Rains, 10 Tex. Rep. 520. The objections must be in writing and notice be given to the opposite party before the trial commences. Ibid., 526. The statute renders the deposition inadmissible, unless they have been filed one entire day before the trial commences. Evans *v.* Hardgrove, 11 Tex. Rep. 210. Cases in which the objections were held to apply to the form and manner of taking the depositions:—Bracken *v.* Neill, 15 Tex. Rep. 109; Chapman *v.* Allen, Ibid., 278; Kottwitz *v.* Bagby, 16 Tex. Rep. 656; Scott *v.* Delk, 14 Tex. Rep. 341; Hopkins *v.* Clark, 20 Tex. Rep. 64.

his interrogatories in the court where said suit is pending, and the Clerk of such court shall thereupon cause a notice to be published in some newspaper for thirty days, stating the number of the suit, the name of the orignal parties, in what court the suit is pending, the name and residence of the witness to whom interrogatories are propounded, and that a commission will issue on or after the thirtieth day after such publication to take the deposition of such witness: at the expiration of which time, such Clerk shall, on the application of the party filing such interrogatories, his agent or attorney, issue a commission, as in other cases; and depositions taken under such notice, shall have the same force and effect as those taken after personal service of the notice and interrogatories upon a party or his attorney.

ART. 463. [16] Such depositions may be returned to the court, either by mail, by a party interested in taking the same, or other private conveyance: If sent by mail, the post-master, or his deputy, mailing the same, shall endorse thereon that he received them from the hands of the officer, before whom they were taken; and the Clerk taking them from the post-office, shall endorse on them that he received them from the post-office, and sign his name thereto: If sent by other conveyance, the person delivering them into Court shall make affidavit before the Clerk that he received them from the hands of the officer before whom they were taken; that they have not been out of his possession since, and that they have undergone no alteration.

Act of March 16, 1848.

Mode of returning depositions.

ART. 464. [17] Depositions taken and returned in the manner provided for by this Act, and an Act entitled "an Act to regulate proceedings in the District Courts," approved May 13th, 1846, may be read as evidence upon the trial of any suit in which they are taken, subject to all legal exceptions which might be made to the interrogatories and answers, were the witness personally present before the court, giving evidence: provided, that no deposition of a witness, except when the witness is a female, shall be permitted to be read in evidence unless the party offering the same, his agent, attorney, or some competent person, shall first make oath that the witness is without the limits of the county where the suit is pending,(*a*) or that such witness is dead, or that by reason of age, sickness, or official duty such witness is unable to attend the court.

Use and effect of depositions taken under this Act.

Not to be read if witness in the county, &c.

ART. 465. [18] When any person may anticipate the institution of a suit in which he may be interested and may desire to perpetuate the testimony of a witness or witnesses to be used in such suit, he, his agent or attorney, may file a written statement in the court of the county where such suit could be instituted, representing the facts and the names of the persons known to be interested adversely to said person, a copy of which statement and writ shall be served on the persons interested adversely, after which depositions may be taken and returned by any of the parties to such statement in like manner as provided for by this Act, and an Act, "entitled an Act to regulate proceedings in the District Courts," approved 13th May, A. D., 1846, and shall be entered on the records of the court, and may be used in any suit or suits which may be thereafter instituted by or between any of the parties to the statement, or those claiming under them, in like manner as if such depositions had been taken after the institution of such suit or suits; and when suits have been instituted, all such depositions so taken and returned shall be subject to like exceptions as all other depositions.

Depositions to perpetuate testimony.

(*a*) The affidavit need not state the fact absolutely. A reasonable presumption that the witness is beyond the limits of the county, is sufficient. O'Shea *v*. Twohig, 9 Tex. Rep. 336.

3. *Records, Office Copies and Written Instruments of Evidence.*

Act of May 13, 1846.

Execution of notes and other instruments presumed, unless, &c.

ART. 466. [86] When any petition, answer, or other pleading, shall be founded, in whole or in part, on any instrument or note in writing, charged to have been executed by the other party or by his authority, and not alleged therein to be lost or destroyed, such instrument or note in writing shall be received as evidence, without the necessity of proving its execution, unless the party by whom or by whose authority such instrument or note in writing is charged to have been executed, shall file his affidavit in writing, denying the execution thereof; and the like rule shall prevail in all suits against endorsers and securities upon any note or instrument in writing; when any such instrument or note in writing is charged to have been executed by any testator or intestate, it shall be received in evidence in like manner, unless some suspicion is cast upon it by the affidavit of the executor or administrator of such testator or intestate.(*a*)

Same subject, where instrument is filed in another court.

ART. 467. [87] If suit be brought on any instrument or note in writing, filed in any suit brought thereupon in any other court of this State, a certified copy of such instrument or note in writing, under the hand and seal of the Clerk of the court in which the original may be filed, shall be admitted in like manner as such original might be; but if the defendant shall plead, and file an affidavit under oath, that such original instrument or note in writing has not been executed by him, or by his authority, the Clerk of the court having the custody of such original shall, on being summoned as a witness, attend with the same on trial of the issue.

Copies of rec'rds of public officers and courts to be *prima facie* evidence.

ART. 468. [89] Copies of the records of all public officers and courts of this State, certified to under the hand and seal (if there be one) of the lawful possessor of such records, shall be admitted as evidence, in all cases where the records themselves would be admissible; (*b*) translated copies of all records in the Land Office, certified to under the hand of the translator, and the Commissioner of the General Land Office, attested with the seal of said office, shall be *prima facie* evidence in all cases where the original records would be evidence.(*c*)

Instruments legally recorded, admitted without proof of execution.

ART. 469. [90]. Every instrument of writing which is permitted or required by law to be recorded in the office of the Clerk of the County Court, and which has been or may be so recorded after being proven or acknowledged in the manner provided for by the laws in force at the time of its registration, shall be admitted as evidence without the necessity of proving its execution:(*d*) provided, that the party who wishes to give it in evidence shall file the same among the papers of the suit in which he proposes to use it, at least three days before the commencement of the trial of such suit, and give notice of such filing to the opposite party or his attorney of record; and unless such

Must be filed three days before trial of suit, &c.

(*a*) The defendant will not be permitted to disprove the execution of the instrument unless he denies the execution under oath. Drew *v.* Harrison, 12 Tex. Rep. 279. Kelly *v.* Kelly, Ibid., 452. Fulshear *v.* Randon, 18 Tex. Rep. 275.

(*b*) To render a certified copy of a record or document admissible in evidence, without other authentication, it must be certified by the officer having charge of the original. York *v.* Gregg, 9 Tex. Rep. 85. Every document of a public nature, which there would be an inconvenience in removing, and which the party has a right to inspect, may be proved by a duly authenticated copy. Ibid.

(*c*) The mesne assignments of land claims, in all cases in which the patent is authorized to issue to the assignee of such claim, when filed in the General Land Office, become records thereof; and copies of the same when certified by the Commissioner, are admissible in evidence as the originals would be. Mason's heirs *v.* M'Laughlin, 26 Tex. Rep. 24. Since the statute has elevated the Land Office copy to the same grade as the original, it is no longer secondary, but is primary evidence, and, consequently, is admissible, without producing or accounting for the non-production of the original. Wheeler *v.* Moody, 9 Tex. Rep. 372. Hubert *v.* Bartlett's heirs, Ibid., 97. Houston *v.* Austin & Williams, 3 Tex. Rep. 390. A certified copy from the General Land Office is inadmissible, unless the original is a public document, of which the Commissioner is the legal custodian. Paschal *v.* Perez, 7 Tex. Rep. 348. See the same case as to what documents are properly archives of the General Land Office.

(*d*) The statute does not apply where the original document is produced and proved as at Common Law; and the document need not be previously filed. Robinson *v.* Martel, 11 Tex. Rep. 149. If the deed is not so authenticated as to make proof of itself, it could not be admitted to record without proof; and the mere filing and notice is not sufficient to authorize it to be read in evidence. Craddock *v.* Merrill, 2 Tex. Rep. 494.

opposite party, or some other person for him shall, within one day after such notice, file an affidavit stating that he believes such instrument of writing to be forged. And whenever any party to a suit shall file among the papers of the suit, an affidavit stating that any instrument of writing recorded as aforesaid has been lost, or that he cannot procure the original, a certified copy of the record of any such instrument shall be admitted in like manner as the original could be.(*a*)

When copies may be read.

Art. 470. [91] Copies of all conveyances and other instruments of writing, between private individuals, which were filed in the office of any Alcalde or Judge, in Texas, previous to the first Monday in February, 1837, shall be admitted as evidence in like manner as the originals might be, and shall have the same force and effect as such originals: provided, such copies shall be certified to under the hand and seal of the officer with whom such conveyance and instrument of writing are now deposited.(*b*)

Copies fil'd with Alcalde or Judge, when admitted.

Art. 471. [92] The printed statute books of this State shall be evidence of the private Acts therein contained; and the printed statute books of the several States and Territories of the United States, purporting to have been printed under the authority of such States and Territories; and a certified copy, under seal of the Secretary of this State, of any act or resolution contained in the printed statute books of any State or Territory of the United States, purporting to be printed under the authority of such State or Territory,—and copies of private bills certified to by the Secretary of State, and attested by his seal of office,—which is deposited in the office of the Secretary of this State, shall be evidence in like manner.(*c*)

Printed statutes evidence of private acts of this State.

Statutes of other States, when admitted.

Art. 472. [1] When the records and papers, or any part thereof, appertaining to the proceedings in any court of this State may have been, or may hereafter be lost or destroyed, the same may be supplied by copies duly certified, which shall have the same force and effect as the originals; and when such copies cannot be produced, then the contents of the records or papers so lost or destroyed may be established by other proof, at the trial of the cause, so that such loss or destruction shall work no injury or alteration in the rights of the parties concerned.(*d*)

Act of Feb'y 1850. Took effect from passage.

Records, lost or destroyed, may be supplied.

Art. 473. [2] Whenever any such loss or destruction of papers or records may occur, any party to the proceedings may file a motion in the cause, which shall be verified by oath, setting forth the loss or destruction, and, when certified copies cannot be produced, the substance of the contents of the writings lost or destroyed, and the cause shall then proceed in the ordinary way.

Mode of supplying.

Art. 474. [10] Whenever in any cause it may be material to prove the assessment of any property for taxes, or the payment of any taxes, the certificate of the Comptroller of this State of such assessment from the rolls deposited in his office, or that the payment of such taxes is shown by the records of his office, shall be admissible in evidence to prove the same.

Act of Feb'y 5, 1858. Took effect July 1, 1858.

Payment of taxes, how proven.

(*a*) The statutory mode prescribed for the admission of secondary evidence of recorded instruments, where the original cannot be procured, must be strictly complied with. Butler *v.* Dunagan, 19 Tex. Rep. 559. The affidavit, if made by any person other than the party to the suit, should exclude the supposition that the party has it in his power to produce the original. If made by an agent, it is not sufficient to state that he (the agent) cannot procure the original. Ibid. See Graham *v.* Henry, 17 Tex. Rep. 164; Peck *v.* Clark, 18 Tex. Rep. 239; Houze *v.* Houze, Ex'r., 16 Tex. Rep. 598; Crayton *v.* Munger, 11 Tex. Rep. 234.

(*b*) York *v.* Gregg, 9 Tex. Rep. 85.

(*c*) Martin *v.* Payne, 11 Tex. Rep. 292. A reprint of a code of statutes of another State, published by authority, and purporting to have been so published, is admissible as evidence. Ellis *v.* Wiley, 17 Tex. Rep. 134.

(*d*) The State *v.* Elliot, 14 Tex. Rep. 423. The State *v.* Womack, 17 Tex. Rep. 237.

4. *Interrogatories to opposite party.*

Act of May 13, 1846. Either party may propound, provided, &c. [See art. 481 to 485.]

ART. 475. [80] Either party to a civil suit may propound written interrogatories to the other: provided, the party propounding them shall make oath before the clerk of the court where suit is pending, or before any of the officers before whom the answers to such interrogatories may be sworn to, that the answers to such interrogatories are material to support his demand, or to aid him in his defence, and that he knows of no other person by whom he can prove the same facts, which may be annexed to or included in the petition or answer; and when not so annexed or included, a copy of such interrogatories shall be served upon the party whose answers are sought, his agent or attorney, at least five days before the commencement of the trial of the suit in which they are propounded: and provided further, that no defendant shall be permitted to propound interrogatories to the plaintiff, unless they are annexed to or included in his answer, until such defendant has first filed his answer.(*a*)

Party shall answer on oath.

ART. 476. [81] The party interrogated shall answer on oath, and categorically each of the questions put to him, unless he cannot do so without criminating himself; and if he refuse or neglect to do so, the facts concerning which he shall have so refused or neglected to answer, shall be taken for confessed.(*b*)

What the answers may contain.

ART. 477. [82] In answering a question, the party shall simply confess or deny the fact, but the party may state such other facts tending to his defence, as are closely connected with the fact on which he has been interrogated; and his declaration in such case shall have as much effect as his answer to the question itself; and if such answers contain other testimony than that permitted by this section, the court, upon exception being made thereto in writing, shall cause so much of said answer as contains such other testimony to be stricken out.(*c*)

Party may except to questions.

ART. 478. [83] The party interrogated may except in writing to any of the questions as not pertinent, and the court shall decide summarily whether he ought to answer or not; if ordered to answer, he shall do so, otherwise the facts unanswered shall be deemed confessed.(*d*)

Answers shall be in writing. [See Commissioners to take Depositions, &c]

ART. 479. [84] The answers to such interrogatories shall be in writing, sworn to and signed by the party answering, and if answered within the county where the suit is pending, may be sworn to before any officer authorized by law to administer oaths, who shall make a certificate thereof; if answered in any other county within the State, they shall be sworn to before some Notary Public, Chief Justice or clerk of the District Court, who shall make a certificate thereof, and affix his seal of office; if answered out of the State, they shall be sworn to before some Judge of a court of record, and have the certificate of such Judge, authenticated with the seal of the court.(*e*)

(*a*) A party should not be permitted to propound interrogatories to the adverse party at a term subsequent to the answer, and within a few days of the calling of the cause for trial, unless it is essential to the justice of the cause, and the delay be satisfactorily accounted for. McMillan *v.* Croft, 2. Tex. Rep. 397.

If the notice is not served on the party, his agent or attorney, the interrogatories may be stricken out upon the calling of the cause for trial. Frosh *v.* Holmes, 8 Tex. Rep., 29. Service on an attorney, not the attorney of record is not sufficient. Ibid.

The answer of a defendant is not evidence for him on the trial, except where it is in response to interrogatories under the statute. Autry *v.* Cannon, 11 Tex. Rep., 110.

(*b*) It is not necessary that the answers should correspond with the interrogatories numerically, if the latter are substantially answered, unless the rights of the opposite party are prejudiced thereby. Harrison *v.* Knignt, 7 Tex. Rep., 47.

Where interrogatories are propounded to one of several defendants, and not answered by him, the other defendants cannot object to the reading of the confessed interrogatories as to the particular defendant. Texas *v.* McDonald, 13 Tex. Rep., 349.

(*c*) Harrison *v.* Knight, *supra.* A defendant interrogated as to the possession and conversion of a certain sum of money, stated that the intestate gave it to him, part for his children and the balance for himself: held that his answer was evidence in his own behalf. 13 Tex. Rep., 263. Teas *v.* McDonald, *supra.* Graham *v.* Stephen, 15 Tex. Rep., 88.

(*d*) It is too late to file exceptions to answers on the day the cause is called for trial, where the answers were filed at a previous term of the court. Dikes *v.* DeCordova, 17 Tex. Rep., 618.

(*e*) The provisions of this act, and that of May 8th, 1846, (see Commissioners to take Depositions,) are not in conflict. The answers may be sworn to, either before a Commissioner or before a Judge of a court of record, who shall certify the same under the seal of his court. Lovett *v.* Casey, 17 Tex. Rep., 594.

ART. 480. [85] The answers of the party interrogated, subject to the exceptions herein provided for, shall be taken entire, and shall be evidence, but they shall not exclude adverse testimony, and may be destroyed by written proof, or by the oath of two witnesses, or of one single witness corroborated by strong circumstantial evidence.(*a*)

Effect of such answers.

ART. 481. [3] Either party to a suit may examine the opposing party as a witness, either personally in court or upon interrogatories filed in the cause, and shall have the same process to compel his attendance or obtain his testimony as in the case of any other witness, and his examination shall be conducted, and his testimony received in the same manner, and according to the same rules which apply in the case of any other witness, except that no party shall be compelled to obey a subpœna unless he is a resident of the county where the suit is pending, or happens to be in said county at the time of trial, and where the testimony is sought to be taken in answer to interrogatories, it shall not be necessary to give notice of the filing of the interrogatories, or to serve a copy thereof on the adverse party before a commission shall issue to take the answers thereto, nor shall it be any objection to the interrogatories, that they are leading in their character.

Act of Feb. 5, 1858. Took effect July 1, 1858.

Either party may be examined personally, or upon interrogatories.

Commission may issue, when

ART. 482. [4] The party interrogated, whether orally or otherwise, may in answer to questions propounded, state any matter connected with the cause, and pertinent to the issue to be tried; and the adverse party may contradict the answers by any other competent testimony, in the same manner as he might contradict the testimony of any other witness.

Answers may be contradicted.

ART. 483. [5] If a party when interrogated, either by written interrogatories or in court, refuse to answer, or answer evasively the intorrogatory so propounded, shall be taken as confessed; or in case the examination be in court, the court may in its discretion compel the party to answer as in case of other witnesses: provided, that no interroga tories shall be taken as confessed unless a commission has first been issued to take the answers of the party, and he shall refuse to answer after being called on in a legal manner to do so, by the proper officer; and in case of such refusal, such officer shall certify to the court such refusal.

When interrogatories shall be taken for confessed.

ART. 484. [6] The answers of a party to interrogatories propounded, may be taken and sworn to before any officer, whether within the State or out of it, who is by law authorized to take depositions, and shall be sealed up with the commission and interrogatories, and returned to the court from which the commission issued, as provided in other cases of depositions.

Before whom answers may be sworn to.

ART. 485. [7] Nothing contained in this act shall effect the rules of practice and procedure as heretofore established by law, for taking the answers of a party to a cause upon interrogatories filed in the cause; but the provisions ot the four preceding sections shall be construed as cumulative.

This act to be cumulative.

IX. CHALLENGE OF JURORS.

Act of Feb. 5. 1858. Took effect July 1, 1858.

ART. 486. [11] In civil suits each party shall be entitled to challenge three jurors without showing any cause therefore.

Peremptory challenges.

(*a*) The answers are not evidence for the defendant unless in response to interrogatories filed by the plaintiff. Autry v. Cannon, 11 Tex. Rep., 110

X. CHARGE OF COURT AND BILLS OF EXCEPTIONS AND NON-SUITS.

Act of May 12, 1846.

After charge either party may ask specific instructions.

[See art. 492.]

Duty of the court.

[See art. 450.]

ART. 487. [100] After the charge of the Judge, either party, or his attorney, may present in writing, but without argument, such charges or instructions as he desires to be given to the jury, which the Judge shall deliver to the jury in whole or in part, or refuse to deliver the same, as he may think proper,(*a*) but where the charge asked, or any part thereof, is refused to be given, the Judge shall write down distinctly what portions of the same he refuses, and what portion he gives, and also subscribe his name thereto, all of which shall be filed by the clerk, and constitute a part of the records of the case, subject to revision for error by the Supreme Court, in the same manner as if a regular bill of exceptions had been signed.

Either party may except, &c.

When Judge refuses to sign bill of exceptions.

ART. 488. [101] Whenever, in the progress of a cause, or of the trial thereof, either party is dissatisfied with a decision or opinion of the court, he may except thereto, and on reducing his exceptions to writing and presenting them to the Judge for allowance, the Judge shall allow and sign his name to the same if they be true, and if he refuses to do so, he shall certify in writing therein, the cause of such refusal.(*b*) If any Judge shall refuse to sign a bill of exceptions, such bill may be signed by three bystanders who are reputable inhabitants of the State, and the court shall permit such bill to be filed; and every bill of exceptions signed by the Judge or bystanders, and filed in the court, shall form a part of the record in the cause in which the same may be filed.(*c*)

When Judge refuses to permit bill of exceptions signed by by-standers to be filed.

ART. 489. [102] When any Judge shall refuse to permit a bill of exceptions, signed by bystanders, to be filed, and shall have certified such bill to be untrue, either party in the suit may take affidavits, giving the adverse party notice of the time and place of taking such affidavits, not exceeding five in number, in relation to its truth; and such affidavits, when taken, shall be filed in the clerk's office within five days after the trial of the suit, and on appeal or writ of error, copies of such affidavits shall be annexed to and form a part of the record in the cause.

Supreme Court shall admit such bill, &c., when.

ART. 490. [103] The Supreme Court shall admit, as a part of the record of the cause, every bill of exceptions taken therein, upon appearing to the satisfaction of the court that the truth of the case is fairly stated in such bills, that the same was taken according to law, and that the court refused to permit such bill to be filed; and the truth of every such bill of exceptions shall be tried by the affidavits required by this act to be taken, and filed in the clerk's office.

Act of February 5, 1853.

Plaintiff shall not suffer a non-suit after the jury retire.

ART. 491. [99] No plaintiff shall be permitted to suffer a non-suit after the jury retire from the bar; but after argument of a cause, the Judge may deliver a charge to them on the law of the case under the following restrictions, viz: He shall not in any case, civil or criminal, charge or comment on the weight of evidence. He shall so frame his charge so as to submit questions of fact solely

(*a*) The parties are required to present the instructions desired by them in writing. Jones *v.* Thurmond, 5 Tex. Rep., 318. It is not legitimate to ask the court to give certain articles or sections of the law in charge to the jury. Ryan *v.* Hall, 11 Tex. Rep., 391. A charge asked must be given if correct and proper in its application to the facts. Earle *v.* Thomas, 14 Tex. Rep., 583.

The court should not charge upon an issue to which there is no evidence before the jury. Austin *v.* Talk, 20 Tex. Rep., 164.

Where the charge is correct, but does not cover the whole ground it is the duty of the parties to ask further instructions if they desire them. Farquar *v.* Dallas, 20 Tex. Rep., 200.

Where the court has sufficiently instructed the jury upon the law of the case, instructions applicable to isolated facts, though correct in point of law should be refused as they would give the particular facts an undue prominance in the minds of the jury. Gray *v.* Burk, 19 Tex Rep., 228.

(*b*) Exceptions to the opinions or rulings of the court should be reduced to writing at the time the opinion is given or ruling made. Houston *v.* Jones, 4 Tex. Rep., 170.

(*c*) As to what a bill of exceptions should show when signed by by-standers, see Houston *v.* Jones, 4 Tex. Rep , 170. If signed by by-standers they should be filed with the knowledge and permission of the Judge Ibid.

to the decision of the jury, deciding on and instructing them as to the law arising on the facts—distinctly separating questions of law from questions of fact. He shall not charge, or instruct the jury in any case, unless the charge shall have been by him first reduced to writing, and signed; and every such charge or instruction shall be given in the precise words in which it shall have been written. All charges or instructions, whether given by the Judge of his own accord, or upon request of counsel or parties, may be carried from the bar by the jury in their retirement; and no Judge shall in any case make any further charge, unless on the application of the jury, or a party, or his counsel.

How charge of the court shall be framed.

Charge shall be in writing and delivered as written.

Judge shall make no other charge, unless.

XI VERDICT.

ART. 492. [104] After verdict of twelve men, judgment shall not be stayed or reversed for want of form.(*a*)

ART. 493. [105] When there are several counts in a petition and entire damages are given, the verdict shall be good, notwithstanding one or more of such counts may be defective.

Good though one or more counts be bad.

ART. 494. [108] In civil suits the jury may find and return a special verdict in writing, in issues made up under the direction of the court,(*b*) declaring the facts proved to them; any verdict so found shall be conclusive between the parties as to the facts found.

Jury may find special verdict.

XII JUDGMENT.

Act of May 11, 1846.

ART. 495. [25] No judgment shall be rendered in any case of attachment, unless the citation has been served in the ordinary mode, or publication, as herein provided.(*c*)

In cases of attachment. [See art. 31.]

Act of March 16, 1848.

ART. 496. [12] In all cases where process has been served according to law, (except such causes as have been brought up from Justices of the Peace,) in which the defendant has not filed his plea on or before the fourth day of the term of the court, the plaintiff may, at any time after said fourth day, have a final judgment against the defendant,(*d*) and if the cause of action is liquidated and proved by any instrument in writing, the clerk shall, unless a jury is asked for by either party, assess the damages of the plaintiff; but if the cause of action is unliquidated, a jury shall be sworn to assess the damages of the plaintiff: provided, however, that in suits when service of the process has been made by publication, no such judgment by default shall be taken at the term of the court to which such process is returnable; but all such suits shall be continued until the next term of the court, when final judgment by default may be taken as in other cases: and, provided, also, in all cases, that if the defendant in person, or by his agent or attorney, shall appear in the case,

By default final if demand is liquidated.

Jury shall assess damages when.

When service has been made by publication.

(*a*) As to the general principles governing verdicts, see the following cases: Burton *v.* Bondies, 2. Tex. Rep., 203; Mays *v.* Lewis, 4 Tex. Rep., 38; Bryan *v.* Bridge, 10 Tex. Rep., 149; Parker *v.* Leman, ibid, 116; Wells *v.* Barnett, 7 Tex. Rep., 584; Hancock *v.* Winans, 20 Tex. Rep., 320; Harrell *v.* Babb, 19 Tex. Rep., 148.

(*b*) The act does not authorize the court to make up issues foreign to, or different from, than those raised by the pleadings of the parties. Guess *v.* Lubbock, 5 Tex. Rep., 535.

(*c*) It seems that where a judicial attachment has issued to compel the defendant to appear and answer, personal service, or service by publication, is not required. Briggs *v.* Smith, 13 Tex. Rep. 269.

(*d*) The defendant has right to file his answer at any time before the plaintiff has taken his judgment by default. Ryburn & Doss *v.* Nail, 4 Tex. Rep. 305.

At any time after the fourth day of the term, if the defendant has not answered, the plaintiff may take judgment. Ibid.

without service of process being made or perfected, then such appearance shall have the same effect as if the service of such process was made or perfected.

Act of Feb. 5, 1858. Took effect July 1, 1858. Judgment where term of court is one week.

ART. 497. [1] In any county where by law the term of the District court is limited to one week, if the defendant in any case has been personally served according to law, (except in cases brought up from the courts of Justices of the Peace) and shall fail to answer before the fourth day of the term of the court to which he has been cited, the plaintiff on or after the fourth day of the term, may have final judgment by default against the defendant. If the cause of action be liquidated and established by an instrument in writing, the clerk may compute the sum due, or it may be found by a jury if asked for by either party. If the cause of action be unliquidated, a jury shall be empanelled to find the sum which the plaintiff is entitled to recover.

Form and nature of

ART. 498. [115.] Judgment in the District Court shall, in all civil cases, be rendered so as to conform to the pleadings, the nature of the case as provided, and the verdict thereon.(*a*)

Act of May 13, 1846. Confession of, without process

ART. 499. [116] Any person, for a *bona fide* debt, may, without process appear in person, or by attorney, and confess judgment for such debt; but in such cases, a petition shall always be filed,(*b*) and the justness of the debt sworn to by the person in whose favor the judgment is confessed; and when confessed by attorney, the warrant of attorney shall be filed.

Confession of, a waiver of errors, except, &c.

ART. 500. [117] Every judgment by confession, duly made, shall operate as a release of all errors in the record thereof, but may at any time be impeached for fraud or other equitable causes, by third parties.(*c*)

When interlocutory judgment against one of several defendants may be taken.

ART. 501. [47.] Where there are several defendants in a suit, and some of them appear and answer, and others make default, an interlocutory judgment by default may be entered against those who do not answer, and the cause may proceed against the others; but only one final judgment shall be given in the suit.(*d*)

In suits by Ex'rs &c., for land, &c, of testator.

ART. 502. [48] Suits for title, or for the possession of lands, or for any right attached to or growing out of the same, or for any injury or damage done thereto, may (be) institute by executors, administrators, or guardians, in like manner as they could have been by their testator or intestate, and judgment in such cases shall be as conslusive as if rendered in favor of their testator or intestate: provided, however, that such judgment may be set aside by any person interested for fraud or collusion on the part of such executor or administrator.

In suits against executors &c.

ART. 503. [118] In suits against executors, administrators, or guardians, for the recovery of the money due from, or damages incurred by their testator, or intestate, or ancestor, when a verdict shall be given against them, or judgment final, by default, shall be taken against them, the judgment shall be that the plaintiff recover his debt or damages, as the case may be, and costs, to be paid in due course of administration; and no execution shall issue on such judgment.(*e*) When the suit is instituted for the enforcement of a specific

Execution shall not issue on.

(*a*) Where the prayer of the petition is for spcific relief only, and the judgment is not expressly authorised by the statute, it is error for the judgment to go beyond the prayer. Moore *v.* Guest, 8 Tex. Rep. 117.

Where the statute prescribes the specific relief to be granted, the judgment should be so rendered, whether it is prayed for or not. Hipp *v.* Huchett, 4 Tex. Rep. 20.

(*b*) The petition must be filed before or at the time the judgment is confessed and not after. Montgomery *v.* Barnett, 8 Tex. Rep. 143. The justness of the debt must be sworn to by the person in whose favor the judgment is rendered. Flanagan *v.* Bruner, 10 Tex. Rep. 257.

The want of the affidavit is error. Hopkins *v.* Howard, 12 Tex. Rep. 7.

(*c*) A confession of judgment is not a waiver of errors, where the confession itself is not in conformity to law. Montgomery *v.* Barnett, 8 Tex. Rep. 143.

(*d*) It may be irregular but not error for the plaintiff, to omit to take judgment by default, against one defendant, who has failed to answer, and upon the final disposition of the case to take a joint judgment against all of the defendants. Peters v. Crittenden, 8 Tex. Rep. 131.

(*e*) The proper judgment against a guardian of a lunatic is that the plaintiff have execution. Adriance, Guardian, *v.* Brooks, 13 Tex. Rep. 279.

lien on personal property, the judgment shall be, that the plaintiff recover his debt and damages and costs, and that the property subject to such lien shall be seized and sold by the Sheriff, if it can be found, and that the proceeds of such sale shall be applied to the judgment and costs, and if there be any excess, after such payment, the same shall be paid to the defendant; and if the proceeds of such sale shall be insufficient to pay such judgment and costs, the balance shall be paid in due course of administration;(*a*) but no execution shall issue thereon. Where the suit is for the foreclosure of a mortgage on real estate or negroes, the heirs interested in the mortgaged property shall be made parties to the suit by due notice served, and the subsequent proceedings shall conform to the rules prescribed as above, in cases of specific liens on personal property.

In cases of specific lien.

In suits to foreclose mortgages, heirs must parties.

ART. 504. [119] All judgments or decrees for the enforcement of specific liens or the foreclosure of mortgages, against persons other than executors or administrators, shall be that the plaintiff recover his debt, damages, and costs, and that an order of sale shall issue to the Sheriff of the county where the property subject to such lien or mortgage can be found, directing him to sell the same, if found, as under execution; and if the proceeds of such sale be insufficient to pay the judgment and costs, or if the property cannot be found, further execution may be issued for such balance, or for the debt, against such defendant, as the case may be.(*b*)

Form of judgment in cases of lien and mortgage.

ART. 505. [120] In all cases where the District or Supreme Courts shall decree a conveyance of real estate, or the delivery of movable property or effects, they may, by decree, pass the title of such property without any act to be done on the part of the defendant, when it shall be proper.

When court decrees conveyance may pass title.

ART. 506. [13] When in the record of any judgment or decree of any court there shall be any mistake, the Judge of said court may in open court, amend such judgment or decree according to the truth and justice of the case, but in all cases the opposite party shall have notice of the application for such amendment.

Act of May 11, 1846.

Mistake in, may be corrected.

ART. 507. [132] When in the record of any judgment, or decree of any District Court, there shall be any mistake, miscalculation, or misrecital of any sum or sums of money, or of any name or names, and there shall be among the records of the proceedings in the suit in which such judgment or decree shall be rendered, any verdict or instrument of writing, whereby such judgment or decree may be safely amended, it shall be the duty of the court in which such judgment or decree shall be rendered, and the Judge thereof, in vacation, to amend such judgment or decree thereby, according to the truth and justice of the case: provided, that the oppposite party, his agent or attorney of record, shall have had reasonable notice of the application for such amendment; and if the transcript of such judgment or decree, at the time of such amendment, or at any time thereafter, shall be removed to the Supreme Court, it shall be the duty of that court, upon inspection of such amended record, to be brought before it by the *certiorari*, if need be, to affirm such judgment, if there be no other error apparent in such record. (*c*)

Act of May 13, 1846.

May be amended, when.

Notice to opposite party.

ART. 508. [133] Where any bond, taken by virtue of any distress for rent, or execution, by miscalculation or mistake, shall be conditioned for a larger sum of money than by law ought to have been required thereby, or where a verdict

Excess of bond —how released, &c., in inferior courts.

(*a*) This article is not affected by the provisions of article 772. Givins *v.* Davenport, 8 Tex. Rep. 451.—Danzey *v.* Swinney, 7 Tex. Rep. 617.

(*b*) There is no necessity for a separate suit on the bond or note. That with the mortgage constitutes but one cause of action; and if there be no bond or note the judgment is still the same; that prescribed by the statute. Duty *v.* Graham. 12 Tex. Rep. 427.

(*c*) This statute does not preclude the Supreme Court from the exercise of its established power to reform judgments. Wortham *v.* Harrison, 8 Tex. Rep. 141. There is no limitation as to the time within which the amendment may be made. Ramsey *v.* McCauley, 9 Tex. Rep. 106. It may be done at the next term of the Court. Swift *v.* Faris, 11 Tex. Rep. 18. The amendment cannot be made by reference to a verdict of the jury which was not received by the court. Messner *v.* Hutchins, 17 Tex. Rep. 597.

shall be rendered for more damages than the plaintiff shall have demanded by his suit, and judgment shall be rendered accordingly, and the court in which such judgment shall be rendered shall have adjourned to another term, without release of such excess having been made, it shall be lawful for the plaintiff, at any time before the record of such judgment shall be removed into the appellate court, at any future term of the court in which such judgment shall be rendered, to release, in open court, any such excess, or he may, in vacation, release the same by deed, under his hand and seal, witnessed by the clerk or deputy clerk of such court, and filed of record among the papers of the court; and such release, made in either of the forms aforesaid, shall cure any error of such excess: if the record of any such judgment shall be removed into the appellate court before such release shall be made, it shall be lawful for the defendant in error to make such release as aforesaid in the appellate court, and thereupon the said court, after revising the judgment, shall proceed to give such judgment as the court below ought to have given, if the release had been made or filed therein.

In appellate court.

In suits by publication, facts to be stated in judgment.

ART. 509. [128] On the rendition of any judgment, in a suit, where notice or service of process has been given or made by publication only, and heard ex parte, the court shall make out and incorporate with the records of the case, a statement of the facts proven therein, on which the judgment was founded. (*a*)

Petition for review of—when to be filed, &c.

ART. 510. [129] When judgment has been rendered in any suit, on notice, or service by publication only, and on ex parte hearing, the party defendant may, at any time within two years after the rendition of such judgment, file his petition of review for the reversal thereof, in the court rendering the judgment; but process on such judgment shall not be suspended unless the petitioner give bond with two or more sureties, to be approved by the clerk, in double the amount of the judgment or value of the property adjudged, payable to the party in whose favor such judgment was rendered, conditioned that he will prosecute his petition for review to effect, and perform such judgment as may be rendered thereon by the court, in case the decision be against him; and in case property has been sold under judgment, before process thereon was superseded by petition and bond, as aforesaid, the same shall not be restored on the reversal of the judgment, but the petitioner shall have judgment for the amount paid or collected thereon, or for damages by him sustained in consequence thereof; minors, married women, and persons *non compos mentis* shall have two years to file such bill of review after their respective disabilities are removed, under the restrictions above stated in this section. (*b*)

XIII. NEW TRIAL AND ARREST OF JUDGMENT.

New trial may be granted on such terms, &c.

ART. 511. [109] New trials may be granted in all civil cases, on such terms and conditions as the court may direct, but not more than two new trials shall be granted to either party in the same cause, except the jury have been guilty of some misconduct, or erred in matter of law. (*c*)

(*a*) The failure to make a statement of the facts upon which an *exparte* judgment is based, where the defendant is cited by publication, is error, for which the judgment must be reversed. Pierpont *v.* Pierpont, 19 Tex. Rep. 227—McFadden *v.* Lockhart, 7 Tex. Rep. 573. Recitals in the judgment of conclusions deduced by the court from the evidence, are not sufficient. Chrisman *v.* Miller, 15 Tex. Rep. 159.

(*b*) The remedy provided by this article, is additional to the remedy by writ of error, and not preclusive of it. Chrisman *v.* Miller, 15 Tex. Rep. 159. Doty *v.* Moore, 16 Tex. Rep. 591. As to Bills of Review, to revise judgments upon service by publication, see Kitchen *v.* Crawford, 13 Tex. Rep. 516—Mussina *v.* Moore, ib. 7.

(*c*) More than two new trials may be granted where the verdicts of the jury are contrary to law. Luckett *v.* Townsend, 3 Tex. Rep. 119. The decision on a motion for a new trial must be final and absolute at the term at which the motion is made. It cannot be granted on conditions of payment of costs, &c. Secrest *v.* Best, 6 Tex. Rep. 199 A new trial cannot be granted after the term at which the trial is had. A motion for a new trial made at that term and continued is discharged by operation of law. McKean *v.* Zillar, 9 Tex. Rep. 58. A new trial may be granted upon absolute terms—as the payment of costs. Houston *v.* Starr, 12 Tex. Rep. 424.

ART. 512. [110] No motion for a new trial shall be allowed after a motion in arrest of judgment. (*a*) Order of motion, &c.

ART. 513. [111] New trials may be granted, as well when the damages are manifestly too small as when they are excessive. May be granted when damages too small.

ART. 514. [112] All motions for new trials, in arrest of judgment, or to set aside a judgment, shall be made within two days after the rendition of verdict, if the term of the court shall continue so long; if not, then before the end of the term, and every such motion shall be accompanied by a written specification of the grounds on which it is founded; and none other than those specified shall be heard. All motions for new trials, in arrest of judgment, or to set aside a judgment, shall be determined at the term of the court at which such motion shall be made. (*b*) When motion shall be made. When determined.

ART. 515. [113] The costs of all new trials may either abide the event of the suit, or shall be paid by the party to whom such new trial may be granted, according to the order of the court, to be made at the time of granting such new trial. (*c*) Costs of new trial.

ART. 516. [114] When any judgment shall be arrested or set aside, the court shall allow the proceedings in which the error was, to be amended in all cases where the same amendment might have been made before trial, and the cause shall again proceed according to the practice of the court; but the party in whose proceedings the first error was committed shall pay the costs incurred thereby. Amendment after arrest of judgment. Costs.

XIV. MOTIONS.

ART. 517. [53] There shall be a motion-docket to be kept by the clerk, in which he shall enter all motions filed in the court; the number of the suit in which they are made, if it relates to a suit pending; the names of the parties, and their attorneys, with a brief statement of the nature of the motion. (*d*) Act of May 13, 1846. Motion docket shall be kept, &c.

ART. 518. [54] All motions relating to a suit pending, which do not go to the merits of the case, may be disposed of at any time before the trial of the cause; but no motion in the nature of a general demurrer, or which relates to the merits of the case, shall be decided before the cause is called in regular order for trial. (*e*) Motions which may be disposed of at any time.

ART. 519. All motions, not relating to a suit pending, shall be taken up and disposed of in the order as other suits are required to be. Certain motions taken up in the order, &c.

ART. 520. [121] On all motions, the court may give or refuse costs, at their discretion, unless where it is otherwise provided by law. Court may allow costs or not, unless.

XV. COSTS.

ART. 521. [8] Every person, whether plaintiff or defendant, who shall make affidavit before the clerk that he is too poor to pay the fees of office, shall be entitled to receive from such clerk all such process as will enable him to prosecute or defend his suit, free of costs. Act of May 13, 1846. Persons too poor to pay costs.

(*a*) Hipp *v.* Ingram, 3 Tex. Rep. 17—The State *v.* Mann, 13 Tex. Rep. 61.

(*b*) Secret *v.* Best, 6 Tex. Rep. 199—McKean *v.* Ziller, 9 Tex. Rep. 58—Bullock *v.* Ballew, ib. 498.

(*c*) See Houston *v.* Starr, *supra*.

(*d*) All motions in the District Court must be in writing and filed. Houston *v.* Jones, 4 Tex. Rep. 170.

(*e*) A motion to dissolve an injunction may be taken up and disposed of at any time. Houston *v.* Berry, 3 Tex. Rep. 235.

When several suits are brought for causes of action which may be joined.

ART. 522. [49] When any plaintiff shall bring, in the same court, several suits, against the same defendant or defendants, for causes of action which may be joined, he shall recover the costs of one action only; and the costs of the other actions shall be adjudged against him, unless sufficient reason appear to the court, for instituting several actions.

In actions for slander, &c., where judgment is under twenty dollars.

ART. 523. [106] In all civil actions of assault and battery, or slander, in the District Court, if the jury find under the sum of twenty dollars, the plaintiff shall not recover costs, but each party shall be taxed with the costs incurred by him.

Judgment shall carry cost, when.

ART. 524. [122] In all cases of law (except motions,) where judgment shall be given for the defendant, or appellee, and have execution for the same; and in all such cases, where judgment shall be given for the plaintiff or appellant, if not otherwise provided by law, he shall recover his costs against the defendant or appellee, and have execution for the same. (a)

Costs of insufficient pleading.

ART. 525. [123] When any plea in abatement shall, upon argument in any court of law, be adjudged insufficient, and when by any interlocutory judgment, any other part of the pleadings shall be judged insufficient, all costs occasioned by such insufficient pleading shall be adjudged against him who committed the fault.

Taxes on law pleading to be included in bill.

ART. 526. [124] All taxes imposed on law pleadings shall be included in the bill of costs.

Law of cost, how interpreted.

ART. 527. [125] The law of costs shall not be interpreted as penal laws.

Each party responsible.

ART. 528. [126] Each party shall be responsible to the officers of court for the costs incurred in any suit by himself. (b)

Fees of but two witnesses to same fact, &c.

ART. 529. [127] There shall not be allowed in any cause or bill of costs the fees of more than two witnesses to any one fact.

Act of March 16, 1848. Took effect Aug. 1, 1848.

Rule for security for.

ART. 530. [1] The plaintiff in any civil suit, at any time before final judgment, upon motion of the defendant or any officer of the court interested in the costs accruing in such suit, may be ruled to give security for the costs; and if such rule be entered against the plaintiff, and he fail to comply therewith, on or before the first day of the next term of the court, the suit shall be dismissed. (c)

Effect of bond for.

ART. 531. [2] All bonds given as security for costs, shall have the force and effect of judgments against all the obligors for the said costs.

Executors and administrators not required to give security for.

[See Art. 558.]

ART. 532. [4] Executors and administrators of deceased persons' estates, shall not be ruled to give security for costs in any suit to recover money due or property belonging to the estate. And no security shall be exacted of executors or administrators of deceased persons' estates, in appeals taken in suing for

(a) The settled and uniform practice of the courts of this country, has been, in rendering final judgment in favor of the defendant, to adjudge the costs of suit against the plaintiff. Jennings *v.* Moss, 4 Tex. Rep. 452. This article extends to cases only, where the entire judgment is given for the plaintiff or defendant—and does not extend to cases, in which judgment, as to a portion of the matters in controversy, is adjudged to one of the parties, and against him as to other matters. Cannon *v.* Hemphill, 7 Tex. Rep. 184. The provisions of the act does not extend to costs of proceedings in the Supreme Court. Ibid.

(b) The plaintiff is not bound for more costs than his own, if he succeeds in the suit, and cannot make the costs out of the defendant. The liability of his surety for costs is the same. Cleaveland *v.* Henderson, 4 Tex. Rep. 182.

(c) To obtain the rule for security for costs, a motion should be made and entered on the motion docket; when the order is made, the rule should be expressed in distinct and appropriate terms, and be entered in the minutes of the court. The entry on the Judge's docket is not sufficient. Shackleford, Sampson, & Co. *v.* Wallace, 4 Tex. Rep. 239. All motions in the District Court must be in writing and filed. Houston *v.* Jones, 4 Tex. Rep. 170. After a first rule has been complied with, the law does not authorize the clerk to call for additional security. Houston *v.* Roberts, 10 Tex. Rep. 348. Where a defendant removes a case from a Justice's Court to the District Court by *certiorari*, the plaintiff or appellee cannot be ruled to give security for costs on motion of defendant or appellant. Foreman *v.* Gregory, 17 Tex. Rep. 193. The rule may be complied with at any time before the case has been actually discussed. Hays *v.* Cage, 2 Tex. Rep. 501—Cook *v.* Beasly, 1 Tex. Rep. 591—Rhodes *v.* Philips, 2 Tex. Rep. 162. The plaintiff must have actual notice of the motion. Houston *v.* Sublett, 1 Tex. Rep. 523. The cause after dismissal may be reinstated, upon a reasonable showing why the rule for costs had not been complied with. 3 Tex. Rep. 9.

such money or property, or in defending suits brought against such estates for money or property. (*a*)

XVI. MARRIAGE OF FEME SOLE.

Art. 533. [40] No suit instituted by a *feme sole*, shall abate by her marriage, but upon a suggestion of such marriage being entered on the record, the husband may make himself a party to such suit, and prosecute the same as if he and his wife had been originally plaintiffs in such suit.

Marriage of *feme sole*, plaintiff not to abate suit.

Art. 534. [41] No suit instituted against a *feme sole* shall abate by her marriage; but upon a suggestion of such marriage being entered on the record, in open court, or upon a petition representing that fact being filed in the Clerk's office, it shall be the duty of the Clerk to issue a *scire facias*(*b*) to the husband of such defendant, and upon the return thereof executed, the husband shall be made a party to such suit, and it shall proceed as [if] such husband and wife had originally been defendants in such suit: provided, that nothing herein contained shall be so construed as to make the husband liable for any debts contracted by said *feme sole* before marriage.

Marriage of *feme sole*, defendant not to abate suit.

Husband not liable for debts of wife, before.

XVII. DEATH OF PARTY.

Art. 535. [36] In all suits where there are two or more plaintiffs or defendants, and one or more of them die, if the cause of action survive to the surviving plaintiff or plaintiffs, and against the surviving defendant or defendants, the suit shall not abate by reason of such death, but upon suggestion of such death being entered upon the record, at the instance of either party, his agent or attorney, the suit shall proceed in the name of the surviving plaintiff or plaintiffs, or against the surviving defendant or defendants, as the case may be.

Act of May 13, 1846.

Not to abate suit if cause of action survive to part of the plaintiffs, &c.

Art. 536. [37] In all suits where either party shall die between verdict and judgment, the judgment shall be entered as if both parties were living.

Death of party between verdict and judgment, not, &c.

Art. 537. [38] In all suits where the plaintiff may die before verdict, if the cause of action survive, the suit shall not abate therefor, but it shall be lawful for the legal representative of such plaintiff, his agent or attorney, to appear, and upon suggestion of such death being upon record, such representative may be made party to such suit, and the same shall proceed in his name;(*c*) but if no such suggestion be made, as aforesaid, at the first term of the court after such death, it shall be the duty of the Clerk, upon the petition of the defendant, his agent or attorney, to issue a *scire facias*, which shall be served upon the legal representative(*d*) of such deceased plaintiff, requiring him to appear and prosecute said suit, and after the service of said *scire* [*facias?*] if he fail so to do, during the first four days after the meeting of the court to which such *scire facias* is returnable, the defendant may, on motion, have such suit discontinued; and in cases where executors or administrators shall be plaintiffs in any suit, and shall die or cease to be such executor or administrator before verdict, the

Not to abate if plaintiff die before verdict and cause of action survive.

Representative, agent or attorney may appear

When *scire facias* to issue.

Death of administrator, &c.

(*a*) This exemption does not extend to proceedings by *certiorari* to Justice's Courts. Ledbetter *v.* Swing, 19 Tex. Rep. 242.

It applies to appeals from the County to the District Court. Battle *v.* Howard, 13 Tex. Rep. 345. Also to appeals to the Supreme Court. Ibid. *But quere?* Does it apply to writs of error to the Supreme Court, since the act of February 5, 1838, art. 558?

(*b*) The process of *scire facias* in our statutes is not an action, and need not be pleaded to. Boone *v.* Roberts, 1 Tex. Rep., 147.

(*c*) The representative cannot become a party until the death of the plaintiff is suggested on the record. Gowings *v.* Loyd, Adm'r, 4 Tex. Rep., 483.

(*d*) The terms "legal representatives," includes heirs, where there is no executor or administrator. Grayson *v.* Winnie, 13 Tex. Rep., 288.

It is irregular to take exceptions to the process by which the representative is brought into court, after he has appeared and continued the cause. Such exceptions, if valid, should be taken before appearance and continuance. Boone *v.* Roberts, 1 Tex. Rep., 147.

suit shall not abate therefor, but the suit may be continued in like manner by the person succeeding him in the administration of the same estate; or the suit may, in like manner, be discontinued.

Death of defendant, when cause of action survives.

ART. 538. [39] In all suits where the defendant may die before verdict, if the action survive, the suit shall not abate therefor, but upon a suggestion of such death being entered upon the record, in open court, or upon a petition of the plaintiff, representing that fact, being filed in the Clerk's office, it shall be the duty of the Clerk to issue a *scire facias* to the legal representative of such defendant, and upon the return thereof executed, such representative shall be made a party to such suit, and the same shall proceed against him; and in case where an executor or administrator shall be the defendant, and shall die, or cease to be such executor or administrator before verdict, the suit shall not abate therefor, but the suit may be continued in like manner against the person succeeding him in the administration of the same.

Scire facias to issue.

Suit shall not abate by death of person suing for the use of, &c.

ART. 539. [42] When a suit has been instituted in the name of one person, for the use of another, and the person in whose name the suit has been instituted, shall die before verdict, it shall not be necessary to revive such suit in the name of the representative of such person, but such suit may be prosecuted in the same manner as though such death had not happened; but such death shall be suggested on the record, and the person for whose use such suit was instituted, shall be responsible for all costs, in the same manner as the person whose name is used would have been; and execution for such costs may be issued against him as in ordinary cases.(*a*)

Act of Feb. 5, 1853.

Death of plaintiff after judgment, execution to issue in the name of survivor or legal representative.

ART. 540. [130] In cases where a sole plaintiff, or one of the several plaintiffs, shall die after judgment, it shall be the duty of the Clerk to issue execution on such judgment, in the name of the legal representative of such deceased sole plaintiff, or in the name of the surviving plaintiffs, and the legal representatives of the deceased plaintiff, as the case may require, without further notice to the defendant, upon an affidavit of such death being entered of record, or filed with the Clerk, by such legal representative, or the attorney of record of such plaintiff, together with a certificate of the appointment of such representative under the hand and seal of the Clerk of the Court where the same was made, and in cases where an executor, administrator, or guardian is plaintiff, and shall die, or cease to be such executor, administrator, or guardian, after judgment, execution shall be issued on each (such?) in the name of the person succeeding him in the administration or guardianship, upon such successor filing of record with the Clerk a certificate of his appointment and qualification as such, under the seal of the court where such appointment was made.

Death of sole defendant after judgment, claim against his estate.

ART. 541. [131] In cases where a sole defendant dies after judgment for money against him, the plaintiff may proceed to establish his claim against the estate, by presenting a certified copy of such judgment, to the executor or administrator of such decedent as directed by law for the settlement of estates of deceased persons, and where there are two or more defendants, one or more of whom die after judgment for money, leaving one or more surviving, then the plaintiff shall be entitled to execution against such survivor or survivors, by filing an affidavit of such death with the Clerk of the Court, and may proceed to establish his claim against the estate of the party deceased in the mode prescribed by law. In all cases of judgments, other than money judgments, where the sole defendant, or one or more of several joint defendants shall die after judgment, the plaintiff shall be entitled to have execution thereon, against the legal representatives of such deceased party or parties, without

Death of one or more joint defendants, execution may issue against survivor

Judgment may be established as a claim against the estate of dec'd, &c.

In other than money judgments, represen-

(*a*) But if the fact does not appear from the petition, that suit is brought for the use of another, the suit must be revived in the name of the representative of the deceased plaintiff. The persons claiming the real interest in the suit, may intervene and contest their rights with the representative. Price *v.* Wiley and others, 19 Tex. Rep., 142.

being required to revive the same by *scire facias* or otherwise, upon an affidavit of such death being filed with the Clerk of the Court; provided, that no defendant shall be deprived of the right to quash or enjoin such execution by showing satisfaction of the same. tative of defendant made party Execution, right to quash, &c.

XVIII. CERTIORARI AND APPEAL FROM COUNTY COURT.

ART. 542. [60] In all appeals from Probate Courts to the District Court, a complete transcript of the record, and of all the proceedings had in the cause below, certified under the hand and seal of the Clerk of the Probate Court, shall be filed with the Clerk of the District Court, on or before the first day of the term to which such appeal is taken; and all such appeals shall be tried *de novo*: upon the application of either party to such appeals, it shall be the duty of the Clerk of the District Court to issue a subpœna *duces tecum* for the Clerk of the Probate Court to bring into the District Court, on the trial of such appeal, all original papers in his office which may be needed on such trial. All judgments upon appeals from the Probate Courts, shall be certified to the Probate Court to be carried into effect. (*a*) Act of May 12, 1846. Appeals from, proceedings in such cases.

ART. 543. [6] The bonds of executors, administrators, and guardians, and the bonds described in the section next preceding, may be put in suit, in the name and at the cost of any person or persons injured by a breach thereof, until the whole penalty shall be recovered thereon, and without the assignment of said bonds being made by the Chief Justice of the County Court. Act of March 16, 1848. Bonds may be put in suit without assignment. (See Limitations.)

ART. 544. [7] Any person interested, desiring to have the proceedings of the County Courts pertaining to the estates of decedents and wards revised and corrected, may do so by application to the Judge of the District Court; and the Judge of the District Court shall, upon such application being made, grant a writ of *certiorari*, to remove the proceedings to the District Court, there to be revised and corrected. (*b*) And such *certiorari* shall not operate as a *supersedeas*, unless such applicant shall give a bond with good and sufficient sureties, payable to the Chief Justice of the County Court, in the same manner as in cases of appeal. *Certiorari* in, cases of decedents and wards, from County Court.

ART. 545. [8] The Clerk of the County Court shall, upon being served with the *certiorari*, make out a certified transcript of the proceeding had at the time of the service of the writ, and transmit the same to the District Court to which the same is returnable. Duty of Clerk in such cases.

ART. 546. [9] Writs of *certiorari* to remove the proceedings of the County Courts, pertaining to the estates of decedents and wards, may be sued out within two years after the proceedings were had, that are sought to be revised and corrected, and not afterwards; saving to persons *non compos mentis*, infants, and *femes covert*, two years after their respective disabilities shall be removed. Within what time writs should be sued out.

(*a*) When the proceedings of the Probate Court are brought into the District Court by *certiorari*, it is the duty of the latter court, either to dismiss the *certiorari*, if it has been improperly awarded, or to try the matter *de novo*, and certify the decree back to the Probate Court, to be carried into execution. Newson, Guard. *v.* Chrisman, 9 Tex. Rep. 113.

(*b*) When a proceeding of the Probate Court is brought into the District Court by *certiorari*, it must be tried *de novo* in all respects, as if it had been removed by appeal. Moore, Adm'r, *v.* Hardison, 10 Tex. Rep. 467; Newson, Guard., *v.* Chrisman, 9 Tex. Rep. 113. It is not necessary that all the creditors or heirs should join in the proceeding, to obtain the revision; it may be done by any one nterested in the estate. Reese *v.* Hicks. 13 Tex. Rep. 162. The death of any one who may have joined as plaintiff. will not abate the proceeding, but the sult may be carried on to judgment in the names of the survivors. Ibid. The remedy given by the statute is concurrent with that of appeal; and to entitle a party to it, he need assign no excuse for not taking an appeal. Ray *v.* Parsons, 14 Tex. Rep. 370. Failing to prosecute an appeal after claiming it. is no objection to a *certiorari* subsequently obtained. The cause of failure to prosecute the appeal need not be shown in the petition. Poag *v.* Rowe, 16 Tex. Rep. 590.

XIX. APPEAL.

Act of May 3, 1838.

State may appeal without bond, etc.

ART. 547. [2] In all cases where the Republic is concerned as a party, either in her own name, or the name of her officers, an appeal may be taken in her behalf, without bond or security. (*a*) (Art. 558.)

Act of May 13, 1846.

Statement of facts to be made out, etc.

(See Art. 557.)

ART. 548. [135] After the trial of any cause, when the party has given notice of appeal, or intends to give such notice, it shall be the duty of the parties, respectively, to make out a clear and explicit statement, or bill of the facts given in evidence on the trial of the cause, and to submit the same to the opposite party, or his attorney, for inspection during the term; and if the parties, or their attorneys, agree as to the facts given in evidence, they shall sign and seal the same, and submit it to the Judge for approval and signature, who shall also sign it, and the statement so made shall be filed as a part of the record of the cause: but if, on inspection of the statement offered, the parties cannot agree, or the Judge do not approve or sign it, then they shall submit their respective statements to the Judge presiding at the trial, who, from the statements so furnished him, and his own knowledge, shall, during the term at which the trial was had, make out a correct and exact statement of the facts of the cause as given in evidence, and shall sign and seal the same, and cause it to be filed in the records of the cause, as a part thereof. (*b*)

Appeal bond.

ART. 549. [136] Any party taking an appeal, shall, within twenty days after the term of the court at which the judgment or decree was rendered, enter into bond with two or more sureties, to be approved by the Clerk of the court, in double the amount of the debt or damages, (*c*) or value of the slaves or other personal property adjudged, conditioned for the prosecution of the appeal with effect, and performing the judgment, sentence, or decree, of the Supreme Court, in case the decision of the said court shall be against the appellant. (*d*)

When given for costs only.

ART. 550. [137] Where the judgment is rendered for the recovery of lands, the judgment below shall operate as a specific lien upon the lands so recovered; but in such case the appeal bond shall only be required for the costs of suit and damages on appeal. (*e*)

Where party is unable to give security.

Duty of Sheriff in such cases.

ART. 551. [138] In case the party be unable to give the appeal bond required, such party may nevertheless appeal, by giving security for no more than the costs and damages of the appeal; but in that case the judgment of the court below shall operate as a lien upon all the property of the appellant, and the Sheriff shall take possession of his personal property, and keep possession of the same, or so much thereof as will be sufficient to satisfy the judgment of the appellate court, during the pendency of the appeal, unless the appellant should execute a bond, made payable to the appellee, with at least one good and sufficient security, whose solvency is to be judged by the Sheriff; conditioned that such personal property shall be forthcoming to be sold in satisfaction, or part satisfaction, of the judgment that may be rendered by the appellate court. (*g*)

(*a*) Where no exceptions are made, the State must prosecute her suits for civil rights in the same way, and under the same forms of remedy, as are prescribed by the laws of the forum for individual suitors. The State *v.* Kroner, 2 Tex. Rep. 492.

(*b*) In the absence of a statement of facts, all presumptions are in favor of the verdict. Portis *v.* Cochrane, 1 Tex. Rep. 77. It is not competent for the Judge to make up a statement of facts, after the adjournment of the court. Withee *v.* May, 8 Tex. Rep. 160. A failure to make out a statement of facts, and have it authenticated, for the purposes of appeal, cannot be supplied by depositions of witnesses as to the evidence on the trial. Garnet *v.* Roberts, 16 Tex. Rep. 555.

(*c*) The entry of approval is a clerical act, and does not invalidate the bond. Burdett *v* Marshall, 3 Tex. Rep. 24.

(*d*) When the appeal bond does not contain the conditions required by the statute, and by reason thereof, does not furnish that security to the rights of the appellee intended to be given by law, the appeal will be dismissed. Doss *v.* Griswold, 1 Tex. Rep. 99. Where the judgment is for costs, and cannot extend beyond, a bond in double the amount of that judgment for costs, will be within the provisions of the law. Scott & Rose *v.* Allen, 1 Tex. Rep. 508. If the appeal bond describes a judgment against two as but against one, it is bad. McGarrah *v.* Burney, 4 Tex. Rep. 287. Hollis *v.* Border, 10 Tex. Rep. 277. To constitute an appeal, notice must be given during the term, and the bond be filed within twenty days thereafter. Burr *v.* Lewis, 6 Tex. Rep. 76. It is not necessary that the bond be signed by the appellant. Shelton *v.* Wade, 4 Tex. Rep. 148. Where there is but one surety to the bond, the appeal will be dismissed. Hooper *v.* Brinson, 10 Tex. Rep. 296.

(*e* McCoy's heirs *v.* Jones, 9 Tex. Rep. 363.

(*g*) Under this article, the bond should show on its face what it is designed for. Doss *v.* Griswold, 1 Tex. 99.

ART. 552. [139] When by appeal or otherwise, a case shall be taken from the District Court to the Supreme Court, the Clerk of the District Court shall immediately make up a full and perfect record of all proceedings in such case(*a*) and shall, on application of either party, give to such party an attested copy of such record, with a taxation of all costs that have accrued thereon, and shall endorse on such copy the day on which it was demanded, and the day on which it is delivered, and sign his name, as Clerk, thereto;(*b*) and if, by reason of delay or neglect of any Clerk, to give a transcript of the record in any case, the same shall not be filed in the Supreme Court in due time, or if the record be erroneously or incorrectly made up, so that the Supreme Court cannot proceed thereon to final judgment, such Clerk shall, in either case, upon conviction thereof before any court of competent jurisdiction, be adjudged guilty of a misdemeanor in office, and shall be fined in a sum not exceeding two hundred dollars, to the use of the State.

Clerk to make out transcript &c.

See art. 557.

ART. 553. [19] That any party to a civil suit, believing himself aggrieved by any final judgment or decree of the District Court may appeal from such final judgment or decree to the Supreme Court during the term of the District Court at which such final judgment or decree was rendered; and notice of such appeal shall in all cases be entered of record.(*c*)

Act of March 16, 1848. Took effect August 1, 1848.

Notice of appeal

XX. WRITS OF ERROR.

ART. 554. [140] The Clerks of the several District Courts, shall grant writs of error upon any final judgment, order, or decree, rendered in their court upon the petition of any party interested. Upon the filing of any such petition, the Clerk shall issue a citation, directed to the Sheriff of the county where the opposite party is alleged to reside, together with a copy of the petition, commanding him to cite such party to be and appear before the Supreme Court, at its next term after the citation is issued, and defend said writ; which citation and copy of petition shall be served by the Sheriff to whom it is directed, and shall be returned to the court from which it issued; and all such citations shall be returnable in thirty days after the issuing thereof; and if the party is a non-resident of the State, or cannot be found, the citation may be served on the attorney of record;(*d*) if any such citation shall not be served, the Clerk shall issue(*e*) an alias, or pluries citation, forthwith. Upon the return of any such citation served, the Clerk shall

Act of Macch 13, 1846.

Writ of error. how obtained.

(*a*) No paper found in the files, should be inserted in the transcript, unless it has been used in the case, and ordered to be made part of the record by the Court, and one insertion of a paper is all that will be allowed. Castro *v.* Illies, 11 Tex. Rep. 39.

The transcript must be certified by the Clerk to be a full transcript of all the proceedings in the case. Martin & Ward *v.* Latimer, Bagby, & Co., 4 Tex. Rep. 335.

(*b*) The appeal will not be dismissed for want of such endorsement. Wilburn *v.* Walker, 11 Tex. Rep. 329.

The requirements of the statute are for the benefit of the party demanding the transcript. Wright *v.* Bonta, 19 Tex. Rep. 385.

(*c*) Notice must be given during the term of the Court at which the judgment or decree is rendered.—Burr *v.* Lewis, 6 Tex Rep. 76.

A party who is surprised by the decision of the Court ruling out his testimony, may take a *non suit*, and an appeal will lie from the refusal of the Court to set aside the non suit and reinstate the cause. Huston *v.* Berry, 3 Tex. Rep. 235.

The judgment must be final to authorize an appeal.—Houston *v.* Starr, 12. Tex. Rep. 424.

When an appeal is taken and security given all proceedings on the judgment are suspended. Shapard *v.* Bailleul, 3 Tex. Rep. 26.

(*d*) The writ of error, as recognized by our law, is one of the modes prescribed for bringing up causes for revision. The whole case, embracing the facts as well as the law, is brought up by this mode as well as by appeal. Luckett *v.* Townsend, 3 Tex. Rep. 119.

A writ of error, can issue only at the instance of the party to the suit, or one whose privity of estate, title or interest appears from the record, or at the instance of the representative of such party. Smith et al *v.* Gerlach et al, 2 Tex. Rep. 424. Thomas *v.* Jones 10 Tex. Rep. 52.

The petition for the writ should allege the residence of the defendant, or that he is not a resident of the State. 10 Tex. Rep. 352. The petition need not state the grounds on which the writ is sought. Turner *v.* Hamilton, 6 Tex. Rep. 250.

(*e*) If the defendant is a resident of the State, the citation should be directed to the county of his residence. If he is a non resident it may be served on his attorney. So also if he is a resident of the State, but cannot be found, which can only be tested by an effort to find him in the county of his residence. Roberts *v.* Sollibellus, 10 Tex. Rep 352. James & Eastman *v.* Gray's heirs, 3 Tex. Rep. 514. Owen *v.* Tankersly, 12 Tex. Rep. 38.

The Coroner is not authorised to serve the citation unless the petition alleges some legal objection to the Sheriff, or that there is no Sheriff. Mays *v.* Forbes, 11 Tex. Rep. 284. See Chambers *v.* Shaw, 16 Tex. Rep. 144. Adkins *v.* Forehand, 10 Tex. Rep. 270.

Transcript to be made out, when. immediately maekout a complete transcript of all the proceedings in there suit upon which the writ is obtained, and also the petition for the writ of error, and the citation issued with the return thereon, and deliver it to either party on application, and under the same rules and penalties as provided in case of appeals: no such writ of error shall operate as a supersedeas, nor shall a supersedeas issue with any such writ, until the party obtaining the same shall have filed with the Clerk issuing such writ of error his obligation, with good and sufficient security, to be approved by the Clerk, payable to the adverse party, in a sum equal to double the value or amount of the judgment, order to decree upon which the writ of error is obtained, conditioned that the party obtaining such writ shall comply with the judgment, order or decree of the Supreme Court upon such writ, and well and truly pay all such damages as may be awarded against him; which bond shall have the force and effect of a judgment against all the obligors, upon which execution may issue; in case of forfeiture.

Not to operate as a supersedeas until, &c.

No writ of, granted after two years. ART. 555. [142] No writ of error shall be granted after the expiration of two years from the rendition of the judgment. Minors, married women, and persons *non compos mentis*, shall have the same time, or two years, after their respective disabilities are removed.

Act of Feb'y 5, 1858. Took effect July 1, 1858.

When an agreed statement shall be sufficient transcript. ART. 556. [12] After trial of any cause, when either party intends to remove the same into the Supreme Court for revision, the parties may, with the consent and approval of the Judge who tried the cause and without the necessity of copying the entire proceedings, agree upon such a statement of the case, and the facts proven, if any, as in their opinion will be necessary to show whether there has been any error in the proceedings; and such statement shall be signed by the Attorneys of the parties, and certified by the Judge, and filed as a part of the record of the cause; and a copy of such statement and of the judgment in the case and the assignment of errors certified by the Clerks of the Court, shall be a sufficient transcript of the proceedings to be taken to the Supreme Court, and to entitle the parties to a trial therein upon the points presented for revision. In all cases proposed to be removed to the Supreme Court, where such agreed statement is not made, approved and filed, as in this section provided, the Clerks shall make out and send up the full transcript of the proceedings as is now provided by law.

Duty of Clerk, when agreed statement.

Writ of error not to issue until &c. ART. 557. [13] No writ of error to remove a cause for the District to the Supreme Court, shall in any case issue unless the plaintiff in error give bond with sufficient security for all the cost which may accrue in the Supreme Court, and which may have accrued in the District Court.

XXI. MISCELLANEOUS PROVISIONS.

Act of May 11, 1846.

Records &c., of Dist. Court of Republic, to be transferred, &c. ART. 559. [26] All records of judgments and all proceedings in suits, heretofore had in the District Courts of the Republic of Texas, shall be transferred to the District Courts of the State, organized under this Act, and the same proceedings may be had thereon as if the said records had been made, and the said suits been commenced, in the District Courts of the State.

Records of County Court of Republic before &c., to be transferred, &c. ART. 560. [27] All records of judgments in the County Courts of the Republic of Texas, made and entered previous to the first day of February 1839, and all papers and proceedings in relation to such judgments, shall be transferred to the District Courts of the same county, organized under this Act, where the same has not already been done, and the same proceedings shall be had thereon in the District Courts as could be, if such judgments had been rendered in such District Court.

ART. 561. [35] No paper shall be considered as filed in the proceedings of any cause, unless the clerk shall have endorsed thereon, the day on which it was filed, and sign his name thereto.(*a*) Act of May 13, 1846. Papers when considered filed.

ART. 562. [43] In all cases where minors may be defendants to a suit, and it shall be shown to the court that such minors have no guardians within the State, it shall be the duty of the court to appoint a guardian to such minors for the purpose of defending such suit.(*b*) When Court may appoint guardian, *ad litem.*

ART. 563. [48] Whenever several suits may be pending in the same court, by the same plaintiff, against the same defendant, for causes of action which may be joined, or where several suits are pending in the same court, for the same plaintiff, against several defendants, which may be joined, the court in which the same are pending, may, in its discretion, order such suits to be consolidated. Consolidation of suits.

ART. 564. [96] Whenever in the commencement or progress of any suit, it shall be necessary to serve any notice on any party to such suit, such notice may be served either by an officer authorized by law to serve original process of the court in which suit is brought or may be pending, or by any person who would be a competent witness upon the trial of such suit; every such notice may be served in like manner as an original writ, either on the party or his attorney of record; and the return of such notice, when made by an officer, or when made by any other person and verified by the affidavit of such person, shall be received as evidence of the facts therein contained, subject however to be repelled by contrary proof. Service of notices.

ART. 565. [97] Whenever, in any suit, it shall appear to the court that an investigation of accounts, or examination of vouchers is necessary, for the purposes of justice between the parties, the court shall appoint an auditor or auditors to state the accounts between the parties, and to make report thereof to the court, as soon as may be; and the report so made shall, under the direction of the court, be given in evidence to the jury, subject, however, to be impeached by evidence from either party; and the court shall award reasonable compensation to such auditors, which shall be allowed and taxed in the bill of costs, to be recovered by the successful party, as in other cases.(*c*) Auditor may be appointed, &c.

ART. 566. [98] The court shall appoint interpreters when necessary, who shall be sworn truly to interpret, and shall be entitled to the same pay therefor as by law is allowed to witnesses; papers read in evidence, although not under seal, may be carried from the bar by the jury in their retirement. Interpreters may be appointed, &c.

ART. 567. [107] All vouchers, views, essoigns, and also trials by wager of battle, and wager of law shall stand repealed. Vouchers, wager of battle, &c, repealed.

ART. 568. [1] The repeal of any statutory provision by this Legislature, shall not affect any act, decree, or right accrued or established, or any proceedings, suit, or prosecution, had or commenced in any civil case, previous to the time when such repeal shall take effect; but every such act, right, and proceedings, shall remain as valid and effectual as if the provisions so repealed had remained in force. Act of May 13, 1846. Repeal of other laws by this act not to affect, &c.

ART. 569. [3] No action, plea, prosecution, or proceeding, civil or criminal,

(*a*) Love & Chappell *v.* McIntyre, 3 Tex. Rep. 10.

(*b*) Thomas *v.* Jones, 10 Tex. Rep., 52.

(*c*) The statute would seem to require that the report should state the items of the respective accounts, as well as the conclusions of the Auditor in respect to the various matters embraced in them. Whitehead *v.* Perie, 15 Tex. Rep., 7.

See the same case as to the duties of the auditor—the requisites of his report and the time and mode of excepting to it.

Proceedings pending, &c., not affected by this act.

pending at the time any statutory provision shall be repealed, shall be effected by such repeal, but the same shall proceed in all respects as if such statutory provision had not been repealed, except that all proceedings had after the taking effect of the statutes passed by the Legislature, shall be conducted according to the provisions of such statutes, and shall be in all respects subject to the provisions thereof, so far as they are applicable.

Act of Feb. 5, 1858. Took effect July 1, 1858. Interest of other States presumed, &c., unless.

ART. 570. [10] In the trial of all causes in the courts of this State, the rate of interest in any other State or Territory of the United States, shall be presumed to be the same as that established by law in this State, unless the rate of interest of such other State or Territory be proven, and may be recovered accordingly, without allegation or proof of the rate of such foreign interest.

XXII. JUDICIAL DISTRICTS AND TERMS OF COURTS.

Act of July 19, 1856. Took effect from passage. 1st District.

ART. 571. [1] From and after the passage of this act, the counties of Matagorda, Wharton, Colorado, Fayette, Austin, Fort Bend and Brazoria, shall compose the first Judicial District of the State of Texas.

Act of Jan. 15, 1858. Terms of courts in.

ART. 572. [2] The District Courts in the first Judicial District shall commence and be held as follows, to-wit: In the county of Brazoria on the first Monday in April and October, and may continue in session two weeks; in the county of Matogorda on the second Mondays after the first Mondays in April and October, and may continue in session one week; in the county of Wharton on the third Mondays after the first Mondays in April and October, and may continue in session one week; in the county of Colorado on the fourth Mondays after the first Mondays in April and October, and may continue in session two weeks; in the county of Fayette on the sixth Mondays after the first Mondays in April and October, and may continue in session three weeks; in the county of Austin on the ninth Mondays after the first Mondays in April and October, and may continue in session two weeks; in the county of Fort Bend on the eleventh Monday after the first Monday of April and on the first Mondays in January, and may continue in session until the business is disposed of.

Act of Feb. 2, 1856. 2d District.

ART. 573. [1] The second Judicial District shall be composed of the counties of Bastrop, Caldwell, Guadalupe, Hays and Travis.

Act of Jan. 15, 1858. Took effect from passage. Terms of courts in.

ART. 574. [1] From and after the passage of this act the District Courts of the second Judicial District shall be held at the times following, to-wit: In Bastrop county on the first Mondays in April and October of each year, and may continue in session three weeks; in Caldwell county on the third Mondays after the first Mondays in Apri. and October, of each year, and may continue in session two weeks; in Guadalupe county on the fifth Mondays after the first Mondays in April and October, of each year, and may continue in session three weeks; in Hays county on the eighth Mondays after the first Mondays in April and October, of each year, and may continue in session one week; in Travis county on the ninth Mondays after the first Mondays in April and October, of each year, and may continue in session until the business is disposed of.

Act of Jan. 19, 1858. 3d District.

ART. 575. [1] The counties of Washington, Brazos, Burleson and Milam, shall hereafter constitute the third Judicial District of Texas.

ART. 576. [2] The terms of the District Court shall be holden in said District at the following times and places, to-wit: In the county of Washington on the first Mondays after the fourth Mondays in March and September, in each year, and may continue in session four weeks; in the county of Brazos on the fifth Mondays after the fourth Mondays in March and September, in each year, and may continue in session one week; in the county of Burleson on the sixth Mondays after the fourth Mondays in March and September, in each year, and may continue in session two weeks; in the county of Milam on the eighth Mondays after the fourth Mondays in March and September, in each year, and may continue in session two weeks. Terms of courts in.

Act of Feb. 1, 1856. Took effect from passage.

4th District.

ART. 577. [1] From and after the passage of this act, the counties of Comal, Kerr, Gillespie and Bexar, shall constitute the fourth Judicial District of this State.

Act of Feb. 2, 1858. Took effect from passage.

Terms of courts in.

ART. 578. [1] The District Court of Bexar county shall hereafter be held as follows, to-wit: The first term of said court to be holden after the passage of this act, shall begin on the second Monday of March, eighteen hundred and fifty-eight, and may continue in session seven weeks; and the subsequent terms of said court shall begin on the first Mondays of March and September, of each year, and may continue in session seven weeks; and the District Courts of the other counties composing the fourth Judicial Districts, shall hereafter be held as follows, to-wit: In the county of Comal, on the eighth Mondays after the first Mondays of March and September, and may continue in session two weeks; in the county of Kerr on the tenth Mondays after the first Mondays of March and September, and may continue in session one week; and in the county of Gillespie on the eleventh Mondays after the first Mondays of March and September, and may continue in session two weeks.

Act of Jan. 30, 1858.

5th District.

Terms of Courts in.

ART. 579. [1] The District Courts of the fifth Judicial District shall be holden at the times hereinafter specified, to wit: in the county of Newton on the fourth Mondays in February and August in each year, and may continue in session one week; in the county of Jasper on the first Mondays after the fourth Mondays in February and August in each year, and may continue in session two weeks; in the county of Sabine on the third Mondays after the fourth Mondays in February and August in each year, and may continue in session one week; in the county of Shelby on the fourth Mondays after the fourth Mondays in February and August in each year, and may continue in session two weeks; in the county of San Augustine on the sixth Mondays after the fourth Mondays in February and August in each year, and may continue in session two weeks; in the county of Angelina on the eighth Mondays after the fourth Mondays in February and August in each year, and may continue in session two weeks; and in the county of Nacogdoches on the first Mondays in January and July in each year, and may continue in session until the business shall be disposed of.

Act of Dec. 18, 1855. Took effect from passage.

6th District.

ART. 580. [1] The following counties shall compose the sixth Judicial District, viz: Wood, Upshur, Harrison, Panola and Rusk.

Terms of Courts in.

ART. 581. [2] The District Courts of the sixth Judicial District shall be held as follows, viz: in the county of Wood on the first Mondays in February and August, and may continue in session two weeks. In the county of Upshur on the second Mondays after the first Mondays in February and August, and may continue in session two weeks. In the county of Harrison on the fourth Mondays after the first Mondays in February and August, and may continue in session six weeks. In the county of Panola on the tenth Mondays after the first Mondays in February and August, and may continue in session three weeks. In the county of Rusk on the thirteenth Mondays after the first Mondays in February and August, and may continue in session five weeks.

Act of February 3, 1858. Took effect March 1, 1858. 7th District.

ART. 582. [1] The counties of Walker, Grimes, Montgomery, Harris and Galveston, shall constitute the seventh Judicial District.

Terms of Courts in.

ART. 583. [2] The District Courts shall commence in the seventh Judicial District, in the county of Grimes, on the third Mondays in April and October, and may continue in session two weeks; in the county of Walker, on the second Mondays after the third Mondays in April and October, and may continue in session two weeks; in the county of Montgomery, on the fourth Mondays after the third Mondays in April and October, and may continue in session two weeks; in the county of Harris, on the sixth Mondays after the third Mondays in April and October, and may continue in session four weeks; in the county of Galveston, on the tenth Mondays after the third Mondays in April and October, and may continue in session until the business is disposed of.

Act of Jan. 14, 1856. Took effect from date. 8th District.

ART. 584. [1] The counties of Red River, Bowie, Cass, Titus, Hopkins, Hunt, Fannin, and Lamar shall compose the eighth Judicial District.

Act of February 16, 1858. Took effect Aug 1858. Terms of Courts in.

ART. 585. [1] The District Courts in said District shall be held in the several counties therein at the times herein specified, to wit: in the county of Bowie on the second Mondays of March and September, and may continue in session two weeks; in the county of Cass, on the second Mondays after the second Mondays in March and September, and may continue in session three weeks; in the county of Titus, on the sixth Mondays after the second Mondays in March and September, and may continue in session two weeks; in the county of Hopkins on the ninth Mondays after the second Mondays in March and September, and may continue in session two weeks; in the county of Hunt, on the eleventh Mondays after the second Mondays in March and September, and may continue in session one week; in the county of Fannin, on the twelfth Mondays after the second Mondays in March and September, and may continue in session two weeks; in the county of Lamar, on the fourteenth Mondays after the second Mondays in March and September, and may continue in session two weeks; in the county of Red River, on the sixteenth Mondays after the second Mondays in March and September, and may continue in session until the business is disposed of.

Act of Dec. 18, 1855. Took effect from passage. 9th District.

ART. 586. [3] The following counties shall compose the ninth Judicial District, viz: Houston, Cherokee, Anderson, Henderson, Kaufman, Van Zandt and Smith.

Act of August 27, 1856. Took effect from passage. Terms of Courts in.

ART. 587. [1] The District Courts of the ninth Judicial District, shall be held as follows, viz: in the county of Houston, on the first Mondays of every March and September, and may continue in session two weeks; in the county of Cherokee, on the second Mondays after the first Mondays in March and September, and may continue in session four weeks; in the county of Anderson, on the sixth Mondays after the first Mondays in March and September, and may continue in session three weeks; in the county of Henderson, on the ninth Mondays after the first Mondays in March and September, and may continue in session one week; in the county of Kaufman, on the tenth Mondays after the first Mondays in March and September, and may continue in session one week; in the county of Van Zandt, on the eleventh Mondays after the first Mondays in March and September, and may continue in session one week; in the county of Smith, on the fourteenth Mondays after the first Mondays in March and September, and may continue in session until the business is disposed of.

ART. 588. [1] The District Courts shall be held in each of the counties composing the tenth Judicial District twice in each year, at the following times, to wit: in the county of Victoria, on the third Mondays in February and August, in each year, and may continue in session two weeks; in the county of Jackson, on the second Mondays after the third Mondays in February and August, and may continue in session one week; in the county of Lavaca, on the third Mondays after the third Mondays in February and August, and may continue in session two weeks; in the county of DeWitt, on the fifth Mondays after the third Mondays in February and August, and may continue in session two weeks; in the county of Gonzales, on the seventh Mondays after the third Mondays in February and August, and may continue in session three weeks; in the county of Calhoun, on the eleventh Mondays after the third Monday in February, and the thirteenth Monday after the third Monday in August, in each year, and may continue in session two weeks; provided, that in case of epidemic, or other cause deemed sufficient, the District Court for Calhoun county may be adjourned to a special term; but said special term shall in no case conflict with a regular term of the District Court for any county in the tenth Judicial District.

Act of Feb. 22, 1858. Took effect from date.

10th District.

Terms of Courts in.

ART. 589. [1] The following named counties shall compose the eleventh Judicial District of the State of Texas, to wit: Presidio, El Paso, and Worth.

[1] The judicial jurisdiction of the county of El Paso, as well civil as criminal, shall be, and the same hereby is extended to and throughout the county of Presidio, until the same shall have been organized according to law; and that all causes of action arising within the said county of Presidio, over which the District Courts would have jurisdiction, shall be tried in the county of El Paso, in the same manner and the same proceedings had thereon as though the said causes of action had arisen in the county of El Paso.

Act of January 1, 1850. In force from passage.

11th District.

Act of February 12, 1852. Took effect from passage.

Presidio coun'y.

ART. 590. [1] The District Courts of the eleventh Judicial District, shall commence in the county of El Paso on the first Mondays in March and September, in each year, and may continue in session until the business is disposed of.

Act of Dec. 28, 1857.

Terms of courts in.

ART. 591. [1] The following named counties shall compose the twelfth Judicial District, to wit: Cameron, Starr, Webb, and Kinney.

Act of Jan. 29, 1850. Took effect Aug. 1, 1850.

12th District.

ART. 592. [1] From and after the passage of this act, the District Courts for the counties composing the twelfth Judicial District shall be begun and holden as follows: In the county of Cameron, on the second Mondays of April and November in every year, and may continue in session four weeks; in the county of Hidalgo on the fifth Mondays after the second Mondays of Aprll and November in every year, and may continue in session one week; in the county of Starr, on the sixth Mondays after the second Mondays in April and November in every year, and may continue in session two weeks; in the county of Webb on the eighth Mondays after the second Mondays in April and November in every year, and may continue in session two weeks; in the county of Zapata* on the tenth Mondays after the second Mondays of April and November in each year, and may continue in session one week.

Act of January 30, 1858.

Terms of courts in.

ART. 593. [1] The thirteenth Judicial District shall be composed of the counties of Madison, Robertson, Falls, Limestone, Hill, Navarro, Freestone, and Leon.

Act of Feb. 5th, 1858.

13th District.

ART. 594. [2] The District Court shall be held in the county of Madison on the third Monday in March and September, and may continue in session one week; in the county of Robertson on the first Monday after the third Monday in March and September, and may continue in session one week; in the county

Terms of Courts in.

* There is no act expressly attaching Hidalgo and Zapata counties to the twelfth District.

of Falls on the second Monday after the third Monday in March and September, and may continue in session one week; in the county of Limestone on the third Monday after the third Monday in March and September, and may continue in session one week; in the county of Hill on the fourth Monday after the third Monday in March and September, and may continue in session one week; in the county of Navarro on the fifth Monday after the third Monday in March and September, and may continue in session two weeks; in the county of Freestone, on the seventh Monday after the third Monday in March and September, and may continue in session one week; in the county of Leon on the eighth Monday after the third Monday in March and September, and may continue in session two weeks.

Act of February 7, 1854. In force from passage. 14th District. ART. 595. [1] The counties of Nueces, San Patricio, Refugio, Goliad, and Karnes, shall hereafter constitute a Judicial District, to be called the Fourteenth Judicial District of the State of Texas.

Act of Dec. 8, 1857. [5] The said county of Bee is hereby attached to the 14th Judicial District.

[10] The county hereby created (Live Oak) shall be attached to and form a part of the Fourteenth Judicial District.

Act of July 24, 1856. 14th District. ART. 596. [2] The District Courts shall be held twice a year in each of the counties composing the fourteenth Judicial District, as follows, to wit: In the county of San Patricio on the first Mondays in April and October, and may continue in session one week; in the county of Live Oak on the first Mondays after the first Mondays in April and October, and may continue in session one week; in the county of Karnes, on the second Mondays after the first Mondays in April and October, and may continue in session two weeks; in the county of Goliad on the fourth Mondays after the first Mondays in April and October, and may continue in session two weeks; in the county of Refugio on the sixth Mondays after the first Mondays in April and October, and may continue in session two weeks; in the county of Nueces on the eighth Mondays after the first Mondays of April and October, and may continue in session until the business is disposed of.

Act of Feb. 12, 1858. [1] The District Courts of the county of Bee shall be commenced on the sixth Mondays after the first Mondays of April and October of each year, and may continue in session to the ends of those weeks respectively; and the courts in Refugio county shall be commenced on the next Mondays respectively, and may continue in session to the ends of those weeks respectivily.

Act of Feb. 16, 1858. In force from passage. 15th District. ART. 597. [1] The counties of Chambers, Liberty, Polk, Trinity, Tyler, Hardin, Jefferson, and Orange, shall constitute the fifteenth Judicial District.

Terms of courts in. ART. 598. [2] The District Courts in the fifteenth Judicial District, shall commence in Chambers county on the second Mondays in March and September, and may continue in session one week; in Liberty county on the third Mondays in March and September, and may continue in session two weeks; in Polk county on the second Mondays after the third Mondays in March and September, and may continue in session two weeks; in Trinity county on the fourth Mondays after the third Mondays in March and September, and may continue in session two weeks; in Tyler county on the sixth Mondays after the third Mondays in March and September, and may continue in session three weeks; in Hardin county on the ninth Mondays after the third Mondays in March and September, and may continue in session one week; in Jefferson county on the tenth Mondays after the third Mondays in March and September, and may continue in session one week; in Orange county on the eleventh Mondays after the third Mondays in March and September, and may continue in session until the business may be disposed of.

[3] This act shall be construed as amendatory of former laws upon the same subject, repealing parts only thereof as may conflict with the provisions herein contained.

ART. 599. [1] The sixteenth Judicial District shall be composed of the counties of Collin, Grayson, Cook, Montague, Clay, Archer, Throckmorton, Young, Jack, Wise, Denton, Tarrant, Parker, Johnson, Ellis, and Dallas. Act of Feb'ry 8, 1858. 16th District.

ART. 600. [2] The District Court shall be held in said counties twice in each year, as follows: In the county of Collin, commencing on the third Mondays in March and September, and may continue in session two weeks; in the county of Grayson on the second Mondays after the third Mondays in March and September, and may continue in session two weeks; in the county of Cook on the fourth Mondays after the third Mondays in March and September, and may continue in session one week; in the county of Montague on the fifth Mondays after the third Mondays in March and September, and may continue in session one week; in the county of Clay on the sixth Mondays after the third Mondays in March and September, and may continue in session one week; in the county of Archer on the seventh Mondays after the third Mondays in March and September, and may continue in session one week; in the county of Throckmorton on the eighth Mondays after the third Mondays in March and September, and may continue in session one week; in the county of Young on the ninth Mondays after the fourth Mondays in March and September, and may continue in session one week; in the county of Jack on the tenth Mondays after the third Mondays in March and September, and may continue in session one week; in the county of Wise, on the eleventh Mondays after the third Mondays in March and September, and may continue in session one week; in the county of Denton on the twelfth Mondays after the third Mondays in March and September, and may continue in session one week; in the county of Tarrant on the thirteenth Mondays after the third Mondays in March and September, and may continue in session two weeks; in the county of Parker on the fifteenth Mondays after the third Mondays in March and September, and may continue in session one week; in the county of Johnson on the sixteenth Mondays after the third Mondays in March and September, and may continue in session one week; in the county of Ellis, on the seventeenth Mondays after the third Mondays in March and September, and may continue in sesssion two weeks; in the county of Dallas on the nineteenth Mondays after the third Mondays in March and September, and may continue in session till the business is disposed of. Terms of courts in.

ART. 601. [1] The seventeenth Judicial District shall be composed of the following counties, to wit: Williamson, Burnett, Llano, San Saba, McCulloch, Brown and Lampasas. Act of Feb'ry 3, 1858. In force from date. 17th District

ART. 602. [2]. The second section of the above recited act be so amended as to read as follows: That the District Court shall be held in the seventeenth Judicial District at the following times and places, to wit: In the county of Williamson on the second Mondays in March and September, and may continue in session three weeks; in the county of Burnett on the third Mondays after the second Mondays in March and September, and may continue in session two weeks; in the county of Llano on the fifth Mondays after the second Mondays in March and September, and may continue in session one week; in the county of San Saba on the sixth Mondays after the second Mondays in March and September, and may continue in session two weeks; in the county of McCulloch on the eighth Mondays after the second Mondays in March and September, and may continue in session one week; in the county of Brown on the ninth Mondays after the second Mondays in March and September, and may continue in session one week; in the county of Lampasas on the tenth Mondays after the second Mondays in March and September, and may continue in session until the business is disposed of. Terms of courts in.

Act of July 22, 1856. Took effect from passage. 18th District.

ART. 603. [1] The counties of Atascosa, Medina, Bandera, Uvalde, Kinney, and Maverick, be, and the same are hereby created into a new Judicial District, to be called the Eighteenth Judicial District.

Act of February 3, 1858. Took effect from date. Term of courts in.

ART. 604. [1] The District Courts shall be held in the counties composing the Eighteenth Judicial District of the State of Texas, as follows, to wit: In the county of Medina, on the second Mondays in March and September, and may continue in session three weeks; in the county of Bandera, on the fourth Mondays after the first Mondays in March and September, and may continue in session one week; in the county of Uvalde, on the fifth Mondays after the first Mondays in March and September, and may continue in session one week; in the county of Atascosa, on the sixth Mondays after the first Mondays in March and September, and may continue in session three weeks; in the county of Kinney, on the ninth Mondays after the first Mondays in March and September, and may continue in session one week; in the county of Maverick, on the tenth Mondays after the first Mondays in March and September, and may continue in session one week.

Act of Dec. 19, 1857. Took effect from passage. 19th District.

ART. 605. [1] The counties of McLennan, Bosque, Erath, Palo Pinto, Buchannan, Comanche, Corryell and Bell shall constitute the Nineteenth Judicial District of the State of Texas.

Terms of courts in.

ART. 606. [2] The District Court shall be holden in said Nineteenth Judicial District at the following times and places, to wit: In the county of McLennan on the third Mondays in March and September in each year, and may remain in session three weeks; in the county of Bosque, on the third Mondays after the third Mondays in March and September in each year, and may continue in session one week; in the county of Erath, on the fourth Mondays after the third Mondays in March and September in each year, and may continue in session one week; in the county of Palo Pinto, on the fifth Mondays after the third Mondays in March and September, in each year, and may continue in session one week; in the county of Buchannan, on the sixth Mondays after the third Mondays in March and September in each year, and may continue in session one week; in the county of Comanche, on the seventh Mondays after the third Mondays in March and September in each year, and may continue in session one week; in the county of Corryell, on the ninth Mondays after the third Mondays in March and September in each year, and may continue in session two weeks; in the county of Bell, on the eleventh Mondays after the third Mondays in March and September, and may continue in session until the business is disposed of.

Act of Jan. 28, 1858. Took effect from date. Hamilton co.

[1] The county of Hamilton be, and the same is hereby made a part of the Nineteenth Judicial District of Texas, and that the Judge of said Nineteenth Judicial District shall hold terms of the District Court in said county on the eighth Mondays after the third Mondays in March and September in each and every year, and may continue in session one week.

DIVORCE AND ALIMONY.

ART. 607. [1] The several District Courts within this Republic shall have jurisdiction to hear and determine suits for the dissolution of marriage, where the causes alleged thereof shall be natural or incurable impotency of body at the time of entering into the marriage contract, and shall have power and authority to decree the marriage to be null and void. *Act of Jan. 6. 1841. District Court—Jurisdiction. Impotency.*

ART. 608. [2] The courts aforesaid are hereby invested with full power and authority to decree divorces from the bonds of matrimony, in the following cases: That is to say, in favor of the husband where his wife shall have been taken in adultery, or where she shall have voluntarily left his bed and board, for the space of three years, with intention of abandonment; in favor of the wife where the husband shall have left her for three years with intention of abandonment, or where he shall have abandoned her and lived in adultery with another woman. *Abandonment. Adultery.*

ART. 609. [3] A divorce by separation from the bonds of matrimony may be decreed in the following cases: That is to say, where either the husband or wife is guilty of excesses, cruel treatment, or outrages towards the other, if such ill treatment is of such a nature as to render their living together insupportable.(*a*) *Excesses—cruel treatment.*

ART. 610. [4] In all suits and proceedings for divorce from the bonds of matrimony, the defendant shall not be compelled to answer upon oath, nor the petition be taken "for confessed" for want of an answer, but the decree of the court shall be rendered upon full and satisfactory evidence, independent of the confession or admission of either party, and upon the verdict of a jury affirming the material facts alleged in the petition; (*b*) and the court pronouncing a decree of divorce from the bonds of matrimony, shall also decree and order a divisien of the estate of the parties in such way as to them shall seem just and right, having due regard to the rights of each party and their children, if any: provided, however, that nothing herein contained shall be construed to compel either party to divest him or herself of the title to real estate or to slaves. (*c*) *Trial, judgment. Division of estate.*

ART. 611. [5] A divorce from the bonds of matrimony shall not in anywise affect the legitimacy of the children thereof, and it shall be lawful for either party, after the dissolution of the marriage, to marry again. *Legitimacy of children. Parties may marry again.*

(*a*) In suits for divorce the acts complained of must be specifically stated as to the time, place and material circumstances,—general charges of cruelty, adultery, excesses, &c., are not sufficient to sustain the action. The acts which constitute the charge must be stated. Proof should not be received to sustain mere general charges without specifications. Wright *v.* Wright, 3 Tex. Rep. 168. The term "outrages," as used in the statute, has reference only to outrages to the person, and does not extend to the alleged commission of theft or other crime Lucas *v.* Lucas, 2 Tex. Rep. 112. The term "insupportable" and "outrageous," is a question of law. Byrne *v.* Byrne, 3 Tex. Rep. 336. The ordinary criterion of "cruelty" is an apprehension of danger to life, or limb, or health. Nogees *v.* Nogees, 7 Tex. Rep. 539. No exact legal definition of cruelty can be given. Ibid.

(*b*) The above provisions exempting the defendant from answering under oath, and rendering the admissions of the parties incompetent as proof, have reference only to the main object of the suit,—the dissolution of the marriage. They do not apply to such statements in the pleadings as relate to the property of the parties. Wright *v.* Wright, 3 Tex. Rep. 168. A demurrer to a plea of justification depicting the general character of the plaintiff, without stating particular acts of bad conduct, does not admit the truth of the charge. Ibid.

(*c*) The most obvious construction of the statute is, that the separate property should be restored to its owner respectively, and that such a division of the community property be made, as may seem just and right; it being understood that due regard must be had to the rights of the parties, that suitable provision must be made for the education and maintenance of the children, if any, and that although the community, if any, is the primary fund, from which such provision should be made, as would render the division just under all the circumstances, yet there may be cases in which the separate property will be subjected to such charges—especially in favor of the wife—as may be equitable and right: provided that the title to lands and slaves be not divested. Fitts *v.* Fitts, 14 Tex. Rep. 444; Trimble *v.* Trimble, 15 Tex. Rep. 18.

Temporary order respecting property.

ART. 612. [6] Pending any suit for a divorce, the court may make such temporary orders respecting the property and parties as they shall deem necessary and equitable.

Either party may appeal.

ART. 613. [7] Either party may take testimony by depositions of witnesses residing within as well as without the county in which the suit is pending, under the same rules, regulations, and restrictions, as exist in other suits; and the court may award costs to the party in whose behalf the sentence or decree shall pass, or that each party shall pay his or her own costs, as to the court shall appear reasonable; and that either party may obtain an appeal to the Supreme Court, from any decree made in any suit under this act, in the same manner as in other suits, without bond and security, if the situation of the party appellant shall render it necessary for the purposes of justice, that an appeal should be thus prosecuted.

Support of wife pending suit.

ART. 614. [8] If the wife, whether complainant or defendant, has not a sufficient income for her maintenance, during the pendency of the suit for a divorce, the Judge may allow her a sum for her support, proportional to the means of the husband, until a final decree shall be made in the case. (a)

Husband not to encumber community after suit.

ART. 615. [9] On and after the day on which the action for divorce shall be brought, it shall not be lawful for the husband to contract any debts on account of the community, nor to dispose of the lands or slaves belonging to the same; and any alienation made by him after that time, shall be null and void, if it be proved to the satisfaction of the Judge and jury that such alienation was made with a fraudulent view of injuring the rights of the wife. (b)

Inventory. Appraisement and injunction.

ART. 616. [10] At any time during a suit for divorce, the wife may, for the preservation of her rights, require an inventory and an appraisement to be made of both the real and personal estate which are in the possession of the husband, and an injunction restraining him from disposing of any part thereof, in any manner. (c)

On ground of adultery.

ART. 617. [11] Where a divorce from the bonds of matrimony is prayed for on the ground of adultery, when the marriage was solemnized abroad, it must clearly and distinctly appear to the satisfaction of the court and jury, that both parties were inhabitants of this Republic at the time the adultery was committed; and to entitle a party to sustain a petition for such divorce, he must be an actual and bona fide inhabitant of this Republic at the time of the adultery committed, and at the time of exhibiting his petition. (d)

Adultery no ground in certain cases.

ART. 618. [12] In any suit for a divorce for the cause of adultery, if it shall be proved that the complainant has been guilty of the like crime, or has admitted the defendant into conjugal society or embraces after he or she knew the criminal fact, or that the complainant (if the husband) allowed of his wife's prostitution, or exposed her to lewd company, whereby she became ensnared to the crime aforesaid, it shall be a good defence and a perpetual bar against said suit; or if it appears to the court and jury that the adultery complained of is occasioned by collusion of the parties, and done with intention to procure a divorce, or where both parties shall be guilty of adultery, then no divorce shall be decreed.

Custody of children.

ART. 619. [13] The several District Courts aforesaid shall have power in all cases of separation, between man and wife, to give the custody and education

(a) Where the wife has a separate income adequate to her maintenance, the husband is not liable for alimony, either under the common law or our statute law. Wright v. Wright, 6 Tex. Rep. 29.

(b) The first clause of the above article is controlled by the latter, and the burden of proving the alienation of land or slaves, as well as of other property, to have been made with a fraudulent view of injuring the rights of the wife, rests upon her in a suit, by her to recover the property from the alinee. Haggerty v. Harwell, et at., 16 Tex. Rep. 663.

(c) Wright v Wright, 3 Tex. Rep. 168.

(d) Simons v. Simons, 13 Tex. Rep. 468.

of the children to either father or mother, as to them shall seem right and proper, having regard to the prudence and ability of the parents, and the age and sex of the child or children, to be determined and decided on the petition of either party; and in the mean time to issue an injunction or make any order that the safety and well-being of any such children may require.

ELECTIONS.

I. GENERAL PROVISIONS.

ART. 620. [1] The County Courts of each county shall, at their first regular session after this act takes effect, and thereafter at their first regular session in each year, if they deem necessary, designate such places for holding elections as may be most suitable and convenient for the people; which places so designated shall be numbered and called election precincts; and they shall also at the same time select and appoint from among the residents at or near each election precinct, some suitable person to be the presiding officer at such precinct in all elections which shall be held thereat, during the year in which he may be appointed.

Act of March 16, 1848. Took effect May 1, 1848.

Precincts to be designated, &c., by County Court.

ART. 621. [2] Forms for notices, writs, and returns of elections, as furnished by the Secretary of State to the Chief Justice of each county, shall be preserved in the office of the County Clerk.

Forms of notices, &c., to be preserved.

ART. 622. [3] The Chief Justices of the several counties, or in case of vacancy in that office, or any inability of the Chief Justice to act, then any two of the County Commissioners shall order all elections in their respective counties.

County elections, by whom ordered.

Ten days notice &c.

ART. 623. [4] Whenever an election may be ordered, except in cases of vacancy in the Legislature, at least ten days' notice of the election shall be given by the officer ordering it, by notice posted up at each election precinct, or by publication in some newspaper, if one be published in the county, specifying the time and places at which such election is to be held, and the officer or officers to be chosen; in cases of elections to fill vacancies in the Legislature, like notices, of not more than ten nor less than five days, shall be given immediately on the receipt of the Governor's proclamation therefor.

Vacancy in county offices.

ART. 624. [5] In all cases of vacancy in any civil office of the county, by death, resignation, or otherwise, which by law is filled by election of the people, the officer or officers authorized by this act to order elections, shall immediately make such order for an election to fill the vacancy, by giving like notice, and issuing writs as prescribed for regulating elections.(*a*)

Writ of, to whom issued.

ART. 625. [6] It shall be the duty of the officer ordering an election, to issue writs of election to the several presiding officers, who may have been previously appointed, as herein directed, or in case of the death, removal, or other inability of any presiding officer, then to some other suitable person, resident at or near the precinct, whom he may select as presiding officer in the place of the one disabled to act, in which writs shall be stated particularly the officer or officers to be chosen, and the day of election; and he shall also send with the writ a copy of the form of election returns furnished by the Secretary of State.

Judges and Clerks of, shall be sworn, &c.

ART. 626. [7] The presiding officer of each precinct shall, on or before the day of election, select two Judges and two Clerks, who, together with the presiding officer, shall be the managers of the election, and he shall administer to each of them an oath, that they will well and truly conduct the election, without partiality or prejudice, and agreeably to law, according to the best of their skill and understanding; and the presiding officer shall be also sworn by a Justice of the Peace, if one be present, if not, by one of the Judges.

If presiding officer fail to attend.

ART. 627. [8] In case the presiding officer appointed as hereinbefore provided, should fail to attend on the day of election, or refuse to act, it shall be lawful for the electors present at the precinct on that day, to appoint a presiding officer to act at that election, and the person so appointed shall be authorized to act as presiding officer as fully as if appointed by the court, or officer ordering the election, and shall be qualified in the same manner: provided, that in such cases the managers shall certify in their returns that the presiding officer failed to attend, or refused to act, and that the person acting as such was duly chosen by the electors present.

Return in such cases.

Voter privileged from arrest, &c., when.

ART. 628. [9] The electors, in all cases, shall be privileged from arrest during their attendance at elections, and in going to and returning from the same,—allowing one day for every twenty miles they may necessarily travel, exclusive of the day of election,—except in cases of treason, felony, or breach of the peace; and service of all other process for any other cause, against any elector, executed during such privilege, shall be void.

Polls opened and closed, when.

ART. 629. [10] The polls shall not be opened before nine o'clock, A. M., nor finally closed before four o'clock, P. M., and not more than one adjournment shall be had during the day; which shall not exceed one hour.

Name and number of voter to be written, &c.

ART. 630. [11] Each of the Clerks shall write and number the name of each voter, at the time of his voting, and in case the voter shall not be entitled to

(*a*) Where the term of office is fixed by the Constitution, at say four years, each succeeding incumbent, although elected to fill a vacancy, is entitled, unless it be otherwise provided in the Constitution itself, to hold the office for the full period. Banton *v.* Wilson, 4 Tex. Rep., 400. The term "regular election," means any election by the people which is provided for by law, for example, to fill that vacancy. Ibid.

vote for all the officers that the election is held for, at that precinct, the Clerk shall set down opposite to his name, the officer or officers for which such voter is entitled to vote, for the purpose of afterwards purging the polls, in case the election shall be contested; and one of the managers shall, in every case, at the time of receiving the ticket or ballot, write upon it the voter's number, corresponding with the Clerk's list; and no manager or other officer of an election shall unfold or examine the vote received, nor shall they examine the endorsements on the tickets when the votes are counted out, nor at any time subsequent to their being received into the ballot-box; and no ticket not thus numbered, shall be counted or noticed in counting out the votes. Duty of officers.

ART. 631. [13] When any person offering to vote shall be objected to, the managers shall examine him upon oath, touching the points objected to; and if he fail establishing his qualifications, to their satisfaction, his vote shall be rejected. Persons offering to vote and objected to.

ART. 632. [17] Whenever it so happens in any election, that there is a tie between two or more candidates for the same office, all of whom cannot be elected, the officer to whom the returns are made, shall declare such election void as between such candidates only, and immediately order a new election for that office, first giving not less than five days' notice thereof. In case of a tie, election void

ART. 633. [3] The several counties which are, or shall be comprised in each Judicial District of this State, shall compose a district for the election of a District Judge and District Attorney. Act of Feb. 11, 1850. Dist. of Judge and Attorney.

[6] All the provisions of the act to which this is a supplement, so far as they can apply, are hereby declared to apply to elections for Governor, Lieutenant-Governor, Justices of the Supreme Court, Representatives to the Congress of the United States, Commissioner of the General Land Office, Attorney-General, Comptroller of Public Accounts, State Treasurer, Judges of the District Courts, and District Attorneys. Act of 1848 shall apply, &c.

ART. 634. [1] It shall be the duty of the Secretary of the Senate, and Chief Clerk of the House of Representatives, on each biennial opening and publishing of the votes for Governor and Lieutenant-Governor, as provided by the Constitution, to record the same in tabular form, by counties alphabetically, in the journals of each house respectively, and also to deposit a certified copy of the same in the State Department; and it is hereby made the duty of the Secretary of State to record the same in the book containing the record of votes for other State officers. Act of Dec. 15, 1857. Took effect from passage. Vote for Governor, &c., to be recorded, where &c.

II. TIME OF HOLDING ELECTION.

ART. 635. [1] The next regular election for Governor, Lieutenant-Governor, members of the State Legislature, Commissioner of the General Land Office, and Representatives to the United States Congress, shall be held on the first Monday in August, Anno Domini, 1849; and elections shall be held for the said officers biennially thereafter, until otherwise provided by law. Act of March 20, 1848. Took effect Ap'l 29, 1848. For Governor, members of the Legislature, &c.

ART. 636. [2] There shall be elected in accordance with the provisions of law on the first Monday in August, Anno Domini 1848, in each county in the State, one Chief Justice, four County Commissioners, one Sheriff, one Coroner, one County Clerk, two Justices of the Peace, and one Constable for each Justice's precinct, and such other county officers as are or may be required by law For Chief Justice, Commissioners, County Clerk, &c.

to be elected by the people; an election shall be held biennially thereafter to fill such offices until otherwise provided by law.

For District Clerk.

ART. 637. [3] There shall be elected in accordance with law, on the first Monday in August, Anno Domini 1850, in each county in the State, one Clerk of the District Court; and elections shall be held on the same day every four years thereafter until otherwise provided by law.

Term of office.

ART. 638. [4] All of the officers elected by authority of the second section of this act, shall hold their offices for two years after their election, and until their successors be duly qualified.

Act of Dec. 5, 1849.

In case of vacancy in office of District Clerk.

ART. 639. [2] On the first Monday in August, in the year eighteen hundred and fifty, and on the first Monday in August every two years thereafter, a regular election shall be held in each and every county where vacancies have already occurred, or may hereafter occur, in the office of the Clerk of the District Court, by death, resignation, removal, or the lapse of four years from the date of the incumbent's election.

Act of Dec. 18, 1849.

Officers shall perform duties of office until.

ART. 640. [1] All officers of the State and of each district and county therein, when the time for which they were respectively elected or appointed shall have expired, shall be hereby authorized and empowered to perform the duties of their respective offices until their successors shall be duly qualified.

Act of Feb. 11, 1850.

Election of Attorney-General, District Attorney, Comptroller, &c.

ART. 641. [4] An election shall be held on the first Monday in August, one thousand eight hundred and fifty, for an Attorney General, Comptroller of Public Accounts, State Treasurer, and one District Attorney for each Judicial District; and it shall be the duty of the Governor, whenever a vacancy shall occur, from any cause, in the office of Justice of the Supreme Court, Judge of the District Court, Commissioner of the General Land Office, Attorney-General, Comptroller of Public Accounts, Treasurer of the State or District Attorney, to order a special election to fill such vacancies, after thirty days' notice; and whenever the term of any of said officers shall expire during the year previous to any regular election for State or county officers, it shall be the duty of the Governor to order an election to be held on the first Monday in August previous to the expiration of said term, and the person so elected shall qualify and enter on his duties at the expiration of such term; and it shall be the duty of the Governor to issue his proclamation, ordering all elections directed under the provisions of this act, at least thirty days before the period established for such election.

In case of vacancy in office of.

Vacancy in Congress.

ART. 642. [22] Whenever a vacancy shall occur in the office of Representative in the Congress of the United States, before the expiration of the term of any such Representative, or whenever there shall be a called session of the Congress of the United States after the expiration of the term of the Representative, and before a regular election shall have been held, it shall be the duty of the Governor to order a special election, after thirty days' notice, and the returns of any such election shall be made within forty days after said election, and in the same form as is prescribed for regular elections for said officers under this act, and all the other provisions of this act relating to regular elections, shall apply to and govern the said special elections so far as they are applicable.

In case of a tie.

ART. 643. [10] In case of a tie in any election for any office mentioned in the fourth section of this act, a new election shall be immediately held, for which purpose the Governor shall issue his proclamation, and therein appoint the time for holding and making returns of the same.

ART. 644. [26] In all cases where a county is not organized, and there is no officer in the same authorized by law to organize such county, the Chief Justice of the nearest county which is organized, may order elections for county officers, in any such disorganized county, and appoint the presiding officers and managers and clerks of election as prescribed by law in other cases. Act of March 16, 1848. Where county is not organized.

ART. 645. [27] If from any cause there should be a vacancy in the office of Chief Justice of any county, a majority of the Commissioners of the County Court shall order a new election to fill such vacancy, to be conducted in the same manner and form as other elections for county officers. Vacancy in office of Chief Justice, &c.

III. RETURNS.

ART. 646. [12] Immediately after closing the polls, the managers of the election shall proceed to count the votes, make out a correct return, signed by the managers, which shall be sealed up and delivered to the Chief Justice of the county, (or in the absence of the Chief Justice, to the Clerk of the County Court, who shall file the same in his office, and deliver the said return to the Chief Justice on the day appointed to open and compare the polls,) by one of the managers, or some other respectable person, who shall swear that he received the package from one of the managers, or the returning officer, and that the seals have not been broken since; which delivery shall be upon oath before the return day of said election; a duplicate of which return shall be kept by the presiding officer. Act of March 16, 1848. Count and returns.

ART. 647. [14] If any manager, or other person, to whom election returns shall have been entrusted, fails or refuses to deliver the same, on oath, to the Chief Justice, or County Clerk, or other officer ordering the election, within ten days of the day of election, such person so offending shall be liable to prosecution, by information or indictment, in the District Court of the county in which he so offends, and on conviction shall forfeit and pay or be fined in a sum not less than fifty nor more than five hundred dollars, to go to the county treasury. Failure to deliver. Quere? Repealed by Criminal Code.

ART. 648. [15] The election returns shall not be opened by the officer to whom they are returned before return day, or tenth day, and exclusive of the day of election; at the expiration of that time, he shall open them and estimate the result, recording the state of the polls of each precinct, in a book to be kept by him for that purpose; and after making such estimate, he shall deliver to the candidate or candidates for whom the greatest number of votes have been polled, a certificate of election, naming therein the office to which he has been elected, the number of votes polled for him, and the day on which the election was held, and shall sign the same, and cause the seal of the County Court to be thereon impressed, and shall also make returns of the result of the election for members of the Legislature to the Secretary of State. When returns shall be opened.

ART. 649. [16] When an election shall have been held for members of the Legislature, in a district composed of more counties than one, the Chief Justice or other officer, to whom the returns in each county may be made, who is not authorized to give certificates of election to such members of the Legislature, shall make out and send complete returns of such election for members of the Legislature in their respective counties, immediately after examining and recording the same, to the Chief Justice of the county who may be so authorized; which returns shall be se sealed up, and the name of the officer forwarding them written across the seal, and the package marked on the outside, "Election Returns," which package may be sent by mail; the Chief Justice to When district is composed of several counties

whom the returns are so forwarded shall upon the twentieth day after the election, which shall be the return day for such elections, open and examine said returns, and after estimating the result and recording the same, give a certificate of election to the candidate for whom the greatest number of votes shall have been polled.

Act of Feb. 11, 1850.

Vote for Governor, &c., to whom returned, &c.

ART. 650. [7] The Chief Justices or County Commissioners, in cases wherein they are authorized by law to discharge the duties of Chief Justices of the several counties of the State, shall promptly make duplicate returns of the elections for Governor and Lieutenant-Governor, carefully sealed up, one of which shall be transmitted to the Seat of Government, and directed to the Speaker of the House of Representatives, endorsed, "Election Returns of ——— county for ———, and the other shall be deposited in the office of the Clerk of the County Court.

Duplicate returns to be made except.

ART. 651. [8] The Chief Justices, or the County Commissioners, in cases wherein they are authorized by law to discharge the duties of Chief Justices of the several counties of the State, or district as the case may be, shall promptly make duplicate returns of elections for officers named in the sixth section of this act, except for Governor and Lieutenant-Governor, carefully sealed up, one of which shall be transmitted by them to the Seat of Government, directed to the Secretary of State, and endorsed, "Election Returns of ——— county for ———; the other shall be deposited in the office of the Clerk of the County Court.

Secretary of State shall open returns when.

ART. 652. [9] On the sixtieth day after every election, as provided for in this act, the Secretary of State, in presence of the Governor and Attorney-General, or in case of vacancy or inability of either of those officers to act, then any two of said officers shall open and count the returns which shall have been made as provided in the preceding section; and the Governor shall therefor deliver a certificate of election to the person or persons who shall have received the highest number of votes for each or any of said offices.

IV. CONTESTED ELECTIONS.

Act of March 16, 1848.

Notice of.

ART. 653. [18] Any person intending to contest the election of any one holding a certificate of election, shall, within ten days after the return day, give him notice thereof in writing, and deliver to him a written statement of the grounds on whichh he relies to sustain such contest; and the person elect as aforesaid, shall, within ten days after receiving such notice, deliver or cause to be delivered his reply to the statement of the contestor.(a)

How served.

ART. 654. [19] The notices and written statements provided for in the foregoing section, shall be served on the opposite party in person if he can be found, if not, then by leaving the same at his usual place of abode or business.

Trial of, for county officers.

ART. 655. [20] If the contest be for the validity of an election for any county officer, a copy of the notices and other papers served on the parties, shall be filed with the Clerk of the County Court; and as soon as convenient the County Court shall convene in special session for the trial of the contest, notice of the time of meeting having been given to the parties; and if on trial any votes be found to be illegal, the court shall subtract such votes from

(a) The party intending to contest the election, to enable himself to do so, must, within the ten days, give the notice and written statement to the opposite party, as required by the act, as the predicate upon which the power of the court is to be set in motion. Lindsey v. Luckett, 20 Tex. Rep., 516.

the poll of the candidate for whom they are given, and shall also hear and consider the evidence given by the parties for and against the grounds assumed by them on their written statement, and no other; and after a full and fair investigation they shall decide to whom the office belongs, or set the election aside, and order a new one, as the case may require.(*a*)

Art. 656. [21] If the contest be for the trial of the validity of an election for members of the Legislature, a copy of the notices and other papers served on the parties as required in the 18th and 19th sections of this act, shall within ten days after the service thereof, be filed with the Chief Justice or officer to whom the returns are made; and he shall envelope the same, together with a copy of the poll-book or register of each precinct or county returned to him, and seal the same, writing his name across the seals, and shall address the packet to the Speaker of the House of Representatives, or President of the Senate, as the case may be; and shall forward the same by mail to the Seat of Government so as to reach there before the convening of the Legislature if possible. For members of the Legislature.

Art. 657. [22] In the cases provided for in the preceding section, so soon as the notice and other papers are filed, either party may apply to the Clerk of the County Court for a commission to be directed to some Notary Public, or two Justices of the Peace, to act as commissioners in taking testimony by deposition, touching the pending contest; of the time and place of taking testimony, both parties shall be notified by the commissioners; no witness shall be examined without such notice, except in the presence of the parties or their attorneys; and the examination shall be conducted according to the rules of evidence; not more than fifteen days from the issuance of the commission shall be allowed to take testimony, and at the expiration of that time the commissioner shall return the testimony written in a fair hand and signed by the several witnesses, and transfer to the Clerk of the County Court, who shall seal the same, and address and send them by mail to the Speaker of the House of Representatives, or President of the Senate, as the case may be, endorsing on the outside what it contains. Depositions may be taken, &c.

Art. 658. [11] Contested elections for the office of District Attorney shall be tried by the District Judge of the District, in the county where the candidate who shall have received the certificate of election shall reside. Act of Feb. 11, 1850. For District Attorney.

Art. 659. [12] Contested elections for the office of District Judge, shall be tried in the county of the adjoining district, the county seat of which is nearest to the residence of the candidate who shall have received the certificate of election, and by the District Judge of such adjoining district. For District Judge.

Art. 660. [13] Contested elections for the office of Justice of the Supreme Court, Commissioner of the General Land Office, Comptroller of Public Accounts, Attorney-General or State Treasurer, shall be tried in the county, and by the District Judge of the district where the Seat of Government shall be located. For Justices of Supreme Court.

Art. 661. [14] Any candidate who shall intend to contest an election for any office mentioned in either of the three preceding sections, shall within thirty days after the certificate of election shall have been made, give notice to the candidate in whose favor such certificate shall have been made, of the grounds upon which he intends to rely on the trial of such contest, and shall within the same period cause a copy thereof to be filed in the office of the District Clerk of the county where such contest is to be tried. When notice to be given.

(*a*) There is no mode of revising the action of the County Court, under this statute, in cases of contested elections of county officers; it is conclusive. O'Docherty *v.* Archer, 9 Tex. Rep. 295.

When answer to be delivered. ART. 662. [15] The party in whose favor the certificate of election shall have been made, shall within twenty days after the receipt of notice, as provided in the preceding section, cause an answer thereto to be delivered to the contesting party, and shall within the same period cause a copy thereof to be filed in the office of the District Clerk of the county where such contest is to be tried.

Commission to take depositions ART. 663. [16] As soon as either party shall have complied with the requirements of the two preceding sections, he may obtain a commission or commissions to take depositions of witnesses in any part of the State, upon the same terms and under the same rules and regulations as are provided for obtaining commissions and returning depositions in civil suits.

Time allowed for taking. ART. 664. [17] In case of a contested election for the office of District Judge or District Attorney, one month shall be allowed; in cases of a contested election for the office of Justice of the Supreme Court, Commissioner of the General Land Office, Comptroller of Public Accounts, Attorney-General, or State Treasurer, three months shall be allowed to each party from the date of the filing of his claim, or answering, for taking testimony.

When returned. ART. 665. [18] It shall be the duty of the District Judge, in the cases named in this act, at the next regular term of the court in the county where any contested election is to be tried, after the expiration of the time allowed for taking testimony, to hear and determine such contested election.

Shall be tried on ART. 666. [19] The trial of every contested election shall be by the Judge, upon the depositions, taken in the mode prescribed in this act.

Appeal. ART. 667. [20] Either party may appeal from the decision of the District Judge to the Supreme Court, and the party against whom the case shall be finally determined, shall pay all the costs of the proceeding, for which judgment shall be rendered as in other cases.

Certified copy of decision, &c. ART. 668. [21] The party receiving a certificate of election shall perform the duties of the office until the contested election is decided; and a certified copy of such decision shall be sufficient evidence for the issuance of a commission to the successful party. No commission shall issue in any case until the time allowed for giving notice of a contested election shall have expired.

ELECTORS FOR PRESIDENT AND VICE PRESIDENT.

Act of March 15, 1848. In force from passage.

Time of election ART. 669. [1] On the Tuesday next after the first Monday in November, A. D. 1848, and on the first Tuesday next after the first Monday in November, every four years thereafter, the qualified electors for members of the House of Representatives of the State Legislature shall elect from among the resident citizens of the State, over twenty-one years of age, and not members of either House of Congress, as many Electors of President and Vice-President of the United States, as the State of Texas may at the time be entitled to.

Mode and places of. ART. 670. [2] Said contemplated election shall be held in the same manner, at the same places, under the same regulations, and by officers and managers appointed in the same way as elections for members of the House of Representatives of this State may be; except that each qualified voter shall be authorized to vote for the whole number of Electors that the State will then be empowered to elect.

Art. 671. [3] The officers conducting said elections, or the managers thereof, at each precinct shall,—under the penalty of one hundred dollars, recoverable in the name of the Governor for the use of the State, on motion made in the District Court by the District Attorney, after ten days' previous notice given to the officer or officers failing to make return—within three days after holding the same, correctly add up and compare the number of votes given for each person there voted for as an Elector; and shall make out in writing, seal up, certify, and transmit the result of said election to the Chief Justice, or other proper officer of their county, in the manner prescribed by the laws regulating elections for members of the State Legislature. Returns of by officers holding.

Art. 672. [4] It shall be and is hereby made the duty of the Chief Justice, or other proper officer, of each county, within four days after the election, under the penalty of five hundred dollars,—recoverable in the name of the Governor for the use of the State, on motion made in the District Court by the District Attorney, after ten days' previous notice given to the officer failing to make return,—to make out in writing, certify, seal up, and transmit by mail, or other expeditious conveyance, a correct statement of the election held at all the precincts in his county, directed to the Secretary of State at the seat of government of the State, as is now required by law in other elections, and endorsed thereon: "Election returns for the county of ———," as the same may be. Returns by Chief Justice, &c.

Art. 673. [5] It shall be the duty of the Secretary of State, in presence of the Governor, Lieutenant Governor, and Attorney General, or any or either of them, on the fourth Monday in November next after said election, to open all the election returns received by him, and correctly add up all the votes cast in the several counties for each of said Electors, and cause the result thereof, with the names of the persons elected, to be forthwith published in some newspaper printed at the seat of government for this State, and in writing notify the persons elected, respectively of their election; and in the event of a failure to perform the duties in this act prescribed, and in the manner specified, said Secretary of State shall forfeit and pay to the Governor for the use of the State, the sum of one thousand dollars, which may be recovered by the Attorney General, upon motion made in the District Court of the county in which the seat of government may be then located, after giving ten days' notice thereof in writing to the Secretary of State. Secretary of State shall open, count, &c.

Art. 674. [6] The Electors so chosen shall convene in the capitol, at the seat of government for the State, on the first Wednesday of December next after their election, and vote for President and Vice-President of the United States, and make return thereof as is required by the laws of the United States. Electors shall convene at the Capitol.

Art. 675. [7] If any person so chosen Elector shall, by death or other disabling cause, fail to attend by the hour of two o'clock in the afternoon of the day pointed out in this act, and vote as hereby required, a majority of the Electors present, after having convened in accordance with the provisions of this act, may appoint some other person to act in the place of the absentee, and shall immediately report their action to the Secretary of State aforesaid. Place of absentee, how suplied.

Art. 676. [8] The Governor shall, on or before the meeting of the Electors, cause three lists of the names of such Electors to be made out and delivered to them as required by act of Congress. List of electors to be delivered, &c.

Gov'r to issue proclamation.

ART. 677. [9] For the purpose of carrying this act into effect, it shall be the duty of the Governor, or in case of his inablity, then of the Lieutenant-Governor, periodically, as herein specified, to issue a proclamation under the seal of the State, and have the same published, for at least six weeks before the election, in some newspaper printed at the seat of government, requiring the Chief Justice or other proper officer of each county in the State to cause an election to be held at each precinct in his county, at the time and for the purpose prescribed in and by this act.

Act of Dec. 1, 1849. Took effect Mar. 23, 1850.

Pay of Electors.

ART. 678. [1] The Electors of President and Vice-President of the United States shall receive the same pay for mileage in travelling to and from the seat of government of the State, and the same pay daily, while engaged there in the performance of the duties required of them by law, as that allowed by law to the members of the Legislature of said State.

ESCHEAT.

Act of March 20, 1848. Took effect Ap'l 29, 1848.

When property escheats.

ART. 679. [1] If any person die seized of any real or possessed of any personal estate, without any devise thereof, and having no heirs; or where the owner of any real or personal estate shall be absent for the term of seven years, and is not known to exist, such estate shall escheat to and vest in the State.

Proceedings when executor does not qualify, and adm'r is appointed.

ART. 680. [2] When the District Attorney shall be informed, or have reason to believe that an executor under the will, has not accepted the trust, and that no administrator with the will annexed, has been appointed; and where said Attorneys shall discover that no letters of administration on the estate of an intestate, who has died without heirs, has been granted, he shall file a petition in behalf of the State, in the District Court of the County where such succession is required to be opened, according to the laws regulating the place of opening successions, which petition shall set forth a description of the estate, the name of the person last lawfully seized or possessed of the same, the names of the tenants or persons in actual possession, if any, and the names of the persons claiming the estate, if any such are known to claim, and the facts and circumstances in consequence of which such estate is claimed to have escheated; praying for a writ of possession for the same in behalf of the State.

Scire facias shall issue, &c.

ART. 681. [3] Such court shall award and issue scire facias against such person, bodies politic or corporate, as shall be alleged in such petition to hold possession or claim such estate, requiring them to appear and show cause why such estate shall not be vested in the State, at the next term of the court.

Service of, and blication of ice.

ART. 682. [4] Such scire facias shall be served ten days before the return day thereof; and the court shall make an order, setting forth briefly the contents of such petition, and requiring all persons interested in the estate to appear and show cause at the next term of said court why the same should not be vested in the State, which order shall be published four weeks in some news paper printed in the State.

ART. 683. [5] All persons, bodies politic, and bodies corporate named in such petition, as tenants or persons in actual possession or claimants of the estate, may appear and plead to such proceedings, and may traverse the facts stated in the petition, or the title of the State to the lands and tenements therein mentioned, at any time on or before the third day after the return of scire facias; and any other person claiming an interest in such estate, may appear and be made a defendant, and plead by motion for that purpose in open court, within the time allowed for pleading. When defendants must plead, &c.

ART. 684. [6] If no person, after notice as aforesaid, shall appear and plead within the time prescribed by law, then judgment shall be rendered, by default, in behalf of the State. Judgment by default.

ART. 685. [7] If any person appear and deny the title set up by the State, or traverse any material fact in the petition, issue shall be made up and tried as other issues of fact; and a survey may be ordered as in other cases where the titles or boundaries of land are drawn in question. Answer—Order of survey, when.

ART. 686. [8] If after the issue and trial, it appears from the facts found or admitted, that the State hath good title to the estate, real or personal, in the petition mentioned or any part thereof, judgment shall be rendered, that the State shall be seized or possessed thereof, and, at the discretion of the court, recover costs against the defendants. Judgment for the State, &c.

ART. 687. [9] If it appear that the State hath no title in such estate, the defendant shall recover his costs, to be taxed and certified by the Clerk; and the Comptroller of Public Accounts, shall, on such certificate being filed in his office, issue a warrant therefor on the Treasury of the State, which shall be paid as other demands on the Treasury. Costs, when paid by State.

ART. 688. [10] When any judgment shall be rendered, that the State be seized or possessed of any estate, such judgment shall contain a description thereof, and shall vest the title in the State. Judgment, what it shall contain.

ART. 689. [11] A writ shall be issued to the Sheriff of the proper county, commanding him to seize such estate, vested in the State; and if the same be personal property, or real estate, he shall dispose thereof at public auction, in the manner provided by law for the sale of property under execution. Property to be sold.

ART. 690. [12] The District Attorney for the district, shall cause two copies of the record and account of sale to be exemplified under the seal of the court, and shall cause one of the same to be deposited in the office of the Comptroller of Public Accounts, and the other to be recorded in the office of the Recorder of the county in which the property was sold; and such record shall preclude all parties and privies thereto, their heirs and assigns. Copies of record to be filed, duty of Dis't Att'y.

ART. 691. [13] Any party who shall have appeared to any proceedings, and the District Attorney, on behalf of the State, shall have the right to prosecute an appeal or writ of error upon such judgment. Appeal and writ of error—right to.

ART. 692. [14] The Comptroller shall keep just accounts of all moneys paid into the Treasury, and of all lands vested in the State under the provisions of this act. Duty of Comptroller.

ART. 693. [15] If any person appear, after the death of the testator or intestate, and claim any money paid into the Treasury under this act, as heir, or devisee, or legatee thereof, he may file a petition in the District Court for the county where the estate was sold, stating the nature of his claim, and praying that such money may be paid to him; a copy of which petition shall Heir or devisee may sue, when.

be served on the District Attorney for the district, at least twenty days previous to the return day of the process, who shall put in answer to the same.

Duty of the court, if claim of heir, &c., be valid. ART. 694. [16] The court shall examine the claim and the allegations and proofs, and if they shall find that such person is an heir, devisee, legatee, or legal representative, whether citizen or foreigner, such court shall make an order, directing the Comptroller to issue his warrant on the Treasury for the payment of the same, but without interest or costs; a copy of which order, under the seal of the court, shall be a sufficient voucher for issuing such warrant; and the same proceedings shall be instituted for the recovery of any money or property heretofore deposited with the Treasurer or Comptroller in accordance with the laws heretofore existing.

Dis't Attorney shall examine proceedings of successions, &c. ART. 695. [17] It shall be the duty of the District Attorney, to examine the proceedings in successions, heretofore opened in any Probate Courts in their districts, and if it appears that any Clerk of the Probate Court, any executor or administrator, has failed to pay over to the Treasurer of the late Republic any moneys or funds, in the manner heretofore provided by law, or has failed to deposit any title papers to land, which have not been claimed by any heir, devisee, or legal representative, he shall notify such person to pay and deliver over the same to him, according to the provisions of this act, and on failure of such persons so to do, institute legal proceedings against him, to carry into effect the object of this act.

Property shall remain subject to, &c. ART. 696. [18] All property escheated under the provisions of this act, shall remain subject to the disposition of the State, as may hereafter be prescribed by law.

ESTATES OF DECEASED PERSONS.

[*See County Court—Marital Rights—Subdivision Community Property.*]

PROBATE OF WILLS—GRANT OF LETTERS TESTAMENTARY AND OF ADMINISTRATION.

(See Wills.)

II. REMOVAL AND RESIGNATION OF EXECUTORS AND ADMINISTRATORS.

III. OATH AND BOND.

IV. APPRAISEMENT AND INVENTORY.

V. PRESERVATION, RENT AND HIRE OF PROPERTY OF THE ESTATE.

VI. DEBTS DUE ESTATE.

VII. ALLOWANCE TO WIDOW AND CHILDREN.

VIII. CLAIMS AGAINST ESTATE.

IX. SALE OF PROPERTY OF ESTATE.

X. PAYMENT OF THE DEBTS OF ESTATE.

XI. PARTITION AND DISTRIBUTION.

(See Partition.)

I. PROBATE OF WILLS—AND GRANT OF LETTERS TESTAMENTARY AND OF ADMINISTRATION.

Act of March 20 1848. Took effect 7th August, 1848.

Letters of administration where granted.

ART. 697. [1] Wills shall be admitted to probate, and letters testamentary or of administration shall be granted in the county where the deceased resided, if he had a domicil, or fixed place of residence in the State: If the deceased had no domicil, or fixed place of residence in the State, but died in the State, then either in the county where his principal property was, at the time of his death, or in the county where he died: If he had no domicil, or fixed place of residence in the State, and died without the limits of the State, then in any county in this State where his nearest kin may reside; but if he had no kindred in the State, then in the county where his principal estate may be situted.

Application in writing, &c.

See wills.

ART. 698. [2] All applications for the probate of wills, and for letters testamentary, or of administration, shall be in writing and filed with the Clerk of the County Court. Upon the filing of any such application, it shall be the duty of the Clerk to give at least ten days' notice thereof, by advertisement posted at the court-house, and at two other public places in the county, not in the same city or town; and proof that such notice has been given, shall be made to the satisfaction of the court before any action shall be had on such application.

Will, how proven.

ART. 699. [3] A written will may be proved by the affidavit in writing of one of the subscribing witnesses thereto, taken in open court, and subscribed by the witness. If all the witnesses are non-residents of the county, or those resident in the county are unable to attend the court, it may be proved by the testimony of any one or more of them, taken by deposition. If none of the witnesses are living, such a will may be probated on proof by two witnesses of the hand writing of the subscribing witnesses, and also of the testator, if he was able to write; which proof may be either by affidavit taken in open court and subscribed by the witnesses, or by deposition: If the will was wholly written by the testator it may be probated on proof by two witnesses of his handwriting, which proof may also be made either by affidavit taken in open court and subscribed by the witnesses or by deposition; such affidavits or depositions shall be filed in the court, and, together with the will shall be recorded by the Clerk; and in any suit that may afterwards be instituted to contest the validity of any such will, such record shall be evidence, if the witness or witnesses be dead or resident without the county. Any person interested in any such will may, within four years after it is admitted to probate, institute suit in the District Court to contest its validity: provided, that infants, *femes covert*, and persons *non compos mentis*, shall have the like period after the removal of their respective disabilities; and, provided, also, that any such will may be attacked for forgery or any other fraud, at the suit of any heir at law of the testator, or any other person interested in his estate, at any time within four years after the discovery of such forgery or other fraud; and infants, *femes covert*, and persons *non compos mentis* shall have a like period after the removal of their respective disabilities. May be contested.

ART. 700. [4] No nuncupative will shall be proved within fourteen days after the death of the testator; nor until those who would have been entitled by inheritance, had there been no will, have been cited to contest the same, if they please; nor shall any such will be probated after six months have elapsed, from the time of speaking the pretended testamentary words, unless the same or the substance thereof shall have been committed to writing within six days after making such will; nor shall any such will be probated unless it be made in the time of the last sickness of the deceased, at his or her habitation, or where he or she hath resided, for ten days next preceding, except when the deceased is taken sick away from home, and dies before he or she returns to such habitation; nor shall any such will be probated unless it be proved by three credible witnesses, that the testator or testatrix called on some person to take notice, or bear testimony that such is his or her will, or words of like import; and whenever any such will may be probated, the evidence of the witnesses shall be committed to writing, sworn to and subscribed, in open court, by the witnesses, and shall be recorded by the Clerk.(*a*) Nuncupative will, how proven.

ART. 701. [5] When application is made for the probate of a will, which has been probated according to the laws of any of the United States or territories, or of any country out of the limits of the United States, a copy of such will and of the probate thereof, attested by the Clerk of the court in which such will was admitted to probate, and the seal of the court annexed, if there be a seal, together with a certificate from the Judge, Chief Justice, or presiding magistrate, as the case may be, that the said attestation is in due form, may be filed and recorded in the court, and shall have the same force and effect as the original will, if probated in said court: provided, that the validity of such will may be contested in the same manner as the original might have been.(*b*) Probate of will, made and probated in another State. May be contested.

ART. 702. [6] Application for the probate of a will, may be made by the testamentary executor, or by any person interested in the estate of the testator. Application, by whom made.

ART. 703 [7] When application is made for the probate of a will, any person interested in the estate of the testator, may, at any time before trial, file his

(*a*) A nuncupative will cannot be sustained in any other cases than those pescribed by the statute. Jones *v.* Norton, 10 Tex. Rep. 120. Mere declaration of a person in good health as to his wishes respecting the disposition of his property in case of his death, which he anticipated might some day suddenly occur, even where his death did occur soon afterwards, are not sufficient to establish a nuncupative will. Ibid.

(*b*) It is not necessary in order to admit a will probated in another State, to record here and give it the effect contemplated by the statute to prove by evidence *aliunde*, that it had been probated according to the laws of such other State. Houze *v.* Houze, Ex'r, 16 Tex. Rep. 598.

Objection to be in writing. Evidence to be taken down in writing. opposition thereto, in writing, and on the trial of the matter, all oral testimony shall be take down in writing and subscribed by the witness or witnesses: copies of all testimony so taken, and also of the testimony of witnesses taken by deposition, shall be admitted in evidence on the trial of the same matter in any other court, when taken there by appeal or otherwise.

Letters to executors. ART. 704. [8] When a will shall have been probated, it shall be the duty of the court to grant letters testamentary to the executor or executors appointed by such will, if any there be, or to such of them as are not disqualified and are willing to accept the trust, and qualify according to law, within twenty days after such probate.

If executors fail to qualify, admr. to be appointed. ART. 705. [9] When any person shall die intestate, or when no executor is named in a will, or when the executor or executors named in a will are disqualified, or shall renounce the executorship, or shall neglect to accept and qualify, within twenty days after the probate of the will, or shall neglect for a period of thirty days, after the death of the testator, to present the will for probate;(*a*) then, administration of the estate of such intestate or administration with the will annexed of the estate of such testator, shall be granted: Who is entitled. first, to the surviving husband or surviving wife: second, to the next of kin, or the principal devisee or legatee of such intestate or testator, or to some one or more of them; and if none of these apply, or, if applying they neglect to qualify for a period of twenty days, after the order for their appointment, then to such other proper person or persons as will accept and qualify.(*b*)

Who shall not administer. ART. 706. [10] Letters testamentary or of administration, shall not be granted to any person who is under twenty-one years of age, or of unsound mind, or who has been convicted of any infamous crime; provided, however, that such letters may be granted to a surviving husband or wife who may be under twenty-one years of age.

Ex'rs. under age may administer when. ART. 707. [11] When the executor or executors named in a will are under age, and letters of administration, with the will annexed, have been granted to any other person or persons, such letters shall, at any time thereafter, be revoked, on the application of such executor or executors, or any one of them, and letters testamentary issued to such executor or executors, or any of them, upon proof being made that he or they have attained the age of twenty-one years; and when two or more persons are named executors in a will, any one or more of whom are minors when such will is admitted to probate, and letters testamentary have been issued to such only as are of full age, such minor or minors, upon attaining the age of twenty-one years, shall be permitted to qualify and receive letters.

Ex'r. absent when the will is proven, &c. ART. 708. [12] Whenever any person named as executor, shall have been absent from the State when the testator died, or when the will was proved, whereby he was prevented from presenting the will for probate within thirty days after the death of the testator, or from accepting and qualifying as executor within twenty days after the probate of the will; or whenever he shall have been prevented by sickness from so presenting the will, or so accepting and qualifying, he shall be allowed to accept and qualify as executor at any time within sixty days after his return to the State, or his recovery from sickness, upon making proof to the court that he was so absent or so prevented by sickness:(*c*) and,

(*a*) The term used as a basis of a penalty or forfeiture must be the neglect of a known duty. Stone *v.* Brown, 16 Tex. Rep. 425. The neglect must be wilful, and not merely a failure caused by ignorance of law.—Ibid.

(*b*) The statute does not give the preference to a creditor over any other suitable person. After the next of kin and principal devisee and legatee, it enjoins upon the court the duty of appointing such persons as will accept and qualify. Cain *v.* Haas, 18 Tex. Rep. 616.

(*c*) This statute does not preclude the executor named in the will and who has neglected to present it for probate within thirty days, in a controversy as to the right to administer from showing a reasonable excuse for not presenting the will for probate within the thirty days. Stone *v.* Brown, 16 Tex. Rep. 425.

if in the meantime letters of administration with the will annexed, have been granted, such letters shall be revoked; provided he shall have first caused the person to whom letters have been granted to be cited to appear before said court, and show cause why said letters should not be revoked. Former adm'r to be cited.

ART. 709. [13] When administration has been granted to any other person or persons than the surviving husband, or surviving wife, of the testator or intestate, upon application being made by him or her, such other person or persons shall be removed from the administration, and letters of administration to such applicant. Surviving husband or wife may be appointed and adm'r removed.

ART. 710. [14] When administration has been granted to any other persons than the surviving husband or surviving wife, or the next of kin, or the principal devisee or legatee, of the intestate, or testator, upon application being made by the next of kin, or the principal devisee or legatee of such intestate or testator or any of them, such other person or persons shall be removed from the administration, and letters shall be granted to such next of kin or principal devisee or legatee or to some one or more of them.(*a*) Next of kin.

ART. 711. [15] Whenever letters of administration shall have been granted upon an estate, and it shall afterwards be discovered that the deceased left a lawful will, such will may be proved in the manner provided in this Act; and if an executor is named in such will he shall be allowed to accept and qualify in the manner herein provided; but if no such executor be named, or if the executor named be disqualified or shall renounce the executorship, or shall neglect to accept and qualify within twenty days after the probate of the will, or shall neglect for a period of thirty days after the discovery of such will to present it for probate, then administration with the will annexed, of the estate of such testator, shall be granted according to the provisions of this Act; and whenever any such executor shall accept and qualify, or whenever any person shall be appointed and qualified as administrator with the will annexed, the letters of administration previously granted shall be revoked; but all acts done by the first administrator, previous to the qualification of the executor or administrator with the will annexed, shall be as valied as if no such will had been discovered.(*b*) Probate of will after grant of letters. Right of executor under it. Letters revoked when.

ART. 712. [16] When a will has been admitted to probate, in any of the United States, or the territories thereof, or of any country out of the limits of the United States, and the executor or executors named in such will, have qualified, and a copy of such will, and of the probate thereof, has been filed and recorded in any court of this State, under the provisions of the fifth section of this Act, and letters of administration with such will annexed, have been granted to any other person or persons than the executor or executors therein named, upon the application of such executor or executors, or any one of them, such letters shall be revoked, and letters testamentary shall be issued to such applicant. Probate of will in any State, or out of the U. S. &c. Letters granted in Texas to be revoked, &c.

ART. 713. [17] When application is made for letters of administration, any person may, at any time before the said application is granted, file his opposition thereto in writing, and may apply for the grant of letters to himself or to any other person; and upon the trial, the court shall grant letters to the person or persons that may seem best entitled to them, having regard to the provisions of this act, without further notice than that of the original application. Application for letters may be contested.

(*a*) A stranger and the next of kin filed applications for letters of administration, and the latter withdrew his application, whereupon the former was appointed, it was held that the next of kin thereby waived his right to the administration, and could not afterwards come in under the statute and have the first appointee removed and himself substituted. Cole *v.* Dial, Adm'r 12 Tex. Rep. 100.

(*b*) Stone *v.* Brown, 16 Tex. Rep, 425.

Administrator *de bonis non*, when appointed.

ART. 714. [18] Whenever an estate is unrepresented, by reason of the death, removal, or resignation of the executor or executors, or administrator or administrators, the court shall grant administration with the will annexed, of the estate not administered, or administration of the estate not administered, as the case may be, in the same manner and under the regulations herein prescribed for the appointment of original administrators.

Clerk to issue letters.

ART. 715. [26] Whenever an executor or administrator has been qualified in the manner required in this act, it shall be the duty of the Clerk to make out and deliver to such executor or administrator, letters testamentary or of administration, as the case may be, which letters shall be signed by the Chief Justice and attested by the Clerk, with his signature and the seal of the court; and either said letters or a certificate of the Clerk, with the seal of the court affixed, that such letters have been issued, shall be sufficient evidence of the appointment and qualification of an executor or administrator, whenever it shall be necessary to make proof thereof.

Wills must be proven and letters granted in open court.

ART. 716. [27] Wills shall be probated, and letters testamentary or of administration, with full powers, shall be granted only in open court at a regular term thereof, after application in writing, and notice, as herein before required; but whenever it may appear to the Chief Justice, that the interest of an estate requires the immediate appointment of an administrator, he shall either in open court or in vacation, by writing under his hand and the seal of the court, attested by the Clerk, appoint some proper person administrator pro tem., with such limited powers as the circumstances of the case may require. Such appointment may be made without notice—shall define the powers conferred, and before being delivered to the person appointed, shall be recorded in the minutes of the court; and the Clerk shall endorse thereon a certificate that it has been so recorded; and until such record and certificate are made, the appointment shall not take effect:(*a*) such appointment shall cease to be of force on the first day of the term of the court next after the date thereof; unless continued in force by an order entered on the minutes in open court; and in no case shall such appointment continue in force beyond the first day of the second term of the court next after the date thereof.

Letters granted in vacation, when.

Duty of Chief Justice pending contested will.

ART. 717. [28] Pending any contest relative to the probate of a will, or the granting of letters of administration, whether such contest be in the County Court, or in any other court on appeal, it shall be the duty of the Chief Justice to appoint an administrator pro tem., in the manner prescribed in the preceding section, and with such limited powers as the circumstances of the case may require: such appointment may continue in force until the termination of the contest, and the appointment of an executor or administrator with full powers.(*b*)

Oath and bond to be filed.

ART. 718. [29] Before the issuance of letters of administration pro tem., under the provisions of the two preceding sections, the person appointed shall take and subscribe an oath and enter into bond; which bond and oath shall be, in substance, the same as the bond and oath required of other administrators, varying the forms to suit the particular case; and such bond and oath shall be filed and recorded in the like manner as other bonds of administrators.

(See arts. 727 and 730.)

One administrator or executor may act when others neglect.

ART. 719. [74] If there be more than one executor or administrator named in the letters, any one or more of them, on the neglect of the rest, may return an inventory as required by this act; and the executor or administrator

(*a*) If the appointment of an administrator *pro tem.* does not conform to the statute, it must be treated as a nullity. Alexander *v.* Barfield and another, 6 Tex. Rep. 400.

(*b*) The designation of an administrator *pro tem.* by the terms "*pendente lite.*" is not fatal to the grant; but the former terms, being those employed in the statute, should be used by the court from which the letters issue. Fisk *v.* Norvell, 9 Tex. Rep. 13.

so neglecting shall not thereafter interfere with the estate, or have any power over the same; but the executor or administrator so returning shall have thereafter the whole administration, unless within two months after the return, the delinquent or delinquents shall assign to the court some reasonable excuse which it shall deem satisfactory.

Rights of administrators *de bonis non.*

ART. 720. [115] When an administrator of the estate not administered has been or shall be hereafter appointed, he shall succeed to all the rights, powers and duties of the former executor or administrator, except such rights and powers conferred on the former executor by the will of the testator, as are different from those conferred by this act on executors generally; and such administrators shall have power to make themselves parties to all suits prosecuted by the former executor or administrator of the estate, and may be made parties to all suits prosecuted against the former executor or administrator of the estate. They shall have power to settle with the former executor or administrator of the estate, and to receive and receipt for all such portion of the estate as remains in their hands; they shall have power to bring suit on the bond or bonds of the former executor or administrator in their own name as administrator for all the estate that has not been accounted for by such former executor or administrator; and they shall proceed to administer such estate in like manner as if their administration was a continuation of the administration of the former executor or administrator, with the exceptions herein before named; but such administrators shall, within one month after their being qualified, return an inventory and list of claims, in like manner as is required in this act, for original administrators; and they shall also in like manner return additional inventories and lists of claims; and whenever an executor shall accept and qualify, after letters of administration shall have been granted, such executor shall in like manner succeed to the previous administrator; and he shall proceed to administer the estate in like manner as if his administration was a continuation of the former one; subject, however, to any legal directions of the testator, in relation to the management of the estate.(*a*)

Shall return inventory in like manner, &c.

Appointment of administrator in place of *pro tem.* shall be party to suits, &c.

ART. 721. [116] Whenever, under the provisions of this act, an administrator *pro tem.* shall have been appointed, and an executor shall afterwards be qualified, or an administrator appointed, such executor or administrator shall succeed and be made a party to all suits and actions prosecuted by or against such administrator *pro tem.*; and such executor or administrator shall have the right to settle with such administrator *pro tem.*, and receive and receipt for all the estate remaining in his hands: and shall have the right to sue in like manner as is provided for in the previous section, on the bond of such administrator *pro tem.* for all the estate not accounted for by him.

(*a*) Where assets have been fraudulently alienated by an administrator, in collusion with the vendee, they may be pursued by an administrator *de bonis non*; and the fact that a judgment has intervened, if obtained through fraud, cannot affect the principle or vary the rights of the parties. DeWitt et al. *v.* Miller's Administrator, 9 Tex. Rep. 239. This section extends to the whole estate in the hands of the former administrator. Miller, Adm'r, *v.* Jasper, 10 Tex. Rep. 513. The cases provided for in this section, are the only cases in which suits can be maintained by an administrator *de bonis non* against the former administrator. Murphy, Adm'r *de bonis non v.* Menard, 11 Tex. Rep. 673. He may maintain a suit against the administrator and the sureties on his bond for the value of assets which came to the hands of such former administrator, and which he failed to account for. Martel *v.* Martel, 17 Tex. Rep. 391. It is not necessary that the abuse of trust on the part of the former administrator should first be established in the Probate Court, analagous to a devastavit, before suit can be brought in the District Court on the administration bond. Francis *v.* Northcote, 6 Tex. Rep. 185. This act confers no jurisdiction on the County Courts over executors or administrators who had resigned under the former law. Ingram *v.* Maynard, 6 Tex. Rep. 130.

II. REMOVAL AND RESIGNATION OF EXECUTORS AND ADMINISTRATORS.

Chief Justice may remove, when.

ART. 722. [34] Executors and administrators shall be removed by the Chief Justice, without notice, in term time, by an order entered on the minutes of the court, in the following cases:

1st. When they neglect to qualify in the manner required by this act, within twenty days after the will is probated, or the order is made for granting of their letters.

2d. When they shall neglect to return to the court, within sixty days after receiving their letters, an inventory of the estate committed to their charge, so far as the same has come to their knowledge.

3d. When they have been required to give a new bond, and neglect to do so within the time prescribed by the court.

4th. When they absent themselves from the State, for a period of three months, without the permission of the court.

With notice, when.

ART. 723. [35] Executors and administrators may be removed by the Chief Justice, of his own motion, or on the complaint of any person interested in the estate, after being cited to answer such complaint or motion in the following cases:

1st. When they shall fail to make to the court any exhibit that they are required to make, by the provisions of this act; or when they shall fail to comply with any order that the Chief Justice is authorized to make against them, under the provisions of the same.

2d. When there shall appear sufficient grounds to believe that they have, or are about to misapply, embezzle, or remove from the State, the property committed to their charge.

3d. When they are proved to have been guilty of gross neglect, or mismanagement, in the performance of any of their duties.

4th. When they fail to obey any order of the court consistent with this act, in relation to the estate committed to their charge:

In the cases enumerated in this section, on proof being made that the executor or administrator has removed from the State, or otherwise endeavored to elude the service of process, on any such complaint or motion; the same may be heard and determined, though the citation be not served; and in all cases where an executor or administrator is removed, the causes of such removal shall be set forth in the order of removal.

Who shall not be appointed.

ART. 724. [36] If any person named as executor, shall have renounced the executorship, or shall have been removed therefrom, he shall not afterwards be appointed administrator of the estate; and whenever any person shall have been removed from the administration of an estate, he shall not afterwards be appointed administrator thereof.

Resignation of Administrator or Executor.

ART. 725. [37] If at any time an executor or administrator, shall wish to resign the administration of the estate that has been committed to his charge, he may present to the court from which his letters issued, a full and complete exhibit of the condition of the estate, together with his administration account —both of which shall be verified by affidavit—and also his application in writing for leave to resign: (*a*) whereupon it shall be the duty of the Clerk to make out a citation, returnable to some regular term of the court; which citation shall state the presentation of such exhibit, account and application, the term of the court to which it is returnable, and shall require all those

(*a*) An executor or administrator cannot resign and become discharged of his trust, until he has first accounted for and delivered the estate to some party entitled to receive it. Ingram *v.* Maynard, 6 Tex. Rep., 130.

interested in the estate to appear and contest such account, if they see proper. Such citation shall be published for at least twenty days in some newspaper printed in the county, if there be one: if not, then by posting copies thereof for a like period at three public places in the county: proof of such publication may be made by the affidavit of the publisher or printer, attached to a copy thereof. At the return term of such citation, or at some other term to which it may have been continued, upon the Chief Justice being satisfied that such citation has been published, or posted, as the case may be, he shall proceed to examine such exhibit and account, and to hear all proofs that may be offered in support of the same, and all objections and exceptions thereto; and shall if necessary, restate such accounts; and shall audit and settle the same. If it shall then appear that such executor or administrator has accounted for all said estate, according to law, the Chief Justice shall order him to deliver the estate, if there be any remaining in his possession, to some person who has given bond for the same, in like manner as herein prescribed for administrators. Upon complying with such order, said executor or administrator shall be permitted to resign his trust and be discharged. Publication to be made, &c. Duty of Chief Justice.

III. OATH AND BOND.

ART. 726. [19] Before the issuance of letters testamentary or of administration with the will annexed, the person named executor or appointed administrator with the will annexed, shall, before the Clerk or Chief Justice, take and subscribe an oath, in form, as follows: I do solemnly swear, that the writing which has been offered for probate, is the last will of ——, so far as I know or believe; and that I will well and truly perform all the duties of executor of the said will or of administrator with the will annexed, of the estate of the said —— as the case may be. Oath of Executor.

ART. 727. [20] Before the issuance of letters of administration, the person appointed administrator shall, before the Clerk or Chief Justice, take and subscribe an oath, in form as follows: I do solemnly swear, that ——, deceased, died without leaving any lawful will, so far as I know or believe; and that I will well and truly perform all the duties of administrator of the estate of said ——. Oath of Administrator.

ART. 728. [21] Before the issuance of letters testamentary or of administration, the person named as executor, or appointed administrator, shall enter into bond with at least two good and sufficient sureties, to be approved by, and payable to, the Chief Justice of the county, in such penalty as he may direct, not less than double the estimated value of the estate of the testator or intestate: provided, however, that when any testator shall direct in his will that no security shall be required of the person or persons named therein, as executor or executors, letters testamentary shall be issued to such person or persons without any bond being required. Bond and security. When no security to be given.

ART. 729. [22] The oath of an executor or administrator may be taken and subscribed or his bond may be given, either in term time or vacation, at any time before the expiration of twenty days from the probate of the will, or the order granting the letters, and all such oaths and bonds, shall be filed and recorded by the Clerk. Executors and Administrators may qualify, when.

ART. 730. [23] The following form may be used for the bonds of executors and administrators: The State of Texas, County of ——, know all men by these presents, That we, A. B. as principal, and C. D. and E. F. as sureties, Form of bond.

are held and firmly bound unto the Chief Justice of the County of ——, in the sum of —— dollars; for the payment of which well and truly to be made unto the said Chief Justice, we bind ourselves, our heirs, executors, and administrators, jointly and severally, firmly by these presents. Signed with our hands and sealed with our seals; the seals being scrawls; the —— day of ——, A. D., 18—. The condition of this obligation is such, that whereas the above bound A. B. has been appointed executor of the last will and testament of J. C., deceased, (or has been appointed by the Chief Justice of the County of ——, administrator, with the will annexed, of the estate of the said J. C., deceased; or, has been appointed by the Chief Justice of the County of ——, administrator of the estate of J. C., deceased, as the case may be:) Now if the said A. B. shall well and truly perform all the duties required of him under said appointment, then this obligation shall be null and void; otherwise to remain of full force and effect.

A. B. [SEAL.]
C. D. [SEAL.]
E. F. [SEAL.]

Husband and wife may qualify jointly.

ART. 731. [24] Whenever a married woman may be appointed executrix or administratrix, and shall wish to accept and qualify as such, she may jointly with her husband, execute such bond as the law requires, and acknowledge the same before the Chief Justice of the court where the will was proved, or letters were granted; and such bond shall bind her estate in the same manner as if she were a feme sole; and whenever an executrix or administratrix may be a married woman, she and her husband shall act jointly in all matters pertaining to her said representative capacity.(*a*)

Surviving wife or husband under age.

ART. 732. [25] Whenever a surviving husband or wife, under twenty-one years of age, shall wish to accept and qualify as executor or executrix, or administrator or administratrix, he or she may execute such bonds as the law requires, and acknowledge the same before the Chief Justice of the court in which the will was proved, or letters of administration were granted, and such bonds shall be as valid as if he or she were of lawful age.

New bond to be given, when.

ART. 733. [30] When the sureties upon an executor's or administrator's bond, or any one of them, shall die, or shall remove beyond the limits of the State, or shall become insolvent, or when, in the opinion of the Chief Justice, the sureties upon any such bond are insufficient; it shall be his duty, either in term time or in vacation, to cause a citation to be issued and served upon such executor or administrator, requiring him to appear and give a new bond, on a day named in such citation, which may be in term time or in vacation.

New security required, when.

ART. 734. [31] Any person interested in an estate may present a petition to the Chief Justice, representing that the bond of the executor or administrator is insufficient, whereupon it shall be the duty of the Chief Justice, either in term time or in vacation, to cause a citation to be issued and served on such executor or administrator, requiring him to appear upon a day named in the citation, which may be either in term time or vacation, and show cause why he should not be required to give a new bond; and, on the return of such citation served, the Chief Justice shall inquire into the truth of the fact alleged, and if satisfied of the insufficiency of the bond, he shall require such executor or administrator to give a new bond.

Security, how released.

ART. 735. [32] The sureties upon the bond of an executor or administrator, or any one of them, may at any time present a petition to the Chief Justice, praying that such executor or administrator may be required to give a new

(*a*) A married woman who is executrix or administratrix, cannot act in anything pertaining to the estate without being joined by her husband; she cannot, therefore, sue alone, in her representative capacity, upon a note payable to her as administratrix. Mitchell & Mitchell *v.* Wright, Admr'x, 4 Tex. Rep., 283.

bond, and that he or they may be discharged from all liability for the future acts of such executor or administrator: whereupon it shall be the duty of said Chief Justice, whether in term time or in vacation, to cause a citation to be issued, and served on such executor or administrator, requiring him to appear, on a day named in the citation, which may be either in term time or in vacation, and give a new bond; and whenever such new bond shall have been given, and approved by the Chief Justice, such sureties shall be discharged from all liability under their bond for the future acts of such executor or administrator.

ART. 736. [33] In all cases where a new bond shall be required from an executor or administrator, under the provisions of this act, an order to that effect shall be entered in the minutes of the court, naming the time within which such new bond shall be given; and until such new bond shall have been given and approved, the order shall have the effect to suspend the powers of such executor or administrator. Order of court and power of Administrator or Executor.

ART. 737. [113] The bond of an executor or administrator of any kind, shall not become void on the first recovery, but may be put in suit and prosecuted from time to time until the whole amount thereof shall have been recovered. Such suit may be brought and prosecuted by any administrator of the estate not administered, in his own name as administrator, whenever the estate he represents has been injured by the breach of the bond of the executor or any previous administrator of the estate; or any other person or persons, injured by a breach of any such bond, may bring suit thereon in their own name; and any number of such persons may join in such suit. Bond not void on first recovery.

ART. 738. [114] All suits, on the bond of any executor or administrator, shall be commenced and prosecuted within four years next after the death, resignation, removal or discharge of such executor or administrator, and not thereafter: provided, however, that infants, *femes covert*, and persons *non compos mentis*, shall have at least two years within which to institute such suits after the removal of their respective disabilities. Limitation of suit on bond.

IV. APPRAISEMENT AND INVENTORY.

ART. 739. [38] Whenever letters testamentary, or of administration, shall be granted, the Chief Justice shall, by an order entered on the minutes of the court, appoint three or more disinterested persons, and citizens of the county, any two of whom may act, to appraise the estate of the deceased. If, from any cause, such appointment be not made; or if the appraisers, or any of them, so appointed, fail or refuse to act; or if, from any other cause, a new appointment is required, the Chief Justice shall, by a like order, either in term time or vacation, appoint another appraiser or appraisers, as the case may require; and, in all cases, any two appraisers may act. Such appraisers shall, each, receive two dollars per day, for every day they may be necessasily engaged, and all reasonable expenses. Appraisers appointed.

ART. 740. [39] Every executor, or administrator, shall, immediately after his appointment, with the assistance of any two or more of the appraisers appointed by the Chief Justice, make, or cause to be made, a full inventory and appraisement of all the estate of the testator or intestate, both real and personal; specifying in such inventory, what portion of such estate is the Inventory, how made, &c.

separate property of the deceased, and what portion, if any, is represented as common property. The appraisement of the property specified in the inventory, shall be sworn to and subscribed by the appraisers making the same, before some officer of the county authorized by law to administer oaths: such executor or administrator shall, also, make and attach to such inventory, a full and complete list of all claims due or owing to the testator or intestate; specifying what portion of such claims is the separate property of the deceased, and what portion, if any, is common property. Such executor or administrator shall also make and attach to such inventory and list, his affidavit in writing, subscribed and sworn to before some officer of the county authorized by law to administer oaths, that the said inventory and list is a full and complete inventory and list of the property and claims of his testator or intestate, that has come to his knowledge. (*a*)

When returned. ART. 741. [40] The inventory and list required to be made by the preceding section, shall be returned to the court, by the executor or administrator, within sixty days after the date of his appointment, and may be returned either in term time or vacation; but when returned, it shall be noticed on the minutes of the court, and shall be recorded by the Clerk.

Additional inventory. ART. 742. [41] Whenever other property or claims of the testator or intestate, than such as may be included in the inventory and list which has been returned, shall come to the knowledge of the executor or administrator, he shall make and return an additional inventory or list of such newly discovered property or claims without delay; which said additional inventory and list shall be made, returned, and recorded, in like manner as original inventories and lists: and any executor or adminsitrator, on complaint of any person interested in the estate, shall be cited by the Chief Justice; and on good and sufficient proof being made, that any property and claims of the estate have not been included in the inventory and list returned, shall be required to make and return an additional inventory and list thereof, in like manner as original inventories and lists. (*b*)

May be given in evidence. ART. 743. [42] Inventories, appraisements, and lists of claims, taken and returned in accordance with the foregoing provisions of this act, may be given in evidence in any suit by or against the executor or administrator; but shall not be conclusive for or against him, if it be shown that there is other property not inventoried; (*c*) or that there are other claims than those named in such lists; or that the property, or any part thereof, was, *bona fide*, sold for more or less than the appraisement; or was not separate or common property, as specified in such inventories and lists.

A new apprisement may be made, when. ART. 744. [43] When any inventory and appraisement has been returned in the manner herein before provided, any person interested in the estate, who may deem such appraisement to be unjust or erroneous, may apply to the Chief Justice for a new appraisement; notice of which application, together with a citation, shall be served on the executor or administrator, requiring him to appear at a regular term of the court, and show cause why a new appraisement should not be made. On the return of such citation served, the Chief Justice shall inquire into the truth of the facts alleged, and, if satisfied that such appraisement was manifestly unjust or erroneous, shall appoint other appraisers, and order a new appraisement to be made, and returned in like

(*a*) On complaint of any person interested in the estate, the administrator may be cited to appear, and, on good and sufficient proof being made that any property or claims of the estate have not been included in the inventory, he may be required to return an additional inventory, &c. White *v.* Shepperd, 16 Tex. Rep. 163

(*b*) This section gives an easy and speedy remedy against an administrator, requiring him to return property not included in his inventory. On proof of property in the deceased, the court will order it to be included in the inventory. Bradshaw *v.* Mayfield, 18 Tex. Rep. 21.

(*c*) Bradshaw, adm'r, *v.* Mayfield, 18 Tex. Rep. 21. White *v.* Shepperd, 16 Tex. Rep. 163.

manner as original appraisements. When such new appraisement is made and returned, it shall be recorded, and shall stand in place of the original appraisement, which shall be as if never made: provided, that not more than one re-appraisement shall be made.

V. PRESERVATION, RENT, AND HIRE, OF PROPERTY OF ESTATE.

ART. 745. [69] It shall be the duty of every executor or administrator to take such care of the property of his testator or intestate, real and personal, as a prudent man would take of his own property; and if there be any buildings or houses belonging to the estate, it shall be his duty to keep the same in tenantable repair, extraordinary casualties excepted: and all reasonable expenses incurred by the executor or administrator, in taking such care of the property, or in making such repairs, on sufficient proof thereof, shall be allowed him by the Chief Justice.

Adm'r or ex'r shall take care of the property,

ART. 746. [70] After the return of the inventory, if there be at any time in the possession of the executor or administrator, a plantation or slaves belonging to the estate, or any other property that may be rented or hired, so as to produce an income to the estate, and the disposition thereof is not specially directed by the will of the testator, or by the provisions of this act; or if the same is not required to be at once sold for the payment of debts, or claims of any kind against the estate, it shall be the duty of the executor or administrator to apply to the Chief Justice for an order to carry on such plantation, or to rent the same and hire out the slaves, and to rent or hire such other property, for the benefit of the estate. Upon such application being made, it shall be the duty of the Chief Justice, either in term time or vacation, to make an order for such executor or administrator either to carry on such plantation, or to rent the same and hire out the slaves, as to the Chief Justice shall appear most for the interest of the estate, and to hire or rent such other property. Such order shall be entered on the minutes of the court, and in making the same, the Chief Justice shall take into consideration the condition of the estate, and the necessity that may exist for future sale of such property, for the payment of debts or claims of any kind against the estate; and shall not extend the time of carrying on such plantation, or for renting or hiring any of the property, beyond what may consist with the speedy settlement of the estate. In carrying on a plantation, or in renting or hiring any such property under such order, all reasonable expenses incurred by the executor or administrator shall be allowed by the Chief Justice, on proper proof thereof; and if any executor or administrator shall fail to make such application, or to obey any such order when made, he and his sureties on his bond shall be liable, at the suit of any person interested in the estate, for the use and benefit of the estate, for such amount as might have reasonably been produced by carrying on such plantation, or by renting or hiring such property. (*a*)

Rent, hire, or sale of property.

Duty of Chief Justice and order of court.

Liability of ex'r or adm'r.

ART. 747. [71] Whenever any property is rented or hired by an executor or administrator, under the provisions of this act, such renting or hiring shall be made at public auction to the highest bidder, after having given at least ten days' notice thereof, by posting a copy of such notice at the court house, and at two other public places in the county where the same is to take place.

Renting or hiring to be at public auction.

(*a*) Hope *v.* Alley *et al.*, 9 Tex. Rep. 394.

VI. DEBTS DUE ESTATES.

Representative, when liable for.

ART. 748. [73] Every executor or administrator shall use ordinary diligence to collect every claim due to the estate he represents, and to recover possession of all property to which the estate has a right; provided there is a reasonable prospect that such claim can be collected, or such property recovered: and if any executor or administrator shall neglect to use such diligence, he and his sureties on his bond shall be liable, at the suit of any person interested in the estate, for the use of the estate, for the amount of such claims, and the value of such property as may have been lost by his neglect to use such diligence.(a)

Appointment of not to release him from his indebtedness.

ART. 749. [75] The naming an executor in a will shall not operate to extinguish any just claim which the deceased had against him; and in all cases when an executor or administrator may be indebted to his testator or intestate, he shall account for the debt in the same manner as if it were so much money in his hands: provided, however, that if said debt was not due at the time of receiving letters, he shall only be required to account for it from the date when it shall become due.

Representative may purchase or take property, &c. when.

ART. 750. [76] Whenever an executor or administrator shall think it will be for the interest of the estate he represents to purchase any property, or take any claims for the use and benefit of the estate, in payment of any debt due to the estate, he may present a petition to the Chief Justice, at a regular term of the court, representing these facts; and if the Chief Justice shall be satisfied that it will be for the interest of the estate to purchase such property, or take such claims, he may make a decree authorizing such executor or administrator to make such purchase, either at public or private sale, or to take such claims for the use and benefit of the estate.

May release the legal title to mortgagor.

ART. 751. [77] When the mortgagee of any property shall die, the executor or administrator of such mortgagee shall be, and he is hereby authorized, on receiving from the mortgagor, or any person for him, the amount due to the estate he represents, to release to the mortgagor the legal title to such mortgaged property, and such release shall be valid.

VII. ALLOWANCE TO WIDOW AND CHILDREN.

One year's allowance, &c.

ART. 752. [44] At the first term of the court, after the original grant of letters testamentary, or of administration, it shall be the duty of the Chief Justice to fix the amount of an allowance to be made for the support of the widow and minor children, if there be either or any, of the deceased, which allowance shall be of an amount sufficient for their maintenance for the term of one year, and shall be paid by the executor or administrator to the widow, if there be one; if not, then to the guardian of the child or children, either in money out of the first funds of the estate that may come to his hands, or in such personal effects of the deceased as such widow or guardian may choose to take at the appraisement, or a part thereof in each, as they may select. If there be no personal effects of the estate that such widow or guardian are willing to take for such allowance, or not a sufficiency of them; and if there be no funds, or not sufficient funds, of the estate in the hands of such executor or administrator to pay such allowance, or any part thereof, then it shall be the

(a) The statute does not, in terms, authorize the sale of claims for money due the estate, but enjoins their collection; and it may well be doubted whether an order of the Probate Court could confer on an administrator, authority to sell the notes and accounts belonging to the estate. Perry v. Booth, 7 Tex. Rep. 493.

duty of the Chief Justice, so soon as the inventory and list of claims are returned, to order a sale of so much of the estate, for cash as will be sufficient to raise the amount of such allowance, or a part thereof, as the case may require: (*a*) provided, however, that when any such widow and minor children shall have separate property adequate to their maintenance, then no such allowance shall be made as is provided for in this section.

Sale may be ordered to raise money for.

ART. 753. [45] At the first term of the court after an inventory and list of claims have been returned, it shall be the duty of the Chief Justice to set apart, for the use and benefit of the widow and children, if there be either or any, of the deceased, all such property as may be exempted from execution or forced sale by the Constitution or laws of the State, with the exception of any exemption of one year's supply of provisions; and in case there should not be among the effects of the deceased, all or any of the specific articles so exempted, it shall be the duty of the Chief Justice to make an allowance in lieu thereof to the widow and children, or such of them as there be, which allowance shall be paid by the executor or administrator, either in money out of the first funds of the estate that may come to his hands, or in any property of the deceased that such widow or children may choose to take at the appraisement, or a part thereof in both as they may select. If there be no property of the deceased that such widow or children are willing to take for such allowance, or not a sufficiency, and there be no funds, or not sufficient funds of the estate in the hands of such executor or administrator to pay such allowance, or any part thereof, it shall be the duty of the Chief Justice, on the application of such widow or children, to order a sale of so much of the estate for cash as will be sufficient to raise the amount of such allowance, or a part thereof, as the case may require. Such allowance shall be paid in the following manner: If there be a widow and no children, the whole to be paid to the widow; if there be a child, or children, and no widow, the whole to be paid to such child, or to be equally divided among such children; if there be a widow and a child, or children, one half to be paid to the widow, and the other half to such child, or to be divided equally among such children: provided, that if the estate of such decedent be not insolvent, nothing in this section contained, shall be so construed as to prohibit the distribution and partition of said estate among the heirs and distributees thereof, including the portion herein provided, to be set aside for the use of the widow and children: and further provided, that a year's provisions shall be exempted from such distribution. (*b*)

Prop'ty exempt from execution to be set apart for.

Widow or children may take property in lieu of deficiency.

Sale of property to supply deficiency.

(*a*) Where the wife, without good cause, voluntarily abandons her husband, for several years, (say three or four,) immediately previous to his decease, she forfeits her claim to the homestead and widow's allowance. Earle *v.* Earle, 9 Tex. Rep. 630.

The object of the statute is to allow a year's support for the widow and the minor children, or for the minor children, if there be no widow, and if there be a widow, she is to receive the whole for the benefit of herself and minor children. As a general RULE, the widow must be regarded as the head of the family, where a homestead has been assigned. James *v.* Thompson, 14 Tex. Rep. 463.

(*b*) It would seem that it is the duty of the Chief Justice, without formal applications, to fix the amount of the year's allowance, and to set apart the property exempt from sale at the times specified in the statute; but it is proper that applications be made, although they need not appear of record; and the requisite information must be afforded, to enable the Chief Justice to perform the duty according to the requirements of the law; at all events, where the Chief Justice has acted, and the widow or children complain of the amount, it cannot be objected to their petition for *certiorari*, that no application was made to the Chief Justice in the premises. Connell *v.* Chandler, Adm'r, &c., 11 Tex. Rep. 249. Considering the policy and object of this provision, the obvious conclusion would be, that the Legislature must have intended primarily, at least, that the family should be secured in the home of the deceased, whether the family consisted of a widow and children, or of either, or whether the children at home be minors or adults. A protection to the family is the reasonable object. Some of the provisions of this section are not entirely reconcilable with this view. James *v.* Thompson, 14 Tex. Rep. 463. The substituted allowance for the widow and children, is to be designated only in cases where the estate is insolvent; or if set apart from a solvent estate, no permanent interest or estate can enure to the beneficiaries; the whole estate, including the portion of the widow and children, is distributable among the heirs and distributees. Green *v.* Crow, Adm'r, 17 Tex. Rep. 180. Where the estate is insolvent, the payment of the allowance to the widow and children is final and absolute, without remainder, or ultimate liability to creditors or others interested in the estate. Ibid. The right of the widow and children, where the estate is insolvent, to the homestead, or substituted allowance, depends on the question whether the domicil of the deceased was in this State, and is not affected by the fact, that the widow and children may have abandoned the State, or may intend to abandon it, as soon as the homestead or substituted allowance is assigned them. Ibid. The homestead may be assigned to the widow on the application of the administrator. Ibid. If the deceased leaves a child, the creditors cannot object to the allowance to the widow and the child on the ground that the widow was not the lawful wife of the deceased; the child would be entitled to the same allowance. Lockhart *v.* White and others, 18 Tex. Rep. 102. If the minor children have property adequate to their support and maintenance, they are not entitled to the allowance of a year's support under the statute. Sloan *v.* Webb, 20 Tex. Rep. 189.

VIII. CLAIMS AGAINST ESTATE.

Published notice to be given

ART. 754. [46] It shall be the duty of executors and administrators, within one month after receiving their letters, to publish in some newspaper printed in the county, where the letters were issued, if there be one; if not, then in some newspaper printed in the State, and nearest the court-house of the county where the letters were issued; a notice requiring all persons having claims against the estate of the testator or intestate, to present the same within the time prescribed by law; which notice shall state the time of the original grant of letters testamentary or of administration, and shall be published once a week for six successive weeks; when no newspaper is printed in the county, a copy of such notice shall also be posted at the court-house. A copy of such printed notice, together with the affidavit of the publisher of the paper, that it was published once a week for six successive weeks, sworn to and subscribed before any Chief Justice, or Notary Public, and attested by his official seal, may be filed and recorded in the court from which the letters were issued; and a copy thereof may be given in evidence in any court, in any action, whether by or against the executor or administrator; and a copy of the notice posted at the court-house, with a certificate of the Clerk that such notice was so posted, may be filed and recorded, and a copy thereof given in evidence in the like manner as provided for the printed notice.

Copy of notice may be given in evidence.

Claims to be presented, when.

ART. 755. [47] Every claim for money against a testator or intestate, shall be presented to the executor or administrator within twelve months after the original grant of letters testamentary or of administration; or the payment thereof shall be postponed until the claims which have been presented within said twelve months and allowed by the executor or administrator, and approved by the Chief Justice, or established by suit, shall have been first entirely paid.(*a*)

Ex'r or adm'r failing to give notice, &c.

ART. 756. [48] If any executor or administrator fail to give the notice required, by the 46th section of this act, to be given, he shall be removed by the Chief Justice at any regular term of the court, on the complaint of any person interested in the estate, after being cited to answer such complaint, unless such executor or administrator shall show to the Court that he has given such notice.

Claim to be verified.

ART. 757. [49] No executor or administrator shall allow any claim for money against his testator or intestate, nor shall any Chief Justice approve of any such allowance, unless such claim is accompanied by an affidavit in writing, that the claim is just, and that all legal offsets, payments, and credits, known to the affiant, have been allowed; (*b*) which affidavit, if made in the county where the

(*a*) It seems that a claim which requires the intervention of a jury, to ascertain the damages, is not such a "claim for money" as the law requires to be presented to the administrator for allowance before instituting suit. Sutton *v.* Page and wife, 4 Tex. Rep. 142. In an action on a title bond, where the petition disclosed that it was not in the power of the defendant to make title, and alleged no special damage, the measure of damages being the purchase money and interest, it was held that the title bond was a "claim for money," within the meaning of the statute. Ibid. See also Dunn *v.* Sublett, Adm'r, 14 Tex. Rep. 521—Hall, Adm'r, *v.* McCormack et al., 7 Tex. Rep. 269. A mortgage is a "claim for money" and must be presented to the administrator for allowance, and to the Chief Justice for approval, before it can be enforced, accompanied by the affidavit required by the statute. Graham *v.* Vining, 1 Tex. Rep. 639. Danzy *v.* Swinney, 7 Tex. Rep. 625. Wright *v.* Henderson, 12 Tex. Rep. 43. Robertson *v.* Paul, 16 Tex. Rep. 472. A demand which accrued after the death of the testator or intestate, must be presented to the administrator for allowance and the Chief Justice for approval. Danzy *v.* Swinney, 11 Tex. Rep. 359. It is not necessary to present a judgment rendered in our own courts, before a suit to revive, where the lien of the judgment has been preserved. Cole *v.* Robertson, 6 Tex. Rep. 356. But otherwise if the judgment has lost its lien. Hall, Adm'r, *v.* McCormack, 7 Tex. Rep. 269. It would seem that the proper practice in allowing or rejecting claims against estates, the Chief Justice should enter an order on the minutes of the court, and not merely to endorse a memorandum on the claim. Davenport *v.* Lawrence, Adm'r, 19 Tex. Rep. 317.

(*b*) The affidavit may be made by the agent or attorney conversant with the facts. Hansell *v.* Gregg, Adm'r, 7 Tex. Rep. 223. If the claim is rejected by the administrator, because the affidavit is not made by the owner, the cause must be specially stated in the rejection. Ibid. Shelton *v.* Berry, Adm'r, 19 Tex. Rep. 154. Dunn *v.* Sublett, Adm'r, 14 Tex. Rep. 521. McIntosh *v.* Greenwood, Adm'r, 15 Tex. Rep. 116. The affidavit need not pursue the language of the statute if the substance be retained. Crosby *v.* McWillie & Moreland, 11 Tex. Rep. 94. An administrator, or heir, may have claims set aside, which were acknowledged in ignorance of the facts, or from fraudulent representations of the holder. Montgomery and wife *v.* Culton, 18 Tex. Rep. 736. Neill *v.* Hodge, 5 Tex. Rep. 487. The statute does not require that the affidavit should be signed by the affiant. Alford, Adm'r, *v.* Cochrane, 7 Tex. Rep. 485.

letters were granted, may be made before any officer of the county authorized to administer oaths; if made in any other county of this State, it shall be made before some Chief Justice, or Notary Public, and shall be attested by his official seal; if made out of this State, it shall be made before some Judge of a Court of Record having a seal, and shall be attested by the seal of his court. (*a*) If any such claim is allowed or approved without such affidavit, such allowance or approval shall be of no force or effect. Before whom.

ART. 758. [50] No holder of a claim for money against the estate of a deceased person, shall bring a suit thereon against the executor or administrator, unless such claim properly authenticated, has been presented to such executor or administrator, and he has refused to allow such claim for the whole amount, or a part thereof; or unless such claim has been presented to the Chief Justice, and he has disapproved of the allowance made by the executor or administrator, or a part thereof. In any suit that may be brought by the holder of any such claim, if he fails to recover thereon a greater amount than has been allowed by the executor or administrator, or than has been approved by the Chief Justice, he shall be liable for all costs of such suit. (*b*) No suit shall be brought on until, &c.

ART. 759. [51] When any claim for money against an estate shall be presented to the executor or administrator, if the same be properly authenticated, in the manner required by this act, he shall endorse thereon, or annex thereto, a memorandum in writing, signed by him, stating the time of its presentment, and that he allows or rejects the claim; or what portion thereof he allows, or rejects, as the case may be. (*c*) If the claim, or a part thereof, be allowed by the executor or administrator, it shall then be presented to the Chief Justice, either in term time or vacation, who shall endorse thereon, or annex thereto, a memorandum in writing, signed by him, stating that he approves or disapproves of such allowance, or what portion of such allowance he approves or disapproves of: (*d*) If all, or any portion of the claim be so allowed and approved, the holder thereof shall be entitled to receive payment of the amount so allowed and approved, in due course of administration. If such claim be rejected by the executor or administrator, either for the whole amount, or a part thereof, or if the allowance, or any part thereof, made by the executor or administrator, be disapproved of by the Chief Justice, the holder of such claim may, within three months after such rejection by the executor or administrator, but not thereafter, bring a suit against the executor or administrator for the establishment thereof, in any court having jurisdiction of the same; and on the trial of such suit, the memorandum in writing of the executor or administrator, or of the Chief Justice, endorsed on, or annexed to, such claim may be given in evidence to prove the facts therein stated, without proof of the handwriting of such executor or administrator, or Chief Justice, unless the same be denied under oath. (*e*) No execution shall issue on a judgment obtained by the plaintiff in any such suit; but such judgment shall have the same force and effect as if the amount thereof had been allowed by the executor or administrator, and approved by the Chief Justice. Claims presented, how endorsed. The holder may sue when the claim is rejected, &c. No execution shall issue on.

ART. 760. [52] When a claim for money against the estate of a deceased person, authenticated in proper form, shall be presented to the executor or administrator within the time prescribed by law; if such executor or adminis- Holder may sue, if ex'r or adm'r refuse to endorse, &c.

(*a*) An affidavit before the presiding Justice of the Court of Pleas and Quarter Sessions, &c., signed and sealed by the Judge, to which was appended the certificate of the Clerk of the Court, attested by his seal of office, was held to be a good affidavit "made out of the State." Moore, Adm'r, *v.* Carson, 12 Tex. Rep. 66.

(*b*) For cases in which it was held that the claim need not be verified by affidavit and presented to the administrator for allowance before suit; see Sutton *v.* Page and wife, 4 Tex. Rep. 142; Merle *v.* Andrews, Ibid. 200; Cole *v.* Robertson, 6 Tex. Rep. 356.

(*c*) Where an administrator verbally admits a claim against the estate to be good, and that it will be paid, and thereby induces a third person to take the claim, he will be estopped from contesting the claim in the hands of such third person. Swenson *v.* Walker, 3 Tex. Rep. 93.

(*d*) The approval by the Chief Justice of the allowance of a claim by an administrator, is a judgment which cannot be impeached collaterally in the County Court. Pitner, Adm'r, *v.* Flanagan, 17 Tex. Rep. 7.

(*e*) A claim once presented to and rejected by an ad

trator fail or refuse to endorse thereon or annex thereto a memorandum in writing, as the previous section requires, such failure or refusal shall be deemed equivalent to a rejection of the claim by the executor or administrator; and shall authorize the holder to bring a suit for the establishment thereof, in like manner as if such claim had been so rejected; and such executor or adminis-

May be removed for failure or refusal.

trator shall be removed by the Chief Justice at any regular term of the court on the complaint of any person interested in such claim, after being cited to answer such complaint, and proof being made of such failure or refusal.

Holder of title bond may file a petition.

ART. 761. [53] When any person shall sell property and enter into bond, or other written agreement, to make title thereto, and shall depart this life without having made such title, the holder of such bond or written agreement, or his legal representatives, may file a complaint in writing in the County Court of the county where letters testamentary or of administration, of such deceased person, were granted, praying that the executor or administrator may be required to make titles, agreeably to the title bond, or other written agreement of the deceased: whereupon, it shall be the duty of the Clerk of said court to issue a citation with a copy of the complaint, to be served on the executor or administrator; and on the return thereof served, at some regular term of the court, the Chief Justice shall, if he find that such sale was legally made, order

Decree for title.

the executor or administrator to make titles, according to the tenor of the bond, or other written agreement, to the property so sold by his testator or intestate; whereupon, it shall be the duty of such executor or administrator to make titles, in compliance with such order: (a) provided, however, that any person interested in such estate may, at any time within two years after the making of any such order, have the same annulled and set aside by a suit in the District Court, upon good cause shown why the same should not have been made: provided also, that married women, minors, and persons of unsound mind

May be set aside.

so interested, shall have a like period of two years, after the removal of their respective disabilities, within which they may in like manner have such order annulled and set aside.

Ex'r or adm'r to return an exhibit of claims allowed, &c., when.

ART. 762. [82] At the first term of the court after the expiration of twelve months from the time of the original grant of letters testamentary or of administration, it shall be the duty of the executor or administrator to return to the court an exhibit, in writing, sworn to and subscribed by him, setting forth a list of all claims against the estate that were presented to him within twelve months after the said grant of letters testamentary or of administration, specifying which have been allowed by him; which have been rejected, and the date when rejected; which have been sued upon, and the condition of the suit; also, setting forth, fully, the condition of the estate; and if any executor or adminis-

Letters to be revoked on failure.

trator shall neglect to return such exhibit at the term of the court named above, it shall be the duty of the Chief Justice to revoke his letters—either in term-time or in vacation—on the complaint of any person interested in the estate, without notice to such executor or administrator.

Further exhibits to be returned.

ART. 763. [84] At the third regular term of the court after the expiration of twelve months from the original grant of letters testamentary or of administration, it shall be the duty of the executor or administrator, to return to the

ministrator, is barred in three months without suit brought, and cannot be revived by a second presentation afterwards. Crosby v. McWillie & Moreland, 11 Tex. Rep. 94. Cobb v. Norwood, Ibid. 556. Arbitration is not a proper mode to establish a rejected claim against an estate. Yarbrough v. Leggett, and another, 14 Tex. Rep. 677.

(a) The authority conferred upon the Probate Court by this statute, is special and limited, and must be strictly pursued, otherwise the acts and proceedings thereon are nugatory, and confer no right. An order requiring an administrator to execute titles to all lands, or which the estate of the deceased stood bound, was held to be a nullity. Jones v. Taylor, 7 Tex. Rep. 240. Peters v. Philips & wife, Adm'r, 19 Tex. Rep. 70.

There is but one case, perhaps, in which litigation on a claim against a deceased person is conducted in the Probate Court, and that is for the enforcement of an executory contract to convey title to lands. In all other cases, the jurisdiction of the District Courts, under the acts now in force, is exclusive. Booth, Adm'r, v. Todd, Guardian, 8 Tex. Rep. 137. The jurisdiction of the county to decree specific performance of written contracts for the sale of lands against the estates of deceased persons, is concurrent with the jurisdiction of the District Courts. Ottenhouse v. Burleson, Adm'r, 11 Tex. Rep. 87. Bridge v. Young, Ex'r, 9 Tex. Rep. 401.

court a further exhibit in writing, sworn to and subscribed by him, setting forth a list of all suits that have been instituted against him since the return of the exhibit required by the eighty-second section of this act; the condition of such suits, and all suits previously instituted; specifying which of said suits are upon claims presented to him within twelve months after such grant of letters; and which upon claims presented after the twelve months; also setting forth a list of all claims that have been presented to him since the expiration of the twelve months from said grant of letters; specifying which have been allowed by him, and which have been rejected, with the date of the rejection. And he shall also, from time to time after the said term, return to the court a further exhibit under oath, setting forth a list of all claims presented to and allowed or rejected by him since the return of his former exhibit, with the date of the rejection; and, also, of all suits instituted against him, and all judgments rendered upon suits against him, since his former return. And any executor or administrator who shall fail to return to the court any exhibit as required by this section, shall be removed by the Chief Justice without notice—either in term time or vacation—on the complaint of any person interested in the estate.

Failure to return, cause for removal.

ART. 764. [88] No claim for money againt his testator or intestate shall be allowed by an executor or administrator, nor shall any suit be instituted against him on any such claim after an order for partition and distribution has been made as provided for in the previous section of this act; but the holder of any such claim not barred by the laws of limitation, shall have his action thereon against the heirs, devisees or legatees of the estate; but they shall not be bound beyond the value of the property they may receive in such partition and distribution.(a)

No claim shall be allowed, &c., after order for partition.

ART. 765. [118] The provisions contained in this act respecting the presentation of claims, shall not be so construed as to apply to the claim of any heir, deivsee, or legatee, when claiming in that capacity; and any devisee or legatee may obtain from the Chief Justice of the court where the will was proved an order for the executor to deliver to him the property devised or bequeathed, whenever it shall appear to such Chief Justice that there will remain in the hands of the executor after such delivery, a sufficient amount of the estate for the payment of all debts against said estate: provided, such devisee or legatee shall have first caused the executor, and the other devisees and legatees, if any, and the heirs, if any of the estate is coming to them, to be cited to appear and show cause why such order should not be made.

Not to apply to heirs, claiming as such.

Property may be delivered, when.

ART. 766. [133] The provisions of this act respecting the presentation of claims shall not be construed to apply to any claim of an executor or administrator against his testator or intestate, that has not been allowed by some previous executor or administrator of the same estate; but any executor or administrator holding any such claims, shall file them in the court from which his letters were granted, on or before the sixth term of the Court after the original grant of letters, or the same shall be barred. The Chief Justice shall, at said term, or at some subsequent term, proceed to examine such claims, and hear all legal evidence that may be offered in support of them, and if satisfied from the evidence that such claims, or any of them, are just, he shall enter on the minutes of the court his approval of such of them as he may think just; and the amount so approved shall be paid in due course of administration, unless, within three months after such approval, some person interested in the estate shall take an appeal from such approval to the District Court; in which case, such account, or so much thereof as may be approved by a jury, shall be paid in due course of administration; if such claims or any of them shall not be approved by the Chief Justice, the executor or administrator may appeal to

Claim of ex'r or adm'r against estate to be filed.

Order of court in such cases.

Appeal to Dis't Court allowed.

(a) The obligation of the heir to pay debts, is commensurate with the amount of assets received from the administrator. Montgomery & wife v. Culton, 18 Tex. Rep. 736.

the District Court in like manner, and such amount as may be approved by a jury, shall be paid in due course of administration. If, in any appeal under the provisions of this section, the executor or administrator shall fail to establish the whole of his claim, he shall be liable for costs; but if he establish the whole amount of his claim, the costs shall be paid out of the estate of the testator or intestate.

IX. SALE OF PROPERTY OF ESTATE.

Application shall be in writing.

ART. 767. [54] It shall be the duty of every executor, or administrator, so soon as he shall ascertain that it is necessary, to apply to the Chief Justice, at some regular term of the court, for an order to sell so much of the property of the estate he represents as he shall think sufficient to pay the expenses of administration and the debts of the estate; such application shall be in writing, and shall be accompanied by a statement in writing, of the estimated expenses of administration, and of all the claims against the estate that have been presented to him, specifying what claims have been allowed by him, what rejected, and those upon which suit has been instituted against him, with the condition of such suit or suits; which statement shall be verified affidavit; upon the presentation of such application and statement, it shall be the duty of the Chief Justice, if satisfied that there is a necessity for such sale, to order the same to be made.(*a*)

Creditor, heir, &c., may apply for order, when.

ART. 768. [55] When any executor or administrator shall neglect to apply for an order to sell sufficient property of the estate he represents to pay the expenses of administration, and the claims against the estate that have been allowed and approved, or established by suit, such executor or administrator shall be required by the Chief Justice, on the application in writing of any creditor of the estate, whose claim has been allowed and approved and established by suits, or any heir, devisee, or legatee of the deceased, to present to the court at some regular term thereof a statement in writing, like that provided for in the preceding section; and upon proof to the court, by any such creditor, heir, devisee, or legatee, that a necessity exists for a sale, to pay the expenses of administration and the debts of the estate, it shall be the duty of the Chief Justice to order such sale to be made: provided, the executor or administrator shall have been first cited.(*b*)

Perishable property may be sold, when.

ART. 769. [56] Whenever there is property belonging to the estate of a deceased person that is perishable or liable to waste, upon the application in writing of the executor or administrator, or any heir, devisee, or legatee of the deceased, or any creditor of the estate whose claim has been allowed and approved, or established by suit, the Chief Justice, by an order entered on the minutes of the court, either in term time or in vacation, may direct the sale of such property, or any part thereof.

ART. 770. [57] The Chief Justice, either in term time or in vacation, may,

(*a*) Where the Probate Court orders a sale of property under the statute, it is the judgment of a court of competent jurisdiction and cannot be collaterally reviewed. Poor *v.* Boyce, 12 Tex. Rep., 440. Toliver and another, Adm'rs, *v.* Hubbell, 6 Tex. Rep., 166. Howard *v.* Bennett, 13 Tex. Rep., 309. Burdett *v.* Silsbee, 15 Tex. Rep., 604. Dancy *v.* Stricklinge & wife, Ibid, 557.

The purchaser at an administrator's sale is not required to go behind the order of sale, to see that the administrator has been duly appointed and continued, and that the proceedings have all been regular. Dancy *v.* Stricklinge & wife, 16 Tex. Rep., 557. Alexander *v.* Maverick, 18 Tex. Rep. 179.

An entry that the final account of an administrator be admitted and filed, and that he be discharged upon paying costs, is not such a final close of the administration as will defeat the title of a bona fide purchaser at a sale by such administrator, upon an order granted eight months afterwards. Alexander *v.* Maverick, 18 Tex. Rep., 179.

(*b*) No proceeding can be maintained in the Probate Court by a creditor whose claim has not been both allowed by the administrator and approved by the Probate Judge; and a proceeding commenced before such approval, it seems, cannot be cured by a subsequent approval. Danzy, Adm'r, *v* Swinney, 7 Tex. Rep., 617.

by an order entered on the minutes of the court, direct the crops belonging to the estate of the deceased person, or any part thereof, to be sold at private sale, upon the application in writing of the executor or administrator, or any heir, devisee, or legatee of the deceased, or any creditor of the estate, whose claim has been allowed and approved, or established by suit: provided that no crops shall be sold under any such order at a price less than their fair or market value. Crop may be sold privately.

ART. 771. [58] All sales for the payment of the debts owing by the estate, shall be ordered to be made of such property as may be deemed most advantageous to such estate to be sold: provided, however, that no order shall be made to sell the slaves belonging to an estate for the purpose aforesaid, until all other property subject to the payment of debts has been first sold, and it shall be shown to the court that the proceeds of such sales are insufficient to pay such debts, unless it shall be necessary to sell such slaves, or a part thereof, for the satisfaction of some debt that is secured by mortgage or other lien, on them, or unless such estate shall, by the exhibit of the executor, or administrator, or by other evidence satisfactory to the court, appear to be insolvent. Slaves not to be sold until, &c.

ART. 772. [59] Any creditor of the estate of a deceased person holding a claim secured by a mortgage, or other lien, which claim has been allowed and approved, or established by suit, may obtain, at a regular term of the court, from the Chief Justice of the county where the letters testamentary or of administration were granted, an order for the sale of the property upon which he has such mortgage, or other lien, or so much of said property as may be required to satisfy such claim, by making his application in writing, and having a copy thereof served upon the executor or administrator, with a citation requiring him to appear and answer such application.(*a*) Mortgage property may be sold, when.

ART. 773. [60] When an application is made to the Chief Justice for an order to sell any property belonging to the estate of a deceased person, for the payment of debts, any person interested in such estate, may, at any time before an order is made thereon, file his opposition in writing to such sale, or may make application in writing for the sale of other property of the estate; and upon the hearing of the matter in controversy, the Chief Justice shall make such order thereon as the circumstance of the case may require, having due regard to the provisions of this act. Application may be opposed.

ART. 774. [61] Whenever any property of an estate is ordered to be sold by the Chief Justice, such order shall be entered on the minutes of the court; shall describe the property to be sold, and shall specify the terms of such sale. Order of sale to be recorded.

ART. 775. [62] Sales of personal property, other than slaves, for the payment of debts, may be ordered either for cash or on such credit as the Chief Justice may direct; and all sales of land or slaves for the payment of debts, shall be made on a credit of twelve months, except when such sales are ordered to raise the amount of the allowance that may be made under the provisions of the forty-fourth and forty-fifth sections of this act, or for the satisfaction of a mortgage or other lien on said land or slaves; in which cases such sales shall be made on such terms as the Chief Justice may direct.(*b*) Personal property to be sold for cash. Land and slaves on a credit, except.

(*a*) See Danzey *v.* Swinney, *supra*. This section of the statute only applies to proceedings in the County Court.

A mortgage debt, except in cases of lien for the purchase money of the property, is postponed by the statute to the payment of the enumerated privileged claims—as funeral expenses, expenses of the last sickness, and expenses of administration—including the allowance to the widow and children and the expenses incurred in the preservation, safe keeping and management of the estate.

A power to sell, contained in a mortgage or deed of trust, to secure the payment of a debt, although not revoked, on general principles, by the death of the constituent, is inconsistent with our statutes respecting the settlement of the estates of deceased persons, and therefore cannot be executed after the death of the constituent. In such case the law requires the presentation of such claim for allowance and approval, and its payment enforced as the statute prescribes. Robertson *v.* Paul, 16 Tex. Rep., 472.

The decree of the District Court enforcing the vendor's lien, should be certified to the Probate Court to be paid in due course of administration; and the order of sale can be obtained under the provisions of the above article. Fortson's Adm'r *v.* Caldwell, 17 Tex. Rep., 627.

(*b*) Where a sale of property is ordered, out of which

Sale shall be to highest bidder.

ART. 776. [63] All sales ordered by the Chief Justice shall be made to the highest bidder, and at public auction, unless otherwise directed, by the will of the testator, or otherwise ordered by the Chief Justice under some provisions of this act.

Sale under a will.

ART. 777. [64] Whenever, in a will, power is given to an executor to sell any property of the testator, no order of the Chief Justice shall be necessary to authorize the executor to make such sale; and when any particular directions are given by a testator in his will, respecting the sale of any property belonging to his estate, the same shall be followed, unless creditors or heirs may thereby be prejudiced in their rights.

Sale, how advertised.

ART. 778. [65] Whenever a public sale of property is ordered under the provisions of this act, if the same be personal property other than slaves, it shall be advertised at least ten days before the day of sale; if the same be land or slaves, it shall be advertised at least twenty days before the day of sale. The manner of advertising shall be by posting a notice of such sale at the court-house, and at two other public places in the county where the sale is to be made, but not in the same city or town. All such public sales shall be made

Time and place of sale.

within the hours of 10 A. M. and 4 P. M.; in case the day set apart for such sale shall be insufficient to complete the same, such sale may be continued from day to day, by giving public notice of the continuance at the conclusion of the sale of each day, and the continued sale shall commence and close within the same hours. All such public sales of personal property other than slaves shall be made at such time and place as may be directed by the Chief Justice in the order of sale; all such public sales of land or slaves shall be made on the first Tuesday of the month, at the court-house door of the county where the letters testamentary or of administration were granted, unless the Chief Justice shall deem it to the advantage of the estate to order the sale in the county in which the property is situated; and in all cases where such public sale is ordered to be made in any other county than that in which the letters testamentary or of administration were granted, such sale shall be advertised in both counties.

Bidder failing to comply with terms of, &c.

ART. 779. [66] When any person shall bid off property offered for sale, rent, or hire, at public auction, by an executor or an administrator, and shall fail to comply with the terms of sale, renting or hiring, such property shall be re-advertised and sold, rented, or hired; and the person so failing to comply, shall be liable to pay to such executor or administrator, for the use of the estate, five per cent. on the amount of his bid; and also the deficiency in price on the second sale, renting or hiring, if any such deficiency there be—to be recovered by such executor or administrator, by action brought before a Justice of the Peace, or in the District Court, according to the amount of such penalty or deficiency.(*a*)

Return of, to be made.

ART. 780. [67] When a sale of property is ordered under the provisions of this act, it shall be the duty of the executor or administrator to make such sale, or cause it to be made in obedience to the order, at the earliest period; and when such sale has been made, it shall be the duty of the executor or administrator, to return to the court that ordered the sale, an account thereof, either in term-time or vacation, within thirty days after the day of sale.(*b*)

an allowance to the widow and children to the amount of the homestead exemption was to be made, the property exceeding in value the amount of the allowance, it was held that the terms of the sale should be cash to the amount of the allowance, to be paid over immediately to those entitled, and a credit of twelve months for the balance. Wood & wife *v.* Wheeler, 11 Tex. Rep., 122.

(*a*) To hold the bidder responsible, the re-sale must be made in a reasonable time. The administrator should proceed to re-advertise and sell as soon as he conveniently can, after the default of the bidder has been fully ascertained. This he may do, it seems, without further order of the court. Short's Adm'r *v.* Ramsey, 18 Tex. Rep., 397. If the bidder offers a note with solvent sureties, according to the terms of the sale, and the administrator refuses the note upon the ground the sureties are insolvent, the bidder may prove their solvency upon the trial as a defence to the action. Hope *v.* Alley, 9 Tex. Rep., 394.

(*b*) The mere failure of the administrator to return the sale within thirty days, unaccompanied with any circumstance showing that the delay had produced any injury to the purchaser or the estate, is not a good ground for setting aside the sale. Brown *v.* Hobbs, Adm'r, 19 Tex. Rep., 167.

Such account of sale shall be in writing, shall specify the property sold, the name of the purchaser, the price for which it was sold, and the terms of sale, and shall be sworn to and subscribed by such executor or administrator, before some officer authorized to administer oaths; whenever such account of sale is returned, such return shall be noted in the minutes of the court; and at the term of the court when it is returned, or if returned in vacation, at the first term thereafter, it shall be the duty of the Chief Justice to inquire into the manner in which such sale was made; and if satisfied that it was fairly made and in conformity with law, he shall cause to be entered on the minutes of the court, a decree confirming it and ordering the account of sales to be recorded by the clerk and a conveyance to be made to the purchaser of either land or slaves, by the executor or administrator; if not satisfied that such sale was so made, he shall cause to be entered in like manner, a decree setting it aside and ordering a new sale to be made. After any such decree of confirmation shall have been made, upon the purchaser complying with the terms of sale, the executor or administrator shall execute and deliver to him a conveyance of the property so sold, if it were either land or slaves, reciting therein the decree confirming the sale, and ordering the conveyance to be made, which conveyance of land or slaves so made, shall vest the right and title that the testator or intestate had, in the purchaser, and shall be *prima facie* evidence that all the requisites of the law have been complied with in making the sale; and such decree of confirmation of the sale of personal property other than slaves, shall in like manner vest the right and title thereof in the purchaser, and shall be like evidence that all the requisites of the law have been complied with in making the sale of such personal property.(*a*)

Duty of Chief Justice.

After confirmation, title to be executed in certain cases.

Art. 781. [68] It shall not be lawful for any executor or administrator to take the estate of his testator or intestate, or any part thereof at its appraised value; or to sell the same or any part thereof unless under the direction of the will or the order of the Chief Justice under the provisions of this act; or to become the purchaser, either directly or indirectly, of any property of the estate sold by him; and if any executor or administrator should, either directly or indirectly, become the purchaser of any of the property of his testator or intestate, at a sale made by him—upon the complaint of any person interested in the estate and service thereof, and of citation on such executor or administrator—such sale shall be declared void by the Chief Justice, and such executor or administrator decreed to hold the property so purchased, in trust as assets of the estate. Nor shall it be lawful for any executor or administrator, either directly or indirectly, to purchase, for his own use, any claim against the estate he represents; and if any executor or administrator should purchase any such claim, upon the complaint in writing of any person interested in the estate and service thereof, with a citation on such executor or administrator, he shall be decreed by the Chief Justice to hold such claim in trust for the use of the estate; and he shall only be entitled to receive from the estate the amount he shall prove to have been paid by him therefor; such amount to be paid *pro rata* with other creditors of an equal degree.

Adm'r or exec'r not to take property at appraised value or, except, &c.

Shall not purchase property of estate.

Nor claims against estate.

Art. 782. [72] Whenever an executor or administrator sells property of the estate he represents on a credit, either under the directions of the will of the

(*a*) Much discretion is left to the Probate Judge in refusing to confirm a sale. If he should believe that the sale was not fair, or that it was not made in conformity with law, it would be his duty to set it aside. He is not required to put his reasons on record, either in confirming or rejecting a sale. Davis *v.* Stewart, Adm'r, 4 Tex. Rep. 223.

A purchaser, at a Probate sale, is aware that he is purchasing subject to confirmation or rejection of the sale by the Probate Judge, and is not entitled to notice before the rejection of the sale. Ibid.

The Probate Judge has no power to revoke a title confirmed at a former term. Ibid. Hurt *v.* Horton, 12 Tex. Rep., 285.

As to the fraudulent representations of an administrator that will vitiate the sale made by him, see Crayton *v.* Munger, 9 Tex. Rep., 285. An estate can neither be charged nor can it charge others, by means of the illegal or fraudulent acts of its legal representative. Ibid.

The maxim, "*caveat emptor*," applies to a sale by an administrator, and mere defect of title cannot avail the purchaser, either as a defence to an action for the purchase money or as a ground for rescinding the contract. Thompson *v.* Munger, 15 Tex. Rep., 523.

Security for personal property sold—mortgage on land and slaves.

testator or under an order of the Chief Justice, he shall take the note of the purchaser for the amount of his purchase, with good personal security; and if land or slaves have been sold, he shall also take a mortgage upon the property sold to secure the payment of the purchase money. And if the executor or administrator shall neglect to take such note, security and mortgage, he and the sureties on his bond shall be liable, at the suit of any person interested in the estate, for the use of the estate, for the amount of such sales; and whenever any executor or administrator shall rent or hire any property of his testator or intestate, on a credit under the provisions of this act, he shall take the note of the person hiring or renting such property, for the amount of the hire or rent, with good personal security; and if he shall fail to take such note and security, he and his sureties shall in like manner be liable for the amount thereof.(*a*)

Liability for neglect.

X. PAYMENT OF THE DEBTS OF ESTATE.

Debts—order of payment.

ART. 783. [78] The debts due from an estate shall be paid by the executor or administrator in the following order:

1st. Funeral expenses and expenses of last sickness.

2d. All expenses of administration, including the allowance that may be made under the provisions of the forty-fourth and forty-fifth sections of this act; and the expenses incurred in the preservation, safe keeping and management of the estate.

3d. Debts secured by mortgage, or having a lien, whether by judgment or execution, or otherwise, so far as the same can be paid out of the proceeds of the property subject to such mortgage or lien; and when more than one of such mortgages and liens, or any of them exist upon the same property, the oldest shall be first paid.

4th. All other debts, and no preference shall be given to debts secured by mortgage, or having a lien by judgment, execution, or otherwise, further than regards the property subject to such mortgage or lien. When there is a deficiency of assets, debts of the fourth class shall be paid only *pro rata;* and no executor or administrator shall be allowed to pay any claims of the fourth class, whether the estate is solvent or insolvent, except with their *pro rata* amount of the funds of the estate that have come to hand.

ART. 784. [80] Executors and administrators, whenever they have funds in their hands belonging to the estate they represent, shall pay—

1st. The funeral expenses and expenses of last sickness.

2d. Expenses of administration, including the allowance that may be made under the provisions of the forty-fourth and forty-fifth sections of this act; and the expenses incurred in the preservation, safe keeping, and management of the estate, when such claims have been allowed, and approved, or established; and if they shall fail or refuse so to do, when required by the holder of such claims, the person holding any such claim may obtain an order from the Chief Justice at a regular term of the court, directing such payment to be made, upon making proof that such executor or administrator has funds of the estate in his hands sufficient to make such payment, and fails or refuses to make it: provided, such executor or administrator shall have first been cited on the complaint of the holder of such claim, to appear and show cause why such order should not be made.

Representative having funds, and failing to pay, &c.

(*a*) That the administrator failed to take the mortgage on the property sold as required by the statute, is no defence to the sureties to the note, in a suit against them to recover the purchase money. Wornell *v.* Williams, 19 Tex. Rep. 180.

Proceeds of mortgage sale to be paid to creditors, when.

ART. 785. [81] Whenever any executor or administrator shall have in his hands the proceeds of a sale that has been made for the satisfaction of a mortgage or other lien, and such proceeds or any part thereof are not required for the payment of any debts against the estate, that have a preference over such mortgage or other lien, it shall be the duty of such executor or administrator immediately to pay over such proceeds, or so much thereof as may not be required for the payment of any debts against the estate that have a preference over such mortgage or other lien, to the creditor or creditors having a right thereto; and if any executor or administrator shall fail or refuse so to do, such creditor or creditors upon proof thereof, may obtain an order from the Chief Justice, in like manner as is provided in the preceding section, directing such payment to be made.

(See art. 1191.)

Payment may be ordered.

ART. 786. [83] Upon the return of the exhibit mentioned in the preceding section of this act, if it shall appear therefrom, or by any other evidence, that the estate is solvent—taking into consideration as well the claims presented before the expiration of twelve months from said granting of letters testamentary or of administration, on which suit has been, or can yet be instituted, as those so presented, allowed, and approved, or established by judgment; and that the executor or administrator has in his hands sufficient funds for the payment of all the aforesaid claims, it shall be the duty of the Chief Justice to order immediate payment to be made of all the claims allowed and approved, or established by judgment. If he has funds in his hands, but not sufficient for the payment of all the said claims; or if the estate be insolvent, and he has any funds in his hands, it shall be the duty of the Chief Justice to order such funds to be applied to the payment of all claims, having a preference in the order of their priority, if they or any of them be still unpaid; and then to the payment, *pro rata*, of the other claims allowed and approved or established; taking into consideration, also, the claims that were presented within the twelve months, and in suit, or on which suit may yet be instituted.(*a*)

Pro rata.

Claims presented after 12 mo's, when paid.

ART. 787. [85] Claims for money against the estate of a deceased person, which may be presented to the executor or administrator after the expiration of twelve months from the original grant of letters testamentary or of administration, and allowed by him, and approved by the Chief Justice, or established by suit, shall be paid by the executor or administrator at any time before the estate is finally closed, when he has funds of the estate in his hands over and above what may be sufficient to pay all debts of every kind against the estate, that were presented within the twelve months and allowed and approved, or established by suit, or that may be so established; and an order for the payment of any such claim, upon proof that the executor or administrator has such funds, may be obtained from the Chief Justice in like manner as is provided in this act, for creditors to obtain orders of payment.

Representative may be required to make an exhibit.

ART. 788. [86] At the third regular term of the court, after the expiration of twelve months from the original grant of letters testamentary or of administration, or at any term of the court after that, any person interested in the estate may, by a complaint in writing, filed in the County Court, cause the executor or administrator to be cited to appear at a regular term of the court, and make an exhibit in writing, under oath, to the court, setting forth fully, in connection with the previous exhibits, the condition of the estate he represents; and if it shall appear to the court by said exhibit, or by other evidence, that such executor or administrator has any funds of the estate in his hands subject to distribution among the creditors

Order of court.

(*a*) The order of the court is not necessary to the validity of a payment of a claim which had been allowed and approved. If an administrator, without an order of court, makes payments to one or more creditors, of a portion or the whole of their claims, he does not thereby render himself personally liable for the debts unpaid; but upon settlement he will only be entitled to credit for the amounts to which such creditors are actually entitled. Lockhart *v.* White, 18 Tex. Rep. 102.

of the estate, it shall be the duty of the Chief Justice to order the same to be paid out to them according to the provisions of this act; or any executor or administrator may voluntarily present such exhibit to the court, and if he has any of the funds of the estate in his hands subject to distribution among the creditors of the estate, a like order shall be made. (a)

XI. PARTITION AND DISTRIBUTION—ART. 823.

[*See Partition.*]

Citation to executor, &c., to show cause, &c. ART. 789. [87] At any time after the first term of the court, after the expiration of twelve months from the original grant of letters testamentary or of administration, the heirs, devisees or legatees of the estate, or any of them, may, by their complaint in writing, filed in the County Court, cause the executor or administrator, and the heirs, devisees or legatees of the estate, to be cited to appear at a regular term of the court, and show cause why a partition and distribution should not be made among the heirs, devisees or legatees, of the residue of the estate, if any there be, after retaining in the hands of the executor or administrator a sufficient portion thereof to pay all debts of every kind against the estate, that have been allowed and approved, or established by suit, or that have been rejected by the executor or administrator, or not approved by the Chief Justice, and may yet be established. And if it shall appear to the Chief Justice, after the service of such citation, that there is any such residue of the estate, he shall order it to be so partitioned and distributed. May be ordered, when.

Final settlement, when made. ART. 790. [89] When all the debts known to exist of every kind against the estate of a deceased person have been paid, or when they have been paid so far as the assets of the estate in the hands of the executor or administrator will permit, the executor or administrator of such estate may present his account to the court, verified by affidavit, for settlement; or, the Chief Justice shall cause him to be cited to present such account, either of his own motion, or on the complaint of any person interested in the estate. Upon the presentation of such account, it shall be the duty of the Chief Justice, either in term time or in vacation, to order at least twenty days' notice to be given by publication in a newspaper, if there be one printed in the county; if not, then by posting such notice at the court house, and at two other public places in the county, for at least twenty days: such notice shall state the presentation of said account, the term of the court when it will be acted on, and shall require all persons interested, to appear and contest said account, if they see proper. The Chief Justice may order such other notice to be given as he shall deem expedient. At the term of the court named in such notice, or at some subsequent term to which the same may be continued, upon proof being made that notice has been given in the manner required by this act and the order of the Chief Justice, it shall be his duty, after examining said account with all the exceptions thereto, and hearing the evidence that may be offered in support of, or against, said account and exceptions, to re-state said account if necessary, and to audit and settle the same; and upon the settlement of said account, if there is none of the estate remaining in the hands of the executor or administrator, he shall be discharged from his trust by an order of the Chief Justice; but if there is any of the estate remaining in the hands of the executor or Proceedings when final account is filed.

(a) That there is "property" in the hands of the administrator, is not sufficient to warrant a peremptory order for the payment of a claim and execution to enforce it. Ray, Adm'r, v. Parsons, 14 Tex. Rep. 370. Until a claim has been allowed by the administrator, and approved by the Probate Court, it has no judicial standing in the Probate Court. Danzey v. Swinney, 7 Tex. Rep. 617.

administrator, and the heirs, devisees, or legatees of the estate, or their assignees, or either or any of them are present or represented in court, it shall be the duty of the Chief Justice to order a partition and distribution of the estate to be made among them, upon satisfactory proof being made that they are entitled to receive it. Discharge of executor, &c.

ART. 791. [90] Upon the settlement of the account of any executor or administrator, as provided for in the preceding section, if the heirs, devisees or legatees of the estate, or their assignees, or either or any of them do not appear or are not represented in the court, and there are any funds of such estate remaining in the hands of the executor or administrator, it shall be the duty of the Chief Justice to order the same to be paid over to the Treasurer of the State; and if there shall be any property of the estate that has not been sold, or any debts due the estate that may be collected, it shall be the duty of the Chief Justice to order such property to be sold on a credit of twelve months, and such debts to be collected; and at the first term of the court, after the expiration of twelve months after such sale, and every six months thereafter, while the estate remains under the control of such executor or administrator, it shall be his duty to render to the court a full exhibit of the condition of such estate, verified by affidavit. And whenever there shall be any funds of the estate in the hands of the executor or administrator, it shall be the duty of the Chief Justice to order the same to be paid to the Treasurer of the State: provided, however, that while such estate, or any portion thereof, remains under the control of the executor or administrator, the heirs, devisees or legatees, or their assignees, or either or any of them, may obtain from the Chief Justice, at a regular term of the court, an order to have the same partitioned and distributed among them according to their respective interests in the same, upon causing the executor or administrator to be cited, and making satisfactory proof to the court of their right to the same; and whenever such estate shall have been so partitioned and distributed and delivered over to the persons entitled thereto, or when the debts due such estate have been collected so far as there is a reasonable prospect of collecting them, and the proceeds paid over to the Treasurer of the State as herein required, such executor or administrator shall be finally discharged from his trust, by an order of the Chief Justice, entered at some regular term. Funds not distributed, to be paid to Treasurer, &c. Property to be sold and proceeds paid to Treasurer, &c., when. May be paid to heirs upon proof.

ART. 792. [91] Whenever an order shall be made by the Chief Justice for an executor or administrator to pay over any funds to the Treasurer of the State under the provisions of this act, it shall be the duty of the Clerk of the court in which such order may be made, to transmit to said Treasurer by mail, a certified copy of such order within one month after said order shall have been made. Whenever the Clerk mails such copy, he shall take from the postmaster with whom it is mailed, a certificate, stating that such certified copy was mailed in his office, directed to the Treasurer of the State, at the seat of government of this State, and the date when it was mailed, which certificate shall be recorded in the minutes of the court; and any Clerk who shall neglect to transmit a certified copy of such order within the time prescribed, and to take such certificate and have it so recorded shall be liable to a penalty of one hundred dollars, to be recovered by an action in the name of the State, before any Justice of the Peace of the county, on the information of any citizen of the county; one half of which penalty shall be paid to the informer, and the other half to the State. Copy of order to be sent to Treasurer, &c. Penalty for neglect.

ART. 793. [92] Whenever any executor or administrator shall pay over to the Treasurer of the State any funds of the estate he represents, under the provisions of this act, he may take from such Treasurer a receipt for such payment, with his official seal attached, and file the same and have it recorded Treasurer's receipt may be taken and filed.

on the minutes of the court by which such funds were ordered to be paid; and a copy of such record shall be evidence of such payment.

Suit may be brought by heirs, &c.

ART. 794. [93] Whenever any funds of an estate shall have been paid to the Treasurer of the State, under the provisions of this act, any heir, devisee, or legatee of such estate, or their assignees, or either or any of them, may recover the portion of such funds to which he or she would have been entitled if the same had not been so paid to the Treasurer. Such recovery may be had in a suit against said Treasurer before any court of competent jurisdiction in the county where the letters testamentary or of administration were granted: but in any such suit the plaintiff shall be liable for all costs of court; and in all cases where any funds belonging to the estate of a deceased person have heretofore been paid into the treasury of the State: or when any title papers belonging to any such estate have been deposited with the Comptroller, such funds or title papers may be recovered in like manner by the person or persons who would have been entitled thereto, if the same had not been so paid over or deposited.

Failure of executor, &c., to pay over to Treasurer.

ART. 795. [94] Whenever any executor or administrator shall fail to pay to the Treasurer of the State any funds of the estate he represents, that he has been ordered by the Chief Justice so to pay within three months after such order has been made, such executor or administrator shall be liable to pay out of his own estate to the State Treasurer damages thereon at the rate of *five per cent.* per month for each month he may neglect to make such payment after the three months from such order. The Treasurer of the State shall have the right, in the name of the State, to apply to the Chief Justice of the court in which such order was made, to enforce the payment of such funds and damages if any have accrued; and it shall be the duty of the Chief Justice to enforce the payment in like manner as other orders of payment are enforced by him; or the said Treasurer shall have the right to institute suit in the name of the State against such executor or administrator and the sureties on his bond, for the recovery of the funds so ordered to be paid, and damages, if any have accrued: which suit may be instituted in any court of competent jurisdiction, in the county where the letters testamentary or of administration were granted.

How enforced.

Failure of executor, &c., to pay over funds.

ART. 796. [95] In all cases where an order shall have been made by any Chief Justice under the provisions of this act, for an executor or administrator to pay over money to any person other than the Treasurer of the State, and such executor or administrator shall neglect to make such payment when it is demanded by the person entitled thereto, his agent or attorney, such executor or administrator shall be liable to pay out of his own estate to the person in whose favor such order of payment was made, damages upon the amount he shall so neglect to pay, at the rate of *ten per cent.* per month for each and every month he shall so neglect to make such payment after the same was so demanded; such damages to be recovered by suit, before any court having competent jurisdiction.

Application for partition and distribution to be in writing, &c.

ART. 797. [96] All applications for the partition and distribution of an estate under the provisions of this act, shall be in writing, and shall be filed with the Clerk of the Court to which the application is made. Upon the filing of any such application, it shall be the duty of the Clerk to issue a citation, returnable to some regular term of the court, which citation shall state the name of the person whose estate is sought to be partitioned and distributed, the term of the court to which such citation is returnable, and shall require all persons interested in the estate to appear and show cause why such partition and distribution should not be made; such citation shall be personally served by caving a copy thereof with each person entitled to a share of the estate,

Proceedings in such cases.

who is known and is a resident of this State; and if there be any person so entitled, who are not known or who are not residents of this State, such citation shall be published for at least four successive weeks in some newspaper printed in the county, if there be one; if not then it shall be published in like manner in one of the nearest newspapers published in the State; a copy of such publication and the affidavit of the publisher or printer attached thereto, stating that it was so published, shall be evidence of the publication. Citation.

ART. 798. [97] At the return term of any such citation as is provided for in the preceding section, or at some succeeding term to which the application may be continued by the court, if it shall appear that such citation has been served and published as required by law, the court shall proceed to ascertain who are the persons, by law, entitled to partition and distribution, and their respective shares; and if there are any persons so entitled, who are known, and are minors, and have no guardian in this State, or whose guardians are also entitled to a portion of such estate, the court shall appoint a guardian, *ad litem*, to represent them in the partition of the estate; and if there are any persons so entitled, who are not known, or not residents of this State, and no person appears who is authorized to represent them, the court shall appoint an attorney to represent them in the partition of the estate: after which, the court shall proceed to ascertain whether advancements have been made to any of the persons so entitled—their nature and value—and require the same to be placed in *hotchpotch*, as required by the law governing descents and distributions; and also to ascertain what estate is liable to partition and distribution: the court shall then enter a decree, which shall state the name and residence if known, of each person entitled to a share of the estate—specifying those who are known to be minors—the name of their guardian or guardians, *ad litem*—the name of the attorney appointed to represent those who are unknown, or are not residents of this State: the decree shall also state the proportional part of the estate to which each is entitled; and shall contain a full description of all the estate to be distributed: if the estate to be distributed shall consist only of money, or debts due the estate, or both, the court shall fix the amount to which each is entitled, and order the payment and delivery thereof by the executor or administrator; but if the estate do not consist entirely of money or debts due the estate, or both, the court shall appoint three or more discreet persons as commissioners to make a partition and distribution of the estate, and shall order a writ of partition to issue, commanding them to proceed forthwith to make such partition and distribution in accordance with the decree of the court, a copy of which shall accompany such writ; and, also, commanding them to make due return of said writ, with their proceedings under it, at some term of the court to be named in the writ. Proceedings after return of citation. Guardian, *ad litem*. Attorney appointed. Decree. Commissioners to make partition. Writ of partition.

ART. 799. [98] It shall be the duty of the Commissioners of partition under this act, to make a fair, just and impartial partition and distribution of the estate in the following order: 1st. Of the land or other real estate by allotment to each distributee, of a part in each parcel, or of parts in one or more parcels or of one or more parcels either with or without the addition of a part or parts of other parcels, as shall be most for the interest of the distributees: provided, the said real estate is capable of being so divided without manifest injury to all or any of the distributees. And the said Commissioners shall have power, if they think it necessary, to call to their aid one or more well qualified surveyors to run the lines of any lands and also divisional lines thereof. If the real estate is not capable of a fair, just, and equal division, in kind, but may be made so, by allotting to one or more of the distributees a proportion of money or negroes, or other personal property to supply the deficiency or deficiencies, the Commissioners shall have power to make, as near as may be, an equal division of the real estate, and supply the deficiency Duty of, and mode of making of any share or shares from the money, negroes, or other property. The Commissioners shall proceed to make a like division in kind as near as may be, of the negroes, supplying the deficiency of any share or shares from the money or other property; and also a like division of the money and other personal property, and shall determine by lot, among equal shares, to whom each particular share shall belong.

Division of negroes.

When property cannot be equally divided, special returns to be made, &c.

ART. 800. [99] When, in the opinion of the Commissioners, the whole, or any portion of any estate, is not capable of a fair and equal division among the distributees, the said Commissioners shall make a special return of such property to the court, with the value thereof duly appraised by them. Upon such return being made to the court, any one or more of the distributees at a regular term of the court by the payment to the executor or administrator of the appraised value of the property so returned as incapable of division; or on the execution of his or their obligations with one or more good and sufficient sureties in favor of each of the other distributees for their share of the appraised value of such property, payable at such time, not exceeding twelve months from the date thereof, as the court may designate; provided, the court may think it for the interest of the distributees to allow a credit; shall have the right to take the said property. Should any one or more of the distributees take the said property as aforesaid, it shall be the duty of the court to enter a decree stating the facts; and on the entry of such decree the property shall vest as fully and absolutely in the person or persons taking the same as the deceased was vested therewith: provided, nevertheless, that when obligations are executed as aforesaid, a lien shall exist upon such property by operation of law, to secure the payment of such obligations; provided, also, that if any of the distributees shall file in the court, his exception to the appraisement of the Commissioners, before any of the distributees shall have so taken such property, a new appraisement of said property shall be made by order of the court. If no distributee take the said property as aforesaid, the court shall order the sale of said property, either for cash, or on a credit, as may be most for the interest of the distributees; and at such sale, if any distributee shall bid off any of said property, he shall be required to pay or secure, as the case may be, only such amount of his bid as may exceed the amount of his share of such property; and the proceeds of sale, when collected, shall be distributed by the court among those entitled thereto.

When distributee may take property at valuation, &c.

If no distributee take, &c., property may be sold.

Report of Commissioners.

ART. 801. [100] Said Commissioners having divided the whole or any part of the estate, shall make to the court a report in writing, subscribed and sworn to by them, containing a statement of the property divided by them; and also a particular description of the property allotted to each distributee, and its value. And if it be real estate that has been divided, said report shall contain a general plat of such land, with the divisional lines plainly set down, and the number of acres in each share. Upon the return of such report, it shall be the duty of the court, at some regular term, to examine said report carefully; and if it be merely informal, to cause said informality to be corrected: and if such division shall appear to have been fairly made according to law, and no valid exceptions are taken to it, the court shall approve it, and order it to be recorded; but if said division shall not appear to have been so made, or any valid exceptions are taken to it, the court shall set aside said report and division, and order a new partition to be made.

When part of estate lies in a distant county.

ART. 802. [101] When any portion of the estate to be partitioned lies in a distant county, and cannot be fairly partitioned without a view thereof, and it is inconvenient for the Commissioners to go and examine such property, they may report such facts to the Chief Justice in writing; whereupon he may at some regular term of the court, if satisfied that the said property cannot be conveniently divided, or that its sale would be more advantageous to the distributees, order a sale thereof for cash, or on a credit of not more than twelve months, at his discretion: and when the proceeds of such sale shall have been collected, they shall be distributed, by him, among those entitled thereto; but if no such proof be made, three or more Commissioners may be appointed in each county where any portion of the estate so reported is situated, and the same proceedings shall be had thereon, as is provided in this act for Commissioners to make partition.

ART. 803. [102] When any husband or wife shall die leaving any common property, the survivor may at any time after letters testamentary or of administration have been granted and an inventory of the estate of the deceased has been returned, make application to the court from which such letters were granted, for a partition of such common property; and if he or she shall execute and deliver to said Chief Justice an obligation with good and sufficient sureties, payable to, and approved by said Chief Justice, for an amount equal to the value of his or her interest in such common property, conditioned for the payment of one-half of all debts existing against such common property; then the Chief Justice shall proceed to make a partition of said common property into two equal moieties, one to be delivered to the survivor and the other to the executor or administrator of the deceased; and all the provisions of this act respecting the partition and distribution of estates, shall apply to any partition made under the provisions of this section so far as the same may be applicable; and whenever such partition may be made, a lien shall exist upon the portion of such survivor to secure the payment of the obligation he may have given as aforesaid; and until a partition shall be applied for as herein provided, the executor or administrator of the deceased shall have the right and it shall be his duty to recover possession of all of such common property, and hold the same in trust to be administered for the benefit of the creditors and others entitled thereto under the provisions of this act. After such partition any creditor of said common property may sue in his own name on such obligation, and shall have judgment thereon for the one-half of such debt as he may establish; and for the other half he shall be entitled to be paid by the executor or administrator of the deceased.(*a*)

Of community property.

Creditor may sue on obligation, when.

ART. 804. [103] In all cases where Commissioners to make partition are appointed under this act, the report of any three of them shall be sufficient. All such Commissioners shall receive two dollars each, for every day they may be engaged, and all their reasonable expenses shall be paid them.

Report and pay of Commissioners.

ART. 805. [104] In any case where the Chief Justice shall appoint a guardian *ad litem* for minors, or any attorney to represent the persons absent from the State or unknown, under the provisions of this act, if such guardian *ad litem*, or attorney shall neglect to attend to the duties of such appointment, the Chief Justice shall appoint others in their places by an order entered on the minutes of the court; and such guardian *ad litem* and attorneys shall be allowed by the Chief Justice a reasonable compensation for their services, which shall be paid out of the estate of the person they represent, and the Chief Justice may order execution to issue for the same.

Guardian *ad litem* and attorney, &c.

ART. 806. [105] That all expenses incurred in the partition of estates shall be paid by the parties interested in the partition, each party paying in proportion to the share he may receive. The portion of the estate allotted to each distributee shall be liable for his or her portion of the expenses; and if not paid, the court shall have power to order execution therefor in the names of the persons entitled thereto.

Expenses of, how paid.

(*a*) The above article must be construed with reference to existing laws upon the subject of exemptions; and be its expressions or constructions what they may, they cannot effect the homestead, guaranteed by the Constitution to every head of a family. Wood and Wife *v.* Wheeler, 7 Tex. Rep., 13.

Who may ask for.

ART. 807. [106] Any person or persons having a joint interest with the estate of a decedent in any property, real or personal, may make application to the County Court from which letters testamentary or of administration have been granted on said estate, to have a partition thereof: whereupon the court shall proceed to make a partition of said property between the applicant or applicants and the estate of the deceased; and all the rules and regulations contained herein in relation to the partition and distribution of estates shall govern partitions under this section, so far as the same may be applicable.

Respective shares to be paid to heirs, &c.

ART. 808. [107] When the report of any Commissioners to make partition shall have been approved and ordered to be recorded, the court shall order the executor or administrator to deliver to the distributees their respective shares of the estate on demand, including all the title-deeds and papers belonging to the same. If any distributee be a minor, his share shall be delivered to his guardian. If any minor distributee, resident of the State of Texas, shall have no guardian, the executor or administrator shall retain his share until a guardian shall be appointed, and he shall be allowed by the court reasonable compensation for taking care of the same. If any executor or administrator shall neglect to deliver to the person entitled thereto, his agent or attorney, when demanded, any portion of an estate so ordered to be delivered, such executor or administrator shall be liable to pay out of his own estate to the person so entitled damages on the amount of his share at the rate of *ten per cent.* per month, for each and every month he shall so neglect to deliver such share, after such demand, which damages may be recovered by suit, before any court of competent jurisdiction.

Executor or administrator to retain, when.

Share not claimed to be paid to Treasurer.

ART. 809. [108] If any person entitled to a portion of an estate shall not demand the same from the executor or administrator, within six months after the report of the Commissioners of partition has been approved and ordered to be recorded, the Chief Justice shall order so much of such portion as may be in money to be paid to the Treasurer of the State; and such portion as may be in other property, the Chief Justice shall order the executor or administrator to sell on such terms as he may think best; and when the proceeds of such sale are collected, he shall order the same to be paid to the Treasurer of the State: in all such cases allowing to the executor or administrator, reasonable compensation for his services.

XII. OF THE COMMUNITY PROPERTY.

Act of August 26, 1856. Took effect from passage.

Community property and debts.

ART. 810. [1] The community property of the husband and wife shall be liable for all the debts contracted during marriage, except in such cases as are specially excepted by law. And in the settlement of community estates it shall be the duty of the survivor, executor, or administrator to keep a separate and distinct account of all the community debts allowed or paid in the settlement of such estates.

Survivor to have control of, without administration.

ART. 811. [2] It shall not be necessary for any surviving husband to administer upon the community property of himself and his deceased wife, but he shall have the exclusive management, control and disposition of the same after her death in the same manner as during her life subject to the provisions of this act.

Duty of husband in case deceased wife leaves children.

ART. 812. [3] It shall be the duty of the surviving husband at the death of his wife, if she have a surviving child or children, to file in the County Court a full, fair and complete inventory and appraisement of all the community property of himself and his deceased wife, to be taken and recorded as in cases of administration, and to have the same force and effect in all suits between parties claiming under it. After which, without any administration or further action whatever in the Probate Court, he shall have the right to manage, control and dispose of said community property both real and personal, in such manner as to him may seem best for the interest of said estate, and of suing and being sued with regard to the same, in the same manner as during the life of the wife. And he shall keep a fair and full account and statement of all exchanges, sales and other disposition of community property, and upon final partition shall account to the legal heirs of his wife for their interest in said community, and the increase and profits in the same after deducting a reasonable commission for the management of the same. And he shall be liable to the amount of said inventory and appraisement at all times for the interest of said heirs in said community property.

ART. 813. [4] Should said surviving husband neglect, fail, or refuse to file said inventory in the County Court as required by the provisions of this act, within sixty days after the death of his deceased wife, the County Court, upon complaint made and satisfactory proof thereof by any one having an interest in said estate either in person or by next friend, may upon its own motion or the motion of any party interested, require him to do so, or otherwise grant administration upon said estate, as in other cases provided by statute. Husband failing to file inventory.

And if upon the filing of said inventory it shall appear to the court, that it is in any way necessary for the protection of the property belonging to said estate, bond and security may be required of said surviving husband in such amount and with such conditions as may be deemed necessary by the Court for the protection of the interests of the creditors and heirs of said estate, and upon failure to execute said bond with security as required by said Court, administration may be granted upon said estate as in other cases. After inventory bond may be required.

ART. 814. [5] Should any of the heirs of the deceased wife, either in person, or by next friend or guardian, represent and show to any court of competent jurisdiction that said surviving husband is wasting or mismanaging or is about to waste or mismanage said community property, or is about to remove it out of the State or otherwise dispose of it in such manner as to injure, or defraud the right of such heir or heirs, the husband may be required to enter into such bond and security for the proper management of such property, and with such other conditions as may be required by the Court, or the Court may appoint an administrator over the estate of the wife as in other cases provided by statute. Proceedings when husband is, or is about wasting community, &c.

ART. 815. [6] Said surviving husband may as each of the surviving heirs of his deceased wife or all of them, become of lawful age, set aside and deliver to him or them, what he considers their equal and equitable share in said community property, exhibiting therewith a full and complete statement of the same for which he may require the receipt of such heir, stating the amount description and value of the property delivered, which said partition and distribution shall be binding, and final upon said heir or heirs, unless proceeding is commenced in some competent court, within two years after said distribution, by such heir to set the same aside. Heirs' coming of age, share to be paid to. Binding, unless.

In which case, any party interested may require a full and fair investigation into the whole of said estate, and said partition and the court entertaining jurisdiction of the same, shall have full discretion to enter all decrees and orders to obtain and carry out a full and fair settlement and partition of said estate, with such heir or heirs as may then be entitled to receive their distributive share. Whole estate, when investigated.

ART. 816. [7.] The surviving wife may retain the exclusive management and control of the community property of herself and her deceased husband, Foregoing provisions apply to surviving wife.

in the same manner, and subject to the same rights, rules and regulations, as provided in the foregoing provisions of this act, until she may marry again. But upon a second marriage she shall cease to have such control and management of said estate, or the right to dispose of the same under the provisions of this act, and said estate shall be subject to administration, as in other cases of deceased persons' estates.

XIII. TRANSFER OF ADMINISTRATION TO NEW COUNTIES.

Act of May 13, 1846. Took effect from passage. Papers relative to estate &c., shall be transmitted.

ART. 817. [1] It shall be the duty of the County Court of Probate of any county from which any county, or part thereof, has been or may hereafter be taken, to transmit all original papers relating to the settlement of estates of deceased persons who were, at the time of their decease, residents of that part of the territory of the county which has been or may hereafter be taken to from (form) any new county, to the Probate Court of such new county, upon the petition of any executor, or administrator, or guardian, or a majority of the heirs of any such estate; and he shall also transmit, with such original papers, a transcript, certified under the seal of the court, of the records of all proceedings had in relation to such estates in his court: provided, that at the time of filing such petition, the party filing it shall pay all fees due on account of such estate.

Shall be first registered.

ART. 818. [2] Previous to the transmission of any such original papers, in the manner provided for in the preceding section, the Judge to whom such petition is presented shall cause a registry of all such original papers as have not been recorded, to be made in his office, for which the same fees shall be allowed as is allowed for other recording.

Act of Jan'y 9, 1852. Force and effect of transcript &c.

ART. 819. [3] In all cases where the papers and proceedings, relating to the settlement of an estate, shall be transmitted to any court in the manner provided for in this act, such estate shall be proceeded in and settled in the Probate Court of such county, in like manner as if the settlement of such estates had been originally commenced in such county, and the transcript of the record transmitted in the manner provided for in this act, shall have the same force and effect in evidence as the record itself might or could have.

XIV. GENERAL PROVISIONS.

Compensation of executor, &c.

ART. 820. [79] Executors and administrators shall be entitled to receive, and may retain in their hands, five per cent. upon the sums they may actually receive in cash; and the same upon all sums they may pay away, in cash, in the course of their adminisiration. All reasonable expenses incurred by an executor or administrator in the preservation, safe keeping, and management of the estate, and all reasonable attorneys' fees that may be incurred in the course of the administration, shall be allowed by the Chief Justice, on proof that there was a necessity therefor. Whenever in the opinion of the Chief Justice, the commission upon the sums received, and paid away, is not sufficient compensation for his services; or if, from the circumstances of the estate, extraordinary services were required to be rendered, the Chief Justice shall allow such further compensation as may seem reasonable.

Receipts for

ART. 821. [109] Whenever any executor or administrator shall file in the court receipts showing that he has disposed of any portion of the estate under the provisions of this Act, the court shall order the same to be recorded; and whenever he shall have so filed rceipts showing that all of the estate has been disposed of by him under the provisions of this Act, he shall be finally discharged from his trust by the Chief Justice. Property disposed of, &c.

ART. 822. [110] Any person capable of making a will, may so provide by his will, that no other action shall be had in the County Court, in relation to the settlement of his estate, than the probate and registration of his will and the return of an inventory of the estate; but in all such cases any person having a debt against said estate may, by complaint in writing, filed in the court where such will was proved, cause all the persons entitled to any portion of such estate under the will, or as heirs at law, to be cited to appear before such court at some regular term, and execute an obligation, with two or more good and sufficient sureties, for an amount equal to the full value of such estate to be ascertained by the inventory; such obligation to be payable to the Chief Justice, and conditioned that the persons who execute the obligation shall pay all debts that may be established against such estate, in the manner herein provided; and on the return of such citations served, unless such persons so entitled to any portion of the estate, or some of them, or some other persons for them, shall execute such obligation to the satisfaction of the Chief Justice, such estate shall be settled under the direction of the court as other estates are required to be settled; but if such obligation shall be executed, it shall be filed and recorded in said court, and no other action shall be had in said court in relation to such estate. All costs of such proceedings shall be paid by the persons so entitled to such estate, according to their respective interests in it. Every creditor of such estate shall have the right to sue on such obligation, and shall be entitled to judgment thereon, for such debt as he may establish against the testator by a verdict of the jury in such suits; or such creditors may have their action against those in possession of the estate.(a)

Testator may will that no action be had in County Court except.

Obligation of heirs may be required.

ART. 823. [111] At any time after the return of the inventory of the estate of a deceased person, any one entitled to a portion of said estate, as heirs, devisee, or legatee, or his or her guardian, if he or she be a minor, may, by a complaint in writing, filed in the court where such inventory has been returned, cause the executor or administrator of the estate to be cited to appear at some regular term of the court and render an exhibit, under oath, of the condition of such estate; and on the return of such citation served, the person so entitled to such estate, or any of them, or any other persons for them may execute and deliver to the Chief Justice, an obligation payable to him, with two or more good and sufficient sureties, to be approved by the Chief Justice, for an amount at least equal to the appraised value of the estate as ascertained by the inventory, conditioned, that the persons who execute such obligation shall pay all debts against the estate not paid, that have been allowed by the executor or administrator, and approved by the Chief Justice, or that have been established by suit against the executor or administrator, or that may be established against the estate by suit in the manner herein provided, and may pay to the executor or administrator any balance that may be decreed to be due to him, on his exhibit, in obedience to said citation; whereupon such obligation shall be filed and recorded in said court; and the court shall on the application of any of the persons so entitled to any portion of the estate, cause a partition and distribution of such estate to be made among the persons entitled thereto, in accordance with the provisions of this Act, respecting the partition and distribution of estates; and a lien shall exist on all of said estate in the hands of the distributees, to secure

Executor &c. may be required to render an exhibit.

Order for delivery of estate over, may be obtained upon giving bond, &c.

Partition shall be ordered.

A lien exist, &c.

(a) A provision in the will and the assent of the heirs are both necessary to take the administration of the estate out of the Probate Court. Unless the heirs comply with the provisions of the statute, the estate must be settled under the directions of the Chief Justice as in other cases. Hogue, Ex'r v. Sims, 9 Tex. Rep. 546.

the ultimate payment of the aforesaid obligation. Any creditor of such estate, whose claim is yet unpaid, and has been allowed by the executor or administrator, previous to the filing of such obligation, and approved by the Chief Justice, or established by suit against the executor or administrator, previous to the filing of such obligation, shall have the right to sue on such obligation in his own name, and shall be entitled to judgment thereon for the amount of his claim: or any other creditor of such estate, whose claim is not barred by the laws of limitation, shall have the right to sue on such obligation, and shall be entitled to judgment thereon, for such debt as he may establish against the estate by a verdict of the jury in such suit: or any of said creditors may sue the distributees, but no one of them shall be liable beyond his just proportion, according to the estate he may have received in the distribution.

In whom property of testator and intestate vests, &c.

ART. 824. [112] When a person dies, leaving a lawful will, all of his estate devised or bequeathed by such will, shall vest immediately in the devisees or legatees; and all the estate of such person, not devised or bequeathed, shall vest immediately in his heirs at law; but all of such estate, whether devised or bequeathed, or not, except such as may be exempted by law from the payment of debts, shall still be liable and subject, in their hands, to the payment of the debts of such testator: and whenever a person dies intestate, all of his estate shall vest immediately in his heirs at law; but, with the exceptions aforesaid, shall still be liable and subject, in their hands, to the payment of the debts of the intestate. But upon the issuance of letters testamentary or of administration, on any such estate, the executor or administrator shall have a right to the possession of the estate, as it existed at the death of the testator or intestate, with the exception aforesaid; and it shall be his duty to recover possession of and hold such estate in trust, to be disposed of under the provisions of this Act.(*a*)

Who shall have possession of, &c

Unsettled estates in Probate Court.

ART. 825. [117] All proceedings in relation to the settlement, partition and distribution of estates, that now remain unsettled in the Probate Courts of the several counties in this State, shall be had in the County Court, and shall, from this time forward, proceed and be concluded, under the provisions of this Act.

Person having possession of testator's will, &c., may be cited, &c.

ART. 826. [119] When complaint shall be made in writing, to any Chief Justice, that any person has the last will of any testator or testatrix, or any papers belonging to the estate of a testator or intestate, said Chief Justice shall cause such person to be cited to appear before him, either in term time or in vacation, and show cause why he should not deliver such will to the court for probate; or why he should not deliver such papers to the executor or administrator; and upon the return of such citation served, unless such will or papers are so delivered, or good cause be shown to the court for not delivering the same, the Chief Justice, if satisfied that such person had such will or papers, at the time of the complaint being filed, may cause him to be arrested and imprisoned until he so deliver them.(*b*)

To whom this Act shall apply.

ART. 827. [120] All the provisions in this Act relative to an executor or administrator, shall apply and extend to an executrix or administratrix, or executors or administrators respectively, unless otherwise expressly provided for; and whenever any party in the singular number, or a male party is mentioned, the rule shall apply to a female, or to two or more having a joint

(*a*) Under our Probate Laws, an estate of a deceased person vests immediately in the heirs subject to administration only; consequently, the heir who takes possession, is not liable in the nature of an executor, *de son tort*, at the suit of a creditor, in the District Court. The proper remedy is administration in the Probate Court. Ansley *v.* Baker, 14 Tex. Rep. 608. Bufford *v.* Holliman, 10 Tex. Rep. 560.

(*b*) In a proceeding under this article, an objection or claim of privilege on the part of the defendant, that he resides in another county, is bad. Pierpont *v.* Threlkeld, 13 Tex. Rep. 244. The section includes previous administrators; but an administrator who has been removed cannot be required to surrender up his own vouchers or papers necessary to his own defence. Miller, Adm'r, *v.* Jasper, 10 Tex. Rep. 513.

interest, or jointly concerned, applying or called upon, so far as the rule can with propriety apply, or so far as is not otherwise directed.(*a*)

Art. 828. [121] Any one interested in the estate of a deceased person, may at any time within two years after the settlement by the Chief Justice of any account of the executor or administrator of such estate, have the same revised and corrected by the District Court of the county in which the letters of such executor or administrator were granted, upon making proof before such District Court, that there was any error or fraud in such account or settlement: provided, that he shall first obtain from the Clerk of the court in which such account was settled, a transcript of all the papers relating to such account and settlement, and file the same with a petition in the office of the Clerk of said District Court, and cause such executor or administrator, or his legal representatives to be cited as in other suits in said District Court. Settlement with Chief Justice may be revised when.

Art. 829. [122] All decisions, orders, decrees and judgments, of the County Court, under the provisions of this Act, shall be entered on the records of the court by the Clerk, at the time such decision, order, decree or judgment shall be made or rendered.(*b*) Decrees, &c., to be recorded.

Art. 830. [123] Any person who may consider himself aggrieved by any such decision, order, decree or judgment, shall have the right to appeal to the District Court of the county: provided, he shall within fifteen days after such decision, order, decree or judgment, shall have been made and rendered, file with the Clerk of said court, a bond for costs and damages, with good and sufficient sureties payable to the Chief Justice in such sum as he shall require, and to be approved by said Chief Justice; conditioned that the appellant shall prosecute said appeal to effect, and perform the decision, order, decree or judgment, which the District Court shall make thereon, in case the cause shall be decided against him.(*c*) Appeal to District Court, how taken.

Art. 831. [124] Upon such appeal bond being filed in the Clerk's office, it shall be his duty immediately to make out a certified transcript of the proceedings in the case, and transmit the same to the District Court. Transcript to be made and returned.

Art. 832. [125] In case the Clerk of the County Court shall be unable for want of time to make out such transcript before the first day of the next term of the District Court of the county, after such appeal is taken, then such transcript shall be transmitted to the next succeeding term of said court. If not time to make, &c.

Art. 833. [126] In all cases where an executor or administrator shall neglect the performance of any duty required by this Act, and shall be cited to appear before the court on account thereof, he shall be liable for all costs of such proceeding out of his own estate; and whenever an executor or administrator shall be removed for any of the causes set forth in this Act, he shall be liable in like manner for all costs attending such removal. Administrator or Executor liable for costs, when.

Art. 834. [127] In all cases where a party shall file any application, complaint or opposition in the court under the provisions of this Act, and on the Persons failing, &c., to be liable, &c.

(*a*) The proceedings under this article, lies at the suit of a creditor, legatee or distributee only. An administrator *de bonis non*, cannot maintain the proceedings against the former administrator. Murphy, Adm'r *de bonis non*, *v.* Menard, 11 Tex. Rep. 673. Hefflefinger *v.* George, 14 Tex. Rep. 569. It is not necessary that the creditors or heirs should join in the proceeding. It may be prosecuted by any one interested in the estate. The death of any one, who may have joined in the suit, will not abate the proceedings, but the suit may be carried to judgment at the instance of the survivors. The judgment should be to pay to each claimant the amount due to him or her respectively. Reese *v.* Hicks, 13 Tex. Rep. 162. Where one of several persons interested in the estate, institutes the proceeding, &c., if successful it enures to the benefit of all persons, similarly interested. Hefflefinger *v.* George, 14 Tex. Rep. 569.

(*b*) It would seem that the proper practice in allowing or rejecting claims against estates, by the Chief Justice, is to enter an order on the minutes of the court, and not merely to endorse a memorandum on the claim. Davenport *v.* Lawrence, Adm'r, 19 Tex. Rep. 317.

(*c*) Davenport *v.* Lawrence, *supra*. This article does not apply to executors and administrators, in their representative capacity, so as to require bonds of them in cases of appeal. Battle *v.* Howard, 13 Tex. Rep. 345. Where a purchaser at a probate sale, believes himself injured by the rejection of the sale by the Probate Judge, his remedy is by appeal to the District Court. Davis *v.* Stewart, Adm'r, 4 Tex. Rep. 223.

trial thereof he shall be defeated or fail in the object for which his application, complaint or opposition was filed, he shall be liable for all costs occasioned by the filing of his application, complaint or opposition.(*a*)

Power of court to enforce obedience to orders. ART. 835. [128] The Chief Justice shall have power to enforce obedience to all his lawful orders against executors or administrators by attachment and imprisonment: provided, no such imprisonment shall exceed three days for any one offence; he shall also have power to order the Clerk to issue execution against the estate of an executor or administrator, in favor of any person to whom money has been ordered to be paid by such executor or administrator: Execution and return. such execution shall be made returnable in sixty days; shall be tested and signed by the Clerk, and sealed with the seal of the court; and may be directed to the Sheriff or other lawful officer of any county in the State; and all proceedings under such executions shall be governed by the laws regulating proceedings under executions issued from the District Court, so far as the same may be applicable.

Depositions. ART. 836. [129] In all proceedings in the County Court, arising under the provisions of this Act, the depositions of witnesses may be taken and read in evidence under the same rules and regulations as in the District Court, and all laws in relation to witnesses and evidence, which govern the District Court, shall apply to all proceedings in the County Court under the provisions of this Act, so far as they are applicable.

Citation to non-residents. ART. 837. [130] In all cases under the provisions of this Act, where it is necessary to cite any person who is out of the limits of this State, and the manner of citing such person is not herein otherwise provided for, such person may be cited by publication in like manner as in the District Court.

Petitions, applications, &c., to be filed. ART. 838. [131] Each Clerk of the County Court shall receive and file all applications, complaints, petitions, and all other papers permitted or required to be filed in said courts under the provisions of this Act, and shall endorse on each the date when it was filed, and sign his name to such endorsement: he shall issue all necessary notices, citations, writs, and process from said court, without any order from the Chief Justice, unless such order is required by some provision of this Act.(*b*)

Property removed may be attached. ART. 839. [132] Whenever complaint in writing, and under oath, shall be made to the Chief Justice by any person interested in the estate of a decedent, that the executor or administrator of such estate is about to remove the same or any part thereof, out of the limits of this State, such Chief Justice shall have power to order a writ to issue, directed to any lawful officer of this State, commanding him to seize such estate or any part thereof, and hold the same, subject to such further order as the Chief Justice may make on such complaint: provided, that no such writ shall issue unless the complainant shall give bond, with good and sufficient security, payable to the executor or administrator, conditioned for the payment of all damages that may be recovered for the wrongful suing out such writ.

May enforce former orders, &c. ART. 840. [134] The Chief Justices of the several County Courts shall have like power to enforce all orders, decrees and judgments heretofore made and rendered in the Probate Court of their county, as they would have if such orders, decrees and judgments had been made or rendered by them under the provisions of this Act.

(*a*) The statute contemplates that any person wishing to contest any matter or proceeding before the court, shall file his complaint or exceptions, and having done so becomes a party, is entitled to the process of the court, and is liable to pay the costs of the case which he makes. Brown *v.* Hobbs, 19 Tex. Rep. 167. There are no regular and formal pleadings in the County Court. Ibid.

(*b*) Brown *v.* Hobbs, *supra.*

ART. 841. [135] The rights, powers, and duties of executors and administrators shall be governed by the principles of the Common Law, where the same do not conflict with the provisions of this Act. Common Law, how far in force, &c.

ART. 842. [136] In all cases where a Chief Justice may have been executor or administrator of an estate, in the county where, and at the time he was elected; or, when a Chief Justice may wish to probate a will, and accept as the executor of the estate of a testator, in the county where he officiates; or, when he may be entitled to a distributive share of an estate that is to be settled in his court, any two of the County Commissioners shall have power to do all acts pertaining to the settlement, partition and distribution of such estates, that might be done by the Chief Justice. When County Commissioners shall act, &c.

ESTRAYS.

ART. 843. [1] Hereafter when any stray horse, mare, colt, mule, jack or jennet shall be found on the plantation or land of any citizen of this State, such citizen shall forthwith advertise the same, describing the animal's color, and specifying the marks and brands, if any, at three public places in the county in which such citizen resides, one of which notices shall be on the court-house door, for at least twenty days; after the expiration of which time, if no owner apply, it shall be lawful for such citizen to appear before some Justice of the Peace in and for said county, and estray the same. Act of Feb'y, 5, 1850. Took effect March 23, 1850. When stray horse shall be advertised, &c.

ART. 844. [2] Any citizen entitled to estray any animal as provided in the first section of this Act, shall make oath that the animal to be estrayed was taken up at his or her residence, or on his or her plantation, or on his or her land adjoining the same; that the marks and brands have not been altered or disfigured since the same was taken up; that notice has been given according to law, and that no owner has been found; which affidavit shall be sworn to and subscribed by the citizen estraying, and filed; whereupon, the Justice shall cause to appear before him, by summons or otherwise, two disinterested householders of his county, commanding them, after being sworn, to value and appraise the same, and certify the valuation, together with a particular description of the animal, including stature, marks, brands, color and age, under oath, which shall be attested by the Justice, who shall thereupon require of the taker up a bond, with two or more solvent securities, for double the appraised value of such animal, payable to the Chief Justice of the county or his successors in office; conditioned, that the taker up shall comply with the provisions of this Act; which affidavit, appraisement and bond shall be transmitted by such Justice to the Clerk of the County Court within twenty days thereafter; for which the said Justice shall receive the same fees that are allowed for similar services by law. Mode of proceeding after advertisement. Affidavit, &c., to be transmitted to County Clerk, &c.

ART. 845. [4] At any time within twelve months, it shall be lawful for the owner of any stray horse, mare, colt, mule, jack or jennet, to prove his or her property by the oath or affidavit of any respectable witness, in a certificate How and when proven by the owner.

containing a particular description of the animal or animals claimed, including the kind, marks, brands, stature, color and age of the same, which certificate shall be sworn to and subscribed before any Justice of the county wherein such animal or animals may have been estrayed, and delivered to the taker up, to be filed by him in the office of the County Clerk of such county; and on the delivery of such certificate, and the payment of all costs incurred in keeping and posting such stray or strays to the taker up, shall be entitled to demand and receive such animal or animals: provided, that when the respectability of the witness aforesaid is not known to the officer administering the oath, the party claiming shall produce satisfactory evidence of the respectabilty of such witness, certified by a Notary Public of the county in which the witness resides: and provided further, that in all cases when the owner and taker up cannot agree upon the charge for keeping such estray or estrays, the Justice before whom such animal or animals may have been posted, shall determine the amount to be paid by the owner to the taker up.

Compensation for keeping, how determined

Party liable, &c., removing or selling, &c.

ART. 846. [6] If any person or persons estraying any horse, mare, colt, mule, jack or jennet, shall send or take away the same out of the State of Texas, through fraud, or swap, sell, or otherwise dispose of the same for the purpose of gain, or for the purpose of holding such property, he, she, or they so offending shall be * * * * * * * * liable upon his, her or their bond in an action for damages, in favor of the party injured.

When stray dies or escapes, duty of taker up.

ART. 847. [9] Whenever any stray animal shall be found dead, or shall escape, the taker up shall, without delay, make report thereof to the Clerk of the County Court, under oath; which report shall be recorded in an estray book: and any person who shall be found guilty of making a false report, shall be liable to an indictment, and punished therefor, as in other cases of perjury; and shall, moreover, be liable on his or her bond for the value of the animal or animals estrayed.

Estray may be used, &c., provided.

ART. 848. [10] Each and every estray shall be kept in the county in which such animal was taken up, and may be used in moderation: provided, that if the same be abused, the taker up shall be liable upon his bond in damages for such abuse, and may be sued therefor, either by the owner or by the Chief Justice, for the use of the county.

Refusal to deliver up.

ART. 849. [11] If any person, having in charge any estray, or estrays, shall refuse to deliver the same to the owner thereof, on his complying with the requisitions of this act, such owner shall be entitled to his action therefor, with damages.

Commissioners to estray, &c., when.

ART. 850. [12] If any estray or estrays, of any kind, shall be found running at large, and not estrayed, and the owner of the same be unknown, it is hereby made the duty of the County Commissioners, or any of them, to return the same, with a full description thereof, to the County Clerks of their respective counties, who shall advertise the same in the manner specified in this act; and if such animal shall not be proved away by the owner within the time allowed by the provisions of this act, the Commissioner returning the same, or his successor in office, shall proceed to sell such animal, or animals, and report the sale thereof to the Clerk of the County Court; and after paying the Clerk's fees, and retaining twenty-five per cent. of the proceeds of such sale, he shall pay the remainder into the county treasury, for the use and benefit of the county.

To be sold, when.

Money paid county, under this act, how appropriated.

ART. 851. [14] All moneys which may be paid into the county treasury, under the provisions of this act, shall be applied to the payment of jurors attending District Courts in their respective counties; and the County Treasurer, after deducting therefrom his legal commissions, shall pay out the same upon the certificates of attendance issued by the Clerk of the District Court to such jurors, after the adjournment of each term, pro rata, if the amount should be insufficient to pay all the jurors.

ART. 852. [15] It shall be the duty of the Chief Justice of those counties in this State bordering on the Rio Grande, to furnish a brand at the expense of the county, with which all animals sold under the provisions of this act shall be branded. Animals sold under this act, on the Rio Grande, to be branded.

ART. 853. [1] It shall be the duty of the Clerk of the County Court, to record the papers transmitted to him, as provided in the second section of said act, in a separate book, to be kept in his office for that purpose, and for which he shall be entitled to demand and receive the same fees that are allowed by law for similar services, to be paid in all cases by the taker up: provided, that when two or more animals are taken up at the same time, and by the same person, they shall be included in the same entry, and the Justice of the Peace and Clerk shall receive no more fees than for one such animal; and each County Clerk shall cause a statement of the appraisement and a description of the animal or animals so estrayed to be advertised, at least three times, in some newspaper published in the county where such animal or animals were estrayed, if there be one; and if there be no newspaper published in the county, then the Clerk shall cause the same to be advertised in the newspaper published nearest to the county, and also by posting up notices at three public places in the county, one of which shall be at the court house door thereof; and the printer of such notice shall furnish a copy of the paper containing the same to said Clerk, whose duty it shall be to file and preserve the same in his office, for the inspection of all persons who may be interested: and for such publication the printer shall be entitled to receive, from the party estraying, the sum of two dollars; to be collected by the County Clerk, and paid to the order of the printer. Act of Dec. 17 1851. Clerk of county court to record papers. Appraisement and description to be published.

ART. 854. [2] The property of every stray horse, mare, colt, mule, jack, jennet, or work ox, taken up as aforesaid, and not proven away by the owner, within twelve months after such appraisement, shall be deemed vested in the county wherein such estray, or estrays, may have been posted; and the taker up shall, immediately thereafter proceed to sell the same, for cash, to the highest bidder, at the court house door of the county, giving notice of the same as required in the case of sheriffs' or constables' sales; and, within ten days after such sale, he shall pay into the county treasury of the county, one-half of the proceeds of the same, and retain the other half for his own use or benefit: provided, that each and every return of sale shall be made to, and filed by, the County Clerk of the county, and sworn to by the taker up: provided, that the owners of property so estrayed may, at any time within six months after such sale, apply to the County Treasurer, and, upon proof of such ownership, shall be entitled to have and receive the amount so deposited, after paying such costs as may be necessary to establish his right thereto. When to be proven away, when sold, &c. Return of sale shall be sworn to. Owner to receive proceeds &c., when.

ART. 855. [3] Any citizen taking up any stray cattle other than work oxen, hogs, sheep, or goats, shall proceed in the same manner as required in the case of horses, &c., except advertising in a newspaper; and any person estraying the same, at the expiration of six months from the date of appraisement, shall proceed to give notice as required in cases of sheriffs' or constables' sales, and to sell such estrays where they were taken up, if not less than three bidders attend such sales; provided, that no animal of the kind enumerated in this section except work oxen, shall be subject to be estrayed, unless the same shall have been on the plantation or land of the taker up, at least twelve months previous to the time of estraying the same: and further provided, that Stray cattle, mode of proceeding, &c.

El Paso and Presidio counties exempt, &c. the counties of El Paso and Presidio be exempt from the provisions of the first section of this act, so far as it relates to the advertisement of estrays in newspapers.

EXECUTIONS.

[*See Judgments.*]

Act of Jan. 27, 1842. Took effect 17th March, 1842. Duty of Clerk to issue, after court rises.

ART. 856. [1] From and after the rising of every court, it shall be the duty of the Clerk to tax the costs of suit in every case incurréd by the successful party, and issue execution, endorsing thereon the several items contained in the bill of costs, in intelligible words and figures.

Clerk to keep Execution Docket.

ART. 857. [2] It shall be the duty of the Clerks of the several courts of this Republic to keep an Execution Docket, in which shall be entered the names of cases, the time at which execution issued, the amount therefor, to whom and when delivered, and the returns which may be made thereon by the Sheriff, or such officer as may receive the execution; which said docket shall be subject to the inspection of any person interested, at any time when required: and any Clerk who shall fail to keep such a docket, or shall neglect to make the entries, shall be liable to a fine of one hundred dollars; to be recovered by the party complaining, by motion before the court, three days' previous notice being given thereof.

To issue before court rises, when.

ART. 858. [3] Should the defendant, in any judgment of the court, be about to remove his or her property from the county in which judgment may be rendered, and before rising of the court, the court shall order execution to be immediately issued, upon an affidavit being made and filed in the court to that effect.

How levy of, to be made, and when returned.

ART. 859. [4] All executions shall be made returnable on or before the first day of the next term of the court, except in Justices' Courts, in which they shall be made returnable in sixty days; and the defendant, or his agent or attorney, in all cases, shall have the right to designate the property to be levied on, provided said property shall be in the county where judgment shall have been rendered, or to which execution may be issued; and if the defendant, his agent or attorney, shall fail or refuse to designate the same, it being his own property, then the levy shall be made in the following manner: first, on personal or movable property; then on uncultivated lands; then on slaves; and, lastly, on the improved lands or homestead of the defendant. (*a*)

(*a*) The defendant has the right, in all cases, to designate property for levy; but should he fail to exercise this privilege, the Sheriff may proceed to levy in the order prescribed by law. The plaintiff has no right, in any case, where the property is to be sold without appraisement, to insist upon making a designation. Bryan *v.* Bridge, 6 Tex. Rep. 137. [See this case as to what is required to constitute a valid levy upon personal

ART. 860. [5] Whenever any property shall have been seized by virtue of an execution, it shall be the duty of the Sheriff, or other officer, to advertise the same, if it be personal property, at least ten days, at three public places in the county, one of which shall be the place where the property is to be sold; if it be slaves or lands, twenty days, by advertisement posted up—one at the court house of the county: provided, that all sales of lands and negroes shall be made at the court house door of the county in which the sales take place, on the first Tuesday of the month, between the hours of 10 o'clock A. M. and 4 o'clock P. M.; and provided, further, that all other property may be sold on the premises where it is seized in execution.(*a*) Advertisement, time and place of sales.

ART. 861. [6] If, on the sale of the property, more money is received than is sufficient to pay the amount of the execution, or executions, in the hands of the Sheriff, or other officer, the surplus shall be immediately paid over to the defendant, his agent, or attorney.(*b*) Surplus after paying debt.

ART. 862. [7] Whenever an execution is levied upon personal property, or slaves, the defendant shall have the right to retain the possession of the same, upon giving bond with good security, payable to the plaintiff, in double the amount of debt and costs, conditioned for the delivery of the property to the Sheriff, or other officer, on the day of sale.(*c*) Delivery bond.

ART. 863. [8] If the defendant shall fail to deliver the property so bonded, it shall be the duty of the Sheriff to return the bond to the Clerk of the court from which execution issued as aforesaid, and endorse thereon, *forfeited*; whereupon, said Clerk shall issue execution against the principal and sureties on the bond, for the amount of the debt and costs; upon which said execution, no delivery-bond shall be taken; which fact shall be endorsed by the Clerk on the execution.(*d*) Failure to deliver property bonded—duty of Sheriff, &c.

ART. 864. [9] It shall be the duty of the Sheriff to endorse, on each execution, the day on which it came into his hands; and, if he received more than one on the same day, and against the same person, he shall number them as received; and, on failure, he shall be liable to pay twenty per cent. on the amount of the execution, together with such damages as the plaintiff in execution may sustain by such failure to number; to be recovered by the plaintiff, from him and his sureties, by motion, on giving three days' notice that a motion will be made to that purpose.(*e*) Sheriff to endorse and number.

ART. 865. [10] Should any Sheriff, or other officer, fail or refuse to pay over money collected under an execution, when demanded by the person entitled to receive the same, he shall be liable to pay ten per cent. per month on the amount so collected, besides interest and costs; which may be recovered of him and his sureties, by motion before the court from which said execution issued, three days' previous notice being given.(*g*) Sheriff failing to pay over money, &c.

property.] Where the principal defendant in the execution fails to point out property, the Sheriff may adopt the designation of his property by his sureties, whereon to make a levy. Martin *v.* Rice, 16 Tex. Rep. 157. Where judgment is obtained in, and execution issues to a county other than that of the defendant's residence, and where he has no agent or attorney to point out property, he cannot complain that he had no notice to point out property. Kendrick *v.* Rice, 16 Tex. Rep. 254. If the defendant should point out property reserved by law for the family, and exempt from execution, the Sheriff cannot properly receive it: it is not subject to levy, though with the consent of the head of the family. Ross *v.* Lister, 14 Tex. Rep. 469.

(*a*) A failure of the Sheriff, or other officer, to sell lands or slaves at the court house door of the county, or on the first Tuesday of the month, is not a mere irregularity which will not vitiate the sale. He has no authority to sell at any other time or place. Howard *v.* North, 5 Tex. Rep. 290.

(*b*) If a Sheriff sell only part of the land levied on, the sale is void. Howard *v.* North, 5 Tex. Rep. 290. The law is mandatory to sell the whole amount of the property levied on, and leaves the officer no discretion to sell the whole or only a portion. Ibid.

(*c*) No person but the defendant can give bond and retain the possession of the property levied on. Harris *v.* Shackleford, Sampson & Co., 6 Tex. Rep. 133. In the absence of fraud, the execution of a delivery bond will estop the defendant from denying the levy; and, under ordinary circumstances, a bond by the defendant's wife to try title, will have the same effect. Portis *v.* Parker, 8 Tex. Rep. 23.

(*d*) The implied judgment on a forfeited delivery bond is not a satisfaction of the original judgment, but is an additional security. Cole *v.* Robertson, 6 Tex. Rep. 356.

(*e*) The penalty does not attach for a failure to date or number, where but one execution is received. De-Witt *v.* Dunn, 15 Tex. Rep. 106.

(*g*) These statutes, authorizing summary proceedings;

Sheriff to keep securely, property levied on.

ART. 866. [11] It shall be the duty of the Sheriff to keep, securely, all property levied on by him, for which no delivery-bond has been given; and if any loss should result to any party interested by his negligence, he shall be liable to pay the value of the property so lost, and ten per cent. damages thereon; to be recovered by the party injured, before any court of competent jurisdiction, three days' previous notice thereof being given.

When execution may issue to another county, &c.

ART. 867. [13] When judgment shall be obtained before the Supreme, District, County, or Justices' Courts, of this Republic, for any debt or damages, and the person against whom such judgment shall be obtained shall not have sufficient property within the county where the judgment shall be rendered, to satisfy the execution of the plaintiff, it shall be lawful to issue execution, directed to the Sheriff or other legal officer of any county in this Republic, where the defendant may have property; which said Sheriff, or other officer to whom said execution may be directed, is hereby empowered and required to serve and execute the same, and shall make return thereof to the court where the judgment was rendered: (*a*) provided, that executions from Justices' Courts, when sent to a different county from that in which they are issued, shall be accompanied by a certificate, under seal of the Clerk of the County Court, that the officer issuing the same is a Justice of the Peace.

Garnishment. (See article 42.)

ART. 868. [14] Whenever a judgment shall have been rendered by any court of this Republic, if the plaintiff, his agent or attorney, shall make affidavit before the Court or Clerk thereof, in which judgment was obtained, that the defendant, or defendants, hath or have no property, within the knowledge of such affiant, in his or their possession, of which the debt can be made; and that such affiant has just reason to believe that another person, or persons, is, or are, indebted to said defendant, or defendants; or hath, or have, effects of such defendant, or defendants, in his or her hands, it shall be lawful for the Court, or Clerk, to cause the person or persons supposed to be indebted to, or supposed to have any effects of said defendant, or defendants, to appear at the next term of such court as garnishee, or garnishees; and the said court shall examine and proceed against said garnishee, or garnishees, in the same manner as prescribed by law, against garnishees in original attachments. (*b*)

Bidder failing to comply with terms of sale, &c., liable for damages.

ART. 869. [15] If any person shall bid off property, at any sale made by virtue of an execution, and shall fail to comply with the terms of the same, he shall be liable to pay to the plaintiff, or plaintiffs, in execution, twenty per cent. on the value of the property thus bid off, besides costs; to be recovered before the court whence the execution issued, by motion, three days' previous notice being given to him, or her, that such motion will be made: and should the property, on a second sale, bring less than on the former, he shall be liable to pay the defendant in execution, all loss which he sustains thereby; to be recovered as above in this section.

Property shall be re-sold if bidder fail, &c.

ART. 870. [16] When the terms of the sale shall not be complied with by the bidder, the Sheriff shall proceed to sell the property again, on the same day, if there be sufficient time; but if not, he shall re-advertise the same for the next succeeding regular day of sale.

and being, in some degree, penal in their character, are to be strictly construed in favor of the party to be affected by them. Hamilton *v.* Ward, 4 Tex. Rep. 356. Where the Sheriff receives the money, after the return day, without having made a levy, the receiving of the money is not an official act, for which he and his sureties can be held liable in a summary proceeding. Ibid. In a summary proceeding against a Sheriff for failing to return an execution, or pay over money, he may show in his defence that there is no judgment, or that it is void. Ibid. Where the Sheriff is in default in several particulars, all the grounds may, and ought to be, joined in one motion. Ibid. An officer is not liable, in nominal damages, in a summary proceeding, where the case does not come within the provisions of the statute itself. Ibid. The motion cannot be sustained against the Sheriff, when the demand for the money, and refusal to pay over the money, is made in the name of, and to a stranger to the execution. Beaver *v.* Batte, 19 Tex. Rep. 111. Nor can it be sustained by the proper party, as to the principal amount even, unless a previous demand be shown. Ibid.

(*a*) If an execution be sent to another county, without a previous return of *nulla bona* in the county in which the judgment is rendered, it is but an irregularity which will not vitiate the title of a *bona fide* purchaser under such execution. Sydnor *v.* Roberts, 13 Tex. Rep. 598.

(*b*) Adams *v.* McCown, 15 Tex. Rep. 349.

ART. 871. [22] When a sale has been made, and the terms thereof complied with, the Sheriff, Coroner, or Constable, shall execute and deliver to the purchaser, a conveyance of all the right, title, interest, and claim, which the defendant in execution had in, and to, the property sold.(*a*)

Conveyance to purchaser.

ART. 872. [23] If any Sheriff, or other officer, shall fail to make return of any execution received by him, on the day and at the place the same shall be made returnable, or shall neglect or fail to make a levy when in his power so to do, being thereto required by the plaintiff, or shall fail to advertise and offer for sale, as required by law, any property levied on by him, he shall be liable to pay to the plaintiff in execution, the full amount of the debt, interest and costs, to be recovered against such Sheriff, or other officer, and his sureties, by motion, in any court having jurisdiction thereof, by giving three days' notice of such motion.(*b*)

Act of Jan. 13, 1844.
Failure to return, &c.

ART. 873. [24] An Act entitled an Act to repeal and amend certain parts or portions of an Act, entitled "An Act concerning Executions," approved twenty-second December, one thousand eight hundred and forty, be, and the same are hereby, repealed; and that nothing in this Act contained shall affect any law heretofore passed, exempting property from execution.

Repealing clause.

II. PROPERTY EXEMPT.

[*See Constitution, Art. 7, Sect. 22.*]

ART. 874. [1] From and after the passage of this act, there shall be reserved to every citizen or head of a family in this Republic, free and independent of the power of a writ of *fieri facias*, or other execution issuing from any court of competent jurisdiction whatever, fifty acres of land or one town lot, including his or her homestead, and improvements not exceeding five hundred dollars in value, all household and kitchen furniture (provided it does not exceed in value two hundred dollars), all implements of husbandry (provided they shall not exceed fifty dollars in value), all tools, apparatus, and books belonging to the trade or profession of any citizen, five milch cows, one yoke of work oxen or one horse, twenty hogs, and one year's provisions; and that all laws and parts of laws contravening or opposing the provisions of this act, be and the same are hereby repealed: provided, the passage of this act shall not interfere with contracts between parties heretofore made.

Act of Jan. 26, 1839.
In force from passage.
Homestead, &c., exempt from.

ART. 875. [1] All lands acquired as headrights, by virtue of the colonization laws of Coahuila and Texas, or by virtue of laws of this Republic, by emigrants from foreign countries, on their settlement in Texas, shall be and are hereby

Act of Feb. 5, 1840.
Took effect March 16, 1840.

(*a*) The bid and payment of the purchase money at an execution sale, constitutes the purchaser's right, the deed is merely evidence of the right. Miller *v.* Alexander, 8 Tex. Rep., 36. As to the purchasers title under a purchase at Sheriff's sale, see Howard *v.* North, 5 Tex. Rep., 290.

(*b*) Although the law does not in express terms admit of any excuse, yet it implies that a reasonable one will be heard. Underwood *v.* Russell, 4 Tex. Rep., 175. When the execution issues to another county, the Sheriff is not bound to return it in person, it is sufficient if he deposit it in the mail, properly directed, and in time to reach the Clerk of the Court from which it issued by the return day. Ibid. Reasonable diligence to execute and return the process is all the law requires. Ibid. The officer may avoid the liability under the statute, by proof showing a reasonable excuse for his failure, or that the plaintiff has sustained no injury. The burden of proof is on the officer. Smith *v.* Perry, 18 Tex. Rep., 510.

The exemption of property from execution by this act, is in favor of "every citizen or head of a family," and extends to all the inhabitants of the State, married or single. Cobbs *v.* Coleman, 14 Tex. Rep., 594. The property so exempt from execution for the family, is not subject to levy, though with the consent of the head of the family. Ross *v.* Lister, Ibid. 469.

The exemption of a horse by the act includes every thing absolutely essential to its beneficial enjoyment, as bridle, saddle, and martingal. Cobbs *v.* Coleman, *supra.*

Under this statute the limitation of the value of the homestead, if in a city or town, is restricted to improvement, whereas, by the Constitution, the valuation is placed upon the lots themselves. See North *v.* Shearn, 15 Tex. Rep., 174.

Headrights exempt from payment of certain debts.

declared exempt from all debts and liabilities contracted by such emigrant anterior to his removal and emigration to Texas; unless such debt was contracted and made with an express reference to the prospective right to be acquired by such emigrant; and proved by written contract: provided, that this act shall not be so construed as to exempt any lands which emigrants may have acquired by purchase, or in any other manner than by virtue of their headright.

Act of Jan. 16, 1843. In force from passage. Property of persons in the army exempt.

ART. 876. [1] From and after the passage of this act, the property of all such persons as are now in the army of Texas, or as may hereafter be mustered into the service of the Republic, by virtue of the law of the land, shall not be liable to forced sales, so long as he or they may remain in said service.

Act of Feb. 2, 1844. In force from passage. No forced sale where owner is a prisoner, &c.

ART. 877. [1] From and after the passage of this act, no forced sale shall be made of any property belonging to any citizen of Texas, who is or may be a prisoner of war, until release or death of said prisoner, or in the event of his death, administration upon his estate.

Act of Feb. 13, 1858. In force from date. Ferry boat exempt, &c.

ART. 878. [1] There shall be reserved to every ferryman in the State, free and independent of any writ of *fieri facias*, or other forced sale, one ferryboat, keel, or flat boat, used as a ferry boat not to exceed in value five hundred dollars: provided, such boats shall always be liable to sale for any damage sustained by the negligence or other improper conduct upon the part of such ferryman.

FEES OF OFFICE.

GENERAL PROVISIONS.

SECRETARY OF STATE—COMMISSIONER OF THE GENERAL LAND OFFICE—COMPTROLLER—TREASURER AND ADJUTANT-GENERAL.

[*See Court of Claims, Art.* 309.]

Act of March 20, 1848. Took effect from passage. Sec'y of State, Com'r G. Land Office, and other officers to furnish copies and certificates.

ART. 879. [1] It shall be the duty of the Secretary of State, Commissioner of the General Land Office, Comptroller, Treasurer, and Adjutant-General, to furnish any person who may apply for the same, with a copy of any paper, document, or record in their respective offices, and also to give certificates, attested by the seals of their respective offices, certifying to any fact or facts contained in the papers, documents, or records of their offices, to any person applying for the same.

ART. 880. [2] It shall be lawful for the said Secretary of State, Commissioner of the General Land Office, Comptroller, Treasurer and Adjutant-General, to demand and receive the following fees for the services mentioned in the preceding section:

Fees of such officers.

For copies of any paper, document, or record in their offices, in the English language, including certificate and seal, for each hundred words, fifteen cents.

For copies of any paper, document, or record in their offices, in any other language than the English, including certificate and seal, for each hundred words, twenty-five cents.

For each translated copy of any paper, document, or record in their offices, including certificate and seal, for each hundred words, thirty cents.

For the copy of any plat or map in their offices, such fee as may be established by the officer in whose office the same is made, to be determined with reference to the amount of labor required.

For each certificate not otherwise provided for, fifty cents.

ART. 881. [3] It shall be the duty of the Secretary of State, Commissioner of the General Land Office, Comptroller, Treasurer, and Adjutant-General respectively, to keep a fee book in their several offices, in which they shall enter all the fees demanded or received, for any of the services named in this act; and they shall quarterly furnish to the Comptroller an account of all fees so demanded and received by them respectively; which account shall be verified by affidavit: and they shall also, at the end of each and every quarter, pay over to the Treasurer of the State, all money received by them respectively, under the provisions of this act.

Shall keep fee book [illegible] account of fees received [illegible] Comptroller quarterly.

ART. 882. [5] Nothing contained in this act shall authorize either of the officers herein named, to demand or receive from any officer of the State, for copies of any papers, documents, or records, in their offices, or for any certificate in relation to any matter in their offices, when such copies or certificates are required in the performance of any of the official duties of such office.

Shall not charge officers of State for copies.

ART. 883. [1] The Commissioner of the General Land Office of this State be, and he is hereby authorized and required to demand and receive, except in cases otherwise directed by any act of the Legislature, of each and every applicant for a land certificate, under the provisions of any act of the Legislature, the following fees, viz: For a league and labor of land, five dollars; for any quantity less than a league and labor, and greater than one third of a league, four dollars; for one-third of a league, three dollars; for any quantity less than one-third of a league, two dollars. Said fees to be paid in par money, and paid into the State Treasury quarterly.

Act of Feb. 1, 1850. Took effect March [illegible], 1850.

Commissioner General Land Office to charge certain fees.

ART. 884. [1] It shall be lawful for the District Attorneys, the Attorney-General, the Clerk of the Supreme Court, the Clerks of the District Courts, the Clerks of the County Courts, the Chief Justices of the County Courts, the Sheriffs, the Coroners, the Justices of the Peace, the Constables, the Notaries Public, the County Surveyors, and the Deputy Surveyors, respectively, to demand and receive the several fees hereinafter mentioned, for services rendered by them respectively in their several offices, and no more:

Act of March 20, 1848. Took effect Aug. 7, 1848.

What officers may demand fees.

TO DISTRICT ATTORNEYS.

ART. 885. [2] For every conviction in cases of felony, twenty dollars.

District Attorney.

For every conviction under the laws against gaming, fifteen dollars.

For every conviction for any other offence against the laws of this State, ten dollars; which fees shall be taxed in the bill of costs against the defendant; but in no case shall be paid by the State.

For all money collected by District Attorneys in suits prosecuted by them in favor of the State, they shall be allowed, on all sums not exceeding five thousand dollars, five per cent.; on all sums after the first five thousand dollars, two and one-half per cent.

TO THE ATTORNEY-GENERAL.

Attorney-General. ART. 886. [3] In each case that may be taken to the Supreme Court, the like fees and commissions as are allowed to District Attorneys; to be taxed and collected in the same manner.

TO THE CLERK OF THE SUPREME COURT.

Clerk of Supreme Court. ART. 887. [4] For entering the appearance of either party, in person or by attorney, to be charged but once, fifty cents.

For docketing each cause, to be charged but once, fifty cents.

For filing the record in each cause, fifty cents.

For entering each rule or motion, twenty-five cents.

For entering the order of the court upon any rule or motion, or for entering any interlocutory judgment, fifty cents.

For administering an oath or affirmation, without a certificate, fifteen cents.

For administering an oath or affirmation, and giving a certificate thereof with seal, twenty-five cents.

For entering each continuance, twenty cents.

For entering every final judgment or decree, one dollar.

For each writ issued, one dollar.

For making out and transmitting the mandate and judgment of the Supreme Court to any inferior court, one dollar and fifty cents.

For making copies of any papers or records in his office, including certificate and seal, when applied for by any person, for each hundred words, fifteen cents.

For recording the opinions of the Judges, for each hundred words, fifteen cents.

For taxing the bill of costs in each case, with copy thereof, fifty cents.

For every service not herein provided for, such fees as may be allowed by the Supreme Court, not to exceed the fees herein allowed for services requiring a like amount of labor. There shall be allowed to said Clerk reasonable office rent, stationery, and furniture for his office, to be paid on the approval and order of the Supreme Court, out of the appropriation for the contingent expenses of said court.

TO THE CLERKS OF THE DISTRICT COURT.

Clerks of the District Courts. ART. 888. [5] For each writ or citation in a civil suit, fifty cents.

For copy of petition, including certificate and seal, for each hundred words, fifteen cents.

For docketing each cause, to be charged but once, fifteen cents.

For filing each paper in a cause, ten cents.

For entering each appearance in person or by attorney, to be charged but once, ten cents.

For entering each continuance, fifteen cents.

For entering each motion or rule not otherwise provided for, with the order, decree, or judgment of the court thereon, fifty cents.

For swearing each witness in a cause, ten cents.

For administering each oath or affirmation, without a certificate, ten cents.

For administering each oath or affirmation, and making a certificate thereof with seal when required, twenty-five cents.

For each subpœna for one witness, twenty-five cents.

For each additional name inserted in such subpœna, ten cents.

For writing and taking a bond in every case where a bond is required to be taken or filed in said court, one dollar.

For each recognizance entered of record, fifty cents.

For swearing and empannelling a jury and receiving and recording the verdict, in each cause tried by a jury, fifty cents.

For assessing the damages in each cause not tried by a jury, fifty cents.

For each commission to take the deposition of one or more witnesses, fifty cents.

For copy of interrogatories, or cross-interrogatories, with certificate and seal, for each hundred words, fifteen cents.

For each *scire facias*, (except against a juror who may be excused,) one dollar.

For entering each interlocutory judgment, not otherwise provided for, fifty cents.

For entering each final judgment in a cause, fifty cents.

For entering each indictment, twenty-five cents.

For arraigning each prisoner and entering his pleas, fifty cents.

For each commitment of a prisoner, seventy-five cents.

For taxing the bill of costs in each cause, with a copy thereof, twenty-five cents.

For each execution, fifty cents.

For each writ of possession or restitution, seventy-five cents.

For each *capias* or other original writ in a criminal cause, fifty cents.

For making out and transmitting the mandate and judgment of the District Court, upon an appeal from the County Court, one dollar.

For entering the return of each writ of execution, possession, or restitution, and recording the return of the officer thereon, fifty cents.

For a transcript of the record and papers in any cause when an appeal or writ of error is taken, with certificate and seal, for each hundred words, fifteen cents.(a)

For copies of all records or papers in their offices, with certificate and seal, for each hundred words, fifteen cents.

For each certificate to any fact or facts contained in the records of his office, with certificate and seal, fifty cents.

For every service not otherwise provided for, such fee as may be allowed by the District Court, not to exceed the fees herein allowed for services requiring a like amount of labor.(b)

There shall be allowed to said clerks, such books, stationery, and office furniture as may be necessary for his office, to be paid on the order of the County Court out of the County Treasury; and a suitable office shall also be provided by the County Court at the expense of the county.

TO THE CLERKS OF THE COUNTY COURTS.

ART. 889. [6] For filing each paper required to be filed in their courts, in relation to the estates of decedents or wards, ten cents. **Of Clerks of the County Court.**

For making out and posting the necessary notices, upon each application for the probate of a will or for the appointment of an administrator or guardian, or in any other case where notices are required to be given in any manner relating to the estates of decedents and wards, fifty cents.

For docketing each application, complaint, petition, or proceeding in relation to the estates of decedents or wards, to be charged but once, ten cents.

For each writ or citation, fifty cents.

For each copy of an application, complaint, or petition that is required to accompany a writ or citation with certificate and seal, fifteen cents for each hundred words.

(a) The Clerk of the District Court is not entitled to demand payment of his fees in advance, as a condition precedent to the delivery of the transcript to either of the parties who may demand it for the purpose of transmission to the Supreme Court. ——— v. Costley, 7 Tex. Rep., 460.

(b) Where an appeal is taken to the Supreme Court, under article 553, the clerk is required to make up a final record and is entitled to his fees for the same. Morgan v. Haldeman, 29 Tex. Rep., 58. Stewart v. Crosby, 15 Tex. Rep., 513.

For making out and attesting letters testamentary or of administration, or of guardianship, fifty cents.

For taking and recording the bond and oath of an executor, administrator, or guardian, one dollar.

For entering each order, judgment, or decree in relation to the estates of decedents or wards, fifty cents.

For recording all papers required to be recorded by them in relation to the estates of decedents or wards, for each hundred words, fifteen cents.

For swearing each witness in court, ten cents.

For administering each oath or affirmation, without a certificate, ten cents.

For administering each oath or affirmation, and giving a certificate thereof, with seal when necessary, twenty-five cents.

For each subpœna for one witness, twenty-five cents.

For each additional name inserted in such subpœna, ten cents.

For each commission to take the deposition of one or more witnesses, fifty cents.

For copy of interrogatories or cross-interrogatories with certificate and seal, for each hundred words, fifteen cents.

For making out a transcript of the papers and records in any cause taken from the County Court to the District Court, with certificate and seal, and transmitting the same, for each hundred words, fifteen cents.

For each execution, fifty cents.

For entering the return of each execution, and recording the return of the officer thereon, fifty cents.

For making copies of any papers or records in their offices, with certificate and seal, for each hundred words, fifteen cents.

For taking the acknowledgment or proof of any deed, bond, power of attorney, or any other instrument of writing, for registration with certificate and seal, fifty cents.

For filing and recording each deed, bond, power of attorney, or any other instrument permitted or required to be recorded by them as recorders, for each hundred words, fifteen cents, including the certificate to such recording with seal.

The recording of all bonds of county officers, shall be paid for by the officer executing the same.

For each marriage license, and receiving and recording the return made thereon, one dollar.

For each license to a ferryman, one dollar.

For every license not otherwise provided for, fifty cents.

For each certificate to any fact or facts contained in the records of his office, with seal, fifty cents.

For every service for individuals, not otherwise provided for, such fee as may be allowed by the County Court; not to exceed the fees herein allowed for services requiring a like amount of labor.

For all county business, in relation to roads, ferries, bridges, elections, and all other county matters not herein provided for, such allowance as may be made by the County Court, be paid out of the County Treasury.

Office, &c., books and stationery at expense of county. The County Court shall, also, furnish said Clerks suitable offices, and such stationery, record books, and office furniture as may be necessary, at the expense of the county.

TO THE CHIEF JUSTICES OF THE COUNTY COURTS.

Of Chief Justices of the County Courts. ART. 890. [7] For taking the probate of a will, two dollars.

For appointing an executor, administrator, or guardian, and approving bond, one dollar.

For each appointment of appraisers, fifty cents.

For each order of sale, fifty cents.

For each approval and confirmation of sale, one dollar.

For each decree for a partition and distribution, two dollars.

For examining and approving or setting aside the report of commissioners of partition or distribution, two dollars.

For removing an executor, administrator, or guardian, one dollar.

For administering any oath or affirmation required to be administered in relation to the estates of decedents or wards, with certificate and seal, when required, twenty-five cents.

For each certificate not otherwise provided for, with seal, fifty cents.

For each order required in relation to the estates of decedents or wards, not otherwise provided for, fifty cents.

They shall also be allowed a commission of one half of one per cent, upon the actual cash receipts of each executor, administrator, or guardian, upon the approval of his annual exhibits and the final settlement of his accounts; but no more than one such commission shall be charged on any amount received by any executor, administrator, or guardian.

For each certificate of election, with seal, fifty cents.

For ordering all elections and doing all other business required of him by law in relation to elections, such sum as may be allowed him by the County Court.

TO SHERIFFS.

ART. 891. [8] For serving each original writ or citation in a civil suit and copy of petition, one dollar. **Of Sheriffs.**

For serving each capias or other writ not otherwise provided for, in a criminal cause, one dollar.

For summoning each witness, fifty cents.

For serving each notice for the taking of depositions, and copy of interrogatories, seventy-five cents.

For serving each *scire facias* (except against a defaulting juror who may be excused,) one dollar.

For levying and returning each writ of attachment or sequestration, two dollars.

For serving each citation and garnishee, one dollar.

For each cause tried in the District Court, a jury fee shall be taxed for the Sheriff, of fifty cents.

For taking each bond of recognizance, and returning the same to the proper court, when necessary, seventy-five cents.

For serving any writ not otherwise provided for, seventy-five cents.

For each commitment or release, one dollar.

For levying each execution, one dollar.

For returning each execution, fifty cents.

For executing and returning each writ of possession or restitution, three dollars.

For all services attending the appraisements of property for sale, under execution, or any order of sale, one dollar.

For posting the advertisements for sales, under execution, or any order of sale, one dollar.

For endorsing the forfeiture of any bond required to be endorsed by him, fifty cents.

For executing a deed to each purchaser of real estate or slaves, under an execution, or an order of sale, two dollars.

For executing a bill of sale to each purchaser of personal property, other than slaves, under an execution or an order of sale, when demanded by the purchaser, one dollar.

For making money, on execution or any order of sale, when the same is made by a sale, for the first hundred dollars, three per cent.; for the second hundred dollars, two per cent.; for all sums over two hundred dollars, one and a half per cent.;—when the money is made without a sale, one half of the said rates shall be allowed.

For executing each death warrant, twenty-five dollars.

For whipping each person, by order of court, two dollars.

For removing a prisoner, for each mile going and returning, including guard and all other expenses, twenty-five cents.

For attending a prisoner on *habeas corpus*, three dollars for each day.

For taking care of property levied on by a writ of execution, sequestration or attachment, all reasonable expenses, to be taxed and allowed by the Court to which such writ is returnable.

For summoning jurors in the District Court, serving all election notices, notices upon Overseers of Roads, attending the District and County Courts, and doing all other public business not otherwise provided for, such sum as may be allowed by the County Court, not to exceed fifty dollars per annum, to be paid out of the County Treasury.

TO CORONERS.

Of Coroners. ART. 892. [9] For summoning a jury, and all other business connected with an inquest upon a dead body, including certifying and returning the same to the proper court, five dollars; to be paid out of the County Treasury; and a Justice of the Peace when performing such service shall receive a like fee, to be paid in like manner.

In all cases where a Coroner shall perform any of the duties of sheriff, he shall be entitled to the same fees as are allowed to Sheriffs.

TO JUSTICES OF THE PEACE.

Of Justices of the Peace. ART. 893. [10] For each citation or writ in civil suits, fifty cents.

For each warrant in criminal cases, fifty cents.

For taking each recognizance in a criminal case, fifty cents.

For taking each bond, not otherwise provided for, fifty cents.

For each subpœna for one witness, twenty-five cents.

For every additional name inserted in a subpœna, ten cents.

For docketing each cause, ten cents.

For each continuance, ten cents.

For swearing each witness in court, ten cents.

For administering an oath or affirmation, without a certificate, ten cents.

For administering an oath or affirmation, with a certificate thereof, twenty-five cents.

For administering the oath, taking bond, and issuing a writ of attachment or sequestration, one dollar.

For causing a jury to be summoned, swearing them, and receiving and recording their verdict in each cause, tried by a jury before them, fifty cents.

For each interlocutory judgment or order in a cause, twenty-five cents.

For each final judgment, fifty cents.

For each application to set aside a judgment by default, or of non-suit, or for new trial, with the final order or judgment of the Justice thereon, fifty cents.

For taking the acknowledgment for a stay in each cause, fifty cents.

For taking each appeal bond, twenty-five cents.

For each commission to take deposition of one or more witnesses, fifty cents.

For copy of interrogatories or cross-interrogatories, for each hundred words, fifteen cents.

For making out and certifying a transcript of the entries on his docket, and filing the same with the original papers of the cause in the District Court, in each case of appeal or certiorari, one dollar.

For each execution, fifty cents.

For each writ of possession or restitution, seventy-five cents.

For receiving and recording the return on each execution, writ of possession or restitution, thirty cents.

For each search warrant, thirty cents.

For each commitment, fifty cents.

For taxing costs and copy thereof in each cause, fifteen cents.

For every certificate not otherwise provided for, twenty-five cents.

For making copies of any papers or records in his office, including certificate, for any person applying for the same, for each hundred words, fifteen cents.

For taking down the testimony of witnesses, swearing them, taking the voluntary statements of persons accused, certifying and returning the same to the proper Court, in examinations for offences, for each hundred words, fifteen cents

TO CONSTABLES.

ART. 894. [11] For serving each writ or citation in a civil suit, fifty cents. Of Constables.

For serving each warrant in a criminal case, fifty cents.

For serving each notice for the taking of depositions, and copy of interrogatories, fifty cents.

For executing a search warrant, fifty cents.

For levying and returning each writ of attachment or sequestration, one dollar

For summoning each witness, twenty-five cents.

For committing a person to jail, seventy-five cents.

For taking each bond, fifty cents.

For levying each execution, fifty cents.

For executing each writ of possession or restitution, one dollar.

For returning each execution, writ of possession or restitution, twenty-five cents.

For summoning a jury in a Justice's Court, one dollar.

For summoning a jury to hold an inquest before a Coroner, to be paid by the county, two dollars.

For advertising sale under execution or any order of sale, fifty cents.

For each appraisement of property for sale under execution, or an order of sale, fifty cents.

For making title to purchaser of real estate under execution or order of sale, one dollar.

For making title to purchaser of personal property under execution or order of sale, when demanded by the purchaser, fifty cents.

For making money under execution or order of sale, when a sale is made, four per centum on the amount.

When the money is made without a sale, two per cent. on the amount.

For conveying a prisoner to jail, including guard and all other expenses, twenty-five cents a mile in going and returning.

For each day's attendance on the District Court, when summoned by the Sheriff, one dollar and fifty cents, to be paid out of the County Treasury.

For taking care of property levied on by a writ of execution, sequestration, or attachment, all reasonable expenses, to be taxed and allowed by the court to which such writ is returnable.

For all services done by Sheriffs in business connected with Justices' Courts, they shall only receive the same fees as are allowed to Constables.

NOTARIES PUBLIC.

ART. 895. [12] For protesting a bill or note for non-acceptance or non-payment, registering and seal, two dollars. Of Notaries Public.

For protest in all other cases, twenty cents for each hundred words, and fifty cents for the certificate and seal.

For taking the acknowledgment or proof of any deed or any other instrument of writing for registration, with certificate and seal, fifty cents.

For administering an oath or affirmation, with certificate and seal, fifty cents.

For taking the acknowledgment of a married woman, to a deed or any other instrument of writing, authorized to be executed by her, with certificate and seal, one dollar and fifty cents.

For all certificates, not otherwise provided for, with seal, fifty cents.

For all notarial acts, not otherwise provided for, fifty cents.

For copies of all records and memorandums in their offices, for each hundred words, with certificate and seal, twenty cents.

TO COUNTY OR DISTRICT SURVEYORS.

Of County or District Surveyor.

ART. 896. [13] For inspection and recording of the field notes and plat of a survey, for any tract of land over one-third of a league, three dollars; for one-third of a league, two dollars; for any quantity of land less than one-third of a league, one dollar.

For each examination of papers and records in his office, at the request of any person wishing to examine them, twenty-five cents.(*a*)

For receiving and filing each application for a location, fifty cents.

For copies of all field notes and plats, or any other papers or records in his office, for each hundred words, twenty cents, including certificate.

For surveying any tract of land, for each English lineal mile actually run, including all expenses of making the survey and returning the plat and field notes of survey, three dollars a mile.(*b*)

GENERAL PROVISIONS.

Fees for taking acknowledgments, depositions, &c.

ART. 897. [14] The several officers and persons authorized to perform any of the services named in this section, shall be entitled to the fees herein allowed for such services, viz.:

For taking the acknowledgment or proof of any deed, or any other instrument of writing for registration, with certificate and seal, fifty cents.

For taking the acknowledgment of a married woman to a deed or any other instrument of writing authorized to be executed by her, with certificate and seal, one dollar and fifty cents.

For taking the deposition of a witness, in answer to interrogatories or cross-interrogatories, under a commission, for each hundred words, twenty-five cents.

For swearing the witness to such answers, making certificates thereof with seal, and all other business connected with taking such depositions, fifty cents.

Fees pertaining to suits, taxed in bill of costs.

ART. 897a. [15] The fees hereinbefore mentioned, pertaining to suits or actions in court, shall be taxed and allowed in the bill of costs against the party cast in each suit or action, wherein any such services shall be rendered; but not more than one copy of any matter shall be allowed in the bill of costs, and if any party or his attorney shall take out copies of his own pleadings, or of papers filed by him in any cause, no charge for such copies shall be allowed in the bill of costs.

Practicing attorneys may examine records without fee.

ART. 898. [16] No Clerk of the Court or Justice of the Peace, shall be allowed to charge any practicing attorney of this State any fee for the examination of any papers or records in his office.

Fee book, &c., of Clerks, Sheriffs, J. Peace & Constable.

ART. 899. [17] Every Clerk of a Court, Sheriff, Justice of the Peace, and Constable in this State shall keep a fee book, and shall enter therein all fees charged for services rendered; which book shall, at all times, be subject to the inspection of any person wishing to see the account of fees therein charged against him.

(*a*) Where certificates are presented to a surveyor for location, and rejected by him, he is not entitled to fees for having searched his records to see whether the certificates should be received by him. The search provided for by the act, is a search made on request, among the records that properly belong to his office. James *v.* Wilson, 7 Tex. Rep. 23[illegible].

(*b*) A surveyor is not entitled to charge fees for surveying lines not actually run by him for the particular occasion. Hays *v.* Stewart, 8 Tex. Rep. 358.

Fees not payable until bill of particulars.

ART. 900. [18] None of the fees hereinbefore mentioned shall be payable by any person whatsoever, until there be produced, or ready to be produced, unto the person owing or chargeable with the same, a bill or account in writing, containing the particulars of such fees, signed by the Clerk or officer to whom such fee shall be due, or by whom the same is chargeable.

No fees, where party is indicted and discharged, when charged.

ART. 901. [19] In all cases where any person shall be presented or indicted by the grand jury, and shall be discharged from such presentment or indictment, neither the Clerks nor Sheriffs shall charge fees for the same; but if the party or parties so presented or indicted shall be convicted, the Clerk or Sheriff shall charge him, her, or them, with all fees accruing thereon.

Penalty for charging higher fees than the law allows.

ART. 902. [20] If any of the officers herein named, shall demand and receive any other or higher fees than are prescribed in this act, for any of the services herein mentioned, he shall be liable to the party aggrieved for fourfold the fees so unlawfully demanded and received, to be recovered in any court of competent jurisdiction. ( )

Execution may issue for fees, when.

ART. 903. [21] It shall be lawful for any Justice of the Peace or Clerk of the Supreme or District Court within this State, when any suits are determined in their respective courts, and the fees are not paid by the party from whom they are due, to make out executions for the same, directed to any lawful officer of the county where the party resides; and it shall be lawful for the Clerks of the County Courts to make out executions in like manner for the fees that may become due the officers of said courts, directed to any lawful officer of the proper county, and the officers to whom any of such executions shall be directed, shall levy and proceed with the same as in other cases: provided, that a bill of the costs shall in all cases accompany such executions. Bill of costs.

Printer's fees for publication.

ART. 904. [22] In all cases where a citation or other process is required to be served by publication in a newspaper, the officer whose duty it may be to make such service shall be furnished with the printer's fee for such publication before he shall be required to have such service made.

Security for costs when may be required.

ART. 905. [23] It shall be lawful for the Clerk of any court or Justice of the Peace, to require security for costs before issuing any process in any suit about to be commenced; unless the party applying for such process, his agent or attorney, shall make oath that the party so applying is unable to give such security.

FENCES.

Act of Feb. 5, 1840. Took effect March 16, 1840. Sufficient fence defined.

ART. 906. [1] Every gardener, farmer, or planter, shall make a sufficient fence about his cleared land in cultivation, at least five feet high, and make such fence sufficiently close to prevent hogs from passing through the same, not leaving a space or more than six inches in any one place for at least three feet high from the surface of the earth.

(a) Demanding and receiving "other or higher" fees than prescribed by the statute does not embrace the demanding and receiving fees for work, or services not performed; but only demanding and receiving of "other or higher" fees than are prescribed by the act for services actually rendered. In the latter case, the action lies for the penalty—in the former, for the amount unlawfully demanded and received. Hays v. Stewart, 8 Tex. Rep. 358. A person from whom illegal fees have been demanded, and paid by him in his capacity as administrator, cannot maintain an action in his personal capacity, either for the penalty, or to recover back the amount paid. Orton v. Engledow, 8 Tex. Rep. 206.

Trespass by cattle, &c., on cleared land of another.

ART. 907. [2] When any trespass shall have been done by any cattle, horse or hogs, on the cleared and cultivated ground of any person, it shall be lawful for such person to complain thereof to any Justice of the Peace for the county where such trespass shall have been done, and such Justice is hereby authorized and required to cause two disinterested and impartial freeholders to be summoned, who, with such Justice, shall view and examine on oath, whether complainant's fence be sufficient or not, and what damages he hath sustained by such trespass, and certify the same under their hands and seals, and if it shall so appear that the said fence be sufficient, then the owner of such cattle, horses or hogs, shall make full satisfaction for the trespass to the party injured, to be recovered before any tribunal having cognizance thereof; but if it shall appear that the said fence be deemed insufficient, then the owner of such cattle, horses or hogs, shall not be liable to make satisfaction for such damages.

Where person maims, &c., any horses, &c.

ART. 908. [3] If any person whose fence shall be adjudged insufficient shall, with guns, dogs, or otherwise, maim, wound or kill any horses, cattle or hogs, or cause or procure the same to be done, such person so offending shall make full satisfaction to the person injured, for all damages by such person sustained; to be recovered before any tribunal having cognizance thereof.(a)

FERRIES.(b)

[*See Article* 877.]

Act of Jan. 23, 1850. Took effect March 23, 1850.

Who entitled to license to keep.

ART. 909. [1] Every person owning the land fronting upon any watercourse, navigable stream, lake or bay, shall be entitled to the privilege of keeping a public ferry over or across such watercourse, stream, lake, or bay; if he owns the lands on both sides or banks, he shall be entitled to the sole and exclusive right of ferriage at such place; if he owns the lands on one side only, he shall have the privilege of a public ferry from his own shore, with the privilege of landing his boat and passengers on the opposite shore, with the consent of the owner of the land on said shore: if such consent cannot be obtained, he may apply to the County Court for the establishment of a public road from said opposite shore; and said court shall act on such application as in other cases.

Shall not be kept for hire, without, &c.

ART 910. [2] No person shall keep any ferry over or across any watercourse, navigable stream, lake, or bay, so as to charge any compensation for crossing the same, without first procuring a license from the County Court of the county in which such ferry is situated.(c)

(a) The statute does not limit the damages to be recovered to compensation only, but contemplates that exemplary or vindictive damages shall be allowed, where the circumstances justify it, as in other cases Cole v. Tucker, 6 Tex. Rep. 266.

(b) The right to keep a ferry and charge ferriage, is a Common Law right, but by our statutes this natural right has been abridged, and it has been made a franchise, to be exercised on giving bond and obtaining a license for its enjoyment. Johnson v. Erskine, 9 Tex. Rep. 1.

(c) Dunlap v. Yoakum, 18 Tex. Rep. 582.

ART. 911. [3] When a watercourse, navigable stream, lake, or bay, makes a part of the boundary line of this State, if any tax or charge shall be assessed or collected by any such adjoining State, for the privilege of a ferry landing on the shore or bank of such State from this State, then the same tax or charge may be assessed and collected by the County Court for the like privilege of landing on the bank or shore of this State. Where stream is part of State boundary, &c.

ART 912. [4] Any person wishing to establish a ferry across any watercourse, navigable stream, lake, or bay in this State, shall apply to the County Court of the county in which such ferry site may be, and on the applicant showing that he is the lawful owner of such land as the ferry is sought to be established on, and also, satisfying the court that the public convenience will be promoted thereby, such court shall grant such license. License, how obtained.

ART. 913. [5] When a County Court shall establish a ferry, they shall state in their record the rates of toll or ferriage, which may be demanded for ferrying passengers, carriages, wagons, carts, beasts, and such other property as is usually transported by ferries; and the said courts may, at their first term in each year, and shall at any other term, upon the petition of twenty respectable citizens of the county, revise, and if deemed expedient, change the rates of toll or ferriage, at all ferries that have been or may be established in their county. All changes of the rates of ferriage shall be entered of record, and notice thereof furnished by the county Clerks to owners of ferries affected by such changes: provided, no change of rate shall take effect until the expiration of thirty days from the day on which said change may be made; and provided, also, that where any owner of a ferry shall refuse to keep up the same at the rates allowed by the County Court, said court may issue a license to any one who will do so; but in all such cases, the party receiving such license shall be bound to take the ferry-boat in use at said ferry, if desired by the owner, at such valuation as two respectable citizens of the vicinity, one to be chosen by each party, shall place upon it. Act of Jan. 5, 1854. Took effect from passage. County Court to establish rates of ferriage. Changes of rates, &c.

ART. 914. [6] The owner or licensed ferrymen of each ferry which has heretofore been established in this State, shall within six months after this act takes effect, apply to the County Court of the county or counties where such ferry is situated, and obtain a license for such ferry, and he shall annually thereafter obtain a renewal of such license. Act of Jan. 23, 1850. License renewed, when.

ART. 915. [7] The owners of all ferries shall annually enter into bond, payable to the Chief Justice of their county, in such sum as the County Court shall direct, not less than one thousand dollars, with good and sufficient sureties to be approved by such Chief Justice, conditioned, that the owner of such ferry will at all times keep good and sufficient boats for the use of such ferry, and will also keep the banks on each side of the ferry in good repair, and so graded and levelled that the rise shall not exceed two feet in every seven feet from the water's edge to the top of the bank, and that said ferry shall be well attended at all times, and that he will comply with all the requisitions of the law relating to, or governing ferries; which bond shall be filed and recorded in the office of the Clerk of the County Court.(a) Bond of owner. See Art. 920.

ART. 916. [8] Upon producing the receipt of the County Treasurer for the payment of the tax assessed by the County Court for the privilege of such ferry, and executing the bond required by this act, such County Court shall grant a license to such applicant for the term of one year from the date of such license; and no license for any ferry that has been, or may hereafter be established, shall be granted, untill such payment shall be made and bond executed. License not to issue, until.

(a) Johnson v. Erskine, 9 Tex. Rep. 1. The decision in that case, was upon the repealed act, passed Dec. 20,1836.

Rates of, to be delivered to person obtaining license.

ART. 917. [9] In all cases where any person shall obtain a license for a ferry, the Clerk of the court shall make out and deliver to such person, a copy of the rates of toll or ferriage established by the court for such ferry, which shall be under his hand and official seal.

Rates of, to be posted at the ferry.

ART. 918. [10] Every owner of a ferry licensed in this State, shall keep a list of the rates of toll or ferriage established for his ferry, posted up either at the ferry or ferry-house, for the inspection of all persons. If any such owner shall fail or neglect to do so, he shall forfeit and pay the sum of four dollars for every such neglect, which may be recovered before any Justice of the Peace of the county, on the complaint of any person; one half of said amount to go to the county, and the other half to the prosecutor: and every week that he shall so fail or neglect, shall be deemed a separate offence, for which he shall be liable as aforesaid.

Where ferryman delays or refuses, &c., to cross person.

ART. 919. [11] If any person licensed to keep a ferry shall, on being tendered his lawful fees, refuse or neglect without a reasonable cause, to cross any person, his horse or other property usually transported by such ferry, every such ferryman shall, for every delay of thirty minutes, forfeit and pay to the person injured the sum of two dollars, to be recovered by action before any Justice of the Peace for the county in which the ferry is situated, with costs of suit; and the oath of the party shall be received in evidence of the fact.

Duties of ferry man.

See Art, 915.

ART. 920. [12] Every licensed ferryman shall at all times keep good and sufficient boats for the use of such ferry, and shall keep the banks on each side of the ferry in good repair, and so graded and levelled that the rise shall not exceed one foot in every seven feet from the water's edge to the top of the bank; and shall give ready and due attendance on all passengers, horses, wagons, and other property.

Where ferryman charges more than, &c.

ART. 921. [13] If any licensed ferryman shall charge and receive from any person a higher rate of toll or ferriage than has been established for his ferry by the County Court, he shall forfeit and pay to such person five dollars for every such offence, to be recovered by action before any Justice of the Peace of the county in which the ferry is established, with costs of suit; and the oath of the complainant shall be received in evidence.

Penalty for keeping, &c., without license

ART. 922. [14] If any person shall keep any ferry over any watercourse, navigable stream, lake, or bay in this State, for which he shall charge any person any money or other valuable thing, without complying with the provisions of this act, in relation to paying the tax, obtaining license and entering into bond, he shall forfeit and pay to every other person having a licensed ferry on the same watercourse, stream, lake, or bay in the same county, five dollars for every person so ferried, and the same sum for every wagon or other article so transported which may be subject to a separate charge, to be sued for and recovered before any Justice of the Peace of the county, with costs of prosecution; and shall, moreover, forfeit and pay a like sum in like manner to the county, which may be sued for and recovered in like manner by the County Treasurer.( )

Proceedings against sureties of ferryman.

ART. 923. [15] In all cases where a recovery shall be had against the ferryman, for violation of this act, if, after judgment, execution shall be returned that no estate of such ferryman can be found whereon to levy and make the money demanded in such execution, the Justice to whom such execution is so returned, shall cite the sureties of such ferryman to appear and show cause why judgment should not be rendered against them for the amount of the

(a) Dunlap v Yoakum, 18 Tex. Rep., 582.

execution that is not satisfied, and unless such cause is shown, judgment shall be so entered, and execution shall issue therefor.

ART. 924. [16] Any person injured by breach of the bond of any ferryman, shall have the right to sue thereon in his own name; and no such bond shall be void on the first recovery, but may be sued on from time to time, until the whole penalty is recovered.(a) Suit on bond of.

ART. 925. [17] Any person wishing to establish a public ferry, between the regular terms of the County Court, may obtain a temporary license for such ferry from the Chief Justice, which shall authorize him to keep such ferry until the next regular term of the County Court for the county, and to charge and receive for such time such rates of toll or ferriage as are charged at other ferries on the same watercourse, stream, lake, or bay. Temporary license.

ART. 926. [18] The County Court of the several counties of this State shall have power to assess and collect an annual tax for the privilege of each and every ferry in their county, which tax shall not exceed one hundred dollars per annum. Tax on.

ART. 927. [19] If any watercourse. navigable stream, lake, or bay shall form a portion of the boundary of any county, so one bank shall be in one county and the other in a different county, at the place where it is proposed to establish a ferry, or where a ferry has been established, then application for a license shall be made to the County Court of each of said counties; but if only one of said counties will grant a license to the applicant, then he shall have the right to ferry under such license alone, and in such case, neither County Court shall assess and collect a tax on such ferry exceeding fifty dollars per annum. Where stream is part of county boundary, &c

---

FISCAL YEAR.

ART. 928. [1] The fiscal year shall hereafter terminate on the 31st day of August of each year, and all officers who by law are required to report annually or biennially to the Legislature or Governor, shall close their books and accounts, and compile their respective reports at the aforesaid time in each year. Act of Dec. 11, 1857. Officers shall close their books and report when.

ART. 929. [2] All biennial reports intended for the use of the Legislature, shall be transmitted by the respective officers to the Secretary of State by the first of September of the year in which the Legislature assembles, whose duty it shall be to furnish the same to the party who may have been elected public printer at the preceding session of the Legislature, and it shall be the duty of such public printer to print said reports, as soon after being furnished therewith as practicable, provided the same shall be completed and ready for distribution by the assembling of the biennial session of the Legislature, next succeeding that for which such reports may have been prepared. Biennial reports to be transmitted, &c., when. Shall be printed.

ART. 930. [3] Fifty copies of the report of the Comptroller, and ten copies of the report of the Treasurer, Commissioner of the General Land Office, Superintendent of the Penitentiary, Commissioner of Claims, and State Engineer, respectively shall be printed for the use of each member of the Legislature, Number of copies to be printed.

(a) Johnson v. Erskine, 9 Tex. Rep. 1.

Duty of the Sec'y of State

and it shall be the duty of the Secretary of State to transmit to the presiding officers of both Houses of the Legislature at the commencement of each session all such reports as may have been published under the provisions of this act, for the use of the members of their respective bodies.

Compensation for printing.

[See Public Printer.]

ART. 931. [4] For the printing of said reports, the same rate of compensation shall be paid that is allowed for printing the laws of the Legislature, and the certificate of the Secretary of State, that the printing has been executed in a satisfactory manner, shall be a sufficient voucher for the accounting officers to audit and pay such claims out of the appropriation made for such purposes.

FORCIBLE ENTRY AND DETAINER. (a)

Act of March 15, 1848. Took effect Ap'l 29, 1848.

What is declared to be.

ART. 932. [1] If any person shall make an entry into any lands, tenements, or other real property, except in cases where entry is given by law, or shall make any such entry by force, or if any person shall wilfully and without force, hold over any lands, tenements, or other real property, after the determination of the time for which such lands, tenements, or other real property were let to him, or to the person under whom he claims, after demand made in writing for possession thereof, (a) by the person or persons entitled to such possession, such person shall be adjudged guilty of forcible entry and detainer, or of forcible detainer (as the case may be,) within the intent and meaning of this act.

Justices of the Peace to have jurisdiction of cases, &c.

ART. 933. [2] Any Justice of the Peace, of any county in this State, shall have jurisdiction of any case arising under this act, and on complaint upon oath of the party aggrieved, or his authorized agent, (b) shall issue his summons to the Sheriff, or any legally authorized officer of his county, commanding him to summon the person against whom such complaint is made, to appear before such Justice, at a time and place, named in such summons, not more than ten, nor less than six days, from the time of issuing such summons, which said summons shall be served at least five days before the return day thereof, by reading the same to the defendant, or by leaving a copy of the same with some free white person over the age of sixteen, at his usual place of abode, and the said Justice shall also, at the same time, issue a precept to the Sheriff or other officer as aforesaid, commanding him to summon a jury of six men, freeholders of the county, to appear before him on the day set for trying said complaint, to hear and try the same; and if any part of the jurors so summoned, shall fail or refuse to attend or be challenged, then the said Justice may order the Sheriff, or other legal officer, to complete the number, by summoning and returning others forthwith.

Summons to issue, &c.

(a) This act superseded the act of 1840, upon the subject of landlord and tenant. Camley v. Stanfield, 10 Tex. Rep. 546.

(a) Where the relation of landlord and tenant has not existed between the parties, it is not necessary to show that a demand of the possession was made in writing before the commencement of the action of forcible entry and detainer. Warren v. Kelly, 17 Tex. Rep. 544.

In an action of forcible entry and detainer under the statute, the right of possession must be the question and not the title to the land. Ibid. One who by violence turns out one, who has the peaceable possession of land, cannot in an action under the statute against him for such forcible entry, set up title either in himself or a third person, but will be compelled to restore the possession, and pursue the due course of law to try his title in the courts and obtain possession, if he has title. Ibid.

(b) The statute does not require that the complaint shall be in writing. That perhaps was the intention. But where the complaint was set out in writing in the summons, accompanied by affidavit, &c., embracing every essential requisite prescribed by the statue, it is too late to object in the District Court, on certiorari, that the complaint had not been filed previous to issuing the summons, when no objection was taken before the Justice. Clay v. Clay, 7 Tex. Rep. 250.

ART. 934. [3] The Sheriff or other officer, shall return to the said Justice, the summons and precept as aforesaid, on the day assigned for trial, and shall state, on the back of said summons, how the same was served, and on the back of said precept the names of the jurors; and if the defendant does not appear, and answer, the justice shall proceed to try the said cause *ex parte*, or may, in his discretion, postpone the trial to a time, not exceeding ten days; and the said Justice shall issue subpœnas for witnesses, and shall proceed to try said cause, as in other cases of trial by jury before Justices of the Peace. Return of summons. Mode of proceeding after return.

ART. 935. [4] The complaint shall describe particularly the lands, tenements, or other possessions in question; and the Justice of the Peace shall keep a record of the proceedings had before him; and if the jury shall find the defendant guilty, he shall give judgment thereon, for the plaintiff to have restitution of the premises and his costs, and shall award his writ of restitution; and if a verdict is given in favor of the defendant, judgment shall be given against the plaintiff for costs, and execution may issue therefor. What complaint shall contain. Judgment of restitution, &c.

FRAUDS AND FRAUDULENT CONVEYANCES.

ART. 936. [1] No action shall be brought whereby to charge any executor or administrator, upon any special promise to answer any debt or damage out of his own estate, or whereby to charge the defendant, upon any special promise to answer for the debt, default or miscarriage of another person (*a*) or to charge any person, upon any agreement made upon consideration of marriage, or upon any contract for the sale of lands,(*b*) slaves, tenements, or hereditaments, or the making of any lease thereof for a longer term than one year, or upon any agreement which is not to be performed within the space of one year from the making thereof;( ) unless the promise or agreement upon which such action shall be brought, or some memorandum thereof shall be in writing Act of Jan. 18, 1840. Took effect March 16, 1840. Certain instruments required to be in writing.

(*a*) To bring the promise to pay the debt of another within the statute, it is necessary that the debt promised to be paid should be a subsisting and continuing one, and that the undertaking be collateral and auxiliary to that debt. Bason *v.* Hughart, 2 Tex. Rep. 476.

If the consideration of the promise is the discharge of a former debt, and the debt is discharged in consequence of the promise, it is an original contract which need not be in writing. Ibid.

It is not necessary that the consideration of the promise should be expressed in writing to make the promise valid. Ellet *v.* Britton, 10 Tex. Rep. 208.

Whenever the main purpose of the promisor is, not to answer for another but to subserve some purpose of his own, his promise is not within the statute. Lemmon *v.* Box, 20 Tex. Rep. 329.

(*b*) An agreement to locate land certificates and procure patents, in consideration of part of the land, is not within the statute, and is not required to be in writing. Watkins *v.* Gilkerson, 10 Tex. Rep. 340. And see, also, Miller *v.* Roberts, 18 Tex. Rep. 16.

Where the purchase money has been paid, and the vendee has taken possession and made valuable improvements, a specific performance will be decreed, although the contract may not have been in writing. Ottenhouse *v.* Burleson, 11 Tex. Rep. 87. Dugan's heirs *v.* Colville's heirs, 8 Tex. Rep. 126. Taylor *v.* Ashley, 15 Tex. Rep. 50.

Payment of part, or even all the purchase money, will not take a case out of the operation of the statute, so as to enable a party to obtain a specific performance of a verbal contract. Gamar *v.* Stubblefield, 5 Tex. Rep. 552. See Fisk *v.* Miller, 13 Tex. Rep. 224.

The statute does not require that the price stipulated to be paid for land should be in writing. Adkins *v.* Watson, 12 Tex. Rep. 199.

A parol agreement that certain real estate shall be substituted in a mortgage for certain other real estate therein described is void under the statute. Castro *v.* Illies, 13 Tex. Rep. 229.

An agreement creating a trust concerning lands need not be in writing. James *v.* Fulcrod, 5 Tex. Rep. 512. Miller *v.* Roberts, 28 Tex. Rep. 16. Mead *v.* Randolph, 8 Tex. Rep. 191. McClenny *v.* Floyd, 10 Tex. Rep. 159.

The petition in a suit, on an agreement concerning land need not allege that the agreement was in writing. Ibid. That the agreement was in writing is a matter of proof. Doggett *v.* Patterson, 18 Tex. Rep. 158. 20 Tex. Rep. 1[illegible]1. See Peters *v.* Phillips, 19 Tex. Rep. 70.

The statute applies to administrator's sale, and the auctioneer is regarded as the agent of the vendor and vendee, with authority to sign for them. Dawson *v.* Miller, 20 Tex. Rep. 171.

A parol agreement by adjoining proprietors upon a line dividing their lands, is not within the statute. Houston *v.* Sneed, 15 Tex. Rep. 307. A parol agreement to partition land is not within the statute. Stuart *v.* Baker, 17 Tex. Rep. 417.

(*c*) Where an agreement is entered into not to be performed within the year, and the parties proceed to act upon the agreement, and one dies before it is executed, the other party is entitled to compensation for labor bestowed during the life time of the other party, which was induced by the contract, although it was not in writing. Ray *v.* Young, 13 Tex. Rep. 550.

and signed by the party to be charged therewith, or some person by him thereunto lawfully authorized.

Certain conveyances declared void as against third persons.

ART. 937. [2] Every gift, grant or conveyance of lands, slaves, tenements, hereditaments, goods or chattels, or of any rent, common or profit out of the same, by writing or otherwise, and every bond, suit, judgment, or execution, had or made, and contrived of malice, fraud, covin, collusion or guile, to the intent or purpose to delay, hinder or defraud creditors of their just and lawful actions, suits, debts, accounts, damages, penalties or forfeitures, or to defraud, or to deceive those who shall purchase the same lands, slaves, tenements or hereditaments, or any rent, profit or commodity out of them, shall be from henceforth deemed and taken only as against the person or persons, his or her, or their heirs, successors, executors, administrators or assigns, and every of them whose debts, suits, demands, estates, interests, by such guileful and covinous devices and practices as is aforesaid, shall or might be, in anywise disturbed, hindered, delayed or defrauded, to be clearly and utterly void; any pretence, color, feigned consideration, expressing of use or any other matter or thing to the contrary notwithstanding;(a) and moreover, if any conveyance be of goods or chattels or slaves, and be not, on consideration deemed valuable in law, it shall be taken to be fraudulent within this act, unless the same be by will duly proved and recorded, or by deed in writing or other instrument acknowledged or proved; if the same deed or instrument of writing include lands also acknowledged or proved in such manner as conveyances of lands are, by law, directed to be acknowledged or proved; or it it be goods and chattels, or slaves only, then acknowledged or proved by two or more witnesses, and recorded in the manner as now established by law, or may hereafter be established for the recording of deeds of conveyance of real estate in this Republic; or unless possession shall really and *bona fide* remain with the donee; and in like manner, when any loan of goods and chattels or slaves shall be pretended to have been made to any person with whom, or those claiming under him, possession shall have remained by the space of three years, without demand made and pursued by due process of law on the part of the pretended lender; or when any reservation or limitation shall be pretended to have been made of a use or property, by way of condition, reversion, remainder or otherwise in goods and chattels, the possession whereof shall have remained in another as aforesaid; the same shall be taken as to the creditors and purchasers, of the persons aforesaid so remaining in possession, to be fraudulent within this act, and that the absolute property is with the possession, unless such loan, reservation or limitation of use or property were declared by will, or by deed in writing, proved and recorded as aforesaid.(b)

Presumption of ownership from three years possession of goods or slaves.

Second section not to refer to conveyances upon good consideration, &c.

ART. 938. [3] The second section of this act shall not extend to any estate or interest in any lands, goods, chattels, slaves, or any rents, common or profit out of the same, which shall be upon good consideration and *bona fide* lawfully conveyed or assured to any person or persons, bodies politic or corporate.

(*a*) A purchase of property with knowledge that the vendor is selling to hinder, delay or defraud his creditors, although for a valuable consideration, is void as against creditors. Walcott *v.* Brander, 10 Tex. Rep. 419. Edrington *v.* Rogers. 15 Tex. Rep. 188.

A bill of sale made to defeat one previously made to defraud creditors, is fraudulent and void, as to all persons except the parties and their privies: but as to them it is valid. McClenny *v.* Floyd, 10 Tex. Rep. 159.

Not only the grantor and his heirs, but all claiming under him with actual notice are bound by a deed made to defraud subsequent purchasers, or to hinder and delay creditors. Fowler *v.* Stoneum, 11 Tex. Rep. 478.

Where property is conveyed by a debtor in failing circumstances, to a third person, and by the latter conveyed by deed of gift to the wife of the former, it is *prima facie* fraudulent and void as to antecedent creditors. Reynolds *v.* Lansford, 16 Tex. Rep. 283.

As to assignments by a merchant in failing circumstances, of his stock in trade, notes and accounts, to a trustee, for the benefit of certain creditors, &c., see Linn *v.* Wright, 18 Tex. Rep. 317.

Neither the parties to a conveyance nor their heirs will be permitted to impeach it, on the ground that it was made to hinder, delay or defraud the creditors of the grantor. Danzy *v.* Smith, 4 Tex. Rep. 411. Nor can an administrator impeach a deed procured to be made by his intestate, on the ground of fraud against creditors. Connell *v.* Chandler, Adm'r, &c., 13 Tex. Rep. 5.

(*b*) A purchaser of slaves from one who had remained in possession of them for more than three years, without demand made by the lender and pursued by due process of law, and where the loan was not declared by will or deed in writing, proved and recorded, acquired the absolute title to the slaves, notwithstanding he had notice at the time of his purchase that the plaintiff set up claim to the slaves, and claimed that the vendor held them under a loan from him. Grumbles *v.* Sneed—decided at Austin, December, 1858.

FREE NEGROES.

ART. 939. All free Africans or descendants of Africans, who were residing within the Republic of Texas at the date of the Declaration of Independence, and their natural issue, are hereby granted and allowed the privilege of remaining in any part of the Republic as long as they choose; on the condition of performing all the duties required of them by law. Joint Resolution, June 5, 1857. Certain free negroes may remain in the Republic.

ART. 940. [1] It shall be lawful for any free person of African descent, now in this State, or who may hereafter be within its limits, being over the age of fourteen years, to choose his or her master, and become a slave, upon the terms and conditions hereinafter named: provided, said slave shall not be subject to forced sales for any debt incurred by, or judgment rendered against the chosen master prior to the period of enslavement. Act of Jan. 27, 1858. In force from March 26, 1858. May choose a master, provided, &c.

ART. 941. [2] Whenever any free person of African descent, as aforesaid, desires to choose a master, such person may file a petition in the District Court of the county in which he or she resides, setting forth his or her desire to choose an owner, and stating the name of such person as he or she desires to select as an owner; which petition shall be signed by the petitioner, in the presence of at least two subscribing witnesses. And thereupon the Clerk of the Court in which such petition shall have been filed, shall give notice thereof, by posting such notice at the court house door for four weeks; and said Clerk shall also issue a summons to the petitioner, and the person designated in the petition as the proposed master, citing them to appear before said court at the term thereof next succeeding the expiration of the publication of said notice, and shall also issue a subpœna for the subscribing witnesses to the petition, which summons and subpœna shall be executed in the same manner as like process in other cases. May petition District Court, &c.,—process, &c.

ART. 942. [3] Upon the appearance in open court of both the petitioner and the person designated in the petition as the desired master, the court shall proceed to examine each party separately, as well as the subscribing witnesses to the petition, and such other person as the court may see fit; and at such examination, the District Attorney shall be present, and see that a full examination is had, and he shall represent the petitioner in such examination. And if upon such examination, the court shall be satisfied that there is no fraud nor collusion between the parties, that the proposed master is a person of good repute, and that there is no good reason to the contrary, the said court shall have power, by decree entered in the records of the court, to grant the prayer of the petitioner; and from the entry of such decree, the property in said person of African descent, as a slave, shall vest in the person so chosen as master, and his rights and liabilities, and the condition of the petitioner shall in all respects be the same as though such petitioner had been born a slave to the master so chosen. Duty of the Court upon the appearance of petitioner, &c. Duty of District Attorney.

ART. 943. [4] When any such petitioner as hereinbefore mentioned, shall be a female having children under fourteen years of age, and shall in her petition ask that such children shall become the slaves of the same person chosen When children of, under fourteen years, may be made slaves.

by her as her master, if the court shall, after examination as in this act before provided, grant the prayer of the petitioner as to herself, it shall also decree such children in like manner, to be the slaves of the same owner; provided, that where the mother of such children of African descent, under the age of fourteen years, shall be deceased, in that case the next friend of such children shall have authority in their behalf, to proceed in the same manner to the selection of a master for them, as the mother might do under the provisions of this act.

Costs by whom paid, &c.

ART. 944. [5] The District Attorney shall be entitled to a fee of ten dollars for each examination attended by him under the provisions of this act, which shall be taxed as costs in the proceedings, and all the costs of the proceedings shall be paid by the master to whom the slave may be decreed, and after a petition shall have been filed under the provisions of this act, and during the pendency of the proceedings under the same, no proceedings shall be had against the petitioner under any law prohibiting free persons of color from remaining in or coming to this State.

GEOLOGICAL AND AGRICULTURAL SURVEY.

Act of Feb. 10, 1858. Took effect from passage.

Governor to appoint Geologist, term of office, and bond.

ART. 945. [1] The Governor is hereby authorized to appoint, as soon as possible, some suitable and competent person as State Geologist, who shall hold his office for two years, and until his successor shall be appointed and qualified, unless removed by the Governor for neglect to perform the duties of his office, or for malfeasance in office, and who shall perform the duties herein prescribed, and during the period of his service shall hold no other office. And before entering upon the discharge of the duties of his office, he shall enter into bond, with security, to be approved by the Governor, in the sum of twenty thousand dollars, conditioned for the faithful discharge of the duties of his office.

Duty of Geologist.

ART. 946. [2] Said State Geologist shall, as speedily as possible, make a thorough and complete geological survey of the State, so as to determine accurately the quality and characteristics of the soil, and its adaptation to agricultural purposes—the species of produce to which the soil, in different sections, is best adapted; its mineral resources—their location, and the best means for their developement; its water powers—their localities and capacities; and generally everything relating to the geological and agricultural character of the State. And for the purpose of carrying out the provisions of this Act, said Geologist shall have power to appoint assistants, with approbation of the Governor—provided, that not more than two assistants shall be appointed.

May appoint assistants.

Office kept at Austin, specimens, &c., to be deposited at Capitol.

ART. 947. [3] Said State Geologist shall keep his office at the city of Austin, but shall not be required to remain in said office except as his duties allow; and shall keep in said office such specimens as he shall deem necessary to convey to such office. He shall also forward to the Governor, from time to time, during the progress of the survey, specimens of rocks, ores, coals, soils, fossils, and other mineral substances, as may be necessary and proper to form a complete cabinet of specimens of the geology and mineralogy of the State; and the

Governor shall cause the same to be deposited, in proper order, in some convenient room at the Capitol of the State, there to be preserved for public inspection. And said Geologist shall make a report to the Legislature, at its regular sessions, of his surveys, explorations, and examinations into the mineral and other natural resources of the State, its climate and agricultural adaptability, accompanied by illustrative maps, charts and drawings, with reference to the same; which report shall be the exclusive property of the State: provided, however, that the said Geologist shall not be prohibited from publishing any such facts, maps, charts and drawings, which it is made his duty to report. And that in making any survey upon the frontier, the Governor or said State Geologist is authorized to request the co-operation of any scientific corps, of the United States army, or navy, and an escort of United States troops.

Report to Legislature.

May publish facts.

Survey on frontier.

ART. 948. [4] Said State Geologist, for the performance of said service, shall receive an annual salary of three thousand dollars, to be paid to him quarterly, after he enters upon the duties of his office; and that the sum of twenty thousand dollars be and the same is hereby appropriated, out of any money in the Treasury not otherwise appropriated, to be expended under the direction of the Governor, for the purposes of carrying into effect this Act, by employing assistants, and in defraying the incidental expenses of his office; and upon presentation, by the State Geologist, of the proper vouchers, approved by the Governor, the Comptroller is hereby authorized to draw his warrant on the Treasury for the cost of any chemical apparatus, or other outfit deemed necessary by the Governor, as well as all other expenses of said survey: provided the amount expended shall not exceed the amount herein specified and appropriated: and provided, further, that the salary of each assistant State Geologist shall not exceed fifteen hundred dollars per annum, for the time he may be engaged.

Salary of Geologist, $20,00 appropriatad to carry this act into effect.

Paid out on vouchers.

Salaries of assistants.

ART. 949. [5] Said State Geologist and his assistants, before entering upon the duties of their respective offices, shall make oath, before some competent officer, that they will not purchase any lands in this State, with a view to speculation, during the time they hold their said offices, and that they will not conceal or suppress any information relative to any valuable discovery which they may make, pertaining to the object of said survey, either from the State, or from individuals upon whose lands said discovery may be made, and will so conduct the survey as to give as much publicity as possible to the important results of said survey.

Oath to be taken by Geologist and assistants.

ART. 950. [6] The Chief Geologist and his assistants, upon their removal or resignation, or at the expiration of his office, shall turn over to his or their successors, or to the Governor, all the minerals, shells, maps, plats and diagrams, which they may collect or make during their term of office, and shall communicate all important geological information to their successors, acquired during such geological survey.

Duty of, upon removal, resignation or expiration of office.

GUARDIAN.

[See County Court—Estates of Deceased Persons—Wills—Idiots and Lunatics.]

I. APPOINTMENT.

Act of March 20, 1848. Took effect Aug. 7, 1848. Who is entitled &c., to appointment.

ART. 951. [1] In all cases not otherwise provided for by law, the father while living, and after his death, and when there shall be no lawful father, and then the mother, if living, shall be entitled to the guardianship of their minor children, and shall have the custody of their persons, education and estates: provided, that if such estates are given to such minor children by any other person than such parent, the father or mother entitled to such guardianship shall give bond with security, take the oath and return an inventory as hereinafter prescribed for other guardians.(*a*)

When Chief Justice may appoint.

ART. 952. [2] If a minor have no parents living, or the parents be adjudged, according to law, incompetent or unfit for the duties of guardian, the Chief Justices, in their respective counties, shall appoint guardians to

(*a*) The power of the natural guardian over the person and estate of the minor child is not assignable by deed, without confirmation by the County Court.—Byrne *v.* Love, 14 Tex. Rep. 81.

such minors under the age of 14 years, and admit those over that age to choose guardians for themselves, subject to the approval of the said Chief Justice. When minor may choose.

ART. 953. [3] Whenever it shall come to the knowledge of any Chief Justice in this State, that there is within his county any minor without any legal or natural guardian, if such minor be under the age of fourteen years, such Chief Justice shall appoint a guardian for such minor; but if such minor shall be over the age of fourteen years, the Chief Justice shall cause a citation to be issued and served on such minor, to appear before him at some regular term of the County Court and choose a guardian; and if such minor, after service of such citation, shall neglect to appear, or to choose a guardian after appearing, the said Chief Justice shall appoint one. If such minor appears and makes choice of a guardian, and the Chief Justice is satisfied that the person chosen is suitable and competent, the person so chosen shall be appointed; but if the choice shall not be approved by the Chief Justice, he shall appoint some competent and suitable person to be guardian for such minor.(a) Where minor is under 14 years, &c., duty of Chief Justice. Where minor is over fourteen.

ART. 954. [4] Whenever the Chief Justice shall be satisfied that it will be for the advantage of a minor to appoint a guardian of the estate of such minor, different from the guardian of the person, he shall have power to make such separate appointment for a minor under the age of fourteen years, and to allow a minor over that age to make such separate choice, subject to the approval of such Chief Justice, as heretofore directed. One for person and one for estate shall be made, when.

ART. 955. [5] When a minor shall be entitled to, or possessed of, any estate not derived from the parent who shall be the natural guardian at the time, and it shall be shown to the Chief Justice of the county that such parent is incompetent to the care of such estate, or is mismanaging or wasting the same, such Chief Justice shall cause a citation to be issued and served on such parent to appear before him at some regular term of the County Court, and show cause why a guardian of the estate of such minor should not be appointed or chosen, and if, after service of such citation, no sufficient cause be shown, such Chief Justice shall appoint a guardian of the estate of such minor, if under fourteen years of age; or, if over that age, admit the minor to choose one in the same manner, and subject to the same restrictions, as herein provided for minors over fourteen years of age. Where parent mismanages estate, &c., not derived from proceedings, &c.

ART. 956. [6] A minor, having a guardian of his person or his estate appointed by the Chief Justice, upon attaining the age of fourteen years, may choose another guardian of his person or of his estate, before the Chief Justice in the county of such minor's residence; and if such Chief Justice is satisfied that the person chosen is suitable and competent, the appointment shall be made accordingly. Where minor, having guardian, attains the age of fourteen, may choose guardian.

ART. 957. [7] If any person who has been appointed a guardian by will, shall fail to appear before the Court where the will was probated, and accept of such appointment and obtain letters of guardianship within six months after the probate of the will, such appointment shall be considered as if it had never been made by the testator. Guardian appointed by will, and failing to appear, &c.

ART. 958. [8] No appointment of a guardian shall be made by the Chief Justice, except at a regular term of the County Court, and after ten days' notice has been given by the Clerk of said court, by posting a notice at the courthouse and two other public places in the county; such notice shall state No appointment shall be made, except.

(a) The appointment of a guardian by the Chief Justice of a county, other than that of the minor's residence, is absolutely void. Munson v. Newsom, 9 Tex. Rep. 109. Testamentary guardians receive their letters from the court where the will is probated. Ibid.

the person for whom a guardian is to be appointed, and the term of the court when an appointment will be made: provided, that this section shall not apply to the appointment of a guardian *ad litem*.

Requisite of letters of, &c. ART. 959. [9] Every appointment of a guardian shall specify whether it be of the person or of the estate, or of both the person and estate of the minor; and every guardian shall continue in office, unless sooner discharged according to law, until the minor, if a male, shall arrive at the age of twenty-one years; and if a female, until her marriage or arrival at the age of twenty-one years, whichever shall first happen. All letters of guardianship Duration of. shall be signed by the Chief Justice, and attested by the Clerk of the County Court with the seal of said court; and such letters, or a certificate of the Clerk of said court, attested by the seal of said court, stating that such letters have issued according to law, shall be evidence of the appointment of a guardian.

Father may appoint by will. ART. 960. [41] The lawful father of any minor under the age of twenty-one years, may, by last will, appoint a guardian of the person, or of the estate, or of both the person and estate of such minor; but no guardian so appointed shall interfere with the estate of such minor, until he shall have qualified and obtained letters of guardianship as herein required. (*a*)

II. OATH AND BOND.

Oath of Gardian. ART. 961. [10] Every person who may be appointed guardian of the estate of a minor, whether by last will or by the Chief Justice, shall before entering upon the duties of his appointment, take and subscribe an oath or affirmation, in substance as follows:—I, A. B., do solemnly swear that I will, well and truly, perform the duties of guardian of the estate, or of the person and estate, as the case may be, of the minor C. D.; which oath or affirmation may be taken and subscribed, either before the Chief Justice or the Clerk of the County Court, in term time or in vacation, and shall be filed and recorded on the minutes of the court.

Bond. ART. 962. [11] Every person who may be appointed guardian of the estate of a minor, whether by last will, or by the Chief Justice, shall, before entering upon the duties of his guardianship, enter into bond with two or more good and sufficient sureties, payable to, and approved by the Chief Justice of the county, in a sum equal to at least double the estimated value of the estate of such minor, conditioned for the faithful discharge of the duties of such guardianship, according to law: provided, however, that when an appointment is made by will, and directions are given in such will that the person so appointed shall not be required to give security, then the Chief Justice may Bond not required of testamentary guardian, when. grant letters of guardianship to the person so appointed, without bond and security. When an oath and bond is required from a parent who is entitled to the guardianship of his or her child, such bond and oath may be in substance the same as the oath and bond prescribed in this Act, for other guardians, varying the form to suit the circumstances of the particular case.

Form of bond. ART. 963. [12] The following form may be used for the bonds of guardians:

(*a*) Byrne *v.* Love, 14 Tex. Rep. 81. The County Court may deny letters of guardianship to a testamentary guardian, but such power should be exercised with caution and delicacy, as where there has been waste, embezzlement, &c., and not where the testamentary guardian has merely proceeded in good faith to carry out the directions of the will, without having first qualified and given bond as required by the statute. Stone *v.* Dorsett, 18 Tex. Rep. 700.

The State of Texas, } Know all men by these presents, that we, B., C., as County of A. } principal, and D. E. and F. G., as sureties, are held and firmly bound unto the Chief Justice of the county of A., in the sum of—— dollars, and —— cents, for the payment of which, well and truly to be made, we bind ourselves, our heirs, executors, and administrators, jointly and severally, firmly by these presents, signed and sealed with our seals, the seals being scrawls, this the —— day of ——, A. D., 18—. The condition of the above obligation is such that whereas the above bounden B. C. has been appointed by the last will of H., deceased, guardian of the estate (or of the person and estate, or has been appointed by the Chief Justice of the county of A., guardian of the estate, or of the person and estate, as the case may be,) of the minor L. M. Now, if the said B. C. shall well and truly perform all the duties required of him by law under said appointment, then this obligation shall be null and void; otherwise to remain in full force and effect.

B. C. [SEAL.]
D. E. [SEAL.]
F. G. [SEAL.]

ART. 964. [13] The bonds of guardians may be taken and approved either in term time or in vacation, at any time within twenty days after the order is made for the appointment of a guardian or for the issuance of letters of guardianship; and should any person appointed a guardian fail to take and subscribe the oath or affirmation, and to give bond in cases where a bond is required, within twenty days after the order of appointment or the order for the issuance of letters is made, such order shall be revoked by the Chief Justice without notice; and all bonds of guardians shall be filed and recorded in the minutes of the court. When bonds may be taken and approved.

ART. 965. [14] The Chief Justices of the several counties of this State, shall have power to require new bonds of guardians in all cases where they have power to require new bonds of executors or administrators, and under the same rules and regulations, and with like effect. New bonds may be required, when.

III. APPRAISEMENT AND INVENTORY.

ART. 966. [15] Every guardian of a minor shall immediately after the commencement of his guardianship, make out, with the assistance of the appraisers, to be appointed by the Chief Justice, an inventory and appraisement of all the estate of his ward that has come to his knowledge; which appraisement shall be sworn to by the appraisers; and such guardian shall also make out a list of all claims and debts owing to his ward; which inventory and list of claims shall be sworn to by such guardian, and returned to the court having jurisdiction of his guardianship, within sixty days after the commencement of his duties; such inventory and list of claims may be returned either in term time or vacation, but when returned, shall be noted on the minutes of the court and shall be filed and recorded by the Clerk. Appraisement and inventory to be made out and returned, when.

ART. 967. [16] Whenever any guardian shall discover any estate of his ward that has not been inventoried and appraised, or any claims or debts owing to his ward that have not been included in the list returned, he shall forthwith make out and return an additional inventory and appraisement of such estate, and list of such claims or debts; and whenever it shall be shown to the Chief Justice that any guardian has not returned to the court an inventory and appraisement of all the estate of his ward, and a list of all the claims and debts owing to his ward, such Chief Justice shall cause such guardian to be cited, either in term time or in vacation, and require him to return an Additional inventory shall be made when. Guardian may be cited to return additional, &c. additional inventory and appraisement of such estate and list of such claims and debts; and all such additional inventories and appraisements and lists of claims and debts, shall be made out, sworn to, returned, and recorded in the manner prescribed by law, for original inventories, appraisements, and lists of claims.

Effect of, when given in evidence. ART. 968. [17] Such inventories, appraisements, and lists of claims may be given in evidence in any suit by or against such guardians, but they shall not be conclusive against the minor if it be shown that there is other property of the minor or other claims or debts due the minor not included therein, or if it be shown that the estate, or claims, or debts were actually worth more than the value at which they are set down in such inventories, appraisements, and lists.

Appraisers, appointment of, &c. ART. 969. [18] The Chief Justice shall appoint appraisers of the estates of minors in the same manner as appraisers of the estates of deceased persons, and all the rules and regulations, respecting appraisers of the estates of deceased persons, shall apply to appraisers of the estates of minors.

IV. POWER AND DUTY OVER PERSON AND ESTATE OF MINOR.

Diligence required of the guardian, &c. ART. 970. [19] Every guardian of the estate of a minor shall use ordinary diligence to collect all claims or debts owing to his ward, and to recover possession of all property to which such ward has a title or claim, provided there is a reasonable prospect of collecting such claims or debts, or of recovering such property; and if any guardian shall neglect to use such diligence, he and the sureties on his bond shall be liable for all damages occasioned by such neglect.

Duty of guardian to manage estate prudently, &c. ART. 971. [20] It shall be the duty of every guardian of the estate of a minor, to take care of and manage such estate in such manner as a prudent man would manage his own estate; and all necessary and reasonable expenses incurred by such guardian in the safe keeping, preservation, and management of his ward's estate, and all necessary and reasonable expenses incurred by him in collecting claims or debts due to his ward, or in recovering property to which his ward has a title or claim, shall be allowed to such guardian by the Chief Justice, on proper proof, to be paid out of the estate of his ward; and every such guardian shall account to his ward for all such rents, and profits, and revenues as the estate would have produced by such prudent management.

Necessary expenses incurred allowed to.

To account to ward, &c.

Guardian of the person entitled to custody of ward. ART. 972. [21] Every guardian of the person of a minor shall be entitled to the charge, custody, and control of the person of his ward, and the care of his education, support, and maintenance; every guardian of the estate of a minor shall be entitled to the possession and management of his estate, shall have authority to receive all debts, rents, and things in action, due or belonging to his ward, to sue and defend for his ward in all suits or actions necessary to be prosecuted for or against him; and in the management of such estate, such guardian shall be governed by the provisions of this act. Every guardian of the person and estate of the minor shall have all the rights and powers, and shall perform all the duties both of a guardian of the person and a guardian of the estate of a minor.

Guardian of estate entitled to possession of estate, with authority, &c.

Duty and liability in regard to money of his ward. ART. 973. [23] Every guardian of the estate of a minor shall put the money of his ward to interest upon mortgage on real estate, to be approved by the Chief Justice, or he may with leave of such Chief Justice, and the assent of his sureties, retain the money in his hands, paying interest therefor; but if no person can be found to take the money upon interest and the guardian should not choose to retain the same paying interest, he shall be liable for the principal only, until the same can be put to interest. Every such guardian shall loan the money of his ward at the highest rate of interest that can be obtained, not exceeding twelve per cent. per annum, and shall account for all interest, which shall be charged in their annual settlement.

ART. 974. [24] The Chief Justice shall order all minors under his jurisdiction to be properly supported and educated, according to the means of such minor, and for that purpose shall from time to time make the necessary appropriations out of the estate of such minors, and when necessary to raise means for the support and education of such minors, or to pay debts against their estate, may order the sale of any personal property of such minor, other than slaves, and the Chief Justice may also order the sale of any perishable property, of a minor, that is liable to waste or to be injured by keeping, if he shall be satisfied that such sale will be for the interest of such minor.

Duty of Chief Justice in regard to support of minor, and management of estate, &c.

ART. 975. [25] Whenever any guardian of the estate of a minor shall represent to the Chief Justice that such minor has not sufficient means for his proper support and education, or to pay the debts against his estate, without a sale of some portion or all of the real estate or slaves of such minor, such Chief Justice, if satisfied of the truth of such representation, shall order a citation to be published in some newspaper printed in the county, if there be one, if not, then in some newspaper printed in the nearest adjoining county where there is one, for four successive weeks, which citation shall state the application for such sale, the property sought to be sold, and the term of the court when the application will be acted on, and shall require all persons interested in the welfare of such minor to appear and show cause why such sale should not be made as applied for; at the term of the court named in such citation, or at some subsequent term of the court to which the application may have been continued, the Chief Justice, if satisfied that the citation has been published according to law, shall proceed to hear the application, and any opposition that may be made thereto, and if satisfied that a necessity exists for a sale of any such property, he shall order it accordingly.

Real estate of minor may be sold when.

Mode of proceedings in such cases.

ART. 976. [26] All sales of a minor's property that may be ordered by the Chief Justice, under the provisions of this act, shall be made by the guardian of the estate of such minor in the same manner, and with the same effect as sales are required to be made by executors and administrators; all the rules, regulations, and provisions respecting sales by executors or administrators shall apply to and govern sales by guardians, so far as the same are applicable and not inconsistent with the provisions of this act.

Sales regulated by what rules.

ART. 977. [27] Every guardian of the estate of a minor shall annually make an exhibit of the condition of the estate of his ward, to the County Court of the county that has jurisdiction of the matter; and shall also annually make a settlement of his account as guardian with such court, beginning at the first term of said court after the end of the year from the commencement of his duties, and at each corresponding annual term, until his final settlement; and the like notice shall be given of such settlement as is required to be given for the settlement of accounts of executors and administrators; and in such settlements, guardians of the persons of the minor shall render a statement under oath, supported by proper vouchers, of the application of all money directed by the Chief Justice to be applied by them to the support and education of their wards; and any guardian, neglecting or refusing to make such settlement and statement on oath, as is herein required, shall be liable to be attached and imprisoned until he shall make such statement and settlement, provided he shall first have been cited to appear and make such settlement and statement.

Annual exhibit and settlement of account of guardian.

Final settlement.

Statement under oath by guardian of the person.

V. GENERAL PROVISIONS.

Death, resignation, &c., of guardian—new guardian—rights, powers and duties of.

ART. 978. [22] Whenever a guardian of the estate of a minor shall die, resign his trust, or be removed in any manner, the person who may be appointed guardian of the estate of such minor shall succeed to all the rights, powers, and duties of the previous guardian; he may be made a party to all suits or actions by, or against any previous guardian; he shall have the right to recover from any previous guardian, all the estate of his ward, and to receipt for the same; and may sue in his own name on the bond of any previous guardian for all such estate of his ward as has not been accounted for by any previous guardian.

When bond may be executed for ward.

ART. 979. [28] Whenever the guardian of the estate of a minor shall consider that it will be for the interest of his ward, that he should execute any bond that may be required by law, in order to obtain a partition of any estate in which such minor may be entitled to a distributive share, he may present a petition to the Chief Justice at some regular term of the court, setting forth such facts; and if the Chief Justice shall be satisfied that the execution of such bond will benefit such minor, he may order him to execute such bond; and any bond executed by a guardian in pursuance of such order, shall bind the estate of such ward in like manner as if executed by himself after he was of full age.

Property may be purchased for in payment of debts.

ART. 980. [29] The Chief Justice may authorize any guardian of the estate of a minor under his jurisdiction to purchase property for the use of his ward, in payment of any debt due to such ward, in all cases where he shall be of opinion that the interest of the ward will be advanced thereby.

Chief Justice may cite guardians to account.

ART. 981. [30] The Chief Justice of every county in this State shall have power to cite any guardian under his jurisdiction, and require him to render an account of his guardianship, as often as he may think such exhibit necessary; and such Chief Justice shall have power at a regular term of the court to remove any guardian whenever he shall be guilty of any gross neglect of duty, or whenever he shall mismanage, misapply or waste the estate of his ward, or whenever he shall remove out of this State, or whenever he shall fail to comply with any lawful order of the Chief Justice in relation to the estate of his ward; but in all such cases the guardian shall be first cited; and they may either in term time, or in vacation, suspend any guardian from the exercise of any of his duties for any of the causes named in this section.

May remove guardian when.

Suspend when.

Ward's property, order to deliver, how enforced.

ART. 982. [31] The several Chief Justices of this State shall have power to order any property or estate that may come to the possession of a guardian as such, and shall be in his possession at the determination of his guardianship, to be delivered to the person who was his ward, his executor or administrator, and to enforce the same by attachment and imprisonment not exceeding three days; and they shall also have power, on the application of any ward, when he shall become entitled to have the possession of his estate, to cite the guardian to such ward to appear and make a final settlement of his guardianship, and to enforce such final settlement and the payment of any balance that may be found to be due from a guardian on such final settlement, either by attachment and imprisonment not exceeding three days, or by execution in like manner as executions are authorized to be issued by them against executors and administrators.

Commission and compensation of guardian.

ART. 983. [32] Each guardian of the estate of a minor, shall be allowed to retain in his hands a commission of five per cent. upon all sums that he actually receives or pays away in cash, for his services as guardian; and in case any such guardian shall control a plantation for his ward, the Chief Justice shall have power to allow him a reasonable compensation for such service. (a)

(a) When a guardian charges his ward with counsel fees paid by him, he must show that the services rendered by the counsel were necesary for the interests of his ward. McGary v. Lamb, 3 Tex. Rep. 342.

ART. 984. [33] In all cases where any guardian and his ward may both be residents of any other State or Territory of the United States, and such ward may be entitled to property of any description in this State, such guardian, on producing to the Chief Justice of the county where such property or the principal part thereof is situated, at some regular term of the County Court, a full and complete transcript from the records of a court of competent jurisdiction in the State or Territory where he and his ward reside, certified as required by the law of the United States, showing that he has been appointed guardian, and has given bond and security in the State or Territory where he and his ward reside, in double the value of the property of such ward; and also showing to such Chief Justice that a removal of the property of such ward will not conflict with the terms or limitations attending the right by which the ward owns the same; then such transcript may be recorded in such court, and such guardian shall be entitled to receive letters of guardianship of the estate of such minor from such Chief Justice, which shall authorize him to demand, sue for, and recover any such property, and remove the same to the place of residence of himself and his ward; and the Chief Justice may order any resident guardian, executor, or administrator, having any of the estate of such ward, to deliver the same to such non-resident guardian; provided, all debts known to exist against such estate have been first paid; and provided, also, that the benefit of this section shall not extend to any citizen of any State or Territory in which a similar law does not now exist, or may not hereafter be passed. Non-resident guardian and wards, property of in this State how removed to State of their residence.

ART. 985. [34] When any guardian of the estate of a minor shall desire to remove the same from one county to another, in this State, the Chief Justice may permit him to do so, by an order entered on the minutes of the court: provided, he shall have first obtained letters of guardianship from the Chief Justice of the county to which he proposes to remove such estate, together with a certificate from such Chief Justice, attested by the Clerk of the court of such Chief Justice and the seal of the county, stating that he has been so appointed, and has given bond and security in double the value of such estate, and has also filed in such court a certified transcript of all the proceedings in relation to his guardianship. Removal of guardianship to another county.

ART. 986. [38] Any guardian may resign his trust in like manner, and with like effect as in the case of an executor or administrator. Guardian may resign.

ART. 987. [39] Appeals may be taken from any decision, order, judgment or decree of the County Court, in relation to the estates of minors, idiots, lunatics, and persons *non compos mentis*, or in relation to their guardians, in the same manner, and under the same rules as provided for appeals from said court in matters relating to the estates of decedents; and any settlement of the account of any guardian may be revised and corrected in the District Court of the county, at any time within two years, after such guardian has ceased his duties, upon proof that there was any fraud or mistake in such settlement: provided, that such guardian, or his legal representative, shall be first cited as in other suits. (*a*) Appeals to District Court allowed.

ART. 988. [42] In all proceedings in the County Court arising under the provisions of this act, the depositions of witnesses may be taken and read in evidence under the same rules and regulations as in the District Courts; and all laws in relation to witnesses and evidence which govern the District Court, shall apply to all proceedings in the County Courts, under the provisions of this act, so far as the same are applicable. Rules of evidence in District Court, apply to proceedings, &c.

(*a*) The revision and settlement of a guardian's accounts in the District Court, under the provisions of this article, is an original proceeding. And the certiorari being designed only to bring up the record of the Probate Court, is unnecessary where a complete transcript of the proceedings of that Court is filed with the petition. Haggerty *v.* Scott, 10 Tex. Rep. 525. A petition which sets up a failure of the guardian to account for certain property belonging to the ward, which came to his hands, is sufficient. Ibid.

Citation by publication.

ART. 989. [43] In all cases under the provisions of this act, when it is necessary to cite any person who is out of the limits of this State, such person may be cited by publication in like manner as in the District Court.

When minor may be bound out.

ART. 990. [44] When a minor shall have no parents living, and no estate, the Chief Justice shall have power, without the appointment of a guardian, to bind out such minor to some suitable person who will undertake the support and education of such minor; if a male, until he shall arrive at the age of twenty-one years; and, if a female, until she shall marry, or arrive at the age of twenty-one years, whichever shall first happen; and when any such minor shall have property, but not sufficient for his support and education, the Chief Justice may authorize the guardian of such minor to bind out such minor under the like rules and regulations.

IDIOTS AND LUNATICS.

[See Guardians—Lunatic Asylum.]

Act of March 20, 1848. Took effect Aug. 7, 1848.

Information, &c.

ART. 991. [35] If information in writing be given to any Chief Justice in this State, that any person in his county is an idiot, or lunatic, or is *non compos mentis*, and is incapable of managing his own affairs, and praying that an inquiry thereinto be had, and such Chief Justice shall believe such information to be true, he shall, at some regular term of the County Court, cause such person to be brought before him, and shall cause twelve competent jurors of the county to be summoned, who shall be sworn to inquire and a true verdict render, whether such person is of sound mind or not; whereupon the matter shall be tried; and if the jury shall return a verdict that such person is not of sound mind, the same shall be recorded, and the Chief Justice shall thereupon appoint a guardian of the person and estate of such idiot, lunatic or person *non compos*, as the case may be, in like manner as provided for minors under fourteen years of age.

Inquisition of idiocy, or lunacy, when to be held.

Guardian to be appointed.

Guardians to continue in office until.

ART. 992. [36] Guardians of idiots, lunatics, and persons *non compos mentis*, shall continue in office, unless sooner discharged according to law, until their ward shall be restored to sound mind, or shall die; and all the provisions of this act respecting guardians, for minors under fourteen years of age, shall apply also to guardians of idiots, lunatics and persons *non compos mentis*.

INDIANS.

ART. 993. [1] The President be and he is hereby authorized and required, at as early a period as practicable, to have surveyed two leagues of land, including the village of the Coshattee Indians, also two other leagues of land including the fenced in village of the Alabama tribe of Indians, for the entire and exclusive use and benefit of said tribe of Indians, until otherwise provided for by law. Act of Jan. 14, 1840. In force from passage. Lands reserved for Coshattee and Alabama Indians.

ART. 994. [2] The surveys of land made for the Indians aforesaid, shall be made conformable to the surveys next adjoining, that is to say, if the surveys next to those to be made for the Indians aforesaid, front one and a half miles on the river, or are square surveys, the surveys to be made for the Indians shall be made in like manner: provided, always, that the improvements of said Indians shall be as near in the centre of the two leagues to be appropriated to the use of each tribe, calculated from the side lines, as practicable. Mode of surveying the same.

ART. 995. [4] The government shall, at all times, exercise exclusive jurisdiction over the soil included in the surveys contemplated by this act, and also criminal jurisdiction over the aforesaid tribes of Indians. Jurisdiction by government retained.

ART. 996. [6] Whenever it shall be deemed expedient to remove said tribes of Indians, and they are actually removed off of said reserved lands, the same shall be held subject to the future disposition of Congress. Disposition of, &c.

ART. 997. [1] Six hundred and forty acres of vacant and unappropriated land situated in Liberty, Polk, or Tyler counties, or any of them, to be selected by the chiefs of the Coshattee tribe of Indians and the Commissioners hereinafter named, be and the same is hereby set apart for the sole use and benefit of, and as a home for the said tribe of Indians; and that the District Surveyor of the District of Liberty, or his legal deputy, be authorized and required, upon the application of said Commissioners, to survey the same and to return the field notes thereof, duly authenticated, to the Commissioner of the General Land Office, who shall thereupon issue a patent to said tribe of Indians for the same; and that said Surveyor shall, for such service, receive the usual fees of office and no more. Act of Aug. 30, 1856. In force from passage. Certain amount of land set apart for use of, &c.

ART. 998. [2] Should said chief and commissioners be unable to select a suitable home for said Indians, on vacant and unappropriated land, then and in that case, the said Commissioners are hereby authorized to purchase six hundred and forty acres of land from the owner or owners thereof, situated in When Commissioners are authorized to purchase land for, &c.

any of the aforesaid counties, at a price not to exceed two dollars per acre, and shall take from the owner or owners of such lands deeds with warranty, conveying the same to said tribe of Indians; which deeds of conveyance shall be acknowledged or proven, and admitted to record in the county in which the land or the greater part thereof is situated, before the purchase money or any part thereof shall be paid. And the said Commissioners are hereby authorized to draw on the Treasurer of the State in favor of the person or persons from whom said land or any part thereof may have been purchased, for a sum of money not to exceed twelve hundred dollars, the amount of which draft the Treasurer shall pay out of any money in the treasury not otherwise appropriated.

Commissioners may draw on Treasurer, &c., when.

Indians not to lease or rent to any person.

ART. 999. [3] Said Indians shall not alien, lease, rent, let, give, or otherwise dispose of said land, or any part thereof, to any person whomsoever. And should the State of Texas hereafter provide a different and permanent home for said tribe of Indians, and settle them thereon, then said six hundred and forty acres of land with its improvements shall become the property of the State.

RESERVATIONS OF LAND.

Act of Feb. 6, 1854. In force from passage.

Extent of reservation.

ART. 1000. [1] Jurisdiction over twelve leagues of land of the vacant domain of the State of Texas, or so much of twelve leagues as the government of the United States may select, be and the same are hereby set apart and appropriated for the use and benefit of the several tribes of Indians residing within the limits of Texas.

United States may have surveyed, &c., three separate districts.

ART. 1001. [2] The government of the United States is hereby authorized to cause to be selected and surveyed of the vacant domain of the State, or to purchase of private individuals and cause to be distinctly marked, three separate districts, or less, each district to be in a form as nearly square as may be, the said three districts not to include exceeding twelve leagues of land.

Duty of District Surveyor of, &c. where land is situated.

ART. 1002. [3] Whenever the proper agent of the government of the United States shall notify the District Surveyor of any land district within the limits of which the land so selected or purchased, may be situated, it shall be the duty of said District Surveyor to cause such land so selected or purchased, to be plainly delineated upon the county map of the county in which the same is situated, and any location or entry upon any vacant land after the same shall have been so designated for Indian purposes, shall be held null and void; provided, no land selected or purchased for Indian purposes under the provisions of this act, shall be situated more than twenty miles south or east of the most northern line of military posts, established by the government of the United States, and extending from Red river to the Pecos river.

Jurisdiction over, ceded to United States, provided, &c.

ART. 1003. [4] The jurisdiction over said twelve leagues of land or any portion thereof, which may be selected for Indian purposes, within the meaning of this act, be and the same is hereby ceded to the government of the United States, so far as to enable it to extend any act of Congress now existing or hereafter to be passed regulating trade and intercourse with the Indian tribes; provided, this cession of jurisdiction shall not be construed so as to deprive the State of Texas of the right of jurisdiction over any person other than an Indian for any offence committed upon the person or property of any one within the limits of this State; and further provided, that all process issuing from any of the courts of this State may be served in the like manner and have the same force and effect as though executed in any other portion of the State.

ART. 1004. [5] The government of the United States, as soon as the above twelve leagues of land, or so much thereof as may be deemed necessary, shall have been selected or purchased and distinctly marked, shall be and it is hereby authorized to establish upon said land whatever agencies and military posts may be deemed necessary, and to settle upon said land such Indian tribes or bands of Indians as belong within the limits of Texas, and shall exercise entire control and jurisdiction over said Indians within said limits, so long as said government shall judge such control and jurisdiction necessary to the well being of said Indians; provided, that whenever the land or any district thereof, selected or purchased as herein provided, shall cease to be used for Indian purposes, the jurisdiction herein ceded shall cease, and such portion of said land as shall be taken from the public domain of this State, shall revert, together with all and singular the improvements made thereon, to the State, to be disposed of in such manner as the Legislature may thereafter see proper; provided, that should the line of the contemplated railroad to the Pacific run through any portion of said territory selected under the provisions of this act, the right of way to three hundred feet in width be and the same is hereby reserved. Agencies and military posts may be established on, &c., by United States, provided, &c.

ART. 1005. [1] Jurisdiction over five leagues of land of the vacant domain of the State of Texas, or so much thereof as the government of the United States may select, be and the same are hereby set apart and appropriated for the use and benefit of the several tribes of Indians residing west of the Pecos river, and within the limits of the State of Texas. Act of Feb. 4, 1856. Took effect from passage. Reservation for Indians west of Pecos river, &c.

ART. 1006. [2] The government of the United States is hereby authorized to cause to be selected and surveyed of the vacant domain of the State, or to purchase of private individuals, and cause to be distinctly marked, one district, containing five leagues as aforesaid or less, which said district shall be located and selected west of the Pecos river, and the said quantity of land may be determined according to English measurement. Where to be located.

ART. 1007. [3] Whenever the proper agent of the government of the United States shall notify the District Surveyor of the land district within the limits of which the land so selected or purchased may be situated, it shall be the duty of said District Surveyor to cause such land, so selected or purchased, to be plainly delineated upon the county map of the county in which the same is situated, and any location or entry upon any vacant land, after the same shall have been so designated for Indian purposes, shall be held null and void. Upon notice District Surveyor shall survey, &c.

ART. 1008. [4] The jurisdiction over said five leagues of land, or any portion thereof, which may be selected for Indian purposes, within the meaning of this act, and the act to which this is a supplement, be and the same is hereby ceded to the government of the United States, so far as to enable it to extend any act of Congress now existing or hereafter to be passed, regulating trade and intercourse with the Indian tribes; provided this cession of jurisdiction shall not be construed so as to deprive the State of Texas of the right of jurisdiction over any person, other than an Indian, for any offence committed upon the person or property of any one within the limits of the State; and further provided, that all process issuing from any of the courts of this State, may be served in like manner and have the same force and effect as though executed in any other portion of this State, and the survey heretofore made by the authority of the United States for Indian reserves, be recognized in the General Land Office of this State according to English measure. Jurisdiction over said reservation ceded to United States, provided, &c.

Certain conditions, &c., shall attach.

ART. 1009. [5] The settlement, conditions and restrictions, named in the fifth section of the act to which this is a supplement, approved February 6th, 1854, be and the same are hereby declared to attach to the grant of jurisdiction herein named.

Act of July 28, 1856. In force from passage.

Intercourse laws extended ten miles from, &c.

ART. 1010. [1] All the intercourse laws of the United States for preventing the introduction, giving or sale of wines or spirituous liquors to Indians within the Indian country, be extended for a distance of ten miles from the boundary line of the Indian reserves in this State, upon which Indians have been or may hereafter be settled by the United States Indian Agents; and may continue in force so long as such reserves are kept for Indian purposes.

Act of Feb. 12, 1858. Took effect April 13, 1858.

Sale of spirituous liquors prohibited.

ART. 1011. [2] All persons are hereby prohibited from selling, bartering or giving spirituous or vinous liquors to an Indian of the Choctaw or Chickasaw territory, bordering on the State of Texas.

Penalty for.

ART. 1012. [2] Any one violating the provisions of this act shall, upon conviction of such violation, be fined not less than fifty, nor more than one hundred dollars.

Persons living within, &c. to give bond.

ART. 1013. [3] All persons living within the above described limits, who are dealing in spirituous liquors, shall be and are hereby required to give bond in a sum of five hundred dollars, with two or more good securities, binding themselves to faithfully carry out the provisions of this act.

Judges to give this act in charge, &c.

ART. 1014. [4] The Judges of District Courts in that portion of our State, contiguous to the Choctaw and Chickasaw Indians, shall give this act in charge to the grand juries.

Joint resolution Approved Feb. 4, 1856.

Intercourse laws, &c., may continue in force as long, &c.

The intercourse laws of the United States for the prevention of the sales of wines and ardent spirits to Indians, be extended for the distance of ten miles from the boundary lines of the Indian Reserves in this State, upon which Indians have been or may hereafter be settled by the United States Indian Agents, and may continue in force so long as such reserves are kept for Indian purposes, and this resolution take effect and be in force from and after its passage.

INJUNCTIONS.

Act of May 13, 1846. Took effect June 22, 1846.

ART. 1015. [149] All petitions for injunction and answers thereto, shall be verified by the oath or affirmation of the party filing the same. (*a*)

Amount for which injunction will be granted.

ART. 1016. [150] No injunction shall be granted to stay any judgment or proceedings at law, except so much of the recovery or cause of action as the complainant shall, in his petition, show himself equitably entitled to be relieved against, and so much as will cover the costs.

(*a*) The rule that the answer of a defendant to an injunction bill must be taken as true, unless contradicted by two witnesses, or one witness with strong corroborating circumstances, has no force under our system of pleading. Autrey *v.* Cannon, 11 Tex. Rep. 110. Where an injunction is not prayed, except on the final hearing, and where the answer seeks no relief or dissolution of the injunction pending the suit, there is no more necessity or reason for the pleadings being verified by affidavit than there is in any other case or where any other measure of relief is sought. Eccles *v.* Daniels 16 Tex. Rep. 136.

Act of Dec. 24, 1851.
Not granted after one year, &c, unless.

ART. 1017. [1] No injunction to stay an execution shall be granted, but within one year after judgment is obtained, unless it shall appear from the oath of the complainant or complainants, to the Judge applied to, that such application has been delayed in consequence of the fraud or false promises of the plaintiff in the judgment, practiced or made at the time of, or after obtaining the judgment, or unless it shall appear on oath, that the complainant or complainants, was or were out of the State at the time of rendering up judgment, so that application could not be made within the time aforesaid, in which cases injunction may be granted at any time within two years. (*a*)

Act of May 13, 1846.
Writs of, where returnable.

ART. 1018. [152] Writs of injunction, granted by any Judge of the Supreme or District Court, if to stay proceedings in a suit, or execution on a judgment, shall be returnable to and tried in the District Court of the county where the suit is pending, or the judgment was rendered; writs of injunction for other causes, where the defendant is an inhabitant of the State, shall be returnable to and tried in the District Court of the county where the defendant, or if there be more than one, where either of the defendants has his domicil. (*b*)

Bond given before issuance of writ.

ART. 1019. [153] No injunction writ shall be issued in any case, until the complainant execute a bond to the adverse party, with good and sufficient security, in such sum as the Judge granting the same shall deem sufficient to secure the amount or matter to be enjoined, and all damages and costs that may be occasioned by such injunction; conditioned that the complainant will abide the decision which may be made therein, and that he will pay all sums of money and costs that may be adjudged against him, if the injunction be dissolved either in whole or in part. The amount of such bond required shall be stated by the Judge, in his order granting the injunction, and the bond shall be taken and the security approved by the Clerk issuing the injunction, who shall file said bond with the petition. (*c*)

Damages when allowed by the court.

ART. 1020. [154] Upon the dissolution of an injunction either in whole or in part when the collection of money has been enjoined, if the court be satisfied that the injunction was obtained only for delay, damages thereon, shall be assessed by the court at ten per cent. on the amount released by the dissolution of the injunction, exclusive of costs; and in all other cases the damages shall be assessed by a jury sworn for that purpose; if neither party require a jury, the damages may be assessed by the court. (*d*)

By the jury.

(*a*) This article has reference to granting of an injunction for causes existing at the time of the rendition of the judgment. It could not have been intended to embrace a case where the injunction was sought upon the ground of payment and satisfaction of the judgment. Beardsly *v.* Hall, 9 Tex. Rep. 119. The time prescribed within which, after judgment, an injunction may be obtained to stay execution, manifestly has no application to an injunction, sought for causes which have arisen subsequent to the rendition of the judgment. Williams *v.* Bradbury, 9 Tex. Rep. 487. Clegg *v.* Varnell, 18 Tex. Rep. 294. For causes existing at the time of the rendition of the judgment, the injunction must be sued out within the time prescribed by the statute. One granted after that time is manifestly against law, and should be dissolved. And if the injunction be the sole object of the suit, the case should be dismissed. Doss *v.* Miller, 6 Tex. Rep. 338.

(*b*) Hendrick *v.* Cannon, 2 Tex. Rep. 259. An application for an injunction to stay proceedings on a judgment, must be made to the court in which the judgment was rendered, unless made by one who is not a party to the judgment, and whose residence is in a different county. Winnie *v.* Grayson, 8 Tex. Rep. 429.

(*c*) Where an injunction bond departs substantially in the condition from the terms prescribed by the statute, it will not have the attributes intended to be imparted by the statute. Hanks *v.* Horton, 5 Tex. Rep. 103. Janes et al., *v.* Reynolds, 2 Tex. Rep. 250. Where the Judge in the order granting an injunction omits to state the amount for which the bond shall be given, a bond given in double the amount of the sum enjoined is good. Dickenson *v.* McDermott, 13 Tex. Rep. 248. If the bond is not conditioned "for the payment of all sums of money," it is error to give judgment against the sureties for ten per cent. damages on the dissolution of the injunction. Pillow *v.* Thompson, 20 Tex. Rep. 206. The defendant is not entitled to damages of course upon the dissolution of the injunction, but only upon proof of damages. Jordan *v.* David, 20 Tex. Rep. 712.

(*d*) The statute evidently contemplates that the assessment of damages may be simultaneous with the dissolution of the injunction. Hammonds *v.* Belcher, 10 Tex. Rep. 271. When the injunction has operated on other matters than the collection of money, the defendant may rightfully prosecute a separate action to have the question of damages and their amount adjudicated. Ibid. The damages sustained by reason of the issue of an injunction may be pleaded in reconvention in the same suit. Ibid. Carlin *v.* Hudson, 12 Tex. Rep. 203. The motion to dissolve may be taken up and disposed of, at any time before the cause is regularly reached on the docket or called for trial. Huston *v.* Berry, 3 Tex. Rep. 235. Smith *v.* Ryan, 20 Tex. Rep. 661. The statute authorizing the Court to award damages on the dissolution of an injunction, has reference to injunctions to restrain the collection of money, obtained by the judgment debtor, or some one who is a party to the judgment. Carlin *v.* Hudson, *supra*. On the dissolution of an injunction restraining the collection of money from the principal in the injunction bond, it is proper for the Court to render judgment against the principal and his sureties for the principal sum enjoined and for the damages assessed. Cook *v.* De La Garza, 13 Tex. Rep. 432.

Interlocutory Judgment. ART. 1021. [155] The court shall enter an interlocutory judgment, or a decree, according to the circumstances of the case, including the damages assessed as aforesaid, against the principal and sureties in the injunction bond, and may award execution thereon, or enforce such decree, in such manner as may be proper according to the rules and practice of the court.(*a*)

Where injunction is dissolved and petition continued over. ART. 1022. [156] Upon the dissolution of any injunction restraining the collection of money by an interlocutory order of the court, if after such interlocutory order of dissolution, the petition shall be continued over for trial, or hearing, as an original petition or suit, it shall be the duty of the court, before whom such case is pending, to require of the defendant or defendants bond and security, payable to the complainant or complainants, in double the amount of the sum enjoined, conditioned to refund to the complainant or complainants the amount of money, interest, and costs, which may be collected of him or them in the suit or proceeding enjoined, in the event of such injunction being made perpetual on final hearing.

Judgment on bond after order of dissolution. ART. 1023. [157] On any bond and security taken in pursuance of the preceding section, in the event of the injunction being perpetuated, on final hearing the court may, on motion of the complainant or complainants, enter up judgment against the principal and sureties for such amount as may be shown to have been collected from or paid by him or them.

INTEREST.(*b*)

Act of Jan. 18, 1840. Took effect March 16, 1840. ART. 1024. [1] The distinction between legal and conventional interest shall be known and recognized by the laws of this Republic.

Legal interest 8 per cent. ART. 1025. [2] On all written contracts ascertaining the sum due, when no specific premium of rate of interest is expressed, interest shall be taken, recovered, and allowed, at the rate of eight per centum per annum, from and after the said sum is due and payable.(*c*)

Conventional, not to exceed 12 per cent. ART. 1026. [3] The parties to any written contract, may agree to and stipulate for any premium or rate of interest, not exceeding twelve per centum per annum on the amount or value of the contract; and the same may be taken, "recovered," and allowed.(*d*)

ART. 1027. [4] All contracts or instruments of writing whatsoever, which may, in any way, directly or indirectly, violate the foregoing provisions of this

(*a*) After the dismissal of the suit for want of prosecution, the court has no jurisdiction, without reinstating the cause, to render judgment against the plaintiff and his sureties in the injunction bond, upon motion under the statute. Wright *v.* Thomas, 6 Tex. Rep. 420. If the bond does not substantially conform to the law, the Court cannot render a summary judgment against the sureties; and a judgment upon such a bond was reversed as to the sureties and affirmed as to the principal. Janes *v.* Reynolds, 2 Tex. Rep. 250. See Cook *v.* De La Garza, *supra.* Kendrick *v*, Rice, 16 Tex. Rep. 254.

(*b*) Interest is the creature of local law, and is governed by the law of the country where the contract is made or the debt incurred. Burton *v.* Anderson, 1 Tex. Rep. 93. It is the creature of positive law, of statute, decree or ordinance of the law making power. Davis *v.* Thorn, 6 Tex. Rep. 482.

(*c*) Interest cannot be recovered on an open account. Cloud *v.* Smith & Adriance, 1 Tex. Rep. 102. Close *v.* Fields, 2 Tex. Rep. 232. To authorize a judgment for interest, the petition should show the debt to be such as under the statute carries interest. Crook & Adriance *v.* McGreal, 3 Tex. Rep. 487. Where goods are contracted to be sold on a credit by an agreement not in writing, interest in the nature of damages cannot be recovered by the seller. Gammage *v.* Alexander, 14 Tex. Rep. 414.

(*d*) Conventional interest does not give place to legal interest at the maturity of the contract, but continues to run until payment. Hopkins *v.* Crittenden, 10 Tex. Rep. 189.

act, by stipulating for allowing or receiving a greater premium or rate of interest than twelve per centum per annum, for the loan, payment, or delivery of any money, goods, wares, merchandise, bonds, notes of hand, or any commodity, shall be void and of no effect for the whole premium or rate of interest only; but the principal sum of money, or the value of the goods, wares, merchandise, bonds, notes of hand, or commodity, may be received and recovered.(*a*)

Contracts for more than 12 per cent. void for the whole interest.

Principal sum may be recovered.

Art. 1028. [5] All judgments of the several courts of this Republic shall bear interest at the rate of eight per cent. per annum, from and after the date of judgment, and the same shall be recovered and allowed: provided, however, that such judgments shall be given only upon contracts hereafter made, in which there may be no more than eight per cent. stipulated in writing.(*b*)

Judgments, interest on.

Art. 1029. [10] In the trial of all causes in the courts of this State, the rate of interest in any other State or Territory of the United States, shall be presumed to be the same as that established by law in this State, unless the rate of interest of such other State or Territory be proven, and may be recovered accordingly, without allegation or proof of the rate of such foreign interest.

Act of Feb'ry 5, 1858. Took effect July 1, 1858.

Interest of other States presumed &c., unless.

IRRIGATION PROPERTY.

Art. 1030. [1] The County Courts be, and they are hereby authorized to order, regulate and control the time, mode and manner of erecting, repairing, cleaning, guarding and protecting, the dams, ditches, roads and bridges, belonging to any irrigation farms and property, and the fences or other like protection in and around such farms; provided, that such farms, dams, ditches and fences be owned conjointly by two or more different persons: and further provided, that the same be situated outside of a corporation having jurisdiction thereof.

Act of Feb'y 10, 1852.

County Court.

Irrigation farms

Art. 1031. [2] Said County Courts shall have power to ordain and establish all the needful police government and civil control over such irrigation farms and property, and said courts may assess and collect fines for breaches of any regulations established by them, or by the joint owners of such farms and property, or recognized by said court as consistent with ancient usage and the law of the State; said courts may order meetings of said joint owners for the election of commissioners and other officers, and for the consideration of any of their other interests, or the said court may proceed and elect said officers, and may regulate the right of way, the stoppage and passage of the water, and the right distribution of the shares of said water; they may forbid the

Power of County Courts over irrigation farms

(*a*) A note given for usurious interest computed on a previous loan, is illegal and void. Stanley *v.* Westrop, 16 Tex. Rep. 200. Contracts made for the payment of usury are void under the statute, and payments of usurious interest, although voluntary, may be applied to the discharge of the principal while any part of it remains unsatisfied. Ware *v.* Bennett, 18 Tex. Rep. 794. See 14 Tex. Rep. 600.

(*b*) All judgments, except those rendered upon contracts in writing, in which the parties have stipulated for a higher rate of interest, bear interest at the rate of eight per cent. per annum, and judgments upon contracts in writing, in which a higher rate of interest is stipulated, not exceeding twelve per cent. per annum, bear interest at the rate of the contract. Jewett *v.* Thompson, 8 Tex. Rep. 437. Finley *v.* Carothers, 9 Tex. Rep. 517. A fine imposed by the judgment of a court on conviction of an offence, does not bear interest under the statute. The State *v.* Steen, 14 Tex. Rep. 396. A claim against an estate, after approval and allowance, is a judgment, and bears interest from the date of approval, although the claim be upon an account. Finley *v.* Carothers, 9 Tex. Rep. 517.

running of stock at large on the common farm; they may fine for taking water out of turn, and for carelessness and wantonness in overflowing roads and neighboring lands, and generally they may do, or cause to be done, what they may consider just and needful or beneficial to the joint owners.

Default of owner of suerte, may fine or lease; leasing.

ART. 1032. [3] If any owner of a suerte or subdivision lot in said farm, shall fail or refuse to do or pay his or her proportion of labor and expense in and on such dam, ditches, fences, bridges and other needful appurtenances to such irrigation farms, the said County Court may, and they are hereby empowered to fine such person, or to lease said suerte: provided, that such leasing shall be at public outcry, after ten or more days of due public notice, and to the persons bidding the shortest term, not to exceed four years, who shall give good security to discharge faithfully all such charge and work.

License to irrigate, when granted.

ART. 1033. [4] Upon the application of the owners of any suitable lands and water, and the assurance and the proper security given to the county, if required by said court, that no injury will result to the public health, the County Courts are hereby authorized, by decree, to license and permit any such owners, to proceed and dam the water, and to ditch, fence, and irrigate their lands: provided, that all such joint owners of new or already established irrigation farms, shall be liable for damages done to the public, or to any person by reason of the overflow of such irrigation water; suit to be brought against the person occasioning the injury, or in such other way as may be sanctioned by said court.

Owners liable for overflow—damages, &c.

Owner of land refusing consent for dam or ditch

ART. 1034. [5] If, in the establishment of any new project of irrigation, or the extension thereof, the County Court deem it of sufficient importance to order a dam or ditch to be made on the lands of any person refusing to consent thereto, the said court, after giving such person actual notice in writing, and full hearing and consideration of his objections, may decree the making of the same, and shall depute two or more discreet and disinterested freeholders of the vicinage to arbitrate and fix the amount of damage permanently sustained by such person, which shall, by that or another such commsssion, be levied upon and paid forthwith by the applicants for such irrigation project, in the ratio of the interest and several shares of the said applicants and joint owners; and the said County Courts may, after like personal notice to parties interested, order the multiplication or extension of any ditches for irrigation, and of irrigation farms at and below, or at the sides of other such property; when it shall be the duty of such court to proceed and assess all just fines and equitable damages, and to fix and direct the rate and amount and kind of work, labor and tax to be paid by any of such applicants and others, according to their interest.

Arbitration and assessment of damages.

Proceedings.

Public health injured, dams, &c., to be discontinued.

ART. 1035. [6] Where the health of the public may be injured by irrigation, or the daming up of water for any purpose, it shall be the duty of the County Courts, after due and mature hearing and consideration, to decree the discontinuance, and they shall proceed and break up and discontinue all such dams, ditches and irrigation, whether the same have been heretofore ever so long in existence, or may be hereafter started.

Regulations where fences may be dispensed with.

ART. 1036. [7] In counties where the County Courts may decree and adjudge that fences around irrigation farms may be dispensed with, they may make all fair, equal and proper regulations for the keeping up or herding of hogs, cattle and other stock, and for the security and protection of the crops and farms: provided, that if ten or more voters shall make written protest against such decree, then the said court shall proceed by notice and a public election, and ascertain if two-thirds of the voters be in favor of dispensing with the use of fences, otherwise it shall not be so decreed.

When not.

JOINT TENANTS.

ART. 1037. [12] When two or more persons hold an estate, real, personal, or mixed, jointly, and one joint tenant dies before severance, his interest in said joint estate shall not survive to the remaining joint tenant or joint tenants, but shall descend to and be vested in the heirs or legal representatives of such deceased joint tenant in the same manner as if his interest had been severed and ascertained.

Act of March 18, 1848. Took effect from passage.

Upon death of one, interest does not survive but descends to his heirs.

JUDGMENTS.

I.

ART. 1038. [8] Hereafter every partition of any tract of land, or lot, made under any order or decree of any court, and every judgment or decree by which the title to any tract of land, or lot, shall be recovered, shall be duly recorded in the clerk's office of the County Court of the county in which such tract of land, or lot, or part thereof shall be; and until so recorded, such partition, judgment, or decree, shall not be received in evidence in support of any right claimed by virtue thereof.(a)

Act of Feb'ry 5, 1840. Took effect March 16, 1840.

Judgment for partition, or for land, shall be recorded—where.

ART. 1039. [2] Where suit is instituted against a parnership, service or process upon one of the partners shall be sufficient notice to all the members of the firm, except that the judgment rendered in case of such service, shall only be enforced against the partnership property, and the separate property of the partner who may have been served.

Act of Feb'ry 5, 1858. Took effect July 1, 1858.

Judgment against partners

II. LIEN OF JUDGMENTS.

ART. 1040. [12] Whenever final judgment shall be rendered, by any of the courts of record of this Republic, it shall operate as a lien on all the real estate of the defendant, situate and being in the same county where the judgment is rendered, from the day of the date of the judgment: provided, that said lien

Act of Jan. 27, 1842. Took effect March 17, 1842.

Judgments of courts of record,

(a) Hearst v Kuykendall, 16 Tex. Rep. 327.

lien on real estate in the county, &c. shall cease to operate if execution be not issued out within twelve months from the date of the judgment.(*a*)

Act of May 13, 1846. Took effect June 22, 1846. When it operates as a specific lien. ART. 1041. [137] Where the judgment is rendered for the recovery of lands, the judgment below shall operate as a specific lien upon the lands so recovered; but in such case the appeal bond shall only be required for the costs of suit and damages on appeal.

III. SUITS ON FOREIGN JUDGMENTS.

[*See Const. U. S., Art. 5, Sec. 1, for Judgments of sister States.*]

Act of June 28, 1845. In force from passage. ART. 1042. [1] In all actions on foreign judgments, the only mode of authentication in the courts of this Republic shall be as follows:

* * * * * * * * * *

Foreign judgments, how authenticated. 3d. All judgments of any other foreign tribunal other than those above named, shall be under the certificates of the Judge and Clerk of the Court, the Chief Executive Government of the country, and a Consul of the Republic.(*b*)

Conditions upon which suit may be brought, on. ART. 1043. [2] No suit shall be allowed to be brought, or be received by the clerk, until a copy of the foreign judgment, authenticated as aforesaid, shall be filed with the petition, and all costs likely to accrue, together with a tax fee of twenty-five dollars cash, for the use of this Republic, be paid to the clerk of the court; and any suit brought without a strict compliance with the provisions of this section, shall be held as if never brought, and without the pale of amendment or correction.

Shall be *prima facie* evidence only. ART. 1044. [3] Foreign judgments, authenticated as aforesaid, shall be regarded as *prima facie* evidence only, and open to all defences that might have been used at any time before judgment.

Suits on, by foreign banking or money corporations. ART. 1045. [5] In all suits on judgments by foreign banking or money corporations, not only shall the costs be so paid as prescribed above, but the act, or copy of the act, of incorporation shall be authenticated as provided for in the first section of this act, according to the divisions of said first section. And in addition thereto, the corporation, if plaintiff, or its assignee, shall prove that a strict and literal compliance was had with the charter in putting the corporation into operation; and the provisions of this section shall apply as well to suits already pending as those hereafter to be brought.(*c*)

(*a*) The lien of a judgment or decree is fixed by law, and can be extended no farther than the limits prescribed by the statute, whether it be attempted so to carry it further by a court or otherwise. It is therefore error to decree that the judgment shall be a lien on slaves or on real estate in another county. Castro *v.* Illies, 13 Tex. Rep. 229.

It is not good cause against the revival of a judgment that execution issued on it within twelve months after its rendition, where by failure to continue the issuance of executions, at proper intervals, the judgment has become dormant. DeWitt *v.* Jones, 17 Tex. Rep. 620. The judgment becomes as dormant by failure to issue executions in the subsequent as it does in the first year of its rendition. Ibid. Bennett & wife *v.* Gamble, 1 Tex. Rep. 124. Scott & Rose *v.* Allen, Ibid. 508. Hall *v.* McCormack, 7 Tex. Rep. 269.

Where execution has been issued on a judgment of a court of record, within the year, and subsequent executions regularly from term to term thereafter, an action on the judgment is not barred until ten years after the last execution. Graves *v.* Hall, 13 Tex. Rep. 379. Where the executions have regularly issued, the omission of the clerk to put them in the form of *alias* and *pluries* is not important. Ibid.

(*b*) This act prescribing the mode of authenticating foreign judgment and limiting suits thereon, was intended to be limited to judgments of a date anterior to its passage, and did not contemplate judgments subsequently to be rendered. Hooper *v.* Nichol, 13 Tex. Rep. 151. Clay *v.* Clay, Ibid. 195. Ingram *v.* Drinkard, 14 Tex. Rep. 351.

(*c*) This act is most clearly intended to apply to cases where the corporation, or the assignee of the corporation is plaintiff. Reynolds *v.* Skelton, 2 Tex. Rep. 516.

The act has reference to suits on foreign judgments, and does not apply to suits brought by a foreign corporation not on a judgment. Field *v.* Gantier, 8 Tex. Rep. 74.

JURY.

[For Grand Jurors see Code of Criminal Procedure.]

I. HOW SELECTED AND SERVICE.

I. HOW SELECTED AND SERVICE.

Act of Feb. 13, 1858. Took effect from passage.

Qualification of, and mode of selecting jurors.

ART. 1046. [1] The County Courts of the several counties of this State, shall provide, and at all times cause to be kept in their respective counties, two jury boxes, numbered one and two; and that said court shall meet on the first Monday in July in each year, when they shall prepare a list of such persons between the ages of twenty-one and sixty years, in their respective counties, as shall be well qualified to serve as jurors, being persons of good moral character, qualified electors in the county under the Constitution, freeholders in the State, or householders in the county, and otherwise qualified as now, or may hereafter be required by law, not including the Governor, Secretary of State, Attorney General, Commissioner of the General Land Office, Clerks in the offices of the various departments of the Government at Austin, State Engineers, Judges, and Clerks of Courts, County Commissioners, and Justices of the Peace, Sheriffs and their deputies, Marshals and their deputies, Constables, Practicing Attorneys and Counsellors at law, practicing Physicians and Surgeons, Postmasters, Revenue Officers, Ferrymen, Schoolmasters, and Ministers of the Gospel, who shall be privileged from serving, which list shall be copied into a well bound book, to be kept by the Clerk of the County Court for that purpose; and the Clerk of the County Court shall make out two duly certified copies of said list, immediately after the adjournment of the court, and file the same, one with the Clerk of the District Court,

Persons exempt from serving on.

and deliver one to the Sheriff of the county; the County Court having written the names on said list upon separate tickets, they shall cause them to be placed in the jury boxes, as hereafter provided, which boxes shall be kept by the Clerk. The persons whose names are entered in the jury book and placed in the jury boxes, shall be liable to serve as jurors.(a)

County Court shall compare the jury list, &c.

ART. 1047. [2] The County Court, at the meeting required by the first section of this act, shall, after preparing the new jury list, as they are required to do, compare the same with the names contained in both of the jury boxes, and shall withdraw from said boxes such names as are not upon the new list; and they shall place in jury box number one, the names upon such new list as were not in either of said boxes.

Act of May 4, 1846. Took effect June 22, 1846. Certain persons excluded from serving on.

ART. 1048. [3] If any person, whose name shall be in the jury box, shall be hereafter convicted of bribery, perjury, forgery, or of any other crime which is by law a disqualification, or who has been convicted of any gross immorality, his name shall be withdrawn from the jury box and erased from the jury book by the County Court.

Act of Feb. 13, 1858. Time and mode of selecting jurors.

ART. 1049. [4] From the jury box number one there shall be drawn by the Clerk of the District Court and the Clerk of the County Court in every county, in the presence of some Justice of the Peace, at least thirty days before the first day of the term of the District Court to be held for the county, the names of twenty-four persons to serve as jurors at such term of the District Court, and as they are drawn, the tickets on which their names are written, shall be placed in jury box number two. Every draft shall be made from jury box number one, and the tickets drawn shall be placed in box number two; and whenever the tickets in box number one are exhausted, then the contents of box number two shall be placed in number one; so that the jury service shall be as nearly as possible equalized. If, in making the draft as before required, any name shall be drawn which is in the list of Grand Jurors selected by the County Court, for the same term of the District Court, the ticket so drawn shall be placed in box number two, but the name of such Grand Juror shall not be counted in the list of twenty-four, and another name shall be drawn.

Act of May 4, 1846. Took effect June 22, 1846. Where name of absent or disqualified juror is withdrawn.

ART. 1050. [5] When the draft is being made, as provided for in the preceding section, if the name of any person shall be drawn, who, within the knowledge of the Clerks, is unable, by reason of his absence from the county, to attend the court, or who has become disqualified to serve as juror since the last revision, or who is privileged by law from serving, the Clerks shall replace the ticket upon which the name of such person is written, in the jury box No. 1, and another shall be drawn in its stead.

Act of Feb. 13, 1858. Names of persons drawn shall be entered in jury book, &c.

ART. 1051. [6] The Clerk of the County Court shall enter the names of the twenty-four persons drawn as before required in the jury book, stating the time of the draft and the term of the Court for which it is made, and shall, together with the Clerk of the District Court, and the Justice of the Peace aforesaid, certify thereto, and in like manner the Clerk of the District Court shall enter the same upon the minutes of the District Court, and with the Clerk of the County Court and Justice of the Peace aforesaid shall certify thereto.

ART. 1052. [7] It shall be the duty of the Clerk of the District Court, immediately after the draft of jurors, as contemplated in the preceding sections

(a) Objections which go to the fitness of jurors may be urged by the party to be affected by their finding; but those which are matters of privilege or exemption merely, can only be urged by the juror himself. That the juror is over sixty years of age or under twenty-one is of the latter class. Breeding v. The State, 11 Tex. Rep. 257.

of this act, has been made, to issue a *venire facias* in due form, directed to the Sheriff or other officer, containing the names of the persons who have been drawn to serve as jurors, and commanding him to summon them to appear and serve as jurors at the next succeeding term of the District Court, naming the day and place where the same is to be held. Act of May 4, 1846. Took effect June 22, 1846. *Venire facias* shall issue.

ART. 1053. [8] The Sheriff or other officer shall execute the *venire* for jurors, either by giving personal notice to them or by leaving a written notice at their usual place of abode, at least five days before the first day of the term of the court at which they are required to appear and serve; and he shall make due returns of the *venire*, certifying how he has executed it. How executed.

ART. 1054. [9] It shall be the duty of the persons summoned, in accordance with the provisions of the foregoing sections of this act, to attend at the time and place to which they have been summoned, and to serve as jurors during the term of the court to which they have been summoned, or until discharged by the court. Duty of persons summoned to attend, &c.

ART. 1055. [10] On the first day of the term of the District Court, or as soon thereafter as the Court may direct, the Sheriff, or other officer in attendance upon the Court, shall call the names of jurors returned upon the *venire*; and thereupon the Court shall organize one or more juries as the business in the opinion of the Court may require. The first twelve persons answering who are not excused, shall constitute petit jury No. 1; the second twelve petit jury No. 2. After the requisite number of persons shall answer to constitute petit jury or juries, the following oath shall be administered to the same: "You, and each of you swear, that in all cases between parties, which shall be to you committed, you will give a true verdict therein, according to the law and evidence given you. So help you God." Act of Feb. 13, 1858. Jury, when organized. Oath of.

ART. 1056. [11] If from any cause no jury has been drawn as contemplated in the preceding sections of this act, or no *venire* has issued, or the *venire* be quashed, or the array challenged, or whenever none of the jurors returned upon the *venire* are in attendance upon the court, the Court shall have power to direct the issuance of a *venire facias* commanding the Sheriff or other officer to summon the requisite number of legally qualified jurors; and such *venire* may be made returnable at such times as the Court may direct, and upon the return thereof the same proceedings shall be had as in cases where the jury has been regularly drawn. Act of May 4, 1846. Took effect June 22, 1846. The District Court may order a *venire* to issue, when.

ART. 1057. [12] In case a portion of the jurors returned upon the *venire* are in attendance upon the court, but not a sufficient number to constitute a petit jury, or two, should the Court think it necessary, the Court shall have power to order the issuance of a *venire facias* commanding the Sheriff or other officer to summon a sufficient number of by-standers to supply the deficiency: provided, no by-stander be summoned unless his name appear upon the list of qualified jurors furnished the Sheriff by the County Court, and of those so summoned, together with the original panel in attendance, the petit jury or juries shall be formed. Act of Feb. 13, 1850. When part of the jurors attend, the Court may order a *venire* to supply, &c.

ART. 1058. [18] Talesmen may be sworn for the trial of the suit or for the day, or for the residue of the term of the court, as the Court may think proper, and such alteration shall be made in the form of the oaths herein prescribed as will meet the circumstances of the case. Act of May 4, 1846. Took effect June 22, 1846. Talesmen may be sworn, when.

ART. 1059. [20] The Court may in its discretion excuse any juror from attendance for a limited time or for the term. Court may excuse jurors.

ART. 1060. [21] It shall be the duty of the Clerk of the District Court,

Names of persons drawn who do not serve, shall be returned to box No. 1.

immediately after the adjournment of said court, to furnish to the Clerk of the County Court the names of those persons who were drawn to serve as jurors at the last term of the court, but not summoned, or who were summoned but did not attend, or who attended but were excused by the Court from serving as jurors; and it shall be the duty of the Clerk of the County Court thereupon to return the tickets upon which the names of such persons are written, from jury box No. 2, to jury box No. 1, making a minute of the same upon the jury book; and such persons shall be liable to another draft and to serve as jurors in the same manner as if their names had not been previously drawn.

Juror failing to attend, liable to fine, &c.

ART. 1061. [26] Every person who shall have been duly summoned as a juror, whether upon a *venire* issued, or as a talesman, who shall fail to attend the court to which he has been so summoned, and serve as a juror, shall be liable to be fined by the Court, in a sum not exceeding one hundred dollars, at the discretion of the court; but where such fine is imposed judgment final shall not be rendered thereon until the defendant has first been cited to appear and show cause why such judgment final should not be rendered against him; and if he appear and show cause, the Court in its discretion, may remit the fine in whole or in part, and with or without payment of costs.

Certificate, &c., evidence of service.

ART. 1062. [27] The certificate of the Clerk of the District Court, shall be evidence of the period of service of each petit juror.

Act of Feb. 16, 1852.

Person who has served one day, shall not be compelled, &c., provided.

ART. 1063. [1] No person who shall have served for more than a single day as a juror at one term of the District Court, shall be compelled to serve as a juror for more than a single day at the next term of such court: provided, that this section shall not apply to jurors summoned on a special venire, unless they shall have actually served on the trial of the cause for which they shall have been summoned: and, provided, further, that this section shall not apply to counties in which there shall not be at the time, two hundred inhabitants liable to do jury duty.

II. JURY FUND.

Act of Feb. 1850. Took effect from passage.

Fines on, &c., shall be paid to clerk.

ART. 1064. [1] All fines imposed on jurors, and all fines imposed for contempt of court, by any District Court of this State, shall be paid to the Clerk of said court.

Jury fee on cases now pending except.

ART. 1065. [2] A jury-fee of three dollars upon all causes now pending in any District Court of this State, except criminal causes, shall be paid to the Clerk of said court before final judgment shall be entered in any such cause.

Jury fee in civil cases shall be paid before judgment is entered.

ART. 1066. [3] A jury-fee of three dollars upon all causes that may hereafter be commenced in any District Court of this State, or that may hereafter be brought to any District Court of this State, by appeal or otherwise, except criminal causes, shall be paid to the Clerk of said court before final judgment shall be entered in any such cause.

Jury fee in criminal cases of $3, when taxed.

ART. 1067. [4] In all criminal causes now pending in any District Court of this State, in which a conviction shall be had, a jury-fee of three dollars shall be taxed in the bill of costs, which fee, when collected, shall be paid to the Clerk of said court: provided, that in no case shall the State be chargeable with such fee.

Of $5, when taxed, &c.

ART. 1068. [5] In all criminal causes that may hereafter be commenced in any District Court of this State, or that may hereafter be brought to any District Court of this State, by appeal or otherwise, in which a conviction shall be had, a jury-fee of five dollars shall be taxed in the bill of costs, which fee when collected, shall be paid to the Clerk of said court: provided, that in no case shall the State be chargeable with such fee.

Clerk shall account for jury fee, when.

ART. 1069. [6] Should any Clerk of the District Court in this State enter a final judgment in any cause, except criminal causes, before he shall have received the jury-fee imposed by this act, such Clerk shall be liable for, and shall account for such fee in like manner as if he received the same; and should the plaintiff in such suit fail to pay the jury-fee in any case, when a verdict has been rendered, on or before the last day of the term at which said verdict may be rendered, a judgment of non-suit shall be entered against the plaintiff, unless the defendant shall pay the jury-fee.

Officers failing to pay over fines and fees collected.

ART. 1070. [7] It shall be the duty of every Sheriff or other officer in this State, to pay over all fines imposed on jurors, and all fines imposed for contempt of court by any District Court, and all jury-fees in criminal causes that may be collected by him, to the Clerk of the District Court, to whom the same is payable; and if any Sheriff or other officer, shall fail so to pay over any such fine or fee so collected by him, or shall fail to use reasonable diligence to collect the same when authority for the collection thereof shall have been placed in his hands, such Sheriff or other officer, and the securities on his bond shall be liable for the amount of such fine or fee, and damages thereon at the rate of ten per cent. per month, from the time such fine or fee was collected, or from the time the same might have been collected by the use of reasonable diligence; which may be recovered by the Clerk of the District Court in which such fine was imposed, by suit against such Sheriff or other officer, and the securities on his bond, before any Justice of the Peace, or court having jurisdiction thereof; and it shall be the duty of each Clerk of the District Court to bring such suit whenever he knows, or is informed that any Sheriff or other officer, and the securities on his bond, are liable to be sued by him.

Jury fund, how constituted.

ART. 1071. [8] All fines imposed on jurors, and all fines imposed for contempt of court, by any District Court of this State, and all jury-fees imposed by this act, shall constitute a jury-fund, to be disposed of by the Clerk of the District Court in the manner provided for in this act; and said Clerk, and the securities on his bond, shall be liable for any misapplication of said fund by said Clerk, or for any failure by said Clerk to apply the same as directed by this act.

Balance of, to whom paid.

ART. 1072. [11] It shall be the duty of each Clerk of the District Court in this State, within ten days after the adjournment of each term of the District Court in his county, to pay over to the County Treasurer of his county any balance of money received under the provisions of this act, that may remain in his hands after reserving a sufficient amount to pay for all jury-service rendered at such term as shown by the statement required to be made under the 6th section of this act; and if any Clerk of a District Court shall fail to pay over any such balance, such Clerk and the securities on his bond shall be liable to pay such balance and damages thereon at the rate of ten per cent. per month from the time such balance should have been paid; which may be recovered by said County Treasurer, in a suit before any Justice of the Peace or court having jurisdiction thereof.

Where clerk has reason to believe former clerk has not accounted and paid over.

ART. 1073. [13] Whenever any Clerk of a District Court shall have reason to believe that any one who has preceded him in said office shall not have accounted for and paid over all money received by him or them, under the provisions of this act, it shall be the duty of such Clerk to collect and apply the same, in like manner as the same should have been collected and applied by the person who so preceded him in said office; and for that purpose he may maintain a suit against any Clerk, who has so failed to account for and pay over any such money, and the securities on his bond, before any Justice of the Peace or court having jurisdiction thereof.

Jury fee shall be taxed in bill of costs.

ART. 1074. [14] Each jury-fee imposed by this act in civil causes, shall be taxed in the bill of costs against the unsuccessful party; and should the said fee have been paid by the successful party, it shall be refunded to him when collected.

Clerk may be indicted for misapplying fund, &c.

ART. 1075. [15] Every Clerk of the District Court, who shall neglect to perform any of the duties required of him by this act, or who shall misapply the jury-fund created by this act, shall be deemed guilty of a misdemeanor, and be liable to indictment therefor in the District Court of his county, and on conviction thereof, shall be removed from office by said court.

Commission of clerk on money received.

Quere? Whether in force.

ART. 1076. [16] Each Clerk of the District Court shall be allowed to retain in his hands a commission of two and one-half per cent. on all moneys received and paid out by him, under the provisions of this act; and shall also be entitled to demand and receive from each juror, to whom he shall give a certificate, under the provisions of this act, a fee of ten cents and no more.

Where party is too poor to pay jury fee.

ART. 1077. [17] The provisions of the second, third, and sixth sections of this act shall not apply to cases in which the party interested in having such judgment entered, shall make affidavit before the Clerk that he is too poor to pay said jury-fee.

Jury fees, fines, &c., to be paid to County Treasurer.

ART. 1078. [18] All fines for contempt of court, and all fines of jurors for non-attendance, or for any other cause, imposed by any court of record of this State heretofore, and all jury taxes or fees in suits which have heretofore been decided in the District Courts of this State, shall continue to be paid into the County Treasury; and it shall not be necessary hereafter for the County Treasurer to keep a separate account of the sums so paid to him.

Sums due jurors for services heretofore rendered, how paid

See Art. 1086.

ART. 1079. [19] All sums due to jurors, who have heretofore served in any of the District Courts of this State, shall be paid out of the Treasury of the county where the service was rendered, in such manner as the County Court shall direct; but no jury-certificate, heretofore issued, shall be receivable for county taxes, unless by an order of the County Court hereafter made.

Act of Feb. 16, 1852. Took effect from passage.

ART. 1080. [7] No more than one jury fee shall be exacted in any cause.

III. PAYMENT OF GRAND AND PETIT JURORS.

Statement of amount due each juror to be made, &c., on last day of term.

ART. 1081. [9] On the last day of each term of the District Court, in every county of this State, it shall be the duty of the clerk of said court, to make out a statement in writing, which shall set forth all moneys received by him, or for which he is liable under the provisions of this act, up to the date of such statement, and since his previous statement, if any such has been made, and also the name of each juror who has served at such term, the number of days he served, and the amount due him for such service at the rate of one dollar and twenty-five cents per day, which statement shall be examined by the Judge holding such court, and if found to be correct, shall be approved and signed by him; should said Judge consider said statement to be erroneous, he shall make such corrections therein as he may think necessary, and shall then approve and sign the same; which statement, when so approved and signed, shall be recorded by the clerk in the minutes of the court.

Art. 1082. [10] It shall be the duty of each clerk of the District Court, after the statement provided for in the preceding section shall have been approved, signed, and recorded, to pay to each juror, who has served at such term, the amount due him for such service, if there shall be a sufficient amount of money in his hands, received under the provisions of this act, to pay all the jurors who served at such term; but if there is not a sufficient amount in his hands for that purpose, then he shall pay to each juror his *pro rata* amount in proportion to his time of service and shall give to each juror a certificate for the balance due him, which certificate shall be paid out of the county treasury, and shall be a sufficient voucher for the county treasurer to pay the amount therein certified to be due; and such certificate shall moreover be receivable for all taxes assessed by the county in which such certificate was given. Jurors to be paid, &c. Certificates shall issue to, &c., when.

Art. 1083. [12] Should any clerk of a District Court fail to pay any juror, who has served in his county, the amount that he is required to pay him under the provisions of this act, when the same is demanded, such clerk and the securities on his bond, shall be liable to pay such juror double the amount he was so required to pay: which may be recovered by such juror in a suit before any Justice of the Peace or court having jurisdiction thereof. Where clerk fails to pay jurors.

Art. 1084. [2] In counties where the term of the District Court shall not exceed one week, grand jurors shall not receive pay for more than three days; in counties where the term of said court shall not exceed two weeks, grand jurors shall not receive pay for more than six days; and in counties where the term of said court shall exceed two weeks, grand jurors shall not receive pay for more than eight days. Act of Feb. 16, 1852. Took effect from passage. Grand jurors shall only receive pay for three days, when.

Art. 1085. [3] It shall be the duty of the clerk of the District Court, within twenty days after the adjournment of every term of said court, to make a report under his hand and official seal to the County Court, to be filed in the office of the clerk of said County Court, stating the number of certificates issued by him to jurors, for services at such term, the amount of each, and to whom issued, which statement shall be entered of record in a separate book, to be provided by the clerk for that purpose. Clerk shall report to County Court in twenty days after, &c.

Art. 1086. [4] Certificates which have been heretofore, or shall hereafter be issued to jurors, under the provisions of the tenth section of the act of February, A. D. 1850, entitled "an act to provide for the payment of grand and petit jurors," shall be receivable for all county taxes in the county in which such certificates have been or shall be issued. Certificates issued to, receiv'd in payment of taxes. Article 1079.

Art. 1087. [5] All such certificates which shall be received by Assessors and Collectors for county taxes, shall be delivered up to the respective County Courts to be cancelled, and at the same time the Assessors and Collectors shall file a statement under oath of the certificates so delivered up. Shall be delivered up by Assessors to County Courts.

Art. 1088. [6] The pay of jurors shall hereafter be one dollar and a half per day, instead of one dollar and a quarter as heretofore. Compensation of jurors.

Art. 1089. [8] The provisions of the act of February, A. D. 1850, entitled "an act to provide for the payment of grand and petit jurors," shall apply to the provisions of this act so far as they may be applicable. Act of 1850 to apply.

JUSTICES' COURTS.

I. ELECTION AND QUALIFICATION OF JUSTICES.

Art. 1090. [1] There shall be elected by the qualified electors of each Justice's precinct, in the several counties of this State, on the first Monday in August, 1848, and every two years thereafter, two Justices of the Peace, who shall hold their offices for the term of two years, and until their successors shall be elected and qualified according to law, and shall be commissioned by the Governor. (*a*) Act of March 20, 1848. Took effect August 7, 1848. When Justices to be elected.

Art. 1091. [2] Before any Justice of the Peace shall enter upon the duties of his office he shall execute a bond, with two or more good and sufficient sureties, in the sum of five hundred dollars, payable to and approved by the Chief Justice of the county, conditioned that he shall well and truly account for and pay over to the County Treasurer of the county, all money that may come to his hands for the use of the county; and also that he shall well and truly account for and pay over to the Treasurer of the State all money that may come to his hands for the use of the State; and, also, that he shall well and truly account for and pay over to the person entitled to receive the same, his agent or attorney, all money that may come to his hands in any suit or action between parties; and he shall also take the oath of office prescribed by law, before some officer authorized to administer oaths, which shall be endorsed on his bond, together with the certificate of the officer who administered the same; such bond and oath shall be returned to and recorded in the office of the Clerk of the County Court of the county in which such Justice was elected. Shall give bond. Bond shall be recorded.

Art. 1092. [3] The bond of a Justice of the Peace may be sued upon, in the name of any party or parties injured by a breach thereof; and shall not be void on a first recovery, but may be sued upon from time to time until the whole amount of the penalty is recovered. Bond may be sued upon.

Art. 1093. [4] Whenever the bond and oath of a Justice of the Peace have been returned to and recorded in the office of the Clerk of the County Court, such Justice may immediately enter upon the duties of his office, and his acts shall be as valid as if he had been commissioned by the Governor. When Justice may enter on duties of his office.

Art. 1094. [5] When any person has been elected a Justice of the Peace, and neglects to execute a bond and take the oath of office, as prescribed by this act, within twenty days after he shall have been declared to be elected, such election shall be deemed void, and the Chief Justice of the county shall immediately order another election. If Justice neglects to give bond, &c., election void.

Art. 1095. [7] Whenever there shall be a vacancy in the office of Justice of the Peace, before the expiration of two years after a regular election, by

(*a*) In the absence of any express authority of law to the contrary, the jurisdiction of Justices of the Peace is restricted to the particular precinct, for which and in which they are elected by the qualified voters thereof. Foster *v.* McAdams, 9 Tex. Rep. 542. A Justice cannot go out of his precinct to hold his court. Ibid.

In case of vacancy, Chief Justice to order an election.

death, resignation, removal, or otherwise, the Chief Justice of the county, where such vacancy exists, shall forthwith order an election to fill such vacancy; and the person so elected, shall hold his office for the unexpired term, and until a successor shall be elected and qualified.

II. DOCKET, BOOKS AND PAPERS OF.

Justice shall keep a docket of criminal cases.

ART. 1096. [8] Every Justice of the Peace shall keep a docket, in which he shall enter all examinations and trials for criminal offences before him, the nature of the offence, the time when the examination was had, stating whether such trial was by a jury or by himself, the verdict of the jury, if any, the judgment rendered by the Justice, and the time when it was rendered, and how the same was executed; he shall also keep a docket, in which he shall enter: first, the titles of all suits commenced before him; second, the time when the first process was issued against the defendant, when it was returnable, and the particular nature thereof; third, the time when the parties or either of them, appeared before him, either without citation, or upon the return thereof; fourth, a brief statement of the nature of the plaintiff's demand or claim, and the amount claimed, and a brief statement of the nature of the defence made by the defendant, (if any;) fifth, every adjournment, stating at whose request, and at what time; sixth, the time when the trial was had, stating whether the same was by a jury or by the Justice; seventh, the verdict of the jury, (if any;) eighth, the judgment rendered by the Justice, and the time of rendering the same; ninth, all applications for setting aside judgments or granting new trials, and the order of the Justice thereon, with the date thereof: tenth, the time of issuing execution, the name of the officer to whom it was directed, and the amount of the debt, damages and costs; and when any execution is returned, he shall note such return on said docket, with the manner in which it was executed; eleventh, all stays and appeals that may be taken, and the time when taken.

Shall keep a docket, &c., in civil cases.

Justice vacating office shall deliver books, &c., to his successor.

ART. 1097. [9] If from any cause whatever, a Justice of the Peace shall vacate his office, all books and papers belonging to, or appertaining to his office, shall be delivered to the person elected, and qualified to fill such vacancy whenever demanded by him; and upon receiving such books and papers, he shall proceed with all judgments, executions and unfinished business therein contained, in like manner, as if the same had been commenced by himself.

If any person refuse to deliver books and papers, may be attached and imprisoned.

ART. 1098. [10] Any person or persons, having the possession of any books or papers, belonging or appertaining to the office of a Justice, that has become vacant, who shall neglect or refuse to deliver them to the person elected and qualified to fill such vacancy, when demanded by him, may upon the motion of any person interested in such books or papers, be attached and imprisoned, by order of any Judge of the District Court of this State, until he shall so deliver such books and papers: provided, that such motion shall be supported by affidavit, and three days' previous notice thereof shall be given to the person or persons against whom such motion is made.

Justice shall demand books and papers of former Justice.

ART. 1099. [11] Whenever any Justice of the Peace shall be elected and qualified under the provisions of this act, he shall demand of his predecessor all books and papers that may be in his possession, belonging or appertaining to his office; and upon receiving such books and papers, said Justice shall proceed, with all executions, judgments, and unfinished business therein contained, in like manner as if the same had been commenced before himself; and any person or persons, having the possession of any such books or papers, who shall neglect or refuse to deliver them, when so demanded, may be proceeded against in like manner as provided for in the previous section. May continue with unfinished business.

III. JURISDICTION.

[*See Code of Criminal Procedure.*]

ART. 1100. [25] Justices of the Peace shall have and exercise jurisdiction to try all suits and actions in behalf of the State, or any county thereof, or any individual to recover penalties, fines and forfeitures, where such penalty, fine, or forfeiture, shall not exceed one hundred dollars; they shall also have jurisdiction to try all suits in behalf of the State, or any county thereof, for any violation of the revenue law of this State, where the matter in controversy shall not exceed one hundred dollars. They shall also have jurisdiction in all suits and actions for the recovery of money on any account, bill, bond, note, or other instrument of writing; of all suits and actions for the recovery of specific articles, or the value thereof; of all suits and actions for torts, trespasses, and other injuries to person or property, where the amount claimed, or the value of the articles, or the damages sought to be recovered, shall not exceed one hundred dollars, exclusive of interest and costs. They shall also have and exercise jurisdiction over all other matters not herein enumerated, that may be cognizable before a Justice of the Peace, under the laws of this State.(*a*) Jurisdiction of Justices.

IV. SUITS, PROCESS, AND SERVICE.

ART. 1101. [30] No person shall be sued before any Justice of the Peace, except in the precinct where such person resides, or in the precinct where the cause of action accrued, (*b*) if in the same county: provided, however, that if there be no Justice of the Peace in the precinct where the defendant resides, then such defendant may be sued in the nearest precinct where there is a Justice: provided, also, that where a defendant has no fixed place of board or residence, he may be sued before any Justice of the Peace in the county; and provided, also, that when a defendant resides in an incorporated city or town, then he may be sued before any Justice of the Peace within the limits of the incorporation.(*c*) In all cases the residence of a married man shall be deemed to be where his family resides, and that of a single man where he boards. Where suit shall be brought.

ART. 1102. [31] All process from a Justice of the Peace, except in criminal cases, shall be under the hand of such Justice, directed to some lawful officer, whose duty it shall be to execute and return the same: all such process shall be returnable, except in cases where it is otherwise provided for by law, to some regular term of such Justices' Court; and shall be served by leaving a Process, how issued, directed, and executed.

(*a*) The jurisdiction conferred by the Constitution upon the District Courts is not exclusive. The jurisdiction conferred upon Justices of the Peace, by the Legislature, over all cases where the matter in controversy is valued at, or amounts to one hundred dollars, exclusive of interests and costs, and no mor, ethe District and Justices' Courts have concurrent jurisdiction. Johnson *v.* Happell, 4 Tex. Rep. 96. See note (*a*) to article 377; also note (*b*) to page 19.

There is no constitutional limit to the jurisdiction of Justices of the Peace. It depends entirely upon legislative enactments. Love & Chappell *v.* McIntyre, 3 Tex. Rep. 10.

(*b*) It may be admitted that the terms "cause of action" are sometimes used in a more limited sense, and that where the cause is founded on contract, the contract itself is denominated the cause of action; but more frequently, and when the terms are used with more precision, they embrace a much wider scope, and include not only the contract, but its performance, if executory, and also the breach of such contract. They are used in the latter sense in the above section. Phillio *v.* Blythe. 12 Tex. Rep. 124.

(*c*) Foster *v.* McAdams, 9 Tex. Rep. 542.

copy thereof with the defendant, at least five days before the return day, exclusive of the day of service and return day.(a)

Absent or transient persons shall be cited by publication.

ART. 1103. [32] Whenever, in any civil suit before a Justice of the Peace, the plaintiff, his agent or attorney, shall make oath in writing, before such Justice of the Peace, that the defendant is absent from this State, or that he is a transient person, so that the ordinary process of law cannot be served upon him, such Justice shall issue a citation, directed to some lawful officer, commanding him to cite the defendant to appear at some regular term of his court, to answer the plaintiff's complaint, stating the nature and amount thereof: such citation shall be returnable at some regular term of such Justice's Court, and shall be published in some newspaper printed in the county, if there be one, for at least three successive weeks before the return day; if there be no newspaper printed in the county, then it shall be published, in like manner, in some newspaper printed in the nearest county where there is one.

Justice may depute any person to execute process, when.

ART. 1104. [57] In cases of emergency, any Justice of the Peace may depute any person of good character to execute any process, civil or criminal: provided, that in every such case, the Justice shall certify on the back of such process, that the person is so deputed by him; and the person so deputed, shall take and subscribe an oath, that he will execute such process according to law: which oath, with the certificate of the Justice that it was administered, shall be endorsed on or annexed to such process.

Cause of action to be inserted in or endorsed on citation.

ART. 1105. [66] The Justice of the Peace, when he issues a citation in a civil suit, shall insert, in the citation, the cause of action, or endorse it thereon.

Act of March 20, 1848. Took effect August 7, 1848.

ART. 1106. [1] In all cases where two or more persons are liable to be jointly sued before a Justice of the Peace, such suit may be brought before any Justice of the Peace in the precinct where either of the defendants may reside.

Act of January 31, 1852. Took effect 31st March, 1852.

Where one or more defendants, jointly liable, reside in different county, how served.

ART. 1107. [1] In all suits brought in a Justice's Court against two or more defendants, jointly liable, and where one or more of the defendants reside out of the county where suit is instituted, the Justice of the Peace before whom suit is brought, shall issue process to the Sheriff, or any Constable, of the county or counties where such defendant or defendants are alleged to reside; and the officer to whom such process is directed, shall serve the same, as in other cases, and make his return to the court from which the process issued.

Where some are served and others not, may dismiss, provided, &c.

ART. 1108. [2] Where there are two or more defendants in a suit, and one or more are served with process in due time, and others not so served, the plaintiff may either discontinue as to those not so served and proceed against those that are, or he may continue the suit until the next term of the court, and take new process against those not served; and no defendant, against whom any suit may be discontinued according to the provisions of this section, shall be thereby exonerated from any liability under which he was, but may at any time be proceeded against, as if no such suit had been brought, and no such discontinuance entered as to such defendants: provided, that this section shall not be so construed as to allow a plaintiff to discontinue as to the principal, and take judgment against the endorser or surety who is jointly sued.

V. CONTINUANCE.

Act of March 20, 1848.

ART. 1109. [46] Any Justice of the Peace, before whom any suit or proceed-

(a) Filing a note with a Justice of the Peace for collection, is not the commencement of a suit. The summons being the leading process, the suit is not commenced until it issues. Keeble v. Bailey, 3 Tex. Rep. 492

ing is pending, may, for good cause shown by either party and supported by affidavit, continue the same to the next term of his court; and if such cause or proceeding is such as can be tried by such Justice at any other time than at a regular term, he shall have the like power to continue the same for a reasonable time.

Continuance may be granted on affidavit, for good cause.

VI. APPEARANCE AND TRIAL.

ART. 1110. [36] When both parties in any suit before a Justice of the Peace, appear in person or by agent or attorney, at the time appointed for the trial thereof, or at the time to which it may have been continued, if the amount in controversy shall not exceed ten dollars, or if the amount in controversy shall exceed ten dollars, and neither party shall make application to have the cause tried by a jury,(*a*) the Justice shall proceed to hear the allegations and proofs of the parties; and the defendant, upon giving notice thereof to the plaintiff before the trial commences, shall be allowed to present and prove any claim or demand not exceeding one hundred dollars, exclusive of interest, against the plaintiff, that is similar in its character to the claim or demand of the plaintiff; and the suit shall be determined by the Justice, as from the testimony shall seem to be right. If it shall appear from the testimony, that the plaintiff is entitled to recover, judgment shall be entered in his favor for such amount as shall appear to be due him with costs; but if it shall appear from the testimony that the defendant is entitled to recover, then judgment shall be entered in his favor for such amount as shall appear to be due him (if any), with costs. If the amount in controversy shall exceed ten dollars, and either party shall make application to have the case tried by a jury, then the same shall be so tried, in like manner as herein-before provided; and upon the return of the verdict of the jury, the Justice shall enter judgment thereon, with costs:(*b*) provided, however, that whenever it shall appear on any such trial, that the defendant's claim or demand was acquired after the commencement of the plaintiff's suit, the defendant shall be liable for all the costs.

If a jury is not demanded, Justice shall try the case.

Set-off may be proved, when.

Judgment, how entered.

If defendant's claim is acquired after suit is brought, he shall pay all costs.

VII. JURY.

ART. 1111. [48] In all proceedings before a Justice of the Peace, in which either party may be entitled to a jury, and shall make application for one, such jury shall be composed of six men; and the Justice shall, forthwith, issue a writ directed to some lawful officer of the county, commanding him to summon forthwith six disinterested freeholders, or householders, to serve as a jury; and if any person so summoned shall fail or refuse to attend, he may be fined by the Justice three dollars, for the use of the county, for such failure or neglect, unless he shall show to such justice good cause for such failure or neglect, after being cited so to do. In all trials for criminal offences, either the person prosecuting, or the accused, may challenge two of such jurors, without assigning any cause therefor; and in all trials, whether civil or criminal, either party may challenge any number of jurors for cause; which cause shall be judged of by the Justice. If, from challenges or any other cause, a sufficient number of the jury do not attend, the Justice shall order some lawful officer

Summons and qualification of jurors.

Challenge of jurors.

(*a*) Under this section the defendant is allowed to prove any claim or demand not exceeding one hundred dollars, exclusive of interest, against the plaintiff, that is similar in its character to the demand of the plaintiff. Fitzhugh *v.* Orton, 12 Tex. Rep. 4.

(*b*) It is the right of the plaintiff [and also of the defendant—COMPS.] to have a trial by jury, on whose verdict it is the duty of the Justice to give judgment. Bailey *v.* Knight, 8 Tex. Rep. 58.

to summon a sufficient number of qualified jurors to make up the jury. When a jury is formed, the Justice shall administer to them an oath or affimation, in form as follows: "You and each of you do solemnly swear, (or affirm, as the case may be,) that you will well and truly try the cause about to be submitted to you, and a true verdict give therein according to the evidence, so help you God."

Same jury shall try all causes on the same day.

ART. 1112. [49] Whenever a jury has been formed in a Justice's Court, the same jury may be called on to try all causes before such Justice, in which a jury is required, on the same day, without the necessity of a new writ in each case: provided, however, that jurors shall be sworn for each cause.

Party applying for a jury shall pay the jury fee, first.

ART. 1113. [50] In all cases before Justices of the Peace, other than prosecutions for offences against the laws of this State, the party applying for a jury shall, before the trial commences, pay a jury fee of three dollars, which shall be equally divided between the jurors trying the cause; and if the party paying such fee shall recover judgment, the jury fee shall be taxed in the bill of costs, and when collected shall be refunded to him; and in all trials before a justice of the Peace which shall be tried by a jury, when the jury fee is not required to be paid before the trial commences, a like jury fee shall be taxed in the bill of costs, and when collected shall be equally divided between the jurors who tried the same.

Jury fee, how and when taxed.

VIII. EVIDENCE.

1. *Witnesses.*

Subpœnas to issue.

ART. 1114. [37] In all suits before a Justice of the Peace, it shall be his duty, on the application of either party, to issue subpœnas for witnesses residing in the county, which subpœnas may be directed to any lawful officer of the county; and all such subpœnas shall be executed by the officer to whom they may be directed, by reading the same to the witness, or leaving a copy thereof at his usual place of abode, and shall be returned on or before the time when the witness is required to attend.

May enforce attendance of witnesses, &c.

ART. 1115. [38] Justices of the Peace shall have power to enforce the attendance of witnesses and to compel them to give evidence in their county, by attachment and imprisonment.

When a party may testify.

ART. 1116. [39] On the trial of any civil suit, before a Justice of the Peace, if either party shall make oath that he knows of no witness by whom he can prove a fact that is material to his claim or defence, except himself; the party making such oath shall be examined touching such fact,(a) and either party to any such suit may cause the other party to be subpœnæd and examined as a witness.

Justice to decide upon exceptions.

ART. 1117. [40] Upon all trials by jury before a Justice of the Peace, if any exceptions are taken to any deposition or evidence, the same shall be decided by the Justice.

ART. 1118. [41] All witnesses who are subpœnæd to attend a Justice's

(a) The act evidently contemplates that the party, proposing to testify in his own case, shall, in his preliminary examination touching his right to do so, state the fact or facts to which he proposes to testify. He is not allowed to testify generally, but only as to such facts as he may be unable to prove by other evidence. Crozier & Rhea v. Kirker, 4 Tex. Rep. 252. When the only witness, by whom a party can prove a fact, is so drunk as to be inadmissible as a witness, and there is no prospect of his being in a better condition, the party may swear that he knows of no person by whom he can prove the fact. McGee v. Currie, 4 Tex. Rep. 217.

Court, shall be entitled to receive one dollar per day for each day's attendance, which, if claimed by the witness at the time of trial, shall be taxed in the bill of costs against the party cast in the suit. Pay of witnesses.

2. *Depositions.*

Art. 1119. [42] Whenever in any civil suit, before any Justice of the Peace, the evidence of a female is required, or the evidence of any witness residing in the county, who is unable by reason of age, infirmities or sickness, to attend the court, or the evidence of a witness residing out of the county, the party interested may take the deposition of any such witness, by filing with the Justice before whom such suit is pending, interrogatories to such witness, and serving a copy of the same on the opposite party, his agent or attorney, with a notice that he intends to apply for a commission to take the answers of the witness to such interrogatories; such notice and copy may be served by any lawful officer of the county, or by any other person; but when served by any other person than an officer, an affidavit shall be endorsed on or annexed to such notice by the person serving the same, stating the fact of the service of such notice and copy of interrogatories; which affidavit, unless disproved, shall be evidence of such service; and the opposite party may file cross-interrogatories with the Justice at any time before the commission issues. When depositions may be taken. Interrogatories to be filed and copy served, &c. Cross interrogatories may be filed.

Art. 1120. [43] At the expiration of five days from the service of any such notice and interrogatories, on the application of the party who filed the same, his agent or attorney, it shall be the duty of the Justice to issue a commission, with a copy of the interrogatories, and cross-interrogatories if any have been filed, directed to some Chief Justice, Notary Public, or Clerk of the District or County Court of the county where such witness resides, requiring such Chief Justice, Notary Public, or Clerk, to take the answers of such witness to the interrogatories and cross-interrogatories that accompany such commission, to cause the witness to be sworn to his answers, and to subscribe them; and every Chief Justice, Notary Public, or Clerk of the District or County Court, to whom any such commissions may be directed, shall execute the same according to the directions therein contained, and for that purpose he shall have like powers as Chief Justices, Notaries Public, and Clerks of the District Court have to execute commissions to take depositions, when issued from the District Court. He shall certify under his hand and official seal the manner in which he has executed such commission, and seal up such certificate and answer, with the commission and interrogatories, write his name across the seal of the envelope, direct the same to the Justice from whom the commission issued, and forward it either by mail or private conveyance. If sent by mail, he shall cause the postmaster, or his deputy mailing the same, to endorse thereon that he received it from the hands of the officer who took such answers; if sent by private hand, the person delivering the same to the Justice shall make affidavit in writing, before such Justice, that he received the package from the hands of the officer who took such answers, and that it has undergone no change since. Commission, to whom issued, how executed and returned.

Art. 1121. [44] All evidence, so taken and returned to any Justice's Court, may be read in evidence on the trial of the suit on which it was taken, and shall have the same force and effect as if the witnesses were examined in open court: provided, the answers are responsive to the intorrogatories; and provided, also, that the interrogatories and answers shall be subject to all legal exceptions; but when such depositions are filed with the Justice before the trial commences, no exceptions shall be heard as to the manner of taking and returning such depositions, unless they are taken before the trial commences. Depositions so taken may be read, provided.

Rules of evidence in District Court to apply, &c.

ART. 1122. [45] All the rules of evidence prescribed for the government of District Courts, where the same do not conflict with the provisions of this act, shall govern the proceedings in the Justices' Courts, so far as the same is applicable.

IX. NEW TRIAL.

May grant new trial, provided.

ART. 1123. [47] Any Justice may, for a good cause shown, supported by affidavit in writing, grant a new trial in any civil suit tried before him, whenever he shall consider that justice has not been done in the trial of such case: provided, however, that all applications for a new trial shall be made within ten days after the rendition of judgment, and one day's notice of the application shall be given to the opposite party, his agent or attorney: provided, also, that not more than one new trial shall be granted to either party; and in all cases where a new trial shall be granted, the cause shall be continued to the next term of the court. (*a*)

X. JUDGMENT.

Shall be given in open court.

ART. 1124. [12] All judgments and final orders, given by any Justice of the Peace, in any suit or prosecution, civil or criminal, shall be given in open court.

May be confessed.

ART. 1125. [33] Any person may appear before any Justice of the Peace and confess a judgment, for any amount within the jurisdiction of a Justice of the Peace, without the issuance of any citation; and all such confessions of judgment shall be recorded in like manner as other judgments. (*b*)

When judgment by default may be rendered on liquidated demand.

ART. 1126. [34] When a defendant, who has been served with a citation, from a Justice of the Peace, according to law, shall neglect to appear, at or before two o'clock, P. M., of the return day of the citation, or at or before the same hour of any day to which the cause may have been continued, the Justice shall proceed in the following manner: 1st. If the plaintiff's cause of action is liquidated, and proved by any instrument in writing purporting to have been executed by the defendant, the Justice shall, whether the plaintiff appear or not, after allowing the proper credits for all payments endorsed on such instrument in writing, render judgment by default, against the defendant, for the amount which shall appear by such instrument in writing, to be due to the plaintiff, together with the costs of suit. 2d. If the plaintiff's cause of action is not liquidated, and the plaintiff appear in person, or by agent or attorney, the Justice shall proceed to hear his allegations and proofs, and shall determine the cause, as shall appear from the testimony to be right; and if it shall appear from such testimony that the plaintiff is entitled to recover, judgment shall be rendered by default against the defendant, for such amount as the testimony shows the plaintiff to be entitled to, with costs; but if it do not appear, that the plaintiff ought to recover, judgment shall be given for the defendant, against the plaintiff for costs. 3d. If the plaintiff fail to appear, at or before 2 o'clock, P. M., of the return day of the citation, or at or before the same hour of any day to which the cause may have been continued, except in the case hereinbefore provided, the Justice shall render judgment of nonsuit against the plaintiff, with costs.

Mode of proceeding when not liquidated.

(*a*) Where a Justice grants a new trial without notice to the adverse party of the application therefor, and the adverse party does not appear at the second trial, he may enjoin the judgment rendered at the second trial, or he may remove the cause to the District Court by *certiorari*; and, in the latter event, it would seem the District Court would not merely set aside the proceedings subsequent to the first judgment, but would try the cause anew on its merits. Aycock *v.* Williams, 18 Tex. Rep. 392.

(*b*) The confession may be in person or by attorney specially authorized. Parker *v.* Pool, 12 Tex. Rep. 86.

ART. 1127. [35] Every Justice of the Peace shall have power, upon good cause shown, supported by affidavit, to set aside a judgment by default, or of nonsuit, at any time within ten days after the same was rendered: provided, that one day's notice of such application shall be given to the opposite party, his agent or attorney, by the party applying, and in such cases the suit shall be continued to the next term of such Justice's Court. Justice may set aside judgment by default, when.

ART. 1128. [61] In all cases where a suit shall be brought before a Justice of the Peace for the recovery of specific articles, on the trial thereof, the jury or justice, as the case may be, shall, if they find for the plaintiff, assess the value of such articles separately; and if the plaintiff recover, judgment shall be rendered for the specific article or articles, if to be had: [illegible] not then for their value; and the Justice shall issue thereon, his writ directed to some lawful officer, commanding him to put the plaintiff in possession of the article or articles so recovered, if to be found: but if not, then to proceed and make the value of such article or articles, with the legal interest from the date of judgment, and costs, as under execution; and every Justice shall, from time to time, when required by a party having a judgment in his court, issue such executions, or other writs, as may be necessary to enforce such judgment, until the same shall have been satisfied. Where suit is for specific articles.

ART. 1129. [65] No Justice shall render a judgment upon any attachment or sequestration, unless the defendant shall have been cited either personally or by publication. In cases of attachment and sequestration.

XI. EXECUTION.

ART. 1130. [52] A Justice of the Peace may grant a stay of execution on any judgment for money, rendered by himself on a civil suit, for three months; provided, the person against whom such judgment was rendered, shall with one or more good and sufficient sureties, to be approved by such Justice, appear before him and acknowledge themselves, and each of them bound to the successful party in such sum as shall secure the amount of the judgment, interest, and costs; which acknowledgment shall be entered by the Justice on his docket, and shall have the force and effect of a judgment against the persons making the acknowledgment; upon which execution shall issue for the amount of the original judgment, interest and costs, in case the same shall not be paid on or before the expiration of such stay: provided, however, that no such stay shall be granted unless the same is applied for within ten days after the entry of the original judgment. Justice may grant a stay of, provided. Must be applied for within ten days.

ART. 1131. [56] All executions issued by a Justice of the Peace, shall be directed to some lawful officer of the State, and shall be returnable to his court in sixty days. It shall be the duty of the officer, to whom any such execution is directed, to execute and return the same, on or before the return day thereof; and all the provisions of the laws regulating executions from the District Courts, where the same are not inconsistent with the provisions of this act, shall apply to and govern executions from Justices of the Peace, so far as the same are applicable. To whom directed and when returnable.

ART. 1132. [1] Hereafter no Justice of the Peace shall issue an execution in any case where the judgment may be for money, except in prosecutions for criminal offences, before the eleventh day after the day on which judgment was rendered; unless the party in whose favor judgment was given, shall have Act of Dec. 20, 1849. Took effect March 23, 1850. Not to issue until, &c.

filed an affidavit with the Justice, setting forth that he believes the party against whom the judgment was rendered, will, within ten days, sell or otherwise dispose of, or remove, his, her, or their property out of the county; whereupon it shall be the duty of said Justice to issue an execution forthwith.

XII. CERTIORARI. (*a*)

Act of March 20, 1848. Took effect Aug. 7, 1848.

When and on what terms to issue.

ART. 1133. [67] No writ of *certiorari* shall be granted by a Judge of a District Court, to remove a cause from a Justice's Court, unless the party applying for the same shall make an affidavit in writing, setting forth sufficient cause to entitle him to such writ; nor shall any such writ be granted after ninety days from the decision of the cause by the Justice of the Peace; and no such writ shall be issued, unless the party applying shall first give bond, with two or more sufficient sureties, payable to the adverse party, for a sum equal to at least double the value of the amount in controversy, conditioned in the same manner as in appeals to the District Court;(*b*) which bond shall be approved by the Clerk of the District Court, and, together with the affidavit, shall be filed in his office; and upon service of such *certiorari* being made on the Justice of the Peace, he shall make out a certified copy of the entries in the cause on his docket, and transmit the same, with the original papers, to the District Court, on or before the first day of the term next thereafter; and the case may be reviewed and tried *de novo;* and if the judgment be affirmed, ten per cent. damages shall be added, and judgment rendered against all the obligors in such bond.(*c*)

Act of Jan. 30, 1858. In force from passage.

May issue within ninety days from, &c.

ART. 1134. [1] When a stay of execution upon any judgment rendered in the Justice's Court is taken, the same shall not prevent the taking of a writ of *certiorari;* but the defendant shall have the right to take out his writ of *certiorari* to the Justice's Court, at any time within ninety days from the decision of the cause by the Justice of the Peace.

(*a*) The constitution having defined the mode by which the District Courts may exercise a general superintendence and control over inferior jurisdictions, viz: by the issue of all writs necessary for that purpose, it is not competent for the Legislature to establish another mode, for example, by appeal. O'Brien *v.* Dunn, 5 Tex. Rep. 570. Titus *v.* Latimer, Ibid. 433.—The writ of *certiorari* is not a writ of right, but is dependent on the sound discretion of the court or Judge; and the petition for the writ should show the error complained of. O'Brien *v.* Dunn, *supra.* The act of the Legislature of February 10, 1852, which attempted to make a *certiorari* a writ of right, issuable in specified cases by clerks, was unconstitutional. Thomas *v.* the State, 9 Tex. Rep. 324.

(*b*) The above section was manifestly intended to authorize a party to employ the writ of *certiorari* for the revision and re-adjudication, in the District Court, of the proceedings of a Justice's Court, upon the merits, upon both the law and the facts, where such proceedings are illegal or erroneous, and where injustice has been done; but it does not appear to have been intended that the writ should be awarded where it is not shown that there is any error or illegality in the judgment; or that any injury or injustice has been done. Mays *v.* Lewis, 4 Tex. Rep. 1. The application for the writ should present facts, with such circumstantial accuracy and distinctness as to enable the Court to determine whether any injury or injustice has, in fact, been done. General allegations of injury and injustice are not sufficient. Ibid. Cotton *v.* Gammon, 4 Tex. Rep. 83. Weihl *v.* Davy, 6 Tex. Rep. 168. Ford *v.* Williams, 6 Tex. Rep. 311. Clay *v.* Clay, 7 Tex. Rep. 250. Johnson *v.* Lane, 12. Tex. Rep. 179. Hooks *v.* Lewis, 16 Tex. Rep. 551. The petition must show that there was an attempt to make the grounds relied on, for the *certiorari*, available upon the trial; or the reasons must be alleged why they were not presented. Clay *v.* Clay, 7 Tex. Rep. 250.—Where a *certiorari* has improvidently issued, the proper practice is, to move to dismiss at the first term of the court after the return of the writ. Ellet *v.* Moore, 6 Tex. Rep. 243. Perdew *v.* Steadham, 8 Tex. Rep 274. Less strictness is required in a petition for *certiorari*, than is exacted by the rules which apply to a motion for a new trial. King *v.* Longcope, 7 Tex. Rep. 236. A motion to dismiss must be made at the return term. 12 Tex. Rep. 31. O'Brien *v.* Dunn, 5 Tex. Rep. 570. A bond with but one surety, however responsible, is not a compliance with the statute. Mays *v.* Lewis, 4 Tex. Rep. 1. A *certiorari* without bond should be dismissed. Cotton *v.* Gammon, 4 Tex. Rep. 83. A bond in double the amount of the judgment sought to be revised, is sufficient. King *v.* Longcope, 7 Tex. Rep. 236. Where the bond was for less than double the amount of the judgment of the Justice, a motion to dismiss was overruled, on condition that a bond in the proper amount should be filed. Smith *v.* Wilson, 15 Tex. Rep. 132. Hooks *v.* Lewis, 16 Tex. Rep. 551. The provision dispensing with security in appeals by executors and administrators, does not extend the exemption to proceedings by *certiorari* to Justices' Courts. Ledbetter *v.* Swing, 19 Tex. Rep. 242 The Clerk has authority to administer the oath to the petition. Smith *v.* Wilson, 12 Tex. Rep. 132. Rollison *v.* Hope, 18 Tex. Rep. 446. The position of the parties is not changed in the District Court, from what it was before the Justice. Latimer *v.* Bagnell, 16 Tex. Rep. 588.

(*c*) The evident meaning of the statute is, that damages shall be added to the sum found to be due upon the trial in the District Court, when it shall be the same as that adjudged by the Justice, or more, thereby affirming the correctness of the decision of the Justice. Lane *v.* Brander, 19 Tex. Rep. 160.

XIII. GENERAL PROVISIONS.

Art. 1135. [51] Every person who shall have a cause of action against another, within the jurisdiction of a Justice of the Peace, who shall make oath in writing before such Justice, that he is too poor to pay the fees of such action, shall be entitled to all process necessary for the trial of such action, and to have a trial thereof, free of costs.

Act of Dec. 20, 1848. Took effect Aug 7, 1848. Where party is too poor to pay fees, &c.

Art. 1136. [58] Justices of the Peace shall have power to administer oaths of office in all cases, and also all other oaths or affirmations, and to give certificates thereof.

Justice may administer oaths, &c.

Art. 1137. [60] No suit shall be brought before any Justice of the Peace where he may be interested, or where he may be related to either the plaintiff or defendant, within the third degree of consanguinity or affinity; but in all such cases, suit shall be brought before the nearest Justice, not so interested or related.

In cases where Justice is related to party, or, &c.

Art 1138. [62] Every Justice of the Peace, upon complaint on oath and in writing, charging any person with an offence against the laws of the United States, shall have power to issue his warrant for the arrest of the accused; and if, upon an examination, to be conducted in the manner herein provided for examinations for offences, such Justice shall think there is probable cause to believe the accused guilty, if the offence is bailable, he may take his recognizance to appear before the court that has cognizance of the offence; but if not bailable, he shall commit him to jail, and certify the fact to said court at its next term.

Where person is charged with an offence against the U. S.

See Code of Criminal Procedure.

Art. 1139. [64] Each Justice of the Peace shall hold a term of his court once in each month, and may transact such business out of said term as is authorized by law; and the Justices of the Peace of each precinct in the State, shall be divided into two classes by the Chief Justices of their respective counties, who shall cause a record of such division to be made in the County Court; and those Justices belonging to the first class shall hold their court on the first Saturday of each month; and those of the second class shall hold their court on the last Saturday of each month.(a)

Time of holding Justice's Courts

Art. 1140. [1] Should the office of Justice of the Peace, within any county of the State of Texas, become vacant by death, resignation or otherwise, it shall be lawful for any Justice of the Peace, within such county, to proceed to try and dispose of all such unfinished business as may be on the docket of such Justice who may have vacated his office as aforesaid, until a successor shall have been elected and qualified.

Act of Feb. 16, 1852. Took effect April 16, 1852. Where office of Justice becomes vacant any Justice may try, &c

Art. 1141. [2] If from sickness, absence from the county, or from any other cause, not amounting to a vacation of his office, any Justice of the Peace shall fail to hold a regular term of his court, then and in that case, any other Justice of the Peace within the same county shall be, and he is hereby authorized to preside in the place and stead of such sick or absent Justice, and to discharge, perform and transact all such business as may be necessary during such absence.

If sick or absent, another Justice may hold his court.

Art. 1142. [3] If from any cause whatever, the regular term of a Justice's Court should not be held at the time fixed by law, the business pending on the Justice's docket shall stand continued until the next regular term thereof; and all business not disposed of at a regular term of such court, shall likewise stand continued until the next regular term thereof.

Business shall stand continued if regular term is not held.

(a) Inge v. Benson, 15 Tex. Rep. 315.

May continue court from day to day, when.

ART. 1143. [4] When any Justice of the Peace cannot dispose of all the business on his docket on the regular days of holding his courts, he shall be, and is hereby authorized to adjourn over and continue his court from day to day until the business of each term is fully disposed of, and he is fully authorized to adjourn any cause on his docket for trial to a particular day by agreement of parties.

Act of Aug. 22, 1856.

When proceedings may be conducted in the Spanish language.

ART. 1144. [1] It shall be lawful in the counties west of the Guadalupe River, except the counties of Nueces, San Patricio and Refugio, to make use of the Spanish language in all judicial proceedings before Justices of the Peace, when neither the Justice of the Peace nor the parties are able to write or understand the English language.

Where one party speaks English only, cause may be removed provided.

ART. 1145. [2] In any case in which one of the parties only speaks the English language, and the Justice or either party is unable to speak the English language, the cause may be removed on motion, to the nearest Justice of the Peace speaking that language: provided, that the English language shall be used in all cases in which any one of the parties interested shall only speak the English language.

LANDS AND GENERAL LAND OFFICE.

I. PUBLIC DOMAIN.

II. COMMISSIONER.

III. CLERKS, DRAFTSMEN AND TRANSLATOR.

IV. LAND DISTRICTS AND SURVEYORS.

V. SURVEYS.

VI. LAND SCRIP AND SURVEYS BY VIRTUE THEREOF.

VII DUPLICATE CERTIFICATES.

VIII. CERTIFICATES, SURVEYS, AND TITLES VALIDATED AND CONFIRMED.

1. *Certificates.*

2. *Surveys.*

3. *Titles.*

IX. PATENTS.

1. *Generally.*

I. PUBLIC DOMAIN.

Act of Dec. 14, 1837. In force from passage.

All vacant lands belong to, &c.

ART. 1146. [26] It is hereby declared that all empresarios' contracts having ceased on the day of the Declaration of Independence, all the vacant lands of Texas are the property of this Republic, and subject alone to the disposition of the Government of the same.

Act of February 10, 1852. Took effect from passage.

If field notes not returned by, &c., land shall become vacant.

ART. 1147. [1] The field notes of all surveys made previous to the passage of this act, shall be made out and returned in the manner now required by law, to the General Land Office, on or before the thirty-first day of August, 1853, or they shall become null and void, and the said surveys shall become vacant land, and be subject to be re-located and surveyed as in other cases, by any persons holding a genuine land certificate, or other legal evidence of claim to land.

Act of August 30, 1856. Took effect from passage.

Where conditional certificate is located and unconditional, &c., is not returned by.

ART. 1148. [1] All owners or holders who have conditional certificates now located, or surveys upon lands, shall return to the General Land Office the unconditional certificates, together with the field notes of the same, on or before the first day of August, 1857; and all unconditional certificates which are not returned by that time, the said locations and surveys shall be null and void, and all such locations and surveys made by virtue of such conditional certificates shall become public domain, and subject to be located upon as other vacant lands.

Act of Aug. 26, 1856. Took effect Oct. 25, 1856.

Pacific Railroad Reserve.

ART. 1149. [1] What is known as the Mississippi and Pacific Railroad Land Reserve shall, from and after the first day of January, A. D. 1857, be subject to location and sale as hereinafter prescribed.

II. COMMISSIONER.

ART. 1150. [6] The Commissioner of the General Land Office be entitled to, and shall keep charge of the seal; and, also, that he be, and is hereby entitled to, and shall have custody and control of all books, records, papers, and original documents appertaining to the titles of lands, heretofore, and by the provisions of the law, denominated archives; and that the said books, records, papers and original documents shall become and be deemed the books and papers of said office. Act of Dec. 14, 1837. In force from passage. To have custody and charge of books, papers, &c., &c.

ART. 1151. [32] The Commissioner of the General Land Office shall, when required by the President of the Republic, or either House of Congress, make a plat of land surveyed under the authority of the Government, and give such information respecting the public lands and concerning the business of his office, as shall be legally required. To make plats, for, &c., when required.

ART. 1152. [1] There shall be established a General Land Office, to be located at the seat of Government of the State of Texas, the chief officer of which shall be styled the Commissioner of the General Land Office; whose duties it shall be to superintend, control, and direct the official conduct of all subordinate officers of the General Land Office, and to execute and perform all acts and things touching or respecting the public land of the State of Texas, or rights of individuals in relation thereto, as may be required of him by law. [See Elections, article 641.] Act of May 12, 1846. In force from passage. To be the chief officer of Land Office, &c.,

ART. 1153. [5] The Commissioner of the General Land Office shall, before he enters upon the discharge of the duties of his office, enter into bond with three or more securities, in the sum of fifty thousand dollars, payable to the Governor of the State of Texas and his successors in office, for the use of the State, conditioned for the faithful discharge of his official duties, and take and subscribe the oath prescribed by the constitution; which bond, after being approved by the Governor, shall, together with the affidavit, be filed in the office of the Secretary of State. Bond to be given, approved, filed, &c.

ART. 1154. [6] The Commissioner of the General Land Office shall procure a seal of office, with the words "General Land Office, the State of Texas," engraved around the margin, and such other device as the Governor of the State shall approve; which approval shall be certified and recorded in the office of the Secretary of State. Seal of Land Office.

ART. 1155. [12] The Commissioner of the General Land Office shall give information to the Governor of this State, or either branch of the Legislature, concerning the public lands, or the General Land Office, from time to time as, may be required. Shall report to the Governor or Legislature.

ART. 1156. WHEREAS, there exists some doubt as to the precise time at which the term of office of the present Commissioner of the General Land Office expires; and whereas it is important that the official acts of that officer should be placed above cavil or doubt; therefore, Act of February 13, 1852. Took effect from passage.

SECTION 1. Be it enacted by the Legislature of the State of Texas, That the official term of Stephen Crosby, Commissioner elect of the General Land Office, shall commence on the first day of March, eighteen hundred and fifty-two, and continue two years; and all his acts as Commissioner, for and during that time, shall be as valid as though no such doubt had existed. When term of office begins, &c.

III. CLERKS, DRAFTSMEN AND TRANSLATOR.

Act of May 12, 1846. Took effect from passage. Appointment of Clerks, &c.

ART. 1157. [3] The Commissioner of the General Land Office shall appoint, for the transaction of the business of the General Land Office, one Chief Clerk, one Spanish Clerk, two Draftsmen, and not more than eight Assistant Clerks. The said Chief Clerk and Spanish Clerk, shall each be required to enter into bond, with three or more securities, in the penal sum of twenty thousand dollars, for the faithful discharge of their official duties, payable to the Governor of the State of Texas and his successors in office, for the use of the State; which bond shall be approved by the Governor and filed in the office of the Secretary of State.

Act of Dec. 14, 1837. In force from passage.

ART. 1158. [3] The said Chief Clerk, * * * * * * * * * * * in case of the absence of the Commissioner of the General Land Office, or in his inability to attend to the duties thereof, shall perform all the duties appertaining to said office.(a)

Act of May 12, 1846. Chief Clerk to perform duties of Commissioner, when.

ART. 1159. [4] In case of the sickness, death or resignation of the Commissioner of the General Land Office, it shall be lawful for the Chief Clerk to act and perform all the duties required of the said Commissioner of the General Land Office.(a)

Act of Dec. 26, 1853. Took effect from passage. Additional Clerks.

ART. 1160. [1] The Commissioner of the General Land Office be authorized to employ two additional Assistant Draftsmen, and ten additional Assistant Clerks.

Salary of officers.

ART. 1161. [2] The salary of the Commissioner of the General Land Office shall be two thousand dollars per annum.

The salary of his Chief Clerk shall be twelve hundred dollars per annum.

The salary of Spanish Clerk shall be twelve hundred dollars per annum.

The salaries of eight Assistant Clerks, each, shall be nine hundred dollars per annum.

The salaries of ten additional Clerks shall be eight hundred dollars each, per annum.

The salary of the principal Draftsman shall be twelve hundred dollars per annum.

The salaries of the first and second Assistant Draftsmen shall be eleven hundred dollars each, per annum, and the salaries of two additional Assistant Draftsmen shall be one thousand dollars each, per annum.

Commissioner to discharge certain clerks.

ART. 1162. [3] It shall be the duty of the Commissioner of the General Land Office, at or before the expiration of twelve months from the adjournment of the present session of the Legislature, to discharge seven of the additional Assistant Clerks, and the two additional Assistant Draftsmen provided for in the preceding sections.

Act of Dec. 14, 1837. Duty of Translator.

ART. 1163. [34] It shall be the duty of said translator, to translate into the English language, and record in a book to be kept by him for that purpose, all the laws and public contracts relative to the titles of land which are written in the Castilian language, and also to translate and record in like manner, all original titles which are written in the Castilian language, which may be on file in the office of the Commissioner of the General Land Office.

(a) The provisions of these two articles are cumulative, and the Chief Clerk of the Land Office may discharge the duties of the Commissioner in any event contemplated by either statute; and when he has acted, the presumption is that one of the contingencies existed, on the happening of which he was authorized to act. Howard and Wife *v.* Perry, 7 Tex. Rep. 259

IV. LAND DISTRICTS AND SURVEYORS.

ART. 1164. [9] There shall be elected * * * * * * * * * * a County Surveyor, who shall reside at the county seat, and whose duty it shall be to receive and examine all field notes of surveys which have been or may hereafter be made in said county and upon which patents are to be obtained, and shall certify the same under his hand to the Commissioner of the General Land Office, after having recorded the same in a book to be kept by him for that purpose, and shall immediately return the same to the President of the Board of Land Commissioners of said county. He shall, before entering upon the duties of his office, enter into bond with three or more securities to be approved by the Board of Land Commissioners of the county, in the sum of ten thousand dollars, payable to the President or his successors in office, conditioned for the faithful performance of his duties, which said bond shall be recorded in the Clerk's office of said county, and the original transmitted to the office of Secretary of State; and the said Surveyor shall hold his office for three years, and be re-eligible. * He shall appoint as many Deputy Surveyors as he may deem necessary for the county; and shall administer to them the oath of office, and take the bond hereinafter prescribed, and shall furnish them such instructions as may be furnished to him from time to time by the Commissioner of the General Land Office; (*a*) and such Deputy Surveyor, before he enters upon the duties of his office, shall enter into bond with two or more securities, to be approved by the County Surveyor, in the sum of five thousand dollars, payable to the President or his successors in office, conditioned for the faithful performance of the duties of his office; and for such appointment of a Deputy Surveyor, the County Surveyor shall be allowed to charge and receive from the person so appointed the sum of five dollars.

Act of Dec. 14, 1837. Took effect from passage.

County Surveyor to be elected

Shall give bond, certify field notes, &c.

See fees.

ART. 1165. [10] It shall be the duty of each Deputy Surveyor to administer an oath to each individual employed by him as chain-carrier or marker, for the faithful performance of his duties as such, in accordance with the instructions given him: and no African, or Indian, or descendant of either, or any person under the age of sixteen years, shall be employed in either of the above capacities; and further, it shall be the duty of said Surveyors to subscribe the name of each of the chain-carriers to his field notes previous to his returning the same to the County Surveyor. He shall also state to the best of his knowledge or belief, the number of labors of irrigable lands, the number of labors of temporal or arable lands, and the number of labors of pasture lands in each survey for that class of claimants who are entitled to land under the Constitution and colonization laws; which shall be plainly written out in the field notes, and also inserted in each patent; and for all such surveys he shall charge and receive three dollars for each English lineal mile actually run.

Duty of, in making survey and returning field notes, &c.

ART. 1166. [17] Any certificate of claim to land, which has been or may be obtained in the manner and form herein prescribed, shall be sufficient evidence to authorize any lawful Surveyor to survey for any person holding such certificates, any lands which he may point out agreeably to all the laws which do

When occupant claim preferred, &c.,—also residents prior to declaration of independence.

(*a*) The instructions of the Commissioner of the General Land Office to the Surveyors, became a part of the law regulating the subject matter to which they referred. Peacock *v.* Hammond, 6 Tex. Rep. 544.—Lewis *v.* Durst, 10 Tex. Rep. 398.

now or may hereafter exist on that subject.(*a*) Provided, also, that where more than one application is made for the same tract of land to be surveyed, the settler or occupant shall have the preference if their claims be otherwise equal. Provided, that no location or improvement made since the declaration of independence, by persons who have since that time arrived in the country, shall be regarded when they come in conflict with the claims of those who were here at the declaration of independence. But those individuals entitled to the six months' preference, shall have the right of locating their lands upon any vacant lands of the Republic, without regard to any improvements made by individuals who have arrived in Texas since the declaration of independence. In all other cases, or in case there be more occupants than one, the conflicting claims shall be summarily tried by the nearest Justice of the Peace and six disinterested jurors summoned for that purpose; and upon their decision the Surveyor shall grant to the successful party the field notes of the tract of land, giving in all cases the preference to the oldest occupant and settler.(*b*) Provided, in all cases, that the claimant shall apply for such certificate in the county in which he or she may reside at the date of the passage of this act; and provided, that persons claiming land by inheritance or assignment shall apply for such certificate in the county where the testator died, or where the assignor lived at the time of making such transfer.

Application for certificate, when to be made.

Joint Resolution, Dec. 20, 1837. Took effect from passage.

When County Surveyor may perform duties of Deputy Surveyors.

ART. 1167. Whenever it shall so happen that the amount of surveying to be done (in any one county) is not more than can be performed by one Surveyor,—which fact shall be determined by the Board of Land Commissioners,—then and in that case the County Surveyor for said county shall be allowed to perform the duties of a practical Surveyor, and perform all the duties as required of the Deputy Surveyors to be appointed under a provision of an act to establish a General Land Office.

Act of Jan. 23, 1839. Took effect from passage.

Compensation for making maps, &c.

ART. 1168. [3] The Auditor is hereby directed to audit, and the Treasurer to pay, all County Surveyors for making complete or connected plats of their respective counties, such amount as the Board of Land Commissioners for the counties in which they reside, shall deem a proper compensation for making said map: provided, the Commissioner General of the Land Office shall approve of the same, both as to execution of the work and the amount of remuneration; and all such certificates shall be sufficient voucher for the action of the Auditor

Act of Dec. 25, 1839. Took effect from passage.

[Quære, if not obsolete? HARTLEY.]

Security of, how released, &c.

ART. 1169. [1] Hereafter it shall be lawful for the security or securities of any County Surveyor, who may wish to be released from such security, to notify, in writing, the Chief Justice of the county in which such County Surveyor may reside, that he or they wish to be released from further responsibility; and it is hereby made the duty of such Chief Justice immediately to notify the County Surveyor, that within ten days he is required to appear before him and enter into a new bond with securities, conditioned, in all respects, according to the provisions of the law in such cases provided.

ART. 1170. [5] So soon as the County Surveyor thus notified shall appear and give the bond required by law, and the same is approved of by the Chief

(*a*) In order that a location and survey should be valid, it is not necessary that the Surveyor should be furnished with a certificate of the recommendation of the certificate. It is sufficient if the fact be proved that the certificate was recommended. Croft *v.* Rains, 10 Tex. Rep. 520.

Where there is no office evidence of a location, nor any act of notoriety from which notice could be presumed, it cannot, after a lapse of a reasonable time for the survey, without any survey being made and returned, claim a preference over a subsequent location—the subsequent location being unaffected with notice of the prior claim. Lewis *v.* Durst, 10 Tex. Rep. 398. Williams *v.* Craig, Ibid. 437. See Morris *v.* Brinlee, 14 Tex. Rep. 285.

(*b*) No appeal lies from the decision of a Justice's Court under this statute. Field *v.* Anderson, 1 Tex. Rep. 437. Cullem *v.* Latimer, 4 Tex. Rep. 329. Prewett *v.* Farris, 5 Tex. Rep. 370. Patton *v.* Skidmore, 19 Tex. Rep 533. The jurisdiction of a Justice of the Peace and six jurors, under the above section, is confined to cases of conflicting claims before the field notes have been delivered to either party; the proceeding is for the information of the Surveyor; if he has delivered the field notes, the case has gone beyond his reach, and the remedy of the subsequent claimant, if any, must be sought in another tribunal. Prewett *v.* Farris, 5 Tex. Rep. 370. Cullem *v.* Latimer, 4 Tex. Rep. 329. The failure of the first class claimant to obtain his certificate and locate his lands, so as to include his improvements within the time left, the land vacant and liable to appropriation by the first applicant. Patton *v.* Skidmore, 19 Tex. Rep. 533.

Justice, that he shall cause the same to be recorded in the County Clerk's office, and the original forwarded to the Secretary of State: but in case the County Surveyor thus notified should fail to appear and give the necessary bond, the Chief Justice is hereby authorized and required, forthwith, to declare the office of County Surveyor in such county vacated, and immediately inform the Commissioner of the General Land Office of the same. Failure to give and renew bond, &c., vacates the office.

ART. 1171. [3] The above enactments shall apply, in all particulars, to the Deputy Surveyors of the different counties: provided, always, that twenty days' notice shall be given to the Deputy Surveyor; and in case of said Deputy refusing or neglecting to appear and renew his bond at the expiration of said notice, it shall be the duty of the County Surveyor to declare, by public notice in writing, that the office of said Deputy is vacated, and shall, as soon as possible, proceed to appoint a Deputy to fill said vacancy. Notice to be given—office of Dep'ty vacated, when.

ART. 1172. [2] Hereafter, when any change may take place in the boundaries of any county, it shall be the duty of the Surveyor of any county from which territory may be so taken, to furnish the Surveyor of the county including such territory, with a full and complete copy of all the field notes of surveys made in the same. Act of Feb. 5th, 1840. Took effect from passage. Change of county boundary, duty of Surveyor.

ART. 1173. [3] It shall be the duty of each County Surveyor in this Republic, to make out and keep in his office, free for the inspection of all persons, a map, on which all the surveys made in his county shall be laid down and properly "connected;" which map shall be corrected at the end of each month. (*a*) Shall keep a map in his office for inspection, &c.

ART. 1174. [5] It shall be the duty of all Deputy Surveyors to make returns of every survey by them made, within three months after making the survey, to the County Surveyor for his approval; * * * * * * and any Surveyor neglecting to do so, shall, moreover, be liable for damages at the suit of any person thereby aggrieved. Act of Feb. 5th, 1840. Took effect March 16, 1840. Deputy Surveyors shall return field notes, &c.

ART. 1175. [2] The County Surveyors of the several counties shall receive a reasonable compensation for all maps, transcripts, etc., forwarded by them to the General Land Office, as required by law—their accounts to be approved by the Commissioner of the General Land Office; and the Auditor is hereby required to audit the same. Act of Feb. 5th, 1841. Took effect March 17th, 1841. Compensation for maps, &c., to County Surveyors.

ART. 1176. [10] There shall be elected by the qualified electors of each Land District, on the day of the first general election of county officers in this State, one District Surveyor for each Land District, whose term of office shall be two years from the date of his election, who shall be entitled to the custody of all books, maps, papers, and such other things as belong to the County Surveyor's office of the county which, by this act, is made a District, upon his entering into bond, with two or more securities, in the penal sum of ten thousand dollars, payable to the Governor of the State of Texas and his successors in office, conditioned for the faithful discharge of the duties of his office; which bond shall be approved by the County Courts of their respective counties, and recorded in the office of the Clerk of the County Court, and filed in the office of the Clerk of the District Court; and a certified copy thereof may be put in suit in behalf of the State, or any citizen aggrieved by the non-performance of its conditions: he shall also take and subscribe an oath to the following effect: That he will faithfully, and to the best of his skill and ability, discharge the duties of his office in accordance with the law; which Act of May 12, 1846. Took effect from passage. Election of District Surveyor, bond, &c. See Elections. Bond may be put in suit.

(*a*) The legislation in relation to the maps of the counties, seems to have been intended, when fully executed, to point out at least *prima facie*, what lands are public and what are private property. Smith *v* Power, 2 Tex. Rep. 57. Horton *v*. Pace, 9 Tex. Rep. 81

shall be filed with his bond in the office of the Clerk of the District Court of their respective counties.

Their duties governed by the law, heretofore, &c.

ART. 1177. [11] The District Surveyors elected under this act shall be governed in the discharge of their official duties, by the provisions of this act and the laws heretofore regulating the duties of County Surveyor, where the same do not conflict with this act, and shall be subject to removal from office by indictment in the District Court of their respective counties, for any abuse, negligence or failure in the discharge of their official duties; and upon their removal from office, or at the expiration of their term of office, shall deliver to their successors, all records, books, papers, maps, and other things appertaining to the office.

Act of March 20, 1848. Took effect from passage.

Two copies of county map, by whom and how made, &c.

ART. 1178. [2] Immediately after the completion of the survey of any county, as contemplated by this act, it shall be the duty of the County Court of the county so surveyed, to appoint a suitable draftsman, who shall proceed to the office of the District Surveyor of the District from which said county may be taken; or if parts of said county be taken from different Districts, then he shall proceed to the District Surveyor's office of each District from which a part of said county may have been taken, and take two correct copies of the map of said county, one of which shall be on good tracing paper; and both of which, as soon as completed, shall be deposited in the office of the Clerk of the County Court of the county for which said maps may have been made, with the certificate of the District Surveyor to each map, if the county be wholly taken from one District; or if taken from more Districts than one, then each District Surveyor shall certify on each map that the part taken from his own District is a true and correct copy of the part of his District represented on said map; and any County Court receiving maps, as provided by this act, shall immediately transmit one copy of said map, under the seal of the County Court, to the Commissioner of the General Land Office, together with a properly authenticated copy of the field notes of the survey of the county boundaries.

Transcripts of Surveyor's records for new counties, by whom and how made, &c.

ART. 1179. [3] It shall be the duty of the County Courts of the several counties that may avail themselves of the benefits of this act, at their first session after the receipt of this act, or as soon thereafter as they can, to appoint some competent person, whose duty it shall be to proceed forthwith to the office or offices of the District Surveyor or Surveyors of the District or Districts in which their respective counties may be situated, and make a true and correct copy of all the records in any District Surveyor's office, of surveys of land situated in the county for which he may have been appointed to take a transcript of records: provided, that after said transcript of records shall have been made out, it shall be the duty of the District Surveyor or Surveyors of the District or Districts, and of the County Clerk or Clerks of the county or counties in which any of said District Surveyors' offices may be situated, carefully to examine such transcript of records, and compare the same with the original records; and when found to be correct, the District Surveyor shall certify in said record-book, at the foot of the last record, over his own proper signature, and the Clerk of the County Court shall certify under his seal of office, that said transcript is a true and correct copy of the original records in the District Surveyor's office; and further provided, that said transcript of records so certified, shall answer all the purposes, and have the same force and effect in law, that the originals could have.

County must pay for transcripts, &c.

ART. 1180. [6] The transcript of records and maps, together with the examination of the same, shall be paid for by the county for the benefit of which they are made, allowing eight cents for every hundred words in copying said records, and three dollars per day for each day the draftsman may be actually and necessarily engaged in copying maps, as provided in this act; and Clerks and District Surveyors, for examining and certifying transcripts of records as required by this act, shall have three dollars per day.

ART. 1181. [1] Whenever an election is held in any land district in this State, for District Surveyor of such district, and the same shall be composed entirely of one county, the returns of said election shall be made to the Chief Justice of such counties, in the same manner as returns are now by law required to be made for county officers; and such Chief Justices shall, in the same manner as in other cases of election, examine such returns and issue certificates of election; but when such land districts embrace more than one county, then the return of the votes given in such elections shall be made to the Chief Justices of those counties in which such votes are given, in the same manner as now provided for county officers, and the several Chief Justices to whom such returns are made shall open and examine the same on the tenth day, exclusive of the day of election, and shall immediately certify and send the result of said election to the Chief Justice of that county from which the land district takes its name, which certificate shall be sealed up and the name of the officer forwarding it written across the seal, and the package marked on the outside "election returns;" which package may be sent by mail: the Chief Justices to whom the certificates are so forwarded shall, upon the twentieth day after election, which shall be the return day for such elections, open and examine said certificates, together with the returns of said election, made from his own county, and after estimating the result and recording the same, give a certificate of election to the candidate or person for whom the greatest number of votes shall have been polled.

Act of Feb. 7, 1853. Took effect April 8, 1853.

Election of surveyors, returns how and to whom made, &c.

ART. 1182. [2] Whenever a vacancy shall occur in the office of District Surveyor, for any land district in this State, and such district be composed entirely of one county, it shall be the duty of the Chief Justice of such county to order an election to fill such vacancy, in the same manner as now provided for county officers; but when such land district shall embrace more than one county, then it shall be the duty of the Chief Justice of the mother county, or that from which the land district takes its name, to issue a notice to the Chief Justices of those counties which are embraced in whole or in part in such land district, which notice may be sent by mail, shall set forth the vacancy and office to be filled, and shall name the day on which said election is to be held, and such day shall be uniform throughout said district, and shall not be less than twenty days after the issuance of such notice. Immediately on the receipt of such notice, the Chief Justice to whom the same shall be directed shall issue orders of election, and notice thereof shall be given in the same manner as provided now for county officers.

Vacancy in the office of—election, by whom ordered.

ART. 1183. [3] Whenever the election of any person to the office of District Surveyor may be contested, like notice shall be given and proceedings had as in case of contested elections for county officers. When the district is composed of one county, the County Court of that county shall be the proper tribunal to try the contest; but where the district is composed of more than one county, then such contest shall be tried in the County Court of the mother county.

Contested election.

Art. 655.

Before what tribunal tried.

ART. 1184. [1] At the next general election for county officers the Chief Justice of every organized county in the State shall order an election for a County Surveyor of said county, by the qualified electors thereof, giving the same notice required for the election of county officers, and requiring the returns to be made at the same time, and in the same manner; provided, that this provision shall not affect those counties, now having Surveyors whose

Act of Jan. 26, 1858. Took effect from passage.

Time of election of county surveyors, provided, &c.

term of office may expire at a different period; and that each county to be organized after the passage of this act shall elect a County Surveyor at the time of electing other county officers. All County and District Surveyors shall hold their offices for two years, and until their successors may be elected and qualified; and in case a vacancy in the office from any cause, the County Court may appoint some person to discharge the duties thereof until twenty days after the then next succeeding August election, at which election a Surveyor shall be elected to serve for two years as in other cases.

Term of office of district and county surveyors.

Qualification and bond of.

Art. 1176.

ART. 1185. [2] When any county shall have elected a Surveyor as provided for in this act, the person so elected shall be qualified in the same manner, and give bond in the same form and amount as now required by law of District Surveyors; and he shall do and perform all the duties now required of them, be governed by the same laws, and liable to the same penalties.

When county becomes a land district.

ART. 1186. [3] When any organized county shall have so elected a Surveyor, and he has given bond and been qualified as above provided, said county shall be a separate land district.

Surveyor not authorized to survey until, &c.

ART. 1187. [4] Before any Surveyor elected under the provisions of this act, in a county not previously a separate land district, shall make any surveys therein, he shall procure a certified map of the surveys in said county, and a certified copy of the files and locations of lands therein from the Surveyor's office of the land districts to which said county belonged, and file the same in his office for the inspection of any one interested in examining the same.

Within what time surveyor shall obtain copies of field notes, &c., in his county.

Art. 1179.

ART. 1188. [5] Said Surveyor shall, within twelve months from the date of his qualification, obtain from the office of the districts from which his county is taken, a transcript of the field notes of surveys in his county, certified to as required by the act to which this is supplementary, and for obtaining which he shall be entitled to ten cents per hundred words, to be paid by the County Court of his county; said transcript of records, so certified, shall answer all the purposes, and have the same force and effect in law that the originals could have.

Each district surveyor shall appoint a deputy, &c.

ART. 1189. [6] It shall be the duty of each District Surveyor of this State, during the month of August, 1858, and thereafter within twenty days after each election for District Surveyor, to appoint as his deputy a special County Surveyor for each unorganized county within his district, who shall hold his office during the term of his principal, unless sooner superseded by the appointment of another as his successor. The District Surveyor shall immediately notify the Commissioner of the General Land Office of every such appointment; each special County Surveyor, so appointed, shall have all the powers, perform all the duties, and be subject to all the penalties appertaining to County Surveyors, and shall keep, in addition to the returns to be made to his principal, a record and map of all the transactions in his office, to become a part of the County Surveyor's records of such county, whenever it may be organized. All such special County Surveyors shall reside and keep their offices in their respective counties, if there be settlements in the same, but if there be no settlements in the county, then at the nearest town to such county. Whenever any county may elect a County Surveyor under the provisions of this act, the District Surveyor, within whose district such county may have been, or may be at the time, and his deputy, shall cease to exercise any official acts within the same; provided, that when any such unorganized county may have been taken from two or more land districts, a special surveyor shall be appointed as herein provided by each District Surveyor, for so much of such county as may have been taken from his district.

ART. 1190. [7] Any person interested for himself, or as agent or friend of another, shall, at all times, have the right to examine the books, papers, plates, maps, or other archives belonging to the office of any District, County, or special Surveyor, on the payment of the fee fixed by law; and whenever an applicant calls upon either a District, County, or special Surveyor, to make an entry for location on his books, and shall be informed that the land indicated by the applicant has already been located, or located and surveyed, the applicant may demand of the surveyor a certificate in writing, setting forth the time at which the entry, location and survey, or either, was made, at whose instance, upon what certificate or warrant, and all the facts in the case, which certificate shall be held good evidence in law and equity against such surveyor, in any suit brought against him, to test the truth of the certificate, and recover damages by the applicant; and any surveyor refusing any examination of his books and archives, or to give the certificates as herein provided, shall be subject to a fine of five hnndred dollars for each offence, to be recovered before the District Court by the party aggressed.

Any person interested, allowed to examine books, papers, &c., of surveyors' office.

ART. 1191. [8] It shall be the duty of every District, County, and special County Surveyor, of this State, once in every three months, to plat upon the map of his district or county, all surveys made to that date, within the three preceding months, and transmit sketches and field notes of the same to the Commissioner of the General Land Office, together with a list of all land certificates or warrants on file in his office, giving the number, date, quantity in acres of each, and stating by whom and to whom the same purports to have been issued; and any surveyor failing or refusing to comply with the provisions of this section, shall be subject to a fine of five hundred dollars for each offence, to be recovered by the State before the District Court, on complaint of any party aggrieved, or of the District Attorney of the district whose duty it shall be to prosecute all such suits. A certificate from a postmaster certifying that a letter or package containing the returns herein provided for, was mailed in his office, addressed to the Commissioner of the General Land Office, shall be evidence of the fact in any suit against a surveyor under this section.

Every three months surveyors shall plat surveys on county map and transmit sketches, &c.

Penalty for neglect, &c.

V. SURVEYS.

ART. 1192. [18] When two or more persons cannot agree to a division line of any land which has never been surveyed agreeably to law, it shall be lawful for either party to apply to any Justice of the county or territory in which the land lies, or if there be no Justice of the Peace in the county or territory, then to the nearest Justice in any county or territory, and make oath that he has tried and has not been able to settle the dispute between himself and one or more other persons (naming them,) concerning a division line, and the said Justice shall issue a warrant to any lawful officer to summon the party or parties defendant, together with six disinterested jurors, to meet upon the premises in dispute—together with such witnesses as either party may choose to have summoned, to give evidence—on a certain day, naming at what time and place. The Justice shall also meet the parties, examine all the testimony before the jury, who shall, on oath, hear and determine the case in dispute, and shall also determine who shall pay the costs of suit. Each juror in such case shall be allowed two dollars per day for such services; the other officers, such fees as have already been established by law for other similar services: provided, that if the land in dispute shall be on a county line, it shall be lawful for a Justice of either county in which part of the land may be, to act in such case; and in case either party be dissatisfied with the decision, they shall

Act of Dec. 14, 1837. Took effect from passage.

In case of dispute as to division line, never run agreeable to law, &c.

Mode of proceeding in such cases.

have the right to appeal to the District Court within ten days, upon giving bond security for the costs.

Notice to be given before division line is run.

ART. 1193. [19] It shall be the duty of the Surveyor in all cases, before he runs a division line between two settlers claiming lands, to notify the party or parties interested, before running the same, in writing. And any survey which may be made contrary to the true intent and meaning of this section of this act, shall not be a lawful one; and the field notes of every survey which shall be returned to any land office hereafter for the purpose of getting a title for the same, shall be under oath of the surveyor, who shall swear it was executed according to law, and shall also swear the same was made prior to the closing of the Land Office by the Consultation, or subsequent to the opening of the same by this act; and if made prior to the closing of the Land Office by the Consultation, the same shall also be proven by at least two respectable witnesses.

Surveys on navigable streams—form of, generally, &c.

ART. 1194. [21] All lands surveyed for individuals lying on navigable water-courses, shall front one-half of the square on the water-course, and the line running at right angles with the general course of the stream, if circumstances of lines previously surveyed under the laws will permit; and all others not on navigable water-courses shall be square if previous lines will permit; and under no circumstances shall any one grant be located in more than two surveys.(*a*)

Act of Dec. 14, 1837. Took effect from passage.

Streams 30 feet wide navigable.

ART. 1195. [42] All streams of the average width of thirty feet shall be considered navigable streams within the meaning of this act, so far as they retain that average width, and that they shall not be crossed by the lines of a survey.(*b*)

Act of Feb. 5, 1840. Took effect April 16, 1840.

ART. 1196. [5] It shall be the duty of all deputy surveyors to make returns of every survey by them made, within three months after making the survey, to the County Surveyor for his approval.

Penalty for surveying for second applicant lands pointed out by a former one, &c.

[See Articles 1203, 1207.]

ART. 1197. [6] It shall be the duty of the several county surveyors, upon the return of the field notes of any surveyor in his county, to examine the same, and if found to be correct, to certify to the same as required by law, and deliver them within ten days after application therefor to the Chief Justice, or to any person interested therein, after having recorded the same in his office; and any surveyor neglecting or refusing so to do, or failing or refusing to survey any lands, the holder of a legal certificate may point out, within a reasonable time, or surveying such lands so designated for any other person, upon a certificate subsequently presented shall be liable for all damages sustained by any person on account of such default.

Act of May 9, 1846. Took effect from passage.

Field notes of national road claims to be recorded.

ART. 1198. [1] It shall be the duty of any county surveyor in this State, to record the field notes which have, or may hereafter be made upon any claim originating under the provisions of an act entitled an act to open and establish a national road, approved 5th February, 1844, upon presentation: provided such survey shall or may have been made by any person legally authorized to survey.

Act of May 9, 1846. Took effect from passage.

In cases where original field notes have been lost, &c.

ART. 1199. [1] When the original field notes of any survey made by authority of law, shall have been heretofore, or may be hereafter, lost or accidentally destroyed, it shall be lawful for the party who owned the same, or his agent, on making affidavit of the loss or destruction of such field notes and filing the same in the office of the county surveyor, to apply to the county

(*a*) This section is directory, and probably would not injuriously affect a survey that did not strictly pursue its directions. Horton *v.* Pace, 9 Tex. Rep. 81—(Special Court.)

(*b*) See Horton *v.* Pace, 9 Tex. Rep. 81.

surveyor of the county where the survey was made and recorded, and obtain from him a certified copy of the record thereof, which copy shall be as valid and efficient in law as the original was, and shall secure to the party all the rights, before the Commissioner of the General Land Office, that the original would have done.

ART. 1200. [1] In all cases where two surveys have been heretofore, or may hereafter be made, by virtue of any headright certificate, bounty warrant, or any other legal evidence of claim to land, and it shall appear by the district or county maps, in the General Land Office, or by a plat or sketch giving a connection of the adjacent surveys, certified by the district surveyor and returned to said office, that all the vacant land, at the place where the second survey was made, has been included therein, without having completed the quantity to which the party was entitled, by the unlocated balance of the claim, the owner or holder thereof shall have a right to a third survey to satisfy the unsurveyed portion of the claim.

Act of Jan. 10 1850. Took effect from passage. When a third survey on unlocated balance, &c., may be made. Art. 1213.

ART. 1201. [1] No certificate of land, land warrant, or evidence of land claim of any kind whatever, shall hereafter be located upon any land heretofore titled or surveyed within the limits of the colonies of Austin, De Witt, and De Leon; and the Commissioner of the General Land Office is hereby prohibited from hereafter issuing a patent on any location hereafter made for any of the lands described in this act; and should any patent be hereafter issued for the same, or a part thereof, contrary to the provisions of this act, the same shall be null and void.

Act of Feb. 5, 1850. Took effect from passage. No certificate shall be located on titled land in certain colonies.

ART. 1202. [1] No certificate of land, land warrants, or evidence of land claim of any kind whatever, shall hereafter be located upon any land heretofore titled or equitably claimed within the limits of what was Milam's colony, and the Commissioner of the General Land Office is hereby prohibited from hereafter issuing a patent on any location hereafter made for any of the lands described in this act, and should any patent be hereafter issued for the same, or any part thereof, contrary to the provisions of this act, the same shall be null and void.

Act of Jan. 10, 1852. Took effect from passage. Same subject.

ART. 1203. [1] The field notes of all surveys made previous to the passage of this act, shall be made out and returned in the manner now required by law, to the General Land Office, on or before the thirty-first day of August, 1853, or they shall become null and void, and the said surveys shall become vacant land, and be subject to be re-located and surveyed as in other cases, by any persons holding a genuine land certificate or other legal evidence of claim to land.

Act of Feb. 10, 1852. Took effect from passage. Certain lands subject to location after 31st Aug., 1853.

ART. 1204. [2] Any person holding a genuine certificate or other legal evidence of right to land under the Republic or State of Texas, and having a survey made by virtue of the same, the field notes of which may not have been returned to the General Land Office before the period prescribed by this act, shall have the right to re-locate the same certificate or other evidence of legal right to land, upon the same survey, but without being compelled to have the same re-surveyed: provided, said survey shall not have been previously located by some other person by right of a genuine land claim.

If field notes not returned, certificate may be re-located on same land, provided.

ART. 1205. [3] Any person wishing to avail him or herself of the privilege of re-locating the same land claim upon the same land, as permitted by the second section of this act, shall present his or her land claim, or cause the same to be done for that purpose, to the district or county surveyor, as the case may be, of the district or county where the field notes were first recorded, who shall duly enter such relocation upon the record of field notes of the office,

Re-location, how made, and field notes when to be filed.

and duly certify the same to the Commissioner of the General Land Office, which shall be sufficient authority for him to issue the patent for the land so re-located, as in other cases; provided, the field notes of survey and certificate of re-location shall be filed in the General Land Office within one year from and after said re-location.

Surveys represented on map void unless.

ART. 1206. [4] All surveys represented upon the maps of the General Land Office, the field notes of which shall not be returned to the General Land Office under the provisions of this act, and for which there are no titles on file in said office, shall be null and void, and be stricken from the maps of said office: provided, this section shall not include surveys made for colonists prior to the closing of the land offices in 1835.

All field notes shall be returned in twelve months.

ART. 1207. [5] The field notes of all surveys hereafter made, shall be returned to, and filed in the General Land Office, within twelve months from the date of survey; provided, that the field notes of surveys made by virtue of certificates issued to claimants in Fisher and Miller's Colony, Castro's, Mercer's or Peters' Colonies, may be returned at any time before the first of March, 1854.

Government dues shall be paid, &c.

ART. 1208. [6] Hereafter all government dues on land shall be paid to the Commissioner of the General Land Office in accordance with the provisions of a joint resolution, approved December 31st, 1849, entitled a joint resolution granting further time for the payment of government dues and the return of field notes.

Fee of, for re-location.

ART. 1209. [7] A fee of one dollar shall be paid to the County or District Surveyor, upon his making record of the re-location of any surveys under the provisions of this act.

Time when surveys shall be made.

ART. 1210. [8] All lands heretofore located by virtue of any genuine claim to land, shall be surveyed within twelve months from the passage of this act, and all lands which may be hereafter located shall be surveyed within twelve months from the date of location, or the said locations, in either case, shall be null and void, and the lands be subject to re-location and survey as other vacant and unappropriated lands.

Penalty, where fees are tendered, for failing to survey, &c.

ART. 1211. [9] If any District or County Surveyor shall fail, neglect or refuse, when the amount of lawful surveying fees of any location of land may be tendered to him by any person legally entitled to the survey, to make, or cause the survey of the same to be made within one month of the time of the tender to him of said surveying fees, he shall be liable on his official bond to the party or parties legally entitled to the same, in the amount of the damages or injury said party or parties may sustain by reason of such neglect, refusal or failure, to be recovered before any competent tribunal: provided, this section shall not apply to any grants made to colonists in the Colonies of Austin, De Witt, De Leon and Milam.

Act of Feb. 16, 1852. Took effect April 18, 1852.

No location shall be made on titled lands, &c.

ART. 1212. [1] Hereafter it shall not be lawful to locate a land certificate, warrant or scrip, on any lands heretofore titled or equitably claimed and situate within the county of Bexar; and the Commissioner of the General Land office is hereby prohibited from hereafter issuing a patent upon a location on any of the lands described in this act, and should a patent be hereafter issued for any of such lands, the said patent shall be null and void.

Act of Feb. 10, 1854. Took effect from passage.

ART. 1213. [1] Surveys of land may be made in more than two places by virtue of any genuine land certificate, bounty warrant, or other legal evidence of claim to land: provided such other places be bounded by previous surveys, and shall be enough to satisfy only a part or the whole of said claim, which fact shall be specially certified to by the surveyor making the survey. Art. 1200.

ART. 1214. [3] Any person holding a genuine land certificate, bounty land warrant, or other headright certificates, or railroad certificates, shall, after the 1st day of March, 1857, have the right to locate the same within the reserve alluded to in this act, as on any other public domain of the State. [See Art. 1147.] Holder of warrant, &c., may locate in reserve after, &c.

ART. 1215. [1] Hereafter, each county and District Surveyor in the State shall keep in his office a well-bound book as a register of entries, in which he shall register entries or applications for land in his county or district. He shall, also, before registering an entry or application, require the applicant to file his land certificate or scrip, or other legal evidence of title to land, together with a written entry or application particularly describing the claim to be surveyed, the date of the entry or application, and the land applied for, in his office, which he shall not allow to be taken from thence, until the same is returned, together with the field notes, to the General Land Office; but the survey shall be made by a copy of the entry, and strictly in accordance with the same: provided, that nothing in this act shall be so construed as to prevent holders of certificates or scrip from having the same surveyed without entry. But such survey shall not have a preference, or give any right over a location or entry of the same land previously made in the proper office. Act of August 30, 1856. Took effect Oct. 30, 1856. Surveyor shall keep a register of entries and applications, &c.

ART. 1216. [2] It shall not be lawful for such surveyor to allow the holder of any land certificate or scrip, or other legal evidence of title to land, to lift or float the same after entry, location, file or survey, when the same is not made upon land previously appropriated. But when a conflict of entries, files, locations or surveys occur, upon a proper showing of the facts, which may be by the certificate of one of his deputies or from his own knowledge, he shall allow the party having his entry, file, location or survey of subsequent date, to lift so much thereof as shall be affected by such conflict. Certificate not to be lifted after entry, except.

ART. 1217. [3] Whenever an entry is made by virtue of a genuine certificate, upon any land which appears to be appropriated, deeded or patented, by the books of the proper Surveyor's office, or records of the County Court or General Land Office, the party making such entry shall abide by the same. And in the event that judgment final shall be rendered against the right of the party making such entry to hold such land, he shall not have the right to lift or re-enter said certificate. But the same shall be forfeited, and so declared to be by the judgment of the court: provided, that nothing in this act shall be so construed as to effect entries or locations heretofore made. Effect of location on a valid claim or title, &c.

VI. LAND SCRIP AND SURVEYS BY VIRTUE THEREOF.

ART. 1218. [1] From and after the first Thursday of August next, all deputy surveyors be, and they are hereby authorized and directed, upon the application of any holder or holders of land scrip under the before recited act, to survey, at the expense of this Government, a sufficient quantity of the vacant land of the public domain within their respective sections,—when said vacant lands shall be pointed out to them,—to satisfy such legal claims of all holders of land scrip sold by this Government agreeably to law in all respects. Act of May 18, 1838. Took effect from passage. Shall be surveyed, on application of holder.

ART. 1219. [1] The provisions of the above recited act do, and they are hereby declared to extend to all land scrip issued and sold by the authority of the Government of Texas, in accordance with law in all respects. Act of May 24, 1838. Took effect from passage.

Act of Feb'y 11, 1858. Took effect from passage. How issued and price of same.

ART. 1220. [1] The Commissioner of the General Land Office is authorized to issue land scrip in certificates of not less than one hundred and sixty acres, (except in the cases hereinafter provided,) which certificates may be sold at the price of one dollar per acre, shall issue in the name of the purchaser, and may be located upon any vacant unappropriated public domain, not being set apart, held in reservation, or the location of which is prohibited by law.

Price of alternate sections.

ART. 1221. [2] The alternate sections of land surveyed and reserved to the State, under the provisions of the laws to encourage the construction of railroads by donations of land, and the act granting land to the Galveston and Brazos Navigation Company, and the islands heretofore reserved, and all other reserved sections may be sold at one dollar and twenty-five cents per acre, except the alternate sections reserved to the State by the Memphis, El Paso and Pacific Railroad Charter, which alternate sections shall not be sold for a less price than two dollars per acre.

Scrip, how issued, and value thereof.

ART. 1222. [3] Any person desiring to purchase the land scrip issued under the first section of this act, shall make application to the Commissioner of the General Land Office, for the certificate or certificates which he desires to purchase; and thereupon the Commissioner of the General Land Office shall deliver to him an order to the Treasurer of the State, directing the Treasurer to receive from him the price of said certificate, stating the name of the purchaser, the number of the certificate, and the quantity of land for which it is to issue; and the Treasurer, upon payment of the price, shall give to the purchaser a receipt in like manner specifying the purchaser's name, and the quantity and number of the certificate; and upon the presentation of said receipt to the Commissioner of the General Land Office, he shall deliver to the applicant the certificate or certificates so paid for.

Purchase of alternate sections, how made.

ART. 1223. [4] Any person desirous of purchasing one or more sections of the lands mentioned in the second section of this act, shall make application to the Commissioner of the General Land Office, stating the section or sections he desires to purchase; and thereupon the Commissioner of the General Land Office shall give to the applicant an order to the Treasurer of the State, directing him to receive from the applicant the price of the section or sections he desires to purchase, stating the name of the purchaser, and describing the section or sections applied for, by number; and the Treasurer, upon payment of the price, shall give to the purchaser a receipt in like manner stating the purchaser's name, and describing the land; and upon presentation of said receipt to the Commissioner of the General Land Office, he shall issue to the purchaser a patent or patents for the lands so purchased and paid for.

Vacant land in quantity less than 160 acres, may be surveyed, &c.

ART. 1224. [5] When there may be any vacant and unappropriated public domain (not being set apart, held in reservation, or the location of which is prohibited by law,) of less quantity than one hundred and sixty acres of land, which is completely surrounded by previous surveys, any one desiring to purchase the same may apply to the surveyor of the county or district in which the land lies, and cause the same to be surveyed, and the field notes of such survey shall be recorded in the office of the said surveyor, and returned to the General Land Office; and the person upon whose application the land was surveyed, shall, for six months after the making of such survey, have a preference to purchase said land; and the sale of the same shall be made in the same manner as is provided for in the fourth section of this act, for the sale of other surveyed lands, and for one dollar per acre, and patented in the same manner: provided, however, that if the person, upon whose application the said land is surveyed, and to whom said preference is given, his heirs or assigns, shall fail, within the said six months from the time of the survey of said land, to file in the office of the District or County Surveyor who surveyed

Preference given to person making application, &c.

the same a certificate from the Commissioner of the General Land Office, stating that he or they had purchased and paid for the same, then said land shall revert to and become part of the public domain, and be subject to location as other lands.

ART. 1225. [6] Land scrip under the provisions of the first section of this act shall be in certificates for one hundred and sixty, three hundred and twenty, six hundred and forty, and twelve hundred and eighty acres, (and no more.) Scrip, in what quantity issued.

ART. 1226. [7] The fourth section of an act to authorize the location, sale and settlement of the Mississippi and Pacific Railroad Reserve, be and the same is hereby repealed: provided, that scrip heretofore issued may be located and patented within said Reserve as though said section were in full force. Rep'ling clause.

ART. 1227. [8] All heads of families, who are settled upon or who may hereafter settle upon any vacant public domain, except those lands the sale of which is provided for in the second section of this act, shall have the privilege of purchasing one hundred nad sixty acres of land, to include his or her improvement, in preference to all others; and also a preference to purchase, in the same manner, one hundred and sixty acres of land adjoining his or her improvement, for every three slaves owned by such person within the State. Preference given to heads families, &c

ART. 1228. [9] Any one desiring to obtain the benefits of the preceding section, shall, within three months of the passage of this act, or of his or her settlement, file with the District Surveyor the affidavit of him or herself, and that of two credible witnesses, made before any officer authorized to administer oaths in the land district in which the settlement is made, that he or she is *bona fide* settled and making improvements upon vacant public domain, the sale of which is contemplated in the first section of this act, and that he or she has not previously had the benefit of said preceding section; and shall, at the same time, file with said surveyor a designation of the land sought to be secured; and said settler shall, within twelve months, have said land surveyed, his field notes recorded, returned to the General Land Office, and scrip applied, or the preference herein provided for shall cease, and said land become vacant and subject to location or purchase: provided, that the sale of any improvement made under the eighth section of this act, shall entitle the purchaser to the same rights possessed by the settler, and none other. Affidavit shall be made by same within 3 months, &c.

ART. 1229. [10] All surveys made under the provisions of this act, previous surveys permitting, shall be made in a square, except on navigable water courses, and upon them they shall not front exceeding one-half the square of the survey. Surveys to be in a square, except

ART. 1230. [11] All moneys received under the provisions of this act, shall be placed with and constitute a part of the Common School Fund. Proceeds of sales part of school fund.

VII. DUPLICATE CERTIFICATES.

ART. 1231. [1] Any person who may have lost any land warrant, discharge or a certificate for a headright claim, emanating from the government, and entitling the holder to a bounty of land, shall be entitled to demand and receive a duplicate of the same so lost, by complying with the provisions hereinafter prescribed by this act. Act of Jan. 14, 1840. Took effect from passage. Lost land warrant, discharge or certificate, duplicate.

ART. 1232. [2] Any person having lost any of the above mentioned certifi-

Publication of loss. cates, or evidences of claim, shall previous to applying for a duplicate of the same, make or cause publication to be made for sixty days, in at least one newspaper, published at the nearest place where the individual resides; which publication shall describe as correctly as possible the paper lost, and give notice that unless intelligence of it is received at the Department of War within three months of the date of publication, he will apply to the proper officers for a duplicate of the paper so lost.

Proof to be made by applicant. ART. 1233. [3] When any person shall apply for a duplicate of any claim against the Government, he shall be required to prove that he has fully complied with the preceding section of this act, and shall take and subscribe an oath to the following effect: That he was the just owner of the claim, that he had never sold, alienated, or transferred the same in any manner, that it has been lost, and that since lost, he has neither known or heard of the same; whereupon it shall be the duty of the Secretary of War, if the claim so lost be a discharge, or a land warrant which had been issued from his department, if no intelligence of the same has been received, to issue to the claimant the same quantity of land as was conferred by the original; and if the claim so lost be a certificate which had issued from any of the Boards of Land Commissioners, of any of the counties of the Republic, and shall have been reported by the Commissioners appointed to investigate and examine the records of the different Land Offices, as genuine and legal, if no intelligence of the same has been received as aforesaid, it shall be the duty of the Commissioner of the General Land Office to issue to the claimant a duplicate entitling him to the same quantity of land as was conferred by the original: provided, that administrators, and the legal representatives of deceased persons shall not be required to take the oath prescribed in this act.

Duplicate to issue.

Proviso in favor of legal representative of deceased persons.

When applicant shall be prosecuted for perjury, and penalty. ART. 1234. [4] Should any land warrant, discharge, or certificate for a headright of land, for which a duplicate had been issued, be ever after presented to the Commissioner of the General Land Office or Secretary of War, and should it appear that such land warrant, discharge, or certificate for a headright of land was not lost, but was sold or in any way alienated by the person who obtained the duplicate thereof, it shall be the duty of the Secretary of War, or Commissioner of the General Land Office to give information of the fact to one of the District Attorneys, who shall prosecute the aforesaid person for perjury; and should he be convicted, in addition to the statutory punishment for that crime, he shall be incapable of ever after holding property within, or enjoying any of the privileges of a citizen of this Republic.

Quere? If repealed by Crim. Code.

Act of May 11, 1846. Took effect from passage.

Duplicates of certain lost claims, how obtained. ART. 1235. [1] Any person who may have lost any land warrant, discharge, certificate for a headright claim emanating from the Government, or any special grant from the Congress of the Republic of Texas, and entitling the holder to a bounty of land, shall be entitled to demand and receive a duplicate of the same, so lost, by complying with the provisions prescribed in the act above recited.

Act of Feb. 7, 1853. Took effect from passage.

Person loosing Land Scrip may obtain duplicate. ART. 1236. [1] Any person who has lost, or who may hereafter loose Land Scrip, be, and they are hereby included in the act authorizing the issuing of duplicate land warrants, discharges and headrights on certain conditions, approved January 14th, 1840, by complying with the conditions specified in the same; provided, that the owner of said land scrip or claim, shall, previous to applying for a duplicate of the same, cause the publication required by said act to be made for sixty days, in some newspaper in the State of Texas.

Provisions of act to apply to party. ART. 1237. [2] The provisions of said act to which this is a supplement, shall apply and be in force in all cases as to the parties applying for and obtaining under this act such duplicate land scrip.

ART. 1238. [3] When headright certificates, land scrip, land warrants, discharges or other claims to land owned by two or more parties may be lost, it shall be lawful for the parties owning the same, to make jointly or severally the affidavit required by the third section of the act to which this is a supplement. Joint owners may make joint or several affidavit.

VIII. CERTIFICATES, SURVEYS AND TITLES VALIDATED AND CONFIRMED.

1. *Certificates.*

ART. 1239. [1] All certificates of headrights issued by the Board of Land Commissioners of Harrison County, on the twentieth, twenty-first, twenty-second, twenty-seventh and twenty-eighth days of April last, to legal claimants, shall be as good and valid as though the same had been issued by said Board previous to the passage of the law limiting the further action of the different Boards of Land Commissioners, passed at the last session of Congress. Act of Jan. 14, 1841. Took effect from passage. Certificates issued in Harrison county validated.

ART. 1240 [2] All Surveyors and officers of the Republic shall respect the said certificates, as though the same had been issued by the said Board of Land Commissioners at their regular session: provided, however, that the provisions of this act shall not give validity to any claim which would not have been otherwise valid, had the same been issued in conformity with law. Certificates to be respected as if issued at regular session—proviso.

ART. 1241. [1] The copy of the original abstract of land certificates, now in the General Land Office, and certified to by the Chief Justice and Sheriff of Jasper County, to be a true copy of the original abstract of land certificates recommended as genuine and legal claims against the Government, by the Commissioners appointed to detect fraudulent land certificates, be, and the same is hereby ratified and validated the same as the original could be; and the Commissioner of the General Land Office is hereby required to issue patents upon the said claims, so certified and returned, in the same manner as though the return had been made by the proper commissioners. Joint Resolution, Dec. 7, 1841. Took effect from passage. Jasper county, copy of abstract of recommended certificates, validated as original.

ART. 1242. [1] All certificates and orders of survey for lands issued by any of the several Boards of Land Commissioners, or District Courts, of the several judicial counties, and all surveys of land which have been made by the several Surveyors or their deputies, of any such counties, and all patents to land issued by the Commissioner of the General Land Office upon such certificate, or order of survey or surveys, so made, shall be held to be good and valid, to all intents and purposes: provided, the same would have been legal, had the same been done by Courts, Commissioners or officers of a constitutional county; and, further provided always, such survey as aforesaid, and patent that may issue thereon, shall not operate against, or prejudice in any manner, the prior vested rights of third parties. Act of July 18, 1842. Took effect from passage. Certificates and orders of survey of judicial counties, &c.

ART. 1243. WHEREAS, the seventh section of an act entitled "An Act to authorize the holding of the District Court in three places in Liberty County and for other purposes," approved January 6th, 1844, was construed by G. W. Miles, former Chief Justice of said county, to authorize him to act in his official capacity without the co-operation of the Associate Justices; and, whereas, acting under that construction of the aforesaid law, land certificates have been issued by the Chief Justice and Clerk, on the proper proof being made: Therefore, Act of March 20, 1848. Took effect April 29, 1848.

SECT. 1 Be it enacted by the Legislature of the State of Texas, That all land certificates, issued by G. W. Miles, former Chief Justice of Liberty County,

Liberty county, certificates issued by G. W. Miles, Chief Justice.

after the passage of the above named law, and which have been issued in all other respects in conformity to law, and have been properly returned to the General Land Office as genuine, shall have the same force and effect as like certificates issued by the Chief Justice and the Associate Justices.

2. *Surveys.*

Act of Dec. 12, 1855. Took effect from passage. Van Zandt county, surveys valid.

ART. 1244. [1] All surveys made in Van Zandt county by the County Surveyor thereof, be and the same are hereby declared to be as valid as if made by a legally authorized Surveyor, and as if said Van Zandt county had been a legal county, having the requisite number of square miles within its territory.

Patents to issue on.

ART. 1245. [2] The Commissioner of the General Land Office is hereby required to issue patents upon said surveys, certified by the said County Surveyor of said Van Zandt county, provided said surveys do not conflict with surveys or locations previously made, and provided further, that no survey shall be made valid by this act, which would have been invalid, if made by a legally authorized Surveyor, and said county had embraced the requisite number of square miles within its territory.

Act of Nov. 12, 1857. Took effect from passage. Karnes District, surveys by Charles A. Russel.

ART. 1246. [1] The election of said Charles A. Russell, to the office of Surveyor of Karnes District, is hereby made legal and valid, and all the official acts of said Russell, done and performed by him since he entered upon the duties of said office, are hereby made legal and valid: provided, that nothing shall be made valid by this act that would not have been valid if performed by a legally authorized Surveyor in said District.

Act of Nov. 24, 1857. Took effect from passage. Hopkins Co., a legal Land Dist.

ART. 1247. [1] The County of Hopkins be and is hereby made a legal Land District with the boundaries according to the map now on file in the General Land Office.

Surveys heretofore made, valid.

ART. 1248. [2] All surveys heretofore made by the County Surveyor of Hopkins County, are hereby made legal and valid: provided, that no survey shall be made valid by this act, which would not have been valid if made in a legally organized Land District.

Act of Feb. 13, 1858. Took effect from passage. Surveys on line between Milam and Bexar Districts, valid.

ART. 1249. [1] All the surveys upon genuine certificates heretofore made in the territory bordering on the supposed line between the Milam and Bexar Land Districts be, and they are hereby made legal and valid, and the Commissioner of the General Land Office be and he is hereby authorized and required to patent all such surveys: provided, that there is no conflict between surveys made by the Surveyors of the said Districts.

On line between Bastrop and Milam, or Bastrop and Burleson Districts.

ART. 1250. [2] All the surveys heretofore made upon genuine certificates and warrants in the territory bordering on the division line between Bastrop and Milam Districts, or Bastrop and Burleson Districts as the case may be, be and they are hereby made legal and valid, and the Commissioner of the General Land Office, be, and he is hereby authorized and required to patent all such surveys, whenever there may be no conflict between surveys made by the Surveyors of the said Districts. The field notes of all surveys mentioned in this act shall be recorded in the county in which the land is situated, and nothing in the first section of this act shall be so construed as to affect the rights of any person who owns or possesses any claim to any of the lands therein referred to or any portion thereof.

3. *Titles.*

Act of Jan. 17, 1852. Took effect from passage.

ART. 1251. WHEREAS, certain grants of land in Vehlin's and Burnet's Colonies were located and surveyed across the boundary line between said colonies, between the Trinity and Neches River—therefore:

SECT. 1. Be it enacted by the Legislature of the State of Texas, That all titles made to colonists or settlers, for their headright claims, provided, that said claims shall not exceed in quantity one league and labor to one individual, located and surveyed as aforesaid, are hereby declared to be as valid as if the same had been located and surveyed wholly in the colony by which they were respectively granted, and the lands embraced by said locations and surveys are hereby relinquished and quit-claimed to the grantees of said titles, their heirs and assigns, in the same manner and to the same extent as if said lands had wholly belonged to the colony from which said titles emanated respectively, and no further; provided, this act shall not affect titles previously acquired by any third party. Titles to certain colonists in Vehlin's and Burnet's Colonies confirmed.

ART. 1252. [1] All titles now on file in the General Land Office, issued by Talbot Chambers, as Commissioner for the Colony of Benjamin R. Milam, to actual settlers or colonists who were, or afterwards became citizens of Texas, shall be as valid as if issued by a legally authorized commissioner; but this act shall not be so construed as to confirm any title which has been obtained by fraud or misrepresentation of the grantee, nor any title or grant over one league and labor; nor shall it extend to any title now in litigation, during the pendency of the suit. Act of Feb. 5, 1852. Took effect from passage. Titles issued by Talbot Chambers in Milam's Colony valid.

ART. 1253. [2] The State of Texas does hereby relinquish to the original grantees, all her right to the lands embraced in the titles validated by the first section of this act. Title relinquished by State.

ART. 1254. [1] All grants made by Commissioners of Austin's second Colony, or Austin and Williams' Colony, and lying in a triangular tract of country south of the upper road from Bexar to Nacogdoches, and between lines drawn north-east and north-west from the western source of the Lavaca river to said road, be and are hereby declared to be as valid as if situated within the undoubted limits of said colonies, and the state hereby releases her claim to the same: provided, that the provisions of this act shall not be so construed as to apply to any grant for a greater amount of land than one league and one labor, nor to any others than those made to colonists for their headrights, or for premium lands to the Empresario. Act of Jan. 25, 1853. Austin's second Colony and Austin and Williams' Colonies, titles confirmed.

ART. 1255. [1] The headrights of land granted to colonists before the thirteenth day of November, A. D. eighteen hundred and thirty-five, and lying and being intersected or crossed by the boundary line of Robertson's colony and Austin's Little Colony, and being part in one of said Colonies and part in the other, are hereby declared to be as valid as if such headrights were lying and being wholly within the colony where such headright grants were issued: provided, that nothing herein contained shall be so construed as to affect the rights of third parties.(a) Act of Feb. 2, 1854. Took effect from passage. Headrights on line of Robertson's and Austin's Little Colony confirmed.

ART. 1256. [2] This act shall not extend to any grant which is fictitious, forged or otherwise fraudulent.* Act not to extend to fictitious &c., claims.

IX. PATENTS.

ART. 1257. [20] The Commissioner of the General Land Office is hereby authorized to grant to all persons holding an order of survey legally obtained previous to the closing of the land offices in one thousand eight hundred and Act of Dec. 14, 1837. Took effect from passage.

* Re-enacted, January, 25, 1856.

(a) The proviso in this statute saved the claim of one who had caused a certificate on part of the land lying without the colony, and surveyed and returned to the General Land Office before the passage of the act of confirmation. Hamilton v. Avery, 20 Tex. Rep. 612.

May issue on surveys made prior to closing of Land Office in 1835, &c. thirty-five, and having a survey which was made agreeably to said order, and in conformity to law in all respects, a patent for the same, upon the holder presenting the certificate of some Board of Land Commissioners, that he is entitled to the quantity of land surveyed, and making such proof to them as is required by law, and upon his paying the several fees as the laws require.

Act of Jan. 20, 1840. Took effect March 16, 1840. On certificates recommended by Travelling Boards &c. ART. 1258. [4] It shall be the duty of the Commissioner of the General Land Office, upon the return of a survey made in accordance with law, and by authority of any certificate that shall be returned as genuine and legal by the commissioners appointed by this act, and as required by this act, to make out and deliver to the rightful owner a patent for the same, unless it shall appear from the records of his office, or from information, on oath given him, that there is some illegality in the claim; in such case he shall refer the matter to the Attorney-General, whose decision in writing shall be sufficient authority for him to issue or withhold the patent, as the case may be.

Not to issue on unrecommend'd certificates, &c. ART. 1259. [5] The Commissioner of the General Land Office is hereby prohibited from issuing a patent upon any survey that shall not have been or may hereafter be made by authority of a certificate returned as genuine and legal by the commissioners appointed by this act, or by authority of a warrant issued for military services, after the same shall have been presented to and approved by the Secretary of War, or by authority of a certificate issued by special act of Congress; and any patent issued contrary to the provisions of this act shall be null and void.

Act of Jan. 19, 1841. Took effect from passage. Shall issue on certificates recommended, &c ART. 1260. [1] The Commissioner of the General Land Office is hereby authorized and required, forthwith to make out patents upon all claims which have been, or may hereafter be returned as genuine, and justly entitled by the different boards of land commissioners appointed under "an act to detect fraudulent land certificates," whether the same has been obtained in strict accordance with law or not. * * * * * *

Map of county to be first returned. ART. 1261. [2] No patent shall be issued upon any claim, unless a map of the county in which the same is situated shall have been returned to the General Land Office by the County Surveyor of the county.

Fees for issuing. ART. 1262. [3] There shall be paid by the patentee for each and every patent issued to him under the provisions of this act, to the Commissioner of the General Land Office, for the use of the Government, for each patent for one league or more, the sum of fifteen dollars; for any less amount, and over one-third of a league, the sum of ten dollars; and for one-third of a league or any less amount, the sum of five dollars, in each case in Texas promisory notes.

Act of Feb. 5, 1841. Took effect from passage. Same subject. ART. 1263. [1] There shall be paid to the Commissioner General of the Land Office, by the patentee in all cases, whether the same is for headright claims, land scrip, or land warrants, the same fees as are directed to be paid for the issuing of patents, by the provisions of the act to which this is a supplement; and this act shall take effect from and after its passage.

Act of Jan 9, 1841. Took effect March 17, 1841. On claims within twenty frontier leagues. ART. 1264. [4] WHEREAS, it appears upon an investigation by a committee of both Houses of Congress, that the location of land claims made prior to the 17th day of March, 1836, on the twenty frontier leagues bordering on the United States of the North, are contrary to law, and there is good reason to believe that the claims, in *their origin*, were for the most part absolutely fraudulent and void; therefore, that the claims of the people within the abovementioned border leagues may be quieted and settled—

Same subject. ART. 1265. [1] Upon the application of any citizen of this Republic to the Commissioner of the General Land Office, for a patent to lands lying and comprehended within the above mentioned twenty frontier leagues, who would have been entitled to a patent had no claim of land been located within the said border leagues prior to the 17th day of March, 1836, the said Commissioner General shall issue a patent to such applicant as if no such location had ever been made.

This act not to prejudice head-rights within, &c.

ART. 1266. [5] Nothing herein contained shall prejudice or invalidate the settlement or headright claims of any citizen residing within the twenty border leagues, heretofore located and surveyed, whose claim shall not exceed one league and labor of land.

Act of April 7, 1846. Took effect from passage.

On land scrip located in two places, &c.

ART. 1267. [1] The Commissioner of the General Land Office be and he is hereby authorized and required to issue patents to the legal owners of land scrip, in all cases where the same has been located in two surveys, where the same is bounded by other surveys: provided, that in every case the patentee shall pay for one of the patents and one of the surveys.

Act of April 29, 1846. Took effect from passage.

Patents issued under Republic validated, &c.

ART. 1268. [1] All patents for lands, issued by the Republic of Texas, which have been sealed with the original seal of the General Land Office, having for device thereon a buffalo under a live oak tree, or which have been sealed with the other seal of said office, having for device thereon a cotton plant, plough, scythe, sheaf of wheat, and meridian sun, shall be as valid as though both of said seals had been devised and adopted by law.

Act of May 9, 1846. Took effect from passage.

On surveys lying in two or more counties.

ART. 1269. [1] The Commissioner of the General Land Office be and he is hereby authorized and required to issue patents, in all cases, upon surveys of land lying in two or more counties, where no conflict between such surveys and others exist, and to which there is no other objection than that of a division in said surveys, occasioned by a county boundary passing through them.

On part, in conflicting surveys, certificate for balance, &c.

ART. 1270. [2] In cases where conflicts exist between surveys, the Commissioner of the General Land Office shall be authorized, and is hereby required, to issue patents to such portions of such surveys as are free from its conflicts, and also to issue a certificate for the residue in each case; upon which certificate County Surveyors shall be authorized and required to survey, as though said certificate had been issued by a board of land commissioners.

Act of May 12, 1846. Took effect from passage.

Requisite of patent.

ART. 1271. [7] All patents for lands, emanating from the State, shall be issued in the name and by the authority of the State, under the seal of the State, and under the seal of the General Land Office, and shall be signed by the Governor, and countersigned by the Commissioner of the General Land Office.

Shall issue on all unconditional certificates, provided, &c.

ART. 1272. [1] The Commissioner of the General Land Office be and he is hereby authorized and required to issue patents upon all unconditional headright certificates for land which have been or which may be granted by any of the boards of land commissioners of the Republic or State of Texas: provided, the same shall have been granted in conformity to law: provided, further, that if a conditional certificate had been previously granted, the same shall be first filed in the General Land Office, unless the party applying for the patent shall make affidavit that the said conditional certificate has been lost, destroyed, or given up to be cancelled by the land board issuing the unconditional certificate, which affidavit shall be filed in the General Land Office.

Act of same date.

To heirs, &c., in certain cases.

ART. 1273. [3] Patents shall in like manner be issued upon all unconditional certificates which have been issued to the heirs or legal representatives of those persons who emigrated to the country, but died citizens of the same previous to having resided the three years required by law.

ART. 1274. [1] The Commissioner of the General Land Office be and he is

To assigns of unconditional headrights, &c., when.

hereby required to issue patents to, and in the names of, the assignees of all unconditional headright land certificates, issued, in conformity to law, by any of the boards of land commissioners of the Republic or State of Texas, upon such assignee presenting a sufficient and properly authenticated chain of transfer, assignment or obligation for title, or a power of attorney, showing such transfer or assignment from the original grantee down to the assignee.

Act of March 18, 1848. Took effect April 29, 1840.

Certificates issued by Sup. and Dist. Court.

ART. 1275. [1] All certificates heretofore, or that may be hereafter issued by the Supreme or District Courts, in accordance with the provisions of an act passed by the fifth Congress of the Republic of Texas, shall be as valid and legal as if issued by any other competent authority.

Patent shall issue on, &c., provided.

ART. 1276. [2] The Commissioner of the General Land Office be and he is hereby required to issue patents upon all surveys made by authority of such certificates; and that a certified copy of the decision of such court or courts, or either of them, be full authority, and sufficient evidence for the same: provided, that the survey is correct and made according to law.

Act of Jan. 10, 1850. In force from passage.

When a third survey may be made under same certificate.

ART. 1277. [1] In all cases where two surveys have been heretofore, or may hereafter be made, by virtue of any headright certificate, bounty warrant, or any other legal evidence of claim to land, and it shall appear by the district or county maps, in the General Land Office, or by a plat or sketch giving a connection of the adjacent surveys, certified by the District Surveyor and returned to said office, that all the vacant land, at the place where the second survey was made has been included therein, without having completed the quantity to which the party was entitled, by the unlocated balance of the claim, the owner or holder thereof shall have a right to a third survey to satisfy the unsurveyed portion of the claim.

Patent on same.

ART. 1278. [2] The Commissioner of the General Land Office is hereby authorized and required to issue patents on claims located in three surveys, as set forth in the first section of this act, as on any other legal surveys.

Certificate for unlocated balance, when to issue, &c.

ART. 1279. [3] Where two surveys have heretofore been made, by virtue of any legal claim to land, and the second survey shall have been patented, if it shall appear as pointed out in the first section of this act, that the first survey is so circumscribed by other surveys that no more vacant land can be obtained in that place, and the two surveys already made do not satisfy the claim, the owner or holder thereof shall have a right to patents on the two surveys already made as in other cases, and a certificate for the unlocated balance of his claim; which certificate shall be sufficient authority for any legally authorized surveyor to survey the same.

Act of Feb. 9, 1854. In force from passage.

Preamble.

ART. 1280. WHEREAS, many citizens who held orders of survey issued under the colonization laws prior to the declaration of independence by the Republic of Texas, under which "orders" surveys had actually been made, in some cases, and other citizens claimed first class headrights; and, whereas, by virtue of the twelfth section of the act of the 14th December, 1837, entitled "An act to reduce into one act and to amend the several acts relating to the establishment of a General Land Office," the claimants to headright certificates and the holders of said "orders of survey" were required to submit their claims and "orders of survey" to the examination of the board of land commissioners created by said act; and, whereas, the said board of land commissioners, in some cases, refused to issue certificates for headrights; in others, refused to issue certificates recognizing the "orders of survey" as valid, from which decision, in many instances, parties appealed to the District Court under the sixteenth section of said act; and, whereas, such appeals were pending in the District Court when the authority of the board of land commissioners to issue certificates under the 16th section of the before recited act was repealed, before the decision of the District Courts on the appeal, and in other cases before the parties could apply for the same; and, whereas, there is no court or person vested with authority to issue certificates in accordance with law, as provided in the 16th section of the aforesaid act. Therefore—

SECTION 1. In all cases where appeals were taken from the decision of the board of land commissioners, under the 16th section of the act referred to in the preamble, when by the decree of the District Court the appellant is declared to be entitled to a specified quantity of land, from which decree no appeal has been taken and prosecuted to effect, or when the decree of the District Court remains unappealed from, in force and unreversed, the Judge of the District Court presiding in the county where such decree was or may be rendered, is hereby authorized, in term time or in vacation, to direct the Clerk of the Court to issue the certificate which was required to be issued by the board of land commissioners under the 16th section of the aforesaid act, which certificate shall be approved by the District Judge and issued under the seal of the court, and the Commissioner of the General Land Office is hereby required to issue patents on certificates so issued as in other cases: provided, the party applying for a certificate shall file with the Clerk of the District Court an affidavit "that no certificate has heretofore been issued under a general or special law, in virtue or on account of the right or claim to land for which I now seek to obtain a certificate." Certificates may be issued by Dist. Clerk, when. Patent may issue on, &c.

ART. 1281. [2] Any certificate issued contrary to the true meaning and intent of this act shall be void. Certificate issued by, when void.

2. *Patents on Certificates, &c., in particular Counties.*

ART. 1282. The President of the Republic and the Commissioner of the General Land Office are hereby authorized and required to issue titles to purchasers of lots on Galveston Island: provided, that the said purchasers shall deliver to the commissioner a certificate of purchase, with a receipt for the payment of the purchase money in full, from the Secretary of the Treasury. Joint resolution May 9, 1838. Took effect from passage. Patent to issue, &c., for lots on Galveston Island.

ART. 1283. [1] The County Surveyor of Smith county be and he is hereby authorized and required to record the field notes of all surveys which have been made within the limits of said county, in conformity to law, by the deputy surveyor of the district of Nacogdoches. Act of Jan. 19, 1850. Took effect from passage. County Surveyor of Smith co.

ART. 1284. [2] The Commissioner of the General Land Office be and he is hereby authorized and required to issue patents upon the same, as if they had been returned and recorded in the office of said District Surveyor of Nacogdoches. Patents to issue on same.

ART. 1285. [1] It shall be the duty of the County Clerk of Robertson county to transmit at the earliest time possible, to the Commissioner of the General Land Office, at the city of Austin, all of the original affidavits or oaths, records, papers, books, and other evidences of the issuance of headright certificates by the Board of Land Commissioners of Robertson county, prior to the 13th day of February, 1846, certifying to the genuineness and authenticity of the same under his hand and seal of office, in such manner as shall be deemed sufficient by the said Commissioner. It shall further be the duty of said Clerk of Robertson county to retain full and complete record transcripts, to be entered in a bound book, of all the above named oaths, papers, records, and evidences above named of the proceedings had before and by the Board of Land Commissioners of Robertson county, regarding the issuing of headright land certificates, duly certifying at the end of said record transcripts to the correctness of the same, which transcript record may be read in evidence to Act of Feb'y 16, 1852. Took effect from passage. Clerk of Robertson county to transmit certain books, &c., to Gen'l L'd Office. Shall retain copies—made evidence, &c.

the same extent to which copies of other records are admissible, the expenses of which copies and transcripts shall be paid by the County Court of Robertson county: provided, the sum shall not exceed fifteen cents per hundred words for each hundred words, inclusive of the certificates thereto made: provided, further, that said County Court shall examine, compare and certify to the correctness of said transcript record of said testimony and evidences.

Patents on certificates issued by Board of L'd Commissioners of Robertson county, when to issue.

ART. 1286. [2] When application shall be made for patents by virtue of any certificate or certificates issued by the Board of Land Commissioners of Robertson county, where the name of the party to whom the certificate was issued shall appear upon the transcript of the original oaths, records and other evidences of the issuing of land certificates by the Board of Land Commissioners in and for Robertson county, transmitted to the General Land Office under the provisions of this act, and where the quantity of land does not appear to be entered of record, or where the number and date of the certificate or certificates are not a matter of record, the applicant for the patent by virtue of any certificate issued in the aforesaid county, shall be entitled to the same in the same manner as if said certificate or certificates had been regularly reported by the Clerk of the County Court for Robertson county as the law directs; and should any doubt arise as to the validity of any certificate purporting to have been issued by the Board of Land Commissioners for Robertson county, it shall be the duty of the Commissioner of the General Land Office to require the party applying for a patent by virtue of any certificate issued in the aforesaid county, to procure satisfactory evidence of the genuineness of said certificate, which said evidence shall be of such a nature and character as may, in the judgment of said Commissioner, be sufficient to establish said certificate to be a legal and genuine certificate, and that the party to whom said certificate was originally granted, was in truth and fact justly entitled to the quantity of land specified in said certificate; upon the production of said evidence it shall be the duty of the Commissioner of the General Land Office to issue patents upon said certificate or certificates as in other cases: provided,

Proviso.

however, that the provisions of this act shall not extend to any certificate which was not recommended as a genuine certificate by the Traveling Board of Land Commissioners for Robertson county.

Act of Aug. 26, 1856. Took effect from passage.

Patents to issue on unconditional certificates issued in, by, &c.

ART. 1287. [1] The Commissioner of the General Land Office be, and he is hereby required to issue patents upon all unconditional certificates issued by the Board of Land Commissioners of Robertson county, under the same conditions and restrictions as is contemplated by the act to which this is a supplement; provided, that nothing in this act shall be so construed as to apply to any other class of certificates than those expressly mentioned in this act.

Act of Feb'y 9, 1852. Took effect from passage.

Preamble.

ART. 1288. WHEREAS, it appears that the Clerk of the Board of Land Commissioners for Upshur county has failed and neglected to make due returns to the Commissioner of the General Land Office, of the certificates issued by said Board: and whereas, it further appears that the records of the Board of Land Commissioners aforesaid have been kept in an imperfect and informal manner, inasmuch as said records do not exhibit the numbers and dates of the certificates issued by said Board, together with the quantities of land for which said certificates were issued, by reason of which neglect and informality in said records, returns cannot now be made in due form to the Commissioner of the General Land Office, of the certificates issued by said Board: and whereas, by reason of the neglect and informality aforesaid, many citizens to whom certificates were issued by said Board, have been prevented from receiving titles for the lands located and surveyed by virtue of said certificates, although said citizens have made all proof required of them by law, and are justly entitled to the lands claimed by them by virtue of the certificates aforesaid; therefore,

SECTION 1. Be it enacted by the Legislature of the State of Texas, That all persons who have received unconditional certificates from the Board of Land Commissioners of Upshur county, and who cannot obtain patents for the reason given in the preamble to this act, may receive their patents from the Commissioner of the General Land Office, upon complying, on their part, with the provisions of an act entitled "an act to authorize the Commissioner of the General Land Office to issue patents on certificates issued by the Board of Land Commissioners of Robertson county, under certain restrictions;" and that the provisions of the above recited act shall apply, so far as the same may relate to, or be in any way applicable to persons desiring to avail themselves of the provisions of this act.

Certain unconditional certificates issued by Commissioners of Upshur county may be patented by complying, &c.

ART. 1289. [1] The Clerk of the County Court of Harris be, and he is hereby authorized and required to transmit to the Commissioner of the General Land Office, the book or register of land certificates issued by the Board of Land Commissioners for the county of Harris, usually known as the lost book; that the said Clerk shall annex to said book a certificate, under the seal of the County Court, that the book transmitted is the lost book, and known and recognised in his office as a genuine record of his office.

Act of Dec'r 2, 1850. Took effect from passage.

Clerk of County Court required to transmit certain book to Com'r, &c.

ART. 1290. [2] The Commissioner of the General Land Office be, and he is hereby required to issue patents on the certificates mentioned and described in said book now on file in his office, which claims have never been acted on or rejected by the Board of Commissioners appointed to detect fraudulent land certificates; and if any certificate mentioned or described in said book has been obtained by fraud or misrepresentation, the patent issued thereon shall be null and void.

Act of Dec'r 8, 1851. Took effect from passage.

Patents on certificates mentioned in same, &c.

ART. 1291. [3] If any certificate mentioned or described in said book has been obtained by fraud or misrepresentation, the patents that may be issued thereon shall be void, as well as every survey made under the same.

Act of Dec'r 2 1850. Took effect from passage.

Patent void, when.

ART. 1292. [2] The application and operation of "an act to authorize the location, sale and settlement, of the Mississippi and Pacific Railroad Reserve," passed August 26th, 1856, shall be governed and controlled by said boundary line as set within the first section of this act: provided, that nothing in this act contained shall be so construed as to prevent the patenting of scrip heretofore issued by authority of the act entitled "an act to authorize the location, sale and settlement, of the Mississippi and Pacific Railroad Reserve," which may have been, or may hereafter be, located north of the boundary line, as herein proposed, and south of the lines as recognised by the General Land Office.

Act of Dec'r 21, 1857. Took effect from passage.

On locations north of Pacific Railroad reserve

See article 1306.

3. *Cancellation of Patents.*

ART. 1293. [1] Where a patent to land has been or may hereafter, through mistake, be issued, upon any valid claim for land which is afterwards found to be in conflict with any older title, it shall be competent for the owner of such patent to return the same to the Commissioner of the General Land Office for cancellation; and should it appear from the records of the General Land Office or from a duly certified copy of a judgment of any court of competent jurisdiction, before which the title to such land may have been adjudicated, that such conflict really exists, and from proper evidence exhibited to said Commissioner, that the party applying is the just and legal owner of the patent thus presented, it shall be lawful for him to cancel the patent and deliver the certificate or other evidence of claim upon which it is issued to the owner for re-location.

Act of Feb'y 3, 1854. Took effect from passage.

Com'r may cancel patent issu'd on valid claim, &c., where there is an older title.

May cancel to extent of conflict.

ART. 1294. [2] In cases where there is only a partial conflict, the Commissioner of the General Land Office may, under like circumstances, and in like manner as is provided for in the first section of this act, cancel any patent presented to him, and issue a patent to the applicant for such portion of the land covered by his patent as may not be in conflict with the older title, where from the field notes the same may be done, and also issue to such applicant a certificate for the unlocated balance of the claim embraced in such canceled patent, which certificate may be located, surveyed under, and patented upon as in other cases.

X. GOVERNMENT DUES.

Act of Jan. 15, 1839. Took effect from passage.

Commissioner authorized to receive.

ART. 1295. [1] The Commissioner of the General Land Office be and he is hereby authorized and required to receive the Government dues upon all surveys that may be returned to his office.

To pay dues into treasury.

ART. 1296. [2] The Commissioner of the General Land Office shall pay into the Treasury of the Republic, all Government dues received by him, at the expiration of every week, as contemplated by the foregoing section of this act.

Act of Jan. 29, 1845. Took effect from passage.

Prices of land.

ART. 1297. [1] The prices of land, as mentioned in the thirty-sixth section of the general land law, passed fourteenth December, eighteen hundred and thirty-seven, be as follows: All those who may have emigrated prior to the second of May, eighteen hundred and thirty-five, shall pay for every labor of irrigable land, the sum of three dollars and fifty cents; for every labor of arable land, two dollars and fifty cents; for every labor of pasture land, one dollar and twenty cents; and all those who emigrated subsequently to the second of May, eighteen hundred and thirty-five, and prior to the declaration of independence, shall pay for every labor of irrigable land, seven dollars; for every labor of arable land, five dollars; and for every labor of pasture land, two dollars and forty cents.

Higher rates paid—may be applied to other lands.

ART. 1298. [2] In all cases where other or higher rates of land dues, than those prescribed in this act, have been exacted and paid by any person, the sum so paid, over and above the rates fixed by this act, may be applied by the person paying the same, in payment of land dues on other lands.

XI. GENERAL PROVISIONS.

Act of Dec. 14, 1837. Took effect from passage.

Officers prohibited purchasing public land.

ART. 1299. [8] No person appointed to an office instituted by this act, or employed in any such office, shall directly or indirectly be concerned in the purchase of any right, title, or interest in any public land, either in his own name, right, or interest for any other person, or in the name or right of any other person, in trust for himself; nor shall take or receive any fee or emolument for negotiating or transacting the business of said office, other than those fees allowed by law.

Joint resolution Feb. 3, 1845. Took effect from passage.

Houston and Jefferson and other counties may transcribe field notes.

ART. 1300. [1] The County Courts of the counties of Houston and Jefferson, and such other counties as shall desire to avail themselves of the benefits of this joint resolution, may employ the County Surveyors of their counties to transcribe the field notes of surveys or other records in their respective counties, in a well-bound book.

ART. 1301. [2] The County Surveyor shall be entitled to ten cents for every hundred words, for making such record, together with the value of the book for such record, to be paid out of the county treasury, upon the certificate of the clerk, after the claim has been audited and allowed by the County Court. Pay for—how paid.

ART. 1302. [3] It shall be the duty of the County Surveyor to certify under his official seal, that the said book contains a full and correct record of all the field notes in his office; and that duly authenticated copies from such record shall be received in evidence, in the same manner as though the record had been made as heretofore required by law. Surveyor to certify book under official seal.

ART. 1303. [1] In all cases instituted by Empresarios, their heirs or legal representatives, which have been, or may be decided by the Supreme Court in favor of the Empresarios, where, by the decree of the court the Empresarios are entitled to land and no title has been heretofore issued, it shall be lawful for the clerk of the Supreme Court to issue certificates for so much land as may be decreed to the parties—which certificates shall be certified by the said clerk under his hand and the seal of said court—and deliver the same to the party interested. The said clerk shall furnish the Commissioner of the General Land Office with a list of certificates issued by him. Act of Feb. 11, 1850. Took effect from passage. Certificates to Empresarios.

ART. 1304. [2] The several surveyors of the State of Texas are hereby directed to receive locations, make surveys and field notes, and record the same for the holder or owner of any such certificates, as in other cases; and the Commissioner of the General Land Office shall issue patents thereon as in other cases of good and valid certificates. Surveyors to receive, &c.

ART. 1305. [1] The owners of deeds issued on paper of the second seal, that have been filed in the General Land Office, shall be, and they are hereby authorized to withdraw said deeds from said office, on leaving a receipt for the same, naming the original grantee of the land therein described and the quantity of land granted by said deed, the date of said deed, and where the land therein described is situated. Act of Feb. 11, 1850. Took effect from passage. Owners of deed on second seal may withdraw them from General Land Office.

ART. 1306. [1] The beginning point on the eastern boundary of Texas, of the northern line of the Pacific Railroad reservation, shall be at the south-west corner of the State of Arkansas and the north-west corner of the State of Louisiana, and thence west to the town of Linden in Cass county, and Dangerfield in Titus county; thence west to Big Cypress; and thence, with south boundary line of Titus county, to the south-east corner of Hopkins county; thence to the south-west corner of said Hopkins county; and thence west, to the south-east corner of Collin county; and thence west, with the south boundary lines of the counties of Collin, Denton, Wise, Jack, and Young, to the south-west corner of Young county; and thence west, to the eastern boundary of New Mexico; and thence south, to the south-east corner of New Mexico; and thence west, with the south boundary line of New Mexico, to the Rio Grande. Act of Dec. 21, 1857. Took effect from passage. Northern boundary of Pacific Railroad Reserve.

ART. 1307. WHEREAS, citizens residing near the boundary line run in the year 1842, between Texas and the United States, North from the point where the 32d parallel of latitude crosses the Sabine, had, in many instances, obtained certificates of headright from the Board of Land Commissioners constituted by virtue of the land law of the 14th December, 1837, and which certificates were conditionally approved by the Board of Investigating Commissioners, previously to the running of said line; and, whereas, the holders of said certificates cannot obtain their patents without proving, before some tribunal yet to be established or authorized by law, to receive these proofs of citizenship, and act upon their claims. Act of Feb. 2, 1852. Took effect from passage. Preamble. Certificates issued to persons on north boundary of State north of point where 32d parallel crosses Sabine.

Holders may apply to District Court—requisites of application.

SECTION 1. Be it enacted by the Legislature of the State of Texas, That all persons who resided near the said boundary line, claiming to be citizens of Texas, before the establishment thereof, and who as such citizens received certificates of headright from any of the original Boards of Land Commissioners constituted by virtue of the land law aforesaid, and whose certificates were conditionally approved by the Investigating Boards, and the heirs and assigns of such persons, may make application by petition to the District Court of the county where the certificate was issued, or any county formed out of any territory of such county, describing the original certificate, and alleging that it was conditionally recommended by the Commissioners appointed to detect fraudulent land certificates, and also the place of residence of the applicant at the time of its issuance, and that he resided within the limits of Texas, and was a citizen thereof; which petition shall be verified by affidavit of the applicant, and together with the proof necessary to establish the facts alleged, shall be submitted to a jury, who shall determine the said facts, and say by their verdict whether the person originally receiving the certificate was or not duly entitled thereto as a citizen of Texas, residing to the west of said line at the time of its issuance.

Petition verified by affidavit, proof—jury—verdict.

District Attorney to defend—fee—costs, &c.

ART. 1308. [2] It shall be the duty of the District Attorney to defend such suits, for which he shall be entitled to a fee of ten dollars; or in his absence or inability to attend, the court shall appoint some competent attorney to defend the same, who shall be entitled to the same fee; and such fee, together with all costs incurred, shall be adjudged against and paid by the applicant in all cases; provided that the costs in any case under this act, shall not be adjudged against any applicant who shall sustain his application.

Judge to cause certificate to issue when.

ART. 1309. [3] It shall be the duty of the Judge, when the jury shall find in favor of the applicant, to cause to be issued to him a certificate thereof, under the seal of the court; and it shall be the duty of the Commissioner of the General Land Office, upon the presentation of said certificate, to issue to the said applicant, his heirs or assigns, a patent for the lands duly surveyed by virtue of the said original certificate of headright.

LAW.

I. COMMON LAW.

II. STATUTES.

I. COMMON LAW.

Act of Dec. 20, 1836.

In its application to juries and evidence adopted.

ART. 1310. [41] The common law of England, as now practiced and understood, shall, in its application to juries and evidence, be followed and practiced by the courts of this Republic, so far as the same may not be inconsistent with this act or any other law passed by this Congress.(*a*)

(*a*) Care must be taken to distinguish between those principles of common law which are incidental to particular forms of action, and those which are independent of the form of action; the latter only being applicable to our system which does not recognize different forms of action. Porter *v.* Miller, 7 Tex. Rep. 468.

ART. 1311. [1] The common law of England, (so far as it is not inconsistent with the Constitution or the acts of Congress now in force), shall, together with such acts, be the rule of decision in this Republic, and shall continue in full force until altered or repealed by Congress.

Act of Jan. 20, 1841. Took effect March 16, 1840. Adopted as the rule of decision,

ART. 1312. [107] All vouchers, views, essoigns, and also trials by wager of battle, and wager of law, shall stand repealed.

Act of May 13, 1846. Certain modes of trial at, repealed.

II. STATUTES.

ART. 1313. [2] Whenever one law which shall have repealed another, shall itself be repealed, the former law shall not be revived without express words to that effect.

Act of Jan. 16, 1840. Repealing law not to revive former repealed law.

ART. 1314. [3] As often as a question shall arise whether a law passed during any session of Congress change or repeal a law passed during the same session, the same construction shall be made as would have been made if this act had never been passed.

Construction of this law as to laws of the same session.

ART. 1315. [1] Every law hereafter made, shall commence and be in force with the commencement of the sixtieth day after the day of the adjournment of the session of the Legislature, at which such law may be passed, unless in the law itself another time for the commencement thereof is particularly mentioned.

Act of Dec. 1, 1849. Took effect March 23, 1850. When laws take effect.

ART. 1316. [1] On the third and last reading of any bill to create a private corporation, in each House of the Legislature, the ayes and noes shall be taken thereon, and if any such bill shall pass both Houses by a majority of two-thirds, the Secretary of the Senate, and the Chief Clerk of the House of Representatives, shall each certify such fact, and their certificates shall accompany the bill, when presented to the Governor for his approval.

Joint Resolution of April 29, 1846. Took effect from passage. Third reading of bill to create private corporation–certificates of Clerks, &c.

LEGISLATURE.*

I. TIME OF BIENNIAL MEETING.

ART. 1317. The Legislature of the State of Texas shall meet at the Seat

* As the present apportionment law will expire after the election in August next, it is omitted.—COMPILERS.

Act of Feb. 18, 1848. Took effect April 29, 1848. of Government thereof and begin their next biennial session on the first Monday in November, A. D. 1849, and biennially thereafter on the same day, until otherwise prescribed by law.

II. ORGANIZATION HOUSE OF REPRESENTATIVES.

Act of April 11, 1846. Took effect 22d June, 1842. Secretary of State to organize House—mode of organizing.

ART. 1318. [1] It shall be the duty of the Secretary of State to organize the House of Representatives at the next, and each subsequent meeting of the Legislature, until otherwise provided by law; for which purpose he shall attend at the time and place designated for the meeting of the Legislature, and after appointing a clerk, who shall have been Chief Clerk of the House the preceding session, if he be present,) to take a minute of the proceedings, he shall have all of the counties of the State called over in alphabetical order, and as the members elect appear and present their credentials, it shall be his duty, or the duty of the clerk under his order and direction, to administer to each the oath prescribed by the Constitution.

Person presenting proper evidence admitted though returns of election be not made, &c.

ART. 1319. [2] Should returns of election in any county or counties for members of the Legislature not be made to the office of Secretary of State, the clerk shall nevertheless call said county or counties, and if any person or persons appear at said call and present the proper evidence of his or their election, he or they shall be admitted or qualified in the same manner as though a return of his or their election had been made to the office of Secretary of State.

Quorum not present on day appointed for meeting.

ART. 1320. [3] Should there not be a quorum in attendance on the day appointed for the meeting of the Legislature, it shall be the duty of the Secretary of State and Clerk to attend from day to day until a quorum shall appear and be qualified as above.

Quorum—election of Speaker.

ART. 1321. [4] When a quorum shall have appeared and been qualified, the House shall proceed to the election of a Speaker, unless a majority of the members present shall think proper to defer said election.

Speaker—necessary officers—oath.

ART. 1322. [5] When an election for Speaker shall have been had, the Speaker elect shall immediately take the chair and the House proceed to its further organization by electing the necessary officers, to whom the Speaker shall administer the oath of office.

In absence of Secretary Attorney-General to act.

ART. 1323. [6] Should there be no Secretary of State, or in case he be absent or unable to attend, from any cause, the Attorney-General shall attend and perform the duties prescribed by this act.

III. PAY OF MEMBERS AND OFFICERS.

Act of Jan. 26, 1854. Per diem and mileage of members.

ART. 1324. [1] The members of the Legislature, at each session hereafter to be held, shall receive from the treasury of the State, as their compensation, five dollars for each day they shall be in attendance on the same, and five dollars for every twenty-five miles they may travel in going to and returning from the place of convening the Legislature.

Joint Resolut'n Feb. 10, 1854.

Per diem of officers.

Art. 1325. The officers of the two Houses of the present Legislature, and the officers of the Legislatures hereafter to assemble, shall each receive five dollars per day, for each day they may serve, and the same shall be paid upon the certificate of the Secretary of the Senate, or Chief Clerk of the House of Representatives, out of any moneys appropriated for that purpose.

IV. VOUCHERS AND PAPERS WITHDRAWN.

Joint Resolut'n of April 25, 1846. Took effect from passage.

Certain papers may be withdrawn, &c.

Art. 1326. [1] In all cases where petitions have been, or may hereafter be presented to the Legislature, and shall not have been granted by that body, the petitioners shall have the privilege of withdrawing the vouchers and other papers accompanying said petitions, at any time, upon application to the Secretary of the Senate, or to the Clerk of the House of Representatives, or, during the recess of the Legislature, to the Secretary of State.

LIMITATION OF CIVIL SUITS.

[*See Trespass to try Title.*]

I. SUITS FOR LAND.

Act of Feb'ry 5, 1841. Took effect 17th March, 1841.

Right of entry, when barred.

ART. 1327. [14] The person who has or shall have right of entry into any real estate, consisting of lands, tenments, or hereditaments, shall make entry therein within ten years next after this right shall have accrued, and on failure shall be forever barred thereafter.(a) Yet, if the person entitled shall have been, or shall be, under the age of twenty-one years, a *feme covert*, or insane; or if forcible occupation of the premises, or county containing them, by a public enemy, prevent entry, the time of such disability shall not be computed as a part of the period of limitation. The death of one, dying possessed of such estate without right, shall not be such descent to the heir of the decedent as to bar entry of the person entitled at the time of the descent, unless such decedent shall have had five years' peaceable possession. Peaceable possession, within the scope of this act, is such as is continuous, and not interrupted by adverse suit to recover the estate.

Peaceable possession, &c. defined.

Possession under title or color of title.

ART. 1328. [15] Every suit, to be instituted to recover real estate, as against him, her, or them, in possession under title, or color of title, shall be instituted within three years next after the cause of action shall have accrued, and not afterwards;(b) but in this limitation, is not to be computed the duration of disability to sue from the minority, coverture, or insanity of him, her, or them having cause of action. By the term *title*, as used in this section, is meant a regular chain of transfer from or under the sovereignty of the soil: and color of title is constituted by a consecutive chain of such transfer down to him, her or them in possession, without being regular; as if one or more of the memorials or muniments be not registered, or not duly registered, or be only in writing, or such like defect as may not extend to, or include the want of intrinsic fairness and honesty; or when the party in possession shall hold the same by a certificate of headright, land warrant or land scrip, with a chain of transfer down to him, her or them in possession; and provided, this section shall not bar the right of the Government.

Title and color of title defined.

Five years peaceable possession under a deed, &c.

ART. 1329. [16] He, she, or they, who shall have had five years' like peaceable possession of real estate, cultivating, using or enjoying the same, and paying tax thereon, if any, and claiming under a deed, or deeds, duly registered, shall be held to have full title, precluding all claims; but shall not bar the Government; and saving to the person or persons having superior right and cause of action, the duration of disability to sue arising from non-age, coverture, or insanity.(c)

Ten years peaceable occupation passed possession.

ART. 1330. [17] Ten years of such peaceable possession and cultivation, use or enjoyment thereof, without any evidence of title, shall give to such naked

(a) It was not intended by this section, as might be supposed from the literal import of the terms, that every owner of real estate must, within ten years from the accrual of his title, make entry upon his lands, or be thereafter debarred of all right therein. Horton *v.* Crawford, 10 Tex. Rep. 382. This section bars the right of entry after ten years from the accrual of the right; but it applies only to cases in which the other party has had an adverse possession. Redding *v.* Redding, 15 Tex. Rep. 249.

(b) Adverse possession taken and held, with the requisites and circumstances specified in 15th, 16th and 17th sections of the act, for the time limited in the section under which the possessor sets up his right, forms an effectual bar to the prosecution of any suit or claim as against such possession. Horton *v.* Crawford, 10 Tex. Rep. 382. The possession must be actual, with a manifest intention to hold and continue it. Wheeler *v.* Moody, 9 Tex. Rep. 372. The limitation of three years applies only to cases where the party is in possession under title or color of title, by transfer from or under the sovereignty of the soil. Mason's Heirs *v.* McLaughlin, 16 Tex. Rep. 24. In so deriving title, no link must be omitted. Castro *v.* Wurzbach, 13 Tex. Rep. 128. To sustain the plea of the statute of three years, the title or color of title by written transfers and the adverse possession must concur for that period. Williamson *v.* Simpson, 16 Tex. Rep. 433.

(c) Jones *v.* Menard, 1 Tex. Rep. 771. Horton *v.* Crawford, *supra*. It seems that the deed contemplated by this section, is an absolute deed, and that an agreement for a title, to be made at a future time, is not sufficient. Castro *v.* Wurzbach, 13 Tex. Rep. 128.

possessor full property precursive of all other claims, in and to six hundred and forty acres of land, including his, her, or their improvement, yet the right of the Government is not to be barred; and there is saved to the person or persons having the title and cause of action the duration of disability to sue from non-age, coverture, or insanity.(*a*) Exceptions.

ART. 1331. [25] This act shall not be construed to prejudice the claims of those, to real estate, that would have been quieted at an earlier time by the twelfth section of "An act organizing the Inferior Courts," &c., approved December the twenty-sixth, eighteen hundred and thirty-six: and the said section shall be considered to continue in full force, whenever it would quiet titles to land at an earlier period than this act. When title would be quieted earlier, &c.

II. AS TO ALIENS.

ART. 1332. [9] In making title to land by descent, it shall be no bar to a party, that any ancestor through whom he derives his descent from the intestate, is or hath been an alien; and every alien, to whom any land may be devised or may descend, shall have nine years to become a citizen of the State and take possession of such land, or shall have nine years to sell the same, before it shall be declared forfeited, or shall escheat to the Government. Act of March 18, 1848. Took effect from passage. Nine years allowed to take possession of inheritance, &c.

III. PERSONAL ACTIONS.(*b*)

ART. 1333. [1] From and after the approval or final passage of this act, all actions of trespass for injury done to the estate, or property of another; all actions for detaining the personal property, and for converting such personal property to one's own use; all actions for taking away the goods and chattels of another; and all actions upon open accounts, other than such accounts as concern the trade of merchandise between merchant and merchant, their factors and servants, shall be commenced and sued within two years next after the cause of such action or suit, and not after.(*c*) All actions for injuries done to the person of another, as of assault, battery, wounding or imprisonment, and all actions for injuries done the character or reputation of another, as of libel or slander, shall be commenced and sued within one year next after the cause of such action or suit, and not after: and all actions of debt grounded upon any contract in writing, shall be commenced and sued within four years next after the cause of such action or suit, and not after. Act of Feb. 5, 1841. Took effect March 17, 1841. For injuries to estate, property or person on open account. On contract in writing.

(*a*) Smith v. Garza, 15 Tex. Rep. 150. Horton *v.* Crawford, 10 Tex. Rep. 382.

(*b*) Statutes of limitations are remedial in their character. Gautier *v.* Franklin, 1 Tex. Rep. 736. Hays *v.* Cage, 2 Tex. Rep. 501. DeCordova *v.* The City of Galveston, 4 Tex. Rep. 470. The first section of the statute of limitations applies as well to contracts then existing as to those subsequently made. DeCordova *v.* The City of Galveston, 4 Tex. Rep. 470. Where the interest falls due before the principal, the statute does not commence running against the claim for interest until the principal falls due, although the creditor may maintain his separate action for the interest. Ibid. Where an agent collects the money of his principal, the statute does not begin to run until demand, &c. Merle *v.* Andrews, 4 Tex. Rep. 200. The entry of a charge in store accounts, "To merchandize, as per bill rendered, $215 70," is in contravention of the provisions of the act of limitations. Love *v.* Doak & Tims, 5 Tex. Rep. 343. Although the terms of our statute do not apply to an action by one partner against another for a balance due after dissolution, yet the same period as is prescribed by the statute in analagous cases will be applied by the court. Leavitt *v.* Gooch, 12 Tex. Rep. 95. Suit on a note over four years due, and to foreclose a mortgage to secure the same debt within four years, the plaintiff had a recovery. Grayson *v.* Taylor, 14 Tex. Rep. 672. "Actions of debt, grounded on any contract in writing," which are required by the statute to be sued on in four years, include all suits brought to recover money for the breach of a contract in writing, without regard to the technical distinction between actions and suits and debt and damages at common law. Robinson *v.* Varnell, 16 Tex. Rep. 382. The statute is not applicable to payments. Williams *v.* Bradbury, 9 Tex. Rep. 487. When the statute begins to run, it continues to run, notwithstanding any supervening disability of the party entitled to sue or be sued. Tyson *v.* Britton, 6 Tex. Rep. 222. Cole *v.* Runnels, 6 Tex. Rep. 272. The statute operates on the cause of action without regard to the residence of the defendant, and whatever may be the mode of proceeding adopted for its recovery.—Love *v.* Doak & Tims, 5 Tex. Rep. 343. If an amendment to a petition sets up a new cause of action, barred at the time of filing the amendment, it will not relate back to the filing of the original petition so as to prevent the bar, Ayres *v.* Cayce, 10 Tex. Rep. 99.

(*c*) The exception in the statute in regard to accounts which concern the trade of merchandize, between merchant and merchant and their factors and servants, does not extend to a case where there is a single transaction, but only to cases of running accounts; and it seems that it only extends to such running accounts as embrace mutual credits, and not where the credit is all on one side. Guichard *v.* Superveile, 11 Tex. Rep. 522.

Judgment, revival of.

ART. 1334. [2] Judgment in any court of record within this Republic, where execution hath not issued within twelve months after the rendition of the judgment, may be revived by scire facias, or an action of debt brought thereon, within ten years next after the date of such judgment, and not after ;(*a*) or where execution hath issued and no return is made thereon, the party in whose favor the same was issued shall and may move against any Sheriff or other officer, or his or their security or securities, for not returning the same, within five years from the day on which it was returnable, and not after; provided, that always when any person or persons entitled to such judgment, when execution hath not issued and no return made, (in either case,) shall be or were under the age of twenty-one years, was a married woman, a person of unsound mind, imprisoned, or not within the Republic, at the time of such judgment being rendered or such execution being returnable, every such person, his or her heirs, executors or administrators, shall and may, notwithstanding the said ten or five years are, or shall have, expired, have the benefit of said judgment where no execution hath issued, by reviving the same by scire facias or by action of debt; and where execution hath issued, and no return made, every such person, his or her heirs, executors or administrators may have the benefit of other executions, or may move against the Sheriff or other officer, or his or their security or securities, for the same, within five years next after such disabilities be removed, and not after.

Motion against Sheriff.

Exceptions.

Actions on store accounts.

ART. 1335. [3] All actions or suits founded upon any account for goods, wares or merchandize sold and delivered, or for any articles charged in any store account, shall be commenced and sued within two years next after the cause of such action or suit, and not after, except that in the case of the death of the creditors or debtors, or removal of the debtor before the expiration of said term of two years, the further term of one year, from the death of such creditor or debtor, shall be allowed for the commencement of any such action or suit: (*b*) provided, that in case of the removal of the debtor out of the county where such debt was created, no act of limitations shall run, unless the person removing shall, ten days previous to his removal, put up a notice in writing at the seat of justice of the county from which he may be about to remove, setting forth his intentions to remove.(*c*)

Debtor removing out of county, statute not to run, unless

How accounts shall be kept, and dates of, &c.

ART. 1336. [4] To prevent imposition or deception herein, the respective times or dates of the delivery of the several articles charged in any such account, or in any receipt taken for the delivery of them, shall be particularly specified; and if any merchant or trader shall wilfully postdate any article or articles, in such account, or the receipt taken for the delivery of them, he shall forfeit and pay ten-fold the article or articles so postdated, to be recovered, with cost, before a Justice of the Peace, where the penalty does not amount to one hundred dollars; and by suit in the District Court, where the penalty may amount to that sum or upwards; the whole of which shall go to the informer or plaintiff in the prosecution.(*d*)

(*a*) The statute applies to judgments of the Justices of the Peace. Wahrenberger *v.* Horan, 18 Tex. Rep. 57. An action upon the judgment of any court in this State, upon which execution has issued within the year, will be barred after the lapse of ten years from the last act of legal diligence. Fessenden *v.* Barnett, 9 Tex. Rep. 475. An action on a judgment of a court of the United States is barred in ten years. Reid *v.* Boyd, 13 Tex. Rep. 241.

(*b*) When a portion of the items of an account are barred and a portion not, the plaintiff is entitled to judgment for those not barred. Alford *v.* Cochrane, 7 Tex. Rep. 485. See Love *v.* Doak & Tims, 5 Tex. Rep. 343. This section is limited to actions upon accounts for goods, wares and merchandize, or for articles charged in a store account, and the exception in the section in favor of the creditor cannot be extended to any other causes than those enumerated. Tyson *v.* Britton, 6 Tex. Rep. 222. The exception in the statute as to accounts between merchant and merchant, includes only accounts current, where there are various credits and charges on each side, and not accounts which consist entirely of charges on one side and payments on the other. Judd *v.* Sampson & Co., 13 Tex. Rep. 19. Love *v.* Doak & Tims, 5 Tex. Rep. 343.

(*c*) The proviso that in case of the removal of the debtor out of the county where the debt was created, &c., extends to cases only where the debt is proven to have been created in the county from which the debtor removed. Judd *v.* Sampson & Co., 13 Tex. Rep. 19.

(*d*) The action under this section for postdating items in an account, is abated by the death of the defendant. Watson *v.* Loop, 12 Tex. Rep. 11. In such action the petition should alledge that the defendant was a merchant or trader at the time. Ibid.

ART. 1337. [5] To prevent evasion hereof in regard to the time of the cause of such action or suit, or the time at which such account became due, it is hereby provided, that no recovery shall be had for any article charged in such account, which was entered, charged or delivered for a term of two years or upwards before the commencement of such action or suit, except in the case of the death of the creditor or debtor, before the expiration of one year from the time of such action or suit; and in that case no article shall be allowed which shall appear to have been charged or delivered three years or upwards before the commencement of such action or suit.

Account when barred—if either party die, &c.

ART. 1338. [6] If in any of the said actions or suits, judgment be given for the plaintiff, and the same be afterwards reversed by error, or a verdict passed for the plaintiff, and upon matter alleged in arrest of judgment, the judgment be given against the plaintiff, that he take nothing by his plaint, petition or bill; in all such cases, the party plaintiff, his heirs, executors or administrators, (as the case shall require,) may commence a new action or suit from time to time, within one year next after such judgment reversed, or such judgment given against the plaintiff, and not after.

New action may be commenced in certain cases within a year.

ART. 1339. [7] If any suit be brought against any executor or administrator or other person having charge of the estate of a testator, or of an intestate, for the recovery of a debt due upon an open account, it shall be the duty of the court, before whom suit shall be brought, to cause to be expunged from such account, every item thereof, which shall appear to have been due two years before the death of the testator or intestate. And if any person shall wilfully postdate any such account, he shall forfeit and pay ten-fold the amount of the articles so postdated, to be recovered before a Justice of the Peace, when the penalty incurred shall be less than one hundred dollars, or by suit in the District Court, when the penaly amounts to that sum or upwards.

Suits against executors or administrators, &c.

ART. 1340. [8] Each and every claim for money, which has been due for more than five years, and less than ten years, an action shall be commenced thereon within one year from the passage of this act, and not thereafter; on each and every claim for money due for ten, and less than fifteen years, action shall be commenced within six months from the passage of this act, and not thereafter; on each and every claim for money due for fifteen years and upwards, action shall be commenced within three months from the passage of this act, and not thereafter; and in each of the cases mentioned in this section, the defendant shall be admitted to plead payment, and to support this plea, may rely upon the circumstances, or the presumption arising from the lapse of time.

Suits on certain claims due before the date of this act.

ART. 1341. [4] All foreign judgments, decrees and adjudications, upon which suits shall be brought in the Courts of this Republic, should the same be of four years' standing and upwards, shall be forever barred and prescribed, unless sued on in sixty days from and after the passage of this act. Those under four and over two years, unless sued on in six months; and those under two years, unless sued on in one year: provided, the original cause of action shall remain unimpaired, and may be sued on at the election of the creditor subject to prescription.

Act of June 28, 1845. Took effect from passage.

Suits on foreign judgments or decrees.

ART. 1342. [1] All actions founded upon any account other than open accounts concerning the trade of merchandise between merchant and merchant, their factors and servants, shall be commenced within two years next after the cause of such action shall have accrued, and not afterwards.

Act of Feb. 10, 1852. Took effect April 17, 1852.

Actions founded on accounts.

IV. ON STATUTORY BONDS.

Act of Feb. 5, 1841. Took effect March 17, 1841. When motion to quash, &c., may be made.

ART. 1343. [18] The obligors or any one or more of them, whose name or names appear to any statutory bond, concerning which it is, or shall be by law provided, that it is to be, or shall become a judgment, or have the effect thereof, shall have one year next after the actual or ostensible forfeiture of the same, to move the proper court, to quash said bond, or otherwise; to move for, and have an issue or issues, and a jury to try the same, or any other matter of fact, which on a regular action on such bond might properly defeat or modify a recovery thereon against such obligor or obligors.

Act of March 16, 1848. Took effect April 29, 1848. Suits on appeal bonds pertaining to estates, &c.

ART. 1344. [5] Suits may be commenced in the District Courts, upon all appeal bonds, given in the County Courts, pertaining to the estates of decedents and wards, and upon all bonds given in the District Courts, to remove causes of the estates of decedents and wards, to the District Courts, within four years next after the right of action shall have accrued on said bonds, and not afterwards; saving to persons *non compos mentis*, infants, and *femes covert* two years after their respective disabilities shall be removed.

Act of March 20, 1848. Took effect August 7, 1848. Suits on guardian's bonds.

ART. 1345. [40] All suits and actions upon the bonds of guardians shall be commenced and sued within four years next after the death, removal, resignation or discharge of such guardian, and not thereafter: provided, that infants, married women, and persons of unsound mind shall have at least two years within which to bring such suits after the removal of their respective disabilities.

Act of March 20, 1848. Took effect August 7, 1848. Suits on executor's or administrator's bond.

ART. 1346. [114] All suits on the bond of any executor or administrator shall be commenced and prosecuted within four years next after the death, resignation, removal or discharge of such executor or administrator, and not thereafter: provided, however, that infants, *femes covert*, and persons *non compos mentis*, shall have at least two years within which to institute such suits, after the removal of their respective disabilities.

V. APPEAL, WRIT OF ERROR AND CERTIORARI.

Act of Feb. 5, 1842. Took effect March 17, 1841. Writ of error, supersedeas, &c. may be granted.

ART. 1347. [9] No writ of error or supersedeas shall be granted, to any judgment at law, nor shall a bill of review be granted to any decree pronounced in equity, after two years from the time such judgment or decree shall have been made final.

Act of May 13, 1846. Took effect June 22, 1846. Same subject.

ART. 1348, [142] No writ of error shall be granted after the expiration of two years from the rendition of the judgment. Minors, married women, and persons *non compos mentis*, shall have the same time, or two years after their respective disabilities are removed.

Act of March 20, 1848. Took effect Aug. 7, 1848. Appeal from order of County Court relating to estates, &c.

ART. 1349. [39] Appeals may be taken from any decision, order, judgment or decree of the County Court, in relation to the estates of minors, idiots, lunatics and persons *non compos mentis*, or in relation to their guardians, in the same manner, and under the same rules as provided for appeals from said court in matters relating to the estates of decedents; and any settlement of the account of any guardian may be revised and corrected in the District Court of the county, at any time within two years after such guardian has ceased his duties, upon proof that there was any fraud or mistake in such settlement: provided, that such guardian, or his legal representatives, shall be first cited as in other suits.

Settlement of guardian when revised.

ART. 1349. [11] Any one interested in the estate of a deceased person, may at any time within two years after the settlement by the Chief Justice of any account of the executor or administrator of such estate, have the same revised and corrected by the District Court of the county in which the letters of such executor or administrator were granted, upon making proof before such District Court, that there was any error or fraud in such account or settlement: provided, that he shall first obtain from the Clerk of the court in which such account was settled a transcript of all the papers relating to such account and settlement, and file the same with a petition in the office of the Clerk of said District Court, and cause such executor or administrator, or his legal representatives, to be cited as in other suits in said District Court. Settlement of executor or administrator may be revised.

VI. GENERAL PROVISIONS.

ART. 1350. [11] If during the coverture a sale of any of the lands or slaves of the wife be illegally effected, no limitation shall commence to run during the coverture; and should the wife survive the dissolution of the marriage, she may sue for and recover such property; should the wife survive the dissolution, but not the time allowed by the law of limitations, then the running of such law shall cease till all the children of the deceased mother shall have arrived at the age of majority, or those under that age shall have married, and the heirs of the wife shall have the unexpired time allowed by the law of limitations, within which to institute their suit for the recovery of said property; and if the wife shall not survive the dissolution of the marriage, the laws of limitations shall not commence running, as to the children of the deceased mother, until all the children shall have arrived at the age of majority, or those under that age shall have married. Act of Jan , 1840. Took effect March 16, 1840. If slave of wife be illegally sold, during coverture, limitation not to run during, &c. Running of limitation against the mother shall cease as to children, until, &c.

ART. 1351. [10] Any person absenting himself beyond sea or elsewhere for seven years successively, shall be presumed to be dead, in any cause wherein his death may come in question, unless proof be made that he was alive within that time; but an estate recovered on such presumption, if in a subsequent action or suit the person presumed to be dead, shall be proved to be living, shall be restored to him who shall have been evicted, and he may moreover demand and recover the rents and profits of the estate during such time as he shall be deprived thereof (with lawful interest.) (*a*) Act of Feb. 5, 1841. Took effect March 17, 1841. Presumption of death.

ART. 1352. [11] No law of limitations, except in the cases provided for in the eighth section of this act, shall run against infants, married women, persons imprisoned, or persons of unsound mind, during the existence of their respective disabilities; and when the law of limitations did not commence to run prior to the existence of these disabilities, such persons shall have the same time allowed them after their removal that is allowod to others by this and other laws of limitations now in force. (*b*) Limitation shall not run against certain persons.

ART. 1353. [12] When an action may appear to be barred by a law of limitations, no acknowledgment of the justice of the claim, made subsequent to the time it became due, shall be admitted in evidence to take the case out of the operation of the law, unless such acknowledgment be in writing and signed by the party to be charged thereby. (*c*) Acknowledgment of claim must be in writing and signed.

(*a*) Primm *v.* Stewart, 7 Tex. Rep. 178.

(*b*) Disabilities cannot be tacked so as to present a continuous obstruction to the running of the statute. White *v.* Latimer, 12 Tex. Rep. 61. Ford *v.* Clements, 13 Tex. Rep. 592. Where a female is under 21 years of age and marries, she is then deemed of full age, and the statute commences running from the date of the marriage. White *v.* Latimer, *supra.*

(*c*) This section does not make any alteration in the legal construction to be put upon the acknowledgment, but merely requires a different kind of proof. Webber *v.* Cochrane, 4 Tex. Rep. 31. The phrase "acknowledgment of the justice of the claim," as used in the statute, imports an admission at the time that the claim is subsisting, unaccompanied by other circumstances, the promise to pay is a necessary inference—Ibid. Coles *v.* Kelsey, 2 Tex. Rep. 541.

Action against immigrant barred or discharged by law of country whence he emigrated.

ART. 1354. [13] No action shall be brought against any emigrant of the Republic, to recover a claim which was barred by the law of limitations of that country or State from which he emigrated; nor shall an action be brought to recover money from an emigrant who was released from its payment by the bankrupt or insolvent laws of the country or State from whence he emigrated. (*a*)

Action against persons without Republic at time action accrued or might have been maintained.

ART. 1355. [22] If any person against whom there is or shall be cause of action, is or shall be without the limits of this Republic at the time of the accruing of such action, or at any time during which the same might have been maintained, then the person entitled to such action shall be at liberty to bring the same against such person or persons after his or their return to the Republic: and the time of such persons' absence shall not be accounted, or taken as a part of the time limited by this act. (*b*)

Repeal of Mexican laws, &c., shall not revise claims barred by previous laws.

ART. 1356. [24] The second section to adopt the common law, &c., approved January the twentieth, one thousand eight hundred and forty, which repealed the laws of limitation or prescription then in force, shall not be so construed as to revive any claim which has been barred by said laws; and all claims against which said laws had commenced to run, shall be barred by the lapse of time which would have barred them had those laws continued in force:

Proviso.

provided, the said time be shorter than that by which they would have been barred by other sections of this act. (*c*)

Act of Feb. 5, 1841. Took effect March 17, 1841.

ART. 1357. [1] To prevent difficulty in the construction of the act of limitation, passed at this session of Congress, it is hereby declared that said act applies no less to foreign than to domestic claims.

Act of Feb. 16, 1852. Took effect April 17, 1852.

Death of person, &c., shall stop running of statute until, &c.

ART. 1358. [2] In case of the death of any person against whom there may be cause of action, the statute of limitation shall cease to run against such cause of action until twelve months after such death, unless an administrator or executor shall have sooner qualified, according to law, upon such deceased person's estate; then and in that case, the said statute of limitation shall only cease to run until such qualification.

Death of owner of cause of action, &c.

ART. 1359. [3] In case of the death of any person in whose favor there may be cause of action, the statute of limitation shall cease to run against such cause of action until twelve months after such death, unless an administrator or executor shall have sooner qualified, according to law, upon such deceased person's estate; then and in that case the said statute of limitation shall only cease to run until such qualification.

Debts incurred prior to removal of person to this State, when barred.

ART. 1360. [4] No demand against any person who shall hereafter remove to this State, incurred prior to his removal, shall be barred by the statute of limitation of this State, until he shall have resided in this State for the space of twelve months: provided, that nothing in this section shall be construed to affect the 13th section of an act of limitation, approved February 5th, 1841.

Statute must be pleaded, &c.

ART. 1361. [5] The statute of limitatation of this State shall not be made available to any person in any suit in any of the courts of this State, unless it be specially set forth as a defence in their answer.

(*a*) Gautier *v.* Franklin, 7 Tex. Rep. 732. Smith *v.* Crosby, 2 Tex. Rep. 514.

(*b*) Where a debt is contracted in another country by a person who afterwards removes to this State, the statute is not suspended until his arrival, but runs against the action from the time of the accrual thereof. Snoddy *v.* Cage, 5 Tex. Rep. 106. Love *v.* Doak & Tims, Ibid. 343. Moore *v.* Hendrick, 8 Tex. Rep, 253. The statute, though suspended while the debtor is absent from the State, commences again to run, upon his death, while so absent. Teal *v.* Ayres, Adm'r, 9 Tex. Rep. 588.

(*c*) All claims, against which the laws of prescription in force previous to the adoption of the common law, had commenced to run, were barred by the lapse of time, which would have barred them had those laws continued in force. Pew *v.* Ward, 10 Tex. Rep. 179.

LUNATIC ASYLUM.

Act of Aug. 28, 1856. Took effect Oct. 28, 1856.

Erection of, appropriation for.

ART. 1362. [1] The sum of fifty thousand dollars of the United States bonds, and the interest accruing thereon, now in the Treasury, be appropriated, set apart and applied, under the immediate direction of the Governor, Comptroller and Treasurer, in the erection of a suitable building for a Lunatic Asylum, which building shall be so constructed that it shall be susceptible of any additions that may be hereafter required.

Commissioners to select a site, &c.

ART. 1363. [2] The Governor be, and he is hereby authorized and required to appoint three commissioners, whose duty it shall be to select a proper site for the Asylum, and secure by donation or purchase not less than fifty nor more than one hundred acres of land, which shall not cost the State more than five dollars per acre. The commissioners shall report their proceedings to the Governor within thirty days after their appointment, together with the deed for the land donated or purchased, which deed shall be duly recorded in the proper office, and filed in the office of the Secretary of State. The commissioners shall receive five dollars per day, while in actual service.

Contract for building.

ART. 1364. [3] The Governor, upon receiving the report of the commissioners, shall, with the Comptroller and Treasurer, let out the contract or contracts for the building of the Asylum, under similar restrictions and liabilities (so far as the same may be applicable) which were in force upon said officers, in the erection of the Treasury buildings and Governor's mansion; and the same requirements which were made of the contractors in every respect, so far as the same may be applicable, shall be made from those who contract to do the work necessary in the construction of the Lunatic Asylum.

Superintendent, appointment and qualification of—assistants, &c.

Semi-annual report, &c.

Art. 1370.

ART. 1365. [4] So soon as he may deem it necessary, the Governor shall appoint a suitable Superintendent, who shall be a skillful physician, and experienced in the treatment of lunatics, and such other assistants, male and female, as may be required to carry out the objects of this act; the Superintendent shall have a salary of two thousand dollars annually; he shall report to the Governor semi-annually all the expenses of the Asylum, with such other information as may show the condition of the Asylum and its inmates. The sum of ten thousand dollars, or so much thereof as may be necessary, of the United States bonds, now in the Treasury, and the accruing interest thereon, is hereby set apart for the expenses of said Asylum until the meeting of the next Legislature.

Act of Feb'y 5, 1858. Took effect from passage. Managers appointed.

ART. 1366. [1] The Governor shall appoint five managers for the State Lunatic Asylum, who shall be citizens of the State. Of those first appointed, one shall serve one year, one two years, one three years, and two four years, and their successors shall be appointed for a term of four years, or in case of vacancy during a term, for the unexpired term.

Powers and duties of managers—may discharge officers, except, &c.

ART. 1367. [2] The managers shall serve without compensation. They shall have general direction and control of the property and business of the Asylum. They shall have power to make, with the approval of the Governor, all necessary by-laws and regulations (not inconsistent with the laws of this State,) for the government of the Institution and of its officers, employees and inmates, and for the admission of visitors. They shall prescribe the duties of all persons employed about the Asylum, and determine their salaries, except in cases specially provided for by law; and may at pleasure discharge any person or officer in the Asylum, except the Superintendent. They may, with the concurrence of the Superintendent, appoint an assistant physician. They may take and hold in trust any gift or devise of real or personal estate for the benefit of the Asylum, and shall make such application thereof as the donor or devisor may prescribe. They shall examine the accounts and vouchers of the Superintendent, and approve of such as may be necessary and proper. They shall exercise a careful supervision over the general operations and expenditures of the Asylum, and direct the manner in which its revenues shall be disbursed.

Shall hold meetings, visit Asylum, keep a journal of proceedings, report, &c.

ART. 1368. [3] The managers shall hold quarterly meetings at the Asylum, when a majority shall constitute a quorum for the transaction of its business. One or more of the managers shall visit the Asylum and inspect the same once in every month, or oftener; and they shall keep a full account of their visits and proceedings in a book to be provided for the purpose, and shall make a report to the Governor on the first day of October of each year, setting forth the condition and wants of the Institution.

Treas'r of State shall be Treas'r of, and report, &c.

ART. 1369. [4] The Treasurer of the State shall act as Treasurer of the Asylum, and shall collect all its dues, and pay out its revenues only in conformity with the laws of the State, and the by-laws of the Institution; and he and the sureties on his official bond shall be liable for any violation or neglect of duty. He shall make a report to the Governor of the condition of its finances and expenditures, on the first day of October of each year.

Superintendent, qualification of, term of office, &c.

ART. 1370. [5] The Superintendent shall be a married man and a skillful physician, experienced in the treatment of the insane. He shall continue in office for the term of four years from the time of his appointment, unless sooner removed by the Governor for incompetency, refusal to discharge any of his duties, or for any misconduct on his part, which might render it improper for him to continue longer in office. He shall reside in the Asylum with his family when required to do so by the managers.

Duties of Superintendent.

ART. 1371. [6] The Superintendent shall be the Chief Executive and medical officer of the Asylum, and shall (subject to the by-laws,) have care and control over everything connected therewith. He shall attend to the enforcement of the laws and by-laws, and see that all persons connected with the Institution faithfully and diligently perform the duties assigned them. He shall, with the consent of the managers, employ such officers, attendants and other persons as may be required for the service of the Institution, and may at pleasure discharge them. He shall receive and discharge patients, and shall annually by the first day of October, cause an inventory of all the personal property belonging to the Asylum to be made out, with an estimate of the value of each article, and submit the same to the managers. He shall be

Ex-officio secretary of, &c.

ex-officio Secretary of the Board of Managers, and shall superintend repairs and improvements, and see that the money intrusted to him is properly and economically expended, and shall keep an accurate account of the same. He shall be the responsible disbursing officer of the Institution, and shall give bond for the faithful performance of his duties, made payable to the State in the sum of the ten thousand dollars, with two or more sufficient sureties, to be approved by the Treasurer.

Bond.

Register to be kept.

ART. 1372. [7] The Superintendent shall keep a register of all patients received and discharged, and of the operations of the Asylum, which may be required by the by-laws, and report the general results to the Governor on the first day of October of each year.

Mode of proceeding where Chief Justice is informed of an idiot or lunatic in his county.

ART. 1373. [8] If information in writing be given to any Chief Justice of a county, that any person in his county is an idiot, or lunatic, or *non compos mentis*, and that the welfare of himself or of others requires that he be placed under restraint, and said Chief Justice shall believe such information to be true, he shall order such person to be brought before him, and twelve competent jurors of the county to be summoned, who shall be sworn to inquire and a true verdict render, whether such person is of sound mind or not; whereupon, the matter shall be tried, and if the jury shall return a verdict that the person is not of sound mind, and that he should be placed under restraint, the same shall be recorded, and the Chief Justice shall thereupon order him to be sent to the Lunatic Asylum, unless some friend (to whom the Chief Justice in his discretion may deliver such person,) will give bond payable to the State, with sufficient security, to be approved by said Chief Justice, with the condition to restrain and take proper care of such person, until the cause of confinement shall cease, or he is delivered to the Sheriff of the county, or other person, to be proceeded with according to law. Upon the trial and inquiry herein provided for, the examination of the insane and the testimony of the witnesses shall be reduced to writing and filed. The proceedings of the Chief Justice in relation to *insane* persons shall be minuted in the record of his court appertaining to estates of deceased persons, &c.

Duty of, on ordering person to Asylum.

ART. 1374. [9] It shall be the duty of the Chief Justice, on ordering a person to be sent to the Asylum, to ascertain,

1. The number of his family, if he has one, and their ability to maintain themselves;

2. The value of his estate, if any; and,

3. The ability of persons legally liable for his support. And he shall make an order specifying the amount which his guardian, if any, shall pay out of the estate of such person, for his support in the Asylum; and shall cause a minute to be made of the facts ascertained.

Before sending person to Asylum, shall forward copy of proceedings to Superintendent.

ART. 1375. [10] Before sending a patient to the Asylum, the Chief Justice shall, without delay, cause authenticated copies to be made of the proceedings, evidence and decree of the original inquisition, and of the record of all subsequent inquisitions and orders, to be forwarded by mail to the Superintendent of the Lunatic Asylum; and in all cases, except those of great emergency, shall, before sending said person, ascertain from the Superintendent by application in writing, that there is a vacancy, and that the officers of the Asylum cannot send for him. Thereupon, the Chief Justice shall issue his warrant to the Sheriff, or other suitable individual, ordering him to convey said person to the Asylum without delay; and when satisfied of the necessity for assistants, he shall prescribe in such warrant the number to be allowed, which in no case shall exceed two; and he shall see that the patient is provided with two good and full suits of summer, and one of winter clothing.

Insane person charged or convicted, &c., shall be sent to, &c. ART. 1376. [11] If any person charged with or convicted of any criminal offence, be found to be insane in the court before which he is so charged, or convicted, said court shall order him to be conveyed to and retained in the State Lunatic Asylum; and he shall be received and retained, until removed by order of the court by which he was committed to the Asylum.

Who shall not be sent to, &c. ART. 1377. [12] No idiot who can be safely kept in the county to which he belongs, nor any person laboring under a contagious or infectious disease, shall be sent to the Asylum.

How admitted, and terms of admission. ART. 1378. [13] Any person may be admitted into and retained in the Asylum as a patient:

1. Upon the order of any court or Judge authorized to send persons to the Asylum.

2. Upon the written request of his legal guardian, near relative, or friend, if he has no guardian, or of the persons or of counties that may be legally liable for their support. Such request shall set forth the name, age and residence of the persons for whom admission is requested, and such other particulars of the case as may be required by the Managers, and shall be signed under oath, and accompanied with a certificate dated within two months, under oath, signed by one respectable physician, of the fact of his being insane; and also, a certificate from the Chief Justice of the county, as to the respectability of the physician so certifying: provided, that for private patients, the friends shall pay six months' board, always in advance, and give such bond and security for the payment of the expenses of such patient, as may from time to time be required by the by-laws of the Asylum. (Private patients.)

Preference of admission, to whom given. ART. 1379. [14] If applications shall be made for the admission of more patients than can be received in the Asylum, preferences, in all instances, shall be given to those made under order of court over private applications; and of the former, to those for cases of less than one years' duration over chronic cases.

Patients, how and when discharged. ART. 1380. [15] Any patient except such as have been committed under the provisions of the eleventh section of this act, may be discharged upon the recommendation of the Superintendent, approved by two of the Managers. Incurable and harmless patients, and such others as the Superintendent may deem proper, may in like manner be discharged whenever it is necessary to make room for recent cases, or when, for any other cause, it may seem expedient.

When discharged uncured. ART. 1381. [16] When the patient is discharged uncured, the Superintendent shall see that a suitable guard is provided to carry him to his friends, or to the county from which he was sent. No patient shall be discharged without suitable clothing, or without money to pay his necessary expenses home.

Rates of boarding. ART. 1382. [17] The amount to be paid for the board of patients admitted into the Hospital, shall be at the rate of two dollars per week for each person supported by the county, and for every other person that the Managers may find not to be possessed of estate sufficient to support him and his family, (or if he has no family himself,) under the visitation of insanity, or that the persons legally liable for his support are in indigent circumstances. For all other persons the Superintendent may make a special contract, at any rate not less than five dollars per week. In all cases, the expenses of removing the patient from the Asylum home, and for the necessary clothing with which he shall be furnished by the Asylum, if not otherwise provided, shall be extra charges. The expenses of persons committed under the eleventh section of this act, shall be defrayed by the State, and the excess of the expenses of those (Expense of removing patient from, &c., extra charges.)

committed by order of the court, and of other patients, over and above what is required in the foregoing rates, shall in like manner be defrayed by the State.

Expense, &c., of persons admitted upon order of Chief Justice, &c.

ART. 1383. [18] The expenses of clothing, maintenance in the Asylum, and removal home therefrom, of every person received upon the order of any Chief Justice, shall be paid by the Treasurer of the county from which he was sent, when and as they become due and payable, according to the by-laws of the Asylum. And the County Court shall have the right to require every individual legally liable for the support of such patient, to reimburse the amount so paid, with interest from the time of paying the same.

Persons chargeable, and about to become chargeable to county, &c.

ART. 1384. [19] No person of unsound mind who is unable to support himself, shall become chargeable to any county, unless he has acquired a legal settlement therein, and shall not be deemed to have acquired such settlement, unless he shall have resided one year in the State, and six months in the county. When any person of unsound mind shall come into the county, who is likely to become chargeable thereto, the Chief Justice of such county may, by warrant, cause such person to be removed to the county wherein he was last legally settled, unless he be so sick or disabled that he cannot be removed without danger of life, in which case he shall be provided for at the expense of the county wherein he is, until he can be so removed.

Duty of County Court in such cases.

ART. 1385. [20] It shall be the duty of the County Court of each county, that shall be chargeable with the support of one or more persons of unsound mind, to make provision therefor in its annual levy of the county tax.

Escape and return of patients.

ART. 1386. [21] If any patient confined in the Asylum shall escape therefrom, it shall be the duty of the Sheriff of any county in which he may be found, to apprehend him; and if required by the Superintendent or Chief Justice, to take him back to the Asylum.

Compensation for carrying patients to, &c.

ART. 1387. [22] The officer complying with the order of the court, or the Superintendent, in carrying a patient to the Asylum, shall, on presentation of the proper vouchers, be paid out of the treasury of the Asylum, at the rate of ten cents per mile for himself, and each guard, (authorized by the court) going and returning, besides tolls and ferriages, and the same for the patient going.

Managers not to be interested in contracts, &c.

ART. 1388. [23] No Manager or other person connected with the institution, shall sell any articles to the Asylum, or have any interest in any contract therewith.

MARITAL RIGHTS.

I. MARRIAGE CONTRACTS.

II. SEPARATE PROPERTY.

III. COMMUNITY PROPERTY.

IV. GENERAL PROVISIONS.

I. MARRIAGE CONTRACT.

Act of Jan. 20, 1840. Took effect March 16, 1840. Marriage contracts may be made, &c., limitations upon, &c.

ART. 1389. [5] Parties intending to enter into the marriage state, may enter into what stipulations they please, provided they be not contrary to good morals, or to some rule of law; and in no case shall they enter into any agreement, or make any renunciation, the object of which would be to alter the legal orders, of descent either with respect to themselves in what concerns the inheritance of their children or posterity which either may have by any other person, or in respect to their common children—nor shall they make any valid agreement to impair the legal rights of the husband over the person of the wife, or the persons of their common children.

Before whom made. Minor may make, &c., when.

ART. 1390. [6] Every matrimonial agreement must be made by an act before a Notary Public and two witnesses; the minor capable of contracting matrimony, may give his or her consent to any agreement which this contract is susceptible of: provided such agreement be made by the written consent of both parents, if both be living; if not, by that of the survivor; if both be dead, then by the written consent of the minor's guardian.(*a*)

Not to be altered, after.

ART. 1391. [7] No matrimonial agreement shall be altered after the celebration of the marriage.

Not good against third persons, unless, &c.

ART. 1392. [8] When the wife, by a marriage contract, may reserve to herself any property or rights to property (whether such rights be in esse or expectancy), for such reservation to be valid as to the subsequent purchasers or creditors of her husband, the said contract must be acknowledged by her husband or proved by at least one witness, and recorded in the Clerk's Office of the County Court of the county in which said married parties may reside.

II. SEPARATE PROPERTY.

Act of March 13, 1848. In force from passage. What shall be the separate property of husband. Of the wife.

ART. 1393. [2] All property, both real and personal, of the husband, owned or claimed by him before marriage, and that acquired afterwards by gift, devise, or descent, as also the increase of all lands or slaves thus acquired, shall be his separate property. All property, both real and personal, of the wife, owned or claimed by her before marriage, and that acquired afterwards by gift, devise, or descent, as also the increase of all lands or slaves thus acquired, shall be the separate property of the wife: provided, that during the marriage the husband shall have the sole management of all such property.(*b*)

(*a*) Burr *v.* Wilson, 18 Tex. Rep. 367. Fitts *v.* Fitts, 14 Tex. Rep. 443.

(*b*) The private property of each partner in the matrimonial union, must, as a general rule, bear its own charges and expences. Womack *v.* Womack, 8 Tex. Rep. 397. The object of this act was to secure the separate property of the wife, and its object would be defeated if she could bind it by her separate contracts during coverture. Kavanaugh *v.* Brown, 1 Tex. Rep. 481. The common law rule respecting the wife's capacity to contract, was not changed by our statute regulating marital rights. Ibid. The admissions of the husband cannot be received in prejudice of the rights of the wife. McKay *v.* Treadwell, 8 Tex. Rep. 176. Where the husband has attempted to convey away the separate property of the wife, the suit should be brought in the name of the wife alone, the husband being joined with the other parties as a co-defendant. Ibid. See note (*a*), page 72. Cartwright *v.* Cartwright, 18 Tex. Rep. 626. The husband may make a donation to the wife, which, if done without injury to creditors, will be her separate property. Higgins *v.* Johnson, 20 Tex. Rep. 389. Reynolds *v.* Lansford, 16 Tex. Rep. 286. The wife may hold separate property without the intervention of a trustee. Reynolds *v.* Lansford, *supra*. The intention of the parties at the time of the execution of the deed, where the purchase money was separate property, is to determine its complexion and character. Smith *v.* Strahon, 16 Tex. Rep. 314. When the separate property of the wife has undergone muta-

III. COMMUNITY PROPERTY.

[*See Estates of Deceased Persons, Articles* 810 *to* 816.—*Descents and Distributions.*]

Act of Jan. 20, 1840. Took effect March 16, 1840.

Property owned at dissolution of marriage, &c.

ART. 1394. [12] All the effects which both the husband and wife reciprocally possess at the time the marriage may be dissolved, shall be regarded as common effects or gains, unless the contrary be satisfactorily proved.

Act of March 13, 1848.

What shall be.

ART. 1395. [3] All property acquired by either husband or wife, during the marriage, except that which is acquired in the manner specified in the second section of this act, shall be deemed the common property of the husband and wife, and during the coverture may be disposed of by the husband only; it shall be liable for the debts of the husband, and for the debts of the wife, contracted during the marriage for necessaries; and upon the dissolution of the marriage by death, the remainder of such common property shall go to the survivor, if the deceased have no child or children; but if the deceased have a child or children, the survivor shall be entitled to one-half of said property, and the other half shall pass to the child or children of the deceased.(*a*)

IV. GENERAL PROVISIONS.

How effects of wife may be sued for.

ART. 1396. [9] The husband may sue, either alone or jointly with his wife, for the recovery of any effects of the wife; and in case he fail or neglect so to do, she may, by the authority of the court, sue for such effects in her name.(*b*)

Where husband fails to support his wife out of proceeds of her separate property.

ART. 1397. [10] Should the husband refuse or fail to support his wife from the proceeds of the lands or slaves she may have, or fail to educate her children as the fortune of the wife would justify, she may, in either case, complain to the County Court, who, upon satisfactory proof, shall decree that so much of such proceeds shall be paid to the wife, for the support of herself and for the nurture and education of her children, as the court may deem necessary.(*c*)

tions, it is indispensible to maintain its separate character, that it be clearly and indisputably traced and identified. Chapman *v.* Allen, 15 Tex. Rep. 278. Rose *v.* Houston, 11 Tex. Rep. 324. Houston *v.* Curl, 8 Tex. Rep. 239. When property is acquired by husband or wife while in the course of migration to this State, and they remove to and reside in this State, the right to such property is regulated by the laws of this State. The State *v.* Barrow, 14 Tex. Rep. 179. See Avery *v.* Avery, 12 Tex. Rep. 54. If the separate funds of either party be employed in the purchase of property, the property so acquired is separate. Houston *v.* Curl, 8 Tex. Rep. 239.

(*a*) Lands acquired by the husband as the head of a family, under the act of January 4th, 1839, formed a part of the community. Wilkinson *v.* Wilkinson, 20 Tex. Rep. 237. Where land is purchased, the funds of the community and the deed is taken in the name of the wife, the presumption is that the land remains community property. But such presumption may be rebutted by proof that the husband declared at the time that his intentions in taking the deed in his wife's name was to make the land her separate property. Higgins *v.* Johnson. 20 Tex. Rep. 389. The increase of cattle during the marriage belonging to the wife, is community property. Howard *v.* York, 20 Tex. Rep. 670. If the husband abandons the wife, the power of managing and selling the common property passes to her. Fullerton *v.* Doyle, 18 Tex. Rep. 3. Check *v.* Bellows. 17 Tex. Rep. 613. Wright *v.* Hays, 10 Tex. Rep. 130. Property acquired by purchase during coverture, by either party, is presumed to be community property, whether the consideration was services rendered or money paid by either party. Chapman *v.* Allen, 15 Tex. Rep. 278. The rights of the husband and wife to property acquired during coverture, are precisely equivalent, the only difference being that he has the management and control of it for the benefit of both. Wright *v.* Hays, 10 Tex. Rep. 130. Property purchased during the marriage is presumed to be community, whether the conveyance be made to the husband or wife separately, or to both of them jointly. Houston *v.* Curl, 8 Tex. Rep. 239. This presumption may be rebutted by clear and satisfactory evidence that the purchase was made with the separate funds of either, in which case it remains the separate property of the party whose funds were employed in the acquisition. Ibid. The community does not embrace property received by either husband or wife in payment of money due them in their separate right; nor does it embrace the increase of slaves owned by either at the time of the marriage or acquired afterwards in his or her individual right. McIntyre *v.* Chappell, 4 Tex. Rep. 187.

(*b*) In a suit by the wife alone, it should be averred and proved that her husband neglected or refused to join her in the suit. McIntyre *v.* Chappell, 2 Tex. Rep. 378. Mitchell *v.* Wright, 4 Tex. Rep. 283. This need not be averred or proved where, by the unauthorized act of the husband, it becomes necessary that suit should be brought against a third person, for her separate property. In that case it is not necessary that the husband should join in the suit, nor that she should obtain the permission of the court to sue alone.—O'Brien *v.* Hilburn, 9 Tex. Rep. 297.

(*c*) Cartwright *v.* Hollis, 5 Tex. Rep. 152.

Provisions as to time of marriage, and what law applies.

ART. 1398. [13] Marriages that may be entered into in this Republic after the passage of this law, shall be governed by the provisions of the same. The marital rights of persons married in other countries, who may remove here after the passage of this act, shall, in regard to property acquired in this Republic during the marriage, be regulated by the provisions of the same. The marital rights of persons married here, before the passage of this act, or of persons married in another country, who removed here before its passage, shall be regulated by the law as it aforetime was.(*a*)

Act of March 13, 1848. Took effect from passage.

Married woman deemed of full age.

ART. 1399. [1] Every female under the age of twenty-one years, who shall marry in accordance with the laws of this State, shall, from and after the time of such marriage, be deemed to be of full age, and shall have all the rights and privileges to which she would have been entitled had she been, at the time of her marriage, of full age.(*b*)

Husband and wife may be jointly sued, &c. when.

ART. 1400 [4] The husband and wife may be jointly sued for all debts contracted by the wife, for necessaries furnished herself or children, and for all expenses which may have been incurred by the wife for the benefit of her separate property.(*c*)

Execution against separate property of wife may be ordered, when.

ART. 1401. [5] Upon the trial of any suit as provided for in the fourth section of this act, if it shall appear to the satisfaction of the court and jury, that the debts so contracted, or expenses so incurred, were for the purposes enumerated in said section; and also that the debts so contracted, or expenses so incurred, were reasonable and proper, the court shall decree that execution may be levied upon either the common property, or the separate property of the wife, at the discretion of the plaintiff.(*c*)

Third and fourth sections of act of 1840 repealed, &c.

ART. 1402. [6] The third and fourth sections of "An act to adopt the common law of England, to repeal certain Mexican laws, and to regulate the marital rights of parties," approved 20th January, 1840, be and the same are hereby repealed; and that nothing contained in this act shall be so construed as to effect any other sections of said act than the said third and fourth sections; but that any other section of said act that may control or affect the said third or fourth sections, shall have the like control and effect over the provisions of this act.

(*a*) Where the place of domicil of both parties is the same at the time of the marriage, the laws of that place control the disposition of personal property possessed by the parties, at the time of the marriage, or acquired by them subsequent thereto and before their change of domicil. McIntyre *v.* Chappell, 4 Tex. Rep. 187. But after their removal to this State, their rights to all property acquired in it, must be governed by our laws. Ibid. See Blanchet *v.* Dugat, 5 Texas Rep. 507.

(*b*) This section applies to marriages which took place before the passage of the act, but not so as to affect or legalize acts done before that time. Chubb *v.* Johnson, 11 Tex. Rep. 469. The statute of limitations commences running from the time of her marriage.—White *v.* Latimer, 12 Tex. Rep. 61.

(*c*) In order to charge the separate property of the wife, under the statute, it is necessary for the plaintiff to bring his case within the terms of the statute. Brown *v.* Ector, 19 Tex. Rep. 346. In order to hold the separate property of the wife liable, under the statute, for necessaries for herself and her children, the debt should be contracted by the wife personally; and if it be made by an agent, her assent must appear; and if the authority arise only by implication, the circumstances must be clear and strong upon which such authority is to be presumed; and the debt so contracted must also be reasonable and proper. Christmas *v.* Smith, 10 Tex. Rep. 123. It is not sufficient that the articles purchased were necessaries for the family. Ibid. A necessary for the husband as a member of the family, will not be chargeable against the wife's separate property, under the statute. Ibid. McFadden *v.* Lockhart, 20 Tex. Rep. 374. The assent of the husband is unnecessary to enable the wife to charge her separate property with debts contracted by her for her support, or for the benefit of her separate property. Booth *v.* Cotton, 13 Tex. Rep. 359. For the powers of the husband over the wife's separate property, and authority to charge the same, see Milburn *v.* Walker, 11 Tex. Rep. 329. The voluntary acts and representations of the wife, made to deceive, and which do deceive others to their prejudice, in regard to her separate property, will be binding upon her. Cravens *v.* Booth, 8 Tex. Rep. 243.—O'Brien *v.* Hilburn, 9 Tex. Rep. 297. The husband is bound to support the wife out of his own property, if able to do so, without resorting to her separate property. Callahan, *v* Patterson, 14 Tex. Rep. 61.

MARKS AND BRANDS.

ART. 1403 [1] Every person in this State who has cattle, hogs, sheep, or goats, shall have an ear-mark and brand, differing from the ear-mark and brand of his neighbors, which ear-mark and brand shall be recorded by the clerk of the County Court, where such cattle, hogs, sheep, or goats, shall be; and no person shall use more than one brand, but may record his brand in as many counties as he may think necessary.

Act of March 20, 1848. Took effect April 29, 1848.

Persons owning hogs, &c., to have ear-mark and brand recorded.

ART. 1404. [2] Cattle shall be marked with the ear-mark, or branded with the brand of the owner, on or before they are twelve months old; hogs, sheep, and goats shall be marked with the ear-mark of the owner on or before they are six months old.

When stock shall be branded, &c.

ART. 1405. [3] If any dispute shall arise about any ear-mark or brand, it shall be decided by reference to the book of marks and brands kept by the clerk of the County Court; and the ear-mark and brand of the oldest date shall have the preference.

Disputes as to, how settled.

ART. 1406. [4] It shall be the duty of the clerks of the County Courts in the respective counties of this State, to keep a well-bound book, in which they shall record the marks or brands of each individual who may apply to them for that purpose; noting in every instance the date on which the brand or mark is recorded; which record shall be subject to the examination of every citizen of the county, at all reasonable office hours, free of charge for such examination.

Record book of marks and brands.

ART. 1407. [5] No brands, except such as are recorded by the officers named in this act, shall be recognised in law as any evidence of ownership, of the cattle, horses, or mules upon which the same may be used.

Brands not recorded.

ART. 1408. [6] Minors owning cattle or hogs, separate from that of the father or guardian, may have a brand and mark, which shall be recorded; the father or guardian shall be responsible for the proper use of such mark and brand of any such minor.

Minors may have brand.

ART. 1409. [7] Persons who have heretofore recorded their mark or brand shall not be required to have the same recorded again under this act in the same county.

Previous record of brand.

MARRIAGE.

ART. 1410. [3] All regular ordained Ministers of the Gospel, Judges of the

Act of June 5, 1837. Took effect from passage.

District Courts, Justices of the County Courts, and all Justices of the Peace of the several counties of this Republic be, and are hereby authorized to celebrate the rites of matrimony between all persons legally authorized to marry: provided, that males under fourteen and females under twelve shall not marry.

License from clerk of County Court.

ART. 1411. [4] Any person desirous of marrying shall apply to the clerk of the County Court, and shall receive from him a license directed to all persons authorized by this law to celebrate the rites of matrimony, which shall be sufficient authority for any one of such persons to celebrate such marriage.

Not to issue without consent of parent or guardian, when.

ART. 1412. [5] No clerk shall issue a license without the consent of the parents or guardians of the parties applying, unless the parties so applying shall be in the case of the male, twenty-one years of age, and in the female eighteen years of age.

License to be recorded. Return of license, &c.

ART. 1413.]6] The said clerk shall record all licenses so issued by him, in a well bound book kept for that purpose; and it shall also be the duty of the persons solemnizing the rites of matrimony to endorse the same on the license, and make return of the same to the office of the clerk of the County Court, within sixty days after the celebration as aforesaid; which return shall also be recorded as aforesaid.

Fee for license.

ART. 1414. [7] For each license so issued the clerk shall charge and receive one dollar.

Act of March 18, 1848. Took effect from passage.

Children of persons subsequ'ntly marrying, &c. Of marriages null in law.

ART. 1415. [10] Where a man having by a woman a child or children, shall afterwards intermarry with such woman, such child or children, if recognised by him, shall thereby be legitimated and made capable of inheriting his estate. The issue also in marriages deemed null in law, shall nevertheless be legitimate.

MECHANICS' LIEN.

I. GENERALLY.

Act of Jan. 23, 1839. Took effect from passage.

Mechanics have a lien, to what extent.

ART. 1416. [1] From and after the passage of this act, master builders and mechanics of every denomination, contracting in writing to put up and erect buildings of any or every description, shall have a lien in the nature of a mortgage on all such buildings as they may put up or erect, or work upon, and also upon the tract, parcel, or lot of land upon which such building or buildings shall be put up and erected, until the price or compensation for services and for materials found shall be fully paid and satisfied, unless a contrary stipulation be made and agreed upon at the time it is entered into:(a)

(a) Where a mechanic furnished material and built a house for another, and the latter moved into it and occupied it as a homestead, it was held that the former retained no lien upon it. It would have been different had the parties contracted under the terms of the statute for a lien upon the house. Merchant *v.* Perez, 11 Tex. Rep. 20.

provided, always, that such lien shall not have a priority over *bona fide* mortgages or legal incumbrances existing anterior to the time of the contract being made, if the said mortgages or legal incumbrances shall duly be recorded according to law: provided, also, that in all cases such builder or mechanic shall have an exclusive lien on all improvements made by him, to the extent of his claim for the same.

ART. 1417. [1] The second section of the above recited act be so amended as to read as follows, to wit: that every contract made and entered into as aforesaid shall be recorded in the County Clerk's office of the county where such building shall have been erected, within thirty days after the contract is made, or otherwise said lien shall be inoperative as to all persons without notice of its existence.

Act of March 15, 1848. Took effect April 29, 1848. Contract to be recorded within.

ART. 1418. [3] When suit shall be brought by any master builder or master builders, mechanic or mechanics, upon any contract made, executed and recorded as aforesaid, and a judgment or decree shall be rendered in favor of such master builder or mechanic, execution for the amount of the same may may be levied upon the tract, parcel or lot of land upon which such building or buildings have been put up and erected, as well as upon the buildings and improvements thereupon erected and made, and all the right, title and interest which the defendant had in and to the said tract, parcel or lot of ground at the time the contract was entered into, as well as the buildings and improvements erected and made thereon, may be sold to satisfy the judgment or decree: provided, nevertheless, that nothing in this act contained shall prevent such master builder or mechanic from levying his said execution upon any other property belonging to the person or persons against whom such judgment or decree shall have been rendered.

Act of Jan. 23, 1839. Took effect from passage. Execution in favor of, how levied.

II. IN INCORPORATED CITIES.

ART. 1419 [1] Every mechanic, workmen or other person, doing or performing any work, or furnishing any kind of materials which are used toward the erection, construction or finishing any building erected under a contract in writing between the owner and builder or other person, whether such work or materials shall be performed or furnished as journeyman, laborer, cartman, sub-contractor, or otherwise, and whose demand for work and labor done and performed, and for materials furnished towards the erection of such buildings, has not been paid and satisfied, may deliver to the owner of such building an attested account of the amount and value of the work and labor, or materials, thus performed or furnished, and remaining unpaid; and thereupon such owner shall retain out of his subsequent payment to the contractor, the amount of such work and labor or materials, for the benefit of the person so performing or furnishing the same.

Act of Feb. 5, 1844. Took effect March 16, 1844. Under workmen and material men may notify owner to retain, &c.

ART. 1420. [2] Whenever any such account of labor performed, or materials furnished, on a building erected under a contract in writing as aforesaid, shall be placed in the hands of the owner of such building, or his authorized agent, it shall be the duty of such owner or agent to furnish his contractor with a copy of such papers, in order that if there shall be any disagreement between such contractor and his creditor, they may, by amicable adjustment between themselves, or by arbitration, ascertain the true sum due; and if the contractor shall not within ten days after the receipt of such papers, give the owner written notice that he intends to dispute the claim, or if in ten days after giving such notice he shall refuse or neglect to have the matter adjusted as

Owner shall notify contractor thereof. Contractor failing to give notice of intention to dispute claim, &c.

aforesaid, he shall be considered as assenting to the demand, and the owner shall pay the same when it becomes due.

When arbitrators shall be chosen. Quære: whether constitutional? ART. 1421. [3] If such contractor shall dispute the claim of his journeyman, or other persons, for work and labor performed, or materials furnished as aforesaid, and if the matter cannot be amicably adjusted between themselves, it shall be submitted, on the agreement of the parties, to the arbitrament of three disinterested persons, one to be chosen by each of the parties, and a third by the two thus chosen; and the decision in writing of such three persons shall be final and conclusive in the case submitted.

If contractor does not pay award within ten days, &c. ART. 1422. [4] Whenever the amount due shall be adjusted and ascertained as above provided, and if the contractor shall not, within ten days after it is so adjusted and ascertained, pay the sum due to his creditor, with the costs incurred, the owner shall pay the same out of the fund, as above provided, and which amount due may be recovered from the said owner by the creditor of such contractor in an action for money had and received to the use of said creditor, and to the extent in value of any balance due by the owner to his contractor, under the contract with him, at the time of the first notice given as aforesaid, or subsequently accruing to such contractor under the same, if such amount shall be less than the sum due from the said contractor to his creditor.

Where owner by collusion pays contractor in advance. ART. 1423. [5] If, by collusion or otherwise, the owner of any building erected by a contract in writing as aforesaid, shall pay to his contractor any money in advance of the sum due on said contract, and if the amount still due to the contractor, after such payment has been made, shall be insufficient to satisfy the demand made in conformity with this act, for work and labor done and performed, or for materials furnished, the owner shall be liable to the amount that would have been due at the time of his receiving the account of such work or materials, in the same manner as if no such payment had been made: provided, that the provisions of this act shall only apply to incorporated cities. This act to apply to, &c.

III. ON DOMESTIC VESSELS.

Act of Feb. 3, 1848. Took effect from passage. Lien on vessel, when. ART. 1424. [1] Every person who may furnish supplies or materials, or do repairs or labor, for or on account of any domestic vessel, owned in whole or in part in this State, shall have a lien on such vessel, her tackle, apparel, furniture, and freight-money, for the security and payment of the same.

Not to affect law of lien for seaman's wages. ART. 1425. [2] The provisions of the first section of this act shall not be construed to alter or affect in any way the general law regulating the liens of seamen on foreign vessels.

MILITIA.

I. GENERALLY.

Act of April 21, 1846. Took effect June 22, 1846.

Who shall do military duty

ART. 1426. [1] Every able-bodied free male inhabitant of this State, between the ages of eighteen and forty-five years, shall be liable to perform military duty, except as herein provided; but no person shall be called upon to perform military duty who shall not, at the time, have resided at least one month in the State, and ten days within the bounds of the company to which he belongs, except in cases of actual or threatened invasion; in which case he shall perform such duty as may be required of other persons, and shall be subject to like fines and penalties.

Persons exempt

ART. 1427. [2] Judges of the Supreme, District, and Probate Courts, Secretary of State, Auditor, Treasurer, and Comptroller, of the State, Clerks of the Supreme and District Courts, Justices of the Peace, Postmasters who have the care of the mails of the United States, Post-riders, Public Millers, Ferrymen on public roads, Teachers and Professors in Academies, shall be exempt from military duty, except in cases of imminent danger, insurrection or invasion.

Division of militia.

ART. 1428. [3] The militia of the State shall be divided into, and compose five divisions. The first division to be composed of the counties of Fannin, Lamar, Red River and Bowie; the second division shall be composed of the counties of Harrison, Shelby, San Augustine, Nacogdoches, Rusk, Houston and Sabine; the third division shall be composed of the counties of Jasper, Jefferson, Liberty, Galveston, Harris, Montgomery, Robertson and Brazos; the fourth division, of the counties of Brazoria, Fort Bend, Austin, Washington, Milam, Travis, Bastrop, Fayette, Colorado and Matagorda; the fifth division shall be composed of the counties of Jackson, Victoria, Gonzales, Bexar, Goliad, Refugio and San Patricio; and each division shall consist of two brigades. The first brigade in the first division shall consist of the counties of

Fannin and Lamar, and the second brigade in the first division, of the counties of Red River and Bowie; and the first brigade in the second division, of the counties of Harrison, Shelby, San Augustine and Sabine, and the second, of the counties of Rusk, Nacogdoches and Houston; and the first brigade in the third division, of the counties of Jasper, Jefferson, Liberty and Galveston, and the second brigade, of the counties of Harris, Montgomery, Robertson and Brazos; and the first brigade in the fourth division, of the counties of Brazoria, Fort Bend, Austin, Washington and Milam, and the second, of the counties of Travis, Bastrop, Fayette, Colorado and Matagorda; and the first brigade in the fifth division, of the counties of Jackson, Victoria and Gonzales, and the second, of the counties of Bexar, Goliad, Refugio and San Patricio; each of which shall be commanded by a Brigadier-General.

Division of militia of each county. ART. 1429.* [4] The militia of each county, when the number of persons therein subject to military duty shall be sufficient to constitute two battalions as hereinafter provided, shall constitute one regiment; but when the number of militia-men in any county shall not be sufficient to constitute two battalions, the militia of such county shall constitute a separate battalion to be formed into independent companies, as may be found most convenient, and when the number in any county shall exceed the whole number hereinafter required to constitute a full regiment, exclusive of any independent companies which may be raised in such county, the same may be divided into two regiments by the Brigadier-General commanding the brigade to which such county may belong, in such manner as he shall direct; each battalion shall consist of not more than four nor less than two companies, and each company, of not more than one hundred nor less than thirty-two non-commissioned officers and privates; and the regiments and battalions shall be numbered by the Commander-in-chief and arranged in numerical order.

Rank of officers. ART. 1430. [5] All commissioned officers shall rank according to their grades, and the date of their commissions; but when officers of the same grade are elected or appointed on the same day, a difference in the date of their commissions shall not determine their rank; the rank of all the field or general officers of this State being of the same grade, and who are elected or appointed on the same day, under the provisions of this Act for the government and organization of the militia of this State, shall be determined by lot to be drawn by the Adjutant-General in the presence of the Governor and Secretary of State; which duty he is required to perform as soon as practicable, and immediately thereafter to transmit to each officer so drawn, the result of such drawing; and it shall be the duty of the Adjutant-General to make an entry in a book kept by him for that purpose, of the grade and rank of each officer, whose rank is determined as specified in this Act.

Same subject. ART. 1431. [6] The rank of Captains and subaltern officers which may hereafter be elected on the same day belonging to the same regiment, shall be determined by lot drawn in presence of the Colonel commandant; and the Adjutant shall make a record of the grade and rank of each officer whose rank is so determined; and each regiment shall be commanded by one Colonel, and each separate battalion and the first battalion in each regiment by a Lieutenant-Colonel; the second battalion in each regiment by one Major; each company by one Captain, one First and one Second Lieutenant, and such non-commissioned officers as are usually appointed to companies in the service of the United States. The Major Generals shall each appoint his Aid-de-camp, and the Governor shall appoint one Aid-de-camp in each Major-General's division, with the rank of Colonel of Cavalry; the Brigadier-Generals each, his Aid-de-camp and Brigade Major; the commanding officer of each regiment and separate battalion, his Paymaster, Judge Advocate, Adjutant, Quartermaster, Sergeant Major and Fife Major; and the Captains, their Drummers and Fifers.

ART. 1432. [7] The Major and Brigadier-Generals of the State shall be allowed to appoint in addition to the Staff allowed them by this act, such other additional Staffs as are allowed to officers of a like grade in the Army of the United States. Appointment of staff.

ART. 1433. [8] The Staffs of the Major-Generals shall rank as Colonels of Infantry; the Staffs of the Brigadier-Generals, as Majors of Cavalry; and the Staffs of Colonels-Commandant shall rank as Captains of Infantry; and the said officers when called into actual service, either by authority of this State or the United States, shall be entitled to the same pay and emoluments as officers of the like grade belonging to the United States Army. Rank of staff.

ART. 1434. [9] The militia of this State, on the election day of civil officers next, at the usual places of holding elections in the several counties, shall elect one Major-General for each division, and one Brigadier-General for each brigade, as contemplated by this act; which election shall be held by the same Judges, conducted in like manner, and returns thereof be made in the same way as the election of civil officers are required by law to be held, conducted and returned; and said returns shall be made to the Governor within thirty days after the election. Election of officers.

ART. 1435. [10] It shall be the duty of each Brigadier-General, so soon as he may be elected and commissioned by the Governor, under the provisions of this act, to proceed without delay to divide his brigade into regiments and battalions, or separate and independent battalions, as the case may be; and said division shall be made as nearly equal and equitable as practicable; and it shall be the duty of the said Brigadier-Generals to proceed to order or cause elections to be held throughout their respective commands, for Colonels-Commandant, Lieutenant-Colonels and Majors for each regiment or separate battalion; which election shall be held according to law, and returns made thereof to the Governor, who shall commission said Colonels, Lieutenant-Colonels, and Majors, as the case may be; and said Colonels, Lieutenant-Colonels, and Majors shall, after receiving their respective commissions as herein contemplated, cause their respective regiments or battalions to be divided into companies as nearly equal as practicable, and cause elections to be holden in each company-beat for Captain, one First Lieutenant, and one Second Lieutenant for each company, and such other officers as are allowed by law in the United States service, giving at least fifteen days' notice of such election; which election shall be held according to law regulating elections for civil officers, and the returns thereof be made to the Colonel commandant or the Lieutenant-Colonel commandant of each separate battalion, as the case may be, within ten days thereafter, whose duty it shall be to keep said election returns, and within five days thereafter to make out an abstract of said election returns under his hand and seal, and transmit the same to the Governor by mail, whose duty it shall be to commission all persons elected as aforesaid; and the term of service of all officers elected under the provisions of this act shall be for four years or until the day of general election of members of the Legislature, in the year 1850: provided, that all officers so elected shall hold their offices until their successors are duly elected and commissioned. Organization of brigade.

ART. 1436. [11] It shall be the duty of the Governor to issue his proclamation requiring elections to be held in each division, brigade, regiment, battalion, and company, throughout the State, for all officers contemplated by this act, to be elected on the day set apart by law for the election of members of the State Legislature, in the year 1850; which elections shall be held at the same places, conducted in the same manner and returned in the same way as elections for civil officers, to the Governor of the State, who shall commission the same. All elections to fill vacancies shall be held as follows: for the Governor to order election.

election to fill a vacancy in the office of Major-General, the Governor shall issue his order, giving sixty days' notice; which election shall be held at the usual places of holding elections for civil officers in each and every county composing the division in which such vacancy may occur; and such election shall be held and conducted in the same manner as hereinbefore provided; and to fill a vacancy in the office of Brigadier-General, the Major-General shall issue his order, giving forty days' notice; to fill a vacancy in the office of Colonel of a regiment or Lieutenant-Colonel commanding a separate battalion, the Brigadier-General shall issue his order giving thirty days' notice; to fill a vacancy in the office of Lieutenant-Colonel or Major of a battalion, [the Colonel] shall issue his order, giving ten days' notice; and to fill a vacancy in the office of First or Second Lieutenant, the Captain shall issue his order, giving five days' notice thereof; and in all cases when elections shall be holden to fill vacancies, the individual so elected shall hold his office for the unexpired term of such office only.

Resignation of officers.

ART. 1437. [12] No person who shall be elected and commissioned in the Military Department of this State, shall resign the same, until he shall have fully organized the militia under his command, and shall have made full returns thereof, of the number of effective men under his command, to his superior officer, under the following penalties: if he be a Major-General, in the sum of one hundred dollars; if a Brigadier-General, in the sum of seventy-five dollars; if a Colonel of a regiment or a Lieutenant-Colonel of a separate battalion, in the sum of fifty dollars; if a Lieutenant-Colonel or Major of a battalion, in the sum of forty dollars; if a Captain, in the sum of thirty dollars; if a First or Second Lieutenant, in the sum of twenty dollars; to be recovered and appropriated as other fines and penalties are by this act directed.

Failure to elect officers, &c.

ART. 1438. [13] In all cases where the militia in any of the military divisions of this State shall fail to elect such officers as they are required to, by law, such division shall be attached to and form a part of some other division which shall have the requisite officers, and shall be subject to perform all military duty by this act required, under the command of the officers of the division to which they may be attached; if the delinquency or failure shall occur in a company division, the militia of such division shall be attached to the next adjoining company in the same battalion, if any company of the battalion to which such division belongs shall have the requisite officers, by order of the Lieutenant-Colonel or Major of such battalion; and if there shall be no company in the battalion, organized and officered as required by this act, the militia of each company of such battalion shall be attached to the most convenient company of the regiment which shall be found to have the requisite officers, by an order of the Colonel of such regiment; and if any regiment or separate battalion shall be found unorganized and without the requisite officers, the militia of such regiment or separate battalion shall be attached to the most convenient regiment or separate battalion in the brigade which shall be found to have the officers and organization required by law, by an order of the Brigadier-General of the brigade to which such regiment or battalion may belong. If any brigade shall be found unorganized and without the requisite officers to command the same, the militia of such brigade shall be attached to the most convenient brigade in the division to which such brigade shall belong, which shall be found to have the officers required by law, by order of the Major-General of such division; and in all cases when the militia of any division shall be attached to any other division, as hereinbefore provided, the militia so attached shall be commanded by the officers of the division to which they shall be attached, and shall be liable to the same duty and subject to the same fines and penalties as if they had previously belonged to such division; and the militia of any division attached to another division, as aforesaid, shall remain subject to such command until they shall be admitted by an order of their superior officer, to whose command they may be attached, to elect the requisite officers to command such division, and shall have reported to him that they have all the requisite officers for the command of their separate divisions duly elected and commissioned; after which the command of the officers of the division to which they shall have been attached shall cease, and shall devolve on the officers of the division, elected and commissioned as aforesaid; and if any division shall be found a second time unorganized and without officers as required by this act, they shall in like manner be again attached to some division having the requisite officers and organization, and shall be debarred the privilege of again separating from the division and command to which they shall be attached, and shall permanently compose a part of said command, anything in this act to the contrary notwithstanding; and the officer whose duty it is made by this act to order the militia of any of the divisions to be attached to some other division, as provided for by this Act, shall at the time of issuing said order, give public notice thereof to the militia of the division to be attached as aforesaid: if it be a company, the notice shall be in writing, put up in at least two of the most public places in the company-beat; if it be a battalion, the like notice shall be put up in at least one of the most public places of each company of the battalion; if a brigade, regiment, or separate battalion, the like notice shall be put up in at least one of the most public places of the brigade, regiment, or separate battalion, or be published for three weeks successively in one or more of the newspapers published in this State; and any notice given as aforesaid shall be deemed in law sufficient, and the militia so notified shall from the time of issuing such order and giving such notice, be considered and treated as part of the division to which they may be attached, and compose a part of the command of the officers of the division to which they are attached, anything in this act to the contrary notwithstanding; and any General Order issued by the Commander-in-Chief, any Major-General, or Brigadier-General, and published in any newspaper printed in this State, for three weeks successively, shall be deemed in law a sufficient notice thereof, to the militia and to all persons to be affected thereby, and shall be to all intents and purposes as valid as if the same were communicated by express or in any other manner whatever.

ART. 1439. [14] All elections in the militia department which may hereafter be contested, shall be determined in the following manner, viz: If the election of a Major-General shall be contested, the party contesting such election shall furnish the Governor a fair statement of his reasons, in writing, upon the receipt of which, he shall order a general court-martial to be held at such place as he may designate in the division to which such Major-General belongs; at which court each militia officer of such division, not under the grade of a field officer, shall be entitled to a seat; and if the election of a Brigadier-General shall at any time be contested, the complainant shall make the like complaint and application to the Major-General of the division to which such brigade belongs, who is, upon the receipt thereof required to order a brigade court-martial, as in other cases; and when the election of a Colonel of a regiment or Lieutenant-Colonel of a separate battalion or Lieutenant-Colonel or Major of a separate battalion, shall be contested, complaint and application shall in like manner be made to the next highest officer in command, who, upon receipt thereof, shall order a regiment court-martial accordingly; if under the rank of a field officer, all complaints and applications shall be made to the commanding officer of the regiment or separate battalion where the contest exists; and in order to explain and fix a principle to govern the several courts-martial in their duties respecting contested elections, it is hereby declared that the person contesting shall in all cases be bound to furnish satisfactory proof to the court that the person whose election Elections, how contested.

is contested did receive a number of illegal votes, which, if deducted, would give a majority to the person contesting; and if the contesting person shall fail to establish his charge, or if the charge shall be sufficiently supported, in either case, the court shall report in favor of the person having the greatest number of legal votes as being duly elected; and the president of each court-martial shall certify, under his hand, the name or names of the person thus duly elected; which certificate, if the officer shall be of the grade of General or field officer, shall be directed and sent to the Governor; if commissioned officers of companies, the certificate shall be signed as aforesaid and be directed and sent to the Colonel of the regiment or Lieutenant-Colonel of the separate battalion and by him to the Governor, who shall issue commissions in either of the above cases; and in order to provide more amply for deciding contested elections, it is hereby declared that when the cause shall arise from any illegal proceedings of any person ordering, conducting or judging said election, on proof thereof being made, satisfactory to the court-martial, such election shall be declared void, and the president by and with the authority of such court-martial shall direct the proper officer to issue an order or orders for an election to fill such vacancy, which election, so ordered, shall in all things be conducted in the same way as other elections to fill vacancies in like offices are by this act directed.

Qualification of officer.

ART. 1440. [15] Each and every officer elected and commissioned under the provisions of this act shall, previous to entering upon the execution of the duties of his office, take the following oath: I ——, do solemnly swear that I will support the Constitution of the United States and of this State, and that I will faithfully and justly execute the duties of the office of —— in the —— company, battalion, regiment brigade, or division, as the case may be, of the militia of this State, according to the best of my skill, power and judgment, so help me God; a copy of which shall be endorsed on the back of the commission, signed by the person taking the same and attested by the officer who administered the oath.

Court-martial, &c.

ART. 1441. [16] If any commissioned officer shall move out of the bounds of his division, brigade, regiment, separate battalion, or company, or offer himself a candidate for any other military appointment, or shall be absent therefrom otherwise than on military duty, for more than twelve months at one time, his office thereby shall become vacated; and if any commissioned officer shall think himself injured by his superior officer, and shall, upon due application made to him, be refused redress, he may complain to the Brigadier-General, who shall order a brigade court-martial, to be held under the rules and regulations prescribed by this Act; if any inferior officer or private shall think himself injured by his Captain or any other superior officer in the regiment or separate battalion to which he belongs, he may complain to the commanding officer of the regiment or separate battalion, who shall order a court-martial, and such court shall determine the complaint agreeably to the nature of the case: provided, that the person complaining shall exhibit his charge in writing supported by oath or affirmation.

Company muster.

ART. 1442. [17] Every Captain or commanding officer shall hold at least two company musters between the months of March and November in each year, and shall require the non-commissioned officers of his company, or such of them as he shall designate, to warn his men of the place of muster, in all cases where notice thereof was not given at the previous muster; and each Captain shall have the right to designate his muster-ground, but shall select some suitable muster-ground as near central as circumstances will permit; and after the first muster the company shall select a place of muster, and every officer, non-commissioned officer, and private, shall appear at his respective muster-field by eleven o'clock in the forenoon, and not leave the parade until permitted by the officer commanding the troops; and at every muster each Captain or commanding officer of the company shall direct the first Sergeant of the company to call the roll, in his presence, between the hours of eleven and twelve o'clock; and the commanding officer of each company shall examine every person belonging to his company, note all delinquencies, make out an accurate statement of the strength and condition of his company, and make returns thereof to the Judge of the County or Probate Court, and to the commanding officer of the battalion to which he belongs, within twenty days thereafter, whose duty it shall be to return the same to the commanding officer of his regiment within ten days thereafter, whose duty it shall be to make out an accurate statement of the condition of his regiment, and return the same to the commanding officer of the brigade, within ten days thereafter, to which he may belong; and the commanding officer of a separate battalion shall make a like return to the commanding officer of the brigade to which he belongs, within the same time; and the Brigadier-General shall make a like return to the Major-General commanding the division to which his brigade belongs, within twenty days thereafter; and the Major-General of a division shall make a like return of the division under his command, to the Adjutant-General of the State, within twenty days thereafter; and it shall be the duty of the Adjutant-General to furnish such blank forms of all the different returns, an explanation of the principles on which they should be made, as shall be approved by the Commander-in-chief; and, also, to receive the returns of the militia throughout the State, from all which he shall make the proper abstract and lay the same before the Commander-in-chief of this State, within twenty days after they shall have been received by him, or sooner if required by the Commander-in-chief; and the Commander-in-chief, when required, shall lay the same before the Legislature of the State.

Disobedience or disorder.

ART. 1443. [18] If any non-commissioned officer, musician, or private, at any muster, shall disobey the legal and proper orders of his superior officer, or act in a disorderly manner; or if, by slanders at any such muster, shall insult or otherwise molest any officer, non-commissioned officer or private, while on parade, or employed in any other service authorized by the laws of this State, the commanding officer of the company may order such person to be arrested and placed under guard for any length of time not exceeding three hours; and the person or persons so offending shall, moreover, be subject to pay such fines as may be imposed in the manner hereinafter provided.

Penalties.

ART. 1444. [19] In order to compel the observance of the provisions of this Act, and for the purpose of introducing a proper degree of subordination and discipline in the operations of the militia of this State, the following penalties shall be incurred and inflicted in the manner hereinafter directed, that is to say: the Adjutant-General, for a neglect or violation of those duties imposed upon him by this act, shall incur a penalty not exceeding one year's pay, nor less than three months' pay; and any commissioned or staff officer for failing to perform the duties required of him by this act, shall forfeit and pay as follows: commandant of a regiment or separate battalion, the sum of fifty dollars; Lieutenant-Colonel or Major of a battalion, the sum of fifty dollars; the commanding officer of a company, or Adjutant, twenty dollars; and those officers respectively, shall moreover be liable to be cashiered at the discretion of a court-martial. Each non-commissioned officer failing to give notice of any muster, when he shall receive orders for that purpose, without a reasonable excuse, shall be fined in the sum of five dollars; each non-commissioned officer, musician or private, failing to attend any muster, or disobeying any order, which by virtue of this act his superior may give, or failing to repair to the prescribed rendezvous, when properly warned so to do, or failing to do his duty when there, or absenting himself without a lawful excuse, shall forfeit and pay such fine as the court-martial shall order under the circumstances of the case, not exceeding the sum of five dollars; every non-commissioned officer appointed in pursuance of this act, shall serve for the term of one year or pay a fine of ten dollars, the payment of which penalty shall, if such person insist on the privilege, exempt him from the duties of such office for the space of two years.

Division of company into classes.

ART. 1445. [20] It shall be the duty of the commanding officers of companies, to proceed forthwith to divide the companies into classes by ballot, from one to three, for the purpose of a regular routine of duty when called into actual service, and to return a roll of each class and its number, in rotation, within thirty days thereafter, to the commanding officer of the battalion, who shall transmit the same to the commanding officer of the regiment, who shall cause the same to be recorded by the Judge Advocate; and the commanding officer of the regiment or separate battalion shall make a return of the same to the Brigadier-General, and those enrolled in the first class shall be subject to perform the first tour of duty, and those in the second class the second tour of duty, and those of the third class the third tour of duty, and so on in rotation. When any Colonel of a regiment or Lieutenant-Colonel of a separate battalion shall be charged with mal-administration or neglect of duty, it shall be lawful for any commissioned officer to exhibit to the Brigadier-General of the brigade, or such other officer as shall at the time have command of the brigade, a fair statement in writing, of the charge or charges and the facts intended to establish the same; and the Brigadier-General is hereby authorized to order a brigade court-martial to consist of at least seven members, none to be under the grade of field officers, who, when assembled, shall take and subscribe the same oath prescribed for regimental courts-martial; and the court, being thus sworn, shall inquire into the nature and truth of the charge or charges; and if the officer accused shall be found guilty of such neglect of duty, he shall forfeit and pay (if guilty of a misdemeanor in office,) any sum not exceeding fifty dollars, and shall be cashiered; and when any Lieutenant, Captain, Lieutenant-Colonel of the first, or Major of the second battalion of any regiment, shall be charged with any misdemeanor in office or neglect of duty, it shall be lawful for any officer, non-commissioned officer or private, to exhibit to the Colonel of the regiment, or Lieutenant-Colonel of a separate battalion, a fair statement of the charge or charges and the facts intended to establish the same; and the Colonel or Lieutenant-Colonel, to whom such complaint is made in writing, may, in his discretion, order a regimental or battalion court-martial, to consist of at least five commissioned officers, who shall take and subscribe the oath directed to be taken by this act, and when sworn, shall inquire into the nature and truth of the charge or charges so exhibited; and if found guilty of a misdemeanor in office, the officer so accused shall be cashiered, and if guilty of neglect of duty shall be fined as prescribed by law; but no sentence of any court-martial, cashiering any officer, shall be final, until the same be laid before the Commander-in-chief and by him approved, if the officer cashiered shall pray an appeal from such decision to him; otherwise the same shall be final.

Substitutes

ART. 1446. [21] If any person shall be called upon to perform a tour of duty, such person shall be acquitted, provided he furnish to his commanding officer an able-bodied substitute in his room or stead; and if any such substitute should be called into actual service in his own term, previous to the expiration of the term for which he shall have enrolled as such substitute, then the person procuring such substitute shall march in his room, or procure another substitute for the remainder of the term, or be liable to the same penalties as if called upon in his own name. Any person called upon to perform a tour of duty as aforesaid, and serving by himself or substitute, or otherwise paying such fine as the court-martial shall adjudge adequate to the offence, shall not be bound to perform any tour of duty until regularly called upon by rotation.

Governor to call militia into service.

ART. 1447. [22] When it may be necessary to call into actual service any part of the militia, on an actual or threatened invasion of this State, or any of the neighboring States or territories, it shall and may be lawful for the Governor to order into the service such part of the militia as the emergency may require; and when any part of the militia of this State shall be called into actual service, it shall be the duty of the Commander-in-Chief to order from the regiment or battalion from which the militia shall be detached, in proportion to the men furnished by the regiment or battalion, a sufficient number of officers, giving preference to senior officers of said regiment or battalion, to officer said detachment; and in all cases the officers of the militia of this State shall be called on to perform their tour of duty, in rotation, in the same manner as is by this act directed for the several classes of the militia: provided, however, that no militiaman shall be compelled to serve more than six months at one time, and sixty days shall be considered a tour of duty.

Invasion or insurrection.

ART. 1448. [23] In case of actual invasion or insurrection, or an invasion threatened or premeditated against this State or any part thereof, it shall be lawful for the Governor, or any officer by him directed, to order into actual service all or any portion of the militia, as the emergency may require, and to discharge such troops as soon as he may judge consistent with the interests of the State; and if a sudden insurrection should be raised, or invasion made upon any county within this State, the commanding officer of the militia of said county is hereby authorized and directed to order out such part of the militia as he may think necessary for suppressing such insurrection, or repelling such invasion; and may, if in his judgment the emergency of the occasion requires it, make a requisition on the commanding officer of the militia of any adjoining county not so invaded or endangered, whose duty it shall be to comply with such requisition: provided, always, it shall be the duty of such officer so ordering out the militia, or any part thereof, to transmit to the Governor, as early as practicable, a statement of his proceedings, setting forth his reasons for exercising such authority; and the militia so called out shall be discharged within thirty days after their rendezvous, except they shall be continued in service for a longer time by the executive authority of this State; and the militia of this State, when in actual service, shall be governed by the rules and articles governing the armies of the United States.

Trial by court-martial.

ART. 1449. [24] Every officer to be tried by a court-martial, shall have ten days' notice given him, of the time and place appointed for the trial, and shall be furnished with a copy of the charges exhibited against him, at least ten days before the sitting of said court. In every court-martial for the trial of an officer, not less than two-thirds of the number present shall agree in the sentence or judgment of said court, otherwise the person charged shall be acquitted; and when the members shall be required to give their votes on a question or decision, they shall begin with the youngest in commission: provided, that no commissioned officer shall be allowed to resign his commission while under arrest.

Assessment and collection of fines of company.

ART. 1450. [25] The captains and subaltern officers of each and every company, or a majority of them, shall, on the muster-day next succeeding the muster of each company, at which there has been any delinquency or delinquencies, hold a court for the adjustment of fines in each company; and the commanding officer of the company shall issue his warrant, directed to any Sheriff or Constable in his beat, which warrant shall have the force and effect of an execution; and said Constable shall proceed to collect the same, in the same manner as if said execution had issued under and by the authority of any civil officer within this State; and all fines collected by virtue of the provisions contained in this section, shall be paid to the Captain of such company, within ten days after the same may be collected, and by him applied to the purchase of a drum, fife, and colors, and for other purposes for the use of the company.

Charges against officers, &c.

ART. 1451. [26] When either the Major-General, Brigadier-General, or Brigade-Major, shall be charged with malfeasance or neglect of duty in office; if a Major-General, it shall be lawful for any militia officer, not under the grade of a field officer, to exhibit to the Governor, for the time being, a fair statement of the charge or charges, with the facts intended to establish the same, who is hereby authorized to order a general court-martial, to consist of at least nine members, none to be chosen under the grade of a field officer, who, when convened, shall take and subscribe the same oath prescribed for regimental courts-martial; the said court thus sworn, shall have power to inquire into the nature of the offence; and if it shall constitute a misdemeanor in office, he shall be removed from the same; if for neglect of duty, he shall forfeit and pay a sum not to exceed one hundred dollars, at the discretion of the court-martial, to be collected as in similar cases of fines; if a Brigadier-General or Brigade Major shall be guilty of either of the aforesaid offences, the charge shall be submitted to the Major-General, who shall issue his order to the senior Colonel commanding in the brigade in which the person charged resides, by virtue of which order the Colonel shall hold a court-martial, and proceed in the same manner as directed for the trial of Major-General: provided, that in all cases of charges exhibited against officers, the officer ordering a court-martial shall, as soon as practicable, furnish the person charged with a copy of the charges exhibited against him; and the president of the court-martial shall give him at least ten days' notice of the time and place appointed for trial, and cause such witnesses as may be required by either party to be summoned by the Adjutant of the regiment in which they reside; and every person summoned and failing to attend, or refusing to be sworn, shall be tried by the court-martial, and if he be an officer, may be cashiered or fined at the discretion of the court-martial, not exceeding fifty dollars; if a non-commissioned officer or private, he may be fined not exceeding twenty dollars, and moreover be confined under guard or put in jail until he will give evidence.

Judge Advocate.

ART. 1452. [27] Each Judge Advocate, previous to entering on the duties of his appointment, shall take an oath to support the Constitution of the United States and of the State of Texas, and also that he will well and truly perform the duties of Judge Advocate, according to law and the best of his skill and abilities; which oath shall be in writing, signed by the Judge Advocate, and attested by the officer who administered the same; the Judge Advocate thus sworn, shall administer the following oath to the officers, previous to their entering on the duties of any court-martial, viz: You, and each of you, do solemnly swear that you will well and truly inquire into the delinquencies which may appear, or returns which may be laid before you, and will assess the fine thereon as may seem just, according to law, without favor or affection, partiality or prejudice; and that you will not disclose or discover the vote or opinion of any particular member of this court, unless required to give evidence thereof in a court of justice, so help you God. It shall be the duty of the Judge Advocate to provide a book, in which he shall record the proceedings of the court-martial, and all other necessary entries for the regiment or separate battalion, which are or shall be required by law, and, for his services, shall be exempt from military duty and be allowed the sum of two dollars per day for attending regimental or battalion courts-martial, which it shall be his duty to attend, to be paid out of the fines arising under this act. If, from any cause, a Judge Advocate shall fail to attend a court-martial, as provided in this act, it shall be the duty of the officers present to appoint a Judge Advocate for the time being; and in case of his death, resignation, or removal out of the county, or from his office, the journals and proceedings shall be kept by the Colonel or commanding officer, until a Judge advocate shall be appointed in his stead.

ART. 1453. [28] All fines and forfeitures imposed by any regimental or battalion court-martial, shall be collected in like manner as fines and penalties are required to be collected by company courts-martial, and paid into the hands of each paymaster of each regiment or separate battalion. It shall be the duty of the commanding officer of the regiment or separate battalion, to appropriate the money arising from fines, in the hands of the paymaster, by order of the court-martial, in the first place to the purchasing of fifes, drums and colors for the use of the regiment or separate battalion; and, secondly, to paying the officers of the regiment or separate battalion for any service for which they may be entitled to pay, under the provisions of this act. Fines and forfeitures of regimental court-martial, &c.

ART. 1454. [29] No officer or private, ordered or directed by this act to appear as aforesaid, shall be liable to be taken or arrested by any officer, in any civil action or process whatsoever, on the day such person is directed to appear or in any reasonable time in going to, continuing at, or returning from the same; and every such arrest is hereby declared void, and shall subject such officer to damages for false imprisonment; and every person required by this act to attend muster, going to and returning from the same, shall be suffered to pass over any bridge, together with his horse, and shall be put over any public ferry, without delay, free of charge; and if any ferryman demand pay for, delay, or refuses to put such person or persons over, or keeper of toll-bridge impede the passing of any person, he shall forfeit and pay for every such offence, the sum of ten dollars, to be recovered by warrant from a Justice of the Peace, one-half to the informer, and the other half to the use of the county where the offence was committed. Arrest of officer or private.

ART. 1455. [30] It shall be lawful for any Colonel of a regiment or separate battalion, upon application of any suitable person, to commission such person to raise by voluntary enlistment, for a period of not more than five years, a company of light infantry or riflemen, a corpse of artillery, or troop of cavalry, in his regiment or separate battalion; which corps, thus formed, shall not consist of less than fifty, nor more than sixty-six privates; and the corps so raised and formed is to remain a part of the same regiment or separate battalion in which it is raised; and when the requisite number shall be enlisted, it shall be lawful for the officer of the regiment or separate battalion to which they belong, to order an election for officers of said companies, to be conducted as other elections, and returns thereof made to said Colonel or commanding officer of the separate battalion, and by him transmitted to the Governor, who shall commission the officers so elected; and the companies so formed shall choose their own uniform, and shall be armed as follows: The rifle corps—the Captain and subaltern officers to be armed with side-arms; the privates, with a good rifle, a shot bag and powder horn, with nine charges of powder and ball suitable to the bore of the rifles; the company of artillery—each Captain and subaltern with side-arms, the artillerists with one field piece with its usual number of cartridges, boxes, balls, &c; the troop of cavalry—the officers and privates shall be furnished with a good horse, bridle, saddle, and martingals, and armed with a sword or cutlass, holsters and holster pistols; and the company of light infantry shall be armed and equipped as like companies are required to be armed and equipped in the armies of the United States; and said corps shall use for instruction and exercise, the system of military discipline adopted in the United States army, for troops of a similar description; and all companies shall have a right to change their uniform from time to time: Commission to raise company.

provided, such change shall not be incompatible with the military regulations of the United States army; and each member of either of the above described corps shall be exempt from the ordinary military duty required of the militia by this act, so long as they may continue so discharge the duties required of them by the provisions of this act, in either of the companies above designated.

Books and forms.

ART. 1456. [31] Every commissioned officer, volunteer or militia, shall be furnished with one copy of this act, at the expense of the State; and every officer shall, when he goes out of office, deliver to his successor in office, all books and forms furnished him by the State, or received from his predecessor in office, and also all books and papers in his possession belonging to his division, brigade, regiment, battalion, or company; and every officer who shall neglect or refuse so to do, shall be fined twenty dollars per month for every month he shall so neglect or refuse, after a demand thereof has been made by his successor, to be assessed by any court-martial having cognizance of the conduct of such officer, and collected and accounted for as other fines imposed upon such officer are by this act directed to be collected and accounted for.

Adjutant-General.

ART. 1457. [32] The Governor shall appoint one Adjutant-General, with the rank of Colonel of Cavalry, who shall do and perform all the duties of Adjutant-General, as required of him by this act, and shall furnish all forms of returns, and keep a book, in which he shall make a fair entry of all returns by him received, which shall be subject to the inspection of the Major-General and Commander-in-Chief; and shall receive for his services the sum of two hundred and fifty dollars per annum, out of any money in the Treasury not otherwise appropriated.

Rules and regulations.

ART. 1458. [33] The system of discipline and exercise which is and shall be ordered to be observed by the regular army of the United States, shall be observed by the militia of this State, and the commanding officers of the several militia divisions shall cause the militia within their respective commands to be disciplined and trained conformably thereto, in all things not otherwise directed by this act; and in all cases not specially provided for by this act, such provisions of law as have been or may be made by Congress, for the government and direction of the army or the militia of the United States in similar cases, shall be binding upon and be observed and conformed to by the militia of this State; and the forms and rules of proceedings of all courts-martial, not provided for in this act, shall be such as are established by the rules and articles of war adopted and used in the militia service of the United States.

New counties.

ART. 1459. [34] Each new county established by this Legislature, shall form a part of the same brigade and division as the county from which such new county, or the greater portion thereof, was taken; and the militia of each new county shall be organized in like manner as the militia of the counties named in this act.

II. VOLUNTEERS.

Act of May 11, 1846. Took effect from passage.

Volunteers, election of officers.

ART. 1460. [1] All volunteers from this State, when called out in defence of the country, shall have the right to elect their own officers, in accordance with the Militia laws of this State, and those regulating volunteers in the United States.

III. MILITARY COMPANIES.

ART. 1461. [1] The Galveston Artillery Company, the Washington Light Guards, of the city of Houston, the Alamo Rifles, of the city of San Antonio, the Milam Rifles, of the city of Houston, the Lone Star Military Company, of Galveston, the Turner Rifles, of the city of Houston, the Refugio Riflemen, and all other uniformed volunteer military companies, now organized, or that may be hereafter organized, in this State, be, and they are hereby constituted bodies politic and corporate, under whatever style and name they may determine, with power to sue and be sued, plead and be impleaded, answer and be answered unto, appear and prosecute unto final judgment, in any court or elsewhere; each to have a common seal with whatever motto and ensign they please, to elect in whatever manner they shall determine the officers necessary to command them, to ordain and establish by-laws for the government and regulation of their affairs, and the same to alter and amend at will; and to hold real estate and personal property, and to dispose of the same: provided, however, that the amount of such real estate and personal property shall at no time exceed thirty thousand dollars, and that said company shall never number less than thirty-two, non-commissioned officers and privates, nor exceed one hundred of the same. Act of Feb. 15, 1858. In force from passage. Companies incorporated, &c.

ART. 1462. [2] The members of said companies shall be exempt from common militia drills, and battalion and regimental reviews. Members exempt from, &c.

ART. 1463. [3] Said companies shall have power by their constitution and by-laws to hold courts of investigation, and courts martial upon their own members, to try all violations of their ordinances, agreed upon by the members of the said companies; to suspend, expel and fine, not to exceed one hundred dollars, those infracting the laws established under this charter. May hold court martial.

ART. 1464. [4] All fines imposed by a court martial, or accruing under the by-laws, shall be collected by a warrant issued by the Secretary, and endorsed by the officers commanding, with the company's seal affixed, the fine collected to belong to the company imposing them; any constable, sheriff, or any city marshall or their deputies, in the beat where said company is established, is empowered to levy said warrant and coerce the payment under the same law that governs such officer in the execution of civil process. Fines imposed, &c.

ART. 1465. [5] Drafts shall never be made from said companies, but it shall be the privilege of their corps, to serve in body under their own officers, and only then when the number of common militia of the battalion is inadequate to meet the demand by draft; and in that case these companies will be selected by lot, to supply the deficiency. Drafts from, not to be made.

ART. 1466. [6] The officers commanding said companies shall consist of a Captain, one 1st and two 2nd Lieutenants, to be commissioned by the Governor, subject when ordered on duty to be trained and governed by the rules and regulations of war as established and ordained by Government. Officers.

ART. 1467. [7] When said company shall be ordered to take the field, they shall be entitled to receive such camp equipage as is usually allowed and furnished the best corps by the Government. Camp equipage allowed, when.

ART. 1468. [8] All companies incorporated by this act shall at all times be subject to the civil authorities of the State, and to the orders of the Governor of the State, in case their services shall be required. Subject to civil authorities, &c.

List of officers and privates to be filed by, &c. ART. 1469. [9] The commanding officers of all such companies shall, on the first day of January in each year, (or as soon thereafter as such company is organized,) file in the office of the County Court, at the county where the company is established, a full list of all the active resident officers and members of said company of that date.

Election of officers, &c. ART. 1470. [10] The officers of said companies shall be elected by the members of the same, in the armory of the company, and the returns of the election made by the 1st Sergeant of the company to the Chief Justice of the county where such company is established, directed to the Governor of the State, who shall commission said officers as soon as he shall have received a certificate of election from the said Chief Justice.

Monthly parades. ART. 1471. [11] Each company incorporated by this act shall have at least one parade in each month, during the year, and as many drills besides as their constitution and by-laws may direct, and no excuse from said parade will be valid, except sickness, or unavoidable absence from the company's beat.

When company entitled to benefit of this act. ART. 1472. [12] Before any such company shall be entitled to the provisions of this act, the commanding officer present shall furnish and have recorded in the office of the County Clerk of the county in which said company may reside, a certificate under oath, showing where such company was organized, and to what arm of the service it may belong, and also the names of all its officers and members at the date of said certificate.

Property, by whom held, &c. ART. 1473. [13] All property, whether personal or real, held by said companies, shall be held by the officers of the same, and their successors in office, as trustees for said company.

List of to be filed in County Court on 1st January, &c. ART. 1474. [14] The commanding officer (present) of all said companies shall on the 1st day of January in each year, file in the office of the County Clerk of the county in which said company is established a full list of all the active resident officers and members of said company at that date.

MORTGAGES.

[*See Registration—Conveyances.*]

I. ON PERSONAL PROPERTY.

I. ON PERSONAL PROPERTY.

Act of May 15, 1838. Took effect from passage. Foreclosure of on personal property. (See arts. 503, 504.) ART. 1475. [2] All mortgages on personal property shall be foreclosed in the following manner: any person or persons holding a mortgage on personal property, and wishing to foreclose the same, shall make application to the Chief Justice of the county, and make affidavit before him of the amount of principal and interest due thereon, which affidavit shall be annexed to such mortgage, and thereupon the Clerk of the County Court shall issue execution as in cases of judgment; which execution being delivered to the Sheriff shall be levied upon the mortgaged property, and after being advertised for at least sixty days in some public gazette, shall be set up and sold to the highest bidder: provided, always, that if any disputes should arise as to the amount due on such mortgage, the Chief Justice of the County Court shall order the sale to be postponed upon the defendant's entering into bond and security in double the amount of the mortgage, for the delivery to the Sheriff of the property so levied upon; and the same shall be returned to and triable at the next term of the court as in other cases. (*a*)

II. ON LAND AND SLAVES.

ART. 1476. [1] From and after the passage of this act, the method of foreclosing mortgages on land or slaves, shall be as follows: any person entitled to foreclose a mortgage on land, or his or their attorney, shall file his petition in the Clerk's office of the District Court of the county where such land, or a part thereof is situated, stating the case and the amount of the demand, and describing the property mortgaged. Whereupon the mortgagor shall be summoned to appear at the next term of the said court to show cause why judgment should not be rendered in favor of the mortgagee for such sum, with interest and costs, as shall be due on such mortgage; which summons shall be served upon the defendant in the manner, and (the) same proceedings shall thereupon be had, as in ordinary cases of civil suits, if the defendant be a resident of the country; if not, then notice of the pendency of said suit shall be given by publication made in some public gazette at least four successive weeks before the commencement of the court in which suit is instituted; and if the defendant should fail to appear at the aforesaid court, or appearing, should show no cause why the mortgage should not be foreclosed, then judgment shall be rendered for said mortgagee so petitioning, and execution issue as in other cases; but if there be any dispute about the amount due on any mortgage, if the mortgagor shall appear within the time prescribed by the rules of pleading, and make affidavit of a just defence, the court shall order a trial of the facts before a jury as in other cases. (*b*)

Act of Feb. 5, 1840. Took effect from passage.

Foreclosing of, on land and slaves.

ART. 1477. [2] The remedy to foreclose mortgages on personal property, shall remain and be as heretofore, and if there should be any dispute as to facts, the trial shall be subject to the same rules and regulations as by law govern the District Courts of this Republic.

Remedy of foreclosure on personal property as heretofore.

(*a*) Representatives of a deceased mortgagor should not be joined with the survivor in a suit to foreclose a mortgage. Martin *v.* Harrison, 2 Tex. Rep. 456. See cases on mortgages generally. Chandler *v.* Fulton, 10 Tex. Rep. 2. Jones *v.* Thurmond, 5 Tex. Rep. 318. Carter *v* Carter, 5 Tex. Rep. 93. Watts *v.* Johnson, 4 Tex. Rep. 311. Stephens *v.* Sherrod, 6 Tex. Rep. 294. Sampson & Keene *v.* Williamson, 6 Tex. Rep. 102. Luckett *v.* Townsend, 3 Tex. Rep. 119. Stampers *v.* Johnson, 3 Tex. Rep. 1. Marshall *v.* Taylor, 7 Tex. Rep. 235. Fowler *v.* Stoneum, 11 Tex. Rep. 478. Gillian *v.* Henderson, 12 Tex. Rep. 47. Duty *v.* Graham, 12 Tex. Rep. 427. Morrison *v.* Bean, 15 Tex. Rep 267. Rankert *v.* Clow, 16 Tex. Rep. 9. Johnson *v.* Murphy, 17 Tex. Rep. 216.

(*b*) The decree of foreclosure in a suit brought against one joint mortgagor, the other being dead, should only direct the sale of the interest of the party sued, in the mortgaged property. Martin *v.* Harrison, 2 Tex. Rep. 456. A mortgage must be presented to an administrator as a claim against an estate. Graham *v.* Vining, 2 Tex. Rep. 433.

NAVIGABLE STREAMS.

Act of Aug. 1, 1856. Took effect from passage. Appropriation. Report of Governor.

ART. 1478. [1] The sum of three hundred thousand dollars be, and the same is hereby appropriated, and set apart as a special fund for the improvement of the navigable rivers, bayous, lakes and bays of Texas, and that the Governor is hereby authorized to draw from the Treasury said fund for the use and benefit of said rivers, bayous, lakes and bays, as hereinafter provided in this act; and to report to the Legislature, at each and every session thereof, his acts and proceedings relative to said fund.

Amount to which each is entitled.

ART. 1479. [2] Any navigable river, bayou, lake or bay, for the improvement of which any specified amount, not less than one thousand dollars, may be raised by private subscription, or other contribution or appropriation, except by the State, shall be entitled to receive, from said fund, four times the amount of said sum so raised and contributed, provided no one river, bayou, lake or bay shall be entitled, under the provisions of this act, to more than fifty thousand dollars of said fund, and provided further, that said sums so contributed by the State and private subscription and appropriation, shall be expended for the improvement of the navigation of such rivers, bayous, lakes and bays, by the removal of all serious obstacles from the mouth up, or on such portion as shall be specially designated on said subscription.

How secured.

ART. 1480. [3] Whenever the citizens interested in the improvement of any navigable river, bayou, lake or bay, may desire to secure the benefits of this act to said river, bayou, lake or bay, they shall have the power, in public meeting, to appoint some good and responsible person as Collector and Treasurer, who shall be authorized to take up a subscription for the benefit of said river, bayou, lake or bay, which subscription must specify for what river, bayou, lake or bay, it is taken. And no subscription shall be received by said Collector and Treasurer, unless at least five per cent. of said subscription is paid in actual cash. That said Collector and Treasurer, before entering upon the duties of his office, shall enter into a bond, with good and sufficient security, in the sum of twenty thousand dollars, payable to the Governor, and his successors in office, for the faithful discharge of the duties of his office, which bond shall be approved by the Governor, and filed with the Secretary of State, and may be sued upon as other bonds. That said Collector and Treasurer shall be entitled to five per cent. on the amount received, and five per cent. on the amount disbursed by him, as hereafter required to be subscribed and raised independent of the amount raised for said rivers, bayous, lakes or bays; and shall be authorized to sue and recover, in his own name, for the benefit of said river, bayou, lake or bay, any amount subscribed for the improvement of the same, as in other cases in law and equity; and shall have the power to call upon said subscribers, at any time, for installments on said

Subscriptions. Treasurer and Collector, their duties, &c.

May sue for subscriptions.

subscription, provided no more than twenty per cent. of said subscription shall be required every sixty days.

ART. 1481. [4] Said Collector and Treasurer shall be required to report quarterly, to the Governor, all accounts collected and disbursed by him, together with a copy of his subscription lists, and all his acts and accounts connected with said business, and shall also be required to keep an accurate record of the same, in a book to be kept for that purpose. Report of Collector and Treasurer.

ART. 1482. [5] There shall be elected, by the Legislature on joint ballot, a State Engineer and Superintendent, who shall receive an annual salary of three thousand dollars, payable quarterly. And said Engineer and Superintendent shall before entering upon the duties of his office, enter into a bond, with good and sufficient security, in the sum of ten thousand dollars, payable to the Governor of the State, and his successors in office, for the faithful discharge of the duties which may be assigned him, and with such other conditions as may be prescribed by the Governor, which bond shall be approved by the Governor, and filed with the Secretary of the State, and may be sued upon as other like bonds. Election of State Engineer, his salary, bond, oath, &c.

And said Engineer and Superintendent shall also take and subscribe the following oath, before any officer legally authorized to administer the same:— "I do solemnly swear (or affirm, as the case may be) that I will well and truly discharge all the duties required of me as State Engineer and Superintendent." And whenever, in the opinion of the Governor, the State Engineer and Superintendent cannot perform the duties required of him, under this act, consistently with his performance of other duties, the Governor may appoint some competent person to superintend the work upon any river, bayou, lake or bay, designated by the Governor, who shall give bond and take an oath of office in the same manner as is required of the State Engineer and Superintendent, and shall receive a compensation of five dollars per day, during the time he is employed in actual service. Governor may appoint assistant, when.

ART. 1483. [6] When the Governor shall be notified that a Collector and Treasurer has been appointed and qualified as provided by this act, and that he has raised a subscription of bona-fide solvent subscribers for as much as the sum of one thousand dollars for one or more rivers, bayous, lakes or bays, and that five per cent. of said subscription has been paid in cash; then said Engineer and Superintendent, shall survey, explore, and lay off the work to be done on said river, bayou, lake or bay, in sections of convenient length, and shall form estimates of the work, and let out the same to the lowest bidder at such time and place as shall be fixed upon by him, and shall enter into written contracts with said contractors, fully specifying the nature of the work to be done, and the time in which the same is to be completed. And said contractors shall enter into bond with securities, to be approved by said Engineer and Superintendent in double the amount of his bid, for the faithful performance of his contract, which bond shall be made payable to the Governor, and may be sued upon and collected as other like bonds. Said Engineer and Superintendent, shall superintend the work, and see that it is done in conformity with the contract, and shall make full and accurate examinations of the same, and shall report quarterly to the Governor all his proceedings and transactions relative to the same, and the condition and progress of all the works of which he is Superintendent. And said Engineer and Superintendent shall not be directly or indirectly interested in any bid or contract whatever, for the improvement of said rivers, bayous, lakes or bays. When rivers, &c., shall be surveyed and contracts let. Bond of Contractors. Engineer's duties. Not to be interested in.

ART. 1484. [7] Said Engineer and Superintendent shall, after, or at the time of, making his quarterly report to the Governor, draw drafts on the Collector and Treasurer for said river, bayou, lake or bay, and also on the Treasurer of the State, in favor of the Contractor or Contractors for such work Drafts on Treasury shall be drawn, provided.

as they may find upon examination to be entitled to. Provided, that in no case shall he draw for more than three-fourths of the work actually done and performed, until the entire contract shall be completed: and further provided, that he shall not draw said drafts, upon the Treasurer of the State until corresponding drafts of one-fifth of the amount have been paid by the Collector and Treasurer for said river, bayou, lake or bay; and the Governor, when satisfied that said corresponding amount has been paid out of the private subscription, shall countersign the drafts so drawn upon the Treasurer, upon which payment shall be made out of said fund, and no payment shall be made upon said drafts upon the Treasurer, until the same are countersigned by the Governor.

In case an appropriation is made by Louisiana to Sabine river, same appropriated by this State, provided, &c.

ART. 1485. [8] Any sum of money, which may be appropriated by the State of Louisiana, for the improvement of the navigation of the Sabine River, shall authorize the Engineer to draw on the Treasurer of this State for the same amount of money, which sum so drawn, shall be appropriated to the improvement of said river, under the provisions of this act; and a certified copy of an act of the State of Louisiana, making such appropriation, shall be sufficient evidence that the appropriation has been made. Provided, the sum drawn from the Treasury of this State shall not exceed fifteen thousand dollars under this provision. And should the State of Arkansas appropriate any sum of money for the improvement of the navigation of Red River, or any amount be raised in the Choctaw Nation for the same purpose, a like amount may be drawn from the Treasury of the State, and used for the improvement of the navigation of Red River above the Northeast corner of the State, under the provisions of this act, provided, the same shall not exceed fifteen thousand dollars. And should the Republic of Mexico, or any of its States bordering on the Rio Grande, appropriate any amount for the improvement of the navigation of the Rio Grande, then a like amount for the same purpose may be drawn from the Treasury of this State, provided, the same shall not exceed fifteen thousand dollars. But no part of said appropriations shall be drawn from the Treasury, under the 8th section of this act, until corresponding appropriations of said adjoining States and Republic have been actually expended upon said streams, and good and satisfactory evidence shall be shown to the Governor of said expenditure.

Persons raising money to construct canals, entitled to benefits of this act, &c, provided.

ART. 1486. [9] Money may be raised in the same manner as provided for in this act for the construction of any canal between any two navigable points, and any canal for the construction of which any amount may be so raised by private subscription or appropriation, shall be entitled and subject to all the benefits and provisions of this act, provided, that no money shall be drawn from the Treasury for the benefit of any such canal, until satisfactory evidence has been shown to the Governor, together with the report of a competent engineer, that the amount raised by private subscription, together with the amount to which said private subscription shall entitle it from the State Treasury, will be amply sufficient to construct and complete said canal so far as to connect two navigable points, with a good navigable channel, and provided that no canal, or any river, bayou, lake or bay, receiving the benefits of the provisions of this act, shall, at any time, receive or collect tolls for the navigation of the same.

Act of Aug. 23, 1856. Took effect from passage.

What waters considered part of bays.

ART. 1487. [1] In the execution of the act to which this is supplementary and amendatory, and of this act, all those bodies of water, in the vicinity of the Gulf of Mexico, locally designated as bays and lakes, shall be considered as parts of the bay through which they have their principal outlet to the Gulf, and all passages between bays, sometimes designated as Bayous, shall be considered as parts of the bays which they connect.

ART. 1488. [2] Not more than fifty thousand dollars shall be drawn from the appropriation made by the act, to which this is supplementary and amendatory, for the improvement of the different bays of the State, and not more than ten thousand dollars shall be drawn for the improvement of any one bay.

Am'nt to which each bay is entitled.

ART. 1489. [3] Each county, or any number of counties, interested in the improvement of any navigable river, bayou, lake or bay, may after general notice, and at a general meeting called for the purpose, appoint a Collector and Treasurer, and any subscription received by any Collector and Treasurer, previous to the approval of his bond by the Governor, shall be as valid and binding as if made afterwards, and the Collectors and Treasurers, appointed under the act to which this is supplementary and amendatory, and under this act, shall return to the Governor before the first day of January, 1857, a list of all subscriptions received by them, with a statement of the amounts paid thereon, and also their bond.

Collectors and Treasurers may be appointed, how.

List of subscriptions to be ret'd to the Governor.

ART. 1490. [4] On or after the first day of January, 1857, the Governor, State Engineer and Comptroller, shall examine the list of subscriptions returned, and if the amount of subscriptions for the improvement of the bays shall be more than sufficient to consume the entire amount of the State appropriation for that object, they shall reduce the subscription for each of said bays in such manner as to secure the benefits of the State appropriation equitably, for the improvement of said bays according to the population accommodated by the same. If the amount of subscription for the navigable rivers, bayous and lakes, shall be more than sufficient to consume the entire amount of the State appropriation for these objects, they shall also reduce the subscription for each of said rivers, bayous and lakes, according to the population accommodated by the same: provided, that in no event shall more than twenty thousand dollars of the State appropriation be applied to the improvement of any streams except the Colorado, Brazos, Trinity and Sabine rivers: and provided further, that no river, bayou or lake, which is not navigable for at least ten miles, shall be entitled to the benefits of this act or the act to which this is supplementary and amendatory.

To be examined by the Governor &c., and if more than will consume appropriation, shall reduce, &c.

ART. 1491. [5] If the State Engineer and Superintendent shall, after surveying, exploring and laying off any river, bayou, lake or bay, find that the appropriation as designated in said several private subscriptions, for such navigable waters, will not effect a permanent, continuous, and valuable improvement upon such navigable water, said Engineer and Superintendent shall have the power to apply said subscriptions and State appropriation to such portions of said navigable waters as he shall be satisfied will effect the most permanent and valuable improvement thereon, and he shall notify the Governor and said Collectors and Treasurers upon what portion of said waters said appropriations will be made.

Engineer to determine the place on, &c., where appropriation, &c., shall be expended.

ART. 1492. [6] Said Engineer and Superintendent shall continue in office two years, or until the election and qualification of his successor in office. And whenever any vacancy occurs in said office, by death, resignation or otherwise, or in the office of any Collector and Treasurer, it shall be the duty of the Governor to fill said vacancy by appointment, which appointment shall continue in office until twenty days after the next regular session of the Legislature.

Engineer and Superintendent, term of office.

Vacancy, how filled.

NOTARIES PUBLIC.

[*See Conveyances, Registration, District Court, Fees of Office.*]

I. APPOINTMENT AND QUALIFICATION.

Act of May 13, 1846. Took effect 22d June, 1846.

Not more than six in each county appointed by Gov., &c., term of office. Vacancies.

ART. 1493. [1] There shall be appointed by the Governor, by and with the advice and consent of two-thirds of the Senate, a convenient number of Notaries Public, not exceeding six for each county; who shall reside in the county for which they are appointed, and shall hold their office for four years, and until their successors are qualified. Should a vacancy occur in the office of Notary Public during the recess of the Senate, the Governor shall fill such vacancy by appointment, which shall continue in force until the end of the next session of the Senate thereafter.

Commission to specify whom Notary succeeds.

ART. 1494. [2] Where a Notary Public is appointed to succeed another, his commission shall specify what Notary he succeeds.

Bond and oath.

ART. 1495. [3] Every person who may be appointed a Notary Public, before he enters upon the duties of his office, shall execute a bond with good and sufficient security, to be approved by the County Court, payable to the Governor and his successors in office, in the sum of two thousand dollars, conditioned for the faithful performance of the duties of his office, and shall also take and subscribe the oath of office prescribed by the Constitution, which shall be endorsed on said bond, with the certificate of the officer administering the same; said bond shall be recorded in the office of the Clerk of the County Court, and deposited in said office, and shall not be void on the first recovery, and may be sued on in the name of any party injured, from time to time, until the whole amount thereof has been recovered.

II. DUTIES AND POWERS OF.

Seal of office.

ART. 1496. [6] Every Notary Public shall provide a seal of office, whereon shall be engraved in the centre, a star of five points, and the words "Notary Public, County of ——, Texas," around the margin; and he shall authenticate all his official acts therewith.

May take acknowledgments.

ART. 1497. [7] Notaries Public may take the acknowledgment or proof of all instruments of writing, in the manner provided for by law, to entitle them to registration in the office of County Recorder, and give certificate of all such acknowledgments and proofs, under their hand and official seals: they may take the examination and acknowledgment of married women to all deeds and instruments of writing, conveying their separate property and their interest in the homestead, in the manner provided by law.

And give certificates.

Same of married women.

ART. 1498. [8] Every Notary Public shall have power to administer oaths and give certificates thereof, under his hand and official seal.

May administer oaths.

ART. 1499. [9] They may take the proof or acknowledgments of all instruments of writing relating to commerce and navigation, and also of letters of attorney and other instruments of writing, make declarations and protests, and certify under their hand and seal, the truth of all matters or things done by virtue of their offices.

Writing relating to commerce, &c., letters of attorney, &c., declarations and give certificates.

ART. 1500. [10] Each Notary Public shall keep a memorandum of all his official acts as Notary Public, in a book to be kept by him for that purpose, and shall give a certified copy of any record in his office, to any person applying therefor, on the payment of all fees thereon.

Memorandum book, certified copies of records.

ART. 1501. [12] Notaries Public shall have power to take the depsitions of witnesses in the manner provided by law, and shall be entitled to the fees allowed to other officers for like services.

Depositions and fees for taking.

ART. 1502. [5] It shall be the duty of every Notary Public who shall protest any bill of exchange or promissory note, for non-acceptance or non-payment, to set forth in his protest and in his notarial record, a full and true statement of what shall have been done by him in relation thereto, according to the facts, by specifying therein whether demand was made of the sum of money in such bill or note specified, of whom, and when, and where such demand was made. It shall also be his duty to make the requisite notices of protest for the drawers and endorsers, who are sought to be made liable; and when any such notice shall be served by him, he shall note in his protest, and notarial record, on whom and when such notice was served; and when such notice shall be deposited in the post-office by him, he shall specify when and where mailed, and to whom, and to where directed; and such protest, or a copy of such notarial record, certified under the hand and seal of such Notary Public, shall be admitted in all the courts of this State, as evidence of the facts therein set forth.

Act of March 20, 1848.

Protests, how made.

Notice of.

Copy of evidence.

ART. 1503. [5] If any Notary Public shall vacate his office in any manner, his record-books and all public papers in his office, and his seal of office, shall be deposited with the Clerk of the County Court of his county, and by him shall be delivered to the successor of such Notary, who shall be bound to pay to the person anthorized to receive the same, the reasonable value of such seal.

When office vacated, books, papers, and seal of office delivered to County Clerk.

ART. 1504. [11] All declarations and protests made, and acknowledgments taken, by Notaries Public, and certified copies of their records and official papers, shall be received as evidence of the facts therein stated, in all the courts of this State.

Official acts, and copies of records, evidence.

ART. 1505. [13] Copies of all records, declarations, protests, and other official acts of Notaries Public, may be certified by their successors, with whom they are deposited, and shall have the same authority as if certified by the Notary by whom they were originally made.

Copies by successor of equal autority.

OFFICERS, OFFICE AND VACANCIES.

Act of Dec. 19, 1849. Took effect from passage. [See Const. Art. 7, Sec. 23.]

ART. 1506. [1] All officers of the State and of each district and county therein, when the time for which they were respectively elected or appointed shall have expired, shall be hereby authorized and empowered to perform the duties of their respective offices until their successors shall be duly qualified.

Act of April 3, 1846. Took effect from passage. Governor may fill certain vacancies.

ART. 1507. [1] The Governor be, and he is hereby authorized to fill all vacancies that may occur during the recess of the Legislature in such offices as have been filled by joint vote of both Houses of the Legislature; also, that he be authorized to fill all vacancies that may occur by death or resignation during the recess of the Legislature, which require the consent of the Senate.

Act of Feb. 11, 1850. *Pro tem.* appointments.

ART. 1508. [5] In case of death, resignation, removal or disability of any present or future incumbent of any of the offices above-mentioned in the preceding section, the Governor shall appoint an officer *pro tem.* in his stead, to discharge the duties of such officer until the same shall be filled by an election under the provisions of this act. In case of vacancy in the office of Comptroller of Public Accounts, or State Treasurer, the Governor shall immediately make a temporary appointment of some suitable person to fill such vacancy, until the person elect shall have been duly qualified; and the person so appointed shall give like bond as is required of those officers, and discharge all such duties as are required of them by law, and be subject to like penalties for malfeascnce in office.

Act of Dec. 24, 1851. Took effect from passage. Qualifications for office.

ART. 1509. [1] No person shall be eligible to any office of honor, profit or trust, in this State, unless he be a qualified elector under the Constitution at the time of his election.

PARTITION.

I. OF LANDS.

II. OF SLAVES AND PERSONAL PROPERTY.

I. OF LANDS.

Act of Feb'ry 5, 1840. Took effect March 16, 1840. Part own'rs may be compelled to make partition.

ART. 1510. [1] All part owners of any estates of inheritance in lands, tenements and hereditaments, in their own rights, or in the rights of other persons, and all part owners who may hold, for a term of life or years, with others who may have estates of inheritance, or freehold in any lands, tenements, or hereditaments, may be compelled to make partition between them, of such lands, tenements and hereditaments as they may hold as part owners, by such lawful method as the party seeking such partition shall choose, or deem expedient; but no such partition between a part owner, or part owners, who hold estates for a term of life, or years, with others who hold equal, or greater estates, shall be prejudicial to those entitled to the reversions, or remainders, after the death of the owners for life, or after the expiration of the years.

Not to prejudice Rev·rs nor or Remainder man

ART. 1511. [4] They who were part owners of the lands, tenements and hereditaments, or any part thereof, before they were divided, shall hold the same of the landlords to whom they shall be allotted by the partition in severalty, under the same conditions, rents, covenants and reservations—and the landlords shall warrant the several parts unto the tenants—as they were bound by leases or grants respectively; and any demandant who was tenant in actual possession, to the tenant to the action, for his purpart of lands, tenements and hereditaments, derived by virtue of a writ of partition, or any part thereof, shall hold for the same term, and under the same conditions and covenants, when it shall be allotted in severalty.

How property shall be held after partition.

II. OF SLAVES AND PERSONAL PROPERTY.

ART. 1512. [1] Part owners of slaves and other personal property may be compelled to make partition between them.

Act of Dec'r 4, 1851. In force from passage.

ART. 1513. [2] The separate value of the slaves or other personal property, and the allotment in kind, to which each party claiming partition shall be entitled, shall be ascertained by the verdict of the jury.

Value ascertained by jury.

ART. 1514. [3] Where partition, in kind, of slaves or other personal property, shall be ordered by the judgment of the Court, execution or executions shall be issued to the proper officer or officers of the county or counties where the property may be, commanding him or them to put the parties in possession of the property allotted each respectively.

Execution when to issue.

ART. 1515. [4] When slaves or other personal property will not admit of partition in kind, the jury shall so find by their verdict, and at the same time ascertain the proportion of the value of such slaves or other personal property, to which each party shall be entitled respectively.

When property will not admit of partition what jury shall find.

ART. 1516. [5] In cases provided for in the next preceding section, execution or executions shall be issued to the proper officer or officers of the county or counties where the property may be, commanding him or them to sell the property as in other cases of execution, and pay over the proceeds of sale to the parties, in proportion ascertained by the judgment of the Court.

Property to be how sold and money partitioned.

ART. 1517. [6] This act shall not affect the mode of proceeding prescribed by law for the partition of estates of deceased persons among the heirs and legatees.

Act not to affect mode of partitioning estates.

(a) The statute is not restrictive; and does not forbid a resort to any other mode known to judicial proceedings, within the general jurisdiction of the District Courts. Payne v. Benham, 16 Tex. Rep. 364. Grassmeyer v. Beeson, 18 Tex. Rep. 753.

Persons having a joint interest with the estate of a deceased person in any property, real or personal, may make application to the County Court, from which letters testamentary or of administration have been granted on said estate, to have partition thereof, or they may sue in the District Court, under the general jurisdiction of that Court. Ellis v. Rhone, 17 Tex. Rep. 131.

It is usual to provide in the decree for partition for the commissioners to report, and upon confirmation of their report to direct conveyances to be made. 18 Tex Rep. 753. But it is competent for the Court to direct the manner of making the partition, and to decree the making of the conveyances without the necessity of a report and decree of confirmation, &c. Ibid.

PARTNERSHIP.

Act of May 12, 1846. Took effect June 22, 1846.

Limited partnerships may be formed.

Art. 1518. [1] Limited partnerships for the transaction of any mercantile, mechanical, manufacturing or other business, except banking, within this State, may be formed by two or more persons, upon the terms, with the rights and powers, and subject to the conditions and liabilities herein prescribed; but the provisions of this act shall not be construed to authorize any such partnership for the purpose of banking or making insurance.

General and special partners.

Art. 1519. [2] Such partnerships may consist of one or more persons, who shall be called the general partners, and who shall be jointly and severally responsible as general partners now are by law, and of one or more persons who shall contribute in actual cash payments a specific sum as capital to the common stock, who shall be called special partners, and who shall not be liable for the debts of the partnerships, beyond the fund so contributed by him or them to the capital.

Special partners.

Who may bind the partnership.

Art. 1520. [3] The general partners only shall be authorized to transact business and sign for the partnership, and to bind the same.

Persons forming, shall sign a certificate, &c.

Art. 1521. [4] The persons desirous of forming such partnerships, shall make and severally sign a certificate, which shall contain—first, the name or firm under which such partnership is to be conducted; second, the general nature of the business intended to be transacted; third, the names of all the general and special partners interested therein, distinguishing which are general and which are special partners, and their respective places of residence; fourth, the amount of capital which each special partner shall have contributed to the common stock; and fifth, the period at which the partnership is to commence, and the period at which it is to terminate.

Shall be acknowledged.

Art. 1522. [5] The certificate shall be acknowledged by the several persons signing the same, before a Judge of the Supreme or District Court, or Notary Public; and such acknowledgment shall be made and certified in the same manner as the acknowledgment of the conveyances of lands.

Certificate shall be filed and recorded.

Art. 1523. [6] The certificate so acknowledged and certified, shall be filed in the office of the Clerk of the court of the county in which the principal place of business of the partnership shall be situated, and shall also be recorded by him at large, in a book to be kept for that purpose, open to public inspection. If the partnership shall have places of business situated in different counties, a transcript of the certificate, and of the acknowledgment thereof, duly certified by the Clerk in whose office it shall be recorded, shall be filed and recorded in like manner in the office of the Clerk of the County Court of every such county.

ART. 1524. [7] At the time of filing the original certificate with the evidence of the acknowledgment thereof, as before directed, an affidavit of one or more of the general partners shall also be filed in the same office, stating that the sums specified in the certificate to have been contributed by each of the special partners, to the common stock, have been actually and in good faith paid in cash. Affidavit shall be filed.

ART. 1525. [8] No such partnership shall be deemed to have been formed until a certificate shall have been made, acknowledged, filed and recorded, nor until an affidavit shall have been filed as above directed; and if any false statement be made in such certificate or affidavit, all the persons interested in such partnership shall be liable for all the engagements thereof, as general partners. Not formed until, &c, Liability for false statement.

ART. 1526. [9] The partners shall publish the terms of the partnership when registered, for at least six weeks, immediately after such registry, in such newspapers as shall be designated by the Clerk in whose office such registry shall be made; and if such publication be not made, the partnership shall be deemed general. Terms of, shall be published.

ART. 1527. [10] An affidavit of the publication of such notice, by the printer of the newspapers in which the same shall be published, may be filed with the Clerk directing the same, and shall be evidence of the facts therein contained. Affidavit of printer filed, evidence of, &c.

ART. 1528. [11] Every renewal, or continuance of such partnership beyond the time originally fixed for its duration, shall be certified, acknowledged and recorded, and an affidavit of a general partner be made and filed, and notice given in the manner herein required, for its original formation; and every such partnership which shall be otherwise renewed or continued, shall be deemed a general partnership. Partnership may be renewed.

ART. 1529. [12] Every alteration which shall be made in the names of the partners, in the nature of the business, or in the capital or shares thereof, or in any other matter specified in the original certificate, shall be deemed a dissolution of the partnership; and every such partnership which shall in any manner be carried on after any such alteration shall have been made, shall be deemed a general partnership, unless renewed as a special partnership, according to the provisions of the last section. When alteration shall be deemed dissolution of special partnership.

ART. 1530. [13] The business of the partnership shall be conducted under a firm in which the names of the general partners only shall be inserted, without the addition of the word "company," or any other general term; and if the name of any special partner be used in such firm, with his privity, he shall be deemed a general partner. Partnership conducted in name of general partners only.

ART. 1531. [14] Suits in relation to the business of the partnership may be brought and conducted by and against the general partners, in the same manner as if there was no special partners. Suits in relation to business of, how brought.

ART. 1532. [15] No part of the sum which any special partner shall have contributed to the capital stock, shall be withdrawn by him, or paid or transferred to him in the character of dividends, profits, or otherwise, at any time during the continuance of the partnership; but any partner may annually receive lawful interest on the sum so contributed by him, if the payment of such interest shall not reduce the original amount of such capital; and if, after the payment of such interest, any profit shall remain to be divided, he may also receive his portion of such profits. Special partner shall not withdraw stock.

When capital of, reduced by payment of interest and profits.

ART. 1533. [16] If it shall appear that by the payment of interest or profits to any special partner, the original capital has been reduced, the partner receiving the same shall be bound to restore the amount necessary to make good his share of the capital, with interest.

Special partner may examine and advise.

ART. 1534. [17] A special partner may from time to time examine into the state and progress of the partnership concerns, and may advise as to their management.

General partners shall account.

ART. 1535. [18] The general partners shall be liable to account to each other, and to the special partners, for their management of the concern, both in law and equity, as other partners now are by law.

Partner guilty of fraud shall be liable, &c.

ART. 1536. [19] Every partner who shall be guilty of any fraud in the affairs of the partnership shall be liable, civilly, to the party injured to the extent of his damage, and shall also be liable to an indictment for a misdemeanor, punishable by fine and imprisonment, or both, at the discretion of the court and jury by which he shall be tried.

Assignment to one creditor, when void

ART. 1537. [20] Every sale, assignment, or transfer of any property or effects of the partnership made by such partnership, when insolvent, or in contemplation of insolvency, or after, or in contemplation of insolvency of any partner, with the intent of giving a preference to any creditor of such partnership, or insolvent partner, over other creditors of such partnership, and every judgment confessed, lien created or security given by such partnership, under the like circumstances, and with like intent, shall be void as against creditors of such partnership.

Effect of such assignment in contemplation of insolvency.

ART. 1538. [21] Every such sale, assignment, or transfer of any of the property or effects of a general or special partner, made by such general or special partner when insolvent, or in contemplation of insolvency, or after, or in contemplation of the insolvency of the partnership, with the intent of giving to any creditor of his own, or of the partnership, a preference over the creditors of the partnership, and every judgment confessed, lien created, or security given by any such partner, under like circumstances, and with like intent, shall be void as against the creditors of the partnership.

Liability for violating the provisions of the two preceding sections.

ART. 1539. [22] Every special partner who shall violate any provision of the last two preceding sections, and who shall concur in or assent to any such violation of the partnership, by any individual partner, shall be liable as a general partner.

Partnership creditors preferred.

ART. 1540. [23] In case of the insolvency or bankruptcy of the partnership, no special partner shall, under any circumstances, be allowed to claim as creditor, until the claims of all other creditors of the partnership shall be satisfied.

Dissolution previous to the time specified in certificate.

ART. 1541. [24] No dissolution of such partnerships, by the acts of the parties, shall take place previous to the time specified in the certificate of its formation, or in the certificate of its renewal, until a notice of such dissolution shall have been filed and recorded, and published once in each week for four weeks, in a newspaper printed in each of the counties where the partnership may have a place of business, if there be such papers; and if there be no newspapers published in such county, then in a newspaper published in the nearest county where there is one.

Act of Feb. 5, 1858. Took effect July 1, 1858.

Process served on one partner, notice to all, except.

ART. 1542. [2] Where suit is instituted against a partnership, service or process upon one of the partners shall be sufficient notice to all the members of the firm, except that the judgment rendered in case of such service, shall only be enforced against the partnership property, and the separate property of the partner who may have been served.

PASSENGERS COMING TO THE STATE.

ART. 1543. [1] Within twenty-four hours after the landing of any passengers from any ship or vessel, arriving at any of the ports of Texas, at which there is an incorporated town, from any of the United States, other than this State, or from any country out of the United States, the master or commander of the ship or vessel, from which such passenger or passengers shall have been landed, shall make a report in writing, on oath or affirmation, to the mayor of such incorporated town, or in case of his absence, or other inability to serve, to the persons discharging the duties of his office; which report shall state the name, place of birth, last legal residence, age and occupation, of every person or passenger, who shall have landed, or been permitted to land, from such ship or vessel, on her last voyage to said port, not being a citizen of the United States, and who shall have within the last preceding twelve months, arrived from any country out of the United States, at any port or place in the United States, and who shall not have paid the commutation money, or been bonded according to the provisions of this act; the said report shall contain a like statement of all such persons or passengers as shall have been put or allowed to go on any ship, vessel or boat, with the intention of proceeding to and landing at any place within the limits of the State of Texas. The said report shall further specify whether any such passengers are lunatic, idiot, deaf, dumb, blind or infirm, and if so, whether they are accompanied by relatives likely to be able or willing to support them; and shall further specify particularly the names, last place of residence and ages of all passengers who may have died during the said last voyage; also, the names and residence of the owner or owners of such vessel. In case any such master or commander of such vessel shall omit or neglect to report as aforesaid, any such person or passenger, with the particulars aforesaid, or shall make any false report or statement in respect to any such person or passenger, or in respect to the owner or owners of such vessel, or in respect to all or any of the particulars herein-before specified, such master or commander shall forfeit the sum of fifty dollars for every such passenger, in regard to whom such omission or neglect shall have occurred, or any such false report or statement shall be made; for which the owner or owners, consignee or consignees, of every such ship or vessel, shall also be liable jointly and severally, and which may be sued for and recovered, before any court of competent jurisdiction.

Act of Feb'y 11, 1850. Took effect March 23, 1850. Report of shall be made by commanders of vessels.

ART. 1544. [2] It shall be the duty of said mayor or other person discharging the duties of his office, by an endorsement to be made upon the said report, to require the owner or consignee of the ship or vessel, from which such persons were landed, to give a several bond, payable to the State of Texas, in a penalty of three hundred dollars, for each and every person or passenger included in such report; such bond being secured as hereinafter provided, and conditioned to indemnify and save harmless, each and every city, town and county in this State, from any cost for the relief or support of the person named within the bond, within five years from the date thereof. Each and every bond shall be secured by two or more sufficient securities, being residents of the county in which it was executed; each of whom shall prove by oath or otherwise, that he is the owner of real estate, situated in such county, of the value of three

Bond required for each passenger mention'd in the report.

hundred dollars, over and above all which is by law exempt from execution and from any claim or lien thereon or against him; including therein any contingent claim, which may accrue from or upon any former bond given under the provisions of this act; or such bond may, at the option of the party, be secured by mortgage of real estate, or by deposit of the amount of the penalty in the treasury of such incorporated city or town. It shall be lawful for any owner or consignee, at any time within three days after the landing of such persons or passengers, to commute for the bond or bonds so required by paying to the Collector or other proper receiving officer, of such incorporated city or town, the sum of one dollar for every passenger reported by him, as by law required; the receipt of which sum shall be deemed a full and sufficient discharge from the requirements of giving bonds as above provided; the said Collector or other officer is required to pay the said money with an account thereof, into the treasury of the corporation of the city or town, for the support and benefit of the Hospital thereof.

Bond may be commuted for one dollar, &c.

If passenger for whom bond is given become chargeable on any city, &c.

ART. 1545. [3] If any person for whom a bond shall have been given, as aforesaid, shall, within the the time specified in such bond, become chargeable upon any city, town or county of this State, or any of the citizens thereof, other than the relatives of such person, the mayor, aldermen, and inhabitants of such incorporated city or town, may bring an action upon such bond, in the name of the State of Texas, and shall be entitled to recover on such bond, from time to time, so much money, not in the whole exceeding the penalty of such bond exclusive of costs, as shall be sufficient to defray the expenses incurred by any such city, town or county, for the maintenance and support of the person for whom such bond was given as aforesaid; and shall be authorized to collect and apply such money, from any of the real or other security mortgaged, pledged or deposited therefor, in conformity with this act.

Penalty for failing or refusing to give bond or pay commutat'n money.

ART. 1546. [4] If any owner or consignee, as aforesaid, shall refuse or neglect to give any such bond or bonds, and security therefor, as required in this act, within three days after the landing of such persons or passengers, or shall not, within that time, have paid the moneys authorized to be received, in cases where such bonds are authorized to be commuted for, every such owner or consignee of such ship or vessel, severally and respectively, shall be subject to a penalty of five hundred dollars, for each and every person or passenger, on whose account such bond may have been required, or for whom such commutation money might have been paid under this act; such penalty to be sued for and recovered in any court of competent jurisdiction.

Recovery and application of penalties.

ART. 1547. [5] The penalties and forfeitures prescribed in and by this act, may be sued for in the name of the State of Texas, and recovered with costs of suit, in any court having cognizance thereof; and, when recovered shall be applied to the support of the hospital or hospitals, or other means provided for the maintenance of destitute, sick, infirm, lunatic, idiot, deaf, dumb or blind persons, or others who may properly become a public charge to the city or town, at which any such penalties or forfeitures may have accrued.

PATROLS.

ART. 1548. [1] The County Court of every county shall, upon application, when necessary, appoint a patrol detachment, to consist of one captain and not more than five privates nor less than three, for each or any district or company division in the county; whose term of service shall be three months from the time of their appointment: provided, that one half of the patrol appointed shall be owners of slaves, or their substitutes. Act of May 9, 1846. Took effect from passage. Appointed by County Court, when.

ART. 1549. [2] The captain and privates of each detachment shall be appointed from among the citizens of the district or division, who are subject to perform militia duty, and who are to patrol the same, and that they shall patrol said district at least once in every month, and as much oftener as the tranquility thereof may require, by visiting the negro quarters and all other places in said district, where it may be suspected that slaves are improperly or unlawfully assembled. Each detachment to be appointed from the district—duties, &c.

ART. 1550. [3] Whenever a detachment, or part of one, may find any slave or slaves off the plantation or other premises of his, her or their master, mistress or employer, strolling about without a pass or other written permission from some person authorized to give the same, said detachment, or part thereof, may give to every slave so offending, any number of lashes not exceeding twenty-five. May punish slave, when.

ART. 1551. [4] Any detachment, or part thereof, shall be authorized under such rules as may be prescribed by law, to search suspected places for harbored, runaway or fugitive slaves; to apprehend and carry the same before a Justice of the Peace in the district, or the nearest Justice out of said district; to be dealt with as the law may direct; and also to apprehend any white person who may be found in any assemblage of slaves, or in or about any negro quarter, associating with, or participating in common with the slaves of such assemblage or quarter, in amusements or associations, without having the permission of the master or owner of such slaves, and carry such person or persons before any Justice of the Peace in such district; who shall be fined for the first offence in a sum not less than five nor more than fifty dollars, and imprisoned not more than thirty days, and for a second offence, shall be liable for double the penalty, and for a third offence, shall be bound by said Justice, to the next District Court, and be subject to indictment and punished as for a misdemeanor. May search suspected places for harbored or runaway slaves—may apprehend white person, when.

ART. 1552. No detachment shall do patrol duty out of the limits of its own district or division, unless by special permission of the County Court, or in case of insurrection or insubordination among slaves, or in case of their assembling at an improper time or place, or unlawfully, or for an improper purpose. Confined to their own districts.

ART. 1553. [6] The captain may divide his detachment, when on duty or about to engage in it, and may require each division thereof to patrol in such part of the district as he may designate: provided, however, that no division shall consist of less than two patrols. Captain may divide detachment.

Duty of captain.

ART. 1554. [7] It shall be the duty of the captain to notify the members of his detachment of their appointment, and of the times when and the places where they will be required to perform patrol duties; and also to prevent each one of them from committing trespasses and all other unlawful acts while engaged in patrolling; but if any member thereof should be guilty of anything herein forbidden, it shall be the duty of said captain to report his name and offence to some Justice of the Peace in his district, or to the nearest Justice in the county, that the offender may be dealt with according to law; and for a failure of said captain so to do, he may, on complaint to said Justice, be fined not less than ten nor more than fifty dollars, for each and every such failure.

Person refusing or failing to do patrol duty.

ART. 1555. [8] If any person liable to do patrol duty, shall after being appointed and notified thereof, fail or refuse to discharge the duties required of him by this act, or shall fail or refuse, when on duty, to obey the detachment officer, he may on conviction before the Justice of the Peace of his district, or the nearest Justice in his county, be fined a sum not less than five nor more than twenty dollars, for each and every failure or refusal: provided, however, that the person so charged shall have the privilege of being heard in his defence.

Officer or member may be removed for cause

ART. 1556. [9] In case of the death or removal from the district, of any member of a detachment, any other member thereof may, on application to the County Court have the vacancy thus occasioned, filled, if necessary; and that any three members of a detachment may on application in writing, for sufficient cause therein shown to said court, have the officer, or any other member thereof removed from said detachment and the vacancy filled as hereinbefore specified.

Captains of militia companies to furnish list, &c.

ART. 1557. [10] Every Captain or Commanding Officer of a Militia Company, shall, within ten days after his muster, file in the office of the Clerk of the County in which he resides, a full and correct list of the persons in his district or division, who are liable to do militia duty; from among whom shall be appointed a patrol detachment, as in this act is provided; and for a failure of said captain or commanding officer, so to do, he shall be subject to a fine of not less than twenty nor more than fifty dollars, recoverable on conviction before a Justice of the Peace, as provided in this act.

County Court to commission officers.

ART. 1558. [11] It shall be the duty of the County Court to commission the officer of said detachment, furnish him with a list of the members thereof, and notify him of the time for which the same were appointed to serve as patrols.

Fees allowed patrol for apprehending runaway.

ART. 1559. [12] Any detachment shall be allowed, for apprehending and taking before a Justice of the Peace, and from thence to the owner or the jail of the county, any runaway slave, the same fees that may be allowed by law to any other person for similar services, and the amount when received shall be equally divided among those who may have performed the services.

Informer against patrol shall be competent witness.

Quære: Whether repealed?

ART. 1560. [13] The informer against any patrol, for malfeasance or for disobedience of orders, shall be a competent witness in the case; and that all fines for breaches of this act, shall when collected, be paid into the County Treasury for county purposes; and that this act shall take effect from and after its passage.

PENITENTIARY.

ART. 1561. [1] The Governor be, and he is hereby authorized and required to appoint, by and with the advice of and consent of the Senate, three competent persons as Commissioners, whose duty it shall be to select a proper site whereon to erect a State Penitentiary, to be convenient to navigable water, having due regard to health, materials for building, the importation of machinery, tools, materials to be wrought or manufactured, and for the transportation of articles made or manufactured by the convicts, to a market for the same. Act of March 13, 1848. Took effect from passage. Commissioners to locate.

ART. 1562. [2] The Commissioners shall secure, by purchase or otherwise, land not exceeding one hundred acres, to include the site selected: provided the land shall not cost the State more than five dollars per acre; and they are authorized to pay a fair value with the consent of the Governor, for any water power adjacent to and connected with the site of the Penitentiary. Site to be secured.

ART. 1563. [3] The Commissioners shall report their proceedings to the Governor within sixty days after receiving notice of their appointment, together with the title deed for the land herein required to be procured, after having the same recorded in the Recorder's office in the county wherein the land lies, which deed shall be recorded and filed in the office of Secretary of State. The Commissioners so appointed shall receive as compensation for their services three dollars per day each, for the time they shall be actually employed in selecting a site and making their report, as herein required. Commissioners to report to Governor. Compensation.

ART. 1564. [4] The Governor, upon the receipt of the reports of the Commissioners, as above prescribed, shall appoint, with the advice and consent of the Senate, a suitable person as Superintendent, whose duty it shall be, in connexion with the Directors herein provided for, to procure and submit a plan of the Penitentiary, to the Governor; which plan, if approved of by him, shall be deposited in the office of Secretary of State; and immediately thereafter, the Superintendent shall be required by the Governor to prepare for the erection of the Penitentiary, upon the plan approved of, and upon the site selected; and the Directors shall be authorized to employ as many mechanics and laborers as they shall deem necessary, in connexion with the convicts delivered to the custody of the Superintendent, to put up so much of the building or buildings as will secure the prisoners and answer the immediate wants of the State; which building or buildings shall be so constructed and arranged as to form a part of the main buildings of the Penitentiary; and upon the erection of said building or buildings, the Superintendent, under the direction of the Directors, shall discharge the hired mechanics and laborers; and the building of the Penitentiary shall be continued by the convicts until the same is completed. The Penitentiary shall be built of substantial materials, and shall be surrounded by a secure wall, to be placed at such a distance from the main building as to enclose a yard of sufficient dimensions to allow room for the erection of workshops and the employment of the convicts at such kind of labor as may be deemed most profitable and useful to the State, and will the Superintendent, Directors, plan. Erection of.

least interfere with the general mechanical industry of the country; the Superintendent shall cause to be erected cells for the solitary confinement of the convicts at night, and at such other times as the Superintendent and Directors shall direct; the Superintendent shall make an annual estimate at the commencement of each year, of all the materials necessary for carrying on the business in the various departments of the Penitentiary, and submit the same to the Directors; and he shall employ under the direction of the Directors, a sufficient number of overseers and guards for the safe keeping of the convicts.

Appointment of Directors.

ART. 1565. [5] The Governor shall appoint with the advice and consent of the Senate, three discreet persons as Directors, any two of whom shall constitute a Board to transact business.

Act of Feb'y 16, 1852. Took effect from passage. Purchasing and disbursing agent.

ART. 1566. [1] The Directors shall, as soon as they are informed of the passage of this act, appoint some suitable person as purchasing, selling and disbursing agent, who shall give bond in the sum of twenty thousand dollars for the faithful performance of the duties of his office, with at least two good and sufficient securities to be approved by the Directors. The agent shall receive from time to time, the moneys appropriated for the support of the Penitentiary: provided, that he shall not receive in any one quarter of the year, more than one-fourth the amount appropriated for the annual support of the Penitentiary. General duties of. He shall, upon the order of the Superintendent, approved by any two Directors, purchase the necessary subsistence and clothing of the convicts, and also such materials as may be necessary for building or manufacturing purposes, except such as can be wrought, made or manufactured by the convicts in the Penitentiary. He shall keep in a well-bound book an account current, specifying the amount of moneys received by him from appropriations, with each particular item of disbursement, for which he shall take receipts. He shall, in the same book, keep an account of each article by him sold, with the price for which the same was sold, which book shall, at all times, be open to the Superintendent, Directors, and such citizens as may desire to examine the same. Book and acc'ts of. He shall annually make out, on or before the first day of November, a transcript from his book of all his disbursements, sales and purchases for the preceding year, and submit the same with his vouchers to the Superintendent and Directors, who shall examine and carefully compare the transcript with the books of the Clerk, and if found correct, they shall transmit the same, certified under their hands, to the Governor of the State, who shall lay the same before the Legislature at each regular session thereof, within ten days after their organization.

Clerk may be removed for fraud &c.

ART. 1567. [2] A majority of the Directors, upon the detection of fraud, negligence or incapacity in the Clerk to perform the duties of his office, may remove him from office, and appoint a successor, who shall demand and receive all the books, moneys and other property, pertaining to the office of his predecessor.

Clerk's salary.

ART. 1568. [3] The Clerk shall receive an annual salary of six hundred dollars, payable quarterly.

Act of Feb'y 11, 1854. Took effect from passage. Cotton manufactory in.

ART. 1569. [1] The Superintendent of the State Penitentiary, under the direction of the Board of Directors, be and he is hereby authorized and directed to erect or cause to be erected, suitable buildings within the walls of the same, as far as practicable, by the labor of the convicts, for the reception of an engine and machinery for the manufacture of coarse cotton and woolen goods, sufficient to employ the labor of at least fifty convicts.

ART. 1570. [2] The Superintendent, under the direction of the Board of

Directors, shall cause to be procured as early as may be necessary, a suitable engine and machinery for the aforesaid purpose; and that the sum of thirty-five thousand dollars, or as much thereof as may be necessary, be, and the same is hereby appropriated to carry this act into effect. Engine to be purchased; appropriation for.

ART. 1571. [3] Said machinery shall be kept constantly at work and in operation, and as much labor applied to the manufacturing of coarse cotton and woolen goods as can be advantageously employed for that purpose. Cotton and woolen goods to be manufactu'd.

ART. 1572. [4] The Superintendent, under the direction of the Board of Directors, shall, if they deem it expedient, employ an engineer and a sufficient number of master workmen to carry the factory system in said Institution into successful operation. Engineer and master workmen.

ART. 1573. [5] Manufactured fabrics are to be sold and disposed of as other articles are disposed of that are now wrought in said Penitentiary, and the proceeds thereof to be applied to the support of said Institution. Sale of fabrics—proceeds.

PILOTS.

I. APPOINTMENT AND QUALIFICATION.

ART. 1574. [1] The Governor be, and he is hereby authorized and required to appoint and commission, for a term of four years, at each of the ports of this State, such number of competent and reputable persons as may be needed at each for the office of Branch Pilot; and he shall, from time to time, make new appointments as aforesaid, when vacancies or an increase of business require it; but until appointments are made pursuant to this act, the Pilots of the several ports, who were in office when the organization of the State Government took place, shall be authorized to continue acting as such, on the authority of their collectoral appointments. Act of April 7, 1846. Took effect from passage. Governor shall appoint Branch Pilots.

ART. 1575. [5] Each Branch Pilot shall give a bond, with two or more securities, made payable to the Governor and his successors in office, for the sum of five thousand dollars, conditioned for the faithful performance of the duties of said Pilot; which bond shall be presented to the Board of Commissioners of Branch Pilots shall give bond, how approved.

Pilots, or if there be none, to the Chief Justice of the county in which the port is situated, and must be approved by said Board or Judge, before said Pilot can exercise the duties of his office; and the bond aforesaid shall be forwarded by said Commissioners or Judge, with their or his approval thereon endorsed, to the Governor.

II. POWERS, DUTIES, AND LIABILITIES.

How Branch Pilots may appoint Deputies.

ART. 1576.' [8] Each Branch Pilot may appoint, subject to examination and approval of the Board of Commissioners, two deputies, for whose acts the Branch Pilot so appointed shall be responsible; and any Branch Pilot who shall appoint a deputy without the approval of said Board, shall forfeit his own appointment; and the said Board shall have authority to restrict all Deputy Pilots from piloting over the bar, vessels of over a certain draft of water.

Penalty of inebriety.

ART. 1577. [10] Any Branch or Deputy Pilot who shall be guilty of taking charge of a vessel, in a state of inebriety, shall, upon proof of the same, for the first offence be suspended for one month, and for the second offence be dismissed, and be rendered incapable of again serving in either capacity; and if any Branch or Deputy Pilot shall wilfully or by neglect, cause the wreck of a vessel, he shall be dismissed, and be rendered incapable of again serving in either capacity, and shall be subject to such punishment as is prescribed by law.

Penalty for acting as, without appointment.

ART. 1578. [11] If any person, not appointed a Branch or Deputy Pilot, shall pilot any ship or vessel out of or into any port of this State, when a Branch or Deputy Pilot has offered such service, the person so piloting shall forfeit and pay to such Branch or Deputy Pilot, the sum of fifty dollars, to be recovered before any court having cognizance of the case.

III. BOARDS OF COMMISSIONERS.

Appointment and Powers.

Governor shall appoint Commissioners.

ART. 1579. [2] The Governor shall appoint, with the consent of the Senate, for each port of the State whose population and circumstances will warrant it, a Board of five persons of respectable standing, under the denomination of Com missioners of Pilots, for such port, three of whom shall be practical seamen, and the other two merchants, who shall be commissioned by the Governor for the term of four years; and the Governor shall, during the recess of the Legislature, be authorized to suspend until the next session of the same, any of said Commissioners, and to fill, until the same period, any vacancies in the Board caused by death, resignation, or otherwise: provided, however, that no member of the Board of Commissioners shall be, directly or indirectly, pecuniarily interested in any Pilot, boat or Branch Pilot in the business of their trust.

Powers and duties of Commissioners.

ART. 1580. [3] Said Board of Commissioners shall be authorized, if they deem it advisable, to examine and decide on the qualifications of any Branch or Deputy Pilot whom they find already appointed at the time of their organization; and it shall be their duty to examine each new applicant for the office of Branch or Deputy Pilot, and to decide on his qualifications, recommending to the Governor, where new appointments are proper, such as are meritorious; and it shall also be their duty to examine into any case of alleged or supposed misconduct, or inefficiency in Branch or Deputy Pilots; and they shall be authorized, after a due hearing of accusation, testimony, and defence, to suspend such Pilot, if sufficient cause appear; and during such suspension, he shall not be allowed to exercise the functions of his office: the Governor shall, however, have power, at his will and pleasure, to remove any Branch Pilot, or to reinstate any one of the same who has been suspended by the Commissioners.

ART. 1581. [4] The Board of Commissioners of Pilots of each port, shall require a certain term of residence in the Republic or State of Texas, not less than two years, to authorize any person to exercise the functions of Branch Pilot for their port; as also to establish a term of probation not exceeding one year as a Deputy Pilot, before any person can exercise the functions of Branch Pilot: provided, however, that the latter requirement shall not apply to those who have been Branch Pilots in the same port, under the laws of the Republic, and are re-appointed under the laws of the State of Texas. Requirements of Branch Pilot.

ART. 1582. [6] The Board of Commissioners of Pilots shall have authority, within the limits provided in this act, to fix the rates of pilotage, and to establish regulations respecting the stations whereat, and the times wherein, Pilots shall be on duty, with provisions for leave of absence; as, also, respecting the class, condition, number and use of pilot-boats, and such other minor regulations, compatible with the provisions of this act, as may be needful for the governance of Pilots, and for the order and good effect of the proceedings of the Board; of which proceedings a record shall be kept: provided, no regulation shall be adopted repugnant to the Constitution of the State. Powers of Board.

ART. 1583. [7] The Board of Commissioners of Pilots shall be authorized and required to hear and determine all disputes that may arise respecting Pilots and pilotage; to award to Pilots extra compensation for extra services to vessels in distress; as also compensation for injurious loss of time incurred by Pilots in waiting on vessels, or by being carried off to sea on vessels by default of the master or owner, when such Pilots might have been landed: provided, always, that no more than three dollars for each day shall be awarded for mere loss of time; and it shall be the duty of said Board to superintend and generally attend to all matters appertaining to Pilots and Pilotage: but from any decision of said Board, an appeal may be taken to the court having cognizance of the case. Same subject.

ART. 1584. At any port whose population and circumstances do not warrant the appointment of a Board of Commissioners of Pilots, in the manner before provided, the Governor may authorize the Chief Justice of the county to appoint a provisional committee of from three to five persons, of good character and maritime experience, who shall be authorized, under this act, to establish the rates of Pilotage and the rules for governing Pilots; to examine the qualifications of Pilots and applicants for the office; to investigate the case of any Pilot charged with misconduct or inefficiency, and to suspend him if sufficient cause appear. Chief Justice of county may appoint provisional Board in certain cases.

IV. PILOTAGE.

ART. 1585. [9] The rate of pilotage on any class of vessels shall not, in any port of this State, exceed three dollars for each foot of water which the vessel, at the time of piloting, draws; and that whenever a vessel, except of the classes below excepted, shall decline the service of a Pilot offered outside the bar, and shall enter the port without the aid of one, she shall be liable to the first Pilot whose services she so declined, for the payment of half-pilotage; and any vessel which, after being brought in by a Pilot, shall go out without employ Rate of pilotage

ing one, shall be liable to the payment of half-pilotage to the Pilot who brought her in; or if she has come in without the aid of a Pilot, though offered outside, she shall, in so going out, be liable for the payment of half-pilotage to the Pilot who had first offered his services before she came in: but if she has come in without the aid of a Pilot, or the offer of it outside, she shall, in case of going out without a Pilot, not be liable to half-pilotage; and when a Pilot takes charge of a vessel twenty miles outside of the bar and brings her to it, he shall be entitled to one-fourth pilotage for such off-shore service, in addition to what he is entitled to recover for bringing her in: but if such off-shore service be declined, no portion of the said compensation for it shall be recovered; and the following classes of vessels shall be free from any charge for pilotage, unless for actual service, to wit: all vessels of twenty tons and under; all vessels of whatsoever burden, owned in the State of Texas, and registered and licensed in the District of Texas, when arriving from or departing to any port of the State of Texas; all vessels of seventy-five tons and under, owned and licensed for the coasting trade in any part of the United States, when arriving from or departing to any port in the State of Texas; all vessels of seventy-five tons and under, owned in the State of Texas, and licensed for the coasting trade in the District of Texas, when arriving from or departing to any port in the United States.

Consignee responsible for pilotage.

ART. 1586. [12] The consignee of any vessel, shall be held responsible for the pilotage of said vessel.

V. FOR MOUTH OF BRAZOS RIVER.

Act of March, 18, 1848. Took effect 29th April, 1848. Pilots for mouth of Brazos river.

ART. 1587. [1] The Governor be, and he is hereby authorized and required to appoint, by and with the advice and consent of the Senate, one or more competent persons to act as Pilots at the mouth of the Brazos river in this State; and the person or persons so appointed shall hold their offices for two years, and until their successors are appointed and qualified, in the manner provided for in this act.

Qualification of.

ART. 1588. [2] Before any person appointed under the provisions of this act shall enter upon the discharge of his duties, he shall execute and deliver to the Chief Justice of Brazoria county, a bond with two or more good and sufficient sureties, to be approved by the said Chief Justice, and payable to the Governor of the State, in the sum of five thousand dollars, conditioned for the faithful performance of the duties of his office, and shall also take and subscribe the oath of office prescribed by the Constitution; which oath shall be endorsed on or annexed to said bond, with the certificate of the officer administering the same. Said bond and oath shall be recorded in the office of the Clerk of the County Court, and deposited therein; and said bond shall not be void on the first recovery, but may be sued on from time to time, in the name of any person or persons injured by a breach thereof, until the whole penalty shall have been recovered.

Vacancies.

ART. 1589. [3] Whenever a vacancy shall happen in either of said offices during the recess of the Senate, the Governor shall have power to make an appointment to fill such vacancy, and the person so appointed shall continue to perform the duties of his office until a successor is appointed and qualified, in the manner provided for original appointments.

Consignees responsible.

ART. 1590. [5] The consignees of any vessel shall be held liable and responsible for the pilotage of said vessel.

Acting as Pilot

ART. 1591. [6] If any person not appointed a Pilot or Deputy Pilot, shall pilot any ship or vessel out of or into said river, when a Pilot or Deputy Pilot has offered such service, the person so piloting shall be liable to pay to the Pilot or Deputy Pilot who offered such service, full pilotage for such vessel, to be recovered by suit before any Justice of the Peace of the county. Without authority.

ART. 1592. [7] Each Pilot appointed under the provisions of this act may, by writing under his hand, appoint a Deputy Pilot to discharge his duties; but he shall be responsible for all official acts of such Deputy, in like manner as if such acts were done by himself. Deputy.

ART. 1593. [1] The said Pilots shall be entitled to three dollars for each foot of water that any vessel may draw, at the time of piloting the same; and whenever a vessel shall decline the services of a Pilot offered outside of the bar, and shall enter said river without the aid of one, the Pilot who first so offers his services, shall be entitled to one-half of the above amount; and if said vessel should also go out without a Pilot, she shall be required in like manner to pay half-pilotage; and any vessel which, after being brought in by a Pilot, shall go out without employing one, shall be liable for the payment of pilotage to the same pilot who brought her in; provided, however, that all vessels of thirty tons burden and under, shall be free from any charge of pilotage, unless for actual services. Act of Feb. 6th, 1850. Rate of pilotage.

PRINCIPAL AND SURETY, AND JOINT OBLIGOR.

ART. 1594. [5] The representative of one jointly bound with another, for the payment of a debt, or for performance or forbearance of any act, or for any other thing, and dying in the lifetime of the latter may be charged by virtue of such obligation, in the same manner as such representative might have been charged, if the obligors had been bound severally as well as jointly. Act of Feb. 5, 1840. Took effect March 16, 1840. Representative of deceased joint obligor, how charged.

ART. 1595. [4] No person shall be sued as an endorser, as guarantor, or as security, unless suit shall have been, or is simultaneously commenced against the principal, except in cases where the principal resides beyond the limits of the State, or in a county that is not organized, or where he is insolvent.(a) Act of May 13, 1846. Surety, guarantor or endorser not sued before principal, except, &c.

ART. 1596. [46] The principal and the endorser or surety upon any instrument in writing, may be joined in the same suit; but no judgment in any such

(a) To entitle a party, as surety, to the privilege under the statute of not being sued first, he must have contracted and been sued as surety. Where the principal is dead, the surety may be sued alone in the first instance. Merriweather *v.* Lewis, 2 Tex. Rep. 340. Ennis & Reynolds *v.* Crump, 6 Tex. Rep. 85. Scott *v.* Dewees, 2 Tex. Rep. 153. Where a person, not the payee, signs his name upon the back of a promissory note, at the time of its inception, without any words to express the nature of his undertaking, he is liable as an original promissor or as surety; but it is competent for the person so signing, to show by oral or other evidence, the real obligation intended to be assumed at the time of signing. Cook *v.* Southwick, 9 Tex. Rep. 615. Lewis *v.* Riggs, 9 Tex. Rep. 164. Campbell *v.* Beckwith, 17 Tex. Rep. 439. Grayson *v.* Taylor, 14 Tex. Rep. 672. Petty *v.* Cleveland, 2 Tex. Rep. 404. The plaintiff in a suit on a promissory note, against the makers and an endorser or guarantor, cannot discontinue as to one of the makers and proceed against the endorser or guarantor, unless he shows that the maker, as to whom he seeks to discontinue, resides beyond the limits of the State, in a county not organized, or is insolvent. Moore *v.* Janes, 6 Tex. Rep. 227. Hawkins *v.* Tinnin, 10 Tex. Rep. 188. Where the endorsee of a note brings suit against the principal, at the first term of the court, the statute is fulfilled; and the rights and liabilities of the parties are remitted to the common law; and at common law, delay, without fraud or agreement with the principal, will not discharge the surety. Cook *v.* Southwick, 9 Tex. Rep. 615.

Principal and security, &c., may be joined, no judgment against latter, unless.

suit shall be rendered against the endorser or surety, unless judgment is at the same time rendered against the principal, except where the plaintiff discontinues as to the principal, because he resides beyond the limits of the State, or because he is insolvent, in which cases he may discontinue and take judgment.(b)

Act of Feb. 5, 1858. Took effect July 1, 1858.

Surety may give notice to principal to bring suit, &c.

ART. 1597. [14] Any person bound as surety upon any contract for the payment of money, or the performance of any act otherwise than by a bill of exchange or promissory note assignable or negociable by law, when the right of action has accrued, may require, by notice in writing, the creditor or obligee forthwith to institute a suit upon the contract.

When surety shall be dis charged after such notice.

ART. 1598. [15] If the creditor or obligee, not being under legal disability, shall fail to bring his suit to the first term of the court thereafter, or to the second term, showing good cause why he did not bring it to the first term, and prosecute the same to judgment and execution, the surety giving such notice, shall be discharged from all liability thereon.

In a joint action how question of suretyship may be tried.

ART. 1599. [16] When any suit is brought against two or more defendants upon any contract, any one or more of the defendants being surety for the others, the surety may, upon a written statement of the matter being set out in his or her answer, cause the question of suretyship to be tried and determined upon the issue made for the parties defendant, at the trial of the cause, or at any time before or after trial, or at a subsequent term; but such proceedings shall not delay the suit of the plaintiff.

Issue in favor of surety, property of principal to be levied on before, &c.

ART. 1600. [17] If the finding of such issue be in favor of the surety, the Court shall make an order directing the Sheriff to levy the execution first upon the property of the principal, subject to execution, and situate in the county in which the judgment is rendered, before a levy shall be made upon the property of the surety: provided, so much property of the principal can be found, as will in the opinion of the Sheriff, be sufficient to make the amount of the execution, otherwise the levy to be made on so much property of the principal as may be found, if any, and upon so much of the property of the surety as may be necessary to make the amount of the execution; and the Clerk shall endorse a memorandum of the order on the execution.

When surety, Sheriff or other officer is compelled to pay debt, remedy against principal.

ART. 1601. [18] When any person being surety in any undertaking whatever, shall be compelled to pay any judgment, or any part thereof, or shall make any payment which is applied upon such judgment, by reason of such suretyship, or when any Sheriff or other officer, shall be compelled to pay any judgment or any part thereof, by reason of any default of such officer, except for failing to pay over any money collected, or for wasting property levied on, the judgment shall not be discharged by such payment, but shall remain in force for the use of the surety, officer, or other person making such payment; and after the judgment creditor is paid, so much of the judgment as remains undischarged, but having been paid by such surety, officer or other person, may be prosecuted to execution for the use of such surety, officer or other person.

(b) There is nothing in the statute which prevents a suit from being brought and maintained against a surety in the first instance, the principal having previously died. The jurisdiction contemplated in the statute has reference to the *person* of the principal, and a party can only be said to be within the jurisdiction of the court when his person is subject to its process. Scott *v.* Dewees, 2 Tex. Rep. 153. Merriweather *v.* Lewis, Ibid. 340. To establish his exemption the surety must plead and prove that his principal is within the jurisdiction of the court. Petty *v.* Cleveland, 2 Tex. Rep. 404. See also Lewis *v.* Riggs, 9 Tex. Rep. 164, and Smith *v.* Doak, 3 Tex. Rep. 215. The plaintiff cannot discontinue as to one of several makers of a promissory note, not served, who does not reside beyond the limits of the State and is not insolvent, and take judgment against an endorser, although he at the same time take judgment against the other makers. Look & Cornelius *v.* Henderson, 4 Tex. Rep. 303. Hawkins *v.* Tinnin, 10 Tex. Rep. 188. The makers and endorsers of a note were joined as defendants in the same suit. The maker appeared and answered by general denial, but the endorsers failed to answer, and judgment by default was rendered against them without further notice of the maker. On error by the endorsers, the judgment was reversed, on the ground that, under the statute, judgment could not be rendered against the endorsers, unless it was at the same time rendered against the maker, except in the cases provided in the statute. Campbell *v.* Beckwith, 17 Tex. Rep. 439.

ART. 1602. [19] Any one of several sureties, having paid and satisfied the judgment creditor, shall have the remedy provided in the preceding section, against the co-sureties, to collect of them the ratable proportion each is equitably bound to pay. Remedy secured to one against other sureties.

ART. 1603. [20] The remedy provided for sureties by this act, extends to endorsers, guarantors, drawers of bills which have been accepted, and every other suretyship, whether created by express contract or by the operation of law. Remedy, to what it extends.

PRISONERS OF WAR.

ART. 1604. [1] From and after the passage of this act, no forced sale shall be made of any property belonging to any citizen of Texas, who is or may be a prisoner of war, until release or death of said prisoner, or, in the event of his death, administration upon his estate. Act of Feb. 2, 1844. Took effect from passage. Property of, exempt from, &c.

ART. 1605. [2] The act of limitations, as far as such prisoner shall be affected, either as debtor or creditor, shall remain suspended during the time of his captivity. Act of limitation suspended as to.

ART. 1606. [3] When satisfactory proof shall be made to the Chief Justice of the county, where any such prisoner had his residence preceding his captivity, that the property of such prisoner is liable to waste, or that his rights may be affected, it shall be the duty of said Chief Justice to appoint a suitable person, under sufficient bond and security as curator of said prisoner, which curator shall take charge of the effects of said prisoner and protect the same to the best of his power and ability. Curators to be appointed to preserve property of.

PROCLAMATIONS OF GOVERNOR.

ART. 1607. [1] Hereafter it shall be the duty of the Governor, in ordering elections, or other proclamations, not particularly required by law to be published in one or more newspapers, to issue in handbill and transmit the same by mail to the proper officer or officers, whose duty it is to carry the proclamation into effect. Act of Feb. 15, 1854. Took effect from passage. Certain proclamations of, issued in handbill.

ART. 1608. [2] In all cases where the Governor is required by law to issue his proclamation, and publish the same in some newspaper or newspapers, he shall cause such proclamation to be published in one paper published at the seat of government, and not exceeding two others in the State, which shall be in different sections of the State. Proclamations in newspapers, &c.

PUBLIC ARMS.

Act of Jan. 19, 1858. Took effect from passage. Gov'r authorized to draw.

ART. 1609. [1] The Governor be, and he is hereby authorized and requested to draw from the United States Government all the arms and accoutrements to which this State is from time to time entitled, for the use of the militia of the State.

May store them at any point he may deem proper.

ART. 1610. [2] The Governor be authorized to store arms and accoutrements at any point he may deem proper, for the convenience of districts, and to save the expenses of transportation.

Arms to uniformed volunteer companies.

ART. 1611. [3] The Governor be authorized to grant arms and accoutrements to each uniformed volunteer military company in the State, as soon as he shall have received a certificate of election of the commissioned officers of the said companies, from the Chief Justice of the county where such company is organized.

Company to consist of, &c.

ART. 1612. [4] Every company that may apply for arms and accoutrements, shall consist of at least thirty-two non-commmissioned officers and privates.

Who responsible for arms—bond, &c.

ART. 1613. [5] The commissioned officers, or four responsible members of any company drawing arms, shall execute a bond to the Governor in double the amount of the value of said arms, for the safe keeping or return of the same; said bond to be approved by the Chief Justice of the county where said company is established.

Arms shall not exceed double number of company.

ART. 1614. [6] No company shall receive a greater number of arms and accoutrements than double the number of the active members of said company.

May be furnished to military colleges and schools, when—bond.

ART. 1615. [7] The Governor be authorized to furnish suitable arms to all military colleges and schools in the State, upon application of the faculty or trustees of the same, and by their executing a bond to him in double the value of said arms, for their safe keeping or return; said bond to be approved by the Chief Justice of the county in which said college or school is established.

Two thousand dollars appropriated.

ART. 1616. [8] Two thousand dollars be, and are hereby appropriated from any money in the treasury not otherwise appropriated, or so much thereof as is necessary for the use of the Governor in defraying the expenses of transportation of the arms and accoutrements drawn from the United States Government.

PUBLIC PRINTING.

[*See Legislature—Fiscal Year—Secretary of State.*]

ART. 1617. [1] There shall be elected by joint vote of the two Houses of the Legislature of the State, at each and every session thereof, some suitable person or persons to print the laws and journals of the respective sessions for which such persons may be elected.

Act of March 8, 1848. Took effect from passage.

Legislature to elect printer.

ART. 1618. [2] There shall be printed by the person or persons so elected to do the public printing, two thousand five hundred copies of the laws of a general nature, and five hundred copies of all acts for private relief, and all acts incorporating towns, cities, institutions of learning, and private associations of every nature, and five hundred copies of the journals of each House, and the same number of copies of the laws and journals of each session hereafter to be held, until otherwise provided by law.

Number of copies of laws and journals to be printed.

ART. 1619. [3] The laws and journals shall be printed on small pica type, the pages to be forty-four lines long, exclusive of the folio, and twenty-seven ems wide, without side notes.

Size of page of laws and journals.

ART. 1620. [4] The person or persons [who] may be elected to print the laws and journals of the present or any future session of the Legislature, shall, within three days after the election, enter into bond, with two or more securities, in the sum of five thousand dollars, payable to the Governor and his successor in office, conditioned that the party so elected shall faithfully execute the duties of his office, in the time and manner prescribed by law; which bond shall be filed in the office of the Secretary of State.

Printer to give bond.

ART. 1621. [5] It shall be the duty of the person or persons elected to do the public printing, to deliver the number of copies of the laws and journals herein or hereafter required to be printed, to the Secretary of State or to his order—the laws within thirty, and the journals within sixty days, from the day on which copies are delivered to him or them—in default of which, the Secretary of State shall forthwith place the bond of the party so failing, in the hands of the District Attorney of the district in which the principal or principals or any of the obligors live; whose duty it shall be to bring suit on the same.

Laws and journals printed to be delivered to the Secretary of State, in what time.

ART. 1622. [6] It shall be the duty of the Secretary of State to superintend the printing of the laws of each session of the Legislature; he shall number all the acts and joint resolutions and keep a register thereof and cause them to be printed in the order in which they are approved, and shall prepare and have printed a minute and comprehensive index to the same, and shall certify at the end thereof, that the laws and joint resolutions as printed are true copies of the original acts and joint resolutions filed in his office; and it shall be his duty also to certify under his hand and seal the day on which the Legislature

Secretary of State to superintend printing—keep register of acts, &c.—Index—certificate—day of adjournment.

adjourned, which shall be printed with the laws of the session named in the said certificate.

Secretary to deliver to printer copies, &c., when.

ART. 1623. [9] Within six days after the passage of any law or joint resolution, it shall be the duty of the Secretary of State, to cause to be delivered to the public printer correct copies of said laws and joint resolutions, in order that the printing may be executed with the least possible delay.

Act of Feb. 16, 1852. Took effect from passage.

Original sheets of journals to be furnished printer—when.

ART. 1624. [3] From and after the passage of this act, it shall no longer be the duty of the Secretary of the Senate and Chief Clerk of the House of Representatives to furnish copies of the journals to the public printer; but instead thereof, the Secretary and Clerk at the time in office, shall furnish the original sheets to the said printer, after the same shall have been approved by the respective Houses, and after they shall have been carefully recorded as provided for in the first section of this act.

Act of Dec. 27, 1851.

Printer, when to be elected.

Prices to be paid for public printing.

ART. 1625. [1] A public printer shall hereafter be elected within three days after the organization of the two Houses of the Legislature, at each regular session thereof, whose duty it shall be to print the laws and journals, in accordance with the act to which this is an amendment, at the following prices, to-wit: One-sixth of a cent per page for the laws, and one-fourth of a cent per page for the journals; one-third of a cent per page for five hundred copies of the message of the Governor, reports of the Secretary of State, Comptroller of Public Accounts, Auditor, Treasurer of the State, Superintendent of the Penitentiary, and all such like printing that may be ordered by the Legislature, or either House thereof, to be printed on the same size sheet and type as is required for the journals, and one-fourth of a cent per page for each additional five hundred copies of said message and other documents; for printing two hundred copies of bills, resolutions or memorials, printed on pica type, the lines numbered on the margin, with a space between the lines of the size of pica, and on foolscap paper, with four pages to a sheet, the sum of two dollars and fifty cents per page, for the number of pages in one copy thereof; for printing Executive proclamations, advertisements and such like documents fifty cents per square of ten lines, for the first insertion, and twenty-five cents per square for each succeeding insertion that may be ordered.

Act of Sept. 5, 1856.

1500 copies additional of General Laws.

ART. 1626. [1] The public printer be, and he is hereby required to print, for the use of the State, fifteen hundred copies of the General Laws of the State Legislature, in addition to the number now required by law to be printed.

Act of Feb. 16, 1858.

After adj'nment work when returned—acc'nts to be audited by Comptroller.

ART. 1627. [1] After the adjournment of the Legislature, the public printer shall return all work to the Secretary of State, which may be required by law, ordered by either House of the Legislature to be done, which, if correct, shall be by him approved, and the account for the same shall be audited by the Comptroller.

QUARANTINE REGULATION.

Act of July 24, 1856.

ART. 1628. [1] The County Courts of the respective counties of this State be, and they are hereby authorized and empowered, whenever in their judgment it may be necessary, to establish quarantine regulations in their respective counties, or any part or parts thereof, not inconsistent with the constitution and laws of this State; and any person offending against any such regulations shall, on conviction thereof before any Justice of the Peace of the county in which the offence was committed, be subject to a fine of not exceeding one hundred dollars, or to imprisonment in the common jail of the county, not exceeding thirty days; and the trial of all such cases shall be had and conducted in the same manner as is provided for the trial of other offences cognizable before Justices of the Peace. *County Court may adopt regulations.*

Art. 1629. [2] The corporate authorities of the respective town and city municipal corporations in this State be, and they are hereby authorized and empowered, whenever in their judgment it may be necessary, to establish quarantine regulations in their respective towns and cities, not inconsistent with the constitution and laws of the State; and any person offending against any such regulations, shall be subject therefor, before any Justice of the Peace of the county where the offence was committed; and the proceedings shall be conducted against such offender in the corporate name of the town or city where the office [offence?] was commited; and on conviction such offender shall be subject to a fine of not more than one hundred dollars, to go to the use of the city or town where the offence was commited, or to imprisonment not more than thirty days in the town or city prison, where the offence was committed; and the trial of all cases arising under the provisions of this section shall be conducted in the same manner as is provided for the trial of other offences cognizable before Justices of the Peace. *City and town corporations may adopt, &c. Before whom offenders may be tried.*

RAILROADS.

I. GENERAL PROVISIONS.

II. LAND GRANTS.

I. GENERAL PROVISIONS.

Act of Feb. 7, 1854.

What railroads governed by this act.

ART. 1630. [1] All railroad companies which have been heretofore incorporated, or which shall hereafter be incorporated, or relieved from the performance of any act required of them, or which shall accept of any donation or loan from this State, or which shall accept of the subscription of any county of this State, shall have all the powers and privileges, and be subject to all the duties, liabilities and provisions contained in this act.

Dividend declared and paid when company insolvent.

ART. 1631. [2] If the directors of any such company shall declare and pay any dividend when the company is insolvent, or any dividend the payment of which would render it insolvent, they shall be jointly and severally liable for all the debts of the company then existing, and for all that shall be thereafter contracted, so long as they shall respectively continue in office; provided, that if any of the directors shall be absent at the time of making the dividend, or shall object thereto, and shall within thirty days thereafter, or after his return, if absent, file a certificate of their absence or objection in writing with the clerk of the company, and with the clerk of the county in which the principal office of said company is located, they shall be exempt from said liability.

Directors absent, or not concurring.

False certificate, report or public notice.

ART. 1632 [3] If any certificate or report made, or public notice given by the officers of any such company, in pursuance of the provisions of this act, shall be false in any material representation, all the officers who shall have signed the same, shall be jointly and severally liable for all the debts of the company contracted while they are officers or stockholders thereof.

Principal office.

ART. 1633. [4] Such corporation shall, as soon as convenient after its organization, establish a principal office at some point on the line of its road, and change the same at pleasure, giving public notice in some newspaper of such establishment and change; and all process against such company shall be served on the President or Secretary, or by leaving a copy at the principal office of the corporation.

ART. 1634. [5] No bridge or other obstruction shall be erected across, in or or over any navigable stream, so as to prevent or unreasonably impede the navigation thereof. Navigable stream, not to be obstructed.

ART. 1635. [6] Such corporation shall erect at all points where its road shall cross any public road at a sufficient elevation from such public road, to admit of the free passage of vehicles of every kind, a sign with large and distinct letters placed thereon to give notice of the proximity of the railroad, and warn persons of the necessity of looking out for the cars; and any company neglecting or refusing to erect such sign shall be liable in damages for all injuries occurring to persons or property from such neglect or refusal. Sign with large letters at crossings of road—penalty for failure.

ART. 1636. [7] Every conductor, baggage-master, engineer, brakeman, or other servant of any such railroad corporation, employed in a passenger train, or at stations for passengers, shall wear upon his hat or cap a badge which shall indicate his office, and the initial letters of the style of the corporation by which he is employed. No conductor or collector without such badge shall demand, or be entitled to receive from any passenger any fare, toll, ticket, or exercise any of the powers of his office, and no other of the said officers or servants, without such badge, shall have any authority to meddle or interfere with the passengers, their baggage or property. Conductor, baggage master, engineer, brakemen, &c., to wear badge.

ART. 1637. [8] If any passenger shall refuse to pay his fare or toll, it shall be lawful for the conductor of the train and the servants of the corporation to put him out of the cars at any usual stopping place which the conductor may select. Passenger refusing to pay fare may be put out.

ART. 1638. [9] Every such corporation shall start and run their cars for the transportation of passengers and property at regular times, to be fixed by public notice, and shall furnish sufficient accommodations for the transportation of all such passengers and property as shall within a reasonable time previous thereto, offer or be offered for transportation at the place of starting, and the junctions of other railroads, and at sidings and stopping places established for receiving and discharging way-passengers and freights, and shall take, transport, and discharge such passengers and property at, from and to such places, on the due payment of the tolls, freight or fare legally authorized therefor. Trains to be regular—notice of—accommodations.

ART. 1639. [10] In case of refusal by such corporation or their agents so to take and transport any passenger or property, or to deliver the same or either of them at the regular or appointed time, such corporation shall pay to the party agrieved, all damages which shall be sustained thereby, with costs of suit. Refusal to transport passengers and property.

ART. 1640. [11] A check shall be affixed to every package or parcel of baggage, when taken for transportation by the agent or servant of such corporation, and a duplicate thereof giving to the passenger or person delivering the same on his behalf; and if such check be refused on demand, the corporation shall pay to such passenger the sum of ten dollars to be recovered in an action of debt; and, further, no fare or toll shall be collected or received from such passenger; and if such passenger shall have paid his or her fare, the same shall be refunded by the conductor in charge of the train; and on producing said check, if his or her baggage shall not be delivered to him or to her, he or she may, himself or herself be a witness in any suit brought by him or her to prove the contents and value of said baggage. Baggage checks. Check refused, penalty.

ART. 1641. [12] In forming a passenger train, baggage or freight or merchandize or lumber cars shall not be placed in rear of passengers cars; and if they or any of them shall be so placed, and any accident happen to life or limb, the officer or agent who so directed, or knowingly suffered such arrange- Passenger trains how formed—penalty for violating.

ment, and the conductor and engineer of the train shall each and all be held guilty of intentionally causing the injury, and be punished accordingly.

Bell or steam whistle, when to be and how used.

ART. 1642. [13] A bell, of at least thirty pounds weight, or a steam whistle shall be placed on each locomotive engine, and the bell shall be rung, or whistle blown, at the distance of at least eighty rods from the place where the railroad shall cross any road or street, and to be kept ringing or blowing until it shall have crossed such road or street, or stopped, under a penalty of fifty dollars for every neglect, to be paid by the corporation owning the railroad; one half thereof to go to the informer, and the other half to the State, and also be liable for all damages which shall be sustained by any person by reason o such neglect.

Engineer or Conductor intoxicated, penalty.

ART. 1643. [14] That if any person shall, while in charge of a locomotive engine, running upon the railroad of any such corporation, or while acting as the conductor of a car, or train of cars on any such railroad, be intoxicated, he shall be guilty of a misdemeanor, and be punished by fine or imprisonment, or both.

Charges for transportation.

ART. 1644. [15] It shall be lawful for the Legislature at any time, to prescribe the rates to be charged for the transportation of persons and property upon any such road, should they be deemed too high; and may exercise the same power every ten years: provided that no reduction shall be made, unless the nett profits of the company for the previous ten years, the expenditures of the company, being bona fide, and not with a view to defeat the operation of this section, shall amount to a sum equal to twelve per centum per annum upon its capital stock, and then so as not to reduce the future probable profits below the said percentum.

Cars of other roads to be drawn over—compensation for, how settled.

ART. 1645. [16] Every such company shall at all reasonable times, and for a reasonable compensation, draw over their road the passengers, merchandize and cars of any other railroad corporation, which may enter and connect with their railroad; and if the respective companies cannot agree upon the compensation aforesaid, it shall be the duty of the President of each company to select one man as a commissioner, and the two commissioners so selected, shall choose a third in case of disagreement, neither of whom shall be a stockholder in either road, or interested therein, and they shall fix the rates, which shall not be changed for one year from the time of going into effect; the said commissioners shall also fix the stated periods at which said cars are to be drawn as aforesaid, having reference to the convenience and interest of said corporations and the public who shall be accommodated thereby; the right or power is specially conferred on any railroad company to enter and connect with any other railroad within the scope of its designated route and branches.

Terms upon which State may purchas road.

ART. 1646. [17] If the Legislature of this State shall at any time make provision by law, for the repayment to any such company of the amount expended by them in the construction of said road, together with all monies for permanent fixtures, cars, engines, machinery, chattels and real property, then in use for the said road, with all monies expended for repairs or otherwise, and interest on such sums at the rate of twelve per centum per annum after deducting the amount of tolls, freights, passage money, and all monies received from the sale of lands donated by the State to said company, with twelve per centum per annum interest on all such sums, then the road with all its fixtures and appurtenances aforesaid, and all the lands donated to the same by the State and remaining unsold, shall vest in and revert to this State: provided, that the State shall not be required to pay, or allow a greater rate of interest on any amount of the money so expended by any company which shall have been borrowed from this State, than the State shall have received for the same from such company.

Proviso. Interest on money borrowed from State.

ART. 1647. [18] Every such corporation shall make an annual report to the Comptroller of Public Accounts of this State of the operations of the year ending on the first day of October, which report shall be verified by the oaths of the Treasurer and acting superintendant of operations, and filed in his office by the twentieth of October in each year, and shall state— Annual report of corporation, what it shall contain.

1st. The capital stock and the amount actually paid in.

2nd. The amount expended for the purchase of land for the construction of the road, for buildings and for engines and cars, respectively.

3d. The amount and nature of its indebtedness, and the amount due the corporation.

4th. The amount received for the transportation of passengers, of property, of the mail, and from all other sources.

5th. The amount of freight, specifying the quantity in tons, of the product of the forest, of animals, of vegetable food, other agricultural products, manufactures, merchandize and other articles.

6th. The amount paid out for repairs, engines, cars, buildings and salaries, respectively.

7th. The number and amount of dividends, and when made.

8th. The number of engine houses, and shops, of engines and cars and their character.

9th. The number of miles run by passenger, freight and other trains, respectively.

10th. The number of men employed and their occupations.

11th. The number of persons injured in life or limb, and the cause of such injuries.

12th. Whether any accidents have arisen from carelessness or negligence of any person in the employment of the corporations, and whether such person is retained in the service of the corporation.

13th. The sales of lands donated by the State, and the quantity remaining unsold.

ART. 1648. [19] Any such corporation, which shall neglect to make such report, shall be liable to a penalty of two hundred and fifty dollars, to be sued for in the name of the State. And any corporation so neglecting, which shall neglect to make such report within three months after notice to the President or any director thereof of such failure by the Comptroller, shall forfeit its charter. Failure to make report.

ART. 1649. [20] Every such corporation shall, when applied to by the Post-Master General, convey the mail of the United States on its road or roads; and in case such corporation shall not agree as to the rate of transportation therefor, and as to the time, rate or speed, manner and condition of conveying the same, it shall be lawful for the Governor of the State to appoint three commissioners, who, or a majority of them, after fifteen days notice in writing of the time and place of meeting to the corporation, shall determine and fix the prices, terms and condition aforesaid; but such price shall not be less for conveying said mails in the regular passenger trains, than the amount which such corporation would receive as freight on a like weight of merchandise, transported in their merchandise trains, and a fair compensation for the post office car; and in case the Post-Master General shall require the mail to be carried at other hours, or at a higher speed than the passenger train be run at, the corporation shall furnish an extra train for the mail, and be allowed an extra compensation for the expenses and wear and tear thereof, and for the services, to be fixed as aforesaid. United States mails. Compensation for transport.

ART. 1650. [21] Every such corporation shall, within a reasonable time after their road shall be located, cause to be made:

Map and profile—to be filed in County Clerk's office. 1st. A map and profile thereof, and of the land taken or obtained for the use thereof, and file the same in the General Land Office of this State, and also like maps of the parts thereof located in different counties, and file the same in the offices of the County Clerk and District Surveyor of the county in which such parts of said road shall be, there to remain as a record forever Every such map shall be drawn on a scale and on paper to be designated by the Commissioner of the General Land Office, and certified and signed by the President of the corporation.

Line of road. 2d. A certificate specifying the line upon which it is proposed to construct the railroad and the grades and curves certified and signed and filed as aforesaid.

Act of Feb'y 11, 1854. ART. 1651. [22] The width of the track or guage of all roads in the State shall be five feet and six inches.

Act of Jan'y 30, 1854. ART. 1652. [23] The Legislature may examine the books of any such company by committee or otherwise, as often as may be deemed expedient.

Brakes and brakemen. [24] Every such company shall have a good and sufficient brake upon the hindmost car on all trains transporting passengers and merchandise, and also permanently stationed there a trusty and faithful brakeman, under a penalty of not exceeding one hundred dollars for each offence, to be recovered by suit in the name of the State.

Proxies. ART. 1653. [25] Every proxy shall be dated within six months previous to the meeting of the stockholders at which said proxy is to be voted on.

Act of Dec'r 19, 1857. Took effect from passage. Stock books kept at principal office on line &c. ART. 1654. [2] Every railroad company heretofore incorporated, or which may hereafter be incorporated, by the Legislature of this State, shall be required to keep its stock books at the principal office of the company on the line of its road, in which books shall be entered all certificates of the capital stock issued by said company, and all transfers of stock shall be entered in such books, which, at all reasonable business hours, shall be open to the inspection of each stockholder, and to any agent or officer of the State, whose duty it may be to inspect such books; and all meetings of the Directors of any railroad company for the transaction of business shall be held at the office of said company, as required to be kept by this section.

Majority of Directors, President, &c., to reside in Texas. ART. 1655. [3] At least a majority of the Directors and the President or Vice President, Treasurer, and Secretary of every railroad company entitled to the benefits and privileges of an act entitled an act to encourage the construction of railroads by a donation of land, approved January 30, 1854, or of an act to provide for the investment of the special school fund, passed August 13, 1856, shall reside within the State of Texas.

By-laws. ART. 1656. [4] Every railroad company shall have the power to make such by-laws as they may think proper for the government of the company, the same not being inconsistent with the objects of its charter, or the laws of the State; and in the enactment of such by-laws the stockholders shall be entitled to one vote for each share of stock held by them, and may vote in person or by written proxy. And it shall require a vote of a majority of not less than two-thirds of the stock of the company to establish such by-laws; and no company shall have the power to make any trust deed or mortgage on the franchise or property of the company, unless the power is expressly given by the by-laws of the company.

One vote for each share of stock. Vote of two-thirds to pass by-laws. Deed of trust or mortgage.

Road, &c., liable to be sold for debts. ART. 1657. [5] The road-bed, track, franchise and chartered rights and privileges of any railroad company in this State, shall be subject to the payment of the debts and legal liabilities of said company, and may be sold in satisfaction of the same; but the said road-bed, track, franchise and chartered powers and privileges shall be deemed an entire thing, and must be sold as such; and in case of the sale of the same, whether by virtue of an execution, order of sale, deed of trust, or any other power, the purchaser or purchasers at such sale, and their associates, shall be entitled to have and exercise all the powers, privileges and franchises granted to said company by its charter, or by virtue of the general laws of this State; and the said purchaser or purchasers and their associates shall be deemed and taken to be the true owners of said charter, and corporators under the same, and vested with all the powers, rights, privileges and benefits thereof, in the same manner and to the same extent as if they were the original corporators of said company; and shall have power to construct, complete, equip and work the road upon the same terms and under the same conditions and restrictions as are imposed by their charter and the general laws of this State. Rights and powers of purchaser under forced sale.

Art. 1658. [6] Whenever a sale of the road-bed, track, franchise, and chartered rights and privileges of any Railroad Company is made by virtue of any deed of trust or power, the same shall be made at the time and place mentioned in the deed of trust or power, and in accordance with the provisions of the same, as to notice, and in other respects; and if the same be not specified, such sale shall be made as hereinafter provided for sales under execution or order of sale. Sale under deed of trust, when and where made.

Art. 1659. [7] Whenever judgment is rendered against any Railroad Company, the party in whose favor such judgment is rendered may have execution thereon, directed to the Sheriff of that county in which the principal office of said company is kept; and if the said company fail to point out other property to satisfy said execution, said Sheriff may, at the request of the plaintiff, levy the same upon the road-bed, track, franchise, and chartered powers and privileges of said company; and said levy shall be held to embrace the whole road-bed and track, and entire line of said railroad, whether situated in the same county or not, and he shall proceed to advertise and sell the same at the court-house door of his county, as in other cases, making the same advertisement as is provided by law in cases of the sale of lands; and upon said sale shall execute to the purchaser a conveyance of the said road-bed, track, franchise, chartered powers, rights and privileges. And the provisions of this section shall be observed, so far as they are applicable, in all cases where, by any decree of a competent court, a sale of the road-bed, track, franchise, and chartered rights of any railroad company is directed to be made: and provided this section shall not be so construed, as to prevent the issuance of execution to another county than that in which judgment is rendered, without first selling the road-bed, track, franchise, and chartered powers. Judgment—Execution. Levy. Advertisement. Sale.

Art. 1660. [8] The sale of the road-bed, track, franchise, and chartered rights, as hereinbefore provided, shall not be held to pass or convey to the purchaser any right or claim to recover from the former stockholders of said company, any sums which may remain due upon their subscriptions of stock, but the said stockholders shall continue liable to pay the same in discharge and liquidation of the debts due by the sold out company, as hereinafter provided. Unpaid stock subscriptions of stock holders of sold out company.

Art. 1661. [9] Whenever a sale of the road-bed, track, franchise, and chartered powers and privileges is made, as hereinbefore provided (unless other persons shall be appointed by the Legislature, or by some court of competent authority,) the Directors or Managers of the sold-out company at the time of the sale, by whatever name they may be known in law, shall be the trustees of the creditors and stockholders of the sold-out company, and shall have full powers to settle the affairs of the sold-out company, collect and pay the outstanding debts, and divide among the stockholders the money and other Directors of sold out company, trustees, with powers, &c.

property that shall remain after the payment of the debts and necessary expenses; and the persons so constituted trustees, shall have authority to sue by the name of the trustees of such sold-out company, and may be sued as such, and shall be jointly and severally responsible to the creditors and stockholders of such company, to the extent of its property and effects that shall come to their hands. And no suit pending for or against any railroad company at the time that the sale may be made of its road-bed, track, franchise, and chartered privileges, shall abate, but the same shall be continued in the name of the trustees of the sold-out company.

Suits not to abate.

This act not to apply to deeds to State under State loans, &c.

ART. 1662. [10] The provisions of this act shall not apply to any debt, execution, or deed of trust, held by the State against any railroad company, because of any loan made by the State to any company, under the provisions of the act to provide for the investment of the Special School Fund, or any other law which authorizes the loan of money to railroad companies; nor shall any creditor of any railroad company be allowed to make the State a party to any suit, brought for the enforcement of any debt, motgage, or deed of trust, or lien, on any railroad, or permitted to require the State to foreclose any lien which it may have upon any road, but the lien of the State, and its right to enforce the same, shall continue as if this act had never been passed, and as if no sale had been made under the provisions of the same.

Not to be made a party.

Roads less than 300 miles to designate termini.

ART. 1663. [11] Every railroad company which has been chartered in this State, the entire length of whose road is less than three hundred miles, shall, previous to the first day of January, 1860, designate the termini of said road, where the same are not fixed in their charters, and the counties through which their road shall pass, following the direction and touching the points established in their charters; and they shall also designate, as near as practicable, the points at which said roads cross the rivers, over which they will pass between said termini. And where any such road is of greater length than three hundred miles, the designation of its said route and crossings, as above required, shall be made for the additional distance of one hundred miles, annually, after said first day of January, 1860: provided, that such railroad companies as shall be hereafter incorporated, shall make the designation of their termini, route and crossings for the first three hundred miles, within two years after the date of their act of incorporation, and one hundred miles annually thereafter, unless it is otherwise provided in their charter. And each of said companies, so designating their termini, route and crossings, shall immediately report the same to the General Land Office of this State, under the seal of said company: provided, further, that whenever any railway company shall have designated the route or line of their road, and thereby secured any reservation of public land under the laws of this State, and such company shall hereafter change said route or line, such change shall in no case authorize the said company to alter, or in anywise change the reservation already secured, or by such alteration or change, to secure a reservation on the line or route so newly designated.

Failure to comply with this act.

ART. 1664. [12] Any railroad company neglecting or refusing to comply with any of the provisions of this act, shall be entitled to none of the benefits granted by "An act to encourage the construction of railroads," approved January 30, 1854, nor of the "act to provide for the investment of the Special School Fund," passed August 13, 1856, and the charter of said company shall be forfeited.

Six months allowed to roads to comply with 2d and 3d sections.

ART. 1665. [13] All railroad companies now chartered and orgrnized, shall have six months to comply with the provisions of the second and third sections of this act.

II. LAND GRANTS.

ART. 1666. [1] Any railroad company chartered by the Legislature of this State, heretofore or hereafter, constructing within the limits of Texas, a section of twenty-five miles or more of railroad, shall be entitled to receive from the State a grant of sixteen sections of land for every mile of road so constructed and put in running order. Act of Jan. 30, 1854. Sixteen sections of land per mile.

ART. 1667. [2] Any railroad company having actually put under contract as much as twenty-five miles of its road or its entire road when the length may not exceed twenty-five miles, upon filing a certified copy of such contract with the Commissioner of the General Land Office, and upon depositing with the Treasurer of the State a bond with two or more good sureties, to be approved by him in favor of the Governor of the State, in the sum of ten thousand dollars, conditioned as hereinafter required, may file an application with any district surveyor of any land district in this State, a copy of which application shall in all cases be forwarded to the Commissioner of the General Land Office by the district surveyor, to survey any quantity of the public domain lying and being in such district, and subject to location and entry, not to exceed eight hundred sections, and said application shall specifically describe the lands applied for and intended to be surveyed; and if said company shall produce and file with the district surveyor a certificate of the Commissioner of the General Land Office, that a copy of its contract has been filed in said office for the construction of twenty-five miles or more of said road; and also a certificate from the Treasurer that a bond as required by this act has been deposited in his office, said application shall exempt the land so designated from any future location, entry or pre-emption privilege, until otherwise directed as hereinafter provided: provided, that no application for a survey of lands under the provisions of this act, shall be made for more than six months before the completion of such section; and if said section be not completed and notice thereof given as herein provided within six months from the time of the application, then such land applied for shall become subject to location and entry as if no such application had been made. Upon what terms, and what amount of land may be surveyed and set apart after contract made for construction of road.

ART. 1668. [3] It shall be the duty of said company to cause to be surveyed the land so designated, into sections of six hundred and forty acres each, and in square blocks of not less than six miles, unless prevented by previous surveys or a navigable stream, which surveys shall be delineated upon a map or maps, the even and odd sections being differently colored and regularly numbered from one upwards to the full number contained in the block, and the field notes of said surveys and map or maps, shall be by said company deposited with the Commissioner of the General Land Office. Survey how made—maps—even and odd sections. Field notes, &c., to be deposited in General Land Office.

ART. 1669. [4] The condition of the bond mentioned in the second section of this act shall be, that said company will cause to be surveyed the land designated and applied for within the time limited for the construction of said section of twenty-five miles by the contract, and in the manner required by the third section of this act; and shall actually construct the said section of twenty-five miles of said road within the time mentioned in said contract, in default of which said land shall become forfeit to the use of the State, which forfeiture shall be declared by the District Court of Travis county, at the first term thereafter, without other formality than as hereinafter provided. Condition of bond. When forfeited. Suit where brought.

ART. 1670. [5] If at the time stipulated in said contract for the completion of said section of twenty-five miles, the field notes and map or maps of the land applied for, be not deposited in the General Land Office as herein required, it

Field notes and maps not deposited, when. Certificate of Commissioner. Lands subject to entry.

shall be the duty of the Commissioner to forward immediately to the Treasurer of the Sate and the District Surveyor of the land district where the land applied for is situate; a certificate of the fact, whereupon the land so applied for shall become subject to location and entry by any one, as if no such application had been made; and it shall be the duty of the Treasurer ten days before the session of the District Court of Travis county, to cause notice of such forfeiture to be advertised in one of the newspapers published at Austin for two successive weeks; and at said session of the District Court, it shall be the duty of the Attorney-General, or in case he be not present, of the District Attorney, to file a motion for the forfeiture of said bond, whereupon said court shall proceed without other citation or notice, to declare said bond absolutely forfeited, and to render judgment against said company and sureties for the amount of said bond, upon which judgment and execution shall issue as in ordinary cases: provided, that it shall be necessary for the Attorney-General or District Attorney to file with said motion a certified copy of said bond under the hand and seal of the Treasurer, and also a copy of the contract deposited in the General Land Office, and a certificate of the Commissioner that said surveys and map or maps of the lands applied for have not been returned.

Suit on bond how and when prosecuted.

When section completed engineer to examine. Report of. Patents to issue for odd sections.

Art. 1671. [6] Any railroad company having completed and put in running order a section of twenty-five miles or more of its road, may give notice of the same to the Governor, whose duty it shall be to appoint some skillful engineer, if there be no State engineer, to examine said section of road, and if upon the report of said engineer, under oath, it shall appear that said road has been constructed in accordance with the provisions of its charter, and of the general laws of the State in force at the time regulating railroads, thereupon it shall be the duty of the Commissioner of the General Land Office to issue to said company patents for the odd sections surveyed in pursuance of the second and third sections of this act; but in case said lands, or any part thereof shall not have been surveyed at the time said section is completed, then it shall be the duty of said Commissioner to issue to said company certificates of 640 acres each, equal to sixteen sections per mile of road so completed, whereupon said company may apply to the District Surveyor of any land district in this State, to survey any quantity of vacant land subject to location and entry in such district, not to exceed twice the quantity of certificates so issued, which surveys shall be made, numbered and colored as directed in the third section of this act, and upon the return of the field notes and map or maps of such surveys to the General Land Office, and the certificates so issued, it shall be the duty of the Commissioner to issue to said company patents for the odd sections of said surveys: provided, that in case the surveys are not applied for before the completion of any section of road, it shall not be necessary to deposit with the Treasurer a bond as required in the second section of this act.

Certificates to issue. Surveys how made and returned.

When bond not required.

Fractional sections.

Art. 1672. [7] Fractional sections, containing more than 320 acres, shall be regarded as whole sections; and two fractional sections, each containing less than 320 acres, shall be taken as a whole section under the provisions of this act; and all the alternate or even sections shall be reserved to the use of the State, until appropriated by law.

Act of Sept. 1, 1856.

Surveys by whom made.

Art. 1673. [8] Surveys under the provisions of this act shall be made by the Deputies or District Surveyors of the district in which the land is situated, and the field notes shall be recorded in such district, and returned to the General Land Office as other surveys.

Act of Jan. 30, 1854.

Roads to alienate lands when.

Art. 1674. [9] Any railroad company in this State acquiring lands or other real estate by virtue of the provisions of this act, or by virtue of the provisions of any other act or charter enacted by the Legislature of the State of

Texas, by purchase, donation or otherwise, shall proceed to alienate the same except so far as may be necessary to the maintenance and running of said road, in six, eight, ten and twelve years; that is, one-fourth shall be alienated in six years, one-fourth in eight years, one-fourth in ten years, and one-fourth in twelve years from the time of acquiring such lands or real estate, in such manner that the whole of such lands or real estate shall pass out of the hands of such company within twelve years from the date of its acquisition: provided, moreover, that said lands and real estate shall in no instance be alienated to any other corporation, except so far as may be necessary for the proper uses and the conduction of the business of such corporation.

ART. 1675. [10] If any company should neglect or fail to alienate its lands or real estate, as herein directed, evidences of which alienations said company shall cause to be filed with the Secretary of State, it shall be the duty of that officer to notify the Comptroller of Public Accounts and Commissioner of the General Land Office of such failure to alienate, whereupon, the Commissioner shall furnish the Comptroller with a list of the lands acquired by said company under this or any other act of the Legislature of the State, and the dates at which such lands were acquired; and the Secretary of State shall also furnish the Comptroller with a schedule of the lands owned and alienated by said company, as the same appears from the last annual return made to his office by said company, in pursuance of the general law of the State regulating railroad companies; and it shall be the duty of the Comptroller of Public Accounts, immediately upon receiving said returns, to cause to be advertised in the newspapers in the city of Austin for sale, sixty days after such advertisement, the lands herein diretced to be alienated, proceeding in the order in which said lands and real estate were granted or deeded to said company; and after deducting all necessary expenses of the sale, the balance shall be deposited with the Treasurer to the credit of said company.

Failure to alienate lands.

Comptroller—how and when to sell the same.

ART. 1676. [11] All the alternate or even sections of land, surveyed in pursuance of the provisions of this act, or of any other act of the Legislature of this State, donating lands to any railroad company, shall be reserved to the use of the State, and not liable to locations, entries, or pre-emption privileges, until otherwise provided by law.

Even sections reserved to the State.

ART. 1677. [12] The provisions of this act shall not extend to any company receiving from the State a grant of more than sixteen sections of land, nor to any company for more than a single-tract road, with the necessary turn-outs; and any company now entitled by law to receive a grant of eight sections of land per mile for the construction of any railroad, accepting the provisions of this act, shall not be entitled to receive any grant of land for any branch road: provided this act shall not be so construed as to give to any company now entitled by law to receive eight sections of land, more than eight additional sections: provided, that no person or company shall receive any donation or benefit under the provisions of this act, unless they shall construct and complete at least twenty-five miles of the road contemplated by their charter within two years after the passage of this act; and such donations shall be discontinued in every case where the company or companies shall not construct and complete at least twenty-five miles of the road contemplated by their charter, each year after the construction of said first mentioned twenty-five miles of road: and further provided, that the proviso herein contained shall not extend to any railroad, the terminus of which is not fixed on the Gulf coast, the bays thereof, or on Buffalo Bayou, and that nothing in this section shall be so construed as to extend the duration of any existing charter: and further provided, that the certificates for land issued under the provisions of this act, shall not be located upon any land surveyed or titled previous to the

This act not to extend to certain companies' branch roads.

passage of this act: and further provided, that this act shall continue in force for the term of ten years from the time it shall take effect, and no longer.

Weight of rails on road hereafter built. ART. 1678. [13] No railroad hereafter to be built shall be entitled to receive the additional sections of land herein granted, unless the railings of such road shall weigh at least fifty-four pounds to the yard.

Act of Jan. 30, 1854. Not more than sixteen sections granted to any road under this act, &c. ART. 1679. [1] No railroad company availing itself of the provisions of the act to which this is a supplement, shall receive more than sixteen sections of land to the mile by virtue of said act, or any proviso therein contained. And no road benefitted by said act, shall receive any donation of land under its charter, or under the act to which this is a supplement, for any work not done within ten years after the passage of this act; and this act shall be in force at the same time that the act to which this is a supplement shall take effect.

Act of Feb. 16, 1858. Took effect from passage. When certificates may issue on graded road. ART. 1680. [1] Any Railroad company in this State, entitled to the benefits of the above recited act, having heretofore graded, or which may hereafter grade, ready for the cross ties, twenty miles of its road, shall be entitled to receive of the Commissioner of the General Land Office, certificates for four sections, of six hundred and forty acres each, per mile, on ten miles of the grade so completed, of the lands contemplated by said act; and on the completion of any additional section of five miles, such company may apply for and receive a like grant of four sections per mile, for five miles, which certificates may be alienated, or located and patented, on any vacant land of the State, in the manner provided for in said act; and if sold, the proceeds to be applied to the further construction of said road: provided, that after the first issue of certificates herein mentioned, no further certificates shall be granted under the provisions of this act, or the act to which this is a supplement, unless satisfactory proof be made before the Commissioner of the General Land Office that the proceeds of the certificates previously issued, or of the lands patented by virtue thereof, if sold, have been applied in aid of the further construction of said road, and also a report of the manner in which such proceeds have been applied, verified by the affidavit of the President or Chief Engineer of said company, be filed in the office of the Secretary of State: and provided further, that no second issue of certificates shall be made under the provisions of this act, unless there be at least ten miles of grade completed in advance of the section on which the certificates are granted.

After first issue of, no further certificates granted, unless, &c.

III. LOAN OF SCHOOL FUNDS.

Act of August 13, 1856. Took effect from passage. Board of School Commissioners. School Fund. ART. 1681. [1] The Governor, Comptroller, and Attorney-General shall, *ex officio*, constitute a board of School Commissioners, whose duty it shall be to draw from the Treasury, the Special School Fund created by the act of January 31st, 1854, entitled an act to establish a System of Schools, and such other amount as may hereafter be added to said fund, and invest the same as provided in this act. And said board shall annually report to the Governor its acts and proceedings relative to the said School Fund, which shall be laid before the Legislature at each and every session thereof.

Annual report to Governor.

Five per cent. indemnity bonds loaned to railroads. ART. 1682. [2] The five per cent. indemnity bonds belonging to said Special School Fund may, and shall be loaned to legally incorporated railroad companies in this State, at their current value, including premium: provided said value shall not be less than par, otherwise at par, for the term of ten years from the date of said loans, at an interest of six per cent. per annum, payable annually upon the terms and conditions specified in this act: provided, that

Six per cent. interest.

one-half of said fund shall be loaned to companies whose works lie east of the Trinity river, and the residue to companies whose works lie west of that river. Half east and half west of Trinity river.

ART. 1683. [3] Said board of Commissioners is hereby authorized to invest said funds, by loaning to any such company which has been heretofore chartered for the purpose of building a railroad in the State, the sum of six thousand dollars per mile, for each and every mile of railroad constructed as hereinafter provided. Said loans to be secured by the bonds of such company for said principal and interest, made and executed to the State of Texas, in the corporate name of such company, signed by the President and countersigned by the Secretary or Treasurer, under the seal of such company; which bonds shall constitute a lien upon the road and charter rights of such company, including the road bed, right of way, grading, bridges, iron rails, equipments, and masonry, and upon all the stock subscribed for in said companies, all the depots and depot stations, and all the property owned by such company, as necessary for its business. And the State of Texas, upon the execution of said bonds, and by the virtue of the same, shall be invested with said lien or mortgage for the payment of said bonds and the interest thereon, as the same becomes due, without the necessity of any deed, special contract, or act of registration. Act of Aug. 26, 1856. Took effect from passage. School funds, how invested. Bonds of company. Lien on road.

ART. 1684. [1] The fourth section of the above recited act shall hereafter read as follows, to wit: "Said Board of Commissioners shall loan said sum of six thousand dollars, for every mile of road completed, to any such company as shall have completed, in a good and substantial manner, and furnished ready for actual use, a continuous section of twenty five miles of the road of said company, and graded an additional consecutive section of twenty-five miles, ready for the cross-ties and other superstructure; and the same amount per mile for every additional section of five miles, which shall be so completed and furnished ready for actual use, there being completely graded and ready for the ties and other superstructure at the time of such loan, not less than five consecutive miles of the road in advance of that on which the loan is proposed to be made; and the same amount per mile for every section of five miles within the limits of this State, which shall be so completed and furnished ready for use, upon any railroad which shall be a continuation of, or connection with any other railroad running from any adjoining State or Territory into the State of Texas; provided, said road shall, together with such continuation or connection, be completed at least twenty-five miles in length. And further provided, that before said loan is drawn upon any completed section of five miles, an additional consecutive section of five miles shall be graded ready for the ties and other superstructure. Act of January 23, 1858. Took effect from passage. When loan may be made.

ART. 1685. [5] Upon the application of any such railroad company to said Board of Commissioners, for said loan, and its representations that section fourth of this act has been complied with, said Board of Commissioners shall appoint some competent Engineer, who shall, at the expense of the company, examine the road of said company, and make a full report upon the condition of the same under oath, and shall report all matters pertaining to the business of said company, which he may deem useful to said Commissioners, in ascertaining the true condition of said road and company. And upon being fully satisfied that any section or sections of said road have been constructed and completed, as provided in the fourth section of this act, and that said section or sections are not subject to any lien whatever, other than such as may be created by this act, in favor of the State, said Board shall draw a warrant on the Treasury of the State, in the name of said company, against said Special School Fund, for such amount of said bonds as it may be entitled to under the provisions of this act; which warrant shall state on account of what work it is drawn, shall be signed by said Board of Commissioners and countersigned by Act of Aug. 13, 1856. Application under fourth section—Commissioners to appoint Engineer: report of. Warrants on Treasury, when to be drawn.

Bonds to be delivered, &c. the Governor, and delivered to the President, or the duly authorized agent of said company.

ART. 1686, [6] Upon the presentation of such warrant or warrants to the Treasury of the State, the amount of said indemnity bonds called for in the same, shall be delivered and transferred according to law, to the President or authorized agent of said company, his receipt taken therefor, and the same charged to the Special School Fund.

Company to give bond to State—amount of, how payable. Lien of, on road. ART. 1687. [7] Before said Board shall deliver to said company said warrant or warrants upon the treasury, it shall require said company to execute and deliver into the treasury the bonds of said company, for said loan or loans, in sums of not more than one hundred and fifty thousand dollars, and not less than fifty thousand dollars each, payable to the State of Texas ten years after date, together with the coupon bonds for the six per cent, interest thereon, payable annually as above stated; which bonds shall be executed in the mode prescribed in the third section of this act, and shall be made payable at the office of the Treasurer of the State, and which shall be a lien in favor of the State, as specified in the third section of this act, and shall have priority over all other claims against said company. That in addition to the annual interest of six per cent., every company accepting any loan under the provisions of this act, shall pay annually at the expiration of each year, from the date of the loan, the further sum of two per cent. upon the amount of the loan, into the treasury of the State for the purpose of establishing a sinking fund, to be applied towards the payment of the loan at its maturity, and the amount so paid for the purpose of such sinking fund with their accumulations, shall be credited to such railroad.

Interest and two per cent. additional annually paid.

No subsequent lien to conflict with that of State. ART. 1688. [8] And after the execution of said bonds upon said first section, or any subsequent constructed section, it shall not be lawful for said company to give, create or convey to any person or persons, or body corporate whatever, any lien, incumbrance or mortgage of any kind which shall have priority over, or come in conflict with the lien herein secured, and any such lien, incumbrance or mortgage, shall be null and void, as against said lien or mortgage, in favor of the State.

Interest where paid. ART. 1689. [9] It shall be the duty of any such company, as the interest becomes due upon said bonds executed as aforesaid, to deposit the same in the treasury of the State, which amount shall be credited to the special school fund, and shall be subject to the immediate appropriation for school purposes, as provided by law. And all railroad companies shall pay said interest so due by them, annually, on the first day of March, out of the first receipts arising from said road, independent of any expenses or other liabilities of said roads, and the coupon bonds of such companies so satisfied, shall be cancelled and delivered up.

Annually on the first day of March.

Bonds of company to be paid in the treasury. ART. 1690. [10] Whenever any of the bonds of said company for the principal loaned thereon shall become due, said company shall deposit said sums so due in the Treasury of the State, and said bonds, when so paid, shall be cancelled and delivered up, and said principal sums so returned into the treasury, shall be credited to the special school fund, and subject to reinvestment by said board as provided in this act.

Failure of company to pay principal or interest. ART. 1691. [11] If any such company shall fail or refuse to pay said principal or interest bonds from time to time, as the same shall become due, the road of said company, together with all the rights and property of said company, specified in section third of this act, shall be sold or caused to be sold by the Governor of the State, for the satisfaction of said bonds so due, as well as the bonds of said company, which may have been given under this act to the State, and the whole of said bonds shall be deemed due if said sale takes place, and the proceeds of such sales shall be deposited in the treasury and credited to the special school fund.

Art. 1692. [12] Upon the failure of any such company to pay said principal or interest bonds, as required in this act, it shall be the duty of the Governor, after the expiration of thirty days, to cause notice of the sale of such road to be advertised in some newspaper published at the seat of government for the term of three months. And after due notice has been given, shall cause the entire road, together with all the rights and property of said company, specified in the third section of this act, to be sold at public auction to the highest bidder for cash, at the door of the capitol of the State, and at the time specified in said advertisement; provided, that if the principal or interest bonds which may have become due before the giving of said notice, and all cost attending said proceedings shall be paid before the day of sale, then said proceedings for sale shall be stopped. Same subject.

Art. 1693. [13] In the event of any sale of any railroad under the provisions of this act, it shall be the duty of the Governor, either in person or by agent, to attend such sale and protect the interest of the special school fund, and shall, if necessary to protect said interest, buy in said road with all the rights and property belonging to said company, in the name of the Board of School Commissioners; provided, he shall not bid more than the amount of the bonds of said company with the interest due thereon, and the cost and expenses attending said sales. And in the event of any such purchase in the name of the Board of School Commissioners, the Governor shall appoint a receiver, who shall be required to enter into such bonds as may be required by the Governor, and whose duty it shall be to take immediate possession of and to control and manage said road, under direction of the Governor, until otherwise disposed of by law, the said Board of School Commissioners shall retain in the treasury of the State, charged to the credit of the school fund, five per cent. of the United States bonds, of all sums loaned, as provided in this act, as a sinking fund, to be used for the "pro rata" appropriation annually due to the several counties for school purposes, in the event of the interest due to the school fund after the sale of any railroad, shall not be paid by said road. In case of sale, Governor in person, or by agent, to attend. Duty of.

Art. 1694. [14] The State of Texas expressly reserves the right to enact hereafter all such laws as may be deemed necessary to protect the interest of the special shool fund, in securing the payment of said bonds and in enforcing the lien reserved thereon. State reserves right to enact laws to protect school fund.

Art. 1695. [15] The provisions of this act shall not extend to any railroad company which may be entitled to receive from the State a larger grant of land than sixteen sections of six hundred and forty acres to the mile, for the construction of such road, nor to any road for more than a single trunk, with the necessary turn-outs, nor to any branch road, nor to any road which shall not be commenced and prosecuted as required by the provisions of its charter. Provided, that no company shall be entitled to a loan under this act for any section of road between the cities of Galveston and Houston, or Galveston and the crossing of Buffalo Bayou, near the city of Houston. What roads not entitled to benefits of this act.

Art. 1696. [16] No railroad which is less than fifty miles in length, according to the terms of its charter, shall be entitled to the benefits of this act, except on the following terms: The Brownsville and Rio Grande Railroad shall be entitled to the benefits of this act on its entire length, as soon as it is completed from Point Isabel to Brownsville; and any other railroad which is less than fifty miles in length, according to the terms of its charter, whenever one half of its entire length has been completed and put in running order, and the Roads less than fifty miles not entitled, except.

other half has been graded ready for the ties and other superstructure, shall be entitled to said loan on said completed section, which shall be expended for the completion of the entire road; and in no event shall said roads be entitled to said loan on more than one half of its entire length.

False affidavit.

ART. 1697. [17] If any person making an affidavit as herein required, shall knowingly swear falsely, he, upon conviction thereof before any court of competetent jurisdiction, shall suffer all the pains and penalties of perjury.

Annual report of railroad companies.

ART. 1698. [18] It shall be the duty of any railroad company receiving the benefits of this act, to make through its proper officers an annual report under oath, to the Governor, containing a full and complete statement of the affairs of said company, together with the receipts, expenditures and liabilities of said companies, and with such other facts as may be necessary, under the general laws regulating railroads and said railroad companies.

Office on line of road.

Superintendent, Directors and President, residence of.

ART. 1699. [19] Every railroad company before it shall be entitled to the privileges of this act, shall establish upon the line of its road an office where books shall be kept, showing the state of its stock and general accounts, and where the company may be legally served with all notices and processes, and the Superintendent or principal manager of the transportation business of the road, shall reside in this State. And whenever a majority of the shares in the capital stock of the company shall be owned in this State, a majority of the Directors, including the President, shall be residents thereof.

REGISTRATION.

VII. PROPERTY OF MARRIED WOMEN.

I. RECORDER.

ART. 1700. [1] The Clerks of the County Courts of the several counties of this State shall be the recorders for their respective counties; they shall provide and keep in their offices well-bound books, in which they shall record, in a fair and legible hand, all instruments of writing authorized or required to be recorded in the recorder's office of their respective counties, in the manner hereinafter provided.

Act of May 12, 1846. Took effect July 13, 1846. Clerks of County Court shall be.

ART. 1701. [2] The seal of the County Court shall be the seal of the recorder, and shall be used for the authentication of all his official acts

Sea.

II. DUTIES.

ART. 1702. [36] It shall be the duty of the Recorder to give attested copies, whenever demanded, of all papers recorded in his office; and the Recorder shall receive for all such copies, and all other writing required of him by virtue of his office, such fees as may be provided by law.

Act of Dec'r 20, 1836. Took effect from passage. Copies of rec'ds shall be given.

ART. 1703. [10] The several Clerks aforesaid shall, on the first day of every term of their respective courts, return to the courts a correct and complete list of all deeds by them admitted to record in the manner aforesaid, since the term last preceding, of their said courts; specifying therein the proof or acknowledgment of such deed before them, (as the case may be,) and also particularly reciting the truth of the case in relation to any deed which may have been admitted to record, upon the certificates of magistrates as aforesaid, and setting forth therein a description of each deed, by the names of the parties thereto, and the kind of property therein mentioned; which list, having been inspected by the court, shall be inserted in the minutes of the proceedings of the day, and read therewith in open court; and the said Clerks shall, moreover, cause a fair copy of such lists of deeds to be set up by ten o'clock, A. M., of the day in which such return is made, at the principal door of their respective court houses.

Act of Feb'y 5, 1840. Took effect March 16, 1840. List of regist'rd deeds to be returned, &c.

ART. 1704. [11] Any Clerk failing to make the return aforesaid, or to advertise a copy thereof in the manner herein prescribed, shall forfeit and pay, for every such neglect of duty, the sum of one hundred dollars, recoverable with costs on action or information, in the District Court of the county in which such Clerk has his office—one moiety to the informer, or person suing for the same, and the other to the Republic.

Penalty for failing, &c.

ART. 1705. [3] Each Recorder shall provide suitable books and presses for his office, and keep regular and faithful accounts of the expenses thereof, and such accounts shall be audited by the County Court and paid out of the County Treasury.

Act of May 12, 1846. Took effect July 13, 1846. Shall provide books, &c.

ART. 1706. [4] It shall be the duty of each Recorder to record in the books provided for his office, all deeds, mortgages, conveyances, deeds of trust, bonds,

Shall record deeds, &c., when

covenants, defeasances, or other instruments of writing, of or concerning any lands and tenements, or goods and chattels, or movable property of any description, in his county, which shall be proved or acknowledged according to law, and delivered to him to be recorded in his office.(*a*)

Shall keep a memorandum of, and give receipt

ART. 1707. [12] When any instrument of writing, authorized by law to be recorded, shall be deposited in the Recorder's Office for record, if the same shall be acknowledged or proved in the manner prescribed by law, for record, the Recorder shall enter in a book to be provided for that purpose, in alphabetical order, the names of the parties and date and nature thereof, the time of delivery for record; and shall give to the person depositing the same, if required, a receipt specifying the particulars thereof.

Shall record without delay in the order presented.

ART. 1708. [13] Each Recorder shall, without delay, record every instrument of writing authorized to be recorded by him, which is deposited with him for record, with the acknowledgments, proofs, affidavits and certificates written or attached to the same, and all other papers referred to and thereto annexed, in the order and as of the time when the same shall have been deposited for record, by entering them word for word and letter for letter, and noting at the foot of such record all interlineations, erasures, and words visibly written on erasures, and noting at the foot of the record, the hour and the day of the month and year when the instrument so recorded was deposited in his office for record.

Record shall take effect from date of deposit.

ART. 1709. [14] Every such instrument of writing shall be considered as recorded from the time it was deposited for record; and the Recorder shall certify and attach to every such instrument of writing so recorded, the hour, day, month and year when he recorded it, and the book and page or pages in which it is recorded; and when recorded, deliver the same to the party entitled thereto, or to his order.

Shall keep alphabetical indexes.

ART. 1710. [15] Each Recorder shall provide and keep in his office a well-bound book, and make and enter therein an index in alphabetical order, to all books of records, wherein deeds, mortgages, or other instruments of writing concerning lands and tenements are recorded, distinguishing the books and pages in which every such deed or writing is recorded.

What they shall contain.

ART. 1711. [16] Such index shall contain the names of the several grantors and grantees in alphabetical order; and in case the deed be made by a sheriff, the name of the sheriff and the defendant in execution; and if by executors or administrators, their names and the names of their testators or intestates; and if by attorney, the name of such attorney and his constituents; and if by a commissioner, the name of such commissioner and the person whose estate is conveyed.

Same subject.

ART. 1712. [17] Each Recorder shall in like manner make and keep in his office a full and perfect alphabetical index to all books of record in his office, wherein all instruments of writing in relation to goods and chattels, or movable property of any description, marriage contracts and powers of attorney, and all other instruments of writing authorized or required to be recorded in his office, are recorded; and a like index of all the books of record wherein official bonds are recorded, the names of the officers appointed, and of the obligors in any bond recorded, and a reference to the book and page where the same are recorded.

Liability of, for neglect, &c.

ART. 1713. [18] If any Recorder to whom any instrument of writing authorized to be recorded by him, and proved or acknowledged according to

(*a*) The recording of instruments, which are not required or affirmatively permitted by law to be recorded, is not notice. Burnham *v.* Chandler, 15 Tex. Rep. 441.

law, which shall be delivered for record, shall neglect or refuse to make an entry thereof, or give receipt therefor, as required by this act, or shall neglect or refuse to record such instrument of writing within a reasonable time after receiving the same, or shall record any instrument of writing affecting the same property, or any part thereof, before another first deposited in his office and entitled to be recorded, or shall record any such instrument incorrectly, or shall neglect or refuse to provide and keep in his office such indexes as required by this act, he shall forfeit and pay any sum not exceeding five hundred dollars, to be recovered on motion in the District Court, one-half to the use of the county, and the other half to the use of the person who shall sue for the same, such clerk having three days' notice of such motion, and shall also be liable to the party for all damages he may have sustained thereby, to be recovered by suit in the official bond of such Recorder, given by him as clerk of the County Court, against such clerk and his securities.

III. OFFICERS TO TAKE PROOF AND ACKNOWLEDGMENTS.

ART. 1714. [11] Proof or acknowledgment of every instrument of writing for record, shall be taken by some one of the following officers: First, when acknowledged or proven within the State, before some Notary Public or clerk of the County Court of any county in the State. Second, when acknowledged or proven without this State, and within the United States or their territories, before some Judge of a court of record having a seal. Third, when acknowledged or proven without the United States, before some Public Minister, Charge d'Affaires, or Consul of the United States; and in all cases the certificate of such acknowledgment or proof, shall be attested under the official seal of the officer taking the same.

Act of May 12, 1846. Took effect July 13, 1846. Before what officers taken, &c.

ART. 1715. [27] The Chief Justice of the County Court shall have power to take the acknowledgment and proof of all instruments of writing for the purpose of being recorded, and they shall also have power to examine and take the acknowledgment of married women to all deeds of their separate property, and all deeds to property for the sale of which their consent is required, in like manner and under the same rules and regulations as are provided for Notaries Public; and all acts so done by any Chief Justice of a County Court in this State, shall have the same force and effect as if done by a Notary Public.

Act of March 16, 1848. Took effect Aug. 16, 1848. Chief Justice may take.

ART. 1716. [1] The several clerks of the County Courts be, and they are hereby authorized to take the separate acknowledgment of deeds executed by married women, under the same rules and regulations as are prescribed for Judges of the Supreme or District Courts, or Notaries Public, in an act entitled, "an act defining the mode of conveying property in which the wife has an interest," approved April 30, 1846.

Act of Dec. 18, 1849. Took effect from passage. County Clerk may take, &c.

IV. DEPUTY CLERKS.

ART. 1717. [1] All deputies regularly appointed by the clerks of the several District Courts of this State, shall have power to take depositions, and to do and perform all other acts that may be lawfully done by said principal clerks.*

Act of Feb'ry 9, 1856. Took effect from passage. Powers of.

* This section should have appeared in the District Court law, but being omitted it is inserted here.

Of Deputy Clerks of County Courts.

ART. 1718. [2] The deputies regularly appointed by the several clerks of the County Courts of this State, have power to take the separate acknowledgments of married women, acknowledging the execution of deeds and other instruments of conveyance, executed by them, in the same manner as the same may be taken by said principal clerks, and that such deputy clerks have power to take proof of the execution of all deeds, mortgages and other instruments of writing that are by law required or allowed to be recorded. And to take the acknowledgments of the persons executing such deeds, mortgages and other instruments of writing, and to do and perform all other acts required to be done by said principal clerks. And that all such acts heretofore done by such deputy clerks are hereby declared to be as valid as if done by said principal clerks.

V. ACKNOWLEDGMENT AND PROBATE.

Act of May 12, 1846. Took effect July 13, 1846.

Acknowledgment of deed, &c.

ART. 1719. [7] The acknowledgment of an instrument of writing, for the purpose of being recorded, shall be by the grantor or person who executed the same appearing before some officer authorized to take such acknowledgment, and stating that he had executed the same for the consideration and purposes therein stated; and the officer taking such acknowledgment shall make a certificate thereof, sign and seal the same with his seal of office.

Proof, by witnesses.

ART. 1720. [8] The proof of any instrument of writing, for the purpose of being recorded, shall be by one or more of the subscribing witnesses personally appearing before some officer authorized to take such proof, and stating on oath that he or they saw the grantor, or person who executed such instrument, subscribe the same; or that the grantor or person who executed such instrument of writing acknowledged in his or their presence, that he had subscribed and executed the same, for the purposes and consideration therein stated, and that he or they had signed the same as witnesses, at the request of the grantor or person who executed such instrument; and the officer taking such proof shall make a certificate thereof, sign and seal the same with his official seal.(a)

When witness is dead, out of the State, &c., how proven.

ART. 1721. [9] When the subscribing witnesses to any instrument of writing may be dead, or their place of residence unknown, or when they reside out of the State, an affidavit thereof may be made and attached to such instrument; after which it may be proved for the purpose of being recorded, by the evidence of the handwriting of the grantor or person who executed such instrument, and at least one of the subscribing witnesses; which evidence shall consist of the deposition of two or more disinterested persons in writing, attached to such instrument: and the officer taking such proof, shall make a certificate thereof, sign and seal the same with his official seal.

When grantor or witness is unknown to the officer.

ART. 1722. [10] Whenever any grantor or person who executed any instrument of writing, or any subscribing witness to any such instrument, shall appear before any officer authorized to take acknowledgments or proofs of such instruments, for the purpose of acknowledging or proving such instrument for record, if such grantor or person who executed such instrument, or subscribing witness, shall be personally unknown to such officer, his identity, and his being the person he purports to be on the face of such instrument of writing, shall be proven to such officer; which proof may be made by witnesses known to such

(a) Where the witness states that he saw the grantor subscribe the instrument, he is not required to show that he subscribed the same as a witness, at the request of the grantor; and the use of the word *execute*, instead of *subscribe*, is not material. Dorn *v.* Best. 15 Tex. Rep. 62.

officer, or the affidavit of such grantor or person who executed such instrument, or subscribing witness, if such officer shall be satisfied therewith; which proof or affidavit shall also be endorsed on such instrument of writing.

VI. INSTRUMENTS REQUIRED TO BE RECORDED.

ART. 1723. [3] All mortgages on real estate shall, upon the usual proof, be recorded in the county where the land is situated, within ninety days from the passage of this act, or from the date of the execution of such mortgage; and upon personal property in the county where the mortgagor lives. No mortgage shall take lien upon property unless so recorded.(*a*)

Act of May 15, 1838. Took effect from passage. Mortgages, when and where to be recorded.

ART. 1724. [2] Copies of all deeds, etc., when the originals remain in the public archives, and were executed in conformity with the laws existing at their dates, duly certified by the proper officers, shall be admitted to record in the county where such land lies.(*b*)

Act of Feb'ry 5, 1840. In force from date. Mortgage lien, when not destroyed.

ART. 1725. [3[All mortgages shall be recorded as heretofore, but the lien created by the making of the mortgage shall not be lost nor destroyed, as between the parties to it, if the mortgagee should fail to have it recorded within the time prescribed by law.

Act of Jan. 19, 1839. In force from passage. Copies of old archives in certain cases.

ART. 1726. [4] All bargains, sales, and other conveyances, whatever, of any lands, tenements and hereditaments, whether they be made for passing any estate of freehold or inheritance, or for a term of years; and deeds of settlement upon marriage, whether land, slaves, money, or other personal thing, shall be settled or covenanted to be left, or paid, at the death of the party, or otherwise; and all deeds of trust, and mortgages whatsoever, which shall hereafter be made and executed, shall be void as to all creditors and subsequent purchasers for valuable consideration without notice, unless they shall be acknowledged or proved, and lodged with the Clerk, to be recorded according to the directions of this act; but the same, as between the parties and their heirs, and as to all subsequent purchasers, with notice thereof, or without valuable consideration, shall nevertheless be valid and binding.(*c*)

Act of Feb. 5th, 1840. Took effect March 16, 1840. Bargains, sales, conveyances, &c., shall be.

ART. 1727. [7] Every title, bond, or other written contract in relation to lands, may be proved, certified, or acknowledged, and recorded, in the same manner as deeds for the conveyance of land; and such proof, acknowledgment, or certificate, and the delivery of such bond or contract to the Clerk of the proper court, to be recorded, shall be taken and held as notice to all subsequent purchasers, of the existence of such bond or contract.(*d*)

Every title, bond, &c., for lands may be.

ART. 1728. [8] Hereafter every partition of any tract of land, or lot, made under any order or decree of any court, and every judgment or decree by which the title to any tract of land, or lot, shall be recovered, shall be duly recorded in the Clerk's office of the County Court of the county in which such tract of land, or lot, or part thereof shall be; and until so recorded, such partition, judgment, or decree, shall not be received in evidence in support of any right claimed by virtue thereof.

Partition of land by order of Court.

ART. 1729. [12] Every deed respecting the title of personal chattels,

(*a*) Crosby *v.* Huston, 1 Tex. Rep. 240.
(*b*) Guilbeau, *v.* Mays, 15 Tex. Rep. 410.
(*c*) This section does not introduce a new rule, but is only declaratory of the law as recognized in the chancery jurisprudence of England and the United States. It is but the declaration of positive law, that the want of registration shall avoid the deed only as to creditors and subsequent purchasers *without notice;* but as to subsequent purchasers with notice thereof, the deed shall nevertheless be valid and binding. Parks *v.* Willard, 1 Tex. Rep. 350. Fowler & Clipper *v.* Stoneum, 6 Tex. Rep. 60.
(*d*) Miller *v.* Alexander, 8 Tex. Rep. 36.

Deed for personal property, where recorded, removal of, &c. hereafter executed, which, by law ought to be recorded, shall be recorded in the Clerk's Office of the County Court of that county in which the property shall remain; and if afterwards the person claiming title under such deed, shall permit any other person in whose possession such property may be, to remove with the same or any part thereof, out of the county in which such deed shall be recorded, and shall not, within four months after such removal, cause the deed aforesaid to be certified to the County Court of the county in which such other person shall so have removed, and to be delivered to the Clerk to be there recorded, such deed, for so long as it shall not be recorded in such last mentioned county, and for so much of the property aforesaid as shall have been removed, shall be void in law as to all purchasers thereof for valuable consideration, without notice, and as to all creditors.

Deeds, &c., valid against subsequent creditors from, &c. ART. 1730. [13] Every conveyance, covenant, agreement, deed, deed of trust, or mortgage, in this act mentioned, which shall be acknowledged, proved, or certified, according to law, and delivered to the Clerk of the proper court to be recorded, shall take effect, and be valid as to all subsequent purchasers for a valuable consideration, without notice, and as to all creditors, from the time when such instrument shall be so acknowledged, proved, or certified and delivered to such Clerk to be recorded, and from that time only.

Act of Feb. 5, 1841. Took effect March 17, 1841. All bargains, conveyances, &c. to be recorded. ART. 1731. [21] Every grant, deed, or instrument, mentioned in the twentieth section of this act, hereafter to be made and recorded, shall be duly registered in the office of the proper county, upon the acknowledgment of the parties or party signing the same, before the Register, or Clerk of the County Court of that county, or Chief Justice of the county, or a Notary Public, * * * * * * * * * * * * or Acknowledgment sufficient, without, &c. proved by a subscribing witness before any such officer, and certified by him for record; and if it be so acknowledged and certified, there need be no subscribing witnesses; and Duty of Register—penalty for neglect. the Register shall certify thereon the day when the same shall be delivered for registration, give a receipt therefor, if required, and record the same within one month thereafter, under the forfeiture to the party injured, for neglecting either particular, of five hundred dollars, and accumulative liability to such party, for recovery of vindictive damages; and such grant, deed, or instrument, so delivered for registration, shall, according to its nature and character, have full effect, validity, and priority, from and after its date of presentation or delivery for registration, against subsequent purchasers and creditors; and such acknowledgment or probate certificate and Notice to subsequent creditors and purchasers. registration, or either, as between the parties and their legal representatives, and all subsequent purchasers, and creditors, with actual notice, or reasonable information of the grant, deed, or instrument, shall not be deemed requisite in order to its full effect, validity, and priority, according to its intrinsic nature.(*a*)

Act of May 12, 1846. Took effect July 13, 1846. Marriage contract, powers of attorney, &c. ART. 1732. [5] Each Recorder shall also record in books to be provided for that purpose, all marriage contracts and powers of attorney, and all official bonds required to be recorded in his office, and all other instruments of writing authorized or required to be recorded in his office, which shall be proved or acknowledged according to law, and delivered to him for record.

Titles issued from Land Office, copies, &c. ART. 1733. [6] Each Recorder shall record all titles issued by the Commissioner of the General Land Office, and copies of all titles recorded in the General Land Office, presented for record: provided, such titles or copies are attested with the seal of the General Land Office. They shall also record all judgments and abstracts of judgments rendered by any court of this State: provided, such judgment or abstracts of judgment are attested under the hand and seal of the Clerks of the court where such judgment was obtained. They

(*a*) Bennet *v.* Cocks, 15 Tex. Rep. 67. Butler *v.* Dunnegan, 19 Tex. Rep. 559.

shall also record all other instruments authorized by law to be recorded by them, which were executed previous to the time this act takes effect, and which are acknowledged or proved in the manner provided for by this act, or by the laws which were in force at the time of such acknowledgment or proof; all of which writings shall be recorded under the same rules and penalties hereinafter prescribed for other instruments.

VII. PROPERTY OF MARRIED WOMEN.

ART. 1734. [8] When the wife, by a marriage contract, may reserve to herself any property or rights to property (whether such rights be in esse or expectancy), for such reservation to be valid as to the subsequent purchasers or creditors of her husband, the said contract must be acknowledged by her husband or proved by at least one witness, and recorded in the Clerk's office of the County Court of the county in which said married parties may reside. Act of Jan. 20, 1840. Took effect March 16, 1840. Reservation under marriage contract &c.

ART. 1735. [2] No covenant or agreement made in consideration of marriage shall be good against a purchaser for a valuable consideration, not having notice thereof, or any creditor, unless the same covenant or agreement be acknowledged by the party to be bound thereby, or proved by two witnesses to be his, her, or their act;—if land be charged, before the court of the county in which the land, or part thereof, lieth;—or if personal estate only be settled, or covenanted or agreed to be paid or settled, before the court of that county in which such personal estate shall remain, and before the court of the county in which the married parties may reside, (if they reside in another county,) or in the manner hereinafter directed, and be lodged with the Clerk of the County Court in which such property may remain, and in which such married parties may reside, to be recorded; and all the provisions of this act shall be complied with, notwithstanding anything that may be contained in the eighth section of the Act to adopt the common law, &c., approved January 20th, 1840. Act of Feb. 5, 1840. Took effect March 16, 1840. Marriage contracts, not good as against subsequent creditors, &c., unless.

ART. 1736. [1] All property, real and personal, owned or claimed by married women, or which may be owned or claimed at the time of marriage, by any woman, or which they may acquire by gift, devise or descent, shall be registered as hereinafter directed. Act of April 29, 1846. Took effect June 22, 1846. Title of property owned at time of marriage shall be, &c.

ART. 1737. [2] Each woman now married, or who may be hereafter married, may present to any officer authorized by law to probate deeds, or other instruments for record, a schedule, particularly describing all the property, real and personal, which she now owns and possesses, or which she may own and possess at the time of her marriage, and make acknowledgment before such officer, that the property described in the schedule is her separate property; and upon such acknowledgment, the officer aforesaid, shall give a certificate of the fact under his hand and seal of office; which certificate shall be sufficient evidence for the Recorder of any county to register the said schedule.(a) May present a schedule of, for record.

ART. 1738. [3] Each married woman, upon coming into possession of any property, real or personal, to which she had claim at the time of her marriage, or which she may afterwards acquire by gift, devise or descent, may have the same registered in the same manner as prescribed in the foregoing section. Of property owned before and acquired after marriage, by, &c.

ART. 1739. [4] The registry of the wife's separate property, herein pro-

(a) This act merely extends a privilege, no penalty is declared in case of failure or neglect of the wife to avail herself of it, nor does the Legislature possess any constitutional power to declare the title of the wife to her property shall be divested for want of registration, nor that for that reason it shall be subjected to the debts of her husband or any other person whomsoever. Edrinton v. Mayfield, 5 Tex. Rep. 363. Warren v. Dickerson, 3 Tex. Rep. 460.

In what county it shall be registered. vided for, shall be made in the county or counties, in which it really may lie; and if there be personal property, then also in the county where the wife may reside; and in case of her removal to another county, the registry may also be made in the county to which she may so remove, within three months after such removal.

Former registrations under, &c. ART. 1740. [5] All registrations of the wife's separate property, which have been made heretofore, shall be deemed good and valid under this act provided, said registrations were made in accordance with the laws then in force.

Registry of schedule, shall be conclusive as against, &c. ART. 1741. [6] The registry of any schedule of a wife's separate property, made in accordance with the provisions of this act, shall be conclusive, as against all subsequent creditors of and purchasers from the husband.

Act of Feb. 5, 1841. Took effect March 17, 1841. Confirmation of defective conveyances heretofore made. ART. 1742. [20] Any grant, deed, or instrument for the conveyance of real estate, or personal, or both, or for the settlement thereof in marriage, or separate property or conveyance of the same in mortgage, on trust to uses, or on conditions, as well as any and every other deed or instrument required, or permitted by law to be registered, and which shall have been heretofore registered, shall, from the passage of this act, be held to have been duly registered, with the full effects and consequences of the existing laws: provided, the same shall have been acknowledged by the grantor or grantors, maker or makers, before any Chief Justice of the County Court, or before any Notary Public, or before the Clerk of the County Court in whose office such record is proposed to be made, or proved before such officer by one or more of the subscribing witnesses, and certified by such officer; any obscurity or conflict in the existing laws, to the contrary notwithstanding.(*a*)

RENTS.(*b*)

Act of January 16, 1843. In force from date. Person granting a lease shall have a lien on the crop. Crop not to be removed, length of lien. ART. 1743. [1] All persons granting a lease of lands or tenements, either at will or for a term shall have a lien upon all the property of the tenant upon such premises, for the payment of the rents becoming due under such lease, whether the same is to be paid in money, cotton, corn, or whatever else may be raised upon the rented premises; and in case where the rent is to be paid in corn, cotton, or other articles raised upon the rented premises, it shall not be lawful for such tenant to remove off the premises any of such corn, cotton, or other article in which such rent is to be paid; and such lien shall continue and be in force so long as such tenant shall occupy the rented premises, and for three months thereafter: provided, however, that such lien shall not attach to any property for more than three months after the same shall be removed off

(*a*) Stramler *v.* Coe, 15 Tex. Rep. 211. Butler *v.* Dunnegan, 19 Tex. Rep. 559.

(*b*) It seems to be clear, beyond dispute, that the authority to resort to the remedy to recover rent by distress warrant, rests upon three distinct grounds, contained in the statute, and separated in it by the disjunctive "or". First, the rent must be due, *or* the tenant is about to remove from the rented premises, *or* about to remove his property from such rented premises. Weir *v.* Brooks. 17 Tex. Rep. 638.

the rented premises; nor to any goods, wares, and merchandize of a merchant or trader, after the same shall be sold in good faith, and removed from the premises.

ART. 1744. [2] When any rent shall become due, or the tenant about to remove from such rented premises, or remove his property from such rented premises, it shall be lawful for the person to whom the rent is payable, his agent, attorney, or assigns, to apply to any Justice of the Peace in the county where the premises is situated, for a distress warrant to seize the property of such tenant: provided such plaintiff, his agent, or attorney, shall make oath that the amount sued for is for rent; or shall produce a writing from such tenant to that effect; and it shall be the duty of such Justice, to issue his warrant of distress to the proper officer, commanding him to seize the property of the defendant, or so much thereof as will satisfy the demand; which warrant shall be, if the sum is not more than one hundred dollars, returnable to said Justice, or to some Justice of the county; but if more than one hundred dollars, the warrant shall be returnable to the District Court; in which case it shall be the duty of the Justice to transmit all the papers of said cause to the District Court, on or before the first day of the next term thereof. A distress warrant may issue, when. How returned

ART. 1745. [3] It shall be the duty of the officer to whom such warrant is directed, to seize the property of such tenant, or so much thereof as shall be of value sufficient to satisfy such debt and cost, and the same in his possession safely keep (unless the defendant will replevy the same) and make due return thereof to the court in which such warrant is returnable, at the next term thereof: provided, that if the property is of a perishable or wasting kind, the Sheriff or other officer, or the plaintiff, or the defendant, may apply to the Justice issuing the warrant, or any other Justice, for an order to sell such property. Duty of the officer. Property seized, if perishable, may be sold.

ART. 1746. [4] It shall be lawful for the plaintiff, at the return of such warrant, to proceed to judgment, as in ordinary cases: provided, that in case the return is to be made to the District Court, the plaintiff shall not be obliged to file his petition before the suing out of such warrant: and provided, further, no other formalities shall be required than those mentioned in this act; and in case the defendant does not apply, the plaintiff may apply to the court where such judgment was rendered, for an order of sale; which sale shall be conducted as sales under execution. Upon return of the warrant, plaintiff may proceed to judgment, provided.

ART. 1747. [1] Landlords shall not have a preference over other creditors, on any portion of the tenant's property, except upon the crop that may be raised on the rented premises. Act of Feb. 3, 1844. In force from date. Landlords shall not have a preference, except.

ART. 1748. [2] The three months' lien provided for in the act to which this is a supplement, shall only apply to the crop raised on the rented premises, and to no other property of the tenant: provided, that in no case shall the lien extend, or continue, beyond the first day of January next after the maturity of the crop, unless the crop subject to said lien be found on said rented premises after said time. Lien shall only extend to the crop, and to 1st January after.

ART. 1749. [3] In all cases, before a distress warrrnt is issued, the party applying for the same, in addition to the requirements in the act to which this is a supplement, shall swear that the writ, or distress warrant, is not sued out for the purpose of vexing and harrassing the defendant; and the person applying for the same, with one good and sufficient security, approved by the Justice of the Peace, shall sign an instrument in substance as follows: "We, or either of us, promise to pay defendant in this suit (naming him) such damages as he may sustain, in case the distress warrant in this case has been illegally and Affidavit to be made before warrant issues.

Bond to be given.

unjustly sued out," which instrument shall be filed among the papers of the cause; and in case the suit shall be finally decided in favor of defendant, he may bring suit against the plaintiff and his security, on such instrument, or either of them, and shall recover such damages as may be awarded to him by the proper tribunal.

This act not to repeal former acts exempting property from execution.

ART. 1750. [4] Said act, or this supplement thereto, shall not be considered as in any manner repealing or affecting any act passed heretofore, exempting property from execution.

If any person except defendant apply for a sale, bond for damages shall be given.

ART. 1751. [5] If any person other than the defendant, apply for an order of sale of the property, as perishable property, the Justice shall not grant such order, uless the person, applying with one good and sufficient security approved by said Justice, shall file with said Justice, a joint and several instrument, signed by them, that they will be responsible to said defendant for such damages as defendant may sustain, in case such sale be illegally and unjustly applied for, or should be illegally and unjustly made.

Special contract as to the lien may be made

ART. 1752. [6] Nothing herein contained shall be so construed, as to prevent landlords and tenants from entering into such stipulations or contracts, in regard to lien, as they may think proper: provided, that the rights of third persons shall not be thereby affected, unless such contract be reduced to writing and put upon record.

RETAILERS OF SPIRITUOUS LIQUORS.(*a*)

Act of Feb'ry 2, 1856. Took effect April 1, 1856.

Privilege to retail, how acquired.

ART. 1753. [1] Any person or firm hereafter wishing to engage in the business occupation of selling spirituous, vinous, or other intoxicating liquors in quantities less than a quart, shall have the privilege of doing so, upon his, her, or their application, in writing, to the County Court of the county where he, she, or they shall reside, stating the house or place where he, she, or they propose to carry on such business and occupation, and for what length of time.

Court to order license, &c.

ART. 1754. [2] Upon the presentation of the written application of the party or parties to the County Court, it shall then be the duty of said court to order the clerk thereof to issue to the applicant a license, authorizing him, her or them to retail spirituous, vinous, or other intoxicating liquors, in quantities less than one quart, at the house or place specified in said written application, and for the length of time applied for upon conditions hereinafter prescribed.

Bond of applicant—condition of bond.

ART. 1755. [3] Before the clerk of the County Court shall issue to the applicant a license to retail spirituous, vinous and other liquors, in quantities less than a quart, he, she, or they, shall make and deliver to the County Trea-

(*a*) This act was not repealed by the Penal Code and Code of Criminal Procedure. Cain *v.* The State, 20 Tex. Rep. 355.

surer, a bond, payable to the Chief Justice of said county, with two or more good and sufficient sureties, to be approved by said Treasurer, in the sum of one thousand dollars, conditioned that the applicant and those acting or attending to said business for him, shall keep an orderly house or place for the retail of spirituous liquors, and that he will not permit a sale of spirituous liquors to be made at his house or place to minors under the age of sixteen years, or students of any institution of learning, or to negro slaves without the written permission of the master, mistress, or overseer of said slave, and that he will not permit any games to be played at the house or place whether licensed or not, which bond upon being approved by the said County Treasurer, shall be filed in his office as an obligation belonging to his county.

ART. 1756. [4] When the party or firm shall have executed the bond with security, as prescribed in the preceding section of this act, and shall have paid into the county Treasury of the county a license tax, at the rate of two hundred and fifty dollars for one year, for the time he, she, or they have applied for the license, and shall produce to the clerk of the County Court the County Treasurer's receipt for the amount of money paid by him, then the said clerk shall issue to him a license to sell at retail any spirituous, vinous or other liquors, in quantities less than a quart, at the house or place, and for the time specified in the application.

When and upon what conditions County Clerk shall issue license.

ART. 1757. [5] If any person or firm shall sell or be in any wise concerned in selling spirituous, vinous, or other intoxicating liquors, in quantities less than one quart, without first having obtained a license therefor, in the manner prescribed by this act, he, she or they shall be deemed guilty of a misdemeanor, and upon conviction thereof, before any District Court, Justice of the Peace, or Mayor of any city or incorporated town, shall be fined in any sum not less than fifty nor more than two hundred dollars, and be imprisoned in the county jail until such fine and the costs be paid, and no person so convicted shall be discharged from such imprisonment before the expiration of thirty days, unless the fine and costs be sooner paid, any law to the contrary notwithstanding.

Penalty for selling in quantities less than quart without license.

ART. 1758. [6] If any person or firm shall sell or be concerned in selling, or shall permit any other person to sell any spirituous, vinous or other intoxicating liquors in quantities of a quart or more and shall permit or suffer the same to be drunk at or about the place or establishment where sold, or at or about any other house provided for that purpose, he, she, or they, upon conviction thereof, before any court mentioned in the next preceding section, shall be fined as therein prescribed.

Selling more than quart to be drank on premises—penalty.

ART. 1759. [7] All fines, forfeitures and penalties and revenues arising under the provisions of this act, shall be exclusively appropriated by the County Treasurer to the payment of general and petit jurors of the county, in accordance with the existing laws regulating the jury-fund of counties: That in all prosecutions for any violations of any of the provisions of this act, it shall be sufficient to allege and prove that the person charged with any such violation, did sell, or was concerned in selling, spirituous, vinous or intoxicating liquors, and it shall not be necessary to allege or prove the kind of liquor sold, the name of the person or persons to whom the same was sold, or that the same was sold without license. This act shall in all cases be liberally and remediably construed.

Fines and penalties under this act to be appropriated to jury fund.

ART. 1760. [8] No license shall be issued by the clerk of the County Court, nor shall the County Court grant a license to any party or firm for a less term than four months.

License not to issue for shorter period than four months.

ART. 1761. [9] If any person or firm shall violate any of the conditions of

Suit on bond—in name of Chi'f Justice—use of jury fund.

the bond required of him, her or them, by the provisions of this act, it shall be the duty of the County Treasurer to institute suit thereupon, in the name of the Chief Justice of the county, for the use and benefit of the jury-fund of the county, and the full amount of the penalty shall be recovered from the principals and sureties, upon proof of a breach of any of the conditions thereof.

Duty of Clerk and County Commissioners to prosecute, &c.

ART. 1762. [10] It shall be the duty of the County Clerk, Treasurer and County Commissioners to prosecute for all violations of the fifth and sixth sections of this act, before the Justices of the Peace of the precinct where they are committed.

Sale without license contrary to public policy, and may be plead in bar of debt.

ART. 1763. [11] If any person or firm shall sell any spirituous, vinous or other intoxicating liquors, in quantities less than a quart whatever, to any person without first having obtained a license therefor according to the provisions of this act, such sale shall be deemed contrary to public policy, and any person or persons who shall be sued upon such contract shall be allowed to plead the same in bar and to prove the same.

Beer, manufacture of.

ART. 1764. [12] No provision of this act shall apply to beer manufactured in the State of Texas.

ROADS.

Act of Feb. 8, 1858. Took effect from passage.

County Court shall classify.

ART. 1765. [1] The County Courts of the several counties of this State shall have full power to order the laying out of public roads, when necessary, and to discontinue or alter any road whenever it shall be deemed expedient, as hereinafter prescribed; and it shall be their further duty to classify all roads running through their several counties; those of the first class shall be clear of all trees, at least thirty feet wide, stumps cut down to six inches of the surface; all causeways laid out at least fifteen feet wide; and those of the second class shall not be less than twenty feet wide, clear of all trees, all stumps cut to six inches of the surface, and all causeways laid out at least twelve feet wide, and all lanes shall be made at least thirty feet wide.

Shall appoint overseers, designate hands, &c.

ART. 1766. [2] The County Courts of the several counties shall lay off their respective counties into road precincts, and shall at their first meeting in each and every year appoint an overseer for each precinct, and shall at the same time designate all the hands liable to work on public roads, under the different overseers in their county; and in case any hand or hands liable to work on roads shall not have been designated by said court, the overseer shall have power to summons them to work on the nearest public road to which they may live, as if they had been designated by the court: provided, thirty days residence be necessary to require the performance of said road service; but if from any cause the court should fail or neglect to perform the duties required in this section, at its first meeting in the year, it shall be competent and legal for it to make such appointment and designation at a called meeting, or at any regular term; and in case a vacancy should occur in any road precinct, by death, removal, or other inability, of any overseer of the road in the county, it shall be the duty of the Chief Justice, immediately upon information of the same, to appoint an overseer to fill such vacancy, who shall be notified of his appointment, as in other cases, and whose duty it shall be to serve until the first regular meeting of the court in the next succeeding year. Vacancy in precinct by death of overseer.

ART. 1767. [3] All public roads and highways that have been laid out and established agreeably to law, except such as have been discontinued, are hereby declared to be public roads, and the said County Court shall in no instance grant an order on any application for any new road, or to discontinue an original one, unless the persons making application for the same, or some one of them, shall have given at least twenty days notice, by advertisement, of their intended application, put up at the courthouse door, and two other public places in the vicinity of the route of the proposed new road, or the road proposed to be discontinued. Public roads, &c., notice of application to change.

ART. 1768. [4] All applications for a new road, and all applications to discontinue an original one, shall be by petition to the County Court, signed by at least eight householders of the precinct, or precincts in which such road is desired to be made or discontinued, specifying in such petition the beginning and termination of such road proposed to be opened or discontinued. Petition for, must be filed.

ART. 1769. [5] All roads hereafter ordered to be made shall be laid out by a jury of householders of the county, to be appointed by the County Court; said jury shall consist of five persons, a majority of whom may proceed to lay out and mark the road so ordered to the greatest advantage to the public, and with as little prejudice to enclosures as may be, after having taken the following oath before some person authorized to administer oaths, to wit: Must be laid out by a jury.

"I,————, do solemnly swear that I will lay out the road, now directed to be laid out by the order to us directed from the County Court, according to law, without favor or affection, malice or hatred, to the best of my skill and knowledge, so help me God." Oath of.

And the jury thus qualified, shall report their proceedings on the same to the next term of the County Court. Jury shall report.

ART. 1770. [6] No public road shall be surveyed or laid out upon or across any farm, lot or enclosure, without first obtaining the written consent of the owner, or owners, his, her, or their agent or attorney, to the same. Consent of owner, &c., required, when.

ART. 1771. [7] If such written consent should be refused, it shall be the duty of the County Court to appoint five disinterested freehold citizens of the county, as commissioners, a majority of whom may act, to review the same, assess the damages incidental to the opening of the road of the first or second class, through any part of said farm, lot or enclosure, as proposed, taking into consideration the advantages and disadvantages accruing to such person from the opening of such road, and report their action in writing, and under oath, to the next regular term of the County Court. If refused, jury shall assess damages, &c.

If owner of unenclosed land protest, &c., jury may assess damages.

ART. 1772. [8] If the owner or owners, his, her, or their agent or attorney, of any unenclosed land, shall file in the County Court a written protest against opening a road viewed and marked out through the same, it shall be the duty of the County Court to appoint five disinterested freehold citizens of the county as commissioners, a majority of whom may act, to review said road, assess the damages, and report in manner and form as provided in the preceding section of this act.

Court may order road opened on paying the damages.

ART. 1773. [9] If, in the judgment of the County Court from the report of the commissioners aforesaid, the road should be deemed of sufficient importance, they may order the survey or opening of the same: provided, that said County Court shall first order the payment of the damages assessed by said commissioners out of the county treasury.

If no objection when report is filed, the road shall be established, &c.

ART. 1774. [10] If no objection be filed upon the report of the jury of view, the court shall proceed to establish and classify such road, appoint an overseer, apportion hands, and order the opening out of such road, as provided in the first section of this act; and the overseer, so appointed, shall report his action upon the same, at the first regular term of the County Court in the next succeeding year, and he shall be liable to the fines imposed upon overseers of roads for the non-performance of duty by the provisions of this act.

Clerks shall make out copies of orders of appointment, &c.

ART. 1775. [11] It shall be the duty of the Clerks of the County Courts to make out copies of all orders of appointment of juries of view and review, and all overseers of roads, in duplicate; and within ten days after such orders of appointment shall have been made, he shall deliver such copies to the Sheriffs of their respective counties, endorsing on the back of the same the date of the issuance of the order; and all orders of appointment of overseers shall embrace the designation of hands liable to work under such overseer, embracing the boundaries of the precincts as laid off by the Court, and the Sheriff shall within twenty days after the reception of the same, deliver to or leave at the common residence of the overseer, or juror of view or review, a copy of the same, and make his return to the Clerk, endorsed on the duplicate, the date of service; and on the Clerks or Sheriffs failing to perform the duties herein required, each shall forfeit and pay for every such failure the sum of ten dollars, which shall be recovered by judgment on motion of the District Attorney in the District Court of the county in which the defaulter may reside; and any juror summoned as aforesaid, to view or review a new road, on his neglect or refusal to perform the service herein required, shall each forfeit and pay for every such failure the sum of ten dollars: provided, all reasonable excuses shall be heard and allowed: and provided, further, that the said viewers or reviewers shall each be exempt from road duty as many days as they are engaged in performing the said services, the same to be recovered by judgment on motion of the District Attorney in the District Court of the county in which the defaulter may reside, said defaulter in all cases having three days notice of said motion.

Duty of Sheriff.

Penalty for neglect.

Reviewers exempt from road duty.

Who is liable to work on roads.

ART. 1776. [12] All free white male persons, between eighteen and forty-five years of age, and all male slaves and other persons of color, over sixteen and under fifty years of age, shall be liable, and it is hereby made their duty, to work on, repair and clear out the public roads of this State, under such provisions and regulations as are hereinafter made: provided, that no licensed Minister of the Gospel, instructor of public or private schools, and all students of common schools, or public institutions, keepers of grist mills that grind for toll, public ferrymen, county commissioners, nor chief justices, shall be liable to work on public roads.

ART. 1777. [13] The overseer of the road shall have power to call out all persons liable to work on public roads, at any time when it may appear necessary to work or repair the roads, or any part of them, in their precinct: provided, that no one person shall be compelled to work on more roads than one, nor more than ten days in each year: and further provided, that every overseer of a road shall work through his precinct at least twice in every year. Overseer shall have power to call out persons liable, &c.

Notice, how given, &c.

ART. 1778. [14] It shall be the duty of the overseer of any road to give three days previous notice, by summons in person or in writing, left at their respective places of abode, to all free male persons as well as to the owners, overseers, or employers of slaves liable to work on the road in his precinct, to meet at such time and place for that purpose as he shall designate, and bring with them such tools to work with as he shall direct: provided, also, that the overseer shall have power to appoint some one to warn in the hands to work on the road, and such person shall be exempt from working on the road as many days as he was engaged in warning the hands.

Penalty if fail to attend, or, &c.

ART. 1779. [15] If any free person, so summoned, shall fail to attend, or send a substitute to work in his place, or when attending, shall fail or refuse to perform his duties as required, such person shall forfeit and pay for each and every day he may so fail to attend, or refuse to work, the sum of one dollar, together with all costs of suit, to be recovered by suit, in the same manner as in cases of debt, before any Justice of the Peace having jurisdiction thereof, in the name of the Chief Justice of the county; and if a slave, the sum of one dollar shall in like manner be recovered from the owner, overseer, or employer, for each and every day such slave shall fail to work as required: provided all reasonable excuses shall be heard and allowed: and provided further, that a list of the defaulting road workers furnished by the overseer, shall be a sufficient showing to authorize the Justice of the Peace to issue writs against the parties liable, upon the return or trial day of which, whether the defaulter was summoned verbally or by writing to work on the road, and if by writing, the testimony of the person leaving the notice shall be necessary, upon which judgment shall be had; but in no event shall the overseer be liable for costs, nor shall he be required to give bond in case he should wish to take an appeal to the District Court.

Penalty, if overseer fail to prosecute, &c.

ART. 1780. [16] If an overseer of a road shall fail or neglect to prosecute any free person, or if a slave, his owner, overseer or employer, who shall fail to attend, or neglect or refuse to perform his duty, when lawfully summoned to work on roads, said overseer shall forfeit and pay, for every such neglect, failure or refusal, the sum of five dollars, to be recovered before any Justice of the Peace having jurisdiction, in the same manner as in action of debt, upon the complaint of any person liable to work upon said road, and the funds accruing under this act to be used and applied to the road where such defaulter resides.

What timber may be used for causeways, &c.

ART. 1781. [17] When to the overseer of the roads it may appear expedient to make causeways and build bridges, the timber most convenient may be used. The earth necessary to cover said causeways shall be taken from both sides so as to make a drain on each side of the causeways, and he shall erect bridges across all such water courses and other places as may appear to him necessary and expedient, and should there be a water course that requires a bridge dividing any two road districts, the overseer of each district shall meet at the same time and place with their hands, and the overseer chosen by the majority present shall superintend the building of such bridges until finished.

Labor of hands exchanged for use of wagon.

ART. 1782. [18] When it may be necessary to use a wagon to haul material for any bridge, causeway, or other purpose in repairing roads, the overseer of such road is authorized to exchange the labor of any hands bound to work on such road for the use of a wagon or wagons, and teams to be employed as aforesaid, also to exchange labor for the making of index boards and mile posts.

Road shall be measured—mile posts and index boards erected, &c.

ART. 1783. [19] It shall be the duty of all overseers of public roads, to measure such parts of roads as fall within their respective precincts or districts, in continuation, and to set up posts at the end of each mile leading from the court house or some noted place or town, and to mark on the said posts in large legible figures the distance in miles to said court house or other noted place, and when a post so erected shall be removed by any means whatever, the overseer of the road shall cause the same to be replaced by another marked as the original one. It shall also be the duty of overseers of roads to affix at the forks of all public roads in their respective districts or precincts, index boards, with directions pointing towards the most noted places to which they lead. And on failure to put up mile posts marked as aforesaid, or index boards, within six months after their appointment, the overseer of such road, for such failure and neglect, shall be liable to indictment, and on conviction thereof before the District Court, shall be fined in the sum of five dollars, and all costs of prosecution.

Penalty for defacing or pulling down.

ART. 1784. [20] If any person shall be guilty of defacing or pulling down any mile post or index board, such person being convicted thereof before any Justice of the Peace for said county, shall forfeit and pay ten dollars for every such offence, and on his failure to pay such fine, he shall be imprisoned in the county jail of the county in which the offence was committed, for ten days, unless sooner paid, to be applied by the overseer to the improvement of such road.

Penalty for altering public road without permission.

ART. 1785. [21] If any person or persons shall alter or change any public road, unless it be done by permission of the County Court, he, she, or they shall on conviction thereof, forfeit and pay the sum of five dollars for each week the road is so turned out of its old course; and if any person or persons shall erect or cause to be erected across any public road, any bar or fence, or fall any tree or brush, or impediment of any kind whatever, and shall not remove such impediment within twenty-four hours, he or they shall forfeit and pay the sum of three dollars for every day the impediment shall remain in such road, upon conviction thereof before any Justice of the Peace in the county having jurisdiction thereof: provided, that the parties so offending shall have at least five days notice, by citation as in other cases: provided, further, that nothing herein contained shall subject the party removing said road, to damages, where the same is done to straighten said road through enclosures, or where the removal shall not render the road more inconvenient to the public.

Person refusing to serve as overseer, &c., may be indicted.

ART. 1786. [22] If any person subject to road duty, shall refuse to serve as overseer on any road, agreeable to the order of the Court in the county in which he resides, he shall be liable to indictment, and on conviction before the District Court, shall be fined in a sum not less than ten, nor more than forty dollars: provided, all reasonable excuses shall be heard by the Court trying the same. And it shall be the duty of every person appointed by the County Court as an overseer of the road, who is lawfully exempt from road duty, to notify the Clerk of his County Court of his non-acceptance within ten days after his being notified of his appointment, and on failure to do so, it shall be considered an acceptance of his appointment, and it shall moreover be the duty of the Clerk to insert on the commission, the duties required of overseers in respect to their non-acceptance. And if any person so appointed shall notify the Clerk of his lawful exemption from road duty, the Clerk shall forthwith report the same to the Chief Justice, who is authorized and required to appoint a successor to serve for the residue of the time, and such new overseer,

Person exempt, who may be appointed, shall notify Clerk of his non-acceptance, when.

so appointed, shall be subject to the same penalties and forfeitures as the overseers appointed by the County Court, and a copy of the order of appointment made by the County Court and certified by the Clerk of said Court, shall be sufficient evidence of the appointment of overseers in all cases of prosecutions under this act: provided, that no person shall be compelled to serve as an overseer for more than one, in every three succeeding years, and shall not be required to serve on juries during the time he serves as overseer. What length of time overseer required to serve.

Art. 1787. [23] If any overseer of a road shall fail, neglect, or refuse to perform the duties as prescribed by the act, or if he should not keep the road, bridges and causeways within his precinct clear and in good order, or if he suffer them to remain uncleared or out of repair for twenty days, at any one time, unless hindered by high water or other sufficient cause, to be judged of by the Court, such overseer shall be liable to indictment, and on conviction thereof by the District Court, shall be fined not less than ten, nor more than twenty-five dollars; said fines shall be paid into the County Treasury, as other fines and forfeitures for the use of the road precinct under the contract of such defaulting overseer. Penalty for failing to keep roads, &c., in good order.

Art. 1788. [24] All fines recovered under the provisions of this act, after deducting therefrom all legal costs, the balance shall be paid over to the overseer of the road, in the precinct where the penalty accrued, for which amount the overseer shall give his receipt, the money to be applied by him to the improvement and keeping in good repair of his road. Fines collected, how applied.

Art. 1789. [25] Every free person liable to work on roads, and if a slave, his master, overseer, or employer, may by calling on the overseer at any time before the day appointed to work on the roads, and paying to said overseer the amount of which he or they might be liable for failing or refusing to work on said road, taking said overseer's receipt for the same shall be exempt from working for every such day so paid for, and also exempt from any penalty for the same. Overseer may excuse a hand by his paying, &c.

Art. 1790. [26] The Overseers of roads shall apply all monies coming into their hands to the improvement of their roads, in an impartial manner, by hiring hands and applying the work equally throughout his precinct, and should said Overseer misapply or fail or refuse to apply the money coming into his hands in manner as provided for in this section of this act, he shall for such refusal or failure be liable for double the amount so misapplied, to be recovered on motion, as provided for in the sixteenth section of this act, and shall be precluded from holding any office in any county in this State, until such monies are fully accounted for: provided, that all reasonable excuses shall be heard and allowed, and provided further, that such monies may be laid out by the Overseer for repairing or building bridges in his precinct, as he may think best. Shall apply all monies to improvement of roads, &c.

Art. 1791. [27] It shall be the duty of all Overseers of roads to report in writing to the County Court, at its first regular session in each year, giving the number of hands and the names of the free white males in his precinct liable to work on roads; the number of days he has worked on his road; the condition the road is in; the amount of fines by him collected, and all the funds received by him for his road. And any Overseer failing or refusing to make such report, shall forfeit and pay five dollars for such failure or refusal, to be recovered on motion, as provided for in the sixteenth section of this act, to be paid into the County Treasury for the use of the road where such penalty accrued. Report of Overseers.

Art. 1792. [28] The Clerks of the several County Courts of this State shall put up in their respective court houses, on the first day of each District Clerks shall put up a list of, &c.

Court, a list of the names and precincts of all the Overseers of the roads in the county, and on neglect shall forfeit and pay for each failure ten dollars, to be recovered on motion made by the District Attorney in the District Court, and paid into the County Treasury.

Judges of District Courts shall give this act in charge. ART. 1793. [29] It shall be the duty of the Judges of the District Courts of the several Judicial Districts in the State, to give this act in charge to the grand jury at the opening of every court held by them.

Persons may petition for private road. ART. 1794. [30] Any person desiring a private road for their own convenience, to any public road, or other public place, may petition the County Court in writing for the same, setting forth their reasons for desiring such road, and designating the place to which such road is desired.

Commissioners to view, &c. ART. 1795. [31] If the court shall think the road necessary, they shall appoint three disinterested householders as commissioners to view out such road, with as little injury as possible to the lands through which it may pass, endeavoring to keep the lines between surveys as much as possible.

Duty of County Court where objection is made. ART. 1796. [32] If objections be made by any person through whose land such road may pass, it shall be the duty of the commissioners appointed to view out the road, to assess the damages done to the person so objecting, and upon the payment of such damages and all other expenses, by the person desiring such road, the court may establish the same as a private road: provided, that the commissioners shall be allowed two dollars per day for each day they may be engaged in such service.

At whose expense opened. ART. 1797. [33] The person desiring such road shall open the same at his own expense, and not wider than is necessary for ordinary purposes for passing: provided, in all cases that private roads may be opened, unless objected to by the owners of the land through which they may pass.

Court may discontinue private roads. ART. 1798. [34] The County Court may discontinue private roads whenever it may be shown that no necessity exists for their longer continuance.

SALARIES.

OF GOVERNOR AND PRIVATE SECRETARY.

ART. 1799. From and after the passage of this act, the annual salary of the Governor of the State of Texas shall be three thousand dollars. Act of Dec. 20, 1855. In force from date. Salary of Gov.

Governor's Private Secretary, nine hundred dollars. Act of Feb. 11, 1854. Of Private Sec.

OF COMMISSIONER AND CLERKS IN LAND OFFICE.

ART. 1800. [2] The salary of the Commissioner of the General Land Office shall be two thousand dollars per annum. Act of Dec. 26, 1833. Took effect from passage. Commissioner.

The salary of Spanish Clerk shall be twelve hundred dollars per annum.

The salaries of eight Assistant Clerks, each, shall be nine hundred dollars per annum. Clerks.

The salaries of ten additional Clerks shall be eight hundred dollars each, per annum.

The salary of the principal Draftsman shall be twelve hundred dollars per annum. Draftsmen.

The salaries of the first and second Assistant Draftsmen shall be eleven hundred dollars, each, per annum; and the salaries of two additional Assistant Draftsmen shall be one thousand dollars, each, per annum.

OF COMPTROLLER AND CLERKS.

ART. 1801. Comptroller, eighteen hundred dollars. Salary of Comp.

Clerk in charge of Tax Bureau, in Comptroller's office, twelve hundred dollars. Sal'ry of Clerks.

Other Clerks in said office, nine hundred dollars.

OF TREASURER.

ART. 1802. Treasurer, eighteen hundred dollars.

OF SECRETARY OF STATE.

ART. 1803. Secretary of State, eighteen hundred dollars.

OF OFFICERS OF PENITENTIARY.

ART. 1804. Superintendent in Penitentiary, twelve hundred dollars.

Clerk in Penitentiary, nine hundred dollars.

OF JUDICIARY.

ART. 1805. [1] The Judges of the Supreme Court of this State shall receive each, a salary of three thousand dollars per annum. Act of February 2, 1856. Took effect from passage. Sup. Judges.

ART. 1806. [2] The Judges of the District Courts of this State shall receive, each, a salary of twenty-two hundred and fifty dollars per annum. District Judges.

ART. 1807. Attorney-General, eighteen hundred dollars. Act of February 11, 1854. Att'y General.

ART. 1808. [1] The several District Attorneys of this State shall receive an annual salary of five hundred dollars, to be paid quarterly. Act of Jan. 24, 1848. Took effect April 13,'48. District Att'ys.

COMMISSIONER OF CLAIMS.

ART. 1809. [1] There shall be elected, by a joint vote of the Legislature, a Commissioner of Claims, who shall hold his office until the first day of September, A. D. 1859. He shall keep his office at the city of Austin, and shall receive an annual salary of two thousand two hundred and fifty dollars. Act of January 16, 1858. Commissioner of Claims. See Art. 301.

CHIEF CLERKS OF DEPARTMENTS.

Act of Feb. 16, 1858. Took effect from passage. Chief Clerks of Departments.

ART. 1810. [1] The Chief Clerk of the General Land Office, the Chief Clerk of the Comptroller's office, the Chief Clerk in the State Department, and the Chief Clerk of the Court of Claims, shall each receive an annual salary of fourteen hundred dollars, and the Chief Clerk of the Treasurer's office shall receive an annual salary of twelve hundred dollars: provided, that the Chief Clerk of the Treasurer's office shall give a bond in the sum of twenty-five thousand dollars, for the faithful performance of his duties.

SALVAGE ON COTTON.

Act of Aug. 30, 1856. Took effect November 1, 1856. Duty of persons taking up cotton afloat, abandoned, &c.

ART. 1811. [1] It shall be the duty of persons taking up cotton afloat, abandoned in rivers, or in the waters of the Gulf of Mexico, on the coast of this State, or in the bays or bayous thereof, to place the same in a secure place out of the weather, and give early notice by advertisement or by other means at the port to which said cotton was destined, if within this State, and if without the limits of the State, or its destination be unknown to the finder, then at the nearest port of entry in this State to the locality where it may be taken up, of the finding of the same, giving a description of the marks or brands on said cotton, together with the place of finding, and the name of the finder.

Shall deliver same to owner, or, &c., when.

ART. 1812. [2] It shall be the duty of the person finding, or other persons having said cotton in his or their possession, to deliver the same to the owner, insurer, or consignee thereof on demand upon being paid the expenses of advertisement, and five dollars upon each bale so saved and delivered up.

If no owner, or, &c., appear in 3 months, same shall be sold, &c.

ART. 1813. [3] If no owner, insurer or consignee of the cotton appear within three months after the time of such advertisement, the person finding shall cause the same to be sold at auction by a legal wreck-master of the county in which said cotton is deposited, to the best bidder therefor; and the said wreck-master shall deduct from the proceeds of said sale, five per cent. upon the dollar upon the amount thereof, for his fees and trouble; and shall also pay the necessary expenses attending the storage, advertising and sale of said cotton, and to the finder the salvage of five dollars for each bale as aforesaid, the remainder he shall hold in trust for the benefit of owner or others concerned. If, at the expiration of one year thereafter, no legal claimant appears therefor, said proceeds shall by said wreck-master be paid over to the treasurer of the county in which the sale took place, and said county treasurer shall immediately pay the same over to the treasurer of the State, who shall pay the same over to the person entitled thereto on proof being made of the right of the claimant in the manner provided for the recovery of money paid into the treasury of the State by executors or administrators of estates, whenever no heirs, devisees or legatees of the estate appear to claim the fund of the estate on the final settlement thereof.

If no legal claimant appear in 1 year after, proceeds shall be paid to, &c.

ART. 1814. [4] In case there shall be no wreck-master in the county in which the cotton is deposited, then it shall be the duty of the County Clerk of the county to perform all the duties required of wreck-masters by this act, and such clerk shall be entitled to receive the same compensation for his services as is allowed to wreck-masters under this act. When duties of wreck-master shall be performed by County Clerk.

ART. 1815. [5] Any person finding a bale or bales of cotton afloat or lodged by the water on the banks of any river, bay, or bayou, or on the beach of the Gulf within this State, who shall secrete the same, or appropriate the same to his own use, or who shall refuse to deliver up the same when required as aforesaid, or who shall having found any cotton afloat without the limits of this State, bring the same into this State, and not comply with the requirements of this act, as in case the same had been found within the State, shall be liable to fine or imprisonment, or both, in the discretion of the District Court for the county in which the said cotton may be found, or stored, in any sum not exceeding five hundred dollars, and imprisonment not exceeding one year. Penalty for secreting or appropriating cotton found, &c., to one's own use.

ART. 1816. [6] Upon affidavit being made before any Justice of the Peace, that the affiant has good reason to believe, and does believe that certain cotton within his county has been so found, or having been found without the same has been brought therein, and that a reasonable time has elapsed, and that the finder has neglected to comply with the requisitions of this act, it shall be the duty of such Justice of the Peace to issue his warrant and cause said cotton or its proceeds to be seized by a legal officer, and deliver to the wreck-master of said county, to be disposed of according to the provisions of this act. Justice of the Peace shall issue warrant to seize, &c., when

---

SEALS AND SCROLLS.

ART. 1817. [1] No scroll or private seal shall be necessary to the validity of any contract, bond or conveyance, whether respecting real or personal property, except such as are made by corporations; nor shall the addition or omission of a scroll or seal in any way affect the force and effect of the same; and every contract in writing hereafter made shall be held to impart a consideration as fully, and in the same manner as sealed instruments have heretofore done. Act of Feb'y 2, 1858. In force from date. Private seal unnecessary.

SECRETARY OF STATE.

[*See Legislature, Public Printing, Reports of Supreme Court, Laws and Journals.*]

REPORTS OF SUPREME COURT—LAWS AND JOURNALS.

Act of May 9, 1846. Took effect from passage.

ART. 1818. [1] A Secretary of State shall be appointed by the Governor, by and with the advice and consent of the Senate, and shall be continued in office during the term of service of the Governor elect.

To keep a register of official acts, &c.

ART. 1819. [2] He shall keep a fair register of all the official acts of the Governor, and when required, shall lay the same and all minutes and other papers in relation thereto, before the Legislature, or either branch thereof.

Office to be kept at seat of Government.

Shall commission officers, &c,

ART. 1820. [3] He shall keep his office at the seat of Government, or other place where the sessions of the Legislature may be held: he shall, in a separate book, suitable for the purpose, keep a complete register of all the officers appointed and elected in the State, and commission the same when not otherwise provided for by law; he shall, in books to be kept in his office, exclusively for the purpose, record depositions and affirmations required by law to be made by resident aliens desirous of holding real estate in this State; he shall arrange and preserve all books, maps, parchments, records, documents, deeds, conveyances, and other papers belonging to the State, that have been or may be properly deposited there, and sealed with the seal of the State, and also similar copies of any act, law, or resolution of the United States, or either of them, from the originals in his office; which copies shall be as legal and conclusive in evidence, and to all intents and purposes, in the courts of this State, as the originals would have been; and he shall, when required, furnish the Governor, the Legislature, or either branch thereof, with such copies, and shall affix the seal of the State to all certificates of official character that may emanate from his office.

Shall attend session of the Legislature for purpose of receiving bills, &c.

ART. 1821. [4] He shall attend at every session of the Legislature for the purpose of receiving bills which have become laws, and immediately after the close thereof shall cause all such bills and all the enrolled joint resolutions of the Legislature to be bound together in a volume to be kept in his office, and the date of the session to be written or stamped thereon; a certified copy of which he shall deliver to the public printer, together with an index of the same; and he shall carefully examine and compare the printed copy with the certified copy and correct all the errors contained in the former.

Shall distribute laws and journals of each session.

ART. 1822. [5] He shall distribute the printed laws and journals of each session of the Legislature, immediately after their publication, as follows: one copy of each to the Governor, Secretary of State, Treasurer, Comptroller of Public Accounts, each member of the Legislature, each Judge and Clerk of the Supreme, District, County and Probate Courts, Attorney-General, and each District Attorney; and a copy of the printed laws to each County Commissioner, each Notary Public, Justice of the Peace, Sheriff, Coroner, Assessor and Collector of taxes, County Treasurer, County Surveyor, Major, Brigadier, Adjutant and Quartermaster-General, and Major; also, three copies to the Secretary of State of the United States, and one copy to each Governor of a State or Territory thereof.

Mode of distributing.

ART. 1823. [6] He shall direct and send to the Clerk of the County Court of each county, all the copies of the laws and Journals which are to be distributed in said county, with instructions to deliver them according to the requisitions of this act; he shall also deposit with said Clerk, for the use of the county, one copy of all the acts of the Congress of the United States which may be received in his office.

ART. 1824. [7] In the absence of the Secretary of State, it shall be competent for the Clerk of the State Department to perform all the duties required by this act from the Secretary of State. Clerk to act in absence of Secretary.

STATE LIBRARY.

ART. 1825. [1] The Governor of the State be, and is hereby authorized and required to forward to the Librarian of Congress, to the Secretary of State of the United States, to the Secretary of the Treasury of the United States, to the Executive Departments of all the States of the Union, to each Foreign Librarian or Government, with whom a system of literary exchange may be established, and to such associations and societies for the promotion of the arts and sciences as he may deem advisable, copies of all laws, judicial reports, maps, charts, and other productions of a literary, scientific, or political character, printed or published by order of the Legislature, or at the expense of the State. Act of March 20, 1848. Took effect from passage. Duty of Governor to forward certain books to Librarian of Congress.

ART. 1826. [2] The Secretary of State be required to safely keep all books, maps, charts, or publications forwarded to or received at his office; the same to constitute a State Library under his control, subject, however, to the inspection and use of all the officers of the State Government, and both branches of the Legislature. Secretary of State shall keep books, &c., safely.

REPORTS OF SUPREME COURT, LAWS AND JOURNALS.

ART. 1827. [1] It shall be the duty of the Secretary of State to distribute the Reports of the Supreme Court, and laws passed by each session of the Legislature, the journals of each session of the Senate and House of Representatives, and all editions of any digest or revision of the laws of the State,—whether such books shall be subscribed for, or published by the State,—in the following manner: Act of Feb. 2, 1850. Took effect from passage. Secretary of State shall distribute Reports, &c.

ART. 1828. [2] Two copies of each volume of the Reports of the Supreme Court shall be forwarded to the Chief Justice of each county, who shall deposit one copy thereof in the office of the Clerk of the County Court, and the other in the office of the Clerk of the District Court, for the use of said courts respectively. How distributed.

ART. 1829. [3] A sufficient number of copies of the volume of the laws of a general nature of each session, shall be forwarded to the Chief Justice of each county, to furnish one copy to each Judge of the Supreme and District Courts, one copy to each Chief Justice, to each Clerk of the Supreme District and County Courts, to each Sheriff and Justice of the Peace, and to each member of the Legislature by which they were passed, that may be a resident of said county; and it shall be the duty of said Chief Justice to deliver one of said copies to each of said officers who may reside in his county. Of general laws.

ART. 1830. [4] A sufficient number of copies of the volume of laws of each session, for private relief, and laws incorporating towns, cities, institutions of learning and private associations, and of the Journals of each House of the Legislature, of each session, shall be forwarded to the Chief Justice of each county, to furnish one copy of each of said books to the Clerk of the County Court, and one copy to each member of the Legislature at such session, who resides in such county; and it shall be the duty of said Chief Justice to deliver one copy of each of said books to each of said persons resident in his county. Of special laws and journals.

ART. 1831. [5] Whenever a Digest or revision of the laws of the State has been, or shall be subscribed for, or published by the State, a sufficient number of copies of each volume thereof, shall be forwarded to the Chief Justice of Of the Digest of Laws, &c.

each county, to furnish one of said copies to each Judge of the Supreme and District Courts, to each Clerk of the Supreme, District and County Courts, and to each Justice of the Peace, that may be a resident in said county; and it shall be the duty of said Chief Justice to deliver one copy of each of said volumes to each of said officers that may reside in said county.

Receipt of officer for, to be taken.

ART. 1832. [6] Whenever the Chief Justice of any county in this State shall deliver any of the books named in this act, to any Judge of the Supreme or District Court, to any Clerk of the Supreme, District or County Court, to any Sheriff or Justice of the Peace, he shall take the receipt of such officer for the same, and shall deposit said receipt in the office of the Clerk of the County Court; and said books shall be deemed to belong to the office of said officer to whom they are delivered, and shall, at all reasonable hours be subject to the inspection and examination of any citizen of this State; and should any of said officers fail or refuse to deliver any of said books to his successor in office, when demanded by him, the officer so failing or refusing shall be liable to pay such successor the costs and charges that may be necessary to supply the office of such successor with any of said books that he shall so fail or refuse to deliver.

Books subject to inspection, &c.,—failure to deliver to successor, &c.

Each executive officer at, &c., entitled to, &c.

ART. 1833. [7] The Secretary of State shall also deliver to each of the executive officers at the seat of Government, one copy of each volume of the public and private laws of each session of the Legislature, and one copy of each volume of any edition of a Digest or revision of the laws of the State,—whether such books shall be subscribed for, or published by the State,—which shall belong to said office; and the officer receiving any such volume shall be bound to deliver it to his successor, and shall be liable to pay his successor the costs and charges that may be necessary to supply the office with any book he may neglect so to deliver.

SEQUESTRATION.

Act of March 15, 1848. Took effect from passage.

By whom and in what cases writs of may be issued.

Art. 423.

ART. 1834. [1] Judges and Clerks of the District Court, and Justices of the Peace, shall, at the commencement, or during the progress of any civil suit before final judgment, have power to issue writs of sequestration, returnable to their respective courts, in the following cases, verified by the affidavit of the party applying for the writ: First, when a married woman sues for a divorce, and makes oath that she fears her husband will waste her separate property, or their common property, or the fruits or revenue produced by either, or remove the same out of the limits of this State, during the pendency of the suit: Second, when a person sues for the title or possession of a slave, or other movable property, or chattels of any description, and makes oath that he fears the defendant, or person in possession thereof, will injure or ill-treat such slave, or waste such movable property or chattels, or remove the same out of the limits of this State during the pendency of the suit: Third, when a person sues for the foreclosure of a mortgage, or the enforcement of a lien upon a slave or movable property of any description, and makes oath that he fears that the defendant, or person in possession thereof, will injure or ill-treat such slave, or waste such movable property, or remove such slave or movable property out of the limits of the county: Fourth, when any person sues for the title or possession of real property, and makes oath that he fears the defendant or person in possession thereof, may make use of his possession to injure such property, or waste the fruits and revenue produced by the same, or convert them to his own use: Fifth, when any person sues for the title or possession of any property from which he has been ejected by force or violence, and shall make oath to such facts.(*a*)

Act of March 15, 1848. Took effect from passage.

By whom and in what cases writs of, may be issu'd Art. 423.

ART. 1835. [2] No writ of sequestration shall issue unless the party applying for the same shall make such affidavit of facts, and shall also file with the clerk of the court, or Justice of the Peace, a bond payable to the defendant for a sum of money equal to double the value of the property to be sequestered, with good and sufficient sureties, to be approved by such clerk or Justice of the Peace, conditioned that the plaintiff or person suing out such writ, will pay to the defendant all such damages as may be awarded against him, in case it shall be decided that such sequestration was wrongfully issued.(*b*)

Affidavit and bond required before, &c.

ART. 1836. [3] Such bond shall not be construed as security for costs: That the writ of sequestration shall command the sheriff or other officer to take into his possession the property described by the affidavit if to be found in the county, and keep the same subject to the future order of the court or Justice of the Peace, unless the defendant or person from whose possession such property is taken shall replevy the same according to law.

Bond not to be construed as security for costs.

ART. 1837. [4] When any person has a mortgage or lien upon a slave or movable property, of any description, and makes affidavit that he fears the defendant or person in possession thereof will injure or ill-treat such slave, or waste such movable property, or remove such slave or movable property out of the limits of the county, a writ of sequestration may issue, although the right of action on such mortgage or lien has not accrued; and the same proceedings shall be had thereon as in other cases of sequestration, except that no final judgment shall be rendered against the defendant until the right of action on such mortgage or lien shall have accrued; but if the property so sequestrated be of a wasting or perishable nature, the same shall, by order of the Judge or Justice of the Peace to whose court the sequestration is returnable, be sold, giving a credit on the sale until such right of action shall accrue, on the purchaser's giving bond, with two or more sufficient sureties, payable to the plaintiff, for the payment of the purchase-money; which bond shall be lodged with the other papers in the cause; and if the money is not paid at the expiration of the time given, the clerk or Justice of the Peace, with whom such bond is lodged, shall issue execution against the principal and sureties, or either of them, and the money when collected shall be paid into the hands of the Clerk or Justice of the Peace to abide the final decision of the cause.

Writ of, may issue in certain cases before cause of action accrues.

If property is of a perishable nature, &c.

ART. 1838. [5] When any property sequestered, on the oath of the plaintiff,

(*a*) This act did not dispense with the provisons of the one hundred and forty-third section of the act of 1846, to regulate the proceedings in the District Court, (See Article 423) In order to obtain a writ of sequestration, it is, therefore, necessary for the party applying to make affidavit of the truth of the matter set forth in his petition. Cheatham *v.* Riddle, 8 Tex. Rep. 162. A writ of sequestration is only an auxiliary process; if erroneously issued, it will not effect the judgment so far as the defendant is concerned. Ibid. A writ of error will not lie from an order quashing a writ of sequestration. Little *v.* Morris, 10 Tex. Rep. 263. A petition claimed the slave as the separate property of the wife, and the writ described him as the property of the husband and the wife, *held* that writ was properly quashed—but that writ was amendable. Porter & wife *v.* Miller, 7 Tex. Rep. 468.

(*b*) Where a writ of sequestration, improperly issued, and the defendant replevies the property, the sureties on the replevy bond should appeal: on appeal by the defendant alone, it is only a question of costs. Cheatham *v.* Riddle, 8 Tex. Rep. 162. The hire or use of property is not one of the enumerated subjects of the liability of a surety on a bond to obtain its release, and the enumeration must be held to include all. McClenny *v.* Floyd, 3 Tex. Tep 114. The liability of the sureties depends upon the principal being condemned to pay for the fruits and revenues of the property replevied. Sartain *v.* Hamilton, 14 Tex. Rep 348. Where the judgment had been affirmed on appeal against the defendant, it was held that the sureties on the replevy bond might nevertheless prosecute their writ of error to the judgment so far as it affected them. Ibid. See Trammell *v.* Trammell, 20 Tex. Rep. 406.

Where property sequestered is likely to be wasted &c.

his agent or attorney, be certified to any Judge or Justice of the Peace, to whose court the sequestration is returnable, to be likely to be wasted or destroyed, by keeping; and the defendant in such sequestration, his agent or attorney, shall not within thirty days after the levy, replevy the property sequestered, then such property shall by order of such Judge or Justice of the Peace, be sold at public sale, by the officer who levied the writ, in the same manner as sales by execution; and the said officer shall within five days after such sale, return the order of sale to the court or Justice of the Peace, to which the sequestration is returnable, with his proceedings thereon; and, also, at the time of making such return, shall pay over into the hands of the Clerk or Justice of the Peace all moneys arising from such sale.

Defendant may retain property and give bond for delivery.

ART. 1839. [6] The defendant whose property has been taken by writ of sequestration, shall have the right to retain the same, by delivering to the Sheriff or other officer executing said writ, his bond payable to the plaintiff, with good and sufficient sureties, to be approved of by the Sheriff or officer taking the same, for an amount of money equal to double the value of the property sequestered; which bond, if the property sequestered be slaves or movable property, shall be conditioned that he will not send away the same out of the county or limits of the State, according to plaintiff's affidavit; that he will not make an improper use of them, and that he will have them forthcoming to abide the decision of the court, or that he will pay the value thereof, in case the suit shall be decided against him. If the property sequestered be real property, the condition of said bond shall be that he will not injure said property, and that he will restore the fruits and revenue produced by the same or pay their value, in case he shall be condemned so to do: such bond shall be returned to the court with the writ, and in case the suit is decided against the defendant, final judgment shall be entered against all the obligors in such bond, jointly and severally.

If defendant fail to replevy within, &c.

ART. 1840. [7] The Sheriff or other officer, while he retains custody of the sequestered property, shall take care of and manage the same in a prudent manner; he may confide the same to the custody of other persons, but he shall be responsible for their acts, and he shall be responsible to the party injured for any neglect or mismanagement by himself or by those whom he has confided the custody or management of such property; and he shall be entitled to receive a just compensation and all reasonable charges therefor, to be determined by the court or Justice of the Peace, and paid out of the proceeds of the property sequestered, if judgment be given in favor of the party suing out the said writ; but if judgment be against such party, then such compensation and reasonable charges shall be paid by him: provided, that if the defendant does not replevy the property sequestered, within thirty days, the Sheriff or other officer shall deliver the property to the plaintiff, upon his giving bond, payable to the Sheriff or other officer, in a sum at least double the value of the property sequestered, with two or more good and sufficient sureties, to be approved by the officer, conditioned that the property shall be forthcoming to abide the decision of the court; which bond, if forfeited, or if the suit be decided against the plaintiff, shall have the force and effect of a judgment; and if the property sequestered be slaves, and the defendant does not within the time prescribed (thirty days) replevy the same, and the plaintiff within the ten days thereafter, it shall be the duty of the Sheriff or other officer to hire out said slaves to the best advantage.

Where neither party replevies.

Petition must be filed before, &c.

ART. 1841. [8] No writ of sequestration shall be issued by any Judge or Clerk of the District Court, unless a petition shall have been first filed in the office of such Clerk.

ART. 1842. [9] No judgment shall be rendered in any suit in which a sequestration has issued, unless the citation has been served in the ordinary mode, or by publication as provided for by law. *No judg'nt shall be rendered, unless.*

SHERIFF.

I. ELECTION.

Art. 1843. [1] There shall be elected by the qualified electors of each county of this State, one Sheriff, who shall hold his office for two years, and until his successor shall be elected and qualified. Should a vacancy occur in the office of Sheriff, the Chief Justice or other officer shall immediately order an election to fill such vacancy, giving at least fifteen days' notice; and the person so elected, after he shall qualify as directed in this act, shall discharge the duties of Sheriff for the unexpired term of his predecessor. *Act of May 12, 1846. Took effect July 13, 1846. One for each county to be elected—vacancy, &c.*

II. BOND AND OATH.

Art. 1844. [2] When any person elected Sheriff shall have given bond, as required by this act, he may enter immediately upon the discharge of his duties; and his acts shall be as valid in law before receiving his commission from the President as afterward.(*a*) *Act of Dec. 20, 1836. Took effect from passage. May enter upon duties of, &c.*

Art. 1845. [2] Every person who may be elected to the office of Sheriff shall, before entering upon the duties of his office, give a bond with two or more good and sufficient securities, to be approved by the County Court of his county, for such sum as may be directed by such court, not less than five nor more than thirty thousand dollars, payable to the Governor and his successors in office, conditioned that he will account for and pay over to the persons authorized by law to receive the same, all fines, forfeitures, and penalties that he may collect for the use of the State, or any county within the State; and that he will well and truly execute, and due return make of all process and *Act of May 12, 1846. Took effect 13th July, 1846. Bond and oath of.*

(*a*) Bryan v. Harvey, 11 Tex. Rep. 311.

precepts to him lawfully directed, and pay over all sums of money collected by him by virtue of any such process or precept, to the persons to whom the same are due, or their lawful attorney; and that he will faithfully perform all such duties as may be required of him by law; and shall also take and subscribe the oath of office prescribed by the constitution, which shall be endorsed on said bond, together with the certificate of the officer administering the same: which bond and oath shall be recorded in the office of the Clerk of the County Court, and deposited in said office. Said bond shall not be void on the first recovery, but may be sued on from time to time, in the name of any person injured, until the whole amount thereof is recovered.

Death, insolvency, &c., of sureties.

ART. 1846. [3] Whenever any of the securities of a Sheriff shall die, remove permanently from the State, or become insolvent, or whenever the County Court shall deem the Sheriff's securities to be insufficient, said court shall cite said Sheriff to appear at a time to be named in such citation, not less than twenty nor more than thirty days after issuing such citation, and give a new bond, with good and sufficient security; and if such Sheriff shall neglect or refuse so to do, his office shall be declared vacant, and election ordered.

Refusal of person elected to qualify.

ART. 1847. [4] Whenever any person elected Sheriff shall neglect or refuse to give bond and take the oath of office, as required by this act, within twenty days after notice of his election, the office shall be deemed vacant, and election ordered.

III. POWER AND DUTIES.(a)

Act of Dec. 20, 1836. Took effect from passage. Shall execute process from a Court of Record or Justice of the Peace.

ART. 1848. [7] Every Sheriff, within his county, by himself or his deputy, shall execute all writs and other process to him legally issued and directed, from any Justice of the Peace or court of record, and shall make due return thereof to the proper court, on the day to which the same is returnable; and any Sheriff who shall fail herein, or shall make a false return on any writ or other process, shall, for every such offence, be fined by the court to which such writ or other process is returnable, in any sum not exceeding one hundred dollars, on motion, reasonable notice thereof being given to each Sheriff. One moiety of said fine shall go to the party aggrieved, and the other moiety to the county treasury; and such Sheriff shall, moreover, be liable to the party injured for all damages he may sustain thereby.

Shall receive persons apprehended by Constables.

ART. 1849. [14] It shall be the duty of the Sheriffs to receive from Constables, and other officers, all persons who shall be apprehended by such Constables or other officers, for offences against the Republic, and keep them, subject to the order of the proper court.

Joint resolution of June 7, 1837. Took effect from passage. May rent houses for safe-keeping of prisoners, &c.

ART. 1850. The Sheriffs of the different counties of this Republic be, and they are hereby authorized to lease or rent suitable houses for the safe-keeping of any prisoners committed to their charge, and, if necessary, to employ a sufficient guard to guard such prisoner or prisoners; and it shall be the duty of the County Courts to allow such accounts, together with all other reasonable and necessary expenses incurred by any Sheriff, in the performance of his duty.

Act of May 12, 1846. Took effect 13th July, 1846.

ART. 1851. [5] Sheriffs shall have power by writing, under their hand and seal, to appoint one or more deputies for their respective counties, to continue in office during the pleasure of the Sheriff; who shall have power and authority

(a) A former Sheriff, after he has gone out of office, may amend a deed executed by him as Sheriff while in office, provided such amendment is only to give to the purchaser more perfect evidence of his right under the deed, and not any new right. Flemming v. Powell, 2 Tex. Rep. 225.

to perform all the acts and duties required of their principals: and every person so appointed, shall, before he enters upon the duties of his office, take and subscribe the oath of office prescribed by the Constitution, which shall be endorsed on his appointment, together with the certificate of the officer administering the same; and such appointment and oath shall be recorded in the office of the County Clerk, and deposited in said office. May appoint deputies.

ART. 1852. [6] Sheriffs shall be responsible for the official acts of their deputies, and they shall have power to require from their deputies, such bond and security; and they shall have the same remedies against their deputies and securities, as any person can have against a Sheriff and his securities. Responsible for acts of.

ART. 1853. [8] Each Sheriff shall execute all process and precepts directed to him by legal authority, and make return thereof to the proper court, on or before the day to which the same is returnable; and any Sheriff who shall fail so to do, or who shall make a false return on any process or precept shall, for every such offence, be liable to be fined by the court to which such process is returnable, as for a contempt, in any sum not exceeding one hundred dollars, at the discretion of the court; which fine shall go to the county treasury: and such sheriff shall also be liable to the party injured, for all damages he may sustain.(*a*) Shall execute and return process and precepts, penalty for failure or false return.

ART. 1854. [10] Whenever a Sheriff, or any of his deputies, shall meet with resistance in the execution of any legal process, they shall call to their aid the power of the county; and any person who shall neglect, or refuse to aid and assist any Sheriff or deputy in the execution of any legal process, when summoned so to do, shall be deemed guilty of a contempt of court, and shall be find in a sum not exceeding ten dollars, to be recovered, on motion of such Sheriff or his deputy, and proof of such neglect or refusal before the court from which such process issued, three days' notice of such motion being given to the party accused. May call out the power of the county, when.

ART. 1855. [13] Each Sheriff shall attend upon all District, County and Probate Courts for his county; and in counties where the Supreme Court shall hold its sessions, the Sheriffs of such counties shall attend upon the Supreme Court. Shall attend on District, County and Supreme Courts.

ART. 1856. [17] Every Sheriff and Deputy Sheriff shall endorse on all process and precepts coming to their hands, the day on which they received them, the manner in which they executed them, and the day when they executed them, and shall sign their return officially.(*b*) Shall endorse process.

ART. 1857. [17] It shall be the duty of each Sheriff, on or before the first day of the District Court of his county, to make out a statement of all moneys by him received or collected on fines, penalties and forfeitures incurred, or judgments in behalf of the State, and paid over by him to the District Attorney for the State, stating particularly in what cases it was collected or received, and to report the same to the Comptroller of Public Accounts. Shall report to Comptroller all moneys paid to, &c.

(*a*) Although the law may not, in express terms, admit of any excuse, yet it implies that a reasonable excuse will be heard; reasonable diligence is all that the law requires. Underwood *v.* Russell, 4 Tex. Rep. 175. Where process is directed to a Sheriff of another county, the law does not require him to return it in person or by deputy; but may deposit it in the mail, properly directed, and in time. Ibid.

(*b*) See article 417, and notes. For insufficient returns see Thompson *v.* Griffis, 19 Tex. Rep. 115. Middleton *v.* the State, 11 Tex. Rep. 255. "Executed Feb'y 1st, 1854, by a certified copy of this writ and copy of petition," held to be a good return on error, from a judgment by default. 15 Tex. Rep 515.

IV. GENERAL PROVISIONS.

Act of Dec. 30, 1840. Took effect from passage. Sheriff *pro tem.* may be appointed.

ART. 1858. [1] Whenever the offices of Sheriff and Coroner both become vacant by death or resignation, or other cause, immediately preceding or during the regular session of the District Court, it shall be the duty of the Judge of the District Court, to appoint a Sheriff *pro tem.*, to hold his office until such time as a successor may be elected by the qualified voters of the particular county.

Act of May 12, 1846. Took effect 13th July, 1846. Unfinished business of, shall be, &c.

ART. 1859. [15] When any Sheriff shall, from any cause, vacate his office, all unfinished business whatsoever, in his hands, shall be transferred to his successor, and completed by him in the same manner as if commenced by himself.

Act of March 16, 1848. Took effect 29th April, 1848. Shall reside at county seat.

ART. 1860. [1] Clerks of the District Court, and Clerks of the County Court of the several counties of this State, shall be and they are hereby required to keep their several offices at the county seats of their respective counties.

Same subject.

ART. 1861. [2] In all cases where the said Sheriff and Clerks do not reside at the county seats of their respective counties, they shall be and are hereby required to have deputies in their several offices, residing in said county seats.

Penalty for not complying with this act.

ART. 1862. [3] Any Sheriff, Clerk of the District Court, or Clerk of the County Court in this State, who shall fail to comply with the provisions of this act, * * * * * * * * * shall be liable to any person injured by such failure, for all damages occasioned by such failure.

Act of Jan. 19, 1850. In force from passage. Where Sheriff is party, or, &c., Constable may execute process.

ART. 1863. [1] In all cases when the office of Sheriff may be vacant, or where the Sheriff is a party to, or interested in any suit pending in the courts of his county, process may be directed to, and served by any Constable in such county.

Constable may act when affidavit is filed, of partiality, &c.

ART. 1864. [2] In all cases where an affidavit shall be filed with the Clerk of any Court in this State, of the partiality, prejudice, consanguinity, or affinity of the Sheriff of the county where suit is brought, or to be brought, or shall have been commenced, such Clerk may issue and direct the original or other process in such suit to any Constable of the county; who shall serve the same in like manner as the Sheriff should do. (See Coroner, Art. 213, 214.)

SHIPPING AND SLAUGHTERING OF CATTLE.

Act of Sept. 5, 1850. Register to be kept of shipped or slaughtered cattle, &c.

ART. 1866. [1] The captains of steamboats or vessels on which cattle are shipped to leave the State, or the proprietor or proprietors or agents of the same of any slaughtering establishments, shall keep, or cause to be kept, a register book, in which the marks, brands and general description of all cattle, of all ages, received on said boats or vessels, or slaughtered at said establishments, shall be registered, together with the names of the person or persons selling them, and the county from which they were driven.

Register shall be presented to County Clerk.

ART. 1867. [2] Said register on the first day of each month, or as near thereto as possible, shall be presented by said captains or proprietors to the

County Clerk of the county where said cattle were shipped or establishments are situated: and said Clerk shall keep a register of the same, and the registers shall at all times be open for inspection; and said captains, proprietors or clerks may charge a fee of fifty cents for each and every inspection thereof.

ART. 1868. [3] Non-compliance with the provisions of this act shall subject said captains, proprietors or clerks to a fine not less than ten dollars nor more than fifty dollars, for each head of cattle shipped or slaughtered, not registered; and said fine with proper proof made shall be recoverable in any court of competent jurisdiction. Penalty for non-compliance with, &c.

SLAVES.

[*See Constitution, Art.* 8.]

I. RUNAWAY SLAVES.

ART. 1869. [1] Where any slave is now in the jail of any county of this Republic, or shall hereafter be committed to the jail thereof, as a runaway, a notice of the apprehension and commitment, with a full description of said slave, shall be published weekly in one of the gazettes at the seat of government, for the space of one month, and printed copies thereof shall be furnished to the Clerk of the County Court of the county in which the commitment is made, to be carefully filed and preserved in his office; and it shall be the duty of the Sheriff or jailor having custody of such slave, to ascertain as nearly as may be, the name of the owner thereof, and to address him or her by regular post, at least twice, giving a full description of said runaway slave, in such manner as may best lead to the discovery and restoration. Act of Feb. 5, 1841. Took effect from passage. Notice of capture, &c., to be published.

ART. 1870. [2] If said runaway slave shall not be claimed and proved by the owner thereof, within six months from the first publication of the commitment of said slave as aforesaid, the Sheriff of the county in which the commitment was made, shall expose said slave to sale at public outcry, at the courthouse of his proper county, upon giving at least thirty days' previous notice of such sale, by advertisement posted up at at least two public places in said county, and published in some gazette of the county in which the sale is to take place, or in the next nearest county having a gazette; and out of the proceeds arising from the sale of any runaway slave as aforesaid, the Sheriff If not claimed in six months from, &c.

shall be entitled to the same commission and fees as are allowed in cases of execution; and the balance, after paying all prison fees, or fees for the maintenance of said runaway while in custody, Clerk's fees, and expenses of advertising and apprehending, shall be paid into the county treasury for the use of the proper county: provided, that if the owner of any runaway thus sold should prove his property in said slave, within three years after said sale, the proper county shall pay to him the amount that shall have been paid into the county treasury, on account of the sale of said slave; but the right to any slave sold as aforesaid shall be and remain vested in the purchaser under the sale made by the Sheriff as aforesaid, any law to the contrary notwithstanding.

If owner prove his property within three years after sale.

Sheriff shall make return of sale.

ART. 1871. [3] The Sheriff making the sale of any runaway slave as aforesaid, shall return a full and clear account and statement of such sale, under his hand and seal, to the Clerk of the County Court, who shall record the same among the record of deeds.

May be lawfully apprehended by any person.

ART. 1872. [4] All runaway slaves shall be lawfully apprehended by any person, and carried before the next Justice of the Peace, who shall either commit them to the county jail, or the custody of the Sheriff, or send them to the owner, if known, who shall pay for every slave so taken up the sum of ten dollars to the person apprehending him or her, and all reasonable costs and damages; and if said owner shall fail or refuse to pay said reward and reasonable expenses, the person apprehending and delivering said runaway slave as aforesaid shall be entitled to have his action for the recovery of the same, before any Justice of the Peace of the district or precinct in which said owner resides, or in which said slave is delivered up to the owner as aforesaid.

II. RUNAWAY SLAVES WEST OF SAN ANTONIO RIVER.

Act of Jan. 27, 1844. Took effect from passage.

Reward for apprehending west of.

ART. 1873. [1] It shall be lawful hereafter for any person or persons who may apprehend and commit to jail any runaway slave or slaves, on or west of the San Antonio River, to demand and receive the sum of fifty dollars for each and every slave so apprehended: provided, said slave or slaves be so secured that the property come safely to the possession of the owner; to be paid upon the delivery of such slave or slaves to the owner thereof, or his authorized agent; and the person or persons apprehending such slave or slaves, shall have a lien on the same until the reward specified as aforesaid be paid.

Further allowance where runaway is delivered to owner, &c.

ART. 1874. [2] In all cases where any slave or slaves shall be apprehended and delivered to the owner at his residence, it shall be lawful for the person apprehending and delivering such slave or slaves, to demand and receive for each slave so apprehended and delivered, in addition to the sum specified as aforesaid, the further sum of two dollars for every thirty miles he may travel in going to and returning from the residence of said owner; the distance to be computed over the shortest route travelled at the time; and to have a lien upon the slave or slaves for the payment of the same, as provided for in the first section of this act.

Same subject.

ART. 1875. [3] The provisions of the second section of this act shall extend to persons apprehending runaway slaves in any part of the Republic: provided, said slaves are delivered by the apprehender, to the owner thereof, at his or her residence.

ART. 1876. [4] If no owner appears and claims any slave or slaves so apprehended, and the same be sold under the provisions of the act to which this is a supplement, then in that case it shall be the duty of the Sheriff to pay over to the person or persons apprehending such slave or slaves, the reward prescribed by the provisions of the first section of this act: provided, that the Sheriff shall take, in writing, the testimony on which the claim to the reward is admitted, and that the same be filed in the office of the Clerk of the County Court. If runaway is sold, Sheriff shall pay over the reward, provided, &c.

III. SLAVES EXECUTED—OWNERS INDEMNIFIED.

ART. 1877. [1] In all cases where a slave, the property of a citizen of this State, shall be convicted of a capital offence by a court of competent jurisdiction, the jury rendering the verdict shall assess the value of such slave. Act of Jan. 24, 1852. Took effect from passage.

ART. 1878. [2] The transcript of the judgment of the court, together with the verdict and appraisement of the jury, and the return of the Sheriff, or other officer authorized to execute the process of said court, that such slave has suffered the penalty of death in accordance with the sentence of the court, shall be sufficient evidence to entitle the owner of any slave so executed to receive from the treasury of the State one half of the appraised value of said slave: provided, that the appraisement shall, in no case, exceed one thousand dollars: and, provided, also, that the owner of said slave shall not attempt to vade or defeat the execution of the law on said slave, which fact shall be found by the jury trying such slave, nor shall a slave be so paid for, who may be condemned for any offence, in the commission of which his owner was either principal or accessary. What shall be sufficient evidence to authorize treasurer to pay for, &c.

IV. PROHIBITED CARRYING GUNS, ETC.

ART. 1879. [1] No slave shall carry a gun or other deadly weapon upon the premises of his master, mistress, or employer, without a written permit from his owner or employer, so to do. Act of Aug. 30 1856. In force from passage.

ART. 1880. [2] No slave shall be permitted to carry a gun or other deadly weapon beyond the premises of his owner or employer, unless accompanied by his owner, employer, or some white person authorized by his owner or employer to have charge of said slave during the time that he carries said gun or other deadly weapon. Not to carry gun, &c., beyond the premises, unless.

ART. 1881. [3] Any gun or other deadly weapon, found in the possession of any slave, contrary to the provisions of the previous sections of this act, may be seized and taken from said slave, by any white person, and said property forfeited to the person seizing and taking the same, provided the same shall not exceed in value the sum of twenty dollars. But any such property may be reclaimed by the owner paying the sum of twenty dollars to the person or persons who may have taken the same. Weapons found unlawfully in possession of, forfeited, &c.

STATE TREASURER.

[*See Fiscal Year.*]

Act of March 19, 1846. Took effect from passage. Bond and oath of the.

ART. 1881a. [1] The first Treasurer of the State of Texas shall, within twenty days from and after the passage of this act, and every subsequent State Treasurer, shall, within twenty days after he shall have received notice of his election, and before he enters upon the duties of his office, give a bond payable to the Governor of the State of Texas and his successors in office, for the use of the State, in the sum of seventy-five thousand dollars, with not less than six good securities, to be approved of by the Governor of the State of Texas; conditioned that he will faithfully execute the duties of his office; and shall take and subscribe the oath prescribed by the Constitution, which, together with the bond, shall be deposited in the office of the Secretary of State; which said bond shall not be void on the first recovery of part, or of the whole of the penalty; but shall thereafter continue in force, for the whole amount of the penalty thereof, and may be sued on from time to time, and shall be deemed to extend to the faithful performance of the duties of his trust, and until his successor shall be duly qualified and shall have entered upon the duties of his office.

Shall receive and receipt for all money, &c.

ART. 1882. [2] The Treasurer shall receive on the warrants of the Comptroller of Public Accounts, all moneys, which shall from time to time be paid into the Treasury of the State, receipting for the same upon duplicate and triplicate warrants, which duplicate shall be deposited with the Comptroller, and the triplicate given to the person depositing such moneys.

Shall countersign and pay warrants drawn by, &c.

ART. 1883. [3] The Treasurer shall countersign and pay all warrants drawn by the Comptroller of Public Accounts on the Treasury, which are authorized by law, and no moneys shall be paid out of the Treasury, except on the warrants of the Comptroller.

Shall keep regular accounts of receipts, expenditures, &c.

ART. 1884. [4] He shall keep true, regular, and methodical accounts of the receipts and expenditures of the public moneys of the Treasury, and close his accounts annually, with the proper and legal vouchers for the same, distinguishing between the receipts and disbursements of each fiscal year.

Shall provide all necessary books and open an account in the name of the State.

ART. 1885. [5] He shall provide, at the expense of the State, all necessary books for the proper keeping of the accounts of the Treasury; and he shall open therein an account in the name of the State of Texas, in which he shall enter the amounts of all moneys, securities, and other property in the Treasury, and which may at any time be received by him; and shall state distinctly the several sources from which the revenue is derived, and the amount received from each.

Also, for all appropriations.

ART. 1886. [6] He shall also open an account in the Treasury for all appropriations of money made by law, so that the appropriations and the application in pursuance thereof, may clearly and distinctly appear.

ART. 1887. [7] The Treasurer shall exhibit to the Governor on the first

Monday of December, of each year, and at such other times as he shall require, an exact statement of the condition and situation of the Treasury, and of the balance of money remaining therein to the credit of the State, with a summary of the receipts and payments of the Treasury during the preceding year, or for such other period of time as may be specially required; and shall exhibit all books, papers, vouchers, and all other matters pertaining to his office for the examination of the Legislature, or either branch thereof, or any committee which may be by them appointed, whenever required by them so to do.

Shall make an annual exhibit to the Governor, &c.

ART. 1888. [8] The Treasurer shall, at the close of his term of office, deliver into the possession of his successor the moneys, securities, and all other property of the State, together with the books, vouchers, papers, and evidences of property in his possession, and all other matters and things which pertain to the office of State Treasurer.

Shall deliver to his successor the moneys, &c.

ART. 1889. [9] The Treasurer shall procure a strong iron safe or safes, in which shall be deposited all moneys or dues received by him on account of the State.

Shall procure iron safes.

SUPREME COURT.

[*See Constitution, Art. 4, Sect. 3.*]

I. ORGANIZATION, POWERS AND JURISDICTION.

Act of May 12, 1846. Took effect from passage.

ART. 1890. [2] The Supreme Court of the State of Texas, shall consist of a Chief Justice and two associates, any two of whom shall form a quorum.

Appellate jurisdiction.

ART. 1891. [3] The Supreme Court shall have appellate jurisdiction over all manner of pleas, plaints, motions, causes and controversies, both civil and criminal, which may be brought before it from the District or any other courts of the State, and which shall be cognizable in the said Supreme Court, according to the laws and Constitution of the State; and when the judgment, or decree of the court below, in civil cases, shall be reversed, the Supreme Court shall proceed to render such judgment or decree as the court below should have rendered, or pronounced, except when it be necessary that some matter of fact be ascertained, or the damages to be assessed or the matter to be decreed is uncertain, in either of which cases the cause or prosecution, as the case may be, shall be remanded, for a more definite decision.(a)

May adjourn from day to day for want of a quorum, &c.

ART. 1892. [16] The said court may adjourn from day to day, or for such longer period as they may think necessary to the ends of justice, and the determination of the business before them; and there shall be no discontinuance of any suit, process, or matter returned to, or depending in the Supreme Court, although a quorum of the court may not be in attendance at the commencement, or any other day of the term; but if a sufficient number of Judges shall not attend on the first day of the term, to hold said court, or shall not attend at any day of the term, any Judge of the court, or the Sheriff attending the same, may adjourn the said court from time to time, for thirty days, at which time, if a majority, or quorum, shall not attend, it shall be the duty of the Judge or Sheriff in attendance to adjourn the court to the next regular term time.

Power to punish contempts.

ART. 1893. [19] The Supreme Court shall have power to punish any person for a contempt of said court, according to the principles and usages of law in like cases, not to exceed one thousand dollars fine, and imprisonment not exceeding twenty days.

May establish rules, &c.

ART. 1894. [20] The Supreme Court shall have power, if necessary, to establish rules of proceedings for the government of said court, and the several District Courts in this State, not inconsistent with the laws and Constitution of the State: provided, that the rules for the government of the District Courts shall not have effect until they have been published at least sixty days in some newspaper published at the seat of Government.

(a) A power in the Supreme Court to grant relief, must either be expressly conferred by law, or it must result from the powers necessarily incident to the exercise of its appellate jurisdiction. Dewees *v.* Hudgeons, 1 Tex. Rep. 192. Where there is no final disposition of the cause by the District Court, the Supreme Court cannot obtain jurisdiction of it by appeal. Hanks *v.* Thompson, 5 Tex. Rep. 6. See McNairy *v.* Castleman, 6 Tex. Rep. 286. Wortham *v.* Harrison, 8 Tex. Rep. 141. See notes to Art. 4, Sect. 3, of the Constitution of the State. The jurisdiction of this court is exclusively appellate. Chambers *v.* Hodges, 3 Tex. Rep. 517.

ART. 1895. [21] The said court, or any Judge thereof, in vacation, may issue writs of habeas corpus, mandamus, and such other writs as may be necessary to enforce the jurisdiction of said court, and also to compel a Judge of the District Court to proceed to trial and judgment in a cause, agreeably to the principles and usages of law, returnable into the Supreme Court on or before the first day of the term, or during the session of the same, or before any Judge of the said court, as the nature of the case may require.(a) Writs of habeas corpus may be issued by.

II. ELECTION OF JUDGES.

ART. 1896. [1] In the election of Judges of the Supreme Court, there shall be elected one Chief Justice and two Associates, to hold their offices under, and in accordance with the provisions of the Constitution of the State: provided, that should there be a tie between two or more persons for the office of Chief Justice, or between three or more persons for Associate Justices, the Governor shall immediately order a new election, giving thirty days notice, to fill the places left vacant by such tie. Act of Dec. 3, 1850. Took effect from passage. Governor shall order new election in case of a tie, &c.

ART. 1897. [2] It shall be the duty of the Governor whenever a vacancy shall occur in the office of Chief Justice or Associate Judges, to order an election for such vacancy or vacancies, which election, when so ordered, shall be held in accordance with the laws regulating elections. Vacancy, special election. See Art. 641.

III. DISQUALIFICATION OF JUDGES AND APPOINTMENT OF SPECIAL JUDGES.

ART. 1898. [17] No Judge of the Supreme Court shall sit in any cause wherein he may be interested in the question to be determined, or where either of the parties may be connected with him by affinity or consanguinity, within the third degree, or where he shall have been of counsel in the cause; and when the Supreme Court, or any two of its members shall be thus disqualified to hear and determine any cause or causes in said court, or when no judgment can be rendered in any case or cases, in said court, by reason of the equal division of opinion of said Judges, the same shall be certified to the Governor of the State, who shall immediately commission the requisite number of persons learned in the law, for the trial and determination of said case or cases. Act of May 12, 1846. Took effect from passage. In case of interest in, &c. See Const. Art. 4, Sect. 14. Special Judges.

ART. 1899. [18] Whenever the Supreme Court shall be equally divided in opinion on hearing any appeal, or other matter, it shall be the duty of the Chief Justice or Presiding Judge of the court, to certify the same to the Governor; also, all other causes of disability of said court, as prescribed in the foregoing section of this act. Cases of equal division, &c., to be certified to the Governor.

IV. CLERK.

ART. 1900. [4] There shall be appointed for the Supreme Court, one Clerk, who shall reside at the place of holding court; the appointment shall be made Shall be appointed by, &c.

(a) Ex parte Thornton, 9 Tex. Rep. 636. Meyer v. Carolan, 9 Tex. Rep. 250. Commissioner, &c., v. Smith, 5 Tex. Rep. 471 Lindsay v. Luckett, 20 Tex. Rep. 516.

by the court, and shall be entered of record in the proceedings of the court; and the person so appointed shall, before he enters upon the duties of his office, take and subscribe the oath prescribed by the Constitution, in open court, and shall enter into a bond with two good securities, to be approved of by the court, payable to the Governor of the State and his successors in office, in the penalty of ten thousand dollars, conditioned for the faithful performance of the duties of his office, and that he correctly record the judgments, decrees, decisions, and orders of the said court, and deliver over to his successor in office all records, minutes, books, and papers, and whatever belongs to his said office of Clerk; which bond and oath shall immediately thereafter be deposited in the office of the Secretary of State, and shall not be void on the first recovery, but may be put in suit, and prosecuted by the party injured, until the amount thereof be recovered, and shall be deemed to extend to the faithful discharge of the duties of his office.

Vacancy in clerkship during vacation.

ART. 1901. [5] If, in vacation, the office of Clerk may become vacant, the appointment shall be made by the Chief Justice and the Associates of said court, or any one of said Associates and Chief Justice; and the person so appointed shall give bond and take the oath as prescribed in the fourth section of this act, the bond to be approved by any Judge of the court; which bond and oath shall be deposited in the same manner as though the appointment had been made in term time, and may be prosecuted and put in suit in like manner; copies of said bond shall be received in evidence in any court in this State, in the same manner as the original would be, were it presented in court; and the said appointment shall continue until the next regular succeeding session of the said court, or until a regular appointment shall be made.

Term of office.

ART. 1902. [6] The Clerk of the Supreme Court shall hold his office for the term of four years from his appointment, but may be removed therefrom for neglect of duty, or misdemeanor in office, by the Supreme Court, on motion, of which the Clerk against whom complaint is made, shall have ten days' previous notice, specifying the particular charges of negligence or misdemeanor in office preferred; and in every such case, the court shall determine both the law and the facts; and whenever the necessity occurs, the Supreme Court may appoint a Clerk *pro tempore*.

Successor of, to receive books, papers, &c.

ART. 1903. [8] The successor in office, of any Clerk, shall receive into his possession all books, papers, stationery, and every thing belonging to the said office; and should any person or persons having possession of the same, refuse to give them up, on demand made, it shall be the duty of said Clerk to give information thereof to the Attorney-General, or the District Attorney of the District in which the said refusal may be made; who shall prosecute such person or persons in the name of the State, before any court having jurisdiction of the same; and, on conviction, the person so offending shall be fined in any sum not less than five hundred dollars, nor more than five thousand dollars, for the use of the State.

Seal of the court

ART. 1904. [12] It shall be the duty of the Clerk of the Supreme Court to procure a seal for the use of the court, which shall have a star of five points, with the words "Supreme Court of the State of Texas," engraved thereon.

Act of Feb'y 11, 1850. Took effect August 1. 1850.

Docket of causes, &c.

ART. 1905. [1] The Clerk of the Supreme Court shall file and carefully preserve the transcripts of all records certified to said court, and all papers relative thereto; and shall docket all causes brought to the court, putting all those from each Judicial District together upon the docket, in the order in which he shall receive them.(*a*)

(*a*) If an appeal or writ of error be not docketed at the term to which it is made returnable, its force and effect is destroyed for every purpose whatever. Wethered *v.* Lee, 3 Tex. Rep. 189. Urbano *v.* Johnson et al., 3 Tex. Rep. 191.

ART. 1906. [2] The said Clerk shall faithfully record the proceedings and decisions of said court, and certify their judgments to the courts from which the causes were brought. Record of proceedings.

ART. 1907. [2] The seventh section of the act entitled an act to organize the Supreme Court of the State of Texas, approved the 12th of May, 1846, be amended so as to read as follows: Section 7th. The Clerk of the Supreme Court shall keep an office at the city of Austin, at the city of Galveston and at the town of Tyler. Said Clerk shall have power to appoint deputies under him, from whom he may require bonds for the faithful discharge of the duties of his office by written appointment under the seal of the court, which shall be filed in the records of the court, to whom he shall administer an oath faithfully to discharge the duties of his office, and for whose official acts he shall in all cases be responsible. The Clerk of the Supreme Court shall appoint a deputy residing in the first, seventh, tenth, or twelfth Judicial Districts, who shall reside at the city of Galveston, and attend at the office of the Clerk of the Supreme Court. He shall also appoint a deputy residing in fifth, sixth, eighth, or ninth Judicial Districts, who shall reside at the town of Tyler, and attend at the office of the Clerk of the Supreme Court, and attend to and discharge the duties of his office during the absence of the Clerk of the Supreme Court, or when the Clerk is present, under his direction. The Clerk of the Supreme Court and his deputies shall have power to administer oaths in all cases incident to the discharge of the duties of his office. Act of Nov. 30, 1850. Took effect from passage. Offices of clerk, where kept—appointment of deputies—powers, &c.

ART. 1908. [1] The Clerk of the Supreme Court be, and he is hereby authorized to have made for the use of said court, two copies of the seal of said court. The one to be used by the said court sitting at Galveston, the other by said court sitting at Tyler, the expenses to be paid out of the contingent fund of said court. Act of Dec. 16, 1853. Took effect Apr. 14, 1854. Two copies of seal to be made.

V. WRITS AND PROCESS.

ART. 1909. [15] All writs and process issuing from the Supreme Court shall bear the test of the Chief Justice of said court, and be under the seal of said court, and signed, by the Clerk thereof, and may be directed to the Sheriff or other proper officer of any county in the State, and shall be by such officer executed according to the commands thereof, and returned to the court from which they emanated: and whenever such writ or process shall not be executed, the Clerk of said court is hereby authorized and required to issue another like process, or writ, upon the application of the party suing out the former writ or process, to the same or any other county; and when any person, plaintiff, or defendant, in any suit pending in said court, shall die, it shall be lawful for the Clerk of the said court, during the recess of the court, upon application by petition, to issue proper process, to enable the court to proceed to a final judgment, or decree, in the name of the representative of such deceased person. Act of May 12, 1846. Took effect from passage. Process—service and return. Death of party pending suit.

VI. PLACES AND TIME OF HOLDING TERMS.

ART. 1910. [1] The Supreme Court shall hold its sessions once in every year at the city of Austin, in the county of Travis; once in every year at the city of Galveston, in the county of Galveston; and once in every year at the town Act of August 28, 1856. Took effect from passage.

Places of holding court, &c., districts, &c. of Tyler, in the county of Smith: that the causes decided in the District Courts of the second, third, fourth, eleventh, thirteenth, sixteenth, seventeenth and eighteenth Judicial Districts, and the counties of Gonzales and Lavaca in the tenth District, when taken up by appeal or otherwise, shall be returnable to the Supreme Court sitting at Austin; that the causes decided in the District Courts of the first, seventh, twelfth, fourteenth, fifteenth and tenth Judicial Districts, with the exception of the county of Gonzales, shall be returnable to the Supreme Court holding its session at Galveston; that the causes decided in the District Courts of the fifth, sixth, eighth and ninth Judicial Districts shall be returnable to the Supreme Court holding its session at the town of Tyler, in the county of Smith: provided that the parties, or their attorneys, may, on filing an agreement for that purpose with the Clerk of any District Court in either of the Judicial Districts, direct the records, accompanied by a certified copy of the agreement to be transmitted, to the Supreme Court holding its sessions either in the city of Austin, the city of Galveston, or at the town of Tyler.

Record may be sent to either court, when.

Act of Dec. 11, 1857. Took effect from passage. Cases appealed, &c., from Lavaca.

ART. 1911. [2] The causes decided in the District Court for the county of Lavaca, of the tenth Judicial District, when taken up by appeal or otherwise, to the Supreme Court, shall be returnable to the Supreme Court holding its session at the city of Galveston.

Act of Dec. 19, 1855. Act of Dec. 19, 1857. In force from date. Appeals from 19th dist., &c.

ART. 1912. [3] * * * * * * * all cases of appeals from the decisions of the District Courts in this District [16th] shall be to the branch of the Supreme Court at the city of Austin; * * * and all appeals from the District Courts of the nineteenth District, shall be to the Austin Term of the Supreme Court.

Act of January 21, 1856.

ART. 1913. [5] All appeals and writs of error from the District Courts of the fifteenth Judicial District, shall be returned to, and considered, and adjudicated by, the Supreme Court holding session at Galveston.

Act of Dec. 3, 1857. Took effect from passage. Times of holding court.

ART. 1914. [1] The sessions of the Supreme Court of the State, shall hereafter be held as follows: At Austin, on the third Monday of October of each year, and may continue in session twelve weeks; at Galveston on the last Monday of January, in each year, and may continue in session ten weeks; at Tyler on the fourth Monday of April in each year, and shall continue in session until the first day of July, unless the causes duly submitted to the Court for determination, shall be sooner decided.

Same subject.

ART. 1915. [3] This act shall regulate all future terms of the Supreme Court, until otherwise provided by law.

VII. PROCEEDINGS IN.

Joint resolution April 25, 1846. Took effect from passage. Appearance by brief.

ART. 1916. [1] Hereafter, when any cause or suit may be taken up from any inferior court to the Supreme Court of this State, whether by appeal, writ, or error, or otherwise, it shall and may be lawful for the attorney or attorneys, both for plaintiffs and defendant, to file in the papers of said suit or cause, his or their written brief or argument; and the Judges of the Supreme Court shall be required to notice the same as much as if it were the personal appearance of such attorney or attorneys; and shall not dismiss any suit or cause, where such brief or argument of counsel is filed with the papers, for want of other or further prosecution.(a)

(a) The act means attorneys, who are known to the court as members of the Supreme Court Bar. Thorn v. Lawson, 6 Tex. Rep. 240.

ART. 1917. [14] In all cases decided by the Supreme Court, the judgment or decree of the court shall be in writing, and pronounced in open court, with the reasons of the court for the same, which shall be recorded by the Clerk of the court in a book kept by him for that purpose. Act of May 12, 1846. Took effect from passage. Opinion shall be in writing, &c.

ART. 1918. [23] There shall be no reversal on an appeal, nor shall the same be dismissed for want of form, provided sufficient matter or substance be contained in the record, to enable the court to decide the cause upon its merits; and where the court shall be of opinion that an appeal or writ of error has been taken for delay, and that there was no good, probable, and sufficient cause for taking such appeal, then, and in that case, the appellant, if he be the defendant in the court below, shall pay ten per cent. on the amount in dispute, as damages, together with the judgment, interest and costs of suit thereon accruing.(*a*) Not to dismiss cause for want of form. Damages, &c.

ART. 1919. [24] In all cases of appeal to the Supreme Court, the trial shall be on a statement of facts, as agreed upon by the parties or their attorneys, certified to by the Judge of the court below; or should the parties fail to agree, then the Judge of the court below shall certify the facts; or on a bill of exceptions to the opinion of the Judge; or on a special verdict; or on an error in law, either assigned or apparent on the face of the record; and in the absence of all these, the appeal shall be dismissed with costs alone, or with costs and damages, at the discretion of the court.(*b*) Mode of trial.

ART. 1920. [25] The appellee shall not be required to file any answer to the assignment of errors or defects as may be insisted on by the appellant, but he shall furnish the court with a brief of his argument, and the authorities on which he relies; and where the appellant does not appear, or furnish the court with a brief of the cause, the appeal may be dismissed; or the appellee may, at his option, proceed *ex parte*. Appellee shall furnish brief. When appellant does not appear, &c.

ART. 1921. [3] Whenever the Supreme Court, on the trial of a cause brought from any District Court, shall affirm the judgment or decree of such District Court; or when said court shall proceed to render such judgment or decree as should have been rendered by the court below, and such judgment shall be for the same or a greater amount, or of the same nature as rendered in the court below, said court shall render judgment against the appellant or appellants, and his, her, or their securities in the appeal bond, a copy of which shall always accompany the transcript of the record; and said Supreme Court shall, in their discretion, also include in their said judgment or decree, such damages, not exceeding ten per cent. on the amount of the original judgment, as the court may deem proper; and the judgment or decree of said court, rendered as contemplated in this section, shall be final, and shall not require any order, decree, or action, on the part of the District Court from which the cause was removed; and the Clerks of the various District Courts, on the receipt of the mandate of the Supreme Court in any such cause, shall proceed to issue execution thereon as in other causes.(*c*) Act of March 13, 1848. In force from passage. Judgment against appellant and sureties, damages, &c.

ART. 1922. [3] Causes on the docket of said court may be tried by Districts, or in such order as to the Judges of said court may seem best calculated to promote the interest and convenience of the parties or their attorneys: pro- Act of Feb. 11, 1850. Took effect 1st Aug. 1850.

(*a*) Where there are no bills of exception or statement of facts, nor error suggested or apparent on the record, it is the duty of the counsel for the appellee or defendant in error, to suggest delay; and even should he omit to do so, the court will usually, under such circumstances, award the damages authorized by law, in cases of frivolous appeals. Chambers *v.* Hodges, 3 Tex. Rep. 517. When a cause is brought into the Supreme Court on a writ of error, without any probable, good and sufficient reason, damages can be assessed for the benefit of the plaintiff in the court below, in like manner as on frivolous appeals. Cheek & Collins *v.* Rogers, 1 Tex. Rep. 440.

(*b*) Hall *v.* Stancel, 3 Tex. Rep. 400. Where the error is apparent on the record, the Supreme Court is authorized to notice it. McNairy *v.* Castleberry, 6 Tex. Rep. 286. Wortham *v.* Harrison, 8 Tex. Rep. 141. Hill *v.* Crownover, 4 Tex. Rep. 8.

(*c*) The power of the Supreme Court to award damages for delay, is not restricted to cases of affirmation, but extends to cases in which the judgment is for the same, or a greater amount than that of the court below. Wortham *v.* Harrison, 8 Tex. Rep. 141. Cheek & Collins *v.* Rogers, 1 Tex. Rep. 440.

Order of trying causes.

vided, that all appeals in criminal cases, shall be called for trial before the civil causes from the same district; and all causes shall be tried at the term they are docketed, unless satisfactory cause be shown for a continuance.

Time when transcript must be filed, &c.

ART. 1923. [4] When an appeal from any final judgment of a District Court has been taken, and an appeal bond has been filed; or when an appeal has been taken in cases where no appeal bond is required; or when a citation has been served on a petition for a writ of error, it shall be the duty of the appellant or plaintiff in error, as the case may be, to file a transcript of the record of the cause with the Clerk of the Supreme Court, in the following manner:

[5] It shall be the duty of the appellant or plaintiff in error, to file a transcript of the record with the Clerk of the Supreme Court, on or before the first of the term of said court next succeeding the time when the appeal was perfected, or the citation on the petition for writ of error was served; or on or before the first day of the time during said term, that may have been designated by the Supreme Court, for the trial of causes from the district in which such appeal or writ of error was taken: provided that such appeal was perfected, or such citation was served, forty days before the said first day of the term next succeeding the taking thereof, or forty days before the first day of the time in said term, designated by said court for the trial of causes brought from said District.(*a*)

If appeal was not perfected or citation served, forty days before, &c.

ART. 1924. [6] If the appeal was not perfected, or the citation on the petition for writ of error was not served, forty days before the first day of the next succeeding term of the Supreme Court, after the taking of such appeal or writ of error, or forty days before the first day of the time that may have been designated by the Supreme Court, for the trial of causes from the district in which such appeal or writ of error was taken, then it shall be the duty of the appellant or plaintiff in error, to file a transcript of the record with the Clerk of the Supreme Court, within forty days after the time when such appeal was perfected, or such citation served: provided, such appeal was perfected, or such citation was served, at any time before the first day of February next, succeeding the taking of the appeal or writ of error; but if such appeal was not perfected, or such citation was not served, forty days before the first day of February next, succeeding the taking of the appeal or writ of error, then it shall be the duty of the appellant or plaintiff in error to file said transcript as directed in the next preceding section.

Where appellant fails to file transcript.

ART. 1925. [7] In case the appellant or plaintiff in error, shall fail to file a transcript of the record as directed in the two preceding sections, then it shall be lawful for the appellee or defendant in error to file with the Clerk of the Supreme Court, a certificate of the Clerk of the District Court in which any such appeal or writ of error may have been taken, attested by the seal of his court, and stating the time when such appeal was perfected or such citation was served; whereupon, it shall be the duty of the Supreme Court, to affirm the judgment of the court below, unless good cause be shown why such transcript was not filed by the appellant or plaintiff in error; and in cases where a bond has been given by the appellant or plaintiff in error, if a copy of such bond accompanies such certificate of the Clerk of the District Court, the judgment shall in like manner be affirmed against the sureties in such bond.(*b*)

(*a*) Citations on writs of error should issue immediately after the writ is sued out; and if not served, *alias* and *pluries* should follow, without unnecessary delay. Roberts & Swisher *v.* Landrum, 3 Tex. Rep. 16. Neither party can have a cause docketed at a term subsequent to which an appeal was taken, or writ of error was returnable. Ibid. If the defendant in the judgment takes an appeal, and does not prosecute it to the next term of the Supreme Court, the supersedeas to the judgment is at an end, and the plaintiff may sue out his execution. Shapard *v.* Baileal, 3 Tex. Rep. 26 When the transcript of a record has been filed with the Clerk of the Supreme Court, but not in the time prescribed by law, the judgment of the court below will be affirmed, on motion of the appellee or defendant in error, without reference to the merits, unless good cause be shown why the transcript was not filed in due time. DeLeon *v.* Owen, 3 Tex. Rep. 153.

(*b*) Upon an application to the Supreme Court to affirm a judgment without reference to the merits, the court will look into the records to determine the question whether the District Court had jurisdiction, but not for the purpose of revising any errors, &c. Able *v.* Bloomfield, 6 Tex. Rep. 263. Where the bond on an-

ART. 1926. [8] In all cases where the Supreme Court shall have affirmed the judgment of the court below, under the provisions of the next preceding section, said court may at any time during the term at which any such judgment was so affirmed, permit the transcript to be filed by the appellant or plaintiff in error, and the case to be tried on its merits: provided, the appellant or plaintiff in error, shall show to the court good cause why the transcript was not filed by him in accordance with the provisions of the fifth and sixth sections of this act; and shall also show to said court, that he has given the appellee or defendant in error, notice of his intention to apply for such permission to file said transcript; and in cases where the Supreme Court shall adjourn within forty days after any judgment shall have been affirmed, under the provisions of the next preceding section, the Supreme Court may permit the appellant or plaintiff in error, to file said transcript on the first day of the next succeeding term, or the first day of the term that may have been designated by said court for the trial of cases from the district in which such appeal or writ of error was taken, and have said cause tried on its merits: provided, said appellant or plaintiff in error, shall show good cause why said transcript was not filed, as directed by the fifth and sixth sections of this act; and shall also show to the court that he has given the appellee or defendant in error, notice of his intention to apply for permission to file said transcript.

How trial on merits may be had after affirmance, &c.

ART. 1927. [9] The appellant or plaintiff in error, shall in all cases file with the Clerk of the court below, an assignment of errors, distinctly specifying the grounds on which he relies, before he takes the transcript of the record from the Clerk's office, and a copy of such assignment of errors, shall be attached to and form a part of the record; and all errors not so distinctly specified, shall be considered by the Supreme Court as waived.(a)

Errors shall be assigned before, &c.

ART. 1928. [1] If any cases argued or submitted to the Supreme Court of this State, during a term holden at one of the places defined by the act to which this is as a supplement, shall be left undecided at the close of said term, it shall be, and is hereby made competent for said Court to decide such case whilst sitting at either of the other two places, and when such decision shall be made, the Court shall cause their judgment and opinion to be transmitted to the Clerk of said Court at the place where the cause was submitted, to be by him entered of record, as in other cases.

Act of Jan. 31, 1852. Took effect from passage.

Cases argued or submitted and undecided at close of term.

VIII. COSTS.

ART. 1929. [2] On the rendition of any final judgment or decree by the Supreme Court, the Clerk of said court shall not be compelled to issue and deliver the mandate of the court, or certify the proceedings to the proper court, until all of the costs accruing on the cause in the Supreme Court shall have been paid. But in case said Clerk shall elect to issue and deliver the mandate of the court or certify the proceedings to the proper court, without such costs having been paid, then he shall make out a correct list of all the costs accruing on said cause in said Supreme Court, and shall issue execution therefor against the party or parties and his, her, or their securities, adjudged to pay the same, directed to the Sheriff of the proper county, from which the original cause

Act of March 18, 1848. Took effect from passage.

Clerk not required to issue mandate until costs are paid.

May issue execution for &c.

peal is not in conformity to the statute, and the appellant fails to file the transcript, the appellee cannot obtain an affirmance without reference to the merits. Chambers v. Miller, 7 Tex. Rep. 75. Mills v. Bagby, 4 Tex. Rep. 320. The judgment will not be affirmed without reference to the merits, unless it appears the citation in error was served. Patton v. Laforce, 14 Tex. Rep. 240. Chambers v. Shaw, 16 Tex. Rep. 143. The term of the Supreme Court next after service of the citation in error is the return term. To this there is an exception where service is perfected during the term, and forty days elapse before the end of it. Chambers v. Shaw, 16 Tex. Rep. 143. Wheeler v. The State, 8 Tex. Rep. 228. Wilson v. Truehart, 13 Tex. Rep. 287.

(a) Flanagan v. McClarty, 10 Tex. Rep. 286.

was removed, or to any county where the person or persons liable under such execution may have property; and it shall be the duty of every Sheriff, on the receipt of any such execution, to execute the same under the same rules, regulations and liabilities as provided for in cases of executions from the District Courts; which execution shall be returnable on or before the next regular term of the Supreme Court; and any Sheriff who shall fail to make due return of any execution herein provided for, or to pay over any costs so collected, when demanded, shall be subject to pay ten per cent. damages per month on the amount of such execution, to the Clerk of the Supreme Court, to be recovered on motion in the District Court of the county to which the execution was issued—such Sheriff having had three days' previous notice of such motion.

Failure of Sheriff to return, &c.

IX. REPORTS OF DECISIONS.

Act of Feb. 3, 1852. Took effect March 17, 1852. Governor may subscribe for.

ART. 1930. [1] The Governor is hereby authorized and required to subscribe for three hundred copies of each succeeding volume of the Reports of the Decisions of the Supreme Court, which shall be prepared under the direction of said court, and for which the Reporter of said Decisions shall be paid the sum of three dollars and a half per page for as many pages as shall be contained in one copy of each volume, and the Comptroller of Public Accounts shall issue warrants for the same, upon the certificate of the Secretary of State, that said books, printed in small pica type, the pages not less in size than those of the reports already published, and neatly bound in law sheep, have been deposited in his office, and specifying the number of pages each volume contains.

X. LIBRARY.

Act of Feb. 4, 1854. Took effect April 14, 1854. Secretary of State to transfer certain books, &c.

ART. 1931. [1] The Secretary of State shall transfer to the control of the Judges of the Supreme Court, all law books and reports of the decisions of the Courts of the several States now in his office, and such as may hereafter be sent to his Department by way of an interchange.

Books, where kept.

ART. 1932. [2] * * * * * The books purchased to be kept at Austin, at Tyler and at Galveston, as the Judges may direct and deem necessary to the investigation of causes pending in the several branches of the Supreme Court.

TAXES.

I. LEVY OF TAXES.

II. PROPERTY EXEMPT FROM.

III. ASSESSOR AND COLLECTOR.

IV. ASSESSMENT OF TAXES.

V. COLLECTION OF TAXES.

VI. TAX ON VOCATION OR CALLING.

VII. GENERAL PROVISIONS.

I. LEVY OF TAXES.

Act of Feb. 16, 1858. Took effect from passage.

Amount of *ad valorem* tax.

ART. 1933. [1] There shall be levied and collected for the use of the State, a direct *ad valorem* tax of twelve and a half cents upon each hundred dollars value of property, real and personal, (except such property as may be exempt by law from taxation.)

Poll tax.

ART. 1934. [2] There shall be assessed and collected of every free male person between the ages of twenty one and fifty years, residents of this State, (idiots and persons *non compos mentis*, excepted,) a poll tax of fifty cents each.

County Court may levy tax.

ART. 1935. [3] The County Courts of the several counties of the State, shall have the power to authorize the assessment and collection of twelve and a half cents on each hundred dollars value of property, real and personal, to be appropriated to the use of the said several counties.

Tax on money loaned.

ART. 1936. [4] There shall be assessed and collected of each person, firm, or public corporation, having money loaned at interest, a tax at the rate of twenty cents on each hundred dollars so loaned; and any person, firm, or public corporation having money loaned at interest, who shall fail or refuse to give in the same for taxation, shall, upon conviction before any court having competent jurisdiction, forfeit the interest on such money loaned at interest, and not given in for taxation, to the use of the informer; that each and every person or firm engaged in the sale of goods, wares and merchandize, vinous and spirituous liquors, when sold in quantities of a quart or more, shall pay a tax of twenty cents on each hundred dollars value of such articles purchased for sale, or received for sale as agent or auctioneer by such person or firm; and it shall be the duty of each Assessor and Collector in this State, once in every three months, or oftener, to call upon such person or firm so occupied or engaged in his county, for an account of such purchases or consignments, to be made under oath; and every person, when so called upon, who shall refuse or fail to furnish such Assessor or Collector with an account of such purchases or consignments during the term for which the assessment is to be made, shall be liable to a penalty of fifty dollars for each failure or neglect, to be recovered on the information of the Assessor and Collector, before any Justice of the Peace of the proper county, by a suit in the name of the State; and the specific tax levied and collected by virtue of this section shall exempt the goods, wares and merchandize from the *ad valoerm* tax levied by this act.

Specific tax on goods, liquors, &c.

Duty of Assessor.

Specific tax, &c. exempt goods, liquors, &c., from *ad valorem* tax.

On theatrical company.

On museum, menagerie, &c.

ART. 1937. [5] There shall be assessed and collected of every theatrical company, exhibiting for pay or emolument, an annual direct tax of one hundred dollars for each and every such establishment; of each and every person or company exhibiting any museum, menagerie, wax works, feats of activity, slight of hand, or any other diversion of like character, an annual direct tax of twenty dollars, in each county in which the same may be exhibited.

Tax on hawkers and pedlars billiard tables, restaurats, race-track and other privileges.

ART. 1938. [6] There shall be assessed and collected of each and every person pursuing the occupation of hawker or pedlar of goods or other articles not manufactured in this State, an annual direct tax of fifty dollars in each and every county in which he may pursue such occupation; of each and every person or firm keeping a billiard table, an annual direct tax of fifty dollars for each and every table so kept; of each and every person or firm keeping a nine or ten pin alley, an annual direct tax of forty dollars for each and every alley so kept; of each and every person or firm keeping a cook-shop, restaurat, or eating house, for pay or emolument, an annual direct tax of sixteen dollars for each and every such establishment; of each and every person or firm keeping a race-track, an annual direct tax of forty dollars; of each and every person or firm pursuing the occupation of real estate broker, ship broker, merchandize or cotton broker, or any commission business, an annual direct tax of twenty dollars for each and every such establishment; of each and every person or firm occupied in the business of auctioneering, an annual direct tax of twenty dollars; of each and every person pursuing the occupation of pawnbroker an annual direct tax of twenty dollars. It shall be the duty of each and every person or firm before entering upon any of the occupations upon which a license tax is imposed by this act, to first call upon the Assessor and Collector of the county in which he may intend to follow such occupation and pay the tax required, and take a receipt for the same, setting forth the occupation and the amount of tax paid, which receipt he shall file with the Clerk of the County Court, who shall thereupon issue to him a license to follow such occupation for the term for which the license tax has been paid. It shall be the further duty of the Clerk to keep a book in which he shall enter the names of all persons obtaining a license, occupation, amount of tax paid, and date of license, which book shall at all times be open to the inspection of the County Court, and to all officers, executive or judicial, of his county, a transcript of which book, certified by the Chief Justice and under the seal of the Court, he shall transmit to the Comptroller on the first day of June in each

To whom tax shall be paid.

Duty of County Clerk.

and every year; for which service the Clerk shall be entitled to a fee of one dollar in each case, to be paid by the party obtaining the license.

ART. 1939. [7] If any person or firm shall pursue any occupation upon which a license tax is imposed by this act, without first having obtained a license, such offender shall forfeit and pay double the amount of the license tax, with costs of suit, recoverable before any Justice of the Peace of the county, or any court of competent jurisdiction, one half to be paid to the Assessor and Collector, which shall be accounted for by him and paid into the State treasury, as other license tax is required to be paid, and the other half shall be paid to the informer. *Penalty for pursuing occupation without license.*

ART. 1940. [8] It shall be the duty of all Sheriffs, Constables and Assessors and Collectors of taxes to arrest all persons that they shall find in their respective counties following any occupation upon which a license tax is imposed, without having first obtained a license therefor, and take him before some Justice of the Peace of his county to be dealt with as provided for in the preceding section of this act. *Duty of sheriffs, constables and assessors to arrest offenders, &c.*

ART. 1941. [9] The taxes assessed in pursuance of this act shall be a lien upon all property, real and personal, belonging to the person or persons so assessed, and upon whom the same be imposed, and upon all property assessed when the owner is unknown, and shall continue to bind such property until the taxes of such person or persons shall be fully settled and paid. *Taxes assessed are a lien on property, &c.*

II. PROPERTY EXEMPT FROM.

ART. 1942. [1] All buildings, with their furniture and library, designed and used solely for purposes of education or public worship, together with the land owned by said institutions of learning or churches, upon which the same may be situated, not exceeding ten acres, shall be, and the same are hereby exempted from taxation. *Act of Dec. 12 1849. Took effect March 23, 1850. Buildings used for education. Public worship.*

ART. 1943. [1] All buildings, furniture, libraries, philosophical apparatus, and lands attached thereto, not exceeding ten acres in each case, owned by, dedicated to, and occupied for, charitable or literary associations, while continued in such ownership, dedication, or use, shall be exempt from taxation. *Act of Jan. 24, 1850. Took effect March 23, 1850. For charitable institutions.*

ART. 1944. [5] All lands (not exceeding ten acres in each case,) held by such Trustees, for any one or all of the purposes above named, together with the buildings, improvements and furniture belonging to the same, shall be held free from taxation until the Legislature shall otherwise direct. *Act of Jan. 30, 1845. Took effect March 15, 1845. Same subject.*

ART. 1945. [6] All lands or other property heretofore conveyed to any church, or denomination of Christians, or association of the people, for the purposes above named, shall enjoy all the benefits of this Act: provided, the amount of lands exempt from taxation, shall not exceed ten acres in each case. *Land owned by churches exempt, provided.*

III. ASSESSOR AND COLLECTOR.

ART. 1946. [1] There shall be elected by the qualified voters of every county within the State of Texas, on the first Monday of August, in the

Act of Feb. 11, 1850. Took effect from passage.

Election and term of office.

year eighteen hundred and fifty, and every two years thereafter, until otherwise provided by law, an Assessor and Collector of taxes, who shall hold his office for and during the term of two years, and until his successor shall have been qualified; and should the office of Assessor and Collector, from any cause become vacant before the expiration of said term, it shall be the duty of the County Court of the county in which such vacancy shall occur, to appoint an Assessor and Collector of taxes, who shall be qualified in the same manner, and subject to a like bond as the Assessor and Collector elected; and the Assessor and Collector so appointed, shall hold his office for and during the unexpired term of his predecessor, and until his successor shall have been qualified.

In case of vacancy.

Bond to the State and oath of.

ART. 1947. [2] Every Assessor and Collector of taxes shall, within twenty days after he shall have received notice of his election or appointment, and before entering upon the duties of his office, give a bond to the "State of Texas," in a sum which the County Court shall consider double the probable amount of the State tax to be assessed in the county for two years, with at least three good and sufficient securities, to be approved by the County Court of his county, and shall take and subscribe the oath prescribed by the Constitution, which, together with said bond, shall be recorded in the Office of the Clerk of the County Court of said county, and be forwarded by the Chief Justice of the county to the Comptroller, to be deposited in his office: said bond shall be deemed to extend to the faithful performance of the duties of his office, as Assessor and Collector, for and during the full term for which he was elected or appointed, and shall not become void upon the first recovery, but suit may be maintained thereon, until the whole amount thereof be recovered. Such Assessor and Collector may be required to furnish a new bond and additional or other securities whenever in the opinion of the County Court it may be advisable. Should any Assessor and Collector fail to give a new bond and additional securities when required, he shall be suspended and dismissed from office by the County Court of his county.

New bond may be required.

Bond of, to the county.

ART. 1948. [3] The Assessors and Collectors of taxes shall give a like bond, with like conditions, to the Chief Justices of their respective counties, and their successors in office, in a sum not less than double the probable amount of the county tax, to be assessed in the county for two years, which bond shall be recorded and deposited in the County Clerk's Office of the county. A new bond and aditional security may be required, and the Assessor and Collector may be removed from office, in the manner prescribed in the second section of this Act

Failure to make and return Assessment roll.

ART. 1949. [11] If any Assessor and Collector of taxes shall fail or refuse to make out and return his assessment-roll as required by the provisions of this Act, he shall forfeit for the use of the State or county, as the case may be, the sum of fifty dollars, in addition to his liabilities under his bond, to be deducted by the Comptroller out of his commissions.

List of delinquent Assessors to be published annually.

ART. 1950. [24] It shall be the duty of the Comptroller, immediately after the day on which the Assessors and Collectors are required to make payment into the Treasury, to make out and publish a list of all delinquent Assessors and Collectors for the past fiscal year, and the amount of their delinquency, in a newspaper printed at the seat of government, and forward copies of the same to the Chief Justice, Sheriff, Assessor and Collector, and Clerks of the County and District Courts, in each county.

Shall not be allowed for insol-

ART. 1951. [25] No allowance shall be made any Assessor and Collector, in the settlement of his accounts, for insolvent tax-payers, unless he shall present a list, certified to by the County Court of his county, as being a correct copy of the list of such insolvent tax-payers, allowed by the court and filed in the office of the County Clerk; and said Assessor and Collector shall thereafter collect, if practicable, the taxes due from the persons named in said list, and make return thereof according to law. vent taxables, unless.

ART. 1952. [26] Every Assessor and Collector of Taxes for the State, in a settlement of his accounts with the Comptroller, shall be entitled to a compensation on the amount by him collected and paid into the Treasury, for the use of the State, of eight per cent. on all sums of one thousand dollars, and less; five per cent. on all sums less than two thousand dollars, and more than one thousand dollars; four per cent. on all sums less than five thousand dollars, and more than two thousand dollars; three per cent. on all sums less than ten thousand dollars, and more than five thousand dollars; and one per cent. on all sums over ten thousand dollars; and on a settlement of his accounts with the County Treasurer of his county, one-half of the like per cent. on the amount collected by him, and paid into the Treasury for the use of the county. Compensation of, for collecting State tax.

ART. 1953. [27] If any Assessor and Collector of taxes shall demand and recive of any person, more than lawful taxes, said officer shall forfeit and pay, upon conviction thereof before any court of competent jurisdiction, to and for the use of the party aggrieved, five times the amount so demanded and received, and be subject to presentment and indictment by the Grand Jury of his county for malfeasance in office, and upon conviction thereof, shall be fined in a sum not less than ten nor more than fifty dollars, at the discretion of the jury trying the same, to be paid when collected into the County Treasury. Penalty for demanding more than lawful taxes.

ART. 1954. [28] If any Assessor and Collector shall fail or refuse to pay into the State Treasury, the amount of taxes by him collected for the use of the State, on or before the day on which the same is made payable, by the provisions of this act, and to pay into the treasury of his county the entire amount collected by him for the use of the county, such Assessor and Collector and his securities shall be liable to be sued upon their bond or bonds, for the damages sustained by the State or county. Failure, &c., to pay over taxes collected.

ART. 1955. [35] If any Assessor and collector shall fail or refuse to surrender up his tax-roll to his successor in office, upon application, he shall, upon conviction in the District Courts, be fined in any sum not less than fifty dollars, for each and every month he may so fail or refuse to surrender up his tax-lists to his successor. Failure to deliver tax-roll to successor.

ART. 1956 [37] The Assessors and Collectors, for going to and returning from the seat of government, when they go for the purpose of settling their accounts, and paying over all moneys due from them as Assessor and Collector, on the settlement of their accounts, they shall be allowed five cents per mile in going to and returning from the seat of government, once in every year. Mileage for traveling to pay over taxes.

Act of Sept. 5, 1850. Took effect from passage.

ART. 1957. [1] Hereafter, no Assessor and Collector of Taxes shall exercise any official function, or perform any official act before he shall have been commissioned. Not to act until commissioned.

ART. 1958. [2] If, after any election for Assessor and Collector, it shall appear that the person elected is a defaulter, it shall be the duty of the Secretary of State, immediately to notify the Chief Justice of the county in which the election was held, of such default, and the amount thereof, who shall forthwith order an election to fill said office; and the said defaulter shall be ineligible at said second election, unless in the meantime he shall have made Where person elected is a defaulter.

his settlement with the Comptroller, and produced said Comptroller's receipt thereof.

Act of Feb. 7, 1853. In force from passage. Where Assessor is in arrearages to county.

ART. 1959. The act to which this is supplementary, shall apply to Assessors and Collectors who are in arrearages to the county, as well as to those who are in arrearages to the State, upon notice of the fact to the Secretary of the State or Comptroller, from the Chief Justice or County Court of the county where said delinquent Assessor and Collector resides.

Act of January 6, 1852. Took effect from passage. May appoint deputies.

ART. 1960. The Assessors and Collectors of this State shall have power to appoint deputies, to assist them in the discharge of their duties; and that the same law which now governs Sheriffs in the appointment of their deputies, shall govern Assessors and Collectors.

Act of August 30, 1856. Took effect from passage. Not to speculate in county paper, &c.

ART. 1961. [1] No Assessor and Collector of Taxes shall, either directly or indirectly, speculate in any county paper, or other fund whatever, made receivable by law for the payment of taxes, nor in any manner invest or use for his own benefit or profit, any moneys or funds received by him in payment of taxes.

Shall keep book of printed receipts, &c., preserve duplicates &c.

ART. 1962. [2] Every Assessor and Collector of Taxes shall keep one or more books, containing printed or written blank receipts, as well as corresponding marginal summaries; and before the delivery of any receipt for taxes, he shall fill up a blank therefor, as well as the corresponding marginal summary in said book, with the dates, name of the person, and amount and character of the fund paid, whether money, county paper, or other fund receivable for State and county taxes; and shall sever said receipt from said book, leaving therein the corresponding marginal summary as a permanent register of his office; which shall be produced before the County Court of his county when required, and shall also be subject to public inspection.

Shall pay taxes to County Treasurer.

ART. 1963. [3] Each Assessor and Collector of Taxes shall pay to the Treasurer of his county, all moneys collected by him for county taxes, in the same funds as received by him.

Penalty for violating this act.

ART. 1964. [4] Every Assessor and Collector of Taxes who shall violate any of the provisions of this act shall, for the first offence, be punished by a fine of not less than fifty nor more than one hundred dollars, to be recovered in the name of the State of Texas, before any court having jurisdiction thereof; of which fine, the informer shall receive the one-half, and the other half shall be paid into the county treasury for county purposes; and for the second offence, he shall be liable to indictment by a Grand Jury, and on conviction, he shall be fined in any sum not exceeding two hundred dollars, and shall be removed from office.

IV. ASSESSMENT OF TAXES.

Act of Feb'y 11, 1850. Took effect from passage. Assessment roll of each county. Time of assessment.

ART. 1965. [4] The assessors and collectors of the several counties of this State shall severally prepare an assessment roll for their respective counties, in which they shall set down in separate columns, in alphabetical order, the names of the taxable inhabitants thereof, the amount and description of the property taxed, real and personal, the value thereof, and the amount of taxes due thereon; for which purpose they shall, between the first days of January and May, in each and every year, call upon each person living in their county, for a list of his or her taxable property, and of all property subject to taxation, held by such person as trustee, guardian, executor, administrator, agent or attorney, within the county or State: provided, that when the assessor and collector shall call at the usual place of abode of the party liable to taxation, in the absence of such person, a written or printed notice to render such list to the assessor, shall serve in lieu of personal notice.

ART. 1966. [5] Whenever any person is assessed as trustee, guardian, executor, administrator, agent or attorney, it shall be done by addition to his name of his representative character; and such assessment shall be carried out in a separate line from his individual assessment. As guardian, agent, attorney &c.

ART. 1967. [6] If any person, when called upon by the assessor and collector of taxes of the county in which such person resides, shall fail or refuse to render a list of his or her property, real or personal, or of that held as administrator, executor, guardian, agent or attorney, which is liable to taxation, such person or persons shall be liable to a fine of not less than ten or more than five hundred dollars, for the use of the State or county, as the case may be, to be recovered before any court of competent jurisdiction; and it shall be the duty of the assessor and collector of every county, to report all such cases to the proper courts, and to attend them as a witness, to prove such failure or refusal. Penalty for failing, &c., to render list of property.

ART. 1968. [7] The list required under the fourth section of this act, shall contain a description of all the taxable property in his or her own right, or held as guardian, executor, administrator, agent or attorney, on the first day of January for the current year; verified by the oath of the party returning the same; made and subscribed before the assessor and collector of taxes, or any Justice of the Peace of the county wherein such parties reside; upon which property so returned, the assessor and collector and the party rendering the same, shall proceed to assess the value; in case they cannot agree as to the amount thereof, each shall have the right to select a respectable freeholder to determine the same; and in case of disagreement between the parties so selected, a third person shall be chosen by them, and a decision of a majority shall be final: provided, that the list of taxable property thus required to be furnished, shall not be construed so as to include the products of the soil of this State, while in the hands of the producer. What the list of property shall contain. Value of, how determined.

ART. 1969. [8] Each person owning or claiming property situated in any other county than that in which he or she resides, may render the same for assessment to the assessor and collector of the county where he or she resides, in the same manner as required by the seventh section of this act; together with a full and complete description thereof, the county wherein the same is situated, if known,—otherwise the former land district,—the name of the original grantee, the class to which the claim belongs, the stream upon which it lies; and when portions only of a grant are rendered, or if personal property, such description as may make its identification easy. And in any case, when in consequence of a vague or imperfect description of property so rendered, the same cannot be identified, and is sold by the assessor and collector of the county, the person making such vague or imperfect description shall be required to redeem, as in other cases where sales are made of the property of delinquents. Person owning property in another county, may render in that of his residence, &c.

ART. 1970. [9] It shall be the duty of each assessor and collector of this State to make out a list of all personal property in his county, which has not been given in for assessment, according to the provisions of this act, and assess the same in the name of the owner, if he be known; and if not, then it shall be assessed by description of the property, owner unknown; and the value of all such property shall be determined by the assessor and collector, who shall assess the same at its cash valuation, and no more; and the same may be sold as in other cases if the tax be not paid in the time prescribed by law. On personal property not given in.

ART. 1971. [10] The assessor and collector of taxes shall, in each and every

Three copies of assessment rolls shall be made out, &c.

year, make out, in alphabetical order, three full and complete copies of his assessment roll, setting forth, in separate columns, the different descriptions of taxable property, real and personal, rendered for taxation, owned or held by any person, firm, or corporate body in his county, and the value thereof; the amount of taxes due thereon; and also a list of unrendered personal property, made as required by the ninth section of this act; one copy of which he shall retain for his own use, one he shall deposit in the office of the Clerk of the County Court of his county, and one he shall cause to be deposited in the office of the Comptroller of public accounts on or before the first day of July in each and every year.

Where person or prop'rty have not been assessed for any past year.

ART. 1972. [12] Whenever any assessor and collector shall ascertain that any taxable inhabitants, lands, town lots, or personal property have not been assessed for any past year, he shall assess the same in his next assessment roll, at the same rate under which such inhabitants and property should have been assessed for such year; and such assessment shall be entered at the end of the assessment roll, stating the years for which such inhabitants or property should have been assessed; and the taxes thereon shall be collected in the same manner as other assessments.

Forms and instructions of Comptrol'r shall be used, &c.

ART. 1973. [13] Every assessor and collector of taxes, in the execution of the duties of his office shall use the forms and pursue the instructions of the Comptroller of public accounts; and after his assessment roll has been completed, upon notification being made to the Chief Justice, by the assessor and collector, it shall be the duty of said Chief Justice of the county to hold a special term of the County Court to examine the same; and after comparing it with the sworn inventories of property rendered, which shall be filed in the office of the Clerk of the County Court; and finding the same correct and true according to the inventories sworn to as required by law, said court shall certify that the assessment made, and the roll deposited in the County Clerk's office of the county is a fair, correct and true assessment thereof. Upon the production of which certificate to the Comptroller, together with the roll, such assessor and collector shall receive a compensation on the amount of the assessment for the use of the State, of eight per cent. upon all sums of one thousand dollars and less; five per cent. upon all sums less than two thousand dollars and more than one thousand dollars; four per cent. on all sums less than five thousand dollars and more than two thousand; three per cent. on all sums less than ten thousand dollars and more than five thousand dollars; and for all sums more than ten thousand dollars, one per cent. upon the amount thereof; and shall receive upon the assessment amount made for the county, one-half of the like per cent.

Compensation for collecting State tax.

For collecting county tax.

Comptrol'r shall compare assessment rolls with abstracts from Land Office, &c.

ART. 1974. [19] It shall be the duty of the Comptroller, upon the receipt of the assessment rolls of the several counties of the State, to proceed to compare said rolls with the abstracts from the General Land Office, filed with him, as required by the provisions of the fourteenth section of this act, and with the maps as furnished by the assessors, and subtract therefrom such tracts, or portions of tracts of land and town lots as may have been rendered, for assessment, to the assessors and collectors, reported by them; and if there shall remain any tract or portion of a tract of land which has not been rendered and assessed, it shall be the duty of the Comptroller to assess the same at the average rate of the land rendered in the county where it is situated; and if town lots, at the average rate of lots rendered for assessment in the town or city in which the same may be situated, and forward it to the assessor and collector of said county, whose duty it shall be, on a failure of payment of the taxes thus assessed, at the time required by the provisions of this act, to levy thereon by virtue of such assessment so made as aforesaid, and sell as directed in other cases: provided, it shall be lawful for any person or persons, non-resi-

Comptrol'r shall assess land at the average value, &c., when

dents of this State, who may own lands or other property liable to taxation, to pay all taxes due upon such property to the Comptroller: provided however, that the tax on said property be paid to said Comptroller on or before the first day of December next after the assessment thereof; and it shall be the duty of the Comptroller to furnish a list of all such taxes so paid to him, together with the names of the persons paying the same, to the assessor and collector of the county for which such taxes were paid, before the first of March thereafter. Non-residents may pay taxes to Comptroller.

Art. 1975. [31] If, from any cause, the direct taxes of any county are not assessed and collected within the period mentioned in this act, the Comptroller shall appoint some other time within which said taxes shall be assessed and collected, and no person shall suffer any of the penalties herein imposed from any failure, caused by such unavoidable change of time; but any person who shall fail to render his or her assessment list, and pay their taxes, within the period so designated by the Comptroller, shall incur all the penalties of this act. If assessment be not made within the time prescribed.

V. COLLECTION OF TAXES.

Art. 1976. [15] Every Assessor and Collector of Taxes, after he has made out and returned the assessment-roll of his county, as required by the provisions of this act, between the first of October and the first of March, shall proceed to collect the taxes therein mentioned; and for that purpose shall call at least once upon every person taxed, or on the agent or attorney of such person, at the usual place of his or her residence, and demand the payment of the taxes charged upon his or her person or property, if the party is to be found; and if not, then a written demand, specifying the amount of taxes due, left at the residence with some member of the family over fourteen years of age, shall be sufficient demand. Within what time Assessor shall collect, etc.

Art. 1977. [16] If any person shall fail or refuse to pay the taxes imposed upon him and his property by law, until the first day of March, next succeeding the return of the assessment-roll of his county, to the Comptroller, the Assessor and Collector shall, by virtue of his tax-list, levy upon so much property liable to taxation, belonging to such person, if to be found in his county, as may be sufficient to pay his or her taxes: provided, however, that if such person, his agent or attorney, shall point out to the Assessor and Collector sufficient property belonging to the party assessed, in said county, to pay said taxes, then the Assessor and Collector shall levy upon the property so pointed out; and in case the property levied on is about to be removed out of the county, the Assessor and Collector shall proceed to take into his possession, so much thereof as will pay the taxes assessed and the costs of collection. When levy on property shall be made. Person taxed may point out property, etc.

Art. 1978. [17] Every Assessor and Collector of Taxes shall give notice of the time and place of the sale of property so levied on, at least thirty days previous to the day of sale, by advertisement in writing, to be posted up, one on the courthouse door of his county, and in two other public places in his county; and such sale shall take place at the courthouse door of the county in which the assessment is made, by public auction; and if the property so levied upon prove to be insufficient to satisfy the taxes due and costs of sale, the Assessor and Collector shall levy upon and sell so much other taxable property belonging to such person, as will be sufficient to satisfy such tax, in the manner prescribed in the preceding part of this section: provided, that when land is offered for sale, and any person or persons shall offer at the sale to pay the dues thereon, aforesaid, for less than the whole quantity of the tract of land advertised, then Sale for taxes.

it shall be stricken off to the lowest bidder; and the part or parcel sold (if less than the entire tract advertised?) shall oe laid off in a square, beginning at the original beginning corner of said tract.

Tax deed shall be *prima facie* evidence, etc., provided.

ART. 1979. [18] The Assessor and Collector shall, when any property has been sold for the payment of taxes, make and execute a deed for said property to the person or persons purchasing the same; which, when recorded according to law, shall be *prima facie* evidence that all the requisitions of the law have been complied with, in making such sale: provided, however, that the owner of such property shall have the right to redeem the same at any time within two years of the day and date of sale thereof, upon paying to the purchaser or assessor and Collector selling the same, or his successor in office, double the amount of taxes for which the same was sold, together with the costs of sale.

Owner may redeem, etc.

Tax on part of lot or tract of land may be received, provided.

ART. 1980. [20] It shall be the duty of the Assessor and Collector, or the Comptroller, as the case may be, to receive the tax on the part of any lot, piece or parcel of land charged with taxes: provided the person paying such taxes shall furnish the Assessor and Collector, or Comptroller, with a particular specification of such part; or if the part on which the tax shall be so paid, be an undivided share, shall state to the Assessor and Collector, or the Comptroller, as the case may be, who the owner of such share is, that it may be excepted in case of sale for tax on the remainder.

Currency receivable for taxes.

ART. 1981. [21] The Assessors and Collectors of Taxes in the State of Texas shall receive, in payment of all taxes imposed, according to law, all coins made current by the laws of the United States, at the rates thereby established.

County taxes collected by Comptroller, or paid to him.

ART. 1982. [23] It shall be the duty of the Comptroller, to pay over to the Assessor and Collector of the county entitled to receive the same, all taxes paid into the treasury under the provisions of the nineteenth and twenty-second sections of this act; and that it shall be the duty of the Assessor and Collector so receiving the same, to account and pay over to the County Treasurer of such county, the amount of tax so received by him as aforesaid.

Where sale does take place at the time appointed.

ART. 1983. [32] If, from any cause, the sale of property seized for taxes shall not take place at the time first appointed, the Assessor and Collector shall appoint some other time, give the like notice, and proceed to sell such property in the manner prescribed in the first instance in this act.

When Assessor shall bid off, &c., for the State.

ART. 1984. [34] When any land or tenement shall be advertised for sale by the Assessor and Collector of Taxes, for any taxes accruing to the State, and such lands or tenements cannot be sold for the want of bidders, it shall be the duty of the Assessor and Collector to bid off the same for the State, for the amount of taxes due; and such lands may be redeemed within two years from the date of sale, by the owner or owners, or some other person for him, paying the amount of taxes, and one hundred per centum thereon, together with costs of sale. When property has been sold for the taxes of any year, and purchased by the State, and remains unredeemed, such property shall not be again assessed or sold for the taxes of any succeeding year; but on the redemption of said property by the owner, he shall be required to pay the taxes which would have accrued on said property, for each successive year, as though the same had been regularly assessed.

Same may be redeemed.

Act of Feb. 9th, 1854. Took effect from passage.

Assessor shall return statemeut every three months to Comptroller, of

ART. 1985. [1] It shall be the duty of every Assessor and Collector, to forward to the Comptroller, every three months, a statement in writing of all monies collected by him for State taxes, and for county taxes on property in counties other than his own, giving the names of persons from whom such taxes were received; and he shall, at all times, pay any drafts drawn on him by the Comptroller or Treasurer, whenever he shall have funds of the State in his hands; and he shall, on or before the first day of June in each and every year, pay over to the Treasurer of the State, all moneys collected by him for State taxes and for county taxes, on property in counties other than his own: it shall also be the duty of every Assessor and Collector, every three months, to return to the County Treasurer of his county, a statement in writing of all amounts collected for county taxes on property situated in his county, with the names of the persons from whom received, distinctly specifying in the said statement, what amounts were received in money, and who from, and what amount in county liabilities which are by law receivable in payment of county taxes, and who from; and he shall also pay over to the County Treasurer of his county, every three months, all county taxes collected by him on property situated in his county, in the money and county liabilities received by him as aforesaid, in the proportion that he received the same from the tax-payer, and on his assessment of taxes for counties other than his own county. The Assessor and Collector shall assess and collect a county tax of one-half of the State tax; and on failure of the said Assessor and Collector to make out and return the statement, and pay over to the County Treasurer, as above provided, such Collector and his sureties shall be liable to be sued upon their bond or bonds, for the damages sustained by any party interested. taxes received, etc. Same to County Treasurer. &c. County tax, amount of, &c.

VI. TAX ON VOCATION OR CALLING.

Art. 1986. [29] Any person wishing to engage in any vocation or calling on which a tax is imposed by law, shall, before engaging therein, pay to the Assessor and Collector of the county in which such vocation or calling is intended to be pursued, the amounts of the tax imposed for the use of the State, and to the County Treasurer, the tax imposed for the use of the county, by the County Court; and the receipt therefor shall entitle such person, on application to the County Clerk, to a license to pursue such vocation or calling during such period, authorized by law, as may be covered by the amounts of said receipt; provided, that when a license to pursue any vocation or calling is desired for a shorter period than one year, and not less than four months, the Assessor and Collector, or the County Treasurer, may receive the amount required, in proportion to the time for which such license is desired; and on filing the receipt of the Assessor and Collector, or the County Treasurer, the Clerk shall issue a license for the time corresponding with the amount which has been paid. Act of February 11, 1850. Took effect from passage. Shall be paid before engaging in.

Art. 1987. [30] When any person shall fail or refuse to pay the tax contemplated by the preceding section of this act, before engaging in any vocation or calling on which such tax is imposed, it shall be the duty of the Assessor and Collector, forthwith, to levy on any property of such person to be found within his county, sufficient to pay the amount of such tax for one year, and all costs; and sell the same at public auction to the highest bidder, for cash, after advertising the same for ten days, by putting up a notice thereof at the court-house door. Where person fails to pay tax on vocation.

VII. GENERAL PROVISIONS.

Art. 1988. [14] It shall be the duty of the Commissioner of the General Land Office to have made out and prepared, from the records and surveys on file in his office, a full and perfect abstract of all the lands, titles or surveys in the State, designating the grantee, the amount of the grant, the class to which

Abstract of all the lands, titles, &c., in the State shall be made out by Commissioner of Land Office, and kept in Comptroller's office.

each belongs, whether headright, bounty, donation or special grant, and the county in which situated; which abstract shall be made up to the first of January, 1851, and deposited in the office of the Comptroller; and on the first day of January in each and every year thereafter, all patents issued and surveys returned during the preceding year shall be furnished by the Commissioner of the General Land Office, and added to said abstract; and for the compilation of which abstract the Commissioner aforesaid shall be authorized to employ such assistance as may be necessary to carry into effect the object of this section; and the Assessors and Collectors shall, in like manner, furnish the Comptroller with maps of the several cities and towns in their respective counties.

Assessors shall furnish maps, &c.

If any officer be sued for any proceeding under authority of this act, &c.

ART. 1989. [33] If any officer is sued or prosecuted in consequence of proceedings made by him, under the authority of this act, or any law in force for the collection of revenue, it shall be lawful for him to plead the general issue, and give this act, or the law under which he has proceeded, as an especial matter in evidence, on the trial of such suit or prosecution.

TOLL-BRIDGES.

Act of Dec. 20, 1836. Took effect from passage. County Court may contract for building of, in certain cases.

ART. 1990. [20] The County Courts through whose county large creeks or water courses shall pass, over which it may be too burdensome for the overseers, with the hands apportioned to them to work on roads, to build bridges, may contract with a proper person or persons to build a toll-bridge, for which the Court shall lay the toll to be levied on all persons, cattle, horses, carriages, &c., passing over the same; to be granted to the undertaker for such a number of years as the said Court may think proper, not to exceed ten years; and the builder or builders, and their successors, shall keep the bridge in constant repair during the term of the contract, and in default thereof shall forfeit all right and claim to the toll of such bridges.

Shall take security from contractors to keep bridge in repair.

ART. 1991. [21] The County Court before granting a license to any person to build a toll-bridge, shall take bond in the sum of one thousand dollars, with good and sufficient securities, conditioned that the undertaker or undertakers shall build and keep in constant repair the bridges so contemplated, for the term of years agreed upon between the undertaker or undertakers and the Court; and if any person or persons shall sustain damages in consequence of the owner or keeper of any toll-bridge not having complied with the conditions of his bond, the person or persons so damaged may bring an action of debt against the owner or keeper of such toll-bridge, on his or their bond, in the name of the Judge of the County Court and his successors in office, of the county in which such license was granted, and recover judgment for the damages so sustained, in the manner prescribed by the seventeenth section of this act.

TOWNS AND CITIES.

I. TOWNS.

Act of Jan. 27, 1858. Took effect from passage.

May be incorporated, when.

ART. 1992. [1] Where a village may contain three hundred free white inhabitants, it may be incorporated as a town, in the manner prescribed by this act.

Mode of proceeding.

ART. 1993. [2] If the inhabitants of such village desire to be so incorporated, at least twenty residents thereof, who would be qualified voters under the provisions of this act, shall file an application for that purpose in the office of the Chief Justice of the County Court of the county in which the village is situated, stating the boundaries of the proposed town, and the name by which it is to be known, if it be incorporated.

County Court to order election to determine, &c.

ART. 1994. [3] If satisfactory proof is made that the village contains the requisite number of inhabitants, it shall be the duty of the County Court to make an order for holding an election on a day therein stated, and at a place designated within the village, for the purpose of submitting the question to a vote of the people.

Officers appointed to hold election.

ART. 1995. [4] The Chief Justice shall appoint an officer to preside at the election, who shall select two judges and two clerks to assist in holding it; and after a previous notice of ten days, by posting advertisements at three public places in the village, the election shall be held in the manner prescribed for holding elections in justices' precincts.

Qualification of electors.

ART. 1996. [5] Every free male person who has attained the age of twenty-one years, and who has resided within the limits of the proposed town for the six months next preceding, and is a qualified elector under the laws of the State, shall be entitled to vote at the election.

Tickets, how endorsed.

ART. 1997. [6] On each ticket the voter must write or cause to be written "corporation" or "no corporation."

Returns of.

ART. 1998. [7] If a majority of the votes are cast in favor of incorporation, the officers holding the election, shall make return thereof to the Chief Justice of the county within ten days after the same was held.

Duty of Chief Justice to make an entry, &c., when.

ART. 1999. [8] The Chief Justice shall, within twenty days after the receipt of the returns, make an entry upon the records of the County Court, that the inhabitants of the town are incorporated within the boundaries thereof, which shall be also designated in the entry, and a certified copy of such entry shall thereupon be recorded in the proper record of deeds of such county.

Powers of corporation.

ART. 2000. [9] When the entry mentioned in the preceding section has been made, the town shall be invested with all the rights incident to such corporations under this act, and shall have power to sue and be sued, plead and be impleaded; and to hold and dispose of real and personal property. Provided, such real property is situated within the limits of the corporation.

Election of Mayor, &c.

ART. 2001. [10] The Chief Justice shall immediately order an election for a Mayor, a Constable and five Aldermen.

Who are eligible for offices.

ART. 2002. [11] No person shall be eligible to any of said offices, nor shall any person be qualified to vote at any election to fill any of them, unless he possesses the requisites prescribed by the fifth section of this act.

Commission of Mayor, &c.

ART. 2003. [12] The Chief Justice shall, immediately after the returns have been made, commission the candidate who received the highest number of votes for the office of Mayor, and shall deliver certificates of election to the other officers elected.

Officers—term of office.

ART. 2004. [13] The Mayor and Constable elected shall hold their respective offices until the first regular election for county or State officers, and until their successors are qualified. The Aldermen shall hold until a sufficient number of the members elected to succeed them shall qualify, to form a quorum for the transaction of business.

Annual election of officers.

ART. 2005. [14] The Chief Justice shall order an election for such officers at every general election, which shall be held in each year after the town has been incorporated, and the officers elected shall be commissioned and receive certificates of election as prescribed by section twelve, and shall continue to discharge their duties for one year, or until another general election for county or State officers, and their successors are qualified as prescribed by the preceding section.

Contested election, how determined.

ART. 2006. [15] The Chief Justice of the county shall determine all cases of contested elections held under this act; and the proceedings, in the event of such a contest, shall be such as are prescribed in cases of contests for county offices, by the act regulating elections.

1. *Powers and duties of the Board of Aldermen.*

Quorum may pass by-laws.

ART. 2007. [16] The Mayor shall be the President of the Board of Aldermen, and shall, with three of the Aldermen, constitute a quorum for the transaction of business; and the quorum shall have power to enact such by-laws and ordinances not inconsistent with the laws and constitution of the State, as shall be deemed proper for the government of the town.

ART. 2008. [17] The Board of Aldermen shall have and exercise control over the streets and other public places in the town; they shall, as far as practicable, prevent any nuisances within the limits of the corporation, and cause such as exist to be removed, at the expense of the persons by whom they were occasioned, or upon whose property they may be found; they may establish and regulate markets, and may do whatever else may be necessary to give effect to the provisions of this act. May prevent and remove nuisances, regulate markets, &c.

ART. 2009. [18] The Board of Aldermen shall have power to levy taxes on persons and property, real and personal, within the town, subject to taxation by the laws of the State; but the tax on persons or property, shall not in any one year, exceed the rate of fifty cents on the one hundred dollars. May levy a tax annually.

ART. 2010. [19] The Board of Aldermen shall have power to prescribe the fine to be imposed by the Mayor for a violation of any by-law or ordinance, which shall in no case exceed one hundred dollars; but no fine shall be imposed except upon the verdict of a jury, should the defendant demand a trial by jury. Aldermen may prescribe the fine, &c.

ART. 2011. [20] When a vacancy shall occur in any of the offices created by this act, or by the Board of Aldermen under its provisions, the acting Aldermen shall fill such vacancy for the unexpired term. Vacancies, how filled.

ART. 2012. [21] The Board of Aldermen shall have power to appoint such officers, other than those mentioned in this act, as shall be deemed necessary to carry out the provisions of the same, to prescribe the duties, and to fix their compensation; and shall also have power to dismiss them at any time, and appoint others in their stead. Additional officers may be appointed.

ART. 2013. [22] The Board must prescribe the bonds and security which the Constable and such other officers as may be appointed, shall give; which shall be executed and approved by the Mayor, before the Constable or other officer shall enter upon the discharge of his duties. Said bond shall be made payable to the Corporation. Board must prescribe amount of bonds, &c.

ART. 2014. [23] If the bond required by the preceding section, is not given within five days after the Constable is elected, or the officer appointed, the Board shall have the power to appoint another Constable or officer in the place of the one so elected or appointed. If bond is not given in five days after, &c.

2. *Duties of the Mayor.*

ART. 2015. [24] The Mayor of a town incorporated under the provisions of this act, shall have the same jurisdiction and power in cases both civil and criminal, that are conferred on Justices of the Peace, and his judgments and final orders therein may be revised in the manner prescribed for revising such judgments and orders, when made in such cases by a Justice of the Peace. Jurisdiction same as Justices of the Peace.

ART. 2016. [25] It shall be the duty of the Mayor to enforce and carry into effect such by-laws and ordinances not inconsistent with the laws of the land, as the Board of Aldermen may from time to time enact for the better regulation of the police of the corporation. Shall enforce by-laws.

ART. 2017. [26] Where the penalty for a violation of a by-law or ordinance has not been fixed by the Board of Aldermen, the Mayor shall have power to enforce fines not to exceed twenty dollars. May fix penalty, when.

Party entitled to a jury when. ART. 2018. [27] In any case or proceeding before the Mayor of a town, any party who will deposit three dollars for paying the jury, or will make an affidavit to the effect that he is too poor to make such deposit, shall have the right to have any question of fact found by a jury.

Fines, how enforced. ART. 2019. [28] It shall be the duty of the Mayor to cause all fines to be enforced by imprisonment not exceeding fifteen days, and by execution against the property of the persons on whom such fines shall be imposed.

Fees of. ART. 2020. [29] The Mayor shall be entitled to such fees as may be allowed to Justices of the Peace for similar services, and to such additional compensation as may be allowed by the by-laws and ordinances of the corporation.

Powers, duties and fees of Constable. ART. 2021. [30] The Constable shall have the same powers within the town that other Constables shall have within their precincts, and shall be entitled to the same fees. He shall discharge all other duties that may be prescribed by the by-laws and ordinances, not inconsistent with the laws of the State, and shall receive therefor such fees as may be fixed by the Board.

Taxes, by whom collected, &c.—sale of property for, &c. ART. 2022. [31] The corporation tax shall be assessed and collected by the Constable, and if the same be not voluntarily paid, he shall have power to make the collection by levying upon, advertising, and selling property, real and personal, in the manner prescribed by the laws regulating executions: provided, that in all cases the property shall be sold within the limits of the corporation, and for cash without appraisement.

Real estate sold, may be redeemed, &c. ART. 2023. [32] Real estate sold for taxes due the corporation may, at any time, within two years from the date of the sale, be redeemed by the payment of the amount of the taxes and costs, for which the property was sold, with interest at the rate of twenty-five per cent. per annum, and all the taxes which have since accrued.

Where purchaser is a non-resident. ART. 2024. [33] Where the purchaser does not reside within the limits of the town, the estate may be redeemed by making the payment into the treasury of the corporation for the benefit of the purchaser.

Ordinance not to be enforced until. ART. 2025. [34] No ordinance or by-law shall be enforced until it has been published at least ten days in three public places in the town or in a newspaper if one be published in the corporation.

Where property is liable for taxes, and owner is unknown. ART. 2026. [35] When any property shall be liable to assessment for corporation taxes, and the owner is unknown, such property shall be valued by the Constable, and assessed by its description, stating that the owner of the property is unknown; unless the taxes are paid the property shall be sold for the payment thereof, as nearly as may be, in the manner in which such property, when duly rendered, is required to be sold, and the sale shall be equally valid.

II. INCORPORATION OF CITIES.

When incorporated as a city. ART. 2027. [36] When a village or town may contain fifteen hundred inhabitants, it may be incorporated as a city, in the manner prescribed in this act, for the incorporation of towns.

Administration of, invested in, &c. ART. 2028. [37] The administration of the fiscal, prudential and municipal affairs of every city incorporated under the provisions of this act, shall be vested in one Mayor and nine Aldermen, to be denominated the City Council.

ART. 2029. [38] The Mayor and Aldermen of a city, and a City Marshal, shall be elected by persons possessing the same qualifications which are required by the fifth section of this act, for electors of towns. Officers, by whom elected.

ART. 2030. [39] All provisions of this act shall apply as well to cities incorporated under it as to towns, and the powers, duties and terms of the Mayors and Aldermen of cities, shall be such as are prescribed for these officers of towns. Provisions of this act to apply to cities.

ART. 2031. [40] In addition to such powers as are by this act vested in a Board of Aldermen of a town, a city council shall have power on the written application of the owners of three-fourths of every square, to prohibit the erection of any except brick, stone, or concrete buildings within the square, and to borrow money on the credit of the city, but not without a direct vote of the people in favor of said loan. Auditorial powers of City Council.

ART. 2032. [41] In addition to the rights, powers and duties prescribed in this act, to town Constables, the City Marshal shall have such rights and powers, and discharge such duties as shall be prescribed by the by-laws and ordinances of the City Council, not inconsistent with the laws of this State. City Marshal.

ART. 2033. [42] The inhabitants of every incorporated town or city, may re-organize under this act, and avail themselves of its provisions, by complying with the regulations herein prescribed for the incorporation of towns and cities, which have not been previously incorporated: provided, that such re-organization shall be adjudged to be a renunciation of all the powers and privileges of the act of incorporation under which such town or city was previously organized. Inhabitants of a town or city may re-organize under this act, provided.

ART. 2034. [43] The act of incorporation under the provisions of this act, shall not be so construed as in any manner to affect the titles to land heretofore granted by the Government to the inhabitants of any town, but the lands so granted shall continue to be held and disposed of by the corporate authorities so created, for the use and benefit of the inhabitants of said town, for the purposes for which they were originally granted. This act not to affect titles to land in, &c.

ART. 2035. [1] Whenever any town or city, already incorporated, shall re-organize under the forty-second section of the act to which this is a supplement, it shall be in the power of the inhabitants, either to contract or extend the limits and boundaries of such town or city: provided, that no town (as defined in the act aforesaid,) shall contain more than twelve hundred and eighty acres, and no city shall contain more than one league and one labor. Act of Feb. 4th, 1858. Took effect from passage. Limits of town or city may be extended, provided.

ART. 2036. [2] The question of the re-organization of any town or city, under the provisions of the act aforesaid and of this act, shall be submitted to the inhabitants, and a vote taken thereupon, in the same manner as in case of original incorporation; and the tickets shall be endorsed—"For Re-organization," or "Against Re-organization." And the same rules shall apply to said election and subsequent proceedings as apply to original incorporations. A vote of shall be taken as to re-organization, &c

ART. 2037. [3] Whenever any town or city is re-organized pursuant to the provisions hereof, and of the act aforesaid, the corporation so re-organized shall succeed to all the rights of property and action which were previously vested in and belonged to the corporation to which it succeeds, and to the right to recover all unpaid taxes due to the old corporation; and it shall also be liable for and bound to satisfy all legal claims or demands, of whatever name or nature, existing against said old corporation at the time of the re-organization. Rights of town or city after re-organization.

TRESPASS TO TRY TITLE.

Act of Feb'ry 5, 1840. Took effect March 16, 1840. Form of action. Mesne profits. Writ of possession.

ART. 2038. [1] All fictitious proceedings in the action of ejectment shall be abolished, and that the method of trying titles to land or tenements in this Republic, shall be by action of trespass, wherein the real names of the plaintiff and defendant shall be used; and if the jury shall find for the plaintiff, they may, in the same verdict award damages for the mesne profits, and judgment shall be entered on such verdict, as well for the damages as for the recovery of the land; and the plaintiff shall, thereupon, be entitled to a writ of possession for the land, and an execution for his damages.

Plaintiff or attorney shall endorse on petition, &c. Shall be tried on the merits.

ART. 2039. [2] In actions of trespass brought to try titles to land, the plaintiff or his attorney, shall always endorse on the original and copy of his petition, that the action is brought as well to try the title as for damages; and the said action shall be tried on their merits conformably to the principles of trial by ejectment.(*a*)

Survey shall be ordered, when. Art. 2052.

ART. 2040. [3] In all actions commenced or prosecuted in any of the courts of this Republic, wherein the right or title to any lands or tenements shall come in question, the presiding Judge of the court wherein the same may be depending, in order for the better finding out and discovering the truth of the matter in difference, shall, either in chambers or in open court, at his own discretion, or on the motion of any of the parties to said suit, appoint a surveyor, who shall survey and return the same on oath at the next sitting of the said court; and if the court shall acquiesce in the return of the surveyor, given in on oath, as aforesaid, the same shall be allowed as evidence.

Where tenant is sued the real owner may enter himself, &c.

ART. 2041. [5] When a tenant is sued for lands of which he is in possession, the real owner, or his agent or attorney, may enter himself on the proceedings as the defendant in the suit, and shall be entitled to make such defence as if he had been the original defendant in the action.

Proof of actual trespass not necessary–certain rights not impaired by this act.

ART. 2042. [6] It shall not be necessary to prove an actual trespass on the part of the defendant to support this action, nor shall this act be so construed as to alter, impair or take away the rights of parties as arising under the laws in force before the introduction of the common law; but the same shall be decided by the principles of the law or laws under which the same accrued, or by which the same were regulated, or in any manner affected.

(*a*) In an action of trespass to try title, it is not material whether the plaintiff's title be a legal or an equitable title. The statute by directing that the action shall be tried "conformably to the principles of trial by ejectment," could not have intended to introduce all the incidents and consequences attached to that form of action in the common law. Its object was not to determine upon what character of title an action may be maintained; but simply to furnish a mode of procedure to ascertain in whom the property resides. Esterling *v.* Blythe, 7 Tex. Rep. 210.

An objection that the petition is not endorsed to the effect that the suit was brought as well to try title as for damages, cannot be taken in arrest of judgment. Shannon *v.* Taylor, 16 Tex. Rep. 413.

ART. 2043. [7] In all actions of trespass to try titles to lands, commenced within the time limited by law, the plaintiff shall proceed with all convenient expedition to the trial of the same; and in case a verdict and judgment shall pass against him in such action, such verdict and judgment shall not be conclusive and definite against the plaintiff, but at any time within one year, the said plaintiff, or any other person claiming under him, shall have a right to commence his action for the recovery of the said lands, *de novo*, and prosecute the same in the manner and with the expedition before directed; but in case a verdict and judgment again pass against such plaintiff, then such second verdict and judgment shall be finally conclusive on the part of every such plaintiff; and he shall be forever barred and excluded from any further action or suit for the recovery of the same lands, and the right of the defendant shall be thenceforth finally settled and established against such plaintiff, his heirs and assigns—excepting persons out of the limits of the Republic, who shall be allowed two years, and *femes covert*, who shall be allowed one year after discoverture, and persons under the age of twenty-one years, who shall be allowed one year after they come to full age, to prosecute their second action in the manner above directed.(*a*)

Plaintiff shall prosecute action with convenient expedition, &c.

May bring a second suit within &c.

Exceptions in favor of certain persons.

ART. 2044. [8] In any action of trespass to try titles, it shall be lawful for the defendant, at any time before the trial of said suit, to suggest to the court that he and those persons whose estate he has in the lands and tenements sued for, have had adverse possession of the same in good faith, for at least one year next before the commencement of such suit; and that he and those persons whose estate he has, have made permanent and valuable improvements on the lands sued for, during the time he or they have had such possession of the same; and the jury trying the suit, if they shall find for the plaintiff, shall at the same time, inquire if the suggestion so made be true or false—if false, they shall return a verdict as in ordinary cases, for the damages sustained—but if true, they shall assess the value of the improvements at the time of the trial, which have been made by the defendant, or by those whose estate he has, and shall assess the value of the land or tenements, without considering the increased value thereof by reason of such improvements as shall have been made by such defendant, or by those whose estate he has; and they shall also assess the value of the use and occupation of the said lands; and if the value of the use and occupation as assessed shall exceed the value of the improvements as assessed, the court shall render a judgment against the defendants for the excess.(*b*)

Where defendant suggests that he is a possessor in good faith, &c.

Art. 2048, 2051.

Damages, how assessed, &c.

ART. 2045. [9] In any suit where the value of the improvements so assessed shall exceed the value of the use and occupation, no writ of possession shall be issued for the term of one year after the rendition of the judgment, unless the plaintiff or his legal representatives shall pay to the clerk of the court, for the defendant, the excess of the assessed value of the improvements over the value of the use and occupation;(*c*) and if the said plaintiff, or his legal representatives, shall neglect, for the term of one year, to pay the excess in value of said improvements, and the said defendant, or his legal representatives, shall within six months after the expiration of said year, pay to the clerk of the court, for said plaintiff, the value of the lands or tenements as assessed by the jury,

Where value of improvements assessed exceed value of the use and occupation.

(*a*) It is no objection to the second action that the first was in the nature of a suit in equity to annul the defendant's title and recover the property—such suit being equivalent to an action of trespass to try title. Allen *v.* Stephanus, 18 Tex. Rep. 658.

(*b*) A party who takes possession under an executory sale and purchase of land, and makes valuable improvements, &c., and elects to be dispossessed rather than pay the purchase money, without showing, in truth, any defect in the vendor's title, cannot claim compensation for such improvements. Allen *v.* Mitchell, 13 Tex. Rep. 373.

It is not sufficient to allege that the defendant believed the land was vacant, without showing that he asserted or attempted to assert a claim of right by location, pre-emption or otherwise. Powell *v.* Davis, 19 Tex. Rep. 380. See Philips and wife *v.* Hill, 3 Tex. Rep. 397.

(*c*) The statute allowing full compensation for improvements, over and above the rents and profits, is not repugnant to the Constitution. Scott *v.* Mather, 14 Tex. Rep. 235.

The statute which secures the possessor of real property in good faith reimbursement from the true owner, for permanent and valuable improvements, is not unconstitutional. Saunders *v.* Wilson, 19 Tex. Rep [illegible]

then the plaintiff shall be forever barred of his writ of possession, and from ever having or maintaining any action whatever against the defendant, his heirs or assigns, for the lands or tenements recovered by such suit; and if the defendant, or his legal representatives, shall not, within the said six months, avail him, or themselves of the benefit of this act, the plaintiff, or his legal representatives, may sue out a writ of possession as in ordinary cases.

Persons out of the State, femes covert and infants shall have, &c.

ART. 2046. [10] Plaintiffs who are without the limits of this Republic, shall have two years to take the benefit of the provisions of this act; and plaintiff *femes covert* and minors, shall be allowed one year after their disability is removed, to take advantage of the same.

Act of Feb'ry 5, 1841. Took effect March 17, 1841.

What is suffic'nt title to maintain action of, &c.

ART. 2047. [1] All certificates for headrights, land scrip, bounty warrant, or any other evidence of right to land recognised by the laws of this Government, which have been located or surveyed, shall be deemed and held as sufficient title to authorize the maintenance of actions of ejectment, trespass, or any other legal remedy given by law; all laws to the contrary notwithstanding.(*a*)

Act of Feb'ry 2, 1844. Took effect Feb. 12, 1844.

If jury find the defendant a possessor in good faith.

ART. 2048. [1] In the trial of all actions of ejectment or trespass to try titles, after the passage of this act, if the jury find the defendant to be a possessor, in good faith, and a verdict go in favor of the plaintiff, for the lands or tenements sued for, the said plaintiff shall not recover pay for the use and occupation of the premises prior to the filing of the suit.

Plaintiff failing in the first, may bring a second action within a year from, &c.

ART. 2049. [3] Section seventh of "an act to provide the mode of trying titles to lands," be so amended as to allow the plaintiff, in case a verdict and judgment should pass against him, and he should determine to appeal to the Supreme Court, and the said Supreme Court should decide against said plaintiff, he the plaintiff shall have one year from the decision of said Supreme Court to bring a second action; and in case a second verdict and judgment should pass against the plaintiff, nothing contained in the act to which this is a supplement shall be so construed as to prevent an appeal from said second verdict and judgment.

Where defendant shows that plaintiff has failed to pay State taxes, &c.

ART. 2050. [4] Should the defendant in any action of ejectment or of trespass to try title, be able to show that the plaintiff has failed to pay the State taxes that may accrue on the lands in controversy, after the passage of this act, or that have accrued by assessments already made, the plaintiff shall forfeit all right to pay for "use and occupation;" and certificates of the Secretary of the Treasury, as to the returns of assessments made, or the want of assessments, in particular instances, or the neglect of payment of the amount assessed, shall be competent evidence, in the trial in all suits contemplated by this act: provided, that other testimony of a legal character shall not be excluded: provided, further, that the defendant, to entitle him to the benefits of this section, shall show that he has paid the taxes due on the land claimed by said defendant during his occupancy of the same.

Plea of "not guilty," only required

Where defendant claims possession in good faith, plaintiff may introduce evidence, &c.

ART. 2051. [5] The plaintiff or his attorney shall not be required hereafter to make any endorsements on the copies of petitions, nor shall the defendant be required to put in any other plea than the one of "not guilty:" and if the defendant, under a suggestion of good faith, introduce evidence as to the value of improvements, the plaintiff shall be permitted by way of rebutting testimony, to show the value of the lands in controversy, without taking into

(*a*) Hughes *v.* Lane, 6 Tex. Rep. 289. Jones *v.* Menard, 1 Tex. Rep. 771.

A survey unaccompanied by the certificate if not sufficient to support a suit. Hart *v.* Turner, 2 Tex. Rep. 374. Kemper *v.* Corporation of Victoria, 3 Tex. Rep. 159.

The authority to sue for land on which the plaintiff has a valid certificate is not a recognition of the fact that the fee, by such location, has passed from the State. It amounts to nothing more than this: that the person holding the incipient title shall recover against and hold against all who cannot show a better title, but does not conclude the State. Hart *v.* Gibbons, 14 Tex. Rep. 213.

consideration the increased value thereof by reason of such improvements as shall have been made by the defendant or those whose estate he has, or under whom he claims by purchase or otherwise; and also the value of the use and occupation of said lands.(*a*)

Survey shall be unnecessary when.

ART. 2052. [6] Where there is no dispute as to the lines or boundaries of the land in controversy, or where the defendant admits that he is in the possession of the lands or tenements included in the plaintiff's claim or title, an order of survey shall be unnecessary, any law to the contrary notwithstanding.

TRIAL OF THE RIGHT OF PROPERTY LEVIED ON.

Act of March 18, 1848. Took effect 29th April, 1848.

When property levied upon is claimed by any person not a party to the writ, &c.

ART. 2053. [1] Whenever any Sheriff or other lawful officer shall levy a writ of execution, sequestration, or attachment, upon any personal property, and such property, or any part thereof, shall be claimed by any person who is not a party to such writ, such person or his agent may make oath in writing, before some Justice of the Peace of the county where the levy was made, that such claim is made in good faith, and present such oath, in writing, to the officer who made such levy, and may also execute and deliver to the officer who made such levy, his bond with two or more good and sufficient sureties, to be approved of by such officer, payable to the plaintiff in such writ, for an amount equal to double the value of the property so claimed, to be assessed by such officer, conditioned that the party making such claim, in case he fails to establish his right to such property, shall return the same to the officer making such levy, or his successor, and shall also pay to the plaintiff in such writ, all damages that may be awarded against him, by the jury, on the trial of the right to such property; whereupon it shall be the duty of the officer receiving such oath and bond, to deliver such property, so claimed, to the person so claiming it.(*b*)

Proceedings where person claiming property makes oath, gives bond, &c.

ART. 2054. [2] Whenever any person shall claim property, and shall make the oath and give the bond, as provided for in the first section of this act, if the writ under which such levy was made, was issued by any Justice of the Peace or court of the county where such levy was made, the Sheriff or other officer receiving such oath and bond, shall endorse on the writ, that such claim has been made, and oath and bond given, stating by whom, and shall also endorse on such bond, the value of the property, as assessed by himself, and shall forth-

(*a*) Under the plea of not guilty the defendant may give in evidence any special matter of defence. Punderson *v.* Love, 3 Tex. Rep. 60. Hunt *v.* Turner, 9 Tex. Rep. 385.

(*b*) Huston *v.* Curl, 8 Tex. Rep. 239. The statutory mode is more simple, and less expensive, than an ordinary suit. Vickers *v.* Ward, 2 Tex. Rep. 312. The owner may interpose his claim under the statute; or he may resort to his common law right, and sue the Sheriff or the plaintiff, if the plaintiff caused the seizure. Moore *v.* Gammel, 13 Tex. Rep. 120. [See Latham *v.* Selkirk, 11 Tex. Rep. 314. Linn *v.* Wright, 18 Tex. Rep. 317.] It is not necessary that the affidavit should state the authority by which the property was levied upon or seized, nor the facts which constitute the claimant's right: it is sufficient for the affidavit to state that the claimant claims the property "as trustee," and that this claim is made in good faith. Wright *v.* Henderson, 10 Tex. Rep. 204. A third party claiming property levied on, cannot, after giving bond under the statute, sustain a distinct action to enjoin the sale, and for damages. Howeth *v.* Mills, 19 Tex. Rep. 295. It seems that giving of the bond to try the right of property levied on, is a waiver of the trespass, commited in making the levy; not merely as to the officer, but also as to the plaintiff in the execution, who directs the levy to be made. Ibid. The damages to be assesed by the jury, under this section, are commutative, and does not preclude the court from assessing damages under art.

with return such bond and oath to the Justice or the Clerk of the Court from which the said writ issued; but if the writ under which such levy was made, was issued by any Justice of the Peace or court of another county than that in which such levy was made, then the Sheriff or other officer receiving such oath and bond, shall endorse on such bond the value of the property, as assessed by himself, and shall forthwith return such bond and oath, with a copy of the writ, to some Justice of the Peace of his county, if the writ was issued by a Justice, or to the District Court of his county, if the writ was issued by any other authority than a Justice of the Peace; and he shall also endorse on the writ, that such claim has been made, and oath and bond given, stating by whom, and to what Justice or court the bond has been returned, and at what time it was so returned; and shall forthwith return such writ to the Justice or court from which it issued.

When oath and bond for trial of the right of property is returned to any other than a Justice's Court.

ART. 2055. [3] Whenever any oath and bond, for the trial of the right of property, shall be returned to any court other than a Justice's Court, as provided for in the second section of this act, it shall be the duty of the Clerk of such court to docket the same in the name of the plaintiff in the writ, as the plaintiff, and the claimant of the property as defendant; and at the first term of the court thereafter, if both parties appear, the court shall direct an issue to be made up between the parties, and tried by a jury, as in other cases;(*a*) but if the plaintiff appears and the defendant fails to appear, or neglects or refuses to join issue under the directions of the court, within the time prescribed for pleading, the plaintiff shall have judgment by default, as in other cases. If the plaintiff does not appear at the said first term, the case shall be continued to the next term, when, if he appears, the like proceedings may be had as at the said first term; but if he does not then appear on or before the first day of said term, he shall be non-suited: provided, that in all such cases, if the property so claimed was taken from the possession of the claimant, then the burden of proof shall be upon the plaintiff in the original writ of execution, sequestration, or attachment; but if the property so claimed, was taken from the possession of any other person than such claimant, then the burden of such proof shall be upon such claimant.(*b*)

When oath and bond for, &c., is returned to a Justice's Court.

ART. 2056. [4] Whenever any oath and bond for the trial of the right of property shall be returned, under the provisions of the second section of this act, to any Justice of the Peace, the plaintiff in the writ may, at any time, apply to such Justice for a citation against such claimant; and on the return thereof executed, a trial of the right to such property shall be had before such Justice, in like manner as other trials are had before Justices of the Peace; but if the property was taken from the possession of the claimant, the burden of proof shall be on the plaintiff; and if it was taken from the possession of the defendant in such writ, or any other person than the claimant, the burden of proof shall be on the claimant.(*c*)

Judgment against claimant for damages in case of failure, &c.

ART. 2057. [5] In all trials of the right of property, under the provisions of this act, if the claimant shall fail to establish his right to the property, the court or Justice trying the same, shall give judgment against all the obligors in the claimant's bond, for ten per cent. damages on the value of the property

(*a*) It is the duty of the court to direct an issue to be formed, so that it may appear from the pleadings, by what authority the plaintiff in the writ had caused the property to be levied on, and by what right the claimant resisted the execution of the writ. Wright *v.* Henderson, 10 Tex. Rep. 204. Linn *v.* Wright, 18 Tex. Rep. 317.

(*b*) Where property was levied on as the property of the husband, and was claimed by the wife, the return of the Sheriff was, that he levied on the "property on the premises of A B.," the husband, it was held that the burden of proof lay on the wife, the claimant. Lott *v.* Keach, 5 Tex. Rep. 394.

(*c*) It is competent for the court to assess ten per cent. damages under this article, in addition to those to be assessed by the jury under art. Latham *v.* Selkirk, 11 Tex. Rep. 314. The judgment may be rendered by the court, without the finding by the jury of either the damages, amount of the execution, or the value of the property, and may properly be rendered against the sureties in the bond, although the bond was only conditioned for the return of the property, and payment of such damages as might be assessed by the jury, that being the condition presented by law. Ibid. [See Gilliam *v.* Henderson, 12 Tex. Rep. 47. Linn *v.* Wright, 18 Tex. Rep. 317.]

claimed; unless such value is greater than the amount claimed under the writ, by virtue of which such property was levied, in which case such damages shall be on the amount claimed under said writ.

ART. 2058. [6] In all trials of the right of property, under the provisions of this act, in any county other than that in which the writ issued under which the levy was made, the copy of the writ required to be returned by the Sheriff or other officer making the levy, shall be received in evidence, in like manner as the original could be. *When copy of the writ shall be evidence, &c.*

ART. 2059. [7] In all cases, when any claimant of property, under the provisions of this act, shall fail to establish his right thereto, and judgment shall be rendered against him, if he shall fail to return such property in as good condition as when he received it, to the officer from whose possession he received it, or his successor, within ten days after the rendition of such judgment, such officer, or his successor, shall certify such failure to the court or Justice by which such judgment was rendered; whereupon, it shall be the duty of the Justice or Clerk having the custody of such bond, to endorse thereon that it has been forfeited; when such bond shall have the force and effect of a judgment against all the obligors, for the value of such property, with legal interest thereon from its date, upon which execution may issue as on other judgments.(a) *Where judgment is against the claimant, and he fails to return the property within, &c.*

ART. 2060. [8] A claim made to property under the provisions of this act, shall operate as a release, by the claimant, of all damages against the Sheriff or other officer who levied on such property.(b) *Claim, &c., shall operate a release of Sheriff for damages.*

ART. 2061. [9] Proceedings for the trial of the right of property under the provisions of this act, shall in no case prevent the plaintiff in the writ from having a levy made upon other property of the defendant than that levied on and claimed, if it can be found. *Claim under this act shall not prevent a levy on other property.*

TRUSTEES FOR MEETING-HOUSES, ETC.

ART. 2062. [1] From and after the passage of this act, it shall be lawful for any denomination of Christians, or the citizens of any neighborhood in this Republic, to appoint a Board or Boards of Trustees, for meeting-houses, camp-grounds, parsonages, and school-houses. *Act of Jan'y 30, 1845. Took effect March 15, 1845. Board of, may be appointed.*

ART. 2063. [2] Each denomination shall be allowed to adopt its own method of appointing Trustees; and that when the citizens of any neighborhood shall be disposed to build a school-house, a public meeting of the citizens shall be called, by giving at least ten days' previous notice; said meeting shall choose a President and Secretary for the time being, and when the meeting is so organized, they shall proceed to elect by a majority of votes, in the manner they may think best, a suitable number of Trustees, not less than three nor more than nine; and a certificate of their election shall be made out and *Mode of appointing.*

(a) Lewis v. Taylor, 17 Tex. Rep. 57. Latham v. Selkirk, 11. Tex. Rep. 314.

(b) Wright v. Henderson, 12 Tex. Rep. 43. Gilliam v. Henderson, Ibid. 47

signed by the President and Secretary of the meeting, and shall within sixty days thereafter be forwarded to the office of Recorder for the county, in which such election shall have taken place; and in case an appointment of Trustees shall be made by any church or denomination of Christians, a like certificate of their appointment shall be made out and signed by the proper officer or officers of the church or denomination making the appointment, and be forwarded for record as above specified.

Certificate of, to be made out and recorded.

Vacancies, how supplied.

ART. 2064. [3] All vacancies in Boards of Trustees shall be filled by each body having jurisdiction in the case: provided, that when a Board of Trustees shall be dissolved by death, resignation or otherwise, it shall be lawful for the party having jurisdiction in the case, to appoint a new Board of Trustees, as provided for in the first section of this act.

Capacities and privileges of the Board of Trustees.

ART. 2065. [4] When a Board of Trustees shall be so constituted, they shall be considered in law and equity a body politic and corporate, capable of making contracts, of suing and being sued, of pleading and being impleaded, of receiving and holding, (in trust,) lands and other property for the purpose of building meeting-houses, camp-grounds, parsonages or school-houses, as the case may be, for the use and benefit of the church or people appointing them; and in all cases said Trustees shall be accountable to the power appointing them, for the faithful performance of their duty; and it shall be lawful for those having jurisdiction to remove them from office, at any time, for delinquent conduct.

Lands held for, &c., ex'mpt from taxation.

ART. 2066. [5] All lands (not exceeding ten acres in each case,) held by such Trustees, for any one or all of the purposes above named, together with the buildings, improvements and furniture belonging to the same, shall be held free from taxation until the Legislature shall otherwise direct.

Lands heretofore conveyed, &c., shall enjoy benefits of this act, provided.

ART. 2067. [6] All lands or other property heretofore conveyed to any church, or denomination of Christians, or association of the people, for the purposes above named, shall enjoy all the benefits of this act: provided, the amount of lands exempt from taxation shall not exceed ten acres in each case.

Other property of, to be given in for taxation, &c.

ART. 2068. [7] It shall be the duty of the President of the Trustees, as contemplated by this act, to give in the lands or other property for taxation, belonging to such Trustees, under oath, except such as are exempt by this act; and the right is hereby reserved to the Legislature, to make such alterations, modifications or restrictions of this act, as may seem to it, to comport with the public interest.

UNITED STATES.

I. JURISDICTION CEDED TO.

II. COAST SURVEY.

III. BREAK-WATERS, JETTYS, DAMS, ETC.

IV. MARSHAL AUTHORIZED TO USE COUNTY JAILS.

I. JURISDICTION CEDED TO.

ART. 2069. [1] The United States be, and they are hereby authorized and empowered to purchase, acquire, hold, own, occupy and possess such land or lands, within the limits of this State, as they shall judge it expedient and shall seek to occupy and hold, as sites on which to erect and maintain light-houses, forts, garrisons, military stations, magazines, arsenals, dock-yards, and other needful buildings, or any of them, as contemplated and provided in the Constitution of the United States; said purchases to be effected either by contract with the owner or owners of said land or lands, or in the manner hereinafter provided.

Act of Dec'r 19, 1849. Took effect from passage. May own land and erect light houses, forts, &c.

ART. 2070. [2] If the executive officer, or other authorized agent employed by the United States to make such purchase or purchases, and the owner or owners of the land or lands contemplated to be purchased as aforesaid, cannot contract or agree for the sale and purchase thereof, it shall be lawful for such officer, or other agent, to apply in writing to the Judge of the District Court of the county in which such land or lands, or the greater portion thereof, may be situated, to estimate the value of such land or lands, in the manner hereinafter mentioned, and to order a conveyance of the same to the United States, for the purposes aforesaid; whereupon it shall be the duty of said Judge, and he is hereby authorized and empowered, after reasonable notice given to said owner or owners, their legal representatives or guardians, to hear and finally determine the value of the land or lands in question, by a competent jury, under oath, to be summoned by the Sheriff, or other proper officer of said court, for that purpose; or by a committee of three persons, such as shall be agreed upon and appointed by the parties aforesaid—such committee, if agreed on and appointed as aforesaid, to be duly sworn faithfully and impartially to value the land or lands last aforesaid; and the value thereof being thus ascertained, to the satisfaction of said Judge, after survey thereof, duly made under the direction of himself, or by consent of said parties, and after such other proceedings in the premises as he shall deem right and proper, he shall order and decree the same to be conveyed in due form to the United States, to be held, owned, and possessed by them for the purposes aforesaid, and none other: provided, that the amount of such valuation, with the reasonable costs of such owner or owners attending such proceedings, shall be paid to him, her or them, or into said court for his, her or their use, before execution or record of said conveyance: and provided, moreover, that if it shall appear to said Judge, upon objection made by said owner or owners, their representatives or guardians, that the quantity of any given tract, parcel or extent of land, sought to be purchased as aforesaid, is greater than is reasonable, he may, in his discretion, refer the matter of such objection to the Governor of this State, for his determination.

May apply to District Court to fix the value of, &c., when.

Mode of proceeding in such cases.

ART. 2071. [3] If the executive officer, or other authorized agent employed by the United States to make such purchase, as contemplated in this act, shall be unable to ascertain who the real owner or owners of such land desired to be purchased, may be; or if it is uncertain in whom the title to such land may be, it shall be lawful for such officer or other agent, to apply to the Judge of the District Court, as contemplated in this act, giving a full description of the land; and after eight weeks' notice of such application shall have been given, by publication in some newspaper printed and published in the county where the land is situated; or in case there is not a newspaper published in

Where agent of, cannot find the owner of, &c.

the county, then in the newspaper published the nearest to said county, such Judge shall call a jury to assess the value of said land, and shall proceed thereon as contemplated in the second section of this act; and the amount of the value of land so ascertained, shall be paid into the Treasury of the State, there to be subject to the order of the owner or owners, when known; and the Clerk of the court shall make a conveyance of the land, under the orders of the court, which conveyance shall be as valid and binding as if the same had been made by the real owner of the land.

Governor may cede jurisdiction over.

ART. 2072. [4] Whenever the United States shall contract for, purchase, or acquire any land or lands, within the limits of this State, for the purposes aforesaid, in either of the modes above mentioned and provided, and shall desire to acquire constitutional jurisdiction over such land or lands, for said purposes, it shall and may be lawful for the Governor of this State, upon application made to him in writing, on behalf of the United States for that purpose, accompanied by the proper evidence of said purchase, contract, or acquisition, of record, describing the land or lands sought to be ceded, by convenient metes and bounds, in the name and behalf of this State, to cede to the United States exclusive jurisdiction over the land or lands so purchased or acquired and sought to be ceded to the United States to hold, use, occupy, own, possess, and exercise said jurisdiction over the same for the purposes aforesaid: provided always, the consent aforesaid is hereby given, and the cession aforesaid is to be granted and made as aforesaid upon the express condition that this State shall retain a concurrent jurisdiction with the United States in and over the land or lands so to be ceded, and every portion thereof, so far, that all process, civil or criminal, issuing under the authority of this State, or any of the courts or judicial officers thereof, may be executed by the proper officers thereof, upon any person or persons amenable to the same, within the limits and extents of the land or lands so ceded, in like manner or to like effect as if this act had never been passed—saving, however, to the United States security to their property within said limits and extent, an exemption of the same and of said land or lands from any taxation, under the authority of this State, whilst the same shall continue to be owned, held, used and occupied by the United States for the purposes above expressed and intended, and not otherwise.

Concurrent jurisdiction of State retained.

Act of Feb. 13, 1854. Took effect from passage.

When Governor may sell land of State, to, &c.

ART. 2073. [1] In all cases where the State of Texas may be the owner of the land which the United States may select, and wish to acquire and occupy for any of the purposes specified in the first section of the act to which this is supplemental, it shall be lawful for the Governor of this State to contract and agree for the sale thereof, and upon the payment thereof by the United States of the purchase money into the treasury of the State, it shall be the duty of the Commissioner of the General Land Office, upon the order of the Governor, to issue a patent to the United States in like manner as other patents are issued.

Governor to cede jurisdiction.

ART. 2074. [2] Whenever the United States shall become the purchaser of any land in the manner pointed out in the preceding section, and shall desire to acquire constitutional jurisdiction over the same, for any of the purposes specified in the first section of the said act to which this is supplemental, it shall be lawful for the Governor of this State to cede said jurisdiction to the United States in the same manner and under the same restrictions as by the fourth section of said act he is authorized to make such cession on lands acquired by the United States in the manner therein authorized.

II. COAST SURVEY.

ART. 2075. [1] Any and every person employed under and by virtue of an act of the Congress of the United States, passed February 10, 1807, and the acts supplementary thereto, concerning the United States Coast Survey, may enter upon lands within this State, and clear and cut timber upon the same, and may erect thereon any works, buildings, stations, monuments, signals or appendages requisite for the purpose of exploring, surveying, triangulation, leveling, or doing any other act requisite or proper to effect the objects of said acts of Congress, without being considered as a trespasser or trespassers: provided, no unnecessary injury be done thereby. Act of Feb. 7, 1853. Took effect from passage. Persons engaged in, may cut timber, &c.

ART. 2076. [2] If the parties interested, namely, the person or persons acting under or representing the Government of the United States in the said Coast Survey, on the coast of Texas, and the person or persons owning or possessing any land so entered upon and to which damage may have been done, cannot agree together upon the amount to be paid for the damages by doing any of the acts aforesaid, either of them may complain in a summary manner to the Chief Justice of the county in which said land is situated, who shall associate with himself two disinterested freeholders of said county, one to be named by each party interested, and the said Chief Justice and freeholders shall, upon hearing the parties and their evidence, and with or without view of the premises, as they may determine, proceed to assess, award and adjudge such damages as may have accrued to the owners or possessors of said land: provided, that said Chief Justice shall so soon as said complaint is made before him, fix a day and a place for the hearing thereof, of which the opposite party shall have at least ten days notice: and provided, further, that if said Chief Justice and freeholders cannot agree as to said damages, the decision of any two of them agreeing shall be their judgment or award. Damages for timber cut, how determined.

ART. 2077. [3] The said Chief Justice and freeholders, or the two of them agreeing, shall enter up in writing a brief statement of the matters in controversy before them, and also their judgment or award, which shall be signed by them or the two agreeing, and shall be within ten days thereafter filed in the office of the Clerk of the District Court of the same county, and upon satisfaction and payment of the said amount of damages, the same shall be conclusive evidence of the assent of said owners and possessors in the premises: provided, that either party shall have the right within ten days after the filing of such judgment or award in the office of said Clerk, to file objections to said judgment or award, of which a copy shall be issued by said Clerk and served upon the opposite party, whereupon the said judgment or award shall be suspended, and an issue shall be made up and a trial had, at the first succeeding term of said District Court, as in other cases: and provided, further, that unless said objections be filed within the said ten days, or satisfaction made of said judgment or award, execution may issue thereon by the Clerk of said Court as in other cases. Award of Chief Justice and freeholders to be filed, provided. When issue shall be made up and tried in District Court.

ART. 2078. [4] Any person or persons so entering upon any land as aforesaid, for the purposes aforesaid, may tender to the party injured sufficient amends for any damage done upon said lands, and if upon examination before said Chief Justice and freeholders as aforesaid, or upon the trial before the District Court as aforesaid, the damages finally assessed shall not exceed the amount so tendered, the person or persons so entering and making tender of amends shall recover his or their costs. Damages may be tendered by, &c., to party injured.

ART. 2079. [5] The costs on any proceedings by virtue of this act, shall be by analogy to the compensation for like services, performed by the same Costs same as for like services.

officers, the said freeholders to be allowed two dollars per day each for every day of necessary service they may perform.

Action for damages, when barred.

ART. 2080. [6] All complaints and actions against any person or persons, entering on any land as aforesaid, shall be forever barred, unless prosecuted within one year from the time the cause of such action or complaint occurred.

Penalty for defacing any signal, &c.

ART. 2081. [7] If any person or persons shall wilfully or wantonly injure, deface or remove any signal, monument, work, building or appendage to any of them used or constructed within the State of Texas, under and by virtue of the acts of Congress aforesaid, he and they shall be liable to indictment for the same, under this statute, for each and every such offence, and upon conviction thereof shall be sentenced to pay a fine not less than fifty nor more than five hundred dollars, one half of which shall go to the prosecutor, and the remainder to the State of Texas, or shall be imprisoned not less than one month, nor more than six months, or both, at the discretion of the jury, and shall also be liable for all damages sustained by the United States of America, by reason of any such injury, defacement or removal, to be recovered by action in any court of competent jurisdiction.

III. BREAKWATERS, JETTYS, DAMS, ETC.

Act of Jan. 8, 1856. Took effect from passage.

United States may erect, &c.

ART. 2082. [1] The United States may exercise all power, rights and privileges, necessary for the erection and construction of breakwaters, jettys, dams and other works for the improvement of harbors, bays, arms of the sea and mouths of the rivers in this State as the United States may deem proper, and to take from the public domain of the State, and from private individuals, on paying just compensation, all stones, timber and earth necessary for such purposes, and to enact all such laws, not being contrary to the Constitution and laws of this State, as may be found necessary and proper for the protection of such works when constructed: provided, the Governor of the State shall have notice of all such contemplated works before the same are commenced, and no work shall be commenced unless the Governor gives his consent to the same.

IV. MARSHAL AUTHORIZED TO USE COUNTY JAILS.

Act of Aug. 30, 1856. Took effect Oct 29, 1856.

May use county jail, &c.

ART. 2083. [1] It shall be lawful for the United States Marshal, for the district of Texas, to use the county jails of the various counties and penitentiary of the State, for the confinement of such persons as may at any time be in his custody, under process from any lawful tribunal or authority, whenever it shall be necessary for him to do so in the discharge of his official duties; and it shall be the duty of the Sheriffs and Jailors of the respective counties, having jails therein to receive such prisoners as may be delivered or tendered to them for safe keeping by the Marshal or his legal deputy, and to safely keep such prisoners until they shall be demanded by the Marshal or his deputy, or discharged by due course of law.

Jail fees shall be paid by.

ART. 2084. [2] The Marshal shall be directly and personally liable to the Sheriff and Jailors for the jail fees, to which they may be entitled for keeping such prisoners as may be committed to their custody by the Marshal or his deputy, under the provisions of this act: provided, that no Sheriff or Jailor shall be entitled to charge or receive any greater compensation for keeping prisoners committed to their custody by the Marshal or his deputy, than they may be entitled to charge and receive for receiving and keeping prisoners under other laws of the State—except when a guard or guards may be necessary, in which case the Marshal shall pay all such additional expenses. Compensation to Sheriffs.

Art. 2085. [3] Any Sheriff or Jailer, in whose county there is a jail, who shall refuse to receive into the jail of his county any prisoner tendered to him by the Marshal or his deputy, as contemplated by the provisions of this act, not having the excuse for such refusal, that there is not room in such jail for the confinement of such prisoner or prisoners, shall be considered guilty of a misdemeanor, and on conviction thereof in the District Court, shall be subject to a fine of not less than fifty dollars. Penalty where Sheriff refuses to receive prisoners.

UNIVERSITY OF TEXAS.

Art. 2086. [4] The President of the Republic be, and he is hereby authorized and required to appoint a Surveyor and have surveyed on and from any of the vacant lands of this Republic, fifty leagues of land, which is to be set apart and is hereby appropriated for the establishment and endowment of two colleges or universities, hereafter to be created; and that the President is hereby authorized to draw upon the Treasury of this Republic for such sum or sums of money as may be necessary for defraying the expenses to be incurred by locating and surveying said lands. Act of Jan. 26, 1839. Took effect from passage. Fifty leagues surveyed for two universities

Art. 2087. [5] Said Surveyor so appointed shall make out a complete description of the land so surveyed, and a neat and correct map of the same, and deposit them together with the field notes in the General Land Office of this Republic; and shall also take and subscribe to this oath or affirmation: I, A B, do solemnly swear (or affirm), that I have well and truly discharged my duties to the best of my knowledge, skill, and ability, and that the field notes and description of said land are as correct as I could make them, so help me God. Which said oath is to be taken before a Chief Justice of the County Court, and deposited in the Land Office; and the Surveyors of the different counties, to survey the lands contemplated by this act, shall take and subscribe the same oath, which shall be recorded in the Clerk's office of the County Court. Duty of the Surveyor, &c

Art. 2088. [6] None of the lands appropriated and set apart by this act for

Lands not to be disposed of except by lease, &c.

the purpose of education, shall be disposed of in any manner except by lease, until the expiration of three years, and none of said lands shall be disposed of by lease for a longer term than three years.

Joint Resolution of Feb. 1, 1850. Took effect from passage.

Defective survey of three leagues of the university lands provided for, &c

ART. 2089. WHEREAS, by an act, entitled "An Act appropriating certain lands for the establishment of a general system of education," approved January 26, 1839, authorizing and requiring the President of the Republic of Texas to employ some County or District Surveyor to survey fifty leagues from any of the vacant or unappropriated lands of the Republic, for the endowment of two colleges or universities; and, whereas, it is ascertained that the field notes of leagues numbers one, two, and three, university lands, purporting to have been surveyed in the district of Nacogdoches, in the year 1839, and now situated in the counties of Rusk and Smith, as represented on the map in the Land Office, have not been returned in accordance with the provisions of the above recited act; and, whereas, since the date of the aforesaid locations, the land above described, in consequence of there being no record, has been surveyed and recorded in the respective counties where the land is situated, and a number of said locations patented in good faith; Therefore,

[1] Be it resolved by the Legislature of the State of Texas, That the Commissioner of the General Land Office be, and he is hereby authorized and required to employ some competent surveyor to survey three leagues, from any of the vacant or unappropriated lands in the State, in lieu of said leagues numbers one, two, and three, university land, hitherto located in the district of Nacogdoches, and said surveyor shall be entitled to the same fees and governed in all respects by the provisions of the above recited act.

Commissioner of the Land Office to have three leagues surveyed, &c.

ART. 2090. [2] The Commissioner of the General Land Office be, and he is hereby, authorized and required to have surveyed the number of leagues named in the fourth section of the above recited act, provided the same has not been surveyed and returned to the Land Office according to law.

Appropriation for.

ART. 2091. [3] The sum of two hundred dollars, or as much as may be necessary, is hereby appropriated, and the Commissioner of the General Land Office authorized to draw upon the Treasurer of the State for the same, to carry out the provisions of this resolution.

Act of Feb. 11, 1858. Took effect from passage.

ART. 2092. WHEREAS, from the earliest times, it has been the cherished design of the people of the Republic and of the State of Texas, that there shall be established, within her limits, an institution of learning, for the instruction of the youths of the land in the higher branches of learning, and in the liberal arts and sciences, and to be so endowed, supported and maintained, as to place within the reach of our people, whether rich or poor, the opportunity of conferring upon the sons of the State, a thorough education, and as a means whereby the attachment of the young men of the State to the interest, the institution, the rights of the State, and the liberties of the people, might be encouraged and increased, and, to this end, hitherto liberal appropriations of the public domain have been made; and, whereas, the increasing population and wealth of the State, and the tendency of events, indicate the fitness of now putting that cherished design into effect, therefore,

University established.

[1] Be it enacted by the Legislature of the State of Texas, That there is hereby established, within this State, an Institution of learning, to be styled "The University of Texas," to be located at such place and in such manner as may be determined by law.

Appropriation of land and money for maintenance of.

ART. 2093. [2] The sum of one hundred thousand dollars of the United States bonds in the Treasury not otherwise appropriated, is hereby set apart and appropriated to the establishment and maintenance of the same. The fifty leagues of land, which, by the Act of January 26, 1839, entitled "An Act appropriating certain lands for the establishment of a general system of education," were set apart and appropriated for the establishment and endowment of two Colleges or Universities, are hereby set apart and appropriated to the establishment and maintenance of the University of Texas. There is hereby set apart and appropriated to the same purpose, one section of land out of every ten sections of land which have heretofore been, or may hereafter be surveyed and reserved for the use of the State, under the provisions of the act of January 30, 1854, entitled "An Act to encourage the construction of railroads in Texas by donations of land," and under the provisions of any general or special law heretofore passed, granting lands to railroad companies, and under the provisions of the act of February 11, 1854, granting lands to the Galveston and Brazos Navigation Company. The Governor of the State shall select the sections hereby appropriated, so that no sections selected shall adjoin, out of the lands now surveyed, as soon as practicable, and out of the lands hereafter to be surveyed, as soon thereafter as practicable, and shall cause a record to be made, in the Land Office of the State, of the sections so selected; and, thereupon, it shall be the duty of the Commissioner of the General Land Office to designate, upon his maps, the sections so selected as University lands. The sale of these sections shall hereafter be regulated by a special law. Governor shall select the sections appropriated, &c.

ART. 2094. [3] The control, management, and supervision of the University and the care and preservation of its property, subject always to the control of the Legislature, is committed to a Board of ten persons, to be styled "The Administrators of the University of Texas," which shall be composed of the Governor of the State of Texas, the Chief Justice of the Supreme Court of Texas, and eight others, who shall be appointed by the Governor, by and with the consent of the Senate, to hold office for four years, and until their successors are qualified. The Administrators shall receive no compensation for their services. Management of, vested in a Bord of Administrators—appointment of, &c.

ART. 2095. [4] The following branches of learning shall be taught at the University, viz: Ancient and Modern Languages, the different branches of Mathematics, pure and physical, Natural Philosophy, Chemistry, Mineralogy, including Geology, the principles of Agriculture, Botany, Anatomy, Surgery and Medicine, Zoology, History, Ethics, Rhetoric and Belles-Lettres, Civil Government, Political Economy, the Law of Nature, of Nations, and Municipal Law. What branches of learning shall be taught.

ART. 2096. [5] The religious tenet of any person shall not be made a condition of admission to any privilege or office in the University; nor shall any course of religious instruction be taught or allowed, of a sectarian character and tendency. The religious tenet of any person not to be made a condition of &c.

ART. 2097. [6] The Administrators shall have the power to appoint the President, Faculty, Instructors, and Officers of the University, and prescribe the course of instruction and discipline to be observed in the University. They shall fix the salaries of the President, Faculty, Instructors, and Officers of the University. Five of the Administrators, with the Governor or the Chief Justice, lawfully convened, shall be a quorum for the transaction of business. They shall meet at least once in every year, for the transaction of business, and shall keep a record of their proceedings. They shall have a Secretary, to be elected by them. They shall have power to make all regulations, which, to them, shall seem expedient for carrying into effect the design contemplated by the establishment of this University, not inconsistent with the laws of the State. Power of Administrators. Appointment of officers, &c.

ART. 2098. [7] The Administrators shall have the right of conferring, on any person whom they may think worthy thereof, all literary honours and degrees known and usually granted by any University or College in the United States or elsewhere. May confer degrees, &c.

Report of. ART. 2099. [8] The Administrators shall report to the Legislature, at each session, the situation of the affairs of the Un versity.

Instruction shall be free. ART. 2100. [9] Instruction at the University shall be free, and the Administrators shall prescribe what degree of proficiencies shall entitle students to admission.

Legislative committee. ART. 2101. [10] A committee, to be appointed by the Legislature at each session, shall attend the annual examinations of the students of the University, and report to the Legislature thereon.

Reasonable expenses of, &c., allowed. ART. 2102. [11] The reasonable expenses incurred by the Administrators and visiting committee, in the discharge of their duties, shall be paid out of the funds of the University.

Treasurer. ART. 2103. [12] The Treasurer of the State shall be Treasurer of the University funds.

Duty of Administrators after location of the University. ART. 2104. [13] So soon as the location of the University is determined upon, it shall be the duty of the Administrators to proceed to the construction of the necessary buildings, and for that purpose, shall procure the services of a competent architect, who shall superintend the work: such plan and design for the buildings shall be adopted, as shall be consistent with the addition of wings or other structures hereafter, without marring the architectural beauty and fitness of the whole. There shall be constructed suitable buildings for the accommodation of the Professors and their families. The contracts for the buildings shall require the performance of the work under ample security for its fitness and faithfulness.

Expenditure for buildings how made, &c., money how drawn. ART. 2105. [14] The expenditures of the University, for the construction of buildings, or otherwise, shall be made under the order of the Administrators; and when money is required for the payment of the same, it shall be drawn upon the warrant of the Governor, countersigned by the Secretary, upon the Treasurer, who shall pay the same out of the University funds.

WEIGHTS AND MEASURES.

Act of May 7, 1846. Took effect from passage. County Court to grant license, &c., to make, provided. ART. 2106. [3] The County Courts of the several counties of this State be and they are hereby authorized and directed to grant and allow a license to such suitable person or persons as they may think proper, to make and vend weights and measures agreeing with the standard furnished by the Governor, under such rules and regulations as they may think proper to prescribe: provided, however, that no such weights and measures shall be sold or distributed unless the same have been first examined and approved by the County Court, or some competent person under their direction and approval.

Legal standard. ART. 2107. [4] The standard of weights and measures adopted and now used by the Government of the United States be and the same is hereby declared the only legal standard of weights and measures for this State.

ART. 2108. [1] The Governor is authorized to procure at the expense of the State, a set of weights and measures in conformity with the standard now used by the Government of the United States, and to cause the same to be deposited with the Treasurer of the State, which shall be safely kept by him, and shall be the only legal standard of weights and measures within the State. Act of Feb. 13, 1858. Took effect from passage. Governor shall procure a set of.

ART. 2109. [2] The Governor is hereby authorized to cause correct copies of such weights and measures when procurred, to be made under such appropriate seal as he may adopt, and to deliver, or cause to be delivered, after the inspection and approval of some competent person by him appointed for that purpose, a full set of such weights and measures to the Chief Justices of the several counties, on their application, and at the cost and expense of their respective counties. Governor shall provide a set for each county.

ART. 2110. [3] The sum of ten thousand dollars, or so much thereof as shall be necessary, is hereby appropriated and set apart to pay the expenses of procuring such set of weights and measures and copies thereof, which may be drawn from the Treasury upon the order of the Treasurer. Appropriation for by State.

ART. 2111. [4] When such copies have been made it shall be the duty of the several County Courts of this State to appropriate a sufficient amount of money to enable the Chief Justice of the respective counties to pay for and procure a full set thereof for the use of their counties, and said Chief Justice shall take charge of and keep the same. Appropriation by county to pay for.

ART. 2112. [5] Any person desirous of having his weights and measures tested may have the same done by applying to the Chief Justice, who, if he find them correct shall seal them with a seal to be provided by the County Court for that purpose, on which shall be the capital letter T. and also the letter with which the name of the county begins. How tested, &c.

ART. 2113. [6] For testing any steelyard, balance or beam, the Chief Justice shall receive from the applicant a fee of fifty cents, and for every weight or measure ten cents. Fees of Chief Justice.

ART. 2114. [7] Any person who shall sell by any weight, balance or measure, that does not correspond to and agree with such copies, or who shall keep the same for the purpose of buying or selling, thereby shall forfeit and pay the sum of ten dollars for every month he may continue to keep the same, one-half of which shall go to the county in which such offence shall have been committed, and the other to the Chief Justice, and it shall be his duty to sue for the penalty incurred by the commission of every such offence. Penalty for selling copies that do not agree, &c.

ART. 2115. [8] If the Chief Justice shall fail to sue for any such penalty within three months after the same shall have been incurred, any other person may sue therefor and recover one-half thereof for his own use and the other for the use of the county. If Chief Justice fail to sue for penalty.

WILLS.

[*See Estates of Deceased Persons—Community Property.*]

Act of Jan. 28, 1840. Took effect March 16, 1840. Who may make a will.

ART. 2116. [1] Every person aged twenty-one years or upwards, being of sound mind, shall have power, at his or her will and pleasure, by last will and testament, in writing, to devise all the estate, right, title, and interest in possession, reversion, or remainder, which he or she hath, or at the time of his or her death shall have of, in or to lands, tenements, hereditaments, or annuities, or rents charged upon or issuing out of them, or shall have of, in or to any personal property whatever, so as such will and testament be signed by the testator, or by some other person in his or her presence, and by his or her direction; and, moreover, if not wholly written by himself or herself, be attested by two or more credible witnesses, above the age of fourteen years, subscribing their names in his or her presence.

Will how made.

Estates for life devisable.

ART. 2117. [2] When any person shall die seized of lands, held for the life of another, such person may, by his or her last will or testament in writing, made and proved as hereinbefore directed, for the devise of lands, &c., devise all his interest in such lands: provided, that if such person, so holding lands by the life of another person, shall not devise away such lands by his or her last will or testament, it shall descend to and vest in the executors or administrators of the person so dying, seized, and be assets in their hands subject to the payment of debts, legacies and distributions.

Revocation of.

ART. 2118. [3] No devise so made, or any clause thereof, shall be revocable but by the testator or testatrix, destroying, canceling, or obliterating the same, or causing it to be done in his or her presence, or by a subsequent will, codicil or declaration in writing, made as aforesaid; but every last will and testament, made when the testator had no child living, wherein any child he might have is not provided for or mentioned, if at the time of his death he leave a child, or leave his wife enceinte of a child which shall be born, shall have no effect, during the life of such after-born child, and shall be void unless the child die without having been married, and before he or she shall have attained the age of twenty-one years. When a testator shall have children born, and his wife enceinte, the posthumous child or children, if unprovided for by settlement, and pretermitted by his last will and testament, shall succeed to the same portion of the father's estate as such child would have been entitled to if the father had died intestate; towards which portion the devisees and legatees shall contribute proportionably out of the parts devised and bequeathed to them by the same will and testament.

Posthumous children.

Children born after making and publication of.

ART. 2119. [4] If a testator leaving a child or children born at the time of making and publishing his last will and testament, shall, at his death, leave a child or children born after the making his last will and testament, the child or children so after-born, if such child or children be unprovided for by settlement, and be pretermitted by the last will and testament, shall succeed to the same portion of the father's estate as such child or children would have been entitled to if the father had died intestate; towards raising which portion the devisees and legatees shall contribute proportionably out of the parts devised and bequeathed to them by the same will and testament, in the same manner as is provided in the case of posthumous children.

ART. 2120. [5] If any testator or testatrix shall or may devise and bequeath any estate of any kind, by last will and testament, to any person being a child or other descendant of such testator or testatrix, and such devisee or legatee shall, during the lifetime of such testator or testatrix, die testate or intestate, leaving a child or children, or one or more descendants of a child or children who shall survive such testator or testatrix, in that case such devise or legacy to such person so situated as above mentioned and dying in the lifetime of the testator or testatrix shall not lapse, but the estate so devised or bequeathed shall vest in such child or children, descendant or descendants of such legatee or devisee, in the same manner as if such legatee or devisee had survived the testator or testatrix and had died unmarried and intestate. Devisees and legacies not to lapse.

ART. 2121. [6] No nuncupative will shall be established unless it be made in the time of the last sickness of the deceased, at his or her habitation, or where he or she hath resided for ten days next preceding, except when the deceased is taken sick from home, and dies before he or she returns to such habitation, nor, when the value exceeds thirty dollars, unless it be proved by three credible witnesses, that the testator or testatrix called on some person to take notice or bear testimony that such is his or her will, or words of like import. Nuncupative will.

ART. 2122. [7] After six months have elapsed from the time of speaking the pretended testamentary words, no testimony shall be received to prove a nuncupative will, unless the testimony or the substance thereof shall have been committed to writing within six days after making the will. No testimony to prove after six months, unless.

ART. 2123. [8] No will in writing, or any devise therein of chattels, shall be revoked by a subsequent will, codicil, or declaration, unless the same be in writing. Revocation in writing.

ART. 2124. [9] Any soldier in actual military service, or any mariner or seaman, being at sea, may dispose of his chattels without regard to the provisions of this act. Soldiers and seamen.

ART. 2125. [10] If any person shall subscribe his name as a witness to a will wherein any bequest is given to him, if the will cannot be otherwise proved, the bequest shall be void, and such witness shall be allowed and compelled to appear and give testimony on the residue of the will, in like manner as if no such bequest had been made; but if such witness would be entitled to any share of the estate of the testator or testatrix, in case the will were not established, so much of his said share shall be saved to him, as shall not exceed the value of the legacy bequeathed. When witness is legatee or devisee.

ARU. 2126. [11] No nuncupative will shall be proved within fourteen days after the death of the testator, nor until those who would have been entitled by inheritance, had there been no will, have been summoned to contest the same if they pleased. Proof of nuncupative will

ART. 2127. [12] All original wills shall be recorded in the Clerk's office of the court wherein they are respectively proved, and shall remain there except during such time as they may be in any courts, having been removed thither for inspection by certiorari or otherwise, after which they shall be returned to said office. Wills shall be recorded.

ART. 2128. [14] Under the name of children are included descendants of

Children. whatever degree they be, it being understood they are only counted for the child they represent.

When father or mother may appoint trustee for estate of child.

ART. 2129. [16] Should any father or mother, in consequence of the idleness, dissipation or extravagance of his or her child or children, apprehend that his, her, or their estate will be squandered if left to their management or control, it shall be lawful for such father or mother, by last will and testament, to leave such estate in the hands of trustees, to be appointed by said will, which trustees shall have the entire management and control of said estate, the profit of which, after deducting expenses of said management, shall be paid over to the child or children entitled to the same for his, her, or their maintenance and support; and it shall be lawful at any time for the Court of Probate in the county where such estate may be situated, or where such trustee or trustees may reside, to take cognizance of the same, and to remove such trustee or trustees from the management of the same: provided, it shall be made to appear that such estate is wasted or improperly managed; and to appoint other trustees for the management thereof, taking bond and security from such trustees, in a sum at least equal to the value of such estate, for the faithful performance of the trust; and if the child or children entitled to such estate, or any part thereof, shall at any time make it appear to the satisfaction of said court that the causes for leaving said estate in trust no longer exist, and that there is no danger of its being squandered by idleness, dissipation, or extravagance, it shall be the duty of said court to dissolve said trust, and place the said estate in the hands of the person or persons who would have been entitled to the same had such trust not been created.

Proviso.

Act of July 24, 1856. In force from passage.

ART. 2130. [1] All persons are hereby authorized and permitted to dispose of their own estate, real or personal, by will or otherwise.

Act of Aug. 26, 1856 Took effect Oct. 25, 1856.

Separate property may be kept together.

ART. 2131. [8] The husband or wife may, by last will and testament, give to the surviving husband or wife the power to keep his or her separate property together, until each of the several heirs shall become of lawful age, and to manage and control the same under the provisions of this act, and such other restrictions as may be imposed by will. Provided the surviving husband or wife is the father or mother, as the case may be, of the minor heirs: and provided, further, that any child or heir entitled to any part of said property shall, at any time upon becoming of age, be entitled to receive his distributive portion of said estate.

WRECK MASTERS.

Act of April 30, 1846. Took effect from passage.

At least one, &c., appointed in each maritime county.

Shall give bond.

ART. 2132. [1] The Wreck Masters of the State of Texas shall hereafter be appointed by the Governor of the State aforesaid, who is required to appoint at least one and not over three persons, of good character, in each maritime county of the State, to act as Wreck Master or Masters within such county; and each person, so appointed, shall give a bond, with two or more good securities, for the sum of five thousand dollars, and conditioned for the faithful discharge of his duties; which bond shall be approved by the Chief Justice of the county from which the Wreck Master is appointed, before he shall be authorized to act as such.

ART. 2133. [2] It shall be the duty of each Wreck Master, so appointed, as soon as practicable after hearing of any wreck in his county, or the portion of it allotted to him, to repair to the place where such wreck has occurred, and if the property so wrecked be abandoned by its owner, or the agent, or factor of the same, or be found abandoned, no such person appearing, it shall be the duty of such Wreck Master to attend to the salving of such property, to use his best endeavors for the preservation of the same, and to attend generally to the interests of the owners of such property or whom it may concern; and such Wreck Master shall have the command and direction of all persons engaged in saving and preserving the property aforesaid. Duty of, after hearing of any wreck.

ART. 2134. [3] The Wreck Master aforesaid, shall in each county be controlled by the Board or Provisional Committee of Pilot Commissioners of the principal port of such county, if such there be, or in default of the same, by the Chief Justice of said county, under the regulation of existing laws. To be controlled by Pilot Commissioners, &c.

ART. 2135. [4] It shall be the duty of each Wreck Master to keep a true account of all property salved by him, or under his direction; to briefly note the circumstances under which it was saved, as well as the names of the persons engaged in salving, and the time that each was so employed, and other circumstances needful for the fair apportionment of salvage; of which, together with the account of sale and of proceeds, commissions, expenses, salvage, balance left, and the condition or disposition of the same, he shall, in due time, or so soon as required, make an abstract report to the Board, Committee, or Chief Justice, under whose control he acts; and he shall also, when required, report the same as well as any other needful information to the court or arbitration before which cases of salvage may come. To keep accounts, make report, &c.

ART. 2136. [5] Each Wreck Master shall take into his custody and attend to the safe keeping of all wrecked property salved by him, or under his direction, or found wrecked and abandoned in his county, or his portion of the same, and after the notice required by law, shall sell, or cause the same to be sold, at public auction, for the benefit of the owners or underwriters, and the salvors, to all of whom he shall faithfully account; and he shall receive a commission of five per cent. upon the amount of sales, after expenses are deducted, and before the part allowed for salvage is appropriated, with such reasonable expenses as may be allowed by the authority which controls him, or the court before which the case may come; which expenses may include the wages and mileage of a crier, at a rate to be fixed by said controlling authority, but no commission for selling, or any other, save that above provided for. To take possession of and sell all wrecked property. Commissions of, on, &c.

ART. 2137. [6] It shall be the special duty of each Wreck Master to prosecute, before the proper tribunal, any person or persons guilty of wasting or embezzling any property coming under the description of wrecked property; and any Wreck Master who shall know of any such offence, and not prosecute, as herein required, shall be subject to a fine not exceeding five hundred dollars, at the discretion of the jury, which may be recovered before any court having competent jurisdiction. Shall prosecute for waste or embezzlement of wrecked property.

THE PENAL CODE.

Act of Aug. 26, 1856. Took effect Feb. 1, 1857.

SECTION 1. This Code is hereby adopted, and shall be known as the Penal Code.

PART I.

GENERAL PROVISIONS RELATING TO THE WHOLE CODE.

TITLE I.

THE GENERAL OBJECTS OF THE CODE, THE PRINCIPLES ON WHICH IT IS FOUNDED, AND RULES FOR THE INTERPRETATION OF PENAL LAWS.

Design of the Code.

ART. 1. The design of enacting this Code is to define in plain language every offence against the laws of this State, and affix to each offence its proper punishment.

Object of punishment.

ART. 2. The object of punishment is to suppress crime and reform the offender.

No person can be punished unless offence is defined by, &c.

ART. 3. In order that the system of penal law in force in this State, may be complete within itself, and that no system of foreign laws, written or unwritten, may be appealed to, it is declared that no person shall be punished for any act or omission as a penal offence, unless the same is expressly defined and the penalty affixed by the written law of this State.

Act of Feb. 12, 1858. Took effect July 1, 1858.

ART. 4. The principles of the common law shall be the rule of construction, when not in conflict with the Penal Code or Code of Criminal Procedure, or with some other written statute of the State.

Act of Aug. 26, 1856.

In cases of conflict.

ART. 5. In the construction of this Code each general provision shall be controlled by a special provision on the same subject, if there be a conflict.

Where provisi'n is defective, &c.

ART. 6. Whenever it appears that a provision of the penal law is so indefinitely framed, or of such doubtful construction, that it cannot be understood, either from the language in which it is expressed, or from some other written aw of the State, such penal law shall be regarded as wholly inoperative.

Where offences are not provided for, duty of the Court.

ART. 7. Whenever a court trying an offence is of opinion that the law is so defective as to have no operation, or when it appears that there has been a failure to provide for any offence, or class of offences, which ought to be made punishable, the Judge of such court shall report the same to the Legislature at its next session, after such defect or omission shall have been discovered.

Attorney-General shall report defects to, &c.

ART. 8. It is also declared to be the duty of the Attorney-General to call the attention of the Legislature in his reports which are required by law to be made to the Governor, to any defects or omissions in the penal law which he may observe, and in like manner the District Attorneys shall communicate to the Attorney General such suggestions as they may deem important touching the same subject.

Act of Feb. 12, 1858. Took effect July 1, 1858.

General rule for construction.

ART. 9. This Code and every other law upon the subject of crime, which may be enacted, shall be construed according to the plain import of the language in which it is written, without regard to the distinction usually made between the construction of penal laws and laws upon other subjects, and no person shall be punished for an offence which is not made penal by the plain import of the words of a law.

Act of Aug. 26, 1856. Took effect Feb. 1, 1857.

ART. 10. Words which have their meaning specially defined, shall be understood in that sense, though it be contrary to their usual meaning.

Presumption of innocence.

ART. 11. Every person accused of an offence shall be presumed to be innocent until his guilt is established to the satisfaction of those whose province it is to try him.

Acts, &c., not punishable unless, &c.

ART. 12. No act or omission can be punished as an offence, unless the law making it penal was in force at the time when such act or omission took place.

When laws defining offences shall take effect.

ART. 13. No law of the Legislature defining an offence, or affixing a penalty thereto, shall take effect until after the expiration of sixty days from the day of the adjournment of the session at which such penal law was enacted.

Ignorance of.

After a law has taken effect, no person shall be excused for its violation, upon the ground that he was ignorant of its provisions.

Effect of modification of by subsequent laws

ART. 14. When the penalty for an offence is prescribed by one law, and is altered by a subsequent law, the penalty of such second law shall not be inflicted for a breach of the law committed before the second shall have taken effect. In every such case the offender shall be tried under the law in force when the offence was committed, and if convicted, punished under that law; except that when by the provisions of the second law, the punishment of the offence is ameliorated, the defendant shall be punished under such last enactment, unless he elect to receive the penalty prescribed by the law in force when the offence was committed.

Effect of repeal.

ART. 15. The repeal of a penal law, where the repealing statute substitutes no other penalty, will exempt from punishment all persons who may have offended against the provisions of such repealed law, unless it be otherwise declared in the repealing statute.

When new penalty is prescribed.

ART. 16. When by the provisions of a repealing statute a new penalty is substituted for an offence punishable under the act repealed, such repealing statute shall not exempt from punishment a person who has offended against the repealed law while it was in force, but in such case the rule prescribed in Article 14 shall govern.

Change of definition by subsequent.

ART. 17. If an offence be defined by one law, and by a subsequent law the definition of the offence is changed, no such change or modification shall take effect as to offences already committed; but all offenders against the first law shall be tried, and their guilt or innocence determined in accordance with the provisions thereof.

No previous offence committed or fine incurred shall be affected, unless.

ART. 18. No offence committed, and no fine, forfeiture, or penalty incurred under existing laws, previous to the time when this Code takes effect, shall be affected by the repeal herein of any such existing laws, but the punishment of such offences and the recovery of such fines and forfeitures shall take place as if the laws repealed had still remained in force; except that when any penalty, forfeiture, or punishment shall have been mitigated by the provisions of this Code, such provision shall apply to and control any judgment to be pronounced after this code shall take effect, for any offence committed before that time, unless the defendant elect to be punished under the provisions of the repealed law.

Not to be considered as creating cumulative penalties.

ART. 19. No penalty affixed to an offence by one law shall be considered as cumulative of penalties prescribed under a former law, and in every case where a new penalty is prescribed for an offence, the penalty of the first law shall be considered as repealed, unless the contrary be expressly provided in the law last enacted.

TITLE II.

DEFINITIONS.

Act of Aug. 26, 1856. Took effect 1st Feb., 1857. Definitions of terms.

ART. 20. The general terms "*whoever*," "*any person*," "*any one*," and the relative pronouns "*he*" and "*they*," as referring to these terms, include females as well as males, unless there is some express declaration to the contrary. The word "*man*," is used to signify a male person of any age; and the word "*woman*," a female person of any age.

Expressing relationship, state, condition, &c.

ART. 21. The use of any word expressive of the *relationship*, *state*, *condition*, *office*, or *trust*, of any person, as of "parent," "child," "ascendant," "descendant," "minor," "infant," "ward," "guardian," or the like; or of the relative pronouns "he" or "they," in reference thereto, includes both *males* and *females*.

What they include.

ART. 22. The use of the singular number includes the plural, and the plural the singular; and words used in the masculine gender include the feminine also, unless, by reasonable construction, it appears that such was not the intention of the language.

Of person.

ART. 23. Whenever any property or interest is intended to be protected by a provision of the penal law, and the general term "*person*," or any other general term, is used to designate the party whose property it is intended to protect; the provision of such penal law, and the protection thereby given, shall extend to the property of the State, and of all public or private corporations.

"Accused."

ART. 24. The word "*accused*" is intended to refer to any person who, in a legal manner, is held to answer for any offence, at any stage of the proceeding, or against whom complaint in a lawful manner is made, charging the commission of an offence, including all proceedings from the order for arrest to the final execution of the law, and the word "*defendant*" is used in the same sense.

ART. 25. A "*criminal action*," as used in this Code, means the whole, and any part of the procedure which the law provides for bringing offenders to justice; and the terms "prosecution," "criminal prosecution," "accusation," and "criminal accusation," are used in the same sense. Criminal action defined.

ART. 26. An accused person is termed a "*convict*" after final condemnation by the highest court of resort, which, by law, has jurisdiction of his case, and to which he may have thought proper to appeal. Convict.

ART. 27. The term "*criminal process*" is intended to signify any *capias*, *warrant*, *citation*, *attachment*, or other written order issued in a criminal proceeding, whether the same be to arrest, commit to jail, collect money, or for whatever other purpose used. Criminal process.

ART. 28. Except where a word, term, or phrase, is specially defined, all words used in this Code are to be taken and construed in the sense in which they are understood in common language, taking into consideration the context and subject matter relative to which they are employed. When construed in common language.

ART. 29. The word "*preceding*" means the next preceding, and the word "*succeeding*," the next succeeding, whenever used, to designate any particular Article, Chapter, or Title of the Code. Preceding.

ART. 30. The word "*writing*" includes *printing*, the word "*oath*" includes *affirmation*. Writing and oath.

ART. 31. The word "*signature*" includes the mark of a person unable to write his name. A mark shall have the same effect as a signature, when the name is written by some other person, and the mark made near thereto, by the person unable to write his name. Signature.

TITLE III.

OF THE PERSONS PUNISHABLE UNDER THIS CODE, AND CERTAIN CIRCUMSTANCES WHICH EXCUSE, EXTENUATE, OR AGGRAVATE.

ART. 32. All free white persons, whether inhabitants of this State or of the United States, or aliens, are amenable to punishment for offences which are defined and made punishable under the provisions of Part II. of this Code. Act of August 26, 1856. Took effect 1st Feb., 1857.

The exceptions to the general rule here laid down, are given in the subsequent Articles of this Title. Persons punishable under the Code.

ART. 33. Slaves and free persons of color are punishable under the provisions of Part III. of this Code, which relates specially to offences committed by persons in that condition. Same subject.

Definition of term "free white persons." ART. 34. All free persons who have less than one-fourth African blood, come within the meaning of the term "*free white persons;* and all free persons who have that, or a greater proportion of African blood, come within the meaning of the terms, "*free persons of color.*"

Word "slaves" and "free persons of color." "*Slaves*" are all such persons of African descent as are held in slavery by the laws of this State, or of any of the States or territories of the United States, or of any foreign country.

Indians, offences committed by, when punishable or not, &c. ART. 35. No act done within the uninhabited portions of the State, by individuals belonging to the several Indian tribes, in their intercourse with each other, or with other tribes, and affecting no other person, is considered as an offence against this Code; but in all other respects, such individuals are upon a footing with free white persons, both as to protection and liability to punishment.

Persons between nine and thirteen years. ART. 36. No person shall, in any case, be convicted of any offence committed before he was of the age of nine years; nor of any offence committed between the years of nine and thirteen, unless it shall appear by proof that he had discretion sufficient to understand the nature and illegality of the act constituting the offence.

Persons under seventeen years. ART. 37. A person, for an offence committed before he arrived at the age of seventeen years, shall in no case be punished with death; but may, according to the nature and degree of the offence, be punished by imprisonment for life, or receive any of the other punishments affixed in this code, to the offence of which he is guilty.

Of married woman committing offence by command, &c., of husband. ART. 38. A married woman who commits an offence by the command or persuasion of her husband, shall not in any case be punished by death, but may be imprisoned for life, or a term of years, according to the nature and degree of the crime; and in cases not capital, she shall receive only one-half the punishment to which she would otherwise be liable.

Minor committing an offence at instance of relative, or, &c. ART. 39. When it shall appear that a minor was aided or instigated in the commission of an offence, by a relation in the ascending line, or by his guardian, or an apprentice under age, by his master, or a wife by her husband, or a slave by a white person; such relation, guardian, master, husband, or white person, shall, at the discretion of the jury in capital cases, be punished by death; and in cases not capital, shall receive double the punishment imposed by law in ordinary cases for the same offence.

Word "minor" defined. ART. 40. The word "*minor*," as here and elsewhere used in this Code, signifies a person under the age of twenty-one years.

Insanity, effect of act done. ART. 41. No act done in a state of insanity, can be punished as an offence. No person who becomes insane after he committed an offence, shall be tried for the same while in such condition. No person who becomes insane after he is found guilty, shall be punished for the offence while in such condition.

How tried ART. 42. The rules of evidence known to the common law, in respect to the proof of insanity, shall be observed in all trials where that question is in issue. The manner of ascertaining whether the insanity is real or pretended, when it is alleged that the defendant became insane after the commission of the offence, is prescribed in Part III., Chapter II., of the Code of Criminal Procedure.

Officer executing process, justified for, &c. ART. 43. A person in the lawful execution of a written process, or verbal order from a court or magistrate, is justified for any act done in obedience thereto.

ART. 44. A peace officer is in like manner justified for any act which he is bound by law to perform, without warrant or verbal order. Peace officer justified, &c.

ART. 45. A person forced by threats or actual violence, to do an act, is not liable to punishment for the same. Such threats, however, must be, Person doing an act from threats, &c., not liable.

1. Loss of life or great personal injury.

2. They must be such as are calculated to intimidate a person of ordinary firmness.

3. The act must be done when the person threatening is actually present.

The violence intended by this Article, must be such actual force as restrains the person from escaping, or such ill-treatment as is calculated to render him incapable of resistance.

ART. 46. No act done by accident is an offence, except in certain cases specially provided for, where there has been a degree of carelessness or negligence which the law regards as criminal. Act done by accident, &c.

ART. 47. No mistake of law excuses one committing an offence; but if a person laboring under a mistake, as to a particular fact, shall do an act which would otherwise be criminal, he is guilty of no offence. No mistake of law excuses.

ART. 48. The mistake as to fact which will excuse, under the preceding Article, must be such as that the person so acting under a mistake, would have been excusable had his conjecture as to the fact been correct; and it must also be such mistake as does not arise from a want of proper care, on the part of the person committing the offence. Mistake of fact.

ART. 49. If one intending to commit a felony, and in the act of preparing for or executing the same, shall, through mistake or accident, do another act, which, if voluntarily done, would be a felony, he shall receive the punishment affixed by law to the offence actually committed. Act done by mistake where intention was to commit a felony.

ART. 50. If one intending to commit a felony, and in the act of preparing for or executing the same, shall, through mistake or accident, do another act which, if voluntarily done, would be a misdemeanor, he shall receive the highest punishment affixed by law to the offence actually committed. Same subject.

ART. 51. If one intending to commit a misdemeanor, and in the act of preparing for or executing the same, shall, through mistake, commit an offence which is by law a felony, he shall receive the lowest punishment affixed by law to the offence actually committed. Act done by mistake, when a misdemeanor.

ART. 52. The intention to commit an offence is presumed, whenever the means used is such as would ordinarily result in the commission of the forbidden act. Intention, &c., presumed.

ART. 53. On the trial of any criminal action, when the facts have been proved which constitute the offence, it devolves upon the accused to establish the facts or circumstances on which he relies to excuse or justify the prohibited act or omission. When accused shall prove his innocence.

PART II.

OF OFFENCES AND PUNISHMENTS.

TITLE I.

DEFINITION AND DIVISION OF OFFENCES.

Act of Aug 26, 1856. Took effect Feb. 1, 1857. ART. 54. An offence is an act or omission forbidden by positive law, and to which is annexed, on conviction, any punisment prescribed in this Code.

Offences divided. ART. 55. Offences are divided into felonies and misdemeanors.

What are felonies. ART. 56. Every offence which is punishable by death or by imprisonment in the penitentiary, either absolutely or as an alternative, is a felony; every other offence is a misdemeanor.

What are capital. ART. 57. Felonies are either capital or not capital. An offence for which the highest penalty is death, is a capital felony.

Petty offences. ART. 58. An offence, which a Justice of the Peace, or the Mayor, or other officer of a town or city, may try and punish, is called a petty offence.

Offences classed. ART. 59. Offences are again subdivided, and classed as follows: they are,

1. Offences against the State, its territory, property and revenue.
2. Offences affecting the Executive, Legislative, and Judiciary departments of the government.
3. Offences affecting the right of suffrage.
4. Offences which affect the free excercise of religious opinion.
5. Offences against public justice.
6. Offences against the public peace.
7. Offences against public morals, decency, and chastity.
8. Offences against public policy and economy.
9. Offences against public health.
10. Offences affecting property held in common for the use of the public.
11. Offences against trade and commerce, and the current coin.
12. Offences against the persons of individuals.
13. Offences against reputation.
14. Offences affectiug slaves and slave property.
15. Offences against property other than slaves.
16. Miscellaneous offences.

TITLE II.

OF PUNISHMENTS IN GENERAL.

ART. 60. The punishments incurred for offences under this Code, are: Act of Aug. 26, 1856. In force Feb. 1, 1857.

1. Death.

2. Imprisonment in the penitentiary for life or for a period of time. Kinds of punishment.

3. Imprisonment in the county jail.

4. Forfeiture of civil or political rights, or suspension from such rights for a limited time.

5. Pecuniary fines.

ART. 61. When an offence of which a person is convicted, is in its nature continuous, there shall also be judgment for its suppression. When offence is continuous, &c.

ART. 62. In case of the execution of a convict under sentence of death, or where he is imprisoned for life, there shall be no forfeiture of any kind to the State, nor shall any cost of prosecution be collected from his estate. No forfeiture to State where person is executed.

ART. 63. When a convict is imprisoned in the penitentiary, his property shall be controlled and managed in the manner directed by law: but there shall, in no case, whether of felony or misdemeanor, be a forfeiture of property of any kind to the State. Or confined in penitentiary.

ART. 64. When the penalty affixed to the commission of an offence is deprivation of political rights, such rights are intended to include the rights of holding office, of serving on juries, and of suffrage. Act of Feb. 12, 1858. In force July 1, 1858. Deprivation of, &c.

ART. 65. Whenever a minimum or maximum punishment is fixed by law, and by reason of any aggravation of the offence, or the existence of any circumstance on account of which the law directs that the punishment be doubled, this shall be construed to mean, that the jury shall not inflict less than double the smallest punishment incurred by the law, nor more than double the greatest punishment so incurred. Act of Aug. 28, 1856. Took effect 1st Feb., 1857. Increase and diminution of.

ART. 66. If fine and imprisonment are the punishments to be incurred for any offence, and it is provided that the punishment be doubled in any particular case, then the jury are to assess not less than double the smallest, and not more than double the largest fine prescribed by law, and not more than double the longest period of imprisonment, nor less than double the shortest period of imprisonment so prescribed. Same subject

ART. 67. When an offence is punishable by either fine or imprisonment, and as an alternative it is declared that the punishment shall be doubled in any particular case, the jury are to assess not less than double the amount of the smallest fine, nor more than double the amount of the largest fine, or as an alternative, they shall assess not less than double the shortest period of imprisonment nor more than double the longest period. This rule applies where there may be more than two kinds of punishment prescribed as alternatives. Same subject.

ART. 68. Where it is directed by law that in any particular case the punishment shall be increased one half, it is to be construed to mean that the jury may, beside the punishment ordinarily prescribed by law, assess such additional punishment as shall not be less than one half the penalty in ordinary cases, and all the rules before prescribed with respect to offences which by law incur alternative punishments, are applicable to cases where the penalty is to be so increased. Same subject.

ART. 69. When it is provided that the punishment in any given case, on account of mitigating circumstances, shall be diminished one half, the jury shall assess only one half of the penalty fixed by law for the offence under ordinary circumstances, and so with regard to any other proportion in which the penalty is directed to be diminished. Same subject.

ART. 70. In the diminution of punishments, the same rule as to two or

Rule in such cases. more penalties, or as to alternative penalties, shall apply which are prescribed with regard to the increase of punishment.

Not applicable in capital cases, &c. ART. 71. The foregoing rules, as to increase or diminution of punishments, have no application to cases where the highest penalty may be death, nor to any case where the penalty is total deprivation of civil or political rights.

Act of Feb. 12, 1858. Took effect July 1, 1858. Discretion of jury where penalty is death or, &c. ART. 71a. Whenever by the provisions of the Penal Code, or other law of the State, it is declared that an offence may be punished by death, or by some other penalty as alternative, the jury may by their verdict find the defendant guilty, and if this be the form of the verdict, sentence of death shall be pronounced thereon. But in the cases above mentioned, the jury may in their discretion assess the lighter penalty prescribed by law within the limits so prescribed, and this, when so intended, shall be specially set forth in the verdict.

Act of Aug. 28, 1856. Took effect Feb. 1, 1857. ART. 72. The punishment of death is inflicted by hanging, as prescribed in the Code of Criminal Procedure.

Imprisonment in, &c., for a term. ART. 73. Whenever the penalty, prescribed for an offence, is imprisonment for a term of years in the Penitentiary, imprisonment to hard labor is intended.

Confinement for life. ART. 74. In cases where the penalty affixed is imprisonment in the Penitentiary for life, the jury may in their discretion direct that the confinement be solitary, or that the whole or any portion of it be to labor.

Officer when to be removed. ART. 75. Whenever an offence is committed by an officer and the same appears to the jury to be a willful violation of duty, they shall so find, and such officer shall be removed from office.

Rule where penalty is confinement in Penitentiary, or fine as alternative. ART. 76. Whenever by the provisions of this Code the penalty for an offence is confinement in the Penitentiary, or fine as an alternative, it shall be in the discretion of the jury to substitute imprisonment in the county jail instead of the Penitentiary.

Jury may extend time of punishment in certain cases. ART. 79. When it may appear to the jury that the time fixed by law for such confinement is not sufficiently long to effect a reformation of the offender, they may in their discretion extend the time, but shall not, under the provisions of this Article, so extend it as that the offender, when discharged, will be more than twenty-one years of age; and nothing in this Article shall be so construed, as to prevent the confinement of a person in the House of Correction, for such length of time as will make his confinement therein reach beyond the period when he is twenty-one years of age, in cases where the longest term fixed by law will, if adopted by the jury, go beyond that period.

TITLE III.

OF THE PENITENTIARY.

CHAPTER I.

ITS ORGANIZATION.

Act of Aug. 28, 1856. Took effect Feb. 1, 1857. ART. 80. The Penitentiary of the State as established, located and organized, under the provisions of an Act of the Legislature of March 13, 1848, with such modifications as are herein set forth, is the place of confinement and punishment for all offenders over the age defined in Article 77, who by sentence of a competent Court are directed to be confined in the Penitentiary. Organiztiion of

ART. 81. The Directors of the Penitentiary shall report to the Governor biennially on the first day of November, the condition of the buildings belonging to the Penitentiary, and shall make such suggestions as they deem advisable relative to any improvements or changes in the plan of the establishment, by means of which it may be better adapted to carry out the objects for which it is designed in accordance with the provisions of this title. Directors shall report.

CHAPTER II.

OFFICERS OF THE PENITENTIARY

ART. 82. The following officers of the Penitentiary shall be appointed by the Governor, by and with the advice and consent of the Senate, to-wit: A Superintendent, three Directors, and a Financial Agent. Act of Aug. 28, 1856. Took effect Feb. 1, 1857.

ART. 83. The officers named in the preceding article shall continue in office for a term of four years, unless removed; but the Governor, when the Legislature is not in session, shall exercise the power of appointing and removing as in other like cases. Term of office.

ART. 84. The Directors, by the vote of a majority, shall appoint a Chaplain, Physician and such number of Overseers and Guards as may be requisite; and they may, when deemed necessary, appoint an Underkeeper. Chaplain.

ART. 85. Nurses may be employed by the Directors, at the suggestion of the Physician of the Penitentiary when required in cases of sickness. Nurses.

ART. 86. The Chaplain, Physician, Underkeeper, (if any,) Overseers and Guards shall be subject to removal at any time by the Directors. What officers may be removed

ART. 87. The officers of the Penitentiary shall be paid as follows: Salary of.

To the Superintendent an annual salary of fifteen hundred dollars;

To the Financial Agent an annual salary of fifteen hundred dollars;

To the Directors, each an annual salary of two hundred and fifty dollars;

To the Chaplain an annual salary of two hundred and fifty dollars;

To the attending Physician an annual salary of five hundred dollars;

To the Underkeeper, if any, and to each Overseer, Guard or Nurse, such compensation as may be agreed upon by contract with the Directors.

ART. 88. The salaries of the Superintendent, Directors, Financial Agent, Physician and Chaplain shall be paid quarterly out of the Treasury of the State, on the warrant of the Comptroller. When paid, &c.

ART. 89. The account of the Superintendent shall be certified to by the Directors. The accounts of the Directors, Financial Agent, Chaplain and Physician, shall be certified to by the Superintendent. Accounts, how certified.

CHAPTER III.

OF CONVEYING PRISONERS TO THE PENITENTIARY.

Act of Aug 28, 1856. Took effect Feb. 1, 1857. Convict conveyed at the expense, &c.

ART. 90. Immediately after final sentence shall have been pronounced, the convict shall be conveyed to the Penitentiary by the Sheriff of the county where the conviction took place, at the expense of the State: provided, that when there are more convicts than one to be transported at the same term of the court, they shall all be conveyed at one time.

Guard, how paid

ART. 91. The Sheriff shall employ a sufficient guard under the direction of the District Judge, whose certificate shall be sufficient evidence for the allowance of the account of the Sheriff, and the same shall be paid by the financial agent, out of the appropriation for the Penitentiary.

Compensation for.

ART. 92. The compensation allowed by law for conveying prisoners to the Penitentiary, shall be paid out of the appropriation for the Penitentiary, upon the certificate of the Superintendent.

Record of conviction, &c., shall be furnished.

ART. 93. The Clerk of the court in which any conviction has been had, shall furnish the Sheriff with a certified copy of the judgment of conviction, and also a certificate showing the name, age and previous occupation, if known, of the convict. The Sheriff shall deliver this certificate to the Superintendent, who shall receipt for the person of the convict; such receipt shall be returned to the Clerk of the proper court and be by him filed. The certified transcript above provided for, is in addition to that contemplated by the provisions of Article 706 of the Code of Criminal Procedure.

CHAPTER IV.

OF THE DUTIES OF THE DIRECTORS.

Act of Aug. 28, 1856. Took effect Feb. 1, 1857. Duties, &c., of Directors.

ART. 94. The Directors of the Penitentiary shall make such rules and by-laws as may be necessary for the government thereof, and for the punishment and control of refractory persons confined therein, and submit the same to the Governor for his approval.

May make rules

ART. 95. They shall cause the rules and by-laws so established to be printed and put in some conspicuous place in the prison, and furnish each convict who can read with a copy.

Appoint officers

ART. 96. They shall appoint all officers and employees of the Penitentiary not otherwise provided for.

Visit Penitentiary.

ART. 97. They shall at all times have access to the Penitentiary, and shall visit the same at least twice in each month, to inquire into the manner in which the convicts are treated.

Examine into any improper conduct.

ART. 98. The Directors have power, and it is their duty, to examine into any improper conduct alleged against the Superintendent, Financial Agent, or any other officer or employee of the Penitentiary.

Shall report to Governor, &c.

ART. 99 They shall report to the Governor any improper conduct on the part of the Superintendent or Financial Agent, and may at discretion remove any officer or employee who has been appointed by them.

May administer oaths, when.

ART. 100. The Directors may call before them, and administer oaths to any person, for the purpose of aiding them in the investigation of any subject within the range of their duties, and they may take other necessary steps to ascertain the truth with respect to any matter of which they have a right to inquire.

May make a difference in treatment of conv'ts.

ART. 101. A distinction shall be made in the treatment of convicts, so as to extend to such as are orderly, industrious and obedient, comforts and privileges according to their merit; and they may establish a system of rewards and punishments not inconsistent with the provisions of this title.

Biennial report.

ART. 102. The Directors shall report to the Governor biennially, on or before the first Monday in November, or oftener if required by him, a comprehensive view of the government, discipline, condition and transactions of the Penitentiary for the preceding two years, or since the time of their last report, and transmit the same, together with the report of the Financial Agent, Superintendent and Physician, which report shall be laid before the Legislature.

Directors—meaning of.

ART. 103. Whenever the term "Directors" is used, it means the three Directors or any two of them.

CHAPTER V.

OF THE DUTIES OF SUPERINTENDENT AND UNDERKEEPER.

1. *Of the Superintendent.*

Act of Aug. 28, 1856. Took effect Feb. 1, 1857.

ART. 104. The Superintendent is to exercise general control over the buildings, grounds, material for labor, erection and completion of the Penitentiary, and of all property of right appurtenant to the Penitentiary.

Control over keepers, &c.

ART. 105. He is to have general supervision of the conduct and management of convicts, and control over the Underkeeper, if any, Overseers, Guards, and other subordinate employees connected with the Penitentiary.

ART. 106. It is his duty to see that all officers under his supervision perform

See that officers perform their duties. their duties, and he shall report any failure on their part, in this respect, to the Directors.

Duty to convicts. ART. 107. He shall visit daily the cells of the prisoners and the places where they are engaged in labor; shall see that they are properly treated; shall give attention to all complaints made by a convict against the Under-keeper, or any Overseer or other subordinate employee. He shall enter into friendly conversation with the convicts, and seek, by the use of kindness, to produce reformation.

Responsible for enforcement of discipline. ART. 108. As the executive officer of the Penitentiary, he shall have all powers necessary to a discharge of his duties, subject only to the instructions of the Board of Directors as provided by law; and he shall be responsible for the manner in which the discipline of the Penitentiary is enforced.

Shall keep a book and register, &c. ART. 109. He shall keep a book in which shall be registered opposite to the name of each convict, all such incidents of importance as may occur respecting the demeanor of any prisoner. He shall also make notes of such occurrences in the course of the discharge of his duties as may seem important.

Residence of. ART. 110. The Superintendent shall reside in the building erected in the plan of the Penitentiary, and known as the Superintendent's house, and shall not absent himself from the Penitentiary enclosure unless by permission of the Directors, or upon business important to the interest of the State, and connected with the duties of his office.

Discharge Financial Agent's duties when. ART. 111. During the absence or inability of the Financial Agent to act, he shall discharge the duties of that officer.

Not to be present when convicts are visited by, &c. ART. 112. The Superintendent shall not be present when the convicts in the Penitentiary are visited by the Directors, or either of them, unless at their request.

Underofficers nominated by, &c ART. 113. The under officers and guards of the Penitentiary, who are to be appointed by the Directors, shall be first nominated for such appointment by the Superintendent. He may nominate several persons for the same appointment, from whom the Directors may select; but in case the Directors do not approve of nominations made by the Superintendent, they may appoint independently of such nominations.

All officers subject to orders of, except. ART. 114. All the officers and employees of the Penitentiary appointed by the Directors, except the Chaplain and the Physician, shall be subject to the orders of the Superintendent, and in case of violation of duty on the part of any of them, the Superintendent shall report such misconduct to the Directors.

Shall make a report biennially. ART. 115. He shall make a written report to the Directors biennially, on or before the first day of November, unless oftener required, upon subjects connected with the duties of his office, and under his management, which shall contain an estimate of the material (if any) for the erection and completion of the Penitentiary buildings, and for the purpose of carrying on the business in the various departments of the Penitentiary, with the amount that may be required (if any) for the purchase of the same, and for the pay of the officers and employees of the Penitentiary, transportation of convicts, rations, clothing and medicines, and advancements to discharge convicts, for which an appropriation would be required out of the State treasury.

Same subject. ART. 116. He shall, also, in his report, distinctly set forth the number of convicts who have been committed since his last report, giving the name, age, sex and place of nativity of each, their habits, education, marital relations, the term of imprisonment, the offences for which they are confined, from what county sent, the number of deaths, escapes, pardons, or discharges by expiration of sentence, with the number then in confinement, the various occupations in which they are employed, and the number employed in each.

ART. 117. In case of escapes, the Superintendent is authorized to offer a reward, not exceeding one hundred dollars, for the apprehension and return of a convict, which shall be paid to the person entitled thereto on the certificate of the Superintendent. May offer rewards.

2. *Of the Underkeeper.*

ART. 118. The Underkeeper of the Penitentiary shall assist the Superintendent in the discharge of his duties, and shall be subject to his directions, and in case of any ill-treatment on the part of the Superintendent, may complain to the Directors. Shall assist the Superintendent.

ART. 119. He shall reside within the walls of the Penitentiary, or at some point immediately adjacent, and shall not on any occasion absent himself from the duties of his office, except by permission of the Superintendent. Residence of, &c.

ART. 120. He shall visit daily the cells of the convicts; shall see that they are provided for according to the requirements of this title and of the rules and by-laws prescribed by the Directors, and during the hours of labor shall occupy his time in personal supervision of the various occupations of the convicts. Shall visit cells of convicts daily.

ART. 121. He shall give attention to all complaints made by a prisoner of ill treatment on the part of an overseer, guard, or other subordinate employee of the Penitentiary, and report the same to the Superintendent. Complaint o prisoner.

ART. 122. He shall superintend in person the overseers and guard of the Penitentiary, and the labor of the convicts; and see that all employees under him perform their duties, and that convicts are kept industriously employed. The Underkeeper shall not be present when the cells of convicts are visited by the Superintendent or Directors, nor when they visit a convict to inquire into the manner in which he is treated. Superintend overseers and guard.

CHAPTER VI.

OF THE DUTIES OF THE FINANCIAL AGENT.

ART. 123. He shall be the purchasing, selling and disbursing agent of the Penitentiary. And before entering on the discharge of his duties, shall give bond in the sum of twenty thousand dollars, for the faithful performance of his trust, with two or more good and sufficient securities, to be approved by the Board of Directors, which shall be recorded in the Directors' book of minutes, and transmitted by them to the State Department for safe keeping, and shall, when not otherwise provided by law, pay all accounts for services rendered and purchases made, on the presentation of proper vouchers; he shall also pay all drafts drawn on him by the Superintendent in favor of a Sheriff, for the transportation of prisoners. Act of Aug. 28, 1854. Took effect Feb'y 1, 1857. Appointment and general duties of.

ART. 124. He shall, from time to time, receive all monies appropriated for

Shall receive appropriations. the purpose of the Penitentiary, or cotton and woolen factories. And on his requisition, approved by the Directors, the Comptroller of public accounts is authorized and required to draw his warrant on the State treasury for the same: provided, he shall not receive, at any one time, more than one-half of the annual amount so appropriated.

Purchase material. ART. 125. He shall, under the advice of the Directors, purchase all such materials as may be necessary for building or manufacturing purposes, subsistence, clothing and medicines for the convicts. He shall also keep an account of each article sold, with the price for which the same was sold. Also, an account specifying the amount of monies received by him, and on what account together with his disbursements. All of which shall be by him entered in well bound books, subject to the inspection of the Superintendent and Directors, or either of them.

Statement of receipts, &c. ART. 126. He shall, every twelve months, furnish the Directors with a written statement of his receipts and disbursements, together with an account of sales.

Biennial report and statement of general transactions. ART. 127. He shall annually furnish the Directors with an abstract statement of his general transactions for the preceding year. And, biennially, on or before the first day of November, he shall furnish the Directors with an abstract of his receipts and disbursements, sales and purchases, for the preceding two years, who shall carefully examine and compare the same with his vouchers and original entries; and if found correct, shall trasmit the same, certified under their hands, to the Governor of the State.

Suit shall be brought in name of. ART. 128. Suits for the recovery of moneys due on account of sales or otherwise, shall be in the name of the Financial Agent, for the use of the Texas State Penitentiary.

Shall perform duties of Superintendent. ART. 129. During the absence of the Superintendent, or his inability to act, the Financial Agent shall discharge the duties of Superintendent.

CHAPTER VII.

DUTIES OF THE PHYSICIAN.

Act of Aug. 28, 1856. Took effect Feb'ry 1, 1857. General duty, ART. 130. It is the general duty of the Physician to visit the Penitentiary at least twice in each week, for the purpose of ascertaining the condition of the health of each convict, and he shall report once in three months, or oftener if required, to the Directors, the sanitary condition of the Penitentiary.

Shall attend convict. ART. 131. He shall attend immediately upon any case of sickness among the convicts, of which he is notified by the Superintendent or Underkeeper.

Examine general health of. ART. 132. He shall examine into the state of health of each prisoner brought to the Penitentiary, before he has been confined in his cell.

ART. 133. He shall notify the Superintendent of each case, in which on account of ill health, it may be deemed advisable to remove a prisoner from the Penitentiary to some other place. Notify Superintendent.

ART. 134. The Physician shall inquire into the mental as well as bodily condition of each convict, and give such advice to the Superintendent as he may deem proper respecting the treatment of all prisoners who may appear to be materially affected either in body, or mind, by any particular mode of treatment; and shall make all proper suggestions touching an alteration in the mode of treatment in any particular case. Examine mental condition.

ART. 135. He shall cause any one suffering under a contagious or infectious disease to be removed, so that other prisoners may not suffer by such contagion or infection, and the directions of the Physician shall be followed by the Superintendent in all such cases. Contagious disease.

ART. 136. When, under Article 134, any particular mode of treatment has been suggested by the Physician to the Superintendent the same shall be followed by him, or he shall report thereon to the Directors for their decision, and shall be governed by their opinion. Special treatment, &c.

ART. 137. If directions be given by the Physician for the removal from the Penitentiary of any person suffering under a contagious or infectious disease, such directions shall be followed and the diseased person removed to some other place, until he shall have died or is restored to health. When diseased person shall be removed.

ART. 138. Convicts when sick shall be kept in the apartment constructed as a hospital by the original plan of the Penitentiary, except when under the advice of the Physician their removal to some other place may become necessary. Convicts when sick, where kept.

ART. 139. The hospital, and all persons employed therein, shall be under the management and control of the Physician. Hospital.

ART. 140. The Physician shall keep a journal, in which he shall regularly enter opposite the name of each prisoner the state of his health, and, if sick, with what disease, and whether he remains within the Penitentiary or has been removed, together with such remarks as he may deem important, which book shall be open at all times for the inspection of the Superintendent and Directors. Physician shall keep a journal.

ART. 141. The treatment prescribed by the Physician for prisoners suffering with disease shall, in all cases, be followed, and only such diet given as is allowed by him. Prescription shall be followed.

ART. 142. A prisoner suffering under a dangerous disease shall not be discharged, except by his own request, while in that condition, though his term of confinement may have expired. Prisoner not to be discharged when diseased, except.

CHAPTER VIII.

DUTIES OF CHAPLAIN.

ART. 143. The Chaplain shall preach at least once on every Sunday to the convicts. Act of Aug. 28, 1856.

Shall visit prisoners, &c.

ART. 144. He shall visit the prisoners at convenient times in the day during their hours of leisure, and is expected to use all the influence he may possess to inculcate sound principles of religion and morality.

May furnish books.

ART. 145. He may furnish the convicts with such books on moral subjects as are approved by the Directors.

May visit prisoners.

ART. 146. He may visit prisoners in case of sickness, by permission of the Physician, and shall always be admitted to see and converse with any convict who has been pronounced by the Physician as beyond reasonable hope of recovery.

Shall not discuss sectarian doctrines.

ART. 147. It is the duty of the Chaplain, in his discourses or conversations with prisoners, to refrain from discussing doctrines merely sectarian, and to teach such pure principles of religion and morality as belong to the creed of all Christian Churches.

All ministers may have access when.

ART. 148. Preachers, Ministers and Priests, of all religious denominations, shall, by consent of the Directors, have access to the Penitentiary, and may, by consent of the Chaplain, preach to the convicts.

Convict of particular form of doctrine.

ART. 149. A convict who is a believer in any particular form or doctrine of religion shall at his own request, at all proper times, be permitted to receive visit from any preacher, minister, or priest, whom he may desire to see.

CHAPTER IX.

OF OVERSEERS AND OTHER SUBORDINATE OFFICERS AND EMPLOYEES.

Act of Aug. 28, 1856

Overseers may be employed.

ART. 150. Overseers may be employed as directed in this title to superintend any particular branch of business carried on by the labor of convicts, or when, from the number of convicts it becomes necessary, they may be employed for the purpose of preserving discipline and securing the safe custody of prisoners.

Shall obey orders, &c.

ART. 151. They shall obey the orders of the Superintendent and Underkeeper, and may complain to the Directors of any ill treatment they may receive from those officers.

Guards may be appointed.

ART. 152. Such number of Guards as are deemed necessary may be appointed to preserve discipline, and prevent escapes of convicts. They shall be subject to the orders of the Superintendent and Underkeeper, and any complaint of ill treatment may be made by them to the Directors.

Neither to be present when &c.

ART, 153. No overseer or guard shall be present when a prisoner is visited by either of the Directors, the Superintendent or the Underkeeper, for the purpose of inquiring into the manner in which the convicts are treated.

CHAPTER X.

OF THE TREATMENT OF CONVICTS AND OF PRISON DISCIPLINE.

1. *General Rules.*

ART. 154. Every convict when received into the Penitentiary shall be carefully searched and deprived of every article by which an escape might be effected. If money be found upon the person of a convict, it shall be delivered by the Superintendent to the board of Directors, and by them be safely kept until the discharge of such prisoner, (if he has no wife or children,) and upon his discharge shall be re-delivered to him, but if the prisoner has a wife or children, the money shall be transmitted to them by the Directors.

Act of Aug. 28, 1856. Convict shall be searched on entering and if money be found &c.

ART. 155. The state of health of the convict shall also be examined by the Physician as directed in chapter VII of this title.

State of health shall be.

ART. 156. The clothes of each convict shall be carefully preserved by the Superintendent during the time of his confinement, and upon his discharge shall be re-delivered to him; and the Superintendent shall give to each convict, on his discharge, twenty dollars, if said convict is without money and otherwise unprovided for.

Clothing of.

ART. 157. The description of each convict when received in the Penitentiary, the name, if known, sex, age, height, color of the eyes and hair, place of nativity and previous occupation, if ascertained, time of conviction, nature of the crime and period of confinement, shall be entered in a book kept by the Superintendent.

Description, &c., shall be entered in book.

ART. 158. All prisoners confined in the Penitentiary are to be treated with humanity, to be provided with suitable clothing of substantial material, and with proper diet, but ardent, malt, or vinous liquors, are not to be allowed except when prescribed by the attending Physician.

Shall be treated with humanity.

ART. 159. The various provisions of this Code are designed to secure to the convicts moral instruction, to provide for their health and extend to them such comforts as are consistent with their situation, and at the same time to require of them a due attention to their various occupations, and a strict observance of the discipline, rules and regulations of the prison.

Object is to secure to moral instruction, &c.

ART. 160. Prisoners who have been reported by the Physician as in a condition of health which requires their removal to some other place, shall be accordingly removed, but in such manner and under such restrictions as will prevent escape.

Where prisoner's health requires removal.

ART. 161. No conversation shall be allowed between convicts except as a reward for good conduct, and while at work together they shall be allowed to speak to each other only when necessary to carry on the labor in which they are engaged, and convicts of different sexes shall at all times be kept separate and apart.

No conversation between convicts allowed.

Uniform dress. ART. 162. The convicts shall be dressed in clothing of uniform make and of coarse but comfortable material, and suited to the season of the year.

Food for. ART. 163. Food of healthy and substantial kind shall be furnished to the convicts; they may be placed upon lighter diet as a punishment for refractory conduct.

May receive instruction when. ART. 164. Convicts who are unable to read when admitted to the Penitentiary, may receive such instruction during hours of leisure as the Chaplain may see proper to give, and for the purpose of aiding in this duty, a teacher may be employed by the Directors.

2. *Of visits to the Penitentiary.*

Who may of right visit. ART. 165. The Governor, Lieut. Governor, Judges of Courts, Magistrates, all other offices connected with the Judiciary, and members of the Legislature have a right to visit the Penitentiary and shall always at proper hours be admitted for the purpose of observing the manner in which the Penitentiary is conducted.

Superintendent may permit. ART. 166. The Superintendent or any Director may give permission to other persons to visit the Penitentiary.

Not to converse with prisoner. ART. 167. No conversation shall be held with a convict by any visitor other than the Governor, except by permission of the Superintendent.

Governor may converse with. ART. 168. The Governor may hold conversations with prisoners apart from the Superintendent or any other officer.

Rules shall apply to all prisoners. ART. 169. The rules prescribed in the foregoing articles of this Chapter apply to prisoners under whatever term of sentence and in whatever manner they are directed by law to be confined, but these rules shall be controlled by others made specially applicable to particular cases.

CHAPTER XI.

OF SOLITARY CONFINEMENT FOR LIFE.

Act of Aug. 28, 1856. ART. 170. Prisoners sentenced to solitary confinement for life shall be strictly confined to their cells. They may, in the discretion of the Directors, be permitted to labor at intervals during their confinement.

Shall receive no visits except. ART. 171. They shall receive no visits except from the Governor of the State, the Directors, Superintendent and other officers of the Penitentiary, including the Physician and Chaplain.

May read the Bible, &c. ART. 172. They may read such selections from the Bible or other works of moral instruction as may be furnished by the Chaplain.

Dress may be changed. ART. 173. Such change may be made with regard to the dress of convicts of this class, as the Directors may think proper.

Cell shall be painted black, &c. ART. 174. The cell in which a prisoner is confined for a crime punishable by solitary imprisonment for life, shall be painted black upon the outside, and some appropriate inscription shall be painted thereon, in plain letters, setting forth the name and age of the offender, the time and place of his conviction, and the crime of which he was found guilty, and that he is enduring in solitary confinement, the penalty for his crime.

CHAPTER XII.

OF PRISONERS CONFINED TO LABOR FOR LIFE OR A TERM OF YEARS.

ART. 175. This class of persons are to be kept at labor from day-light until twenty minutes before sunset, with the exceptions stated in the succeeding articles. Act of Aug. 28, 1855. Working hours

ART. 176. No labor shall be required of a convict on Sunday. Sunday excep'd

ART. 177. There shall be allowed an interval of one hour's rest at breakfast, and an hour and a half at dinner. Hours of rest.

ART. 178. The particular occupation and employment in which a convict is to engage shall be determined by the Superintendent after consultation with the Directors. Occupation to be followed, &c.

ART. 179. If a prisoner, prior to his conviction, has been engaged in any particular mechanical employment, he shall be set to labor in the same occupation, provided the trade be one which is or may be carried on in the Penitentiary. When employ'd at former trade.

ART. 180. No greater amount of labor shall be required of a convict than a due regard to his physical strength and health may render proper. Amount of labor required.

CHAPTER XIII.

OF THE RULES TO BE PRESCRIBED BY THE DIRECTORS.

ART. 181. The authority given to the Directors of the Penitentiary to establish rules and By-Laws, is intended to supply any defects in the law with regard to prison discipline, and to provide for such details as are not embraced within the rules laid down in this Title. Object of authority to Directors.

ART. 182. These rules and By-Laws shall be reported to the Governor whenever adopted, and all changes and amendments as they are made. By-Laws, amendments to.

ART. 183. The Directors have the same authority to make rules and By-Laws in regard to the House of Correction, as they have with respect to the other department of the Penitentiary. Authority to make By-Laws.

ART. 184. The rules and By-Laws shall be made with a view to carry out the general principles on which the penal laws are founded, and the designs for which the different systems of imprisonment are established. Object of By-Laws

Rewards to convicts.

ART. 185. The rewards to be bestowed upon convicts who evince a purpose of reformation and a disposition to obey the rules of discipline, shall consist of an extension of social privileges, permission to read, write, and such other mitigations of the severity of punishment as may not be inconsistent with proper discipline. No written communication from a convict shall, however, in any case, be sent out without the permission of the Superintendent, nor until it has been read by him.

Punishments prescribed by Directors.

ART. 186. The punishments to be prescribed by the Directors of the Penitentiary, shall consist of closer imprisonment, confinement in irons, deprivation of privileges enjoyed by other prisoners, and punishments of the like kind. Whipping shall not be resorted to except by special order of the Directors in the particular cases, nor shall shaving the head of a convict be in any instance allowed.

TITLE IV.

OF THE HOUSE OF CORRECTION.*

CHAPTER I.

ITS ORGANIZATION AND OFFICERS.

[*See Penitentiary.—Convicts.*]

Act of Aug. 28, 1856.

House of, where built

ART. 187. There shall be built by the State, convenient and adjacent to the Penitentiary grounds, a place of confinement to be called the House of Correction.

Superintendent, principal officer of.

ART. 188. The Superintendent of the Penitentiary shall be also the Superintendent and principal officer of the House of correction, and all duties assigned him with respect to the management of the affairs of the Penitentiary are also to be performed in regard to the House of Correction.

Directors of.

ART. 189. The Directors of the Penitentiary shall in like manner be the Directors of the House of Correction; shall exercise all powers and perform all duties in respect to the affairs of the House of Correction, which are prescribed to them in like cases in the control and supervision of the Penitentiary.

Assistant Superintendent, &c., compensation of.

ART. 190. The Directors may appoint an Assistant Superintendent, and such subordinate officers and guards as may be deemed necessary, for the proper management of the House of Correction, who shall be paid such compensation as is agreed upon by contract with the Directors.

How appointed.

ART. 191. The appointment of Assistant Superintendent, subordinate officers and guards, shall be made upon the nomination of the Superintendent, under the rules which are prescribed in the preceding Title for the appointment of officers by the Directors.

Physician and Chaplain, duties

ART. 192. The Physician and Chaplain of the Penitentiary shall exercise their respective offices as Physician and Chaplain of the House of Correction, and in case it becomes necessary, or is deemed proper, the Directors may appoint an Assistant Chaplain and Physician, upon such terms as they may think reasonable: provided that the compensation of such assistants shall not exceed that allowed the Physician and Chaplain respectively.

ART. 193. The general rules prescribed in the preceding Title, as to the management of the pecuniary affairs of the Penitentiary, shall also apply to the House of Correction. Finances of

ART. 194. There shall be appointed by the Directors a teacher, whose duty it shall be to give instruction to the convicts in the House of Correction. The compensation of the teacher shall be fixed by agreement with the Directors. Teacher of convicts.

ART. 195. Competent mechanics shall be chosen by the Directors to give instruction in any branch of mechanical business which may appear to be suited to a convict in the House of Correction. Mechanical instruction of.

ART. 196. The duties of Teacher may be performed by the Chaplain, or Assistant Chaplain, and an additional compensation allowed therefor, by the Directors. Who may perform duties of Teacher.

ART. 197. The duties of instructor in mechanical pursuits may be performed by such convicts in the Penitentiary as are qualified, and as may appear to the Superintendents and Directors to be suitable, by having given evidence of sincere reformation. Who may be mechanical instructor.

CHAPTER II.

ITS GENERAL OBJECTS.

ART. 198. The principal design of the House of Correction is to reform and improve the moral condition and character of juvenile offenders. Act of Aug. 28, 1856.

ART. 199. All officers charged with duties in the management and discipline of the House of Correction, are required to use kind and persuasive measures to produce a reformation of the convicts under their care. Officers to use kindness.

ART. 200. To carry out the objects designed, the Directors may establish rules and by-laws for the government of the persons confined in the House of Correction. Object of By Laws of.

CHAPTER III.

OF DISCIPLINE AND TREATMENT OF CONVICTS.

ART. 201. All rules prescribed in the preceding Title for the humane treat- Act of Aug. 28, 1856.

ment of prisoners in the Penitententiary, shall equally apply to those confined in the House of Correction.

Time given to instruction of mechanics. ART. 202. Three hours of each day shall be devoted to the instruction of convicts in reading, writing, grammar and arithmetic. Such convicts as are already sufficiently instructed in these, may be taught the higher branches of learning.

Time to rest. ART. 203. One hour at breakfast time, and one hour and a half at dinner, shall be allowed for rest and leisure, from labor or instruction.

Time for labor. ART. 204. The remaining portion of the day, between sunrise and sunset, except Sundays, shall be devoted to labor and instruction in mechanical pursuits.

Books for instruction. ART. 205. The Directors have the right to prescribe the kind of books to be used in the instruction of convicts.

Teachers and instructors. ART. 206. All persons engaged in teaching or superintending the instruction of convicts, are expected to inculcate principles of morality, to advise kindly, and exhort convicts to a course of reformation and good behavior.

Visits to prisoners. ART. 207. The rules prescribed in the preceding Title respecting visits to prisoners by officers or other persons, shall apply to convicts in the House of Correction.

Punishments. ART. 208. The punishment in the House of Correction for refractory conduct, shall be the same as in the Penitentiary, except that moderate correction by whipping may be resorted to when necessary, in the case of offenders under the age of fifteen.

Rewards. ART. 209. Rewards appropriate to the case shall be bestowed upon such as are worthy, which shall be by allowing privileges of social intercourse, the perusal of books, visits from friends, and other like privileges.

Convicts shall not converse, except, &c. ART. 210. As a general rule convicts in the House of Correction shall not converse together, except in the hearing of the Superintendent, Assistant Superintendent, Chaplain, Physician, Teacher, or one of the Directors. Those, however, who manifest an improvement of character, may be allowed social intercourse with each other.

Shall not communicate with convicts. ART. 211. The convicts in the Penitentiary shall have no communication with those in the House of Correction, except when one of the former is made an instructor of one of the latter, and then only in the presence of some officer of the Penitentiary.

Ill treatment of convict by officer, how punished. ART. 212. Any ill treatment by a subordinate officer or guard towards a convict, shall be punished by the Directors by deducting from the pay of such officer, or, in cases where it is proper, by prosecution before a Magistrate, or by dismissal from office.

Complaints by convicts, how investigated. ART. 213. All complaints made by a convict shall be promptly investigated by the Superintendent or Directors, and the proper remedy applied.

TITLE V.

OF PRINCIPALS, ACCOMPLICES, AND ACCESSARIES.

CHAPTER I.

PRINCIPALS.

ART. 214. All persons are principals who are guilty of acting together in the commission of an offence. Act of Aug. 28, 1856. Who are principals.

ART. 215. When an offence is actually committed by one or more persons, but others are present, and knowing the unlawful intent, aid by acts, or encourage by words or gestures, those actually engaged in the commission of the unlawful act; or who, not being actually present, keep watch so as to prevent the interruption of those engaged in committing the offence, such persons so aiding, encouraging, or keeping watch, are principal offenders, and may be prosecuted and convicted as such. Same subject.

ART. 216. All persons who shall engage in procuring aid, arms, or means, of any kind, to assist in the commission of an offence while others are executing the unlawful act, and all persons who endeavor, at the time of the commission of the offence, to secure the safety or concealment of the offenders, are principals, and may be convicted and punished as such. Same subject.

ART. 217. If any one, by employing a child or other person, who cannot be punished, to commit an offence, or by any means, such as laying poison where it may be taken, and with intent that it shall be taken, or by preparing any other means by which a person may injure himself, and with intent that such person shall thereby be injured, or by any other indirect means, cause another to receive an injury to his person or property, the offender, by the use of such indirect means, becomes a principal. Same subject.

ART. 218. Any person who advises or agrees to the commission of an offence, and who is present when the same is committed, is a principal thereto, whether he aids or not in the illegal act. Same subject.

ART. 218a. If the master of a slave instigates, aids, encourages, advises, or wilfully permits such slave to commit an offence, he may be considered and prosecuted, either as a principal or as an accomplice, and shall be punished in the manner prescribed in Article 223 of the Penal Code. Act of Feb. 12, 1858. Master instigating slave to commit offence.

CHAPTER II.

ACCOMPLICES.

ART. 219. An accomplice is one who is not present at the commission of an offence, but who, before the act is done, advises, commands or encourages another to commit the offence; or, Act of Aug. 28, 1856.

Accomplice, who is. Who agrees with the principal offender to aid him in committing the offence, though he may not have given such aid; or,

Who promises any reward, favor, or other inducement; or threatens any injury in order to procure the commission of the offence; or,

Who prepares arms, or aid of any kind, prior to the commission of an offence, for the purpose of assisting the principal in the execution of the same.

It is sufficient that the offence be of same nature. ART. 220. To render a person guilty as an accomplice, it is not necessary that the precise offence which he may have advised, or to the execution of which he may have given encouragement or promised assistance, should be committed; it is sufficient that the offence be of the same nature, though different in degree, as that which he so advised or encouraged.

Punishment of. ART. 220a* Accomplices shall, in all cases not otherwise expressly provided for, be punished in the same manner as the principal offender.

When one offence is attempted and another committed. ART. 221. If, in the attempt to commit one offence, the principal shall by mistake or accident commit some other under the circumstances set forth in Articles 49, 50, and 51, the accomplice to the offence originally intended shall, if both offences are felonies by law, receive the punishment affixed to the lower of the two offences; but, if the offence designed be a misdemeanor, he shall receive the highest punishment affixed by law to the commission of such misdemeanor, whether the offence actually committed be a misdemeanor or a felony.

Where principal is under the age of seventeen. ART. 222. If the principal in an offence less than capital be under the age of seventeen years, the punishment of an accomplice shall be increased, so as not to exceed, however, double the penalty affixed to the offence in ordinary cases.

Where accomplice is parent, master, &c., to principal. ART. 223. If the accomplice stands in the relationship of parent, master, guardian, or husband, to the principal offender, he shall, in all such cases, receive the highest punishment annexed to the offence, and the same may in felonies less than capital, be increased by the jury to double the highest penalty which would be suffered in ordinary cases.

Who may be accomplice. ART. 224. There may be accomplices to all offences, except manslaughter and negligent homicide.

CHAPTER III.

ACCESSARIES.

Act of Aug. 28, 1856.

Who is an accessary. ART. 225. An accessary is one who, knowing that an offence has been committed, conceals the offender, or gives him any other aid in order that he may evade an arrest or trial, or the execution of his sentence. But no person, who aids an offender in making or preparing his defence at law, or procures him to be bailed, though he afterwards escape, shall be considered an accesary.

Who cannot be. ART. 226. The following persons cannot be accessaries:

1. The husband or wife of an offender.
2. His relations in the ascending or descending line, by consanguinity or affinity.
3. His brothers and sisters.
4. His slaves.

How punished. ART. 227. Accessaries to offences shall be punished by the infliction of the lowest penalty to which the principal in the offence would be liable.

CHAPTER IV.

TRIAL OF ACCOMPLICES AND ACCESSARIES.

ART. 228. An accomplice may be arrested, tried, and punished, before the conviction of the principal offender, and the acquittal of the principal shall not bar a prosecution against the accomplice, but on the trial of an accomplice, the evidence must be such as would also have convicted the principal. Act of Aug. 28, 1856. Accomplice may be tried.

ART. 229. An accessary may, in like manner, be tried and punished before the principal, when the latter has escaped; but if the principal is arrested, he shall be first tried, and, if acquitted, the accessary shall be discharged. Accessary, &c.

ART. 230. Persons charged as principals, accomplices, or accessaries, whether in the same indictment or by different indictments, cannot be introduced as witnesses for one another, but they may claim a severance; and if any one or more be acquitted, they may testify in behalf of the others. May be witnesses, when.

TITLE VI.

OF OFFENCES AGAINST THE STATE, ITS TERRITORY, PROPERTY, AND REVENUE.

CHAPTER I.

TREASON.

ART. 231. Treason against the State shall consist only in levying war against it, or in adhering to its enemies, giving them aid and comfort. [Cons. Art. 7, Sec. 2.] Act of Aug. 28, 1856. Treason defined.

ART. 232. If any citizen of this State be guilty of treason, he shall suffer death, or imprisonment in the penitentiary for life, at the discretion of the jury. How punished.

CHAPTER II.

MISPRISION OF TREASON.

ART. 233. Whoever shall know that another person has committed treason, or is intending so to do, and shall not, within five days from the time of his having come to such knowledge, give information of the same to the Governor, or to some magistrate or peace officer of the State, shall be deemed guilty of misprision of treason. Definition of.

ART. 234. The punishment for misprision of treason is confinement in the Penitentiary a time not less than two nor more than seven years. Act of Feb. 12, 1858. How punished.

CHAPTER III.

EMBEZZLEMENT OR MISAPPLICATION OF PUBLIC MONEY.

Act of Feb. 12, 1858. Officer embezzling public money, how punished.

ART. 235. If any officer of the Government, who is by law a receiver or depository of public money, or any clerk or other person employed about the office of such officer, shall fraudulently take, or misapply, or convert it to his own use, any part of such public money, or secrete the same with intent to take, misapply, or convert to his own use, or shall pay or deliver the same to any person, knowing that he is not entitled to receive it, he shall be punished by confinement in the Penitentiary for a term not less than two nor more than ten years.

Person receiving and concealing it, how punished.

ART. 236. If any person shall, knowingly and with fraudulent intention, receive or conceal any public money which has been taken, or converted to his own use by an officer or employee, as set forth in the preceding Article, he shall be punished by confinement in the Penitentiary, for a term not less than two nor more than five years.

Act of Aug. 28, 1856. Officer of, &c., defined.

ART. 237. Under the term "officer of the Government," as used in Article 235, are included the State Treasurer and all other heads of Departments who, by law, may receive or keep in their care public money of the State, Assessors and Collectors, and all other officers who, by law, are authorized to collect, receive or keep money due to the government.

CHAPTER IV.

COLLECTION OF TAXES AND OTHER PUBLIC MONEY.

[*See Extortion—Public Money—Riots—Unlawful Assemblies.*]

Act of Aug. 28, 1856. Penalty for extortion.

ART. 238. If any person authorized to collect or receive taxes or other money due the State, shall extort, or attempt to extort from any one, a larger sum than is due, or shall receive any sum of money or other reward as a consideration for granting any delay in the collection of such dues, or for doing any illegal act, or omitting to do any legal act in relation to the collection of such money, he shall be punished by fine not exceeding five hundred dollars, and shall be dismissed from office, and rendered incapable forever of holding the same office.

Exacting usurious interest on taxes advanced.

ART. 239. If any Assessor and Collector of Taxes shall advance for a person owing taxes to the government the amount of money so due, and shall charge therefor a rate of interest greater than twelve per centum per annum, he shall be punished in the manner provided in the preceding Article.

Where Assessor assumes taxes, &c.

ART. 240. Within the meaning of Article 239, is included the case of an Assessor and Collector who fails to collect taxes due, and assumes to be responsible to the government therefor, and receives for such act any compensation or reward.

ART. 241. If any person shall, by force or threats of force, prevent, or attempt to prevent, the collection of taxes or other money due the State by an officer authorized to enforce such collection, he shall be punished by fine, not less than one hundred nor more than five hundred dollars, and by imprisonment in the county jail, not less than three months nor more than one year. Person preventing the collection of taxes.

When the means used to prevent the collection are such as to amount to a riot, or unlawful assembly, the punishment shall be that which is prescribed in Title XI., Article 367.

CHAPTER V.

DEALING IN FRAUDULENT LAND CERTIFICATES.

ART. 242. If any person shall make or issue any fraudulent or forged certificate for land, or shall knowingly purchase or sell any such certificate, or locate any such certificate, or be in any manner directly or indirectly concerned in the making, or issuing, purchasing, selling, or locating any such certificate for land, knowing the same to be fraudulent, he shall be punished by confinement n the Penitentiary, for a term not less than two nor more than five years. Act of Feb. 12, 1858. Penalty for dealing in.

ART. 243. It shall not be lawful for any District or Deputy Surveyor to locate any certificate for land, or to survey any land for any person holding a head-right certificate of the first or second class, unless it be certified under the hand and seal of the Clerk of the County Court of the county where the certificate was issued, or the county where it is proposed to be located, or under the hand and seal of the Commissioner of the General Land Office, that the same has been reported by the Commissioners appointed under an act of Congress to detect fraudulent land certificates, &c., passed January, 1840, as a genuine and legal claim against the Government of Texas; and any Surveyor offending against the true intent and meaning of this Article, shall be deemed guilty of a high misdemeanor, and on conviction shall be fined in any sum not more than five thousand dollars. District or deputy surveyor prohibited from locating, &c.

CHAPTER VI.

DEALING IN PUBLIC LANDS BY OFFICERS.

ART. 244. If any person who is an officer or Clerk in the General Land Office, or a District Surveyor, or Deputy District Surveyor, shall directly or indirectly be concerned in the purchase of any right, title, or interest, in any public land, in his own name, or in the name of any other person; or shall take or receive any fee or emolument for negotiating or transacting any business connected with the duties of his office, other than the fees allowed by law, he shall be removed from office, and fined in any sum not exceeding five hundred dollars, and be excluded from holding any other office under the State. Act of Aug. 28, 1856. Certain officers prohibited from buying public lands, &c.

CHAPTER VII.

FORGERY OF PATENTS, LAND CERTIFICATES, &C. &C.

Act of Aug. 28, 1856. Forging of patents, &c.

ART. 245. If any person shall forge any concession, patent, or certificate, bounty warrant, donation, or land scrip for land within this State, he shall be punished by confinement in the Penitentiary not less than five nor more than twenty years.

Preceding Art. construed.

ART. 246. The preceding Article is intended to include any and all instruments of writing, or documents of whatever name or description, which purport to grant, concede, give, or convey any right or interest in any land, emanating from any former Government of Texas, or from the State, whether such claim or title for land be perfect or imperfect.

Forging of any instrument to procure from State, warrant, &c.

ART. 247. If any person shall forge an instrument of writing of any description whatever, with intent that the same may be used for the purpose of obtaining from any of the public departments or offices of the State at the seat of government, any bounty or donation warrant, or land scrip, or patent for any public land of this State; or that the same may be used to obtain any money or property of the State, he shall be punished by confinement in the Penitentiary, not less than five nor more than twenty years.

Act of Feb. 12, 1858. Using such forged instrument.

ART. 248. If any person shall wilfully and knowingly pass or use, or attempt to pass or use, any such false document or instrument as is mentioned in the three preceding articles, he shall be punished by confinement in the Penitentiary, not less than two nor more than five years.

Act of Aug. 28, 1856. Rules prescribed in, &c., shall apply.

ART. 249. The Rules prescribed in Title XVI., Chapter I. of this Code, defining the offence of forgery, apply to the offences enumerated in the four preceding articles.

TITLE VII.

OF OFFENCES AFFECTING THE EXECUTIVE, LEGISLATIVE AND JUDICIARY DEPARTMENTS OF THE GOVERNMENT.

CHAPTER I.

BRIBERY.

[*See Auditor, Arbitrator, Juror, Umpire, Referee, Sheriff, Attorney, Clerk, Peace-Officer, Elections.*]

Act of Feb. 12, 1858. Bribery of certain officers.

ART. 250. If any person shall bribe, or offer to bribe, any executive, legislative, or judicial officer, after his election or appointment, and either before or after he shall have been qualified or entered upon the duties of his office, with intent to influence his act, vote, opinion, decision, or judgment, on any matter, question, cause, or proceeding which may be then pending, or may thereafter by law be brought before such officer in his official capacity, he shall be punished by confinement in the Penitentiary, for a term not less than two nor more than five years.

ART. 251. Any legislative, executive, or judicial officer, who shall accept a bribe under an agreement, or with an understanding that his act, vote, opinion, or judgment, shall be done or given in any particular manner, or upon a particular side of any question, cause or proceeding, which is or may thereafter by law be brought before him, or that he shall make any particular nomination or appointment, shall be punished by confinement in the Penitentiary not less than two nor more than ten years. Accepting bribe by.

ART. 252. Under the name of executive, legislative and judicial officers, are included the Governor, Lieutenant Governor, Comptroller, Auditor, State Treasurer, Commissioner of the General Land Office, Members of the Legislature, Judges of the Supreme and District Courts, Attorney General, District Attorneys, Chief Justices of the County Courts, Justices of the Peace, Mayors and Judges of such City Courts as may be organized by law. Act of Aug. 28, 1856. What officers are included.

ART. 253. If any person shall bribe, or offer to bribe, any clerk or other officer of either branch of the legislature, or any clerk or secretary in any department of the State Government, with the intent to influence such officer to make any false entry in any book or record pertaining to his office, or to mutilate or destroy any part of such book or record, or to violate any other duty imposed upon him as an officer, he shall be punished by confinement in the Penitentiary a term not less than two nor more than five years. Act of Feb. 12, 1858. Bribery of legislative officer or any clerk.

ART. 254. If any officer named in the preceding article shall accept a bribe so offered, he shall be punished by confinement in the Penitentiary not less than two nor more than five years. Penalty for accepting bribe.

ART. 255. By a "*bribe*," as used in this Title, and throughout this Code, is meant any gift, advantage or emolument, bestowed for the purpose of inducing an officer or other person to do a particular act in violation of his duty, or as an inducement to favor, or in some manner aid the person offering the same, or some other person in a manner forbidden by law. Act of Aug. 28, 1856. Bribe defined.

ART. 256. The gift, advantage or emolument need not be direct; it may be hidden under the semblance of a sale, wager, payment of a debt, or in any other manner designed to cover the true intention of the parties. The offer or gift of the bribe must precede the act which it is intended to induce the person bribed to perform. Gift, &c., need not be direct.

TITLE VIII.

OF OFFENCES AFFECTING THE RIGHT OF SUFFRAGE.

CHAPTER I.

BRIBERY AND UNDUE INFLUENCE.

ART. 257. If any person shall bribe, or offer to bribe, any elector, for the purpose of influencing his vote at any public election, he shall be punished by fine, not exceeding five hundred dollars. Act of Aug. 28, 1856. Bribery of elector.

ART. 258. If any elector shall accept a bribe offered as set forth in the preceding article, he shall be punished in like manner as is provided with respect to the person offering the bribe. Voter accepting bribe.

Bribery of officer of election.

ART. 259. If any person shall bribe, or offer to bribe, any manager, judge, or clerk of a public election, or any officer attending the same, as a consideration for some act done or omitted to be done, or to be done or omitted contrary to his official duty in relation to such election, he shall be punished, by fine, not exceeding five hundred dollars.

Officer of election accepting bribe.

ART. 260. If any manager, judge or clerk of an election, or officer attending thereon, shall accept a bribe offered as set forth in the preceding article, he shall be punished in the same manner as is provided in reference to the persons offering the bribe.

Bribing person to influence voters.

ART. 261. If any one shall offer or give a bribe to any person whatever, for the purpose of inducing him to persuade, or by means not amounting to bribery, to procure persons to vote at any public election, for or against any particular candidate, the person so giving or offering, and the person so accepting, shall be punished by fine, not exceeding two hundred dollars.

Furnishing money to be used in.

ART. 262. If any person shall furnish money to another, to be used for the purpose of promoting the success or defeat of any particular candidate, or of any particular question submitted to a vote of the people, he shall be punished by fine, not exceeding two hundred dollars.

Attempting to influence voter by violence or threats.

ART. 263. If any person shall procure, or endeavor to procure, the vote of any elector, or the influence of any person over other electors, by means of violence, or by threats of violence, or of any injury to the person or property of such elector or person threatened, he shall be punished by fine, not exceeding five hundred dollars.

CHAPTER II.

OFFENCES BY JUDGES AND OTHER OFFICERS OF ELECTIONS.

Act of Aug. 28, 1856.

Officer of, making false entry.

ART. 264. If any Manager, Judge or Clerk of an election, shall knowingly make or consent to any false entry on the list of voters, or put into the ballot box, or permit to be put in, any ballot not given by a voter, or take out of such box, or permit to be taken out, any ballot deposited therein, except in the manner prescribed by law, or change any ballot given by an elector, or make any false return as to the number of votes given for or against any particular candidate, the person so offending shall be punished by fine, not less than one hundred dollars nor more than one thousand dollars.

Officer opening ballot, &c.

ART. 265. Any Judge, Clerk or Manager of an election, who without the consent of an elector, shall open and read, or permit to be opened and read, any ballot offered by such elector, except in counting the votes given, as provided by law, shall be punished by fine, not exceeding one hundred dollars.

Officer refusing corruptly to receive vote.

ART. 266. If any Manager or Judge of an election, shall corruptly refuse to receive the vote of any qualified elector, who shows by his own oath, that he is entitled to vote, when his vote is objected to, such Manager or Judge shall be punished by fine, not exceeding two hundred dollars.

Attempting to influence vote, &c.

ART. 267. Any Manager, Judge or Clerk of an election, who shall, while discharging his duties as such, attempt to influence the vote of an elector, for or against any particular candidate, shall be punished by fine, not exceeding two hundred dollars.

ART. 268. Any Manager, Judge or Clerk of an election, who shall, while in discharge of his duties as such, by violence or threats of violence, attempt to influence the vote of an elector for or against any particular candidate, shall be punished by fine, not exceeding one thousand dollars. Officer using violence, &c.

ART. 269. If any officer authorized by law to give a certificate of election, shall, knowingly and corruptly, give any false certificate thereof, he shall be punished by fine, not exceeding three hundred dollars. Officer giving false certificate, &c.

ART. 269a. Any officer or person having custody or charge of ballots cast in an election, who shall open and read any ballot, or who shall permit it to be done, without the consent of the elector who cast it, except when such ballot has been decided to be illegal by the lawful tribunal deciding a contested election, shall be punished by fine, not exceeding five hundred dollars. Act of Feb. 12, 1858. Officer opening ballot.

CHAPTER III.

ILLEGAL ACTS OF MAGISTRATES AND PEACE OFFICERS.

ART. 270. If any Magistrate or peace officer shall, knowingly, cause an elector to be arrested in attending upon, going to, or returning from an election, except in cases of treason, felony, or breach of the peace, he shall be punished by fine, not exceeding three hundred dollars. Arresting elector.

CHAPTER IV.

RIOTS AND UNLAWFUL ASSEMBLIES AT ELECTIONS, VIOLENCE USED TOWARDS ELECTORS.

ART. 271. If any riot be committed at the place of holding a public election, or within one mile of such place, with a design to disturb or influence such election, every person engaged therein shall be punished by fine not exceeding one thousand dollars. Act of Aug. 28, 1856. Riot at the place of election.

ART. 272. If any unlawful assembly meet at the place of holding an election, or within a mile thereof, for the purpose of preventing the holding of such election, all persons engaged in such unlawful assembly shall be punished by fine not exceeding five hundred dollars. Unlawful assembly, to prevent.

ART. 273. If any person, by force, or threats of force, shall prevent, or attempt to prevent, any person from voting at a public election, he shall be punished by fine not exceeding five hundred dollars. Preventing any person from voting, &c.

ART. 274. When the means used amount to a riot or unlawful assembly, the persons engaged therein are punishable according to the provisions of Articles 271 and 272. How punished.

CHAPTER V.

MISCELLANEOUS OFFENCES AFFECTING THE RIGHT OF SUFFRAGE.

[*See Election-riots, Electors, Unlawful Assemblies, Bribery.*]

Act of Aug. 28, 1856.

Illegal voting. ART. 275. If any person knowing himself not to be a qualified voter, shall, at any election, vote, or offer to vote, for any officer to be then chosen, he shall be fined in a sum not exceeding one hundred dollars for each offence.

Person advising illegal voting. ART. 276. Every person who shall procure, aid, assist, counsel, or advise another to give his vote at any election, knowing that the person is not duly qualified to vote, shall be fined in a sum not exceeding two hundred dollars.

Voting more than once at the same election. ART. 277. If any voter shall knowingly give in more than one ballot at any one time of balloting at any election, or if he shall vote, or offer to vote, more than once at the same election, he shall for every such offence be fined in any sum not exceeding three hundred dollars.

False swearing by elector. ART. 278. If any person challenged as unqualified, shall be guilty of wilful and corrupt false swearing, in taking any oath prescribed by law, he shall be punished by confinement in the Penitentiary, for not less than one nor more than five years.

Procuring to swear falsely. ART. 279. Every person who shall wilfully and corruptly procure any person to swear falsely, as spoken of in the preceding Article, shall be punished by confinement in the Penitentiary for any time not exceeding three years, or by fine, not exceeding three thousand dollars.

Altering ballots, &c. ART. 280. If any person shall fraudulently alter or obliterate, or wilfully secrete, suppress, or destroy any ballots, election return, or certificate of election, he shall be punished by fine, not exceeding three thousand dollars.

Failing to deliver returns. ART. 281. If any person entrusted with the transmission of an election return, shall wilfully do any act that shall defeat the delivery thereof, or shall wilfully neglect to deliver the same, as directed by law, he shall be punished by fine not exceeding one thousand dollars.

Taking returns, to prevent. ART. 282. If any person shall take away such election return from any person entrusted therewith, either by force or in any other manner, or shall wilfully do any act that shall defeat the due delivery thereof, as directed by law, he shall be punished by fine not exceeding two thousand dollars.

Officer guilty of wilful neglect of duty. ART. 283. If any officer on whom a duty is enjoined, in any statute relating to elections, shall be guilty of a wilful neglect of such duty, or shall act corruptly, or with partiality, in the discharge of such duty, in any matter not provided for in this Title, he shall be fined in a sum not less than one hundred nor more than one thousand dollars.

TITLE IX.

OF OFFENCES WHICH AFFECT THE FREE EXERCISE OF RELIGIOUS OPINION.

ART. 284. If any person shall maliciously disturb any congregation assembled for religious worship, and conducting themselves in a lawful manner, whatever may be the religion professed by such congregation, he may be put under restraint by any peace officer present, during the continuance of such religious worship. And, in addition thereto, he shall, on conviction, be fined a sum not less than five dollars nor more than one hundred dollars. Act of Aug. 28, 1856. Disturbing religious congregation.

ART. 285. If complaint be made to any magistrate, that a person has committed the offence mentioned in the preceding Article, he may be, at the discretion of the magistrate, bound over to keep the peace, and to refrain from any like disturbance for a term of one year. Complaint of such offence.

ART. 286. Double the fine prescribed in Article 284, shall be imposed for any subsequent offence of the same kind. Subsequent offence.

TITLE X.

OF OFFENCES AGAINST PUBLIC JUSTICE.

CHAPTER I.

OF PERJURY AND FALSE SWEARING.

ART. 287. Perjury is a false statement, either written or verbal, deliberately and wilfully made, relating to something past or present, under the sanction of an oath, or such affirmation as is by law equivalent to an oath, where such oath or affirmation is legally administered, under circumstances in which an oath or affirmation is required by law, or is necessary for the prosecution or defence of any private right, or for the ends of public justice. Act of Aug. 28, 1856. Definition of perjury.

ART. 288. A false statement made through inadvertence or under agitation, or by mistake, is not perjury. What is not perjury.

ART. 289. The oath or affirmation must be administered in the manner required by law, and by some person duly authorized to administer the same in the matter or cause in which such oath or affirmation is taken. Oath, how administered.

ART. 290. The false statement must be of something past or present—oaths of office, or any other promissory oaths, are therefore not included in the definition of perjury, except that part of the official oath prescribed by the Constitution which relates to duelling. Perjury relates to something past or, &c.

ART. 290a* All oaths or affirmations legally taken in any stage of a judicial proceeding, civil or criminal, in or out of court, are included in the description of this offence. Perjury further defined.

ART. 291. The statement of any circumstance wholly immaterial to the matter in respect to which the declaration is made, is not perjury. Immaterial* statement not perjury.

Penalty. ART. 292. The crime of perjury is punished by imprisonment in the penitentiary for a term not more than ten years nor less than five years.

Perjury in capital cases. ART. 293. When the perjury is committed on a trial of a capital felony, and the person guilty of such perjury has, on the trial of such felony, sworn falsely to a material fact tending to produce conviction, and the person so accused of the capital felony is convicted and suffers the penalty of death, the punishment of the perjury so committed shall be death.

Penalty for voluntary false swearing. ART. 294. If any person shall deliberately and wilfully, under oath or affirmation legally administered, make a false statement by a voluntary declaration or affidavit, which is not required by law, or made in the course of a judicial proceeding, he is guilty of "false swearing," and shall be punished by imprisonment in the Penitentiary not less than two nor more than five years.

False swearing relates to. ART. 295. The false swearing must, as in regard to perjury, be relative to something past or present.

Penalty for inducing. ART. 296. If any person shall designedly induce another to commit perjury or false swearing, he shall be punished as if he had himself committed the crime.

Penalty for attempting to, &c. ART. 297. If any person shall, by any means whatever, corruptly attempt to induce another to commit the offence of perjury, he shall be punished by imprisonment in the Penitentiary not less than two nor more than five years.

Act of Feb. 12, 1858. Penalty of attempting to procure false swearing. ART. 298. If any person shall, by any means whatever, corruptly attempt to induce another to commit the offence of false swearing, he shall be punished by imprisonment in the Penitentiary for a term not less than two nor more than five years.

CHAPTER II.

BRIBERY.

[*See Auditor, Arbitrator, Juror, Umpire, Referee, Sheriff, Attorney, Clerk, Peace-Officer, Elections.*]

Act of Feb. 12, 1858. Bribing Auditor, Juror, &c. ART. 299. If any person shall bribe, or offer to bribe any Auditor, Juror, Arbitrator, Umpire, or Referee, with intent to influence his decision, or bias his opinion in relation to any cause or matter which may be pending before, or may thereafter by law be submitted to such Auditor, Juror, Arbitrator, Umpire or Referee, he shall be punished by imprisonment in the Penitentiary not less than two nor more than five years.

Accepting a bribe by. ART. 300. If any Juror, Auditor, Arbitrator, Umpire or Referee, shall accept a bribe offered for the purpose of biasing or influencing his opinion or judgment, as set forth in the preceding Article, he shall be punished by confinement in the Penitentiary not less than two nor more than five years.

Act of Aug. 28, 1856. ART. 301. To complete the offences mentioned in Articles 299 and 300, it is not necessary that the Auditor, Umpire, Arbitrator or Referee, shall have been actually selected or appointed, it is sufficient if the bribe be offered or accepted with a view to the probable appointment or selection of the person to whom the bribe is offered, or by whom it is accepted. Nor is it necessary that the Juror shall have been actually summoned; it is sufficient if the bribe be given or accepted in view of his being summoned as a Juror or selected as such, to sit in any particular case, civil or criminal. Offering or accepting, &c., sufficient.

Act of Feb. 12, 1858. Bribing an attorney, &c.

Art. 302. If any person shall bribe, or offer to bribe, any attorney at law, or attorney in fact, charged with the prosecution or defence of a suit, with intent to induce him to divulge any secret of his client, or any circumstance which came to his knowledge as counsel, to the injury of his client, or with intent to induce him to give counsel, or in any way advise or assist the opposite party, to the injury of his client, in any cause civil or criminal, or to neglect the interest of his client, he shall be punished by imprisonment in the Penitentiary not less than two nor more than five years.

Act of Aug. 28, 1856. Accepting a bribe, &c.

Art. 303. If any attorney, at law or in fact, charged as above stated with the management of any cause, civil or criminal, shall accept a bribe offered to induce him to divulge any secret of his client, or any circumstance which came to his knowledge as counsel, to the injury of his client, or to give counsel or in any way advise or assist the opposite party to the injury of his client, or to neglect the interest of his client, he shall be punished in the manner provided in the preceding Article.

Act of Feb. 12, 1858. Bribing clerk, &c.

Art. 304. If any person shall bribe, or offer to bribe, any clerk or deputy clerk of any court of record, to induce such officer to alter, destroy or mutilate any book, record, or paper, pertaining to his office, or to surrender to the person offending any book, record, or paper, for any unlawful purpose, he shall be punished by imprisonment in the Penitentiary for a term not less than two nor more than five years; and the officer accepting such bribe shall be punished in the same manner.

Any clerk accepting.

Art. 305. If any clerk, or deputy clerk, of any court of record in this State shall accept a bribe offered for the purposes enumerated in the preceding Article, he shall be punished by imprisonment in the Penitentiary for a term not less than two nor more than five years.

Bribing or offering to bribe clerk, &c.

Art. 306. If any person shall bribe, or offer to bribe, any officer named in Article 304, to do any other act not enumerated in said Article, in violation of the duties of his office, or to omit to do any other act incumbent on him as an officer, he shall be punished by imprisonment in the Penitentiary, not less than two nor more than five years.

Bribing Sheriff, &c.

Art. 307. If any person shall bribe, or offer to bribe, any Sheriff or other peace officer, to permit any prisoner in his custody to escape, he shall be punished by imprisonment in the Penitentiary, for a term not less than two nor more than five years.

Same subject.

Art. 308. If any person shall bribe, or offer to bribe, any Sheriff, or other peace officer, in any case, civil or criminal, to make a false return upon any process directed to him, or to fail to return any such process, or to summon, or fail to summon, any one to serve on a jury, with a view to produce a result favorable to a particular side, in any cause, civil or criminal, he shall be punished by confinement in the Penitentiary, not less than two nor more than five years.

Same subject.

Art. 309. If any person shall bribe, or offer to bribe, a Sheriff, or any other peace officer, to do any other act not heretofore enumerated, contrary to his duty as an officer, or to omit to do any duty incumbent upon him as an officer, he shall be punished by confinement in the Penitentiary, not less than two nor more than five years.

Act of Aug. 28, 1856. Sheriff accepting bribe, &c. ART. 310. If any Sheriff, or other executive officer, shall accept a bribe offered, as mentioned in Articles 308 and 309, he shall receive the same punishment as is affixed to the offence of giving or offering a bribe in the particular case specified.

Offenders deprived of political rights. ART. 311. A person convicted of any one of the offences enumerated in the preceding Articles of this Title, shall, in addition to the punishments prescribed in respect to such offence, be also deprived of his political rights.

CHAPTER III.

OFFENCES RELATING TO THE ARREST AND CUSTODY OF PRISONERS.

[*See Convict, Penitentiary, Escape Jail.*]

Act of Aug. 28, 1856. Officer permitting escape in capital cases. ART. 312. Any Sheriff, or other officer, having the legal custody of any person accused or convicted of a capital offence, who wilfully permits such person to escape, or to be rescued, shall be punished by confinement in the Penitentiary not less than two nor more than ten years.

In felonies, less than capital. ART. 313. Any Sheriff, or other officer, who has the legal custody of any person accused or convicted of a felony less than capital, who wilfully permits such person to escape, or to be rescued, shall be punished by imprisonment in the Penitentiary for a term not less than two and not exceeding five years.

In misdemeanor cases. ART. 314. Any Sheriff, or other officer, having the legal custody of a person accused or convicted of a misdemeanor, who wilfully permits such person to escape, or to be rescued, shall be fined not exceeding one thousand dollars.

Negligently permitting, in capital cases. ART. 315. Any Sheriff, or other officer, who has the legal custody of a person accused or convicted of a capital offence, and who negligently permits such person to escape, or to be rescued, shall be punished by fine not exceeding two thousand dollars.

In felony, less than capital. ART. 316. Any Sheriff, or other officer, who has the legal custody of a person accused or convicted of a felony less than capital, and who negligently permits such person to escape, or to be rescued, shall be punished by fine not exceeding one thousand dollars.

In misdemeanor cases. ART. 317. Any Sheriff, or other officer, who has the legal custody of a person accused or convicted of a misdemeanor, and who negligently permits such person to escape, or to be rescued, shall be punished by fine not to exceed five hundred dollars.

ART. 318. Any Sheriff, or other officer, who wilfully refuses to execute any lawful process in his hands, requiring the arrest of a person accused of a felony, or wilfully omits to execute such process, whereby such person escapes, or wilfully refuses to receive in a jail under his charge, or to receive into his custody, any person lawfully committed to such jail, and ordered to be confined therein on an accusation of felony, or lawfully committed to his custody on such accusation, shall be fined not exceeding two thousand dollars. Sheriff refusing to arrest in felony cases.

ART. 319. Any Sheriff, or other officer, who wilfully refuses to execute any lawful process in his hands, requiring the arrest of a person accused of a misdemeanor, or wilfully omits to execute such process, whereby the accused escapes, or who wilfully refuses to receive into a jail under his charge, or to receive in his custody any person lawfully committed to such jail on an accusation of misdemeanor, or lawfully committed to his custody on such accusation, shall be punished by fine not exceeding five hundred dollars. In misdemeanor cases.

ART. 320. If any private person, appointed with his own consent, to execute a warrant of arrest, shall be guilty of any one of the offences heretofore enumerated in this Chapter, he shall be punished in the same manner as an officer in a like case. Private person guilty of offences, &c., when.

ART. 321. If any person shall convey into any jail, any disguise, instrument, arms, or any other thing useful to aid any prisoner in escaping, with intent to facilitate the escape of a prisoner lawfully detained in such jail, on an accusation of felony, or shall, in any other manner calculated to effect the object, aid in the escape of a prisoner legally confined in jail, he shall be punished by imprisonment in the Penitentiary, not less than two nor more than five years. Act of Feb. 12, 1858. Conveying arms to prisoner, &c.

ART. 322. If any person, to effect the rescue or escape of a prisoner in jail shall break into the jail, he shall be punished by imprisonment in the Penitentiary for a term not less than two nor more than six years. Act of Aug. 28, 1856. Breaking jail to rescue.

ART. 323. If any person shall, by any of the means contemplated by Article 321, aid in the escape of a person legally confined in jail upon an accusation for a misdemeanor, he shall be fined not exceeding five hundred dollars. Aiding the escape from jail.

ART. 324. If any person, for the purpose of aiding in the escape of a prisoner, so confined, shall break into the jail, he shall be fined not exceeding one thousand dollars. Same subject.

ART. 325. If any person shall wilfully aid in the escape of a prisoner from the custody of an officer by whom he is legally held in custody on an accusation for a felony, by doing any act calculated to effect that object, he shall be punished by imprisonment in the Penitentiary, not less than two nor more than seven years; and if, in aiding in the escape, he shall make use of arms, he shall be punished by imprisonment in the Penitentiary, for a term not less than two nor more than ten years. Act of Aug. 28, 1856. Aiding prisoner to escape from officer.

ART. 326. If any person shall wilfully aid a prisoner to escape from the custody of an officer, by whom he is legally detained in custody on an accusation for a misdemeanor, by doing any act calculated to effect that object, he shall be punished by fine, not exceeding five hundred dollars; and if, in aiding in the escape, he shall make use of arms, he shall be punished by fine not exceeding one thousand dollars. Act of Aug. 28, 1856. Penalty for.

ART. 327. If any person shall prevent or defeat the execution of any process in a civil cause, by any means not amounting to actual resistance, but which

Preventing execution of process in civil cause.

are calculated to prevent the execution of such process, he shall be punished by fine not exceeding five hundred dollars; evading the execution of such process is not an offence under this Article.

Offence complete without, &c.

ART. 328. The offences enumerated in Articles 321, 322, 323, 324, 325 and 326, are complete without the actual escape of the prisoner.

When retaken, person aiding may be prosecuted.

ART. 329. Any person accused of the offences enumerated in Articles 321, 322, 323, 324, 325 and 326, may be prosecuted and tried, although the person escaping may be retaken, and although after being retaken, he may be brought to trial and acquitted.

Person escaping may be retaken without warrant.

ART. 330. Any person legally confined in a jail, who escapes therefrom, may be pursued, and if taken, may be again imprisoned without warrant, notwithstanding the term for which he was imprisoned may have expired at the time he was so taken, and shall remain imprisoned until discharged in due course of law, and the period elapsing between his escape and the time he is retaken, is not to be computed as a portion of the term of his imprisonment.

Act of Feb. 12, 1858.

Person resisting the execution of process in felony cases.

ART. 331. If any person shall wilfully oppose and resist an officer in executing, or attempting to execute, any lawful warrant for the arrest of another person, in a case of felony, he shall be punished by confinement in the Penitentiary, for a term not less than two nor more than five years; and if arms be used in such resistance, he shall be punished by imprisonment in the Penitentiary, not less than two nor more than seven years.

Act of Aug. 28, 1856.

In case of misdemeanor.

ART. 332. If any person shall wilfully oppose and resist an officer in executing, or attempting to execute, any lawful warrant for the arrest of another person in a case of misdemeanor, he shall be punished by fine not exceeding five hundred dollars; and if arms be used, the punishment shall be doubled.

In a civil cause.

ART. 333. If any person shall wilfully resist and oppose an officer in executing, or attempting to execute, any process in a civil cause, he shall be fined not exceeding five hundred dollars; and if arms be used in such resistance, the punishment shall be doubled.

Where accused resists execution of process.

ART. 334. If the party against whom a legal warrant of arrest is directed in any criminal case, resist its execution, when attempted by any person legally authorized to execute the same, he shall be fined not exceeding five hundred dollars; and if arms be used in making the resistance, in such manner as would make him liable for an assault and battery, or assault with intent to murder, or any other offence against the person, he shall receive the highest penalty affixed by law for the commission of such offence in ordinary cases.

Who are guilty of resisting criminal process.

ART. 335. To render a person guilty of any of the offences included within the meaning of articles 331 and 332, the warrant or process must be executed, or its execution attempted in a legal manner.

Definition of "accusation," &c.

ART. 336. The word *accusation*, as used here, and in every part of this Code, means a charge made in a lawful manner against any person, that he has been guilty of some offence which subjects him to prosecution in the name of the State. A person is said to be *accused* of an offence from the time that any *criminal action* shall have been commenced against him.

A legal arrest without warrant;

A complaint to a magistrate;

A warrant legally issued; an Indictment, or an Information, are all examples of *accusations*, and a person proceeded against by either of these, is said to be *accused*.

Definition of

ART. 337. A person is "*legally confined in jail,*" or "legally detained in custody," when he has been committed or arrested upon a legal warrant, or arrested in any of the modes pointed out in the Code of Criminal Procedure. Words "legally confined in jail," &c.

ART. 338. The word *jail*, means any place of confinement used for detaining prisoners. Definition of jail.

ART. 339. By "Officer," as used in this Chapter, is meant any peace officer, as Sheriff, Deputy Sheriff, Constable of a beat, Marshal or Constable of a city or town, or any person specially authorized by warrant to arrest. Officer, meaning of.

ART. 339a. If any person, being called on by a magistrate, or peace officer, shall fail or refuse to aid such officer in any matter in which by law he may be rightfully called on to aid or assist, in the execution of a duty incumbent upon such magistrate, or peace officer, he shall be punished by fine not exceeding one hundred dollars. Act of Feb. 12, 1858. If person called on refuse to aid officer.

CHAPTER IV.

FALSE CERTIFICATE, AUTHENTICATION OR ENTRY BY AN OFFICER.

1. *Commissioner of Deeds.*

ART. 340. If any person, being a Commissioner of Deeds and Depositions, who is residing out of this State, and acting as such Commissioner under authority of a law of the State, shall fraudulently certify to the execution of any instrument of writing which was never in fact acknowledged or proved before him as the same purports to have been acknowledged, or proved, he shall be punished by imprisonment in the penitentiary, not less than two nor more than five years. Act of Aug 28, 1856. False certificate, &c.

ART. 341. By "instrument of writing," is meant any deed, conveyance, transfer, release, obligation, or other written instrument of any kind or description whatever, which such Commissioner is, by the law, authorized to authenticate for record. Instrument of writing, meaning of.

ART. 342. If any such Commissioner shall falsely certify to any deposition purporting to have been taken before him, and to be used in any cause pending in a Court of this State, he shall be punished in the same manner as is prescribed in Article 340. As to depositions.

ART. 343. If any such Commissioner shall falsely certify to any affidavit purporting to have been made before him, and which by law he is authorized to take, he shall be punished as prescribed in Article 340. As to affidavit.

2. *Clerk of a Court.*

ART. 344. If any Clerk of a Court in this State, shall knowingly make any False entry by.

false entry upon the records of his Court, which may prejudice or injure the rights of any person, he shall be punished by confinement in the penitentiary, not less than two nor more than five years.

False certificate. ART. 345. If any such Clerk shall give a false certificate, stating that any person has done any act whatever, to which he has a right to certify, or that such person is entitled to any right whatever, when such Clerk may, by law, give such certificate if the same were true, he shall be punished as directed in the preceding Article.

3. *Authentication of Deeds or Depositions by Notary Publics, or other like officers.*

False certificate to instrument, &c. ART. 346 If any Notary Public, Chief Justice of a county, or other officer authorized by law, shall give a false certificate for the purpose of authenticating any instrument of writing for registration, he shall be punished by imprisonment in the penitentiary, for a term not less than two nor more than five years.

Act of Feb. 12, 1858. As to depositions, Affidavits, &c. ART. 347. If any officer authorized by law to take depositions, or administer oaths, in this State, shall falsely certify that any deposition was sworn to before him, or any oath made, or shall with fraudulent intent place his certificate, signature, or seal, to any affidavit which is drawn with blanks as to any matter of substance, he shall be punished by imprisonment in the penitentiary, for a term not less than two nor more than five years, and shall be dismissed from office. Within the meaning of this Article, shall be included the case of an officer who, with design that the same may be filled up and used for fraudulent purposes, attaches his signature or seal of office to any paper wholly blank. Certificate to a blank paper, &c.

4. *General Provisions.*

Act of Aug. 28, 1856. Took effect Feb. 1, 1857. Officer corruptly refusing to issue or execute process. ART. 348. Whenever any officer, who is by law charged with the issuance or execution of process, either in civil or criminal actions, corruptly and wilfully refuses to issue or execute such process, or corruptly and wilfully refuses to perform any other duty enjoined upon him by law, he shall, when the act or omission is not otherwise provided for or punished, be deemed guilty of a misdemeanor, and shall be fined not exceeding five hundred dollars, and may, in the discretion of the jury, be imprisoned in the county jail not exceeding one year.

Rule where officer is declared guilty of, &c. ART. 349. Wherever, in the Code of Criminal Procedure, it is declared that an officer is guilty of an offence on account of any particular act or omission, and there is not, in the Penal Code, any punishment assigned for the same, such officer shall be deemed guilty of a misdemeanor, and shall be fined, not exceeding two hundred dollars.

Malfeasance in office. ART. 350. All offences committed by officers of the law, when not otherwise designated, are known under the general name of *malfeasance in office.*

Officer of the law is, &c. ART. 351. An officer of the law is any Magistrate, Peace Officer, or Clerk of a Court.

CHAPTER V.

EXTORTION BY OFFICERS.

Extortion by. ART. 352. If any officer, authorized by law to demand or receive fees of office, or any person employed by such officer, shall wilfully demand or receive higher fees than are allowed by law, he shall be punished by fine not exceeding one hundred dollars for each offence.

ART. 353. The preceding Article applies to all persons holding any office to which fees are attached, and to the heads of the Departments of the Government, in whose offices fees may be chargeable. To whom applicable.

ART. 354. If any Justice of the Peace, Sheriff, or other Peace Officer, shall wilfully neglect to return, arrest, or prosecute any person committing a breach of the peace, or other crime or misdemeanor, which has been committed within his view or knowledge, or shall wilfully and knowingly absent himself from any place where such crime or misdemeanor is being committed, or is about to be committed, for the purpose of avoiding seeing or having a knowledge of the same, he shall be guilty of a misdemeanor, and, on conviction, shall be fined not less than seventy-five dollars, nor more than five hundred dollars, and may, in the discretion of the Court, be removed from office. It shall be the duty of the District Courts to give this Article specially in charge to the Grand Jury. Officers wilfully neglecting to arrest, &c. May be removed from office.

CHAPTER VI.

EMBEZZLEMENT BY OFFICERS OF COURTS.

ART. 354a. If any sheriff or other officer, entitled to collect money for a party to a suit, shall without the consent of the party entitled, unlawfully convert the same, or any part thereof, to his own use, collected by him and justly belonging to such party, he shall be punished as provided in Articles 756 and 757. Act of Feb. 12, 1858. Embezzlement by.

CHAPTER VII.

UNLAWFULLY DEALING IN JURY SCRIPT AND WITNESS FEES.

ART. 354b. No Clerk or Deputy Clerk, of any District or County Court, Sheriff or his Deputy, Constable or Coroner, or Justice of the Peace, shall hereafter be permitted to purchase, or otherwise acquire from the party interested, any Jury Script or the fees coming to any witness, in any proceeding whatever, before either the District or County Court, or the Court of any Justice of the Peace, or before any Coroner's Inquest; and any officer above mentioned, guilty of such unlawful dealing, shall be punished by fine not exceeding one hundred dollars. Shall not deal in.

TITLE XI.

OF OFFENCES AGAINST THE PUBLIC PEACE.

CHAPTER I.

UNLAWFUL ASSEMBLIES.

Act of Aug. 28, 1856.

What is unlawful assembly.

ART. 355. An unlawful assembly is the meeting of three or more persons, with intent to aid each other by violence, either to commit an offence, or illegally to deprive any person of the enjoyment of any right.

To prevent holding election.

ART. 356. If the purpose of the unlawful assembly is to prevent the holding of any public election, or to prevent any particular person, or number of persons, from voting at a public election, the punishment shall be that which is prescribed in Article 272.

To prevent execution of court decree, or,

ART. 357. If the purpose of the unlawful assembly be to oppose or prevent the execution or enforcement of any law of the State, or the lawful decree or judgment of a court in a civil action, the punishment shall be a fine not exceeding five hundred dollars.

To effect a rescue of prisoner convicted of capital offence.

ART. 358. If the purpose of the unlawful assembly be to effect the rescue of a prisoner lawfully convicted of a capital offence, the punishment shall be fine not exceeding one thousand dollars.

Less than capital.

ART. 359. If the purpose of the unlawful assembly be to effect the rescue of any person lawfully convicted of a felony less than capital, the punishment shall be fine not exceeding five hundred dollars.

Rescue before conviction.

ART. 360. If the purpose of the unlawful assembly be to rescue any person arrested or imprisoned for a capital offence before trial, the punishment shall be fine not exceeding five hundred dollars.

Same subject.

ART. 361. If the purpose of the unlawful assembly be to rescue any person lawfully arrested or imprisoned for any felony less than capital, the punishment shall be fine not exceeding three hundred dollars.

Same subject.

ART. 362. If the purpose of the unlawful assembly be to rescue a person accused of a misdemeanor, the punishment shall be fine not exceeding two hundred dollars.

To prevent holding of court, &c.

ART. 362a.* If the purpose of the unlawful assembly be to prevent or oppose the sitting of any lawful Court, Board of Arbitrators or Referees, the punishment shall be fine not exceeding one thousand dollars.

To prevent the collection of Taxes.

ART. 363. If the purpose of the unlawful assembly be to prevent the collection of taxes, or other money due the State, the punishment shall be fine not exceeding five hundred dollars.

Any other illegal purpose.

ART. 364. If the purpose of the unlawful assembly be to effect any illegal object other than those mentioned in the preceding Articles of this Chapter, all persons engaged therein shall be liable to fine, not exceeding two hundred dollars.

Certain meetings not within the meaning of.

ART. 365. No public meeting for the purpose of exercising any political, religious, or other lawful rights; no assembly for the purpose of lawful amusement or recreation, is within the meaning of this Chapter.

CHAPTER II.

RIOTS.

ART. 366. If the persons unlawfully assembled together do, or attempt to do, any illegal act, all those engaged in such illegal act are guilty of riot.

Definition of.

ART. 367. If the purpose of a riot be to prevent the collection of taxes, or other money due the State, any persons engaged therein, shall be punished by fine not less than two hundred dollars, and not exceeding one thousand dollars, although the purpose of the riot be not effected; and if such illegal purpose be effected, in addition thereto, imprisonment in the county jail, not exceeding two years, may be added.

To prevent the collection of taxes, &c.

ART. 368. If any person, by engaging in a riot, shall prevent the execution or enforcement of any law of the State, or the lawful decree or judgment of any court, in a civil cause, he shall be punished by imprisonment in the county jail, not exceeding two years, and by fine, not less than two hundred nor more than one thousand dollars.

Execution of a law.

ART. 369. If any person, by engaging in a riot, shall rescue another lawfully convicted, or under lawful sentence of death, he shall be punished by imprisonment in the penitentiary, not less than five nor more than ten years.

To rescue a person convicted of capital offence.

ART. 370. If any person, by engaging in a riot, shall rescue any prisoner lawfully convicted of felony, less than capital, or lawfully under sentence for such offence, he shall be punished by imprisonment in the penitentiary, not less than two nor more than seven years.

Rescue where felony is less than, &c.

ART. 371. If any person, by engaging in a riot, shall rescue any person lawfully arrested or imprisoned for a capital felony, he shall be punished by confinement in the penitentiary, not less than two nor more than seven years.

Rescue of person imprisoned for capital felony.

ART. 372. If any person, by engaging in a riot, shall rescue any person lawfully arrested or imprisoned for a felony less than capital, he shall be punished by confinement in the penitentiary, not less than two nor more than seven years.

Act of Feb. 12, 1858.

Less than capital.

ART. 373. If any person, by engaging in a riot, shall commit any illegal act, other than those mentioned in Articles 367, 368, 369, 370, 371, and 372, he shall, in addition to receiving the punishment affixed to such illegal act, by other provisions of this Code, be also punished by confinement in the county jail, not exceeding one year, or by fine, not exceeding one thousand dollars.

Act of Aug. 28, 1856.

Other illegal acts.

ART. 374. When the purpose of the riot was to effect any of the illegal acts mentioned in the eight preceding articles, and such unlawful object is not effected, the punishment may, in the discretion of the jury, be diminished to half the penalty affixed to such riot, where the illegal purpose was effected.

Where object is not effected.

All who engage in, are guilty, &c.

ART. 375. A person engaged in any riot, whereby an illegal act is committed, shall be deemed guilty of the offence of Riot, according to the character and degree of such offence, whether the said illegal act was in fact perpetrated by him, or by those with whom he is participating.

Rule where purpose was first lawful.

ART. 376. Where the persons engaged in any unlawful assembly, met at first for a lawful purpose, and afterwards agreed upon an unlawful purpose, they are equally guilty of the offence defined in Article 355.

Same subject.

ART. 377. Where the assembly was at first lawful, and the persons so assembled afterwards agree to join in the commission of an act which would amount to a riot, if it had been the original purpose of the meeting, all those who do not retire when the change of purpose is known, are guilty of riot.

Any one engaged in, may be prosecuted before.

ART. 378. Any one person engaged in an unlawful assembly or riot, may be prosecuted and convicted before the others are arrested, but the indictment or information must state, and it must be proved on the trial, that three or more persons were assembled, and their names given, if known, if not known, it must be so alleged.

Indictment in such cases.

ART. 379. The indictment or information must likewise state the illegal act which was the object of the meeting, or which they proceeded to do, if the assembly was originally lawful.

Duty of peace-officers to suppress.

ART. 380. If any persons shall be unlawfully or riotously assembled together, it shall be the duty of any magistrate, or peace officer, so soon as it may come to his knowledge, to go to the place of such unlawful or riotous assembly, and command the persons assembled to disperse; and all who continue so unlawfully assembled, or engaged in a riot, after being warned to disperse, shall be punished by the addition of one-half the penalty to which they would otherwise be liable, if no such warning had been given.

CHAPTER III.

AFFRAYS AND DISTURBANCES OF THE PEACE.

Affray defined.

ART. 381. If any two or more persons shall fight together in a public place, they shall be punished by fine not exceeding one hundred dollars.

Disturbance of the peace, &c.

ART. 382. If any two or more persons shall assemble in any public place, without such intent as would make the meeting an unlawful assembly or riot, and shall, by loud and vociferous quarrelling, disturb the inhabitants of the place in the prosecution of their lawful business, any person engaged in such disturbance shall be fined, not exceeding twenty-five dollars.

What constitutes a public place.

ART. 383. A public place within the meaning of the two preceding Articles, is any public road, street, or alley, of a town or city, inn, tavern, store, grocery, work-shop, or any place to which people commonly resort for purposes of business, recreation, or amusement.

TITLE XII.

OFFENCES AGAINST PUBLIC MORALS, DECENCY AND CHASTITY.

CHAPTER I.

UNLAWFUL MARRIAGE.

ART. 384. If any person who has a former husband or wife living, shall marry another in this State, such person shall be punished by imprisonment in the Penitentiary for a term not exceeding three years. When former husband, or, &c., is living.

ART. 385. The provisions of the preceding Article shall not extend to any person whose husband or wife shall have been continually remaining out of the State, or shall have voluntarily withdrawn from the other and remained absent for five years, the person marrying again not knowing the other to be living within that time. Nor shall the provisions of said Article extend to any person who has been legally divorced from the bonds of matrimony. Not punishable, when.

ART. 386. If any white person shall, within this State, knowingly marry a negro, or a person of mixed blood, descended from negro ancestry, to the third generation inclusive, though one ancestor of each generation may have been a white person, or having so married in or out of this State, shall continue within this State to cohabit with such negro, or such descendant of a negro, he or she shall be punished by confinement in the Penitentiary not less than two nor more than five years. Act of Feb. 12, 1858. Marriage of white person with a negro, &c.

ART. 387. In trials for the offences named in the three preceding Articles, proof of marriage by mere reputation shall not be sufficient. Act of Aug. 28, 1856. Proof of.

CHAPTER II.

OF INCEST AND ADULTERY.

ART. 388. All persons who are forbidden to marry by the succeeding Articles, who shall intermarry or carnally know each other, shall be punished by imprisonment in the Penitentiary, not less than two nor more than ten years. Act of Feb. 12, 1858. Punishment.

ART. 389. No man shall marry his mother, his father's sister or half sister, his mother's sister or half sister, his daughter, the daughter of his brother or sister, or of his half brother or sister, the daughter of his son or daughter, his father's widow, his son's widow, his wife's daughter, the daughter of his wife's son or daughter. Act of Aug. 28, 1858. Certain marriages prohibited.

ART. 390. No woman shall marry her father, her father's brother or half brother, her mother's brother or half brother, her brother, her son, the son of her brother or sister, or of her half brother or sister, the son of her son or daughter, her mother's husband after the death of her mother, her daughter's husband after the death of her daughter, her husband's son, the son of her husband's son or daughter. Same subject.

Relationship, how proved.

ART. 391. Upon a trial for incest, the fact of the relationship between the parties may be proved in the manner in which that fact is established in civil suits, and proof of cohabitation or carnal knowledge, shall be, in all cases, sufficient, without proof of marriage.

Act of Feb. 12, 1858. Adultery, punishment.

ART. 392. Every man and woman who shall live together in adultery, or fornication, shall be punished by fine, not less than one hundred nor more than one thousand dollars.

Act of Aug. 28, 1856. Proof.

ART. 393. It is sufficient to prove in trials for living in adultery that the parties cohabit together, and that one of them is married to some other person. The proof of marriage, in such cases, may be made by the testimony of any person who was present at such marriage, or who has known the husband and wife to live together as married persons.

Definition of.

ART. 394. Where two persons live together in a state of cohabitation, one of them being married, they are both guilty of adultery according to the sense in which the term is here used, though only one of them be married.

Single act of, not sufficient.

ART. 395. A single act of adultery is not sufficient to bring the offence within the meaning of this Chapter, unless proof be made that the parties live together.

Act of Feb. 12, 1858. Adultery with a negro, &c.

ART. 395a. Every white person who shall live in adultery or fornication with a negro, or a person of mixed blood, descended from negro ancestry, to the third generation inclusive, though one ancestor of each generation may have been a white person, shall be punished by fine, of not less than one hundred nor more than one thousand dollars.

CHAPTER III.

DISORDERLY HOUSES.

Definition of.

ART. 396. A disorderly house is one kept for the purpose of public prostitution, or as a common resort for prostitutes, vagabonds, free negroes, or slaves.

Act of Aug. 28, 1856. Same subject.

ART. 397. Any room or part of a building appropriated for either of the purposes above enumerated, is a disorderly house within the meaning of this Chapter.

Act of Feb. 12, 1858. Penalty for keeping.

ART 398. Any person who shall keep a disordely house, as defined above, shall be punished by fine, not less than one hundred nor more than five hundred dollars.

CHAPTER IV.

OF INDECENT EXHIBITIONS AND PUBLICATIONS.

Act of Aug. 28, 1856. Punishment.

ART. 399. If any person shall make, publish or print, any indecent and obscene print, picture or written composition, manifestly designed to corrupt the morals of youth, or shall designedly make any obscene and indecent exhibition of his own or the person of another, in public, he shall be fined, not exceeding one hundred dollars.

CHAPTER V.

DISTURBANCE OF GRAVES AND DEAD BODIES

Act of Feb. 12, 1858. — Punishment for disturbing, &c.

ART. 399a. If any person shall wrongfully destroy, mutilate, deface, injure, or remove any tomb, monument, grave-stone, or other structure in any place used or intended for the burial of the dead, or any fence, railing, or curb, for the protection of such structure, or any enclosure for any such place of burial, or shall wrongfully injure, cut, remove, or destroy any tree or shrub growing within any such enclosure, he shall be punished by imprisonment in jail, not exceeding six months, or by fine, not exceeding five hundred dollars.

For disinterring, &c.

ART. 399b. If any person not authorized by law, or by a relative or friend, for the purpose of re-interment, shall disinter, remove, or carry away any human body, or the remains thereof, or shall conceal the same, knowing it to be so illegally disinterred, he shall be punished by fine, not exceeding two thousand dollars.

TITLE XIII.

OF OFFENCES AGAINST PUBLIC POLICY AND ECONOMY.

CHAPTER I.

ILLEGAL BANKING AND PASSING SPURIOUS MONEY.

Act of Aug. 28, 1856. — Issuing bills within the State

ART. 400. If any person within the State shall issue any bill, promissory note, check, or other paper intended to circulate as money, he shall be fined, not less than ten dollars, nor more than fifty dollars, for each bill, promissory note, check, or other paper so issued.

If any officer of, &c., sign bills, &c.

ART. 401. Any officer of any banking company or body corporate who signs his own name, or that of another, by the authority of such other, to any bank bill, promissory note, check, or other paper, being evidence of a promise to pay, and intended to circulate as money is guilty of the offence punishable by the preceding Article.

Endorsing of bank bills, &c.

ART. 402. Any person who may bring into this State any bank bill, purporting to be issued by any bank in any other State or Territory of the Union, or in any foreign country, and shall sign or endorse the same to be circulated as money in this State, shall be deemed guilty of the offence mentioned in Article 400.

Act of Feb. 12, 1858. — Passing broken bank paper, &c.

ART. 403. If any person shall fraudulently pass or transfer, or offer to pass or transfer, any paper purporting to be bank paper, and to be issued by any bank which having once existed, has since broken, or the money of the same become valueless, he shall be punished by confinement in the Penitentiary, not less than two nor more than five years.

CHAPTER II.

OF LOTTERIES AND RAFFLES.

Act of Aug. 28, 1856. Penalty for establishing. ART. 404. If any person shall establish a lottery, or dispose of any estate, real or personal, by lottery, he shall be fined not less than one hundred dollars, nor more than one thousand dollars.

For selling tickets, &c. ART. 405. If any person shall sell, offer for sale, or keep for sale, any ticket or part ticket in any lottery, he shall be fined not less than ten dollars nor more than fifty dollars.

Penalty for establishing a raffle. ART. 406. If any person shall establish a raffle for, or dispose by raffle, of any estate, real or personal, exceeding five hundred dollars in value, he shall be fined, not less than one hundred, nor more than one thousand dollars.

Selling tickets for. ART. 407. If any person shall offer for sale, or keep for sale, any ticket or part ticket in any raffle, of estate real or personal, exceeding five hundred dollars in value, he shall be fined, not less than ten nor more than fifty dollars.

CHAPTER III.

OF SELLING TO INDIANS AND FREE PERSONS OF COLOR.

Selling arms, liquor, &c., to. ART. 408. If any person shall sell, give or barter, any ardent spirits, arms or ammunition, to an Indian of the wild or unfriendly tribes, or shall sell, barter or give to a free person of color, any ardent spirits, arms or ammunition, he shall be fined, not less than ten, nor more than one hundred dollars. Justices of the Peace and Mayors shall have jurisdiction under this Chapter.

CHAPTER IV.

GAMING.

Playing cards at house for retailing, or other public place. ART. 409. If any person shall play at any game with cards, at any house for retailing spirituous liquors, store-house, tavern, inn, or any other public house, or in any street, highway, or other public place, or in any out-house where people resort, he shall be fined not less than ten nor more than twenty-five dollars.

What houses are included. ART. 410. All houses commonly known as *public*, and all gaming houses, are included within the meaning of the preceding Article. Any room attached to such public house, and commonly used for gaming, is also included, whether the same be kept closed or open. A private room of an inn or tavern is not within the meaning of a public place, unless such room is commonly used for gaming.

ART. 411. Upon the trial of any person accused of offending against the provisions of the two preceding Articles, either in the District Court, or Justices' or Mayors' Courts, it shall not be necessary to prove that any money, or article of value, or the representative of either, was bet at such game. The offence is complete without such proof: * * * * * Proof necessary. Proviso repealed.

ART. 412. If any person shall keep or exhibit, for the purpose of gaming, any gaming table or bank of any name or description whatever, or any table or bank used for gaming which has no name, or shall be in any manner interested in keeping or exhibiting such table or bank, at any place whatever, he shall be fined not less than twenty-five dollars, nor more than one hundred dollars. Keeping table or bank for, how punished.

ART. 413. It being intended by the foregoing Article to include every species of gaming device known by the name of table or bank of every kind whatever, this provision shall be construed to include any and all games which in common language are said to be *dealt, kept or exhibited.* Definition of gaming table, &c.

ART. 414. Lest any misapprehension should arise as to whether certain games are included within the meaning of the foregoing Articles, it is declared that the following games are within the meaning and intention of said Articles, viz: "Faro;" "Monte;" "Viente-un;" "Rouge et Noir;" "Roulette;" "A. B. C.;" "Chuck Luck;" "Keno;" "Pool," and "Rondo;" but the enumeration of these games specially, shall not exclude any other properly within the meaning of the two preceding Articles. Any game played for money upon a billiard table, or table resembling a billiard table, other than the game of billiards licensed by law, is punishable under the provisions of this Chapter. Certain games enumerated.

ART. 415. In any indictment or information for the class of offences named in the three preceding Articles, it is sufficient to state that the person accused kept a table or bank for gaming, or exhibited a table or bank for gaming, without giving the name or description thereof, and without stating that the table or bank, or gaming device, was without any name, or that the name was unknown. Indictment or, &c., when sufficient.

ART. 416. In proceedings before the District Court, or before Justices of the Peace, Mayors, and Recorders, on the trial of offences under Articles 412, 413 and 414, it is sufficient to prove that any game therein mentioned was *played, dealt,* or *exhibited,* without proving that money or other articles of value was won or lost thereon. Proof necessary.

ART. 417. The words "played and "dealt", have the meaning attached to them in common language. The word "exhibited" is intended to signify the act of displaying the bank or game, for the purpose of obtaining betters. Definition of "dealt," "played," &c.

ART. 418. If any person shall bet at any gaming table, or bank, such as are in the six preceding Articles mentioned, he shall be fined not less than ten, nor more than twenty-five dollars. Betting at, &c., how punished.

ART. 419. If any person shall permit any game, prohibited by the provisions of this Chapter, to be played in his house, or a house under his control, he shall be fined not less than ten, nor more than one hundred dollars. Permitting game to be played.

ART. 420. If any person shall rent to another a room or house, for the purpose of being used as a place for playing, dealing, or exhibiting, any of the games prohibited by the provisions of this Chapter, he shall be fined not less Renting room for purpose of.

than twenty-five, nor more than one hundred dollars. It shall be presumed that a room, or house, was let for the purpose of being used for gaming, whenever the lessor knew that to be the object for which it was rented.

Act of Feb. 12. 1858. Grand Jury, &c., may compel attendance of witnesses. ART. 420a. The Grand Juries, Justices of the Peace, Mayors and Recorders, having jurisdiction of violations of the provisions of the preceding Articles, are empowered to send for persons, and compel their attendance as witnesses to give evidence of a violation of any of the provisions of the foregoing Articles; and any such person so made a witness, shall be exempt from liability for any violation of said Articles of this Code, of which he is compelled to give evidence.

CHAPTER V.

BETTING ON ELECTIONS.

Penalty for. ART. 421. If any person shall, whether before or after the happening of any public election, held within this State, wager or bet in any manner whatever upon the result of any such election, he shall be fined, not less than twenty-five nor more than one thousand dollars.

Act of Aug. 28, 1855. Public election, meaning of. ART. 422. A public election within the meaning of the preceding Article, is any election for a public officer under the authority of the Constitution and Laws of the United States or of this State.

Nature of the bet. ART. 423. The bet or wager may be of money, or of any article of value; and any device in the form of purchase, or sale, or in any other form, made for the purpose of concealing the true intention of the parties, is equally within the meaning of a bet, or wager.

CHAPTER VI.

NEGLECT OF OFFICERS TO ARREST OR PROSECUTE IN GAMING CASES.

Act of Feb. 12, 1858. Neglect by Justice of Peace, Mayor, &c. ART. 423a. If any Justice of the Peace, Mayor, or Recorder, shall know the fact that an offence against the Gaming Laws has been committed by any person, and shall fail or neglect to cause such person to be arrested and prosecuted for the same, he shall be punished by fine, not less than twenty-five nor more than one hundred dollars.

Neglect by peace officer. ART. 423b. If any peace-officer shall know that any person has committed an offence against the Gaming Laws, and shall neglect or fail to give information thereof to some Justice of the Peace, Mayor, or Recorder, having jurisdiction to try such offence, he shall be punished by fine, not less than twenty-five nor more than one hundred dollars.

Offence defined, &c. ART. 423c. By the term offence against the Gaming Laws, as used in the two preceding Articles, is meant any offence included within the provisions of Title 13, Chapter 4, of the Penal Code.

CHAPTER VII.

RETAILING LIQUOR WITHOUT LICENSE.

Art. 423 d If any person or firm shall sell, or be in any way concerned in selling spirituous, vinous, or other intoxicating liquors, in quantities less than one quart, without first having obtained license therefor, in the manner prescribed by "An act to authorize the County Courts of this State to grant license for the retail of spirituous, vinous, and other intoxicating liquors, in quantities less than one quart, and imposing a license tax for such privilege," approved 2d February, 1856, or in violation of any other law hereafter passed, regulating licenses for the sale of liquor, or shall violate any other provision of said act of 2d February, 1856, such person, or firm, shall be punished by fine, not less than fifty nor more than two hundred and fifty dollars. Retailing in less quantities than a quart, penalty.

Art. 423 e. If any person, or firm, shall sell, or be in any way concerned in selling spirituous, vinous, or other intoxicating liquors, in quantities of a quart or more, and shall permit the same to be drank at the place, or establishment where sold, or any other place provided by said person or firm for that purpose, he shall be punished as provided in the preceding Article. Retailing by quart, or more, and permitting same to be drank at.

Art. 423 f. Where persons are jointly indicted, or otherwise prosecuted for selling liquor in violation of law, or for any other offence against said act of 2d February, 1856, it shall be sufficient to show by general reputation, that they are understood to be members of the firm. Persons jointly indicted, proof.

Art. 423 g. Any one member of a firm may be separately prosecuted for the offence of selling liquor in violation of the law, or for any other offence against said act of 2d February, 1856, unless it be shown by evidence, and under a special plea, that the defendant was notoriously in partnership with some other person, and that such other person was, at the time of commencing the prosecution, a resident of the county where the same is instituted. Any one member of, may be prosecuted, unless.

Art. 423 h. Where any establishment for the sale of liquor is conducted without the name of the owner being known, any and all persons who may be found selling liquor in such establishment, in violation of law, shall be subject to prosecution as separate offenders. Where owner, &c., is unknown.

Art. 423 i. When a firm is prosecuted for a violation of the law relating to the sale of liquor, the fine shall be assessed against the parties jointly, but each defendant shall be liable for the whole amount; and in cases of prosecution against a firm, if all the defendants be not arrested, a verdict and judgment for the full amount of the fine may be rendered against any one or more who may be tried. Fine against firm assessed jointly.

Art. 423 k. Each separate act of selling shall constitute a separate offence under the six preceding Articles. Each act a separate offence.

Art. 423 l. No fines, forfeitures, or penalties, which have accrued, and no prosecution which is pending for unlawfully selling liquor, shall be affected by the provisions of the seven preceding Articles, nor shall the provisions of this act affect any other sections, or parts of the act of 2d February, 1856, above recited, except the fifth and sixth sections of the same. Pending prosecutions, &c., not affected, &c.

CHAPTER VIII.

PEDDLING WITHOUT LICENSE.

Penalty for.

ART. 423m. If any person shall, without first obtaining license therefor, pursue the occupation of a peddler, he shall be punished by a fine of fifty dollars; and prosecutions under this Article may be instituted before any Justice of the county where the offence is committed.

TITLE XIV.

OF OFFENCES AFFECTING PUBLIC HEALTH.

CHAPTER I.

OF OCCUPATIONS INJURIOUS TO HEALTH.

Penalty for carrying on.

ART. 424. If any person shall carry on any trade, or business, injurious to the health of those who reside in the vicinity, or shall suffer any substance which shall have that effect to remain on premises in his possession, he shall be punished by fine, not less than ten dollars nor more than one hundred dollars; and each separate day of carrying on such business or trade, or of permitting such substance to remain on the premises, shall be considered a separate offence.

CHAPTER II.

SALE OF UNWHOLSOME FOOD, DRINK, OR MEDICINE.

Selling unwholsome food.

ART. 425. If any person shall knowingly sell the flesh of any animal, dying otherwise than by slaughter, or slaughtered when diseased; or shall sell any kind of corrupted, diseased, or unwholsome substance, whether for food or drink, without making the same fully known to the buyer, he shall be fined not less than twenty nor more than one hundred dollars.

Adulterated food, liquor, &c.

ART. 426. If any person shall fraudulently adulterate, for the purpose of sale, any substance intended for food, or any spiritous, vinous, or malt liquor, intended for drink, with any substance injurious to health, he shall be punished by fine, not less than fifty dollars nor more than five hundred dollars.

Adulterated medicine.

ART. 427. If any person shall fraudulently adulterate, for the purpose of sale, any drug or medicine, in such manner as to change the operation of such drug or medicine, or render the same worthless, or injurious to health, he shall be punished by fine, not less than fifty dollars nor more than five hundred dollars.

TITLE XV.

OF OFFENCES AFFECTING PROPERTY HELD IN COMMON FOR THE USE OF THE PUBLIC.

CHAPTER I.

OBSTRUCTION OF NAVIGABLE STREAMS.

ART. 428. If any person shall obstruct the navigation of any stream which can be navigated by steam, keel, or flat boats, by cutting and felling trees, or by building a dyke, mill-dam, or other obstruction of a like kind, he shall be fined, not less than fifty nor more than five hundred dollars. *Penatly for.*

ART. 429. If any person shall erect any fence, or building, or dig any ditch, or throw up any mound of earth, in any street, or public road, or square, or do any other act not authorized by law, that shall obstruct the public use thereof, or shall unlawfully destroy, injure or obstruct the passage over any bridge erected thereon, he shall be fined, not less than three nor more than ten dollars, for each day such unlawful obstruction shall remain. *Penalty for.*

ART. 430. The County Courts may make such regulations as they deem proper, relative to removing obstructions from public roads and bridges; and all persons guilty of any offence named in the preceding Article, shall also be subject to such regulations. *County Court may make regulations, &c.*

TITLE XVI.

OF OFFENCES AGAINST TRADE AND COMMERCE, AND THE CURRENT COINS.

CHAPTER I

OF FORGERY AND OTHER OFFENCES AFFECTING WRITTEN INSTRUMENTS.

ART. 431. He is guilty of forgery who, without *lawful authority*, and with intent to *injure* or *defraud*, shall make a false *instrument in writing*, purporting to be the act of *another*, in such manner that the false instrument so made, would (if the same were true) have created, increased, diminished, discharged, or defeated any *pecuniary obligation*, or would have transferred, or in any manner have affected any *property* whatever. *Act of August 28, 1856. Forged instruments.*

ART. 432. He is also guilty of forgery who, without lawful authority, and with intent to injure or defraud, shall *alter* an instrument in writing, then already in existence, by whomsoever made, in such manner that the alteration would (if it had been legally made) have created, increased, diminished, discharged, or defeated any pecuniary obligation, or would have transferred, or in any manner have affected any property whatever. *Alteration of written instruments.*

ART. 433. If any person be guilty of forgery, he shall be punished by confinement in the Penitentiary, not less than two years nor more than seven years. *Punishment.*

Definition of "instrument of writing." ART. 434. The words "instrument in writing," as used in Article 431 and 432, and elsewhere in this Chapter, include every writing purporting to make known or declare the will or intention of the party whose act it purports to be, whether the same be of record, or under seal or private signature, or whatever other form it may have. It must be upon paper or parchment, or some substance made to resemble either of them. The words may be written, printed, stamped, or made in any other way, or by any other device. And the words "in writing," "write," "written," include all these modes of making. An instrument partly printed or stamped, and partly written, is an instrument in writing. In order to come within the definition of forgery, the signature, when made otherwise than by writing, must be made to resemble manuscript.

Who are guilty of making or altering, &c. ART. 435. He is guilty of making or altering, as the case may be, under Articles 431, and 432, who, knowing the illegal purpose intended, shall write, or cause to be written, the signature, or the whole or any part of the forged instrument. All persons engaged in the illegal act, are deemed guilty of forgery.

Filling up over signature. ART. 436. It is forgery to make, with intent to defraud or injure, a written instrument, by filling up over a genuine signature, or by writing on the opposite side of a paper, so as to make the signature appear as an indorsement.

Rule where authority is believed sufficient. ART. 437. When the person making, or altering an instrument in writing, acts under an authority which he has good reason to believe, and actually does believe, to be sufficient, he is not guilty of forgery, though the authority be in fact insufficient and void.

Definition of the word "alter." ART. 438. The word "alter," in the definition of forgery, means to erase or obliterate any word, letter, or figure, to extract the writing altogether, or to substitute other words, letters, or figures, for those erased, obliterated or extracted, to add any other word, letter or figure, to the original instrument; or to make any other change whatever, which shall have the effect to create, increase, diminish, discharge, or defeat, a pecuniary obligation, or to transfer, or in any other way affect any property whatever.

Instrument must purport to be the act of "another." ART. 439. The instrument must purport to be the act of "another," and within the meaning of this word, as used in defining forgery, are included this State, the United States, or either of the States or Territories of the Union; all the several branches of the government of either of them; all public and private bodies, politic and corporate; all courts; all officers, public or private, in their official capacity; all partnerships in professions or trades; and all other persons, whether real or fictitious, except the person engaged in the forgery.

"Pecuniary obligation," meaning of. ART. 440. "Pecuniary obligation" means every instrument having money for its object, and every obligation for the breach of which a civil action for damages may be lawfully brought.

Definition of the words, "transferred, or," &c. ART. 441. By an instrument, which would "have transferred, or in any manner have affected" property, is meant every species of conveyance, or undertaking in writing, which supposes a right in the person purporting to execute it, to dispose of, or change the character of property of every kind, and which can have such effect when genuine.

Must be done with intent to injure, &c. ART. 442. The false making, or alteration, to constitute forgery, must be done with intent to injure or defraud, and the injury must be such as affects one pecuniarily, or in relation to his property.

ART. 443. If any person shall knowingly, pass as true, or attempt to pass as true, any such forged instrument in writing as is mentioned and defined in the preceding Articles of this Chapter, he shall be punished by imprisonment in the Penitentiary, not less than two, nor more than five years. Passing forged instrument.

ART. 444. Whoever shall prepare, in this State, any implements or materials, or engrave any plate for the purpose of being used in forging the notes of any bank, whether within this State or out of it, and whether the same be incorporated or not; or who shall have in his possession, in this State, any such implements, materials, or engraved plate, with intent to be used for the purpose above mentioned, shall be imprisoned, in the Penitentiary, not less than two, nor more than five years. Preparing implements for purpose of forgery, or, &c.

ART. 445. If any person shall knowingly have in his possession any instrument of writing, the making of which is by law an offence, with intent to use or pass the same as true, he shall be punished by confinement in the Penitentiary, not less than two, nor more than five years. Act of Feb. 12, 1858. Possession of forged instrument, with intent to pass.

ART. 446. Upon the trial of any indictment for the forgery of any bank bill, or for passing, or attempting to pass, any such bill as true, or for knowingly having in possession any such forged bank bill, evidence that bills or notes, purporting to be issued by any bank, are commonly received as currency, or proof of the existence of such bank by parol testimony, shall be deemed sufficient to show its legal establishment and existence. Act of Aug. 28, 1856. Proof as to forging of bank bills.

ART. 447. If any one, with intent to defraud, shall, either by falsely reading, or falsely interpreting, any pecuniary obligation, or instrument in writing, which would in any manner affect property, or, by misrepresenting its contents, induce any one to sign such instrument as his act, or give assent to it in such manner as would make it his act, if not done under mistake, the person so offending shall be imprisoned, in the Penitentiary, not less than two, nor more than five years. False reading, &c., of written instruments.

ART. 448. If any person, with intent to defraud, shall substitute one instrument of writing for another, and by this means induce any person to sign an instrument materially different from that which he intended to sign, he shall be punished by imprisonment, in the Penitentiary, not less than two, nor more than five years Substitution of false instrument for.

ART. 449. If any one shall falsely personate another, whether bearing the same name or not, and, in such assumed character, shall give authority to any person to sign such assumed name to any instrument of writing, which, if genuine, would create, increase, diminish, or discharge any pecuniary obligation, or would transfer, or in any way affect any property, he shall be imprisoned, in the Penitentiary, not less than two, nor more than seven years. Falsely personating another.

ART. 450. If any person shall falsely personate another, whether bearing the same name or not, and in such assumed character shall, before any officer authorized by law to authenticate instruments of writing for registration, acknowledge the execution of any instrument of writing, purporting to convey, or in any manner affect, an interest in property, such instrument purporting to be the act of the person whose name is so assumed, and the acknowledgment thereof being such as would entitle the instrument to be registered, he shall be punished, by confinement in the Penitentiary, not less than two, nor more than ten years. Same subject.

CHAPTER II.

OF COUNTERFEITING AND DIMINISHING THE VALUE OF CURRENT COIN.

Of gold or silver.

ART. 451. He is guilty of counterfeiting who makes, in the semblance of true gold or silver coin, any coin of whatever denomination, having in its composition a less proportion of the precious metal of which the true coin intended to be imitated is composed, than is contained in such true coin, with intent that the same should be passed in this State or elsewhere.

Altering coin.

ART. 452. He is also guilty of counterfeiting, who, with like intent, alters any coin of lower value, so as to make it resemble coin of higher value.

Resemblance need not be perfect.

ART. 453. The resemblance between the true and the false coin need not be perfect to constitute the offence of counterfeiting.

Punishment.

ART. 454. Any person who shall counterfeit any gold or silver coin, shall be punished by imprisonment in the Penitentiary not less than five, nor more than ten years.

Passing counterfeit coin.

ART. 455. If any person, with intent to defraud, shall pass, or offer to pass, as true, or bring into this State, or have in his possession, with intent to pass as true, any counterfeit coin, knowing the same to be counterfeit, he shall be punished by imprisonment, in the Penitentiary, not less than two, nor more than five years.

Making or having moulds, &c., in possession.

ART. 456. If any person, with the intention of committing the offence of counterfeiting, or of aiding therein, shall make, or repair, or shall have in his possession, any die, mould or other instrument whatever, designed or adapted, or usually employed for making coin, or shall prepare, or have in his possession, any base metal prepared for coinage, with intent that the same may be used for the purpose of counterfeiting, he shall be punished, by imprisonment in the Penitentiary, not less than two, nor more than five years.

Act of Feb. 12, 1858.
Passing coin of diminished weight.

ART. 457. If any person shall, with intent to profit thereby, diminish the weight of any gold or silver coin, and shall afterwards pass it for the value it would have had before it was so diminished, or send it to any place, whether in the State or out of it, with the intent that the same may be passed, he shall be punished by imprisonment in the Penitentiary, not less than two, nor more than five years.

Act of Aug. 28, 1856.
Definition of gold or silver coin.

ART. 458. By the gold or silver coin, mentioned in this Chapter, is meant any piece of gold or silver of which one of those metals is the principal component part, and which passes as money in the United States, either by law or usage, whether the same be of the coinage of the United States or of any foreign country.

Definition of "passing or attempting to pass."

ART. 459. It is sufficient to constitute the offence of passing, or attempting to pass, under the provisions of this Chapter, if the counterfeit coin be delivered or offered to another, with the intention of defrauding, or enabling such other person to defraud, although such counterfeit coin be not delivered or offered at the full value which it would bear if genuine.

CHAPTER III.

OF OFFENCES WHICH AFFECT FOREIGN COMMERCE.

ART. 460. If any person shall export from this State, or ship, for the purpose of exportation to any one of the United States, or to any foreign port, any article of commerce, which, by any law of the State, may be required to be inspected by a public inspector, without having caused such inspection to be made according to law, he shall be fined, not exceeding one hundred dollars. Shipping articles without being inspected, &c.

ART. 461. If any one shall counterfeit, or alter the mark, brand, or stamp, directed by any law of the State to be put on any article of commerce, or on the box, cask or package, containing the same, he shall be punished by fine, not exceeding one thousand dollars, or by imprisonment in the County Jail, not exceeding one year. Altering marks on, &c.

ART. 462. If any person shall, with intent to defraud, put into any hogshead barrel, cask or keg, or into any bale, box or package, containing merchandize or other commodity usually sold by weight, any article whatever of less value than the merchandize with which such bale, box, package, hogshead, barrel, cask or keg, is apparently filled, or with intent to defraud, shall sell or barter, give in payment, or expose to sale, or ship for exportation, any such hogshead, barrel, cask, keg, box, bale, or package of merchandize, or other commodity, with any such article of inferior value concealed therein, he shall be punished, by confinement in the County Jail, not exceeding one year, or by fine, not exceeding one thousand dollars. False packing, &c.

ART. 463. If any person shall with intent to deceive and defraud, conceal within any hogshead, cask, barrel, box, bale, keg or package, containing merchandize or other commodity, any merchandize or commodity of a quality inferior to that with which such hogshead, cask, barrel, bale, keg or package, is apparently filled, or any substance of less value, he shall be fined not exceeding five hundred dollars. Act of Feb. 12, 1858. Concealing merchandize of inferior quality, in, &c.

ART. 464. If any person shall cause insurance to be made in this State, on any merchandize, or other commodity, represented to be already shipped, or about to be shipped, at any place, whether within this State or out of it, and shall, with intent to defraud the insurer, ship articles of value less than one-half the represented value of those insured, or of a different kind from those insured, he shall be punished, by fine, in any sum not exceeding the amount for which such merchandize or commodity may be insured. Act of Aug. 28, 1856. Fraudulent insurance.

ART. 465. The municipal authorities of incorporated towns and cities being shipping ports, may make such regulations as are deemed proper for the punishment of keepers of boarding houses and others, who knowingly lodge, entertain, or conceal, seamen who have deserted from any merchant vessel in their respective ports. But they shall not affix a higher penalty for such offence than a fine of fifty dollars, or imprisonment, in Jail, for thirty days. For boarding deserting seamen.

CHAPTER IV.

FALSE WEIGHTS AND MEASURES.

Use of, how punished.

ART. 466. If any person shall use a false balance, weight, or measure, in weighing or measuring anything whatever, purchased, or sold by himself, or bartered, shipped, or delivered by him for sale, or bartered, or pledged, or given in payment, knowing the same to be false, and with intent to defraud, he shall be punished, by fine, not exceeding three hundred dollars.

Definition of.

ART. 467. A false weight or measure is such as is not in conformity with the standard which is or may be established by a law of this State.

Shall be seized and destroyed by, &c.

ART. 468. When a warrant of arrest is issued in case of offences under this Chapter, the Magistrate shall direct the false balances, weights, or measures, to be seized, and kept by the Sheriff until the trial of the defendant, and, in case of conviction, the same shall be destroyed.

CHAPTER V.

OF OFFENCES BY PUBLIC WEIGHERS.

Use of false balance by.

ART. 469. If any person, appointed Public Weigher by authority of any law of the State, shall fraudulently use any false balance or instrument for weighing, or shall, in the exercise of his official duties, fraudulently give the wrong weight of any article weighed by him, he shall be punished by fine, not less than one hundred dollars, nor more than five hundred dollars, or by imprisonment, in the County Jail, not exceeding one year.

CHAPTER VI.

MISCELLANEOUS OFFENCES.

False certificate &c., by Notary Public.

ART. 470. If any Notary Public shall make any false certificate as to the proof or acknowledgment of any instrument of writing relating to commerce or navigation, to which, by law, he is authorized to certify; or shall make any false certificate as to the proof or acknowledgment of any letter of attorney, or other instrument of writing relating to commerce or navigation, to which he may by law certify, he shall be punished by confinement, in the Penitentiary, not less than two years, nor more than five years.

False declaration or protest by

ART. 471. If any Notary Public shall make any false declaration or protest, respecting any matter or thing relating to commerce or navigation, or to commercial instruments, where, by law, he is authorized to make such declaration or protest, he shall be punished as prescribed in the preceding Article.

ART. 472. The provisions of the two preceding Articles are intended to embrace all acts of a Notary Public, done in an official capacity, within the proper sphere of his duties, and which arise out of transactions respecting navigation or commerce. What acts embraced.

ART. 473. If any master or other officer of a vessel, with intent to defraud, shall make a false declaration or protest, as to the loss or damage of any vessel or cargo, he shall be punished by confinement, in the Penitentiary, not less than two, nor more than five years. False declaration or protest by master of vessel.

ART. 474. If any person with intent to defraud, shall make or cause to be made, any false entry in any book kept as a book of accounts; or shall, with like intent, alter or cause to be altered, any item of an account kept or entered in such book, he shall be fined, not less than one hundred dollars nor more than one thousand dollars, or be punished by confinement in the Penitentiary, not less than two nor more than five years Act of Feb. 12, 1858. Keeping false accounts.

TITLE XVII.

OF OFFENCES AGAINST THE PERSONS OF INDIVIDUALS.

CHAPTER I.

OF ASSAULT AND BATTERY.

1. General Provisions and Definitions.

1. *General Provisions and Definitions.*

ART. 475. The use of any unlawful violence upon the person of another, with intent to injure him, whatever be the means or the degree of violence used, is an assault and battery. Any attempt to commit a battery, or any threatening gesture showing in itself or by words accompanying it, an immediate intention, coupled with an ability to commit a battery, is an assault. Act of Aug. 28, 1856. Definition of,

ART. 476. When an injury is caused, by violence to the person, the intent to injure is presumed, and it rests with the person inflicting the injury to show the accident or innocent intention. The injury intended may be, either bodily pain, constraint, a sense of shame, or other disagreeable emotion of the mind. Intent, &c., presumed.

ART. 477. An assault, or an assault and battery, may be committed, though the person actually injured thereby was not the person intended to be injured. May be committed, &c.

ART. 478. An assault, or assault and battery, may be committed by the use of any part of the body of the person committing the offence, as of the hand, foot, head; or by the use of any inanimate object, as a stick, knife, or anything else capable of inflicting the slightest injury; or by the use of any animate object, as by throwing one person against another, or driving a horse or other animal against the person. Means used to commit.

Other means of committing. ART. 479. Any means used by the person assaulting, as by spitting in the face, or otherwise, which is capable of inflicting an injury, comes within the definition of an assault or an assault and battery, as the case may be.

Degrees of assault, &c. ART. 480. An assault is either a simple assault, an aggravated assault, or an assault with intent to commit some other offence.

Class of persons referred to. ART. 481. Assaults and assaults and batteries, as here spoken of, have reference to such offences when committed against a free white person.

Definition of the words "coupled with an ability to commit." ART. 482. By the terms "coupled with an ability to commit," as used in Article 475, is meant,

1. That the person making the assault must be in such a position that, if not prevented, he may inflict a battery upon the person assailed.

2. That he must be within such distance of the person so assailed as to make it within his power to commit the battery by the use of the means with which he attempts it.

It follows, that one who is, at the time of making an attempt to commit a battery, under such restraint as to deprive him of the power to act, or who is at so great a distance from the person assailed, as that he cannot reach his person by the use of the means with which he makes the attempt, is not guilty of an assault. Pointing an unloaded gun, or the use of any like means with which no injury can be inflicted, cannot constitute an assault.

When violence does not amount to. ART. 483. Violence used to the person does not amount to an assault or battery in the following cases:

1. In the exercise of the right of moderate restraint or correction given by law to the parent over the child, the guardian over the ward, the master over his servant or apprentice, the teacher over the scholar.

2. For the preservation of order in a meeting for religious, political, or other lawful purposes.

3. For the preservation of the peace, or to prevent the commission of offences.

4. In preventing or interrupting an intrusion upon the lawful possession of property.

5. In making a lawful arrest and detaining the party arrested, in obedience to the lawful order of a Magistrate or Court, and in overcoming resistance to such lawful order.

6. In self-defence, or the defence of another, against unlawful violence offered to his person or property.

Degree of force which may be used. ART. 484. In all the cases mentioned in the preceeding Article, where violence is permitted to effect a lawful purpose, only that degree of force must be used which is necessary to effect such purpose.

Verbal provocation, &c. ART. 485. No verbal provocation justifies an assault and battery, but insulting and abusive words may be given in evidence in mitigation of the punishment affixed to the offence.

Battery, in what sense used. ART. 486. The word battery is used in this Code in the same sense as "*assault and battery.*"

2. *Punishment of Simple Assault and Battery.*

Punishment. ART. 487. The punishment for a simple assault, or for assault and battery, unattended with circumstances of aggravation, shall be a fine, not to exceed one hundred dollars.

CHAPTER II.

OF AGGRAVATED ASSAULTS AND BATTERY.

Art. 488. An assault or battery becomes aggravated when committed under any of the following circumstances: Act of Feb. 12, 1858. Becomes aggravated when,

1. When committed upon an officer in the lawful discharge of the duties of his office, if it was known or declared to the offender that the person assaulted was an officer discharging an official duty.

2. When committed in a court of Justice, or in any place of religious worship, or in any place where persons are assembled for the purpose of innocent amusement.

3. When the person committing the offence goes into the house of a private family, and is there guilty of an assault and battery.

4. When committed by a person of robust health, or strength, upon one who is aged or decrepid.

5. When committed by an adult male upon the person of a female, or child, or by an adult female upon the person of a child.

6. When the instrument or means used is such as inflicts disgrace upon the person assaulted, as an assault or battery with a whip or cowhide.

7. When a serious bodily injury is inflicted upon the person assaulted.

8. When committed with deadly weapons, under circumstances not amounting to an intent to murder or maim.

9. When committed with premeditated design, and by the use of means calculated to inflict great bodily injury.

Art. 489. The circumstances of aggravation mentioned in the preceding Article are of different degrees, and the jury are to consider these circumstances in forming their verdict and assessing the punishment. Act of Aug. 28, 1856. Degrees of aggravation.

Art. 490. Upon an indictment for an aggravated assault or battery, the jury may find the defendant guilty of simple assault, or assault and battery, and assess the punishment therefor, as prescribed in this Code. Discretion of Jury.

2. *Punishment.*

Art. 491. The punishment for an aggravated assault or battery, shall be fine, not less than one hundred, nor more than one thousand dollars, and the jury may, in addition thereto, find a verdict for the imprisonment of the defendant, in the county jail, not exceeding two years. Punishment of aggravated.

CHAPTER III.

OF ASSAULTS WITH INTENT TO COMMIT MURDER, RAPE, ROBBERY OR OTHER CRIME.

Art. 492. If any person shall assault another with intent to commit the

Act of Feb. 12, 1858. — Assault with intent to maim. offence of maiming, he shall by punished by fine, not exceeding one thousand dollars, or by imprisonment in the Penitentiary, not less than two nor more than five years.

Act of Aug. 28, 1856. — To commit murder, &c. ART. 493. If any person shall assault another with intent to murder, he shall be punished by confinement in the Penitentiary, not less than two years, nor more than seven years. If the assault be made with a bowie-knife, or dagger, the punishment shall be doubled.

Intent to commit rape. ART. 494. If any person shall assault a woman, with intent to commit the offence of rape, he shall be punished, by confinement in the Penitentiary, not less than two years, nor more than seven years.

Act of Feb. 12, 1858. — Robbery. ART. 495. If any person shall assault another, with intent to commit the offence of robbery, he shall be punished by confinement in the Penitentiary, not less than two, nor more than five years.

Burglary. ART. 496. If any person in attempting to commit burglary shall assault another, he shall be punished by confinement in the Penitentiary, not less than two nor more than five years.

Act of Aug. 28, 1856. — Intent to murder. ART. 497. Whenever it appears upon a trial for assault with intent to murder, that the offence would have been murder had death resulted therefrom, the person committing such assault is deemed to have done the same with that intent.

Discretion of jury. ART. 498. The jury, in every case arising under this Chapter, may acquit the defendant of the offence charged in the indictment, and may, according to the facts of the case, find the defendant guilty of an aggravated assault, or of assault and battery, or of a simple assault, and affix the proper penalty to which such offence is liable by law.

Rule as to what constitutes assault with intent to commit another offence. ART. 499. An assault, with intent to commit any other offence, is constituted by the existence of the facts which bring the offence within the definition of an assault, coupled with an intention to commit such other offence, as of maiming, murder, rape, or robbery.

CHAPTER IV.

OF MAIMING, DISFIGURING AND CASTRATION.

1. *Definition.*

Act of Aug. 28, 1856. — Maiming defined. ART. 500. To maim, is to cut off or otherwise deprive a person of the hand, arm, finger, foot, leg, nose or ear; to put out an eye, or in any way to deprive the person of any other member of his body.

ART. 501. To disfigure, is to place any mark, by means of a knife, or other instrument, upon the face or other part of the person. Of disfiguring.

ART. 502. To castrate, is to deprive any person of either, or both, or of any part of either or both of the testicles. Of castration.

2. *Punishment.*

ART. 503. If any person shall commit the offence of maiming, he shall be punished, by confinement in the Penitentiary, not less than two nor more than ten years. For maiming.

ART. 504. If any person shall disfigure another, he shall be punished by confinement in the Penitentiary, not less than two nor more than five years, or by fine not exceeding two thousand dollars. Act of Feb. 12, 1858. For disfiguring.

ART. 505. If any person shall commit the offence of castration, he shall be punished, by confinement in the Penitentiary, not less than five, nor more than fifteen years. Act of Aug. 28, 1856. For castration.

ART. 506. The offence of maiming, or of castration, when committed upon a slave or free person of color, shall be punished in the same manner as if committed upon a free white person. When committed on slave, &c.

ART. 507. Upon the trial of any indictment for either of the offences named in this Chapter, the jury may, according to the facts of the case, acquit the defendant of the offence charged, and find him guilty of an assault with intent to commit the offence charged in the indictment. Discretion of jury.

CHAPTER V.

OF FALSE IMPRISONMENT, KIDNAPPING AND ABDUCTION.

1. *False Imprisonment.*

ART. 508. False imprisonment is the wilful detention of another against his consent, and where it is not expressly authorized by law, whether such detention be effected by an assault, by actual violence to the person, by threats, or by any other means which restrains the party so detained from removing from one place to another as he may see proper. Act of Aug. 28, 1856. Definition of

ART. 509. The assault or violence may be such as is spoken of in defining the offence of assault and battery. Violence same as, &c.

Detention. ART. 510. The impediment must be such as is in its nature calculated to detain the person, and from which he cannot by ordinary means relieve himself.

Threats. ART. 511. The threat must be such as is calculated to operate upon the person threatened, and inspire a just fear of some injury to his person, reputation or property, or to the person, reputation or property of another; and the jury are to consider the age, sex, condition, disposition or health of the person threatened, in determining whether the threat was sufficient to intimidate, and prevent such person from removing beyond the bounds in which he was detained.

What detention does not constitute. ART. 512. It is not an offence to detain a person in the cases and for the objects mentioned in Article 483, as justifying the use of force, but whenever it is assumed as a justification that such circumstances existed, it must be shown also that the detention was necessary to effect any of the objects set forth in said Article.

Punishment. ART. 513. Any person who shall be guilty of the offence of false imprisonment, shall be fined not exceeding five hundred dollars, and may be confined in the County Jail not exceeding one year.

In cases of *habeas corpus*. ART. 514. If any officer or other person shall hold or detain, in any manner, any one who has been ordered to be discharged by any Court or Judge, upon the hearing of a writ of habeas corpus, he shall suffer double the punishment prescribed in the preceding article.

2. *Of Kidnapping.*

Act of Feb. 12, 1858. Definition of ART. 515. When any person is falsely imprisoned for the purpose of being removed from the State, or for the purpose of being sold, or detained as a slave, (the person being free,) or if a minor under the age of seventeen years, for the purpose of being concealed, or taken from the lawful possession of a parent, or guardian, such false imprisonment is kidnapping. If the person kidnapped be under the age of fifteen years, it is not necessary that there should be force to constitute the offence.

Act of Aug. 28, 1856. Punishment. ART. 516. The punishment of kidnapping shall be imprisonment, in the Penitentiary, not less than two, nor more than five years, or fine not exceeding two thousand dollars.

Same subject. ART. 517. If the person so falsely imprisoned is actually removed out of the State, or sold as a slave, the punishment shall be imprisonment in the Penitentiary, not less than two, nor more than ten years.

3. *Of Abduction.*

Definition of ART. 518. Abduction is the false imprisonment of a woman, with intent to force her into a marriage, or for the purpose of prostitution.

Of female under fourteen. ART. 519. If a female under the age of fourteen be taken, for the purpose of marriage or prostitution, from her parent, guardian, or other person having the legal charge of her, it is abduction whether she consent or not, and although a marriage afterwards take place between the parties.

When complete ART. 520. The offence of abduction is complete if the female be detained as long as twelve hours, though she may afterwards be relieved from such detention without marriage or prostitution.

Act of Feb. 12, 1858. Punishment. ART. 521. Any person who shall be guilty of abduction shall be punished by fine not exceeding two thousand dollars. If by reason of such abduction, a woman be forced into marriage, the punishment shall be confinement in the

Penitentiary, not less than two nor more than five years; and if by reason of such abduction a woman be prostituted, the punishment shall be confinement in the Penitentiary, not less than three nor more than ten years.

ART. 522. The jury in a prosecution for kidnapping or abduction, may find a verdict acquitting the defendant of the offence charged in the indictment, and finding him guilty of false imprisonment, if the facts authorize such verdict, and in such case they shall affix the penalty prescribed for the last named offence. Act of Aug. 28, 1856. Discretion of jury.

CHAPTER VI.

OF RAPE.

ART. 523. Rape is the carnal knowledge of a woman without her consent, obtained by force, threats, or fraud, or the carnal knowledge of a female under the age of ten years, with or without consent, and with or without the use of force, threats or fraud. Act of Aug. 28, 1856. Definition.

ART. 524. The definition of force, as applicable to assault and battery, applies also to the crime of rape, and it must have been such as might reasonably be supposed sufficient to overcome resistance, taking into consideration the relative strength of the parties, and other circumstances of the case. Definition of force.

ART. 525. The threat must be such as might reasonably create a just fear of death, or great bodily harm, in view of the relative condition of the parties, as to health, strength, and all other circumstances of the case. Threats.

ART. 526. The fraud must consist in the use of some stratagem by which the woman is induced to believe that the offender is her husband, or in administering without her knowledge or consent, some substance producing unnatural sexual desire, or such stupor as prevents or weakens resistence, and committing the offence while she is under the influence of such substance. It is a presumption of law which cannot be rebutted by testimony, that no consent was given under the circumstances mentioned in this Article. Fraud.

ART. 527. Penetration only is necessary to be proved upon a trial for rape. Proof of penetration.

ART. 528. No person under the age of fourteen, at the time the offence is charged to have been committed, can be convicted of rape, or assault with intent to commit the offence. Person under fourteen years cannot be convicted.

ART. 529. Whoever shall be guilty of rape, shall be punished by confinement, in the Penitentiary, not less than five, nor more than fifteen years. Punishment.

ART. 530. If it appear on the trial of an indictment for rape, that the offence, though not committed, was attempted by the use of any of the means spoken of in Articles 524, 525, and 526, but not such as to bring the offence within the definition of an assault with intent to commit rape, the jury may find the defendant guilty of an attempt to commit the offence, and affix the punishment prescribed in Article 494. Where offence was only attempted, &c.

CHAPTER VII.

OF ABORTION.

Act of Aug. 28, 1856.

Produced by consent of woman, or, &c.

ART. 531. If any person shall designedly administer to a pregnant woman, with her consent, any drug or medicine, or shall use towards her any violence, or any means whatever, externally or internally applied, and shall thereby procure an abortion, he shall be punished, by confinement, in the Penitentiary, not less than two, nor more than five years; if it be done without her consent the punishment shall be doubled.

Person furnishing the means of, &c.

ART. 532. Any person who furnishes the means for procuring an abortion, knowing the purpose intended, is guilty as an accomplice.

Act of Feb. 12, 1858.

Attempt to produce.

ART. 533. If the means used shall fail to produce an abortion, the offender is nevertheless guilty of an attempt to produce abortion, provided it be shown that such means were calculated to produce that result, and shall be punished by fine not less than one hundred nor more than one thousand dollars.

Act of Aug. 28, 1856.

Murder of, &c.

ART. 534. If the death of the mother is occasioned by an abortion so produced, or by an attempt to effect the same, it is murder.

Destroying life of child during parturition, &c.

ART. 535. If any person shall, during parturition of the mother, destroy the vitality or life in a child, in a state of being born, and before actual birth, which child would otherwise have been born alive, he shall be punished, by confinement in the Penitentiary, for life, or any period not less than five years, at the discretion of the jury.

Procured by medical advice, &c.

ART. 536. Nothing contained in this Chapter shall be deemed to apply to the case of an abortion procured or attempted to be procured by medical advice for the purpose of saving the life of the mother.

CHAPTER VIII.

OF ADMINISTERING POISONOUS AND INJURIOUS POTIONS.

Act of Aug. 28, 1856.

Administering.

ART. 537. If any person shall mingle any poison, or any other noxious portion or substance, with any drink, food or medicine, with intent to kill or injure any other person, or shall wilfully poison any spring, well, cistern, or reservoir of water, with such intent, he shall be punished, by imprisonment in the Penitentiary, not less than two, nor more than ten years.

Act of Feb. 12, 1858.

Person causing another to inhale injurious substance, &c.

ART. 538. If any person shall, with intent to injure, cause another person to inhale, or swallow any substance injurious to health, or any of the functions of the body, or if such substance was administered with intent to kill, he shall be punished by confinement in the Penitentiary, not less than two nor more than five years.

Act of Aug. 28, 1856.

ART. 539. If, by reason of the commission of the offences named in the two preceding Articles, the death of a person be caused within one year, the offender shall be deemed guilty of murder, and punished accordingly. Death from, within a year.

ART. 540. If any person engaged in the practice of medicine, and claiming to be a physician, shall, by the use of any noxious substance, administered in a grossly ignorant manner, produce death, or other great bodily injury, he shall be punished for the offence, as any other person would be who had given such substance, knowing it to be injurious, and intending to kill or injure. When administered by physician through gross ignorance.

CHAPTER IX.

OF HOMICIDE.

ART. 541. Homicide is the destruction of the life of one human being by the act, agency, procurement, or culpable omission of another. Act of Aug. 28, 1856. Definition.

ART. 542. The destruction of life must be complete by such act, agency, procurement, or omission; but although the injury which caused death might not, under other circumstances, have proved fatal, yet if such injury be the cause of death, without its appearing that there has been any gross neglect, or manifestly improper treatment of the person injured it is homicide. Destruction of life must be complete, &c.

ART. 543. The foregoing Article, in what is said of gross neglect or improper treatment, has reference to the acts of some person other than him who inflicts the first injury, as of the physician, nurse, or other attendant. If the person inflicting the injury, which makes it necessary to call aid in preserving the life of the person injured, shall wilfully fail or neglect to call such aid, he shall be deemed equally guilty as if the injury were one which would inevitably lead to death. Where death is caused from neglect, when injury was not mortal.

ART. 544. No person shall be convicted of any grade of homicide unless the body of the deceased, or portions of it, are found, and sufficiently identified to establish the fact of killing. Body of deceased must be found, &c.

ART. 545. The person upon whom the homicide is alleged to have been committed, must be in existence by actual birth. It is homicide, however to destroy human life actually in existence, however frail such existence may be or however near extinction from other causes. Person must be in existence.

ART. 546. Although it is necessary, to constitute homicide, that it shall result from some act of the party accused, yet, if words be used which are reasonably calculated to produce, and do produce an act which is the immediate cause of death, it is homicide; as, for example, if a blind man, a stranger, a child, or a person of unsound mind, be directed, by words, to a precipice, or other dangerous place, where he falls and is killed; or if one be directed to take any article of medicine, food, or drink, known to be poisonous, and which does produce a fatal effect; in these, and like cases, the person so operating upon the mind or conduct of the person injured, shall be deemed guilty of homicide. When produced by words.

CHAPTER X.

OF JUSTIFIABLE HOMICIDE.

Act of Aug 28, 1856. — Justifiable when.

ART. 547. Homicide is justifiable in the cases enumerated in the succeeding Articles of this Chapter.

1. *Of a Public Enemy.*

Killing of public enemy.

ART. 548. It is lawful to kill a public enemy not only in the prosecution of war, but when he may be in the act of hostile invasion, or occupation of any part of the State. A public enemy is any person acting under the authority or enlisted in the service of any government at war with this State, or the United States. Persons belonging to hostile tribes of Indians who habitually commit depredations upon the lives or property of the inhabitants of this State, and all persons acting with such tribes are public enemies, and this, whether found in the act of committing such depredations, or under circumstances which sufficiently show an intention so to do.

By poison not justifiable.

ART. 549. Homicide of a public enemy by poison, or the use of poisoned weapons, is not justifiable.

Bearer of flag of truce, &c., not.

ART. 550. Homicide of a public enemy who is a deserter, or a prisoner of war, or the bearer of a flag of truce, is not justiable.

2. *Of a Convict.*

Execution of convict.

ART. 551. The execution of a convict for a capital offence by a legally qualified officer, under the warrant of a Court of competent jurisdiction, is justsfiable when the same takes place in the manner authorized by law and directed by the warrant.

3. *By officers in the performance of a duty, and by other persons under certain circumstances.*

ART. 552. Homicide by an officer in the execution of the lawful orders of Magistrates and Courts, is justifiable when he is violently resisted, and has just ground to fear danger to his own life in executing the order. By officer when resisted in discharge of his duty.

ART. 553. The officer is justifiable, though there may have been an error of judgment on the part of the Magistrate or Court, if the order emanated from a proper authority. Justifiable though order be erroneous.

ART. 554. The rule set forth in the two preceding Articles is subject to the following restrictions: Rules as to homicide by officers.

1. The order must be that of a Magistrate or Court having lawful authority to issue it.

2. It must have such form as the law requires to give it validity.

3. The person executing the order must be some officer duly authorized by law to execute the order, or some person specially appointed in accordance with law for the performance of the duty.

4. If the person executing the order be an officer, and performing a duty which no other person can by law perform, he must have taken the oath of office and have given bond, where such is required by law.

5. The order must be executed in the manner directed by law, and the person executing the same must make known his purpose and the capacity in which he acts.

6. If the order be a written one, and the person against whom it issues, before resistance offered, wishes to see the same, or hear it read, the person charged with its execution shall produce the order and show it or read it.

7. In making an arrest, under written order, the person acting under such order shall, in all cases, declare to the party against whom it is directed the offence of which he is accused, and state the nature of the warrant, unless prevented therefrom by the act of the party to be arrested.

8. The officer, or other person executing an order of arrest, is required to use such force as may be necessary to prevent an escape when it is attempted, but he shall not, in any case, kill one who attempts to escape, unless in making, or attempting such escape, the life of the officer is endangered, or he is threatened with great bodily injury.

9. In overcoming a resistance to the execution of an order, the officer, or person executing the same, may oppose such force as is necessary to overcome the resistance; but he shall not take the life of the person resisting, unless he has just ground to fear that his own life will be taken, or that he will suffer great bodily injury in the execution of the order.

10. A prisoner under sentence of death, or of imprisonment in the Penitentiary, or attempting to escape from the Penitentiary, may be killed by the officer having legal custody of him, if his escape can in no other manner be prevented.

ART. 555. The order referred to in this chapter may be either written or verbal, where a verbal order is allowed for the arrest of a person. Order may be written or verbal, &c.

ART. 556. Under written orders are included all process in a criminal or civil action, which directs the seizure of the person or of property. Written orders defined.

ART. 557. No officer, or other person ordered verbally to arrest another, is justified in killing, except the arrest be in a case of felony, or for the prevention of a felony. Verbal orders, &c.

ART. 558. Persons called in aid of an officer, in the performance of a duty, are justified in the same manner as the officer himself. Persons called in aid of.

Persons opposing.

ART. 559. All persons opposing the execution of the order, or aiding in an escape, may be treated in the same manner as the person against whom the order is directed, or who is attempting to escape.

As United States officers.

ART. 560. Officers acting under the authority of the laws or Courts of the United States, have the rights and are liable to the rules prescribed in this chapter.

In suppressing riots.

ART. 561. Homicide is justifiable when necessary to suppress a riot, when the same is attempted to be suppressed in the manner pointed out in the Code of Criminal Procedure and can in no way be suppressed except by taking life.

In cases of adultery.

ART. 562. Homicide is justifiable when committed by the husband upon the person of any one taken in the act of adultery with the wife, provided the killing take place before the parties to the act of adultery have separated.

Same subject.

ART. 563. Homicide cannot be justified by reason of the existence of the circumstances spoken of in the preceding article, where it appears that there has been, on the part of the husband, any connivance in, or assent to the adulterous connection.

4. *Homicide of a Slave when justifiable.*

Of a slave when justifiable.

ART. 564. Homicide committed upon a slave is justifiable in the following cases:

1. When a slave is in a state of insurrection.

2. When a slave forcibly resists any lawful order of his master, overseer, or other person having legal charge of him, in such manner as to give reasonable fear of loss of life, or great bodily harm, in enforcing obedience to such order.

3. Where a runaway slave forcibly resists a person attempting to arrest him, in such manner as to cause reasonable fear of loss of life, or of great bodily harm, in making such arrest.

4. Where a slave forcibly resists any lawful order of any patrol or officer of the law, in such manner as to cause reasonable fear of loss of life, or great bodily harm in executing such order.

5. When a slave uses weapons calculated to produce death, in any case other than those in which he may lawfully resist with arms, under the provisions of Part III, of this Code.

Rule as to homicide of a slave.

ART. 565. A slave is said to be in a state of insurrection when he is acting in concert with at least four others, and they are armed with the intention of freeing one or more of their number from a state of slavery.

Same subject.

ART. 566. Flight on the part of a slave, except when in a state of insurrection, does not justify homicide by either the master or any other person; and the killing of a slave under any other circumstances except those above enumerated, is the same offence as the killing of a free person.

5. *In defence of person or property.*

In defence of person or property. [See 570]

ART. 567. Homicide is permitted in the necessary defence of person or property, under the circumstances and subject to the rules herein set forth.

In preventing murder, rape, &c., when.

ART. 568. Homicide is permitted by law, and subject to no punishment, when inflicted for the purpose of preventing the offences of murder, rape, robbery, maiming, arson, burglary, and theft at night, whether the homicide be committed by the party about to be injured, or by some person in his behalf, when the killing takes place under the following circumstances:

1. It must reasonably appear by the acts, or by words, coupled with acts of

the person killed, that it was the purpose and intent of such person to commit one of the offences above named.

2. The killing must take place while the person killed was in the act of committing the offence, or after some act done by him, showing evidently an intent to commit such offence.

3. It must take place before the offence committed by the party killed is actually completed, except that, in case of rape, the ravisher may be killed at any time before he has escaped from the presence of his victim, and except also in the cases hereafter enumerated.

4. Where the killing takes place to prevent the murder of some other person, it shall not be deemed that the murder is complete so long as the offender is still inflicting violence, though the mortal wound may have been given.

5. If homicide takes place in preventing a robbery, it shall be justifiable, if done while the robber is in presence of the person robbed, or is flying with the money or other article taken by him.

6. In case of maiming, the homicide may take place at any time while the offender is mistreating with violence the person injured, though he may have completed the offence of maiming.

7. In case of arson, the homicide may be inflicted while the offender is in or at the building or other property burnt, or flying from the place before the destruction of the same.

8. In cases of burglary and theft by night, the homicide is justifiable at any time while the offender is in the building, or at the place where the theft is committed, or is within reach of gun-shot from such place or building.

ART. 569. When the homicide takes place to prevent murder or maiming, if the weapons or means used by the party attempting or committing such murder or maiming are such as would have been calculated to produce that result, it is to be presumed that the person so using them designed to inflict the injury. Presumption, &c., from weapons used.

ART. 570. Homicide is justifiable, also, in the protection of the person or property against any other unlawful and violent attack besides those mentioned in the preceding article, and in such cases all other means must be resorted to for the prevention of the injury, and the killing must take place while the person killed is in the very act of making such unlawful and violent attack, and any person interfering in such case, in behalf of the party about to be injured, is not justifiable in killing the aggressor, unless the life or person of the injured party is in peril by reason of such attack upon his property. In protecting person or property from other violent attacks. Person interfering in behalf of party injured.

ART. 571. The party whose person or property is so unlawfully attacked, is not bound to retreat in order to avoid the necessity of killing his assailant. Injured party not bound to retreat.

ART. 572. The attack upon the person of an individual, in order to justify homicide, must be such as produces a reasonable expectation or fear of death, or some serious bodily injury. Attack must produce fear, &c.

ART. 573. When, under Article 570, a homicide is committed in the protection of property, it must be done under the following circumstances: Rule as to homicide in the protection of property.

1. The possession must be of corporeal property and not of a mere right, and the possession must be actual and not merely constructive.

2. The possession must be legal, though the right of the property may not be in the possessor.

3. If possession be once lost, it is not lawful to regain it by such means as result in homicide.

4. Every other effort in his power must have been made by the possessor, to repel the aggression, before he will be justified in killing.

Simple assault, &c., does not justify. ART. 574. Simple assault and battery, or mere trespass upon property, will not justify homicide, nor will any offence not accompanied by force, such as theft, except in the night time, and from some house or place, such as defined in Articles 680 and 681.

CHAPTER XI.

OF EXCUSABLE HOMICIDE.

Act of Aug. 28, 1856. When death ensues by accident. ART. 575. Homicide is excusable when the death of a human being happens by accident or misfortune, though caused by the act of another, who is in the prosecution of a lawful object by lawful means.

Must be done when party is prosecuting lawful object, &c. ART. 576. The lawful act, causing the death of another, must be done by lawful means, and used in a lawful degree. Though lawful for the parent, guardian, schoolmaster, or master, to chastise the child, ward, scholar, or slave, or apprentice; yet if this be done with an instrument likely to produce death, or if with a proper instrument the chastisement be cruelly inflicted, and death result, it is murder.

CHAPTER XII.

HOMICIDE BY NEGLIGENCE.

Definition of. ART. 577. Homicide by negligence is of two kinds:

1. Such as happens in the performance of a lawful act; and
2. That which occurs in the performance of an unlawful act.

I. *In the performance of a lawful act.*

In the performance of lawful act. ART. 578. If any person, in the performance of a lawful act, shall, by negligence and carelessness, cause the death of another, he is guilty of negligent homicide of the first degree.

Definition of lawful act. ART. 579. A lawful act is one not forbidden by the penal law, and which would give no just occasion for a civil action.

Must be apparent danger, of, &c. ART. 580. To constitute this offence, there must be an apparent danger of causing the death of the person killed, or some other.

Degree of care, &c. ART. 581. The want of proper care and caution distinguishes this offence from excusable homicide. The degree of care and caution is such as a man of ordinary prudence would use under like circumstances.

ART. 582. Throwing timbers by a workman from the roof or upper part of a house into a public street or highway, or where a number of persons are known to be around the house.* Throwing timbers, &c.

Discharging firearms in a public street or highway, in such manner as would be likely to injure persons who might pass, are examples of negligent homicide of the first degree. Discharging fire-arms, &c.

But if, by the corporate laws of any town or city, the firing of arms be forbidden, the act is unlawful, and the offence will be of a higher degree.

ART. 584. To bring the offence within the definition of homicide by negligence, either of the first or second degree, there must be no apparent intention to kill. Must be no apparent intention to kill.

ART. 585. The homicide must be the consequence of the act done or attempted to be done. Homicide must be consequence of, &c.

ART. 586. Negligent homicide of the first degree, shall be punished by confinement in the county jail, not exceeding one year, or by fine, not exceeding one thousand dollars. How punished.

2. *In the Performance of an Unlawful Act.*

ART. 587. The definitions, rules and provisions of the preceding Articles of this Chapter, with respect to negligent homicide of the first degree, apply also to the offence of negligent homicide in the second degree, or such as is committed in the prosecution of an unlawful act, except when contrary to the following provisions: Definitions, rules, &c., applicable in second degree.

ART. 588. Negligent homicide of the second degree can only be committed when the person guilty thereof is in the act of committing, or in attempting the commission of an unlawful act. Homicide can only be committed when, &c.

ART. 589. Within the meaning of an unlawful act, as used in this Chapter, are included— Unlawful act defined.

1. Such acts as by the penal law are called misdemeanors; and,
2. Such acts, not being penal offences, as would give just occasion for a civil action.

ART. 590. When one in the execution of, or in attempting to execute, an act made a felony by the penal law, shall kill another, though without an apparent intention to kill, the offence does not come within the definition of negligent homicide. Rule when the act, &c., is a felony.

ART. 591. When the unlawful act attempted, or executed, is one known as a misdemeanor, the punishment of negligent homicide committed in the execution of such unlawful act, shall be imprisonment in the county jail not exceeding three years, or by fine not exceeding three thousand dollars. When it is a misdemeanor.

ART. 592. If the act intended is one for which an action would lie, but not an offence against the *penal* law, the homicide resulting therefrom is a misdemeanor, and may be punished by fine, not exceeding one thousand dollars, and by imprisonment in the county jail, not exceeding one year. When not a penal offence.

CHAPTER XIII.

OF MANSLAUGHTER.

1. *Definition.*

Act of Aug. 28, 1856. Definition of.

ART. 594. Manslaughter is voluntary homicide, committed under the immediate influence of sudden passion arising from an adequate cause, but neither justified or excused by law.

Definition of phrase "under the immediate influence of sudden passion."

ART. 596. By the expression "under the immediate influence of sudden passion" is meant—

1. That the provocation must arise at the time of the commission of the offence, and that the passion is not the result of a former provocation.

Act must be the result of.

2. The act must be directly caused by the passion arising out of the provocation. It is not enough that the mind is merely agitated by passion arising from some other provocation, or a provocation given by some person other than the party killed.

(See 615.)

3. The passion intended is either of the emotions of the mind, known as anger, rage, sudden resentment, or terror, rendering it incapable of cool reflection.

"Adequate cause."

ART. 597. By the expression "adequate cause" is meant, such as would commonly produce a degree of anger, rage, resentment or terror, in a person of ordinary temper, sufficient to render the mind incapable of cool reflection.

What are not, &c.

ART. 598. Insulting words or gestures, or an assault and battery, so slight as to show no intention to inflict pain or injury, or an injury to property, unaccompanied by violence, are not *adequate causes.*

What are deemed adequate causes.

ART. 599. The following are deemed adequate causes:

1. An assault and battery by the deceased, causing pain or bloodshed.

2. A serious personal conflict, in which great injury is inflicted by the person killed, by means of weapons, or other instruments of violence, or by means of great superiority of personal strength, although the person guilty of the homicide were the aggressor, provided such aggression was not made with intent to bring on a conflict, and for the purpose of killing.

3. Adultery of the person killed, with the wife of the person guilty of the homicide, provided the killing occur as soon as the fact of an illicit connection is discovered.

(See 599b, 599d.)

4. Insulting words or conduct of the person killed, towards a female relation of the party guilty of the homicide.

Act of Feb. 12, 1858. To reduce homicide to manslaughter, it must appear, &c.

ART. 599a. When it is sought to reduce the homicide to the grade of manslaughter, by reason of the existence of the circumstances specified in the fourth subdivision of Article 599 of the Penal Code, it must appear that the killing took place immediately upon the happening of the insulting conduct, or the uttering of the insulting words, or so soon thereafter as the party killing may meet with the person killed, after having been informed of such insults.

ART. 599b. In every case where the defence spoken of in the preceding Article is relied on, it shall be competent to prove the general character of the female insulted, in order to ascertain the extent of the provocation. General character of female may be proved.

ART. 599c. The jury shall be at liberty to determine in every case, whether, under all the circumstances, the insulting words or gestures were the real cause which provoked the killing. Discretion of jury in, &c.

ART. 599d. Any female under the permanent or temporary protection of the accused, at the time of killing, shall also be included within the meaning of the term *relation*. Who are included by term, "*relation*."

ART. 600. In order to reduce a voluntary homicide to the grade of manslaughter, it is necessary not only that adequate cause existed to produce the state of mind referred to in the third subdivision of Article 596, but also that such state of mind did actually exist at the time of the commission of the offence. Act of Aug. 28, 1856. State of mind must actually exist at, &c.

ART. 601. Though a homicide may take place under circumstances showing no deliberation, yet if the person guilty thereof provoked a contest with the apparent intention of killing, or doing serious bodily injury to the deceased, the offence does not come within the definition of manslaughter. Rule, when person killed, provoked a contest.

2. *Punishment.*

ART. 602. Manslaughter is of various degrees of culpability, according to the circumstances under which it was committed. It shall be punished by imprisonment in the Penitentiary, not less than two nor more than five years. Act of Feb. 12, 1858. Punishment.

CHAPTER XIV.

OF DUELLING.

ART. 603. Any citizen of this State who shall fight a duel with deadly weapons, or send or accept a challenge to fight a duel with deadly weapons, either within this State or out of it, or who shall act as second, or knowingly aid or assist in any manner those thus offending, shall be deprived of holding any office of trust or profit under this State. Act of Aug. 28, 1856. How punished when engaged in by a citizen of the State.

ART. 604. If any person not being a citizen of this State, shall, within this State, commit either of the offences named in the preceding Article, he shall be fined in an amount not less than one thousand dollars, and be imprisoned in the county jail, not exceeding twelve months. By a citizen of another State within this State.

ART. 605. If, in any duel hereafter fought within this State, either of the combattants be killed, or receive a wound from which he afterwards dies within three months, the survivor shall be deemed guilty of manslaughter, and punished accordingly. When punished as manslaughter.

ART. 606. It is the duty of all magistrates, when they have probable grounds to suspect that a duel is about to be fought, or that persons are going out of the State for that purpose, to issue a warrant of arrest, and have all persons concerned, either as principals or seconds, and all persons aiding or assisting in such duel, brought before them, and upon examination, according to the facts of the case, to require of such persons to enter into bond, with sufficient secu- Duty of magistrates to prevent.

rity, to keep the peace; and a bond so taken shall be recoverable upon suit brought, and the breach thereof proved in the same manner as provided for bonds taken under Article 81 of the Code of Criminal Procedure.

CHAPTER XV.

OF MURDER.

Act of February 12, 1858. Offence of, defined. ART. 607. Every person with a sound memory and discretion, who shall unlawfully kill any reasonable creature in being within this State, with malice aforethought, either express or implied, shall be deemed guilty of murder. Murder is distinguishable from every other species of homicide, by the absence of the circumstances which reduce the offence to negligent homicide or manslaughter, or which excuse or justify the homicide.

In the first and second degree. ART. 608. All murder committed by poison, starving, torture, or with express malice, or committed in the perpetration, or in the attempt at the perpetration of arson, rape, robbery, or burglary, is murder in the first degree, and all murder not of the first degree, is murder of the second degree.

Jury shall determine the degree, &c. ART. 609. If the jury shall find any person guilty of murder, they shall also find by their verdict whether it is of the first or second degree; and if any person shall plead guilty to an indictment for murder, a jury shall be summoned to find of what degree of murder he is guilty, and in either case, if they shall find the offence of murder to be of the second degree, they shall also find the punishment.

Act of Aug. 28, 1856. Killing with bowie knife or dagger. ART. 610. If any person be killed with a *bowie knife* or *dagger*, under circumstances which would otherwise render the homicide a case of manslaughter, the killing shall nevertheless be deemed murder, and punished accordingly.

Definition of. ART. 611. A "bowie knife" or "dagger," as the terms are here and elsewhere used, means any knife intended to be worn upon the person, which is capable of inflicting death, and not commonly known as a pocket knife.

Act of Feb. 12, 1858. Threats of deceased may be proved—effect of. ART. 612. Where a defendant accused of murder, seeks to justify himself on the ground of threats against his own life, he may be permitted to introduce evidence of the threats made, but the same shall not be regarded as affording a justification for the offence, unless it be shown that at the time of the homicide, the person killed by some act then done, manifested an intention to execute the threat so made. In every instance where proof of threats has been made, it shall be competent to introduce evidence of the general character of the deceased. General character of deceased may be proved, when. Such evidence shall extend only to an enquiry as to whether the deceased was a man of violent or dangerous character, or a man of kind and inoffensive disposition; or whether he was such a person as might reasonably be expected to execute a threat made.

2. *Punishment.*

Murder, how punished. ART. 612a. The punishment of murder in the first degree shall be death, and the punishment of murder in the second degree shall be confinement in the Penitentiary for not less than five years.

CHAPTER XVI.

GENERAL PROVISONS AS TO OFFENCES AGAINST THE PERSON.

ART. 613. The instrument or means by which a homicide is committed, are to be taken into consideration, in judging of the intention of the party offending; if the instrument be one not likely to produce death, it is not to be presumed that death was designed, unless from the manner in which it was used, such intention evidently appears. Act of Aug. 28, 1856. Rule as to means, &c., used in perpetrating.

ART. 614. If an injury be inflicted in a cruel manner, though with an instrument not likely under ordinary circumstances to produce death, the killing will be manslaughter or murder, according to facts of the case. If done in a cruel manner, &c.

ART. 615. Where a homicide occurs under the influence of sudden passion, but by the use of means not in their nature calculated to produce death, the person killing is not deemed guilty of the homicide, unless it appear that there was an intention to kill, but the party from whose act the death resulted, may be prosecuted for, and convicted of any grade of assault and battery. Homicide under sudden passion, &c. [See 596.]

ART. 617. Where the circumstances attending a homicide show an evil or cruel disposition, or that it was the design of the person offending to kill, he is deemed guilty of murder or manslaughter, according to the other facts of the case, though the instrument or means used may not in their nature be such as to produce death ordinarily. Rule when circumstances show a cruel disposition, &c.

TITLE XVIII.

OF OFFENCES AGAINST REPUTATION.

CHAPTER I.

OF LIBEL.

ART. 618. He is guilty of libel, who, with intent to injure, makes, writes, prints, publishes, sells or circulates any malicious statement affecting the re- Act of Aug. 28, 1856.

Who is guilty of. putation of another, in respect to any matter or thing pointed out in this Chapter.

Punishment. ART. 619. If any person be guilty of libel, he shall be punished, by fine, not less than one hundred dollars, nor more than two thousand dollars, or by imprisonment, in the county jail, not exceeding two years; and the Court may enter up judgment and issue an order thereupon, directing the Sheriff to seize and destroy all the publications, prints, paintings, or engravings, constituting the libel as charged in the indictment or information.

By circulating false writing, purporting to be the act of another. ART. 620. If any person, with intent to injure the reputation of another, shall without lawful authority, make, publish or circulate, a writing, purporting to be the act of some other person, and which comes within the definition of libel, as given in this chapter, he shall be punished in the same manner as if the act purported to be his own; and the rules with respect to libel apply also to the making and circulation of such false writing.

What constitutes a party the "maker" of. ART. 621. He is the maker of a libel, who originally contrived, and either executed it himself, by writing, printing, engraving, or painting, or dictated or caused it to be done by others.

Who is the publisher of. ART. 622. He is the publisher of a libel, who, either of his own will, or by the persuasion or dictation of another, executes the same in any of the modes pointed out as constituting a libel; but if any one by force or threats is compelled to execute such libel, he is guilty of no offence.

"Circulating," definition of, ART. 622a*. He is guilty of circulating a libel, who, knowing its contents, either sells, distributes or gives, or who, with malicious design, reads or exhibits it to others.

What idea must be conveyed by the published statement. ART. 623. The written, printed or published statement to come within the definition of libel, must convey the idea, either,

1. That the person to whom it refers has been guilty of some penal offence; or,

2. That he has been guilty of some act or omission, which, though not a penal offence, is disgraceful to him as a member of society, and the natural consequence of which is to bring him into contempt among honorable persons; or,

3. That he has some moral, vice or physical or mental defect or desease, which renders him unfit for intercourse with respectable society, and such as should cause him to be generally avoided; or,

4. That he is notoriously of bad or infamous character; or,

5. That any person in office, or a candidate therefor, is dishonest; and therefore unworthy of such office, or that while in office he has been guilty of some malfeasance rendering him unworthy of the place.

May be either written, printed &c. ART. 624. A libel may be either written, printed, engraved, etched or painted, but no verbal defamation comes within the meaning thereof; and whenever a defendant is accused of libel, by means of a painting, engraving or caricature, it must clearly appear therefrom that the person said to be defamed was, in fact, intended to be represented by such painting, engraving or caricature.

Must be circulated or posted, &c. ART. 625. In order to render any manuscript a libel, it must be circulated, or posted up on some public place.

Editor, printer, or publisher who issues or sells, is guilty, &c. ART. 626. If the libel be in printed form, and issues or is sold in any office or shop, where a public newspaper is conducted, or where books or other printed works are sold or printed, the editor, publisher and proprietor of such newspaper, or any one of them, or the owner of such shop, is to be deemed guilty of making or circulating such libel, until the contrary is made on the trial to appear.

ART. 627. The editor, publisher or proprietor of a public newspaper, may avoid the responsibility of making or publishing a libel by giving the true author of the same, provided such author be a resident of this State, and a person of good character, except in cases where it is shown that such editor, publisher or proprietor caused the libel to be published with malicious design. May avoid responsibility by, &c.

ART. 628. No person shall be convicted of libel merely on evidence that he has made a manuscript copy of a libel, or has performed the manual labor of printing it, unless it be shown positively that such person was actuated by a malicious design against the person defamed. But the person for whose account, or by whose order it was printed, shall be presumed to have known the intent of the publication, and shall be liable for the offence. Manual labor, &c., not sufficient, unless.

ART. 629. It is sufficient to constitute the offence of libel, if the natural consequence of the publication of the same is to injure the person defamed, although no actual injury to his reputation has been sustained. When natural consequence is to injure, tho'gh none be proved.

ART. 630. The intent to injure is to be presumed if such would be the natural consequence of the libel, though no actual proof be made that the defendant had such design; and, in all trials for libel, the jury are to judge from the facts proved relative to the malicious design of the defendant, as to what penalty ought to be imposed under the restrictions herein prescribed. Intent to injure, when presumed.

ART. 631. It is no offence to make true statements of fact, or express opinions as to the integrity or other qualifications of a candidate for any office or public place, or appointment. True statements concerning candidates, &c., no libel.

ART. 632. It is no offence to publish true statements of fact as to the qualifications of any person for any occupation, profession or trade. Same of tradesmen and professional men.

ART. 633. It is no offence to publish any criticism or examination of any work of literature, science or art, or any opinion as to the qualifications or merits of the author of such work. Criticism of works of literature, &c.

ART. 634. To constitute libel, there must be some injury intended to the reputation of *persons;* and no publication as to the Government, or any of the branches thereof, as such, is an offence under the name of seditious writings, or any other name. Injury must be to the reputation of persons. Publication against Government.

ART. 635. It is no libel to make publication respecting the merits or doctrines of any particular religion, system of morals, or politics, or of any particular form of government. Respecting religious systems, &c.

ART. 636. It is no libel to make any publication respecting a body politic or corporate as such. Bodies politic, &c.

ART. 637. It is no libel to publish any statement respecting any legislative or judicial proceedings, whether the statement be in fact true or not, unless in such statement a charge of corruption is made against some person acting in a legislative or judicial capacity. Legislative or judicial proceedings.

ART. 638. Where any person, by virtue of his office, is required to record the proceedings of any department of the Government, or of any body corporate or politic, or of any association organized for purposes of business, or as a religious, moral, benevolent, literary, or scientific institution, he cannot be charged with libel for any entry upon the minutes or records of such department, body, or association, made in the course of his official duties. Records of proceedings of a department of the Government.

Of the proceedings of a corporate body, or, &c.

ART. 639. If any false statement be entered upon the minutes or record of proceedings of any corporate body or association, included within the meaning of the preceding article, which would be libel if written, printed, published or circulated by an individual, according to the previous articles of this chapter, the persons being members of such body or association, who assent to, and direct such libellous statement to be made, are guilty of libel, under the same rules as if the false statement had been written, published or circulated, in any other manner than as a part of the record or proceedings of such body or association; subject, however, to the restrictions contained in the succeeding article.

Same subject.

ART. 640. The libellous statement referred to in the preceding article, is not to be presumed to have been made with intent to injure, from the mere fact that such would be the natural result thereof, unless it appear from other facts that the statement was in fact made with that intention.

Definition of word "malicious."

ART. 641. The word "malicious" is used to signify an act done with evil or mischevious design; and it is not necessary to prove any special facts, showing ill feeling on the part of the person who is concerned in making, printing, publishing or circulating a libellous statement against the person injured thereby.

Statement made in legislature.

ART. 642. No statement made in the course of a legislative or judicial proceeding, whether true or false, although made with intent to injure, and from malicious purposes, comes within the definition of libel.

Truth of statement may be shown in justification, when.

ART. 643. In the following cases the truth of any statement charged as a libel, may be shown in justification of the defendant.

1. Where the publication purports to be an investigation of the official conduct of officers or men, in a public capacity.

2. Where it is stated in the libel that a person has been guilty of some penal offence, and the time, place and nature of the offence is specified in the publication.

3. Where it is stated in the libel that a person is of notoriously bad or infamous character

4. Where the publication charges any person in office, or a candidate therefor, with a want of honesty, or of having been guilty of some malfeasance in office, rendering him unworthy of the place. In other cases the truth of the facts stated in the libel cannot be enquired into.

Province of jury in cases of libel.

ART. 644. The jury in every case of libel are not only the judges of the facts and of the law, under the direction of the Court, in accordance with the Constitution, but they are judges of the intent with which a libel may have been published or circulated, subject to the rules prescribed in this chapter, and in rendering their verdict they are to be governed by a consideration of the nature of the charge contained in the libel, the general reputation of the person said to be defamed, and the degree of malice exhibited by the defendant in the commission of the offence.

When law of is regulated by the Code.

ART. 645. This title regulates the law with regard to libel, when prosecuted as a penal offence, and is not intended to have any operation upon the subject so far as relates to civil remedies for the recovery of damages.

CHAPTER II.

OF FALSE ACCUSATION AND THREATS OF PROSECUTION.

ART. 646. If any two or more persons shall combine falsely to accuse another of an offence, and shall, in pursuance of such combination, make such accusation before a court or magistrate, or in any newspaper or other public print, or by the circulation of handbills, or in any other public manner, by writing, they shall be punished by fine, not exceeding two thousand dollars, or by imprisonment, in the county jail, not exceeding two years. Act of Aug. 28, 1856 Combinations to make.

ART. 647. If the purpose of such combination be to extort money or any pecuniary advantage, the punishment shall be fine, not to exceed two thousand dollars, and imprisonment, in the Penitentiary, not to exceed three years. To extort money.

ART. 648. If any person, with intent to extort money, or any pecuniary advantage, shall threaten to accuse another of a felony, before any court, or to publish any other statement respecting him which would come within the meaning of a libel, he shall be punished in the manner set forth in Article 646. Threats of prosecution to extort money.

ART. 649. If any person shall, in any newspaper, or handbill, or by notice posted up in any place, publish another as a coward, or use towards him other opprobrious language, he shall be fined in an amount not exceeding two hundred dollars; and if such publication or posting be in consequence of a refusal to fight a duel, the punishment shall be fine, not exceeding five hundred dollars. Publishing another as a coward.

TITLE XIX.

OF OFFENCES AFFECTING SLAVES AND SLAVE PROPERTY.

CHAPTER I.

EXCITING INSURRECTION OR INSUBORDINATION.

ART. 650. Any person who shall aid in any insurrection of slaves against the free inhabitants of this State, who shall join in any secret assembly of slaves in which such insurrection shall be planned, with design to promote it, or shall excite or persuade any slaves to attempt any such insurrection, shall be punished by confinement in the Penitentiary, not less than ten years or for life. Punishment for.

ART. 651. By "insurrection of slaves" is meant an assemblage of three or more, with arms, with intent to obtain their liberty by force. Insurrection of slaves defined.

ART. 652. The term excite, as here used, means to offer any persuasion, or inducement, which has insurrection for its immediate object. Definition of term "excite."

ART. 653. Any person who shall, by words or writing addressed to a slave, endeavor to render such slave discontented with his state of slavery, shall be punished by confinement in the Penitentiary, not less than five years nor more than fifteen years. Rendering slaves discontented.

CHAPTER II.

ILLEGAL TRANSPORTATION OF SLAVES.

How punished. ART. 654. The master, or any other officer, or any of the crew, of any steamboat or other vessel, who shall carry, or cause to be carried, out of any county, a slave or slaves, without the consent of the owner or employer, with intent to deprive the owner or owners of his or their property in such slave, or slaves, or who shall knowingly receive on board of his vessel any runaway slave, and permit him to remain on board, without proper effort to apprehend him, shall be confined in the Penitentiary, not less than ten nor more than thirty years.

CHAPTER III.

STEALING OR ENTICING A SLAVE.

How punished. ART. 655. Any person who shall steal or entice away any slave, the property of another, shall be confined in the Penitentiary, not less than five, nor more than fifteen years.

Attempt to steal—how punished. ART. 656. Any person who shall attempt to steal, or entice away a slave, the property of another, shall be confined in the Penitentiary, not less than five nor more than fifteen years.

Definition of. ART. 657. The offence of stealing a slave is complete within the meaning of Article 655, by taking the slave into possession, either by his consent or forcibly, and removing him a distance however short, from the possession or premises of his employer or owner, with the design to claim the ownership of such slave, or otherwise dispose of the same.

What constitutes "enticing away a slave." ART 658. The offence of enticing away a slave consists in inducing a slave through persuasion, or by means of any reward, to leave the possession or premises of his owner or employer, and to accompany the person so offending for the purpose of escaping from servitude to his owner, but the offence is not complete unless such slave shall have actually abandoned such possession or premises.

Definition of words "attempt to steal." ART. 659. By the words "*attempt to steal*," as used in Article 656, is meant the use of any means, either forcible or persuasive, which may be directly calculated to enable the party offending to steal the slave.

Enticing a slave defined. ART. 660. An attempt to entice away a slave is the use of any means forcible or persuasive, which may be calculated to induce such slave to abandon the service of his master or employer, and accompany the offender, with the view to deprive the owner of his property.

CHAPTER IV.

OFFENCES RESPECTING RUNAWAY SLAVES.

ART. 661. If any person advise a slave to leave the service of his master or employer, or aid such slave in so leaving, by procuring for or delivering to him a pass, or other writing, or by furnishing him with money, clothes, provisions, or other facility, and such slave do actually abscond, he shall be confined in the Penitentiary, for not less than three nor more than ten years. Punishment for advising a slave to leave service of his master.

ART. 662. The offence mentioned in the preceding Article differs from that of enticing, or attempting to entice away a slave, in this, that the offence of aiding or advising a slave to leave the service of his master or employer, is complete when the slave shall have left his owner or employer, but not in the company of the person so aiding or advising. Differs from enticing away a slave.

CHAPTER V.

IMPORTING SLAVES GUILTY OF CRIME.

ART. 663. If any person shall knowingly import, or bring into this State, a slave who shall be a fugitive from justice, or who shall have been sold or convicted of crime beyond the limits of this State, he shall be fined not less than one hundred dollars, nor more than one thousand dollars. Fugitive from justice, &c.

CHAPTER VI.

HARBORING AND CONCEALING.

ART. 664. If any person shall harbor any runaway slave, he shall be fined, not less than one hundred dollars, nor more than five hundred dollars. How punished.

ART. 665 If any person shall conceal, or aid in concealing, any runaway slave, he shall be punished as prescribed in the preceding Article. Same.

ART. 666. Any person convicted of a second offence, under either of the two preceding articles, shall be punished by confinement in the Penitentiary, not less than three nor more than ten years. Second offence, how punished.

ART. 667. By the term *harboring*, is meant the act of maintaining and concealing a runaway slave; the person so harboring having knowledge of the fact that he is a runaway. Definition of term *harboring*.

CHAPTER VII.

TRADING WITH SLAVES.

Selling liquors to slaves.

ART. 668. If any person who deals in intoxicating liquors, either by wholesale or retail, shall sell to a slave without the written consent of his master, mistress, overseer, or employer, any intoxicating liquors, or shall give to any such slave, and without such written consent, any intoxicating liquors, he shall be fined, not less than fifty nor more than two hundred dollars.

Buying from slaves.

ART. 669. If any person shall buy from a slave any valuable produce, or other article whatever, without the written consent of the master, mistress overseer, or employer of such slave, he shall be fined not less than twenty nor more than two hundred dollars.

CHAPTER VIII.

CRUEL TREATMENT OF SLAVES.

Punishment for cruel treatment, &c.

ART. 670. If any person shall unreasonably abuse, or cruelly treat a slave whether his own property or the property of another, he shall be fined not less than one hundred nor more than two thousand dollars.

What is unreasonable abuse.

ART. 671. It is unreasonable abuse of a slave to inflict a chastisement by whipping, or otherwise greatly disproportioned to the nature of the offence which provoked such chastisement, or to beat with unusual implements any such slave.

What is cruel treatment.

ART. 672. It is cruel treatment of a slave to inflict an unusual degree of punishment without just provocation, or to torture or to cause unusual pain and suffering to a slave by the use of any means, or to subject such slave to punishment so severe as to become injurious to his health, or calculated greatly to depreciate his value, or for the person having the charge of any slave to fail to supply him with comfortable clothing, or a sufficient quantity of wholesome food.

Maiming a slave, &c.

ART. 673. When by abuse or cruel treatment, a slave is maimed or disfigured, the offence comes within the definition of maiming or disfiguring; but a person indicted for either of the last named offences may be convicted on the trial thereof of the offence of unreasonably abusing or cruelly treating a slave.

Murder, when.

ART. 674. If, by reason of abuse or cruel treatment to a slave, death shall result, the offence is murder.

Punishment for whipping slave, the property of another.

ART. 675. If any person, not authorized by law, and without sufficient provocation, shall whip or strike any slave not his own property, he shall be punished, by fine, not exceeding one hundred dollars.

Patrols, &c.

ART. 676. Patrols and Police Officers, who, under the police regulations of any county, city or town, inflict the punishment of whipping upon a slave come within the meaning of persons "authorized by law," as set forth in the preceding Article; but if the chastisement be unreasonably or cruelly inflicted, such persons are guilty of an offence under the previous Articles of this Chapter.

ART. 677. Any person who has the control or management of slaves, as heir, employer, executor, administrator or guardian, or in any other lawful capacity, is not within the meaning of Article 675. Executors, &c.

ART. 678. Insulting language or gestures from a slave to a free white person will justify reasonable chastisement, whether such person has lawful control over the slave or not. Justifiable, when.

TITLE XX.

OF OFFENCES AGAINST PROPERTY OTHER THAN SLAVES.

CHAPTER I.

OF ARSON.

ART. 679. Arson is the wilful burning of any house included within the meaning of the succeeding Articles of this Chapter. Definition of

ART. 680. A house is any building, edifice, or structure, enclosed with walls and covered, whatever may be the materials used for building. House defined.

ART. 681. A dwelling house is any house within which some person habitually sleeps or eats his meals, though it may be used for other purposes, as a store house, office, mill-house, or the like; a tent or open shed does not come within the meaning of a dwelling house. Dwelling house defined.

ART. 682. An outhouse is any house adjacent to, communicating with, or on the same premises with a dwelling house. Outhouse defined.

ART. 683. A public building is any court house, county clerk's, sheriff's, assessor and collector's office, meeting house, church, college, academy, school house, town house, jail, or any other building used for purposes of religious worship, political meetings, amusement, or as a place of confinement for prisoners. Public building defined.

ART. 684. The burning is complete when the fire has actually communicated to a house, though it may neither be destroyed nor seriously injured. Burning, when complete.

ART. 685. It is of no consequence by what means the fire is communicated to a house, if the burning is with design. It may be by setting fire to any combustible material communicating therewith, by an explosion, or by any other means. Design constitutes the arson, however done.

ART. 686. When fire is communicated to a house by means of the burning of another house, or some combustible matter, it shall be presumed that the intent was to destroy every house actually burnt, provided there was any apparent danger of such destruction. Intent presumed, when.

Explosions. ART. 687. The explosion of a house by means of gun-power, or other explosive matter, comes within the meaning of arson.

When not arson ART. 688. A house blown up, or otherwise destroyed, for the purpose of saving another house from fire, is not within the meaning of arson.

Owner may destroy, when ART. 689. The owner of a house may destroy it by fire or explosion, without incurring the penalty of arson, except in the cases mentioned in the succeeding article.

Owner guilty of arson, when, ART. 690. When a house is within a town or city; or when it is insured; or when there is within it any property belonging to another; or when there is apparent danger by reason of the burning thereof, that the life or person of some individual, or the safety of some house belonging to another will be endangered; the owner, if he burn the same, is guilty of arson, and shall be punished according to the description of the house so burnt.

Part owner may not burn, ART. 691. One of the part owners of a house is not permitted to burn it.

Punishment. ART. 692. If any person shall wilfully burn a dwelling house or outhouse, he shall be punished by confinement in the Penitentiary, not less than five, nor more than fifteen years.

Punishment for burning storehouse, &c. ART. 693. If any person shall wilfully burn any storehouse, warehouse, gin house, mill house, when such house does not also come within the definition of a dwelling house, or any public building, as defined in Article 683, he shall be punished, by confinement in the Penitentiary, not less than four, nor more than ten years.

Burning the Capitol, &c. ART. 694. If any person shall wilfully burn the Capitol building of the State the Treasury building, or Comptroller's Office of the State, the Executive mansion of the State, the building in which the Executive or Secretary of State shall keep their offices, or the General Land Office of the State, he shall be punished by confinement in the Penitentiary for life.

Burning a building other than a dwelling house. ART. 695. If any person shall wilfully burn a building other than a dwelling house, he shall be punished, by confinement in the Penitentiary, not less than three, nor more than seven years.

Definition of the term, building. ART. 696. By the term "building or other than a dwelling house," is meant any building coming within the definition of a house, and not included within the meaning of some other Article of this Chapter.

CHAPTER II.

OF OTHER WILFUL BURNING.

Rules applicable to arson, apply also to wilful burning. ART. 697. The rules and definitions contained in the preceding Chapter, with respect to arson, apply also to wilful burnings under the provisions of this Chapter, where they are not clearly inapplicable.

Other buildings hay, corn, &c. ART. 698. If any person shall wilfully burn any building not coming within the description of a house as defined in the preceding Chapter; or shall wilfully burn any stack of corn, hay, fodder, grain or flax, or any pile of boards, lumber or wood, the property of another, he shall be punished by confinement in the Penitentiary, not less than two nor more than five years, or by fine not exceeding two thousand dollars. Act of Feb. 12, 1858.

ART. 699. If any person shall wilfully burn any ship or other vessel, or any boat, flatboat or raft, which, with its cargo, is of the value of one hundred dollars or more, he shall be punished, by confinement in the Penitentiary, not less than two, nor more than seven years, or by fine, not exceeding two thousand dollars. Act of Aug. 28, 1856. Ship or other vessel, &c.

ART. 700. This offence is complete only when some person other than the person offending has an interest in the property by insurance, or otherwise, at the time the burning takes place. Offence, when complete.

ART. 701. If any person shall wilfully burn any bridge, which by law or usage is a public highway, he shall be punished, by imprisonment in the Penitentiary, not less than two, nor more than seven years, or by fine not exceeding five thousand dollars. Act of Feb. 12, 1858. Bridge.

ART. 702. If any person shall wilfully burn, or cause to be burned, any woodland or prairie not his own, at any time between the 1st of July and the 15th of February, succeeding, he shall be fined not less than fifty dollars, nor more than three hundred dollars. Act of Aug. 28, 1856. Woodland or prairie, the property of another

ART. 703. The offence named in the foregoing Article is complete where the person offending sets fire to his own woodland or prairie, and the fire communicates the woodland or prairie of another. When offence complete.

ART. 704. If any person with intent to defraud, shall wilfully burn any personal property owned by himself, which shall be at the time insured against the loss or damage from fire, he shall be punished by confinement in the Penitentiary, not less than two, nor more than five years. Act of Feb. 12, 1858. Person burning property of his own, which is insured, &c.

ART. 705. If any person shall wilfully burn any personal property belonging to another, he shall be fined, not exceeding five times the value of the property destroyed. A t of Aug. 28, 1856. Personal property belonging to another.

ART. 706. If any bodily injury, less than death, is suffered by any person, by reason of the commission of any of the offences named in this and the preceding Chapter, the punishment may be increased by the jury, so as not to exceed double that which is prescribed in cases where no such injury is suffered. When bodily injury ensues, punishment may be doubled.

ART. 607. Where death is occasioned by any of the offences described in this and the preceding Chapter, the offender is guilty of murder. Where death ensues, it is murder.

CHAPTER III.

OF ATTEMPTS TO COMMIT ARSON, OR OTHER WILFUL BURNING.

ART. 708. If any person shall, by any means calculated to effect the object, attempt to commit any of the offences enumerated in the two preceding Chapters, he shall receive such punishment as may be assessed by the jury, not to exceed one-half of the penalty which would have been affixed in case the offence attempted had been actually committed; *provided*, that, when the punishment shall have been confinement in the Penitentiary, in no case shall the lowest term be less than two years. Act of Feb. 12, 1858. unishment.

CHAPTER IV.

MALICIOUS MISCHIEF

Act of Feb. 12, 1858. Wilfully sinking vessel, &c. how punished.

ART. 709. If any person shall wilfully and maliciously cast away, sink, or destroy, in any way other than by fire, any vessel or boat, which, together with its cargo, if any, shall be of the value of one hundred dollars or more, he shall be punished by imprisonment in the Penitentiary not less than two nor more than five years, or by fine not exceeding two thousand dollars. If the life of any person is lost by such act, the offender is guilty of murder.

Act of Aug. 28, 1856. Telegraph wire, breaking, cutting, &c.

ART. 710. If any person shall intentionally break, cut, pull, or tear down, misplace, or in any other manner injure any telegraph wire, post, machinery, or other necessary appurtenance to any telegraph line, or in any way wilfully obstruct or interfere with the transmission of messages along such telegraph line, he shall be punished by confinement in the Penitentiary, for a term not exceeding five years, or by fine, not less than one hundred nor more than two thousand dollars.

Obstructing railway, &c., how punished.

ART. 711. If any person shall wilfully place any obstruction upon the track of any railroad, or remove any rail therefrom, or in any other way injure such road, or shall do any damage to any railroad, or car, whereby the life of any person might be endangered, he shall be punished by imprisonment in the Penitentiary, not less than two nor more than seven years. If the life of any person is lost by any such unlawful act, the offender is guilty of murder.

Felling boundary trees, &c.

ART. 712. If any person shall fell, cut, alter, or remove, or cause to be cut, felled, altered, or removed, any boundary tree, or any landmark established upon the line or corner of, or as a bearing tree to, any tract or lot of land, without the consent of the owner, and with fraudulent intent, he shall be punished by imprisonment in the county jail, not exceeding three years, or by fine, not exceeding one thousand dollars.

Act of February 12, 1858. Wilfully killing, maiming, &c., horse, &c.

ART. 713. If any person shall wilfully kill, maim, wound, poison, or disfigure, any horse, mare, gelding, jack, jennet, mule, colt, cattle, sheep, goat, swine, or dog, of another, with intent to injure the owner thereof, he shall be fined not less than three times the amount of the injury done to the owner by such offence, and not exceeding ten times the amount of such injury.

Act of August 28, 1856. Same.

ART. 714. If any person shall wilfully and wantonly kill, maim, wound, poison, or cruelly and unmercifully beat and abuse any dumb animal, such as is enumerated in the preceding Article, he shall be fined, not exceeding two hundred and fifty dollars.

Act of Feb. 12, 1858. Removing buoy, beacon, light, &c.

ART. 715. If any person shall wilfully and mischievously remove any buoy, beacon, light, or any other mark or signal, erected for the purpose of indicating the channel in any bay, river, lake, or other navigable water within the State; or shall erect any false buoy, beacon, light, or mark, or signal, to indicate the channel in any such bay, river, lake, or other navigable water, with intent to mislead or deceive, he shall be punished by confinement in the penitentiary, not less than two nor more than five years, or by fine not exceeding two thousand dollars; and if death occurs by reason of such unlawful conduct, the offender is guilty of murder.

Act of Aug. 28, 1856.

Injuring or destroying growing fruit, &c.

Art. 716. If any person shall wilfully and mischievously injure or destroy any growing fruit, corn, grain, or other agricultural product, or property, real or personal, of any description whatever, in such manner as that the injury does not come within the description of any of the offences against property otherwise provided for by this Code, he shall be punished by fine, not exceeding five times the value of the property so destroyed, or five times the amount of the injury done.

CHAPTER V.

OF CUTTING AND DESTROYING TIMBER.

Act of Aug. 28, 1856.

Cutting timber, how punished.

Art. 717. If any person without the consent of the owner, shall knowingly cut down or destroy any tree or timber, upon any land not his own; or shall knowingly and without such consent, carry away any such timber, he shall be punished by fine, not exceeding three times the value of the timber so unlawfully cut down, destroyed, or carried away.

Not necessary to state name of owner in indictment.

Art. 718. If the offence spoken of in the preceding Article be prosecuted in the District Court, it shall not be nesessary for the indictment, or information, to state the name of the owner of such timber, but it shall be sufficient to charge that the timber was not the property of the person so offending.

Act of Feb. 12 1858.

How State may prove ownership to be in third party.

Art. 718a. Upon the trial of any case coming within the provisions of Article 717, the State may prove the ownership of the land to be in some person other than the defendant, by either of the following modes:

1st. By the copy of a grant duly certified from the General Land Office.

2d. By a deed, or a copy of a deed, or other evidence of title, duly certified, from the office of the Clerk of the County Court of the county where the prosecution is pending.

3d. By a certificate from the Comptroller's office, or from the Assessor and Collector of the county, that some person other than the defendant pays taxes on the land.

4th. By verbal testimony of title, or of notorious use and possession of the land by some person other than the defendant; and such proof shall be held sufficient, until contradicted by competent evidence on the part of the defendant, that he is the owner of the land.

Act of Aug. 28, 1856.

Art. 719. Each day's cutting, destruction, or carrying away of timber, in violation of the provisions of this act, shall be regarded as a separate offence.

May be prosecuted before Justice of Peace when.

Art. 720. An offence under the provisions of this Chapter, may be prosecuted before a Justice of the Peace, when three times the amount of the damage done by the unlawful act, does not exceed one hundred dollars.

When in District Court, &c.

Art. 721. The District Court shall have exclusive jurisdiction of the offence defined in this Chapter, when the fine exceeds one hundred dollars, and shall have concurrent jurisdiction with the Justice's Courts, where the fine does not exceed that amount.

When used for repairing public road. ART. 722. Nothing in this Chapter contained shall render any person guilty of an offence, who cuts or uses timber for the purpose of making or repairing any public road or bridge passing over, or immediately adjacent to, the land on which such tree or timber may be found, or who uses a reasonable amount of wood standing outside of an enclosure, for the purpose of making fires while traveling upon the road.

Shall not exempt from penalty affixed to theft. ART. 723. Nothing contained in this Chapter shall exempt a person from the penalty affixed to the offence of theft, whenever timber is taken in such manner as to come within the definition of that offence.

CHAPTER VI.

OF BURGLARY.

Act of Aug. 28, 1856. — Definition of. ART. 724. The offence of burglary is constituted by entering a house by force, threats, or fraud, at night, or, in like manner, by entering a house during the day and remaining concealed therein until night, with the intent in either case of committing a felony.

Same subject. ART. 725. He is also guilty of burglary who, with intent to commit a felony by breaking, enters a house in the day time.

Definition of term "entry." ART. 725a*. The entry into a house, within the meaning of Article 724, includes every kind of entry, but one made by the free consent of the occupant, or of one authorized to give such consent; it is not necessary that there should be any actual breaking to constitute the offence of burglary, except when the entry is made in the day time.

Same subject. ART. 726. The entry is not confined to the entrance of the whole body; it may consist of the entry of any part for the purpose of committing a felony; or it may be constituted by the discharge of fire-arms or other deadly missile, into the house, with intent to injure any person therein; or it may be constituted by the introduction of any instrument for the purpose of taking from the house any personal property, although no part of the body of the offender should be introduced.

Definition of term "breaking." ART. 727. By the term breaking, as used in Article 725, is meant, that the entry must be made with actual force. The slightest force, however, is sufficient to constitute breaking; it may be by lifting the latch of the door that is shut, by raising a window, the entry at a chimney, or other unusual place, the introduction of the hand or any instrument to draw out the property through an aperture made by the offender for that purpose.

Definition of term "house." ART. 728. A "house" within the meaning of this Chapter, is any building or structure erected for public or private use, whether the property of the United States, of this State, or of any public or private corporation or association, or of any individual, and of whatever material it may be constructed.

ART. 729. A "dwelling house," within the meaning of this Chapter, is any house where any person habitually sleeps. Definition of term "dwelling house."

ART. 730. Where the house entered is a dwelling house, the punishment of burglary shall be imprisonment in the Penitentiary not less than three nor more than ten years. Where the house entered is not a dwelling house, the punishment shall be confinement in the Penitentiary not less than two nor more than five years. Act of Feb. 12, 1858. Punishment for.

ART. 731. If the entry into a house be effected by force, the punishment for the offence shall be increased to not more than double the punishment which would otherwise be affixed to the offence. Force, within the meaning of this Article, is any violence whatever, opposed to any person or to any part of the house, for the purpose of effecting an entrance. Act of Aug. 28, 1856. If force be used, punishment double. Force defined.

ART. 732. If the burglary consist of the discharge of arms, as specified in Article 726, the punishment shall be confinement in the Penitentiary, not less than two nor more than seven years. Act of Feb. 12, 1858. Discharge of arms, how punished.

ART. 733. If any person shall, after entering a house in any of the modes spoken of in this Chapter, commit the offence of theft, he shall be punished by confinement in the Penitentiary, not less than two years, nor more than seven years. Act of Aug. 28, 1856. Theft after entering house, how punished.

ART. 734. If a house be entered in such manner as that the entry comes within the definition of burglary, and the person guilty of such burglary shall, after so entering, commit theft, or any other offence, he shall be punished for burglary, and also for whatever other offence is so committed. Act of Feb. 12, 1858. Burglary, and other offence committed after entry, both punished.

ART. 735. If the burglary was effected for the purpose of committing one felony, and the person guilty thereof shall, while in the house, commit another felony, he shall be punishable for any felony so committed as well as for the burglary. Act of Aug. 28, 1856. Same subject.

ART. 736. An entry into a house for the purpose of committing theft, unless the same is effected by actual breaking, is not burglary when the same is done by a domestic servant or other inhabitant of such house; and a theft committed by such person after entering a house is only punishable as simple theft. Entry by domestic servant, for purpose of theft, not burglary, &c., unless, &c.

ART. 737. By the terms "day time" is meant, any time of the twenty-four hours from thirty minutes before sunrise, until thirty minutes after sunset. Definition of term "day time."

CHAPTER VII.

OF OFFENCES ON BOARD OF VESSELS AND STEAMBOATS.

ART. 738. If any person, by any of the means enumerated in Article 724, shall, at night, enter a ship or other sail vessel, or a steamboat, with intent to commit a felony, he shall be punished by confinement in the Penitentiary, not less than two nor more than five years. Act of Feb. 12, 1858. Entry of ship, &c., at night, with intent to commit, &c.

ART. 739. If any person shall, in the day time, by breaking, enter a vessel or Act of Aug. 28, 1856.

Same in daytime, how punished. steamboat, with intent to commit a felony, he shall be punished as prescribed in the preceding Article.

If theft be committed after entry, how punished. ART. 740. If theft be committed on board a vessel or steamboat, by any person who has entered in the manner and for the purpose specified in the two preceding articles, he shall be punished by confinement in the Penitentiary, not less than two nor more than seven years.

Definitions, rules, &c., how applicable. ART. 741. The definitions, rules and explanations of terms given in the preceding Chapter, are applicable to such terms in this Chapter; and the rules prescribed in articles 724, 725, 726, and 727, of the preceding Chapter, shall also apply to similar cases on board of vessel or steamboat.

Theft on steamboat by servant or employee, how punished. ART. 742. A theft on board a steamboat, committed by a servant or employee thereof, except in cases where there has been an actual breaking in, is punishable as simple theft.

CHAPTER VIII.

OF ROBBERY.

Act of Aug. 26, 1956.
Definition of. ART. 743. If any person, by assault or by violence, and putting in fear of life or of bodily injury, shall fraudulently take from the person of another any property, with intent to appropriate the same to his own use, he shall be punished by confinement in the Penitentiary, for a term not less than two nor more than ten years. *How punished.*

Act of Feb. 12, 1858.
Same subject. ART. 744. If any person, by threatening to do some illegal act injurious to the character, person or property of another, shall fraudulently induce the person so threatened to deliver to him any property, with intent to appropriate the same to his own use, he shall be punished by confinement in the Penitentiary, not less than two nor more than five years.

CHAPTER IX.

OF THEFT.

1. *Of Theft in general.*

2. *Of Theft from the Person.*

1. *Of Theft in General.*

ART. 745. Theft is the fraudulent taking of corporeal personal property, belonging to another, from his possession, or from the possession of some person holding the same for him without his consent, with intent to deprive the owner of the value of the same, and to appropriate it to the use or benefit of the person taking. Act of Aug. 28, 1856. Definition of.

ART. 745 a. If any person shall receive or conceal property, which has been acquired by another in such manner as that the acquisition comes within the meaning of the term theft, knowing the same to have been so acquired, he shall be punished in the same manner as by law, the person stealing the same would be liable to be punished. Act of Feb. 12, 1858. Receiver of stolen property punished in same manner.

ART. 746. The property must be such as has some specific value, capable of being ascertained. It embraces every species of personal property capable of being taken. Act of Aug. 28, 1856. Property must have some specific value.

ART. 747. To constitute "taking" it is not necessary that the property be removed any distance from the place of taking, it is sufficient that it has been in the possession of the thief, though it may not be removed out of the presence of the person deprived of it; nor is it necessary that any definite length of time shall elapse between the taking and the discovery thereof; if but a moment elapse, the offence is complete. What constitutes "taking," &c.

ART. 748. The taking must be wrongful, so that if the property came into the possession of the person accused of theft by lawful means, the subsequent appropriation of it is not theft; but if the taking, though originally lawful, was obtained by any false pretext, or with an intent to deprive the owner of the value thereof, and appropriate the property to the use and benefit of the person taking, and the same is so appropriated, the offence of theft is complete. The taking must be wrongful, &c., but if by any false pretext, the offence of theft is complete.

ART. 749. It is not necessary, in order to constitute theft, that the possession and ownership of the property be in the same person at the time of taking. Possession and ownership in same person, not necessary to constitute theft

ART. 750. Possession of the person so unlawfully deprived of property, is constituted by the exercise of actual control, care, or management of the property, whether the same be lawful or not. Possession of person unlawfully defined, how constituted.

ART. 751. No person can be guilty of theft by taking property belonging to himself, except in the following cases: Person not guilty of theft by taking property belonging to himself, except, &c.

1. Where the property has been deposited with the person in possession, as a pledge or security for a debt.

2. Where it is in the possession of an officer of the law, by process from a court of competent jurisdiction.

3. Where the property is in the possession of an executor or administrator, for the purpose of administration.

4. In all other cases where the person so deprived of possession is, at the time of taking, lawfully entitled to the possession thereof as against the true owner.

If the person accused be part owner, the taking no theft, unless, &c.

ART. 752. If the person accused of theft be part owner of the property, the taking does not come within the definition of theft, unless the person from whom it is taken be wholly entitled to the possession at the time.

Definition of the term property.

ART. 753. The term property, as used in relation to the crime of theft, includes money, bank bills, goods of every description commonly sold as merchandize, every kind of agricultural produce, clothing, any writing containing evidence of an existing debt, contract, liability, promise or ownership of property, real or personal, any receipt for money, discharge, release, acquittance, any printed book or manuscript, and in general, any and every article commonly known as, and called personal property, and all writings of every description, provided such property possess any ascertainable value.

Act of Feb. 12, 1858.

Taking record book, &c., from Clerk's office, &c., made theft, and how punished.

ART. 753 a. If any person shall take and carry away any record book or filed paper from any Clerk's office, public office, or other place where the same may be lawfully deposited, or from the lawful possession of any person whatsoever, with intent to destroy, suppress, alter, or conceal, or in any wise dispose of the same, so as to prevent the lawful use of such record book or filed paper, he shall be deemed guilty of theft, and punished by imprisonment in the Penitentiary, not less than three nor more than seven years.

Theft of certain particular kinds of property, &c.

ART. 754. Theft of certain particular kinds of property, as of a slave, horse, property wrecked, &c., have a punishment affixed, differing from the general punishment of the crime of theft; whenever, therefore, the law provides a particular punishment for theft, committed in regard to a special kind of property, theft of such property is not included within the law affixing a general penalty to the offence; but in other cases, whenever it is declared to be an offence to steal or otherwise fraudulently appropriate property, the provision is intended to include any and every species of personal property, according to its general and broadest signification.

Animals of domestic breed within the meaning of personal property.

ART. 755. Within the meaning of personal property, which may be the subject of theft, are included all animals of domestic breed, when they are proved to be of any specific value.

Theft of property of the value of twenty dollars, or over

ART. 756. Theft of property, of the value of twenty dollars or over, shall be punished by confinement in the Penitentiary, for a term not less than two, nor more than ten years.

Theft of property under &c.

ART. 757. Theft of property under the value of twenty dollars, shall be punished by confinement in the Penitentiary, for a term of two years.

Act of Aug. 28, 1856.

Two preceding Articles do not apply, &c.

ART. 758. The two preceding Articles do not apply to theft of property from a house or from the person, nor to cases of theft of any particular kind of property, where the punishment is specially prescribed.

Act of Feb. 12, 1858.

When property is voluntarily returned.

ART. 759. If property, taken under such circumstances as to constitute theft, be voluntarily returned within a reasonable time, and before any prosecution is commenced therefor, the punishment shall be by fine not exceeding one thousand dollars.

Act of Aug. 28, 1856.

Definition of 'steal' or stolen.

ART. 760. Fhe words "steal" or "stolen," when used in this Code in reference to the acquisition of property, include property acquired by theft.

Stealing growing corn, &c.

ART. 761. The stealing or feloniously taking of any growing, standing, or ungathered Indian corn, wheat, cotton, potatoes or rice, shall hereafter be deemed theft; and any person who shall hereafter steal or feloniously take, pluck, sever, or carry away, any Indian corn, or wheat, cotton, potatoes or rice, growing, standing, or remaining ungathered in any plantation, field or other ground, shall on conviction thereof, be deemed guilty of theft, and suffer punishment as in other cases of theft.

2. *Of Theft from the Person,*

ART. 762. If any person shall commit theft by privately stealing from the person of another, he shall be punished by confinement in the Penitentiary, not less than two, nor more than seven years.

Theft from the person, how punished.

ART. 763. To constitute this offence, it is necessary that the following circumstances concur:

Definition of,

1. The theft must be from the person; it is not sufficient that the property be merely in the presence of the person from whom it is taken.

2. The theft must be committed without the knowledge of the person from whom the property is taken, or so suddenly as not to allow time to make resistance before the property is carried away.

3. It is only necessary that the property stolen should have gone into the possession of the thief, it need not be carried away in order to complete the offence.

3. *Of Theft from a House.*

ART. 764. If any person shall steal property from a house, in such manner as that the offence does not come within the definition of burglary, he shall be punished, by confinement in the Penitentiary, not less than two, nor more than seven years.

Theft from a house, how punished.

4. *Theft of Animals.*

ART. 765. If any person shall steal any horse, gelding, mare, colt, ass, or mule, he shall be punished by confinement in the Penitentiary not less than five nor more than fifteen years.

Act of Feb. 12, 1858.

Theft of horse, gelding, &c., how punished.

ART. 766. If any person shall steal any neat cattle, sheep, goat, or hog, he shall be punished by confinement in the Penitentiary not less than two nor more than five years.

Theft of neat cattle, sheep, goat, &c., how punished.

5. *Illegal Marking and Branding, &c.*

ART. 767. Every person who shall mark, or brand, any horse, gelding, mare or colt, mule, ass, or neat cattle, or who shall mark any sheep, goat or hog, not being his own, and without the consent of the owner, and with intent to defraud, shall be punished, by fine, not exceeding one hundred dollars.

Act of Aug. 28, 1856.

Illegal marking or branding, how punished.

ART. 768. Every person who shall alter or deface the mark or brand of any horse, gelding, mare, or colt, mule, ass, or neat cattle, or shall alter or deface the mark of any sheep, goat, or hog, not being his own property, and without the consent of the owner, and with intent to defraud, shall be punished in the same manner as if he had committed a theft of such animal.

Act of Feb. 12, 1858.

Illegal altering or defacing mark or brand, how punished.

ART. 769. If any person shall remove the hide, or any part thereof, from any neat cattle not his own, and without the consent of the owner of said cattle, he shall be deemed guilty of a misdemeanor, and on conviction thereof, before any Court of competent jurisdiction, shall be fined not less than twenty, nor more than fifty dollars.

Act of Aug. 28, 1856.

Person removing the hide, or any part of any neat cattle, not his own, how punished.

6. *Of Wrecks.*

ART. 770. If any person, with intent to deprive the true owner of the value

Person appropriating to his own benefit property taken from vessel wrecked, &c., how punished.

thereof, shall appropriate to his own use, or dispose of to his own benefit, any property taken or driven on shore, from any vessel wrecked, stranded, or burnt, on the sea shore, or on any river, bay or harbor of the State, he shall be punished, by confinement in the Penitentiary, not less than two, nor more than five years.

CHAPTER X.

EMBEZZLEMENT OF PROPERTY BY PRIVATE PERSONS.

Act of Feb. 12, 1858.

By agent or clerk of incorporated company, &c., how punished. By consignee or bailee of money or property. By clerk or agent of private person or co-partnership.

ART. 771. If any officer, agent, or clerk, of any incorporated company, or institution, or of any city, town, or county; or if any clerk, or agent, of any private person or co-partnership; or if any consignee or bailee of money or property, shall embezzle, or fraudulently misapply or convert to his own use, without the consent of his principal or employer, any money or property of such principal or employer, or the proceeds of such property, after sale, which shall have come to his possession, or shall be under his care by virtue of such office, agency or employment, he shall be punished as prescribed in Articles 756 or 757, according to the amount of, or value of such money or property so embezzled.

By factor or commission merchant, of money, goods, &c

ART. 771a. If any factor or commission merchant shall embezzle, or fraudulently misapply, or convert to his own use, any money, goods, produce, commodity, or other property, which shall have come into his possession, or shall be under his care by virtue of his office, agency, or employment, he shall be punished as prescribed by Articles 756 or 757, according to the amount of the value of the money, goods, produce, commodity, or other property so embezzled or misapplied.

By carrier, or any other person.

ART. 772. If any carrier, to whom any money, goods, or other property, shall have been delivered, to be carried by him; or if any other person, who shall be entrusted with such property, shall embezzle or fraudulently convert to his own use any such money, goods or property, either in the mass, as the same were delivered, or otherwise, he shall be deemed guilty of theft, and shall be punished as prescribed by Articles 756 or 757, according to the amount of the value so embezzled or misapplied.

CHAPTER XI.

FRAUDULENT DISPOSITION OF MORTGAGED PROPERTY.

1. *Fraudulent Disposition of Mortgaged Property.*

Act of Feb. 12, 1858.

ART. 773. If any person has given, or shall hereafter give, any mortgage, deed of trust, or other lien, in writing, upon any personal or moveable property, and shall remove the same or any part thereof out of the State, or shall sell, or otherwise dispose of the same, with intent to defraud the person having such lien, either originally or by transfer, he shall be punished by imprisonment in the penitentiary not less than two nor more than five years. Selling or removing same out of the State how punished.

Art. 773a. Swindling is the acquisition of any personal or movable property, money, or instrument of writing conveying or securing a valuable right, by means of some false or deceitful pretence or device, or fraudulent representation, with intent to appropriate the same to the use of the party so acquiring, or of destroying or impairing the rights of the party justly entitled to the same. Definition of swindling.

Art. 773b. Within the meaning of the term swindling are included the following wrongful acts: Swindling, further defined.

1. The exchange of property upon the false pretence that the party is the owner or has the right to dispose of the property given in exchange.

2. The purchase of property upon the faith and credit of some other person, upon the false pretence that such other person has given the accused the right to use his name or credit in making the acquisition.

3. The obtaining, by false pretences, the possession of any instrument of writing, certificate, field notes, or other paper relating to lands, the property of another, with the intent that thereby the proper owner shall be defeated of a valuable right in such lands.

4. The special enumeration of cases of swindling, above set forth, shall not be understood to exclude any case which, by fair construction of the language, comes within the meaning of the preceding Article. The special enumeration of cases herein not to exclude others.

Art. 773c. Within the meaning of money, as used in the two preceding Articles, are included, also, bank bills, or other circulating medium, current as money. Definition of "money," &c.

Art. 773d. It is not necessary, in order to constitute the offence of swindling, that any benefit shall accrue to the person guilty of the fraud or deceit, nor that any injury shall result to the persons intended to be defrauded, if it is sufficiently apparent that there was a wilful design to receive benefit or cause an injury. Not necessary to constitute the offence, that any benefit shall accrue to the accused

Art. 773e. Where property, money, or other articles of value enumerated in the definition of swindling, are obtained in such manner as to come within the meaning of theft, or some other offence known to the law, the rules herein perscribed, with regard to swindling, shall not be understood to take any such case out of the operation of the law which defines such other offence. If the act constitutes any other offence than swindling, &c.

Art. 773f. If any executor, administrator, or guardian, having charge of any estate, real, personal, or mixed, shall unlawfully and with intent to defraud any heir, legatee, ward or distributee, interested in such estate, convert the same, or any part thereof, to his own use, he shall be deemed guilty of the offence of swindling. Executor, administrator, &c., guilty of swindling, when

Art. 773g. Every person, guilty of swindling, within the meaning of Article 773a, or 773f, shall be punished by confinement in the Penitentiary not less than two, nor more than five years. How punished.

CHAPTER XII.

OFFENCES AGAINST PROPERTY COMMITTED IN ANOTHER STATE OR TERRITORY.

Act of Aug. 28, 1856. Bringing stolen property into this State, &c.

ART. 774. If any person, who shall have committed an offence, in any foreign Country, State or Territory, which if committed in this State would have been robbery, theft, or receiving of stolen goods or property knowing the same to have been stolen, shall bring said property into this State, he shall be deemed guilty of robbery, theft, or receiving of stolen goods, knowing the same to have been stolen as the case may be, and shall be punished as if the offence had been committed in this State.

Must be an offence by the law of the State, &c. from which property was taken

ART. 775. To render a person guilty, under the preceding Article, it must appear that by the law of the State or Territory, from which the property was taken, and brought to this State, the act committed would also have been robbery, theft, or receiving of stolen goods.

CHAPTER XIII.

ESTRAYS.

Act of Feb. 12, 1858. Fine of double the value of, for unlawfully selling or removing

ART. 775a. If any person shall unlawfully remove, sell, or in any other manner dispose of any animal which has been taken up by him as an estray, he shall be punished by fine not exceeding double the value of the property so unlawfully disposed of.

Punishment for using, &c., without complying with the law, taking, &c. theft in certain cases.

ART. 775b. If any person shall, without complying with the laws regulating estrays, take up and use, or otherwise dispose of any animal coming within the meaning of an estray, he shall be punished as prescribed in the preceding Article. If the unlawful taking or disposition of an estray animal be effected in such manner as to come within the meaning of theft, the person guilty of the same shall be punished for that offence.

TITLE XXI.

OF MISCELLANEOUS OFFENCES.

CHAPTER I.

OF CONSPIRACY.

Act of Aug. 28, 1856. Definition.

ART. 776. A conspiracy is an agreement entered into between two or more persons, to commit any one of the offences hereafter named in this Chapter.

ART. 777. The offence of conspiracy is complete, although the parties do not proceed to effect the object for which they have so unlawfully combined. *When offence complete,*

ART. 778. Before any conviction can be had for the offence of conspiracy, it must appear that there was a positive agreement to commit an offence. It will not be sufficient that such an agreement was contemplated by the parties charged. *What must appear before conviction.*

ART. 779. A threat, made by two or more, acting in concert, will not be sufficient to constitute conspiracy. *Threats, by two or more, insufficient.*

ART. 780. The agreement to come within the definition of conspiracy, must be to commit one or more of the following offences: Murder, Robbery, Arson, Burglary, Rape, or Theft. *Must be agreement to commit what crimes.*

ART. 781. Conspiracy to commit murder, shall be punished by confinement in the Penitentiary, not less than two nor more than ten years. Conspiracy to commit any of the other offences named in the preceding article, shall be punished by one half the punishment affixed by law to the commission of the offence so intended by the parties: Provided, that in no case, the punishment by confinement in the Penitentiary be for less than two years. *Act of Feb. 12, 1858. Punishment of, to commit murder or other offences.*

ART. 782. A conspiracy to kill a human being shall be deemed a conspiracy to commit murder. *Act of Aug. 28, 1856. To kill same as to murder.*

ART. 783. A conspiracy entered into in this State, for the purpose of committing an offence in any other of the States or Territories, of the Union, or in any foreign Territory, shall be punished in the same manner as if the object was to commit the offence in this State. *When to commit, in another State or foreign country.*

CHAPTER III.

OF THREATS TO COMMIT OFFENCES.

ART. 784. If any person shall threaten to take the life of a human being, or to inflict upon him any serious bodily injury, he shall be punished by imprisonment in the Penitentiary, not less than two, nor more than five years, or by fine not exceeding two thousand dollars. *Act of Feb. 12, 1858. Punishment of to take life or, serious injury.*

ART. 785. In order to render a person guilty of the offence provided for in this Chapter, it is necessary that the threat be seriously made. *Act of Aug. 28, 1856. Seriously made.*

ART. 786. It is for the Jury to determine in every case of prosecution under this Chapter, whether the threat was seriously made, or was merely idle. *Jury to determine when seriously made.*

ART. 787. A threat that a person will do any act merely to protect himself, or to prevent the commission of some unlawful act by another, does not come within the meaning of this Chapter. *When not within the meaning of this Chapter.*

CHAPTER III.

SEDUCTION.

Act of Feb. 12, 1858.
Punishment of, female under twenty-five years old.

ART. 788. If any person, by promise to marry, shall seduce an unmarried female, under the age of twenty-five years, and shall have carnal knowledge of such female, he shall be punished by imprisonment in the Penitentiary, not less than two, nor more than five years, or by fine not exceeding five thousand dollars.

Act of Aug. 28, 1856.
Definition.

ART. 789. The term seduction is used in the sense in which it is commonly understood.

Marriage cancels offence, unless committed by defendant while married.

ART. 790. If the parties marry each other at any time before the conviction of the defendant, or if the defendant, in good faith, offer to marry the female so seduced, no prosecution shall take place, or, if begun, it shall be dismissed; but the benefits of this Article shall not apply to the case of a defendant who was in fact married at the time of committing the offence.

No offence if marriage is known to party seduced.

ART. 791. No person who was, at the time of committing the offence, married, and the fact of marriage known to the woman, shall be held liable for the offence defined in this Chapter.

CHAPTER IV.

ISSUING MARRIAGE LICENSES UNLAWFULLY.

Act of Feb. 12, 1858.
Punishment for

ART. 791 a. If any Clerk of a County Court, or other officer, authorized by law to issue a license of marriage, shall without the consent of the parent or guardian of the party applying, issue a marriage license to a male person under the age of twenty-one, or to a female under the age of eighteen years, he shall be punished by a fine of five hundred dollars.

When consent of father alone suffient.

ART. 791 b. Where both parents of any minor may be alive, the consent of the father alone shall be sufficient to authorize the issuance of license to the minor.

TITLE XXII.

REPETITION OF OFFENCES.

Act of Aug. 28, 1856.
On conviction second and third times.

ART. 792. If it be shown on the trial of misdemeanor that the defendant has been once before convicted of the same offence, he shall, on a second conviction, receive double the punishment prescribed for such offence in ordinary cases, and upon a third, or any subsequent conviction for the same offence, the punishment shall be increased, so as not to exceed four times the penalty in ordinary cases. If it be shown, on the trial of a felony, less than capital, that the defendant has been before convicted of the same offence, or of one of the same nature, the punishment, on such second or other subsequent conviction shall be the highest which is affixed to the commission of such offence in ordinary cases.

ART. 793. Any person who shall have been three times convicted of a felony, less than capital, shall, on such third conviction, be imprisoned to hard labor for life, in the Penitentiary. Punishment on third conviction for felony.

ART. 794. A person convicted a second time of any offence to which the penalty of death is affixed as an alternative punishment, shall not receive, on such second conviction, a less punishment than imprisonment for life in the Penitentiary. On second conviction for offence where death is an alternative punishment.

PART III.

OF OFFENCES COMMITTED BY SLAVES AND FREE PERSONS OF COLOR.

TITLE I.

GENERAL PROVISIONS.

ART. 795. The definition of offences as contained in the first and second Parts of this Code, are applicable to all such offences therein enumerated, as may be committed by slaves or free persons of color, except when otherwise provided in this Part of the Penal Code. Act of Aug. 28 1856. Definitions of offences, unless otherwise provided.

ART. 796. An offence committed by a slave or free person of color, is known as a felony. When the punishment therefor is death, all other offences committed by either of these classes of persons are called petty offences. Act of Feb. 12, 1858. Offence by, when felony.

ART. 797. The District Court alone has jurisdiction to try felonies committed by either slaves or free persons of color; the jurisdiction for the trial of petty offences, belongs to the Courts of Justices of the Peace, Mayors and Recorders. Act of Aug 28, 1856. Jurisdiction of offences by slaves and free persons of color.

ART. 798. On the trial before a Justice, Mayor or Recorder, of any offence committed by a slave or free person of color, if the offence be of a higher grade than theft of property not equal in value to twenty dollars, the defendant is entitled to be tried by a jury. Entitled to be tried by jury, when.

ART. 799. The grade of offences is determined by the amount of punishment; an offence, therefore, to which the punishment affixed is greater than that which is affixed to theft of property, of less amount than twenty dollars, is said to be of higher grade than such theft. How grade of offence determined.

ART. 800. All general provisions in the first and second Parts of this Code having reference to rules of evidence, or of construction, and all special rules for ascertaining the nature and degree of crime, are equally applicable to offences committed by slaves and free persons of color, subject to such modifications as are provided in this Part of the Code. Rules of evidence and construction, &c., applicable to.

When to be treated as persons.

ART. 801. A slave or free person of color when tried for a penal offence, is in law a person, but his personal rights are to be controlled by the provisions of this Part of the Penal Code, and are subject to rules different from those which would be applied in the case of a free white person, arising from the peculiar position of these classes of persons in society.

TITLE II.

RULES APPLICABLE TO OFFENCES AGAINST THE PERSON WHEN COMMITTED BY SLAVES OR FREE PERSONS OF COLOR.

Act of Feb. 12, 1858.
When committed against a free white person.

ART. 802. The offences enumerated in Title 17 of the Second Part of this Code, when committed by slaves, or free persons of color, against a free white person, are subject to different rules from such as are prescribed in defining such offences when committed by a free white person, and the guilt or innocence of the accused is to be ascertained by a consideration of the following general principles:

Killing the master, murder, when.

1st. The right of the master to the obedience and submission of his slave, in all lawful things, is perfect, and the power belongs to the master to inflict any punishment upon the slave, not affecting life or limb, and not coming within the definition of cruel treatment, or unreasonable abuse, which he may consider necessary for the purpose of keeping him in such submission, and enforcing such submission to his commands; and if, in the exercise of this right, with or without cause, the slave resists and slay his master, it is murder.

Master's right to kill or injure slave, when.

2d. The master has not the right to kill his slave, or to maim or dismember him, except in cases mentioned in article 564 of this Code.

Master's right to correct slave, when.

3d. A master, in the exercise of his right to perfect obedience on the part of the slave, may correct in moderation, and is the exclusive judge of the necessity of such correction; and resistance by the slave under such circumstances, if it result in homicide, renders him guilty of murder.

Insolence of slave to white man, punishment.

4th. The insolence of a slave will justify a white man in inflicting moderate chastisement, with an ordinary instrument of correction, if done at the time when the insolent language is used, or within a reasonable time after; but it will not authorize an excessive battery, as with a dangerous weapon.(a)

Rules as to manslaughter inapplicable, when.

5th. The rules respecting manslaughter, as given in the second part of this Code, apply only to equals, and not to the case of offences by slaves, or free persons of color, against free white persons.

Murder not mitigated to manslaughter, when.

6th. An assault and battery, not inflicting great injury, committed by a free white person upon a slave, will not be a sufficient provocation to mitigate a homicide of the former by the latter, from murder to manslaughter, although it be in a case where the law does not expressly justify such assault and battery.

(a) Insolence of slave, matter of defence State v. Stephenson, 20 Tex. Rep. 151.

8th. If a slave, by insolence, provoke chastisement, and then slay the person chastising him, it will be murder. Killing by slave, murder, when.

9th. In the following cases it is lawful for a free white person to inflict chastisement upon a slave by moderate whipping: Lawful for free white person to inflict punishment on slave, when

1st. If a slave, without the consent of the white person, be found upon his premises at night.

2d. If the slave, against the orders of the white person, be found upon his premises at any time.

3d. If a slave be found using improper language, or guilty of indecent or turbulent conduct in the presence of white persons.

4th. If the slave be guilty of rude or unbecoming conduct in the presence of a free white female.

5th. If a slave use insulting language or gestures towards a white person.

6th. If a slave commit any wilfull act, injurious to the property or person of a free white person, or of any member of his family.

7th. If a slave be found drunk, and making a disturbance in any public place, or upon the premises of a free white person.

Art. 803. The term master includes the person having lawful control of a slave as executor, administrator, or guardian, and the hirer of a slave upon a lawful contract.(*a*) Act of Aug. 28, 1856. Term "master" includes what.

Art. 804. Patrols or others, authorized by law to punish slaves, may inflict moderate chastisement, and the rights and duties of a slave, under such circumstances, are governed by the same rules which would apply to the case of the master enforcing lawful obedience. Rules as to master, applicable to patrols, &c.

Art. 805. The rules prescribed in article 802, with respect to the conduct of slaves, under particular circumstances, are also applicable to the case of free persons of color residing in this State, whether with or without authority of law, except so much of said article as refers particularly to the relationship of master and slave. When same rules relates to slaves and free persons of color.

Art. 806. A free person of color residing in the State in violation of law, is, in all respects, upon a footing of equality, as to his personal rights, with a slave. Rights of slave and free person of color the same, when.

Art. 807. In every case of offences committed by slaves against the person of free persons of color, or of free persons of color against the persons of slaves, the parties are deemed to stand upon terms of equality. The same.

Art. 808. If it shall appear on trial of any slave or free person of color, for the killing of, or personal injury to a white person, that the person killed or injured was in the habit of association with slaves or free negroes, and by his general conduct placed himself upon an equality with these classes of persons, the rights of the slave or person of color are to be governed by the same rules which would apply if the offence had been committed upon the person of a slave or free person of color, except in cases where the person injured is a minor, under the age of eighteen years. White person associating with slaves or free negroes treated as their equal in what cases.

Art. 809. The preceding article does not apply where the injury was done to the master of the slave, or to any member of the family of the master. 808 not applicable to master and his family.

Art. 810. When it shall appear on trial of any slave, before a Justice or Mayor, for an offence punishable only by whipping, that such slave has been chastised by his master, or under his orders, to the extent which the law would authorise, in case of his conviction, no further punishment shall be Punishment by master relieves from punishment by Justice or Mayor, when.

a Includes also superintendent or overseer who has control of hired slave. Echols *v.* Dodd, 20 Tex. Rep. 190.

inflicted by the Justice or Mayor; and in like manner, where by law a person other than the master of the slave is authorised to inflict chastisement by whipping, and it appears that such chastisement, to the extent authorised by law has been inflicted for a petty offence, punishable by whipping only, such slave shall not be subject to further punishment by the Justice or Mayor.

TITLE III.

OF PUNISHMENT OF SLAVES AND FREE PERSONS OF COLOR.

CHAPTER I.

OF SLAVES.

1. *General Provisions.*

Act of Aug. 28, 1856. — Slaves not punishable by fine or imprisonm'nt

ART. 811. Slaves are not punishable by fine, or by imprisonment in the Penitentiary or House of Correction.

Act of Feb. 12, 1858. — Punishable by death or whipping.

ART. 812. Slaves are subject to the following punishment—

1. Death.
2. Whipping.

Act of Aug. 28, 1856. — Death inflicted by hanging.

ART. 813. The punishment of death is inflicted by hanging, in the same manner as in the case of free white persons.

Act of Feb. 12, 1858. — Whipping, how done, by whom fixed, not to endanger life.

ART. 816. Whipping is inflicted upon the bare back, and in all cases the number of lashes shall be fixed by the Jury, Justice, Mayor, or Recorder, who try the case; provided the whipping allowed by this article shall not be such as to permanently injure or endanger the life of the slave.

Act of Aug. 28, 1856. — Whipping, in public or private, at discretion of court or jury.

ART. 817. When it is not otherwise directed, whipping shall be inflicted in public, or in private, at the discretion of the jury or court trying the offender, and the judgment shall direct the manner of inflicting the chastisement.

2. *Of the Punishment of Particular Offences.*

Act of Feb. 12, 1858. — What offences committed by slaves punishable with death.

ART. 819. The following offences when committed by slaves, shall be punished by death: first, murder; second, insurrection; third, arson; fourth, rape upon a free white woman; fifth, robbery when committed upon a free white person; sixth, assault with intent to commit murder, rape or robbery upon a free white person; seventh, an attempt to commit a rape upon a free white woman; eighth, assault with a deadly weapon upon a free white person.

What by whipping.

ART. 821. All offences not specially enumerated, when committed by slaves, shall be punished by whipping, which may be public or private, at the discretion of the jury or court.

CHAPTER II.

OF FREE PERSONS OF COLOR.

1. *Of Free Persons of Color.*

Act of Feb. 12, 1858.

Punished by death, &c.

ART. 822. Free persons of color are subject to the following punishments: 1. Death; 2. Whipping; 3. Labor upon any public works of a county.

Capitally punished in same cases as slaves.

ART. 823. All offences which by law may be capitally punished, in the case of a slave, shall be punished capitally, when committed by a free person of color.

Aiding in insurrection and, &c.

ART. 824 Aiding in an insurrection of slaves, and kidnapping a free white woman, when committed by a free person of color, shall be punished by death.

Act of Aug. 28, 1856.

Punished with branding, when.

ART. 825. For any of the offences named in the two preceding Articles, if the defendant be sentenced to the penitentiary, branding may be also added as a part of the punishment.

Act of Feb. 12, 1858.

All other offences, how punished.

ART. 829. For all other offences not herein provided for, a free person of color, may be punished by whipping, and by being forced to work upon the roads, or other public works of the county where he is convicted, under the directions of the county court, for a term not exceeding twelve months.

Schedule of repealed acts.

SECTION 2. The following acts and parts of acts, to-wit:

An act punishing crimes and misdemeanors, passed December 21, 1836.

An act supplementary to an act for the punishment of crimes and misdemeanors, passed December 21, 1836.

An act to suppress gambling, passed May 26, 1837.

An act amending the judiciary laws of the Republic, passed December 18 1837.

The eighth and ninth sections of an act to legalize certain marriages, to provide for the celebration of marriages, and for other purposes, passed June 5, 1837.

An act to punish certain offences therein named, passed January 15, 1839.

An act to prohibit the driving of cattle from that part of the country west of the Guadalupe, passed January 19, 1839.

An act to amend the judiciary laws of the Republic, passed January 23, 1839.

An act to provide for the punishment of horse thieves, passed January 26, 1839.

An act to suppress duelling, passed January 28, 1840.

An act to punish swindling and other offences therein named, passed February 5, 1840.

An act to suppress gaming, passed February 5, 1840.

An act to punish persons concerned in making, selling and locating fraudulent land certificates, passed February 5, 1840.

An act concerning slaves, passed February 5, 1840.

An act to amend an act to suppress gaming, passed December 24, 1840.

The fifth section of an act regulating the sale of runaway slaves, passed February 5, 1841.

An act to make certain offences therein named grand larceny, and to prescribe their punishment, passed February 4, 1841.

An act to amend the criminal laws of the Republic of Texas, passed January 16th, 1844.

An act to prevent the obstruction of navigable rivers and streams, passed February 3, 1844.

An act to fix the currency in which fines and forfeitures shall be recoverable, passed January 17, 1844.

An act to protect religious meetings, passed April 23, 1848.

An act to exclude from office, serving on juries, and from the rights of suffrage, all persons who may be hereafter convicted of bribery, perjury, subornation of perjury, forgery, counterfeiting, larceny or other felony or treason, against this State, or the United States, passed April 2, 1846.

An act regulating appeals to the Supreme Court in criminal cases, passed May 13, 1846.

An act requiring juries in certain criminal cases to assess the amount of fine to be imposed, or punishment to be inflicted, passed April 30, 1846.

The fourteenth, fifteenth, sixteenth, twenty-second, twenty-third, twenty-fourth and twenty-fifth sections of an act regulating juries, passed May 4, 1846.

An act to amend the seventeenth and nineteenth sections of an act regulating juries, passed March 16, 1848.

An act to prevent confusion in judicial proceedings arising from a repeal of laws under which they were had or occurred, passed May 13, 1846.

An act giving concurrent jurisdiction to the District and inferior Courts, in certain cases, passed May 11, 1846.

An act to amend the forty-third section of an act punishing crimes and misdemeanors, approved December 21, 1836, passed March 15, 1848.

An act to amend the third section of an act entitled an act concerning slaves, approved February 5, 1840, passed February 14, 1848.

An act to prevent burning the woods and prairies, passed March 18, 1848.

An act prescribing the punishment for cutting down, carrying away or destroying trees, or timber, upon any land, without the consent of the owner, passed March 20, 1848.

An act concerning crimes and punishments, passed March 20, 1848.

An act prescribing in what cases the Governor may remit fines and forfeitures, passed February 26, 1848.

An act appropriating certain fines and forfeitures, passed March 18, 1848.

Joint Resolution for the punishment of vagrants, passed January 10, 1839.

The fourth section of an act defining the duties of District Attorneys, passed March 13, 1846.

The fourth and fifth sections of an act defining the duties of the Attorney General of the State of Texas, passed May 11, 1846.

The fifth, sixth and seventh sections of an act defining the office and duties of Constables, passed May 12, 1846.

An act supplementary to an act concerning crimes and punishments, approved March 20, 1848, passed February 11, 1854.

An act concerning offences against life or person, passed January 31, 1854.

An act to prohibit individuals from issuing bills, checks, promissory notes, or other paper, to circulate as money, passed April 7, 1846.

An act to give the right of appeal in cases of Habeas Corpus, passed Feb. 5, 1853.

An act to establish a State Penitentiary, passed March 13, 1848, except the first, second, third and fourth sections of said act, and except also so much of the fifth section of said act as provides for the appointment of three Directors of the Penitentiary.

An act supplementary to an act to establish a State Penitentiary, approved March 13, 1848, passed February 16, 1852.

An act concerning free persons of color, passed February 5, 1840.

An act to provide for the punishment of crimes and misdemeanors, committed by slaves and free persons of color, passed December 14, 1837.

An act supplementary and amendatory of certain acts therein named, passed January 22, 1841.

An act to prevent slaves from hiring their own time, or their owners from hiring them to other slaves, free negroes, or mulattoes, passed May 11, 1846.

An act concerning offences committed by negroes, passed February 3, 1853.

Together with all other laws and parts of laws relating to crimes and punishments, are hereby repealed.

Act of Feb. 12, 1858.

What articles and portions of articles of Penal Code repealed.

The following Articles and portions of Articles of the Penal Code are hereby repealed, to-wit: Articles seventy-seven, seventy-eight, five hundred and ninety-three, five hundred and ninety-five, six hundred and sixteen, eight hundred and fourteen, eight hundred and fifteen, eight hundred and eighteen, eight hundred and twenty, eight hundred and twenty-six, eight hundred and twenty-seven, eight hundred and twenty-eight, and the provisions to Article four hundred and eleven, and the seventh subdivision of Article eight hundred and two. This act to take effect from and after the first day of July, A. D. 1858.

THE CODE

OF

CRIMINAL PROCEDURE.

AN ACT

TO ESTABLISH A CODE OF CRIMINAL PROCEDURE FOR THE STATE OF TEXAS.

WHEREAS, it is the duty of every Government to prescribe plain rules in reference to the prevention and prosecution of crime, by means of which the rights of citizens shall be protected, the innocent acquitted and the guilty brought to certain punishment, which rules ought to be definite and easy of comprehension, so that every officer may understand his duties and every citizen his rights. Therefore— Act of Aug. 26, 1856. Took effect Feb. 1, 1857*.

Be it enacted by the Legislature of the State af Texas,

SECTION 1. The following Code is hereby established, and shall be called The Code of Criminal Procedure. Adoption of.

* The Code of Criminal Procedure was approved August 26th, 1856, and took effect February 1st, 1857. The amendments were approved February 15th, 1858, and took effect July 1st, 1858.

INTRODUCTORY TITLE.

CHAPTER I.

CONTAINING GENERAL PROVISIONS.

Act of Feb. 15, 1858.

Its objects.

ART. 1. It is hereby declared that this Code is intended to embrace rules applicable to the prevention and prosecution of offences against the laws of this State, and to make the rules of proceeding in respect to the prevention and punishment of offences intelligible to the officers who are to act under them, and to all persons whose rights are to be affected by them.

Act of Aug. 26, 1856.

It seeks, 1st. To adopt measures for preventing the commission of crime.

2d. To exclude the offender from all hope of escape.

3d. To ensure a trial with as little delay as shall be consistent with the ends of justice.

4th. To bring to the investigation of each offence, on the trial, all the evidence tending to produce conviction or acquittal.

5th. To ensure a fair and impartial trial, and,

6th. The certain execution of the sentence of the law when declared.

The same.

ART. 2. In order to collect together, for the convenience of officers and all others charged with the enforcement of the laws, the material provisions of the Constitution of this State respecting the prosecution of offences, the following provisions of said instrument are here inserted:

Trial by due course of law secured.

ART. 3. No citizen of this State shall be deprived of life, liberty, property or privileges, outlawed, exiled, or in any manner disfranchised, except by due course of the law of the land. [*Bill of Rights, Section* 16.

Rights of accused persons.

ART. 4. In all criminal prosecutions, the accused shall have a speedy public trial by an impartial jury; he shall not be compelled to give evidence against himself; he shall have the right of being heard by himself or counsel, or both; shall be confronted with the witnesses against him, and shall have compulsory process for obtaining witnesses in his favor; and no person shall be holden to answer for any criminal charge, but on indictment or information, except in cases arising in the land or naval forces, or offences against the laws regulating the militia. [*Bill of Rights, Section* 8.

Protection against searches and seizures.

ART. 5. The people shall be secure in their (persons,) houses, papers and possessions from all unreasonable seizures or searches; and no warrant to search any place or seize any person or thing shall issue without describing them as near as may be, nor without probable cause supported by oath or affirmation. [*Bill of Rights, Section* 7.

ART. 6. All prisoners shall be bailable by sufficient sureties, except for capital offences when the proof is evident or the presumption great; but this provision shall not be so construed as to prohibit bail after indictment found, upon an examination of the evidence by a Judge of the Supreme or District Court, upon the return of a writ of habeas corpus, returnable in the county where the offence is committed. [*Bill of Rights, Section* 9. Bail in certain cases.

ART. 7. The privilege of the writ of habeas corpus shall not be suspended, except when, in case of rebellion or invasion, the public safety may require it. [*Bill of Rights, Section* 10. Writ of habeas corpus.

ART. 8. Excessive bail shall not be required, nor excessive fines imposed, nor cruel or unusual punishment inflicted. All courts shall be open, and every person, for an injury done him in his lands, goods, person or reputation, shall have remedy by due course of law. [*Bill of Rights, Section* 11. Excessive bail, fines, &c., forbid. Open court.

ART. 9. No person, for the same offence, shall be twice put in jeopardy of life or limb, nor shall a person be again put upon trial for the same offence, after a verdict of not guilty; and the right of trial by jury shall remain inviolate. [*Bill of Rights, Section* 12. No trial after acquittal. Trial by jury shall remain inviolate.

ART. 10. In prosecutions for the publication of papers investigating the official conduct of officers or men in a public capacity, or when the matter published is proper for public information, the truth thereof may be given in evidence. And in all indictments for libels the jury shall have the right to determine the law and the facts, under the direction of the court, as in other cases. [*Bill of Rights, Section* 6. Liberty of speech and of the press.

ART. 11. Electors, in all cases, shall be privileged from arrest during their attendance at elections, and in going to and returning from the same, except in cases of treason, felony, or breach of the peace. [*State Const., Art.* 3, *Sec.* 3. Privilege of electors.

ART. 12. Senators and Representatives shall, in all cases, except in treason, felony, or breach of the peace, be privileged from arrest during the session of the Legislature, and in going to and returning from the same, allowing one day for every twenty miles such member may reside from the place at which the Legislature is convened. [*State Constitution, Art.* 3. *Sec.* 16. Privilege of members of the legislature.

ART. 13. Justices of the Peace shall have such civil and *criminal* jurisdiction as shall be provided for by law [*State Constitution, Art.* 4, *Sec.* 17. Justices' jurisdiction.

ART. 14. In all cases where Justices of the Peace, or other judicial officers of inferior tribunals, shall have jurisdiction in the trial of causes, where the penalty for the violation of law is fine or imprisonment, (except in cases of contempt,) the accused shall have the right of trial by jury.(*a*) [*State Constitution, Art.* 4, *Sec.* 19. Accused entitled to jury trial in inferior tribunals in all cases except, &c.

ART. 15. The style of all writs and process shall be "The state of Texas." All prosecutions shall be carried on in the name and by the authority of the "State of Texas," and conclude "against the peace and dignity of the State." [*State Constitution, Art.* 4, *Sec.* 9. Style of process, prosecutions how carried on.

ART. 16. In the prosecution of slaves for crimes of a higher grade than petit larceny, the Legislature shall have no power to deprive them of an impartial trial by a petit jury. [*Constitution, Art.* 8, *Sec.* 2. Trial by jury secured to slaves.

ART. 18. No person for the same offence can be twice put in jeopardy of life or limb. This is intended to mean that no person can be subjected to a No person shall be tried twice

(*a*) This section applies to mayors' courts. Burns *v.* The Town of Lagrange, 17 Tex. Rep. 415. Smith *v.* The City of San Antonio, ibid, 643.

for the same offence.

second prosecution for the same offence, after having been once prosecuted in a Court of competent jurisdiction and duly convicted.

In what cases accused may be tried, &c., after conviction.

Art. 19. The foregoing article will exempt no person from a second trial, who has been convicted upon an illegal indictment or information, and the judgment thereupon arrested, nor where a new trial has been granted to the defendant, nor where a jury has been discharged without rendering a verdict, nor for any case other than that of a legal conviction.

Same subject.

Art. 20. By the provisions of the Constitution, an acquittal of the defendant exempts him from a second trial, or a second prosecution for the same offence, however irregular the proceedings may have been; but if the defendant shall have been acquitted upon trial, in a Court having no jurisdiction of the offence, he may, nevertheless, be prosecuted again in a Court having jurisdiction.

Officer may use sufficient force to detain prisoner.

Art. 21. Before conviction, a person imprisoned or detained in custody shall be subjected only to sufficient restraint to prevent his escape; but it is the duty of the officer having charge of such person to use the necessary force for his detention and to ensure his being brought to trial.

When person is entitled to trial by jury, conviction can be had only, &c.

Art. 22. When a person is entitled to a trial by jury, he cannot be convicted of an offence except upon a plea of *guilty*, or upon the verdict of a jury duly rendered and recorded.

Trial shall be public.

Art. 23. The proceedings and trials in all Courts shall be public.

Defendant shall be confronted by witnesses, except.

Art. 24. The defendant, upon a trial, shall be confronted with the witnesses, except in certain cases provided for in this Code, where depositions have been taken.

Construction of the Code.

Art. 25. The provisions of this Code shall be liberally construed, so as to attain the objects intended by the Legislature, the prevention, suppression and punishment of crime.

Defendant may waive any legal right, except.

Art. 26. The defendant to a criminal prosecution for any offence may waive any right secured to him by law, except the right of trial by jury when he has pleaded not guilty.

Act of Feb. 15, 1858.

When rules of common law shall govern.

Art. 27. Whenever it is found that this Code fails to provide a rule of procedure in any particular state of case which may arise, and is therefore defective, the rules of the common law shall be applied and govern.

CHAPTER II.

THE GENERAL DUTIES OF OFFICERS CHARGED WITH THE ENFORCEMENT OF THE PENAL LAWS.

1. *The Attorney General and the District Attorney.*

2. *Magistrates.*

3. *Peace Officers.*

1. *The Attorney General and the District Attorney.*

Act of Feb. 15, 1858.

Attorney-General shall represent the State, &c.

ART. 28. It is the duty of the Attorney-General to represent the State in all criminal cases in the Supreme Court, except in cases where he may have been employed adversely to the State, previously to his election; and he shall not appear as Counsel against the State in any court.

Act of Aug. 26, 1856.

Shall represent the State before examining court when.

ART. 29. He shall, also, in cases of felony, represent the State in proceedings before an examining court, or on the hearing of applications under habeas corpus, if he be in the county where such proceeding takes place, and be notified thereof.

Act of Feb. 15, 1858.

District Attorney shall represent the State, &c.

ART. 30. It is the duty of each District Attorney to represent the State in all criminal cases in the District Courts of his District, except in cases where he has been, before his election, employed adversely, and he shall not appear as counsel against the State, in any court, and he shall not after the expiration of his term of office, appear as counsel against the State, in any case in which he may have appeared as counsel for the State.

Act of Aug. 26, 1856.

To represent the State before examining court.

ART. 31. He shall, also, when any criminal proceeding is had before an examining court, or before a Judge upon habeas corpus, represent the State, if he is at the time within the county where such proceeding is had.

2. *Magistrates.*

Shall preserve the peace, issue process, &c.

ART. 32. It is the duty of every officer, known in this Code as a "Magistrate," to preserve the peace within his jurisdiction, by the use of all lawful means; to issue all process intended to aid in preventing and suppressing crime; to cause the arrest of offenders, by the use of lawful means, in order that they may be brought to punishment.

Failure of certain officers to issue process, &c.

ART. 33. A Chief Justice of a county, County Commissioner, Justice of the Peace, or Coroner, who, when legally applied to, refuses to issue process, or who knowingly and corruptly refuses to discharge a duty imposed upon him by the provisions of this Code, is guilty of an offence for which he is subject to removal, upon trial and conviction.

3. *Peace Officers.*

Duty and power of peace officers.

ART. 34. It is the duty of every peace officer to preserve the peace within his jurisdiction. To effect this purpose he shall use all lawful means. He shall, in every case where he is authorized by the provisions of this Code, interfere without warrant to prevent or suppress crime. He shall execute all lawful process issued to him by any magistrate or court. He shall give notice to some magistrate of all offences committed within his jurisdiction, where he has good reason to believe there has been a violation of the penal law. He shall arrest offenders without warrant in every case where he is authorized by law, in order that they may be taken before the proper magistrate or court, and be brought to punishment.

Wilful neglect of, to execute process, &c.

ART. 35. Any peace officer who wilfully neglects to execute process in a criminal case, or who wilfully fails or refuses to interfere for the preservation of the peace, or for the arrest of offenders, when authorized by law to do so, is guilty of an offence, for which, on conviction, he is liable to be removed from office, and shall incur such other punishment as may be prescribed by law.

By whom warrant may be executed. ART. 36. A warrant of arrest may be executed by any peace officer into whose hands it may come, except in certain special cases provided for in this Code.

Sheriff to be keeper of jail. ART. 37. Each Sheriff is the keeper of the jail of his county, and responsible for the safe-keeping of all prisoners committed to his custody.

Shall place in jail every person committed by lawful authority. ART. 38. When a prisoner is committed to jail by lawful warrant from a magistrate, or court, he shall be placed in jail by the Sheriff; and it is a violation of duty on the part of any Sheriff to permit a defendant so committed to remain out of jail, except that he may, when a defendant is committed for want of bail, or when he arrests after indictment or information in a bailable case, give the person arrested a reasonable time to procure bail, but in the meanwhile he shall so guard the accused as to prevent escape.

Sheriff shall notify Dist. Att'y of prisoners, &c. ART. 39. The Sheriff shall, at each term of the court, give notice to the District Attorney, as to all prisoners in his custody, and of the authority under which he detains them.

May appoint a jailor, who shall be responsible. ART. 40. The Sheriff may appoint a jailor to take charge of the jail, and supply the wants of a person therein confined; and the person so appointed is responsible for the safety of prisoners, and liable to punishment as provided by law, for negligently or wilfully permitting a rescue or escape. But the Sheriff shall, in all cases, exercise a supervision and control over the jail.

Shall be paid by County Court for keeping prisoners. ART. 41. The Sheriff shall be paid by the county Court fifty cents a day for each prisoner committed to his custody, during the time such prisoner is in jail.

Compensation for guards. ART. 42. When it becomes necessary to employ a guard for the safe-keeping of prisoners, the Sheriff shall be allowed one dollar a day for each person employed as a guard, and an additional allowance for the board of such guard.

May rent room and employ guard, when. ART. 43. When there is no jail in a county, the Sheriff may rent a suitable house and employ guards, all of which expenses shall be paid by the County Court of the proper county.

May summon aid when resisted. ART. 44. Whenever a peace officer meets with resistance in discharging any duty imposed upon him by law, he shall summon a sufficient number of citizens of his county to overcome the resistance, and all persons summoned are bound to obey; and if they refuse are guilty of an offence.

Person refusing to obey, liable to prosecution. ART. 45. The peace officer who has summoned any person to assist him in performing any duty, shall report such person if he refuse to obey, to the District Attorney of the proper district, in order that he may be prosecuted for the offence.

Deputy may perform duties of Sheriff. ART. 46. Wherever a duty is imposed by this Code upon the Sheriff, the same duty may lawfully be performed by his deputy; and when there is no Sheriff in a county, the duties of that office, as to all proceedings under the criminal law, devolve upon the officer, who, under the law, is empowered to discharge the duties of Sheriff, in cases of vacancy in the office.

4. *Clerk of the District Court.*

District Clerk shall file all papers, issue process, &c. ART. 47. It is the duty of every Clerk of the District Court to receive and file all papers in respect to criminal proceedings, to issue all process in such cases, and to perform all other duties imposed upon him by this Code, or the penal laws of the State, and a willful failure to perform any such duties renders him liable to prosecution for an offence, in accordance with the provisions of the Penal Code.

ART. 48. Wherever a duty is imposed upon the Clerk of the District Court the same may be lawfully performed by his deputy. Power of Deputy Clerk.

CHAPTER III.

CONTAINING DEFINITIONS.

ART. 49. All words and phrases used in this Code are to be taken and understood in their usual acceptation in common language, except where their meaning is particularly defined by law. Act of Feb. 15, 1958. Words and phrases how understood.

ART. 50. The words and terms made use of in this Code, unless herein specially excepted, have the meaning which is given to them in the Penal Code, and are to be construed and interpreted as therein declared. Act of Aug. 26, 1856. Same Subject.

ART. 51. A criminal action is prosecuted in the name of the State of Texas against the person accused, and is conducted by some officer or person acting under the authority of the State, in accordance with its laws. Criminal action prosecuted in name of the State.

ART. 52. Either of the following officers is a "Magistrate" within the meaning of this Code: the Judges of the Supreme Court, the Judges of the District Court, the Chief Justice of the County, either of the County Commissioners, the Justices of the Peace, the Mayor or Recorder of an incorporated city or town, and, in certain special cases, the Coroner. Act of Feb. 15, 1858. Who are "Magistrates."

ART. 53. The following are "Peace Officers:" the Sheriff and his deputies, Constable, Coroner, the Marshall and Constable of an incorporated town or city, and any private person specially appointed to execute criminal process. Who are "Peace Officers."

ART. 54. The general term "officers" includes both magistrates and peace officers. Act of Aug. 26, 1856.

ART. 55. When a Magistrate sits for the purpose of enquiring into a criminal accusation against any person, this is called an "Examining Court." "Examining Court," definition of.

CHAPTER IV.

DIVISIONS OF THE CODE.

ART. 56. This Code is divided into five parts. Act of Aug. 26, 1856. Divided into five parts.

The first relates to the courts having original jurisdiction of criminal actions, and defines their jurisdiction.

The second relates to the prevention of offences, and the suppression of such as are in their nature continuous, and defines specially the mode of proceeding under the writ of habeas corpus.

The third relates to proceedings in such criminal actions as are by law subject to be prosecuted by indictment or information in the District Court, including all proceedings had from the time of the commission of the offence to the final execution of the sentence of the law.

The fourth relates to proceedings in inferior tribunals in cases of offences which they have jurisdiction to try, and to certain special proceedings of a criminal nature.

The fifth relates to costs in criminal proceedings.

PART I

OF THE COURTS HAVING ORIGINAL JURISDICTION IN CRIMINAL ACTIONS.

Act of Aug. 26, 1856.

What Courts have original jurisdiction.

ART. 57. The following Courts have original jurisdiction in criminal actions

1. The Supreme Court.
2. The District Courts.
3. The Justices' Courts, and the Mayors' and other Courts of incorporated towns and cities.

TITLE I.

OF THE SUPREME COURT.

Act of Aug 26, 1856

Original jurisdiction of, in criminal cases.

ART. 58. The Supreme Court, or either of the Judges thereof, has original jurisdiction to enquire into the cause of the detention of persons imprisoned or detained in custody, and for this purpose may issue the writ of habeas corpus, and upon the return thereof may remand such person to custody, admit to bail, or discharge the person imprisoned or detained, as the law and the nature of the case may require.

TITLE II.

OF THE DISTRICT COURTS.

Act of Aug. 26, 1856.

Jurisdiction of.

ART. 59. The District Courts have original jurisdiction of all criminal actions. By virtue of this general jurisdiction, they have power:

1. To enquire, by the intervention of a grand jury, of all offences committed or triable within their respective jurisdictions.

2. To hear and determine all prosecutions in the name of the State, by indictment or information, for all offences committed within their respective jurisdictions.

3. To enquire into the cause of the detention of persons imprisoned in the jails of their respective counties, and make all necessary orders for their recommitment, discharge, or admission to bail, by the writ of habeas corpus, or in such other manner as may be prescribed by law.

4. To exercise all other powers conferred by this Code.

Jurisdiction of Judge of.

ART. 60. Each District Judge has power to issue the writ of habeas corpus, and have brought before him any person imprisoned or otherwise illegally detained in custody, in any county, whether within or out of his district, and make such order on the return of the writ as the law and the facts of the case may require, whether the person detained has been indicted or not, under the restrictions herein prescribed.

TITLE III.

OF THE JUSTICES, MAYORS AND RECORDERS COURTS.

Art. 61. Justices of the Peace have jurisdiction to try and determine criminal actions against persons accused of the following offences: Act of Feb. 15, 1858. Jurisdiction of Justices of the Peace.

1st. Simple assaults and batteries.

2d. Affrays.

3d. Violations of the penal laws with regard to gaming, where the highest penalty does not exceed one hundred dollars.

4th. Petty offences committed by slaves and free persons of color.

5th. Cases of vagrants and disorderly persons.

Art. 62. The jurisdiction of Justices' Courts is concurrent with that of the District Courts as to the offences named in the preceding Article, except as to the jurisdiction conferred in the 5th and sixth subdivisions thereof, in which cases the Justices of the Peace have exclusive jurisdiction. Act of Aug. 26, 1856. Jurisdiction of, when concurrent, &c.

Art. 63. The Justices' Courts have no jurisdiction to try offences where deadly weapons were used, or attempted to be used, by the party accused. When deadly weapons are used.

Art. 64. They have all such other jurisdiction in criminal actions as is conferred by this Code, under the rules and regulations prescribed by the law. Jurisdiction over other criminal actions.

Art. 65. Justices of the Peace may sit at any time to try criminal causes over which they have jurisdiction. Mayors and Recorders of incorporated towns and cities have the same jurisdiction as Justices of the Peace within the limits of their respective incorporations, and all the provisions of this Title have reference to Mayors and Recorders as well as to Justices' Courts. May set at any time to try criminal case.

PART II.

OF THE PREVENTION AND SUPPRESSION OF OFFENCES, AND THE WRIT OF HABEAS CORPUS.

TITLE I.

OF PREVENTING OFFENCES BY THE ACT OF A PRIVATE PERSON.

Art. 66. The commission of offences may be prevented either Act of Aug. 26, 1856. May be prevented, how.

1. By lawful resistance, or

2. By the intervention of the officers of the law.

Resistance to the offender may be made as hereinafter pointed out, either by the person about to be injured, or by some person in his behalf.

Rules as to prevention of, by resistance.

ART. 67. Resistance by the party about to be injured may be used to prevent the commission of any offence, which, in the Penal Code, is classed as an "offence against the person."

Same subject.

ART. 68. Resistance may also in like manner be made by the person about to be injured, to prevent any illegal attempt by force to take or injure property in his lawful possession.

Resistance must be in proportion to, &c.

ART. 69. The resistance which the person about to be injured may make, to prevent the commission of the offence, must be proportioned to the injury about to be inflicted. It must be only such as is necessary to repel the aggression.

Same subject.

ART. 70. If the person about to be injured in respect either to his person or property, uses a greater amount of force to resist such injury than is necessary to repel the ageressor and protect his own person or property, he is himself guilty of an illegal act, according to the nature and degree of the force which he has used.

When other person, &c., may prevent.

ART. 71. Any person other than the party about to be injured may, also, by the use of necessary means, prevent the commission of the offence.

Act of Aug. 26, 1856.

Same rules shall govern in such cases as, &c.

ART. 72. The same rules which regulate the conduct of the person about to be injured, in repelling the aggression, are also applicable to the conduct of him who interferes in behalf of such person. He may use a degree of force proportioned to the injury about to be inflicted, and no greater.

TITLE II.

OF PREVENTING OFFENCES BY THE ACT OF MAGISTRATES AND OTHER OFFICERS.

CHAPTER I.

THE DUTY OF MAGISTRATES AND OTHER OFFICERS.

Duty of Magistrate to prevent.

ART. 73. It is the duty of every Magistrate when he may have heard, in any manner, that a threat has been made by one person to do some injury to the person or property of another, immediately to give notice to some peace officer, in order that such peace officer may use lawful means to prevent the injury.

Same subject.

ART. 74. Wherever, in the presence or within the observation of a Magistrate, an attempt is made by one person to inflict an injury upon the person or property of another, it is his duty to use all lawful means to prevent the injury. This may be done either by verbal order to a peace officer to interfere and prevent the injury, or by the issuance of an order of arrest against the offender, or by arresting the offender; for which purpose he may call upon all persons present to assist in making the arrest.

Same subject.

ART. 75. If within the hearing of a Magistrate one person shall threaten to take the life of another, he shall issue a warrant for the arrest of the person making the threat, or, in case of emergency, he may himself immediately arrest such person.

ART. 76. When the person making such threat is brought before the Magistrate, he may compel him to give security to keep the peace, or commit him to custody, in the manner hereafter provided. May compel offender to give security.

ART. 77. It is the duty of every peace officer, when he may have been informed in any manner that a threat has been made by one person to do some injury to the person or property of another, to prevent the threatened injury, if within his power, and in order to do this he may call in aid any number of citizens in his county. He may take such measures as the person about to be injured might, for the prevention of the offence. Duty of peace officer to prevent.

ART. 78. Whenever, in the presence of a peace officer, or within his view, one person is about to commit an offence against the person or property of another, it is his duty to prevent it, and for this purpose he may summon any number of citizens of his county to his aid. He must use the amount of force necessary to prevent the commission of the offence, and no greater. Same subject.

ART. 79. The conduct of peace officers, in preventing offences about to be committed in their presence, or within their view, is to be regulated by the same rules as are prescribed to the action of the person about to be injured. They may use all force necessary to repel the aggression. Conduct of, &c., how regulated.

CHAPTER II.

PROCEEDINGS BEFORE MAGISTRATES FOR THE PURPOSE OF PREVENTING OFFENCES.

ART. 80. Whenever a Magistrate is informed upon oath, that an offence is about to be committed against the person or property of the informant, or of another, or that any person has threatened to commit such offence, it is his duty immediately to issue a warrant for the arrest of the accused, that he may be brought before such Magistrate, or before some other named in the warrant. Act of Aug. 26, 1856. Magistrate shall issue warrant to prevent, when.

ART. 81. When the person accused has been brought before the Magistrate, he shall hear proof as to the accusation, and if he be satisfied that there is just reason to apprehend that the offence was intended to be committed, or that the threat was seriously made, he shall make an order that the accused enter into bond in such sum as he may in his discretion require, conditioned that he will not commit such offence, and that he will keep the peace towards the person threatened, or about to be injured, and towards all others, for one year from the date of such bond. Proceedings when defendant is brought before Magistrate.

ART. 82. If the defendant refuse to give bond, he shall be committed to the jail of the county, or if there be no jail, to the custody of the Sheriff. If defendant refuses to give bond.

ART. 83. The warrant issued by a Magistrate in cases provided for in Articles 75 and 80, shall be sufficient if it state the name of the defendant, or, Sufficiency of warrant.

if unknown, describe him, and set forth in plain words the nature of the accusation against him, be signed by the Magistrate and dated.

Sufficiency of bond.

ART. 84. The bond taken by the Magistrate in the cases provided for in Article 81, shall be sufficient if it be payable to the State of Texas, recite plainly the nature of the accusation against the defendant, be for some certain sum, and be signed by the defendant and his surety, and dated.

No error of form shall vitiate such bond, and no error in the proceedings, prior to the execution of the bond, shall be available as a defence in an action thereupon.

May discharge defendant, when

ART. 85. If the Magistrate be of opinion from the evidence, that there is no good reason to apprehend that the offence was intended or will be committed, or that no serious threat was made by the defendant, he shall discharge the person so accused, and may in his discretion, tax the cost of the proceeding against the party making the complaint.

Same subject.

ART. 86. If the accused be committed for refusing or failing to give bond, he shall be discharged by any Magistrate upon his afterwards entering into bond in such amount as was fixed by the Magistrate who committed him.

Suit may be brought on bond.

ART. 87. If the condition of the bond be forfeited, it shall be sued upon in the name of the State of Texas, by the District Attorney, and the full amount of the same may be recovered against the principal and sureties.

Suit shall be commenced on, within two years, &c.

ART. 88. Actions upon such bonds shall be commenced within two years from the breach of the same, and shall be governed by the rules applicable to civil actions, except that the sureties may be sued without joining the principal. It shall only be necessary in order to entitle the State to recover, to prove that the defendant did commit the offence which he bound himself not to commit, or failed to keep the peace according to his undertaking.

How surety may exonerate himself from.

ART. 89. A surety upon any such bond may, at any time before a breach thereof, exonerate himself from the obligations of the same, by delivering to the magistrate the person of the defendant, and the magistrate shall, in that case, again require of the defendant bond with other surety, and the same proceedings be had as in the first instance.

Duty of magistrate as to amount of bond.

Oath by surety to.

ART. 90. Magistrates taking bonds under the provisions of this Chapter, shall be governed as to the amount of the bond by the pecuniary circumstances of the accused, and the nature of the offence threatened or about to be committed. And they shall require the sureties of a defendant to make oath as to the value of their property, in the manner pointed out with regard to recognizances and bail bonds.

Shall require a bail bond when the life of a person has been threatened.

ART. 91. When the information given to the magistrate is that the defendant has threatened the life of a person, he shall, in addition to the bond heretofore spoken of, require also of the defendant a bail bond with security, conditioned that he will appear at the next term of the District Court of the county to answer the accusation, which bail bond shall be filed with the Clerk of the District Court, shall have the same force as other bail bonds, and may be forfeited in the same manner.

May direct that the person or property threatened shall be protected.

ART. 92. When, from the nature of the case and the proof offered to the magistrate, it may appear necessary and proper, he shall have a right to order any peace officer to protect the person or property of any individual threatened; and such peace officer shall have the right to summon aid by requiring any number of citizens of his county to assist in giving the protection.

ART. 93. The District Court, when in session, may, upon complaint made cause the arrest of any person who might be arrested by a magistrate under the provision of any of the preceding Articles, and require such person to enter into recognizance for the same purposes for which a magistrate may require bond, may commit in default of security or discharge, according to the nature of the case. District Court may cause arrest to prevent threatened offence, &c., when.

ART. 94. All persons have a right to prevent the consequences of theft, by seizing any personal property which has been stolen, and bringing it with the supposed offender, if he can be taken, before a magistrate for examination, or delivering it to a peace officer for tha purpose. To justify such seizure there must, however, be reasonable grounds to suppose the thing to be stolen, and the seizure must be openly made, and the proceedings had without delay. All persons have a right to prevent the consequences of theft, &c.

ART. 95. If any person shall make oath, and shall convince the magistrate that he has good reason to believe that another is about to publish, sell, or circulate, or is continuing to sell, publish, or circulate any libel against him, or any such publication as is made an offence by the Penal Law of the State, the person accused of such intended publication may be required to enter into bond not to sell, publish, or circulate such libellous publication, and the same proceedings be had as in the cases before enumerated in this Chapter. In case the accused is found subject to the charge and required to give bond, the cost of the proceeding shall be taxed against him. May require bond of person charged with libel, &c.

CHAPTER III.

OF THE SUPPRESSION OF RIOTS.

ART. 96. When any officer authorized to execute process, is resisted, or when he has sufficient reason to believe that he will meet with resistance in executing the same, he may command as many of the citizens of his county as he may think proper, and the Sheriff may call any military company in the county to aid him in overcoming the resistance, and, if necessary, in seizing and arresting the persons engaged in such resistance, so that they may be brought to trial. Act of Aug. 26, 1856. Officer may require aid of citizens and military when he apprehends resistance.

ART. 97. It is a misdemeanor to refuse to obey an officer, when summoned by him for the purposes set forth in the preceding article. Misdemeanor to refuse to obey.

ART. 98. If it be represented to the Governor in such manner as to satisfy him that the power of the county is not sufficient to enable the Sheriff to execute process, he may, on application, order any military company of volunteers from another county to aid in overcoming such resistance. Governor may order military to aid in executing process.

ART. 99. Whenever a number of persons are assembled together in such a manner as to constitute a riot, according to the Penal Law of the State, it is the duty of every Magistrate or peace officer to cause such persons to disperse. This may either be done by commanding them to disperse, or by arresting the persons engaged, if necessary, either with or without warrant. Duty of Magistrate and peace officers to suppress, &c.

Officer may call to his aid the power of the county. ART. 100. In order to enable the officer to disperse a riot, he may call to his aid the power of the county in the same manner as is provided where it is necessary for the execution of process.

Where officers fail to suppress. ART. 101. If a Justice of the Peace, Mayor, or any peace officer shall have notice of a riot, and shall fail to take measures necessary to suppress it, he is guilty of a misdemeanor.

What means may be adopted to suppress. ART. 102. The officer engaged in suppressing a riot, and those who aid him, are authorized and justified in adopting such measures as are necessary to suppress the riot, but are not authorized to use any greater degree of force than is requisite to accomplish that object.

Unlawful assembly. ART. 103. All the articles of this chapter, relating to the suppression of riots, apply equally to an unlawful assembly, as defined by the Penal Code.

Conduct of the military in suppressing riots. ART. 104. Whenever, for the purpose of suppressing riots or unlawful assemblies, the aid of military companies is called, they shall obey the orders of the civil officer who is engaged in suppressing the same. Arms shall only be used where the rioters themselves are armed, and are using their arms. Nor shall it be permitted to fire upon the rioters except in cases of imminent peril, and in order to preserve the lives of the force engaged in suppressing the riot or other unoffending citizens.

When use of arms in, &c., is an offence. ART. 105. The use of arms in suppressing a riot, if wantonly resorted to, or resorted to when it might have been suppressed without their use, is an offence.

Suppression of riot, unlawful assembly, &c., at election. ART. 106. For the purpose of suppressing riots, unlawful assemblies and other disturbances at elections, any Magistrate may appoint a sufficient number of special Constables. Such appointments shall be made to each special Constable, shall be in writing, dated and signed by the Magistrate, and shall recite the purposes for which such appointment is made, and the length of time the appointment is to continue, and before the same is delivered to such special Constable, he shall take an oath before the Magistrate to suppress, by lawful means, all riots, unlawful assemblies and breaches of the peace of which he may receive information, and to act impartially between all parties and persons interested in the result of the election.

Power of spec'l Constable in such cases. ART. 107. Special Constables so appointed, shall, during the time for which they are appointed, exercise the powers and perform the duties properly belonging to peace officers.

TITLE III.

OF THE SUPPRESSION OF OFFENCES IN THEIR NATURE PERMANENT.

CHAPTER I.

OFFENCES WHICH AFFECT PUBLIC HEALTH.

Act of Aug. 26, 1856. ART. 108. After an indictment or information has been presented against

Court may enjoin a person not to carry on an occupation injurious to health &c.

any person for carrying on a trade injurious to the health of those in the neighborhood, if it be charged in the indictment or information that any person has actually suffered in health on account of the carrying on of such trade or business, the Court shall have power, on the application of any one interested, and after hearing proof, both for and against the accused, to enjoin the defendant in such penalty as may be deemed proper not to carry on such occupation, or may make such order respecting the manner and place of carrying on the same, as may be deemed advisable; and, if, upon trial, the defendant be convicted, the injunction shall be made perpetual, and the party be required to enter into bond not to continue such occupation. If he refuse to give the bond, the Court may either commit the party to jail, or make an order requiring the Sheriff to seize upon the implements of trade, or the goods and property used in conducting the business, and destroy the same. After conviction for selling unwholesome food or liquor, or adulterated medicine, the Court shall enter up an order to the Sheriff to seize and destroy such as remains in the hands of the defendant, which order shall forthwith be executed by the Sheriff.

If he refuse to give bond, may be committed to jail, or &c.

After conviction for selling unwholesome food or liquor, Sheriff shall seize and destroy such as remains, &c.

Upon breach of bond it may be sued on in name of the State, and recovery had as pointed out in Arts. 87 and 88.

ART. 109. If bond be given, it shall be payable to the State of Texas in a reasonable amount, to be fixed by the Court; upon the breach thereof, it may be sued in the name of the State, by the District Attorney, and recovery had, upon proving the breach, in the manner pointed out for suing on bonds, in Articles 87 and 88; and the full amount shall be recovered.

Carrying on occupation, after execution of bond, a breach thereof, &c.

ART. 110. It is sufficient proof of the breach of any bond taken under the provisions of this Chapter, to show that the party continued, after executing the same, to carry on the occupation which he bound himself to discontinue.

CHAPTER II.

SUPPRESSION OF OFFENCES WHICH ARE INJURIOUS TO PROPERTY HELD IN COMMON FOR THE USE OF THE PUBLIC.

Act of February 15, 1858.

ART. 111. Whenever any building or other property is for the use of the public, it is unlawful for any person to place an obstruction which shall prevent the free use of such public property.

Act of Aug. 26, 1856.

Unlawful to obstruct road, bridge, &c.

ART. 112. Whenever any road, bridge or the crossing of any stream, is made by the proper authority a public highway, it is unlawful for any person to place an obstruction across such highway, or in any manner prevent the free use of the same by the public.

After indictment, &c District Judge, upon hearing proof, may issue an order to remove obstruction, &c., but person giving the information shall give bond to indemnity accused, &c.

ART. 113. After indictment or information presented against any person for violating any provision of the two preceeding Articles, any one in behalf of the public may apply to the Judge of the District Court of the proper county, and, upon hearing proof, such Judge, either in term time, or in vacation, may issue his written order to the Sheriff of the county, directing him to remove the obstruction, but the person giving the information shall be required to give bond with security, in an amount to be fixed by the Judge, to indemnify the accused, in case of acquittal, for the loss he sustains.

ART. 114. If the defendant to any such indictment, or information, be acquit-

If the defendant be acquitted, he may maintain a civil action against the applicant in injunction, and his sureties, &c.

ted, after a trial upon the merits of the case, he may maintain a civil action against the applicant in injunction and his sureties, and may recover the full amount of the bond, or such damages less than the full amount thereof as may be assessed by a jury provided he shows on the trial, that the building or other property, in fact, belonged to him and not to the public, or in case the defendant was charged with obstructing a public highway, that the same was not, in fact, at the time he placed the obstruction or impediment thereupon, a public highway, established by proper authority, but was in fact his own property.

No defect of form &c.

ART. 115. No mere defect of form shall vitiate any order or proceeding of the County Court in establishing a public highway.

CHAPTER III.

SUPPRESSION OF OFFENCES AFFECTING REPUTATION.

Act of Aug. 26, 1856.

On conviction for selling libel, &c.

ART. 116. On conviction for selling and publishing a libel, the Court may, if it be shown that there are in the hands of the defendant, or other person, copies of such libel, intended for sale, publication or distribution, order all such copies to be seized by the Sheriff and destroyed.

CHAPTER IV.

OF THE SUPPRESSION OF OFFENCES AGAINST PERSONAL LIBERTY.

4. *General Provisions.*

ART. 117. The writ of habeas corpus is the remedy to be used when any person is restrained of his liberty.

Act Feb. 15, 1858. Writ of habeas corpus.

I. *Definition and Object of the Writ.*

ART. 118. A writ of habeas corpus is an order issued by a Court or Judge of competent jurisdiction, directed to any one having a person in his custody, or under his restraint, commanding him to produce such person, at a time and place named in the writ, and show why he is held in custody, or under restraint.

Act of Aug. 26, 1856. What a writ of habeas corpus is, &c.

ART. 119. The writ, as all other process, runs in the name of "The State of Texas." It is to be addressed to the person having another under restraint, or in his custody, describing, as near as may be, the name of the office, if any, of the person to whom it is directed, and the name of the person said to be detained. It shall fix the time and place of return, and be signed by the Judge, or by the Clerk, with his seal, where issued by a Court.

To whom directed, &c.

ART. 120. The writ of habeas corpus is not invalid, nor shall it be disobeyed for any want of form, if it substantially appear that it is issued by competent authority, and the writ sufficiently show the object and design of its issuance.

Not invalid for want of form.

ART. 121. Every provision relating to the writ of habeas corpus shall be most favorably construed, in order to give effect to the remedy, and protect the rights of the person seeking relief under it.

Provisions relating to, how construed.

2. *By whom and when granted.*

ART. 122. The Supreme Court, or either of the Judges, the District Courts, or either of the Judges, have power to issue the writ of Habeas Corpus; and it is their duty, upon proper application, to grant the writ under the rules herein prescribed.

Act of Aug. 26, 1856. By whom granted.

ART. 123. Before indictment found, the writ may be made returnable to any county of the State.

Before indictment, writ returnable where, &c.

ART. 124. After indictment found, the writ must be made returnable in the county where the offence has been committed, on account of which the applicant stands indicted.

After indictment, returnable where, &c

Who may apply for the writ, when, and to whom.

ART. 125. In all cases where a person is confined on a criminal accusation, and indictment has been found against him, he may apply to the Judge of the District Court for the District in which he is indicted, or if there be no Judge within the district, then to the Judge of any district whose residence is nearest to the courthouse of the county in which the applicant is held in custody.

Proceedings under the writ.

ART. 126. When application has been made to a Judge, under the circumstances set forth in the preceding Article, it shall be his duty to appoint a time when he will examine the cause of the applicant, and issue the writ returnable at that time, in the county where the offence is charged in the indictment to have been committed. He shall also specify some place in the county where he will hear the application.

Time appointed for hearing.

ART. 127. The time so appointed shall be the earliest day which the Judge can devote to hearing the cause of the applicant, consistently with his other duties.

Who may present petition for relief.

ART. 128. Either the party for whose relief the writ is intended, or any person for him, may present a petition to the proper authority, for the purpose of obtaining relief.

The word *applicant* refers to.

ART. 129. The word *applicant*, as used in this Chapter, refers to the person for whose relief the writ is asked, though, as above provided, the petition may be signed and presented by any other person.

What the petition must state.

ART. 130. The petition must state substantially:

1. That the person for whose benefit the application is made is illegally restrained in his liberty, and by whom—naming both parties, if their names are known—or, if unknown, designating and describing them.

2. When the party is confined, or restrained by virtue of any writ, order or process, or under color of either, a copy shall be annexed to the petition, or it shall be stated that a copy cannot be obtained.

3. When the confinement or restraint is not by virtue of any writ, order or process, the petition may state only that the party is illegally confined or restrained of his liberty.

4. There must be a prayer in the petition for the writ of Habeas Corpus.

Petition must be sworn to.

5. Oath must be made that the allegations of the petition are true, according to the belief of the petitioner.

The writ shall be granted without delay, unless, &c.

ART. 131. The writ of Habeas Corpus shall be granted without delay, by the Judge or Court receiving the petition, unless it be manifest by the statements of the petition itself, or some documents annexed to it, that the party is entitled to no relief whatever.

District Judge may issue the writ without application, when.

ART. 132. A Judge of the District Court who has knowledge that any person is illegally confined, or restrained in his liberty within his district, may issue the writ of Habeas Corpus, without any application being made for the same.

When there is good reason to believe that person will be removed out of the State, or when the writ has been disregarded, the court may issue warrant, &c.

ART. 133. Whenever it shall be made to appear by satisfactory evidence, to a Judge of the Supreme or District Court, that any one is held in illegal confinement or custody, and there is good reason to believe that he will be carried out of the State, or suffer some irreparable injury, before he can obtain relief in the usual course of law, or whenever a writ of Habeas Corpus has been issued and disregarded, the Supreme or District Court, or either of the Judges, may issue a warrant to any officer of the law, or to any person specially named by said Court or Judge, directing him to take and bring such person before him, to be dealt with according to law.

ART. 134. Where it appears by the proof offered, under circumstances mentioned in the preceding Article, that the person charged with having illegal custody of the prisoner, is by such act guilty of an offence against the law, the Judge may, in the warrant, order that he be arrested and brought before him; and upon examination, he may be committed, discharged, or held to bail, as the law and the nature of the case may require. The person having custody of the prisoner may be arrested, when.

ART. 135. The officer charged with the execution of the warrant, shall bring the persons therein mentioned before the Judge or Court issuing the same; who shall inquire into the cause of the imprisonment or restraint, and make an order thereon, as in cases of Habeas Corpus, according to the rules laid down in this Chapter, either remanding into custody, discharging, or admitting to bail, the party so imprisoned or restrained. Proceedings under the writ.

ART. 136. The same power may be exercised by the officer executing the warrant, (and in like manner), in cases arising under the foregoing Articles, as is exercised in the execution of warrants of arrest, according to the provisions of this Code. Officer executing the warrant may exercise same power, &c.

ART. 137. The words "confined," "imprisoned," "in custody," "confinement," "imprisonment," refer not only to the actual, corporal and forcible detention of a person, but likewise to any and all coercive measures by threats, menaces, or the fear of injury, whereby one person exercises a control over the person of another, and detains him within certain limits. The words 'confined,' 'imprisoned,' &c., refer to, &c.

ART. 138. By "restraint," is meant that kind of control which one person exercises over another, not to confine him within certain limits, but to subject him to the general authority and power of the person claiming such right. By 'restraint,' is meant, &c.

ART. 139. The writ of Habeas Corpus is intended to be applicable to all such cases of confinement and restraint, where there is no lawful right in the person exercising the power, or where, though the power in fact exists, it is exercised in a manner or degree not sanctioned by law. The writ of habeas corpus is intended to be applicable, when, &c.

ART. 140. Where a person claiming to be free is held as a slave, he may be relieved by Habeas Corpus; and if, upon any such application, the person so held is discharged, his discharge shall be evidence of his freedom against the person claiming him, unless such claimant shall, within three months thereafter, bring suit to establish his right to the services of the person so claimed Where a free person is held as a slave, he may be relieved, &c.

ART. 141. Where a person has been committed to custody for failing to enter into bond, he is entitled to the writ of Habeas Corpus, if it be stated in the petition that there was no sufficient cause for requiring bail, or that the bail required is excessive; and if the proof sustains the petition, it will entitle the party to be discharged, or have the amount of the bail reduced, according to the facts of the case. A person committed for failing to enter into bond, is entitled to the writ, when, &c.

ART. 142. When a Judge or Court authorized to grant writs of Habeas Corpus shall be satisfied, upon investigation, that a person in legal custody is afflicted with a disease which will render a removal necessary for the preservation of his life, an order may be made for the removal of the prisoner to some other place, where his health will not be likely to suffer, or he may be admitted to bail when it appears that any species of confinement will endanger his life. A person in legal custody afflicted with disease may be removed, when, &c.

3. *Service and return of the Writ, and Proceedings thereon.*

Act of Aug. 26, 1856.

ART. 143. The service of the writ may be made by any free white person capable of giving testimony in court. Who may serve the writ.

ART. 144. The writ may be served by delivering a copy of the original to

How the writ may be served and returned.

the person who is charged with having the party under restraint, or in custody, and exhibiting the original if demanded; if he refuse to receive it, he shall be informed verbally of the purport of the writ. If he refuse admittance to the person wishing to make the service, or conceal himself, a copy of the writ may be fixed upon some conspicuous part of the house where such person resides, or conceals himself, or of the place where the prisoner is confined; and the person serving the writ of Habeas Corpus shall, in all cases, state fully, in making return, the manner and time of the service of the writ.

The return shall be made under oath, if made by a person other than an officer.

ART. 145. The return of a writ of Habeas Corpus under the provisions of the preceding Article, if made by any person other than an officer, shall be under oath.

The person on whom the writ is served, shall obey same, &c.

ART. 146. The person on whom the writ of Habeas Corpus is served, shall immediately obey the same, and make the return required by law, upon the copy of the original writ served on him, and this whether the writ be directed to him or not.

How the return shall be made.

ART. 147. The return is made by stating in plain language upon the copy of the writ, or some paper connected with it:

1. Whether it is true or not, according to the statement of the petition, that he has in his custody or under his restraint, the person named or described in such petition.

2. By virtue of what authority, or for what cause he took and detains such person.

3. If he had such person in his custody or under restraint at any time before the service of the writ, and has transferred him to the custody of another, he shall state particularly to whom, at what time, for what reason, or by what authority he made such transfer.

4. He shall annex to his return the writ or warrant by virtue of which he holds the person in custody, if any writ or warrant there be.

Must be signed and sworn to.

ART. 148. The return, as provided in Articles 146 and 147, must be signed and sworn to by the person making it.

The person in custody shall be brought before the Judge, &c.

ART. 149. The person on whom the writ is served, shall bring also before the Judge, the person in his custody or under his restraint, unless it be made to appear that by reason of sickness he cannot be removed, in which case another day may be appointed by the Judge or Court for hearing the cause, and for the production of the person confined; or the application may be heard and decided without the production of the person detained, by the consent of his counsel.

The court shall allow reasonable time, &c.

ART. 150. The Court or Judge granting the writ of Habeas Corpus, shall allow reasonable time for the production of the person detained in custody.

Person having the illegal custody of another, who refuses to obey the writ, &c., shall be punished, how, &c.

ART. 151. When service has been made in either of the modes pointed out in Article 144, upon a person charged with the illegal custody of another, if he refuses to obey the writ and make the return required by law, or where he refuses, as mentioned in Article 144, to receive the writ, or conceals himself, the Court or Judge issuing the writ shall issue a warrant directed to any officer or other suitable person willing to execute the same, commanding him to arrest the person charged with the illegal custody or detention of another, and bring him before such Court or Judge; and when such person shall have been arrested and brought before the Court or Judge, if he still refuse to return the writ, or do not produce the person in his custody, he shall be committed to prison and remain there until he is willing to obey the writ of habeas corpus, and until he pays all the costs of the proceeding.

ART. 152. Any person disobeying the writ of habeas corpus, shall also be liable to a civil action at the suit of the party, and shall pay in such suit fifty dollars for each day of illegal detention and restraint, after service of the writ, to be recovered in any court of competent jurisdiction; and it shall be deemed that a person has disobeyed the writ who detains a prisoner a longer time than three days after service thereof, and one additional day for every twenty miles he must necessarily travel in carrying the person held from the place of his detention to the place where the application is to be heard, unless where further time is allowed in the writ for making the return thereto. Person disobeying the writ, shall be liable to a civil action, &c., and it shall be deemed that a person has disobeyed the writ, when, &c.

ART. 153. In case of the disobedience of the writ of habeas corpus, the person for whose relief it is intended may also be brought before the Court or Judge having competent authority, by an order for that purpose issued to any peace officer or specially named. In case of disobedience to the writ, the person in custody may be brought before the Court, how, &c.

ART. 154. It is a sufficient return to the writ of habeas corpus, that the person once detained has died, or that by some superior force he has been taken from the custody of the person making the return; but where any such cause shall be assigned for not producing the applicant, the Court or Judge shall proceed to hear testimony, and the facts so stated in the return shall be proved by satisfactory evidence. What is sufficient return to the writ.

ART. 155. When a prisoner confined in jail shall die, the officer having charge of him shall forthwith report the same to the Coroner of the county, or any Justice of the Peace, and an inquest shall be held to ascertain the cause of his death; which may be done by calling in any number of physicians and surgeons. All the proceedings had in such cases shall be certified and returned to the District Court of the proper county, and be filed by the Clerk, a certified copy of which proceedings shall be sufficient proof of the death of the prisoner, at the hearing of an application under habeas corpus. A prisoner in jail dying, inquest shall be held, &c. The proceeding in such case returned to the District Court.

ART. 156. Whenever the District Attorney of the proper district is in the county where a cause is heard under habeas corpus, it is his duty, if the defendant is accused of a felony, to be present at the hearing, and represent the State; for which service he shall be paid the fee allowed by law. And if the District Attorney is not present at the hearing of such cause, the Judge shall appoint some well qualified practising attorney to represent the State, who shall be paid the same fee as is allowed District Attorneys for like services. The District Attorney to be present where cause is heard under habeas corpus. In absence of District Attorney, the Court shall appoint an attorney to represent the State.

ART. 157. The Judge or Court before whom a person is brought by writ of habeas corpus, shall examine the writ and the papers attached to it, and if no legal cause be shown for the imprisonment or restraint, or if it appear that the imprisonment or restraint, though at first legal, cannot, for any cause, be lawfully prolonged, the applicant shall be discharged. The Court shall discharge prisoner, when, &c.

ART. 158. If it appear by the return and papers attached, that the party stands indicted for a capital offence, the Judge or Court shall nevertheless proceed to hear such testimony as may be offered, on the part both of the applicant and the State, and may either remand the defendant or admit him to bail, as the law and the facts of the case may justify. If the party stands indicted for a capital offence.

ART 159. In all cases where no indictment has been found, it shall not be deemed that any presumption of guilt has arisen from the mere fact that a criminal accusation has been made before a competent authority. Where no indictment has been found, &c.

ART. 160. The Judge or Court after having examined the return and all documents attached, and heard the testimony offered on both sides, shall, according to the facts and circumstances of the case, proceed either to remand the party into custody, admit him to bail, or discharge him: provided that no defendant shall be discharged after indictment, without bail. The Court shall remand into custody, &c. Defendant shall not be discharged after indictment without bail.

If the commitment be informal or void, &c.

ART. 161. If it shall appear that the applicant is detained or held under a warrant of commitment which is informal or void, yet, if from the document on which the warrant was based, or from the proof on the hearing of the habeas corpus, it appear that there is probable cause to believe that an offence has been committed by the prisoner, he shall not be discharged, but shall be committed or held to bail by the Court or Judge trying the application under habeas corpus.

If there be probable cause to believe an offence has been committed, &c.

ART. 162. Where, upon an examination under habeas corpus, it shall appear to the Court or Judge that there is probable cause to believe that an offence has been committed by the prisoner, he shall not be discharged, but shall be committed, or admitted to bail, according to the facts and circumstances of the case

The Court may summon the magistrate, who issued the warrant.

ART. 163. For the purpose of ascertaining the grounds on which an informal or void warrant has been issued, the Judge or Court may cause to be summoned the magistrate who issued the warrant, and may, by an order, require him to bring with him all the papers and proceedings touching the matter. The attendance of such magistrate, and the production of such papers, may be enforced by warrant of arrest, if necessary.

A written issue, in case under habeas corpus, not necessary.

ART. 164. It shall not be necessary, on the trial of any cause arising under habeas corpus, to make up a written issue, though it may be done by the applicant for the writ. He may except to the sufficiency of, or controvert the return or any part thereof, or allege any new matter in avoidance. If written denial on his part be not made, it shall be considered, for the purpose of investigation, that the statements of said return are contested by a denial of the same, and proof shall be heard accordingly, both for and against the applicant for relief.

The applicant shall open and conclude the argument.

ART. 165. The applicant shall have the right to open and conclude, by himself or counsel, the argument upon the trial under habeas corpus.

Costs of the proceeding, how disposed of.

ART. 166. The Court or Judge, trying a cause under habeas corpus, may make such order as is deemed advisable or right, concerning the cost of bringing the defendant before him, and all other costs of the proceedings, awarding the same either against the person to whom the writ was directed, the person seeking relief, or may award no costs at all.

If the Court be in session, the Clerk shall record the proceedings.

ART. 167. If a writ of habeas corpus be made returnable before a Court in session, all the proceedings had shall be entered of record by the Clerk thereof, as would be done in any other case pending in such Court; and when the application is heard out of the county where the offence was committed, or in the Supreme Court, the Clerk shall transmit a certified copy of all the proceedings upon the application to the Clerk of the District Court of the county where the offence was committed or is triable.

If the proceedings be had before a Judge in vacation, &c.

ART. 168. If the return is made and the proceedings had before a Judge of a Court in vacation, he shall cause all the proceedings to be taken down, shall certify to the same, and cause them to be filed with the Clerk of the District Court of the county where the offence was committed or is triable, whose duty it shall be to keep them safely.

Provisions of the two preceding Articles, refer to, &c.

ART. 169. The provisions of the two preceding Articles refer only to cases where an applicant is held under accusation for some offence; in all other cases, the proceedings had before the Judge shall be filed and kept by the Clerk of the District Court of the county where the application is heard.

ART. 170. The Court or Judge granting a writ of habeas corpus may grant all necessary orders to bring before him the testimony taken before the examining Court, and may issue all process for enforcing the attendance of witnesses, which is allowed in any other proceedings in a criminal action. The Court may grant all necessary orders, &c.

ART. 171. The word "Return," as used in Article 144 and 145, refers to and means the report made by the officer or person charged with serving the writ of habeas corpus; and the same word as used in other Articles of this Chapter, means the answer made by the person accused of having another illegally in custody or under restraint, setting forth the cause for which he holds such other person in custody or under restraint. The word "Return" means, &c,

4. *General Provisions.*

ART. 172. Where a person, before indictment found against him, has been discharged or held to bail on habeas corpus, by order of a Court or Judge of competent jurisdiction, he shall not be again imprisoned or detained in custody on an accusation for the same offence until after he shall have been indicted, unless delivered up by his bail in order to release themselves from their liability. Act of Aug. 26, 1856. A person discharged before indictment, shall not again be imprisoned, until, &c.

ART. 173. Where a person once discharged, or admitted to bail, is afterwards indicted for the same offence, for which he has been once arrested, he may be committed on the indictment, but shall be again entitled to the writ of habeas corpus, and may, notwithstanding the indictment, be admitted to bail, if the facts of the case render it proper, but in cases where after indictment found, the cause of the defendant has been investigated on habeas corpus, and an order made either remanding him to custody, or admitting him to bail, he shall neither be subject to be again placed in custody, unless when surrendered by his bail, or when the trial of his cause commences before a petit jury, nor shall he be again entitled to the writ of habeas corpus, except in the special cases mentioned in article 175. Act of Feb. 15, 1858. A person once discharged or admitted to bail, may be committed, when, &c.

ART. 174. If the accusation against the defendant for a capital offence has been heard on habeas corpus before indictment found, and he shall have been committed after such examination, he shall not be entitled to the writ unless in the special cases mentioned in the next Article. Act of Aug. 26, 1856. A person committed for a capital offence, shall not be entitled to the writ, unless, &c.

ART. 175. A party may obtain the writ of habeas corpus a second time, by stating in the application therefor that since the hearing of his first application important testimony has been obtained, which it was not in his power to produce at the former hearing. He shall also set forth the testimony so newly discovered, and if it be that of a witness, the affidavit of the witness shall also accompany such second application. A party may obtain the writ a second time, when, &c.

ART. 176 The preceding Article shall not apply where there has been an appeal to the Supreme Court from the decision of a District Court or Judge upon the first application. The preceding Art. shall not apply where there has been an appeal to the Supreme Court.

ART. 177. Any officer to whom a writ of habeas corpus or other writ, warrant or process, authorized by this Chapter, shall be directed, delivered or tendered, who shall refuse to execute the same according to its directions, or who shall wantonly delay the service or execution of the same, is guilty of an offence, and shall be punished according to the provisions of the Penal Code; he shall also be liable to fine as for contempt of Court. An officer refusing to execute the writ, shall be punished, how, &c.

ART. 178. Any one having another in his custody, or under his power, control or restraint, who refuses to obey a writ of habeas corpus, or who evades the service of the same, or places the person illegally detained under the control of another, removes him, or in any other manner attempts to evade the Any one having the custody of another who refuses to obey the writ, &c., shall be punished, how.

operation of the writ, is guilty of a penal offence, and shall be punished as provided in the Penal Code.

Any Jailor, &c., who refuses to furnish copy of process under, &c.

ART. 179. Any Jailor, Sheriff, or other officer, who has a prisoner in his custody, and refuses upon demand to furnish a copy of the process under which he holds the person, is guilty of an offence.

Person shall not be discharged under writ of habeas corpus, when.

ART. 180. No person shall be discharged under the writ of habeas corpus, who is in custody by virtue of a commitment for any offence exclusively cognizable by the Courts of the United States, or by order or process issuing out of such Courts in cases where they have jurisdiction, or who is held by virtue of any *legal* engagement or enlistment in the army, or who being *rightfully* subject to the rules and articles of war is confined by any one *legally* acting under the authority thereof, or who is held as a prisoner of war under the authority of the United States.

This Chapter applies to what cases.

ART. 181. This Chapter applies to all cases of habeas corpus for the enlargement of persons illegally held in custody, or in any manner restrained of their personal liberty; for the admission of prisoners to bail; and for the discharge of prisoners before indictment, upon a hearing of the testimony. Instead of the writ of habeas corpus in other cases where heretofore used, a simple order shall be substituted.

PART III.

OF PROCEEDINGS IN CRIMINAL ACTIONS PROSECUTED BY INDICTMENT OR INFORMATION IN THE DISTRICT COURT.

TITLE I.

THE TIME AND PLACE OF COMMENCING AND PROSECUTING CRIMINAL ACTIONS.

CHAPTER I.

The time within which criminal actions may be commenced.

Act of Feb. 15, 1858.

For forgery, ten years.

ART. 182. An indictment for forgery may be presented within ten years from the time of the commission of the offence, and not afterwards.

Act of Aug. 26, 1856.

For theft, &c., five years.

ART. 183. An indictment for theft punishable as a felony, arson, burglary, robbery and counterfeiting, may be presented within five years, and not afterwards.

For rape, one year.

ART. 184. An indictment for the offence of rape may be presented within one year, and not afterwards.

Act of Feb. 15, 1858.

Other felonies except murder.

ART. 185. An indictment for all other felonies except murder, may be presented within three years from the commission of the offence, and not afterwards.

Act of Aug. 26, 1856.

For all misdemeanors.

ART. 186. For all misdemeanors an indictment or information may be presented within two years from the commission of the offence, and not afterwards; except misdemeanors which Justices' Courts have concurrent jurisdiction to try, in which cases the indictment may be presented within one year, and not afterwards.

ART. 187. The time during which a person accused of an offence is absent from the State shall not be computed in the period of limitation. Absence from the State not computed.

ART. 188. An indictment is to be considered as "presented" when it has been duly acted upon by the grand jury and received by the Court. An indictment is "presented," when.

ART. 189. An information is to be considered as presented when it has been filed by the proper officer in the proper court. An information is presented, when.

CHAPTER II.

OF THE COUNTY WITHIN WHICH OFFENCES MAY BE PROSECUTED.

Act of Aug. 26, 1856.

ART. 190. Prosecutions for offences committed wholly or in part without, and made punishable by law within this State, may be commenced and carried on in any county in which the offender is found. For offences committ'd wholly or in part without the State.

Act of Feb. 15, 1858.

ART. 190a. The offence of forgery may be prosecuted in any county where the written instrument is forged, or where the same is used or passed, or attempted to be used or passed; and the offence of counterfeiting may be prosecuted in any county where the offence is committed, or where the counterfeit coin is passed, or attempted to be passed. The offences of forgery or counterfeiting, prosecuted where.

Act of Aug. 26, 1856.

ART. 191. An offence committed on the boundary of any two counties, or within four hundred yards thereof, may be prosecuted and punished in either county, and the indictment or information may allege the offence to have been committed in the county where it is prosecuted. Offences committed on the boundary of two counties.

ART. 192. If any person, being at the time within this State, shall inflict upon another, also within the State, an injury of which such person afterwards dies without the limits of this State, the person so offending shall be liable to prosecution in the county where the injury was inflicted. Person dying out of the State of an injury inflicted in the State, &c.

ART. 193. If a person, being at the time within this State, shall inflict upon another out of this State, an injury by reason of which the injured person dies without the limits of this State, he may be prosecuted in the county where he was when the injury was inflicted. Person within the State inflicting injury on another out of the State, where prosecuted.

Person without the State inflicting an injury on one within the State, where prosecuted.

ART. 194. If a person being at the time without the limits of this State, shall inflict upon another who is at the time within this State, an injury causing death, he may be prosecuted in the county where the person injured dies.

An offence committed on a stream the boundary of this State, where prosecuted.

ART. 195. If an offence be committed upon any river or stream, the boundary of this State, it may be prosecuted in the county the boundary of which is upon such stream or river, and the county seat of which is nearest the place where the offence was committed.

Person receiv'g an injury in one county and dying in another, offender where prosecuted.

ART. 196. If a person receive an injury in one county and die in another by reason of such injury, the offender may be prosecuted in the county where the injury was received or where the death occurred.

An offence committed on a stream &c., the boundary between two counties, punishable, where.

ART. 197. Where a river or other stream or highway is the boundary between two counties, any offence committed on such river, stream, or highway, at a place where it is such boundary, is punishable in either county, and it may be alleged in the information or indictment, that the offence was committed in the county where it is prosecuted.

Property stolen in one county and carried to another, offender prosecuted, where.

ART. 198. Where property is stolen in one county and carried off by the offender to another, he may be prosecuted either in the county where he took the property, or in any other county where he may be found with it.

Citizen of this State who fights a duel out of this State, prosecuted, where.

ART. 199. A citizen of this State who fights a duel with deadly weapons out of this State, or who sends or accepts a challenge to fight a duel with deadly weapons out of this State, or who acts as second, or knowingly aids and assists any other person engaged in a duel, may be prosecuted in any county of this State where he may be found.

Offences committed out of the State by Commissioner of Deeds, prosecuted, where.

ART. 200. Offences committed out of this State by a Commissioner of Deeds, or other officer acting under the authority of this State, may be prosecuted in any county of this State.

Offences committed on vessels within the State prosecuted, where.

ART. 201. Where an offence is committed on board a vessel which is, at the time, upon any navigable water within the boundaries of this State, the jurisdiction for the prosecution of the offence is in any county through which the vessel is navigated in the course of her voyage, or in the county where the voyage commences or terminates.

Offence of bringing into this State a slave convicted of an offence in another State, where prosecuted.

ART. 202. The offence of bringing into this State a slave that has been convicted in another State, of an offence which is capital by the laws of this State, may be prosecuted in any county where the offender may be found, or into which he may have brought such slave.

Offence of embezzlement prosecuted, where.

ART. 203. The offence of embezzlement may be prosecuted in any county in which the offender may have taken or received the property, or through or into which he may have undertaken to transport it.

Act of Feb. 15, 1856.

False imprisonment, kidnapping, and abduction prosecuted, where.

ART. 204. The jurisdiction for the trial of the offences of false imprisonment, kidnapping, and abduction, belongs either to the county in which the offence was committed, or to any county through, into, or out of which the person falsely imprisoned, kidnapped, or taken in such manner as to constitute abduction, may have been carried.

Act of Aug. 26, 1856.

Conviction or acquittal in another State, bar to prosecution in this State.

ART. 205. When an act has been committed out of this State by an inhabitant thereof, and such act is an offence by the laws of this State, and is also an offence by the laws of the place where the same was done, a conviction or acquittal of the offender, under the laws of the place where the offence was committed, is a bar to the prosecution in this State. Where the escape of a prisoner occurs, the Sheriff or other person having lawful custody of him may be prosecuted therefor, either in the county where the escape has or may occur, or in the county where the prisoner was under prosecution or trial for the offence. Where prisoner escapes, sheriff, &c., may be prosecuted, where.

ART. 206. Where different counties have jurisdiction of the same offence, a conviction or acquittal of the offence in one county, is a bar to any further prosecution in any other county. Conviction, &c., in one county bar to prosecution in another, when.

ART. 207. In all cases mentioned in the foregoing articles of this chapter, the indictment or information, or any proceeding in the case, may allege that the offence was committed in the county where the prosecution is carried on; and to sustain the allegation of venue, it shall only be necessary to prove that by reason of the facts existing in the case, the county where such prosecution is carried on, has jurisdiction. Act of Feb. 15, 1858. Proof of jurisdiction sufficient to sustain allegation of venue, when.

ART. 208. In all cases except those enumerated in previous articles of this chapter, the proper county for the prosecution of offences, is that in which the offence is committed. Act of Aug. 26, 1856. Offences not enumerated prosecuted, where.

TITLE II.

OF ARREST, COMMITMENT AND BAIL.

CHAPTER I.

OF ARREST WITHOUT WARRANT.

ART. 209. A peace officer, or any other person, may, without warrant, arrest an offender, when the offence is committed in his presence, or within his view, if the offence is one classed as a felony, or as an "offence against the public peace." Act of Aug. 26, 1856. Arrest without warrant, when.

ART. 210. A peace officer may arrest without warrant when a felony or breach of the peace has been committed in the presence or within the view of a magistrate, and such magistrate shall verbally order the arrest of the offender. Same subject.

ART. 211. The municipal authorities of towns and cities may establish rules authorizing the arrest without warrant, of persons found in suspicious places, and under circumstances which reasonably show that such persons have been guilty of some felony or breach of the peace; or threaten, or are about to commit some offence against the laws. Municipal authorities may authorize arrest without warrant, when.

ART. 212. Where it is shown by satisfactory proof to a peace officer, upon the representation of a credible person, that a felony has been committed, and that the offender is about to escape, so that there is no time to procure a warrant, such peace officer may, without warrant, pursue and arrest the person accused. May arrest without warrant, when felony has been committed, &c.

ART. 213. In all the cases enumerated where arrests may be lawfully made without warrant, the officer or other person making the arrest, is justified in adopting all the measures which he might adopt in cases of arrest under warrant, as provided in this Code. In all such cases the officer may adopt the same measures as, &c.

In such cases must take the offender before nearest magistrate.

ART. 214. In all the cases enumerated in this chapter, the person making the arrest shall immediately take the person arrested before the magistrate who may have ordered the arrest, or before the nearest magistrate where the arrest was made, without an order.

CHAPTER II.

OF ARREST UNDER WARRANT.

Act of Aug. 26, 1856.

Definition of warrant of arrest.

ART. 215. A warrant of arrest is a written order directed to a peace officer, or some other person specially named, commanding him to take the body of the person accused of an offence, to be dealt with according to law.

Is sufficient if it have, &c.

ART. 216. It issues in the name of "The State of Texas," and shall be deemed sufficient, without regard to form, if it have these substantial requisites:

1. It must specify the name of the person whose arrest is ordered, if it be known; if not known, then some reasonably definite description must be given of him.

2. It must state that the person is accused of some offence against the laws of the State, naming the offence.

3. It must be signed by the magistrate, and his office be named in the body of the warrant, or in connection with his signature.

4. It may be directed to "any peace officer," or private person, by name.

Magistrates may issue warrants of arrest, when.

ART. 217. Magistrates may issue warrants of arrest in all cases in which they are, by law, authorized to order verbally the arrest of offenders.

Same subject.

ART. 218. Magistrates may issue warrants of arrest, also, in the following cases:

1. When any person shall make oath before such magistrate, that another has committed some offence against the laws of the State.

2. In other cases named in this Code, where they are specially authorized to issue such warrants.

Complaint is, what.

ART. 219. The affidavit made before the magistrate, which charges the commission of an offence, is called a *complaint*.

Complaint must be in writing and signed.

ART. 220. The complaint shall be reduced to writing, and signed by the person making it, if he is able to write his name, otherwise he may place his mark at the foot of the complaint.

Warrant from Supreme or District Judge shall extend, &c.

ART. 221. A warrant of arrest issued by a Judge of the Supreme or District Court, shall extend to every part of the State.

How a warrant of arrest may be directed, &c.

ART. 222. A warrant of arrest may be directed to "any peace officer," but when issued by a magistrate other than a Supreme or District Judge, if the offender escape from the county where the offence was committed, the warrant may be made effectual in any county of the State, by procuring the endorsement of the same by a magistrate of such county. The endorsement may be in these words, "Let this warrant be executed in the county of ——," signed by the magistrate, with the name of his office. Any other words expressing the same meaning, will be sufficient. A District or Supreme Judge may, by endorsement of a warrant, authorize it to be executed in any part of the State.

ART. 223. In cases where it is made known by satisfactory proof to the magistrate, that a peace officer cannot be procured to execute a warrant of arrest, or that so much delay will be occasioned in procuring the services of a peace officer, that a person accused will probably escape, the warrant of arrest may be directed to any suitable person who is willing to execute the same, and in such case his name shall be set forth in the warrant. Warrant may be issued to any suitable person, when.

ART. 224. No person other than a peace officer can be compelled to execute a warrant of arrest; but if any person shall undertake the execution of the warrant, he shall be bound to do so under all the penalties to which a peace officer would be liable. He has the same rights, and is governed by the same rules, as are prescribed to peace officers. Cannot be compelled to execute warrant, &c.; has same rights as peace officer.

ART. 225. The officer or person executing a warrant of arrest, shall take the person whom he is directed to arrest, forthwith, before the magistrate who issued the warrant, unless he is directed in the warrant to take such person before some other magistrate. How warrant is executed, &c.

ART. 226. If any person be arrested in one county for felony committed in another, he shall in all cases be taken before some magistrate of the county where it was alleged the offence was committed; but if the arrest be for a misdemeanor, he shall be taken before a magistrate of the county where the arrest takes place, who shall be authorized to take bail, and whose duty it shall be to transmit immediately the bond so taken, to the Clerk of the District Court of the county in which the offence was committed. If the arrest be for felony committed in another county, &c., but if the arrest be for a misdemeanor.

ART. 227. A person is said to be arrested when he has been actually placed under restraint, or taken into custody by the officer or person executing the warrant of arrest. A person is said to be arrested, when.

ART. 228. An arrest may be made on any day, or at any time of the day or night. An arrest may be made, when.

ART. 229. In making an arrest, all reasonable means are permitted to be used to effect it. No greater force, however, shall be resorted to than is necessary to secure the arrest and detention of the accused. What force may be used.

ART. 230. In cases of felony, the officer may break down the door of any house for the purpose of effecting an arrest, if he be refused admittance after giving notice of his authority and purpose. In case of felony may break door, &c.

ART. 231. In executing a warrant of arrest, it shall always be made known to the person accused, under what authority the arrest is made, and if requested, the warrant shall be exhibited. Authority to arrest must be made known.

ART. 232. If a person arrested shall escape or be rescued, he may be re-taken without any other warrant; and for the purpose of re-taking the person so escaping or rescued, all the means may be used which are authorized in making the arrest in the first instance. Prisoner escaping, &c., may be re-taken without warrant.

CHAPTER III.

OF THE COMMITMENT OR DISCHARGE OF THE ACCUSED.

Act of Aug. 26, 1856.

Proceeding when brought before a Magistrate.

ART. 233. When a person accused of an offence has been brought before a Magistrate, that officer shall proceed to examine into the truth of the accusation made, allowing the accused, however, sufficient time to procure the aid of counsel.

Act of Feb. 15, 1858.

When examination postponed for reasonable time—custody and disposition of the accused during that time.

ART. 234. The magistrate may at the request of the prosecutor or person representing the State, or of the defendant, postpone, for a reasonable time, the examination, so as to afford an opportunity to procure testimony; but the accused shall, in the meanwhile, be detained in the custody of the Sheriff or other duly authorized officer; unless he give bail to be present from day to day before the magistrate, until the examination is concluded, which he may do in all cases except murder and treason.

Act of Aug. 26, 1856.

Witnesses examined before voluntary statement of accused witnesses placed under rule upon application.

ART. 235. Before the accused has made any voluntary statement, the witnesses, both for and against him, shall be sworn and examined. But the Magistrate shall, if requested by the accused or his counsel, or by the person prosecuting, have all the witnesses placed in charge of an officer, except the witness who is testifying, so that the testimony given by any one witness shall not be heard by any of the others.

Right of counsel to examine witness.

ART. 236. If any person appear to prosecute as counsel for the State, he shall have the right to put the questions to the witnesses on the direct or cross-examination, and the accused or his counsel has the same right.

Act of Feb. 15, 1858.

Accused may make voluntary statement when —witness placed under rule upon application by either party.

ART. 237. The accused may make a voluntary statement before the witnesses, both for and against him, are sworn and examined; and the Magistrate shall, if requested by the accused or his counsel or by the person prosecuting, have all the witnesses placed in charge of an officer, except the witness who is testifying, so that the testimony given by any one witness, shall not be heard by any of the others.

Act of Aug. 26, 1856.

Testimony reduced to writing.

ART. 238. The testimony of all the witnesses shall be reduced to writing, signed by them with their names or marks; and all the testimony thus taken shall be certified to by the Magistrate.

Manner of postponing examination to procure testimony.

ART. 239. After examining the witnesses in attendance, if it satisfactorily appear to the Magistrate that there is other important testimony which may be had by a postponement of the examination, he shall, at the request of the prosecutor or of the defendant, postpone the further examination for a reasonable time, to enable such testimony to be procured; but in such case the accused shall remain in the custody of the proper officer until the day fixed for such further examination. No postponement shall take place unless a statement on oath be made by the defendant or the person prosecuting, setting forth the name and residence of the witness, and the facts which it is expected will be proved; or if it be testimony other than that of a witness, the statement made shall set forth the nature of the evidence.

ART. 240. The examination of the witnesses shall be in the presence of the accused. Examination in presence of accused.

ART. 241. Before the examination of the witnesses the magistrate shall inform the defendant that it is his right to make a statement relative to the accusation brought against him, but shall, at the same time, also inform him that he cannot be compelled to make any statement whatever. Act of Feb. 15, 1858. Defendant shall be informed of his right to &c.

ART. 242. If the accused shall desire to make a voluntary statement, the same shall be reduced to writing by the Magistrate or some one under his direction, and shall be signed by the accused. Where the accused prefers to write out altogether his statement, he is at liberty to do so, and of this he shall be informed by the Magistrate; should the accused be unable to write, he may affix his mark to the statement. Act of Aug. 26, 1856. Statement of accused reduced to writing.

ART. 243. The Magistrate shall in every case attest, by his own certificate and signature, the execution and signing of the statement. Certified by Magistrate.

ART. 244. The Magistrate has the power to issue an attachment for the purpose of enforcing the attendance of a witness; and this he may do without having previously issued a subpœna for that purpose. Magistrate may attach witnesess

ART. 245. The officer to whom the attachment is issued shall execute it forthwith, by bringing before the magistrate the witness named. Attachment when executed.

ART. 246. Witnesses may be brought by attachment before the examining Magistrate, from any county, in case of felony, and it shall not be necessary to tender the expenses of such witnesses, but no attachment shall issue to a county other than that where the prosecution is being conducted, unless oath be made by the party applying for the process, that the presence of the witness is material and his testimony important for the prosecution or defence, as the case may be; and the affidavit shall further set forth the facts which it is expected will be proved by the witness. An examination may be postponed a reasonable time for the purpose of bringing in a witness. May issue to any county, when, Examination postponed.

ART. 247. Should no counsel appear either for the State or for the defendant, the Magistrate may examine the witnesses, and the accused has the same right. Act of Feb. 15, 1858.

ART. 248. Upon examination of a person accused of a capital offence, no Magistrate other than a Judge of the Supreme or District Court, or Chief Justice of a county, shall have power to discharge the defendant. Any Magistrate may admit to bail, unless in capital cases where the proof is evident or the presumption great. Act of Aug. 26, 1856. Who has power to discharge accused, &c.

ART. 249. Where it is made to appear by complaint on oath to a Judge of the Supreme or District Court, or Chief Justice of a county, that the bail taken in any case is insufficient in amount, such Judge or Chief Justice shall issue a warrant of arrest, and require of the defendant additional security, according to the nature of the case. When insufficient bail has been taken.

ART. 250. After the voluntary statement of the accused, if any, and the examination of the witnesses has been fully completed, the magistrate shall proceed to make an order committing the defendant to the jail of the proper county, if there be one, discharging him or admitting him to bail, as the law and facts of the case may require. Act of Feb. 15, 1858. When committed, discharged, or admitted to bail.

Act of Aug. 26, 1856.

When no safe jail, &c.

ART. 251. Where there is no safe jail in the county in which the prosecution is carried on, the Magistrate may commit to the nearest safe jail of any other county.

To whom warrant is directed in such case.

ART. 252. The warrant of commitment in the case mentioned in the preceding Article shall be directed to the Sheriff of the county to which the defendant is sent, but the Sheriff of the county from which the defendant is taken, shall be required to deliver the prisoner into the hands of the Sheriff of the county to which he is sent.

What is warrant of commitment, &c.

ART. 253. A warrant of commitment is an order, signed by the proper Magistrate, directing a Sheriff to receive and place in jail the person so committed. It will be sufficient if it have the following requisites:

1. That it run in the name of "The State of Texas."

2. That it be addressed to the Sheriff of the county, to the jail of which the defendant is committed.

3. That it state, in plain language, the offence for which the defendant is committed, and give his name, if it be known, or if unknown, contain an accurate description of the defendant.

4. That it state to what Court, and at what time, the defendant is to be held to answer.

5. When the prisoner is sent out of the county where the prosecution arose, the warrant shall state that there is no safe jail in the proper county.

When prisoner sent to jail of another county, &c.

ART. 254. In every case where, for want of a safe jail in the proper county, a prisoner is committed to the jail of another county, the last named county shall have the right to recover, by civil action, in a court of competent jurisdiction, of the county from which the prisoner was sent, an amount of money, not exceeding seventy-five cents per day, on account of the expenses attending the custody and safe keeping of a prisoner.

Duty of Sheriff in reference to prisoner.

ART. 255. It is the duty of every Sheriff to keep safely a person committed to his custody. He shall use no cruel or unusual means to secure this end, but shall adopt all necessary measures to prevent the escape of a prisoner. He may summon a guard of sufficient number, in case it become necessary, to prevent an escape from jail or the rescue of a prisoner.

Discharge shall not prevent &c.

ART. 256. A discharge by a Magistrate upon an examination of any person accused of an offence, shall not prevent a second arrest of the same person for the same offence.

CHAPTER IV.

OF BAIL.

1. *General Rules applicable to all cases of Bail.*

2. *Surrender of Principal by his Bail.*

3. *Bail before Examining Court.*

4. *Bail by Witnesses.*

1. *General Rules Applicable to all Cases of Bail.*

ART. 257. Bail is the security given by a person accused of an offence that he will appear and answer before the proper Court, the accusation brought against him. Act of August 26, 1856. Definition of bail.

ART. 258. This security is given by means of a recognizance, or a bail bond. Either recognizance or bail bond.

ART. 259. A recognizance is an undertaking entered into before the Supreme or District Court by the defendant to a criminal action and his sureties, by which they bind themselves respectively, in a sum fixed by the Court, that the defendant will appear for trial before the proper Court upon the accusation preferred against him. The undertaking of the parties, in such case, is not signed, but made a matter of record in the Court where the same is entered into. What is recognizance.

ART. 260. A bail bond is an undertaking entered into by the defendant and his sureties for the same purpose as a recognizance; it is written out, and signed by the defendant and his sureties. What is bail bond.

ART. 261, A bail bond is entered into, either before a Magistrate, upon an examination of a criminal accusation against a defendant, as provided in Chapter III of this Title, or before a Judge, upon an application under habeas corpus; or it is taken from the defendant by a peace officer who has a warrant of arrest or commitment, as hereafter provided. When bail bond given.

ART. 262. Wherever the word bail is used with reference to the security given by the defendant, it is intended to apply as well to recognizances as to bail bonds. Bail includes both recognizances and bail bonds.

When a defendant is said to be "on bail," or to have "given bail," it is intended to apply as well to recognizances as to bail bonds.

ART. 263. A recognizance shall be sufficient to bind the principal and sureties, if it contain the following requisites: Act of Feb. 15, 1858. Requisites of a recognizance.

1. If it be acknowledged that the defendant is indebted to the State of Texas in such sum as is fixed by the Court, and the sureties are in like manner indebted in such sum as is fixed by the Court.

2. That it state the name of the offence with which the defendant is charged.

3. That it appear by the recognizance that the defendant is accused of an offence against the laws of this State.

4. That the time and place when and where the defendant is bound to appear, be stated, and the Court before which he is bound to appear.

Requisites of bail bond.

ART. 264. A bail bond shall be sufficient if it contain the following requisites:

1. That it be made payable to the State of Texas.

2. That the obligors thereto bind themselves that the defendant will appear before the proper court to answer the accusation against him.

3. That the offence of which the defendant is accused be distinctly named in the bond, and that it appear therefrom that he is accused of some offence against the laws of the State.

4 That the bond be signed by the principal and sureties, or in case all or either of them cannot write, then that they affix thereto their marks.

5. That the bond state the time and place when and where the accused binds himself to appear, and the Court before which he is to appear. In stating the time it is sufficient to specify the term of the court; and in stating the place it is sufficient to specify the name of the court and of the county.

Act of Aug. 26, 1856.

Rules in this chapter applicable to all cases where bail is taken.

ART. 265. The rules laid down in this Chapter respecting recognizances and bail bonds are applicable to all such undertakings when entered into in the course of a criminal action, whether before or after indictment or information, in every case where authority is given to any Court, Judge, Magistrate, or other officer, to require bail of a person accused of an offence, or of a witness in a criminal action.

How forfeitures recovered.

ART. 266. The manner of recovering, in behalf of the State, the amount of such recognizances and bonds, is laid down in Part III, of this Code, Title IV, Chapter IV.

Bail bond and recognizance, how construed.

ART. 267. A recognizance or bail bond, entered into by a defendant, and which binds him to appear at a particular term of the District Court, shall be construed to bind him and his sureties, for his attendance upon the Court from term to term, and from day to day, until his final acquittal or conviction and sentence.

Minor or marr'd woman cannot be security of bail.

ART. 268. A minor or married woman, cannot be surety on a recognizance or bail bond, but if either of these classes of persons be the accused party, the undertaking shall be binding both upon principal and surety.

In what manner bail shall be taken.

ART. 269. It is the duty of every Court, Judge, Magistrate, or other officer, taking bail, to require evidence of the sufficiency of the security offered; but in every case one surety shall be sufficient, if it be made to appear that such surety is worth at least double the amount of the sum for which he is bound, exclusive of all property exempted by law from execution, and of debts or other incumbrances; that he is a resident of this State, and has property therein liable to execution, worth the sum for which he is bound.

Prop'ty exempt from sale shall not be liable for satisfaction, &c.

ART. 270. The property secured by the Constitution and laws from forced sale, shall not in any case be held liable for the satisfaction of a recognizance or bail bond, either as to the principal or sureties.

How sufficiency of security shall be ascertained.

ART. 271. In order to test the sufficiency of the security offered to any recognizance or bail bond, unless the Court or officer taking the same is fully satisfied as to the sufficiency of the security, the following oath shall be made in writing, and subscribed by the surety: "I, A. B., do swear, (or affirm as the case may be,) that I am worth in my own right, at least the sum of [here insert the amount in which the surety is bound,] after deducting from my property all that which is exempt by the Constitution and Laws of the State, from forced sale, and after the payment of all my debts of every description, whether individual or security debts, and after satisfying all incumbrances upon my property which are known to me; that I reside in ——— county, and have property in this State liable to execution, worth [amount for which he offers to be bound] or more.

Dated —— and attested by the Judge of the Court, Clerk, Magistrate or Sheriff. [Signed by the surety.]

Which affidavit shall be filed with the papers of the cause, or criminal proceedings.

ART. 272. The amount of bail to be required in any case, is to be regulated by the Court, Judge, Magistrate, or officer taking the bail; they are to be governed in the exercise of this discretion by the Constitution of this State, and by the following rules: Rules for fixing amount of bail.

1. The bail shall be sufficiently high to give reasonable assurance that the undertaking will be complied with.
2. The power to require bail is not to be used in such manner as to make it an instrument of oppression.
3. The nature of the offence and the circumstances under which it was committed, are to be considered.
4. The pecuniary circumstances of the accused are to be regarded, and proof may be taken upon this point.

2. *Surrender of the Principal by his Bail.*

ART. 273. Those who have become bail for the accused, or either of them, may at any time relieve themselves of their undertaking, by surrendering the accused into the custody of the Sheriff of the county where he is prosecuted. Securities may surrender accused to the Sheriff.

ART. 274. Should a surrender of the accused be made during a term of the Court to which he has bound himself to appear, the Sheriff shall take him before the Court; and if he is willing to give other bail, the Court shall forthwith require him to enter into recognizance. Any surety desiring to surrender the accused may, upon making a written affidavit of such intention, obtain a warrant for his arrest, which shall be executed as in other cases. When during the term of the Court.

ART. 275. If the surrender be made while the Court is not in session, the Sheriff may himself take the necessary bail bond. When Court is not in session.

ART. 276. If the accused fail or refuse to give bail, in case of a surrender, during a term of the Court, the Court shall make an order that he be committed to jail until the bail be given; and this shall be a sufficient commitment without any written order or warrant to the Sheriff. When accused is surrendered by securities in term time, failure to give bail sufficient, &c.

ART. 277. Where the surrender is made at any other time than during the session of the Court, and the defendant refuses to give other bail, the Sheriff shall take him before the nearest Magistrate, and such Magistrate shall issue a warrant of commitment, reciting the fact that the accused has been once admitted to bail, has been surrendered and now refuses to give other bail. Duty of Sheriff in such case, when surrender is made in vacation.

ART. 278. The rules laid down in Chapter III, of this Title, with respect to the sending of an accused person to the jail of another county, shall also apply to cases where the party has been surrendered by his bail. When sent to jail of another county.

ART. 279. The Sheriff, in cases of misdemeanor, has authority, at all times, whether during the term of the Court, or in vacation, where he has a defendant in custody under a warrant of commitment, or where the accused has been surrendered by his bail, to take of the defendant other bail. Sheriff may take bail in cases of misdemeanor.

In cases of felony, Sheriff cannot take bail in term time.

ART. 280. In cases of felony, the Sheriff cannot, during the term of the Court, take the bail, but must bring the accused before the Court, that he may there enter into recognizance.

Act of Feb. 15, 1858.

Securities shall be severally bound, if jointly—does not render bond void—surrend'r by one, discharge of all.

ART. 281. Sureties shall in all cases be severally bound, and when a surrender of the defendant is made by one or more of them, all the sureties shall be considered discharged: and in such cases the defendant shall be required to give other security in place of the persons so discharged. But if in any recognizance or bail bond, the parties either as principal or security, be in whole or in part bound jointly, the obligation shall nevertheless be valid.

Art. 281 applies to all bonds in criminal cases.

ART. 283. The provisions of article 281 apply to all bonds authorized to be taken for the prevention or suppression of offences.

3. *Bail before the Examining Court.*

Act of Aug. 26, 1856.

Rules in relation to bail, and of a general nature, applicable in this Court.

ART. 284. The rules laid down in the preceding articles of this chapter, relating to the amount of the bail—the number of sureties—the person who may be surety—the property which is exempt from liability—the form of bail bonds—the responsibility of parties to the same—and all other rules in this chapter of a general nature, are applicable to bail taken before an examining Court.

Proceedings when bail is granted.

ART. 285. After a full examination of the testimony, the Magistrate shall, if the case be one where bail may properly be granted and ought to be required, proceed to make an order that the accused execute a bail bond with sufficient security, conditioned for his appearance at the next term of the District Court for the proper county.

Bail, matter of right, when.

ART. 286. All persons accused of offences less than capital, are entitled to bail as a matter of right.

When it cannot be allowed.

ART. 287. In capital cases *where the proof is evident or the presumption great,* bail cannot be allowed.

When amount shall be fixed.

ART. 288. In making the order, admitting to bail, the Magistrate shall fix the amount of the sum in which the accused and his sureties shall be respectively bound.

Reason'ble time given to procure bail.

ART. 289. Reasonable time shall be given the accused to procure security.

When giving bail is delayed.

ART. 290. If, after the allowance of reasonable time, the security be not offered, the Magistrate shall make an order committing the accused to jail, to be there kept safely until the required bail be given, and he shall issue a warrant of commitment, directed to the Sheriff of the county in which the prosecution is pending, or in cases provided for in articles 251 and 278 to the Sheriff of some other county, which warrant of commitment shall, however, set forth that the defendant is entitled to be released upon giving bail to the Sheriff in whose custody he may be, in the amount fixed by such Magistrate.

How bail shall be taken by Magistrate.

ART. 291. If the party accused be ready to give bail, the Magistrate shall prepare, or cause to be prepared, a bail bond, which shall be signed by the accused and his surety, the Magistrate first enquiring into the sufficiency of the security offered, and requiring one or more sureties according to the wish of the accused or the solvency of the sureties offered.

No form of bond necessary.

ART. 292. There is no particular form for a bail bond, but it must contain the substantial requisites prescribed in the preceding part of this Chapter.

ART. 293. The accused is to be set at liberty so soon as he has complied with the order of the Magistrate, by giving the bail required.

Accused liberated when bond is given.

ART. 294. Where a defendant is committed for failing to give bail, he shall be discharged by the officer in whose custody he is, upon executing the proper bail bond. The officer to whose charge he is committed having the right, in all such cases, to take the bond.

When committed for failure to bail, officer has the right to take bond.

ART. 295. The Magistrate before whom an examination has taken place, upon a criminal accusation, shall certify to all the proceedings had before him, and transmit them, sealed up, to the Court before which the defendant is subject to be tried upon indictment or information, writing his name across the seals of the envelop containing the proceedings. The voluntary statement of the defendant—the testimony of the witnesses—bail bonds, and all and every other proceeding in the case, shall be thus delivered to the Clerk of the District Court.

Magistrate shall certify proceedings to District Court—how done.

ART. 296. It is the duty of a Magistrate, as well where a party has been discharged as where he has been held to bail or committed, to cause the proceedings before him to be certified and delivered to the District Court; and he shall, likewise, where a complaint has been made to him of the commission of an offence, and there has been a failure from any cause to arrest the accused, file with the proper clerk the warrant of arrest and complaint.

The same subject.

4. *Bail by Witnesses.*

ART. 297. Witnesses on behalf of the State or defendant may be required by the Magistrate, upon the examination of any criminal accusation before him, to give bail for their appearance to testify before the District Court; and if a witness make oath that he is unable to give security, or deposit a sufficient amount of money in lieu thereof, then his individual bond shall be taken, and shall have the same force and effect against him as a bail bond.

Witnesses required to give bail or recognizances, when.

ART. 298. The amount of security to be required of a witness, is to be regulated by his pecuniary condition, and the nature of the offence with respect to which he is a witness.

Of amount of security required of a witness.

ART. 299. Bonds given by witnesses may be forfeited and recovered upon in the manner pointed out in Part III, Title IV, Chapter IV, Section 2, of this Code.

How bonds of witnesses forfeited.

TITLE III.

OF SEARCH WARRANTS.

CHAPTER I.

GENERAL RULES.

ART. 300. A search warrant is a written order, issued by a Magistrate and directed to a peace officer, commanding him to search for personal property, and to seize the same and bring it before such Magistrate; or it is a like written order, commanding a peace officer to search a suspected place where it is alleged stolen property is commonly concealed, or implements kept for the purpose of being used in the commission of any designated offence.

Act of Aug 26, 1856.

Definition.

For what purposes it may be issued.

ART. 301. A search warrant may be issued for the following purposes and no others:

1. To discover property acquired by theft, or in any other manner which makes its acquisition a penal offence.

2. To search suspected places, where it is alleged property so illegally acquired is commonly kept or concealed.

3. To search places, where it is alleged implements are kept for the purpose of being used in forging or counterfeiting.

4. To search places, where it is alleged arms or munitions are kept or prepared for the purpose of insurrection or riot.

5. To seize and bring before a Magistrate any such property, implements, arms or munitions.

Object is to procure goods for the owner, and arrest the party guilty of the theft.

ART. 302. A warrant to search for and seize stolen property is designed as a means of obtaining possession of the property, for the purpose of restoring it to the true owner, and detecting any person guilty of the theft or concealment of the same.

Definition of word "stolen."

ART. 303. The word "stolen, as used in this Title, is intended to embrace also the acquisition of property by any means forbidden and made penal by the law of the State.

When asked for, in reference to property not stolen.

ART. 304. When it is alleged that the property, to search for which a warrant is asked, was acquired in any other manner than by theft, the particular manner of its acquisition must be set forth in the complaint and in the warrant.

These rules applicable to all cases where property sought, is acquired contrary to provisions of "Penal Code."

ART. 305. The mode of proceeding, directed to be pursued in applying for a warrant, to search for and seize *stolen* property, and the rules prescribed for officers in issuing such warrants, and executing the same, the disposition of the property seized, and all other rules herein prescribed on the subject, shall apply and be pursued, when the property to be searched for was acquired in any manner in violation of the provisions of the Penal Code.

CHAPTER II.

WHEN AND HOW A SEARCH WARRANT MAY BE ISSUED.

Act of Aug. 26, 1856.

Contents of application for search warrant.

ART. 306. A warrant to search for and seize property alleged to be stolen and concealed at a particular place, may be issued by a Magistrate whenever complaint in writing and on oath is made to such Magistrate, setting forth—

1. The name of the person accused of having stolen or concealed the property, or if his name be unknown, giving a description of the accused; or stating that the person who stole or concealed the property is unknown.

2. The kind of property and its probable value, alleged to be stolen or concealed.

3. The place where the property is alleged to be concealed.

4. The time, as near as may be, when the property is alleged to have been stolen.

Contents of application for

ART. 307. A warrant to discover and seize property alleged to have been stolen, or otherwise acquired in violation of the penal law, but not alleged to be concealed at any particular place, may be issued whenever complaint is made in writing and on oath, setting forth— Warrant to discover and seize.

1. The name of the person suspected of being the thief, or an accurate description of him if his name be unknown, or that the thief is unknown.

2. An accurate description of the property, and its probable value.

3. The time, as near as may be, when the property is supposed to have been stolen.

4. That the person complaining has good ground to believe that the property was stolen by the person alleged to be the thief.

ART. 308. A warrant to search any place suspected to be one where stolen goods are commonly concealed, or where implements are kept, for the purpose of aiding in the commission of offences, may be issued by a Magistrate when complaint is made in writing and on oath, setting forth— Contents of application for warrant to search suspected place.

1. A description of the place suspected.

2. A description of the kind of property alleged to be commonly concealed at such place, or the kind of implements kept.

3. The name, if known, of the person supposed to have charge of such place, when it is alleged that it is under the charge of any one.

4. When it is alleged that implements are kept at a place for the purpose of aiding in the commission of offences, the particular offence for which such implements are designed, must be set forth.

ART. 309. The Magistrate, at time of issuing a search warrant, may also issue a warrant for the arrest of the person accused of having stolen the property, or of having concealed the same, or of having in his possession or charge, property concealed at a suspected place, or of having possession of implements designed for use in the commission of the offence of forgery or counterfeiting, or of having the charge of arms or munitions prepared for the purpose of insurrection, or of having prepared such arms or munitions, or who may be in any legal manner accused of being accomplice or accessory to any of the offences above enumerated. Warrant to arrest, may issue with search warrant in certain cases.

ART. 310. The search warrant may, in addition to commanding the peace officer to seize property, also require him to bring before the Magistrate the person accused of having stolen or concealed the property. Search warrant may command officer to bring party accused before the magistrate.

ART. 311. A search warrant to seize property stolen and concealed, shall be deemed sufficient if it contain the following requisites: Requisites of a search warrant.

1. That it run in the name of "The State of Texas."

2. That it be directed to the Sheriff of the proper county.

3. That it describe the property alleged to be stolen or concealed, and the place where it is alleged to be concealed, and order the same to be brought before the Magistrate.

4. That it name the person accused of having stolen or concealed the property, or if his name be known, that it describe him with accuracy, and direct the officer to bring such person before the Magistrate, or state that the person who stole or concealed the property is unknown.

5. That it be dated and signed by the Magistrate.

ART. 312. A warrant to search a suspected place shall be deemed sufficient if it contain the following requisites: Requisites of a warrant to search suspected place.

1. That it run in the name of "The State of Texas."

2. That it describe with accuracy the place suspected.

3. That it describe, as near as may be, the property supposed to be commonly concealed in such suspected place, or the implements alleged to be there kept for the purpose of aiding in the commission of offences, and state the particular offence for which such implements are designed.

4. That it name the person accused of having charge of the suspected place, if there be any such person, or if his name is unknown, that it describe him with accuracy and direct him to be brought before the Magistrate.

5. That it be dated and signed by the Magistrate, and directed to the Sheriff of the proper county.

CHAPTER III.

OF THE EXECUTION OF A SEARCH WARRANT.

Act of Feb. 15, 1858. Shall be executed, &c.

ART. 313. Any officer to whom a search warrant is delivered, shall execute the same without delay.

Act of Aug 26, 1856. Officer may call in aid, when.

ART. 314. In the execution of a search warrant, the officer may call in aid any number of citizens in his county, who shall be bound to aid in the execution of the same.

Officer shall give notice of purpose to execute warrant.

ART. 315. The officer, shall, upon going to the place ordered to be searched, or before seizing any property for which he is ordered to make search, give notice of his purpose to the person who has charge of, or is an inmate of the place, or who has possession of the property described in the warrant.

In case of resistance.

ART. 316. If an officer, in the execution of a search warrant, is resisted, he may use such force as is necessary to overcome the resistance, but no greater.

When officer may enter house by force.

ART. 317. In the execution of a search warrant, the officer may break down a door or window of any house which he is ordered to search, if he cannot effect an entrance by other less violent means; but when the warrant issues only for the purpose of discovering property stolen or otherwise obtained in violation of the Penal Law, without designating any particular place where it is supposed to be concealed, no such authority is given to the officer executing the same.

Shall seize person accused and property, and take them before Magistrate.

ART. 318. When the property, implements, arms or munitions, which the officer is directed to search for and seize, are found, he shall take possession of the same and carry them before the Magistrate. He shall also arrest any person whom he is directed to arrest by the warrant, and forthwith take such person before the Magistrate.

Warrant shall be executed in three days or less.

ART. 319. A search warrant must be executed within three days from the time of its issuance, and forthwith returned to the proper Magistrate; but the Magistrate may, in the warrant, direct that the same may be executed within a shorter period.

Officer shall give receipt of property to person from whom taken.

ART. 320. An officer taking any property, implements, arms or munitions, shall receipt therefor to the person from whose possession the same may have been taken.

How return made.

ART. 321. Upon returning the search warrant, the officer shall state on the back of the same or on some paper attached to it, the manner in which it has been executed, and shall likewise deliver to the Magistrate an inventory of the property, implements, arms or munitions, taken in his possession under the warrant.

CHAPTER IV.

PROCEEDINGS ON THE RETURN OF A SEARCH WARRANT.

ART. 322. When property is taken under a search warrant and delivered to a Magistrate, he shall, if it appear that the same was stolen or otherwise acquired in violation of the Penal Law, dispose of it according to the rules prescribed in Part III, Title VIII, Chapter III, of this Code. Act of Aug. 26, 1856. How property seized shall be disposed of.

ART. 323. When a warrant has been issued for the purpose of searching a suspected place, and there be found any such implements, arms or munitions, as are alleged to have been there kept or concealed, the same shall be safely kept by the Sheriff, subject to the order of the District Court of the proper county. In what cases kept by Sheriff, subject to order of Dist. Court.

ART. 324. The Sheriff shall, in every case arising under the preceding Article, furnish the Magistrate who issued the warrant, with a certified schedule of the articles in his possession. Sheriff shall furnish schedule of property to Magistrate.

ART. 325. Arms or munitions, taken under a warrant in accordance with the provisions of this Title, shall become forfeited to the State, and shall be so adjudged by the District Court, upon the conviction or escape of any person accused of having had possession of, or of having concealed them. How arms or munitions taken under warrant shall be forfeited to the State.

ART. 326. Implements intended to be used for forging or counterfeiting, shall, upon the conviction or escape of the person accused of having had or concealed them, be destroyed by the Sheriff under the order of the Court. Implements for forging or counterfeiting, destroyed by Sheriff.

ART. 327. When implements, supposed to be designed for forging or counterfeiting, are in the hands of the Sheriff, and the person accused of having had possession of, or of having concealed such implements, has been discharged by the Magistrate, the District Attorney shall cause the fact to be made known to the Court, who, (if satisfied upon investigation that they were designed for such purpose) shall cause them to be destroyed by the Sheriff, in the same manner as if the accused person had been convicted or had escaped. How disposed of when person accused shall have been discharged.

ART. 328. When it appears upon investigation, that the implements seized were not such as might be or are commonly used for forging or counterfeiting, they shall be delivered to the person from whom they were taken. When delivered to the person from whom they were taken.

ART. 329. The investigation spoken of in the preceding Articles, may be made by the District Judge, by hearing proof before a jury. Investigation, by whom made.

ART. 330. The Magistrate, upon the return of a search warrant, shall proceed to try the questions arising upon the same, and shall take testimony, as on other examinations before him, and be governed by like rules. Upon return of search warrant, shall proceed to try, how.

ART. 331. If the Magistrate be satisfied there was good ground for issuing

Shall give bail, &c., when, — the warrant, he shall require the person arrested to give bail, as in other cases, to answer the accusation against him before the proper Court.

Shall discharge defendant, when — ART. 332. If the Magistrate be not satisfied that there was good ground for the issuance of the warrant, he may discharge the defendant and order restitution of the property or articles taken from him, except implements which appear to be designed for forging or counterfeiting; and in such case the implements shall be kept by the Sheriff, subject to the order of the proper Court. (Sheriff shall report to District Attorney, &c.) It shall be the duty of the Sheriff to report to the District Attorney all cases in which such implements are in his possession, and the accused person discharged.

Bail bonds in such cases, same requisites as, &c. — ART. 333. Bail bonds taken in such cases shall have the same substantial requisites which are prescribed for other bail bonds taken before the Magistrates, and may be recovered upon in the same manner.

Magistrate shall keep a record, &c., and file original papers with District Clerk. — ART. 334. The Magistrate shall keep a record of all the proceedings had before him in cases of search warrants, and shall file with the Clerk of the District Court, before the next term of said Court, all the original papers relating thereto.

TITLE IV.

OF THE PROCEEDINGS SUBSEQUENT TO COMMITMENT OR BAIL, AND PRIOR TO THE TRIAL.

CHAPTER I

THE ORGANIZATION OF THE GRAND JURY.

Act of Aug. 26, 1956. County Court shall select Grand Jury, when. — ART. 335. The County Court, consisting of the Chief Justice and County Commissioners, or a quorum of that body, shall meet on the first Monday of January and the first Monday in July of each year, for the purpose of selecting the Grand Jurors, to serve at the next succeeding term of the District Court, in each county of the State.

A quorum for the purpose shall consist, &c. — ART. 336. A quorum, for the purposes specified in the preceding Article, shall consist of any three of the Commissioners, or of the Chief Justice and any two Commissioners.

In case a quorum be not in attendance, — ART. 337. In case a quorum of the court be not in attendance at the time fixed in Article 335, any one or more of the members of the court who may be present, may adjourn from day to day for one week, until the attendance of a quorum be had; and in case of a failure to hold a court during said week, the Chief Justice of the county or (in case of his absence, or failure to discharge the duty then,) any two of the County Commissioners may call a meeting of the court, at as early a day as practicable after the first Monday of January and July, for the purpose of selecting the Grand Jury for the next succeeding term of the District Court.

ART. 338. The court, when assembled at a regular or called term, as above provided, shall proceed to select a number of persons, not less than fifteen nor more than twenty, to serve as Grand Jurors. The court shall select, how.

ART. 339. The court shall take care to select persons having the following qualifications, they shall be: Act of Feb. 15, 1858. The persons selected shall have the following qualifications, &c.

1 Citizens of the State and of the county in which they are to serve, and qualified under the constitution and laws to vote in said county.

2. Freeholders within the State, or householders within their respective counties.

3. Their names shall be upon the jury list required to be made out by said court, according to the laws regulating juries.

ART. 340. The proceedings of the County Court, in selecting the Grand Jurors, shall be entered of record upon the minutes of said court, which entry shall particularly state the names of the persons selected. Act of Aug. 26, 1856. The proceedings of the court to be recorded.

ART. 341. It is the duty of the County Court, to see that the persons so selected be men of good moral character and intelligence; and they shall be distributed, as to residence, as nearly as may be through the different parts of the county. Jurors shall be men of good moral character, &c.

ART. 342. At each term of the County Court, when a Grand Jury is selected as herein provided, the names of the persons so selected shall be placed on a list to be kept in the office of the Clerk of said court, in order that the same persons may not be compelled to serve at any two successive terms of the District Court. Jury list shall be kept.

ART. 343. The County Court shall, as far as practicable, so regulate the Grand Jury service in each county, (taking into consideration the amount of population,) as that such service may be equally divided among the citizens of the county, qualified to discharge the duty. Jury service equally divided &c.

ART. 344. The Clerk of the County Court shall furnish to the Clerk of the District Court, a certified list of the persons selected as Grand Jurors, within ten days after they have been selected. Certified list furnished District Clerk.

ART. 345. The Clerk of the District Court shall issue a writ to the Sheriff of the county, directing him to summon the persons whose names have been furnished him as Grand Jurors, to attend at the proper term of the court. Writ to Sheriff to summon Grand Jurors.

ART. 346. The Sheriff shall give notice to each person whom he is directed to summon, at least ten days before the meeting of the District Court. This notice may be given verbally in person to each juror, or by leaving a written notice at the house of such person, with some free white person over the age of fourteen years, who is an inmate of such house; and if any person so notified shall fail to attend as a juror, he may be fined by the court not exceeding the sum of fifty dollars. Sheriff shall give notice to jurors, &c. Juror failing to attend, may be fined.

ART. 347. If, for any cause, there should be a failure to select and summon a Grand Jury, as herein directed, or when none of those summoned shall attend, the District Court shall, on the first day of the organization thereof, In case of failure to select Grand Jury.

direct a writ to be issued to the Sheriff, commanding him to summon any number of persons not exceeding twenty, to serve as Grand Jurors.

If fifteen jurors be in attendance, &c., shall be impannelled. ART. 348. If as many as fifteen persons shall be in attendance on the District Court, who have been selected by the County Court in accordance with the provisions of this Chapter, the court shall proceed to impannel a Grand Jury.

Shall be interrogated touching qualifications. ART. 349. Each person who is presented to serve as a Grand Juror, shall, before being impannelled, be interrogated on oath by the District Judge, or under his direction, touching his qualifications

Act of Feb. 15, 1858.

Shall be asked these questions, &c. ART. 350. In trying the qualification of any person to serve on the Grand Jury, he shall be asked these questions:

1. Are you a citizen of this State and county, and a qualified voter for members of the Legislature in this county?

2. Are you a freeholder in this State or a householder in this county?

And the Court shall cause the jury list to be examined to ascertain whether the name of the person be upon the same.

What constitutes qualifications. ART. 351. If by the answer of the person interrogated, and the examination of the jury list, it appears that he is a citizen of the State and county, where the court is held; is qualified by the Constitution and laws to vote for members of the Legislature; and is either a freeholder in the State or a householder in the proper county, and that his name is upon the jury list, he shall be deemed a competent Grand Juror.

Act of Aug. 26, 1856.

ART. 352. Any person summoned who does not possess the requisite qualifications, shall be excused by the Court from serving.

Shall be impannelled, unless, &c. ART. 353. If it be found that there are as many as fifteen of those summoned to attend as Grand Jurors who are present and possess the proper qualifications, they shall be impanelled as the Grand Jury, unless the array or some particular member be challenged, as hereinafter provided, and by reason of such challenge the whole body of Grand Jurors is set aside, or a sufficient number to reduce it below the number of fifteen.

If less than fifteen be present &c. ART. 354. When a number less than fifteen are found to be in attendance, of persons qualified to serve as Grand Jurors, the Court shall require such additional number to be summoned as may be deemed necessary, so that a legal Grand Jury may be organized, of at least fifteen persons.

If the jury be reduced to less than fifteen by challenges, &c. ART. 355. When, by challenges to particular individuals of those summoned less than fifteen persons remain, or when from any cause whatever, it is found that less than that number are present, the Court shall direct the Grand Jury to be completed as provided in the preceding Article.

Act of Feb. 15, 1858.

Foreman appointed—his oath. ART. 356. When the Grand Jury is completed, one of their body shall be appointed foreman, and the following oath shall be administered to each of said Jurors:

"You solemnly swear, (or affirm as the case may be,) that you will diligently enquire into, and true presentment make of all such matters and things as shall be given you in charge, the States counsel, your fellows and your own you shall keep secret. You shall present no person from envy, hatred or malice, neither shall you leave any person unpresented for love, fear, favor, affection or hope of reward, but you shall present things truly as they come to your knowledge, according the best of your understanding; so help you God."

Act of Aug. 26, 1856. ART. 357. After the Grand Jury has been sworn, the Court shall give them instruction as to their duty.

ART. 358. One or more bailiffs may be sworn to attend upon the Grand Jury. The oath taken by a bailiff shall be to keep secret the proceedings of the Grand Jury. Bailiffs, their oaths.

ART. 359. A bailiff is to obey the instructions of the foreman, to summon all witnesses, and generally to perform all such duties as are required of him by the foreman; where two bailiffs are appointed, one of them shall be always with the Grand Jury. Bailiff's duties.

ART. 360. A Grand Juror is said to be impannelled after his qualifications have been tried, and he has been sworn. By the word panel is meant the whole body of Grand Jurors. Words *impannelled* and *panel* defined.

ART. 361. In case of the absence of the foreman of the Grand Jury, from sickness or other cause, the Court may appoint in his place, some other member of the body. Absence of foreman, &c.

ART. 362. Any person, before the Grand Jury have been impanelled, may challenge the array of Jurors, or any person presented as a Grand Juror. Any person may challenge the array, &c.

ART. 363. A challenge to the array may be made for these causes only: A challenge to the array may be made, for what causes.

1. That the list of persons summoned by the Sheriff was not in fact selected by the County Court.

2. In case of a Grand Juror summoned by order of the District Court, where there has been a fa lure to act by the County Court, or a failure to attend on the part of the person summoned, that the Sheriff has acted corruptly in summoning any one or more of the Jurors.

ART. 364. A challenge to a particular Grand Juror may be for the following causes: A challenge to particular juror for what cause.

1. That he is under twenty-one years of age.

2. That he is not a citizen of the State, and a qualified voter under the laws.

3. That he is not a freeholder of the State, or a householder of the county.

4. That since the last term of the Court he has been prosecuted, and is under accusation, for some offence, indictable in the county, where he is about to be placed on the Grand Jury.

5. That he is the prosecutor upon an accusation against the person making the challenge.

6. That he is related by consanguinity or affinity to some person who has been held to bail, or who is in confinement upon a criminal accusation.

ART. 365. When a challenge to the array or to any individual has been made, the Court shall hear proof and decide in a summary manner whether the challenge be well founded or not. The Court shall decide challenges, how.

ART. 366. If the challenge to the array be sustained, the Court shall, as in Article 347, direct another Grand Jury to be summoned. If the challenge to the array be sustained, &c.

ART. 367. If by challenge to any particular individual, the number of Grand Jurors be reduced below fifteen, the panel shall be completed by summoning others under the orders of the Court as provided in Articles 354 and 355. If challenge to individual be sustained, &c.

ART. 368. By the array of Grand Jurors is meant the whole body of persons summoned to serve as such, before they have been impannelled. The array of Grand Jurors means &c.

ART. 369. The proper time for a challenge to the array is before the Jurors have been interrogated as to their qualifications. A challenge to any particular individual is to be made after the qualifications of the Grand Jurors have been tested by their own oaths. Challenge to the array, when made, &c.

ART. 370. Twelve members shall be a quorum for the purpose of discharging any duty or exercising any right properly belonging to the Grand Jury. Twelve members constitute quorum.

CHAPTER II.

OF THE DUTIES, PRIVILEGES AND POWERS OF THE GRAND JURY.

Act of Aug. 26, 1856.

Suitable place to be prepared for Grand Jury.

ART. 371. The Grand Jury, after being organized, shall proceed to the discharge of their duties, and some suitable place shall be prepared by the Sheriff for their sessions.

Deliberations shall be secret.

ART. 372. The deliberations of the Grand Jury shall be secret, and any member of the body or bailiff who divulges any thing transpiring before them in the course of their official duties, shall be liable to a fine, as for contempt of the court, not exceeding one hundred dollars, and to imprisonment, not exceeding five days.

District Attorney may go before Grand Jury.

ART. 373. The District Attorney may go before the Grand Jury at any time, except when they are discussing the propriety of finding a bill of indictment, or voting upon the same.

May send for District Attorney.

ART. 374. When any question arises before a Grand Jury, respecting the proper discharge of their duties, or any matter of law, about which they may require advice, it is their right to send for the District Attorney, and take his advice thereon.

District Attorney may examine witnesses, &c.

ART. 375. The District Attorney may examine the witnesses before the Grand Jury, and may advise as to the proper mode of interrogating them, if desired, or if he thinks it necessary.

Grand Jury may seek advice from the Court.

ART. 376. The Grand Jury may also seek and receive advice from the Court, touching any matter before them, and for this purpose shall go into court in a body; but they shall so guard the manner of propounding their questions, as not to divulge the particular accusation that is pending before them; or they may propound their questions in writing, upon which the Court may give them the desired information in writing.

Grand Jury shall meet and adjourn, when.

ART. 377. The Grand Jury shall meet and adjourn at times agreed upon by a majority of the body, but they shall not adjourn at any one time for more than three days, and shall, as near as may be, conform their adjournments to those of the Court.

Duties of Grand Jury.

ART. 378. It is the duty of the Grand Jury to inquire into all offences liable to indictment, of which any of the members may have knowledge, or of which they shall be informed by the District Attorney or any other credible person.

Foreman may issue summons for witnesses.

ART. 379. The foreman of the Grand Jury may issue a summons for any witness in the county where they are sitting, which summons need only require the witness to appear before them at a time fixed or forthwith, without stating the matter in respect to which the witness will be called upon to testify.

ART. 380. If a person notified by written summons, to appear before the Grand Jury as a witness, refuses or fails to obey the summons, the bailiff shall make return of that fact upon the summons, and file the same with the Clerk of the District Court, who shall, thereupon, issue an attachment, which shall authorize the bailiff or Sheriff to arrest the witness and take him before the Grand Jury. If witness refuses to attend, attachment may issue.

ART. 381. When a witness brought in any manner before a Grand Jury, refuses to testify, such fact shall be made known to the District Attorney or to the Court, and the Court may compel the witness to answer the question, if it appear to be a proper one, by imposing a fine not exceeding one hundred dollars, and by committing the party to jail until he is willing to testify. If witness refuse to testify, &c.

ART. 382. Witnesses shall first be sworn by the foreman not to divulge, either by words or signs, any matter about which they may be interrogated, and to keep secret all proceedings which may be had in their presence. Witnesses shall be sworn to, what.

ART. 383. The Grand Jury in propounding questions to witness, shall direct the examination to the person accused or suspected, shall state the offence with which he is charged, the county where the offence is said to have been committed, and as nearly as may be, the time of the commission of the offence, but should the jury think it necessary, they may ask the witness in general terms, whether he has knowledge of the violation of any particular law, by any person. Act of Feb. 15, 1858. How questions shall be propounded to witnesses.

ART. 383a. When a felony has been committed in any county within the jurisdiction of the Grand Jury, and the name of the person guilty thereof is unknown, or where it is uncertain by whom the same was committed, the Grand Jury may ask any pertinent question relative to the transaction, in such manner as to ascertain who is the guilty party. When a felony has been committed, &c.

ART. 384. The duty of Grand Jurors is to enquire of offences against the laws indictable within their respective counties. Duty of Grand Jurors.

ART 385. After all the testimony which is accessible to the Grand Jury shall have been given in respect to any criminal accusation, the vote shall be taken as to the presentment of a bill of indictment, and if twelve members concur in finding the bill, the foreman shall make a memorandum of the same, for the purpose of enabling the District Attorney to write the indictment. Act of Aug. 26, 1856. Indictment found, if twelve members concur. Memorandum furnished District Attorney.

ART. 386. The memorandum, furnished the District Attorney, shall state the name of the defendant, if known, the nature of the offence, the time and place of its commission, and the name of the witnesses on whose testimony the accusation is sustained. Memorandum shall state what.

ART. 387. The District Attorney shall prepare all indictments which have been found by a Grand Jury, with as little delay as possible, and when so prepared shall deliver them to the foreman. District Attorney shall prepare indictments.

ART. 388. When the Grand Jury shall have acted upon any accusation before them, and the indictment has been prepared with the requisite form, they shall, in open Court, deliver the indictment to the Judge of the Court, a quorum at least being present on such occasions. Jury shall deliver indictment in open Court, &c.

ART. 389. The fact of the presentment of the indictment, in open Court, by the Grand Jury, shall be entered upon the minutes of the proceedings of the Court, noting briefly the style of the criminal action, and the offence charged. Fact of presentment shall be entered on the minutes, &c.

CHAPTER III.

OF INDICTMENTS AND INFORMATIONS.

Act of Aug. 26, 1856.

ART. 390. All felonies shall be presented by indictment only, except in cases specially provided for.

Misdemeanors presented by indictment or, &c.

ART. 391. All misdemeanors may be presented by either information or indictment.

All offences must be presented by indictment or information.

ART. 392. All offences known to the Penal Law of this State, must be prosecuted either by indictment or information. This provision does not include fines and penalties for contempt of Court, nor special cases in which inferior courts exercise jurisdiction.

An indictment is, what.

ART. 394. An indictment is the written statement of a Grand Jury accusing a person, therein named, of some act or omission, which, by law, is declared to be an offence.

Act of Feb. 15, 1858.

Shall be deemed sufficient if it has, &c.

ART. 395. An indictment shall be deemed sufficient if it has the following requisites:

1. It shall commence "in the name and by the authority of the State of Texas."

2. It must appear therefrom that the same was presented in a Court having jurisdiction of the offence set forth.

3. It must appear to be the act of a Grand Jury of the proper county.

4. It must contain the name of the accused, or state that his name is unknown.

5. It must show that the place where the offence was committed is within the jurisdiction of the Court in which the indictment is presented.

6. The time mentioned must be some date anterior to the presentment of the indictment, and not so remote that the prosecution of the offence is barred by limitation.

7. The offence must be set forth in plain and intelligible words.

8. The indictment must conclude "against the peace and dignity of the State."

9. It shall be signed officially by the foreman of the Grand Jury.

Act of Aug. 26, 1856.

Not necessary to state, &c.

ART. 396. It is not necessary to state in an indictment anything which it is not necessary to prove.

The certainty required.

ART. 398. The certainty required in an indictment, is such as will enable the accused to plead the judgment that may be given upon it, in bar of any prosecution for the same offence.

Particular inten—intent to defraud.

ART. 399. Where a particular intent is a material fact in the description of the offence, it must be stated in the indictment. But in any case where an intent to defraud is required to constitute an offence, it shall be sufficient to allege an intent to defraud, without naming therein the particular person intended to be defrauded.

ART. 400. When by law the District Court of more than one county has jurisdiction of the same offence, the indictment may allege the offence to have been committed in the county where the same is prosecuted, or in any county or place where the offence was actually committed. Allegation of venue, &c.

ART. 401. No objection shall be heard by motion, plea, exception, or in any other manner to an indictment, on the ground that the Grand Jury finding the same was not legally constituted. Any objection to the qualification of one or all of the Grand Jurors may be made available in the manner provided in Article 363, and following Articles, and in no other way. Objection by motion, &c., to constitution of Grand Jury not heard. How taken.

ART. 402. An *information* is a written statement filed and presented in behalf of the State by the District Attorney, accusing the defendant therein named of an offence which is by law subject to be prosecuted in that manner. Definition of term *information*.

ART. 403. An information is sufficient if it has the following requisites: Act of Feb. 15, 1858. Information sufficient if it has these requisites, &c.

1. It shall commence "in the name and by the authority of the State of Texas."

2. That it shall appear to have been presented in a court having jurisdiction of the offence set forth.

3. That it appear to have been presented by the proper officer.

4. That it contain the name of the person accused, or be stated that his name is unknown.

5. It must appear that the place where the offence is charged to have been committed is within the jurisdiction of the court where the information is filed.

6. That the time of the commission of the offence be some date anterior to the filing of the information, and that the offence does not appear to be barred by limitation.

7. That the offence be set forth in plain and intelligible words.

8. That the information conclude "against the peace and dignity of the State."

ART. 404. An information shall not be presented by the District Attorney, until oath has been made by some credible person, charging the defendant with an offence. This oath shall be reduced to writing and filed with the *information*. It may be sworn to before the District Attorney, who, for that purpose, shall have power to administer the oath, or it may be made before any officer authorized by law to administer oaths. Act of Aug. 26, 1856. Before information, oath must be made, charging an offence, &c.

ART. 406. The rules laid down in articles 398, 399, 400 and 401 with respect to indictments, are applicable also to informations. Act of Feb. 15, 1858.

ART. 406a. When an indictment has been lost or mislaid, the District Attorney may suggest the fact to the Court, and the same shall be entered upon the minutes of the Court, and in such case another indictment may be substituted upon the written statement of the District Attorney that it is substantially the same as that which has been lost, or mislaid. Or another indictment may be presented to the Grand Jury; and in such case, the period for the commencement of the prosecution shall be dated from the time of making such entry. When indictment has been lost.

CHAPTER IV.

OF PROCEEDINGS PRELIMINARY TO TRIAL.

1. *Of enforcing the attendance of the Defendant, and of forfeiture of Bail.*

2. *Of Witnesses and of the manner of enforcing their attendance.*

3. *Service of a copy of the Indictment.*

4. *Of arraignment and of proceedings where no arraignment is necessary.*

5 *Of the pleadings in criminal actions.*

6. *Of the Argument and decision of Motions, Pleas and Exceptions.*

1. *Of enforcing the attendance of Defendant, and of forfeiture of Bail.*

Art. 407. Wherever a defendant is bound by recognizance or bail bond, to appear at any term of a Court, his name shall be called at the door of the Court House, on the day set apart for taking up the criminal docket, or on any subsequent day when his case comes up for trial, and if he fail to appear, a forfeiture of his recognizance or bail bond shall be taken. *Act of Aug. 26, 1856. Defendant called at the door of the court house, &c., and forfeiture, &c.*

Art. 408. Recognizances and bail bonds are forfeited in the following manner: The name of the defendant and of his sureties, shall be called distinctly at the door of the Court House, and if the defendant do not appear within a reasonable time after such call is made, judgment shall be entered that the State of Texas recover of the defendant the amount of money in which he is bound, and of his sureties the amount of money in which they are respectively bound, which judgment shall state that the same will be made final unless good cause be shown, at the next term of the Court, why the defendant did not appear. *Recognizances and bail bonds forfeited, how.*

Art. 409. After the adjournment of the Court at which the proceedings set forth in the last two articles have been had, a citation shall issue from the Court, notifying the sureties of the defendant, that the recognizance or bond has been forfeited, and requiring them to appear at the next term of the Court, and show cause why the same should not be made final; but it shall not be necessary to give notice to the defendant. *Notice to sureties of forfeiture.*

Art. 410. At the next term of the Court after forfeiture of the recognizance or bond as provided for in articles 407 and 408, if the sureties have been duly notified, or at the first term of the Court after the service of such notice, the sureties shall answer in writing, and show cause why the defendant did not appear, which answer may be filed within the time limited for answering in a civil action. *Sureties shall answer at next term, &c.*

Art. 412. Sureties shall be entitled to notice by service of a citation, the length of time, and in the manner required in civil actions; and, if any surety fail to appear after such notice, and show sufficient cause for the non-attendance of the defendant, the judgment against him shall be made final, at any time after the expiration of the time allowed for answering in a civil suit. *Surety shall be entitled to, what notice—If he fail to appear, &c.*

Causes which will exonerate from liability.

ART. 413. The following causes will exonerate the defendant and his sureties from liability upon the recognizance or bail bond.:

1. The death of the defendant before the term of the court at which the forfeiture was taken.

2. The sickness of the defendant, or some uncontrollable circumstance, which prevented his appearance at court; and it must, in every case, be shown that his failure to appear arose from no fault on his part.

3. Failure to present an indictment or information at the first term of the court which may be held after the defendant has been admitted to bail, in cases where the party was bound over before indictment or information, and the prosecution has not been continued by order of the court, as prescribed in Article 537.

Same subject.

ART. 414. The causes mentioned in the second subdivision of the preceding Article, shall not be deemed sufficient to exonerate the defendant or his sureties, unless he appear before final judgment on the bond or recognizance.

The court may remit, when.

ART. 415. If, before final judgment is entered against the bail, the defendant appear, or be arrested and lodged in the jail of the proper county, the court may, at its discretion, remit the whole or part of the sum specified in the bond or recognizance.

If defendant appears before final judgment, &c.

ART. 416. When the defendant appears before the entry of final judgment, and sufficient cause is shown for his failure to appear before the forfeiture taken, and a trial is had of the criminal action pending against him, he shall be entitled to have the forfeiture set aside, and the criminal action against him shall stand for trial, but the State shall not be forced to try the same until reasonable time has been allowed to prepare for trial; and the State shall, in such case, be entitled to a continuance of the cause.

If no sufficient cause be shown.

ART. 417. When, upon a trial of the issue presented by the answers of the sureties, no sufficient cause is shown for the failure of the defendant to appear, the judgment shall be made final against him and his sureties, for the amount in which they are respectively bound; and the same shall be collected by execution, as in civil actions. Separate executions shall issue against each party for the amount adjudged against him, and the costs be equally divided between the sureties, if there be no more than one.

Separate executions shall issue.

Where defendant fails to appear, &c., capias shall issue.

ART. 418. Where a defendant has been held to bail, or recognized to appear, and has failed to appear when called as prescribed in Article 407, a capias shall be issued, for his arrest.

Where defendant has not been arrested, &c., capias shall issue.

ART. 419. In cases where the defendant has not been arrested or held to bail, before indictment or information is presented, there shall be issued a capias for his arrest, as provided in the succeeding articles.

A capias is, what.

ART. 420. A capias is a writ issued by the Clerk of the District Court, and directed "To any Sheriff of the State of Texas," commanding him to arrest a person accused of an offence, and bring him before that court forthwith, or on a day, or at a term stated in the writ.

Sufficient if have, &c.

ART. 421. A capias shall be held sufficient, if it have the following requisites:

1. That it run in the name of "The State of Texas."

2. That it name the person whose arrest is ordered, or, if unknown, describe him.

3. That it specify the offence of which the defendant is accused, and it appear thereby that he is accused of some offence against the penal law of the State.

4. That it name the day or term when the same is returnable, or be made returnable forthwith.

5. That it be dated and signed by the Clerk, with his seal of office annexed.

ART. 422. A capias shall be immediately issued upon each indictment or information presented, except in cases where the defendant is already in custody or on bail. A capias shall be issued on each indictment, &c., except, &c.

ART. 423. A capias shall not lose its force or virtue, if not executed and returned at the time fixed in the writ, but may be executed at any time afterwards, and return made; and all proceedings under such capias shall be as valid as if the same had been executed and returned within the time specified in the writ. A capias may be executed at any time, &c.

ART. 424. When a defendant indicted for felony is not arrested during the term at which the indictment is presented, the court, in all bailable cases, shall, before adjourning, fix the amount of the bail to be required, and the same shall be entered upon the minutes; and in issuing the writ, the Clerk shall specify therein the amount of the bail to be taken: but in case of neglect to comply with either of the requirements of this Article, the arrest of the defendant and the bail bond taken by the Sheriff, shall be as legal and valid as if there had been no such omission. Defendant indicted for felony who is not arrested during the term, &c.

ART. 425. A defendant may be arrested under a capias, by any peace officer; but, when so arrested, he shall be delivered to the Sheriff (together with the writ under which he was taken) to be dealt with as the law requires. Who may arrest under capias.

ART. 426. The Sheriff has authority in cases of misdemeanor, at all times, whether during a term of a court, or in vacation, to take bail of the defendant; and he may take bail in cases of felonies less than capital, when he makes an arrest under capias during vacation. The Sheriff may take bail, when.

ART. 427. In cases of arrest for felony, during a term of the court, the Sheriff cannot take bail, but must forthwith bring the defendant before the court, that he may be dealt with according to law. Cannot take bail for felony, during term.

ART. 428. Where an arrest is made under a capias during vacation, the Sheriff shall, in a capital case, confine the defendant in jail, and the capias shall, for that purpose, be a sufficient warrant of commitment. Arrest in a capital case, in vacation, &c.

ART. 429. When, in accordance with the provisions of Articles 424 and 425, the Sheriff is authorized to take bail, he shall require of the defendant to enter into bond with one or more sureties, in the amount specified in the writ; and if no amount is specified, then in such sum as he may deem reasonable. Sheriff shall take bail, how.

ART. 430. The provisions of Articles 426, 427, 428, and 429, refer to arrests made in the county where the prosecution is pending. Arrests in the county where prosecution, &c.

ART. 431. In every capital case, when a defendant is arrested, under capias, in a county other than that in which the prosecution is pending, it is the duty of the Sheriff who arrests, or to whom the defendant is delivered by some other peace officer, to convey him forthwith to the county from which the capias issued, for which service he is entitled to be paid according to the provisions of Article 952; and a failure to discharge the duty herein imposed, renders the Sheriff guilty of an offence. Defendant arrested in capital case, in a county other than that in which prosecution is pending, &c.

ART. 432. When an arrest is made out of the county in which the prosecution is pending, in cases of felony less than capital, and of misdemeanor, the Sheriff is authorized to receive from the defendant, bail according to the directions of the capias, or if no amount be fixed in the writ, then in some reasonable amount; and he shall transmit, through the mail, to the Clerk of the proper court, the bail bond and the capias, with his return thereon. But a Sheriff may, in any case, convey the defendant and deliver him to the Sheriff of the proper county. Defendant arrested, in cases less than capital, in a county other, &c.

In such case, if defendant refuse to give bail, &c.

When defendant is imprisoned out of the county, &c.

ART. 433. When a defendant, in a bailable case, is arrested under capias, out of the county of the prosecution, and refuses to give bail, the Sheriff may place him in the jail of the county where the arrest is made, or he may convey him to the proper county, and deliver him to the Sheriff thereof. When the defendant is placed in jail out of the county of the prosecution, it is the duty of the Sheriff making the arrest, immediately to give notice through the mail, of such arrest and confinement, to the Sheriff of the county where the prosecution is pending, whose duty it shall be to convey such defendant, without delay, to the jail of his county.

Defendant imprisoned out of the county shall be discharged, when.

ART. 434. If a defendant be placed in jail, out of the county of the prosecution, he shall be discharged from custody if not applied for and taken by the Sheriff of the proper county, before the end of ninety days from the time of his commitment: provided, that this Article shall not apply to cases where the defendant has been placed in jail out of the county of the prosecution, under some provision of this Code, for want of a sufficient or safe jail in the county of the prosecution.

2. *Of Witnesses, and the manner of enforcing their attendance.*

Subpœna issued to any county.

ART. 435. A subpœna may be issued to any county, on application to the Clerk, for witnesses either for the State or defendant.

Act of Feb. 15, 1858.

In case of felony, attachment may issue, when.

ART. 436. In cases of felony, after indictment found, the State or the defendant shall be entitled, on application to the Clerk of the Court, to obtain an attachment against the person of a witness, to compel his attendance upon any particular day of the court, if the witness resides in the county of the prosecution, provided that no attachment shall issue, unless the witness has failed to obey a subpœna.

Attachment for witness out of the county.

ART. 437. Where the witness resides out of the county where the prosecution is pending, the defendant shall be entitled, on application to the court, for an attachment to compel the attendance of such witness, such application shall be in writing under oath, and state the name of the witness, the county of his residence, and the facts expected to be proved by such witness or witnesses; and if it appear to the court that such testimony is material, the attachment shall issue: the State shall also be entitled to attachments under the provisions of this article, upon the written application of the District Attorney, which shall contain the same requisites as required of the defendant under this article.

Act of Aug. 26, 1856.

Definition of *subpœna.*

ART. 438. A subpœna is a writ issued to the Sheriff, or other proper officer, commanding him to summon a person therein named, to appear at a certain term of the court, or on a certain day, to testify in a criminal action, or upon any proceeding before an examining court, Coroner's inquest, the Grand Jury, or before a Judge hearing an application under habeas corpus. If issued by the Clerk of the District Court to another county, (but in no other case,) it shall be authenticated by his official seal.

Definition of *attachment.*

ART. 439. An attachment is a writ issued by a Clerk of the District Court, or by any magistrate upon examination of criminal accusation, or in any other proceeding before him when authorized by law, or by a Judge sitting in cases of habeas corpus, commanding some peace officer to take the body of a witness and bring him before such court, magistrate, or Judge, on a day named, to testify in behalf of the State or of the defendant, as the case may be; when issued by a Clerk, it shall be authenticated by his official seal.

No attachment in case of misdemeanor, &c.

ART. 440. No attachment shall be issued for a witness, in a case of misdemeanor, until it has been shown that he refuses to obey a subpœna, or that he fails to attend on some day set apart for the criminal docket, after having entered into recognizance or bond, whether with or without security.

ART. 441. It shall be understood that a witness refuses to obey a subpœna: 1. If he is not in attendance on the Court, on the day set apart for taking up the criminal docket, or any day subsequent thereto, and before the final disposition or continuance of the particular case in which he is a witness. Witness understood to refuse to obey a subpœna, when.

ART. 442. Witnesses on behalf of the State or defendant may, at the request of either party, be required to enter into recognizance in the District Court, to appear and testify in a criminal action. Witness recognized, when.

ART. 443. A witness who makes affidavit that he is unable to give security, or to deposit a sufficient amount of money in lieu thereof, shall be recognized, or give bond, without security. Witnesses recognized without security, when.

ART. 444. If a witness refuse to obey a subpœna, in a capital case, he shall be fined, at the discretion of the Court, not exceeding five hundred dollars. Judgment may be entered on motion, of either the District Attorney or the defendant, or his counsel, against such defaulting witness, which, however, shall not be made final, until the witness has been duly notified to show cause why he did not appear. Witness refusing to obey a subpœna in a capital case, shall be fined, &c.

ART. 445. A refusal to obey a subpœna in case of felony, less than capital, shall subject the witness to a fine not exceeding two hundred dollars; and in cases of misdemeanor, to a fine not exceeding one hundred dollars. In cases less then capital.

ART. 446. Before a fine is entered against a witness, for disobedience to a subpœna, it must be made to appear to the Court, by the oath of the defendant, or some other credible person, or the statement of the District Attorney, that the testimony of such witness was material, either to the prosecution or defence. Before fine entered, it must be made to appear, &c.

ART. 447. When a fine is entered against a witness, for a failure to appear and testify, the judgment shall be conditional, and a citation shall issue to him to show cause why the same should not be made final; and such citation shall be served in the manner, and for the length of time prescribed for citations in civil actions. Judgment on fine, conditional.

ART. 448. Witnesses cited to show cause, as provided in the preceding Article, may do so in writing or verbally, at any time during the term of the Court next after they are cited. Witness may show cause, how and when.

ART. 449. When a fine has been entered against a witness, but no trial of the cause takes place, and such witness afterward appears and testifies upon the trial thereof, it shall be discretionary with the Judge, though no good excuse be rendered, to reduce the fine or to remit it altogether; but he shall, nevertheless, be adjudged to pay all the costs accruing in the proceeding against him by reason of his failure to attend. Where witness appears and testifies, after fine.

ART. 450. When a witness has given bail either in the District Court, or before the Magistrate, for his appearance, the recognizance or bail bond may be enforced against such witness and his sureties, in the manner pointed out in Articles 407, 408, 409, and 410, for recovery upon the recognizance or bail bond of the defendant. Recognizance of witness enforced, how.

ART. 451. When no security was given by a witness, but his individual recognizance or bond was taken, judgment final may, upon his failure to appear, be entered against him for the amount in which he is bound; which judgment, however, he may have set aside by showing, at any time within twelve months after the rendition thereof, sufficient cause for his failure to attend. Judgment, where no security was given.

Act Feb. 15, 1858.

ART. 452. It shall be in the discretion of the Court to judge of the sufficiency of an excuse rendered by a witness.*

Act of Aug. 26, 1856.

ART. 453. The sureties of a witness have no right in any case, to discharge themselves by the surrender of such witness, after the forfeiture of their recognizance or bond.

Fees of witnesses in criminal cases.

ART. 454. Witnesses in criminal cases shall be allowed one dollar and fifty cents a day, for each day they are in attendance upon the Court, and six cents for each mile they may travel in going to or returning from the place of trial. But the State shall in no case pay costs as witness fees.

Act of February 15, 1858.

ART. 455. The State shall in no case pay witness fees.†

Act of Aug. 26, 1856.

ART. 457. Upon conviction, in all cases, the costs accruing from the attendance of witnesses, shall be taxed against the defendant.

3. *Service of a Copy of the Indictment.*

Copy of indictment delivered to defendant, in case of felony.

ART. 458. In every case of felony, when the accused is in custody, or as soon as he may be arrested, it shall be the duty of the Clerk of the Court, where an indictment has been presented, immediately to make out a correct copy of the same, and deliver such copy to the Sheriff, who shall immediately deliver the same to the defendant.

Act of Feb. 15, 1858.
May demand a copy, in misdemeanors.

ART. 459. In misdemeanors it shall not be necessary before trial to furnish the defendant with a copy of the indictment or information; but he or his counsel may demand a copy, which shall be given at as early a day as possible.

When defendant is on bail, in felony.

ART. 460. When the defendant in cases of felony is on bail at the time the indictment is presented, it is not necessary to serve him with a copy; but the Clerk shall deliver a copy of the same to the defendant or his counsel when requested, at the earliest possible time.

4. *Of Arraignment, and of Proceedings where no Arraignment is necessary.*

Act of Aug. 26, 1856.

ART. 461. There shall be no arraignment of a defendant except upon an indictment for a capital offence.

An arraignment for what purpose.

ART. 462. An arraignment takes place for the purpose of reading to the defendant the indictment against him, and hearing his answer thereto.

No arraignment until two days after service of copy, &c.

ART. 463. No arraignment shall take place until the expiration of at least two entire days after the day on which a copy of the indictment was served on the defendant, unless the right to such copy or to such delay be waived, or the defendant was on bail.

Act of Feb. 15, 1858.
Court shall appoint counsel, when.

ART. 466. When the defendant is brought into court for the purpose of being arraigned, if it appear that he has no counsel and is too poor to employ counsel, the Court shall appoint one or more practising attorneys to defend him, and the counsel so appointed shall have at least one day to prepare for trial.

Name as stated in indictment.

ART. 468. When the defendant is arraigned, his name, as stated in the indictment, shall be distinctly called; and, unless he suggest by himself or counsel, that he is not indicted by his true name, it shall be taken that his name is truly set forth, and he shall not thereafter be allowed to deny the same by way of defence.

ART. 469. If the defendant, or his counsel for him, suggest that he bears

* Amended Art. 455, is Art. 452 in the enrolled copy. † Amended Art. 458, is Art. 455 in the enrolled copy.

some name different from that stated in the indictment, the same shall be noted upon the minutes of the Court, the indictment amended, the style of the cause changed, so as to give his true name, and the cause proceed, as if the true name had been first recited in the indictment. If defendant suggest different name.

ART. 470. If the defendant allege that he is not indicted by his true name, and refuse to say what his real name is, the cause shall proceed as if the name stated in the indictment were true, and the defendant shall not be allowed to contradict the same by way of defence. If defendant refuse to give his real name.

ART. 471. Where a defendant is described as a person whose name is unknown, he may have the indictment so corrected as to give therein his true name. Act of Feb. 15, 1858. Where name is unknown, &c.

ART. 472. The name of the accused having been called, if no suggestion, such as is spoken of in the four preceding Articles, be made, or being made, is disposed of as before directed, the indictment shall be read, and the defendant asked whether he is guilty or not, as therein charged. Act of Aug. 26, 1856. Indictment read.

ART. 473. If the defendant answer that he is not guilty, the same shall be entered upon the minutes of the Court; if he refuse to answer, the plea of not guilty shall in like manner be entered. Plea of not guilty entered on the minutes of the Court.

ART. 475. If the defendant plead guilty, he shall be admonished by the Court of the consequences; and no such plea shall be received, unless it plainly appear that he is sane, and is uninfluenced by any considerations of fear, by any persuasion or delusive hope of pardon prompting him to confess his guilt. Plea of guilty not received, unless, &c.

ART. 476. Where a defendant persists in pleading guilty, if the punishment of the offence is not absolutely fixed by law, and beyond the discretion of the jury to graduate in any manner, a jury shall be impannelled to assess the punishment, and evidence submitted to enable them to decide thereupon. If defendant plead guilty, jury impannelled, &c.

ART. 477. The preceding article refers to offences of every description whether felonies or misdemeanors. Act of Feb. 15, 1858.

ART. 479. The same proceedings shall be had in cases of felony less than capital, with respect to the name of the defendant, and the amendment of the indictment, as are provided in Articles 468, 469, 470 and 471, with respect to such proceedings in capital cases. Act of Aug. 26, 1856. Same proceedings in cases less than capital

ART. 480. The plea of not guilty shall, in every criminal action, be entered where the defendant refuses to answer; and in all cases of felony, when a plea of guilty is offered, like proceedings shall be had as are directed in Articles 475 and 476, in relation to capital offences. Act of Feb. 15, 1858. Where defendant refuses to answer, plea of not guilty.

5. *Of the Pleadings in Criminal Actions.*

ART. 481. The primary pleading in criminal actions on the part of the State, is the indictment or information. Act of Feb. 15, 1858. Indictment, &c.

ART. 482. On the part of the defendant the following are the only pleadings: Act of Aug. 26, 1856. Pleadings on part of defendant.

1. The motion to set aside the indictment or information.

2. A special plea, setting forth one or more facts, as cause why the defendant ought not to be tried upon the indictment or information presented against him.

3. An exception to the indictment or information, for some matter of form or substance.

4. A plea of guilty.
5. A plea of not guilty.

Motion to set aside indictment, &c., for what causes, only.

ART. 483. A motion to set aside an indictment or information, shall be based on one or more of the following causes, and no other:

1. That it appears by the records of the Court, that the indictment was not found by at least twelve Grand Jurors, or that the information was not presented after oath made as required in Article 404.

2. That some person not authorized by law, was present when the Grand Jury were deliberating upon the accusation against the defendant, or were voting upon the same, and the issue of fact arising thereon, shall be tried by the Judge without a jury.

Only special pleas for defendant.

ART. 484. The only special pleas which can be heard for the defendant are:

1. That he has been before convicted, legally, in a court of competent jurisdiction, upon the same accusation, after having been tried upon the merits, for the same offence.

2. That he has been before acquitted by a jury, of the accusation against him, in a court of competent jurisdiction, whether the acquittal was regular or irregular.

3. That the Court before whom he is prosecuted has no jurisdiction to try the cause.

Special plea must be verified.

ART. 485. Every special plea shall be verified by the affidavit of the defendant.

What pleas tried by the Court, and what by a jury.

ART. 486. The plea to the jurisdiction shall be tried by the Court; all issues of fact, presented by a special plea, shall be tried by a jury.

Exceptions to the substance of an indictment.

ART. 487. There is no exception to the substance of an indictment or information, except:

1. That it does not appear from the face of the same, that any offence against the law was committed by the defendant.

2. That it appears from the indictment or information that a prosecution for the offence is barred by a lapse of time; or that the offence was committed after the finding of the indictment.

3. That it contains matter which is a legal defence or bar to the prosecution.

Exceptions to the form of an indictment.

ART. 488. Exceptions to the form of the indictment or information, may be taken for the following causes only:

1. That the indictment or information does not appear to have been presented in the proper Court, as required by Article 395 or 403.

2. The want of any other requisite of form prescribed by Articles 395 and 403, except the want of the signature of the foreman of the Grand Jury.

Act of Feb. 15, 1858. All motions, &c.

ART. 489. All motions to set aside an indictment or information, all special pleas and exceptions, shall be in writing.

Act of Aug. 26, 1856. Two days allowed defendant to plead, when.

ART. 490. Two entire days after the service of a copy of the indictment, shall be allowed in every case, (where the law requires such service to be made;) before the defendant can be compelled to file written pleadings.

Same subject.

ART. 491. In cases where no service of a copy is required, two entire days shall be allowed after the presentment of the indictment or information, for the defendant to file written pleadings.

Same subject.

ART. 492. The two preceding Articles refer to cases where a defendant has been arrested before indictment found, and is, at the time of the presentment of the same, on bail, or in custody.

ART. 493. If a criminal action be continued by the State, or by operation of law, the defendant may file his pleadings at any time on or before the second day of the term after such continuance, except in cases where an arraignment has already taken place. If case be continued by the State.

ART. 494. Two entire days as here and elsewhere used, mean two days exclusive of all fractions of a day. Two days mean, &c.

ART. 495. Where a defendant has never been arrested before indictment or information, and is arrested during the term of the Court at which the prosecution is commenced, he shall be allowed two entire days after his arrest, in which to file written pleadings; or if it be a case in which he is entitled to be served with a copy of the indictment, he shall be allowed to two entire days after service of a copy thereof. Where defendant is arrested during term, &c. time allowed for pleading.

ART. 496. If, after the adjournment of the Court, the arrest takes place, a defendant shall be allowed to file written pleadings at any time on or before the second day of the next term of the Court in which the prosecution is pending; where he is entitled to be served with a copy of the indictment, he may file such pleadings within two days after the service thereof; and if the service be made during vacation, he may file such pleadings at any time on or before the second day of the term of the Court next after receiving a copy of the indictment. Defendant arrested after adjournment, &c, time allowed for pleading.

ART. 496a. The time allowed the defendant in which to file his pleadings, as provided in articles 490, 491, 492, 493, 495, and 496, shall not be so construed as to preclude him from filing his pleadings at any time before the case is ready for trial, except in cases that may occur under the provisions of article 529 of this Code. Act of Feb. 15, 1858. May file pleadings before, &c.

ART. 497. The plea of "not guilty" shall be made orally, and noted upon the minutes of the Court. It shall be construed to be a denial of every material allegation in the indictment. Under the plea of "not guilty," evidence to establish the insanity of the defendant, and every fact whatever tending to acquit him of the accusation may be introduced, except such facts as, by Article 484, are proper for a special plea. Act of Aug. 26, 1856. Plea of "not guilty," made orally, construed to be, &c., what evidence admissable under it.

ART. 497a. The Court shall in all criminal cases dispose of the pleadings of the defendant in their order as at common law. Act of Feb. 15, 1858.

6. *Of the Argument and Decision of Motions, Pleas and Exceptions.*

ART. 498. In every case where a motion to set aside an indictment or information, or a special plea or exception, has been filed, the Court shall decide upon such pleadings at the earliest possible day consistent with a due administration of justice; and for that purpose shall, on the day set for the trial of the criminal docket, take up for argument and decision all such pleadings as are then filed. Act of Aug. 26, 1856. Court shall decide at earliest day possible, motions to set aside, &c.

ART. 499. The provisions of the preceding Article shall not preclude the hearing and determination at any other time, of all written pleadings which are to be tried by the Court. The same.

ART. 500. The counsel of the defendant has the right to open and conclude the argument in such cases. Defendant opens and concludes, when

ART. 501. Where the matters involved in any such written pleading, depend in whole or in part upon testimony either written or verbal, and not altogether upon the record of the Court, every process known to the law may be obtained, either on behalf of the State, or of the defendant, or the purpose of procuring Process of procuring testimony.

such testimony; but there shall be no delay on account of the want of the testimony; unless it be shown to the satisfaction of the Court, that all the means given by law have been used to procure the same.

Exceptions, special pleas, &c., heard together.

ART. 502. The motion to set aside an indictment, all exceptions and such special pleas as are to be tried by the Judge without a Jury, shall be heard together, and shall be decided without delay.

Special pleas setting forth matter of fact.

ART. 503. Such special pleas as set forth matter of fact proper to be tried by a Jury, shall be submitted and tried with the plea of "not guilty."

Where motion to set aside, &c. is sustained, in misdemeanor.

ART. 504. Where the motion to set aside an indictment, or information, or an exception to the same, is sustained, the defendant, in a case of misdemeanor, shall be discharged, but may be again prosecuted within the time allowed by law.

Act of Feb. 15, 1858.

In cases of felony.

ART. 505. If the motion to set aside, or the exception to the indictment or information in cases of felony be sustained, the defendant shall not therefore be discharged, but may be immediately recommitted by order of the Court, upon motion of the District Attorney, or without motion, and proceedings may afterwards be had against him as if no prosecution had ever been commenced.

Act of Aug. 26, 1856.

Shall be fully discharged, when.

ART. 506. Where, after the motion or exception is sustained, it is made known to the Court, by sufficient testimony that the offence of which the defendant is accused, will be barred by limitation before another indictment or information can be preferred, he shall in every case be fully discharged.

When exception is, that no offence is charged.

ART. 507. If an exception to an indictment or information, is made upon the ground that there is no offence against the law charged therein, the defendant shall be discharged, unless an affidavit be filed accusing him of the commission of an offence punishable by law.

When exception is on account of form.

ART. 508. When the exception to an indictment or information is merely on account of form, the same shall be amended, if decided to be defective, and the cause proceed upon such amended indictment or information.

Exception to special plea.

ART. 509. Where a special plea is filed by the defendant, the District Attorney may except to its sufficiency for substantial defects; and if the exception be sustained, the plea may be amended.

If plea be not excepted to.

ART. 510. If the plea be not excepted to, it shall be considered that issue has been taken upon the same.

Plea of former conviction, &c., in Justice's Court.

ART. 511. When a special plea alleges that the defendant has been before acquitted or convicted of the same offence, upon a trial in a Justice's Court, and it appears on the trial, from the facts proved, or the law governing the case, the Court had no jurisdiction, the former conviction or acquittal shall have no effect whatever, and it is not necessary for the District Attorney to reply to the plea in order to present the question of jurisdiction.

Plea of not guilty allowed, where motion, &c., has been overruled.

ART. 512. Judgment shall in no case be given against the defendant, where his motion, exception, or plea is overruled; but he shall in all cases be allowed to plead not guilty. If he refuse to plead, it shall be considered as if the plea were offered, and be noted accordingly.

7. *Of Continuance.*

Continuance by operation of law when.

ART. 513. Criminal actions are considered as continued by operation of law, when there is not sufficient time for trial at any particular term of a Court, or where the defendant has not been arrested.

ART. 514. The trial of a criminal action may be postponed on the written application of the State or of the defendant, upon sufficient cause shown. May be continued, when.

ART. 515. Upon the first application by the District Attorney, he shall make a statement in writing, in which he shall set forth the cause for continuance; and if the same be asked on account of the absence of a witness, he must set forth that the testimony is material, and that the process authorized by law has been issued or applied for, or must show some sufficient excuse for failing to apply therefor. The issuance of, or application for a subpœna, shall not be considered due diligence in cases where the law authorizes the issuance of an attachment. First application by District Attorney.

ART. 516. The District Attorney, on any subsequent application for a continuance must also set forth in writing, the facts he expects to establish by the witness, and must state that he expects to be able to procure his attendance at the next term of the Court. Subsequent application by District Attorney.

ART. 517. If the cause of continuance be any other than the want of attendance on the part of a witness, the District Attorney shall distinctly set it forth in his written application. If the cause of continuance be, &c.

ART. 518. It shall be sufficient, upon the first application by the defendant, for a continuance, if the same be for want of a witness, to state: First application by defendant shall state.

1. The name of the witness and his residence, if known, or that his residence is not known.

2. The diligence which has been used to procure his attendance; and it shall not be considered sufficient diligence to have caused to be issued, or to have applied for a subpœna, in cases where the law authorizes the issuance of an attachment.

3. The facts which are expected to be proved by the witness; and it must appear to the Court that they are material.

4. The witness is not absent by the procurement or consent of the defendant.

5. That the application for continuance is not made for delay.

ART. 519. Subsequent applications for continuance, on the part of the defendant shall, in addition to the requisites in the preceding article, state also: Act of Feb, 15, 1858. Subsequent applications by defendant.

1. That the testimony cannot be procured from any other source.

2. That the defendant has a reasonable expectation of procuring the same at the next term of the Court.

ART. 520. A criminal action may be continued on the application of the defendant, for good cause other than the absence of a witness; but he shall in all cases set forth fully and distinctly the ground on which the continuance is asked. Act of Aug. 26, 1856. Other causes for continuance.

ART. 521. All applications for continuance on the part of the defendant, must be sworn to by himself. Applications by defendant must be sworn to.

ART. 522. It shall not be necessary to file any written motion for continuance; the motion based upon the written statement may be made orally. Written motions not necessary.

ART. 524. If a defendant in a capital case demand a trial, and it appear that more than one continuance has been granted to the State, and that the defendant has not before applied for a continuance, he shall be entitled to be admitted to bail, and unless it appear from the written statement of the District Attorney, or by the oath of some credible person, that a material witness of the State had been prevented from attendance by the procurement of the defendant or some person acting in his behalf. Act of Feb. 15, 1858. If more than one continuance has been granted to the State, in capital case, &c.

ART. 526. A continuance may be granted on the application of the defendant

Continuance after trial commenced, when. or District Attorney after the trial has commenced, when it is made to appear to the satisfaction of the Court, that by some unexpected occurrence the trial commenced, which no reasonable diligence could have anticipated, the defendant or District Attorney is so taken by surprise that a fair trial cannot be had, or the trial may be postponed to a subsequent day of the term.

8. *Change of Venue.*

Act of Feb. 15, 1858. Change of venue, when granted on applicat'n of defendant.

ART. 527. A change of venue may be granted on the written application of the defendant, supported by his own affidavit, and the affidavit of at least two credible persons, residents of the county where the prosecution is instituted, for either of the following causes, the truth and sufficiency of which the Court shall determine:

1. That there exists in the county where the prosecution is commenced so great a prejudice, against him that he cannot obtain a fair and impartial trial.

2. That there is a dangerous combination against him instigated by influential persons, by reason of which he cannot expect a fair trial.

Act of Aug. 26, 1856. Where jury cannot be procured for trial of felony.

ART. 528. Where an unsuccessful effort has been once made in any county to procure a jury for the trial of a felony, and all reasonable means have been used, if it be made to appear to the Court, by the written affidavit of the District Attorney, or any other credible person, that no jury can probably be had in that county, the Court may order a change of venue, and cause the reasons therefor to be placed upon the minutes of the proceedings.

Act of Feb. 15, 1858. Venue shall not be changed until

ART. 529. The venue shall not in any case be changed on the written application of the defendant, until after all motions, special pleas, and exceptions have been filed and acted on by the Court, and if overruled the plea of not guilty entered.

Act of Aug. 26, 1856. Venue changed to nearest county, unless.

ART. 530. Upon the grant of a change of venue, the criminal cause shall be removed to some adjoining county, the court house of which is nearest to the court house of the county where the prosecution is pending, unless it be made to appear in the application that such nearest county is subject to some objection, sufficient to authorize a change of venue in the first instance.

Court may exercise discretion, when.

ART. 531. If it be shown in the application for a change of venue or otherwise, that all the counties adjoining that in which the prosecution is pending, are subject to some valid objection, the cause may be removed to such county as the Court may think proper.

Clerk's duties in case of change of venue.

ART. 532. When an order for a change of venue has been made, the clerk of the court, where the prosecution is pending, shall make out a true transcript of all the orders made in the cause, and shall transmit the same to the proper county, and shall send the original papers also with the transcript.

The same.

ART. 533. The clerk shall also make a correct copy of all the original papers where a change of venue is ordered, and shall retain such copy in his office, to be used in case the originals, or any of them be lost.

If defendant be on bail shall be recognized.

ART. 534. When a change of venue is ordered, and the defendant is on bail, he shall be required to enter into recognizance forthwith, conditioned for his appearance before the proper Court, at the next succeeding term thereof; or if the Court of the county to which the cause is taken be then in session, he shall be recognized to appear before said Court, on a day fixed, and no change of venue shall take effect until after the defendant has been so recognized.

If defendant be in custody.

ART. 535. When the venue is changed in any criminal action, if the defendant be in custody, an order shall be made for his removal to the proper county, and his delivery to the Sheriff thereof before the next succeeding term of the District Court of the county to which the case is to be taken; and he shall be removed by the Sheriff accordingly, and delivered as directed in the order.

ART. 536. If the District Court of the county to which the case is removed be then in session, the defendant shall be removed forthwith, and delivered to the Sheriff of such county. If the court to which the case is removed be in session.

9. *Of Dismissing Prosecutions.*

ART. 537. When a defendant has been detained in custody, or held to bail for his appearance to answer any criminal accusation before the District Court, the prosecution unless otherwise ordered by the Court, for good cause shown, supported by affidavit, shall be dismissed and the bail discharged, if indictment or information be not presented against such defendant at the next term of the Court which is held after his commitment or admission to bail. If defendant be held to bail, &c., if no indictment be presented, &c., shall be discharged.

ART. 538. The District Attorney may, by permission of the Court, dismiss a criminal action at any time. Dist't Attorney may dismiss.

TITLE V.

OF TRIAL AND ITS INCIDENTS.

CHAPTER I.

OF THE MODE OF TRIAL.

ART. 539. The only mode of trial upon issues of fact, in the District Court, is by a jury of twelve men, unless in cases specially excepted. Act of Aug. 26, 1856. By a jury of, &c.

ART. 540. In all prosecutions for felonies the defendant must be personally present on the trial; and he must likewise be present in all cases of indictment or information for misdemeanors where the punishment is imprisonment in jail. Defendant must be present on trial, when.

ART. 541. In all other cases of misdemeanor the defendant may appear by counsel if he has given bail, and the trial proceed without his personal presence; and he may, by consent of the District Attorney, appear by counsel in such cases where he has not given bail. Need not be present, when.

ART. 542. When the defendant, in a case of felony, is on bail, he shall, before the trial commences, be placed in the custody of the Sheriff, and his bail be considered as discharged. If on bail, in felony, shall be placed in custody of Sheriff.

ART. 543. If there be a mis-trial in a case of felony, the original sureties of the defendant shall be still held bound for his appearance until they surrender him in open Court. Act of Feb. 15, 1858. In case of mis-trial, &c.

ART. 544. There shall be kept by each District Clerk a criminal docket, in which shall be set down the style of each criminal action, the nature of the offence, the names of counsel and the proceedings had at each term of the Court. Act of Aug. 26, 1856. Criminal docket shall be kept.

Court on first day of term shall fix a day for taking up criminal docket

ART. 545. The District Court shall, on the first day of its organization at each term, fix a day for taking up the criminal docket, which shall be noted on the minutes; but in case of failure to make such order the criminal docket may be taken up on any day not earlier than the third day of the term.

In cases less than capital, defendant shall plead, &c.

ART. 546. In cases of felony less than capital and of misdemeanor, the defendant is required, when his cause is called for trial, before it proceeds further, to plead by himself or counsel whether or not he is guilty.

Term "called for trial" defin'd

ART. 547. By the term "called for trial" is meant the stage of the cause when both parties have announced that they are ready, or when a continuance being applied for has been denied.

CHAPTER II.

FORMATION OF THE JURY.

Act of Aug. 26, 1856.

In capital cases, District Attorney may apply for special venire.

ART. 548. When there is pending in any District Court, a criminal action for a capital offence, the District Attorney may, at any time after indictment found, on motion, obtain an order for summoning any number of persons not less than thirty-six nor more than sixty, as may be deemed advisable, from whom the jury for the trial of such capital case is to be selected.

Special venire facias.

ART. 549. The Clerk shall, upon this order, forthwith issue a writ to the Sheriff, commanding him to summon the number of persons named in the order to appear on a certain day therein named, to act as jurors. This writ is called "a special venire facias."

Court shall caution Sheriff to summon, &c.

ART. 550. The court, in granting the order, shall, in every case, caution and direct the Sheriff to summon such men as have legal qualifications to serve on juries, informing him of what those qualifications are; and shall further direct him, as far as he may be able, to summon men of good character, and such as are not prejudiced against the defendant or biased in his favor, if he knows of the existence of such bias or prejudice.

Sheriff who shall wilfully summon, &c.

ART. 551. Any Sheriff who shall wilfully summon, under a special venire facias, persons whom he knows to be biased or prejudiced in favor of, or against the defendant, is guilty of an offence.

Sheriff shall summon jurors.

ART. 552. The Sheriff, so soon as he receives the order, shall proceed to summon the jurors, and make return of the same to the Clerk of the Court.

Copy of persons summoned delivered to defendant.

ART. 553. The Clerk, immediately upon receiving the list of the names of the persons summoned under a special venire facias, shall make a copy thereof, and shall furnish the same to the Sheriff, who shall deliver such copy to the defendant.

One day's service of copy before trial.

ART. 554. No defendant, in a capital case, shall be brought to trial, until he has had one day's service of a copy of the names of persons summoned under a special venire facias, except where he waives the right. But the service may be made at any time after indictment found, whether before or after arraignment.

ART. 555. When any capital case is called for trial, the list of persons summoned as jurors shall be called at the courthouse door, and such as are not present may be fined by the court a sum not exceeding fifty dollars. Juror failing to attend.

ART. 556. In forming the jury, the names of the persons summoned shall be called in the order they stand upon the list, and, if present, shall be tried as to their qualifications, and, unless challenged, shall be impannelled. How jury formed.

ART. 557. When any person is not present at the time his name is called in the proper order, an attachment may, at the request of the State, or of the defendant, issue for him; but no cause shall be unreasonably delayed on account of the absence of such person. Attachment may issue for absent juror.

ART. 558. A person summoned, who is not present, may, upon his appearance before the jury is completed, be impannelled as a juror, unless challenged. Appearing before jury is complete may be impannelled.

ART. 559. In impannelling the jury, the person to be tried as to his qualifications shall first be sworn in every case to answer questions, and shall be interrogated touching his qualifications, as pointed out in Chapter III, of this Title. Juror examined under oath, touching qualification.

ART. 561. The regular jury for the term shall try all offences not capital, unless challenged for cause, in which event the pannel shall be filled by surrounding talesman; and if more jurors are required to enable the court to proceed with the business of the term, the Sheriff shall supply them from the bystanders. Act of February 15, 1858. Regular jury shall try all offences, unless.

ART. 563. The oath administered to a juror in criminal cases, shall be as follows: The oath of juror.

"You solemnly swear that in the case of the State of Texas against (A. B.) the defendant, you will a true verdict render according to the law and evidence, so help you God."

ART. 565a. Where the list of persons summoned for the trial of a criminal cause is exhausted by challenges or otherwise, or where the persons summoned do not attend, talesmen shall be summoned upon the verbal order of the court, until the jury is completed. Where pannel is exhausted.

CHAPTER III.

OF CHALLENGES.

ART. 566. A challenge is an objection to the impannelling of a Juror, made either by the State or by the defendant. Act of Aug. 26, 1856.

ART. 567. A challenge is either to the array or to a single Juror. Either to the array or to Juror.

State may challenge array, when.

ART. 568. The array of Jurors summoned for the trial of any criminal action, may be challenged by the State, when it can be shown that the officer summoning the Jurors has acted corruptly, and has wilfully summoned Jurors with a view to securing an acquittal.

Defendant may challenge array, when.

ART. 569. The defendant may challenge the array for the following cause only:

That the officer summoning the Jury has acted corruptly, and has wilfully summoned persons upon the Jury known to be prejudiced against the defendant, and with a view to cause him to be convicted.

Two kinds of challenges.

ART. 570. Challenges to individual Jurors are of two kinds, *peremptory* and *for cause.*

A peremptory challenge.

ART. 571. A peremptory challenge is made to a Juror without assigning any reason therefor.

Number of challenges in capital cases.

ART. 572. In capital cases the defendant shall be entitled to twenty peremptory challenges, and the State to ten, and where there are more defendants than one tried together, each defendant shall be entitled to twelve peremptory challenges, and the State to six for each defendant.

In felonies not capital, number of challenges.

ART. 573. In prosecutions for felonies not capital, the defendant shall be entitled to ten peremptory challenges and the State to five, and where more defendants than one are tried together, each defendant shall be entitled to six peremptory challenges, and the State to three for each defendant.

In misdemeanors.

ART. 574. In misdemeanors, the State and defendant shall be each entitled to five peremptory challenges; and if there are more defendants than one tried together, each defendant shall be entitled to three peremptory challenges.

A challenge for cause is. May be made for what reasons

ART. 575. A challenge for cause is an objection made to a particular Juror, alleging some fact which renders him incapable or unfit to serve on the Jury. It may be made for either of the following reasons:

1. That the juror has been convicted of some offence which, by law, disqualifies him from serving on a Jury.

2. That his name is not upon the list required to be kept by the County Court from which Jurors are drawn.

3. That he is not twenty-one years of age, a qualified elector under the Constitution and Laws, a resident of the proper county and a householder in that county, or freeholder in the State.

4. That he is insane, or has such a defect in the organs of seeing, feeling or hearing, or such bodily or mental defect or disease as renders him unfit for jury service.

These are called principal causes of challenge.

Act of Feb. 15, 1858.

Causes of challenge to Juror.

ART. 576. The following are also causes of challenge to a juror:

1. That he is related by consanguinity or affinity to the defendant, or is his master or guardian.

2. That he is related by consanguinity or affinity to the person injured by the commission of the offence, or to the private prosecutor, if there be one.

3. That he served on the Grand Jury which found the indictment.

4. That he served on the petit jury in a former trial of the same case.

5. That he has a bias or prejudice in favor of or against the defendant.

6. That, from hearsay or otherwise, there is established in the mind of the juror, such a conclusion as to the guilt or innocence of the defendant as will influence him in his action in finding the verdict.

For the purpose of ascertaining whether the last cause of challenge exists, the juror shall be first asked, whether in his opinion the conclusion, so established, will influence his verdict. If he shall answer in the affirmative, he shall be discharged. If he answer in the negative he shall be further examined by the Court, or under its directions, as to how his conclusion was formed, and the extent to which it will affect his action; and if the court is not satisfied, from such examination, that he is impartial, the juror shall be discharged.

7. That the juror has conscientious scruples in regard to the infliction of the punishment of death, for crime. This cause of challenge is only applicable to capital cases.

ART. 577. In testing the qualifications of a Juror, he shall himself be sworn to answer questions, and any other proof may be also heard touching the subject; but a Juror shall not be asked a question the answer to which may show that he has been convicted of an offence which disqualifies him. *Act of Aug 26, 1856. Testing the qualification of Juror.*

ART. 578. No Juror shall, on the trial of any criminal action for felony, be impanneled when it appears that he is subject to either the first, third or fourth cause of challenge mentioned in Article 575, although both parties may consent, and it is the duty of the Court, in every case of felony, to cause questions to be asked the Juror for the purpose of testing his qualifications, under the second and third subdivisions of said Article. *Shall not be impannelled, when.*

ART. 579. The Court is the Judge, after proper examination, of the qualifications of a Juror. *The Court is Judge of qualifications.*

CHAPTER IV.

OF THE TRIAL BEFORE THE JURY.

ART. 580. A jury having been impannelled in any criminal action, the cause shall proceed to trial in the following order: *Act of Aug 26, 1856. Order of proceedings in trial.*

1. The indictment or information shall be read to the jury by the District Attorney.

2. The special pleas, if any, shall be read by the defendant's counsel, and if the plea of not guilty is also relied upon, it shall also be so stated.

3. The District Attorney, or the counsel prosecuting in his absence, shall state to the jury the nature of the accusation and the facts which are expected to be proved by the State in support thereof.

4. The testimony on the part of the State shall be introduced.

5. The nature of the defences relied upon shall be stated by the counsel of the defendant, and what are the facts expected to be proved in their support.

6. The testimony on the part of the defendant shall be offered.

7. Rebutting testimony may be offered on the part of the State, and of the defendant.

Testimony allowed at any time before, &c., if, &c.

ART. 581. The Court shall allow testimony to be introduced at any time before the argument of a cause is concluded, if it appear that it is necessary to a due administration of justice.

Witnesses placed under rule.

ART. 582. At the request of either party, the witnesses on both sides may be sworn and placed in the custody of an officer, and removed out of the court room to some place where they cannot hear the testimony as delivered by any other witness in the cause. This is termed placing witnesses under rule.

Witnesses under rule kept separate, or.

ART. 583. When witnesses are placed under rule, those summoned for the prosecution may be kept separate from those summoned for the defence; or they may be all kept together, as the Court shall direct.

Shall be attended by an officer.

ART. 584. Witnesses, when under rule, shall be attended by an officer, and all their reasonable wants provided for, unless the Court in its discretion direct that they be allowed to go at large.

Order of argument regulated by the Judge; but State shall conclude.

ART. 585. When a criminal cause is to be argued, the order of argument may be regulated by the presiding Judge; but in all cases, the State's counsel shall have the right to make the concluding address to the jury.

In prosecutions for felony, two addresses on each side.

ART. 586. In prosecutions for felony the Court shall never restrict the argument to a less number of addresses than two on each side.

Defendants may sever.

ART. 587. Where two or more defendants are jointly prosecuted, they may sever on the trial, at the request of either.

District Attorney may dismiss as to one, who may be witness.

ART. 588. The District Attorney may at any time dismiss a prosecution, as to one or more defendants, jointly indicted with others; and the person so discharged, may be introduced as a witness by either party.

Where there is no evidence against a defendant, jointly prosecuted.

ART. 589. When it is apparent that there is no evidence against a defendant, in any case where he is jointly prosecuted with others, the jury may be directed to find a verdict as to such defendant; and if they acquit, he may be introduced as a witness in the case.

Where it appears the Court has no jurisdiction, &c.

ART. 590. Where it appears in the course of a trial that the Court has no jurisdiction of the offence, or that the facts charged in the indictment do not constitute an offence, the jury shall be discharged.

In such case Court may commit, when.

ART. 591. If the want of jurisdiction arises from the fact that the defendant is not liable to prosecution in the county where the indictment was presented, the Court may, in cases of felony, order the defendant into custody for a reasonable length of time, to await a warrant for his arrest from the proper county; or if the offence be bailable, may require the defendant to enter into recognizance to answer before the proper Court.

In misdemeanor where Court has no jurisdiction.

ART. 592. In cases of misdemeanor, where it appears on the trial that the Court has no jurisdiction, the defendant shall be discharged.

The jury are judges of facts.

ART. 593. The jury are the exclusive judges of the facts in every criminal cause, but not of the law in any case. They are bound to receive the law from the Court, and be governed thereby.

ART. 594. After the argument of any criminal cause has been concluded, the Judge shall deliver to the Jury a written charge, in which he shall distinctly set forth the law applicable to the case; but he shall not express any opinion as to the weight of evidence, nor shall he sum up the testimony. This charge shall be given in all cases of felony, whether asked or not. Charge to the jury.

ART. 595. It is beyond the province of a Judge sitting in criminal causes, to discuss the facts or use any argument in his charge, calculated to rouse the sympathy or excite the passion of a jury. It is his duty to state plainly the law of the case. Judge shall not discuss the facts.

ART. 596. After or before the charge of the court to the jury, the counsel on both sides may present written instructions, and ask that they be given to the Jury. The court shall either give or refuse these charges, with or without modification, and certify thereto; and when the court shall modify a charge, it shall be done in writing, and in such manner to clearly show what the modification is. Instructions asked by the parties.

ART. 597. The general charge given by the court, as well as those given or refused at the request of either party, shall be certified by the Judge, and, in case of appeal, constitute a part of the record of the cause. Charges shall be certified by the Judge.

ART. 598. In criminal actions for misdemeanor, the court is not required to charge the jury, except at the request of the counsel on either side; but, when so requested, shall give or refuse such charges, with or without modification, as are asked in writing. No charge in misdemeanors, except

ART. 599. No verbal charge shall be given in any case whatever, except in cases of misdemeanor; and then only by consent of the parties. No verbal charge, except.

ART. 600. When charges are asked, the Judge shall read to the jury only such as he gives. Judge shall read to jury only such charges as he gives.

ART. 601. If the jury request it, a copy of the charges given shall be taken with them to their room; but in cases where charges have been asked, and some have been given and some refused, the Clerk shall copy for them such as were given; and those refused shall in no case be given to the jury. Copy of charges given to jury, when.

ART. 602. Whenever it appears by the record in any criminal action, taken to the Supreme Court upon appeal by the defendant, that the instructions given to the jury were verbal, (except where so given by consent in a case of misdemeanor,) or that the District Judge has departed from any of the requirements of the eight preceding articles, the judgment shall be reversed, provided it appears by the record, that the defendant excepted to the order or action of the court at the time of the trial. Where verbal instructions are given, &c.

ART. 603. On the trial of any criminal action, the defendant, by himself or counsel, may tender his bill of exceptions to any decision, opinion, order or charge of the court; and the Judge shall sign such bill of exceptions, under the rules prescribed in civil suits, in order that such decision, opinion, order or charge may be revised upon appeal to the Supreme Court. Bill of exceptions.

ART. 604. A statement of the facts in a criminal action, shall be agreed upon by the Disirict Attorney and the defendant, or his counsel; and when they fail to agree, the same shall be made out and certified, as directed in civil suits. In preparing a statement of facts, the rules in civil suits shall apply, as to the manner and form of preparing and sending up the same. Statement of facts.

ART. 605. After a jury has been sworn and impannelled to try any case of felony, they shall not be permitted to separate until they have returned a In case of felony, jury shall not separate, unless. verdict, unless by permission of the court, with the consent of the District Attorney and the defendant, and in charge of an officer.

Sheriff shall provide jury with, &c. ART. 606. It is the duty of the Sheriff to provide a suitable room for the deliberation of the jury, in all criminal cases, and to supply them with such necessary food and lodging as he can obtain; but no spirituous, vinous, or malt liquor, of any kind, shall be furnished them.

No person shall converse with juryman, except. ART. 607. The Sheriff shall take care that no person converses with a juryman after he has been impannelled to try a criminal action, except in the presence and by permission of the court.

Bailiff shall attend jury. ART. 608. In order to supply all the reasonable wants of the jury, and for the purpose of keeping them together and preventing intercourse with any other person, the Sheriff shall see that one or more bailiffs are constantly in attendance upon them.

Officer shall not be in room with jury. ART. 609. No officer who is in attendance upon the jury, shall be permitted to be in the room with them while they have a case under consideration. The officer, however, shall always remain sufficiently near to answer to any call made upon him by the jury.

Jury shall take all papers in the case. ART. 610. The jury may take with them, on retiring to consider of their verdict, all the original papers in the cause, and any papers used as evidence.

Foreman appointed. ART. 611. The jury, in all cases, shall appoint one of their body foreman, in order that their deliberations may be conducted with regularity and order.

Jury may communicate with the court. ART. 612. When the jury wish to communicate with the court, they shall make their wish known to the Sheriff, who shall inform the court thereof, and they may be brought into the court house.

How communicate. ART. 613. When a jury comes into the court house, for the purpose of communicating with the Judge, they shall, through their foreman, state their object.

Jury may ask further instruction. ART. 614. The jury, after having retired, may ask further instruction of the Judge touching any matter of law, which shall be given them in writing; but no charge shall be given, except upon the particular point on which it is asked.

Jury may have witness re examined, when. ART. 615. If the jury disagree as to the statement of any particular witness, they may, upon applying to the court, have such witness again brought upon the stand, and he shall be directed by the Judge to detail his testimony in respect to the particular point of disagreement, and no other; and he shall be further instructed to make his statement in the language used upon his examination as nearly as he can.

If a juror has knowledge of a fact connected with the cause. ART. 616. If any juror has knowledge of a fact connected with the cause on trial, it is his duty to make it known before the cause is finally submitted. Should he fail to do this, he may come into the court with the other jurors, after their retirement, and shall be sworn as a witness, and give his testimony.

Defendant shall be present, when. ART. 617. In every case of felony, the defendant shall be present in the court when any such proceeding is had, as mentioned in the three next preceding articles. His counsel shall also be called. In cases of misdemeanor, the defendant need not be personally present.

If juror become sick, after retirement. ART. 618. If, after the retirement of the jury, any one of them become so sick as to prevent the continuance of his duty, or any accident or circumstance occur to prevent their being kept together, the jury may be discharged.

ART. 619. The jury may be discharged after the cause is submitted to them, when they cannot agree, and both parties consent to their discharge, or where they have been kept together for such time as to render it altogether improbable they can agree; in this latter case, the court, in its discretion, may discharge them. *Disagreement of jury.*

ART. 620. A final adjournment of the court, before the jury have agreed upon a verdict, discharges them. *Final adjournment of court discharges jury.*

ART. 621. In all the cases enumerated in articles 618, 619, and 620, where the jury is discharged without giving a verdict, the cause may be again tried at the same or another term. *When jury is discharged, case continued.*

ART. 622. The court may, during the retirement of the jury, proceed to any other business and adjourn from time to time, but shall be deemed open for all purposes connected with the case before the jury. *During retirement of jury, court may proceed, &c.*

CHAPTER V.

OF THE VERDICT.

ART. 623. When the Jury have agreed upon a verdict they shall be brought into Court by the proper officer; and if, when asked, they answer that they have agreed, the verdict shall be read aloud by the Clerk; and if in proper form, and no Juror dissents therefrom, and neither party requests to have the Jury polled, the verdict shall be entered upon the minutes of the Court. *Act of Aug. 26, 1856. When the jury have agreed upon a verdict.*

ART. 624. It is the right either of the State or of the defendant, to have the Jury polled, which is done by calling separately the name of each Juror, and asking him if it is his verdict. If all, when asked, answer in the affirmative the verdict shall be entered upon the minutes; but if any Juror answer in the negative, the Jury shall retire again to consider of their verdict. *Polling the jury.*

ART. 625. In cases of felony, the defendant must be present where the verdict is read, unless he escape after the commencement of the trial of the cause; but in cases of misdemeanor it may be received and read in his absence. *Defendant must be present when*

ART. 626. The verdict in every criminal action, must be general; when there are special pleas upon which the jury are to find, they must say in their verdict that the matters alledged in such pleas are either true or untrue; where the plea is not guilty, they must find that the defendant is either "guilty" or "not guilty;" and in addition thereto they shall assess the punishment in all cases where the same is not absolutely fixed by law, to some particular penalty. *The verdict must be.*

ART. 627. If the jury find a verdict which is informal, their attention shall be called to it; and with their consent, the verdict may, under the direction of the Court, be reduced to proper form. *Informal verdict.*

ART. 628. If the Jury refuse to have the verdict altered, they shall again retire to their room to deliberate, unless it manifestly appear that the verdict *If jury refuse to alter verdict.*

is intended as an acquittal; and in that case, the judgment shall be rendered accordingly, discharging the defendant.

Judgment on acquittal, judgment on conviction.

ART. 629. In every case of acquittal, judgment shall be entered immediately upon the verdict discharging the defendant. But in case of a conviction for a felony, no judgment shall be rendered on the verdict, until the expiration of the time allowed for making a motion for a new trial, or in arrest of judgment.

Where offence of different degrees is charged

ART. 630. Where a prosecution is for an offence consisting of different degrees, the Jury may find the defendant not guilty of the higher degree, (naming it,) but guilty of any degree inferior to that charged in the indictment.

Act of Feb. 15, 1858.

Offences of different degrees.

ART. 631. The following offences include different degrees:

1. Murder, which includes all the lesser degrees of culpable homicide.

2. Maiming, which includes disfiguring, wounding, aggravated assaults and batteries, and simple assaults and batteries.

3. Arson, which includes every malicious burning made penal by law.

4. Burglary, which includes every species of house-breaking, and of theft from a house.

5. Theft, which includes all unlawful acquisitions of personal property, punishable by the penal code.

6. Every offence against the person, includes within it, assaults with intent to commit said offence, when such assault is a violation of the penal law.

7. Every offence includes within it an attempt to commit the offence, when such attempt is made penal by law.

Act of Aug. 26, 1856.

ART. 632. Where several defendants are tried together, the Jury may convict such of the defendants as they deem guilty and acquit others.

Where several defendants are tried together.

ART. 633. Where the Jury, on the trial of several defendants, agree to a verdict as to one or more, and cannot agree as to others, they may find a verdict as to those in regard to whom they agree, and judgment shall be rendered accordingly; and the case, as to the rest may be tried by another Jury.

Where verdict of guilty in felony.

ART. 634. When a verdict of guilty is rendered in any case of felony, the defendant shall remain in custody to await the judgement of the Court thereon.

In case of acquittal.

ART. 635. In all cases of acquittal the defendant shall be immediately discharged, unless he is held in custody on some other criminal accusation.

Acquittal for insanity.

ART. 636. When the defendant is acquitted on the ground of insanity, the Jury shall so state in their verdict.

Verdict on a plea of guilty, plea of "guilty" by person insane.

ART. 637. When a jury has been impannelled to assess the punishment upon a plea of "guilty," they shall say in their verdict what the punishment is which they assess; but where the Jury are of opinion that a person pleading guilty is insane, they shall so report to the Court, and an issue as to that fact shall be tried before another Jury; and if upon such trial it be found that the defendant is insane, such proceedings shall be had as are directed in Chapter II, Title VIII, Part III, of this Code.

CHAPTER VI.

OF EVIDENCE IN CRIMINAL ACTIONS.

1. *General Rules.*

Act of Aug. 26 1856.

Rules of common law shall govern, except.

ART. 638. The rules of evidence known to the common law of England, both in civil and criminal cases, shall govern in the trial of criminal actions in this State, except where they are in conflict with the provisions of this Code or of some Statute of the State.

Rules of the statute law shall govern, when.

ART. 639. The rules of evidence prescribed by the Satute Law of this State, in civil suits, shall so far as applicable, govern also in criminal actions, when not in conflict with the provisions of this Code or of the Penal Code.

Defendant presumed to be innocent, reasonable doubt.

ART. 640. A defendant in a criminal cause is presumed to be innocent until his guilt is established by legal evidence; and in case of reasonable doubt as to his guilt he is entitled to be acquitted.

Defendant may be convicted of lower degree of crime, than charged.

ART. 641. Where a defendant is prosecuted for an offence which includes within it lesser degrees of crime, he may, if the evidence be sufficient, be convicted of any of the lower degrees included within the higher.

Conviction of a lower, considered as acquittal of higher offence.

ART. 642. If a defendant prosecuted for an offence which includes within it lesser degrees, be convicted of an offence lower than that for which he is indicted, and a new trial be granted him, or the judgment be arrested for any cause other than the want of jurisdiction, the verdict upon the first trial shall be considered an acquittal of the higher offence; but he may upon a second trial be convicted of the same offence of which he was before convicted, or any other inferior thereto.

Jury the judges of facts, except.

ART. 643. The Jury in all cases are the exclusive judges of the facts proved and of the weight to be given to the testimony, except where it is provided by law that proof of any particular fact is to be taken as either conclusive or presumptive proof of the existence of another fact, or where the law directs that a certain degree of weight is to be attached to a certain species of evidence.

2. *Of Persons who may Testify.*

Act of Feb. 15, 1858. Persons incompetent to testify.

ART. 644. The following persons only are incompetent to testify in criminal actions:

1. Insane persons, who are in an insane condition of mind at the time when they are offered as witnesses, or who were in that condition when the events happened of which they are called to testify.

2. Children, or other persons who, after being examined by the Court, appear not to possess sufficient intellect to relate transactions with respect to which they are interrogated, or who do not understand the obligation of an oath.

3. A slave or free person of color shall not testify, except where the prosecution is against a person who is a slave or free person of color.

4. In prosecutions for seduction, under the provisions of the penal code, the female alledged to have been so seduced.

5. All persons who have been, or who may be convicted of felony in this, or in any other State of the United States, or in any other State or Kingdom, notwithstanding such person or persons may have been pardoned for such crime, unless the pardon so obtained shall, by its terms, specifically restore his competency to testify in a Court of Justice, or unless his competency be otherwise restored by the proper authorities of this State.

Act of Aug. 26, 1856. Court may interrogate witness touching competency.

ART. 645. The Court may, upon suggestion made, or of its own option, interrogate a person who is offered as a witness, for the purpose of ascertaining whether he is competent to testify, according to the rules laid down in the preceding Article, or any other Article of this Code.

All other persons competent witnesses.

ART. 646. All other persons except those enumerated in the preceding Article, whatever may be the relationship between the defendant and witness, are competent to testify, except that an Attorney at law, shall not disclose a communication made to him by his client during the existence of that relationship.

Husband or wife shall not testify as to, &c.

ART. 647. Neither husband or wife shall, in any case, testify as to communications made by one to the other while married; nor shall they, after the marriage relation ceases, be made witnesses as to any such communication made while the marriage relation subsisted, except in a case where one or the other is prosecuted for an offence, and a declaration or communication made by the wife to the husband, or by the husband to the wife, goes to extenuate or justify an offence for which either is on trial.

Common law rules not applicable, when. Husband and wife shall not testify against each other, except, &c.

ART. 648. No rule of the common law which excludes a witness on account of the existence of any particular relationship to the defendant, as of husband and wife, shall have any force, except where it is in express accordance with the provisions of this Code or of some other Statutory Law of the State. The husband and wife can in no case testify against each other, except in a criminal prosecution for an offence committed by one against the other; but they may, in all criminal prosecutions, be witnesses for each other.

Witness not incompetent on account of religious belief.

ART. 649. No witness is incompetent to testify on account of his having any particular faith upon religious subjects, provided he believes in the existence of a Supreme Being.

Judge of the Court a competent witness.

ART. 650. The Judge of the Court trying an offence is a competent witness for either the State or defendant, and may be sworn upon the trial. But in such case it is in his discretion to order the trial to be postponed and to take place before some other Judge.

ART. 651. When it is proposed to offer the testimony of a Judge, in a cause pending before him, he is not required to testify if he declares that there is no fact within his knowledge important in the cause. Judge not required to testify when.

ART. 652. When the Judge of a Court is offered as a witness, the oath may be administered to him by the Clerk. Oath administered to the Judge by the Clerk.

ART. 653. A conviction cannot be had upon the testimony of an accomplice unless corroborated by other evidence tending to connect the defendant with the offence committed; and the corroboration is not sufficient if it merely shows the commission of the offence. Testimony of accomplice not sufficient to convict, unless, &c.

3. *Evidence as to Particular Offences.*

ART. 654. No person can be convicted of treason, except upon the testimony of at least two witnesses to the same overt act, or upon his own confession in open Court. In treason, two witnesses, or confession necessary to conviction.

ART. 655. Evidence shall not be admitted, in a prosecution for treason, as to an overt act not expressly charged in the indictment. Nor shall any person be convicted under an indictment for treason unless one or more overt acts are expressly charged therein. Overt act must be expressly charged.

ART. 656. In all cases where, by law, two witnesses, or one with corroborating circumstances, are required to authorize a conviction, if the requirement be not fulfilled, the Court shall instruct the Jury to render a verdict of acquittal, and they are bound by the instruction. Court shall instruct jury to render verdict of acquittal, when.

ART. 657. In trials for perjury, no person can be convicted, except upon the testimony of two credible witnesses, or of one credible witness, with strong corroborating circumstances. In perjury, two witnesses necessary.

ART. 658. In trials for forgery, the person whose name is alleged to have been forged is a competent witness. In forgery, person whose name is forged, competent witness.

ART. 659. In trials for forgery, it need not be proved that the defendant committed the act with intent to defraud any particular person. It shall be sufficient to prove that the forgery was in its nature calculated to injure or defraud any of the sovereignties, bodies corporate or politic, officers or persons named in Article 439 of the Penal Code in defining forgery. What proof necessary to convict in forgery.

4. *Of Dying Declarations and of the Confessions of the Defendant.*

ART. 660. The dying declarations of a deceased person may be offered in evidence either for or against a defendant charged with the homicide, under the restrictions hereafter provided. To render the declarations of the deceased competent evidence, it must be satisfactorily proved: Dying declarations admissible against person charged with homicide, when.

1. That at the time of making such declarations he was conscious of approaching death, and believed there was no hope of recovering.

2. That the declaration was voluntarily made, and not through the persuasion of any person.

3. That such declaration was not made in answer to interrogatories calculated to lead the deceased to make any particular statement.

4. That he was of sane mind at the time of making the declaration.

ART. 661. The confession of a defendant may be used in evidence against him, if it appear that the same was freely made without compulsion or persuasion, under the rules hereafter prescribed. Confession of defendant admissible against him, if.

ART. 662. The confession shall not be used, if, at the time it was made, the

The confession shall not be used, if.

defendant was in jail, or other place of confinement, nor while he is in custody of an officer, unless such confession be made in the voluntary statement of the accused, taken before an examining Court in accordance with law, or be made voluntarily after having been first cautioned that it may be used against him.

The confession of a slave shall not be used against him, when.

ART. 663. The confession of a slave shall never be used in evidence against him, when made after whipping or other chastisement has been inflicted or threatened, on account of the offence of which he is accused.

5. *Miscellaneous Provisions.*

When part of an act, declaration, &c., is given in evidence, the whole may be required.

ART. 664. When part of an act, declaration or conversation, or writing, is given in evidence by one party, the whole on the same subject may be enquired into by the other, as, when a letter is read, all other letters on the same subject, between the same parties, may be given. And when a detailed act, declaration, conversation or writing is given in evidence, any other act, declaration or writing, which is necessary to make it fully understood, or to explain the same, may also be given in evidence.

Written part of an instrument shall control, &c.

ART. 665. When an instrument is partly written and partly printed, the written shall control the printed portion, when the two are inconsistent.

When subscribing witness denies execution, &c, of instrument.

ART. 666. When a subscribing witness denies or does not recollect the execution of an instrument to which his name appears, its execution may be proved by other evidence.

Evidence of handwriting by comparison.

ART. 667. It is competent, in every case, to give evidence of handwriting by comparison, made by experts or by the Jury; but proof by comparison only shall not be sufficient to establish the handwriting of a witness who denies his signature.

The rule that a party shall not attack the testimony of his own witness, modified.

ART. 668. The rule that a party introducing a witness shall not attack his testimony, is so far modified as that any party, when facts stated by the witness are injurious to his cause, may attack his testimony in any other manner, except by proving the bad character of the witness.

TITLE VI.

OF PROCEEDINGS AFTER VERDICT.

CHAPTER I.

OF NEW TRIALS.

Act of Aug. 26, 1856.
A new trial, &c.

ART. 669. A new trial is the rehearing of a criminal action, after verdict, before another jury.

Cannot be granted where verdict is for def't.

ART. 670. A new trial can in no case be granted where the verdict has been rendered for the defendant.

Must be applied for within two days after verdict, except.

ART. 671. A new trial must be applied for within two days after the verdict is returned; but for good cause shown, the Court, in cases of felony, may allow the application to be made at any time before the adjournment of the term at which the verdict was found. When a Court adjourns before the expiration of two days from the return of verdict, the motion shall be made before the adjournment.

ART. 672. New trials, in cases of felony, shall be granted for the following causes, and for no other: May be granted in cases of felony, for what causes.

1. Where the defendant has been tried in his absence or has been denied counsel.

2. Where the Court has misdirected the jury as to the law, or has committed any other material error calculated to injure the rights of the defendant.

3. Where the verdict has been decided by lot, or in any other manner than by a fair expression of opinion by the jurors.

4. Where a juror has received a bribe to convict, or has been guilty of any other corrupt conduct.

5. Where any material witness of the defendant has, by force, threats or fraud, been prevented from attending the Court, or where any written evidence tending to establish the innocence of the defendant, has been intentionally destroyed or removed, so that it could not be produced upon the trial.

6. Where new testimony material to the defendant has been discovered since the trial. A motion for a new trial based on this ground shall be governed by the same rules as those which regulate civil suits.

7. Where the jury, after having retired to deliberate upon a case, have received other testimony; or where a juror has conversed with any person in regard to the case; or where any juror, at any time during the trial or after retiring, may have become so intoxicated as to render it probable his verdict was influenced thereby. But the mere drinking of liquor by a juror shall not be sufficient ground for granting a new trial.

8. Where, from the misconduct of the jury, the Court is of opinion that the defendant has not received a fair and impartial trial, and it shall be competent to prove such misconduct by the voluntary affidavit of a juror; and a verdict may, in like manner, in such cases, be sustained by such affidavit.

9. Where the verdict is contrary to law and evidence. A verdict is not contrary to the law and the evidence, within the meaning of this provision, where the defendant is found guilty of an offence of inferior grade to, but of the same nature as, the offence proved.

ART. 673. If a new trial be refused, a statement of facts may be drawn up and certified, and placed in the record as in civil suits. Where the defendant has failed to move for a new trial, he is nevertheless entitled, if he appeals, to have a statement of the facts certified and sent up with the record. Statement of facts.

ART. 674. The effect of a new trial is to place the cause in the same position in which it was before any trial had taken place. The former verdict shall be regarded as no presumption of guilt, nor shall it be alluded to in the argument. Effect of a new trial.

CHAPTER II.

ARREST OF JUDGMENT.

ART. 675. A motion in arrest of judgment is a suggestion to the Court on the part of the defendant that judgment cannot be legally rendered upon the Act of August 26, 1856.

A motion in arrest of judgm't, is what. May be orally or in, &c.

verdict against him. The motion may be made orally or in writing, and the record must show the grounds of the motion

Must be made in two days after verdict.

ART. 676. The motion must be made within two days after the verdict is returned; or if the Court adjourn before the expiration of two days from such return of verdict, then it may be made at any time before judgment is entered.

Court may hear at any time.

ART. 677. The Court may, for good cause shown, hear a motion in arrest of judgment at any time.

Shall be granted for what cause.

ART. 678. A motion in arrest of judgment shall be granted upon any ground which would be good upon exception to an indictment or information, for any substantial defect therein.

Shall not be, &c.

ART. 679. No judgment shall be arrested for want of form.

Effect of arresting a judgment.

ART. 680. The effect of arresting a judgment is to place the defendant in the same position he was before the indictment or information was presented. And if the Court be satisfied from the evidence, that he may be convicted upon a proper indictment or information, he shall be remanded into custody, or bailed, as the case may require.

Court may discharge defendant, when.

ART. 681. Where the Court is not satisfied from the proof that upon a proper indictment or information the defendant may be convicted, he shall be discharged.

CHAPTER III.

JUDGMENT AND ITS INCIDENTS.

1. *Judgment in Cases of Felony.*

Act of Aug. 26, 1856.

In cases of felony, sentence pronounced, when.

ART. 682. If a new trial is not granted, nor the judgment arrested, the judgment of the Court, in cases of felony, shall be entered, and sentence pronounced in presence of the defendant, at any time after the expiration of the time allowed for making the motion for a new trial, or the motion in arrest of judgment.

In case of an appeal, sentence shall not be pronounced.

ART. 683. In cases of felony, where an appeal is taken, sentence shall not be pronounced, but shall be suspended until the decision of the Supreme Court has been received.

Where two days do not intervene before adjournment.

ART. 684. In cases where a verdict of conviction takes place so late in the term of the Court as not to allow the time given by Articles 671 and 676 for making a motion for a new trial, or in arrest of judgment, the judgment may be entered and sentence pronounced at any time before th Court finally adjourns; provided that in every case at least six hours shall be allowed for making either of these motions.

Art. 685. If, at the time a verdict is returned into Court, there be less than six hours remaining before the Court by law must adjourn, it shall be lawful and shall be the duty of the District Judge, to sit during the whole of Saturday night and Sunday, for the purpose of enabling the defendant to move for a new trial or in arrest of judgment, and prepare his cause for the Supreme Court. This Article shall not require the District Judge to sit longer than six hours after verdict rendered, if a motion for a new trial, or in arrest of judgment, shall not have been filed. Where less than six hours remain before adjournment.

Art. 686. Where, from any cause whatever, a verdict of conviction has been returned, and there is a failure to enter judgment and pronounce sentence during the term, the judgment may be entered and sentence pronounced at the next succeeding term of the Court, unless a new trial has been granted, or the judgment arrested, or an appeal has been taken. Where there is a failure to enter judgment or pronounce sentence.

Art. 687. Before pronouncing sentence in a case of felony, the defendant shall be asked whether he has any thing to say why judgment should not be rendered and sentence pronounced against him. Before pronouncing judgment, defendant shall be asked, &c.

Art. 688. The only reasons which can be shown on account of which sentence cannot be passed, are: Reasons why sentence cannot be passed.

1. That the defendant has received a pardon from the proper authority; on the presentation of which, legally authenticated, he shall be discharged.

2. That the defendant is insane; and if sufficient proof be shown to satisfy the Court that the allegation is well founded, no sentence shall be pronounced. And where there is sufficient time left, a jury may be impannelled to try the issue. Where sufficient time does not remain, the Court shall order the defendent to be confined safely until the next term of the Court, and shall then cause a jury to be impannelled to try such issue.

3. Where there has not been a motion for a new trial, or a motion in arrest of judgment made, the defendant may answer that he has good grounds for either or both of these motions, and either or both motions may be immediately entered and disposed of, although more than two days may have elapsed since the rendition of the verdict.

4. When a person who has been convicted of felony escapes between verdict and judgment, or between the time of rendering the judgment in the District Court and sentence thereon, after affirmance of the same in the Supreme Court, and an individual supposed to be the same has been arrested, he may, before sentence is pronounced, deny that he is the person convicted, and an issue be accordingly tried before a jury as to his identity.

Art. 689. Where the sentence of death is pronounced against a convict, a time shall be set for the execution of the same not earlier than thirty days from the date of the sentence. Time set for the execution of convict.

Art. 690. The Clerk of the District Court shall issue a warrant for the execution of the sentence of death, which shall recite the fact of conviction, setting forth specifically the offence and the judgment of the Court, the time fixed for its execution, and the manner in which it is to be executed. Warrant for the execution, shall recite.

2. Judgment in Cases of Misdemeanor.

Art. 691. The judgment in cases of misdemeanor may be rendered in the absence of the defendant. May be rendered in absence of defendant.

Art. 692. When the defendant has not given bail, and is not in custody, the

Act of Feb. 15, 1858.

Capias may issue, after verdict, when.

District Attorney may, in case a pecuniary fine has been imposed, have a capias issued, and the Sheriff shall execute the same by placing the defendant in jail until the fine is paid; from which confinement he may be released after remaining in jail the length of time prescribed in Article 694, upon making oath before the Sheriff that he is unable to pay.

Defendant discharged upon payment of fine and costs.

ART. 693. When the punishment assessed by the jury is a pecuniary fine only, the defendant, if in custody, may be discarged therefrom upon the payment of the fine and costs.

Defendant may be committed to jail, to remain until.

ART. 694. If the defendant is in custody he may be committed to jail, to remain until the fine and costs are paid, unless he make oath that he is unable to pay the fine and costs, in which case he shall be committed to jail for a term not exceeding ten days; and if the fine and costs exceed twenty dollars, then one additional day for every three dollars over twenty to which the fine and costs may amount.

Act of Aug. 26, 1856.

Proceedings after verdict, where defendant is not in custody.

ART. 695. When the defendant is not in custody, but has given bail, the District Attorney may, in any case of misdemeanor, take a forfeiture of his recognizance or bail bond, or he may, in case of a mere pecuniary fine, have execution issued against the defendant, to be collected and returned as in civil actions.

Act of Feb. 15, 1858

Where the punishment is imprisonment, and the defendant is not in custody, a capias may issue.

ART. 696. Where the punishment imposed, or any part thereof, is imprisonment, and the defendant is not in custody, a capias may be issued to take the defendant, and the Sheriff shall execute the same, by placing the defendant in jail, to remain the length of time fixed by the judgment, and until the costs and the fine if any has been imposed, in addition to the imprisonment, are paid, unless he be discharged according to the provisions of Article 694.

Act of Aug. 26, 1856.

ART. 697. Where a defendant makes his escape from custody, either before or after verdict, a capias shall be issued for his arrest.

CHAPTER IV.

EXECUTION OF JUDGMENTS.

1. *Collection of Pecuniary Fines.*

2. *Enforcing the Judgment in Misdemeanors where the Penalty is Imprisonment, and in Felonies less than Capital.*

3. *Execution of the Penalty of Death.*

1. *Collection of Pecuniary Fines.*

Act of Aug. 26, 1856.

ART. 698. Where a defendant is committed to the custody of the Sheriff, or taken under a capias, for the purpose of enforcing the collection of a pecuniary fine, it is the duty of the Sheriff to place him in jail.

ART. 699. A copy of the judgment of the Court imposing the fine, certified to by the Clerk of the District Court, is sufficient authority for the Sheriff to commit a defendant to the jail of his county, in cases where, by the judgment, it is directed that he be committed until the fine and costs be paid. What sufficient authority to place defendant in jail.

ART. 700. Where it is directed in the judgment of the Court that a capias issue to enforce the collection of a fine, the Clerk of the District Court shall issue the writ to the Sheriff, reciting the existence and character of the judgment, and commanding the Sheriff to take the body of the defendant, and hold him in custody until the fine and costs are paid. This writ is sufficient authority to justify the commitment of the defendant to jail. The same.

ART. 701. In cases where an execution is ordered to be issued in a criminal cause, to enforce a judgment, it is the duty of the Sheriff to collect the same as in civil suits. Execution, as in civil suits, to enforce a judgment.

ART. 702. All recognizances, bail bonds and undertakings of any kind, whereby a party becomes bound to pay money to the State, shall be deemed payable in gold or silver; and all fines and forfeitures of a pecuniary character shall be collected in that currency only. Gold and silver only receivable by the State.

ART. 703. The Sheriff shall make a written report, under oath, of all money collected by him, under execution or other process, in criminal actions, and file the same at each term of the District Court. Written report by Sheriff of moneys collected.

2. *Enforcing the Judgment in Misdemeanors where the Penalty is Imprisonment, and in Felonies less than Capital.*

ART. 704. When, by the judgment of the Court, a defendant is to be imprisoned in jail, as the penalty, or a part of the penalty of the offence, a copy of the judgment is sufficient to authorize the Sheriff to execute the same, by such imprisonment of the defendant. Copy of judgment sufficient authority to imprison defendant.

ART. 705. When a capias is directed to be issued for the apprehension and commitment of a person convicted of a misdemeanor, the penalty of which is imprisonment in jail, the writ shall recite the judgment, and command the Sheriff to place the defendant in jail, to remain the length of time therein fixed, and this writ shall be sufficient to authorize the Sheriff to enforce such judgment. Warrant of commitment shall recite, what.

ART. 706. When the defendant has been sentenced to the Penitentiary, a certified copy of the judgment shall be sufficient to authorize the Sheriff to convey such convict and deliver him to the proper officer of the same. Copy of judgment sufficient authority to commit convict to penitentiary.

ART. 707. Prisoners shall be conveyed to the Penitentiary in the manner, and under the rules prescribed in the act of March 13, 1848, entitled "An Act to establish a State Penitentiary," as the same is amended and set forth in the Penal Code. Prisoners conveyed to penitentiary, how.

3. *Execution of the Penalty of Death.*

ART. 708. When sentence of death is to be executed, a warrant shall be issued by the Clerk of the District Court, directed to the Sheriff of the proper county, which may be carried into effect, at any time after eleven o'clock and before sunset, on the day stated in such warrant. Warrant shall be issued by Clerk, where sentence of death is to be executed.

ART. 709. The sentence of death shall be executed by hanging the convict by the neck until he is dead. How executed.

Shall take place within the walls of the jail, when.

ART. 710. Where there is a jail in the county, and it is so constructed that a gallows can be erected therein, the execution of the sentence of death shall take place within the walls of the jail.

Who shall be present.

ART. 711. Where the sentence of death is executed within the walls of the county jail, the Sheriff shall notify any number of physicians or surgeons, not exceeding six, any number of Justices of the Peace of his county, not exceeding four, and any number of freeholders in the county, not exceeding six, any or all of whom may be present, together with such deputies of the Sheriff as he may require to be in attendance when the penalty of death is executed.

Reasonable request of convict.

ART. 712. The Sheriff shall comply with with any reasonable request of the convict; and where the execution takes place within the walls of the county jail, shall permit such persons to be present (not exceeding five) as he may name.

No torture shall be inflicted.

ART. 713. No torture or ill treatment, or unnecessary pain shall be inflicted upon a prisoner to be executed under the sentence of the law.

Sheriff may order military company to aid.

ART. 715. The Sheriff may, when he supposes there will be a necessity, order such number of citizens of his county, or any military company, to aid in preventing the rescue of a prisoner, or to prevent persons not authorized to be present from intruding themselves within the place of execution.

Body of a convict shall be buried, how.

ART. 716. The body of a convict shsll be buried at the expense of the county, unless demanded by his relatives or friends, in which case it shall be given to them, and shall never, unless by consent of the convict himself, before execution be delivered to any person for dissection.

Sheriff shall return the warrant, stating therein.

ART. 717. The Sheriff shall immediately return the warrant, stating therein:

1. The fact, time, place and mode of execution.

2. If the execution do not take place within the jail, the return shall state that there is no jail, or that it is not so constructed that a gallows can be erected therein.

3. If the execution take place within the jail, the return shall state the names of the physicians, Justices of the Peace, and freeholders notified to be present, and the names of the persons present, if any, by request of the convict.

4. If the execution do not take place within the jail, the return shall state the names of five freeholders of the county who were present.

5. That the body of the convict was buried, or delivered to his relatives or friends, or to a physician or surgeon, by consent of the convict.

TITLE VII.

OF APPEALS.

Art. 718. An appeal may be taken from the District to the Supreme Court by the State, in the following cases, and in no others: Act of Aug. 26 1856. State may appeal in following cases.

1. When the District Court sustains an exception of the defendant to the indictment or information.

2. Where the District Court sustains a motion of the defendant in arrest of judgment.

Art. 719. An appeal may be taken by the defendant in every case where judgment of conviction has been rendered against him in the District Court, or where such a Court or a Judge thereof, or a Judge of the Supreme Court, has decided against an application of the defendant under habeas corpus. Defendant may appeal, when.

Art. 720. Where the State appeals no security can be required. No security, &c

Art. 721. Where the defendant appeals in any case of felony, he shall be committed to Jail until the decision of the Supreme Court can be made; and if the jail of the county is unsafe, or there be no Jail, the Judge of the District Court may, either in term time, or in vacation, order the prisoner to be committed to the Jail of the nearest county in his district which is safe. Where defendant appeals in felony, shall be committed to jail.

Art. 722. When the defendant appeals in any case of misdemeanor, he shall be committed to jail, unless he enter into recognizance to appear before the District Court, to abide the judgment of the Supreme Court. In misdemeanors, shall be committed or recognized.

Art. 723. The defendant shall also be required, when the State appeals, to enter into recognizance to appear before the District Court to answer the criminal accusation against him, in case the judgment of the District Court be reversed. Act Feb. 15, 1858. When State appeals, defendant recognized.

Art. 724. An appeal on behalf of the State must be taken so soon as the order is made which is appealed from. Act of Aug. 26, 1856.

Art. 725. An appeal may be taken by the defendant at any time during the term of the Court at which the conviction is had. Defendant may appeal, when.

Art. 726. An appeal is taken by giving notice thereof in open Court, and having the same entered of record. An appeal is taken, how.

Art. 727. The effect of an appeal is to suspend and arrest all further proceedings, until the judgment of the Supreme Court has been received by the District Court. Effect of an appeal.

Art. 728. Where the defendant fails to appeal until after sentence has been pronounced, the appeal shall nevertheless be allowed if demanded, and has the effect of superceding the execution of the sentence and all other proceedings, as fully as if taken at the proper time. Defendant may appeal after sentence.

Art. 729. It is the duty of the Clerk of the District Court to prepare,

Transcript for Supreme Court. immediately after the adjournment of each term of Court a transcript in every case where an appeal is taken; which transcript shall contain all the proceedings had in the case. The transcripts in criminal cases shall be made out before those in civil actions decided at the same term.

Transcript in misdemeanors, shall be delivered, to whom.

ART. 730. The transcript of the record in cases of misdemeanor must be delivered to the party appealing, or his counsel, when the defendant appeals, or to the District Attorney, or any counsel associated with him, when the State appeals. But if not applied for before the twentieth day before the commencement of the term of the Supreme Court to which the appeal is returnable, the Clerk shall transmit the same by mail, paying the postage thereon, to the Clerk of the Supreme Court.

Transcripts in felonies shall be sent by mail to Clerk of the Supreme Court.

ART. 731. Transcripts of record in all cases of felony shall, so soon as prepared be sent by mail addressed to the Clerk of the Supreme Court, at the place where the session of the Supreme Court is held, to which the appeal is returnable. The District Clerk shall deposit each transcript so addressed and securely enveloped, and shall pay the postage upon the same; and the amount paid shall be taxed as a part of the costs in each case.

A list of appealed cases shall be made by the Clerk, and shall show.

ART. 732. The District Clerk shall immediately after the adjournment of the Court, at which appeals in criminal actions may have been taken, make out a certificate under ~~his seal of~~ office, exhibiting a list of all such causes which have been decided, and in which either the State or defendant has appealed. This certificate shall show the style of the cause upon the docket—the offence of which the defendant stands accused—the day on which judgment was rendered, and the day on which the appeal was taken—which certified list he shall transmit, post paid to the Clerk of the Supreme Court at the proper place.

Clerk of the Supreme Court shall file said list.

ART. 733. The Clerk of the Supreme Court shall file the certificate provided for in the preceding article, and notify the Attorney-General that the same has been received.

When transcript, in misdemeanor, is not filed within time.

ART. 734. When it appears by such certificate that an appeal has been taken by the defendant in a criminal action for misdemeanor, and the transcript is not filed within the time required by law for filing transcripts in civil actions, such cause may be entered upon the docket on motion of the Attorney-General and the judgment of the District Court shall be affirmed.

When transcript, in felony, is not filed within time.

ART. 735. When it appears by the certificate of the Clerk of the District Court, that an appeal has been taken by the defendant in any criminal action for felony, and no transcript thereof is filed in the Supreme Court within the time required by law, the Clerk of the Supreme Court shall notify the Attorney General of the same, and shall also immediately, by mail, inform the Clerk of the proper District Court that such transcript has not been received.

Judgment in felony shall not be affirmed, unless the record is filed.

ART. 736. No judgment of the District Court in a case of felony shall be affirmed unless the record of the cause is before the Supreme Court, and it is the duty of the Clerk of the Supreme Court, to notify the counsel of the accused, through the mail, if he knows the residence of such counsel, whenever there has been a failure to receive the transcript of record in any case of felony.

Clerk of District Court shall prepare another transcript, &c.

ART. 737. The Clerk of the District Court, when informed that a transcript has not been received by the Clerk of the Supreme Court, shall immediately prepare and transmit another, as directed in article 731.

ART. 738. When an appeal is taken by the State, and the transcript of the record is not filed in the Supreme Court within the time limited for filing transcripts in civil actions, the defendant's counsel may suggest the facts to the Court, and upon exhibiting the certificate of the District Clerk that such appeal was taken by the State, the cause shall be docketed and the judgment of the District Court affirmed, unless good cause be shown why the transcript has not been filed. When transc'pt is not filed in time, on appeal by the State.

ART. 738a. An appeal may be taken either by the State or defendant, from every final judgment rendered upon a recognizance, bail bond, or bond taken for the prevention or suppression of offences, and the proceedings in such cases shall be regulated by the same rules which are prescribed in civil suits, except that no security shall be required of the State. Act of Feb. 15, 1858. Appeals, by the State or defendant, from judgment on bail bonds, &c.

ART. 738b. Judgment final, in the cases mentioned in the preceding article, may be also taken to the Supreme Court by Writ of Error, as in civil suits, except that the defendant shall in all cases, be required to give bond to comply with the judgment or order of the Supreme Court. Writ of Error in same cases

ART. 739. The Clerk of the Supreme Court shall receive, file and docket appeals in criminal actions, under the same rules which govern appeals in civil actions, except that it shall be in the discretion of the Court, in cases of felony, to permit a transcript to be filed at any time during the term to which an appeal is taken. Act of Aug. 26, 1856. Appeals shall be controlled by rules which govern in civil actions, except.

ART. 740. The defendant to a criminal action need not be personally present upon the hearing of his cause in the Supreme Court, but he may appear in person in cases where by law he is not committed to jail upon appeal. Defendant need not be present in Supreme Court.

ART. 741. The Court shall hear and determine appeals in criminal actions at the earliest time it may be done with due regard to the rights of parties and a proper administration of justice. Court shall determine appeals at the earliest conven'nt time.

ART. 742. The judgment in a criminal action, upon appeal, may be wholly reversed and dismissed when brought up by the defendant, or affirmed and dismissed when brought up by the State; the judgment may be reformed and corrected, or the cause may be remanded for further proceedings in the District Court, as the law and the nature of the case may require. Judgment may be affirmed, reversed, dismissed, &c.

ART. 743. As soon as the judgment of the Supreme Court is rendered, the Clerk shall make out the proper certificate of the proceedings had and judgment rendered, and transmit the same by mail, to the Clerk of the District Court, or deliver the mandate to the counsel of the defendant when the decision is favorable to the defendant, if requested to do so, unless he is instructed by the Court to withhold the mandate to any particular time. Clerk shall make out and transmit mandate.

ART. 744. The Supreme Court may revise the judgment in a criminal action, as well upon the law as upon the facts; but when a cause is reversed for the reason that the verdict is contrary to the weight of evidence, the same shall in all cases be remanded for a new trial. Cases shall be remanded for new trial, when.

ART. 745. The Supreme Court may make rules of procedure, as to the hearing of criminal actions upon appeal; but in every case at least two counsel for the defendant shall be heard, if they desire it, either by brief or by oral or written argument, or by both, as such counsel shall deem proper. Court may make rules of procedure.

ART. 746. When the certificate of the judgment and proceedings in the Supreme Court shall be received by the Disttict Clerk, he shall file the same with the original papers of the cause. District Clerk shall file mandate.

ART. 747. In cases where the judgment of the District Court is affirmed upon an appeal by the defendant, if the mandate be received during the session District Court shall pronounce sentence upon receipt of mandate. of the District Court, that Court shall proceed to pronounce sentence, in cases of felony, during the term at which the mandate is received.

The same. ART. 748. If the mandate be received in vacation, and the judgment in a case of felony has been affirmed, sentence shall be pronounced during the term of the Court next succeeding the time at which the same was received.

In misdemeanors, no proceedings necessary after filing mandate. ART. 749. In cases of misdemeanor, where no formal sentence is to be pronounced, no proceedings need be had after filing the mandate in the District Court, but the cause shall stand as it would have stood in case no appeal had been taken, and the recognizance of the defendant may be forfeited, or a capias issued to enforce the punishment adjudged, whether of fine or imprisonment, or both, in the same manner as if no appeal had been taken.

Where Supreme Court awards a new trial. ART. 750. Where the Supreme Court awards a new trial to the defendant, the cause shall stand as it would have stood in case the new trial had been granted by the District Court.

Where motion in arrest should have been sustained. ART. 751. Where the defendant's motion in arrest of judgment was overruled, and it is decided on appeal that the same ought to have been sustained, the cause shall stand as if the motion had been sustained in the Distric Court, unless the Supreme Court in its judgment direct the cause to be dismissed and the defendant wholly discharged.

When the State appeals from a judgment sustaining exception to the indictment, &c. ART. 752. If the appeal was taken by the State, from a judgment of the District Court, sustaining an exception to the indictment or information, or sustaining a motion in arrest of judgment, and the judgment is reversed, the cause shall stand as if the exception or the motion in arrest had been overruled by the District Court.

Where Supreme Court dismisses a cause, defend'nt shall be discharged. ART. 753. Where the Supreme Court reverses a judgment of the District, Court, and directs the cause to be dismissed, the defendant, if in custody, must be discharged; and the Clerk of the Supreme Court shall transmit to the officer having custody of the defendant an order to that effect.

Appeal in case of habeas corpus. ART. 754. When the defendant appeals from the judgment rendered on the hearing of an application under habeas corpus, a transcript of the proceedings in the cause shall be made out and certified to, together with all the testimony offered, and shall be sent up to the Supreme Court for revision. Who shall make transcript. This transcript, when the proceeding takes place before the District Court in session, shall be prepared and certified by the Clerk thereof, but when had before a Judge of the Supreme Court or of the District Court not in session, the transcript may be prepared by any person under the direction of the Judge and certified by such Judge.

The Supreme Court shall make such judgment, &c. ART. 755. The Supreme Court shall hear the appeal upon the facts and law arising upon the record, and shall enter such judgment and make such orders as the law and the nature of the case may require.

Decision of an incidental question not revised by Supreme Court. ART. 756. The opinion of a District or Supreme Judge shall not be revised as to any incidental question which may have arisen on the hearing of the application for habeas corpus. The only design of the appeal being to do substantial justice to the party appealing.

Habeas corpus cases heard at the earliest, &c. ART. 757. Cases of habeas corpus taken to the Supreme Court by appeal shall be heard at the earliest practicable time.

The Supreme Court may allow costs in habeas corpus, &c. ART. 758. The Supreme Court may make such order relative to the costs in cases of habeas corpus as may seem right, allowing costs and fixing the amount, or allowing no costs at all.

ART. 759. The judgment of the Supreme Court, in appeals under habeas corpus, shall be final and conclusive, and no further application in the same case can be made for the writ. The judgment of the Supreme Court shall be certified by the Clerk thereof to the officer holding the defendant in custody, or, when he is held by any person other than an officer, to the Sheriff of the proper county. Judgment of Supreme Court in appeals under habeas corpus final.

ART. 760. If an officer, holding a person in custody, fails to obey the mandate of the Supreme Court, he is guilty of an offence, and punishable according to the provisions of the Penal Code. Officer failing to obey mandate of, penalty for.

ART. 761. If the appellant, in a case of habeas corpus, be detained by any person other than an officer, the Sheriff shall, upon receiving the mandate of the Supreme Court, immediately cause the person so held to be discharged, and the mandate shall be sufficient authority therefor. Where appell'nt in a case of habeas corpus is detained by, &c.

ART. 762. The defendant need not be personally present upon the hearing of an appeal in cases of habeas corpus. Defendant need not be present at the hearing.

ART. 763. When, by the judgment of the Supreme Court, upon appeal in cases of habeas corpus, the applicant for relief is ordered to give bail, such judgment shall be certified to the officer holding him in custody; and if he be the Sheriff, the bail bond may be executed before him; if any other officer, he shall take the person detained before some Magistrate, who may receive a bail bond, and shall file the same in the District Court of the proper county, and such bond shall have the same force and effect as a recognizance, and may be forfeited and enforced in the same manner. Where applic'nt for relief is ordered to give bail—bond, how executed.

TITLE VIII.

MISCELLANEOUS PROCEEDINGS.

CHAPTER I.

DEPOSITION OF WITNESSES.

1. *When taken.*

Act of Aug. 26, 1856.

ART. 764. Whenever an examination takes place in a criminal action before a magistrate, the defendant may have the deposition of any witness taken by any officer or officers hereafter named in this Chapter; but the State or person prosecuting shall have the right to cross-examine the witnesses, and the defen- In an examination before a magistrate, depositions may be taken.

dant shall not use the deposition for any purpose, unless he first consent that the entire evidence or statement of the witness may be used against him by the State, on the trial of the case.

May be taken at the request of defendant in these cases.

ART. 765. Depositions of witnesses may also, at the request of the defendant, be taken in the following cases:

1. When the witness resides out of the State.
2. When the witness is aged or infirm.

2. *Persons authorized to take Depositions, and the manner of taking and returning them.*

Depositions of witnesses within the State may be taken, by whom.

ART. 766. Depositions of witnesses within the State may be taken by a Supreme or District Judge, or before any two or more of the following officers: the Chief Justice of a county, Notary Public, Clerk of the District Court, and Clerk of the County Court.

May be taken out of the State, by whom.

ART. 767. Depositions of a witness residing out of the State may be taken before the Judge or Chancellor of a Superior Court of law or equity, or before a Commissioner of deeds and depositions for this State, who resides within the State where the depsition is to be taken.

Deposition of non-resident witness temporarily within the State.

ART. 768. The deposition of a non-resident witness, who may be temporarily within the State, may be taken under the same rules which apply to the taking of depositions of other witnesses in the State.

Shall be taken as in civil cases.

ART. 769. The rules prescribed in civil cases for taking the deposition of witnesses shall, as to the manner and form of taking and returning the same, govern in criminal actions, when not in conflict with the requirements of this Code.

Same objections to depositions as in civil cases.

ART. 770. The same rules of procedure, as to objections to depsitions, shall govern in criminal actions which are prescribed in civil actions, when not in conflict with this Code.

How defendant shall proceed in taking deposition of witness.

ART. 771. When the defendant desires to take the deposition of a witness, at any other time than before the examining court, he shall, by himself or counsel, file with the Clerk of the District Court, a statement on oath, setting forth the facts necessary to constitute a good reason for taking the same, and in addition thereto, state in his affidavit, that he has no other witness whose attendance on the trial can be procured, by whom he can prove the facts he desires to establish by the deposition.

Written interrogatories shall be filed, and notice given, as in civil cases.

ART. 772. In cases arising under the preceding Article, written interrogatories shall be filed with the Clerk of the District Court, and a copy of the same served on the District Attorney of the proper District, the length of time required for service of interrogatories in civil actions.

Certificate of officer taking deposition.

ART. 773. In every case where depositions are taken, under commission in criminal actions, the officer or officers taking the same shall certify that the person deposing is the identical person named in the commission; or, if they cannot certify to the identity of the witness, there shall be an affidavit of some person attached to the deposition, proving the identity; and the officer or officers shall certify that the person making the affidavit is known to them, and is worthy of credit.

Where two officers act, each shall sign and seal.

ART. 774. In cases where it is required that two officers shall act in executing a commission to take depositions, the official seal and signature of each shall be attached to the certificate authenticating the deposition.

Deposition be-

ART. 775. The deposition of a witness taken before an examining Court, may

be taken without interrogatories; but whenever a deposition is so taken, it shall be done by the proper officer or officers, and there shall be allowed both to the State and to the defendant, full liberty of cross-examination.

fore examining court may be taken without interrogatories.

Art. 776. The depositions of witnesses taken before an examining court may be taken without a commission; and if such examining court be held by a Supreme or District Judge, he shall, upon request, proceed to take depositions of the witnesses.

May be taken without commission.

Art. 777. Where any of the officers, other than a Supreme or District Judge, are called upon to take a deposition before an examining Court, it is their duty to attend and take the same.

Duty of officer to attend.

Art. 778. A deposition taken in an examining court shall be sealed up and delivered by the officer or officers, or one of them, to the Clerk of the District Court of the county having jurisdiction to try the offence; in all other cases, the return of depositions may be made as provided for depositions in civil actions.

How deposition shall be returned

3. *Of reading Depositions in Criminal Actions.*

Art. 779. Depositions taken in criminal actions shall not be read, unless oath be made that the witness resides out of the State; or, that since his deposition was taken, the witness has died; or that he has removed beyond the limits of the State; or that he has been prevented from attending the court through the act or agency of the defendant; or by the act or agency of any person whose object was to deprive the defendant of the benefit of the testimony.

Deposition shall not be read, unless oath be made that, &c.

Art. 780. When the deposition is sought to be used by the State, the oath prescribed in the preceding article may be made by the District Attorney, or any other credible person; and when sought to be used by the defendant, the oath shall be made by him in person.

District Attorney may make oath.

CHAPTER II.

OF INQUIRY AS TO THE INSANITY OF THE DEFENDANT.

Art. 781. If it be made known to the court at any time after conviction, or if the court has good reason to believe that a defendant is insane, a jury shall be impannelled to try the issue.

Act of Aug. 26 1856.

After conviction.

Art. 782. Information to the court as to the insanity of a defendant may be given by the written affidavit of any respectable person, setting forth that there is good reason to believe that the defendant has become insane.

Information as to, may be given on oath, &c.

Art. 783. The court shall direct the Sheriff to summon twelve men, qualified jurors, for the purpose of trying the question of insanity.

Jury summon'd to try question of.

No special formality required on trial. ART. 784. No special formality is necessary in conducting the proceedings authorized by this Chapter. The court shall see that the inquiry is conducted in such manner as to lead to a satisfactory conclusion.

Challenges by either party. ART. 785. In trials of an issue as to the insanity of a defendant, each party shall be entitled to six peremptory challenges, and may challenge also for the same causes which are made good ground of challenge on the trial of criminal actions.

Def't's counsel may open and conclude. ART. 786. The counsel for the defendant has the right to open and conclude the argument upon the trial of an issue as to insanity.

Court shall appoint counsel, when. ART. 787. If the defendant has no counsel, the court shall appoint counsel to conduct the trial for him.

Judgment of conviction to be suspended, when. ART. 788. When an inquiry as to the insanity of a defendant takes place, before judgment is rendered, and it is found that the defendant is insane, the judgment shall be suspended until he becomes sane.

Execution of judg't to be suspended, when. ART. 789. Where an inquiry as to insanity has taken place after judgment, and the defendant is found to be insane, the execution of the judgment shall be suspended until he becomes sane.

Judg't to be rendered ag't defendant, when. ART. 790. When, upon the trial of an issue as to insanity, it is found that the defendant is sane, judgment shall be rendered upon the verdict of conviction as if no such issue had been tried.

Execution of judg't to follow, when. ART. 791. When the inquiry takes place after judgment, and the defendant is found to be sane, the execution of the judgment shall follow as if no such inquiry had been made.

Duty of County Court as to insane persons. ART. 792. It is the duty of each County Court to make provision for the safe keeping and proper treatment of persons who become insane, until a lunatic asylum shall be provided by the State.

Order of Dist. Court in cases of. ART. 793. Whenever it is found that a defendant is insane, upon inquiry, as directed in this Chapter, the court shall make an order that he be placed in the charge of the County Court until a lunatic asylum shall be provided by the State.

CHAPTER III.

DISPOSITION OF STOLEN PROPERTY.

Act of Aug. 26, 1856. Subject to order of proper court. ART. 794. When any property alleged to have been stolen comes into the custody of an officer, he must hold it subject to the order of the proper court or magistrate.

Restored, on trial for theft, to proper owner. ART. 795. Upon the trial of any criminal action for theft, or for any other illegal acquisition of property, which is by law a penal offence, the court before whom the trial takes place shall order the property to be restored to the person appearing by the proof to be the owner of the same.

ART. 796. When an officer seizes property alleged to have been stolen, it is his duty immediately to file a schedule of the same and its value, certifying that the property has been seized by him, and the reason therefor. Schedule of, to be filed by officer.

ART. 797. Upon examination of a criminal accusation before a magistrate, if it is proved to the satisfaction of such magistrate that any person is the true owner of property alleged to have been stolen, and which is in the possession of a peace officer, he may, by written order, direct the property to be restored to such owner. May be restor'd to owner, &c., when.

ART. 798. If the Magistrate have any doubt as to the ownership of the property, he may require of the person claiming to be the owner a bond with security for the re-delivery of the same, in case the property should thereafter be shown not to belong to such claimant, or he may, in his discretion, direct the property to be retained by the Sheriff until further order respecting the possession thereof. When delivered bond may be required of the person receiv'g.

ART. 799. A bond, under the provisions of the preceding article, shall be taken, payable to the Sheriff from whose custody it is received. To whom payable.

ART. 800. If stolen property be not claimed within six months from the conviction of a defendant accused of the theft, the same shall be by the Sheriff sold, for cash, after advertising for ten days, and the proceeds paid into the treasury of the county where the defendant was convicted. If not claimed within six months.

ART. 801. Advertisement, as provided for in the preceding article, shall be made by posting up a notice on the Court House door of the proper county; and the sale shall take place at the county seat and before the Court House door. Advertisement relative to.

ART. 802. If the property stolen consist of money, the same shall be paid into the county treasury, if not claimed by the proper owner within six months. Money, how disposed of.

ART. 803. The real owner of the property or money disposed of, as provided in article 800 and 802, shall have twelve months to present his claim to the County Court to which the money held or realized from the sale has been paid, and if his claim be denied he may sue the County Treasurer, and upon sufficient proof recover the same. Owner may present his claim to County Court, within twelve months.

ART. 804. If the property stolen be a written instrument of any description, and is not claimed before the trial of the cause, the same shall be filed by the Clerk of the District Court, subject to the claim of any person who may afterwards establish his right thereto, and any person claiming such written instrument shall, by advertisement in a newspaper published in the proper county, or in a newspaper nearest the county seat of such county, for eight successive weeks, give notice of his claim, and may afterwards, at any succeeding term of the Court, establish by proof his right thereto. Written instrument stolen to be filed with District Clerk. Owner of, may establish his claim, how.

ART. 805. All the provisions of this chapter relating to stolen property apply as well to property acquired in any manner which makes the acquisition a penal offence. As to property acquired in any manner which makes the, &c.

CHAPTER IV.

APPROPRIATION OF FINES AND MONEYS COLLECTED UPON RECOGNIZANCES, BAIL BONDS, AND OTHER LIKE UNDERTAKINGS.

Act of Aug. 26, 1856.

Fines and forfeitures collec'd on bail bonds, &c., to whom payable.

ART. 806. Every officer charged with the collection of money, upon forfeited recognizances, bail bonds, and other obligations recovered upon in the name of the State, under the provisions of this Code, shall pay over all money collected to the County Treasurer of the proper county. And all fines collected by virtue of any process issued to the Sheriff from any Court having jurisdiction in criminal actions, shall in like manner be paid over when collected.

Fines and forfeitures in criminal cases, &c., to be paid to County Treasurer.

ART. 807. All fines and forfeiture of money upon any proceeding in criminal cases, including fines against the defendant and against defaulting witnesses, money recovered upon recognizances, bail bonds, and all other undertakings in a criminal case, whether of a defendant or of a witness, or the sureties of either, and all fines against defaulting jurors, and for contempts of Court shall be paid into the County Treasury, and shall constitute a fund for the payment, first, of expenses incurred by the county in the keeping of prisoners, and the payment of the expenses of juries in cases of felony, and, secondly, for the payment of jurors in attendance upon the Court at each term.

Fee of District and County Court Attorney and Sheriff, for collecting.

ART. 808. The District Attorney shall be entitled in each case to a fee of five per cent. upon the whole amount of any fine, forfeiture or other money collected under the provisions of this chapter. If there be an Attorney appointed by the County Court to represent the interest of any county in judicial proceedings, he shall be also entitled to a fee of five per cent. for assisting in the collection of money so accruing to the connty; and the Sheriff shall retain five per cent. as compensation for his own services in collecting the same, which several amounts shall be deducted from the amount collected, and the balance paid over to the County Treasurer as before directed.

CHAPTER V.

OF REMITTING FINES AND FORFEITURES, COMMUTATION OF PUNISHMENTS AND REPRIEVES.

Act of Aug. 26, 1856.

Governor may remit fines after conviction.

ART. 809. After conviction, the Governor of the State shall have power, without restriction, to remit fines and forfeitures of a pecuniary character; but he shall report to the Legislature all cases in which he has remitted such penalties, with his reasons for the same.

Governor may remit forfeitures of land, &c., when.

ART. 810. After conviction, the Governor shall have power to remit forfeitures of lands, or of rights and privileges, or forfeitures of any character whatever known to the laws of the State, whenever he shall be memorialized by the Legislature in a joint resolution, setting forth the forfeiture which they may wish remitted.

ART. 811. The Governor shall have authority to commute the punishment in every case of capital felony, by changing the penalty of death into that of imprisonment for life, or for a term of years, either with or without hard labor, which may be done by his warrant to the proper Sheriff commanding him not to execute the penalty of death, and directing him to convey the prisoner to the Penitentiary, stating therein the time for which and the manner in which the defendant is to be confined, which warrant shall be sufficient authority to the Sheriff to deliver, and to the proper officers of the Penitentiary to receive the convict. Governor may commute capital punishment to imprisonment, how.

ART. 812. The Governor may also reprieve and delay the execution of the penalty of death to any day fixed by him in a warrant to the Sheriff. Governor may reprieve.

PART IV.

OF PROCEEDINGS IN INFERIOR TRIBUNALS, AND OF CERTAIN SPECIAL PROCEEDINGS OF A CRIMINAL NATURE.

TITLE I.

OF PROCEEDINGS IN JUSTICES AND MAYORS COURTS.

CHAPTER I.

General Provisions.

ART. 813. The Mayor, or the officer by law exercising the duties usually incumbent upon the Mayors of incorporated towns and cities, and Recorders thereof, shall exercise within the corporate limits of their respective towns or cities, the same criminal jurisdiction which belongs to Justices of the Peace within their jurisdiction, under the provisions of this Code. Act of Aug. 26, 1856. Mayors shall exercise criminal jurisdiction.

ART. 814. The proceedings before Mayors or Recorders shall be governed by the same rules which are prescribed for Justices of the Peace, and every provision of this Title with respect to a Justice shall be construed to extend to Mayors and Recorders within the limits of their jurisdiction. Mayors or Recorders governed by same rules as Justices of the Peace.

ART. 815. The jurisdiction given to Mayors and Recorders of incorporated towns and cities shall not prevent Justices of the Peace from exercising the criminal jurisdiction conferred upon them. But in all cases where there is an incorporated town or city within the bounds of a county, the Justices, and the Mayor and Recorder, shall have concurrent jurisdiction within the limits of such town or city. Mayors and Justices of the Peace have concurrent jurisdiction.

ART. 816. Warrants issued by a Mayor or Recorder are directed to the Marshal or other proper officer of the town or city where the criminal proceeding is had; but in case there be no such officer, the process issued by a Mayor or Recorder shall be directed to any peace officer within the city, town or county, and shall be executed by such officer. Warrants issued by Mayor directed to whom.

ART. 817. Each Justice of the Peace, Mayor and Recorder, shall keep a book in which he shall enter the proceedings had before him in a criminal action, noting the time of issuing his warrant, the name of the defendant, the Justice of the Peace shall keep record book.

accusation against him, a minute of the trial, verdict, judgment, and all proceedings had in the cause.

County Attorney has the right to prosecute in Justices Courts.

ART. 818. In every county of the State where an Attorney has been appointed by the County Court to represent the interests of the county, such Attorney shall have the right to prosecute, in the name of the State, all persons guilty of offences cognizable before Justices of the Peace.

CHAPTER II.

OF THE ARREST OF THE DEFENDANT.

Act of Aug. 26, 1856.

Justice may issue warrant of arrest, when.

ART. 819. Whenever a criminal offence which a Justice of the Peace has jurisdiction to try, shall be committed within the view of such Justice, he may issue his warrant for the arrest of the offender.

Complaint shall be written and sworn to.

ART. 820. Whenever any credible person complains to a Justice of the Peace that an offence has been committed which, by law, such Justice has jurisdiction to try, he shall cause the complaint to be reduced to writing and sworn to, and such complaint shall be attested by the Justice and filed.

Justice shall issue warrant upon complaint, which shall recite.

ART. 821. The Justice shall, immediately upon receiving the complaint, issue his warrant to any peace officer, commanding him to arrest the defendant and bring him before such Justice. The warrant shall be dated and signed by the Justice; it shall set forth in intelligible terms the nature of the offence of which the defendant is accused, and name the place of trial.

How warrant is executed.

ART. 822. Any peace officer into whose hands a warrant may come shall execute the same, by arresting the person accused, and bringing him forthwith before the Justice of the Peace.

CHAPTER III.

OF THE TRIAL AND ITS INCIDENTS.

Act of Aug. 26, 1856.

Justice shall try cause without delay.

ART. 823. When the defendant is brought before the Justice he shall proceed to try the cause without delay, unless good ground be shown for a postponement thereof, in which case, he may postpone the trial to any time not longer than five days, and may, if he deem proper, require the defendant to give bail for his appearance. And if, when required, he fails to give bail, he shall be kept in custody until the final determination of the cause.

ART. 824. If the warrant has been issued upon a complaint made to the Justice, the complaint and warrant shall be read to the defendant. If issued by the Justice without previous complaint, he shall state to the defendant the accusation against him.

Complaint and warrant shall be read to defendant.

ART. 825. A defendant shall not be discharged by reason of any informality in the complaint or warrant; and the proceeding before the Justice shall be conducted without reference to technical rules.

Informality in complaint or warrant, not material.

ART. 826. The Justice shall issue to the Constable, or other peace officer, directing him to summon a jury of twelve men for the trial of the case before him, unless the defendant waive the right of a trial by jury, and consent that in case of conviction, the Justice may assess the fine and imprisonment, or either. Any person summoned as a juror, who fails to attend, may be fined by the Justice as for contempt, in a sum not exceeding twenty dollars.

Act of Feb. 15, 1858.

Justice shall issue order to summon jury.

ART. 827. The defendant and the complainant, or any counsel prosecuting for the State, shall be entitled to four peremptory challenges each.

Act of Aug. 26, 1856.

ART. 828. Either party may challenge any number of Jurors for the following causes:

1. That the Juror is not a freeholder in the State or householder in the county.
2. That the Juror is not a qualified elector of the county.
3. Relationship by consanguinity or affinity, between the Juror and the defendant or complainant.
4. That the Juror has been convicted of some offence which, by law, disqualifies him from sitting on a Jury.

Either party may challenge for following causes.

ART. 829. After impannelling the Jury, the defendant shall be required to plead, and he may plead "guilty" or "not guilty," or the special plea named in the succeeding Article.

The defendant shall plead.

ART. 830. The only special plea allowed is that of former acquittal or conviction for the same offence.

Only special plea allowed.

ART. 831. All pleading in the Justice's Court, in criminal actions, is oral; but the Justice shall note upon his minutes the nature of the plea offered.

Pleadings oral.

ART. 832. If the defendant plead "guilty," proof shall be offered to the Jury, as to the offence; and they shall assess the amount of fine.

If defendant plead "guilty," jury shall assess the fine.

ART. 833. If the defendant refuse to plead, the Justice shall enter the plea of "not guilty," and the cause proceed accordingly.

If defendant refuse to plead.

ART. 834. The following oath shall be administered by the Justice of the Peace to the Jury:

"You swear that you will well and truly try the issue before you, between the State and the defendant, according to law and evidence, so help you God."

Oath administered to the jury

ART. 835. If the State be represented by counsel he may examine the witnesses and argue the cause to the Jury; if the State is not represented the witnesses shall be examined by the Justice.

Who shall examine witnesses for the State.

ART. 836. The defendant has a right to appear by counsel as in all other cases, but not more than one Attorney shall conduct either the prosecution or defence; and the counsel for the State may open and conclude the argument to the Jury.

Defendant may appear by counsel. State shall open and conclude.

Rules of evidence in District Court shall govern. ART. 837. The rules of evidence which govern the trials of criminal actions in the District Court shall apply also to such actions in Justice's Courts.

Jury shall be kept together till they agree. ART. 838. When the cause is submitted to the Jury they shall retire in charge of some officer, and be kept together until they agree to a verdict or are discharged.

If the jury fail to agree, shall be discharged. ART. 839. If a Jury fail to agree upon a verdict, after being kept together a reasonable time, they shall be discharged; and, if there be time left on the same day, another Jury shall be impannelled to try the cause; or the Justice may adjourn for not more than two days, and again impannel a Jury for the trial of such cause.

When court adjourns, the defendant shall enter into bail. ART. 840. In case of an adjournment the Justice shall require the defendant to enter into bail for his appearance; and upon his failure to give bail the defendant may be held in custody.

Bail bonds may be sued upon in the name of the State. ART. 841. Bail bonds taken in accordance with any of the preceding Articles of this Chapter may be sued on in the name of the State before the District Court, and recovery had as provided in Article 87.

When the jury have agreed upon a verdict. ART. 842. When the Jury have agreed upon a verdict, they shall bring the same into Court, and the Justice shall see that it is in proper form.

Justice shall enter verdict upon his books. ART. 843. The Justice shall enter the verdict upon his minute book, and render the proper judgment thereon.

Defendant may be placed in jail, when. ART. 844. Wherever, by the provisions of this Title, the peace officer is authorized to retain a defendant in custody, he may place him in jail or any other place where he can be safely kept.

CHAPTER IV.

OF THE JUDGMENT AND EXECUTION.

Act of Aug. 26, 1856. Judgment. ART. 845. The judgment, in case of conviction in a criminal action before a Justice of the Peace, shall be that the State of Texas recover of the defendant the fine assessed by the Jury and costs, and that the defendant remain in custody of the Sheriff until the fine and costs are paid, and further, that execution issue to collect the same.

Act of Feb. 15, 1858. Defendant may be discharged from jail, how. ART. 848. If a defendant be placed in jail, on account of failing to pay the fine and costs, he can be discharged on *Habeas Corpus*, by showing: 1st. That he is too poor to pay the fine and costs; and further: 2d. That he has remained in jail a sufficient length of time to satisfy the fine at the rate of three dollars for each day; but the defendant shall, in no case under this Article, be discharged until he has been imprisoned at least ten days; and a Justice of the Peace may discharge the defendant upon his showing the same cause, by written application, presented to such Justice, and upon such application being granted, the Justice shall note the same on his minute-book.

Act of Aug. 26, 1856. Execution shall issue. ART. 849. In every case of conviction before a Justice there shall be issued an execution for the collection of the fine and costs, which shall be enforced and returned in the manner prescribed by law in civil actions before Justices.

ART. 850. Every peace officer is bound to execute all process directed to him from a Justice of the Peace. Peace officer bound to execute process.

TITLE II.

OF CORONERS' INQUESTS.

ART. 851. It is the duty of the Coroner to hold inquests in the following cases: Act of Aug. 26, 1856. Coroners shall hold inquests in the following cases.

1. When any person dies in prison.

2. When any person is killed, or from any cause dies an unnatural death, except under sentence of the law.

3. When the body of any human being is found, and the circumstances of his death are unknown.

4. When the circumstances of the death of any person are such as to lead to suspicion that he has come to his death by violent means.

ART. 852. When a body upon which inquest ought to have been held has been interred, the Coroner may cause it to be disinterred for the purpose of holding such inquest. May cause to be disinterred.

ART. 853. The Coroner shall act in such cases upon verbal or written information given him by any credible person, or upon facts within his own knowledge. Upon what information he shall act.

ART. 854. It is the duty of the Sheriff, and of every keeper of any prison, to inform the Coroner of the death of any person confined therein. Sheriff shall inform Coroner of death of a prisoner.

ART. 855. The Coroner may summon a jury of inquest himself, or may direct an order to any peace officer for that purpose. Jury of inquest summoned, how.

ART. 856. A jury of inquest shall consist of six men, citizens of the proper county, freeholders or householders and qualified electors. Shall consist of six men—qualifications.

ART. 857. A person summoned as a juror in such cases who refuses to obey the summons, may be fined by the Coroner, not exceeding ten dollars. Juror refusing to obey summons.

ART. 858. The Coroner shall, so soon as a jury is summoned, proceed with them to the place where the dead body may be, for the purpose of inquiring into the cause of the death. Coroner shall proceed.

ART. 859. The following oath shall be by the Coroner administered to the jury: "You swear that you will diligently inquire into the cause, manner, time and circumstances of the death of the person whose body lies before you, Oath administered to the jury and that you will thereupon make presentment of the truth, the whole truth and nothing but the truth, so help you God."

Coroner shall issue subpœnas.

ART. 860. The Coroner shall have power to issue subpœnas to enforce the attendance of witnesses upon an inquest; and in case of disobedience or failure to attend, may issue attachments for such witnesses.

Testimony reduced to writing.

ART. 861. The testimony of each witness shall be reduced to writing, under the direction of the Coroner, and subscribed by the witness.

Inquest may be private. Coroner or juror, only, shall ask questions, unless.

ART. 862. A Coroner's inquest may be held in private if deemed proper. If other persons than the Coroner and the jury be present, they shall not interfere with the proceedings; and no question shall be asked a witness, except by the Coroner or one of the jurors, unless, as in cases provided for in Article 865, some person is present, who has been accused of killing the deceased. In all such cases the accused may interrogate the witness.

Verdict of the jury.

ART. 863. After having examined into the cause, time, manner and place of the death of the deceased, the jury shall form their verdict, setting forth distinctly the facts relating thereto, which they find to be true; which verdict shall not be valid unless signed by the Coroner and each of the jurors.

Coroner shall keep a minute book, wherein shall be set forth.

ART. 864. The Coroner shall keep a book, in which he shall make a minute of all the proceedings relating to every inquest held by him. Such minute shall set forth—

1. The nature of the information given the Coroner, and by whom given, unless he acts upon facts within his own knowledge.
2. The time and place when and where the inquest is held.
3. The name of the deceased, if known, or, if not known, as accurate a description of him as can be given.
4. The verdict of the jury of inquest.
5. If any arrest is made of a suspected person before inquest held, the name of the person and the fact of his arrest, as well as every thing material which relates thereto, shall be noted.

Where the killing was the act of any person.

ART. 865. When the Coroner has knowledge that the killing was the act of any person, or when an affidavit is made that there is reason to believe that such person has killed the deceased, a warrant may be issued for the arrest of the person accused, before inquest held, and the accused shall have the right to be present when the same is held.

Peace officer shall execute warrant of arrest.

ART. 866. Any peace officer to whose hands the Coroner's warrant of arrest shall come, is bound to execute the same without delay; and he shall detain the person arrested until his discharge is ordered by the Coroner, or some Judge upon habeas corpus.

Warrant shall be sufficient, if.

ART. 867. A warrant of arrest in such cases shall be sufficient if it issues in the name of "The State of Texas," recites the name of the accused, or describes him when his name is unknown, sets forth the offence charged in plain language, and is signed officially by the Coroner.

If the verdict find that a person killed the deceased.

ART. 868. If it be found by the verdict of the jury of inquest that a person already arrested did in fact kill the deceased, or was an accomplice or accessary to the death, the Coroner may, according to the facts of the case, commit him to jail, or require him to execute a bail bond with security for his appearance before the proper court to answer for the offence.

Bail bond shall be sufficient, if.

ART. 869. A bail bond taken before a Coroner shall be sufficient if it recite the offence of which the party is accused, be payable to the State of Texas, be dated and signed by the principal and his surety.

Coroner shall file papers with Clerk of District Court.

ART. 870. The Coroner shall file with the Clerk of the District Court of the proper county the warrant of arrest, the testimony taken, the bond and other papers relating to the inquest. If the District Court be in session, the papers shall be forthwith filed; if not in session, they shall be filed on or before the first day of the next term of the court.

Bail bond may be forfeited, &c.

ART. 871. A bail bond taken in accordance with the directions of this Title, may be forfeited and judgment recovered thereon as in cases of other bail bonds.

When the verdict finds that a person not in custody killed deceased, Coroner shall issue warrant.

ART. 872. When, by the verdict of a jury of inquest, it is found that any person not in custody killed the deceased, or was an accomplice to the death, the Coroner shall issue his warrant to the Sheriff, or other peace officer, commanding him to arrest the person accused, and take him before some magistrate to be named in the writ.

Warrant shall be sufficient, if.

ART. 873. The warrant issued in accordance with the provisions of the preceding Article, shall be sufficient if it run in the name of "The State of Texas," give the name of the person accused, or describe him when his name is unknown, recite the offence with which he is charged in plain language, and be dated and signed officially by the Coroner.

Peace officer shall execute the warrant, how.

ART. 874. The peace officer into whose hands such warrant may come, shall forthwith execute the same by arresting the defendant and taking him before the magistrate named in the warrant; and the magistrate shall proceed to examine the accusation, and the same proceedings shall be had thereon as in other cases where persons accused of offences are brought before him.

Duties of Coroner performed by Justice of the Peace, when.

ART. 875. When there is no Coroner in a county, or he is absent or unable to serve, or resides more than ten miles from the place where any dead body is found, the duties prescribed in this Title to be performed by him, may be performed by any Justice of the Peace of the county, who shall proceed in holding the inquest according to the rules prescribed for the government of the Coroner.

Coroner shall certify to the verdict.

ART. 876. When a jury of inquest have agreed to a verdict, it is the duty of the Coroner or Justice holding the inquest, to certify that the same is the verdict of the jury.

Magistrate may proceed against person accused.

ART. 877. Nothing contained in this Title shall prevent proceedings from being had, for the arrest and examination of an accused person before a magistrate, pending the holding of an inquest. But when a person accused of an offence has been already arrested under a warrant from the Coroner, he shall not be taken from the hands of the peace officer by a warrant from any other magistrate.

TITLE III.

OF FUGITIVES FROM JUSTICE.

ART. 878. A person charged in any other State or Territory of the United

Act of Aug. 26, 1856.

Fugitive from justice delivered up, when.

States with treason, felony, or other crime, who shall flee from justice and be found in this State, shall, on demand of the executive authority of the State or Territory from which he fled, be delivered up to be removed to the State or Territory having jurisdiction of the crime.

Judicial and peace officers shall aid in the arrest.

ART. 879. It is declared to be the duty of all judicial and peace officers of the State, to give aid in the arrest and detention of a fugitive from any other State or Territory, that he may be held subject to a requisition by the Governor of the State or Territory from which he may have escaped.

Fugitive shall not be delivered up, if offence was committed prior to 16th Feb., 1846.

ART. 880. No person shall be arrested, or if arrested, shall be delivered up, on the requisition of the Governor of any other State or Territory, where it appears that the offence with which he is charged was committed prior to the sixteenth day of February, A. D. 1846.

Governor of this State can demand fugitive from justice, how.

ART. 881. Whenever the Governor of this State may think proper to demand a person who has committed an offence in this State, and has fled to another State or Territory, he may commission any suitable person to take such requisition; and the accused person, if brought back to the State, shall be delivered up to the Sheriff of the county in which it is alleged he has committed the offence. A reasonable compensation for his services shall be paid to the person so commissioned, out of the treasury of the State.

Magistrate shall issue warrant for arrest of fugitive, when.

ART. 882. Whenever complaint on oath is made to a magistrate, that any person within his jurisdiction is a fugitive from justice from another State or Territory, it is his duty to issue a warrant of arrest for the apprehension of the person accused.

Complaint shall be sufficient if it recite.

ART. 883. The complaint shall be sufficient if it recite:

1. The name of the person accused.
2. The State or Territory from which he has fled.
3. The offence committed by the accused.
4. That he has fled to this State from the State or Territory where the offence was committed.
5. That the act alleged to have been committed by the accused, is a violation of the penal law of the State or Territory from which he fled.

Warrant of arrest from magistrate shall direct, what.

ART. 884. The warrant of a magistrate to arrest a fugitive from justice, shall direct a peace officer to apprehend the person accused, and bring him before such magistrate.

Shall require bail or commit accused, when.

ART. 885. When the person accused is brought before the magistrate, he shall hear proof, and if satisfied that the defendant is charged in another State or Territory with the offence named in the complaint, he shall require of him bail to appear before such magistrate at a specified time; and in default of such bail, he may commit the defendant to jail, to await a requisition from the Governor of the State or Territory from which he fled.

Certified transcript of indictment evidence.

ART. 886. A properly certified transcript of an indictment against the accused, shall be evidence to show that he is charged with the crime alleged.

Person arrested shall not be committed or.

ART. 887. A person arrested under the provisions of this Title, shall not be committed or held to bail for a longer time than six months.

Magistrate shall give notice to Dist. Attorney.

ART. 888. The magistrate by whose warrant an accused person is arrested, shall forthwith give notice to the District Attorney of the District in which the arrest is made, who shall forthwith, through the mail, give notice to the Governor of the State or Territory from which the defendant is charged to have fled.

ART. 889. If the defendant is not arrested under a warrant from the Governor of this State before the expiration of the time for which he is committed, or held to bail, he shall be discharged. Defendant shall be discharged, when.

ART. 890. A person who shall have been once arrested under the provisions of this Title, and discharged under the provisions of the preceding Article, or by habeas corpus, shall not be again arrested upon a charge of the same offence, except by a warrant from the Governor of this State. Shall not be arrested a second time, except.

TITLE IV.

OF VAGRANTS.

ART. 891. A vagrant is an idle person, living without any visible means of support, and making no exertion to obtain a support by any honest employment. Act of Aug. 26, 1856. Definition of vagrant.

ART. 892. It is the duty of each Chief Justice of a county and Justice of the Peace, to order the arrest of vagrants; which may be done by warrant, directed to any peace officer. Chief Justice and Justice of the Peace shall order arrest of vagrants.

ART. 893. A warrant to arrest a vagrant may be issued upon complaint made on oath by any three credible persons, householders of the county where the complaint is made. Warrant of arrest may issue, when.

ART. 894. A peace officer shall arrest a vagrant when directed by warrant, and take him before one of the magistrates named in Article 892. Peace officer shall arrest vagrant.

ART. 895. When a person arrested is taken before the magistrate, he shall proceed to ascertain whether he is a vagrant within the meaning of the law; and if it be found that he is, the magistrate shall make an order that such vagrant be put to labor in such manner as the County Court may direct. If magistrate find that person arrested is a vagrant, he shall order that, &c.

ART. 896. The magistrate trying a case of vagrancy shall certify to the County Court his order, in every case where he has adjudged a person to be a vagrant. Magistrate shall certify his order to County Court.

ART. 897. The County Court of each county shall, by general regulation, provide for the manner in which vagrants are to be employed, and the kind of labor to which they shall be put, which may be upon any road, bridge, or other public work of the county. County Court shall provide for employment of vagrants.

ART. 898. The County Court shall so regulate the disposal of vagrants, as that they may be compelled to labor for the first offence not more than one week, and for the second, or any subsequent offence, not more than three weeks, during which time the person so compelled to work shall be supported, and, if deserving thereof, shall be paid an additional compensation, at the discretion of the County Court, out of the county treasury. Time vagrant shall labor.

ART. 899. The municipal authorities of incorporated towns and cities may make like regulations, respecting cases of vagrancy within their respective Municipal authorities of incorporated cities may make like regulations respecting vagrants.

jurisdictions, and vagrants may be arrested and dealt with under the warrant of the Mayor or Recorder of such town or city; may be compelled, in like manner, to labor upon any street or public work of such town or city, and shall be supported and compensated therefor out of the treasury of the corporation, at the discretion of such municipal authorities.

Vagrant may demand a trial by jury.

ART. 900. A person arrested as a vagrant may demand a trial by jury, and the magistrate shall thereupon cause a jury of twelve householders, or freeholders, to be summoned and sworn, for the trial of such person, and render such judgment as the verdict authorizes.

TITLE V.

OF DISORDERLY PERSONS.

Act of Aug. 26, 1856.

Municipal authorities may make regulations regarding disorderly persons.

ART. 901. The municipal authorities of each city or town may make such regulations as may be deemed expedient for the arrest and punishment of disorderly persons; and the County Court of each county may provide for the employment in labor, upon public works, of all persons arrested and adjudged by a Magistrate to be disorderly persons.

The following are disorderly persons.

ART. 902. The following are disorderly persons within the meaning of this Title:

1. Strolling persons who go about proposing to tell fortunes, or exhibiting in public any cheating tricks or apparatus.

2. Keepers of bawdy houses, or houses for the common resort of prostitutes, vagabonds or free negroes.

Disorderly persons may be dealt with as vagrants.

ART. 903. Disorderly persons may be arrested and dealt with as vagrants are directed to be treated by the provisions of Title IV, Part IV, of this Code; and like proceedings as in cases of vagrants may be had before Magistrates, in ascertaining whether a person arrested is a disorderly person.

May be fined and imprisoned.

ART. 904. A person adjudged by the Magistrate to be a disorderly person may also be fined, not exceeding twenty-five dollars and imprisoned in jail, not exceeding ten days.

May demand a trial by jury.

ART. 905. Disorderly persons may demand a trial by Jury, in the same manner as vagrants.

TITLE VI.

OF PROCEEDINGS AGAINST FREE PERSONS OF COLOR REMAINING IN THE STATE IN VIOLATION OF LAW.

ART. 906. A person of color is one who has at least one-eighth African blood. Act of Feb. 15, 1858. Who is a person of color.

ART. 908. No free person of color can lawfully emigrate to, or remain in this State, except where special permission is given by the Constitution and Laws of the State. Act of Aug 26, 1856. Free person of, shall not emigrate, &c.

ART. 909. Where a free person of color, who is not specially permitted by law to reside in the State, is found within its limits, any Magistrate may, from his own knowledge, or upon information given him by a credible person, issue his warrant for the arrest of such free person of color. Magistrate may issue his warrant for arrest of.

ART. 909a. When a free person of color is arrested under a warrant issued by a Magistrate, he shall be brought by the officer making the arrest before such Magistrate. Act of Feb. 15, 1858. Shall be brought before.

ART. 910. And thereupon the Magistrate shall give a written order to the Sheriff of the county to take such free person of color, and hire him for the term of six months to the highest bidder, at the court-house of the county, giving notice of the hiring by advertisement posted up at two or more public places in the county. Act of Aug. 26, 1856. Shall be hired for six months.

ART. 911. The proceeds of the hire of a free person of color shall be collected by the Sheriff, and after deducting costs of the proceedings and expenses, the remainder shall be paid over to such person to enable him to leave the State, and the Sheriff shall notify him to leave within thirty days from the time he receives the money. Proceeds of the hire dispose of, how.

ART. 912 If a free person of color does not leave the State within thirty days from the time the proceeds of his hire is paid to him as directed in the preceding Article, he may be arrested by the Sheriff of the county, upon the warrant of a Magistrate, and may be hired at public outcry to the highest bidder, for cash, for the term of five years, unless he can show, when brought before the Magistrate, that he was prevented from leaving the State by sickness, or other unavoidable casualty, in which case an additional time of thirty days shall be given him to leave the State; and if he be found in the State after the expiration of that time he shall be proceeded against as above directed in this Article. Shall be hired for five years, when.

ART. 913. One-half of the proceeds of the hiring provided for in the preceding Article, shall be paid into the County Treasury, and the balance to the free person of color, after deducting five per cent. of the whole amount as compensation for the services of the Sheriff. Proceeds of the hire disposed of, how.

ART. 914. At the expiration of the term of five years, for which any free person of color is hired as herein directed, the portion of the proceeds of the hire to which he is entitled shall be paid to him, and he shall be again warned by the Sheriff to leave the State. Shall be warned to leave the State.

ART. 915. If after the expiration of thirty days from the time when the money is paid to a free person of color he be found in the State, a warrant of arrest may be again issued, and he may be brought before a Magistrate, and unless he can make it appear satisfactorily that he was prevented from leaving by force, or by reason of sickness, or some unavoidable casualty, the Magistrate shall issue an order to the Sheriff for the sale of such free person of color, by virtue of which the Sheriff shall, after advertising for ten days, by public notice in some newspaper in the county, if there be one published in the county, or by notices posted up at two or more public places, if there is no newspaper published in the county, sell such free person of color as a slave for life, to the highest bidder, for cash. Shall be sold as a slave for life, when.

Proceeds of the sale disposed of, how.

ART. 916. The ownership of said person of color shall by such sale be fully vested in the purchaser. The proceeds of the sale shall be paid into the County Treasury, after deducting five per cent. as compensation for the services of the Sheriff.

While hired, shall be treated as a slave.

ART. 917. A free person of color, while hired under the provisions of any of the foregoing Articles, shall in all respects for the term of the hiring be considered and treated as a slave.

TITLE VII.

OF PROCEEDINGS BEFORE JUSTICES OF THE PEACE AND MAYORS, AGAINST SLAVES WHO HIRE THEIR TIME, OR ARE HIRED TO OTHER SLAVES, OR TO FREE PERSONS OF COLOR.

Act of Aug. 26, 1856.

Slave shall not hire his time, &c.

ART. 918. It shall not be lawful for the master of any slave to permit such slave to hire his time, or to hire him to any other slave, or to any free person of color.

The term master includes.

ART. 919. The term master, as used in this Title, includes all persons having the charge, control, or management of slaves for any period of time.

By the term, "hire his time" is meant.

ART. 920. By the term "hire his time," as used in this Title, is meant any contract between the master and slave, by which such slave agrees to pay any stipulated price for his time, and during such time regulates his own conduct in respect to labor to be performed by him, or make contracts as to such labor.

Slave may go one day, &c.

ART. 921. The provisions of this Title shall not prevent the master of a slave from permitting such slave to go at large for one day at a time in search of employment.

Peace officer shall arrest slave hiring time.

ART. 922. It is the duty of every peace officer, and any other person has the right, to arrest a slave who may be found hiring his time, or hired to any free person of color or slave contrary to the provisions of this Title.

Justice of the Peace, Mayor, &c.

ART. 923. Any Justice of the Peace, Mayor, or Recorder of a town or city, may, by order, either verbal or written, directed to a peace officer, cause the arrest of a slave who hires his time, or is hired to another slave, or to a free person of color.

Slave arrested shall be carried be carried before Justice, &c.

ART. 924. When a slave is arrested by a peace officer or other person, under the provisions of the two preceding Articles, he shall be taken before a Justice of the Peace, Mayor, or Recorder. The jurisdiction of a Justice of the Peace, in such cases, shall extend to his county, and that of Mayors or Recorders to the limits of their respective corporations.

ART. 925. The Justice, Mayor, or Recorder, shall proceed, in a summary manner to examine into the facts, and if it be found that such slave has been permitted to hire his time, or has been hired to a slave or free person of color, he shall commit such slave to the county Jail, to remain until discharged as hereinafter provided. Slave shall be committed to county jail, &c.

ART. 926. The Justice, Mayor, or Recorder, shall assess a fine of not less than ten, nor more than one hundred dollars, against the slave who shall have been found hiring his time, or hired to another slave, or free person of color, and shall cause notice to be given to the master of such slave, if he reside within the county where the arrest takes place, or if he resides without the county, or be temporarily absent therefrom, then to his agent, if he has one in the county. Fine assessed against the slave and notice to master.

ART. 927. If the master of the slave, or any person for him, shall pay to the Sheriff of the county the amount of the fine assessed by the Justice or Mayor against the slave, such slave shall be discharged from custody. Slave discharged upon payment of fine by master.

ART. 928. If a slave, arrested and committed under the provisions of this Title, remains in Jail for a time exceeding five days, it shall be the duty of the Sheriff to hire such slave for a term of thirty days at public outcry, giving one day's notice thereof, by posting an advertisement at the court-house door of the proper county; such hiring shall be for cash, payable before the slave is delivered into the hands of the hirer. Sheriff shall hire such slave out, when.

ART. 929. The hirer of a slave under the provisions of the preceding Article, and under Article 931, shall be entitled to his services, and shall, during the time for which he is hired, exercise all the rights of ownership over such slave; and at the expiration of the thirty days shall deliver the slave into the hands of the Sheriff. Hirer shall exercise rights of ownership.

ART. 930. If the master, before or immediately upon the expiration of the time for which the slave was hired, make application to the Sheriff, the slave shall be delivered to him so soon as the time shall have expired for which the hiring took place, upon his paying the fine assessed and all costs accruing by reason of the proceeding. Slave delivered to master, when

ART. 931. If no application by the master be made, or he refuse to pay the fine and cost, the Sheriff shall proceed, after giving five days' notice by advertisement, posted at three public places, one of which shall be the court-house door, to hire such slave for a term of twelve months to the highest bidder, for cash, payable before the slave is delivered into the hands of the hirer; at the expiration of the time of hiring such slave shall be delivered into the hands of the Sheriff. Slave hired for twelve months, when.

ART. 932. If, before or at the expiration of the time for which a slave was hired, under the preceding Article, the master make application to the Sheriff, such slave shall be delivered to him so soon as the time has expired for which the hiring took place, upon his paying to the Sheriff the fine assessed and the costs that have accrued by reason of the proceeding. May be deliver'd to master after time expires.

ART. 933. If no application be made, as provided for in the preceding Article, the Sheriff shall give public notice for thirty days, by posting advertisements at three of the most public places in the county, one of which shall be at the court-house door, and no two of which shall be in the same town or city, (except the city of Galveston.) This notice shall state the facts as to the previous apprehension of the slave, and the proceedings which have taken place; shall contain a full description of such slave, and further state that unless claimed by some person duly authorized to receive the slave, he will be Slave sold, when sold to the highest bidder, for cash, at the court-house door, on a day to be fixed by the notice. If there be a newspaper published in the county, this notice shall also be inserted therein, and if there be no newspaper in the county, then the same shall be published in a newspaper nearest to the county seat of the county where the proceedings have taken place.

Delivered to master, upon demand, before sale. ART. 934. The Sheriff shall deliver the slave, if demanded by his master, at any time before the sale has taken place, upon payment of the fine assessed and the costs that have accrued.

Title of purchaser good. ART. 935. If no demand be made, as before provided, or the person demanding refuse to pay the fine and costs, the slave shall be sold on the day appointed to the highest bidder, for cash, and the title of the purchaser shall be good and valid against all persons whatever.

Proceeds of hire or sale disposed of, how. ART. 936. All fines assessed, and all money received for the hire or sale of a slave, under the provisions of this Title, shall be paid into the County Treasury of the proper county, after deducting twenty per cent. therefrom as compensation to the Sheriff for his services.

Fees of Sheriff. ART. 937. The Sheriff shall also be entitled to be paid, as costs, fifty cents a day for the time he may have the custody of any slave arrested under the provisions of this Title. He shall safely keep any such slave, and for that purpose may place him in jail during any time when the slave is in his possession, by delivery from the hirer under Articles 929 and 931.

If the right of the person applying be doubtful. ART. 938. When any person shall apply for a slave as his master, under the provisions of this Title, the Sheriff may, if he has doubt as to the right of the person applying, require him to file suit in the District Court to establish his claim; and the claimant shall be entitled to damages in such suit, if it appear that the Sheriff was clearly wrong in refusing to deliver the property upon his demand.

If the owner apply within 5 years, the County Court shall pay value of slave. ART. 939. If any person shall appear before the County Court within five years from the time of the sale of a slave under the provisions of this Title, and establish to the satisfaction of the court his right as the owner of the slave sold, the County Court shall pay to such owner, out of any money in the treasury, the amount which was received by the county from the proceeds of a sale of the slave; and if the County Court refuse to pay the same, the owner may bring his suit against the county, in the District Court, to establish his right.

The term "owner" means ART. 940. The term "owner," as here used, means the person having the rightful property in a slave, either in his own right, or as executor, administrator or guardian.

Demand may be made, by whom. ART. 941. The application or demand, for the possession of a slave, spoken of in Articles 930, 932, 934, and 938, may be made by any duly authorized agent of the person who is master or owner of the slave, and shall have the same effect as if made by such owner or master in person.

Sufficient proof that slave hires his time. ART. 942. Upon any investigation before a Justice, or Mayor, under the provisions of this Title, if it be proved that a slave is in the habit of making contracts for himself, with regard to his labor, without the subsequent ratification by the master, or that he lives off the premises of his master, and conducts any business or labor not under the immediate superintendence of the master, it shall be deemed sufficient proof that he hires his time.

If it appear that negro arrested is a free person ART. 943. If it appear to the Justice, or Mayor, that a negro arrested as a slave is in fact a free person of color, who resides within this State in violation of law, such proceedings shall be had as are directed in Title VI, of Part IV. If it appear upon such examination that a slave arrested is a runaway, he shall be dealt with as directed by law in the case of runaway slaves. of color or runaway.

TITLE VIII.

OF REPORTS RELATIVE TO CRIME.

ART. 944. Each Clerk of the District Court shall, within twenty days after the adjournment of a term of the Court, make out and transmit to the Attorney General a report setting forth: Act of Aug. 26, 1856. District Clerks shall make reports to Attorney General, setting forth.

1. The number of indictments and informations presented to the last term of the Court, and for what offences.

2. The number of arraignments, convictions and acquittals for each offence, and the penalties assessed in each case.

3. The number of indictments and informations which have been disposed of without the intervention of a petit jury, with the cause and manner of such disposition.

4. The amount of money collected and reported by the Sheriff under any criminal process.

ART. 945. The Attorney General shall furnish to each Clerk of the District Court forms for reports in the cases provided for in the preceding Article. Attorney General shall furnish forms to District Clerks.

ART. 946. Each Justice of the Peace shall report in like manner, to each term of the District Court, the number of causes which have been tried and determined before him, with the disposition made of the same in all cases where he has jurisdiction to try offences; and the Clerk of the District Court shall send a copy of such report to the Attorney General, accompanying his own report, as required by Article 944. Justices of the Peace shall report to each term District Court.

ART. 947. The Attorney General shall, on the first Monday of December of each year, communicate to the Governor of the State all the information which he has received from the District Clerks under the provisions of Articles 944 and 946, with such suggestions thereon as he may deem useful respecting the penal laws of the State and the enforcement of the same. Attorney General shall report to Governor each year.

ART. 948. The information thus communicated to the Governor shall be by him laid before the Legislature at its regular or any called session. Governor shall report to the Legislature.

TITLE IX.

OF SPECIAL PROCEEDINGS AGAINST RAILROAD COMPANIES.

ART. 948a. If any railroad corporation shall wilfully neglect to perform any duty enjoined by "An Act to regulate Railroad Companies," approved Feb- Act of Feb. 15, 1858.

Railroad company may be prosecuted in any county through which road passes. ruary 7, 1853, or by any other law of the State, that is now or may hereafter be enacted, such Company may be prosecuted in the name of the State, in the District Court of any county through which said road may pass; or of any county where the route of such road in actual operation may commence or terminate.

Such prosecutions governed by rules in civil suits. ART. 948b. Prosecution in such cases shall be regulated by the rules which govern civil suits, as to the form of the petition and other pleadings, and the service of process, and as to the trial before the jury.

If the verdict be for the State. ART. 948c. If the verdict be for the State, such damages shall be assessed as are prescribed by the laws heretofore or hereafter to be passed, relating to such illegal acts, and the judgment of the Court shall be rendered against the company in its corporate name, and execution may be levied against any property belonging to such company.

Where act or omission operates a forfeiture of a charter. ART. 948d. The three preceding Articles have no reference to cases where any act or omission of a Railroad Company operates as a surrender or forfeiture of its charter.

PART V.

OF COSTS IN CRIMINAL ACTIONS.

TITLE I.

TAXATION OF COSTS.

Act of Feb. 15, 1858.

Fee book shall be kept by, what officers. ART. 949. The Clerk of the Supreme Court, each Clerk of the District Court, and each Justice of the Peace and Mayor or Recorder of an incorporated city or town, shall keep a book called a fee-book, in which they shall tax the costs accruing in each criminal action or proceeding before them.

Act of Aug. 26, 1856.

If officer charge higher fee than is allowed by law. ART. 950. When, as hereafter provided, costs are to be paid by the State, the fees allowed in Title II, of this Part, shall be charged in criminal proceedings; and if any one of the officers named in the preceding Article shall charge, either for himself or any other persons entitled to costs, higher rates than are allowed by law, he is guilty of a penal offence, and subject, on conviction, to be removed from office.

The same. ART. 951. When, as hereafter provided, costs are to be paid by the defendant, the fees allowed in Title III, of this Part, shall be taxed; and no officer entitled to fees shall charge higher rates than those allowed under the penalty prescribed in the preceding article.

TITLE II.

OF COSTS PAID BY THE STATE.

ART. 952. Costs in accordance with the rates herein fixed, shall be paid by the State to the following persons and in the following cases: — Act of Aug. 26, 1856. The State shall pay costs as follows.

* * * * * * * *

To the Sheriff shall be paid in each case of felony, where the defendant is brought to trial, whether he be convicted or acquitted:

For executing each warrant of arrest or capias, or for making arrest without warrant, one dollar.

For summoning or attaching each witness, fifty cents.

For summoning jury two dollars.

For conveying prisoners to the Penitentiary, for each mile going and coming, ten cents; for each guard employed by him in conveying such prisoners, the same amount; and for the support of each prisoner ten cents for each mile travelled in going to the Penitentiary. For conveying a prisoner taken under criminal process, ten cents for each mile traveled in going to and returning from the place to which he is required to convey such prisoner, and the like sum for one person employed as a guard in such cases; and for the support of the prisoner ten cents for each mile traveled in going to the place to which he is required to convey such prisoner—the distance to be computed over the most commonly travelled route.

For executing death warrant, twenty-five dollars.

For each mile he may be compelled to travel in executing criminal process, or in summoning or attaching witnesses, six cents.

ART. 952d. Costs shall be paid by the State as follows: to the Attorney General in every case of felony, where the defendant appeals and the judgment is affirmed, twenty dollars; to the District Attorneys in every case of conviction for felony in the District Court, where the defendant does not appeal, or where upon appeal the judgment is affirmed, twenty dollars; to the Clerk of the Supreme Court, in every case of felony upon which an appeal is taken, ten dollars; to the Clerks of the District Courts in every case of felony, whether the defendant is acquitted or convicted, ten dollars; but in cases where the defendant is indicted for a felony and by the verdict of a jury is convicted of an offence less than felony, no cost shall be paid by the State. — Act of Feb. 15, 1858. Costs shall be paid by the State, as follows.

ART. 953. When services have been rendered by any peace officer other than a Sheriff, in cases where the State is liable for costs, such peace officer shall receive the same fees as are allowed the Sheriff. — Act of Aug. 26, 1856. Peace officer, as Sheriff, &c.

ART. 954. The fees accruing to peace officers other than the Sheriff, shall be taxed as Sheriff's costs, the clerk noting the name of the peace officer. Such costs shall be collected by the Sheriff as a part of his own, and he shall be liable to pay the same to the proper person so soon as he has received it from the State; and if he refuse to pay the same when demanded he shall be liable in a civil action before a Justice of the Peace to pay five times the amount of such fees. — Peace officers' fees taxed as Sheriffs.

ART. 955. The fees allowed Sheriffs and Clerks shall be audited and paid by the officers of the State Treasury, upon the certificate of the Judge of the District Court attached to the bill of costs. — Fees paid by State Treasurer upon certificate of District Judge.

Costs paid by State a charge against defendant, except.

ART. 956. The costs and fees, paid by the State under this title, shall be a charge against the defendants in cases where they are convicted, except in cases of capital punishment, or of sentence to the penitentiary for life; and when collected, shall be paid into the Treasury of the State.

TITLE III.

OF COSTS TO BE PAID BY COUNTIES AND THE MANNER OF ENFORCING COLLECTION.

Act of Aug. 26, 1856. County shall be liable for, what costs.

ART. 957. Each county shall be liable for all the expenses incurred on account of the safe keeping of prisoners confined in their respective jails or kept under guard.

Shall be responsible for food and lodging of Jurors.

ART. 958. Each county shall be liable for the expenses of food and lodging for Jurors impannelled in a case of felony; but in such cases no scrip shall be issued or money paid to the Jurors whose expenses are so paid.

Juror may pay his own expenses and draw scrip.

ART. 959. A Juror may pay his own expenses and draw his scrip, but the county is responsible in the first place for all the expenses incurred by the Sheriff in providing suitable food and lodging for the Jury, not to exceed, however, one dollar and twenty-five cents a day.

Sheriff shall receive from county, what costs.

ART. 960. The Sheriff shall receive from the county one dollar a day for each guard he employs, and also the reasonable expenses of such guard, not exceeding one dollar a day, and for the support and maintainance of each prisoner in his custody, fifty cents a day during the time he has charge of such prisoner.

Sheriff shall pay what expenses, and be reimbursed by county.

ART. 961. It is the duty of the Sheriff to pay the expenses of Jurors impannelled in cases of felony, (except when they are paid by the Juror himself,) the expense of employing and maintaining a guard, and to support and take care of all prisoners; for all of which he shall be reimbursed by the county according to the rates fixed in the two preceding Articles.

Sheriff shall present account to District Judge.

ART. 962. At each term of the District Court of his county the Sheriff may present to the District Judge presiding, his accounts for the keeping of persons and maintaining guards since the last term of the Court, and also for all expenses incurred by him for food and lodging of Jurors in cases of trials for felony during the term at which his account is presented, which account shall be verified by the oath of the Sheriff.

Judge shall allow it, when.

ART. 963. If the account does not exceed the amount allowed by Articles 959 and 960, and the same appears to the Judge to be correct, he shall allow it; and such account shall be filed with the District Clerk.

Judge shall give Sheriff draft upon county treasurer.

ART. 964. The District Judge shall give to the Sheriff a draft upon the County Treasurer for the amount of each account allowed by him; and the same when presented to the County Treasurer shall be paid out of any money in his hands.

ART. 965. The Coroner shall be entitled to receive for summoning a Jury and all other business connected with an inquest upon a dead body, including certifying and returning the same to the proper Court, five dollars, to be paid out of the County Treasury; and when a Justice of the Peace acts as Coroner, he shall be paid a like fee for the same services. Coroner's fees—to be paid by county.

ART. 966. Services performed under the last Article shall be proved by the affidavit of the Coroner or Justice, and presented to the District Judge, who shall, if the account be allowed, give his draft upon the County Treasurer, and the same shall stand upon the same footing and be paid as provided for drafts to the Sheriff. How proved.

ART. 967. The fund raised in accordance with Articles 806 and 807, shall not be appropriated by the County Court for any purpose other than the payment of costs due officers in criminal proceedings, and for which the counties are liable, and it is the duty of the County Treasurer to reserve said fund for that purpose, and pay out of it any draft drawn upon him by a District Judge. What fund reserved for costs due officers.

ART. 968. Drafts drawn by a District Judge on the County Treasurer, shall, without any action of the County Court, or acceptance by the County Treasurer, be receivable for all county taxes at par. They may be transferred by delivery, and no ordinance, rule or regulation whatever, made by the County Court, shall postpone or defeat the right of a holder of such draft to pay county taxes therewith. Drafts drawn by Judge on county treasurer.

ART. 968a. Each member of a Coroner's Jury shall be allowed one dollar and twenty-five cents a day, while serving upon the same, to be paid by the County, and the certificate of the Coroner shall be sufficient evidence for the allowance of the claim. Act of Feb. 15, 1858. Coroner's jury allowed, what.

TITLE IV.

OF COSTS PAID BY THE DEFENDANT.

CHAPTER I.

IN THE SUPREME AND DISTRICT COURTS.

ART. 969. In every case of misdemeanor, where the defendant is convicted, the costs shall be paid by him; and the same shall be taxed by the Clerk, and collected under execution or other process as provided in Articles 698, 699, 700 and 701. Act of Aug. 26, 1856. Costs paid by defendant, convicted in misdemeanor.

ART. 970. Costs, when adjudged against the defendant, shall be allowed as follows: To the Attorney-General shall be paid for every conviction for offences against the Penal Laws relating to gaming, where the judgment is affirmed, or where the appeal is dismissed, fifteen dollars; for every case of appeal by the State in gaming cases, where the judgment is reversed, fifteen dollars; for every like case of affirmance of judgment in favor of the State, or of dismissal of the appeal of the defendant, or of refusal where the State appeals in other cases of misdemeanor, ten dollars. Act of Feb. 15, 1858. Costs against defendant allowed as follows.

ART. 971. To the District Attorney shall be paid,

In every case of conviction for violation of the laws against gaming, where no appeal is taken or where the judgment on appeal is affimed, fifteen dollars. Act of Aug. 26, 1856.

Fees of District Attorney.

For every like conviction and affirmance of judgment in other misdemeanors, ten dollars.

To the Clerk of the Supreme Court shall be paid,

In every appeal by the State in a case of misdemeanor, where the judgment is reversed, and in every appeal by the defendant where the judgment is affirmed, ten dollars.

Fees of District Clerk.

ART. 972. To the District Clerk shall be paid,

For issuing each capias, subpœna, attachment, or other process, fifty cents.

Entering appearance, ten cents.

Docketing cause to be charged once, fifteen cents.

Swearing and impannelling Jury, thirty cents.

Swearing each witness, ten cents.

Entering each order, thirty cents.

Receiving and recording verdict, thirty cents.

Entering judgment, fifty cents.

Each transcript on appeal, ten cents a hundred words.

Copy of indictment or information, when asked by defendant, fifty cents.

Fees of Sheriff.

ART. 973. To the Sheriff shall be paid,

For executing warrant of arrest or capias, one dollar.

Summoning or attaching witness, fifty cents.

For each Jury, one dollar.

For executing search warrant, two dollars.

For each execution, two dollars.

For each commitment or release, one dollar.

For each bond, one dollar.

For attending prisoner on habeas corpus, three dollars a day.

For each mile necessarily traveled in executing any criminal process, including subpœnas and attachments for witnesses, six cents.

CHAPTER II.

IN JUSTICES' COURTS.

Act of Aug. 26, 1856.

In misdemeanors before Justices of the Peace, Mayors, &c.

ART. 974. In every case of misdemeanor tried before a Justice of the Peace, Mayor or Recorder, the defendant upon conviction shall pay costs according to the rates herein fixed, and in every proceeding under this Code, where a Justice of the Peace, Mayor or Recorder, acts for the purpose of preventing or suppressing crime, costs shall be paid as herein provided.

Costs of Justices of the Peace, Mayors and Recorders.

ART. 975. Justices of the Peace, Mayors and Recorders shall be allowed costs as follows:

Issuing warrant of arrest, warrant of commitment, search warrant or other process against a defendant, one dollar.

Issuing subpœna or attachment, fifty cents.

Taking bail, one dollar.

Swearing witness, twenty-five cents.

Administering oath, where complaint is made to him relative to crime, fifty cents.

Swearing and impannelling jury, one dollar.

Receiving and entering verdict and judgment, one dollar.

For each execution, one dollar.

For making copies of any papers or entries on his dockets, including certificate for any person applying for same, fifteen cents for each hundred words.

ART. 976. The Constable or other peace officer shall receive in all cases before a Justice of the Peace for misdemeanors, the following fees. Fees of Constable or other peace officer.

For executing warrant of arrest, or of commitment, one dollar.

Summoning jury, two dollars.

Serving Subpœna or attachment, fifty cents.

For each commitment, one dollar.

For each execution, one dollar.

For conveying prisoner to jail, including guard and all other expenses, twenty-five cents a mile.

For every mile he may necessarily travel in executing criminal process, including subpœnas and attachments for witnesses, six cents a mile.

In every case of violation of the law against gaming tried before a Justice of the Peace, Mayor or Recorder, five dollars in addition to the above fees.

ART. 977. To the Sheriff, in addition to the fees allowed in the preceding article, shall be allowed: Sheriff's fees additional.

For executing search warrant, two dollars.

For taking bail, one dollar.

ART. 978. The rules as to the rate of cost allowed to Justices of the Peace, Mayors and Recorders, and to peace officers, are to apply to proceedings before Justices, Mayors and Recorders, in cases of vagrancy and of other special proceedings of a criminal nature; and where the defendant is not able to pay in cases of vagrancy, or of disorderly persons, the same shall be a tax upon the county, and shall be allowed and paid by the County Court. Fees in cases of vagrancy.

ART. 978a. In case of the conviction of a slave for a petty offence, the costs shall be adjudged against the master, or person in whose employment the slave may be at the time of the conviction, to be collected under execution as in ordinary cases. Act of Feb. 15, 1858. Where slave is convicted of petty offence, master pays costs.

ART. 978b. When a free person of color is convicted of a petty offence, and the cost is not paid by him, or he is unable to pay the same, it shall be paid by the county, and the defendant may be compelled by the County Court to labor upon any public work of the county, for the reimbursement of the same, or he may be hired out under the direction of the County Court until his earning will pay the same. Where free person of color is convicted of petty offence.

TITLE V.

OF COSTS TO BE PAID BY A WITNESS.

ART. 979. In all criminal cases where a witness has been subpœnaed and fails to attend, he shall be liable for the costs of an attachment, unless good cause be shown to the Court or Magistrate why he failed to obey the subpœna. Act of Aug. 26, 1856. Witness liable for costs, when.

FINAL TITLE.

Act of Aug. 26, 1856.

Suits pending not effected by this Code, except.

ART. 980. No action, plea, prosecution or proceeding in any criminal cause now pending, or which may be pending when this act takes effect, shall be affected by the repeal of the laws under which it originated, but the same shall proceed in all respects as if no such repeal had taken place; except that all proceedings had after the time this act takes effect shall be conducted according to its provisions.

Regulation of proceedings in crimin'l actions, &c.

ART. 981. The provisions of this Code shall regulate proceedings in all criminal actions, and shall be the rule on all subjects of which it treats, from and after the first day of February, A. D. 1857.

ART. 982. This act shall take effect on the first day of February, 1857, and from and after that time all laws and parts of laws now in force which regulate or refer to the prevention, suppression, prosecution and proceedings for the punishment of crime shall stand repealed.

Act of Feb. 15, 1858.

Repealing clause.

ART. 983. So much of article nine hundred and fifty-two as refers to costs of Clerks, article seventeen, twenty-nine, two hundered and eighty-two, three hundred and ninety-three, three hundred and ninety seven, four hundred and five, four hundred and fifty-six, four hundred and sixty-four, four hundred and sixty-five, four hundred sixty-seven, four hundred and seventy four, four hundred and seventy-eight, five hundred and twenty-three, five hundred and twenty-five, five hundred and sixty, five hundred and sixty-two, five hundred and sixty-four, five hundred sixty-five, seven hundred and fourteen, eight hundred forty-six, eight hundred and forty-seven, of the Code of Criminal Procedure, are hereby repealed.

NOTE.—The Penal Code was approved August 28th, 1856, and took effect February 1st, 1857. The amendments were approved February 12, 1858, and took effect July 1, 1858.
The Code of Criminal Procedure was approved August 26th, 1856. and took effect February 1st, 1857. The amendments were approved February 15, 1858, and took effect July 1, 1858.

REPEALED

AND

OBSOLETE LAWS OF THE REPUBLIC

AND

STATE OF TEXAS,

BY, THROUGH OR

UNDER WHICH RIGHTS HAVE ACCRUED.

PLAN AND POWERS

OF THE

PROVISIONAL GOVERNMENT OF TEXAS.

ARTICLE 1. There shall be, and there is hereby created, a Provisional Government for Texas, which shall consist of a Governor, a Lieutenant-Governor, and a General Council, to be elected from this body, one member from each municipality, by the majority of each separate delegation present; and that the Governor and Lieutenant-Governor shall be elected by this body. Nov. 13, 1836. Provisional government established.

ART. 2. The Lieutenant-Governor shall be President of the Council, and perform the duties of Governor in case of death, absence, or from other inability of the Governor, during which time a President "pro tem." shall be appointed to perform the duties of the Lieutenant-Governor in Council. Lieutenant-Governor.

ART. 3. The duties of the General Council shall be, to devise ways and means, to advise and assist the Governor in the discharge of his functions: they shall pass no laws except such as, in their opinion, the emergency of the country requires—ever keeping in view the army in the field, and the means necessary for its comfort and support: they shall pursue the most effective and energetic measures to rid the country of her enemies, and place her in the best possible state of defence: two-thirds of the members elect of the General Council shall form a quorum to do business; and in order that no vacancy shall happen in the Council, if any member, from death or other casualty, shall be incapacitated to act, the Governor shall immediately, on information thereof, notify the member elected to fill the place; and, on his default, any member who has been elected to this body from the same jurisdiction. The Governor and Council shall be authorized to contract for loans, not to exceed one million of dollars, and to hypothecate the public lands and pledge the faith of the country for the security of the payment: that they have power to impose and regulate impost and tonnage duties, and provide for their collection under such regulations as may be most expedient. They shall have power, and it is hereby made the duty of the Governor and Council, to treat with the several tribes of Indians concerning their land claims, and, if possible, to secure their friendship. General Council, powers of the, &c.

They shall establish post-offices and post-roads, and regulate the rates of postage, and appoint a Postmaster-General, who shall have competent power for conducting this department of the Provisional Government, under such rules and regulations as the Governor and Council may prescribe: they shall have power to grant pardons, remit fines, and to hear and judge all cases usual in high Courts of Admiralty, agreeably to the law of nations. Post-offices and post-roads.

They shall have power to appoint their own Secretary and other officers of their own body; also, that they have the power to create and fill such offices as they may deem proper: provided, nevertheless, that this power does not extend to officers heretofore rejected by this House. Offices.

That the Governor and Council have power to organize, reduce, or increase the regular forces, as they may deem the emergencies of the country require.

ART. 4. The Governor, for the time being, and during the existence of the Provisional Government, shall be clothed with full and ample executive powers, and shall be Commander-in-chief of the Army and Navy, and of all the mili- Governor, powers and duties of the.

tary forces of Texas, by sea and land; and he shall have full power by himself, by and with the consent of the Council, and by his proper commander or other officer or officers, from time to time, to train, instruct, exercise, and govern the militia and navy; and for the special defence and safety of the country, to assemble in martial array, and put in warlike attitude the inhabitants thereof; and to lead and conduct them by his proper officers, and with them to encounter, repel, resist, and pursue by force of arms, as well by sea and by land, within or without the limit of Texas; and, also, to destroy, if necessary, and conquer by all proper means and enterprises whatsoever, all and every such person or persons as shall, at any time, in a hostile manner, attempt or enterprise the destruction of our liberties, or the invasion, detriment, or annoyance of the country; and by his proper officers, use and exercise over the army and navy, and the militia in actual service, the law martial in time of war, invasion or rebellion; and to take and surprise by all honorable ways and means consistent with the law of nations, all and every such person or persons, with their ships, arms, ammunition, and goods as shall, in a hostile manner, invade or attempt the invading or annoying our adopted country; and that the Governor be clothed with all these and all other powers which may be thought necessary by the Permanent Council, calculated to aid and protect the country from her enemies.

Provisional judiciary constituted. ART. 5. There shall be constituted a Provisional Judiciary in each jurisdiction represented, or which may hereafter be represented in this House, to consist of two judges, a first and second, the latter to act only in the absence or inability of the first, and be nominated by the Council and commissioned by the Governor.

Jurisdiction and powers of Judges. ART. 6. Every Judge so nominated and commissioned, shall have jurisdiction over all crimes and misdemeanors recognised and known to the common law o *Habeas corpus.* England: he shall have power to grant writs of "habeas corpus" in all cases known and practised to and under the same laws; he shall have power to grant *Remedial writs.* writs of sequestration, attachment, or arrest, in all cases established by the *Testamentary powers.* "Civil Code" and "Code of Practice" of the State of Louisiana, to be regulated by the forms thereof; shall possess full testamentary powers in all cases; and *Conveyances.* shall also be made a court of records for conveyances which may be made in English, and not on stamped paper; and that the use of stamped paper be, in *Notaries public.* all cases, dispensed with; and shall be the "Notary Public" for their respective municipalities: all office fees shall be regulated by the Governor and Council. *Sheriffs, alcaldes, &c.* All other civil proceedings at law shall be suspended until the Governor and General Council shall otherwise direct. Each municipality shall continue to elect a sheriff, alcalde and other officers of ayuntamientos.

Trial by jury. ART. 7. All trials shall be by jury, and in criminal cases the proceedings *Common law in criminal cases.* shall be regulated and conducted upon the principles of the common law of England; and the penalties prescribed by said law, in case of conviction, shall be inflicted, unless the offender shall be pardoned, or fine remitted; for which purpose a reasonable time shall be allowed to every convict to make application to the Governor and Council.

Officers. ART. 8. The officers of the Provisional Government, except such as are elected by this House, or the people, shall be appointed by the General Council, and all officers shall be commissioned by the Governor.

Commissions, pardons, &c. ART. 9. All commissions to officers shall be, "In the name of the People, free and sovereign," and signed by the Governor and Secretary; and all pardons and remissions of fines granted, shall be signed in the same manner.

ART. 10. Every officer and member of the Provisional Government, before *Oath of office.* entering upon the duties of his office, shall take and subscribe the following oath of office: "I, A. B., do solemnly swear (or affirm), that I will support the republican principles of the Constitution of Mexico of 1824, and obey the Declarations and Ordinances of the Consultation of the chosen Delegates of all Texas in General Convention assembled, and the Ordinances and Decrees of the Provisional Government; and I will faithfully perform and execute the duties of my office agreeably to law, and to the best of my abilities, so help me God."

Impeachment. ART. 11. On charges and specifications being made against any officer of the Provisional Government for malfeasance or misconduct in office, and presented to the Governor and Council, a fair and impartial trial shall be granted, to be conducted before the General Council; and if, in the opinion of two-thirds of the members, cause sufficient be shown, he shall be dismissed from office by the Governor.

Organization, &c., of Governer and Council. ART. 12. The Governor and Council shall organize and enter upon their duties immediately after the adjournment of this House, and hold their sessions at such times and places as, in their opinion, will give the most energy and effect to the objects of the people, and to the performance of the duties assigned to them.

ART. 13. The General Council shall appoint a Treasurer, whose duties shall be clearly defined by them, and who shall give approved security for their faithful performance. Treasurer.

ART. 14. That all land-commissioners, empressarios, surveyors, or persons in anywise concerned in the location of land, be ordered, forthwith, to cease their operations during the agitated and unsettled state of the country, and continue to desist from further locations until the land offices can be properly systematised by the competent authorities which may be hereafter established; that fit and suitable persons be appointed to take charge of all the archives belonging to the different land offices, and deposit the same in safe places, secure from the ravages of fire or devastations of enemies; and that the persons so appointed be fully authorized to carry the same into effect, and be required to take and sign triplicate schedules of all the books, papers, and documents found in the several land offices, one of which shall be given to the Governor and Council, one left in the hands of the officers of the land office, the other to be retained by the said persons, and they are enjoined to hold the said papers and documents in safe custody, subject only to the orders of the Provisional Government, or such competent authority as may hereafter be created. And the said persons shall be three from each department as commissioners to be forthwith appointed by this House, to carry this resolution into full effect, and report thereof to the Governor and Council; that the political chiefs immediately cease their functions. The different archives of the different primary judges, alcaldes, and other municipal officers of the various jurisdictions, shall be handed over to their successors in office, immediately after their election and appointment; and the archives of the several political chiefs of Nacogdoches, Brazos, and Bexar shall be transmitted forthwith to the Governor and Council, for their disposition. Closing of the land offices. Archives of land offices. Political chiefs. Archives of municipal officers.

ART. 15. All persons, now in Texas, and performing the duties of citizens, who have not acquired their quantum of land, shall be entitled to the benefit of the laws of colonization under which they emigrated; and all persons who may emigrate to Texas during her conflict for constitutional liberty, and perform the duties of citizens, shall also receive the benefits of the law under which they emigrated. Their lands secured to individual grants.

ART. 16. The Governor and Council shall continue to exist as a Provisional Government until the reassembling of this consultation, or until other delegates are elected by the people and another government established. Duration of provisional government.

ART. 17. This Convention, when it may think proper to adjourn, may stand adjourned, to meet at the town of Washington, on the first day of March next, unless sooner called by the Executive and Council. Next meeting of the Convention.

ART. 18. All grants, sales, and conveyances of lands, illegally or fraudulently made by the Legislature of the State of Coahuila and Texas, located, or to be located, within the limits of Texas, are hereby solemnly declared null, void, and of no effect. Certain grants of land declared void.

ART. 19. All persons who leave the country in its present crisis, with a view to avoid a participation in its present struggle, without permission from the alcalde, or judge of their municipality, shall forfeit all or any lands they may hold, or may have a claim to, for the benefit of this government: provided, nevertheless, that widows and minors are not included in this provision. Forfeiture of lands for leaving the country.

ART. 20. All moneys now due, or that may hereafter become due, on lands lying within the limits of Texas, and all public funds or revenues, shall be at the disposal of the Governor and General Council, and the receipt of the Treasurer shall be a sufficient voucher for any and all persons who may pay moneys into the Treasury; and the Governor and Council shall have power to adopt a system of revenue to meet the exigencies of the country. Land dues.

ART. 21. Ample powers and authority shall be delegated, and are hereby given and delegated to the Governor and General Council of the Provisional Government of all Texas, to carry into full effect the provisions and resolutions adopted by "the Consultation of the chosen Delegates of all Texas in General Convention assembled," for the creation, establishment and regulation of said Provisional Government. General grant of powers.

OF THE MILITARY.

ART. 1. There shall be a regular army created for the protection of Texas during the present war. Regular army.

Commander-in-chief. ART. 2. The regular army of Texas shall consist of one Major-General, who shall be Commander-in-chief of all the forces called into public service during the war.

Appointment, &c. ART. 3. The Commander-in-chief of the regular army of Texas shall be appointed by the Convention, and commissioned by the Governor.

Subject to orders. ART. 4. He shall be subject to the orders of the Governor and Council.

Staff of Commander-in-chief. ART. 5. His staff shall consist of one Adjutant-General, one Inspector-General, one Quarter-Master-General, one Paymaster-General, one Surgeon-General, and four Aides-de-Camp with their respective ranks, as in the United States Army in time of war, to be appointed by the Major-General and commissioned by the Governor.

Rugular army. ART. 6. The regular army of Texas shall consist of men enlisted for two years, and volunteers for and during the continuance of the war.

Rules and Regulations. ART. 7. The regular army of Texas, while in the service, shall be governed by the rules, regulations, and discipline, in all respects applicable to the regular army of the United States of America, in time of war, so far as applicable to our condition and circumstances.

Rank and file. ART. 8. The regular army of Texas shall consist of eleven hundred and twenty men rank and file.

Rangers. ART. 9. There shall be a corps of Rangers under the command of a major, to consist of one hundred and fifty men, to be divided into three or more detachments, and which shall compose a battalion, under the Commander-in-chief when in the field.

Militia. ART. 10. The militia of Texas shall be organized as follows: all able-bodied men over sixteen, and under fifty years of age, shall be subject to militia duty.

Companies of militia. ART. 11. Every inhabitant of Texas, coming within purview of the preceding Article, shall, on the third Monday of December next, or as soon there after as practicable, assemble at each precinct of their municipality and proceed to elect one captain, one first lieutenant, and one second lieutenant to every fifty-six men.

Commissions of captains. ART. 12. When said election shall have taken place, the judges shall certify to the governor, forthwith, the names of the respective officers elected, who shall, as soon as practicable, make out and sign, and transmit commissions for the same; that if there shall be found to exist in any municipality, more than three companies, the captain, or commandants, on giving due notice thereof, shall call together the subalterns of said companies, and proceed to elect one major; if of four companies, one lieutenant-colonel; if of five or more companies, one colonel for the command of said companies, which shall constitute a regiment of said municipality; that if there shall be found to exist more than one regiment in said municipality, the whole number of field and company officers, shall, on due notice, proceed to elect a brigadier-general out of their number who shall command the whole militia in said municipality. (Battalions. Regiments. Brigades.)

BRANCH TANNER ARCHER, President.

Municipality of Austin.—Wyly Martin, R. Jones, Jesse Burnham, William Menifee.

Municipality of San Augustine.—A. Houston, William N. Sigler, A. E. C. Johnson, A. Horton, A. G. Kellogg.

Municipality of Gonzales.—Wm. S. Fisher, J. D. Clements, George W. Davis, James Hodges, Wm. W. Arrington, Benjamin Fuqua.

Municipality of Columbia.—Henry Smith, John A. Wharton, Edwin Waller, John S. D. Byrom.

Municipality of Washington.—Philip Coe, E. Collard, Jesse Grimes, Asa Mitchell, Asa Hoxey.

Municipality of Viesca.—Samuel T. Allen, A. G. Perry, A. G. W. Pierson, Alexander Thompson, James W. Parker.

Municipality of Nacogdoches.—Samuel Houston, James W. Robinson, William Whittaker, Daniel Parker, William N. Sigler.

Municipality of Mina.—D. C. Barrett, J. S. Lester, R. M. Williamson.

Municipality of Liberty.—Henry Millard, B. Woods, A. B. Hardin.

Municipality of Harrisburg.—Lorenzo De Ravalla, C. C. Dyer, John W. Moore, M. W. Smith, David B. Macomb, George M. Patrick.

Municipality of Bevil.—S. H. Everitt, John Bevil, Wyatt Hanks.

Municipality of Jefferson.—Claiborne West.

Municipality of Matagorda.—R. R. Royal, Charles Wilson.

Municipality of Tenehaw.—Martin Parmer.

P. B. DEXTER, Secretary.

CONSTITUTION

OF THE

REPUBLIC OF TEXAS.

WE, the People of Texas, in order to form a government, establish justice, insure domestic tranquility, provide for the common defence and general welfare; and to secure the blessings of liberty to ourselves and our posterity, do ordain and establish this Constitution. Adopted March 17, 1836

ARTICLE I.

SECT. 1. The powers of this government shall be divided into three departments, viz: legislative, executive, and judicial, which shall remain for ever separate and distinct. Division of the powers of government.

SECT. 2. The legislative power shall be vested in a Senate and House of Representatives, to be styled the Congress of the Republic of Texas. Legislative power.

SECT. 3. The members of the House of Representatives shall be chosen annually, on the first Monday of September each year, until Congress shall otherwise provide by law, and shall hold their offices one year from the date of their election. Time of election and term of office of members of the House of Representatives

SECT. 4. No person shall be eligible to a seat in the House of Representatives until he shall have attained the age of twenty-five years, and shall be a citizen of the Republic, and shall have resided in the county or district six months next preceding his election. Qualifications of members of the House of Representatives.

SECT. 5. The House of Representatives shall not consist of less than twenty-four, nor more than forty members, until the population shall amount to one hundred thousand souls, after which time the whole number of Representatives shall not be less than forty, nor more than one hundred: *Provided*, however, that each county shall be entitled to at least one Representative. House of Representatives shall consist, &c. Each county, one representative.

SECT. 6. The House of Representatives shall choose their Speaker and other officers, and shall have the sole power of impeachment. House choose officers, &c.

SECT. 7. The Senators shall be chosen by districts, as nearly equal in free population (free negroes and Indians excepted), as practicable; and the number of Senators shall never be less than one-third nor more than one-half the number of Representatives, and each district shall be entitled to one member and no more Senators shall be chosen by districts. Number of Senators.

SECT. 8. The Senators shall be chosen for the term of three years, on the first Monday in September; shall be citizens of the Republic, reside in the district for which they are respectively chosen at least one year before the election; and shall have attained the age of thirty years. Senators, their election, term of office, and qualifications.

SECT. 9. At the first session of Congress after the adoption of this Constitution, the Senators shall be divided by lot into three classes, as nearly equal as practicable; the seats of the Senators of the first class shall be vacated at the end of the first year; of the second class, at the end of the second year; the third class, at the end of the third year, in such a manner that one-third shall be chosen each year thereafter. At first session Senators shall be classified.

SECT. 10. The Vice-President of the Republic shall be President of the Senate, but shall not vote on any question, unless the Senate be equally divided. Vice-President shall be President of the Senate, &c.

Officers of the Senate.

SECT. 11. The Senate shall choose all other officers of their body, and a President pro tempore, in the absence of the Vice-President, or whenever he shall exercise the office of President; shall have the sole power to try impeachments, and when sitting as a court of impeachment, shall be under oath; but no conviction shall take place without the concurrence of two-thirds of all the members present.

Senate shall try impeachments, &c.

Judgment in cases of impeachment.

SECT. 12. Judgment in cases of impeachment shall only extend to removal from office, and disqualification to hold any office of honor, trust, or profit under this government; but the party shall nevertheless be liable to indictment, trial, judgment, and punishment according to law.

Each house judge of the election, &c., of members.

A quorum.

SECT. 13. Each House shall be the judge of the elections, qualifications, and returns of its own members. Two-thirds of each House shall constitute a quorum to do business, but a smaller number may adjourn from day to day, and may compel the attendance of absent members.

Each house may adopt its own rules, &c.

SECT. 14. Each House may determine the rules of its own proceedings, punish its members for disorderly behaviour, and with the concurrence of two-thirds, may expel a member, but not a second time for the same offence.

Compensation of members of Congress.

SECT. 15. Senators and Representatives shall receive a compensation for their services, to be fixed by law, but no increase of compensation, or diminution, shall take effect during the session at which such increase or diminution shall have been made. They shall, except in case of treason, felony, or breach of the peace, be privileged from arrest during the session of Congress, and in going to and returning from the same; and for any speech or debate in either House they shall not be questioned in any other place.

Privileges of members of Congress.

Punishment of disrespect to Congress, &c.

SECT. 16. Each House may punish, by imprisonment, during the session, any person not a member, who shall be guilty of any disrespect to the House, by any disorderly conduct in their presence.

Journals.

Yeas and nays.

SECT. 17. Each House shall keep a journal of its proceedings, and publish the same, except such parts as in its judgment require secrecy. When any three members shall desire the yeas and nays on any question, they shall be entered on the journals.

Adjournments.

SECT. 18. Neither House, without the consent of the other, shall adjourn for more than three days, nor to any other place than that in which the two Houses may be sitting.

Vacancies.

SECT. 19. When vacancies happen in either House, the Executive shall issue writs of election to fill such vacancies.

Passage of bills.

SECT. 20. No bill shall become a law until it shall have been read on three several days in each House, and passed by the same, unless, in cases of emergency, two-thirds of the members of the House where the bill originated shall deem it expedient to dispense with the rule.

After a bill has been rejected.

SECT. 21. After a bill shall have been rejected, no bill containing the same substance shall be passed into a law during the same session.

Style of laws.

SECT. 22. The style of the laws of the Republic shall be. "Be it enacted by the Senate and House of Representatives of the Republic of Texas, in Congress assembled."

Persons holding office not eligible to Congress.

SECT. 23. No person holding an office of profit under the government shall be eligible to a seat in either House of Congress, nor shall any member of either House be eligible to any office which may be created, or the profits of which shall be increased during his term of service.

Holder or collector of public money not eligible until, &c.

Protest.

SECT. 24. No holder of public moneys or collector thereof, shall be eligible to a seat in either House of Congress, until he shall have fully acquitted himself of all responsibility, and shall produce the proper officer's receipt thereof. Members of either House may protest against any act or resolution, and may have such protest entered on the journals of their respective Houses.

No money shall be drawn from the treasury except, &c.

SECT. 25. No money shall be drawn from the public treasury but in strict accordance with appropriations made by law; and no appropriations shall be made for private or local purposes, unless two-thirds of each House concur in such appropriations.

Act of Congress shall be approved and signed by the President, before it becomes a law.

SECT. 26. Every act of Congress shall be approved and signed by the President before it becomes a law; but if the President will not approve and sign such act, he shall return it to the House in which it shall have originated, with his reasons for not approving the same, which shall be spread upon the journals of such House, and the bill shall then be reconsidered, and shall not become a law unless it shall then pass by a vote of two-thirds of both Houses. If any act shall be disapproved by the President, the vote on the reconsideration shall be recorded by ayes and noes. If the President shall fail to return a bill within five days (Sundays excepted) after it shall have been presented for his approval and signature, the same shall become a law, unless the Congress prevent its return within the time above specified by adjournment.

SECT. 27. All bills, acts, orders, or resolutions, to which the concurrence of both Houses may be necessary, (motions or resolutions for adjournment excepted,) shall be approved and signed by the President, or being disapproved, shall be passed by two-thirds of both Houses, in manner and form as specified in section twenty. All bills, &c., shall be approved and signed by the President, &c.

ARTICLE II.

SECT. 1. Congress shall have power to levy and collect taxes and imposts, excise and tonnage duties; to borrow money on the faith, credit and property of the government, to pay the debts and to provide for the common defence and general welfare of the Republic. Powers of Congress.

SECT. 2. To regulate commerce, to coin money, to regulate the value thereof and of foreign coin, to fix the standard of weights and measures; but nothing but gold and silver shall be made a lawful tender. To coin money, regulate commerce, &c.

SECT. 3. To establish post offices and post-roads, to grant charters of incorporation, patents and copy-rights, and secure to the authors and inventors the exclusive use thereof for a limited time. To establish post offices, &c. To grant charters, patents, &c.

SECT. 4. To declare war, grant letters of marque and reprisal, and to regulate captures. To declare war, &c.

SECT. 5. To provide and maintain an army and navy, and make all laws and regulations necessary for their government. To provide and maintain an army and navy.

SECT. 6. To call out the militia to execute the law, to suppress insurrections, and repel invasion. To call out the militia.

SECT. 7. To make all laws which shall be deemed necessary and proper to carry into effect the foregoing express grants of power, and all other powers vested in the government of the Republic, or in any officer or department thereof. General powers of Congress.

ARTICLE III.

SECT. 1. The executive authority of this government shall be vested in a chief magistrate, who shall be styled the President of the Republic of Texas. The President.

SECT. 2. The first President elected by the people shall hold his office for the term of two years, and shall be ineligible during the next succeeding term; and all subsequent Presidents shall be elected for three years, and be alike ineligible; and in the event of a tie, the House of Representatives shall determine between the two highest candidates by a viva voce vote. Term of the presidency. Ineligible to consecutive terms. In case of a tie.

SECT. 3. The returns of the elections for President and Vice-President shall be sealed up and transmitted to the Speaker of the House of Representatives, by the holders of elections of each county; and the Speaker of the House of Representatives shall open and publish the returns in presence of a majority of each House of Congress. Returns of elections for President and Vice-President.

ARTICLE IV.

SECT. 1. The judicial powers of the government shall be vested in one Supreme Court, and such inferior courts as the Congress may, from time to time, ordain and establish. The Judges of the Supreme and inferior Courts shall hold their offices for four years, be eligible to re-election, and shall, at stated periods, receive for their services a compensation, not to be increased or diminished during the period for which they were elected. Judicial powers of the government.

SECT. 2. The Republic of Texas shall be divided into convenient judicial districts, not less than three, nor more than eight. There shall be appointed for each district a Judge, who shall reside in the same, and hold the courts at such times and places as Congress may by law direct. Judicial districts. District Judges.

SECT. 3. In all admiralty and maritime cases, in all cases affecting ambassadors, public ministers, or consuls, and in all capital cases, the District Courts shall have exclusive original jurisdiction, and original jurisdiction in all civil cases when the matter in controversy amounts to one hundred dollars. Jurisdiction of the district Courts.

SECT. 4. The Judges, by virtue of their offices, shall be conservators of the peace throughout the Republic. The style of all process shall be, "The Republic of Texas;" and all prosecutions shall be carried on in the name and by the authority of the same, and conclude, "against the peace and dignity of the Republic." Judges shall be conservators of the peace, &c. Style of process, &c.

SECT. 5. There shall be a District Attorney appointed for each district, whose duties, salaries, perquisites, and term of service shall be fixed by law.

Clerks of the district courts. SECT. 6. The clerks of the District Courts shall be elected by the qualified voters for members of Congress, in the counties where the courts are established, and shall hold their offices for four years, subject to removal by presentment of a grand jury, and conviction of a petit jury.

The Supreme Court. SECT. 7. The Supreme Court shall consist of a Chief Justice and Associate Judges; the District Judges shall compose the Associate Judges, a majority of whom, with the Chief Justice, shall constitute a quorum.

Jurisdiction of Supreme Court. Its sessions, &c. SECT. 8. The Supreme Court shall have appellate jurisdiction only, which shall be conclusive, within the limits of the Republic; and shall hold its sessions annually, at such times and places as may be fixed by law: provided, that no Judge shall sit in a case in the Supreme Court tried by him in the court below.

Election of Judges. SECT. 9. The Judges of the Supreme and District Courts shall be elected by joint ballot of both Houses of Congress.

County courts and justices' courts. SECT. 10. There shall be in each county a County Court, and such Justices' Courts as the Congress may, from time to time, establish.

Counties. SECT. 11. The Republic shall be divided into convenient counties, but no new county shall be established, unless it be done on the petition of one hundred free male inhabitants of the territory sought to be laid off and established; and unless the said territory shall contain nine hundred square miles.

Justices of the peace. Sheriffs, coroners, and constables. SECT. 12. There shall be appointed for each county, a convenient number of Justices of the Peace, one Sheriff, one Coroner, and a sufficient number of Constables, who shall hold their offices for two years, to be elected by the qualified voters of the district or county, as Congress may direct. Justices of the Peace and Sheriffs shall be commissioned by the President.

Common law of England shall be introduced. SECT. 13. The Congress shall, as early as practicable, introduce, by statute, the common law of England, with such modifications as our circumstances, in their judgment, may require; and in all criminal cases, the common law shall be the rule of decision.

ARTICLE V.

Ministers of the Gospel not eligible to the presidency nor to Congress SECT. 1. Ministers of the Gospel being, by their profession, dedicated to God and the care of souls, ought not to be diverted from the great duties of their functions: therefore, no minister of the Gospel, or priest of any denomination whatever, shall be eligible to the office of the Executive of the Republic, nor to a seat in either branch of the Congress of the same.

Oath of office of members of Congress. SECT. 2. Each member of the Senate and House of Representatives shall, before they proceed to business, take an oath to support the Constitution, as follows:

"I, A. B., do solemnly swear, (or affirm, as the case may be,) that, as a member of this general Congress, I will support the Constitution of the Republic, and that I will not propose or assent to any bill, vote, or resolution, which shall appear injurious to the people."

Oath of office. SECT. 3. Every person who shall be chosen or appointed to any office of trust or profit shall, before entering on the duties thereof, take an oath to support the Constitution of the Republic, and also an oath of office.

ARTICLE VI.

Qualifications of the President. SECT. 1. No person shall be eligible to the office of President who shall not have attained the age of thirty-five years, shall be a citizen of the Republic at the time of the adoption of this Constitution, or an inhabitant of this Republic at least three years immediately preceding his election.

Term of office of the President. SECT. 2. The President shall enter on the duties of his office on the second Monday in December next succeeding his election, and shall remain in office until his successor shall be duly qualified.

Compensation of the President. SECT. 3. The President shall, at stated times, receive a compensation for his services, which shall not be increased or diminished during his continuance in office; and before entering upon the duties of his office, he shall take and subscribe the following oath or affirmation:

Oath of office of the President. "I, A. B., President of the Republic of Texas, do solemnly and sincerely swear (or affirm, as the case may be,) that I will faithfully execute the duties of my office, and to the best of my abilities preserve, protect, and defend the Constitution of the Republic."

President shall SECT. 4. He shall be Commander-in-chief of the army and navy of the

Republic, and militia thereof, but he shall not command in person without the authority of a resolution of Congress. He shall have power to remit fines and forfeitures, and to grant reprieves and pardons, except in cases of impeachment. be commander-in-chief of the army, &c. Remit fines, &c.

SECT. 5. He shall, with the advice and consent of two-thirds of the Senate, make treaties; and with the consent of the Senate, appoint ministers and consuls, and all officers whose offices are established by this Constitution, not herein otherwise provided for. He shall make treaties, appoint ministers and other officers, &c.

SECT. 6. The President shall have power to fill all vacancies that may happen during the recess of the Senate; but he shall report the same to the Senate within ten days after the next Congress shall convene; and should the Senate reject the same, the President shall not re-nominate the same individual to the same office. Vacancies during the recess of the Senate.

SECT. 7. He shall, from time to time, give Congress information of the State of the Republic, and recommend for their consideration such measures as he may deem necessary. He may, upon extraordinary occasions, convene both Houses, or either of them. In the event of a disagreement as to the time of adjournment, he may adjourn them to such time as he may think proper. He shall receive all foreign ministers. He shall see that the laws be faithfully executed, and shall commission all the officers of the Republic. President shall give congress information, &c. He may convene both, &c. In event of disagreement, &c. He shall see the laws faithfully executed, &c.

SECT. 8. There shall be a seal of the Republic which shall be kept by the President, and used by him officially; it shall be called the great seal of the Republic of Texas. Seal of the Republic.

SECT. 9. All grants and commissions shall be in the name and by the authority of the Republic of Texas, shall be sealed with the great seal, and signed by the President. Form of grants and commissions.

SECT. 10. The President shall have power, by and with the advice and consent of the Senate, to appoint a Secretary of State and such other heads of executive departments as may be established by law, who shall remain in office during the term of service of the President, unless sooner removed by the President, with the advice and consent of the Senate. Secretary of State and other heads of executive departments.

SECT. 11. Every citizen of the Republic who has attained the age of twenty-one years, and shall have resided six months within the district or county where the election is held, shall be entitled to vote for members of the General Congress. Qualified electors.

SECT. 12. All elections shall be by ballot, unless Congress shall otherwise direct. Elections shall be by ballot, &c.

SECT. 13. All elections by joint vote of both Houses of Congress shall be viva voce, shall be entered on the journals, and a majority of the votes shall be necessary to a choice.

SECT. 14. A Vice-President shall be chosen at every election for President, in the same manner, continue in office for the same time, and shall possess the same qualifications of the President. In voting for President and Vice-President, the electors shall distinguish for whom they vote as President, and for whom as Vice-President. Vice-President. Voting for President and Vice-President.

SECT. 15. In cases of impeachment, removal from office, death, resignation, or absence of the President from the Republic, the Vice-President shall exercise the powers and discharge the duties of the President until a successor be duly qualified, or until the President, who may be absent or impeached, shall return or be acquitted. Vice-President shall act as President, when.

SECT. 16. The President, Vice-President, and all civil officers of the Republic shall be removable from office by impeachment for, and on conviction of, treason, bribery, and other high crimes and misdemeanors. All civil officers removable by impeachment.

SCHEDULE.

SECT. 1. That no inconvenience may arise from the adoption of this Constitution, it is declared by this convention that all laws now in force in Texas, and not inconsistent with this Constitution, shall remain in full force until declared void, repealed, altered, or expire by their own limitation. Laws now in force shall remain in force, until, &c.

SECT. 2. All fines, penalties, forfeitures and escheats, which have accrued to Coahuila and Texas, or Texas, shall accrue to this Republic. Fines, &c.

SECT. 3. Every male citizen, who is, by this Constitution, a citizen, and shall be otherwise qualified, shall be entitled to hold any office or place of honor, trust or profit under the Republic, anything in this Constitution to the contrary notwithstanding. Every male citizen entitled to hold office, &c.

SECT. 4. The first President and Vice-President that shall be appointed after the adoption of this Constitution, shall be chosen by this Convention, and shall immediately enter on the duties of their offices, and shall hold said offices until First President and Vice-President.

their successors be elected and qualified, as prescribed in this Constitution, and shall have the same qualifications, be invested with the same powers, and perform the same duties which are required and conferred on the executive head of the Republic by this Constitution.

Writs of election.

President, &c., shall hold their offices until their successors are qualified.

SECT. 5. The President shall issue writs of election directed to the officers authorized to hold elections of the several counties, requiring them to cause an election to be held for President, Vice-President, Representatives, and Senators to Congress, at the time and mode prescribed by this Constitution, which election shall be conducted in the manner that elections have been heretofore conducted. The President, Vice-President and members of Congress, when duly elected, shall continue to discharge the duties of their respective offices for the time and manner prescribed by this Constitution, until their successors be duly qualified.

Representative districts.

SECT. 6. Until the first enumeration shall be made, as directed by this Constitution, the precinct of Austin shall be entitled to one Representative; the precinct of Brazoria to two Representatives; the precinct of Bexar two Representatives; the precinct of Colorado one Representative; Sabine one; Gonzales one; Goliad one; Harrisburg one; Jasper one; Jefferson one; Liberty one; Matagorda one; Mina two; Nacogdoches two; Red River three; Victoria one; San Augustine two; Shelby two; Refugio one; San Patricio one; Washington two; Milam one; and Jackson one Representative.

Senatorial districts.

SECT. 7. Until the first enumeration shall be made, as described by this Constitution, the Senatorial districts shall be composed of the following precincts; Bexar shall be entitled to one Senator; San Patricio, Refugio and Goliad one; Brazoria one; Mina and Gonzales one; Nacogdoches one; Red River one; Shelby and Sabine one; Washington one; Matagorda, Jackson, and Victoria one; Austin and Colorado one; San Augustine one; Milam one; Jasper and Jefferson one; and Liberty and Harrisburg one Senator.

All judges, &c. shall continue in office, until, &c.

SECT. 8. All Judges, Sheriffs, Commissioners, and other civil officers shall remain in office, and in the discharge of the powers and duties of their respective offices, until there shall be others appointed or elected under the Constitution.

GENERAL PROVISIONS.

Disfranchisement of persons convicted, &c.

SECT. 1. Laws shall be made to exclude from office, from the right of suffrage, and from serving on juries, those who shall hereafter be convicted of bribery, perjury, or other high crimes and misdemeanors.

Returns of elections of certain officers.

SECT. 2. Returns of all elections for officers who are to be commissioned by the President, shall be made to the Secretary of State of this Republic.

Offices of President, &c., shall be kept at the seat of government, unless, &c.

SECT. 3. The Presidents and heads of departments shall keep their offices at the seat of Government, unless removed by the permission of Congress, or unless in cases of emergency in time of war, the public interest may require their removal.

Temporary seal of the Republic.

SECT. 4. The President shall make use of his private seal, until a seal of the Republic shall be provided.

Education.

SECT. 5. It shall be the duty of Congress, as soon as circumstances will permit, to provide by law a general system of education.

Naturalization.

SECT. 6. All free white persons who shall emigrate to this Republic, and who shall, after a residence of six months, make oath before some competent authority that he intends to reside permanently in the same, and shall swear to support this Constitution, and that he will bear true allegiance to the Republic of Texas, shall be entitled to all the privileges of citizenship.

There shall be a penal code formed on the principles of reformation, &c.

SECT. 7. So soon as convenience will permit, there shall be a penal code formed on principles of reformation, and not of vindictive justice; and the civil and criminal laws shall be revised, digested, and arranged under different heads; and all laws relating to land titles shall be translated, revised, and promulgated.

Persons leaving the country to avoid participation in the struggle.

SECT. 8. All persons who shall leave the country for the purpose of evading a participation in the present struggle, or shall refuse to participate in it, or shall give aid or assistance to the present enemy, shall forfeit all rights of citizenship, and such lands as they may hold in the Republic.

Congress shall pass no laws to prohibit emigrants from bringing slaves into the Republic, &c.

SECT. 9. All persons of color who were slaves for life previous to their emigration to Texas, and who are now held in bondage, shall remain in the like state of servitude: provided, the said slave shall be the bona fide property of the person so holding said slave as aforesaid. Congress shall pass no laws to prohibit emigrants from bringing their slaves into the Republic with them, and holding them by the same tenure by which such slaves were held in the United States; nor shall Congress have power to emancipate slaves; nor shall any slaveholder have power to emancipate his or her slave or slaves without the consent of Congress, unless he or she shall send his or her slave or slaves without the limits of the Republic. No free person of African descent, either in whole or in part, shall be permitted to reside permanently in the Republic, without the consent of Congress; and the importation or admission of Africans or negroes into this Republic, excepting from the United States of America, is for ever prohibited, and declared to be piracy.

Terms on which owners of slaves may emancipate them, &c. Importation of Africans or negroes, excepting from the United States, declared to be piracy.

SECT. 10. All persons (Africans, the descendants of Africans and Indians excepted,) who were residing in Texas on the day of the Declaration of Independence, shall be considered citizens of the Republic, and entitled to all the privileges of such. All citizens now living in Texas, who have not received their portion of land in like manner as colonists, shall be entitled to their land in the following proportion and manner: Every head of a family shall be entitled to one league and labor of land; and every single man of the age of seventeen and upwards, shall be entitled to the third part of one league of land. All citizens who may have previously to the adoption of this Constitution, received their league of land as heads of families, and their quarter of a league of land as single persons, shall receive such additional quantity as will make the quantity of land received by them equal to one league and labor, and one-third of a league, unless by bargain, sale, or exchange, they have transferred or may henceforth transfer their right to said land, or a portion thereof, to some other citizen of the Republic; and in such case, the person to whom such right shall have been transferred shall be entitled to the same, as fully and amply as the person making the transfer might or could have been. No alien shall hold land in Texas, except by titles emanating directly from the government of this Republic. But if any citizen of this Republic should die intestate or otherwise, his children or heirs shall inherit his estate, and aliens shall have a reasonable time to take possession of and dispose of the same, in a manner hereafter to be pointed out by law. Orphan children whose parents were entitled to land under the colonization laws of Mexico, and who now reside in the Republic, shall be entitled to all the rights of which their parents were possessed at the time of their death. The citizens of the Republic shall not be compelled to reside on the land, but shall have their lines plainly marked.

Who were citizens of the Republic.

Citizens who have not received their quantum of land.

Augmentation.

Assignee entitled to the augmentation.

Aliens shall not hold land, except, &c.

All orders of survey legally obtained by any citizen of the Republic, from any legally authorized commissioner, prior to the act of the late consultation closing the land offices, shall be valid. In all cases the actual settler and occupant of the soil shall be entitled, in locating his land, to include his improvement, in preference to all other claims not acquired previous to his settlement, according to the law of the land and this Constitution: provided, that nothing herein contained shall prejudice the rights of any other citizen from whom a settler may hold land by rent or lease.

Orders of survey obtained prior to the closing of the land offices.

Priority in favor of actual settler.

And, whereas, the protection of the public domain from unjust and fraudulent claims, and quieting the people in the enjoyment of their lands, is one of the great duties of this Convention; and, whereas, the Legislature of Coahuila and Texas having passed an act in the year 1834, in behalf of General John T. Mason of New York, and another on the 14th day of March, 1835, under which the enormous amount of eleven hundred leagues of land has been claimed by sundry individuals, some of whom reside in foreign countries, and are not citizens of the Republic—which said acts are contrary to articles fourth, twelfth and fifteenth of the laws of 1824 of the General Congress of Mexico, and one of said acts, for that cause has, by said General Congress of Mexico, been declared null and void: It is hereby declared that the said act of 1834, in favor of John T. Mason, and of the 14th March, 1835, of the said Legislature of Coahuila and Texas, and each and every grant founded thereon, is, and was from the beginning, null and void; and all surveys made under pretence of authority derived from said acts, are hereby declared to be null and void; and all eleven league claims, located within twenty leagues of the boundary line between Texas and the United States of America, which may have been located contrary to the laws of Mexico, are hereby declared to be null and void. And, whereas, many surveys and titles to lands have been made whilst most of the people of Texas were absent from home, serving in the campaign against Bexar, it is hereby declared that all the surveys and locations of land made since the act of the late Consultation closing the land offices, and all titles to land made since that time, are, and shall be null and void.

Certain grants of land declared void.

Eleven league claims located within the border leagues contrary to law, declared void.

Surveys and titles made since closing of the land offices declared void.

Operations of land office and whole land system suspended.

And, whereas, the present unsettled state of the country and the general welfare of the people demand that the operations of the land office, and the whole land system shall be suspended until persons serving in the army can have a fair and equal chance with those remaining at home, to select and locate their lands, it is hereby declared, that no survey or title which may hereafter be made shall be valid, unless such survey or title shall be authorized by this Convention, or some future Congress of the Republic. And with a view to the simplification of the land system, and the protection of the people and the government from litigation and fraud, a general land office shall be established, where all the land titles of the Republic shall be registered, and the whole territory of the Republic shall be sectionized, in a manner hereafter to be prescribed by law, which shall enable the officers of the government or any citizen, to ascertain with certainty the lands that are vacant, and those lands which may be covered with valid titles.

Land titles shall be registered, and territory of Republic sectionized.

Amendments may be proposed, &c.

SECT. 11. Any amendment or amendments to this Constitution may be proposed in the House of Representatives or Senate, and if the same shall be agreed to by a majority of the members elected to each of the two houses, such proposed amendment or amendments shall be entered on the journals, with the yeas and nays thereon, and referred to the Congress then next to be chosen, and shall be published for three months previous to the election; and if the Congress next chosen as aforesaid shall pass said amendment or amendments by a vote of two-thirds of all the members elected to each house, then it shall be the duty of said Congress to submit said proposed amendment or amendments to the people, in such manner and at such times as the Congress shall prescribe; and if the people shall approve and ratify such amendment or amendments by a majority of the electors qualified to vote for members of Congress voting thereon, such amendment or amendments shall become a part of this Constitution: provided, however, that no amendment or amendments be referred to the people oftener than once in three years.

DECLARATION OF RIGHTS.

Reservation of rights not herein delegated.

This declaration of rights is declared to be a part of this Constitution, and shall never be violated on any pretence whatever. And in order to guard against the transgression of the high powers which we have delegated, we declare that every thing in this bill of rights contained, and every other right not hereby delegated, is reserved to the people.

Equal rights asserted; exclusive privileges denied.

First. All men, when they form a social compact, have equal rights, and no men or set of men are entitled to exclusive public privileges or emoluments from the community.

All political power is inherent in the people.

Second. All political power is inherent in the people, and all free governments are founded on their authority, and instituted for their benefit; and they have at all times an inalienable right to alter their government in such manner as they may think proper.

Religious liberty and toleration.

Third. No preference shall be given by law to any religious denomination or mode of worship over another, but every person shall be permitted to worship God according to the dictates of his own conscience.

Liberty of speech and of the press.

Fourth. Every citizen shall be at liberty to speak, write, or publish his opinions on any subject, being responsible for the abuse of that privilege. No law shall ever be passed to curtail the liberty of speech or of the press; and in all prosecutions for libels, the truth may be given in evidence, and the jury shall have the right to determine the law and fact, under the direction of the court.

Seizures and searches.

Fifth. The people shall be secure in their persons, houses, papers and possessions, from all unreasonable searches and seizures, and no warrant shall issue to search any place or seize any person or thing, without describing the place to be searched or the person or thing to be seized, without probable cause, supported by oath or affirmation.

Rights of accused persons.

Sixth. In all criminal prosecutions the accused shall have the right of being heard, by himself, or counsel, or both; he shall have the right to demand the nature and cause of the accusation, shall be confronted with the witnesses against him, and have compulsory process for obtaining witnesses in his favor. And in all prosecutions by presentment or indictment, he shall have the right to a speedy and public trial, by an impartial jury; he shall not be compelled to give evidence against himself, or be deprived of life, liberty, or property, but by due course of law. And no freeman shall be holden to answer for any criminal charge, but on presentment or indictment by a grand jury, except in the land and naval forces, or in the militia when in actual service in time of war or public danger, or in cases of impeachment.

Seventh. No citizen shall be deprived of privileges, outlawed, exiled, or in any manner disfranchised, except by due course of the law of the land. No citizen deprived of privileges &c., except

Eighth. No title of nobility, hereditary privileges or honors, shall ever be granted or conferred in this Republic. No person holding any office of profit or trust shall, without the consent of Congress, receive from any foreign State any present, office, or emolument of any kind. Titles of nobility, &c., not to be granted. Offic'rs shall not receive presents, &c.

Ninth. No person, for the same offence, shall be twice put in jeopardy of life or limbs. And the right of trial by jury shall remain inviolate. Same offences. Trial by jury inviolate.

Tenth. All persons shall be bailable by sufficient security, unless for capital crimes, when the proof is evident or presumption strong; and the privilege of the writ of "habeas corpus" shall not be suspended, except in case of rebellion or invasion the public safety may require it. Bail. Habeas corpus.

Eleventh. Excessive bail shall not be required, nor excessive fines imposed, or cruel or unusual punishments inflicted. All courts shall be open, and every man for any injury done him in his lands, goods, person, or reputation, shall have remedy by due course of law. Excessive bail and unusual punishments prohibited. Courts open.

Twelfth. No person shall be imprisoned for debt in consequence of inability to pay. No imprisonment for debt.

Thirteenth. No person's particular services shall be demanded, nor property taken or applied to public use, unless by the consent of himself or his representative, without just compensation being made therefor according to law. No person's services or property applied to public use, &c.

Fourteenth. Every citizen shall have the right to bear arms in defence of himself and the Republic. The military shall at all times and in all cases be subordinate to the civil power. Right to bear arms. Military subordinate, &c.

Fifteenth. The sure and certain defence of a free people is a well-regulated militia; and it shall be the duty of the Legislature to enact such laws as may be necessary to the organizing of the militia of this Republic. The militia.

Sixteenth. Treason against this Republic shall consist only in levying war against it, or adhering to its enemies, giving them aid and support. No retrospective or ex post facto law, or laws impairing the obligation of contracts, shall be made. Treason. Retrospective, ex post facto law, or law impairing the obligation of contracts.

Seventeenth. Perpetuities or monopolies are contrary to the genius of a free government, and shall not be allowed; nor shall the law of primogeniture or entailments ever be in force in this Republic. Perpetuities, monopolies, primogeniture, &c.

The foregoing Constitution was unanimously adopted by the delegates of Texas, in convention assembled, at the town of Washington, on the seventeenth day of March, in the year of our Lord one thousand eight hundred and thirty-six, and of the Independence of the Republic, the first year. Adopted March 17, 1836.

In witness whereof, we have hereunto subscribed our names.

RICHARD ELLIS,
President and Delegate from Red River.

ALBERT H. S. KIMBLE, *Secretary.*

C. B. Stewart, James Collinsworth, Edwin Waller, A. Brigham, John S. D. Byrom, Francis Ruis, J. Antonio Navarro, William D. Lacy, William Menifee, John Fisher, Matthew Caldwell, William Motley, Lorenzo de Zavala, George W. Smyth, Stephen H. Everett, Elijah Stepp, Claiborne West, William B. Leates, M. B. Menard, A. B. Hardin, John W. Bunton, Thomas J. Gazley, R. M. Coleman, Sterling C. Robertson, George C. Childress, Baily Hardiman, Robert Potter, Charles Taylor, John S. Roberts, Robert Hamilton, Collin McKinney, A. H. Latimore, James Power, Sam Houston, Edward Conrad, Martin Palmer, James Gaines, William Clark, Jun., Sydney O. Pennington, Samuel P. Carson, Thomas J. Rusk, William C. Crawford, John Turner, Benjamin Briggs Goodrich, James G. Swisher, George W. Barnet, Jesse Grimes, E. O. Legrand, David Thomas, S. Rhoads Fisher, John W. Bower, J. B. Woods, Andrew Briscoe, Thomas Barnett, Jesse B. Badgett, Stephen W. Blount.

REPEALED LAWS.

CONVEYANCES OF PROPERTY OF MARRIED WOMEN.

Act of Feb. 3, 1841. Repealed by Act of April 30, 1846.

Conveyance—privy examination of the wife.

ARTICLE 1. [1] From and after the passage or approval of this Act, when a husband and his wife have sealed and delivered a writing purporting to be a conveyance of any estate or interest in any land, slave or slaves, or other effects, the separate property of the wife, if she appear before any Judge of the District Court, or Chief Justice of the County Court, and being examined privily and apart from her husband, shall declare that she did freely and willingly seal and deliver the said writing (to be then shown and explained to her,) and wishes not to retract it, and shall acknowledge the said writing so again shown to her, to be her act; such privy examination, acknowledgment and declaration, the said Judge or Chief Justice shall certify under his hand and seal by a certificate annexed to said writing, and to the following effect, or substance thereof, that is to say:

Form of certificate.

Republic of Texas, } I, A. B., Chief Justice of the county aforesaid, do hereby County of ———, } certify, that E. F., the wife of G. H., parties to a certain deed, bearing date on the —— day of ———, and hereunto annexed, personally appeared before me, the Chief Justice of the county aforesaid, and having been examined by me privily and apart from her husband, and having the deed aforesaid fully explained to her, she, the said E. F., acknowledged the same to be her act and deed, and declared that she had willingly signed, sealed, and delivered the same, and that she wished not to retract it.

Given under my hand and seal, this ——— day of ———.

[SEAL.]

But any certificate showing that the requisitions of the law have been complied with, shall be as valid as the form here prescribed; and such conveyance shall pass all the right, title, and interest, which the husband and wife, or either of them may have in or to the property therein conveyed.

COUNTY COURTS.

Act of Dec. 20, 1836. Repealed Jan. 26, 1839.

County Court established.

ART. 2. [1] There shall be established, in the several counties of this Republic an inferior court of law, which shall be styled the County Court of the County of ———; to be composed of one Chief Justice, who shall be elected by joint ballot of both Houses of Congress, and shall hold his office for a period of four years, and two Associate Justices, who shall be selected by a majority of the Justices of the Peace of each county, from among their own body, at the beginning of each and every year; and the Justices so selected shall attend said County Courts, or pay a fine to be assessed by the Chief Justice, not exceeding one hundred dollars.

ART. 3. [2] The Chief Justices of said court shall be commissioned by the President, and may be sworn into office by any primary Judge, heretofore appointed by law, or any legally authorized person. Chief Justice.

ART. 4. [6] The several County Courts of this Republic shall have original jurisdiction of all suits and actions for the recovery of money, founded on any bond, bill, promissory note, or other written contract, covenant, or agreement whatsoever, or any open account, where the sum demanded shall exceed one hundred dollars; and shall have concurrent jurisdiction with the District Courts, in all such suits and actions: provided that no suit relative to the title of land shall be tried and determined in said court; and generally to do and perform all other acts, and exercise all other powers, lawfully pertaining to a County Court, within this Republic. Jurisdiction.

ART. 5. [13] Any party may appeal from any final judgment or decision of any County Court, provided the amount in controversy shall exceed two hundred dollars, to the District Court, for said county, in the same manner and under the same restrictions as provided in the sixteenth section of an "Act establishing the jurisdiction and powers of the District Court," and the forty-second section of the aforesaid act, shall apply equally to the County Courts, so far as is consistent with this act. Appeal to District Court.

ART. 6. [18] The said courts shall have power to hear and determine all motions, reasonable notice being given to the adverse party, against Sheriffs or other officers for money received on execution or other process from said court, which they have neglected to pay on demand, to the party entitled to the same; and all motions against attorneys and counsellors at law for neglecting or refusing to pay money received for their clients in any case instituted in said courts, and award judgment and execution for the same. The Chief Justices of the County Courts shall have power to grant the same remedial process as a District Judge, provided that no such writ or process shall extend to any act of a District Judge; or relate to any business pending before a District Court, or which may be exclusively cognizable before it. Motions against Sheriffs and other officers for money received under execution.

ART. 7. [1] All probate business heretofore pending before the Primary Courts, the original papers thereof, or the papers relative to each and every estate or succession, shall be forthwith transferred by the Clerk of any Court, or person in possession of said papers, to the Clerks of the Probate Courts, where the deceased had his domicil at the time of his death; or if he had no fixed domicil, then to the Clerk of the Probate Court where the deceased died, or where the majority of the property of the deceased is situated. Act of Jan. 26, 1839. Repealed May 13, 1846. Probate business transferred to court of deceased's domicil.

ART. 8. [24] The Chief Justices of the County Courts shall be Judges of Probate for their respective counties, shall take the probate of wills, grant letters of administration on the estates of persons deceased, who were inhabitants of, or resident in said county, at the time of their decease; shall appoint guardians to minors, idiots, and lunatics; and in conjunction with the Associate Justices, shall examine and settle the accounts of executors, administrators, and guardians; and said Chief Justices shall have full jurisdiction of all testamentary and other matters appertaining to a Probate Court, within their respective counties. Act of Dec. 20, 1836. Repealed May 13, 1846. Jurisdiction and powers.

ART. 9. [25] The Chief Justice shall hold a Probate Court at the Court-house of their respective counties, on the last Monday of every month in the year, except in cases when the County Courts shall be held on the last Monday in any month; and in such case the Probate Court shall be held on the Monday next preceding, and they may hold a special court for the transaction of any business within their jurisdiction, provided ten days' notice is given by advertisement, at three of the most public places in different parts of the county, of the time of holding said court, and of all business to be acted on at such special term. To be held last Monday of every month—special terms.

ART. 10. [26] Any person may appeal from any decision or decree of any Court of Probate, within ten days after such decision or decree shall have been rendered to the District Court of the county: provided such appellant shall give bond with good and sufficient security, to be approved by said Court of Probate, conditioned that said appellant shall prosecute said appeal to effect, and perform the sentence, judgment, or decree which the said District Court shall make therein, in case the cause be decided against said appellant. Appeals to District Court.

ART. 11. [27] When any appeal shall be taken on any decision or decree of a Court of Probate, the Clerk of such court shall immediately make out a full Same subject.

and perfect record of all the proceedings in such case; and shall, on the application of either party, give to such party an attested copy of such record, which shall be transmitted to the District Court; and the said District Court shall, at the next succeeding term, hear and determine such appeal; and the decision of the District Court shall be certified to the Court of Probate, which shall carry the same into effect.

Duties of Clerk. ART. 12. [30] The Clerks of the County Courts shall be Clerks of the Courts of Probate for their respective counties, and shall record all wills and testaments, and other instruments of writing required by law to be recorded in their offices; shall give certified copies of all papers in their offices to any person applying for the same; and shall receive for all duties required to be performed by them, by virtue of their offices, such fees as may be prescribed by law.

Business of Primary Courts transferred to. ART. 13. [31] All probate business heretofore pending before the Primary Courts, shall be transferred to, and completed in the Probate Court for the county, established by this Act; and any of the Primary Judges heretofore acting, who shall refuse or neglect to transmit all such business, and all records and papers appertaining thereto, shall be proceeded against in the same manner and under the same penalties as provided in the eleventh section of the act establishing the jurisdiction and powers of the District Court.

Estates heretofore administered on. ART. 14. [32] It shall be the duty of the several Probate Courts to compel a settlement of all estates heretofore administered on, within twelve months; and may require new security to be given, if by them deemed necessary, within six months from the passage of this law.

Records, papers &c. ART. 15. [33] It shall be the duty of the Judge of the first instance, of each and every county, to deposit in the office of the Clerk of the County Court of his county, every matter of record, paper, document, or thing heretofore filed in the office, not by law required to be transmitted to the District Court, or to Justices of the Peace.

Act of July 19, 1842 ART. 16. [1] That hereafter the Probate Courts of the several counties, in this Republic, shall have authority to continue their session from day to day, until the business shall be disposed of.

DESCENTS AND DISTRIBUTION.

Act of December 18, 1837. Supplied Jan. 28, 1840. ART. 17. [2] In case any husband or wife shall die intestate, and leaving no heirs, the survivor shall be the heir and shall inherit the estate of the deceased spouse.

Act of Jan. 28, 1840. Repealed March 18, 1848. ART. 18. [1] The estates of suicides shall descend or vest as in cases of natural death; if any person shall be killed by casualty, there shall be no forfeiture by reason thereof.

Estates, how to descend. ART. 19. [2] When any person having title to any estate of inheritance, either real, personal, or mixed, shall die intestate, as to such estate, it shall descend and pass in parcenary to his or her kindred, male and female, in the following course, that is to say:

ART. 20. [3] To his or her children or their descendants, if any there be.

ART. 21. [4] If there be no children, nor their descendants, then to his or her father and mother in equal proportions; but if only the father or mother survive the intestate, then his or her estate shall be divided in two equal portions, one of which shall pass to such survivor, and the other shall pass to the brothers and sisters of the deceased, and to their descendants, or to such of them as there be; but if there be none such, then the whole estate shall be inherited by the surviving father or mother.

ART. 22. [5] If there be neither father nor mother, then the whole of such estate shall pass to the brothers and sisters of the intestate, and to their descendants, or to such of them as there be.

ART. 23. [6] If there be none of the kindred aforesaid, then the inheritance shall be divided into two moieties, one of which shall go to the paternal and the other to the maternal kindred in the following course, that is to say—to the grandfather and grandmother in equal portions; but if only one of these be living, then the estate shall be divided in two equal parts, one of which shall go to the survivor and the other shall go to the descendant or descendants of such deceased grandfather or grandmother; if there be no such descendant or descendants, then the whole estate shall be inherited by the surviving grandfather or grandmother; if there be no grandfather or grandmother, then the whole of such estate shall go to their descendants, or to such of them as there be; and so on without end, passing in like manner to the nearest lineal ancestors and to their descendants, or to such of them as there be.

ART. 24. [7] Where any person shall die intestate, and without issue, having title to any estate of inheritance, either real, personal, or mixed, derived by gift, devise, or descent from the father, and there be living, at the death of such intestate, his father, or any brother or sister of such intestate on the part of the father or paternal grandfather or grandmother of the intestate, or any brother or sister of the father, or any descendant of any of them, then such estate shall descend and pass to the paternal kindred without regard to the mother or maternal kindred of such intestate, in the same manner as if there had been no such mother or other maternal kindred. When no issue: estate derived from father.

ART. 25. [8] When any person shall die intestate and without issue, having title to any estate of inheritance, either real, personal, or mixed, derived by gift, devise, or descent from the mother, and there be living at the death of such intestate, his mother, or any brother or sister of the intestate on part of the mother, or the maternal grandfather or grandmother of the intestate, or any brother or sister of the mother, or any descendant of any of them, then such estate shall descend and pass to the maternal kindred without regard to the father or other paternal kindred, in the same manner as if there had been no such father or other paternal kindred living at the death of such intestate. When from mother.

ART. 26. [9] No right in the inheritance shall accrue to any persons whatsoever, other than to children of the intestate, unless they be in being and capable in law to take as heirs at the time of the intestate's death. Persons not in *esse*.

ART. 27. [10] Where, for want of issue of the intestate, and of father, mother, brothers and sisters, and their descendants, the inheritance is directed to go by moieties to the paternal and maternal kindred, if there should be no such kindred on the one part, the whole shall go to the other part; and if there be no kindred either on the one part or the other, the whole shall go to the wife or husband of the intestate; and if the wife or husband be dead, it shall go to her or his kindred in the like course as if such wife or husband had survived the intestate, and then died entitled to the estate. Default of paternal or maternal kindred.

ART. 28. [11] In cases before mentioned, where the inheritance is directed to pass to the collateral kindred of the intestate, if part of such collaterals be of the whole blood to the intestate, and the other part of the half blood only, those of the half blood shall inherit only half so much as those of the whole blood; but if all be of the half blood, they shall have whole portions. Collaterals of half blood.

ART. 29. [12] Where the children of the intestate's brothers and sisters, uncles and aunts, or any other relations of the descendant standing in the same degree, come into the partition, they shall take *per capita*, that is to say, by persons; and where a part of them being dead and a part living, the issue of those dead have a right to partition—such issue shall take *per stirpes*, or by stocks, that is to say, the shares of their deceased parent. *Per capita—per stirpes.*

ART. 30. [13] Where any of the children of a person dying intestate, or their issue, shall have received from such intestate, in his lifetime, any real, personal, or mixed estate, by way of advancement, and shall choose to come into the partition and distribution of the estate with the other parceners and distributees, such advancement of real, personal, and mixed estate shall be brought into hotchpotch with the whole estate, real, personal and mixed, descended; and such party returning such advancement as aforesaid, shall thereupon be entitled to his or her portion of the whole estate so descended, real, personal, and mixed: and, provided, that it shall be sufficient to account for the property so brought into hotchpotch as at the time it was advanced; and when money and negroes shall have been advanced, the interests of the one or the increase of the other need not be brought into hotchpotch. Hotchpotch.

ART. 31. [14] In making title to land by descent, it shall be no bar to a party that any ancestor through whom he derives his descent from the intes- Alienage of ancestor—9 years to aliens.

tate, is or hath been an alien; and every alien to whom any land may be devised or may descend, shall have nine years to become a citizen of the Republic and take possession of such land; or shall have nine years to sell the same before it shall be declared to be forfeited, or before it shall escheat to the government.

Bastards. ART. 32. [16] Bastards shall be capable of inheriting or of transmitting inheritance on part of their mother, and shall also be entitled to a distributive share of the personal estate of any of their kindred on the part of their mother, in like manner as if they had been lawfully begotten of such mother.

Act of March 17, 1842. Father and mother. ART. 33. [1] The seventh and eighth sections of the above entitled act shall be controlled and governed by the provisions of the fourth section of said act; and, farther, that should there be either father or mother of the intestate surviving, instead of the estate of the intestate taking the direction indicated in said seventh and eighth sections, the whole shall be inherited and descend upon such surviving parent, or both, in equal moieties, should both survive; and such surviving parent or parents, shall not be excluded, no matter in what manner the estate may have been acquired by the intestate.

DOWER.

Act of Jan. 26, 1839. Repealed Feb. 5, 1840. Widow may claim. ART. 34. [1] The widow may in all cases waive the provision made for her in the will of her deceased husband, and claim her dower, which shall be assigned her accordingly; in which case she shall receive no part of such provision, unless it appears plainly by the will that the testator intended it in addition to her dower.

Estate insolvent. ART. 35. [2] When the estate of any testator or intestate shall be represented to be insolvent, and shall not be sufficient both personal and real to pay the just debts, the widow of such testator or intestate shall nevertheless have maintenance for life, to be determined by the Probate Court.

Time to dissent from will. ART. 36. [3] When any person shall die intestate, or shall make his last will and testament, and not therein make any express provision for his wife by giving and devising unto her such part or parcel of his real and personal estate as shall be satisfactory to her, such widow may signify her dissent thereto in the Probate Court in the county where the succession is opened, at any time within six months after the probate of such will; and then, and in that case, she shall be entitled to dower in the following manner, to wit: one-third part of all the lands, tenements, and hereditaments, of which her husband died seised and possessed, which third part she shall be entitled to for life, in which said third part shall be comprehended the dwelling-house in which her husband shall have been accustomed most generally to dwell next before his death, together with the offices, out-houses, buildings, house and kitchen furniture, and other improvements thereunto belonging or appertaining: provided, that if it should appear to the court to whom application is made, that the whole of said dwelling-house, out-houses, buildings, and other improvements, thereunto appertaining, cannot be applied to the use of the widow without manifest injustice to the children and other heirs, then and in that case such widow shall be entitled to such part thereof only as the court may deem reasonable and just. (Dower in real estate.)

Personal estate. ART. 37. [4] When a husband dies intestate, or shall make his last will and testament and not make provision therein for his wife, as expressed in the first section of this act, she shall be entitled to share in the personal estate in the following manner, to wit: if there be but one child, she shall be entitled out of the residue left after paying the debts of the deceased, to one-half; if there be more than one child, but not more than four, in that case she shall be entitled to a child's part; but if there be more than four children, then and in that case she shall be entitled to one-fifth.

ART. 38. [5] When a husband dies intestate, or shall make his last will and testament and not make provision therein for his wife, as expressed in the first section of this act, and shall die without legitimate heirs of his body, or their descendants, she shall be entitled for life to one-half of all her husband's estate, both real and personal. Husband dies without heirs.

ART. 39. [6] It shall be lawful after the passage of this act, for any widow claiming dower, to file her petition in the Probate Court in the county in which the succession is commenced, setting forth the nature of her claim, and particularly specifying the lands, tenements, and hereditaments of which she claims dower, and praying that her dower may be allowed to her; whereupon the said court shall appoint three discreet freeholders as commissioners, connected with the parties neither by consanguinity or affinity, and entirely disinterested, who upon oath, (which oath the Sheriff is hereby authorized to administer,) and in connection with said Sheriff, shall allot and set off by metes and bounds to the said widow, one-third part, according to quality and quantity, of all the lands, tenements, and hereditaments in said county, and shall put her in possession of the same. And when she has claim to dower to land being in different counties, she may proceed in the same court as above directed, and setting forth the county in which the lands are situated; and it shall be the duty of the Clerk, under the order of the court, to transmit to the Probate Court in the county in which the said lands are situate, a certified copy of the petition and order of the court; which papers, when received by the court of the county in which the land lies, shall be sufficient authority for said court to proceed to the appointment of commissioners, who shall execute the decree of the court in the manner provided in the first part of this section, and make return of the same to the Clerk of the said court; and said Clerk shall, under his hand and seal, transmit a copy of the return of said commissioners to the court in which the succession was opened. Dower, how assigned.

ART. 40. [7] The court at its first term after such petition for dower is filed, shall proceed to hear and determine as to them shall seem just and right: provided, that the party petitioning for dower, shall give ten days' previous notice to the executors or administrators, or children of such deceased person, or to their representatives, or to their guardians, if they be minors, by services as in other cases; and where there are no executors, or administrators, or children, or their representatives, or when the widow is the executrix or administratrix, then she shall give notice by advertisement in the newspapers published nearest the county in which the succession is carried, and once a week for four weeks. Court shall determine, &c.

ART. 41. [8] It shall be lawful for the widow to retain full possession of the dwelling-house in which her husband most usually dwelt next before his death, together with the out-houses, offices or improvements, and plantation thereunto belonging, free from molestation and rent, until she shall have her dower assigned her. Dwelling-house, &c.

EXECUTIONS.

Act of Jan. 23, 1839. Repealed Feb. 5, 1840. Time of sales.

ART. 42. [1] From and after the passage of this act, all Sheriffs' sales, and administrators' or executors' or guardians' sales of real estate or personal property, or a right growing out of the same, shall be made on the first Tuesday in every month; which sales shall take place between the hours of ten o'clock A. M., and four o'clock P. M., at the court-house door of the county in which said sales are made.

Advertisements of.

ART. 43. [2] All such sales of real estate shall be advertised thirty days in some public gazette or newspaper, before the sale takes place, and all personal property shall be advertised in like manner for twenty days before the day of sale: provided, there is a public gazette or newspaper published in the county, or in an adjoining county to where such sale takes place; and said sales shall also be advertised at the court-house door of the county in which said sale takes place and at other public places; and all laws and parts of laws contrary to the true intent and meaning of this act be, and the same are hereby repealed.

Act of Jan. 26, 1839. Repealed Feb 5, 1840. Clerk to issue.

ART. 44. [1] From and after the rising of every court, it shall be the duty of the clerk thereof to tax the costs of suit incurred by the successful party, and for which judgment is rendered, distinguishing between the plaintiff's, attorney's, and sheriff's fees, and issue execution in the following form:

The Republic of Texas to the Sheriff (or Coroner, as the law may require,) of ——— county:

Form of.

Whereas A. B., on the —— day of ———, in the year of our Lord eighteen hundred and ———, at our ——— court hath recovered against C. D. for debt, (if debt, designate the debt, interest and costs, or if damages, say damages,) and which to the said A. B. now adjudged; these are therefore to command you, that of the goods, chattels, and estates of the said C. D., you cause to be made the full amount of this execution, after deducting therefrom the legal fees and commissions for collecting the aforesaid amount; and that you have then this writ at the clerk's office of said court on the return day hereof, certifying how you have executed the same.

Given under my hand this ——— day of ———, 18—.

T. H.,
Clerk.

Execution book.

ART. 45. [2] The clerk shall keep an Execution Book, in which it shall be his duty to record an abstract of all the executions, together with a copy of the return of the sheriff, showing the amount, and file the same in the office, subject to the order of the plaintiff in the execution, or his attorney; and when delivered it shall be the duty of the clerk to endorse the delivery in the margin of the Execution Book, and to whom; which endorsement shall be recorded evidence of that fact.

May issue before rising of court, when.

ART. 46. [3] Should the defendant in any judgment of court be about leaving the county in which judgment may be rendered, and before rising of the court, the court shall order execution to be immediately issued, upon an affidavit being made and filed with the court of that fact.

Return. Levy.

ART. 47. [4] All executions shall be made returnable within ninety days from the date of their issue; and the defendant or his agent shall have the right in all cases to designate the property; and if the defendant shall fail or refuse to designate the same, then the levy shall be made in the following manner: first on personal or movable property, then on slaves, and then on lands.

Advertisement.

ART. 48. [5] Whenever property shall have been seized by virtue of an execution, it shall be the duty of the sheriff or other officer to advertise the same, if it be personal property, twenty days, if it be slaves or lands, thirty days, by advertisements posted up, one at the court house of the county, and at least two others at two or more of the most public places in the county.

Appraisement.

ART. 49. [6] Upon the day of sale the plaintiff may choose one and the defendant another appraiser, who being first duly sworn by the sheriff, shall proceed to appraise the property seized at its fair cash value in that kind of money or paper demanded; and in case of their disagreement, then an umpire shall be appointed by the clerk or deputy clerk of the court from which the execution may have issued, or in his absence, by the Chief Justice of the county where the sale is to be made, or in his absence, by the nearest Justice of the Peace, which person so chosen shall be duly sworn in the manner aforesaid, and proceed to decide between the appraisers. But if either party fail to attend either in person or by agent, then and in that case it shall be the duty of the sheriff to choose an appraiser or appraisers for the absentee or absentees.

ART. 50. [7] The sheriff or other officer shall then offer for sale the property to the highest bidder for cash, and if the bid amounts to two-thirds of the appraised value of the property, then the sheriff or other officer shall deliver up the property to the highest bidder, and on receiving the money shall execute a title to him therefor.

ART. 51. [8] If the bids do not amount to two-thirds of the appraised value, then the Sheriff or other officer shall again advertise the same, in the manner required by this law; and on the day of sale the property shall be sold on a twelve months' credit, for whatever it will bring, the purchaser being required to give bond, with good and sufficient security, payable to the plaintiff, which bond shall be returnable to the Clerk's office of the court from which the execution shall have issued, and shall, have the force and effect of a judgment against the principal and the securities; and upon the maturity of the bond, if it shall not be punctually paid, execution shall issue thereon against the principal and securities, and the Sheriff or other officer, by virtue of this execution, shall proceed to seize and sell sufficient property to pay the amount thereof, and costs for cash without appraisement, which fact shall be endorsed on this execution. When on twelve months' credit.

ART. 52. [10] Whenever an execution is levied upon any property, the defendant shall have the right to retain the possession of the same upon giving bond with good security, payable to the plaintiff, in double the amount of the debt and costs, conditioned for the delivery of the property to the sheriff on the day of sale. Delivery bond.

ART. 53. [11] If the defendant shall fail to deliver the property so bonded, it shall be the duty of the Sheriff to return the bond to the Clerk of the court from which execution issued, as forfeited; whereupon said clerk shall issue execution against the principal and the securities on the bond for the amount of the debt and costs, upon which said execution no delivery bond shall be taken; which fact shall be endorsed by the Clerk on the execution. (*a*) Failure to deliver property.

ART. 54. [12] It shall be the duty of the Sheriff to endorse on the execution the day on which it came into his hands, and if he receive more than one on the same day, and against the same person, he shall number them as received, and on failure he shall be liable to pay twenty per cent. on the amount of the execution, to be recovered by the plaintiff from him and his securities, upon giving five days' notice that a motion will be made to this purpose at the next term of the Court, from which the execution issued. Sheriff to endorse and number.

ART. 55. [13] Should any sheriff or other officer fail or refuse to pay over money collected under execution, when demanded by the person entitled to receive the same, he shall be liable to pay ten per cent. per month on the amount so collected, besides interests and costs; which may be recovered of him and his securities by motion before the court from which said execution issued, five days' previous notice thereof being given. Officer failing to pay over money.

ART. 56. [15] In levying on land, the Sheriff or other officer shall first levy on the wild land, and lastly on the domicil and improved land; and in case the land be more than sufficient to pay the execution and costs at two-thirds of its appraised value, the appraisers shall take off so much of the land at one corner of the survey as will at the aforesaid valuation, satisfy the said execution and all costs and thereupon the Sheriff or Coroner, shall offer the land for sale in satisfaction of the debt, costs, &c.; and whoever will pay the said execution, together with costs and commissions, for the fewest number of acres, shall be the purchaser. Mode of levy and sale of land.

ART. 57. [17] Whenever a final judgment shall be rendered by any court of record of this Republic, it shall operate as a lien upon the lands of the defendant, from the day of the date of the judgment; and executions shall operate as a lien upon the personal property and slaves of the defendant, from the day on which it issues. Lien of judgment and execution.

ART. 58. [18] If any sheriff or other officer shall fail to make return of any execution received by him, which return shall be made five days before the ensuing court to which the same is returnable, or if he shall make a false return, or shall neglect or fail to make a levy when in his power so to do, being thereto specially required by the plaintiff, or shall fail legally to advertise and offer for sale any property levied on, he shall be liable to pay to the plaintiff in execution the amount of the debt, interest, and costs, with twenty per cent. damages thereon, which may be recovered of him and his securities by motion in the competent court, upon giving five days' notice thereof. Sheriff failing to return, &c.

ART. 59. [1] From and after the rising of every court it shall be the duty of the Clerk thereof to tax the costs of suit in every case incurred by the success- Act of Feb. 5, 1840.

(*a*) Cole, Admx., *v.* Robertson, 6 Tex. Rep. 356.

Repealed Jan. 27, 1842. ful party, and for which judgment shall be rendered, and issue execution, and endorsing on each execution issued, the several items contained in the bill of costs, in intelligible words and figures.

Clerk to issue, when.

When to issue before rising of Court. ART. 60. [3] Should the defendant in any judgment of the court, be about to leave the county in which judgment may be rendered, and before rising of the court, the court shall order execution to be immediately issued, upon an affidavit being made and filed with the court, of that fact.

Levy and return Proviso Repealed Dec. 22, 1840. ART. 61. [4] All executions shall be made returnable at the next term of the court, and the defendant or his agent in all cases shall have the right to designate the property, and if the defendant shall fail or refuse to designate the same, then the levy shall be made in the following manner: First on personal or movable property, then on uncultivated lands, then on slaves, and lastly on the improved lands or homestead of the defendant: provided, that in no case shall the judgment be sent out of the county where the judgment is obtained, unless there is not sufficient property within the limits of the same to satisfy the amount of the judgment, interest, and costs.

Not to be sent out of county, unless, advertisement sale. ART. 62. [5] Whenever any property shall have been seized by virtue of an execution, it shall be the duty of the Sheriff or other officer to advertise the same, if it be personal property, at least ten days, by advertising the same at three public places in the county, one of which shall be the place where the property is sold; if it be slaves or land, twenty days, by publication in some newspaper, if there be any published in the county, and also by advertisements posted up, one at the court-house in the county: provided, that all sales of lands and negroes shall be made at the court-house door of the county in which the sales take place, on the first Tuesday, or the following day, of the month, between the hours often o'clock, A. M., and sundown: and provided further, that all other property may be sold on the premises where it is seized in execution.

Delivery bond. ART. 63. [7] Whenever an execution is levied upon property, the defendant shall have the right to retain the possession of the same, upon giving bond with good security, payable to the plaintiff, in double the amount of debts and costs conditioned for the delivery of the property to the plaintiff [Sheriff?] on the day of sale.

Failure to deliver property. ART. 64. [8] If the defendant shall fail to deliver the property so bonded, it shall be the duty of the Sheriff to return the bond to the Clerk of the court, from which execution issued as aforesaid; whereupon the Clerk shall issue execution against the principal and sureties on the bond for the amount of the debt and costs, upon which said execution, no delivery bond shall be taken; which fact shall be endorsed by the Clerk on the execution.

Sheriff to endorse and number. ART. 65. [9] It shall be the duty of the Sheriff to endorse on the execution the day on which it came into his hands, and if he received more than one on the same day and against the same person, he shall number them as received, and on failure he shall be liable to pay twenty per cent. on the amount of the execution, together with such damages as the plaintiff in execution may sustain by such failure to number; to be recovered by the plaintiff from him and his sureties, by giving five days' notice that a motion will be made to this purpose at the next term of the court from which the execution issued.

Officer failing to pay over money. ART. 66. [10] Should any Sheriff, or other officer, fail or refuse to pay money collected under an execution, when demanded by the person entitled to receive the same, he shall be liable to pay ten per cent. per month on the amount so collected beside interest and costs; which may be recovered of him and his sureties, by motion before the court from which said execution issued; five days' previous notice being given.

Property levied on to be kept securely. ART. 67. [11] It shall be the duty of the Sheriff to keep securely all property levied on by him for which no delivery bond has been given, and if any loss should result to any party interested by his negligence, he shall be liable to pay the value of the property so lost, and ten per cent. damages thereon, to be recovered by the party injured, before any court of competent jurisdiction; five days' previous notice thereof being given.

Lien of judgment. ART. 68. [12] Whenever final judgment shall be rendered by the Supreme, District, or County Courts of this Republic, it shall operate as a lien on all the property of the defendant, situated and being in the same county where judgment is rendered, from the day of the date of the judgment: provided, that said lien shall cease to operate, if execution be not issued out within twelve months from the date thereof, and due diligence be not used to collect the same.

ART. 69. [13] When judgment shall be obtained before the Supreme, District, County, or Justice's court of this Republic, for any debt or damages, and the person against whom such judgment shall be obtained shall not have sufficient property within the county where the judgment shall be rendered to satisfy the execution of the plaintiff, it shall be lawful to issue execution, directed to the Sheriff or other legal officers of any county in this Republic where the defendant may have property, which said Sheriff or other officer to whom said execution may be directed, is hereby empowered and required to serve and execute the same, and shall make return thereof to the court where the judgment was rendered. When to issue to other county.

ART. 70. [14] Whenever a judgment shall have been rendered by any court of this Republic, if the plaintiff, his agent or attorney, shall make affidavit before the court or the clerk thereof in which judgment was obtained, that the defendant or defendants hath or have no property within the knowledge of such affiant, in his or their possession, and that such affiant has just reason to believe that another person or persons is or are indebted to said defendant or defendants, or hath or have effects of such defendant or defendants in his or her hands, it shall be lawful for the court or the clerk to cause the person or persons supposed to be indebted to, or supposed to have any effects of said defendant or defendants, to appear at the next term of such court as garnishee or garnishees, and said court shall examine and proceed against said garnishee or garnishees in the same manner as prescribed by law against garnishees in original attachments. Garnishment.

ART. 71. [15] When the day of sale shall have arrived, it shall be the duty of the clerk of the District Court, or in his absence, the Chief Justice of the County Court, or in his absence the clerk of the County Court, or in his absence some Justice of the Peace, at the request of the sheriff, coroner, or constable, to appoint three discreet, disinterested men, citizens and freeholders of the county, to appraise the property levied on by virtue and authority of an execution, which appraisers shall be sworn by the sheriff, coroner or constable, or by any officer authorized to administer an oath, and shall assess the value of the property taken under execution at its fair cash price, which assessment shall be reduced to writing, signed by the appraisers or a majority of them, and be returned with the execution. Appraisement.

ART. 72. [16] The property levied on shall then be offered for sale for cash, to the highest bidder, and if the property be improved lands or slaves, it must bring two-thirds of the appraised value or no sale shall be made for cash; but any other species of property may be sold if the highest bid amounts to one-half the appraisement. Sale for cash

ART. 73. [17] If the highest bid does not amount to two-thirds of the appraised value in cash, the sheriff, coroner, or other officer shall then advertise the same again for the ensuing sale day, if practicable; and that the same shall be sold to the highest bidder for what it may bring, on a credit of twelve months, bearing the same rate of interest as that recovered on the judgment; and the purchaser shall be required to give bond with two good securities for the payment of the purchase-money; which bond shall be returned with the execution to the court from which the same issued; shall be a mortgage on the property purchased, and shall have the force and effect of a judgment, upon which execution may issue without any other formality against the principal and securities to the same, if the same be not punctually paid; and by virtue of this execution the property first sold, or any other property belonging to the principal and sureties may be seized and sold for cash without any appraisement; and upon this execution the clerk shall endorse that no delivery bond or security whatever shall be taken. Sale on twelve months' credit

ART. 74. [18] If any person shall bid off property at any sale made by virtue of an execution, and shall fail to comply with the terms of the same, he shall be liable to pay to the plaintiff or plaintiffs in execution, twenty per cent. on the value of the property thus bid off, besides costs, to be recovered before the court whence the execution issued, by motion, five days' previous notice being given to him or her that such motion will be made; and should the property on a second sale bring less than on the former, he shall be liable to pay to the defendant in execution, all loss which he sustains thereby, to be recovered as above in this section. Bidder failing to comply.

ART. 75. [19] When the terms of the sale shall not be complied with by the bidder, the sheriff shall proceed to sell the property again on the same day, if there be sufficient time, but if not, he shall re-advertise the same for the next succeeding regular day of sale. Re-sale of property.

Sale on credit—bond of purchaser.

ART. 76. [20] When the property is sold on a credit of twelve months, if the proceeds is more than sufficient to pay the execution, interests and costs, the purchaser shall also execute a bond as provided in the section of this act, payable to the defendant in execution, for the excess; on which the same summary remedy may be had as is provided in favor of plaintiff in execution; and the property may be seized and sold in like manner.

Conveyance to purchaser.

ART. 77. [21] When a sale has been made and the terms complied with by payment of the price or executing the contemplated bond, the sheriff, coroner or constable shall make and deliver to the purchaser, a conveyance of all the right, title, interest or claim, which the defendant in execution had in and to the property sold.

Executions from Justices' Courts.

ART. 78. [22] Justices of the Peace shall have power, and they are hereby authorized to issue executions against lands and tenements as well as goods and chattels; and when such execution shall be levied upon lands and tenements, the same proceedings shall be had thereon as provided for executions in the hands of Sheriffs by this act; but when levied upon goods and chattels, the same proceedings shall be had thereon as now required by law, adhering nevertheless to the mode of advertising prescribed in this act.

Act of Dec. 22, 1840. Repealed Jan. 22, 1842.

Appraisement.

ART. 79. [1] When the day of sheriff's sale shall have arrived, it shall be the duty of the Chief Justice of the County Court, or in case of his absence, any disinterested magistrate of the beat where such sale may take place, or of an adjoining beat, at the request of the Sheriff, Coroner, or Constable, to appoint three discreet men, citizens, freeholders, or householders of the county, to appraise the property levied on by virtue of execution, at a fair cash price, which valuation shall be reduced to writing, and signed by [the] appraisers, or a majority of them, and returned to the Sheriff.

No sale, when.

ART. 80. [2] The property so levied on and appraised, shall then be offered for sale to the highest bidder; and if the same (be it real or personal property) shall not bring two-thirds of the valuation returned by the appraisers, there shall be no sale, and the execution shall bind the property.

Re-sale.

ART. 81. [3] The property so offered and unsold, may, at any time subsequent, be exposed again to sale, at the instance of the plaintiff, upon previous notice of twenty days being given, in the manner pointed out by law.

When plaintiff to pay costs.

ART. 82. [4] If there be no sale of the property executed in the manner pointed out in the third section of this act, the plaintiff shall pay the costs of said last-mentioned exposure to sale; provided, always, that either party shall be entitled to have a new appraisement of the property once in every six months after the first attempt to sell the same.

Constable's sales.

ART. 83. [6] The provisions of the foregoing act shall be construed to relate also to Constables' sales, under executions.

Act of January 21, 1841. Repealed Jan'y 27, 1842.

Place of sale.

ART. 84. All public sales in the Republic by Sheriffs, Constables, administrators, and other persons, may be held at the residence of the owner of the property, or at the late residence of a deceased person, or at any other place by consent of the parties interested, which will be most advantageous to the sale of the property: provided, always, that real estate and slaves shall be sold at the court-house of the respective counties, unless an order of the court be had to sell at some other place, any law to the contrary notwithstanding.

Act of January 27, 1842.

Obsolete.

ART. 85. [17] Upon the day of sale, the plaintiff may choose one, and the defendant another, appraiser, who, after being duly sworn by the Sheriff, shall proceed to appraise the property levied on, at its fair cash value; and, in case said appraisers shall not be able to agree, they shall choose an umpire, who, after being duly sworn in like manner, shall proceed to decide between them: but if either party fail to attend or make his selection, either in person or by agent, it shall be the duty of the Sheriff to appoint an appraiser, or appraisers, for the absentee, or absentees. The appraisement shall be reduced to writing, and signed by the appraisers, or a majority of them: the Sheriff, or other officer, shall then proceed to offer the property so levied on and appraised, for sale, to the highest bidder, for cash; and if the highest sum bid does not amount to two-thirds of the valuation made by the appraisers, there shall be no sale: provided, that if the property so levied on and appraised, be personal property or slaves, the defendant shall give bond, as specified in the seventh section of this act, conditioned for the delivery of the property to the Sheriff, or other officer, whenever thereto required; and that he shall not, in the mean time, remove said property out of the county in which said levy is made.

Appraisement.

No delivery bond. Perishable property.

ART. 86. [18] When any defendant shall fail, or refuse, to give bond, as hereinbefore provided, or when the property levied upon shall be clearly of a wasting or perishable nature, and likely to be destroyed by keeping, it shall be lawful for the Chief Justice of the county in which such levy is made, on the application of the Sheriff, or either of the parties, supported by the affidavit of some credible person, to order such property to be sold, after due notice, on a credit of nine months, for whatever it will bring—the purchaser being required to give bond, with good security, for the purchase money, payable to the plaintiff; which bond shall be returned by the Sheriff, or other officer, to the Clerk's office of the court from which the execution issued, and shall have the force and effect of a judgment: and if, at the maturity of such bond, it shall not be punctually paid, execution shall issue thereon against both the principal and securities, upon which the Clerk shall endorse that "no appraisement shall be had, and no security, of any kind, shall be taken;" and the Sheriff, or other officer, by virtue of such execution, shall proceed to seize and sell sufficient property to pay the amount thereof, for cash without appraisement.

ART. 87. [19] In case there be no sale of property taken in execution, as contemplated in the seventeenth section of this act, it shall be lawful for the Sheriff, or other officer, after the expiration of three months, to proceed to make a second levy upon such property as the defendant may point out to him, not being the same levied upon in the first instance; and in case the property so levied upon in the second instance shall not bring two-thirds of its appraised value, then it shall be lawful, after the expiration of three months from the last-mentioned sale day, for the plaintiff in execution, his agent or attorney, to designate such property of the defendant as he may think proper, to be levied on; and if the property so pointed out shall not bring its full appraised value, there shall be no sale; and it shall not be lawful for the Sheriff, or other officer, to levy the same execution upon any property of the defendant, for the space of twelve months thereafter; after which time the plaintiff may again point out property to be sold under the provisions above specified, in cases of property pointed out by plaintiff: provided, that each levy and sale of property pointed out by the plaintiff, shall be at his own expense. Proceedings in case of no sale, &c.

ART. 88. [20] The provisions of this act shall apply to all sales under execution, whether by Sheriffs, Coroners, or Constables, except sales for public dues, which shall be positive without appraisement. Act to apply, to what sales.

ART. 89. [21] The provisions of the seventeenth, eighteenth, and nineteenth sections of this act shall apply only to debts, and other legal liabilities, contracted and incurred prior to the first day of March next; and that all sales by virtue of executions issued on judgments founded on debts, and other legal liabilities, contracted and incurred after the first day of May next, shall be made for cash, without appraisement; and the Clerk, or other officer issuing any execution, shall endorse thereon, whether the sale shall be made with or without appraisement. To what debts act applies.

ART. 90. [1] The twenty-first section of the above recited act be so amended as to read, that the provisions of the seventeenth, eighteenth, and nineteenth sections of this act shall apply only to debts and other legal liabilities contracted and incurred prior to the first day of May, one thousand eight hundred and forty-two, instead of March, as mentioned in said section of the above recited act. Same subject.

ESTATES OF DECEASED PERSONS.

ESTATES OF DECEASED SOLDIERS.

Ordinance and decree of Jan. 22, 1836. Took effect from passage. Repealed Feb. 5, 1840.

ART. 91. [3] All proceedings relative to successions, matters of probate, *et cetera*, shall be regulated and governed agreeably to the principles and laws in similar cases in the State of Louisiana: provided, that no Judge shall act as administrator; but in all cases of intestacy, the next of kin, and other principles of the common law shall prevail in the appointment of administrators and guardians. And the Judges shall proceed to complete all unfinished business which remains on file or of record, of their predec essors, under the laws of Coahuila and Texas, including all appeals which have been taken from their respective municipalities to the Supreme Court, the records of which shall be returned to the courts of their respective municipalities, and trials thereon be had *de novo:* provided, that in all cases where new municipalities have been created, taken from one or more municipalities, it shall be the duty of the Clerk of the court of the old municipality to transmit all original papers, documents, and transcripts of proceedings had in each case or suit, and all original papers and proceedings relative to successions, testamentary business of every kind, and all unfinished business and proceedings whatever, belonging to or connected with the citizens of the new municipality, to the Clerk of the court of the said municipality, to be regulated by the rules of practice in suits, as heretofore existed in the country.

Laws of Louisiana to govern, when. Unfinished business under the laws of Coahuila and Texas, &c.

Right of administration, how determined.

ART. 92. [1] When any person shall die intestate, the executors named in any testament shall renounce the executorship, or refuse or neglect, for the space of thirty days after the death of the testator, to exhibit such testament for probate, then administration of the succession of such intestate or such testator, with the testament annexed, shall be granted—first to the surviving husband or surviving wife; then the next of kin of such intestate or testator, or to some of them: and in case of their and each of their refusal, then to a principal creditor or creditors of such intestate or testator; and if none of them will accept, then to such other proper person or persons as will accept the same.

Act of Feb. 5, 1840. Took effect 16th March, 1840.

To whom administration shall be granted, when executor fails, &c., to qualify.

ART. 93. [2] Before issuing letters testamentary, or letters of administration with the will annexed, such executor or executrix, with the will annexed, shall take, and the Judge shall administer, the following oath, viz:—"You swear that the writing which has been offered for probate, is the last will of ——— as far as you know or believe, and that you will well and truly execute said will according to law, and the directions thereof, so far as the estate of the said ——— will extend; and that you will return a true inventory of all said estate, whether real or personal, of the deceased, so far as the same may come to your knowledge; a true account of sales, and your said administration, as required by law; and before issuing any other letters of administration, such administrator or administratrix shall take, and the Judge shall administer, the following oath:—"You swear that ———, deceased, died without any lawful will as far as you know or believe; and that you will well and truly administer all and singular the succession of the said deceased, and return a true inventory thereof, so far as the same may come to your knowledge; and a just account of sales, and of your administration, as required by law." But when letters testamentary, or of administration, shall be granted on any authenticated copy of a will, and in such other cases as, in the opinion of the Judge, may require a change in the form of the oath, the oath may be administered in such form as, in the opinion of the Judge, is suitable to the nature of the case; and when the testator fails to appoint an executor, or in case the executor appointed may refuse or fail to prove the will and qualify, or may die before he has fully executed the will, then the legatee under the will; and in case there be more legatees than one, then that legatee the court may deem best qualified; shall have right to letters of administration upon the estate of the testator, to the exclusion of every other person; but should all the legatees be minors, then the court shall be governed in the appointment of an administrator, by the provisions of this act.

Oath of administrators, &c.

ART. 94. [3] When application is made for probate of a will, or for letters of administration, ten days' notice of such application shall be given, by order of the Judge of Probate by advertisement posted on the door of the court house, and in two other public places in the county, before the said probate is made, or letters of administration granted; and the said will may be admitted to probate on the deposition of a single witness—the said deposition shall be taken in writing; and, if the will be subsequently attacked, shall be considered good evidence of the facts therein set forth, if the witness be dead or removed from the Republic. But any person interested in the will may, within four years afterwards, require it to be proved in solemn form, or contest its validity before the Psobate Court, and the final judgment thereon given, shall be conclusive: provided, that infants, feme coverts, and persons *non compos mentis*, shall have the like period, after the removal of their respective disabilities.

Notice of application of probate of will, and probate of the same.

ART. 95. [4] In all cases of granting of letters testamentary, or of adminis-

Bond of executor, administrator, or guardian. tration or guardianship, the executor or executrix, administrator or administratrix, or guardian, shall enter into bond with at least two good and sufficient securities, approved by the Judge, payable to him and his successors in office, in such penalty as they may direct; which shall, at least, be equal to double the estimated value of the estate, with a condition as follows:—"The condition of the above obligation is such, whereas, the above bound —— has been duly appointed administrator of the estate of —— or administrator or executor or executrix of the last will of ——, or guardian of —— (as the case may be); now if the said —— shall well and truly perform all the duties that are or may be required of him, her, or them, as such administrator or administratrix, executor or executrix, or guardian, (as the case may be,) then the above obligation to be void; otherwise, to remain in full force Such bond shall not become void on the first recovery, and may be put in suit and prosecuted from time to time, against all, or any one, or more, of the obligors, in the name and at the cost of any person or persons injured by a breach thereof, until the whole penalty shall be recovered thereon; and if the Judge of the Probate Court shall fail to take the bond, with the security as aforesaid, such Judge shall be liable to be sued for all the damages arising from such neglect, by any person interested in the estate.

Further security may be required. ART. 96. [5] The Probate Court shall have full power, when letters of administration shall be granted upon insufficient security, to order and direct such administrators to give further security by bond, in the usual form; and if it appear, upon examination, that any administrator hath embezzled, wasted, or misapplied all, or any part, of the deceased's estate, or shall refuse or neglect to give bond, with security, as aforesaid, the said court may forthwith revoke or repeal the letters of administration, and thereupon grant letters of administration to such other person or persons having a right thereto, as will give bond in manner and form aforesaid, who may institute a suit for such goods and chattels as came to the possession of the former administrators, and were withheld, wasted, embezzled, detained, misapplied, by any of them, and no satisfaction made for the same.

Same subject. ART. 97. [6] Any executor, executrix, administrator or administratrix, or guardian, may be ordered to give further security, on complaint of his, her, or any of their securities, or any of their representatives; or when there shall appear sufficient grounds to believe that he, she, or they, are about to misapply, embezzle, or remove from the Republic, the property committed to his, her, or their charge; or proof of gross neglect in the performance of any of the duties of him, her, or them, enjoined by law; or that his, her, or their securities have become insufficient, as well as for the causes heretofore specified; and on proof that such executor or executrix, administrator or administratrix, or guardian, has removed from the Republic, or otherwise endeavored to elude the service or process on any such complaint, the same may be heard and determined, though the citation be not executed.

Removal of executors, &c. ART. 98. [7] If any executor of any last will and testament, or administrator of an intestate's estate, shall remove out of this Republic, or refuse, or neglect, after due notice from the Probate Court, to render his account and make settlement of such estate with creditors, legatees, or heirs, or their legal representatives; or if any executor or administrator shall become insane, or if any administrator becomes otherwise incapable of, or evidently unsuitable to discharge the trust reposed in him, the said Probate Court is authorized and empowered, in each of the said cases mentioned in this section, to grant letters of administration, with the will annexed, or otherwise, as the case may require, to such person or persons as may be entitled to the same, and as to the said court shall seem meet; and the administrator thus appointed shall have the same power and authority to administer the estate of the deceased, not administered upon by such former executor or administrator, and be subject to the same duties, in as full and as ample a manner as if the executor or administrator so removed, as aforesaid, were actually dead.

Discharge original sureties. ART. 99. [8] Wherever security shall be ordered or taken from any executor or executrix, administrator or administratrix, or guardian, the Judge may direct such alteration in the condition of the bond, as the case may require, and may order the original securities to be discharged entirely, or from the time of taking such new security, as to him shall seem proper.

Resignation of executors, &c., ART. 100. [9] Any executor, executrix, administrator or administratrix, or guardian, may, by writing, by him or her, subscribed and delivered into the

Clerk's office, resign his or her authority; but in such case he, she, or they, and his, her, or their securities, shall be bound for all the assets or effects which shall not have been duly administered or applied, or shall not be delivered to their successors respectively. Liability, &c.

ART. 101. [10] Where no one shall have been admitted and qualified as an executor, executrix, administrator or administratrix, within three months after the death of the deceased, or when the executorship or administration shall have become vacant by death, resignation or removal, the Judge having jurisdiction of the case, may commit the administration to the Sheriff, or some Justice of the Peace, of the county where the succession is opened; the said Sheriff, or Justice, shall take the oath, and give the bond and security required of executors and administrators in other cases; and such bond may be sued, and judgment from time to time recovered thereon, in the same manner as may be provided by law in case of other bonds of executors, or administrators, or guardians. The administration so committed to any Sheriff or Justice of the Peace, may, at any time, be revoked, on the application of any of the executors, kindred, or creditors of the deceased, and the executor permitted to qualify, or another administrator appointed; during any contest about the validity of a will, the infancy or absence of the executor or administrator, and in such other cases not otherwise provided for, as may so require, the Judge may appoint an administrator or administratrix, with such limited authority as the case may require; and where the necessity of the case may require, such administration may be granted or revoked forthwith, without any citation. Administration committed to sheriff or justice, when. Revoked on application of kindred. Administrator *pro tem.*

ART. 102. [11] Every Probate Court, granting letters testamentary, or letters of administration, shall nominate, and, by warrant, appoint three or more judicious and discreet persons, appraisers of the estate of the deceased, who shall return their appraisement on oath, in such time as the court shall appoint, of all the real and personal estate of such deceased as may come to their knowledge; which appraisement, if subscribed and sworn to by the executor or administrator, may be considered as an inventory of such part of the estate as had heretofore come to hand; and inventories, which the executors or administrators, in all cases, shall return at the time limited by the court, and appraisements may be given in evidence in any suit, by or against the executor or admistrator; but shall not be conclusive for or against him, if it be shown that the estate was really worth, or was, *bona fide*, sold for more or less than the appraisement. Appraisers and appraisement, &c.

ART. 103. [12] Where the effects, whether real or personal, of the deceased be in different counties, the Court of Probate, granting letters testamentary, or of administration, shall order appraisement, and appoint appraisers in each; and the said appraisement, when made and sworn to by the appraisers and executor, or administrator (as the case may be,) shall be transmitted to the Court of Probate, where the will was recorded, or administration granted; and every executor or administrator shall, upon oath, be bound to produce and show to the appraisers appointed by the court for that purpose, or a majority of them, all, and singular, the goods and chattels of the said testator, or intestate, which has come into their, or either of their hands, possession, or knowledge; and he shall, also, in a like manner, point out and exhibit to the said appraisers, all, and singular, the lands and land claims belonging to the decedent, and he shall cause to be made, a true and just appraisement and inventory, upon oath, of all, and singular, the lands, tenements, hereditaments, goods, and chattels, rights and credits, of the said testator or intestate, together with a list or schedule of the books of account of such testator, or intestate, with the number of pages in each book—to which books, all parties concerned shall have, at all convenient times, free access; and every such executor and administrator shall be chargeable with so much of the said credits only as he shall, after due and proper diligence, recover and receive. When effects in different counties. Inventory and appraisement shall be made.

ART. 104. [13] If there be, in the estate of the deceased, effects, whether real or personal, which belong entirely to the deceased, and others which belong to him in part only, this distinction must be made in the inventory; and especially the distinction between the separate property of the decedent, and that held in common with a surviving husband, or wife, (as the case may be.) Distinction between several and joint property in inventory.

ART. 105. [14] No formalities, except those required by this law, shall be necessary to make a valid inventory; and all guardians of infants, idiots, lunatics, and persons *non compos mentis*, shall be required, by the Judge of the Probate Court granting letters of guardianship, to make an appraisement and Inventory—requisites of.

inventory of the estates of persons committed to their charge, in the same manner that inventories of the estates of deceased persons are required by this Act to be made.

Appraised--pay of. ART. 106. [15] The appraisers shall be allowed three dollars,—and such additional compensation as the Judge may allow, if the appraisement be laborious,—each per day, whilst employed in appraising any estate, to be paid out of the estate so appraised.

Claims not presented in a year, barred. ART. 107. [16] It shall be the duty of executors and administrators, within two months after granting letters testamentary, or letters of administration, to publish, in some newspaper printed in this Republic, a notice requiring all persons having claims against the estate of their testator, or intestate, to exhibit the same within the time limited by law, or the same shall be barred; which notice shall state the time of granting such letters testamentary, or letters of administration, and shall continue to be published once a week for six weeks; and the claimants shall have twelve months from the date of letters testamentary, or of administration, to present their demands.

Shall not sue before presentation of claim. ART. 108. [17] No bearer of a claim for money against a succession, administered by an executor, or administrator, shall commence an action against such succession before presenting his claim to the executor or administrator.

Claims app'ved shall be endorseed. ART. 109. [18] If such claim be acknowledged by the executor or administrator, he shall endorse or annex to the claim a declaration signed by him, stating that he has no objection to the payment of such claim; after which the bearer of such claim shall submit it to the Judge, that it may be ranked among the acknowledged debts of the succession.

Claims not approved may be sued. ART. 110. [19] If the claim be not acknowledged and approved by the executor or administrator, the owner of said claim, for the establishment thereof, may bring his action against the executor or administrator before a Justice of the Peace, or the District Court of the county where the said succession is opened, and may obtain judgment as in ordinary cases.

No property allowed such claims except. ART. 111. [20] The creditor who has obtained such judgment, or the acknowledgment of debt, can only obtain the payment of it currently with the other creditors of the succession, unless it be such a privileged claim as ought to be paid without delay.

Order of paying debts. ART. 112. [21] The debts due by any testator or intestate shall be paid by his executor or administrator in the order following, to wit: funeral and other expenses of last sickness, charges of probate will, or of letters of administration, judgments, mortgages, and executions, the oldest first, then all other debts; and no preference whatever shall be given to creditors in an equal degree, when there is a deficiency of assets, except in the case of funeral expenses and those of the last sickness, and costs of court, judgments, executions, and mortgages, the oldest of which shall be first paid, or in those cases when a creditor may have a lien on any particular part of the estate.

Sales, how to be made. ART. 113. [22] It shall not be lawful for any executor or executors, administrator or administrators, guardian or guardians, to take the estate, or any part thereof, of any intestate or testator, or ward, at the appraised value, or to dispose of the same at private sale, except when the same is directed by the will of the testator; but in all cases when it may be necessary to sell the whole, or part of the estate of any testator or intestate, it shall be the duty of the executor, administrator, or guardian to apply to the Probate Court of the proper county for an order of sale, and sell the same at public auction; and any sale made otherwise than herein directed shall be null and void.

Same subject. ART. 114. [23] All sales made by an executor or executrix, administrator or administratrix, shall commence and close at the hours required by law; but in case the day or days set apart for such sale shall be insufficient to complete the sale of such estate intended to be sold, the same may be continued from day to day, by giving public notice thereof to the attending company at the conclusion of the sale of each day of such continuance, which continued sale shall commence and close within the hours prescribed by law.

Sales, return of. ART. 115. [24] Executors and administrators within three months after their appointment, shall return to the Clerk's office a full inventory of the estate, real and personal of the deceased which has come to his knowledge or possession; and within one month after the sale of any property of the estate, he shall in like manner return an account thereof; and the said accounts of sales shall be subscribed and sworn to by the executor or administrator, in the same manner that inventories are required to be sworn to and subscribed.

ART. 116. [25] The Chief Justice of the Probate Court of the county in which said Justice resides, besides presiding in the Probate Court in the term time, is empowered and required to take, receive and audit all accounts of executors, administrators, and guardians, to receive will exhibited for probate, applications for administration, inventories and appraisements duly made and sworn to (to be recorded), to cause to be issued all citations and other necessary process returnable to the next term of said court; and the said Chief Justice after examining and auditing said accounts, and causing them to be properly stated, shall report the same for allowance to the next term of the Probate Court,—the executor, administrator, or guardian, giving at least twenty days' notice of his intention of having such account presented to the said court for allowance at such term, by posting up notice thereof in three of the most public places in the county, or advertising the same for three weeks at least, in some public newspaper in this Republic, whichever the said Chief Justice shall have directed,—and the court, on due proof of notice aforesaid, and no exception being made to the accounts as stated, may decree an allowance of the said account; but if any person or persons interested in the settlement of the said account shall, by himself or attorney, appear and make exception to the account, the court shall either proceed to hear the proofs and allegations, and correct or amend the mistakes or errors in the accounts as reported, or refer the same to auditors, who shall examine and restate the account after hearing the parties and witnesses, and report to the next or some subsequent term of the said court for confirmation or allowance as aforesaid. Proceedings in vacation, confirmation of accounts of executors, &c.

ART. 117. [26] Whenever any executor or executrix, administrator or administratrix, or guardian, shall be cited by the Probate Court to appear and settle his accounts as executor, administrator, or guardian, and shall fail to appear in obedience to the citation, the said Probate Court shall have power to issue an attachment against the person or persons so failing, in the same manner as the District Courts of this Republic might or could do for disobedience to any order, judgment, or decree of said court. Attachments to compel settlements of account.

ART. 118. [27] Where two or more persons have letters of administration granted to them of any intestate's estate, and one or more of them take all or the greatest part of such estate, and refuse to pay the debts or funeral expenses of such intestate, or refuse to account with the other administrator; in such case the administrator so aggrieved may have his action of account, or bill in equity against the other administrator or administratrix, and recover such proportional share of such estate as shall belong to him; and any executor, being residuary legatee, may have an action of account, or a bill in equity against his co-executors, and receive his part of the estate in the hands of his co-executor or co-executors; and any other residuary legatee may have the like remedy against the executors; and any person having a legacy bequeathed in any last will and testament may sue for and recover the same at common law. One administrator, &c, may sue another. Legatee may sue.

ART. 119. [28] When any suit may have commenced on behalf of or against the personal representative or representatives of any testator or intestate, the same may be prosecuted by, or against any person or persons who may afterwards succeed to the administration or executorship, and such person or persons may at any time be made parties on motion, and the cause shall proceed in the same manner, and judgment be had thereon in all respects as effectual as if the same were prosecuted by or against the parties originally named; when any personal representative or guardian shall be displaced, all moneys due to him or her in such right by execution or otherwise, shall be paid to his or her successor. Substitution of administrators, &c., in suits.

ART. 120. [29] Every executor or administrator is bound, within three months after his appointment, to petition the Court of Probate, granting letters testamentary or administration, for the sale of all the perishable property belonging to the succession, and all or such portion of the other personal property except slaves, as may be shown to the court to be necessary for the payment of debts against said estate; and in case, or if on further information, he finds that the proceeds of the sale of the personal property will not be sufficient for the payment of the said debts, he shall then, within six months after his appointment, or as soon as he ascertains the said deficiency, petition the Probate Court for the sale of the slaves and real estate of the decedent, or so much thereof as may be necessary for the payment of the said debts; and the said court, on full and satisfactory proof of the existence of the debts, and the necessity of the sale, shall order the same on cash or credit as may be most advantageous to said estate, or as the nature of the claims against said estate may require. Executor, &c., bound to petition Court of Probate, &c.

ART. 121. [30] Should the executor or administrator fail to petition the court for the sale of property as directed by the above section of this Act, If executor, &c., fail to apply for order of sale.

then it may be lawful for any one of the creditors of the said estate, whose claims have been acknowledged or established, to petition the court for the sale of the property for the payment of the debts against the said succession; and the court shall thereupon proceed and make such order and decree as if the petition had been filed by the executor or administrator.

Privileged claims, when paid, account rendered at the end of twelve months, &c.

ART. 122. [31] The executor or administrator shall, within six months after the granting the letters testamentary or of administration, if he have sufficient funds belonging to the estate, pay the funeral expenses, costs of court, expenses of the last sickness, or other debts, the payment of which cannot be retarded; and, at the end of twelve months after the granting of the letters testamentary or of administration, he shall render to the Probate Court granting said letters, a just and true account, upon oath, of the receipts and expenditures of the estate administered upon within the preceding year; he shall also be bound to file a statement mentioning the names and places of residence of the creditors of the succession, and the amount due to each as acknowledged, established or claimed; and also the character of the claims respectively,—as also the amount of funds on hand; and shall fully account for all his proceedings in relation to said estate; and the court shall, thereupon, order payment of the claims of creditors, either in whole or in part, according to the extent of the funds of the estate,—paying the debts according to the order of their privilege as laid down in this law; and if the funds be not sufficient for the payment of all the debts, then the debts of an equal degree shall be paid *pro rata*.

Term of administration, may be extended, executor may settle with heirs &c., when.

ART. 123. [32] The term for the administration of the succession is fixed at one year from the day of appointment of the administrator, or the granting letters testamentary, but the Probate Court may extend the time, on good causes shown; and nothing in this Act shall prevent an executor or administrator, when the estate is not indebted,—or only to a small extent,—from settling with the heirs, devisees, and legatees, and delivering up the estate to them before the end of twelve months. And should the said executor or administrator fail to render his account to the Court of Probate, at or before the end of the first term of the Probate Court, after the expiration of twelve months from the grant of letters testamentary or of administration, or should he fail to pay the creditors according to the order of the Court of Probate made in relation thereto, within ten days after granting said order, then execution may issue from the Probate Court in the name of the creditors whom he has failed to pay, against the property of said executor or administrator, and his or her securities, which shall be sold after the usual advertisements, for what it will bring in cash.

Terms of granting administration to creditors.

ART. 124. [33] No letters of administration shall be granted to any person whatsoever as principal creditor or creditors, but upon special trust and confidence, and for the benefit of all the rest of the creditors; and all debts of an equal nature shall be discharged by such administrator in average and proportion, as far as the assets of the intestate shall extend, and no preference shall be given among the creditors in an equal degree; and every such administrator shall be obliged to sue for such debts as he may reasonably expect to recover; or at the request and proper charge of any of the creditors of the intestate, assign and empower them, or any of them, to sue for the debts outstanding to the estate of such intestate.

Collection of debts in such cases.

Appointment of debtor executor, not to operate as remission.

ART. 125. [34] If any person shall, by will, appoint his debtor to be his executor, such appointment shall not, in law and equity, be construed to be a release or extinguishment of the debt, unless the testator shall, in his will, expressly declare his intention to release the same.

When Chief Justice is appointed, &c.

ART. 126. [35] Where the Chief Justice of any county is appointed executor of the last will and testament of any person deceased, within his jurisdiction, and chooses to take upon himself the burthen and execution thereof, he shall prove said last will and testament, and qualify as executor thereof, before the Judge of the District Court of the said county either during term of vacation; and where he may seek or require administration of the succession of any person dying intestate, within his jurisdiction, or administration with the will annexed, the Judge of the District Court of said county, either in term time or during vacation, may have jurisdiction of and determine respecting the same, and grant letters of administration, if the said Chief Justice shall be thereto entitled, and take bonds for due administration, and do all other acts thereunto incident: and the said Chief Justice, when acting as executor or administrator, shall account for the execution of the will, and the management of the estate so committed to him, before the Judge of the District Court for the said county, in the same manner that executors and administrators are required to account before the Courts of Probate; and the said Chief Justice shall be required to file, among the records of the Probate Court of which he is the Judge, the last will and testament aforesaid, and probate thereof, and letters of administration, and all other proceedings in cases testamentary and of administration, in the same manner as is practised in cases where they may not be interested or concerned, after the same shall have been recorded in the office of the Clerk of the District Court, where such will shall be proved or administration granted as aforesaid.

ART. 127. [36] The place where the succession shall be opened is fixed as follows, viz: in the county where the deceased resided, if he had a fixed domicil or residence in the Republic; in the county where the deceased owned real estate, if he had neither domicil nor residence in the Republic; or in the county in which the principal effects of the deceased are, if he have effects in different counties; or in the county in which the deceased has died, if he had no fixed residence, nor any immovable effects within the Republic at the time of his death. Place of opening succession.

ART. 128. [37] It shall be lawful for any person entitled to a distributive share of any succession, whether real or personal, or may hold property in common with said succession, who shall have arrived at the age of twenty-one years, or be married, or who, if an infant, shall have a guardian legally appointed, to petition the Court of Probate for the county where the said succession was opened, or where lie the principal effects of the said succession, for a summons, to be issued and directed to all persons interested or in possession of such estate, commanding them to appear at the next term of the Probate Court—which summons must be served at least ten days before the said court—to show cause why a writ of partition, to be directed to certain commissioners, authorizing and requiring them to divide said estate, shall not be awarded by the said court; and if, on the return of such summons, sufficient cause be not shown to the contrary, the said court shall decree the partition of said estate, and order a writ of partition to be issued, directed to three or more discreet persons, commanding them, or a majority of them, being first duly sworn, fairly and impartially to discharge their duty, to proceed to execute the said writ, and return the same to said court within a time to be fixed and specified in the writ. Distribution and partition, how enforced, in, &c.

ART. 129. [38] When the said estate cannot, in the opinion of the commissioners, be fairly and equally divided amongst the parties interested therein, without manifest injury to them, or some of them, they shall make a special return of the whole property and the value thereof duly appraised, and certify their opinion to the court, whether it will be most for the benefit of all parties interested therein, to deliver to one or more of them the property which cannot be fairly divided, upon the payment of a sum of money to be assessed by the said commissioners, or to sell the same at public auction; and the court shall proceed to consider and determine the same; and if it shall appear to the court that the said estate cannot be equally and fairly divided, and that it will be for the benefit of all the parties interested in the said estate, that the same shall be vested in one or more persons, entitled to a portion of the same, on the payment of a sum of money, they shall determine accordingly; and such person or persons, on payment of the consideration money, shall be vested with the estate so adjudged to them, as fully and absolutely as the deceased was vested therewith; but if it shall appear to the court to be more for the interest of the parties that the same should be sold, it shall direct a sale to be made on such a credit, and on such terms as to it shall seem right; and the proceeds of said sale shall be distributed among those interested in said estate, according to the respective shares or interests in the same. Where partition would not be advantageous.

ART. 130. [39] The service of the summons in partition shall be proved on oath, by the person making the same; and if the defendants, or any of them, be minors, having no guardian legally appointed, the court shall appoint a guardian or guardians *ad litem*, to defend their interests in said partition; and if the defendants, or any one of them, be absent from and beyond the limits of this Republic, the court, in term time or vacation, shall order publication to be made in one or more newspapers printed in the Republic, for the space of three months, or longer, should the same by the court be deemed necessary, commanding the defendant or defendants to appear and answer the plaintiff's petition; and if the said defendant or defendants do not appear within the time specified, either personally, by guardian, or attorney, then the court shall appoint a guardian *ad litem* to defend the interests of the absentees, and shall proceed to divide the estate as if they were personally present. Service of summons in partition—Guardian *ad litem*.

Partition of.

ART. 131. [40] The persons who shall be appointed to make such partition, or a majority of them, may, if they shall think it necessary, call in to their aid one or more surveyors to run the lines of any lands, and also the divisional lines thereof; and the commissioners are hereby authorized and required, in the admeasurement aforesaid, to have regard to the true and real value of the lands in question; and when any tract of land has been divided, they, or a majority of them, shall return to the Court of Probate a general plat of the said land, in which the division lines shall be plainly set down, and with a certificate thereon in writing, under their hands, describing the manner in which the division has been made; and all expenses that may be incurred in making said partition shall be paid by the parties interested in said division, and the portion of the estate allotted to each of the distributees shall be held liable to the payment of his or her portion of the said expenses; and if not paid, the Court of Probate may issue execution therefor, in the names of the persons entitled thereto, and sell the said portion of the said distributee for cash, after the usual advertisements.

Same subject

ART. 132. [41] All questions in relation to the settlement of the accounts of the estate with the administrator, or with the heirs or any one of them, or in relation to the collection or return of advancements made by the ancestor, and all others of a similar nature, shall be decided by the judges before the issuing of the writ of partition; and in the writ special instructions shall be given to the commissioners, and particularly there must be set forth the partition of the estate to be allotted to each one among whom the property is to be divided; and it is hereby made the special duty of the Court of Probate to guard and protect the interests of minors and absentees; and their guardians shall be allowed out of their estates all reasonable and necessary expenses incurred in protecting and defending the same; and all sales to effect partition shall be made by the Clerk of the Probate Court issuing the order of sale; and the portion of moneys, or evidence of debts, belonging to minors, shall be paid to their guardians then or thereafter appointed, or shall be retained by the said Clerk until a guardian is appointed, or until the minor arrives at the age of twenty-one years; and in the case of absentee minors or adults, the said Clerk shall pay over all moneys due them as fast as the same can be collected, to the Treasury of the Republic of Texas, to be held by the same in trust for the said absentees, their guardians or attorneys, legally appointed; and the said Clerk and his securities shall be liable on his official bond for the faithful performance of the duties herein required of him, or he may be required to give further bond if, by the court, deemed necessary; and on either bond he may be sued from time to time, and judgment recovered thereon, in the same manner as is provided by law in case of bonds of executors and administrators, or guardians; and the said Clerk shall be allowed, for all sales under decree of the Probate Court, three per cent. on all sums under three hundred dollars; and one per cent. on all sums above the first three hundred; and for every conveyance made to purchasers, he shall be allowed the sum of five dollars.

Court to protect minors and absentees.

When the effects lie in different counties.

ART. 133. [42] Where the effects, whether real or personal, of the estate to be divided, lie in several counties, the Judge of the Court of Probate of the county where the succession has been opened, shall order division, and direct a writ of partition to commissioners appointed in each; and the same proceedings shall be had by the said commissioners, and by the court, as are directed by the above law, in cases where the estate lies in the county where the Court of Probate is held: provided, always, that where the property to be divided lies in any county other than where the succession is opened, or where the proceedings for partition are had, then it may be lawful for the court, without appointing commissioners, when it shall be satisfied by sufficient proof, which must be taken in writing and filed with the records of the court, that the said property cannot be conveniently divided, or that its sale would be more advantageous to the parties interested, to order the sale of the said property after the usual advertisements; and should it be impossible or inconvenient for the Clerk of the Probate Court making said order of sale, to attend to the execution thereof, then it shall be lawful for the Probate Court to appoint some prudent and discreet person to make the said sale; the individuals so appointed shall give bond in double the estimated amount of the property to be sold, payable to the Judge of the Court of Probate, with at least two good securities, conditioned for his faithfully executing the said order of sale, in the manner pointed out by law; and the individual so appointed shall proceed to conduct the said sale, pay over the proceeds thereof to the parties interested, and the Treasurer of the Republic, in the manner pointed out for the Clerks of the Probate Court, by this law; and they shall receive the same commissions, and their necessary expenses, and be subject to the same liabilities to which the said Clerks are subjected by this law.

Appeal to District Court.

ART. 134. [43] If any person shall think himself aggrieved by the judgment, sentence, decree, or determination of any Probate Court, such person shall be at liberty to appeal therefrom to the District Court, within twenty days, next after such judgment, decree, determination, or order shall have been given—the applicant giving the usual bond in the case of appeal; and on the trial of such appeal, testimony, in addition to that taken in the Court of Probate, shall be heard.

Compensation of executors, &c.

ART. 135. [44] Executors, administrators and guardians, shall, for their care, trouble and attention, in the execution of their several duties, receive or retain in their hands the sum of five dollars for every hundred dollars they may receive, and the like sum of five dollars in every hundred dollars they may pay away in credits, debts, legacies, or otherwise, during the course or continuance of their administration; and should they not be satisfied with the legal commissions, they may, in case of having extraordinary trouble in the management of estates under their care, be at liberty to bring an action in the District Court for compensation for their services; but no judgment shall be given for more than ten per centum over and above the sum hereinbefore allowed.

Sale on forfeit'd bond of purchasers at administrator's sales.

ART. 136. [56] In all cases where property is sold at a sale of a succession of any deceased person, or of the property of minors, idiots, lunatics, and persons, *non compos mentis*, the property of the purchaser, or his securities, may be seized and sold on execution, for cash, to the highest bidder, without the necessity of appraisement.

Process, when served.

ART. 137. [57] In all cases where not otherwise directed, process from the Probate Court shall be served five days before the session of the Probate Court at which the said process is to be returned.

Executors, &c., not required to give appe'l bond —frivolous appeal.

ART. 138. [58] In all cases of appeal from any court in this Republic, it shall not be necessary for executors, administrators, or guardians, to give the bond and security required of applicants in other cases; but in all cases of appeals pronounced frivolous by the court trying the appeal, the costs shall be paid out of the private property of the executor, administrator, or guardian.

Former administrations to be settled.

ART. 139. [60] The respective Judges of Probate, upon the passage of this act, shall be required to cause all executors, administrators and guardians, to whom letters of administration or guardianship have been granted twelve months previous to the passage of this act, to appear before them and account for their proceedings in relation to the estates which they may have administered, and settle their accounts as executors, administrators, and guardians are required to settle by this law; and all executors, administrators, or guardians, to whom letters of administration and guardianship may have heretofore been granted, shall, at the expiration of twelve months from the granting of such letters of administration or guardianship, be required to come forward and settle as above; and any administrator or executor, failing to comply with the provisions of this section, shall be liable to the penalties prescribed by this act, for defaulting administrators or executors.

When provision is made by will for sale of property.

ART. 140. [61] Whenever express provisions are made, or directions given, in any will or testament, for the sale, or other disposition of any property belonging to the estate of the deceased, the executor or executrix of such will shall not be required to obtain from the Probate Court an order for such sale, or other disposition of such property, but may proceed to sell, or otherwise dispose of the same, as directed in such will or testament, and make return thereof as required by law.

Balance due heirs after settlement, &c.

ART. 141. [62] When an administrator has accounted for his proceedings in relation to an estate committed to him, and has settled his account with the same, if there be a balance due the heirs of said estate, the same shall be paid to the heirs thereof, according to their respective interests in said estate; or if the heirs be minors, or absent, then to their guardians or attorneys, legally appointed; but in the event that there be no guardians to the said minors, appointed as the law directs—whether the said minors be within or beyond the limits of this Republic—or that adult absentees have no attorneys or agent within this Republic, then it shall be the duty of the said administrator to pay the said balance, or the share thereof due the said minors or absentees, within thirty days after the final settlement of said estate, to the Treasurer of this Republic, who shall deliver to the said administrator duplicate receipts, making mention of the sum received, and the name of the succession or heirs, on whose account it has been paid.

Copy of judg m'nt to be transmitted to Treasurer of Republic.

ART. 142. [63] It shall be the duty of the Judge who has determined definitely the balance due to minors who have no guardians, and to absentees, within fifteen days after the date of said judgment, to transmit a copy thereof to the Treasurer of the Republic; and the Judge shall allow, in the accounts of administrators, the costs of two copies of said judgment—one to be retained by the administrator, and the other forwarded to the Treasurer as aforesaid. The administrator who has paid the said balance of his account, or the portion thereof required by this law, into the Treasury of the Republic, shall deposit one of the receipts delivered to him in the Probate Court: and it is only on the exhibition of this receipt that he or his securities can be discharged from his administration.

Papers, &c., to be deposited in Court, when.

ART. 143. [64] When a succession, the heirs of which, or a part of whom, are absent from, and not represented in this Republic, if there remain in the hands of the administrator, any letters or papers belonging to the said succession or heirs, the Judge shall order them to be deposited in court, in order that they may be delivered to the said heirs, their guardians or attorneys in fact.

Funds of estate to be paid to Treasurer.

ART. 144. [65] The funds of estates psid into the Treasury of the Republic, shall remain in deposit until claimed by their heirs, or those having a right to them.

Persons claiming after close of administration.

ART. 145. [66] After payment into the hands of the Treasurer of the Republic, and the discharge of the administrator, any one who has a right to claim the succession, or the payment of any debts due him by the deceased—such heir must cause his quality to be recognized before the Probate Court; and such creditor must cause his claim to be established before a competent court, in the county where the succession is opened; and in both cases the court must appoint an attorney, *ad litem*, to defend the interests of absent heirs, who shall deny the pretensions of such person, as heir or creditor, and discharge his duty under the strictest responsibility.

Treasurer of Republic to pay over, when.

ART. 146. [67] If the demand of the person claiming the succession, a portion of it, or the payment of a debt, be established by a judgment, the Treasurer of the Republic shall pay to such claimant, on his exhibiting an authentic copy of said judgment, the amount due him, either as heir or creditor, if there be a sufficient amount of said succession deposited in the Treasury to satisfy his demands.

Administrators failing to pay to Treasurer.

ART. 147. [68] If administrators, within three months after the date of the judgment rendered on their accounts, neglect to pay the portion of the succession hereby required of them to be paid into the Treasury of the Republic, then it shall be the duty of the Treasurer of the Republic to denounce them to the District Attorney of the district where the succession is opened, who shall, in the name of the Republic, take out an execution for the amount which should have been paid to the Treasurer, from the Probate Court where the estate has been settled, against the said administrator and his securities; and their property, after the usual advertisements, shall be sold for cash to the highest bidder, without the necessity of appraisement.

Where estates were closed at the passage of this act.

ART. 148. [69] Where estates have been already closed, and there remain any funds in the hands of administrators belonging to minors without guardians, or to absentees, the said administrators are required within three months after the passage of this act, to pay over the said funds to the Treasurer of the Republic, under the penalties prescribed by the above section, against defaulting administrators; and every Judge of the Probate Courts of this Republic is required to transmit a copy of every decree heretofore made, settling the accounts of administrators in which a balance has been decided to be due to minors or absentees: provided, that it may be in the power of the said administrator, to show that he has heretofore paid out the said succession to the persons entitled to the same.

Repealing clause.

ART. 149. [72] All laws and parts of laws conflicting with, and contrary to the provisions of this act, be, and the same are hereby repealed.

Sales regulated by execution laws.

ART. 150. [1] All sales, whether by order, judgment, or decree of any Probate Court, or Court of Chancery, shall be regulated and governed by the laws governing sales under execution; and all laws which relate to sales under execution, shall be applicable to such sales as above stated.

Sales to be on a credit of twelve months.

ART. 151. [1] All sales of the property of any deceased person, made by any administrator, curator, or guardian, under or by the order, judgment or decree of any Probate Court, or Court of Chancery, shall be made on a credit of twelve months; any conflict in the act to which this is a supplement to the contrary notwithstanding.

ART. 152. [1] All sales of the property of any deceased person, made by any administrator, executor, or guardian, under or by order of any judgment or decree of any Probate Court, or Court of Chancery, shall be made upon a credit of twelve months, with security to the satisfaction of such administrator, executor, or guardian, or for cash, as the said Probate Court, or Court of Chancery shall deem most advisable for the interest of the estate of said deceased person, and of the creditors thereof: provided, that all such sales for cash shall be made upon appraisement, and shall not be made for less than two-thirds of the appraised value of the property to be sold: and provided, that in case any property ordered to be sold for cash, shall not sell for two-thirds of its appraisement, it shall be within the discretion of the Judge to re-order the sale, on a credit of twelve months. Terms and conditions of.

ART. 153. [2] A like notice, as that required for sales under execution, shall be given for all sales to be made by virtue of this act; and that on all sales for cash, by virtue of this act, the Chief Justice of the county where such sales are to be made, or in his absence, the Associate Justices, shall, on the day of such sales, or a day previous, appoint three appraisers, who shall on oath appraise the value of the property to be sold: provided, that the heirs or legatees of such estate, if present in person, or by attorney, or guardian, shall have the right of appointing one of said appraisers, by making said appointment in writing, filed in the Clerk's office of the Probate Court of the county where said sale is to take place, at least three days before the day of sale: and provided, that all such appraisers shall be freeholders of the county where such sale is to be made. Advertisement and appraisement, if for cash

ART. 154. [3] All laws and parts of laws contrary to, or conflicting with this act be, and the same are hereby repealed. Repealing clause.

Act of Jan. 9th, 1843.

ART. 155. [1] Hereafter, when any person shall die intestate, or shall not expressly forbid it by will, the same amount of property, and the same kind, if so much belong to the estate in kind, that is exempt from sale under fieri facias, or execution, by an act approved twenty-fifth January, one thousand eight hundred and thirty-nine, entitled "An act to exempt certain property therein named from execution," be, and the same is hereby declared to be exempt from sale by order of any Probate Court. Property exempt from sale.

ART. 156. [2] When an inventory is made out and returned to the Probate Court, of the property and effects belonging to a succession, the Judge thereof shall set apart the property and articles as contemplated in the preceding section, for the sole use and benefit of the widow and children of the deceased. Property set apart for widow

ART. 157. [3] The appraisers required to appraise property previous to its sale, be appointed by the Probate Judge at the time of issuing the order of sale, or on some day previous to the sale; and that they be sworn by any person legally authorized to administer an oath. Appraisers appointed, by whom.

ART. 158. [4] So much of the probate law as authorizes administration to be granted to the Sheriff or a Justice of the Peace be, and the same is hereby repealed. Laws granting letters to sheriffs repealed.

ART 159. [5] Any testator by his last will may so provide, that no other action than the probate and registration of the will, in whatsoever county he may designate, shall be had in the Probate Courts. Testator may restrict action of Probate Courts.

ART. 160. [6] All laws conflicting with the provisions of this act be, and the same are hereby repealed. Repealing clause.

Act of Jan. 16, 1843.

ART. 161. [1] In no case shall any administrator, executor, or guardian, be required to sell any other property than that of a perishable nature, belonging to the estate of any deceased person or ward, nor be required to render and settle their accounts, except upon application, by petition of some creditor or creditors, heir or heirs, legatee or legatees, or of some next friend of the ward, any law now in existence to the contrary notwithstanding. Executors, &c., not required to sell and settle accounts, except &c.

Act of Jan. 18, 1844.

ART. 162. [1] In any case where an executor, administrator, or guardian, is plaintiff in execution, under which an appraisement is necessary, before a sale can be made, it shall be lawful for said plaintiff, upon the written decree of the Probate Judge, authorizing the same to purchase the property which may be levied on by execution, either at the first, or any subsequent offering: provided, that no bid shall have been made by any other person, sufficiently high to make a sale under the former existing laws; and the property thus purchased shall be considered as a part of the mass of the estate which he represents, and may be disposed of as in other cases. Executors, &c., allowed to purchase property for estate, when.

Act of Feb. 2, 1844.

ART. 163. [1] When further time, after the expiraiion of onc year, is granted to any administrator, or executor, to settle the estate of his testator, or intestate, such executor, or administrator, shall not be required to execute a new Where term of administration is extended, new bond, &c., not required, except. bond for the faithful performance of his duties, but the original bond of such executor, or administrator, shall be deemed and held as sufficient, and binding, until the final settlement of the estate, except in cases where new security is specially required by the existing probate laws.

Where there are outstanding title bonds against estate. ART. 164. [2] Whenever there may be outstanding bonds, obligations, or contracts in writing, for the conveyance of lands or tenements, against the estate of any deceased person, which it may be to the interest of said estate should be lifted, or complied with, it shall be the duty of the Probate Court where the succession was opened, or where the same was or may be administered, upon an application by petition of the executor or executrix, administrator or administratrix, or guardian, where all the heirs are minors and have such guardian, after full proof of the existence of such bond, obligation, or contract in writing, and upon satisfactory evidence that a compliance with the requirements of said bond, obligation, or contract, would be beneficial to the interests of said estate, to decree that the person thus applying, shall fully comply with the same; and any deed, or tender of deed, made under such decree, shall be as valid and binding as if it had been made or tendered by the testator or intestate, himself.

Where estate is exonerated from responsibility, &c. ART. 165. [3] Such bond or contract, thus complied with, or tendered to be complied with, shall exonerate the estate from all liability or responsibility on such instrument; and the Probate Court shall take possession of such instrument of writing, and file it among the papers of the court; and where the same is complied with, it shall be cancelled by the Probate Judge; and all the testimony heard under the second section of this act, shall be taken down in writing, signed by each of the witnesses, and preserved among the records of the court: provided, that minors, and all persons laboring under disabilities recognized by the statute of limitations, shall have three years after such disabilities are removed, to set aside all deeds or judgments made by virtue of this act, for fraud, covin, and collusion, or any other causes that should vitiate the same.

Where there are title bonds in favor of the estate. ART. 166. [4] When bonds or obligations are outstanding against any deceased person, for the conveyance of lands, suits may be brought in the District Courts, against the executor, administrator, or guardian (as the case may be), and upon full proof being made of the justness of the same, the courts shall decree a title in favor of [against?] the heirs of said estate, or wards (as the case may be), and such title shall be as good as if made by the original obligor.

Executors, &c., may sue on such bonds. ART. 167. [5] Executors, administrators, or guardians, may bring and sustain all actions for the recovery of titles upon such bonds, obligations, or contracts, and all actions necessary to recover the possession of lands which are held by any person, or persons, adversely to the estate which he represents.

Act of Feb. 2, 1844.

Repeal of law allowing commissioners, &c. ART. 168. [1] So much of the fortieth section of the above-recited act, as authorizes persons who shall be appointed to make partition, or a majority of them, "to call in one or more surveyors to run the lines of any lands, and also the divisional lines thereof," be and the same is hereby repealed.

Allowed to call in County Surveyor. ART. 169. [2] The persons who shall be appointed to make the partition contemplated in said act, be, and they are hereby authorized to call in the County Surveyor, or his legal deputy, to run the lines, &c., contemplated in said act, for which services the said Surveyor shall receive the same pay as now allowed by law.

Act of Feb. 3, 1844.

Notice to creditors in certain cases. ART. 170. [1] In all cases in which there may be debts due the estate of any deceased person, or property sold by the executor or administrator thereof, prior to the first day of May, eighteen hundred and forty-two, or upon contracts made by the deceased, in his lifetime, and prior to said first day of May, 1842, it shall be the duty of the Chief Justice of the Probate Court, upon a representation of the facts, by petition, by the administrator or executor, to cause the creditors of the estate to be notified to appear at some specified term of the court, and have their claims settled, which notice shall be personal, or by publication in some newspaper, nearest the place of the opening of the succession, for three weeks successively.

Credits of estate transferred to creditors in such cases. ART. 171. [2] When the time for said settlement shall arrive, the court, after ascertaining the amount due to each, and what proportion of their respective claims the estate will be able to pay, shall cause the executor or administrator (as the case may be) to transfer to each of the several creditors, so much of the credits thereof, at their appraised value, as may appear to be their respective proportion: provided, that the same shall be taken and held to be in full and perfect satisfaction of their claims, to the amount received.

Art. 172. [3] Should any of the creditors be unwilling to receive said credits, in satisfaction of their claims, the court shall set apart such proportion thereof as they may be entitled to, and the settlement shall take place as to the other creditors; the claims thus set apart shall be retained by the executor or administrator, or filed in the Probate Court Clerk's office, until the same can be collected, and the proceeds thereof paid over to the creditors entitled to receive the same. Creditors declining to receive their proportion.

Art. 173. [4] Executors and administrators shall, in the settlement of their accounts, be allowed all payments made in compliance with the provisions of this act. Payments made &c., allowed executors.

Art. 174. [5] All laws and parts of laws contravening the provisions of this act be, and the same are hereby repealed. Repealing clause.

Art. 175. [1] It shall be the duty of the County Court of Probate of any county from which any county, or part thereof, has been or may hereafter be taken, to transmit all original papers relating to the settlement of estates of deceased persons who were, at the time of their decease, residents of that part of the territory of the county which has been or may hereafter be taken to from [form] any new county, to the Probate Court of such new county, upon the petition of any executor, or administrator, or guardian, or a majority of the heirs of any such estate; and he shall also transmit, with such original papers, a transcript, certified under the seal of the court, of the records of all proceedings had in relation to such estates in his court: provided, that at the time of filing such petition, the party filing it shall pay all fees due on account of such estate. Act of May 13, 1846. Original papers may be transferred to new counties, when.

Art. 176. [2] Previous to the transmission of any such original papers, in the manner provided for in the preceding section, the Judge to whom such petition is presented shall cause a registry of all such original papers as have not been recorded, to be made in his office, for which the same fees shall be allowed as is allowed for other recording. Duty of the court before.

Art. 177 [3] In all cases when the papers and proceedings relating to the settlement of an estate, shall be transmitted to any court, in the manner provided for in this act, such estates shall be proceeded in and settled in the Probate Court of such county in like manner as if the settlement of such estate had been originally commenced in such county; and the transcript of the record, transmitted in the manner provided for in this act, shall have the same force and effect in evidence as the record itself might or could have: provided that the provisions of this act shall not extend to the counties of Jackson, Victoria, Gonzales, Bexar, Goliad, Refugio, San Patricio and Colorado. How proceeded in after transfer. Certain counties excepted.

Art. 178. [1] There shall be established in each county in this State a Probate Court, consisting of one Judge whose term of office shall be two years, and who shall be elected by the citizens of said county, who are legally qualified to vote for the representatives thereof in the Legislature. Act of May 11, 1846. Organization of Probate Courts.

Art. 179. [2] The Judge of Probate shall have power in open court, on due notice given, to receive proof of wills, to order the same to be recorded and to grant letters of executorship or of administration thereon, with the will annexed; to grant letters of administration in the following order: first, to the surviving husband or wife; second, to the next kin of the intestate or testator; third, if none such claim, or, claiming, are unable to give security, then to such resident citizen of the county where such succession is opened, as can give sufficient bond, and who, in the judgment of the Judge of Probate, will well and faithfully discharge the duties of the trust; to grant letters of guardianship, and if for minors under the age of fourteen years, first, to the surviving husband or wife; second, to the testamentary guardian or next of kin, or if they fail to claim, or are unable to give security, then to such resident citizen of the county where the succession is opened, as can give the required bond, and who, in the judgment of the Judge, will well and faithfully discharge the duties of the trust; to grant letters of guardianship for minors over fourteen years of age, at their request made in person in open court; to order inquisition to be made by a jury, of idiocy, lunacy, and of persons of unsound mind; to grant letters of guardianship for idiots, lunatics, and persons *non compos mentis*; to order inventories of the estates of such persons, and of such as are under guardians or trustees; and on due notice served, after good cause shown, to revoke letters of administration or of guardianship, not testamentary, and to dismiss trustees; to order the sale of property for costs of court, and where proven necessary for the payment of debts of the intestate or Powers and jurisdiction of.

testator, or the payment of taxes, or the support or education of minors; and to direct the partition of property of estates. The court shall have power, either in term-time or vacation, to demand any will, papers, or property, of the deceased person, or belonging to those subject to, or under guardianship; to appoint and remove, without notice, administrators with limited powers, and also to suspend the action of administrators, upon good cause shown, by petition of any party interested; to order the sale of perishable property; to appoint appraisers; to order all writs to issue that may be necessary to enforce his jurisdiction; to approve or disapprove of claims acknowledged by an executor, administrator, or guardian; to approve or reject bonds; to require additional security on such as have been approved; to examine accounts; to administer oaths or affirmations; to supervise, correct and approve the minutes of the proceedings of the court, as kept by the Clerk. The court shall in no case grant letters of executorship, administration, or guardianship to the Clerk of the Court of Probate; but if such Clerk be interested in the estate of the deceased, or is named executor, or is entitled to guardianship, he may apply to the District Court for letters of administration, testamentary, or guardianship, and in all cases in which the Probate Judge or Clerk may be so interested, the District Court shall have and exercise exclusive jurisdiction.

Clerk of County Court *ex officio* Clerk of Probate.

ART. 180. [3] The Clerk of the County Court shall, ex-officio, be Clerk of the Probate Court; it shall be his duty to receive all petitions directed to the Judge of Probate, endorsing on them the time of their filing; he shall issue the notices prayed for in said petitions, and also such writs and warrants as the Judge shall direct, in special cases; he shall issue all subpœnas for witnesses, and commissions to take depositions that may be made returnable to said court; he shall for each regular term, keep a docket for probate cases, numbered in the order in which they were filed; he shall take minutes of the proceedings of the court during each day of its session, and keep separately in different books, all items of costs against each estate, and submit the same to the Judge for correction and approval; he shall make a final record of all petitions, inventories, appraisements, orders, accounts of sale, of final accounts rendered by executors, administrators, and guardians, and keep the papers belonging to each estate separately and properly endorsed, as archives of his office. The Clerk shall also procure a seal at the expense of the county, on which shall be engraved a star of five points with the words, "Probate Court, County of ——" around the margin, which shall be kept by him and used officially for the authentication of process, copies of records and other acts done by the Probate Court.

Duties of, &c.

Terms of Probate Courts.

ART. 181. [4] Six regular terms of the Court of Probate shall be held in each year, in the court-house of each county, unless the District Court be in session there; and in that event said Probate Court shall, for such time, hold its session in some other suitable building, at the seat of justice of the county; each term may continue for one week; the regular terms of the court shall commence on the last Mondays of January, March, May, July, September and November.

County for opening successions.

ART. 182. [5] The proper county for opening successions shall be determined by proof, giving preference in the following order: first, in the county where the deceased had a fixed domicil, or fixed residence; second, in the county where the deceased owned real estate; third, where the deceased had his principal effects; fourth, where the deceased died.

Petition for letters of administration, &c.

ART. 183. [6] Each executor accepting the trust, and each applicant for letters of administration or of guardianship, shall file in the office of the Clerk of the Probate Court, a petition, directed to the Judge of Probate, plainly stating therein the nature of the case submitted, and the action thereon desired.

Application for probate of will, &c., to be advertised.

ART. 184. [7] When application is made for the probate of will, for letters of guardianship, or of the appointment of trustees, ten days' notice of such application shall be given by the Clerk, by advertisement in writing, posted up, one on the court-house door, and one at three several public places in the county, not in the same town or city.

Mode of proving will—*prima facie* evidence of validity.

ART. 185. [8] A will may be proved by the testimony of one of the subscribing witnesses thereto, taken in open court, establishing the fact that the testator, being of sound mind and disposing memory, of his own free will, signed and acknowledged the said will in the presence of the witness, as his last will and testament; such testimony shall be taken in writing, and be subscribed to by the witness, and shall be sufficient to admit said will to record, and be *prima facie* evidence in favor of the validity of the will; but any person claiming an interest in the estate of the testator, in his own right, or in the right of any one he represents, or any attorney on behalf of the State, may, within four years after the same is recorded, institute suit in the District Court, to contest the validity of said will; minors, married women, persons *non compos mentis* may commence suit at any time, within four years after their respective disabilities are removed, and not thereafter; no *nuncupative* will shall be valid, unless made by a soldier while in actual military service, or by a mariner while at sea; a will made by an unmarried woman, shall be deemed to be revoked by her subsequent marriage; nor shall a *nuncupative* will deprive the wife or children of the deceased of inheriting his or her estate.

ART. 186. [9] Each executor and testamentary guardian, when not exempted by the will, each administrator and guardian, before receiving letters testamentary, or of administration, or guardianship, shall give a bond, with two or more good securities, payable to the Judge of Probate and his successor in office, for the use of any one interested in the estate, in a penalty at least double the amount of the estimated value of the estate, conditioned for the faithful performance of the duties of his trust; such bond shall not be void on the recovery of a part of the penalty, but may be put in suit from time to time, and shall be deemed in force to cover all breaches of such trust; and a right of action thereon shall not be barred until four years from and after the time that the youngest heir attains majority; the form of such bond shall be directed by the Judge. Executors, &c., to give bond, &c. except.

ART. 187. [10] Each executor, administrator, guardian, or trustee, shall take an oath of office, to be administered by the Judge. Oath of executor, guardian, &c.

ART. 188. [11] All appraisements shall be made after a view of the property for that purpose, and shall be made by citizens residing in the county in which the same is situated; the appraisement shall be made in writing, and shall be sworn to before any officer of the county, who is authorized by law to administer oaths, or if made out of the county in which the succession is opened, then it shall be sworn to before a notary public of the county in which it shall have been made. Mode of making appraisements.

ART. 189. [12] It shall be the duty of executors and administrators, immediately after they are qualified to act, to publish for six successive weeks, in some newspaper in the county, a notice to all persons who have claims against the estate they represent, to present them for acknowledgment within twelve months after the date of such publication, and to all persons indebted to the estate to make payment; if there be no newspaper published in the county, the notice herein required shall be published in the nearest paper printed in the State, and by written advertisements posted up, one at the court-house door, and three others at three several public places, not in the same town or city, but in the county where the estate is opened; a copy of said notice, certified to by the Judge, shall be filed with the papers of the estate, and a full copy of the same included in the final record. Notice to debtors, and creditors to be published.

ART. 190. [13] Every claim for money, or personal property, or for land, before it can be acknowledged, must be verified by the affidavit of the owner before the Judge of Probate or a Notary Public, stating what part is due and unpaid and not satisfied; and when thus verified and presented, the executor or administrator shall endorse thereon his acceptance or rejection, with the date of presentation. Claims to be verified

ART. 191. [14] All claims accepted by executors or administrators, shall be presented to the Judge, who shall endorse on the same his approval or non-approval. Accept'd claims to be presented to Judge.

ART. 192. [15] No action shall lie on a claim before its presentation for acknowledgment, but if a claim be rejected by the executor or administrator, or if accepted by him and disapproved by the Judge, the owner of such claim may, for the establishment thereof, institute suit against such executor or administrator, before a Justice of the Peace, or the District Court of the county where the succession is opened; but no judgment thereon shall give such claim priority, but it shall be paid currently with other claims of the same degree. No suit on, before presentation

ART. 193. [16] Any party interested in his own right, or as representative in right of another, may, by giving security for the costs and damages, appeal to the District Court from any judgment, decree, or order of the Probate Court, rendered in term time, within twenty days from the date of said judgment, decree, or order; executors, administrators, and guardians, and the attorney for the State, may appeal without security. Appeal to Dist. Court.

ART. 194. [17] When a sale of land or negroes becomes necessary for the

Order for sale of land or negroes. payment of debts, application shall be made therefor by petition in writing, filed with the clerk. The petition shall first set forth the amount of personal property that has come to the hands of the executor, administrator, or guardian, stating its nature and kind; second, the manner in which any portion of said property has been applied; third, the debts that have been paid, and those that are still due and unpaid, the amount of each, and the names of the parties to whom payable; fourth, the description of the real estate, where situated, and whether vacant or occupied, and if occupied, the names of the occupants; fifth, the names, sexes, and ages of the negroes, by families, and their number; sixth, the names of the heirs and legatees, and if minors, the names of their representatives; on which petition citation shall issue and be personally served on the heirs and legatees, and if minors, on their representatives, and on the occupants of the land, living in the county. If no such heirs or legatees are in the State, or if in the State, are not known, publication shall be made in a newspaper printed in the county, if there be one—if there be none, then by publication in the nearest newspaper published in the State—at least four weeks before the return thereof, and such newspapers in other counties where any person interested in the estate may reside, as the Judge, on due inquiry, may direct, and by personal notice served on the attorney to represent the State; to which petition answer may be filed by the parties interested, showing their objections. The Judge may order the executor or administrator to make the aforesaid exhibit, on the petition of the creditors. At the return term of said notice, the Judge shall determine whether, or not, a sale be necessary; and if ordered, returns of the sale shall be made under oath; and the Judge may examine testimony relating thereto, and if any fraud has been committed, or any irregularity has taken place, to the prejudice of the estate, he shall vacate such sale, and may order a new one; if the sale be approved, he shall endorse on the return thereof his approval, and order a confirmation of the same to be recorded, and a conveyance to be made. The conveyance shall recite the order of sale, the sale, and the confirmation, and order of conveyance; which recital shall be a copy from the records of the court. Lands and negroes sold shall not be subject to liens existing at the time of the death of the deceased.

No sale to pay debts before fourth term of the court—perishable property may be sold at discretion.

ART. 195. [18] No sales shall be ordered for the payment of debts before the fourth regular term of the court after letters have been granted; but sales of perishable property, sales for the support of the family of the deceased, or for the education of minors, and sales made to avoid expenses incidental to the preservation of personal property, and for taxes, are hereby left to the discretion of the Judge. The land and slaves, and other property, shall in all cases, upon a proper showing by the heirs, be, for their benefit, kept together, without sale or hiring, when a sale thereof is not absolutely necessary.

Land and slaves kept together in certain cases.

ART. 196. [19] All sales by executors may be made in accordance with the directions of the testator in relation thereto, expressed in the will; and all sales not so directed shall be made at public auction in accordance with the law regulating sales under execution. The terms of the sales of personal property are hereby left to the discretion of the Judge; but in all cases, land and negroes shall be sold on a credit of twelve months, with approved security, retaining a lien on the same for the payment of the purchase money, unless otherwise directed by the testator.

Manner and terms of sales by, &c.

No executor, &c., shall purchase claim ag't estate.

ART. 197. [20] No executor, administrator, guardian, or trustee, qualified under this act, shall either directly or indirectly, become the purchaser of any bond, note, or other demand against the estate for his own use, or for the use of another, or of any property of the estate he represents; the Judge may in his discretion order him to purchase, at public auction, for the use and benefit of the estate, property in payment of debts due to the estate.

Inventories, accounts of sales, &c.

ART. 198. [21] Inventories and accounts of sales shall always be returned under oath, either in open court or in vacation, at such times as the Judge shall direct; and at the sixth regular term of the court, after letters issued, a full statement of the condition of the estate shall be returned; and at the sixth regular term of the court, after letters issued, notice shall issue, to be served on the creditors and the next of kin of the deceased, and the legatees, if any, and if there be none, on the attorney for the State, to appear before the court at the next regular term thereof, to attend the settlement of the accounts of the estate; which notice shall be executed in the manner pointed out in section 17 of this act.

Order of paying claims.

ART. 199. [22] The owners of claims which have been presented, acknowledged, and approved, or which have been established by judgment, shall be entitled, in the following order, to a full or a pro rata payment at the sixth regular term of the court, after granting the letters: first, funeral expenses; second, debts due the late Republic of Texas; third, debts due the Government of the United States; fourth, taxes assessed for the State; fifth, recorded mortgages and liens on specific property, then judgments of the courts of this State, the oldest first; sixth, all other debts,—and debts not due after deducting a discount of legal interest, shall be classed and paid as debts that are due; claims in suit shall be taken into the pro rata estimate, and claims not presented within twelve months from the publication of notice, shall be postponed in their payment until those presented have been paid; they shall be finally barred, however, only by the general law of limitations.

ART. 200. [23] The Judge may, upon proof that the condition of the estate requires it, continue the administration of the estate, as the condition of the same in the opinion of the Judge may require, upon good cause shown by the administrator in writing and verified by affidavit. Administration may be continued.

ART. 201. [24] After the payment of the debts and expenses, and after due notice given, as provided in the 17th section of this act, of the distribution of the estate, the same shall be distributed under the direction of the Judge, to the parties legally entitled thereto. If there be no heirs or legatees, the administrator or executor shall pay the money in hand into the Treasury of the State, and deliver to the Comptroller of Public Accounts all papers and documents relating to real estate, taking receipts therefor; and the receipts for the same of the Treasurer and Comptroller severally, shall be filed with the papers of the estate in the Probate Court. Distribution of estate—when paid to Treas'r.

ART. 202. [26] Whenever an inventory of any estate may be made out and returned to the court, the Judge thereof shall set apart for the sole use and benefit of the widow and children, if there be either or any, of the deceased, all such property as by the Constitution and laws of the State, has been or shall be declared not to be subject to forced sale, for debts contracted after the 16th day of February, 1846; and in case there should not be among the effects of the deceased, all or any of the specific articles which are by the Constitution and laws of the State exempt from forced sale, it shall be the duty of the Probate Judge to order a sale of a sufficiency of the other effects belonging to the estate of such deceased person as will, under the direction of such Judge, procure for the use of the wife and children, or wife in case such person have no children, or child or children in case such person have no wife, the specific articles which may, at the time of the death of such person, be exempt by law from forced sale under execution; and that any testator, by his last will and testament, may so provide that no other action than the probate and registration of said will and testament, and an inventory of the estate shall be had in the Probate Court. Exempt property set apart to widow and children. Testator may provide that no action except probate of his will, &c., be had

ART. 203. [27] All laws and parts of laws heretofore in force relative to the duties of Probate Courts and the settlement of successions, be and the same are hereby repealed; and the unfinished business of all estates now pending shall be conducted from this date in accordance with the provisions of this act. Repeal'g clause.

ART. 204. [1] The third section of an act providing for the transfer of records of administrators to new counties, approved 13th May, A. D. 1846, be so amended as to read as follows, to-wit: In all cases when the papers and proceedings, relating to the settlement of an estate, shall be transmitted to any court in the manner provided for in this act, such estate shall be proceeded in and settled in the Probate Court of such county, in like manner as if the settlement of such estate had been originally commenced in such county, and the transcript of the record transmitted in the manner provided for in this act, shall have the same force and effect in evidence as the record itself might or could have: provided, that the provisions of this act shall not extend to the counties of Jackson, Victoria, Gonzales, Bexar, Goliad, Refugio, and San Patricio. Act of Feb'y 14, 1848. Transfer of records to new counties. Certain counties excepted.

ESTATES OF DECEASED SOLDIERS.

ART. 205. [1] All persons who have, or may hereafter administer upon the estate of deceased soldiers or officers shall, before the auditor is allowed to audit the claims, or the Secretary of War, or Board of Land Commissioners, of any county, be authorized to grant bounty warrants, or land certificates, enter into bond with approved security as the court may direct, for the faithful Administrators of, to give bond.

performance of the duties of such administration; a copy of which bond and all the proceedings in such case duly certified under the hand and seal of the Chief Justice of such county, shall be returned to the Secretary of War.

Publication of, &c., to be made at, &c. ART. 206. [2] Hereafter no letters of administration shall be granted, nor any further action be had under those that have already been granted, until publication of such application for letters, or the existence of such letters of administration shall have been made at least sixty days in one of the public gazettes, published at the seat of government.

No sale of effects of deceas'd except. ART. 207. [3] No sale of any of the effects of any deceased soldier or officer shall be made, unless by order of the court granting letters of administration, approved by the Secretary of War, and published in some newspaper sixty days; and all sales made contrary to the provisions of this section, (unless by heirs of full age,) shall be entirely null and void.

Adm'r to return inventory and make annual report. ART. 208. [4] It shall be the duty of all administrators on the estates of deceased soldiers to return to the court granting letters, within ninety days, an inventory of all the effects of such deceased soldier, and annually at the Probate Court in January of each year, to make return of all his proceedings, unless by special leave of the court, longer time be granted; a copy of which said inventory and returns shall be immediately transmitted to the Secretary of War.

Administrator's names to be published. ART. 209. [5] It shall be the duty of the Secretary of War, once in every three months, to publish in some public gazette the names of all administrators (and on whose estate) that may be returned to him.

Foregoing act not to apply to citizen soldiers. ART. 210. [1] The above recited act shall not be so construed as to apply to the duty of any administrator upon the estate of any deceased citizen soldier, who was a citizen of Texas, in the full exercise of his rights as such at the time of his death.

Certificate of Clerk or Judge to be evidence. ART. 211. [2] The certificate of the Judge or Clerk of Probate before whom administration shall have or may hereafter be commenced, shall be evidence to all whom it may concern, any laws to the contrary notwithstanding.

Act of Dec. 17, 1851.

WHEREAS, doubts have arisen whether the several acts of the Congress of the Republic of Texas relating to the estates of deceased soldiers, were repealed by the act to organize Probate Courts, approved May 11, 1846, and unauthorized persons have administered upon many of such estates, and sold the lands intended to be granted to the heirs of such soldiers, contrary to the intent of such acts: therefore,

Act of May 18, and Dec'r 24, 1838, repealed, and act of Jan. 14, 1841, declar'd to be in force. ART. 212. [1] "An act to provide for the settlement of deceased soldier's estates," approved May 18, 1838, and "an act to amend said act," approved December 24, 1838, be, and the same are hereby repealed; and that the "act to protect the rights of the heirs and next of kin to the members of the Georgia Battalion, and other volunteers from foreign countries, who have fallen in the battles of the Republic, or otherwise died in the limits of the same," approved January 14, 1841, be, and is declared to be in full force and effect.

Administration on estate of foreign volunteer—to whom granted. ART. 213. [2] No administration shall be granted on the estate of any person who served as a volunteer, from another State or country, who may have fallen in the battles of the Republic, or otherwise died in the limits of the same, or elsewhere, to any person who shall not show himself entitled to the same as next of kin, or shall not produce an authority from the heirs or next of kin of such deceased soldier, authorizing him to take administration.

Administrator shall not receive patent, unless, &c. ART. 214. [3] When administration has heretofore been granted on the estates of deceased soldiers, without the authority contemplated by this act, it shall not be lawful for such administrator to receive from any officer of the State or other person, any patent or land claim, money or evidence of debt, to which such deceased soldier may have been entitled, nor to sell the lands, or land claims of such deceased, without the consent of the heirs of such deceased soldier; and the proof relied on as evidence of such consent shall be recorded in the court granting the order to sell, before such order is made.

Adm'r shall file his authority from next of kin to administer, &c. ART. 215. [4] In all cases where administration has been granted on estates of deceased soldiers, without the authority contemplated by this act, it shall be the duty of the Chief Justices of the County Courts granting the same, to cause the administrators to be notified, as in other cases, to file in court the authority or consent aforesaid; and in case of failure so to do, they shall order the removal of such administrators, and also, to require them to deliver to the Property to be delivered to heirs. Clerk of the Court all the property and title papers in their possession, belonging to the estate; and it shall be the duty of such administrators, or Clerk of the Court having possession of said property, to deliver the same to the heirs of such deceased soldier, or their legally authorized agent, on demand.

GUARDIANS.

ART. 216. [46] Any guardian so appointed by the last will and testament of any person admitted to probate in any court, shall, before the exercise of any authority over the minor, or his estate, declare openly in said court, his acceptance of said guardianship, which shall be recorded; and he shall give bond and security in the manner required of executors and administrators by this act; and the said guardian, and all guardians appointed by the Probate Court, before letters of guardianship are issued, shall take an oath for the faithful discharge of the duties of his trust. *Act of Feb. 5, 1840. Repealed May 11, 1846. Testamentary guardian. Bond and oath.*

ART. 217. [47] The Probate Judge in each county, when, and as often as there may be occasion, is hereby empowered to appoint guardians that shall be chosen by minors of fourteen years of age, in open court, who shall be appointed, unless there be good and sufficient cause for their rejection; and it shall be lawful for the said court to appoint guardians to such as shall be within or under that age—the father or mother, the brothers and sisters, and the next of kin, in the order enumerated, are entitled to the guardianship of the minor; but if there be neither father nor mother, sisters or kindred; or in the event that the brother or sister, or next of kin, do not apply for the guardianship of the minor, or are not able or refuse to give sufficient security, then the court may appoint any suitable person to the guardianship. The father or mother shall not be compelled to give security for the guardianship of their minor children, except when required by the court, or when the mother may marry a second time; and it shall be lawful for the Probate Court, with the consent of the person entitled to the guardianship of the minor, to appoint any suitable person as said guardian: the person appointed as guardian, before the minor arrives at fourteen years of age, shall continue to act as such after that time until a guardian is chosen by said minor; and when a minor above fourteen years of age shall be cited by the Probate Court to choose a guardian, and such minor shall refuse or neglect so to do, or any guardian, chosen by such minor, shall be unable to give sufficient security, or shall refuse the trust; in every such case the Probate Court shall have the same power to appoint a guardian, as though such minor was under the age of fourteen years. *Appointed for minors.*

ART. 218. [48] Every guardian shall, within three months after his appointment and acceptance of such office, return to the court appointing him an inventory, on oath, of all the estate, real and personal, which he shall have received or taken possession of, or which has come to his knowledge, (to be entered of record,) in the manner directed by this law, for the making and return of inventories by executors and administrators. And the said guardian shall, once in every year, and oftener, if hereunto lawfully required, render an account of his management of said estate and the proceeds thereof, and of the sale and disposition of each product, and generally of the receipts and expenditures of said estate; which accounts being examined and audited in the same manner as executors' and administrators' accounts, and reported fairly stated, and supported by vouchers, and approved of by the court, shall be recorded in the said court. *Annual reports.*

ART. 219. [49] Any guardian who shall not deliver in such inventory, or render such account, shall by order of the court to which he is answerable, be summoned, and, if he remain in default, be compelled to perform his duty, or be displaced; and the said court may, for any good and sufficient cause, displace a guardian, giving such guardian fourteen days' previous notice, by citation, to appear and show cause why he should not be displaced; and the Probate Court, at any time it shall know or have cause to suspect that the securities of a guardian, or any of them, are in failing or dubious circum- *Inventory and report, failure to make.*

stances, shall require and compel such guardian to give additional security or securities; and if he refuses or neglects to do so, shall displace him.

Petition to sell personal property. ART. 220. [50] Within a month after closing the inventory, the guardian shall petition the sale of the personal property (except slaves) of the minor, unless the Judge, for any sufficient reason, should authorize the guardian to preserve the said property, in kind, in whole or in part; in which case the guardian shall return to the minor the estimated value of said property which he cannot restore in kind, or which he has suffered to deteriorate for want of care.

Land and slaves not to be sold unless, &c. ART. 221. [51] The land and slaves of the minor cannot be sold, or mortgaged, unless on the application of the guardian for that purpose, and on the testimony, on oath, of at least three discreet persons, to be taken in open court, and to be put on record in said court, that they believe such sale is of absolute necessity, or of evident advantage to the minor; and all private sales of the property of a minor, by a guardian, shall be absolutely null and void.

Price of property—Terms of credit. ART. 222. [52] The minor's property cannot be sold for less than a price to be fixed by order of the court, which shall not be greater than the amount of the appraised value of said property, nor less than two-thirds of said appraisement; and the Judge shall have the authority of granting such terms of credit, and giving such other facilities as shall secure prompt and advantageous sale of the property of the minor.

When slaves and land may be sold. ART. 223. [53] The prohibition of alienating the slaves and real property of a minor does not extend to the case in which a judgment is to be executed against him, or where property is to be sold for a division between co-heirs and co-proprietors.

Guardians for idiots, lunatics, &c. ART. 224. [54] It shall and may be lawful for the Court of Probate to appoint guardians for idiots, lunatics, and persons *non compos mentis*, on full proof of the idiotcy, madness or incompetency of the person prayed to be interdicted; and the rules respecting the guardianship of the minor, concerning the oath, the inventory and security, the mode of administering the property, the sale of the estate, the commissions of the guardian, the granting and the deprivation of the guardianship, the mode of rendering the accounts, and other obligations apply with respect to the guardianship of idiots, lunatics, and persons *non compos mentis*, and the said guardian or guardians are hereby empowered to collect, sue for and recover all just debts due to such idiot or lunatic, or person *non compos mentis*, and to bring, prosecute, and defend any action in any court of law or equity, which the said idiot, lunatic, or person *non compos mentis* might bring, prosecute, or defend were he or she sane or competent to the discharge of his or her business; and they shall pay all just debts of such persons' contracting when they were of sound mind, and before his or her distraction or lunacy, out of the personal estate; or if that be insufficient, then out of the real estate, in such way and manner as executors and administrators may by law discharge the debts of deceased persons when the personal estate is insufficient.

When restored to reason. ART. 225. [55] If any idiot, lunatic or person *non compos mentis*, shall be restored to the use of his or her reason and sanity of mind; and if the same shall be made to appear to the Probate Court, who shall judge thereof, the residue of his or her estate, both real and personal, shall be returned and delivered to him or her; and the guardian or guardians of persons interdicted, as well as the guardians of minors, shall have the same compensation and commissions as are allowed to executors by the provisions of this law.

Property of purchaser sold without appraisement. ART. 226. [56] In all cases where property is sold at a sale of a succession of a deceased person, or of the property of minors, idiots, lunatics, and persons *non compos mentis*, the property of the purchaser, or his securities, may be seized and sold on execution for cash to the highest bidder without the necessity of appraisement.

No bond required on appeal. ART. 227. [58] In all cases of appeal from any court in this Republic, it shall not be necessary for executors, administrators, or guardians to give the bond and security required of applicants in other cases; but in all cases of appeals pronounced frivolous by the court trying the appeal, the costs shall be paid out of the private property of the executor, administrator, or guardian.

Guardians appointed before passage of this act. ART. 228. [60] The respective Judges of Probate, upon the passage of this act, shall be required to cause all executors, administrators, and guardians, to whom letters of administration or guardianship have been granted twelve months previous to the passage of this act, to appear before them and account for their proceedings in relation to the estates which they may have administered, and settle their accounts as executors, administrators and guardians are required to settle by this law; and all executors, administrators, or guardians, to whom letters of administration and guardianship may have heretofore been granted, shall, at the expiration of twelve months from the granting of such letters of administration or guardianship, be required to come forward and settle as above; and any administrator or executor, failing to comply with the provisions of this section, shall be liable to the penalties prescribed by this act for defaulting administrators or executors.

LIMITATIONS.

Act of Dec. 20, 1836. Supplied by act of Feb. 5, 1841. On suits for land.

Art. 229. [39] Any actual settler, who is a citizen of this Republic, who may have and hold peaceable possession of any tract or parcel of land under a color of title duly proven and recorded in the proper county, for a term of five years from and after recording of said color of title or titles, his, her, or their claim shall be considered good and valid, barring the claim or claims of any and every person or persons whatsoever,—minors, feme coverts, and persons *non compos mentis* excepted, who shall have, and be allowed two years after their maturity, marriage, or return to sound mind, to demand and commence an action for his, her or their claims, and no more. A peaceable possession can only be interrupted by an actual suit being instituted and prosecuted agreeably to the due forms of law, against the holder or holders thereof. Provided, that this Act shall not effect the rights of any person who may have been prevented from complying with the provisions of this law, by reason of an enemy having had possession of the country, or for want of a proper court or officer having been established in due time: and provided, further, that this Act shall not give validity to claims unlawfully obtained from Government.

MARITAL RIGHTS.

Act of Jan. 20, 1840. Repealed March 13, 1848. Separate property of the wife.

Art. 230. [3] Neither the lands nor slaves which the wife may own, or to which she may have any right, title, or claim at the time of her marriage, nor the lands nor slaves to which she may acquire, during the coverture, any right, title, or claim, by gift, devise, or decent, nor the increase of such slaves in each case, nor the paraphernalia, as defined at common law, which the wife may have at the time of the marriage or which she may acquire during the coverture as aforesaid, shall, by virtue of the marriage, become the property of the husband, but shall remain the separate property of the wife: provided, however, that during the continuance of the marriage, the husband shall have the sole management of such lands and slaves.

Community property.

Art. 231. [4] All property which the husband or wife may bring into the marriage, except land and slaves and the wife's paraphernalia, and all the property acquired during the marriage, except such land or slaves or their increase, as may be acquired by either party, by gift, devise, or descent, and except also the wife's paraphernalia, acquired as aforesaid and during the time aforesaid, shall be the common property of the husband and wife, and during the coverture may be sold or otherwise disposed of by the husband only; it shall be first liable for all the debts contracted by the husband during the marriage, and for all debts contracted by the wife for necessaries during the same time; and upon the dissolution of the marriage, by death, after the payment of all such debts, the remainder of such common property shall go to the survivor, if the deceased have no descendant or descendants; but if the deceased have a descendant or descendants, the survivor shall have one-half of such common property, and the other half shall pass to the descendant or descendants of the deceased.

MARRIAGE.

Ordinance and Decree of Jan. 16, 1836. Temporary. Who may celebrate, and mode. Marriages declared valid.

ART. 232. [9] All Judges, Alcaldes, Commissarios, and regularly accredited Ministers of the Gospel, of whatever denomination, shall have the power to celebrate the rites of matrimony in their respective municipalities, which shall be done in the presence of not less than three disinterested and reputable witnesses; certificates of which shall be made and signed by the said Judge, Alcalde, Commissario, or Minister of the Gospel, who may celebrate the same, tested by two or more witnesses present, one of which shall be given to the bride, and the other filed with the archives of said municipality; and all marriages so celebrated, shall be valid to all intents and purposes, in law and in equity. And all marriages heretofore celebrated by bond or otherwise, under the heretofore existing laws, are, in like manner declared and decreed to be valid: provided, that all officers who have attended to the same, shall, on the application of either party or the friend of either party, file the bond or other evidence of such marriage, with the archives and records of the court of their respective municipality; and on failure to do so, within ten days after application is made, shall be fined, in a summary way, in the sum of one hundred dollars—to be paid to the injured party—and to be, in the same manner, fined from time to time within ten days after each application, until the same is done: provided, also, that all marriages heretofore entered into, under the heretofore existing laws, shall be, and are hereby declared legal, and the issue of the parties legitimate.

Act of June 5, 1837. Temporary. Certain informal marriages.

ART. 233. WHEREAS, in many parts of Texas no person legally authorized to celebrate the rites of matrimony has existed; and whereas, from that cause, many persons have resorted to the practice of marrying by bond, and others have been married by various officers of Justice, not authorized to celebrate such marriages; and whereas, public policy and the interests of families require some legislative action on the subject: therefore,

Be it enacted by the Senate and House of Representatives of the Republic of Texas, in Congress assembled, That all persons who have so intermarried be, and they are hereby authorized to go before any of the persons hereinafter provided for, and publicly solemnize the rites of matrimony; and all marriages so solemnized are hereby declared of legal and binding effect, from the period the persons had previously intermarried agreeably to the custom of the times; and the issue of such persons are hereby declared legitimate children: provided, however, that such marriages shall be celebrated within six months from the passage of this law; and provided, further, that no legal bar exists to such marriage.

Children legitimate.

ART. 234. [2] In cases where persons have intermarried as aforesaid agreeably to the customs of the country, and either the husband or wife has died previous to the passage of this law, then and in that case, all such marriages are declared of legal and binding effect, and the issue of the same are hereby legitimatized: provided, that such parties lived together as man and wife at the said death of either party.

Act of Feb. 5, 1841. Temporary. Certain marriages declared legal. Children legitimate.

ART. 235. [1] WHEREAS, many persons heretofore, previous to the passage of an Act approved June the fifth, eighteen hundred and thirty-seven, regulating marriages, and for other purposes, had, for the want of some person legally qualified to celebrate the rites of matrimony, resorted to the practice of marrying by bond; and others have been married by various officers of justice, not authorized to celebrate such marriages; and whereas, public policy and the interests of families require a further legislative action on the subject: Therefore all such marriages are declared legal and valid, to all intents and purposes; and the issue of such persons are hereby declared legitimate children, and capable of inheritance.

Same subject.

ART. 236. [2] In cases where persons have so intermarried, agreeably to the custom of the times, and where husband or wife has since died, previous to the passage of this Act, then and in that case, the issue of such marriages are hereby legitimatized.

ART. 237. [1] When any unmarried persons who have heretofore lived together as husband and wife, and who have had a child or children born out of wedlock, shall have intermarried with each other, or shall hereafter intermarry within twelve months from and after the passage of this Act, such child or children so born out of wedlock, shall be, and the same are hereby declared to be, legitimate, and entitled to all the rights and privileges of children born in wedlock.

Act of Nov. 29, 1841.

Children legitimated by subsequent marriage of parents.

LANDS.

EMPRESSARIOS.

HEADRIGHTS.

CONDITIONS ANNEXED TO.

FANNIN, WARD, TRAVIS, GRANT AND JOHNSON HEADRIGHTS.

BOUNTIES.

LAND SCRIP.

EMPRESSARIOS.

Act of June 12, 1837. Repealed Dec'r 14, 1837. Archives in possession of.

ART. 238. [6] It is hereby made the duty of all empressarios, commissioners, political chiefs, alcaldes, and other persons, to deliver over to the Commissioner of the General Land Office all titles, surveys, books, papers, documents, or other things in their possession or charge, belonging to this Republic, or which by this act is made public property, and so contemplated to be delivered over as aforesaid, on the application in person of said Commissioner, or to his order in writing.

Joint resolution Dec. 14, 1837. Same subject.

ART. 239. [1] It shall be the duty of every person or persons, who may have in his or their possession or control any titles or documents whatever, which relate to lands, and which by the laws now or hereafter [heretofore?] existing in Texas, have been and are considered "Archives," to deliver the same to the Commissioner of the General Land Office, on his order, within sixty days after the final passage of this act.

May institute suits against President, &c.

ART. 240. [27] In order to settle the claims of empressarios, each and every one of the same are hereby authorized to institute a suit against the President of the Republic of Texas; which suit or suits shall be tried in the county in which is situated the seat of government, and shall be tried as all other land suits are required to be tried. And should any empressario who should thus sue, fail to establish the claim for which he sues, he shall pay all the costs of said suit: provided, that neither aliens nor the assignees of aliens shall be entitled to the benefits of this act.

Attorney General and counsel to defend.

ART. 241. [28] It shall be the duty of the Attorney General to attend to all such suits, in behalf of the Republic of Texas; and the President is hereby authorized to employ such additional counsel as in his opinion he may deem proper, the expense of which shall not exceed one thousand dollars in each case.

May sue the State.

ART. 242. [1] In all cases in which parties were authorized by the laws, to commence suit against the President of the Republic of Texas, or against the Republic, prior to the adoption of the State Constitution, such parties may now commence such suits against the Governor or against the State of Texas.

HEADRIGHTS.

Act of Dec. 22, 1836. Repealed Dec'r 14, 1837.

Emigrants after Jan. 1st. 1837.

Art. 243. [24] Every emigrant who arrives in this Republic, from and after the first day of January next, who is a free white person, and is the head of a family, and who shall actually reside within the government with his family, shall be entitled to a conditional grant for twelve hundred and eighty acres of land, by paying the fees of office and for surveying. The conditions of said grant shall be, that the grantee shall remain and reside here, and his or her family, both within this government, and do and perform all the duties required of other like citizens, for a term of three years; after which time and several acts, he or she shall have and receive an unconditional patent for said land; and in no case whatever, shall a grant of that description be patented, unless it be satisfactorily proven, that all the conditions of the grant have in fact and in good faith, been complied with. And all single free white men, who may emigrate to the country after the first day of January next, shall be entitled to six hundred and forty acres of land, and so soon as they shall marry, they shall receive an additional quantity of six hundred and forty acres of land, upon the same conditions above named; and all laws contrary to the purview and meaning of this act, are hereby repealed and declared null and void, so far as regards their future operation.

Act of Dec. 14, 1837.

Volunteers under 17 years of age.

Art. 244. [22] Each and every individual under the age of seventeen, who have volunteered in the service of their country, and who have received honorable discharges, shall be entitled to the same quantity of land as a headright, that they would be though they were twenty-one years of age, and upon the same conditions.

Volunteers arriving between March 2, and Aug. 1, 1838.

Art. 245. [29] Every volunteer who arrived in this Republic after the 2d day of March, 1836, and before the 1st of August, 1836, and has received or may hereafter receive an honorable discharge and has taken the oath prescribed by the Constitution, or who may have died, shall receive the quantity of land by this act secured to original colonists: provided, that the priority of location mentioned in the thirty-eighth section of this act shall be adhered to: and further provided, that none but the person who served, or his heirs, shall be entitled to the benefit of this provision, and all augmentation shall accrue to the original claimants, and not to the person to whom it may have been transferred: provided, no person who is entitled to the benefit of the first part of this section of this act, shall be entitled to the benefits of the latter part of the same; every person who has arrived in this Republic since the declaration of independence, and previous to the 1st of October, 1837, who is a free white person, and the head of a family, and who actually resides within the government with his family, shall be entitled to a conditional grant of twelve hundred and eighty acres of land, by paying the fees of office and surveying. The conditions of said grant shall be that both grantee and his or her family shall remain and reside within this Republic, and do and perform all the duties required of other like citizens, for the term of three years; after which time, he or she shall receive an unconditional deed for said land; and in no case whatever shall a grant of that description be made unless it be satisfactorily proven that all the conditions and provisions of the law have been complied with. And all single free white men who have emigrated to this Republic since the declaration of independence, and previous to the 1st of October, 1837, shall be entitled to six hundred and forty acres of land, and if they married before the 1st day of October, 1837, they shall be entitled to an additional quantity of six hundred and forty acres of land upon the same conditions as above named; and all laws contrary to the meaning and provisions of this section are hereby repealed.

Immigrants after March 2, 1836, and before Oct. 1st, 1837.

Act of Jan. 4, 1839.

Immigrants after October 1st, 1837, and before January 1, 1840.

Art. 246. [1] Every person who emigrated to this Republic since the first day of October, Anno Domini one thousand eight hundred and thirty-seven, or who may emigrate to this Republic by the first day of January, one thousand eight hundred and forty, who is a free white person and the head of a family, and who actually resides within the Government with his or her family, shall be entitled to a conditional grant of six hundred and forty acres of land, by paying the fees of office and surveying. The conditions of the said grant shall be, that both grantee and his or her family shall remain and reside permanently within this Republic, and do and perform any and all duties required of other citizens, for the term of three years; after which time he or his legal representatives shall receive from the Government, an unconditional deed for said grant of land: provided that no sale of said claim to land, by the individual entitled to the same, of this Government shall be valid in law and binding upon the person selling the same, until an unconditional deed shall be obtained by the grantee for said land; and in no case whatever shall a grant of that description be made, unless it be satisfactorily proven that all the conditions and provisions of the law have been complied with. And all single free white male persons, of the age of seventeen and upwards, who have emigrated to this Republic since the first day of October, one thousand eight hundred and thirty-seven, or who may emigrate to this Republic by the first day of January, one thousand eight hundred and forty, shall be entitled to three hundred and twenty acres of land: and all laws and parts of laws contrary to the meaning and provisions of this act are hereby repealed.

Resident citizens of 17 years between same dates.

ART. 247. [2] All permanent resident citizens of Texas, who have or may arrive to the age required of emigrants by the above section of this act, shall be entitled to the same quantity of land as emigrants, upon the same conditions that emigrants are.

Act of Feb. 4, 1841.

Heads of families after Jan. 1, 1840, and before January 1, 1842.

Every head of a family who has emigrated to this Republic since the first of January, one thousand eight hundred and forty, or who may emigrate before the first of January, one thousand eight hundred and forty-two, with his family, and who is a free white person, shall be entitled to six hundred and forty acres of land: provided he settle and actually reside on the same for the term of three years, and cultivate an amount of the same not less than ten acres: and further provided, he shall have his land surveyed and plainly marked, so as to include his improvements.

Single men between the same periods.

ART. 248. [2] Each single man over the age of seventeen, who has or may emigrate as provided in the first section of this act, shall be entitled to three hundred and twenty acres of land, upon the same conditions and restrictions as the heads of families.

AUGMENTATION OF.

Act of Dec. 14, 1837.

Single men who were citizens on the 20th March, 1836, and since married, &c.

ART. 249. [23] All single men who were in the Republic at the date of the declaration of independence, and entitled under the Constitution to one-third of a league of land, and who have since married, or may marry within the next twelve months, shall be entitled to the additional quantity of two-thirds of a league and a labor of land: provided, that the benefits of this section shall only extend to those who have contributed to the support and defence of their country: and provided, this additional quantity shall not be allowed to any whose wife has received a league of land of this government.

Volunteers arriving after March 2, and before August 1, 1836.

ART. 250. [30] All officers and soldiers who engaged in the service of Texas previous to the 1st of March, 1837, whose families are now here or may arrive within twelve months from the date of their discharges, shall be entitled to the same quantity of land as they would have been entitled to, if their families had emigrated with them to the country.

Officers and soldiers whose families arrive by Jan. 1, 1840.

ART. 251. [3] All officers and soldiers who engaged in the service of Texas previous to the first of March, one thousand eight hundred and thirty-seven, whose families are now here, or may arrive here by the first day of January, one thousand eight hundred and forty, shall be entitled to the same quantity of land that they would have been if their families had emigrated to the country with them.

CONDITIONS ANNEXED TO.

Act of Dec. 22, 1836.

Conditions cancelled.

ART. 252. [21] Whereas many persons have received titles under the colonization laws, as colonists, from the different commissioners of the country: and whereas many conditions were, by the laws, attached to said titles—that all such conditions be, and are hereby cancelled, and the titles to all such lands be, and are hereby ratified and confirmed: provided, that such persons shall pay, or cause to be paid into the office of the Receiver of the Land office of the District where such land may be situated, or into the office of the Secretary of the Treasury, within six months after the opening of the Land office, all money which may be due or owing on the same: provided, that the conditions of remaining in the country, and the provision prohibiting a sale to aliens, shall not be repealed by this law: and further provided, that no title by this act shall be confirmed, which was illegal or invalid *ab initio*: and be it further provided, that it shall not affect the rights of third persons: and further provided, this act shall not extend to the benefit of any grantee or individual, for a greater amount of land than one league and one labor, or that granted to like citizens by the Constitution of this Republic.

ART. 253. [24] Whereas many persons have received titles under the colonization laws, as colonists from the different commissioners of the county; and whereas many conditions were by the law attached to said titles; that all such conditions be, and are hereby cancelled, and the titles to all such lands are hereby ratified and confirmed: provided, that such persons shall pay, or cause to be paid, to the President of the Board of Land Commissioners of the county where such land may be situated, within six months after the opening of the Land Office, all money which may be due or owing on the same: provided, that the condition of remaining in the country, and the provision prohibiting the sale to aliens, shall not be repealed by this law: and further provided, that no title by this act shall be confirmed, which was illegal or invalid *ab initio*: and further provided, that this act shall not extend to any grantee or individual for a greater amount of land than one league and one labor. Same subject.

ART. 254. [13] All those volunteers who arrived in this Republic from the second of March, one thousand eight hundred and thirty-six, to the first of August, one thousand eight hundred and thirty-six, as mentioned in the twenty-ninth section of the land law of one thousand eight hundred and thirty-seven, shall be exempted from the conditions as mentioned in the same for the second and third class of claimants. Certain volunteers exempt from conditions, &c.

FANNIN, WARD, TRAVIS, GRANT AND JOHNSON HEADRIGHTS.

ART. 255. [1] The Adjutant-General shall, as early as practicable after the passage of this act, make out from the records of his office, copies of the muster rolls of the several companies that were under the command of Fannin and Ward, and a list of the names of those who fell in the Alamo with Travis, and a list of those who fell with Grant, and under the command of Johnson, during the war with Mexico, in the year eighteen hundred and thirty-six, and deliver the same, certified under his seal of office, to the Commissioner of the General Land Office; who shall file the same among the archives appertaining to his office. Adjutant Gen'l to make out copy of muster roll.

ART. 256. [2] As soon as the copies of muster rolls, and lists mentioned in the first section of this act, shall have been filed in accordance with the provisions of this act, the Adjutant-General shall, and he is hereby required to issue to the heirs of those who fell with Fannin, Ward, Travis, Grant, or Johnson, their heirs or legal representatives, attorneys or assigns, certificates for headrights in right of those who were heads of families, for one league and labor of land—and in right of those who were single men, for one-third of a league of land. Certificates to be issued to heirs, &c.

ART. 257. [3] Said certificates shall be issued in the names of the parties originally interested, and as [heirs of ?] those who fell with Fannin, Ward, Travis, Grant, or Johnson, as the case may be; shall be signed by the Adjutant-General, and certified under his seal of office, and countersigned by the Commissioner of the General Land Office. To whom issu'd and signed and countersigned, &c.

ART. 258. [4] This act shall extend only to the heirs of those who fell as mentioned in the second section of this act, and of them, only to those in whose right no certificates for headrights have been issued. To whom this act extends.

ART. 259. [5] The name appearing on the muster rolls, or the lists filed in accordance with the first section of this act, and the name not appearing on the list of certificates approved by the Traveling Board of Land Commissioners, or on the several lists returned by clerks of the District Courts, in cases where parties have received their certificates in suits instituted in the several District Courts, shall be sufficient evidence that the parties in interest are entitled to, and have not received their certificates. What shall be suffic't evidence

ART. 260. [6] When it may appear from the list of land certificates, approved by the Traveling Board of Land Commissioners, or the lists returned by any of the several clerks of the District Courts, that a certificate has been issued to an administrator, or to the heirs of a person of the same name with one whose name is on the muster rolls or lists mentioned in the first section of this act, then and in that case, the Adjutant-General and the Commissioner of When it appe'rs certificate has heretofore is'u'd the General Land Office shall constitute a Board of Investigation, and may sit at any time to hear the evidence produced by the applicants; and upon full and satisfactory proof that the said certificate issued in right of a person of the same name, but who was not with those who fell with Fannin, Ward, Travis, Grant, or Johnson, a certificate shall be issued for the quantity of land to which the applicant is entitled.

Proof required of applicants.

ART. 261. [7] The applicants for land certificates under this act, who claim a league and labor, shall file in the office of the Adjutant-General, the affidavit of two respectable witnesses, sworn to and subscribed before any Judge of the District Court, Judge of the Supreme Court, Adjutant-General, or any Commissioner appointed by the Governor of the State, stating and affirming that the individual in whose right the claim is made, was a man of family; the officer administering the oath shall certify, that of his own knowledge, or from satisfactory proof produced to him, the witnesses who swear are respectable persons, and entitled to credit; and in all cases where such affidavit is not filed and certified as aforesaid, the certificate shall issue for one-third of a league.

In case there is no list on file, &c.

ART. 262. [8] In case there is no list on file in the office of the Adjutant-General, of the names of those who fell with Grant and under Johnson, then and in that case, the applicant shall apply to the Adjutant-General and Commissioner of the General Land Office, who shall sit as a Board of Investigation, as mentioned in the fifth section of this act, and produce the affidavit of two respectable witnesses, sworn to and certified as in the seventh section of this act required and directed, stating that the individual in whose right the claim is made, was actually with said Grant and Johnson; that they were killed by the Mexicans, or that they have never been heard of since they were under the command of Grant or Johnson; and that the fifth section shall apply to applicants under this section so far as it is applicable.

Certificates to issue free of charge.

ART. 263. [9] The acts required to be done by the Adjutant-General and the Commissioner of the General Land Office, shall appertain to the duties of their respective offices; that certificates shall issue free from charge, and patents shall issue on surveys made under such certificates as in other cases, in the name of the party originally entitled to the same.

BOUNTIES.

Ordained and decreed Nov. 24, 1835.

Members of regular army.

ART. 264. [5] Every non-commissioned officer and private of the Regular Army of Texas shall receive, and it is hereby granted to him, his heirs, legal representatives, or assigns, one mile square, or six hundred and forty acres of land in Texas, after he shall have received an honorable discharge, to which he shall be entitled for a faithful service, agreeably to the terms of his enlistment.

Drummer and fifer entitled, &c

ART. 265. [6] [One drummer and one fifer to be enlisted for each company, and be entitled to same bounty land, &c.]

Ordained and decreed Dec. 5, 1835.

Volunteers.

ART. 266. [5] All volunteers, who shall enter the service agreeably to the provisions of this decree, shall be entitled to one mile square, or six hundred and forty acres of land, to be selected out of the public domain of Texas; and all volunteers, who shall become disabled in the service of Texas, and who shall be discharged therefor before the expiration of the term for which they volunteered, in consequence of inability or disability, shall receive the aforesaid one mile square, or six hundred and forty acres of land as a bounty.

Volunteer dies bounty to descend to heirs.

ART. 267. [6] If any volunteer or volunteers shall die in the service of Texas, then, and in that case, it shall be and is hereby declared that their bounty of land shall descend to their heirs and legal representative or representatives, with all the benefits which the said volunteer could have claimed had he been living.

Auxiliary volunteer corps entitled, &c.

ART. 268. [10] All volunteers for three months, in the Auxiliary Volunteer Corps of Texas, shall be entitled to a bounty of three hundred and twenty acres of land after receiving an honorable discharge.

Ordained and decreed Dec. 11, 1835

Same subject.

ART. 269. There shall be, and there is hereby granted to each volunteer in the Army of the People of Texas, his heirs, or legal representative, who may have been or may hereafter be killed in battle, or shall come to his death by sickness, or any accident whatever, in going to or returning from the Volunteer Army of the People of Texas, one mile square, or six hundred and forty acres of land in Texas.

ART. 270. All persons entitled to a bounty by the fifth and sixth sections of an ordinance and decree to raise a Regular Army, passed on November the twenty-fourth, eighteen hundred and thirty-five, shall be entitled to an additional bounty, over and above the bounty already given, of one hundred and sixty acres of land, and twenty-four dollars in money—one-half of said (money) twenty-four dollars, to be paid to each soldier upon being mustered at headquarters of the Regular Army, and the other half at the first quarterly payment thereafter. Same subject.

ART. 271. [5] The volunteers of said division shall enjoy the same emoluments, benefits, and privileges for their services, and be subject to the same rules and regulations heretofore provided for volunteers. Ordained and decreed Jan. 7, 1836. Same subject.

ART. 272. [2] The provisions of the Ordinance granting the lands to volunteers from the United States and elsewhere, be so construed as to extend to all who have rendered service as volunteers in the army of the Republic of Texas. Joint resolution Nov. 24, 1836. Same subject.

ART. 273. [3] All volunteers who have entered the service of the Republic of Texas since the first day of July last, shall be entitled to the same pay and bounties of land as those who entered the service prior to that time. Same subject.

ART. 274. [1] The President be and he is hereby required to raise, with as little delay as possible, a battalion of mounted riflemen, to consist of two hundred and eighty men, for the protection of the frontier, to be officered in like manner as the balance of the army. Act of Dec. 5, 1836. Frontier battalion.

ART. 275. [3] The pay, emoluments, and bounty of said corps shall be the same as that provided for other corps of the army, with this addition, that the sum of fifteen dollars per month be allowed for the furnishing of the horses and arms. Pay of said corps same as, &c.

ART. 276. [1] Each and every mounted rifleman, who has entered the ranging service, and not otherwise provided for, be, and is hereby entitled to twenty-five dollars per month as pay, and the same bounty of land as other volunteers in the field. Act of Dec. 10, 1836. Mounted riflemen.

ART. 277. [2] The pay of officers in the above service shall be as follows: a captain shall be entitled to receive seventy-five dollars per month, a first lieutenant shall receive sixty dollars per month, a second lieutenant, fifty dollars per month, and the orderly sergeant, forty dollars per month; the said officers shall also be entitled to the same bounties of land as officers of the same grade and rank in the volunteer army. Pay of officers.

ART. 278. [3] All officers and soldiers, who have been actually engaged in the ranging service since July 1835, shall be included in this Act, and shall receive pay for the time he is in service. Who included.

ART. 279. [1] A corps of mounted gunmen, consisting of six hundred mounted men, rank and file, shall be raised by voluntary enlistment, for a term of six months, dating from the time of rendezvous, and officered in the following manner, viz.: one colonel, one lieutenant-colonel, one major, ten captains, ten first and second lieutenants; all of whom shall be appointed by the President, by and with the advice and consent of the Senate. Act of June 12, 1837. Corps of mounted gunmen to be raised.

ART. 280. [3] The officers shall receive the same pay as is fixed in the corresponding rank in the ranging service; and the privates twenty-five dollars per month, and officers and men a bounty of land of six hundred and forty acres each. Pay of.

ART. 281. [9] [In cases of dishonorable discharge, all right to pay and bounty land forfeited.] Same subject.

WHEREAS, much difficulty exists in reconciling the various conflicting laws granting bounty lands to the soldiers and officers who have served in the army, and the allowance does not bear an equal proportion in many cases to the services rendered; for remedy whereof— Act of Dec. 4, 1837.

ART. 282. [1] Be it enacted by the Senate and House of Representatives of the Republic of Texas in Congress assembled, That the laws in existence granting bounty lands to those who have served in the army be so amended as to grant to all who have served three months in the army, three hundred and twenty acres of land; to all who have served for six months, six hundred and forty acres; to all who have served for nine months, nine hundred and sixty acres; and to all who have served twelve months or upwards, twelve hundred and eighty acres. Bounty lands to soldiers, &c.

ART. 283. [1] Thomas William Ward, James C. Neill, James Belden, John Thomas, Washington Somers, and all others who have been permanently Act of Dec. 18, 1837.

Persons disabled, &c. disabled by loss of eye, arm or limb, or such other bodily injury as by certificate of the Board of Land Commissioners shows his incapacity for bodily labor, by wounds received in the service of Texas, be, and they are hereby declared to be entitled to one league of land each, as a testimony of the gratitude of this Republic.

Included in class of preference claimants. ART. 284. [2] The lands hereby granted shall be included within that class of claimants to whom six months preference has been given.

Act of Dec. 21, 1837.

Soldiers in the battle of San Jacinto, and other battles, &c. ART. 285. [1] All persons who were actually engaged in the battle of San Jacinto, on the twenty-first day of April, eighteen hundred and thirty-six, and all persons who were wounded on the twentieth of the same month, so as to prevent them from participating in the battle on the twenty-first day of April, eighteen hundred and thirty-six, and all persons who were detailed by special order of the commanding general to guard the baggage at the camp near Harrisburg, be, and they are hereby entitled to six hundred and forty acres of bounty land, on the following conditions, to wit: that each soldier claiming land under the provisions of this act shall produce a certificate to the Secretary of War, signed by the commandant of the company to which said soldier belonged, and countersigned by at least one field officer, accompanied by an affidavit by the person claiming land under the provisions of this act, that his claim is just, true, and original, and that he has never presented a claim of a like nature for liquidation.

Secretary of War to issue warrant. ART. 286. [2] The Secretary of War be authorized and required to issue a land warrant for six hundred and forty acres of bounty land to all persons presenting a certificate as is required in section first of this act.

What warrants and patents shall state. ART. 287. [3] The bounty warrants, and also the patents issued thereon, shall state on the face thereof for what said warrant or patent was granted.

Lands shall not be sold. ART. 288. [4] The lands granted by this act shall not be subject to sale or alienation, mortgage or execution, during the lifetime of the person to whom such warrant or patent shall be granted.

Upon what evidence party entitled. ART. 289. [5] All commissioned officers coming under the provisions of this act, by producing a certificate signed by at least one superior officer, accompanied by an affidavit as is required in first section of this act, shall be entitled to the benefits of this law, on the same conditions as is required in the fourth section of this act.

Soldiers who entered Bexar and who were in other battles. ART. 290 [6] All persons who entered Bexar from the morning of the fifth to the tenth of December, one thousand eight hundred and thirty-five, and who actually took part in the reduction of the same; also, those who were in the action of the nineteenth of March, one thousand eight hundred and thirty-six, under the commands of Colonels Fannin and Ward; also, all those who fell at the Alamo, under the command of Bowie and Travis, shall be entitled to the same quantum of land as specified in this bill given to those engaged in the battle of San Jacinto, subject to the same rules, regulations and restrictions, and entitled to all its benefits: provided, always, that any person who may have participated in both battles shall only receive as a donation one tract or parcel of land, of six hundred and forty acres, and no more.

Heirs of. ART. 291. [7] The legal representatives of those who fell in the storming of Bexar be entitled to select and perfect titles for their benefit, by themselves or agent, to six hundred and forty acres.

Act of May 24, 1838.

Conditions cancelled. ART. 292. [1] The conditions contained in the first section of the act to which this is a supplement, so far as relates to the individuals who were in the action of the 19th March, 1836, under the commands of Colonels Fannin and Ward, and also those who fell at the Alamo under the commands of Bowie and Travis, are hereby cancelled.

Secretary of War to issue warrants. ART. 293. [2] The Secretary of War is hereby authorized and required to issue land warrants agreeably to all the provisions of the aforesaid act, which is not repealed by this act, to the legal representatives, in the name of the heirs of all persons embraced in the first section of this act, upon the production of satisfactory testimony that the persons whom they represent were among those who fell in either of the two actions above named.

Act of Dec. 30, 1840.

Preamble. ART. 294. WHEREAS, it appears that all the Secretaries of War, previous to the appointment of General Johnston, had granted to all soldiers who had served against San Antonio, and were engaged in the storming of that place, in the Fall of one thousand eight hundred and thirty-five, a bounty warrant for three hundred and twenty acres of land; and it also appears that nearly all of said soldiers had obtained their bounty land previous to the appointment of General Johnston, and there now remains but a few who have not obtained their claims, General Johnston and his successor having refused to grant said claims on account of the law not being sufficiently explicit, and it is but just that the few who have not obtained their claims should be relieved; therefore—

Art. 295. [1] All those soldiers who entered Bexar between the fifth and tenth of December, one thousand eight hundred and thirty-five, and actually assisted in the reduction of that place, and remained there until the surrender of General Cos, and honorably discharged from the service, shall be entitled to three hundred and twenty acres of land, the same as though they had served out their time of three months. Land granted to all soldiers who entered Bexar.

Art. 296. Whereas, the soldiers enlisted under an "Act entitled an act to provide for the protection of the northern and western frontier," approved twenty-first December, one thousand eight hundred and thirty-eight, were, under the provisions of the tenth section of said act, entitled to a bounty of one hundred and sixty acres of land, to be surveyed to them contiguous to the posts to which they were respectively attached; and, whereas, by a supplement to the above recited act, approved the fifth February, one thousand eight hundred and forty, said bounty was augmented to two hundred and forty acres, in the event it could not be had contiguous to the posts; and, whereas, the provisions of the above-named acts were not carried into effect, the regiment disbanded, and the soldiers discharged prior to the expiration of their term of service; therefore— Joint Resolution of Dec. 10, 1841.

Art. 297. [1] Be it resolved by the Senate and House of Representatives of the Republic of Texas, in Congress assembled, That the Secretary of War be and he is hereby authorized and required to issue certificates for two hundred and forty acres each, to all soldiers who shall produce honorable discharges, signed by the proper officers. Secretary of War to issue certificates.

Art. 298. [2] The soldiers so receiving certificates are hereby authorized to locate the same upon any unappropriated lands belonging to the Republic at their own expense and in conformity to law: provided, always, said certificates shall only be granted to the original holder, or soldier, his heirs and legatees. May be located, &c.

LAND SCRIP.

Art. 299. [1] The Secretary of the Treasury, under the direction of the President, be and he is hereby authorized to pay out of the first available means which may be at the disposal of this Government, all the debts and lawful demands against this Government, now owned by William Bryan, Esq., of New Orleans, or for which the said Bryan is in any way liable to any individual or individuals, for or on account of this Government. Joint resolution Dec. 6, 1836. Claims against the government in favor of Wm. Bryan.

Art. 300. [2] The President be and he is hereby authorized to place in the hands of said William Bryan, Esq., and authorize him to sell a sufficient quantity of land scrip to pay all the demands named in the foregoing resolution, and that he instruct him to apply the proceeds of the sale of said scrip to that special purpose: provided, that said scrip shall not be sold at a less price than fifty cents per acre; and that the said Bryan be required to file in the office of the Secretary of the Treasury, proper vouchers for all said debts. Authorized to be paid. Price of scrip.

Art. 301. [1] From and after the passage of this Act, that there shall be, and is hereby established, an agency in the city of Mobile, in the State of Alabama, United States of America. Act of Dec. 10, 1836. Agency at Mobile for sale of.

Art. 302. [2] David White, of the city of Mobile, is hereby made the agent of the government of Texas. The said agent be and is hereby fully authorized to dispose of land scrip, at not less than fifty cents per acre; the proceeds of which shall be applied exclusively to the benefit of this government. David White empowered to sell scrip.

Art. 303. [3] The President of this Republic be, and is hereby required to deliver over to the said agent, scrip to the amount of one hundred thousand dollars, in due form; and the said agent shall be responsible to this government for the net proceeds of the sale of all scrip which he may receive; and it shall be his duty to report monthly to the President of this Republic, all his transactions in any manner touching his agency. Amount issued to.

Art. 304. [4] The said agent shall receive as a compensation for his services, five per cent, on all moneys received, and disbursements two and one half per cent. Commission of agent.

Sale to be stopped, when. ART. 305. [5] If, in the opinion of the President of this Republic, our Commissioners should succeed in making a negotiation, or negotiations to a sufficient amount of money to defray the expenditures of this government, then, and in that case, the President of this Republic is authorized and required forthwith to stop the sale of said scrip by said agent.

Joint resolution Dec. 10, 1836. ART. 306. [1] The President be, and he is hereby authorized and empowered to borrow twenty thousand dollars, for the purpose of purchasing ammunition and munitions of war; and that he be authorized to stipulate for such an amount of interest, payable at such time, as he may be best able to contract for; and that the principal shall be redeemed at such time as may be agreed on.

President to raise twenty thousand dollars by sale of. ART. 307. [2] The President is hereby authorized to sell sufficient land scrip to raise the said sum of twenty thousand dollars: provided, that in procuring said twenty thousand dollars, no lands shall be sold for less than fifty cents per acre.

Joint resolution Dec. 10, 1836. Scrip issued to Thomas Toby, at New Orleans, for sale. ART. 308. [1] The President be, and he is hereby authorized and required to sign land scrip to the amount of five hundred thousand acres, and transmit the same to Thomas Toby, of New Orleans, for the purpose of being sold: provided, that said scrip shall not be sold for a less sum than fifty cents an acre; and further provided, that should the bonds of this government, to the amount of five hundred thousand dollars, be previously sold, then and in that case it shall be the duty of the President to recall said scrip, and forbid the further selling of the same.

Proceeds of, how to be applied. ART. 309. [2] The said Toby, with the proceeds arising from the sale of said scrip be, and is hereby authorized and required to fulfill all legal obligations into which he may have entered as agent of this government, on the faith of the authority given him by the President "ad interim," for the selling of land scrip; and that he be authorized and required to pay all legal debts contracted on the faith of the same.

Act of Dec. 3, 1837. Scrip issued to James Erwin, and others. ART. 310. WHEREAS, Stephen F. Austin, Branch T. Archer, and William H. Wharton, as Commissioners of the government and people of Texas, did, on the twentieth day of January, eighteen hundred and thirty-six, contract with James Erwin and others in the city of New Orleans for a loan of fifty thousand dollars, all of which was paid at the time; and whereas, existing circumstances render it impossible for the government to comply strictly with the conditions of the aforesaid contract; and whereas, the holders of the aforesaid loan, have voluntarily expressed a willingness to release the government from conditions that would be unjust and ruinous to the interests of the country; and the Congress of Texas being desirous of executing, in good faith all its obligations: therefore,

Duty of Secretary of Treasury when scrip is surrendered. ART. 311. [1] The Secretary of the Treasury be, and he is hereby directed, upon the surrender of the scrip issued by the Commissioners to the parties to the loan aforesaid, or any of them, to calculate interest at the rate of eight per centum per annum, on the amount the party so surrendering may be entitled to, from the day and date of the loan to the day of surrender; and shall issue to the person or his assignee, land scrip at the rate of fifty cents the acre, in tracts of six hundred and forty acres each; and the said Secretary shall issue scrip to the amount of twenty thousand acres, to be divided and distributed to the parties aforesaid, in the ratio that the amount they respectively hold bears to fifty thousand dollars in tracts of six hundred and forty acres each: provided, that the said scrip shall not be located on land except by its legal subdivisions.

Duty of owner, before receiving. ART. 312. [2] Before the parties or any of them shall be entitled to receive his scrip under the provisions of this Act, he shall file in the office of the Secretary of the Treasury, by himself or a legally authorized agent or attorney, a copy of the original contract, and also file a relinquishment on his part, of all further claim upon the government or the Commissioners growing out of the contract aforesaid, and accept and receive the same scrip in lieu of all liabilities whatever: and the parties who may not now file their relinquishment aforesaid shall have six months to accept of the provisions of this Act and be entitled to all its benefits.

Certain claims to have a preference over scrip. ART. 313. [3] Scrip issued by virtue of this Act, shall not in any manner interfere with the rights or claims of those entitled to lands as citizens of Texas at the day of the declaration of independence, but shall be placed on equal footing with all other existing claims, as to the time and mode of locating the same; and after the first day of October, eighteen hundred and thirty-seven, shall have preference over all claims originating after that time, and shall not be subject after location to a higher rate of taxation than that imposed by law on citizens holding lands of like quality.

ART. 314. [4] The parties holding the scrip, issued under the authority of this Act, may transfer the same, by assignment, and the assignees shall have all the rights and privileges of the original holders: and the lands located shall not be subject to forfeiture for want of cultivation or improvement, and may be held by aliens: they are to be located at the expense of the government, and titles be issued in the same manner and held upon the same terms as if the holders thereof were citizens of the Republic: provided, that no lands granted by this government, shall be located on salt springs, gold or silver mines, copper or lead, or other minerals, or any island of the Republic. Scrip may be transferred.

ART. 315. [5] Any of the holders of the loan shall have the right to surrender their scrip within six months from the passage of this Act and receive from the Secretary of the Treasury, whose duty it shall be to issue the same, a bond from the government for the principal and interest at the rate of twelve and a half per centum per annum, pledging the faith of the government for its redemption, and redeemable at their pleasure. May be surrendered, within what time.

ART. 316. [6] The form of the scrip issued by virtue of this Act, shall be such as expresses in substance the provisions of this Act. Form of scrip.

ART. 317. [6] The President is authorized to sell five hundred thousand acres of land scrip, the proceeds of which shall be paid into the Treasury, to be out only for the redemption of these promissory notes of the government: provided, that this scrip shall be disposed of at not less than fifty cents per acre: and, provided further, that the agents appointed to sell the scrip shall give bond and approved personal security in double the value of the scrip so delivered to him for the faithful discharge of his duty as agent. Act of June 9, 1837. President to sell five hundred thousand acres.

ART. 318. The President be authorized to appoint an agent to proceed to the United States with instructions to receive the unsold land scrip, and to settle with the different agents heretofore appointed by the Government; and that he be also directed to sell any scrip he may receive for cash, at not less than the minimum price, and the proceeds be deposited in bank, subject to the order of the Secretary of the Treasury, except such portion thereof as the agent may deem expedient to expend for provisions, arms, clothing, or ammunition for the use of this Republic. Joint resolution June 9, 1837. Agent to sell, to proceed to United States.

ART. 319. [1] The President be, and he is hereby authorized and required to issue his proclamation forthwith recalling our agent sent to the United States for the sale of land scrip, and forbidding the sale of any more. Act of Dec. 14, 1837. Recal of agent.

ART. 320. [2] The said agent be required forthwith to return to the Secretary of the Treasury all the land scrip in his possession, and should he fail or refuse to do so, four months after the first day of January next, he shall be considered guilty of a high misdemeanor, and on conviction before any court shall be fined in a sum not less than five thousand dollars, nor more than twenty thousand dollars,—which fine shall go to the use of the Republic,—and shall be liable and subject with his securities, to be sued on his bond also. Refusal to obey, Penalty.

ART. 321. [3] All sales of land scrip made by said agents after receipt of the President's proclamation shall be null and void. Sale of, when void.

ART. 322. To fulfil and carry into effect the contract of compromise made on the first day of April, 1836, between the Government *ad interim* of Texas and the stockholders in the first loan negotiated by the Commissioners of Texas in New Orleans, on the 11th day of January, 1836, the President of the Republic be, and he is hereby authorized to issue to the said stockholders, the land scrip as stipulated in said contract of compromise: provided, the said scrip shall not be located until after the first Thursday in August next: and further provided, that no interest shall be allowed on said loan, but that the land hereby authorized to be given, shall be in full payment and liquidation of said loan. Act of May 24, 1838. Scrip issued to stockholders in first loan.

ART. 323. [1] From and after the passage of this act, any individual who shall present to the Secretary of the Treasury any promissory notes, bonds, funded debt, or other liquidated demands against the Republic of Texas, shall be entitled, upon the cancelling of the same, to receive from the Secretary of the Treasury, a certificate of the fact that so much has been deposited and cancelled; upon the presentation of which certificate to the Commissioner of the General Land Office, he shall be authorized and required to issue to the said holder, land scrip to the amount thereof, at the price of two dollars per acre. Act of February 5, 1841. In exchange for promissory notes, &c., of Republic. Suspended by joint resolution of June 25, 1845.

ART. 324. [2] The said land scrip shall be in such form as shall be approved Form of, &c.

by the President, shall be signed by the Commissioner of the General Land Office, and countersigned by the Secretary of the Treasury.

Size of certificates, &c. ART. 325. [3] The said land scrip shall be in quantity not less than six hundred and forty acres, and three hundred and twenty acres; shall be located, surveyed, and patented according to the law now in existence: provided, that said three hundred and twenty acres shall only be issued to actual citizens of the Republic.

Act of January 29, 1842. Scrip issued to George M'Intosh for sale. ART. 326. The President be authorized and requested to place in the hands of George S. M'Intosh, nine thousand six hundred acres of land scrip, which the said M'Intosh is hereby authorized to sell, and use the proceeds, accounting to the Government therefor.

Act of Feb. 11, 1850. Took effect 1st May, 1850. In liquidation of public debt. ART. 327. [1] Any legal holder of any of the liabilities of the late Republic of Texas, that have been audited and reported to the Legislature by the Auditor and Comptroller of the State of Texas, under the provisions of an act to provide for ascertaining the public debt of the late Republic of Texas, approved 20th March, in the year eighteen hundred and forty-eight, may, by surrendering the same to the Commissioner of the General Land Office, receive in lieu therefor land certificates, under the seal of the Land Office, for the same, at the rate of fifty cents per acre, to the satisfaction of his, her, or their claim; and the said Commissioner of the General Land Office is hereby authorized and required to issue land certificates for the same, under the regulations and restrictions hereafter provided in this act.

Persons surrendering, &c., entitled to. ART. 328. [2] Any person or persons surrendering their claims as provided for in the first section of this act, shall be entitled to and receive a certificate for the same: provided, his or her claim shall amount to three hundred and twenty acres; and that no certificate shall issue for a less number of acres than six hundred and forty, where the party's claim amounts to that much; and no certificate shall issue for a less number of acres than twelve hundred and eighty, where the party's claim shall amount to that much; but certificates may issue for any number of acres between the numbers here given, to the satisfaction of the claims exceeding the minimum and falling under the number of acres here given.

Record and report of, to be made. ART. 329. [3] The Commissioner of the General Land Office shall keep a correct record of all land certificates issued by him under the provisions of this act, with the date of said issue, number of the certificate, the amount in acres, and the person to whom issued; and he shall report the same to the Governor every six months; and he shall also deposit in the office of Secretary of State, all claims for which he has issued land certificates every six months, [and] take his receipt for the same; and the claims so filed with the Secretary of State shall, within five days thereafter, be publicly burned in the presence of any three respectable persons, to be selected by the Secretary of State, who shall certify on oath that the said claims, specifying each, were then and there wholly destroyed by fire in their presence.

How surveyed, patented, &c. ART. 330. [4] All land certificates issued under the provisions of this act, shall be located, surveyed and patented according to the laws now in force regulating the same: provided, that said certificates may be transferred by endorsement and delivery, at any time before the same have been located and surveyed.

This act to be published, &c. ART. 331. [5] The Governor shall cause this act to be published in some newspaper printed at the seat of government of this State, and also in some newspaper published at the city of New Orleans, Louisiana, for three successive months immediately after its passage.

Public liabilities not presented, &c., shall cease to draw interest. ART. 332. [6] All liabilities of the late Republic of Texas, whether the same have or have not been presented to the Auditor and Comptroller, under the provisions of the act to provide for ascertaining the debt of the late Republic of Texas, approved March, A. D. 1848, shall cease to draw interest from and after the first day of July, in the year one thousand eight hundred and fifty.

Repealing clause. ART. 333. [7] All laws contrary to the provisions of this act be, and the same are hereby repealed.

PRE-EMPTIONS.

Act of January 22, 1845. ART. 334. [1] All individuals who have settled upon and improved, or who may hereafter settle upon and improve a portion of the vacant public domain which has been neither filed upon, entered, located, nor surveyed, by virtue of some genuine, legal, and valid certificate, or other evidence of title to land previous to such settlement and improvement, shall have the privilege of locating and surveying a tract of land not exceeding three hundred and twenty acres, so as to include said settlement and improvement, in preference to all other claims or claimants; and all files, entries, locations, or surveys made so as to interfere with the preference granted by this act, shall be null and void. Settlers to have 320 acres.

ART. 335. [2] It shall be the duty of all settlers contemplated by this act, who intend to avail themselves of the benefits of its provisions, to have the lands including their improvements covered with a valid certificate, within three years from the passage of this act, or within three years from the commencement of their settlement; and the laws now in force in regard to the surveying and procuring of lands shall be observed, where the same do not conflict with the provisions of this act. Must be covered by certificate within three years.

ART. 336. [3] Any genuine headright certificate, land scrip, bounty warrant, or other genuine evidence of a claim to land, issued by the authority of this Government, may be located on such improvements; and the Commissioner of the General Land Office is hereby authorized and required to issue land certificates to any settler requiring the same, on his paying at the rate of two dollars per acre in the old promissory notes, bonds, funded debt, or other liquidated demands against the Republic of Texas, in accordance with the provisions of an act approved February fifth, eighteen hundred and forty-one, or fifty cents in par funds, per acre: provided, that to actual settlers, as contemplated by this act, certificates or land scrip to the amount of eighty acres may be issued, but not for a less amount. What certificates may be located on.

ART. 337. [4] All sales made of improvements contemplated by this act, previous to survey or patent, except to those who may actually settle upon and occupy said improvements, shall be null and void; and the purchasers of such improvements shall be subject to the same conditions, restrictions, and limitations, as if the original settler had remained in possession. Of sales of improvements before survey, &c.

ART. 338. [5] Nothing herein contained shall be so construed, as to prevent the locations of certificates on such improvements containing more than three hundred and twenty acres: provided, that the preference shall be only construed to apply to the amount of three hundred and twenty acres: and any Surveyor disregarding or violating the provisions of this act, shall, on conviction thereof before the District Court, be fined or imprisoned, at the discretion of the court, and dismissed from office. Where improvements contain more, &c., May be located upon, &c. Penalty for violating this act.

ART. 339. [6] It shall be the duty of the County Surveyors of each and every county in this Republic, to keep a record book to be devoted exclusively to pre-emption claims; and settlers within eight months from the passage of this act, or within eight months from the commencement of such settlement hereafter made, shall cause to be surveyed the amount of land for which they intend to claim pre-emption; and on application being made by such settler, to a Surveyor, to have his land surveyed to include his improvements, he shall not be compelled to furnish the Surveyor with any land certificate, but he shall take an oath, which may be administered to him by said Surveyor, that he believes he is settled upon vacant land, as contemplated in the first section of this act; upon which the survey, not exceeding three hundred and twenty acres, may be made, and the field notes shall be returned, with the aforesaid affidavit of the settler, to the County Surveyor of the county in which the land lies, who shall have the same recorded in said pre-emption book; for which services the said Surveyor and County Surveyor may charge the fees now allowed by law for such services, and no more; provided, that when a proper certificate may be subsequently obtained by the settler, the same may be applied to such survey without running or marking the lines anew. Surveyor to keep a book of pre-emption claims. When survey shall be made.

ART. 340. [7] Should any settler die previous to procuring a patent for the land, including the settlement and improvement, as provided by this Act, the widow (if there be one,) and the heirs, or the heirs alone (if there be no widow,) shall be entitled to the same preference as the deceased would have been, according to the provisions of this Act. When settler dies, who entitled.

ART. 341. [1] All individuals who have settled upon any of the public domain of this State, and have had the same surveyed prior to the first day of January, eighteen hundred and fifty-one, in accordance with the provisions of "an act," passed on the twenty-second day of January, eighteen hundred and forty-five, "granting to settlers on the public domain, pre-emption privileges," are hereby authorized and empowered, to have, hold and enjoy the same until Act of Feb. 10, 1852. Time extended to settlers to cover land by certificate.

the first day of January, eighteen hundred and fifty-four, without having their land covered by a certificate prior to that time.

Privileges forfeited on what condition. ART. 342. [2] Should any pre-emption claimant or claimants fail to have the land he, she or they may be entitled to, covered by a valid land certificate, land scrip, or bounty warrant, or other genuine evidence of a claim to land, by the said first day of January, eighteen hundred and fifty-four, said claimant or claimants shall forfeit and lose all the rights and privileges granted by this act, and by the act passed January the twenty-second, eighteen hundred and forty-five, "granting settlers on public domain pre-emption privileges."

Act of Feb. 7, 1853. ART. 343. [1] The provisions of the above recited act, [act of January 22d, 1845,] be so modified as to read as follows, to wit:

320 acres granted. That each and every settler who have availed themselves of the provisions of said law, upon any of the public domain of the State, shall be entitled, not to exceed three hundred and twenty acres of land, upon the conditions and restrictions hereinafter set forth.

On what conditions. ART. 344. [2] To entitle any settler to a patent not to exceed three hundred and twenty acres of land, he must produce a certificate from the clerk of the County Court wherein he resides, that he or his assigns has resided upon and cultivated the same for the space of three years, and complied fully with the provisions of an act to which this is a supplement.

Must pay fees and $20 for 320 acres. ART. 345. [3] Each and every settler or applicant, at the time he applies for a patent, not to exceed three hundred and twenty acres, shall pay to the Commissioner of the General Land office the usual fees, and additional sum of twenty dollars for the use and benefit of the State, for every patent thus issued.

Fees and $10 for less quantity. ART. 346. [4] Each and every patent issued under the provisions of this act, for any less number than three hundred and twenty acres, shall pay the usual fees, and ten dollars for each and every patent so issued.

Proof to entitle party to certificate. ART. 347. [5] To entitle the party to a certificate from the County Clerk of the County Court, he must prove by two respectable citizens, known to the County Clerk, that he has fully complied with the provisions of this act.

Repealing clause. ART. 348. [6] All laws and parts of laws that conflict with the provisions of this act, be and the same are hereby repealed.

Act of Jan. 7, 1854. ART. 349. [1] Nothing in the act passed tenth day of February, 1852, entitled "an act concerning surveys of land," shall be so construed as to

The act of Feb. 10, 1852, not to affect pre emption surveys on or to Jan. 1, 1851. embrace the field notes of surveys made prior to the first day of January, 1851, for pre-emption claimants, in virtue of an act passed on the twenty-second day of January, 1845, "granting to settlers on the public domain pre-emption privileges;" but the Commissioner of the General Land Office shall issue patents on the same in conformity to law; provided, that the field notes are returned by or before the first day of January, eighteen hundred and fifty-five.

Act of Feb. 12, 1854. Repealed Aug. 26, 1856. ART. 350. [1] All individuals who have settled upon and improved, or may hereafter settle upon and improve a portion of the vacant public domain, which has been neither filed upon, entered, located or surveyed by virtue of some genuine, legal and valid certificates or other evidence of title to land, previous to such settlement and improvement, shall have the privilege of locating and

Pre-emption to 160 acres granted. appropriating a tract of such vacant land not exceeding one hundred and sixty acres, so as to include said settlement or improvement, in preference to all other claims or claimants, and all files, entries, locations or surveys made so as to interfere with the preference granted by this act shall be null and void.

Duty of county and district surveyors in relation to. ART. 351. [2] It shall be the duty of the county and district surveyors of each and every county and district, to keep a record book to be devoted exclusively to pre-emption claims, and such settlers shall each, within eight months from the passage of this act, or within eight months from the commencement of any such settlement, which may hereafter be made, cause to be surveyed the amount of land for which said settler intends to claim pre-emption privileges. And on application being made by such settler to a surveyor to have his or her said land surveyed, to include his or her improvements, he or she shall not be required to furnish the surveyor with any land certificate or other claim against the government for land, but he or she shall make an affidavit, which may be administered by such surveyor, that he or she believes that he or she has settled upon vacant land, as contemplated in the first section of this act; upon which the survey for not exceeding one hundred and sixty acres may be made, and the field notes thereof shall be returned to the county or district surveyor of the district or county in which the land lies, who shall record the same together with the said affidavit of the settler in his pre-emption book, for which services the said surveyors may charge the fees now allowed by law for such services and no more.

ART. 352. [3] Each and every such settler shall prove before the Chief Justice of the County Court of the county in which he or she resides, by the testimony of two respectable citizens of the same county, known to said Chief Justice, that he or she is bona fide settled upon vacant land, and that he or she has resided upon and cultivated the same for the space of three years next preceding the time of making such proof, and that he or she was a resident of the State of Texas at the time of the passage of this act, and the said Chief Justice shall, after recording in a book to be kept by him for that purpose, the application of such settler, the proof taken in support of the same and the names of the witnesses, shall deliver to such settler a certificate under the seal of his office, upon receiving a fee of two dollars therefor. Proof to be made by pre-emptor.

ART. 353. [4] Should any such settler die previous to procuring a patent for the land, including his or her settlement and improvement as provided by this act, his or her heir or heirs shall be entitled to the same preference and privileges as the deceased would have been according to the provisions of this act. That each and every such settler, upon presenting to the Commissioner of the General Land Office the field notes of his or her survey, together with a duly authenticated copy from the record of the county or district surveyor of his or her said affidavit, and also his or her certificate, made in accordance with the third section of this act, shall be entitled upon paying to said Commissioner the usual patent fee and no more, to a patent upon and for his or her said survey of land: provided the same does not exceed one hundred and sixty acres. Death of settler heirs entitled. Patent to issue, when.

ART. 354. [5] An act approved January twenty-second, A. D. eighteen hundred and forty-five, entitled an act granting to settlers on vacant public domain pre-emption privileges, and an act approved February seventh, A. D. eighteen hundred and fifty-three, entitled an act supplementary to an act granting to settlers on public domain pre-emption privileges, be and the same are hereby repealed, saving to all persons who have settled on the public domain as pre-emptioners, all rights which have accrued to them under the provisions of said acts, and allowing to all such pre-emptioners, who have not obtained patents for their lands, the option of perfecting their titles thereto, either according to the requirements of said acts, or according to the provisions of this act: provided, that the provisions of this act shall not extend to any person who did not emigrate to the State prior to the passage of this act. Act of Jan. 22, 1845, and act of Feb. 7, 1845, repealed, saving, &c.

ART. 355. [6] All land which may be settled upon under the provisions of this act, shall be liable for the State and county taxes from the time of making such survey, and no patent shall issue thereon, until all such taxes shall have been paid. And no individual shall be entitled or allowed to appropriate or secure more than one tract or survey of land under the provisions of this act. Lands liable for taxes, &c.

ART. 356. [7] The provisions of this act shall not be so construed as to grant a pre-emption right to any land which by law is now reserved from location or entry: provided, that all those who have settled upon the public domain since the seventh day of February, eighteen hundred and fifty-three, and previous to the passage of this act, shall be permitted to perfect their titles to three hundred and twenty acres of land, according to the provisions of an act supplementary to an act granting to settlers on public domain pre-emption privileges, approved February seventh, eighteen hundred and fifty-three. Lands reserved not liable to pre-emption, provided, &c.

Act of Jan'y 26, 1856.

ART. 357. [1] All persons who settled as pre-emptors within the limits of the colony granted to W. S. Peters and others prior to the twenty-first day of December, 1853, shall be entitled to the amount of land granted to pre-emption settlers by the law in force at the date of their said settlement by complying with all the provisions of the same: provided, that when the lands have been surveyed by any legally authorized surveyor, it shall not be necessary to have the same re-surveyed: and provided further, that in all cases of conflict of title, whether by location or pre-emption, the oldest genuine claim shall have the preference. Settlers in Peter's colony entitled.

Act of Aug, 15 1856.

ART. 358. [1] All persons who have heretofore settled within the limits of Peter's colony, as pre-emptionists, and have complied with the requirements of the laws in force at the time of their settlement, shall be as fully entitled to the benefits of the pre-emption laws under which they made their settlements as pre-emptionists in any part of the State, any reservation for colonial purposes to the contrary notwithstanding: provided, such pre-emption settlements do not conflict with any legal locations or surveys previously made. Same subject.

ART. 359. [2] All pre-emptionists who failed to have their land surveyed

Time extended for surveys. within eight months after their settlement, shall have eight months further time to do so; and twelve months after the passage of this act, in which to return the same to the General Land Office. And where no field notes of a survey were made out, a certified copy of the surveyor's record of survey shall be sufficient in lieu of such field notes.

First and sec'd sections apply to settlers outside of Peter's colony. ART. 360. [3] Sections one and two of this act shall apply to pre-emptors outside of Peter's colony, as well as to those within it: provided, that this act shall not be construed to confer any rights or grant any relief to those persons who have settled as pre-emptors within the Pacific Railroad Reservation, since twenty-first day of December, eighteen hundred and fifty-three, whether they have settled within or without Peter's colony.

Act of Aug. 30. 1856. WHEREAS, the book of records of pre-emption claims for the Houston Land District, including the counties of Houston, Trinity, and part of the county of Henderson, has been lost or destroyed, by which it is placed out of the power of many bona fide pre-emption settlers within said district to obtain their patents; therefore,

Settl'rs in Houston Land Dist. SECTION 1. Be it enacted by the Legislature of the State of Texas, That all persons who settled upon the public domain within said district as a pre-emptor, and had his land surveyed by the surveyor of said district, may make oath before some officer having a seal; that the land he claims as a pre-emptor was actually surveyed by a surveyor of said district, together with the date of said survey as near as he can in accordance with the laws in force, at the date thereof, and prove the same facts by one or more witnesses, and may have his said claim re-surveyed.

Survey to relate back. ART. 362. [2] Said re-survey shall relate back to the date of said original survey and pre-emption location.

When Com'r shall issue patent. ART. 363. [3] The Commissioner of the General Land Office shall issue patents to said claimants for the amount of land they may be entitled to, upon the applicant making the proof hereinbefore required in addition to the proof now required by law to be made.

Death of settler, heir to make proof. ART. 364. [4] In case the original settler may be dead, his heirs or legal representatives may make the proof herein required of the settlement and survey.

Time to return field notes extended. ART. 365. [5] Said pre-emption settlers shall have the further time of eight months from the passage of this act, to return their field notes to the General Land Office, and shall in all respects be entitled to the benefits of the pre-emption laws under which they settled, and also those in force in this State, provided that nothing in this act shall be so construed as to legalize the settlement of surveys or patents within the reserve known as the Mississippi and Pacific Railroad reserve, made after the twenty-first of December, eighteen hundred and fifty-three.

Act of Feb. 10, 1858. Time to return field notes extended to Jan'y 1, 1859. ART. 366. [1] All pre-emption settlers and their assignees who have succeeded the original settlers in continued occupancy under any of said acts, who would be entitled to their pre-emption claims by virtue of the settlement and improvement thereof, under any or all of the following acts, to-wit: The act of the 22d January, 1845; the act of the 7th February, 1853; and the act of the 13th February, 1854: provided, they had returned their field notes for patent within the time prescribed by law, shall have until the first day of January, 1859, to return for patent to the Commissioner of the General Land Office, the field notes of their surveys. All of said settlers and their assignees who would have been entitled to their pre-emption under said acts, provided they had caused their land to be surveyed within the time prescribed by law; and all of those who having caused their lands to be surveyed within the time prescribed, failed through the neglect of the surveyor, or from any other cause whatever, to have their field notes returned and recorded in the surveyor's

Same time to perfect, &c., certain surveys. office of the county in which their land is located, shall have the same time to cause to be surveyed or re-surveyed, as the case may be, their pre-emption claims, and to return their field notes for patent, to the Commissioner of the General Land Office: provided, however, that said settlers and their assignees have complied in all other respects with the law under which they may claim:

Failure to comply, claim forfeited. and provided further, that the land so claimed remains unlocated by virtue of any genuine land claim against the State: and provided further, that if said settlers shall fail to comply with this act, within the time prescribed, their claims shall be forfeited, and their lands subjected to location as other public domain.

ART. 367. [2] All those actual settlers or their assigns, who are required by an act, passed August 26th, 1856, for location, settlement and survey of the

Pacific Railroad Reservation, and an act supplemental thereto, passed for the relief of said actual settlers by the 7th Legislature, to pay fifty cents per acre, shall have until the first day of January, 1859, to have their surveys made and field notes returned to the General Land Office. In Pacific Railroad survey, time extended to January 1, 1859.

ART. 368. [3] Occupation of the premises up to the time of issuing the certificate by the clerk of the County Court or Chief Justice of the county, as provided for in said acts, shall not be necessary to entitle said settlers or their assignees to said certificates: provided, that said settlers and their assignees shall be required to prove in accordance with the law under which they may claim, that they resided upon and improved their lands, in accordance with the law under which they settled, for three consecutive years: and provided further, that the widows and children of settlers or their assignees, who died upon their pre-emption, shall be entitled to the benefits of this act by complying with the provisions thereof. Occupation of premises, &c.

ART. 369. [4] It shall be the duty of the Commissioner of the General Land Office to issue patents upon all field notes returned in accordance with the provisions of this act. Patents to issue

ART. 370. [5] All laws and parts of laws, conflicting with the provisions of this act, are hereby repealed. Repealing sec'n.

COLONIES.

ART. 371. [4] The President of the Republic be, and he is hereby authorized to make a contract with W. S. Peters, Daniel S. Carroll, Alexander M'Red, Rowland Gibson, Robert Espie, William H. Oldmixon, Daniel Spillman, Robert Hume, John Salmon, W. Byrne, Henry Richards, Robert D. Stringer, W. C. Peters, John C. Bansamen, John Peters, William Scott, Phineas J. Johnson, H. S. Peters, Timothy Cray, and Samuel Browning, collectively, for the purpose of colonizing and settling a portion of the vacant and unappropriated lands of the Republic, on the following conditions, to wit: the said contractors, on their part, agree to introduce a number of families, to be specified in the contract, within three years from the date of the contract: provided, however, they shall commence the settlement within one year from the date of said contract. President authorized to contract with Peters and others.

ART. 372. [5] The said contract shall be drawn up by the Secretary of State, setting forth such regulations and stipulations as shall not be contrary to the general principles of this law and the Constitution; which contract shall be signed by the President and the party or parties, and attested by the Secretary of State, who will also preserve a copy in his department. Contract to be drawn by Secretary of State—Stipulations, &c.

ART. 373. [6] The President shall designate certain boundaries, to be above the limits of the present settlements, within which the emigrants under the contract must reside: provided, however, that all legal grants and surveys that may have been located within the boundaries so designated previously to the date of said contract, shall be respected; and any locations or surveys made by the contractors or their emigrants on such grants and surveys, shall be null and void. President to designate boundaries.

ART. 374. [7] Not more than one section of six hundred and forty acres of land, to be located in a square, shall be given to any family comprehended in said contract; nor more than three hundred and twenty acres to a single man over the age of seventeen years. Six hundred and forty acres to heads of families—320 to single men over 17 years of age.

ART. 375. [8] No individual contract made between any contractor and the families or single persons which he may introduce, for a portion of the land to which respectively they may be entitled, by way of recompense for passage, expense of transportation, removal or otherwise, shall be binding, if such contract embrace more than one half of the land which he, she, or they, may be entitled to under this law; nor shall any contract act as a lien on any larger portion of such land; nor shall any emigrant be entitled to any land, or receive a title for such land until such person or persons shall have built a good and comfortable cabin upon it, and shall keep in cultivation, and under good fence, at least fifteen acres on the tract which he may have received. Contracter not to stipulate with colonists for more than half their land.

ART. 376. [9] All the expenses attending the selection of the land, surveying, title, and other fees, shall be paid by the contractor to the persons respectively authorized to receive them: provided, however, that this provision Expenses of selection and survey.

shall not release the colonist from the obligation of remunerating the contractor in the amount of all such fees, so soon as it can be done, without a sale of their land; and, further, the President may donate to every settlement of one hundred families, made under the provisions of this act, one section of six hundred and forty acres of land, to aid and assist the settlement in the erection of a building for religious public worship.

Sections reserved for religious purposes. ART. 377. [10] The President may allow the contractors a compensation for their services, and in recompense of their labor and expense attendant on the introduction and settlement of the families introduced by him, ten sections for every hundred families; and in the same ratio of half sections for every hundred single men introduced and settled; it being understood that no fractional number less than one hundred, will be allowed any premium.

Premium lands, &c. ART. 378. [11 The premium lands must be selected from the vacant lands within the territorial limits defined in the contract; and, further, all fees incidental to the issue of patents for lands acquired under the provisions of this law, shall be paid to the Commissioner of the General Land Office, for the use and benefit of the Public Treasury.

Colonist shall be entitled. ART. 379. [12] A failure on the part of the contractors, and a forfeiture of their contract, shall not be prejudicial to the rights of such families and single persons as they may introduce; who shall be entitled to their respective quotas of land, agreeable to the provisions of this law.

Time in which families shall be introduced. ART. 380. [13] The contractors shall be required to have one-third of the whole number of the families and single persons for which they contract, within the limits of the Republic before the expiration of one year from the date of the contract, under the penalty of a forfeiture of the same; and it shall be the duty of the Secretary of State forthwith, after the expiration of such term, and failure on the part of the contractors to comply with this provision, to publish and declare said forfeiture; unless the President, for good and sufficient reasons, shall extend the term six months, which he can do; and all substitutions of families living within the limits of the Republic, by the contractors, shall not entitle them to any premium for such families, nor shall it operate in favor of them, for the number of families which they are bound to introduce.

Joint resolution Jan. 16, 1843. Terms and conditions and modifications of new contracts. ART. 381. WHEREAS, by an act passed by the Congress of Texas, entitled, "An act granting land to emigrants," and bearing date the fourth day of February, 1841, a grant was made to Daniel Joseph Carroll, Henry J. Peters and others, their associates, therein named, for the introduction and settlement of emigrants within the territory of this Republic, and upon the terms and conditions therein provided; and, whereas, by said act, the President of this Republic was authorized to make a contract with said Daniel J. Carroll, Henry J. Peters, and their associates aforesaid, collectively, in conformity with the provisions of the same; and, whereas, in pursuance of such authority, the President did make a contract with the aforesaid grantees, which was duly executed in their behalf, by their attorney, Samuel Browning, and which bears date the thirtieth day of August, 1841; and, whereas, the President did make a further contract with the same parties, which bears date the twentieth day of November, 1841; and, whereas, the President did make a yet further contract with the same parties, through their attorney, Horace Burnham, which bears date the twenty-sixth day of July, 1842, said last two contracts being supplementary to, and making one with the said first contract; and, whereas, it is deemed expedient to modify some of the provisions of said act and contracts, and to extend some of the privileges therein granted; now, therefore—

Resolved by the Senate and House of Representatives of the Republic of Texas in Congress assembled, That the President be, and he is hereby authorized and required to make such modification of the aforesaid contracts, or such further contract or contracts, with the grantees named in the aforesaid act, or with their assigns or legal representatives, as shall be deemed by him for the benefit of this Republic, and as shall not be inconsistent with the provisions of the said act:

Provided, however, that he shall have full power and authority to extend the time to the grantees named in the aforesaid act, or to their assigns or legal representatives, for the introduction and settlement of emigrants in this Republic, to a period not exceeding five years from the first day of July next; and that he shall be authorized to prescribe the limits within which the grantees or their assigns or legal representatives shall be permitted to introduce and settle any number of families, not exceeding ten thousand, within the whole time limited; that he shall be authorized to make the title and conveyance of each section of six hundred and forty acres of land which has been or shall be acquired under any contract made or to be made, by the President of this Republic, with the grantees or their assigns, or legal representatives, to the said grantees or their assigns, or legal representatives direct: provided, that said grantees, their assigns or legal representatives, shall survey the land assigned to them, as provided in the act aforesaid; and shall be required to settle or receive such lots only as are of fair quality for agricultural purposes, and not too far situated in the interior of a prairie for such purposes; and whenever they shall have completed the surveys of any number of sections, and built a corresponding number of small comfortable houses, or cabins of logs or other materials, thereon, and placed families therein, they shall receive a title from this government to one section of six hundred and forty acres for each family so introduced and settled; and shall be required to immediately convey to the legal representative of said family, not less than one hundred and sixty, nor more than six hundred and forty acres of said land; conditioned that said family shall remain upon said land so conveyed, and enclose with fence and cultivate fifteen acres, for at least three years; and in default thereof, shall forfeit the same to the Republic:

Provided, further, that in the contract to be made by the President of this Republic with the said grantees, or with their assigns, or legal representatives, they shall be required to settle each year, within the territory prescribed, or to be prescribed to them, at least two hundred and fifty families, reckoning from and after the first day of July next, and including the families which shall then have been settled on the tract prescribed; and in default of introducing and settling such number of families, their contract shall be forfeited:

Provided, however, that they shall be allowed to introduce and settle any number of families, not exceeding ten thousand in all, on the same terms and conditions; and,

Provided, further, that they shall be permitted to settle all the sections within any limits prescribed, or to be prescribed, and not located previous to the time of defining such limits; and that for every alternate section of six hundred and forty acres which shall be conveyed to them, they shall pay into the treasury of this Republic twelve dollars in specie, on receiving the title from the government; and,

Provided, further, that in case of forfeiture, the party shall only be affected prospectively, anything in the aforesaid act, or contracts, to the contrary notwithstanding:

Provided, further, that the Cherokee lands shall be exempt from the provisions of this act.

REGISTRATION.

Act of Dec. 20, 1836.

County Clerks shall record all deeds, &c., provided.

ART. 382. [35] The Clerks of the County Courts shall be the recorders for their respective counties; and it shall be their duty to record all deeds, conveyances, mortgages, and other liens, and all other instruments of writing required by law to be recorded in their offices, which are presented to them: provided one of the witnesses, of the number required by law, shall swear to the signature of the signer, or he himself shall acknowledge the same; which shall be certified by the Recorder, and form part of the record: and all deeds, conveyances, mortgages, and other liens shall be recorded in the county where the property is situated.

Claims proven and recorded.

ART. 383. [37] Any person who owns or claims land of any description, by deed, lien, or any other color of title, shall, within twelve months from the first day of April next, have the same proven in open court, and recorded in the office of the Clerk of the County Court in which said land is situated; but if a tract of land lies on the county line, the title may be recorded in the county in which part of said land lies.

All titles, or color of, must be proven by two witnesses. ART. 384. [38] All titles, liens, mortgages, or other color of title, before they can be admitted upon record, must be proven by at least two subscribing witnesses, if living in the county, and if not so living in the county, then the hand-writing shall be proven either before some county Judge, or before the Clerk of the County Court in whose office such record is proposed to be made; and in all cases the certificate of any county Judge, that the said witness appeared before him and acknowledged his signature, or that the hand-writing of the same was duly proven, shall be sufficient evidence to authorize the Clerk of the County Court to enter such title, lien, mortgage, or other color of title, upon record; and the said Clerk, for recording the same, shall be entitled to charge and receive the sum of twenty cents for every hundred words.

Proof of, sufficient evidence to authorize, &c.

Rights of third parties must be proven. ART. 385. [40] No deed, conveyance, lien, or other instrument of writing, shall take effect as regards the interests and rights of third parties, until the same shall have been duly proven and presented to the court, as required by this act, for the recording of land titles: and it shall be the duty of the Clerk to note particularly the time when such deed, conveyance, lien, or other instrument is presented, and to record them in the order in which they are presented.

Clerk note time when, &c.

Act of January 19, 1839.

Duty of County Clerks to record, &c. ART. 386. [1] It shall be the duty of the Clerks of the County Courts to record all deeds, conveyances, mortgages, and other liens affecting the titles to land and immovable property situated within the same, which shall be presented to them for record: provided, one of the subscribing witnesses shall swear to the signature of signer, or he himself shall acknowledge the same; which proof or acknowledgment shall be made either before some County Court or Chief Justice of the same, or before the Clerk in whose office such instrument is proposed to be recorded, a certificate of which shall be made upon such instrument by the proper officer, and become a part of the record: and all laws contrary to or conflicting with this act be, and the same are hereby repealed, so far as they conflict with, or are contrary to, the same.

Act of February 5, 1840.

Clerk shall admit to record any conveyance, &c. ART. 387. [5] The Clerks of the several County Courts of this Republic, and their deputies, shall be, and they are hereby authorized and required to admit to record, at any time, in the form required by this act, any conveyance, either on the acknowledgment of the party or parties, or the proof, on oath, of such acknowledgment by the legal number of witnesses thereto made, in the offices of the respective Clerks; or upon the certificate of some District Judge or Chief Justice, or Notary Public of a county, with the seal of his office thereunto annexed, that such acknowledgement was made, or the execution of the instrument proven as required above; and any conveyance so recorded, shall have the same legal validity, in all respects, as if it were proven in open court.

Deed admitted to record upon certificate of justices of the peace. ART. 388 [6] Any deed may in like manner be admitted to record upon the certificate, under seal, of any two Justices of the Peace for any county in this Republic, annexed to such deeds, and to the following effect, to wit: "Republic of Texas, County of ———, We, A. B. and C. D., Justices of the Peace in the county aforesaid, do hereby certify that E. F., a party, (or E. G. and G. M., &c., parties,) to a certain deed bearing date on the ——— day of ———, and hereto annexed, personally appeared before us, in our county aforesaid, and acknowledged the same to be his (or their) act and deed, and desired us to certify the said acknowledgment to the Clerk of the county of ———, in order that the said deed may be recorded. Given under our hands and seals this ——— day of ———.

A. B. [L. S.]
C. D. [L. S.]

WILLS.

Act of Dec. 18, 1837. Repealed July 24, 1856. See art. 2130.

ART. 389. [1] Legitimate descendants alone shall hereafter be considered forced heirs: and all persons having no legitimate descendants are hereby authorized to dispose by will or otherwise of their estate; any law heretofore existing to the contrary notwithstanding.

Act of Jan. 28 1840.

ART. 390. [13] No father or mother shall, by last will and testament, disinherit his or her child or children for any cause except for personal violence committed by such child or children on the testator or testatrix, at any time after such child or children shall have arrived at the age of sixteen years, or for the attempt of such child or children, at any time after arriving at said age, to slander or defame the said testator or testatrix, by imputing to them or either of them, offences punishable by law, or ascribing to them, or either of them acts calculated to bring them, or either of them, into disrepute and disgrace in the community; and if any father or mother shall, by last will and testament, disinherit his or her child or children for either of said causes, such cause shall be assigned in said last will and testament, as the reason for such disinherison; and if said child or children should afterward, and within four years after said will is admitted to probate, contend for his, her, or their rights to the estate, by denying the existence of said cause, it shall be incumbent upon the person or persons taking said estate, to the exclusion of such child or children, to prove that such cause did exist during the lifetime of said testator or testatrix; otherwise, said last will and testament shall be declared void, as to such child or children, and they shall be as capable of inheriting as though no such will and testament had been made. Disinherison, when lawful.

ART. 391. [15] This Act shall not be so construed as to prevent any parent from the free disposition of one-fourth of his or her property, by last will and testament, or by donation in last sickness. One-fourth of estate may be disposed of, when.

ART. 392. [45] Any father or surviving mother, may by deed or last will and testament, (either of them being executed in the presence of two creditable witnesses) grant or devise the custody of a minor child which had never been married, although it be not born, during any part of the infancy of such child, to whomsoever he or she will; and such grant or devise shall give the grantee or devisee full power over the person of a child, and authorize him by action to recover the child with damages, for the wrongful taking of him or her, for his or her use; and for the same use to undertake the care and management, and receive the profits of the ward's estate, real and personal; and prosecute and maintain all necessary action and suits concerning the same. Act of Feb. 5, 1840. Repealed May 11, 1846. May appoint guardians for minor children.

TAX SALES AND TAX TITLES.

ART. 393. [3] On the failure of any person or persons to attend and punctually pay the amount of taxes that may be due the Government, then and in that case the Sheriff shall proceed and take an execution (to be issued by any Justice of the Peace for said county,) against the goods and property of said delinquent or delinquents, and proceed to sell so much of the same as will satisfy debts and costs. Act of Dec. 21, 1837. Sale on failure to pay taxes.

ART. 394. [4] It shall be the duty of the several Clerks and Sheriffs of the several counties to report to the Secretary of the Treasury on or before the first day of September in each year, and pay over the amount of public moneys that may have come into their hands, into the Treasury of the Republic. Clerks and Sheriffs shall report.

ART. 395. [5] The several Clerks and Sheriffs of the several counties shall be allowed five per cent. on all moneys that may be so collected or received by them, and that each and every applicant for license for retailing, &c., shall pay to the Clerk as his fee the sum of one dollar. Clerks and Sheriffs entitled to, &c.

Act of May 24, 1838. Sale of lands. May be redeemed.

ART. 396. [11] In all cases where there is no personal property to be found, whereon to distrain for taxes on lands and lots, the Sheriff shall report all such lands and lots to the County Court, whose duty it shall be to enter up judgment against the same, and the owners thereof, for the amount of taxes, costs, and charges thereon; and an order of sale shall issue to the Sheriff, requiring him to sell the same; and the return of the Sheriff on such order shall be good in law, as all other sales made on a fieri facias; all lands and lots so sold may be redeemed by the original owner, within twelve months from the day of sale by paying fifty per cent. on the amount.

Act of Jan. 29, 1839. Non payment of taxes--execution—sale—redemption.

ART. 397. [4] On the failure of any person or persons to pay punctually the taxes due the Government, the Sheriff shall forthwith take out an execution (to be issued by any Justice of the Peace, if the amount of tax due, be within his jurisdiction; and if it be not, by the Clerk of the District Court,) against the property of the delinquent or delinquents, and shall sell for cash to the highest bidder at public auction, after giving public notice for thirty days, so much of such goods or property as will pay the amount of the taxes due, and all costs; and any real estate which shall be sold under a tax-execution, may be redeemed by the original owner at any time within two years from the day of sale, by paying to the purchaser double the sum for which it was sold under such execution.

Act of Jan. 16, 1840. Mode of sales under.

ART. 398. [12] During the month of November, the Sheriff of each and every county throughout this Republic, shall make his returns to the Secretary of the Treasury, and pay over to him the amount of moneys which he may have collected for taxes due to the Republic, under the provisions of this law; and all those who shall not have paid their quota of taxes to the Sheriff of the respective county, when [where ?] it may be due, by the time in which, under this section, it is made the duty of the Sheriff to make returns to the Secretary of the Treasury, shall be considered as delinquents; and a list of them shall be made out, expressing names and amount of taxes due by each, from the list in possession of the Sheriff (which he received from the Assessor,) by an officer of the Treasury Department, under the direction of the head of that Department, and to which shall be affixed a certificate of the Secretary for its correctness, and shall then be handed to the respective Sheriff, (and a copy of it shall be published by order of the Department) whose duty it shall be, within one month after he shall have received it from the Department, to present and deliver it to the Clerk of the District Court; and it is hereby made the duty of said Clerk, on receiving such list of delinquents, to issue execution against the property of such delinquents, when the amount of tax due requires the intervention of that court; and such execution shall be handed to the Sheriff, who shall levy upon the property assessed or on any other property belonging to such delinquent, for double the amount of the tax and costs; from the list of delinquents furnished by the Treasury Department, the Sheriff shall draw a list of all those delinquents, from whom the amount of tax due, comes within the jurisdiction or cognizance of a Justice of the Peace, and deliver the same to that officer, who, upon receiving it shall immediately issue execution against the property of such delinquents, and hand the same over to the Sheriff, who shall levy, as provided for under the executions to be issued by the District Courts, for double the amount of tax and costs; and if the property levied upon, under the provisions of this section, be real estate, it shall be advertised in a public newspaper for forty days previous to the day of sale; should execution be levied on personal property, it shall be advertised at three or more public places in the county, for twenty days previous to the day of sale, and then sold for the amount of double taxes and costs; and if the property seized and sold be real estate, it may be redeemed at any time within two years, on payment being made of double the amount of purchase-money, subsequent tax paid, and interest thereon at twenty per cent. per annum as damages and penalty.

Where person owing tax moves out of county.

ART. 399. [23] If any person or persons liable to pay taxes, may after being assessed, remove from the county in which he, she or they may have been so assessed, not having paid their taxes, the Sheriff as Tax Collector of the county in which he, she or they may have been so assessed, is hereby required to send certified under his hand, a transcript from his tax list, to the Collector of the county where such delinquent or delinquents may be; and the Sheriff of such last mentioned county, as Tax Collector, is authorized upon such transcript, to proceed to make the money by distress and sale as provided in other cases, and immediately transmit the amount so made, to the Sheriff who sent the said transcript; for which services, the Sheriff, making the said money, shall receive five per centum as a compensation for his services.

ART. 400. [24] The taxes imposed by virtue of this Act, shall be preferred to all incumbrances and securities whatever; and if any person between the time of rendering a list of his taxable property to the Assessor and the time at which the Sheriff as Collector, is authorized to levy or make distress, shall be about to remove without the limits of his county, the Sheriff upon receiving information thereof, shall immediately make distress of the goods and chattels of the person about to remove, sufficient to satisfy the amount of taxes that he may owe, and sell the same, upon giving notice as hereinbefore directed; and all taxes assessed on any person or persons under this Act, shall be a lien upon his real property, lying within the county in which the assessment was made, until the taxes be paid. *When about to be removed.*

ART. 401. [25] Every Sheriff, who as Tax Collector under this Act, shall sell any real estate, to satisfy any tax imposed by this law, shall make and execute to the purchaser or purchasers thereof, a deed of conveyance immediately; which deed shall be good and effectual, both in law and equity; and in every such deed the Sheriff, as Collector, making the same, shall recite that the real estate thereby conveyed was sold for taxes, and the consideration; but no deed given in manner aforesaid, shall be recorded until the expiration of two years from the date thereof; but it may nevertheless, be proved; and if the person whose land has been sold, or his legal representative, agent or attorney, shall within the two years, tender to the purchaser, or his legal heirs, representative, or agent, and if such person be absent from the Republic, then to the Sheriff who sold the same, or to his successor in office, double the amount of purchase-money, (or the amount of consideration,) and the amount which the purchaser may have paid for taxes on such real estate, and twenty per centum per annum as damages, penalty and interest thereon from the date of such payment until such tender be made, the deed given for such real estate thus sold and conveyed, shall be made void and be given up. *Sheriff may make deed.*

ART. 402. [26] When any Sheriff, as tax-collector, shall have advertised for sale any lands or tenements to raise the taxes due, and such lands or tenements so advertised could not be sold for want of bidders, he may adjourn any such sale from time to time until the same be sold; and any sale made on an adjourned day, shall be valid as if the same had been made on the day fixed in the advertisement. *Sheriff may adjourn sale from day to day.* *Sale on adjourned day of sale, valid.*

ART. 403. [7] When any lands or tenements shall be advertised for sale, by the collector of taxes, for any taxes or other dues accruing to the Republic, and such lands or tenements cannot be sold for the want of bidders, it shall be the duty of the collector to bid off the same for the Republic at the amount of the tax so due on said lands; and which lands shall be specially reserved to the Government, and not subject to location or other appropriation, until otherwise directed by law. *Act of Feb. 5, 1842.* *Lands to be bid off to Republic, when.*

ART. 404. [12] Upon the failure of any person or persons to pay their quota of taxes when it may be due, it shall not be necessary for the Sheriff to take out execution against such person or persons, but the Assessor's list in his possession shall operate as, and have the force and effect of, an execution; and he shall advertise for sale all property, the taxes upon which have not been paid on or before the first day of December, by posting up notices in three public places in the county where the property is situated—one of which places shall be the county seat—for sixty days previous to the sale; and shall sell the said property on the first Monday of March and succeeding days, at the court-house door, if there be one, and if not, at the place where the court of said county may be held, for the taxes, costs, and charges; and if any person or persons shall offer, at the sale, to pay the dues aforesaid, for less than the whole quantity of the tract of land advertised, then it shall be stricken off to the lowest bidder; and the part or parcel sold, if less than the entire tract advertised, shall be laid off in a square, beginning at the beginning corner of said tract. *Act of Feb. 5, 1842.* *On failure to pay, Sheriff may sell without execution.*

ART. 405. [13] Upon said sale said tax collector shall give a receipt to the purchaser or purchasers of said land, entitling them to a deed in fee simple, if the same is not redeemed in one year, by the owner or owners, or any other person paying the amount of said sale, and one hundred per centum thereon; and shall also return to the Secretary of the Treasury the land stricken off to the Republic, which, if not redeemed as before stated, shall be considered as relinquished, and held as heretofore provided; and the Tax Collector or his successor in office, at the expiration of one year, as before provided, upon the production of the receipt given to the purchaser or purchasers at said sale, and *Sheriff's receipt to purchaser, &c.* *Collector to make deed, &c.*

in the event said land is not redeemed as aforesaid, shall make to said persons a quit-claim deed, transferring all the interest that said party had in and to said tract of land, to said purchaser; which deed shall be *prima facie* evidence that all the requisites of the law have been complied with.

Act of May 13, 1846.

Taxes not paid, Collector to levy.

ART. 406. [17] If any person shall neglect or refuse to pay the tax imposed on him and his property, by law, until the first day of January in each year, the Assessor and Collector shall levy by virtue of his tax list, upon so much property liable to taxation, belonging to such person, to be found in his county, as may be sufficient to pay such taxes.

Mode of sale.

ART. 407. [18] Every Assessor and Collector of Taxes shall give notice of the time and place of the sale of the property so levied upon to be sold, at least thirty days previous to the day of sale, by advertisement in writing, to be posted up at the court-house door of his county, and at least three other public places therein; and every such sale shall take place at the court-house of the county in which such levy is made, and shall be by public auction; and if the property so levied upon, prove to be insufficient to satisfy the amount of taxes due, the Assessor and Collector shall levy upon and sell so much other taxable property, belonging to such person, as will be sufficient to satisfy such taxes, in the manner prescribed in the preceding part of this section; and paying the taxes, the surplus, if there be any, shall be paid over to the person for the payment of whose taxes the levy and sale shall have been made.

Tax deed.

ART. 408. [19] It shall be the duty of the Assessor and Collector, when any property shall be sold for the payment of taxes, to make and execute a deed to the person purchasing the same, conveying all the right, title, and interest, which the person assessed had in and to the same; which, when recorded according to law, shall be as binding and as valid as any other instrument of conveyance: provided, however, that the owner of such property shall have the right to redeem the same within twelve months of the day and date of the sale thereof, upon payment of double the amount of the taxes for which the same was sold.

Owner may redeem.

Act of March 20, 1848.

If not paid by first November, Collector to levy.

ART. 409. [14] If any person shall fail or refuse to pay the tax imposed upon him and his property, by law, until the first day of November, in each year, the Assessor shall levy, by virtue of his tax list, upon so much property, liable to taxation, belonging to such person, to be found in his county, as may be sufficient to pay his or her taxes; and in case such property is about to be removed out of the county, the Assessor and Collector shall, in like manner, proceed to take into his possession, so much property as will pay the taxes assessed, and costs of collection.

Mode of sale.

ART. 410. [15] Every Assessor and Collector of taxes shall give notice of the time and place of the property, so levied upon, to be sold, at least thirty days previous to the day of sale, by advertisement in writing, to be posted up at the court-house door of his county, and in two other public places in his county; and such sale shall take place at the court-house door of the county in which the assessment is made, by public auction; and if the property so levied upon, prove to be insufficient to satisfy the amount of taxes due and costs of sale, the Assessor and Collector shall levy upon and sell so much other taxable property belonging to such person as will be sufficient to satisfy such taxes, in the manner prescribed in the preceding part of this section; and after paying the taxes, the surplus, if any, shall be paid over to the person for the payment of whose taxes the levy and sale shall have been made.

Tax deed.

ART. 411. [16] The Assessor and Collector shall, when any property has been sold for the payment of taxes, make and execute a deed for said property to the person or persons purchasing the same; which, when recorded according to law, shall be prima facie evidence that all the requisitions of the law have been complied with in making such sale: provided, however, that the owner of such property shall have the right to redeem the same at any time within twelve months of the day and date of the sale thereof, upon payment of double the amount of the taxes for which the same was sold, and costs of sale.

Where sale does not take place at time appointed.

ART. 412. [29] If from any cause the sale of property seized for taxes shall not take place at the time first appointed, the Assessor and Collector shall appoint some other time, give the like notice, and proceed to sell such property in the manner prescribed in the first instance by this act.

When Collector shall bid off lands for the State.

ART. 413. [31] When any lands or tenements shall be advertised for sale by the Assessor and Collector of taxes for any taxes or other dues accruing to the State, and such lands or tenements cannot be sold for the want of bidders, it shall be the duty of the Assessor and Collector to bid off the same for the State, for the amount of taxes so due; and when such lands are not redeemed within one year from the date of sale, by the owner or owners, or some other person, paying the amount of such taxes and costs of sale, and one hundred per centum thereon, it shall then become public domain and subject to location by any person holding a legal land warrant against the State, by such person paying the amount of tax for which such land was sold and costs of sale, with one hundred per centum thereon. And it shall be the duty of the Commissioner of the General Land Office to issue patents on all surveys of land sold in conformity of this act, on a legal return and showing being made to him of the same.

COLONIZATION LAWS

OF

MEXICO,

COAHUILA AND TEXAS,

WHICH WERE IN FORCE BEFORE THE

DECLARATION OF INDEPENDENCE

BY TEXAS.

COLONIZATION LAWS

OF

MEXICO, COAHUILA AND TEXAS, WHICH WERE IN FORCE BEFORE THE DECLARATION OF INDEPENDENCE.

COLONISATION LAW OF 1823.

[No. 5.]

AUGUSTIN, by divine providence, and by the congress of the nation, first constitutional emperor of Mexico, and grand master of the imperial order of Guadalupe; To all who shall see these presents: Know ye, That the junta nacional instituyente of the Mexican empire, has decreed, and we sanction the following:

The Junta Nacional Instituyente of the Mexican empire, being convinced by the urgent recommendations of the government, of the necessity and importance of giving to the empire a general law of colonisation, have thought proper to decree as follows:

ART. 1. The government of the Mexican nation will protect the liberty, property and civil rights, of all foreigners who profess the Roman Catholic apostolic religion, the established religion of the empire.

ART. 2. To facilitate their establishment, the executive will distribute lands to them, under the conditions and terms herein expressed.

ART. 3. The empresarios, by whom is understood those who introduced at least two hundred families, shall previously contract with the executive, and inform it what branch of industry they propose to follow, the property or resources they intend to introduce for that purpose, and any other particulars they may deem necessary, in order that with this necessary information, the executive may designate the province to which they must direct themselves, the lands which they can occupy with right of property, and the other circumstances which may be considered neccessary.

ART. 4. Families who emigrate, not included in a contract, shall immediately present themselves to the ayuntamiento of the place where they wish to settle, in order that this body, in conformity with the instructions of the executive, may designate the lands corresponding to them, agreeably to the industry which they may establish.

ART. 5. The measurement of land shall be the following; establishing the *vara*, at three geometrical feet; a straight line of five thousand *varas* shall be a league; a square, each of whose sides shall be one league, shall be called a sitio; and this shall be the unity of counting one, two, or more sitios; five sitios shall compose one hacienda.

ART. 6. In the distribution made by government, of lands to the colonists, for the formation of villages, towns, cities, and provinces, a distinction shall be made between grazing lands, destined for the raising of stock, and lands suitable for farming or planting, on account of the facility of irrigation.

ART. 7. One labor shall be composed of one million square varas, that is to say, one thousand varas on each side, which measurement shall be the unity for counting one, two or more labors. These labors can be divided into halves and quarters, but not less.

ART. 8. To the colonists, whose occupation is farming, there cannot be given less than one labor, and those whose occupation is stock raising there cannot be given less than one sitio.

ART. 9. The government of itself, or by means of the authorities authorized for that purpose, can augment said portions of land as may be deemed proper, agreeably to the conditions and circumstances of the colonists.

ART. 10. Establishments made under the former government which are now pending, shall be regulated by this law in all matters that may occur, but those that are finished shall remain in that state.

ART. 11. As one of the principal objects of laws in free governments, ought to be to approximate, so far as possible, to an equal distribution of property; the government, taking into consideration the provisions of this law, will adopt measures for dividing out the lands, which may have accumulated in large portions, in the hands of individuals or corporations, and which are not cultivated, indemnifying the proprietors for the just price of such lands, to be fixed by appraisers.

ART. 12. The union of many families at one place, shall be called a village, town or city, agreeably to the number of its inhabitants, its extension, locality, and other circumstances which may characterise it, in conformity with the law of that subject. The same regulations for its internal government and police, shall be observed as in the others of the same class in the empire.

ART. 13. Care shall be taken in the formation of said new town, that, so far as the situation of the ground will permit, the streets shall be laid off straight, running north and south, east and west.

ART. 14. Provinces shall be formed, whose superfice shall be six thousand square leagues.

ART. 15. As soon as a sufficient number of families may be united to form one or more towns, their local government shall be regulated, and the constitutional ayuntamientos and other local establishments formed in conformity with the laws.

ART. 16. The government shall take care, in accord with the respective ecclesiastical authority, that these new towns are provided with a sufficient number of spiritual pastors, and in like manner, it will propose to Congress a plan for their decent support.

ART. 17. In the distribution of lands for settlement among the different provinces, the government shall take care that the colonists shall be located in those which it may consider the most important to settle. As a general rule, the colonists who arrive first, shall have the preference in the selection of land.

ART. 18. Natives of the country shall have a preference in the distribution of land; and particularly the military of the army, of the three guarantees, in conformity with the decree of the 27th of March, 1821; and also those who served in the first epoch of the insurrection.

ART. 19. To each empresario who introduces and establishes families in any of the provinces designated for colonization, there shall be granted at the rate of three haciendas and two labors, for each two hundred families so introduced by him, but he will lose the right of property over said lands, should he not have populated and cultivated them in twelve years from the date of the concession. The premium cannot exceed nine haciendas, and six labors, whatever may be the number of families he introduces.

ART. 20. At the end of twenty years the proprietors of the lands, acquired in virtue of the foregoing article, must alienate two-thirds part of said lands, either by sale, donation, or in any other manner he pleases. The law authorises him to hold in full property and dominion one third part.

ART. 21. The two foregoing articles are to be understood as governing the contracts made within six months, as after that time, counting from the day of the promulgation of this law, the executive can diminish the premium as it may deem proper, giving an account thereof to Congress, with such information as may be deemed necessary.

ART. 22. The date of the concession for lands constitutes an inviolable law, for the right of property and legal ownership; should any one through error, or by subsequent concession, occupy land belonging to another, he shall have no right to it, further than a preference in case of sale, at the current price.

ART. 23. If after two years from the date of the concession, the colonist should not have cultivated his land, the right of property shall be considered as renounced; in which case, the respective ayuntamiento can grant it to another.

ART. 24. During the first six years from the date of the concession, the colonists shall not pay tithes, duties on their produce, nor any contribution under whatever name it may be called.

ART. 25. The next six years from the same date, they shall pay half tithes, and the half of the contributions, whether direct or indirect, that are paid by the other citizens of the empire. After this time, they shall in all things relating to taxes and contributions, be placed on the same footing with the other citizens.

ART. 26. All the instruments of husbandry, machinery, and other utensils, that are introduced by the colonists for their use, at the time of their coming to the empire. shall be free, as also the merchandise introduced by each family, to the amount of two thousand dollars.

Art. 27. All foreigners who come to establish themselves in the empire, shall be considered as naturalised, should they exercise any useful profession or industry, by which, at the end of three years, they have a capital to support themselves with decency, and are married. Those who with the foregoing qualifications, marry Mexicans, will acquire particular merit, for the obtaining letters of citizenship.

Art. 28. Congress will grant letters of citizenship to those who solicit them, in conformity with the constitution of the empire.

Art. 29. Every individual shall be free to leave the empire, and can alienate the lands over which he may have acquired the right of property, agreeably to the tenor of this law, and he can likewise take away from the country, all his property, by paying the duties established by law.

Art. 30. After the publication of this law, there can be no sale or purchase of slaves which may be introduced into the empire. The children of slaves born in the empire, shall be free at fourteen years of age.

Art. 31. All foreigners who may have established themselves in any of the provinces of the empire, under a permission of the former government, will remain on the lands which they may have occupied, being governed by the tenor of this law, in the distribution of said lands.

Art. 32. The executive, as it may conceive necessary, will sell or lease the lands, which, on account of their local situation, may be the most important, being governed with respect to all others, by the provisions of this law.

This law shall be presented to his Imperial Majesty for his sanction, publication and fulfilment.—Mexico, 3d January, 182—3d of the independence of the empire.—Juan Francisco, Bishop of Durango, President.—Antonio de Mier, Member and Secretary.—Juan Batista de Arispe, Member and Secretary.

Therefore, we order all tribunals, judges, chiefs, governors, and all other authorities, as well civil as military and ecclesiastical, whatever class or dignity they may be, to comply with this decree, and cause it to be complied with in all its parts; and you will cause it to be printed, published and circulated.—Given in Mexico, 4th January, 1823.—Signed by the Emperor.—To Don Jose Manuel de Herrera, Minister of Interior and Exterior Relations.

[No. 20.] (Decree No. 72.) NATIONAL COLONISATION LAW.

The Supreme Executive Power, provisionally appointed by the general sovereign Constituent Congress—To all who shall see and understand these presents: Know ye—that the said Congress has decreed as follows:—

Art. 1. The Mexican nation offers to foreigners, who come to establish themselves within its territory, security for their persons and property, provided, they subject themselves to the laws of the country.

Art. 2. This law comprehends those lands of the nation, not the property of individuals, corporations, or towns which can be colonized.

Art. 3. For this purpose the legislatures of all the states will, as soon as possible, form colonisation laws, or regulations for their respective states, conforming themselves in all things, to the constitutional act, general constitution, and the regulations established in this law.

Art. 4. There cannot be colonised any lands, comprehended within twenty leagues of the limits of any foreign nation, nor within ten leagues of the coasts, without the previous approbation of the general supreme executive power.

Art. 5. If for the defence and security of the nation, the federal government should deem it necessary to use any portion of these lands, for the construction of warehouses, arsenals, or other public edifices, they can do so, with the approbation of the general congress, or in its recess, of the council of government.

Art. 6. Until after four years from the publication of this law, there shall not be imposed any tax whatever, on the entrance of foreigners, who come to establish themselves for the first time in the nation.

Art. 7. Until after the year 1840, the general congress shall not prohibit the entrance of any foreigner, as a colonist, unless imperious circumstances should require it, with respect to the individuals of a particular nation.

ART. 8. The government, without prejudicing the objects of this law, shall take such precautionary measures as it may deem expedient, for the security of the confederation, as respects the foreigners who come to colonise.

ART. 9. A preference shall be given in the distribution of lands, to Mexican citizens, and no other distinction shall be made in regard to them except that which is founded on individual merit, or services rendered the country, or under equal circumstances, a residence in the place where the lands to be distributed are situated.

ART. 10. The military who in virtue of the offer made on the 27th March, 1821, have a right to lands, shall be attended to by the states, in conformity with the diplomas which are issued to that effect, by the supreme executive power.

ART. 11. If in virtue of the decree alluded to, in the last article, and taking into view the probabilities of life, the supreme executive power should deem it expedient to alienate any portion of land in favor of any officer, whether civil or military of the federation, it can do so from the vacant lands of the territories.

ART. 12. It shall not be permitted to unite in the same hands with the right of property, more than one league square of land, suitable for irrigation, four square leagues in superficies, of arable land without the facilities of irrigation, and six square leagues in superficies of grazing land.

ART. 13. The new colonists shall not transfer their property in mortmain (*manus muertos.*)

ART. 14. This law guarantees the contracts which the empresarios make with the families which they bring at their own expense, provided they are not contrary to the laws.

ART. 15. No person who by virtue of this law, acquires a title to lands, shall hold them if he is domiciliated out of the limits of the Republic.

ART. 16. The government in conformity with the provisions established in this law, will proceed to colonise the territories of the Republic.

MEXICO, 18th August, 1824.

CAYETANO IBARRA, President.
PEDRO DE AHUMADA, Member and Secretary.
MANUEL DE VILLAY COCIO, Member and Secretary.

Therefore, we command it to be printed, circulated, and obeyed.

NICHOLAS BRAVO,
VICENTE GUERRERO,
MIGUEL DOMINGUEZ.
Members of the Supreme Executive Power.

[No. 21.] COLONIZATION LAW OF THE STATE OF COAHUILA AND TEXAS.

The Governor provisionally appointed by the Sovereign Congress of this State; to all who shall see these presents: Know, that the said congress, have decreed as follows:

Decree No. 16. The constituent congress of the free, independent and sovereign state of Coahuila and Texas, desiring by every possible means, to augment the population of its territory; promote the cultivation of its fertile lands; the raising and multiplication of stock, and the progress of the arts and commerce; and being governed by the constitutional act, the federal constitution, and the basis established by the national decree of the general congress, No. 72, have thought proper to decree the following LAW OF COLONIZATION:

ART. 1. All foreigners, who in virtue of the general laws of the 18th August, 1824, which guarantees the security of their persons and property, in the territory of the Mexican nation, wish to remove to any of the settlements of the state of Coahuila and Texas, are at liberty to do so; and the said state invites and calls them.

ART. 2. Those who do so instead of being incommoded, shall be admitted by the local authorities of said settlements, who shall freely permit them to pursue any branch of industry, that they may think proper, provided they respect the general laws of the nation, and those of the state.

ART. 3. Any foreigner, already in the limits of the state of Coahuila and Texas, who wishes to settle himself in it, shall make a declaration to that effect, before the ayuntamiento of the place, which he selects as his residence, the ayuntamiento in such case, shall administer to him the oath, which he must take to obey the federal and state constitutions, and observe the religion which the former prescribes; the name of the person, and his family if he has any, shall then be registered in a book kept for that purpose, with a statement of where he was born, and whence from, his age, whether married, occupation, and that he has taken the oath prescribed, and considering him from that time, and not before, as domiciliated.

ART. 4. From the day in which any foreigner has been enrolled, as an inhabitant, in conformity with the foregoing article, he is at liberty to designate any vacant land, and the respective political authority will grant it to him in the same manner as to a native of the country, in conformity with the existing laws of the nation, under the condition that the proceedings shall be passed to the government for its approbation.

ART. 5. Foreigners of any nation, or a native of any of the Mexican states, can project the formation of new towns on any lands entirely vacant, or even on those of an individual, in the case mentioned in the 35th article; but the new settlers who present themselves for admission, must prove their christianity, morality, and good habits, by a certificate from the authorities where they formerly resided.

ART. 6. Foreigners who emigrate at the time in which the general sovereign congress may have prohibited their entrance, for the purpose of colonising, as they have the power to do, after the year 1840, or previous to that time, as respects those of any particular nation, shall not then be admitted; and those who apply in proper time, shall always subject themselves to such precautionary measures of national security, which the supreme government, without prejudicing the object of this law, may think proper to adopt relative to them.

ART. 7. The government shall take care, that within the twenty leagues bordering on the limits of the United States of the North, and ten leagues in a straight line from the coast of the Gulf of Mexico, within the limits of this state, there shall be no other settlements, except such as merit the approbation of the supreme government of the Union, for which object, all petitions on the subject, whether made by Mexicans or foreigners, shall be passed to the superior government, accompanied by a corresponding report.

ART. 8. The projects for new settlements in which one or more persons offer to bring at their own expense, one hundred or more families, shall be presented to the government, and if found conformable with this law, they will be admitted; and the government will immediately designate to the contractors, the land where they are to establish themselves, and the term of six years, within which they must present the number of families they contracted for, under the penalty of losing the rights and privileges offered in their favor, in proportion to the number of families which they fail to introduce, and the contract totally annulled if they do not bring at least one hundred families.

ART. 9. Contracts made by the contractors or undertakers, *Empresarios*, with the families brought at their expense, are guaranteed by this law, so far as they are conformable with its provisions.

ART. 10. In the distributions of land, a preference shall be given to the military entitled to them, by the diplomas issued by the supreme executive power and the Mexican citizens who are not military, among whom there shall be no other distinction, than that founded on their individual merit, or services performed for the country, or in equal circumstances, a residence in the place where the land may be situated; the quantity of land which may be granted, is designated in the following articles:

ART. 11. A square of land, which on each side has one league or five thousand varas, or what is the same thing, a superficies of twenty-five million varas, shall be called a sitio, and this shall be the unity for counting one, two, or more sitios; and also the unity for counting one, two, or more labors, shall be one million square varas, or one thousand varas on each side, which shall compose a labor. The vara for this measurement shall be three geometrical feet.

ART. 12. Taking the above unity as a basis, and observing the distinction which must be made between grazing land, or that which is proper for raising of stock, and farming land, with or without the facility of irrigation; this law grants to the contractor or contractors, for the establishment of a new settlement, for each hundred families which he may introduce and establish in the state, five sitios of grazing land, and five labors at least, the one-half of which, shall be without the facility of irrigation, but they can only receive this premium for eight hundred families, although a greater number should be introduced, and no fraction whatever, less than one hundred, shall entitle them to any premium, not even proportionally.

Art. 13. Should any contractor or contractors in virtue of the number of families which he may have introduced, acquire in conformity with the last article, more than eleven square leagues of land, it shall nevertheless be granted, but subject to the condition of alienating the excess, within twelve years, and if it is not done, the respective political authority shall do it, by selling it at public sale, delivering the proceeds to the owners, after deducting the costs of sale.

Art. 14. To each family comprehended in a contract, whose sole occupation is cultivation of land, one labor shall be given; should he also be a stock raiser, grazing land shall be added to complete a sitio; and should his only occupation be raising of stock, he shall only receive a superfice of grazing land, equal to twenty-four million square bars.

Art. 15. Unmarried men shall receive the same quantity when they enter the matrimonial state, and foreigners who marry native Mexicans, shall receive one-fourth more; those who are entirely single, or who do not form a part of some family whether foreigners or natives, shall content themselves with the fourth part of the above mentioned quantity, which is all that can be given them until they marry.

Art. 16. Families or unmarried men who, entirely of their own accord, have emigrated and may wish to unite themselves to any new towns, can at all times do so, and the same quantity of land shall be assigned them, which is mentioned in the last two articles, but if they do so in the first six years from the establishment of the settlement, one labor more shall be given to families, and single men in place of the quarter designated in the 15th article, shall have the third part.

Art. 17. It appertains to the government to augment the quantity indicated in the 14th, 15th, and 16th articles, in proportion to the family, industry and activity of the colonists, agreeably to the information given on these subjects by the ayuntamientos and commissioners; the said government always observing the provision of the 12th article, of the decree of the general congress on the subject.

Art. 18. The families who emigrate in conformity with the 16th article shall immediately present themselves to the political authority of the place which they may have chosen for their residence, who finding in them the requisites, prescribed by this law for new settlers, shall admit them, and put them in possession of the corresponding lands, and shall immediately give an account thereof to the government; who of themselves, or by means of a person commissioned to that effect, will issue them a title.

Art. 19. The Indians of all nations, bordering on the state, as well as wandering tribes that may be within its limits, shall be received in the markets, without paying any duties whatever for commerce, in the products of the country; and if attracted by the moderation and confidence, with which they shall be treated, any of them, after having first declared themselves in favor of our religion and institutions wish to establish themselves in any settlements that are forming, they shall be admitted, and the same quantity of land given them, as to the settlers, spoken of in the 14th and 15th articles, always preferring native Indians to strangers.

Art. 20. In order that there may be no vacancies between tracts, of which, great care shall be taken in the distribution of lands; it shall be laid off in squares, or other forms although irregular, if the local situation requires it; and in said distribution, as well as the assignation of lands for new towns, previous notice shall be given to the adjoining proprietors, if any, in order to prevent dissentions and law suits.

Art. 21. If by error in the accession, any land shall be granted, belonging to another, on proof being made of that fact, an equal quantity shall be granted elsewhere, to the person who may have thus obtained it through error, and he shall be indemnified by the owner of such land, for any improvements he may have made; the just value of which improvements shall be ascertained by the appraisers.

Art. 22. The new settlers as an acknowledgement, shall pay to the state, for each sitio of pasture land, thirty dollars; two dollars and a half for each labor without the facility of irrigation, and three dollars and a half for each one that can be irrigated, and so on proportionally according to the quantity and quality of the land distributed; but the said payments need not be made, until six years after the settlement, and by thirds; the first within four years, the second within five years, and the last within six years, under the penalty of losing the land, for a failure, in any of said payments; there are excepted from this payment, the contractors, and military, spoken of in the 10th article; the former, with respect to lands given them, as a premium, and the latter, for those which they obtained, in conformity with their diplomas.

ART. 23. The ayuntamientos of each municipality (*Comarco*,) shall collect the above mentioned funds, gratis, by means of a committee, appointed either within or without their body; and shall remit them as they are collected, to the treasurer of their funds; who will give the corresponding receipt, and without any other compensation than two and a half per cent., all that shall be allowed him, he shall hold them at the disposition of the government, rendering an account every month of the ingress and egress, and of any remissness or fraud, which he may observe in their collection, for the correct management of all which, the person employed, and the committee, and the individuals of the ayuntamientos who appoint them, shall be individually responsible, and that this responsibility may be at all times effectual, the said appointments shall be made viva voce, and information shall be given thereof, immediately to the government.

ART. 24. The government will sell to Mexicans, and to them only, such lands as they may wish to purchase, taking care that there shall not be accumulated in the same hands more than eleven sitios; and under the condition, that the purchaser must cultivate what he acquires by this title within six years from its acquisition, under the penalty of losing them, the price of each sitio, subject to the foregoing condition, shall be one hundred dollars, if it be pasture land; one hundred and fifty dollars, if it be farming land without the facility of irrigation; and two hundred dollars if it can be irrigated.

ART. 25. Until six years after the publication of this law, the legislature of this state, cannot alter it as regards the acknowledgement, and price to be paid for land, or as regards the quantity and quality, to be distributed to the new settlers, or sold to Mexicans.

ART. 26. The new settlers, who within six years from the date of the possession, have not cultivated or occupied the lands granted them, according to its quality, shall be considered to have renounced them, and the respective political authority shall immediately proceed to take possession of them, and recall the titles.

ART. 27. The contractors and military, heretofore spoken of, and those who by purchase have acquired lands, can alienate them at any time, but the successor is obliged to cultivate them in the same time, that the original proprietor was bound to do; the other settlers can alienate theirs when they have totally cultivated them, and not before.

ART. 28. By testamentary will, made in conformity with the existing laws, or those which may govern in future, any new colonist, from the day of his settlement, may dispose of his land, although he may not have cultivated it, and if he dies intestate, his property shall be inherited by the person or persons entitled by the laws to it; the heirs being subject to the same obligation and condition imposed on the original grantee.

ART. 29 Lands acquired by virtue of this law, shall not by any title whatever, pass into mortmain.

ART. 30. The new settler who wishing to establish himself in a foreign country, resolves to leave the territory of the state, can do so freely, with all his property; but after leaving the state, he shall not any longer hold his land, and if he had not previously sold it, or the sale should not be in conformity with the 2‑th article, it shall become entirely vacant.

ART. 31. Foreigners who in conformity with this law, have obtained land, and established themselves in any new settlement, shall be considered from that moment, naturalised in the country; and by marrying a Mexican, they acquire a particular merit to obtain letters of citizenship of the state, subject however to the provisions which may be made relative to both particulars, in the constitution of the state.

ART. 32. During the first ten years, counting from the day on which the new settlements may have been established, they shall be free from all contributions, of whatever denomination, with the exception of those which, in case of invasion by any enemy, or to prevent it, are generally imposed, and all the produce of agriculture or industry of the new settlers, shall be free from excise duty *Alcabala*, or other duties, throughout every part of the state, with the exception of the duties referred to in the next article; after the termination of that time, the new settlements shall be on the same footing as to taxes, with the old ones, and the colonists shall also in this particular, be on the same footing with the other inhabitants of the state.

ART. 33. From the day of their settlement, the new colonists shall be at liberty to follow any branch of industry, and can also work mines of every description, communicating with the supreme government of the confederation, relative to the general revenue appertaining to it, and subjecting themselves in all other particulars, to the ordinances or taxes, established or which may be established on this branch.

ART. 34. Towns shall be founded on the sites deemed most suitable, by the government, or the person commissioned for this effect, and for each one, there shall be designed four square leagues, whose area may be in a regular or irregular form, agreeably to the situation.

ART. 35. If any of the said sites should be the property of an individual, and the establishment of new towns on them, should notoriously be of general utility, they can, notwithstanding, be appropriated to this object, previously indemnifying the owner for its just value, to be determined by appraisers.

ART. 36. Building lots in the new towns shall be given gratis, to the contractors of them, and also to artists of every class, as many as are necessary for the establishment of their trade; and to the other settlers they shall be sold at public auction, after having been previously valued—under the obligation to pay the purchase money by instalments of one-third each; the first in six months, the second in twelve months, and the third in eighteen months; but all owners of lots, including contractors and artists, shall annually pay one dollar for each lot, which, together with the produce of the sales, shall be collected by the ayuntamientos, and applied to the building of churches in said towns.

ART. 37. So far as practicable, the towns shall be composed of natives and foreigners, and in their delineations great care should be taken to lay off the streets straight, giving them a direction from north to south, and from east to west, when the site will permit it.

ART. 38. For the better location of the said new towns, their regular formation and exact partition of their lands and lots, the government on account of having admitted any project, and agreed with the contractor or contractors, who may have presented it, shall commission a person of intelligence and confidence, giving him such particular instructions as may be deemed necessary and expedient; and authorising him under his own responsibility, to appoint one or more surveyors to lay off the town scientifically, and do whatever else may be required.

ART. 39. The governor in conformity with the last fee bill *Arancel*, of notary publics of the ancient audience of Mexico, shall designate the fees of the commissioner, who, in conjunction with the colonists, shall fix the surveyor's fees; but both shall be paid by the colonists, and in the manner which all parties among themselves may agree upon.

ART. 40. As soon as at least forty families are united in one place, they shall proceed to the formal establishment of the new towns, and all of them shall take an oath to support the general and state constitutions; which oath will be administered by the commissioner, they shall then, in his presence, proceed for the first time to the election of their municipal authority.

ART. 41. A new town, whose inhabitants shall not be less than two hundred, shall elect an ayuntamiento, provided there is not another one established within eight leagues, in which case, it shall be added to it. The number of individuals which are to compose the ayuntamiento, shall be regulated by the existing laws.

ART. 42. Foreigners are eligible, subject to the provisions which the constitution of the state may prescribe, to elect the members of their municipal authorities, and to be elected to the same.

ART. 43. The municipal expenses, and all others which may be considered necessary, or of common utility to the new towns, shall be proposed to the governor, by the ayuntamientos through the political chief, accompanied with a plan of the taxes *arbitrios*, which in their opinion may be just and best calculated to raise them, and should the proposed plan be approved by the governor, he shall order it to be executed, subject however to the resolution of the legislature, to whom it shall be immediately passed with his report and that of the political chief, who will say whatever occurs to him on the subject.

ART. 44. For the opening and improving of roads and other public works in Texas, the government will transmit to the chief of that department the individuals who, in other parts of the state, may have been sentenced to public works as vagrants, or for other crimes, these same persons may be employed by individuals for competent wages, and as soon as the time of their condemnation is expired, they can unite themselves as colonists to any new settlement, and obtain the corresponding lands, if their reformation shall have made them worthy of such favor in the opinion of the chief of the department, without whose certificate they shall not be admitted.

ART. 45. The government in accord with the respective ordinary ecclesiastics, will take care to provide the new settlements with the competent number of pastors, and, in accord with the same authority, shall propose to the legislature for its approbation, the salary which the said pastors are to receive, which shall be paid by the new settlers.

ART. 46. The new settlers as regards the introduction of slaves, shall subject themselves to the existing laws, and those which may hereafter be established on the subject.

ART. 47. The petitions now pending relative to the subject of this law, shall be despatched in conformity with it, and for this purpose, they shall be passed to the governor, and the families who may be established within the limits of the state, without having any land assigned them, shall subject themselves to this law, and to the orders of the supreme government of the Union, with respect to those who are within twenty leagues of the limits of the United States of America, and ten leagues in a straight line of the coast of the Gulf of Mexico.

ART. 48. This law shall be published in all the villages of the state, and that it may arrive at the notice of all others throughout the Mexican confederation, it shall be communicated to their respective legislatures, by the secretary of this state; and the governor will take particular care to send a certified copy of it, in compliance with the 161st article of the federal constitution, to the two houses of congress, and the supreme executive power of the nation, with a request to the latter to give it general circulation through foreign states, by means of your ambassadors.

The governor pro tem. of the state will cause it to be published and circulated.—Saltillo, 24th March, 1825.—Signed,

RAFAEL RAMOS Y VALDEZ, President.
JUAN VICENTE GAMPOS, Member and Sec'y.
JOSE JOAQUIN ARCE ROSALES, Member and Sec'y.

Therefore, I command all authorities, as well civil as military and ecclesiastical, to obey, and cause to be obeyed, the present decree in all its parts.

RAFAEL GONZALES, Governor.

INSTRUCTIONS TO THE COMMISSIONER APPOINTED BY THE LEGISLATURE OF THE STATE.

EXECUTIVE DEPARTMENT OF THE STATE OF COAHUILA AND TEXAS.

Instructions by which the commissioner shall be governed in the partition of lands to the new colonists, who may establish themselves in the state, in conformity with the colonisation law of the 24th March, 1825.

ART. 1. It shall be the duty of the commissioner, keeping in view the contract which an empresario may have entered into with the government, and also the colonisation law of the 24th March, scrupulously to examine the certificates or recommendations which foreign emigrants must produce from the local authorities of the place where they removed from, accrediting their christianity, morality, and steady habits, in conformity with the 5th article of said law, without which requisite they shall not be admitted in the colony.

ART. 2. In order to prevent being imposed on by false recommendations, the commissioner shall not consider any as sufficient without a previous opinion in writing as to their legitimacy, from the empresario, for which purpose they shall be passed to him by the commissioner.

ART. 3. The commissioner shall administer to each of the new colonists the oath in form, to observe the federal constitution of the united Mexican states, the constitution of the state, the general laws of the nation, and those of the state which they have adopted for their country.

ART. 4. He shall issue in the name of the state the titles for land, in conformity with the law, and put the new colonists in possession of their lands, with all legal formalities, and the previous citation of adjoining proprietors, should there be any.

ART. 5. He shall not give possession to any colonists who may have established, or who may wish to establish themselves within twenty leagues of the limits of the United States of the north, or within ten leagues of the coast, unless it should appear that the supreme government of the nation had approved thereof.

ART. 6. He shall take care that no vacant lands be left between possessions, and in order that the lines may be clearly designated, he shall compel the colonists, within the term of one year, to mark their lines, and to establish fixed and permanent corners.

ART. 7. He shall appoint, under his own responsibility, the surveyor, who must survey the land scientifically, requiring him previously to take an oath truly and faithfully to discharge the duties of his office.

ART. 8. He shall form a manuscript book of paper of the 3d stamp, in which shall be written the titles of the lands distributed to the colonists, specifying the names, the boundaries, and other requisites, and legal circumstances, and a certified copy of each title shall be taken from said book on paper of the 2d stamp, which shall be delivered to the interested person on his title.

ART. 9. Each settler shall pay the value of the stamp paper used in issuing his title both for the original and copy.

ART. 10. This book shall be preserved in the archives of the new colony, and an exact form of it shall be transmitted to the government, specifying the number of colonists, with their names, and the quantity of land granted to each one, distinguishing that which is farming land with or without the facilities of irrigation, and that which is granted as grazing land.

ART. 11. He shall select the site which may be the most suitable for the establishment of the town or towns, which are to be founded agreeably to the number of families composing the colony, and keeping in view the provisions of the law of colonisation on this subject.

ART. 12. After selecting the site destined for the new town, he shall take care that the base lines run north and south, east and west; and he will designate a public square one hundred and twenty varas on each side, exclusive of the streets, which shall be called the *principal, or constitutional square*, and this shall be the central point from which the streets shall run, for the formation of squares and blocks in conformity with the model hereto annexed.

ART. 13. The block situated on the east side of the principal square shall be destined for the church, curate's house, and other ecclesiastical buildings. The block on the west side of said square shall be designated for public buildings of the municipality. In some other suitable situation a block shall be designated for a market square, another for a jail and house of correction, another for a school and other edifices for public instruction, and another beyond the limits of the town for a burial ground.

ART. 14. He shall, on his responsibility, cause the streets to be laid off straight, and that they are twenty varas wide, to promote the health of the town.

ART. 15. Mechanics, who at the time of founding a new town, present themselves to settle in it, shall have the right of receiving one lot a piece without any other cost than the neccesary stamp paper for issuing the title, and the light tax of one dollar annually for the construction of the church.

ART. 16. The lots spoken of in the preceding article shall be distributed by lot, with the exception of the empresario, who shall be entitled to any two lots he may select.

ART. 17. The other lots shall be valued by appraisers according to their situation, and sold to the other colonists at their appraised value. In case there should be a number of applicants for the same lot, owing to its situation or other circumstances, which may excite competition, it shall be decided by lot as prescribed in the preceding article; the product of said lots shall be appropriated to the building of a church in said town.

ART. 18. He shall, in union with the empresario, promote the settlement of each town by the inhabitants belonging to its jurisdiction, who take lots in it, and cause them to construct houses on said lots within a limited time under the penalty of forfeiting them.

ART. 19. He shall form a manuscript book of each new town, in which shall be written the titles of the lots which are given as a donation, or sold, specifying their boundaries and other neccessary circumstances, a certified copy of each one of which on the corresponding stamp shall be delivered to the interested person as his title.

ART. 20. He shall form a topographical plan of each town that may be founded, and transmit it to the government, keeping a copy of it in the said register book of the colony.

ART. 21. He shall see that at the crossing of each of the rivers on the public roads, where a town is founded, a ferry is established at the cost of the inhabitants of said town, a moderate rate of ferriage is established to pay the salary of the ferryman and the costs of the necessary boats, and the balance shall be applied to the public funds of the town.

ART. 22. In places where there is no towns, and where ferries are neccessary, the colonists who may be settled there shall be charged with the establishment of the ferry, collecting a moderate ferriage until such ferries are rented out for the use of the state. Any colonist who wishes to establish a ferry on the terms above indicated, shall form an exact and certified account of the costs which he may be at for the building of boats, and also an account of the produce of the ferry, in order that when said ferry is rented out for the use of the state, he shall have a right to receive the amount of said expenses which had not already been covered by the produce of the ferry, which for the present he will collect.

ART. 23. He shall preside at the popular elections mentioned in the 40th article of the colonisation law for the appointment of the ayuntamiento, and shall put the elected in possession of their offices.

ART. 24. He shall take special care that the portions of land granted to the colonists by articles 14, 15, and 16, shall be measured by the surveyors with accuracy, and not permit any one to include more land than is designated by law, under penalty of being personally responsible.

ART. 25. Should any colonist solicit, in conformity with the 17th article of the law, an augmentation of land beyond that designated in the preceding articles, on account of the size of the family, industry, or capital, he shall present his petition in writing to the commissioner, stating all the reasons on which he founds his petition, who shall transmit it to the governor of the state, together with his opinion, for which opinion he shall be responsible in the most rigid manner, in order that the governor may decide on the subject.

ART. 26. All the public instruments, titles, or other documents issued by the commissioner, shall be written in Spanish, the memorials, decrees, and reports of the colonists or empresarios, on any subject whatever, shall be written in the same language, whether they are to be transmitted to the government, or preserved in the archives of the colony.

ART. 27. All public instruments or titles of possession, and the copies signed by the commissioner, shall be attested by two assistant witnesses.

ART. 28. The commissioner shall be personally responsible for all acts or measures performed by him contrary to the colonisation law, or these instructions.

A copy.—Saltillo, September 4th, 1827.

TIJERINA, } Secretaries of the
ARCINIEGA, } Legislature.
A copy, JUAN ANTONIO PADILLA,
Secretary of State.

DECREE NO. 190.

The Congress of the State of Coahuila and Texas has thought proper to decree as follows:

ART. 1. To any Mexicans, who on the publication of this law shall resolve to settle any of the vacant lands thereof, the state hereby tenders its protection and aid.

ART. 2. Any Mexican or Mexicans who offer to effect at their own expense the removal of ninety families at least, shall present themselves to the executive, with whom they shall ratify their contracts according to this law, and shall fulfill the said contracts within the term of four years. Those who do not settle the aforementioned number of families shall forfeit the rights and privileges granted them by this law.

ART. 3. As soon as thirty families are collected, the formal establishment of the new town shall be commenced on the site most appropriate in the judgment of the executive, or person commissioned by him for the purpose; and four square leagues shall be assigned for each new town, whose area may be of a regular or irregular figure, as the local situation shall require.

ART. 4. Should any of the sites designed for founding a new town consist of land already appropriated, and the establishment be of evident general utility, it may be taken notwithstanding, observing the provision made by the constitution in restriction fourth, of article 113.

ART. 5. The executive, pursuant to the contract ratified by the empresario or empresarios, and for the better situation and formation of the new towns, and exact distribution of lands, lots, and water, shall commission a person of his confidence, a Mexican born, to act agreeably to the instructions of the 4th of September, 1827, so far as they are not opposed to this law.

ART. 6. In towns which admit of canals (for irrigation,) said canals shall be made at the expense of the persons interested. The commissioner shall divide them into channels or drains, procuring to have them made half a vara in width at least, and the same in depth, assigning one for the use of the town, and the rest for that of the fields in cultivation.

ART. 7. In the distribution of lands and waters, the empresario and new settler shall be subject to no other expense than the legal charges paid to the commissioner and surveyor.

ART. 8. To each of the families comprised in the contract mentioned in article 2, one day for watering, and one labor shall be granted, or two labors, should the land be temporal, (land cultivated during ordinary rains) and a lot of sixty yards square, whereon said family shall erect a dwelling within two years, otherwise they shall forfeit the privilege. Should a family have neat stock, horse kind, or small stock, exceeding one hundred head of the two former kinds, or six hundred of the latter, the same shall be entitled to one sitio of grazing land.

ART. 9. A square of land measuring one league, consisting of five thousand varas on each side, or what is the same thing, a superficies of twenty-five million square varas shall be called a sitio, and this shall be the unit for enumerating one, two or more sitios, in the same manner as one million square varas, or one thousand varas, on each side, which shall constitute a labor, shall be the unit for reckoning one, two or more labors. The vara for this measure shall consist of three geometrical feet.

ART. 10. This law shall grant to empresarios, for every ninety families they settle in the new town, four sitios of grazing land, and three watering days from the aqueducts or canals that can be applied to the cultivation of the land pertaining to their *empresa*; but they shall receive premium only in the ratio of ninety families, although they should introduce more, and they shall be entitled to no prize land for a fraction not amounting to ninety.

ART. 11. Neither the commissioner or any other authority shall grant another lot to the same person until he shall have built upon the first.

ART. 12. Any empresario who, in consideration of the families he settles, shall acquire agreeable to article 10, more than eleven sitios, shall alienate the excess within nine years, and should he not, the respective political authority shall sell the same at public auction, and deliver the proceeds to the owners thereof, after deducting the costs of sale.

ART. 13. The government may sell to Mexicans the lands they solicit, taking care that more than eleven leagues are not united in the same, hands, and on the positive condition that, by the fourth year from the acquisition thereof, the purchaser shall have introduced upon said land at least thirty head of large or two hundred of small stock for each sitio. The purchaser shall deliver one-fourth of the value of the land granted, to the state treasury or where the executive designates, at the time of the sale; ond the remaining three-fourths shall be paid, the first on the second, the second on the third, and the last on the fourth year, under penalty of forfeiting the right acquired in the part wherein this provision is not fulfilled.

ART. 14. Within the ten littoral leagues upon the coast of the Gulf of Mexico the price of each sitio shall be two hundred dollars for grazing and three hundred for tillage land, not irrigable. In the rest of the department of Bexar, the price thereof shall be one hundred dollars for the former, and one hundred and fifty for the latter kind of land; and that of the other vacant lands of the state fifteen dollars a sitio for the former, and twenty for the latter.

ART. 15. Lands, whose local situation admits of canals, and not designed for towns may be sold by the executive, to Mexicans only, at three hundred dollars each sitio in the department of Bexar, and at two hundred in the others of the state; to be paid as article 13 provides, and under the same penalty imposed therein; on the express condition that by the fourth year from the acquisition thereof the purchaser shall have cultivated one-eighth of the land, and the same shall be observed with respect to the tillage land not irrigable mentioned in the preceding article.

ART. 16. No change shall be made with respect to the contracts which the executive has ratified, or the concessions stipulated to purchasers or settlers by virtue of decree No. 16, of the 24th of March, 1825; but the executive shall take care that, within eighteen months from the publication of this law, the purchasers enter in possession of the land which he has granted them. Those who shall hereafter ratify new contracts, or acquire new concessions by purchase, shall be required, the former to have introduced one-sixth of the families contracted within eighteen months from the ratification of the contract, and the latter to enter in possession of the land acquired, within the same term; under penalty of forfeiture for the non-fulfilment thereof.

ART. 17. All new towns shall be free from taxes of whatever denomination for the term of ten years, reckoned from the time they are founded, with the exception of those that may be generally levied to prevent or repel foreign invasion.

ART. 18. Families that remove to any of the new towns to settle therein shall always be permitted to do so, and in consideration thereof shall be entitled to the privileges granted to new settlers by this law, for which purpose they shall appear before the commissioner, and in his default, the respective political authority, that the subject may be communicated to the executive, and their corresponding concession accorded.

ART. 19. No new settler, Mexican or foreigner, shall under any title or pretence sell or alienate the land or water that fall to his share, until after six years from the time of taking possession.

ART. 20. Mexicans or foreigners who undertake to colonize with foreign families, whose introduction is not prohibited by the general law of the 6th of April, 1830, shall be entitled to the privileges granted by article 6th of the present law.

ART. 21. The distribution of lands and waters to the foreign families mentioned in articles 18 and 20, shall be made agreeably to article 8, should they possess the merit required by this law, and they shall pay the state for the same one-third less than the price specified in article 14, and in the following manner—one-half the amount in two, and the remainder in six years from the time of taking possession.

ART. 22. To the families mentioned in the preceding article, should they possess the number of head of large and small stock, required in the second part of article 8, half a sitio of grazing land shall be granted.

ART. 23. The Ayuntamienta, each in its own limits, shall collect the aforesaid funds gratis, by a committee appointed from within or without their own body, and remit them as fast as collected to the depository or treasurer of their funds and means, who shall give the corresponding receipt for no other compensation than two and a half per cent., which is all that shall be paid him, and who shall hold the said funds at the disposal of the executive, giving an account monthly of the amounts received and remitted, and of any negligence or fraud he observes in their collection. For the management of the treasurer and committee, these officers themselves, and, furthermore the individuals of the Ayuntamienta that shall appoint them shall be held responsible with their property; and that this responsibility may always be effectual the said appointments shall be made viva voce, and notice thereof shall immediately be given to the executive.

ART. 24. Foreigners, to be admitted as new settlers, shall furnish adequate proof to the commissioner, and under his responsibility, of their christianity and good moral character: these indispensable requisites shall be made to appear in the manuscript mentioned in article 9, of the instructions of the fourth of September, 1827.

ART. 25. The executive shall take care that, within twenty border leagues fronting upon the United States line, and ten littoral leagues upon the coast of the Gulf of Mexico, no settlements are made that are not composed of two-thirds Mexicans, previously obtaining by request the approval of the national executive, to whom he shall forward all petitions made on the subject, accompanied by his report, whether the empresarios are Mexicans or foreigners.

ART. 26. In the distribution of lands native Mexicans shall be preferred to foreigners, and no other distinction shall be made between the former than such as is founded in their special merit and services rendered the country, or in equal circumstances, a residence in the place where the lands are situated.

ART. 27. The Indians of all nations bordering on the State, as well as the wandering tribes within the same, shall be admitted in market exempt from all duties in their traffic in the effects of the country; and should any of the same being attracted in this manner, and by the mildness and confidence with which they shall otherwise be treated, wish to establish themselves in any of the settlements, after declaring themselves in favor of our institutions and religion, they shall be admitted, and share the same quantity of land as the other settlers mentioned in this law, native Indians to be distinguished as Mexicans, and border Indians as foreigners, and the former shall not be required to furnish any stock.

ART. 28. That no vacancies be left between the tracts, which shall be carefully avoided in the distribution of lands, they shall be distributed in squares or other forms, although irregular should the locality so require, and to prevent litigation and dispute, in making the distribution aforesaid, as well as in the designation of sites, whereon new towns are to be founded, the adjoining proprietors, should there be any, shall be previously notified.

ART. 29. The survey of vacant lands that shall be made upon the borders of any river, running rivulet or creek, or lake, shall not exceed one-fourth of the depth of the land granted, should the land permit

ART. 30. Should any appropriated land be taken possession of through error in the concession, on proof thereof an equal quantity of land entirely vacant shall be granted to the person who obtained the same, and moreover he shall be indemnified by the owner of the land aforesaid, agreeably to a just estimate made by competent judges, and according to law, for the expense he has incurred in the improvements that appear thereon.

ART. 31. Every new settler from the time of his settlement, shall be permitted to dispose of his land, although it shall not be cultivated, by testament made in conformity to the laws that are now, or shall be hereafter in force; and should he die intestate, his lawful heir or heirs shall succeed him in the enjoyment of his rights and property, assuming in both cases the obligations and conditions incumbent on the respective grantee.

ART. 32. Land acquired by virtue of this law shall from no cause be transferred in mortmain, and those who have acquired by purchase shall not alienate their land without having complied with the provision made in article 13 of the present law.

ART. 33. New settlers, who shall resolve to leave the State to establish themselves in a foreign country, shall be at liberty to do so with all their property, but after thus leaving they shall no longer hold their land; and should they not have previously disposed of the same, or should not the alienation be in conformity to art. 19, it shall become entirely vacant.

ART. 34. The executive in connection with the respective vicarial ecclesiastics, shall take care that the new towns are adequately supplied with curates, and with the concurrence of the said authority, shall propose their salary to congress, which shall be paid by the new settlers.

ART. 35. The new settlers, in respect to the introduction of slaves, shall conform to the laws that are now, or shall be hereafter enacted on the subject.

ART. 36. Servants and day laborers, hereafter introduced by foreign colonists, cannot be obligated by any contract to continue in the service of the latter longer than ten years.

ART. 37. The commissioner or commissioners, who shall be appointed agreeably to this law, shall not be suspended in their functions by any other authority than that of the executive. The judges, within whose jurisdiction the commissioners officiate, shall confine themselves to giving information with respect to the bad management they observe in said commissions.

ART. 38. Decree No. 16, of the 24th of March, 1825, is hereby repealed.

For its fulfilment, the Governor of the State shall cause it to be printed, published, and circulated.

Given in the city of Leona Vicario on the 28th of April, 1832.

JOSE J. GRANDE, President.
MANUEL MUZQUIZ, D. S.
CESARIO FIGUEROA, D. S. *ad interim*.

FORGING INSTRUMENTS TO BE USED AT ANY OF THE PUBLIC OFFICES OF THE STATE.

ART. 829a. If any person or persons shall falsely make, counterfeit, forge, or fraudulently alter or change any instrument of writing, or printing, or document of any kind, with the intent, and for the purpose of being used or made for use, in or at any of the public departments or offices of this State, at the Seat of Government, or at any of the public offices of any county of this State, with intention of obtaining from any such public office of said State or county, any certificate, county or donation warrant or land scrip, or patent for any of the public lands of the State, or with the intent of obtaining any money or property belonging to the State or county, then he, she, or they, shall be deemed guilty of fraud and forgery, and upon conviction thereof, shall be imprisoned in the Penitentiary not less than five nor more than twenty years. Act of Feb. 2, 1856. Took effect from passage. Forgery of instrument for purpose of receiving land or money from the state. Penalty for.

ART. 829b. Any authentic copy of a proclamation which the Governor shall issue, offering a reward for the arrest of any person charged with having committed any such fraud or forgery, as described in the first section of this act, or for the arrest of any person who may be charged with wilful and malicious burning of any building, containing the books, papers, records, archives and documents of any such public office, shall be sufficient authority to any officer or citizen holding any such authentic copy, to arrest, and hold, and carry such person or persons, from the place of arrest, through any county or counties, to the place of prosecution and trial, without the necessity of having any other warrant, or other criminal process. Governors proclamation sufficient authority to arrest for forgery or arson.

ART. 829c. The sum of ten thousand dollars be, and the same is hereby appropriated out of any money in the Treasury of the State, for the purpose of paying the expenses of arresting any such offenders, and carrying them to the county or counties where the prosecution is commenced, and for the compensation of such witnesses who shall be summoned in behalf of the State upon such trials, and for the safe keeping of such offenders in custody, until the final trials thereof, and for the payment of such other expenses, concerning the prosecution of such offenders as the Governor and Attorney General, or the Governor and District Attorney of any Judicial District shall deem necessary, and shall certify to be just and reasonable, without regard to former laws. Appropriation to aid in prosecution of offenders.

ART. 829d. This act shall be given in charge by the District Judges of the several Districts to the Grand Juries of the several Counties of this State. To be given in charge to grand juries.

DEFACING THE WALLS OF PUBLIC BUILDINGS.

ART. 829e. Any person or persons who may write, scratch upon, in any manner deface or disfigure the walls of the State Capitol, or any other public buildings belonging to the State, either inside or outside of the same, or of any of the rooms, halls, steps, columns, banisters, galleries, doors or other appurtenances in any manner belonging or pertaining to the same, shall be deemed guilty of a misdemeanor and subject to a fine of not exceeding fifty nor less than five dollars. Act of Aug. 1 1856. Took effect from passage. Defacing public buildings. Penalty for.

ART. 829f. The Mayor of the city of Austin, or any Justice of the Peace in said city, shall have and exercise jurisdiction in all offences under the first section of this act, and that whenever information shall be given to said Mayor or Justice of the Peace that an offence has been committed within the meaning of this act, he shall issue his warrant directed to any Marshal or Constable of said city or beat, commanding the arrest of said offender or offenders. The Mayor, or any Justice of the Peace of the city of Austin to have jurisdiction, &c.

ART. 829g. Whenever any person or persons shall be found guilty of any offence under this act, and shall fail to pay the fine and costs adjudged against him or them, then and in that case, said Mayor or Justice of the Peace, before whom said offender shall be tried, shall have the power of imprisoning said person or persons so found guilty, in the county or city jail until the fine and costs of When offender fails to pay fine and costs.

* The Articles numbered 829a to 829h, (pages 773 and 774) were inadvertently omitted. They should have come in at the end of the Penal Code.—COMP.

Term of imprisonment. prosecution be paid. Provided said imprisonment shall not exceed forty days. And that in all prosecutions under this act, the said Mayor, Justice of the Peace, Marshal or Constable shall be allowed the same fees as are by law. Fees of officers. allowed in prosecutions for misdemeanors, in the District Court, said fees in all cases to be taxed against the defendant. And all fines collected under this Fines paid to city Treasury. act shall be paid by said Mayor or Justice of the Peace into the Treasury of the city of Austin, for the use and benefit of said city.

IMPORTATION OF FREE NEGROES PROHIBITED.

Act of Aug. 25, 1856. Took effect from passage. Importation of free negroes prohibited. ART. 829h. The ninth section of the above recited act is hereby amended, so that the same shall hereafter read as follows, to-wit: That it shall not be lawful for any master of a vessel, or owner thereof, nor for any other person whatsoever, to bring, import, induce or aid or assist in the bringing, importing or inducing any free person of color, within the limits of the State of Texas, directly or indirectly. And any person so offending shall be deemed guilty of a misdemeanor, and on conviction thereof in the District Court, shall be fined in a sum of not less than one hundred dollars, nor more than two thousand Penalty for. dollars for each offence.

INDEX OF CIVIL STATUTES.

INDEX TO THE PENAL CODE.

INDEX TO THE CODE OF CRIMINAL PROCEDURE.

INDEX TO THE REPEALED LAWS.

INDEX TO THE COLONIZATION LAWS.

The following act was accidentally overlooked in the preparation of the head to which it appropriately belongs:

AN ACT TO ENCOURAGE THE RECLAMATION OF SLAVES, ESCAPING BEYOND THE LIMITS OF THE SLAVE TERRITORIES OF THE UNITED STATES.

SECT. 1. Any person or persons capturing, or causing the capture of any slave or slaves who may have escaped beyond the limits of the slave territory of the United States, and who shall deliver such slave or slaves to the Sheriff of Travis county, shall be entitled to receive from the Treasury of the State thirty-three and one-third per cent. on the value of such slave or slaves.

SECT. 2. Any person capturing a slave or slaves, as provided for in the first section of this act, shall, after arriving within the limits of this State in the first organized county which he may reach, go before a Judge of the District Court, Chief Justice, Notary Public, or Clerk of the District or County Court, and make proof to the satisfaction of such officer, by at least two witnesses, that the slave or slaves so captured were taken beyond the limits of the slave territory of the United States; whereupon such officer shall certify to the fact of said proof, under his hand and seal, if he have one, and deliver the same to the party so appearing before him. Upon arriving at the city of Austin, in the county of Travis, the captor shall deliver such slave or slaves to the Sheriff of said county, who shall without delay summon two freeholders, citizens of said county, to appraise such slave or slaves under oath, and he shall append to the certificate of proof said appraisement, together with his certificate that they have been delivered to him and are in his custody, and upon presentation of the same to the Comptroller, that officer shall issue his warrant on the Treasurer for the amount of said thirty-three and one-third per cent. on the appraisement, to be paid out of any money in the Treasury not otherwise appropriated.

SECT. 3. It shall be the duty of the said Sheriff to advertise such slave or slaves in the official paper of the State for three months, giving therein a full description of the same, the appraised value, and the name of the reputed owner; and should the owner appear and prove his property according to law, he or they shall be entitled to receive the same upon paying the one-third appraised valuation, with interest thereon at the rate of eight per cent. per annum, and also five per cent. of the appraised value of said slaves, which five per cent. shall remain in the Treasury as an accumulating fund to be applied to the purposes contemplated by this act, and all other legal charges.

SECT. 4. Should the owner of said slave or slaves fail to prove property and pay charges, prior to the expiration of said three months, it shall be the duty of the Sheriff aforesaid to advertise such slave or slaves for sale, giving thirty days notice in some newspaper of the city of Austin, and at the expiration of said period shall sell the said slave or slaves at auction to the highest bidder for cash; and after paying all the necessary and legal charges, shall pay the remainder over to the Treasurer, who shall reimburse the State for the amount originally paid for their apprehension, and shall retain the remainder subject to the order of the owner or owners of such slaves.

SECT. 5. It shall not be lawful for any officer of the State to charge more than the legal fees for services or expenses incurred under this act.

SECT. 6. Any person capturing a slave as contemplated by the preceding sections of this act, who shall deliver the same to the owner in any portion of this State, shall be entitled to receive the same compensation as if delivered to the Sheriff of Travis county, and shall be entitled to hold possession of such slave or slaves, as security therefor until paid. And that this act take effect after its passage.

Approved February 13, 1858.

www.ingramcontent.com/pod-product-compliance
Lightning Source LLC
LaVergne TN
LVHW062241200926
848484LV00006B/1588